MW00999976

Texas Master Naturalist Statewide Curriculum

Texas A&M AgriLife Research and Extension Service Series

Craig Nessler and Douglas L. Steele, General Editors

Texas Master Naturalist Statewide Curriculum

Edited by
Michelle M. Haggerty
Master Naturalist State Program Coordinator
Texas Parks and Wildlife Department

and

Mary Pearl Meuth
Master Naturalist Assistant State Program Coordinator
Texas A&M AgriLife Extension Service

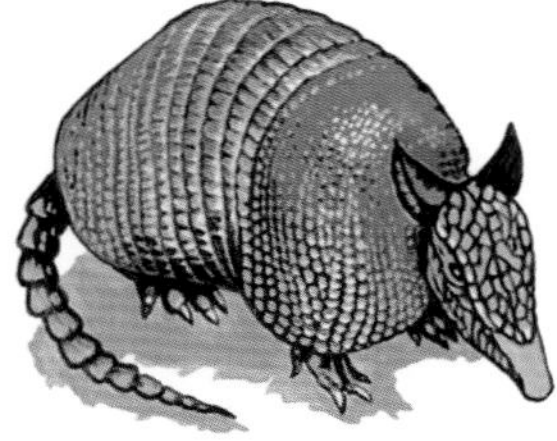

TEXAS A&M UNIVERSITY PRESS COLLEGE STATION, TEXAS

Manufactured in China
by Everbest Printing Co.
through FCI Print Group

First edition

This paper meets the requirements of ANSI/NISO Z39.48–1992 (Permanence of Paper).
Binding materials have been chosen for durability.
♾♲

General editors for this series are Craig Nessler, director of Texas A&M AgriLife Research, and Douglas L. Steele, director of Texas A&M AgriLife Extension Service.

LIBRARY OF CONGRESS CATALOGING-IN-PUBLICATION DATA
Names: Haggerty, Michelle M., 1974– editor. | Meuth, Mary Pearl, editor.
Title: Texas Master Naturalist statewide curriculum / edited by Michelle M. Haggerty and Mary Pearl Meuth.
Other titles: Texas A&M AgriLife Research and Extension Service series.
Description: First edition. | College Station, Texas : Texas A&M University Press, [2015] | Series: Texas A&M AgriLife Research and Extension Service series | Includes bibliographical references and index.
Identifiers: LCCN 2015044739| ISBN 9781623493400 (hardcover (printed case) ; alk. paper) | ISBN 9781623493448 (ebook)
Subjects: LCSH: Conservation of natural resources—Texas—Citizen participation. | Naturalists—Education—Curricula—Texas. | Texas Master Naturalist (Program)
Classification: LCC S944.5.C57 T48 2015 | DDC 333.7209764—dc23 LC record available at http://lccn.loc.gov/2015044739

Contents

Preface

Find your place on the planet. Dig in, and take responsibility from there.
—Gary Snyder

Questions, not answers, stimulate the mind.
—Richard Paul

Everything is bigger in Texas! With over 268,000 square miles of territory and an ever-growing population of nearly 27 million residents, there are ample opportunities for those seeking to go outdoors and get involved with the "natural Texas."

From north to south Texas spans 801 miles, and east to west it spans 773 miles. The highest point of elevation is Guadalupe Peak on the border with New Mexico, and the lowest is at sea level along the 367 miles of Gulf of Mexico coastline. Texas is generally considered to be one of the most ecologically diverse states in the United States. Texas has 10 climatic regions, 15 soil regions, and 11 distinct ecological regions and 56 subregions. There are more than 180 species of mammals, 635 of birds, 30,000 of invertebrates, 5,200 of plants, 240 of fishes, and 210 of reptiles and amphibians found within the state's borders.

This diversity of the ecological regions, geography, flora, and fauna has always been of interest to naturalists. Discovery in Texas has progressed from that of early naturalists who were not native to the area and spent time identifying the diverse flora and fauna, to discovery by those who decided to stay and stake a claim on the land. Next came those who grew up with Texas over multiple generations and craved an understanding of the interactions between the wildlife they observed and their agricultural-based livelihood. From that generation emerged a group of men and women who desired a higher level of education from the formal institutions in early Texas. This distinguished them from the observational naturalists and created a standard of in-depth education and field-based research about the state's native flora and fauna. The passion of these early naturalists, who were also educators in their own communities, has spread to today's growing culture of community-centered learning and natural resource conservation, a prelude for the Texas Master Naturalist program.

The mission of the Texas Master Naturalist program from its inception in 1997 has been to develop a corps of well-informed volunteers to provide education, outreach, and service dedicated to the beneficial management of natural resources and natural areas within their communities for the State of Texas. Many communities and organizations in Texas rely on these citizen-volunteers for implementing youth education programs; for operating parks, nature centers, and natural areas; and for providing leadership in local natural resource conservation efforts. In fact, a short supply of dedicated and well-informed volunteers is often cited as a limiting factor for community-based conservation efforts. But the Texas Master Naturalist program is training volunteers to help in these conservation efforts. From its early beginnings of just 4 chapters and 400+ volunteers, the program has grown to include more than 44 chapters and 9,000+ volunteers who provided about 400,000 hours of service valued at $9 million to the state in 2014 alone. To date the program has provided more than 2.4 million hours of service valued at about $65 million. More than 4.1 million people have been reached through Texas Master Naturalist–sponsored volunteer outreach and educational events. Texas Master Naturalists have made an impact on nearly 220,000 acres with their stewardship and technical guidance services, while roughly 1,850 miles of interpretive trails have been developed and cared for by these volunteers. The program and its chapters have established partnerships with about 400 organizations that share a similar mission and vision. The program has been recognized with more than 35 local, state, national, and international awards for its efforts and accomplishments.

None of this would have been possible without a good foundation, and the Texas Master Naturalist program owes its good fortune to the statewide partnership developed between the Texas Parks and Wildlife Department and Texas A&M AgriLife Extension Service. Part of that foundation is a good training curriculum that enables our members to feel knowledgeable, confident, and successful in their program endeavors.

Development of the *Texas Master Naturalist Statewide Curriculum* has brought together a well-articulated, academia-level resource guide for the program's volunteers and their communities, who needed and wanted to enhance their natural resource education and conservation. It is designed as a training tool and reference resource for the Texas Master Naturalist volunteers as they strive to address the education of our public, along with the conservation and management needs of our natural resources for the State of Texas.

We have found that Texas Master Naturalist volunteers are better able to find relevance in natural history and ecological information if it is presented as "answers" to broadly posed questions like our historical "master naturalists" would have asked. By presenting consistent basic ecological and biological information to chapters and members across the state, with the local ecological diversity highlighted by each chapter's training, the volunteers are better able to gain a working understanding of the interactions among species, habitats, and human activities. The curriculum stresses ecosystem dynamics—the ways in which ecological systems change and adapt over time and space. In most instances, the training instructors will teach above and beyond what is presented in the curriculum unit and customize their presentations to the specific issues, resources, and case studies of the local ecological area being addressed by that Texas Master Naturalist chapter.

Developing this book has been no small feat. As a program team in 2000, with the numerous requests we received from our ever-growing list of trained naturalists and our newly developed Texas Master Naturalist chapters, we embarked upon developing an official statewide Texas Master Naturalist curriculum. Many members and leaders of established and newly establishing chapters told us that having such a resource would catapult their and their trainee's development and enhance the program's preservation for the future. Thus, our state program launched into the development of a comprehensive curriculum for our members and chapters to use statewide.

The first drafts of the curriculum drew from the many resources of our early chapters, and in some cases, the chapters' early instructors were asked to write a specific unit with statewide applicability for the work. Over the next few years, the book began to take form with the assistance of many authors, contributors, reviewers, curriculum coordinators, student workers, Texas Master Naturalist volunteers, and others. The curriculum was developed as *the* basis of training for Texas Master Naturalist volunteers throughout the state and thus as *the* reference book required for all of the program's volunteers, therefore establishing a consistent baseline of knowledge among our program participants.

Our first edition of the *Texas Master Naturalist Statewide Curriculum* made its debut in 2004 as a black-and-white, 22-unit, 742-page document in a three-ring binder after years of development, editing, and layout. Despite its humble beginnings and shoestring budget, the curriculum received high praise from professionals, our volunteers, and laypersons from Texas and nationally for its comprehensiveness and exhaustive academia-level reference materials presented. Several units have even been adopted and adapted with our permission (and proper credit) by several Master Naturalist programs in other states.

After 10 years of being "ground-truthed," used, reviewed, and edited by our program participants, naturalists, program staff, partners, and instructors, we set out to establish a second edition that included all of those updates; new units focusing on emerging issues of natural resource concern; further discussions on stewardship and ethics; and much, much more. Just as nature is dynamic, so is our program curriculum. It, too, will continue to develop for years to come.

This curriculum could not have come to fruition without our dedicated Texas Master Naturalist volunteers. They are the people who make this program special. They are the people who make this program unique and recognized. Without their dedication and willingness to make a difference in our state's natural resource future, the Texas Master Naturalist program would not be as successful as it is. On behalf of our sponsoring agencies of the Texas Parks and Wildlife Department and the Texas A&M AgriLife Extension Service, it is with great excitement and pleasure that we are providing this product to our program participants. The development of the second edition of the *Texas Master Naturalist Statewide Curriculum* was a huge undertaking by numerous individuals. Thank you to each of the individuals involved in this lengthy publication project—both those mentioned and unmentioned. And thank you, the Texas Master Naturalist volunteers, for taking the steps to "be the change you wish to see in the world!"

—Michelle M. Haggerty
—Mary Pearl Meuth
Texas Master Naturalist
Program Coordinators

Acknowledgments

The *Texas Master Naturalist Statewide Curriculum* has a lot of people to thank for their contributions, encouragement, expertise, and reviews. From its original authors, editors, and compilers, to the latest edition's review and updates by many more, the work as a whole has been a team effort across the state.

First and foremost, the original focus group that came together from across the state to spearhead the production of the curriculum included John Davis, Diana Foss, Elizabeth Gregory, Michelle Haggerty, Billy Kniffen, Julie Massey, Patricia Morton, Jennifer Pestovic, Barron Rector, and Neal Wilkins. The efforts made from these original contributors laid the groundwork for the cooperation and partnership of the two sponsoring organizations, Texas Parks and Wildlife Department (TPWD) and Texas A&M AgriLife Extension Service.

The original curriculum, written in 2004, was brought together under the leadership of Michelle Haggerty and Neal Wilkins, with the coordination done by Jennifer Pestovic, Texas A&M AgriLife Extension Service. The original prototype layout and design were developed by Elizabeth Gregory, Texas A&M AgriLife Communications & Marketing, and completed by Alexandra D. Manning and Garrett L. Anderson, both working as students for the Texas A&M AgriLife Extension Service. Bethany Foshee was a contributor to the original content and layout of the curriculum while also assisting as a curriculum resources and information coordinator as a student in the Wildlife and Fisheries Department at Texas A&M University.
The curriculum would also not have been originally possible without the financial contributions from the Exxon Mobil Corporation and from the Texas Parks and Wildlife Department, Wildlife Division; the Renewable Resources Extension Act; and the Texas A&M AgriLife Wildlife & Fisheries Sciences Extension Unit. In 2012, Kathi Camp of the Blackland Prairie Chapter of the Texas Master Naturalist program began the huge undertaking of making grammatical and factual edits and minor revisions to the original manuscript, preparing it for the second edition. In 2014, the second-edition production—with a complete review and update of units by each of their authors—was coordinated by Mary Pearl Meuth, Texas A&M AgriLife Extension Service, under the leadership of Michelle Haggerty, TPWD, and James Cathey, Texas A&M AgriLife Extension Service. An instrumental part of the revision process can also be very tedious at times; Ashley Steinbach, a student worker with the Texas Master Naturalist program was vital in accomplishing these tasks by preparing the manuscript files, compiling the image database of over 600 images, and adjusting the graphic quality of the new work. This new revision would have been impossible without the guidance, patience, and expertise of the Texas A&M University (TAMU) Press team of editors, managers, and copyeditors: Shannon Davies, Donna Boswell, Patricia Clabaugh, Cynthia Lindlof, and all the others behind the scenes who reviewed it as it slowly morphed into a real book.

Each unit was individually authored with multiple contributors and reviewers. We thank each one separately for their contributions made.

A huge thanks to the author and expert who wrote the **Land Stewardship** unit, Jim Stanley, a member of the first class of the Hill Country Chapter of the Texas Master Naturalist program. His unit brings answers to the most philosophical question in natural resource conservation: What is stewardship? We also thank his team of reviewers, who all had high praises for Jim's work in the arena of stewardship and conservation: Steve Nelle, Natural Resources Conservation Service; Don Steinbach, Texas A&M AgriLife Extension Service; David Langford, DKL Photography; and Jenny Sanders, Temple Ranch.

The **Archaeology** unit owes its success to the team of Herbert Uecker, Archeological Consultant, and Todd McMakin, TPWD. Diane Dismukes, TPWD, also gave reviews and praise for the unit in its second update. At a last-minute request, Chris Lintz, TPWD, provided a heavy hand to the unit in its second edition updates and was vital to bringing the unit to publication.

Thanks to the original Texas Naturalists unit **Prior to World War II** author, Horace Burke, Department of Entomology, TAMU. Without his extensive library of knowledge and expertise, these important figures would be lost in obscurity to all those who follow in their steps. Burke contributed his unit with thanks to his colleagues Stanley D. Casto and Rollin H. Baker, who, as he said, "willingly lent their knowledge and time."

Thanks to the lead authors of the rewritten **Historical Naturalists** of Texas unit, Kristen Tyson and Mary Pearl Meuth, Texas A&M AgriLife Extension Service, and author of the preface, David Schmidly, President, University of New Mexico. This unit's unique group of essays were provided by a wide range of Master Naturalists from different chapters around the state, including Karen and Allen Ginnard, Gideon Lincecum Chapter; Wallace Stapp, Capital Area Chapter; Al McGraw, Archeologist; Deborah Canterbury, Blackland Prairie Chapter; Charlie Grindstaff, Indian Trail Chapter; Mary Ann Melton, Goodwater Chapter; Mark Tyson, Texas A&M AgriLife Extension Service; and Steve Houser, North Texas Master Naturalist. The unit was edited by Valerie Taber, a member of the Rio Brazos Chapter, without whom the unit would be in pieces.

The **Ecological Regions** of Texas unit was written by David Riskind, TPWD, with contributions from Bethany Foshee, originally a student intern with TAMU Wildlife and Fisheries Department and now with Houston Audubon Society, and Michelle Haggerty, TPWD.

Thanks to Louis Verner, retired TPWD Urban Wildlife Biologist and retired Virginia Department of Game and Inland Fisheries Biologist, for authoring the **Ecological Concepts** unit, with contributions from Debbie Reid, Antoinette Villarreal, and Mark White. In the updated manual, thanks go to Doug Slack, Wildlife & Fisheries Sciences Department, TAMU; and Richard Heilbrun, TPWD, for reviewing and updating the text.

Thank you to Barron Rector, Extension Range Specialist, Department of Ecosystem Science and Management, for putting his energy and expertise into the **Ecosystem Concepts and Management** unit, with reviews made by Larry White, Texas A&M AgriLife Extension Service.

The **Geology and Soils** unit was authored by Chris Mathewson, Department of Geology/Geophysics, TAMU, who also made the reviews and updates. Thanks are also owed to Jon Brandt, Geologist and Texas Master Naturalist volunteer, for reviewing the original submission. The original unit as submitted was also reviewed and given contributions from select staff members of the Natural Resources Conservation Service and William A. Foss, Registered Professional Geologist.

Thank you to the authors who wrote, reviewed, and updated the **Weather and Climate** unit: John Neilson-Gammon, Texas State Climatologist and Professor of Meteorology, Department of Atmospheric Sciences, TAMU; Billy Kniffen, Texas A&M AgriLife Extension Service; and Troy Kimmel Jr., University of Texas.

In the development of the second edition of the curriculum, several new units were proposed for addition. The first of these, **Texas Water Resources**, was written with the high interest in water sources and the hot topic of water conservation and rights.

Under the guidance of a team from both the Texas Water Resources Institute and the Texas A&M AgriLife Extension Service, Kevin Wagner, Nikki Dictson, Allen Berthold, Diane Boellstorff, Clare Entwistle, Drew Gholson, Lucas Gregory, Chelsea Hawkins, Kirstin Hein, Brian Jonescu, and Aubrey Wolff deserve a special thank you.

The **Nature of Naming** unit owes its creation to Barron Rector, Texas A&M AgriLife Extension Service, with reviews from William Foxx III, Texas A&M AgriLife Extension, and Jason Singhurst, TPWD. Thank you to Matthew R. McClure, Lamar State College–Orange, for his review of the text and clarification of the terminology.

Thanks to Barron Rector, Texas A&M AgriLife Extension Service, for authoring the unit on **Plants**, with reviews made by Larry White, Texas A&M AgriLife Extension Service, and Jason Singhurst, TPWD. Matthew R. McClure, Lamar State College–Orange, also provided revisions of the charts and taxonomic levels.

Thanks to Charles Jack Randel III, Department of Wildlife & Fisheries Sciences, TAMU, author of the **Ornithology** unit. Thanks also to Jennifer Pestovic and Nova Silvy, Department of Wildlife & Fisheries Sciences, TAMU, who provided contributions. The final unit was reviewed and updated with help from Keith Arnold, Department of Wildlife & Fisheries Sciences, TAMU; Mary Ann Weber, Houston Audubon Society; and Mark Lockwood, TPWD.

Thanks to the **Entomology** unit author, Will Godwin, Jarvis College, for his thorough exploration of the insects of Texas and their study. The unit was also reviewed and updated by the Texas A&M AgriLife Extension Entomology Specialists team: Charles Allen, Molly Keck, Wizzie Brown, and Mike Merchant. Thank you also to Mike Quinn of texasento.net for contributing images and experience.

The **Ichthyology** unit was authored by John McEachran, Department of Wildlife & Fisheries Sciences, TAMU, with reviews by Kevin Conway, Biodiversity Research and Teaching Collections, and Billy Higginbotham, Texas A&M AgriLife Extension Service.

Thanks to Lee Fitzgerald, Department of Wildlife & Fisheries Sciences, TAMU, for putting extensive hours into the **Herpetology** unit, with reviews by the late Jim “Doc” Dixon, Department of Wildlife & Fisheries Sciences, TAMU; Andy Gluesenkamp, TPWD; John Karges, The Nature Conservancy; and Toby Hibbitts, Biodiversity Research and Teaching Collections, TAMU. Also thank you to Gage Dayton for reviewing the manuscript and offering suggestions.

Thanks to the author of the **Mammalogy** unit, John Young, TPWD, with contributions made by Kevin Herriman, TPWD, and Jonah Evans, TPWD, and initial reviews contributed by Paul Robertson, TPWD.

Thanks to Kathy Flannery, Texas Forest Service, as the original **Forest Ecology and Management** unit author, along with original reviewer, Neal Wilkins, Texas A&M AgriLife Extension Service. In the updated version, John Warner, Urban District Forester, and his team from the Texas Forest Service across the state made substantial updates and contributions to the text. Thanks to Donna Work, Lufkin; Oscar Mestas, El Paso; Mark Kroeze, San Antonio; Michael Merritt, Houston; Gretchen Riley, College Station; and Leslie Kessner, College Station. The unit was also reviewed by Steve Houser, Texas Tree Trails and North Texas Master Naturalist.

The original **Aquatic Systems Ecology and Management** unit was written by Michael Masser, Department of Wildlife & Fisheries Sciences, TAMU; with second-edition reviews and updates by Michael Masser; Todd Sink, Texas A&M AgriLife Extension Service; and Jeff Henson, TPWD.

Thanks to the team who brought together the update and review of the **Wetland Ecology and Management** unit, originally written by Jeff Raasch, TPWD. This team includes reviewers and contributors Matthew

Symmank, Tom Heger, Ryan McGillicuddy, Anne Rogers, and Cappy Smith, TPWD.

The **Rangeland Ecology and Management** unit was produced by Texas Master Naturalist Program Advisor Barron Rector, with reviews by colleague Dale Rollins, Texas A&M AgriLife Extension Service.

In the first printing of the curriculum, the **Urban Systems** unit was compiled by John Davis, TPWD, and used with great success. In the update and second publishing, the unit underwent a change of title and a redraft of the information. The unit is now titled **Urban Ecosystems**. Big thanks to Clark Adams, Department of Wildlife & Fisheries Sciences, TAMU, and coauthor Kieran J. Lindsey, Virginia Tech University, for taking on this task and making this newly revised unit.

Thank you to Michael Mitchell, TPWD, who created a new unit, **Laws, Regulations, and Ethics**, with the reviews and critique from Richard Heilbrun, TPWD; Jessica Alderson, TPWD; and Diane Dismukes, TPWD.

Thanks to Shirley Jones, TPWD, for her insight in the writing of the **Volunteers as Teachers** unit. And thanks to Teri Gerst and Tamara Trail, a partner from the Texas Wildlife Association, for her review.

Thanks for the new **Citizen Science** unit go to author Cullen Hanks and reviewers Marsha May, TPWD; Michael Warriner, TPWD; and Rob Stevenson, Department of Biology, University of Massachusetts Boston.

Sonny Arnold, Texas Master Naturalist Program Assistant Coordinator, TPWD, was also instrumental in reviewing and preparing the original curriculum for its second-edition editing. For more than seven years Sonny took great responsibility of handling curriculum inventory and coordinating additional edits to the curriculum sent in by our Texas Master Naturalist volunteers. Thanks, Sonny, for your dedication to the Texas Master Naturalist program, both as a county administrator and as a Texas Master Naturalist program leader.

Special thanks also go to Ray C. Telfair III for his extensive review of the curriculum's first edition in preparation for the second. He also provided extensive updates to many of the references in several of the curriculum units prior to the second edition.

Thank you to our statewide chapter sponsors and partners and the professionals in the field who deliver our basic and advanced training to our Texas Master Naturalist trainees and volunteers. You are the people who bring the curriculum to life—and even expand it—when educating our Texas Master Naturalist volunteers. Thanks for your dedication and willingness to advance our version of the modern naturalist.

Thank you to Texas Parks and Wildlife Department and Texas A&M AgriLife Extension Service and their leadership teams who have supported the Texas Master Naturalist program and its curriculum continuously.

Finally, the Texas Master Naturalist program cannot and would not function without its ever-growing, ever-moving, and ever-involved membership of volunteers. With more than 9,000 volunteers trained in the first 15 years of existence, and a growth from one chapter in the city of San Antonio to 44 chapters that cover over 75% of Texas' counties, the Texas Master Naturalist volunteer efforts are far reaching. Their tireless dedication to conservation, outreach, education, and improvement and their lifelong continuation of learning have made the program a model for success and one that has been copied in other states across the nation. Thank you for making it all possible!

In the words of Carter Smith, Executive Director of Texas Parks & Wildlife Department:

"Their talents are many.
Their time is a godsend.
And, if they were an army, they would
be a formidable one."

Texas Master Naturalist Statewide Curriculum

Introduction to the Texas Master Naturalist Program

MICHELLE M. HAGGERTY
Master Naturalist State Program Coordinator
Texas Parks and Wildlife Department

MARY PEARL MEUTH
Assistant Master Naturalist State Program Coordinator
Texas A&M AgriLife Extension Service

Unit Goals

After completing this unit, volunteers should be able to

- describe what a Master Naturalist is
- identify and communicate the mission and goals of the Master Naturalist volunteer program
- identify and communicate the requirements and responsibilities of a Texas Master Naturalist

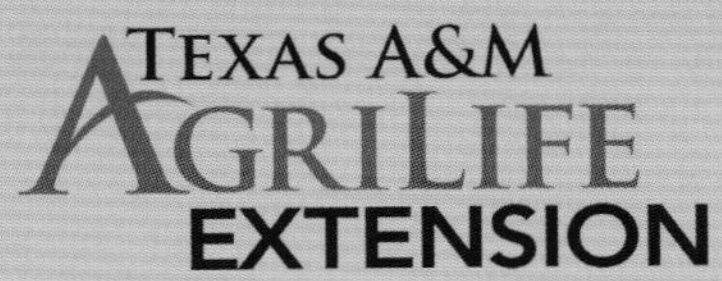

Welcome to the Texas Master Naturalist Program!

"Never doubt that a small group of thoughtful, committed citizens can change the world. Indeed, it's the only thing that ever has."
—Margaret Mead

The Texas Master Naturalist program is a natural resource–based, educational volunteer training and development program jointly sponsored statewide by the Texas A&M AgriLife Extension Service and the Texas Parks and Wildlife Department (TPWD). The ultimate goal is to help improve Texas residents' natural resource understanding and conservation management activities. Therefore, these state agencies have made the overall mission of the Texas Master Naturalist program "to develop a corps of well-informed volunteers who provide education, outreach, and service dedicated to the beneficial management of natural resources and natural areas within their local communities for the State of Texas." The program has the following goals and objectives:

1. **Improve public understanding of natural resource ecology and management** by developing a pool of local knowledge about natural resource ecology and management that can be used to enhance land management, education, and outreach efforts within local communities
2. **Enhance existing natural resources education and outreach activities** by providing natural resources training at the local level, thereby developing a supply of dedicated and informed volunteers
3. **Develop a Texas Master Naturalist volunteer network that is efficient and effective** by developing and supporting local Master Naturalist chapters at the state level as a network of locally directed volunteer training and development programs adhering to a set of guidelines, objectives, procedures, and minimum requirements set by the state program. At the state level, the program is sponsored and supported by both the TPWD and

Texas horned lizard (*Phrynosoma cornutum*) on a Texas Master Naturalist baseball hat. Courtesy of John English, Big Country Chapter, www.johnenglishphoto.com

Texas A&M AgriLife Extension Service, with occasional outside financial support provided by grants and/or private donors. However, it is a program based on the local natural resource community, the partners of each local chapter, and the program's volunteers, who provide ownership of the program.

The Texas Master Naturalist program would not be possible without extensive partnerships at the state and local levels, which are crucial to the success of the overall program and our mission. These partnerships include other public agencies as well as private organizations whose interests align with the mission of the program. The partnerships formed in each local chapter bring together a variety of expertise, experience, networks, resources, and other opportunities in a "one for all and all for one" approach to ultimately train and certify each volunteer member as a Master Naturalist through their respective local chapter. Quite literally, this program is owned by no single organization.

As the program developed, it was guided by a Statewide Advisory Committee made up of Certified Texas Master Naturalist Volunteers, as well as statewide sponsor representatives from TPWD and Texas A&M AgriLife Extension Service. The state committee set the minimum program standards, policies, procedures, and curriculum requirements, in addition to reviewing and approving each local chapter's development and curriculum to ensure effective and efficient operation of the overall statewide effort.

Why Was the Master Naturalist Program Developed?

In a nutshell, the Master Naturalist program in Texas was developed to address a growing need:

- Texas has a population of more than 26 million people, and more than 86% of those people live in urban and urbanizing areas of the state. Many of these residents and landowners are two to three generations removed from direct land management (farming, ranching, or forestry), and they rarely seek traditional forms of outreach and extension prior to making their land management decisions.
- Texas contains 144 million acres, 240,000 farming and ranching operations in the state, and a constantly changing shift in demographics and land use.
- Texas has more than 180 species of mammals, 639 species of birds, 230 species of reptiles and amphibians, and 240 species of fishes. In fact, about three-fourths of all species found in the United States have been found in Texas.
- Texas is one of the most ecologically diverse states in the nation, but there is only a handful of resource management professionals compared to the state's size.
- Due to variations in geology and climate Texas has 11 ecological regions that are further divided into 56 distinct ecological subregions. Each of these areas has a unique natural history with native plant and animal communities that distinguishes it from any other area.
- Texas has several local natural resource

and conservation organizations with education, outreach, and service missions that depend on well-trained adult volunteers to conduct youth education programs; to operate parks, nature centers, and natural areas; and to provide leadership for local natural resource conservation efforts.

We are clearly facing broadening and complex natural resource challenges that require an understanding of complex ecological dynamics at a local level.

"Great things are done when men and mountains meet."
—William Blake

"To be whole. To be complete. Nature reminds us what it means to be human, what we are connected to rather than what we are separate from."
—Terry Tempest Williams

Taking care of Texas is everyone's business. Conservation and stewardship are not spectator sports. Texas needs an involved and educated citizenry willing to demonstrate their commitment to conserving and managing the natural and cultural resources of the state. Citizens such as Master Naturalist volunteers are essential to the conservation and management of a better Texas. We need more citizen-volunteers bringing together diverse sets of personal and professional skills to creatively tackle our natural resource challenges and accomplish more for regarding these resources.

This cannot be done alone. The development of a culture of conservation with the help of volunteers has resulted and will continue to result in each Texan bearing personal responsibility for the management and conservation of the natural and cultural resources of the state. Through outreach, education, interpretation, and recreation these volunteers can help lead Texans to a better understanding of the responsibilities of stewardship, resource management, and conservation.

Dick Benoit, Galveston Bay Area Chapter member surveying a native prairie.

History of the Master Naturalist Program

Efforts for the program began in early 1997 with the development of the first Master Naturalist chapter in San Antonio. Representatives from the San Antonio Parks and Recreation Department and TPWD decided it would be beneficial to create a corps of trained volunteers to assist at local parks and natural areas.

Then, in 1998, using a similar approach, a Master Naturalist organization began operating in the Dallas–Fort Worth area. The effectiveness and popularity of the program among other volunteers and agency personnel prompted TPWD and the Texas A&M AgriLife Extension Service to develop a statewide partnership and organize a Statewide Advisory Committee later that year. This committee, consisting of local representatives from TPWD, Texas A&M AgriLife Extension, and Texas Master Naturalist volunteers, developed an expanded statewide training curriculum, a statewide marketing and identity plan, and a set of standards and direction for a Texas Master Naturalist program and its chapters.

As a result of the committee's statewide program development, new chapters centered in Austin and Houston developed in early 1999. Today, the program is ever growing with numerous chapters and volunteers statewide.

What Is a Naturalist?

Naturalists are students of natural science or natural history. For most, becoming a naturalist can be a lifelong goal. Learning never stops, as the natural world presents an infinite number of things to investigate. Yet many would agree that "natural history" is an almost obsolete term for the study of things in nature—plants, animals, minerals. In fact, the term "naturalist" brings to mind such historic figures as Carl Linnaeus, John Muir, John Burroughs, and Aldo Leopold. So, are naturalists outdated, old-fashioned types of investigators, students, and teachers? Hardly! Although natural history may have begun as a somewhat unsystematic approach to investigating the environment and its inhabitants, modern naturalists are scientists in the truest sense. They interact with the environment through careful observation, study, and analysis.

Before the current trend toward specialization, in which scientists tend to know more and more about less and less, professional scientists were naturalists in a broad sense. In the past and today, naturalists are people characterized by knowing something about the whole of nature—they are generalists. Although usually trained in one discipline, they delve into a variety of subjects, including botany, entomology, ornithology, mammalogy, herpetology, and geology.

Heartwood Chapter member sketching and journaling about nature during a nature walk discussing foraging in Conroe, Texas.

Naturalists emphasize field investigations rather than laboratory work. A naturalist is someone who possesses extensive knowledge of the natural world. More important, modern naturalists understand that in nature rarely anything stands alone. The interconnectedness of all living things to each other and to their environment is the essence of the study of natural history. Therefore, naturalists also become ecologists, ethologists, and environmentalists. They are people who understand that the natural world is not separate from human existence—we are surrounded by nature and we act upon it.

But naturalists are not just trained scientists. They are people with a real appreciation and respect for nature. They are people equipped with the tools necessary to be a naturalist—and not just a quirky hat and binoculars. A desire to ask questions and seek answers, resources for naming and identifying things, a concern for the environment, and an awareness of the threats to nature are a few of the naturalist's tools.

"Study nature, love nature, stay close to nature. It will never fail you."
—Frank Lloyd Wright

"The environment is not only more complex than we think; it is more complex than we can think."
—Anonymous

The term "Master Naturalist," as used in this program, describes the scope of the training and the areas of knowledge. The natural world comprises a variety of complicated, interrelated subjects, and many questions still remain unanswered. None of us can truly master all of the disciplines pertaining to the natural world. But we can master the skills of those that came before us, including careful observation, note taking or journaling, asking questions, experimenting and evaluating, and teaching others. Our volunteers wear the title as a representation of this program but understand that becoming a true Master Naturalist is a goal that can be only approached, never attained. Naturalists work to gain the wisdom of those who came before them, build on that knowledge, and teach those who will come after them.

What Is a Texas Master Naturalist?

Texas Master Naturalists are volunteers with the interest and desire to learn more about the natural world around them and to give back to their local natural resource community. The Texas Master Naturalist program has three components (a "three-legged stool"): training, volunteer service hours, and advanced training.

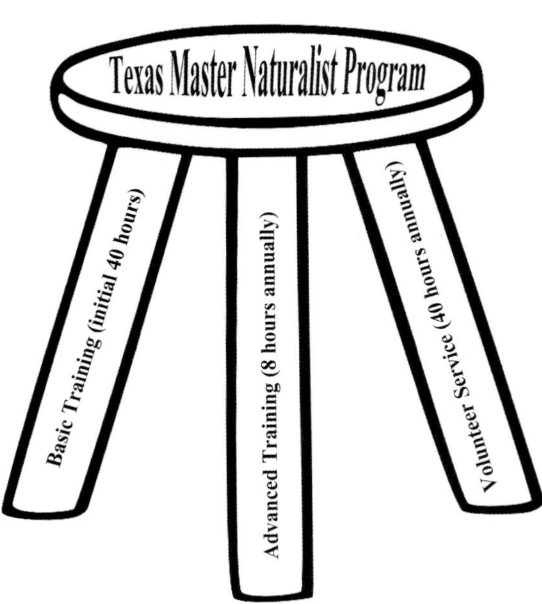

A three-legged stool showing "Training," "Service," and "Advanced Training" as the pillars of the program.

Texas Master Naturalist Certification

As set by state standards, completion of 40 hours of approved basic training, 40 hours of approved natural resource volunteer service, and 8 hours of approved advanced training certifies each participant as a Texas Master Naturalist. The state program has established statewide minimum requirements for certification. However, local chapters

Ron Hood, a Hill Country Chapter member, receiving his 10,000-hour volunteer service award. Below, he is conducting a bird survey as part of his service to the program.

Texas Master Naturalist Certification Requirements
In the first year a trainee must complete

- 40 hours of approved basic training
- 8 hours of approved advanced training
- 40 hours of approved volunteer service

Certification maintenance requires a minimum of 40+ hours of service and 8+ hours of advanced training annually. Local chapters may require higher training, volunteer service, and/or advanced training standards.

may opt to exceed the minimum requirements.

During the first year of involvement in the Texas Master Naturalist program, each trainee is expected to complete a combination of at least 40 hours of hands-on classroom and field experiences delivered by resource experts, professionals, and specialists and designed to give an understanding of natural history and ecological processes influencing their local ecosystems. In return for this training and prior to certification as a Texas Master Naturalist, each trainee will complete at least 40 hours of volunteer service while supplementing training and service with a minimum of at least 8 additional hours of advanced training.

After becoming Certified Texas Master Naturalists, they are expected to continue volunteer efforts through active membership in their local Texas Master Naturalist chapters. To retain certification each year thereafter, volunteers are required to perform a minimum of 40 hours of service and 8 hours of advanced training annually.

Texas Master Naturalist Training

The Texas Master Naturalist training program provides the volunteers a broad-based curriculum that covers a wide variety of topics from botany, ecology, and geology, to conservation, communication, and leadership skills. The overall goals of the curriculum are to provide nonbiased natural resource information and materials in an interesting format to create volunteer naturalists and inspire them to become stewards of the state's natural resources and share that information and enthusiasm with others.

This curriculum was designed by resource professionals from state fish and wildlife agencies, universities, and nongovernmental partners to provide Texas Master Naturalist volunteers with basic hands-on knowledge in the function, management, and interpretation of the ecosystems and natural resources of the state. The training benefits all who are interested in becoming Texas Master Naturalist volunteers—from professionals to the general public. Texas Master Naturalists are people who want to make a difference in Texas' natural resource future by giving back to the natural resource community around them while also increasing the scope of their knowledge.

Because Texas has such diversity in climate, population, and land types, the natural resources (and their uses) in each area of the state are unique. Therefore, each local chapter has organized and customized the following training categories to fit its natural resource systems and needs with hands-on field and classroom experiences and case studies specific to the chapter's local ecoregion. Additionally, each chapter's training outline and agenda are pre-approved by the Texas Master Naturalist State Program.

All chapters cover through their training, at a minimum, the following topics:

- **Roles, responsibilities, and benefits of being a Texas Master Naturalist:** To understand the purpose and mission of the program—and commit to participate as a volunteer.
- **Historical perspectives of naturalists in Texas and elsewhere:** Naturalists were frontiersmen, pioneers, observers, interpreters, and teachers. They were important in the history of our state. The Master Naturalist training should include pro-

grams designed to create an appreciation for the role that these early naturalists played in Texas and US history. Because many of the early naturalists kept accurate records of what they observed, this study can provide an interesting way for people to realize the changes in our landscapes over time. Also, studying those early "master naturalists" creates a sense of appreciation that goes along with the title of Texas Master Naturalist.

- **Traditional disciplines of a naturalist:** The original naturalists were botanists, entomologists, ornithologists, mammalogists, herpetologists, paleontologists, and geologists. Professionals within these disciplines from local universities, state agencies, nature centers, and research centers will eagerly share their disciplines with members in training.
- **Ecological concepts:** Ecological concepts may be discussed in a classroom situation but may also be combined with case studies and/or field demonstrations to take on meaning that is more relevant. Volunteers will come away from the training sessions with an accurate baseline understanding of what is meant by some of the ecological concepts and ideas that need to be understood in order to manage natural resources. These include the functional definitions of ecosystems, landscapes, communities, species diversity, populations, and biodiversity. The training sessions will also expose each trainee to the dynamics of natural systems, including succession, natural and human disturbances, recovery and restoration.
- **Ecoregions of Texas:** As a Texas Master Naturalist, each new member will be trained to understand the basic differences among the various ecoregions of the state. In addition, volunteers will be trained to understand the unique characteristics and interactions among the geology, climate, water, soils, flora, fauna, and major land uses in their local ecoregion.
- **Management of natural systems:** Trainees are exposed to the management of natural systems, including forest ecology and management, rangeland ecology and management, wetland ecology and management, urban ecology and management, and aquatic ecology and management. These applied fields are each represented by natural resource professionals with the qualifications to lead these sessions. Because not all parts of the state have land types suitable for these managed systems, training sessions will focus on those managed systems that are a dominant feature in each chapter's local ecosystem.
- **Interpretation and communications:** As Master Naturalists, trainees may often represent their efforts to the public. Through the training, each trainee will be given an opportunity to develop presentation skills and active learning techniques. Each Texas Master Naturalist chapter will function as a reservoir of teaching resources and materials for its members' use. The availability and effective use of these resources should be reviewed as part of the initial training.
- **Natural Resource Stewardship, Laws, Regulations, Ethics, and Citizen Science:** The Texas Master Naturalist Program curriculum should include an introduction to the history of land conservation, stewardship, and land management ethics, focusing on the local regions and habitats of the Chapter. New member training should promote a discussion of ethics, with each trainee being encouraged, through the use of best practices, to develop their own conservation ethic. Emphasis should be placed on the interconnected relationship between good land management practices, habitat, and all wildlife survival. Appropriate local, state, and national laws and regulations pertaining to conservation and the protection of natural resources should be emphasized. Citizen Science and its role in the Master Naturalist volunteer pro-

gram, as a means to contribute to natural resource research, better management practices and conservation efforts in Texas, should also be presented.

As a Master Naturalist in training (i.e., trainee or intern), each volunteer can begin earning volunteer service hours once he or she begins the Texas Master Naturalist training—or in some cases—once a volunteer is an enrolled and fully accepted member of an official chapter's training class.

Two Typical Curriculum Training Schedules

There are two typical training-schedule approaches practiced throughout the chapters around the state: the "systems approach" and the "-ologies approach."

The **systems approach** is a useful training design tool for chapters wanting to feature each of the major Texas ecoregions or systems as a learning environment for studying the major flora and fauna typically found within that system. The chapter curriculum coordinator or new class director will schedule the training around the ecosystem of interest, and each session will be dedicated to learning about all of the flora and fauna typically found within that region or system. For example, a wetland systems training session may dedicate the first half of the class to learning about the typical ecosystem processes found within the wetland environments, the water, and wetland plant life. The second half may be dedicated to the most common fauna found within that system—reptiles, birds, mammals, and so on—and their adaptations and roles within that environment. One benefit to the systems approach is that the chapter trainees will be able to organize their knowledge of the flora and fauna per ecoregion within a close proximity to their chapter. One of the difficulties with this training style is that the classes may take a more skilled presenter to provide the information of the flora and fauna per system or may take more than one presenter or session to cover the full system.

The **-ologies approach** is a more academic-based approach, where each classification unit and curriculum unit is examined within the context of the multiple ecoregions of the chapter's service area. For example, in the training session learning about mammalogy, the study of mammals, the presenter will discuss the typical mammals found within the different ecoregions or systems of the local area or even around the state, comparison of mammals of wetlands and rangeland systems, or comparison of mammals of the Gulf Coast and the Hill Country. One benefit to this approach is that it is simpler to complete with one presenter teaching each "-ology" and classification per region or system. It also lines up better with the way in which the curriculum book is laid out. However, one thing to consider with this training style is the feeling of jumping around ecoregions within each session.

There is also a third approach to designing the training schedule, a **hybrid approach**, with each session scheduled around the systems found within the chapter's local region and addressing the "-ologies" relative to that system. This organization style relies more on the field studies incorporated into the class schedule.

Advanced Training

The minimum annual requirement of 8 hours of advanced training promotes continued learning, exploring, and development just as historical naturalists practiced. Through the initial 40 hours of Master Naturalist training, each trainee will learn a little about a lot. Many say that after their Master Naturalist training, they really begin to realize just how little they actually know. Ideally, advanced training should cover in more depth a subject area of the initial training that is of specific interest to each volunteer. Advanced training should not only give volunteers in-depth information but should also enable or prepare them to be a better volunteer in their area of natural resource interest when conducting their Master Naturalist service. Ultimately, the purpose of advanced training is to provide Texas Master Naturalists an opportunity to focus their interests on one, or several, specific topics. Also, advanced training on an annual basis promotes continued learning and development.

Advanced training is a benefit in itself, providing the trained Master Naturalist with tools to work in more advanced volunteer efforts. Advanced training opportunities are available through a variety of places, such as the statewide program, the local chapter, and the local chapter partners, or each Master Naturalist volunteer can seek out such opportunities. However, every oppor-

Kip Kiphart, a Hill Country Chapter member, conducting field studies.

"Down the Rabbit Hole." Trail marking at John Bunker Sands Wetland Center by North Texas Master Naturalist volunteers is an example of a Texas Master Naturalist service project. Courtesy of Carol Mayhew, North Texas Chapter

tunity is required to be pre-approved by the local chapter. Although the Texas Master Naturalist program may occasionally provide statewide or regional advanced training opportunities, it is generally the responsibility of the chapter to ensure that there are sufficient advanced training opportunities offered so that members can attain their 8-hour minimum requirement.

In addition, each local chapter should be a clearinghouse for notifying members of approved advanced training opportunities that exist both inside and outside the chapter boundaries. Watching television shows and reading books are not accepted as advanced training. However, with the advancement of online media, live webinars with specialized topics, expert presenters, and an interactive feature allowing audio and text question/answer sessions may be accepted for advanced training hours.

When a volunteer submits an advanced training topic for consideration, the chapter will ask if the advanced training opportunity

- promotes continued learning and development of naturalist skills
- provides Master Naturalists with knowledge and skills to work in volunteer efforts
- direct-trains volunteers toward specific programs in need of their services
- provides practical information and training for application in volunteer efforts
- takes advantage of local partnerships
- provides Master Naturalists an opportunity to focus their interests on one or a few specific topics
- builds on the core curriculum initially provided by the local chapter
- provides natural resource management issues and information applicable to

Texas and the member's area of ecological training

"Do what you can, with what you have, where you are."
—Theodore Roosevelt

Service Projects

In return for the training and in order to attain and/or maintain certification, Master Naturalists are required to provide service back to the program, its state sponsors, and local chapter partners and affiliates. Good-quality natural resource service projects are never in short supply, nor is there a service project that does not fit some volunteer's interests, skills, or abilities. Service projects can be identified through the local partners, by the volunteer, by the statewide program and program coordinators, or through local chapters. This service can be a short, one-time project, such as participating on a speaker's bureau providing valuable information to Texas residents and communities, or the service can be a long-term project, such as overseeing a park or prairie restoration.

Service project involvement also ranges from a single Master Naturalist project developed and carried out by an individual to chapters or training classes developing and carrying out "signature projects" and working on them as a group. Whatever the project or number of people involved, all service is generally performed within the geographic area served by the Master Naturalist chapter in which volunteers were trained. Additionally, all projects must be pre-approved through each local chapter.

The nature and structure of the Texas Master Naturalist program are such that volunteer hours can be contributed to many different projects involving natural resource agencies, schools, local governments, private landowners, parks, and nature centers. No matter where members are volunteering, as long as the service is an approved project of their chapter, then they are always representing themselves as a Texas Master Naturalist volunteer. Many projects and volunteer opportunities already exist and are in need of people, but this should not stifle a member's creativity. There are many new and exciting ideas for projects still out there to be discovered.

Currently, a number of specific projects and areas of need exist in which volunteers may participate. The future, however, will undoubtedly bring many new and exciting projects. Following are some of the current and typical service projects that take place in almost every chapter across the state:

- development and maintenance of wildscapes and demonstration areas at parks, nature centers, and municipal areas
- construction and maintenance of interpretive nature trails
- stream bank, marsh, prairie, and rangeland restorations
- brush and exotic plant and wildlife control
- fish, wildlife, and plant inventories and surveys
- native plant seed collections and rescues
- outreach and education programs
- instructors or mentors for natural resource youth camps

Ray and Kris Kirkwood of the Mid-Coast Chapter working on a bird banding project.

- docents for nature centers and natural areas
- interpretive tour leaders
- serving on the local Master Naturalist chapter's committees or other leadership positions

What Are the Benefits of Being a Texas Master Naturalist?

Texas Master Naturalist volunteers receive many benefits from being involved in the program. Some of the most rewarding, as indicated by our volunteers, include

- helping to make a difference for Texas' natural resources both now and in the future
- having the opportunity to learn from experts in the field through Master Naturalist training and advanced training
- having the opportunity to provide important and valuable natural resource information to others
- gaining an appreciation for and understanding of natural environments and their management
- having the opportunity to build new friendships and working relationships with people sharing the same interests
- having the opportunity to earn individual awards and recognition offered by the state program

Mary Frances Anderson, an Alamo Area Chapter member, gets in the dirt on a habitat restoration project.

What Are the Responsibilities of a Texas Master Naturalist?

The title "Master Naturalist" and "Texas Master Naturalist" can be used only by individuals volunteering and active in the Texas Master Naturalist program. When an individual no longer actively participates in the program, the individual's designation as a Master Naturalist and/or Certified Master Naturalist becomes void.

The Texas Master Naturalist name, title, and certification should never be displayed as an endorsement, advertisement, or credentials; in a place of business; or identified with any particular political viewpoint and/or political advocacy. The Master Naturalist program is a public service program established to provide unbiased and scientifically based information and management practices. Therefore, the title can be used only when conducting unpaid, pre-approved Master Naturalist and Master Naturalist chapter approved volunteer service.

As a Master Naturalist member, each volunteer is a representative of the TPWD and the Texas A&M AgriLife Extension Service. With that in mind, volunteers should consult with and follow the recommended management practices of the TPWD and Texas A&M AgriLife Extension Service as the Texas Master Naturalist program's statewide sponsors. Master Naturalist volunteers should also recognize the autonomy of the various program partners when coordinating and implementing projects.

In addition, Master Naturalists should follow and respect the proper ethics, guidelines, laws, and responsibilities as they relate to collecting specimens, species permits, landownership, and landowner's rights when conducting volunteer projects.

Attaining and maintaining Master Naturalist Certification is each volunteer's personal responsibility. And an important part of that responsibility is record keeping.

Documenting their observations, research, training, service, and advanced training hours and the number of people or amount of the resources they were able to reach or affect can help to document and maintain their certification as well as track their success and growth as Master Naturalists—just as early historical Texas naturalists did. These data from Master Naturalist volunteers are very valuable to the TPWD and Texas A&M AgriLife Extension Service. Well-maintained, accurate records provide a written account of the ways the agencies and the program are serving the public and making an impact on our natural resources in Texas. These records also ensure the strong support of the program and its volunteers.

Master Naturalist volunteers make it possible for TPWD and Texas A&M AgriLife Extension Service employees to conserve and manage even more natural resources and natural areas and to reach even more people with natural resource programs. In short, Master Naturalist volunteers make these agencies more effective and efficient. As equally important, Master Naturalists also need to strive to manage their own programs by taking on coordinating, committee, and/or leadership opportunities within their local chapter.

However, all volunteers occupy their time and talents as Master Naturalist volunteers, they all have fun with it, and they know that the program sponsors and our resources are grateful for their time and dedication.

"When you change the way you look at things, the things you look at change."
—Wayne Dyer

Website Resources

Texas A&M AgriLife Extension Wildlife and Fisheries Unit: http://wildlife.tamu.edu/

Texas A&M Institute of Renewable Natural Resources: http://irnr.tamu.edu/

Texas Land Trends: http://texaslandtrends.org/

Texas Master Naturalist Program: http://txmn.org/

Texas Parks and Wildlife's Wildlife Diversity Program: http://www.tpwd.state.tx.us/huntwild/wild/wildlife_diversity/

Texas State Historical Association Texas Almanac: http://www.texasalmanac.com/

UNIT 1

Land Stewardship

JIM STANLEY
Texas Master Naturalist

Unit Goals

After completing this unit, volunteers should be able to

- define land stewardship
- discuss the role of private and public land management in conservation
- describe the five management tools outlined by the naturalist Aldo Leopold
- be encouraged to develop their own land ethics

What is a Land Steward?

In this unit you will learn about the ethical and moral aspects of land management, the importance to the landowner and to society as a whole that land be well managed, some of the problems a good land steward may encounter, and things he or she can do to help mitigate the problems.

Merriam-Webster's Collegiate Dictionary defines *stewardship* as "the careful and responsible management of something entrusted to one's care." Perhaps the best definition of **land stewardship** is contained in the Texas Master Naturalist mission statement: "beneficial management of natural resources and natural areas." Land management can be good or bad, but land stewardship implies good or "beneficial" management.

The idea of people taking care of the land is not a new one:

> In the primitive state of the country, the mountains and hills were covered with soil and there was an abundance of timber. The plains were full of rich earth, bearing an abundance of food for cattle. Moreover, the land reaped the benefit of the annual rainfall, having an abundant supply of water in all places; receiving the rainfall into herself and storing it up in the soil. The land let off the water into the hollows which it absorbed from the heights, providing everywhere abundant fountains and rivers. Such was the state of the country, which was cultivated by true husbandmen, who made husbandry their business, and had a soil the best in the world and abundance of water. (Plato, a description of ancient Greece, 400 BC)

One does not have to go back as far as Plato's time to find a philosopher and advocate for land stewardship. The voluminous writings of Aldo Leopold in the first half of the twentieth century are filled with discussions of the importance that the land be well managed, even though he seldom used the term "land stewardship."

Aldo Leopold (1887–1948) was trained as a forester but was much more—a naturalist, an expert on game management, a philosopher, and an advocate for the conservation of soil, forests, grasslands, and wildlife. He is best known for his book *A Sand County Almanac*, published in 1949, a year after his death. The lessons that Leopold most tried to teach were that (1) everything in nature is interconnected and interdependent and (2) every part is important to the health and survival of the whole. He emphasized that soil, water, plants, and animals, including humans, were part of the whole and that

Aldo Leopold sitting on rimrock with quiver and bow at Rio Galilean in Mexico, 1938. Courtesy of the Aldo Leopold Foundation

humankind has an ethical and moral obligation to treat this community with respect and to protect and conserve it as much as possible.

This was a hard sell to the population in Leopold's time, when the prevailing attitude toward the land was to use it, even abuse it, and when the land became worn out and unproductive, to simply move on to more unspoiled land. Even though we now live in a time when there are very little unspoiled areas left, it is still a hard sell to the great majority of people living in cities who feel unconnected to nature and the land.

Leopold wrote about the importance and the ethics of good land management, which formed what he called the "**land ethic**":

> "We abuse land because we regard it as a commodity belonging to us. When we see land as a community to which we belong, we may use it with love and respect. There is no other way for land to survive the impact of mechanized man. . . .
>
> That land is a community is the basic concept of ecology, but that land is to be loved and respected is an extension of ethics." (A. Leopold 1949, xviii)
>
> "A land ethic, then, reflects the existence of an ecological conscience, and this in turn reflects a conviction of individual responsibility for the health of the land. Health is the capacity of the land for self-renewal. Conservation is our effort to understand and preserve this capacity." (Ibid., 258)
>
> "There must be born in the public mind a certain fundamental respect for living things, and for the epic grandeur of the processes which created them. Society must see itself not as the terrestrial end-result of a completed evolution, but as the custodian of an incomplete one." (A. Leopold 1933b)
>
> "Conservation is a state of harmony between men and land. By land is meant all of the things on, over, or in the earth. Harmony with land is like harmony with a friend; you cannot cherish his right hand and chop off his left. That is to say you cannot love game and hate predators; you cannot conserve waters and waste the ranges; you cannot build the forest and mine the farm. The land is one organism." (L. Leopold 1993, 145–46)
>
> "Ecology tells us that no animal—not even man—can be regarded as independent of his environment. Plants, animals, men and soil are a community of interdependent parts, an organism." (A. Leopold 1934, 209)
>
> "We end, I think, at what might be called the standard paradox of the twentieth century: our tools are better than we are, and grow better than we do. They suffice to crack the atom, to command the tides. But they do not suffice for the oldest task in human history: to live on a piece of land without spoiling it." (A. Leopold 1938, 254)

Leopold was the first person to use the term "ethic" in the context of the way humans treat the land. When we think of ethics, or morality, or philosophy, we tend to think of what is right or wrong in terms of relationship between humans or with human society as a whole. Most people probably have some feeling of ethics or right and wrong in the way humans treat animals. And certainly the average American has an aversion to anything we might call cruelty to animals and probably considers such actions morally wrong.

But Leopold took the concept two steps further. First, he believed that there were ethically right and wrong actions in the way humans manage land, meaning not only the animals but the soils, water, and plants as well. Second, he believed humankind should be considered along with the other animals as being a part of the "land" or "community." He did not mean to imply that humans do not occupy a special place in the universe or even that their needs do not take priority over those of the other inhabitants. But he believed that people should consider themselves members of the total land community with which they have to coexist in harmony. I think this new philosophy is probably more easily accepted today than in Leopold's time, but that does not imply it is a universally accepted concept, far from it (Stanley 2014, 13–14).

We can all agree, I hope, that if you bring children into this world, you have a certain moral obligation to nurture and protect them for as long as necessary. Likewise, I would argue, if you adopt a puppy or a kitten, you have a similar obligation. I would further suggest that a somewhat similar obligation pertains to buying a piece of land. People and puppies have finite lifetimes, but the land lives on forever, so our actions with respect to the land have a longer-lasting effect than how we raise our kids or pets.

Being a good steward of the land should be as much a requirement of a good citizen as being a good parent. Regardless of what the laws and the books in the courthouse say, we do not really own the land; we are just the current tenants who are taking care of the place for a brief time before passing it on to the next generation. Common sense and common courtesy require that we leave the land in at least as good a condition as we found it.

Landownership in Texas

Larry White of Texas A&M AgriLife Extension Service at Texas A&M University (retired) put the idea somewhat differently:

> As a rancher/landowner you manage an entire ecosystem of interrelated factors and resources. . . . Your Land Ethics and Stewardship Goals determine what you select to do.
>
> Land Ethics is the moral philosophy, standards of conduct and moral judgment related to the land/natural resources/environment.
>
> Land Stewardship is assuming the responsibilities for the care and use of the land resource. (White ca. 2006)

Texans have a strong attitude that "it's my land, and I will do what I want to on it." As a consequence, we have few laws regulating what you can in fact do with your land. Zoning laws are very few in rural areas, as are most any other legal restrictions. Good land stewards, however, tend to concentrate as much on their landowner responsibilities as on their landowner rights.

About 95% of the land area in the state of Texas is privately owned. In spite of some great state parks and magnificent national parks, we have a smaller percentage of public land than most other states. The relevance of this fact is, simply, that if land is to be conserved and managed well, it will have to be done by private landowners. And given the lack of any rules or restrictions in this area, it will have to be done voluntarily. Thus, to use Larry White's terms, the land

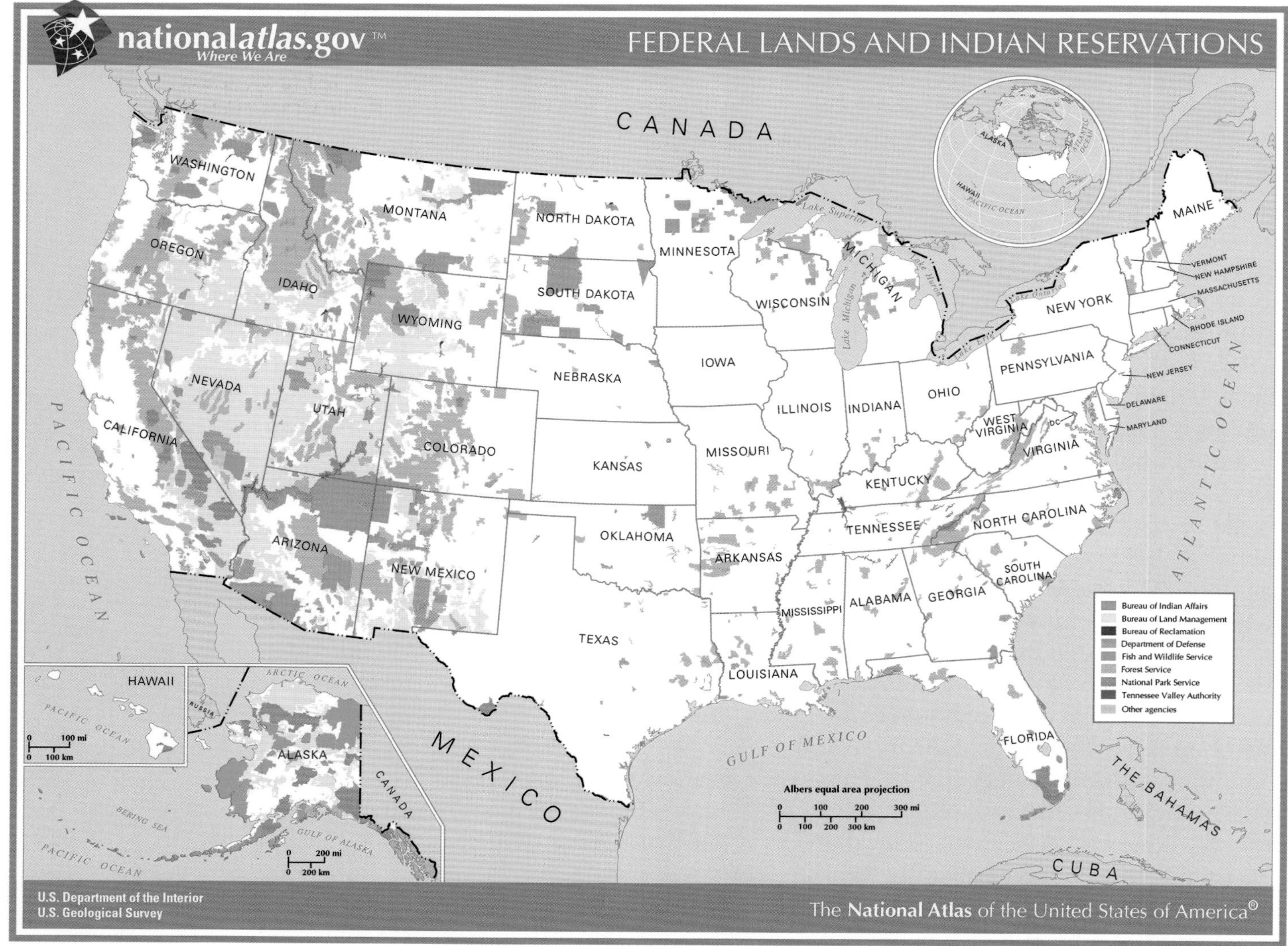

Maps showing federally owned and privately owned lands across the United States and in the state of Texas (facing page). Courtesy of the National Atlas of the USA

ethics and land stewardship of individual landowners are critical to keeping Texas looking like Texas.

Private Landowners

We proceed on the assumption that there is at least general agreement about the ethical responsibilities that apply to owning a piece of property and that we all want to "take care" of our land, to "manage it well," and to "leave it in better shape than we found it." But well-meaning people with the best of intentions can do damage if they do not know what are, in fact, good or poor land management practices. But before landowners can decide what actions constitute good land stewardship, they must first answer the question, What is our goal?

When asked that question, some intelligent, well-intentioned folks might answer that they want "nature to take its course." This sounds good; who could be against nature, after all? The problem is that this is not really a vision of what they want the land to look like but rather a laissez-faire management style that accepts whatever results. In many areas, what would result might not be what the landowner dreamed of at all.

Other folks might answer that they want the land to look like it did before Europeans began settling the area, that is, before about 1830. At first thought, this sounds like a great

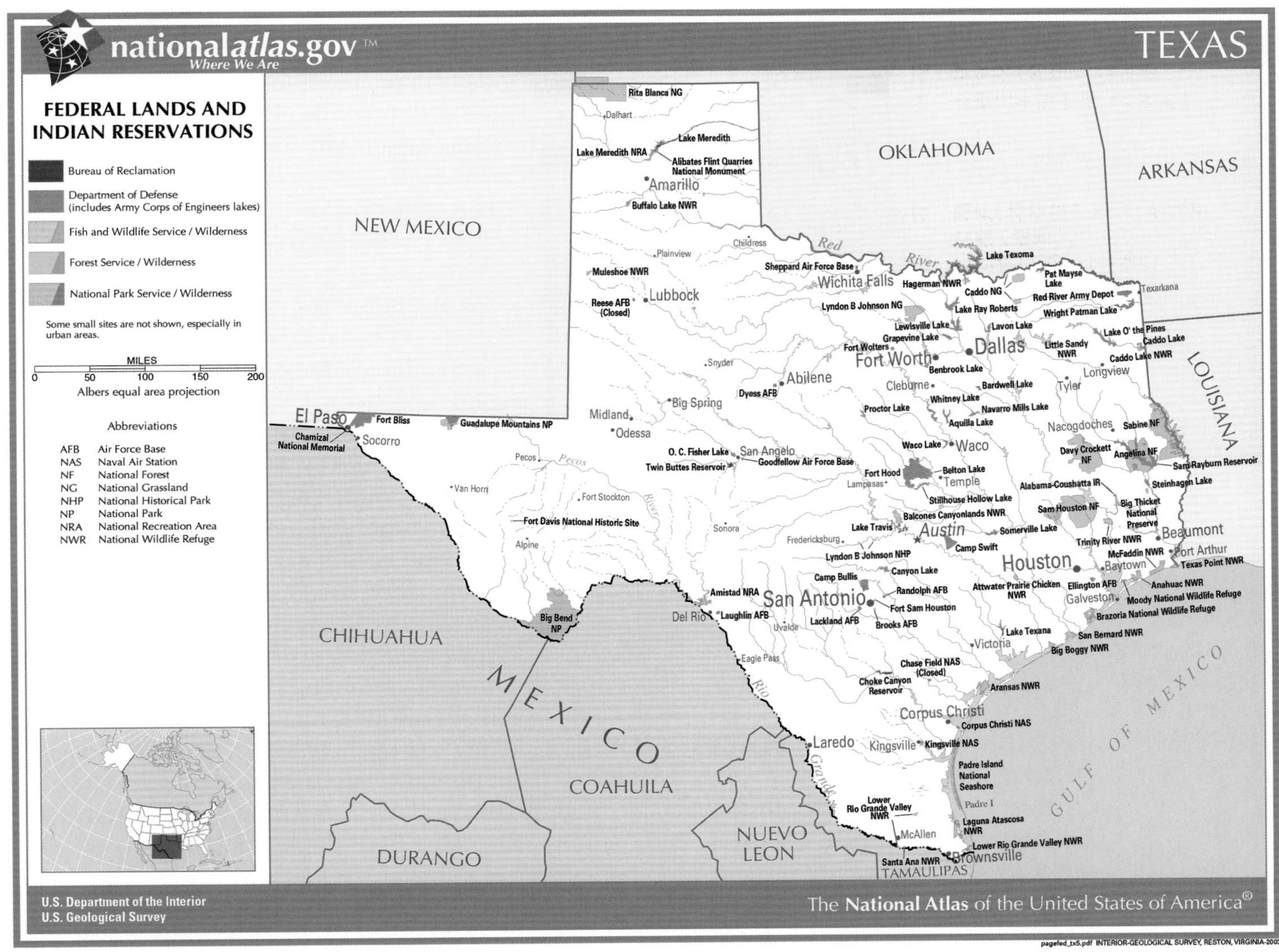

vision also. But to do that, we would have to stop farming and let the land revert to grassland, take down all the fences, and bring back huge herds of bison. We would also have to bring back the black bear, the wolf, and larger numbers of mountain lions. We would have to let wildfires burn themselves out. Clearly, that is not going to happen.

So what would describe an ideal landscape? Probably the best answer is to think about the land as a biologist would and invoke two of the most powerful concepts in biology and ecology: diversity and sustainability. **Diversity** has to do with variety, in terms of both numbers of plant and animal species and sizes and ages of the longer-lived species. **Sustainability** has to do with the ability of the ecosystem to continue long term in the current state. *Merriam-Webster's Collegiate Dictionary* defines *sustainable* in this context as "a method of harvesting or using a resource so that the resource is not depleted or permanently damaged." An ecosystem is sustainable if there is a balance in the numbers of each species so that consumers consume only as much as the land can produce or replace over the long term. No one species crowds out any others, no species becomes overpopulated, and none is eliminated.

You will notice that these definitions do not list which species should or should not be present or any specific stocking rate or crop, because there may be many different collections of species that will work in dif-

A fence line can separate habitat managers and land stewards. Courtesy of David K. Langford, *Hillingdon Ranch: Four Seasons, Six Generations*

ferent ecosystems throughout the state. No two pieces of property are exactly alike; no two will have exactly the same percentage of each species (Stanley 2009, 1–5).

• • • • • • • • • • • • • • • • • •

CHANGING TEXAS: PLACES, PEOPLE, AND PERSPECTIVES

Roel Lopez, Texas A&M Institute of Renewable Natural Resources

When thinking about management of Texas' natural resources, we often jump to the scenic or physical elements that make up the landscape, like rolling hills, flowing rivers, oak tree stands, or even the wildlife that inhabits these areas. Less obvious factors often not considered that can also greatly impact our natural resources include human population growth and the ensuing infrastructure, changes in ownership of rural lands, agriculture and timber industries, and changing landowners' perspectives.

Texas is facing unique challenges, never before encountered where human populations are not only growing but are expanding around and moving into urban areas. The tradition of passing down the family land is now being tested by the pressures of encroaching development, increasing land values, and even a generational shift of feelings of connectedness outdoors. Farming, ranching, and timber industries also are experiencing impacts of a changing society, as populations' needs rise and the rural land base shrinks. Understanding general land trends occurring now and projected into the future can ultimately help us make critical natural resource management decisions today, to hopefully have a positive impact on the Texas landscape for years to come. This section provides an overview of these changing Texas demographics.

Changing Places

Texas is a large state comprising 171 million acres, of which 142 million acres are private rural working lands. While the majority of Texas is 95% privately owned, statistics also

171 Million Acres...

5% PUBLIC vs

95% PRIVATE

17% DEVELOPED vs

83% RURAL

...142 Million Acres

Private Working Lands

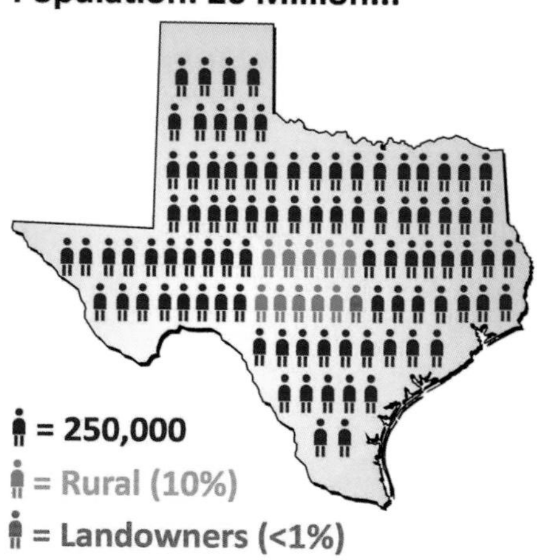

Present-day breakdown of Texas rural lands and population. Courtesy of Texas Land Trends, Texas A&M Institute of Renewable Natural Resources, 2014

highlight the fact that less than 1% of the population actually owns rural lands (i.e., farms, ranches, etc.). A growing number of small landowners in various parts of the state are neither farmers nor ranchers but own significant and growing amounts of rural natural areas. The concept of "land stewardship," when viewed from this perspective, begins to illustrate the significant and important role private landowners can play from a natural resource sustainability perspective.

Between 1980 and 2014, Texas has gained over 10 million new residents, resulting in urban sprawl around major city centers and increased needs for natural resources and their associated ecosystem services from neighboring rural communities. The majority of these population increases occur around Texas' major cities (e.g., Dallas, San Antonio). Surrounding rural lands, once productive, are subsequently engulfed by the expanding cities and converted from rural to urban areas.

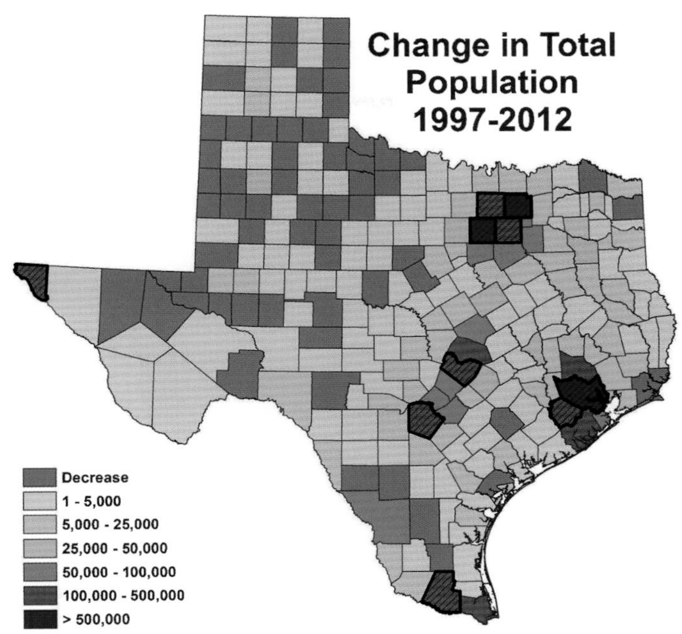

Texas population changes by county, 1997 to 2012. Courtesy of US Census and the Office of the Texas State Demographer

Changing People

Nearly 86% of all Texans live in urban centers or major cities in the state. This trend has continued to increase over the last several decades further dividing the connection of the general public to the value of private land stewardship. This trend will continue to be a challenge in the future management of natural resources.

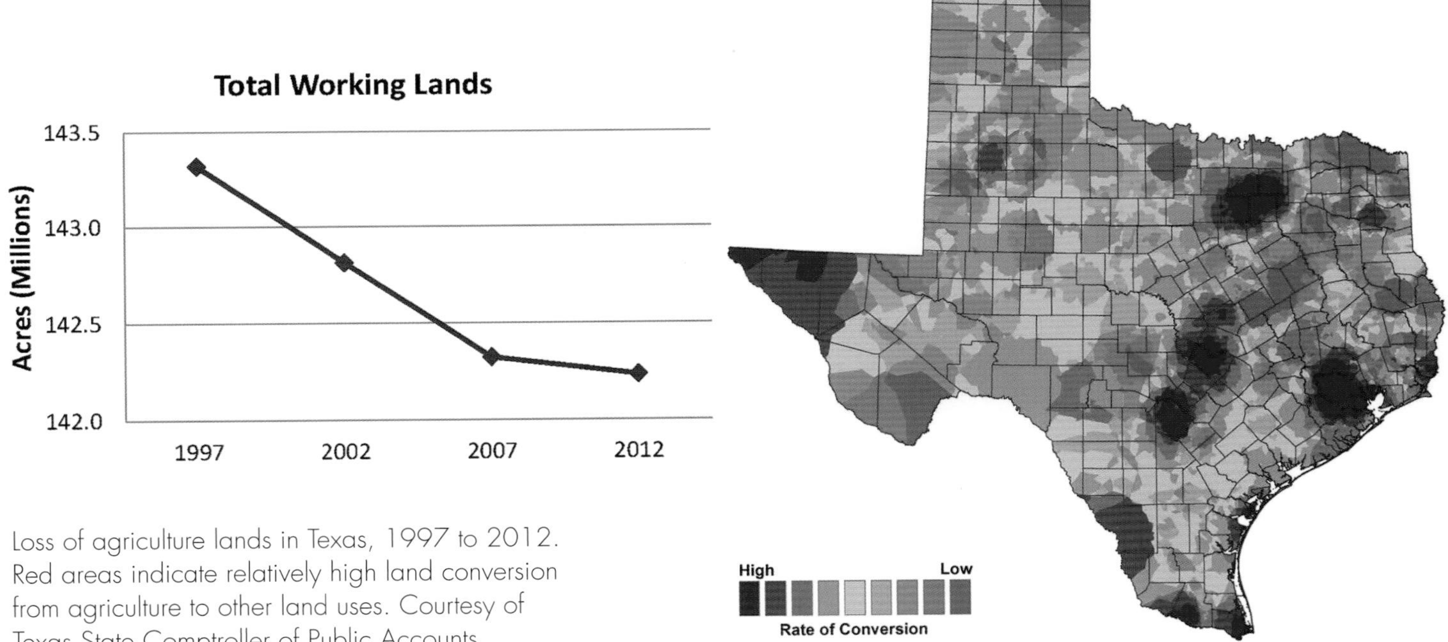

Loss of agriculture lands in Texas, 1997 to 2012. Red areas indicate relatively high land conversion from agriculture to other land uses. Courtesy of Texas State Comptroller of Public Accounts

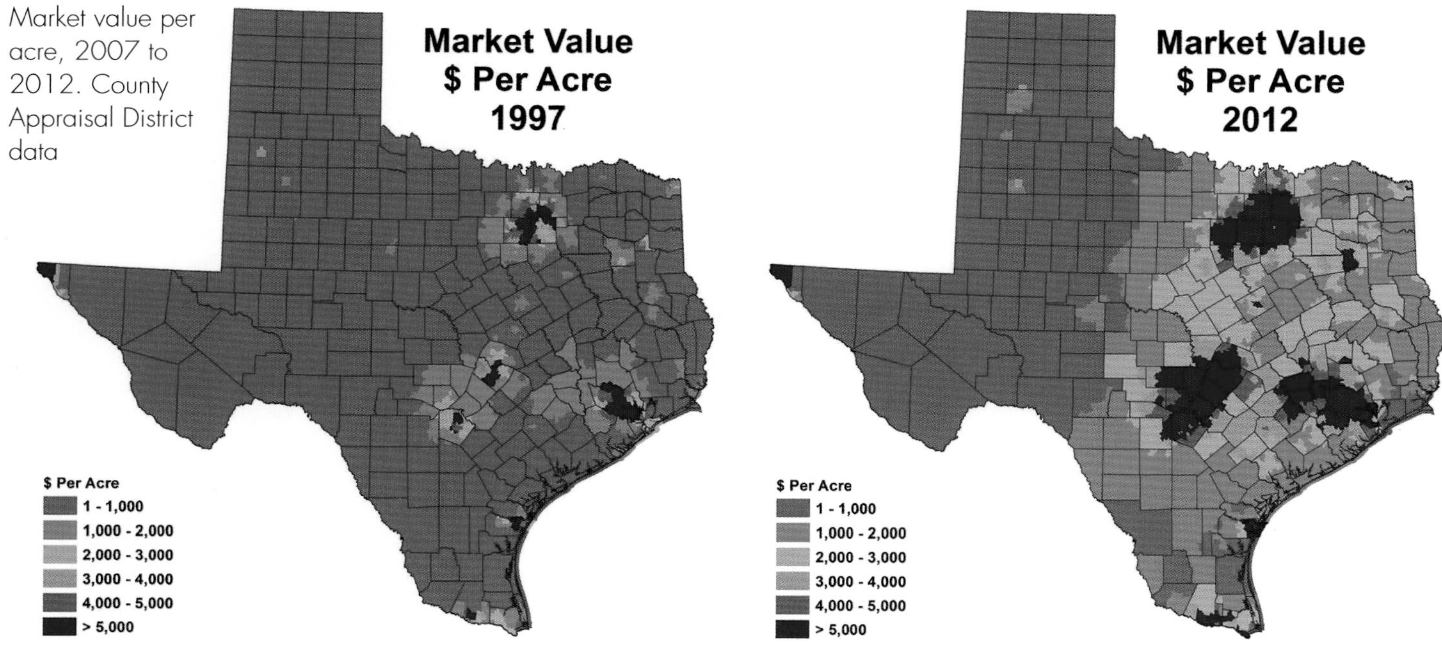

Market value per acre, 2007 to 2012. County Appraisal District data

Changing Perspectives

Private landowners in Texas have long contributed to our state's natural resources but in recent years have been faced with increased pressures to parcel out their lands while market value of land has increased, especially around the larger cities. Younger generations of landowners are opting out of their family legacy businesses (e.g., farming, ranching) in exchange for large monetary payouts. As these larger, privately owned properties are sold as smaller parcels of land, numerous issues arise that may affect not only the property itself but Texas' communities as well. Smaller properties traditionally have a much harder time supporting any sort of profitable agriculture business; thus, dividing the landscape into smaller sections limits the agriculture industry (from the reduction in businesses), which also limits supply in a time of ever-increasing demand.

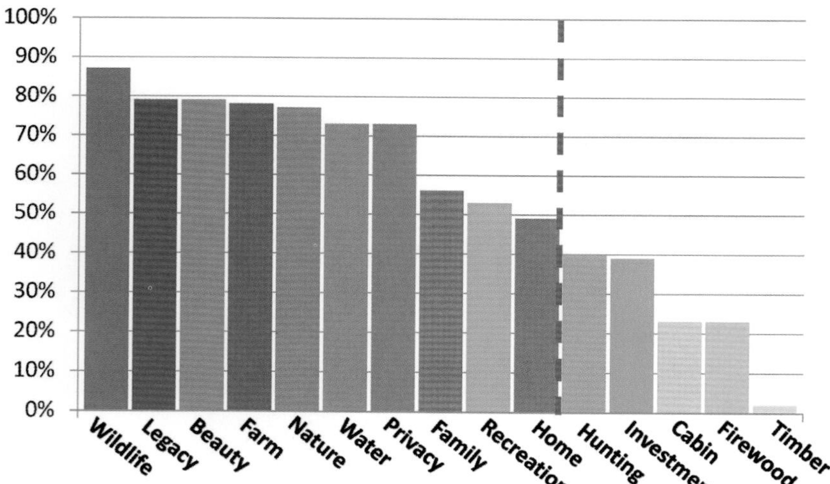

Reasons for owning land in East and West Texas. Courtesy of Texas Land Trends, Texas A&M Institute of Renewable Natural Resources, 2014

Land fragmentation can also indirectly affect wildlife habitat and ecosystem services. Approximately 41%–48% of rural landowners are now what is termed "absentee landowners," meaning they own property in rural areas but mainly reside in cities. These landowners use their properties primarily for recreational purposes with little to no intent to use the land for production reasons. This poses a challenge and will greatly affect how natural resources are managed across the state. In addition, landowner goals and objectives are also changing, moving to land uses that can be considered "nontraditional."

In the case of land stewardship, it is apparent that we will need to incorporate new tactics for natural resource management, as rural lands in Texas continue to fundamentally change. Integrating land trend topics into management discussions will benefit the decision-making process, promoting positive impacts on our natural resources as well as our state economy.

• • • • • • • • • • • • • • •

The Importance of Good Land Management to All Texans

The condition of the land in Texas is important for everyone, not just for the individual landowner. Range scientists rate the condition of rangeland as either healthy, at risk, or unhealthy/degraded. The same rating could be applied to all natural areas. While applying the term "health" to land may be a new concept for some readers, Leopold used the term often.

Healthy rangelands are worth more and can produce more livestock, thus potentially contributing more to the income of the landowner and to the general economy than unhealthy ones. For example, healthy habitats can produce healthier deer, which hunters will pay more to hunt, again a general economic advantage. Healthy land areas are the best at capturing rainwater and preventing erosion, providing more available clean water for all Texans and preventing pollution and silting of lakes and rivers. And finally, although intangible but not inconsequential, healthy natural areas are more beautiful than degraded landscapes.

For the landowner, land in good condition is better wildlife habitat, better grazing land, better able to withstand droughts and floods, less susceptible to plant and animal diseases, and generally more productive. Well-managed land is also more valuable, keeps or increases its value better over time, and will thus be more desirable to future owners. Well-managed land is less susceptible to erosion and more fertile, with good stands of native grasses that help maintain soil health. Healthy land has diverse native flora and fauna populations and is sustainable long term.

For society as a whole, well-managed land provides a greater quality and quantity of water, year-round, because of improved rainwater capture and infiltration. Well-managed land harbors greater diversity and density of native wildlife. Well-managed land produces a more aesthetically pleasing landscape, conserves greater diversity of native plants, and provides for a generally improved quality of life.

If nothing just described sounds like the typical suburban landscape with chinaberry and Chinese pistache trees, vitex shrubs, and St. Augustine lawns, there is a reason for that. That landscape is poor habitat for most all native wildlife and very far from most experts' ideas of what Texas looked like before Europeans arrived. People certainly have the right to manage their property as they see fit, but hopefully most people will learn as much as they can about their land and what practices would be most beneficial to the health, diversity, and sustainability of their property.

In summary, good land stewardship is accomplished by management practices that result in a healthier, more diverse, and sustainable native habitat. This is a big part of land stewardship, but others may concentrate on the ethical aspect and think of good land stewardship as the moral guiding principles that determine what management practices are conducted. Both views have the same goals and, we hope, arrive at the same end point.

Hopefully, this discussion has informed readers of the ethical aspects of owning land and convinced them of the importance that the land be well managed. The following sections discuss some of the common problems that landowners face and what actions good land stewards can use to help mitigate these problems.

Common Problems of Land Management

The following are some of the major issues or potential problems that Texas rural landowners may encounter:

- overgrazing, past and/or present
- overbrowsing
- brush encroachment
- erosion
- exotics, both plant and animal
- poor water catchment and management

Knowing how to improve the condition on the land requires first understanding what problems may exist on the land. Challenges will vary in number and complexity by ecoregion and property. Owning a piece of rural land inherently brings different problems than most people encounter in suburbia or cities. How landowners manage the problems matter for the following reasons:

- Land with good stands of native plants of many different species give rise to more fertile, healthy, porous soil that best allows rainfall to infiltrate into the ground to nourish plants and recharge water tables and aquifers rather than run off and cause erosion.

The leaves are beginning to fill out the trees on Skyline Ridge. Photo by David K. Langford, *Hillingdon Ranch: Four Seasons, Six Generations*

- Natural areas with diverse native species of trees, shrubs, and vines and without significant browse lines caused by excessive browsing animals make the best habitat for almost all native wildlife and ensure that young replacement plants survive to become mature, reproducing individuals.
- Encroachment of brush species, native or exotic, that crowds out other native vegetation and reduces the diversity of plants results in poorer wildlife habitat and grazing land than property without such encroachment.
- The loss of soil through wind or water erosion, usually beginning with bare ground because of poor vegetative cover, is a permanent, irreplaceable loss and degradation of the future health and productivity of the land. Erosion of riparian areas because of degradation of the streamside vegetation not only requires many years or decades to recover but may continue degrading as a result of poor upstream land management. A degraded creek on one landowner's property could cause problems for all landowners downstream.
- Exotic plants can become invasive, crowding out native riparian and upland plants, resulting in poorer habitat for native animals, and may require expensive, destructive work to remove them. Many exotic plants, especially lawn grasses, use much more water and fertilizers than natives and provide less wildlife habitat. Exotic animals compete with native wildlife and cause destruction to native vegetation. It is often said that the introduction of exotics is the second-greatest cause, worldwide, of species extinction. Habitat destruction is first.
- Allowing water carrying silt to run off the land, channelizing creeks to speed the flow of water, and using water for vanity lakes or other unimportant uses is a serious waste of a precious resource belonging to everyone.

Late afternoon's light and shadows enhance the view from the big hill in the Loma Chiva pasture. Courtesy of David K. Langford, *Hillingdon Ranch: Four Seasons, Six Generations*

Learning about these issues and understanding how they affect the property condition and management decisions are the obligation of every landowner, regardless of size or location of the property. It is especially important for landowners in natural areas to practice good land stewardship if we are to protect those lands from degradation and pass healthy habitats on to an ever-increasing new generation (Stanley 2014, 20–24). One yardstick that can be used to judge whether a property is well managed is how thoughtful is the landowner's consideration of the challenges just described and the management strategy employed to mitigate them.

Virtually all of the state has been overgrazed at some time in the past, and unless a range has been unusually well managed for a number of years, the effects of overgrazing can still be seen in terms of the composition and amount of native grasses and forbs found on the property. A good land steward will prevent overgrazing by controlling livestock and browsing wildlife numbers and the length of time and season the animals are allowed to graze any specific pasture. The total number of animal units should be kept below the carrying capacity of the range, and the animals should be rotated among several pastures to allow the grass time to recover between grazing events. This is essential to maintain a healthy, sustainable grassland.

While landowners are in control of the number of livestock and when and where they are allowed to graze, the same cannot necessarily be said for the number of exotic animals and deer on the property. Controlling exotics and white-tailed deer numbers can be especially difficult for small landowners. Deer and most all of the exotics can jump low fences, and most regularly roam over several hundred acres, so what is happening on the neighbor's property may well conflict with a landowner's efforts to control these animal numbers.

A good land steward will work to control the population of browsers, including domestics (sheep and goats), exotics (axis

An example of abused habitat found in the Texas Hill Country. Courtesy of Max Traweek, Texas Parks and Wildlife Department (retired)

and fallow deer, blackbuck antelope, etc.), and native white-tailed and mule deer. If the combination of these species becomes excessive in number, they will destroy the understory habitat by eating all palatable vegetation below the browse line. This results in a lack of habitat for many birds and small animals that use low-growing vegetation for both cover and food. If browser populations become excessive, the animals will exceed the carrying capacity. As a result they will be malnourished, and recruitment of plants, including hardwoods, will decline.

A good land steward will control the encroachment of unwanted brush to maintain healthy native habitats consisting of a variety of vegetative types, including shrubs and vines that frequently make up the majority of understory plants. However, if past management practices have allowed any one species to spread and invade the habitat to the exclusion of others, diversity is lost and the quality and health of the habitat are degraded. A good land steward will maintain a program of brush management to prevent excessive growth of any one species.

A good land steward will work to eradicate and/or prevent the incursion of exotic vegetation or the frequent visitation by exotic animals. Exotic species that outcompete and crowd out natives may cause significant disruption of the native habitat, and sometimes the damage is already done before the problem is discovered. Planting exotic grasses or other types of plants should be avoided.

A good land steward will maintain a healthy native grass cover to prevent erosion. The loss of soil is the worst and most permanent damage to the health of the land. Good grass cover serves to prevent the beginning of erosion by intercepting raindrops, slowing down any sheet flow across the land, and maintaining the soil porosity to allow for greater infiltration into the ground and thus less runoff. A good land steward will also prevent animal traffic from creating gullies and from destroying riparian areas.

What Would an Ideal Native Habitat Look Like?

Obviously, no single specific description of an ideal native habitat applies to all areas of the state, because Texas is composed of many different ecosystems. Here are some generalities that should be kept in mind and applied to your local area.

An ideal twenty-first-century native habitat would contain a diversity of healthy, sustainable native plants that have historically lived in the area, including natural populations of grasses, forbs, and woody plants. The land should, in most cases, be uncultivated and contain little bare ground and no browse line. The habitat would be home to (or at least occasionally frequented by) a collection of native animals from insects to reptiles to birds to small mammals and herbivores. The populations of the animals and plants should be sustainable long term. The ideal natural area would be free of any exotic plants or animals as well as pesticides and herbicides. If the habitat has riparian areas, these areas would contain a collection of different types and species of vegetation to maintain a healthy, functioning riparian system.

The specific plant and animal species, as well as their density, will vary according to the part of the state and the specific ecosystem of the property. Note that the previous description does not exclude livestock in sustainable numbers, nor does it include the reintroduction of extirpated species such as wolves or buffalo or the elimination of fences. Some accommodation to twenty-first-century practicality is required.

This ideal land description serves as a goal to keep in mind and to which consideration should be given in all management decisions. It does not mean it will be likely attained completely on most properties or that if your property is far from the ideal that you should be discouraged. Striving in the direction of goodness is more important than how far away the goal appears (Stanley 2014, 25–26).

Basic Land Management Principles

In theory, one starts with the belief that an ecosystem that has been completely untouched and unaffected by modern humans would represent the ideal collection of plants and animals for that area. It is assumed that this collection of plants and animals are what would "naturally" be growing or living on this spot if modern humans have not done something to prevent or change it.

All of the native organisms evolved to be in that place together, and, presuming no recent major change in the environment, have been doing so for a long time. This would be the ideal flora and fauna community and the perfect example of a healthy habitat for that given area. Looking back 200 years would give an ideal natural habitat for management to strive to achieve on the land. (However, this goal has its limits. No one would suggest cutting down native oak trees just because the habitat was a more open grassland in the early 1800s, or bringing back the bison and large carnivores.)

In Texas, we normally think about the time before substantial numbers of European settlers arrived (early 1800s) as our best model of what each of the areas in the state looked like before significant changes were caused by modern humans. Fortunately, this is also the beginning of the time when we have many records describing various areas of the state, written by numerous explorers and settlers.

It is, of course, true that American Indians had an impact on the landscape. They certainly traveled throughout the state, hunting animals and collecting native edible plants; some even did small-scale farming. They also impacted the land by starting fires, both intentionally and accidentally, which burned large areas periodically. These fires certainly affected the plant community composition, such as helping to maintain open grasslands in places where a more wooded community would have otherwise developed. But because of their smaller numbers and their lack of the tools Europeans had (horses, guns, plows), their effects on the landscape were relatively minor. So the American Indians had a much smaller impact on the landscape than the new European settlers, what we would call today a smaller footprint on the land.

If modern humans interact with such an ecosystem by removing or adding species or by altering the distribution of native species, then the functioning, health, and stability of the system are altered, as may be the food web and the carbon and hydrologic cycles. Human-made alterations usually take place over an extremely short time period, compared to the much slower pace of natural changes, such as climate change and evolution; therefore, the biosystems have more difficulty adapting to such changes.

It is unlikely that there are any places in

Texas today that completely fit the unaltered or unspoiled condition of the state in the early 1800s. So from a purely practical standpoint, we have to start with areas that we believe to be the *least* affected by humans, and using historical and archeological records and information from surrounding areas, try to put together a picture of what flora and fauna should naturally occur in any area.

We get a good idea of what an area might have originally looked like from individual properties today that have been well managed, long term, in ways we believe best mimic the early nineteenth-century conditions. What we know about the early nineteenth-century landscape is that, in general, except for the far eastern parts of the state and parts of the Panhandle and Trans-Pecos regions, there were somewhat more open grasslands or grassland savannas. In much of the state there would have been less woody cover (fewer trees per acre), including junipers, mesquite, and other shrubs. And, of course, none of the state would have been plowed. (Do not overinterpret this description to mean that Texas used to be a "sea of grass with no trees"—it has always had lots of trees.)

There would have been occasional bison herds migrating, periodically grazing much of the state but moving on to fresh ranges and not returning to any one spot for some months or years. This pattern would have allowed the grass time to recover from being grazed. We also know that there would have been occasional wildfires sweeping through many parts of the state; some scientists speculate fires burned many areas on an average of every 3 to 10 years. In addition to the bison, there would have been elk and pronghorn grazing the grasslands and deer in the wooded areas, along with wolves, bears, cougars, coyotes, and bobcats. There is evidence that these conditions persisted for thousands of years, indicating that this mixture of plants and animals, predators and prey, represented stable, healthy ecosystems (Stanley 2014, 43–47).

Riparian Area Management

Riparian areas require special management practices. A **riparian area** is defined as the creek area itself, as well as the creek banks and the floodplain above the banks. **Floodplains** include those areas that normally flood at least every two or three years, but not necessarily areas that are only very seldom flooded.

Because water is such an essential part of any habitat, and the land area alongside the creeks is a unique habitat all its own, the health of riparian areas is more important than any other parts of the landscape. It is also, however, the most sensitive and easily abused habitat and, unfortunately, the one most often abused. A healthy riparian area should perform the following functions:

- dissipate the energy of flowing water
- stabilize creek banks
- reduce erosion
- trap sediment
- store water
- sustain creek baseflow

In order for these functions to be performed, the riparian area must have certain characteristics: a collection of different vegetation types with different properties in sufficient density. For example, different kinds of vegetation that can grow in the water, to the water's edge, to areas farther up the floodplain are required. Vegetation that is good at colonizing and holding newly bare soil exposed by erosion or deposited as sediment is one type of desired vegetation. Another is a species able to hold the soil in place and stand up to floods so that the creek banks are stabilized. Single species of either type are never as beneficial as collections of several species.

When a riparian area is healthy, sufficient vegetation of the described types can help dissipate the energy produced during floods and stabilize the soils along the banks and throughout the floodplain, therefore reducing erosion. In addition, abundant vegetation traps sediment washing down from upstream, thus building up the banks and the floodplain. The resulting sediment being held in place by plant roots makes for a very porous soil referred to as the "riparian sponge," which becomes the shallow water table responsible in large measure for maintaining the baseflow of the creek.

Common vegetative species to be found along riparian areas are sedges, rushes, and grasses with extensive root systems, such as Emory sedge, spikerush, sawgrass, bushy bluestem, switchgrass, eastern gamagrass, and Lindheimer muhly. Forbs and shrubs such as American water-willow and buttonbush, and trees such as cypress, black willow, and sycamore add more stability.

Problems arise, however, when people or their livestock overuse a riparian area, thus removing the vegetation. Without the proper vegetation, the creek will be subject to extensive erosion in times of floods, washing away the creek banks and widening the creek bed, resulting in shallower, warmer water that is poor habitat for fish and other aquatic animals.

Ranchers need water for their livestock, so the easiest thing to do is to just let the animals have constant access to the creek, which means they not only drink but trample, graze, and defecate all along the creek bank. Once the vegetation is gone, the creek banks that formerly held water that fed the creek will be eroded away, and the creek baseflow will diminish. There are ways to prevent the animals from having access to the whole riparian area full-time. These methods require more fencing and other infrastructure that require more maintenance, but it is possible to raise livestock and not destroy the riparian vegetation.

Landowners without livestock also frequently degrade good riparian areas. Too often, landowners with creek-side property remove all vegetation except short grasses, which they mow frequently so they can see the water and have easy access to it. Short, lawn-type grasses are very poor at holding the soil and preventing erosion.

In the past, much of the mechanics of stream flow and riparian areas was not well understood, and many common management practices were actually detrimental. People frequently purposefully removed vegetation in the mistaken belief that if the vegetation were removed, the floodwaters could move along faster and thus cause less damage. In practice, however, more erosion takes place, flooding zones are increased, and the creek banks are washed away, large amounts of riparian sponge are lost, and flooding is passed along to downstream landowners. Attempting to "reshape" the creek banks with a bulldozer usually makes the situation much worse.

The general prescription for maintaining a healthy riparian area is to leave all native vegetation along the creek bank alone, to leave any large downed wood where it lies, to graze it only a few days a year, and to not mow anywhere close to the creek. The more native plants, from the smallest sedges to the largest trees, that one has, the healthier the riparian area and the better it can withstand floods without erosion and maintain a good baseflow (Stanley 2014, 116–19).

Wildlife Management

In the 1933 book *Game Management*, Aldo Leopold said, "The central thesis of game management is this: game can be restored by the *creative use* of the same tools that heretofore destroyed it—axe, plow, cow, fire and gun. . . . Management is their purposeful and continuing alignment" (vi).

Of course, we have a lot more tools available to us today than in Leopold's time. In place of the axe, we have chain saws, skid steer tractors with shears, and bulldozers and, from a functional standpoint, even herbicides. These can all be used to control excessive, unwanted brush, thus allowing for a better diversity of vegetation. On some

The five tools of land management according to Aldo Leopold.

A prescribed burn being done as a habitat management tool.

properties, brush "sculpting" can be done to make better habitat for a variety of species. In Leopold's time, much of the axe use was clearing land for farming, which destroyed much natural habitat for many species. When used properly, the axe can remedy some of the past destructive uses of the same tools.

The use of the plow in Leopold's time was detrimental to wildlife, as it was generally used to plow under native prairies and plant row crops that were less valuable to wildlife. Today, this same tool can be used to plant food plots for deer or stimulate growth of native plants.

Grazing can reduce tall grasses and generate bare ground from hoof traffic, which encourages the germination of forbs that provide food for many different species of animals and insects. Grazing a pasture can also reduce the likelihood of uncontrolled fire destroying the vegetation. Well-managed cattle grazing has little effect on deer habitat or food sources, so the two species are generally compatible. In Leopold's time fire was often considered detrimental because it was not well understood and thought to destroy wildlife habitats. Foresters burned the underbrush of a forest to prevent crown fires in commercial timberlands. Burning the underbrush also meant burning deer food, so the idea was controversial then, as it still is today to some extent.

Prescribed burning of areas under the right conditions, however, can be an inexpensive way to manage brush. This practice also stimulates some species to germinate while setting back the growth of brush, thus changing the species mix and creating a more diverse habitat, so it can be a very beneficial practice.

In Leopold's time, guns were used in two ways: to kill predators and thus provide for more game to hunt and to harvest game. Ideally, the goal for the use of guns should be to balance predator and prey numbers while assuring healthy habitats. However, in areas with excessive deer populations, hunting is not as effective as many would like.

Leopold understood that game could be

either protected or decimated by the use of the same tools (axe, plow, cow, fire, and gun). In fact, it is frequently not the tool that a landowner uses but how and when it is used that determines whether the outcome is beneficial or detrimental. There is a saying that "those who do not understand nature are destined to deplete it, but those who understand nature best are compelled to conserve it" (Nelle 2013). Understanding the problem and its causes is essential to good land stewardship, or as Leopold wrote, "The urge to comprehend must precede the urge to reform" (A. Leopold 1953, 60).

Hunting and Land Stewardship

Aldo Leopold was an avid hunter all of his life and spent much of his time in the effort to improve game numbers and hunting opportunities.

> I have congenital hunting fever and three sons. As little tots, they spent their time playing with my decoys and scouring vacant lots with wooden guns. I hope to leave them good health, an education, and possibly even a competence. But what are they going to do with these things if there are no more deer in the hills, and no more quail in the coverts? . . . no more piping of widgeons and chattering of teal as darkness covers the marshes; no more whistling of swift wings when the morning star pales in the east!" (L. Leopold 1993, 173)

While land stewardship is ultimately the responsibility of the landowner, nonlandowners such as hunters, birders, and nature photographers have indirect influence on the way land is managed as well. Currently in Texas, many ranchers derive a significant income from hunting leases, predominantly for deer and quail. Because hunters are willing to pay more for leases on properties that have the most or the best-quality game, landowners have an incentive to manage their land to achieve those goals. The best-quality bucks and numbers of quail can be achieved only on well-managed land. The result is that most ranchers now manage their land not only to provide better grazing for livestock but also to provide the best wildlife habitat. And part of that management, the management of deer populations and sex ratios, is largely accomplished for the landowner by the hunters themselves.

Leopold struggled much of his life trying to find a balance between too many deer and too few predators and the opposite situation, too many predators and too few deer. Today in most parts of Texas the big predators are largely gone or very few in numbers, so hunters are the last significant predators of the white-tailed deer. In many areas the numbers of deer taken by hunters is very much below that necessary to maintain the population at a healthy level.

This is not a recent problem, as evidenced by Leopold's words more than 50 years ago:

> I have lived to see state after state extirpate its wolves. I have watched the face of many a newly wolfless mountain, and seen the south-facing slopes wrinkle with

Red wolf (*Canis rufus*). From John James Audubon, *The Viviparous Quadrupeds of North America* (New York, 1945)

Aldo Leopold writing at Shack with dog Flick, ca. 1940. Courtesy of Aldo Leopold Foundation

> a maze of new deer trails. I have seen every edible bush and seedling browsed, first to anemic desuetude, and then to death. I have seen every edible tree defoliated to the height of a saddle horn. Such a mountain looks as if someone had given God a new pruning shears and forbidden Him all other exercise. In the end the starved bones of the hoped-for deer herd, dead of its own too-much, bleach with the bones of the dead sage, or molder under the high lined junipers.
>
> I now suspect that just as a deer herd lives in mortal fear of its wolves, so does the mountain live in mortal fear of its deer. And perhaps, with better cause, for while the buck pulled down by wolves can be replaced in two or three years, a range pulled down by too many deer may fail of replacement in as many decades. (A. Leopold 1949, 139–40)

And in recent years it is not just hunters that influence landowner's management decisions. Birders, nature photographers, and other groups of nature-oriented folks are also willing to pay money to spend time in a natural area to view wildlife. These people would not pay to visit an overgrazed, overbrowsed, brush-covered property, but they do pay to visit healthy native habitats. Leopold commented on this situation:

> The objective of the conservation program for non-game wildlife should be exactly parallel [to that of game management] to retain for the average citizen the opportunity to see, admire and enjoy, and the challenges to understand, the varied forms of birds and mammals indigenous to his state. It implies not only that these forms be kept in existence, but that the greatest possible variety of them exist in each community. (A. Leopold 1933a, 403–4)

Public Lands

As mentioned previously, since 95% of the land area in Texas is privately owned, it stands to reason that if good land steward-

Block Creek at dawn in the milk cow pasture. Courtesy of David K. Langford, *Hillingdon Ranch: Four Seasons, Six Generations*

Fall reflections on Chalet Creek, an image of a functioning riparian system. Courtesy of David K. Langford, *Hillingdon Ranch: Four Seasons, Six Generations*

ship is to be effective, it has to be practiced by private landowners. But that does not mean that public lands do not play a role in the beneficial management of native areas in Texas.

Good land stewardship is needed on public lands as well. Texas has 125 state parks, historic sites, and natural areas that total approximately 600,000 acres. In addition, there are 51 wildlife management areas with 756,000 acres owned or leased. National forests, national parks, and US Fish and Wildlife Service wildlife refuges make up another 2.25 million acres. Additionally, US Department of Defense land and municipal- and county-owned parkland total almost another 1 million acres. Thus, the total land area in public domain in Texas is about 4.5 million acres, or about 2.6% of the land area. With the exception of Department of Defense land, most all of the other public land is accessible to everyone, although some areas have restrictions on access.

Government lands provide about the only places where the average citizen can experience anything like a "natural area." State parks provide places for people to camp, hike, swim, boat, fish, hunt, and enjoy the outdoors. For many people, it is the only time they are actually in such a place. This fact alone more than justifies the existence of every park, forest, seashore, recreational area, refuge, and wildlife management area we currently have, as well as any other such areas that can be acquired in the future.

Leopold's view was that while private land being managed to help protect wildlife was essential for wildlife to survive, it was also important for society to have places where the average citizen could go to experience nature. He also understood that the only way that right—and he believed it was a right—could be assured was by having public lands available to all (Stanley 2014, 153–54).

In addition to state parks and state natural areas, many of the state wildlife management areas have been and continue to be laboratories for studies of various land management issues. These state facilities are great sources of examples of land stewardship. They serve as educational resources for private landowners as well as demonstration areas to illustrate new land management techniques applicable to local conditions.

Conclusion

It is hoped that Master Naturalists will now understand the importance of good land stewardship not only for the landowner but for society and future generations as well and be able to educate their friends and neighbors on the subject. The future of native habitats in Texas depends on it. All landowners need to develop their own "land ethic" and to learn which of Leopold's "tools" are available and how to use these tools to better manage their property.

References

Leopold, A. 1933a. *Game Management.* Dehradun, India: Natraj Publishers.

———. 1933b. The Social Consequences of Conservation. Unpublished manuscript.

———. 1934. The Arboretum and the University. *Parks and Recreation* 2 (3): 4–5.

———. 1938. Engineering and Conservation. Lecture at University of Wisconsin, April 11.

———. [1949] 1966. *A Sand County Almanac. With Essays on Conservation from Round River.* Reprint, New York: Ballantine Books, Oxford University Press.

———. 1953. Conservation. In *Readings in Wildlife Conservation,* edited by J. A. Bailey, W. Elder, and T. D. McKinney, 55–61. Washington, DC: The Wildlife Society, 1974.

Leopold, L. B., ed. 1993. *Round River: From the Journals of Aldo Leopold.* New York: Oxford University Press.

Nelle, S. 2013. Presentation to the Hill Country Chapter of the Texas Master Naturalist.

Stanley, J. P. 2009. *Hill Country Landowner's Guide.* College Station: Texas A&M University Press.

———. 2014. *A Beginner's Handbook for Rural Texas Landowners: How to Live in the Country without Spoiling It.* Denver, CO: Outskirts Press.

White, L. ca. 2006. Presentation to the Hill Country Chapter of the Texas Master Naturalist.

UNIT 2

Archaeology

HERBERT G. UECKER
Archeological Consultant

CHRIS LINTZ
Archeologist, Texas Parks and Wildlife Department

TODD MCMAKIN
Archeological Consultant

Unit Goals

After completing this unit, volunteers should be able to

- understand archeological concepts and methods
- become familiar with Texas cultural history
- become familiar with the Texas archeological regions
- become familiar with antiquities laws

"It's not what you find, it's what you find out."
—David Hurst Thomas, Curator of Anthropology, American Museum of Natural History

Introduction

As keen observers of nature, we understand that humans play an integral role in shaping the world around us. The Texas Master Naturalist program (TMN) not only trains volunteers to identify and help protect our natural resources; it also provides training to recognize and protect our cultural resources. Archaeology (also spelled archeology) helps us appreciate a shared cultural heritage as we work to protect a shared environment. In this unit we focus on studying humans as *part* of the natural environment.

From study of diet and subsistence to cultural history and environmental reconstruction, archeologists research the way people lived in the past and how they made their living on the landscape. What resources did these ancient peoples have to exploit for their basic needs: food, clothing, shelter, and security? Through public archaeology, professional and avocational archeologists will be invited to work with TMN chapters to offer opportunities for volunteers to assist in field or laboratory settings and/or to attend presentations, workshops, and site tours as part of TMN training.

Archaeology Defined

Archaeology is the scientific study of the material remains from past human cultures. The discipline as a science is only about 150 years old. In the United States, archaeology is a subdiscipline of anthropology—the study of humankind. Anthropologists also study sociocultural anthropology (the study of living cultures), biological/physical anthropology (the study of human evolution and biological diversity), and linguistics (the study of hu-

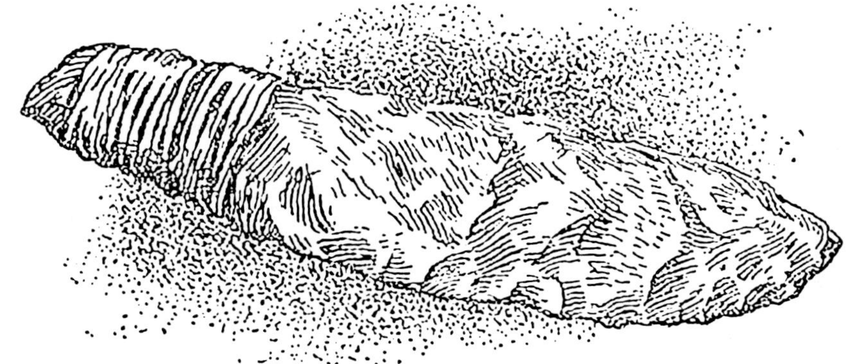

Artists depiction of an Early Historic Indian encampment of Coahuiltecan Indians in south Texas. Painting by Frank Weir, courtesy of texasbeyond history.net

man language). In contrast, archaeology in England and Canada is a distinct discipline not associated with anthropology.

For our purposes, **archaeologists** focus on peoples and cultures in **prehistory** (prehistoric, before written records) and the **historic** past. Multidisciplinary research approaches are used to study, collect, and analyze **material culture** (e.g., pottery, stone tools, animal bones, hearths, structures) to understand human lifeways; **noncultural materials** (e.g., geological, botanical, climatic) to shed light on past environments and human ecology. Archaeology is often lumped with **paleontology**, a subdiscipline of geology focusing on the history of the earth through the analysis of ancient plant and animal fossils such as those of dinosaurs. Paleontologists do *not* study morphologically modern humans but often contribute to archeological research by investigating environmental samples (e.g., fossil pollen) to help reconstruct diet or climate change.

French, Spanish, and American Indian artifacts from Fort St. Louis. Photo by Susan Dial, courtesy of texasbeyondhistory.net

Archeologists do not collect artifacts or dig sites just for the fun of it, nor do they sell artifacts. That would be treasure hunting. Cultural resources are protected by state and federal laws such as the National Historic Preservation Act of 1966, much like the legislation that protects our natural resources—land, water, soil, plants, and animals—such as the National Environmental Policy Act and Endangered Species Act.

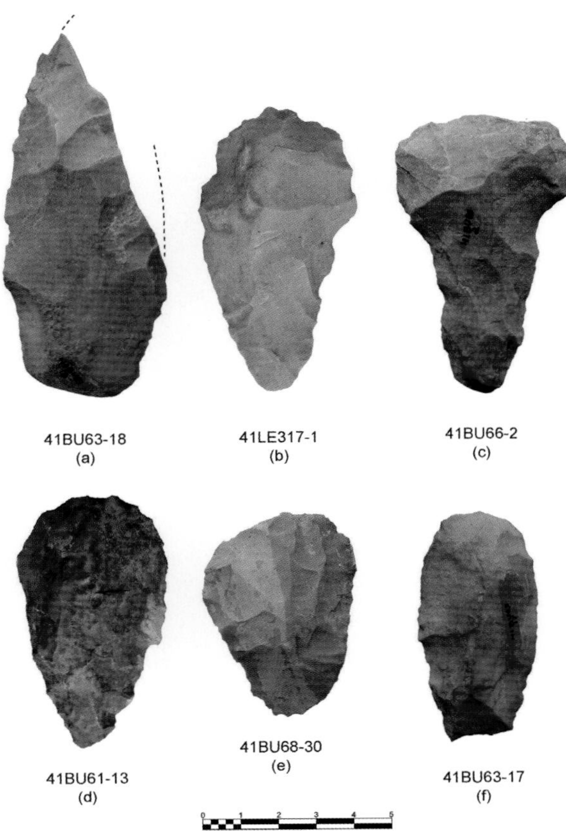

American Indian wood working tools. Photo by Alston Thoms

The Science of Archaeology

Archeologists use several methods and techniques to study the past, and the relevance of archaeology as a science is far reaching. The interrelationships between archaeology and other sciences like biology, chemistry, and geology is known as **archeometry**. **Remote sensing** using aerial photography, satellite imagery, or ground-penetrating radar is standard practice. Experimental or **ethnoarchaeology** is another approach to studying past human behaviors and processes. Good methodology balances science *and* a humanistic approach in archaeology, especially when dealing with descendant groups whose ancestors are the focus of inquiry.

Research Design

Archeologists start by formulating a set of research questions. To answer these questions, they develop a **research design**, laying out their methodology and strategy for data recovery. Permits will usually be required at the federal, state, and even local levels. Once all of the necessary permits are obtained, the fieldwork begins and may include a combination of survey, testing, and mitigation/excavation. Research designs outline project-specific research questions and lay out the methods that will be used to excavate and analyze the data. A thorough review of the existing literature and records about the project area and cultural history is done—aerial photographs, topographic maps, geological surveys, site reports, archival documents, and ethnographies are common sources to review. Other researchers and specialists who have knowledge of the history and area are also contacted. To assure that professional standards are met, the key players at this stage are the archeologist(s) (e.g., university-based or private consultant), state or federal agencies and/or private landowners that own or manage the land, and the state archeologist. A state antiquities permit is usually required to excavate on public lands. Federal- and state-permitted projects may also require government-to-government consultation with American Indian tribes or other noteworthy stakeholders during the project planning process.

Texas was home to several hundred groups of American Indians (alliances, bands, clans, confederations, families and tribes) such as Karankawa, Caddo, Apache, Comanche, Wichita, Coahuiltecan, Neches, and Tonkawa. Today, there are three Indian reservations in Texas:

Alabama-Coushatta Tribe of Texas, Livingston, Texas
Kickapoo Traditional Tribe of Texas, Eagle Pass, Texas
Ysleta del Sur Pueblo, El Paso, Texas

Archaeologists conducting a pedestrian survey and flagging artifacts (inset). Photos by Alston Thoms

Whether the archeologist is conducting a prehistoric or historic archeological investigation, the same basic archeological principles and techniques are used. One difference, however, is that historic-era investigations also rely on written or archival records. Indeed, the existence of books, journals, diaries, ledgers, maps, deeds, censuses, tax rolls, birth and death certificates, and church rosters can be a great advantage to inform and contextualize the historic archaeological record.

Survey and Testing

The research design may call for a **field survey**, **surface collection**, and/or **site testing** to be undertaken. For a survey, depending on the terrain and vegetative cover, the field crew will systematically walk over the entire survey area using evenly spaced transects (sections). Cut banks are often examined to understand the natural stratigraphy of the land and to determine how well preserved the archeological record is. Information is systematically recorded about the location and distribution of archeological materials and the general overlay of the landform. Shovel probes or strategically placed test pits may be dug to search for artifacts and any evidence of past human activity. A backhoe might also be used to dig trenches in key locations as another means to understand

Archaeological testing often includes digging shovel probes and screening the dirt to record and/or recover material culture. Photo by Alston Thoms

site stratigraphy. Sites determined to have limited potential will usually require little or no additional work. Potentially significant sites that might yield new findings may be partially or completely excavated to address the research design questions. Sites deemed to have important significance might also be left undisturbed, if at all possible.

Sites are officially recorded using TexSite, a site data recording program developed by the State of Texas to register archeological sites. The Texas Archeological Research Laboratory (TARL) (http://www.utexas.edu/cola/orgs/tarl/registering-sites-at-tarl/registering-sites-at-tarl.php) will assign a trinomial number when all of the required site information and documentation is complete. There is a fee for registering sites, except for site forms submitted by avocational or student archeologists or from pro bono research projects.

Trinomial Number

Site Number 41BX831
Texas (41)
Bexar County (BX)
Next number in line indicating this is the 831st site recorded in Bexar County (831)

Excavation

Most people are familiar with archeological **excavation**, which can be exciting as clues to the past are revealed. Vegetation is cleared from the site either mechanically or by hand. A **site grid** is laid out, and a **site datum** is established as a reference from which all measurements in the excavation block are taken. Archeologists set up the grid using a **transit** or **electronic distance measurer**, measuring tapes, stakes, and strings. Squares are measured in 1 or 2 m grids and staked off at each corner with the string. Each square is identified as a **unit** and is assigned a unique number identifying its location and grid coordinates. A site excavation map is either hand drawn on graph paper or, if using an electronic transit, generated using mapping software.

Using shovels, trowels, picks, and screens,

Excavation block with units laid out in meter squares; unit fill in the wheelbarrows will be screened and the contents systematically collected. Photo by Alston Thoms

researchers carefully record, map, draw, photograph, and/or collect all artifacts, ecofacts, features, and samples that were excavated from each unit. Everything that is going back to the laboratory carries **provenience** information: site number/name; content (e.g., all screened material, dart point, charcoal sample); spatial location within the grid system; level and depth (units are usually dug in 10 cm levels or by natural stratigraphy); date and excavator name; and any other information important for processing. Buckets of excavated dirt are shaken or washed through mesh screens, and everything left in the screen is collected for further sorting and analysis. Once excavation work is completed, the site is usually back-filled with the screened dirt and other fill.

Laboratory

Archaeologists spend more time in the laboratory analyzing artifacts and data than they do in the field. The kinds of analyses conducted will depend on project specific research questions and additional investigations as needed. **Archeological laboratories** can be set up in the field or are established in universities, museums, consulting firms, or governmental agencies. The preliminary stages of cleaning, cataloging, and preserving collected materials as well as processing collected samples are done in the lab. Field records (e.g., field notes, level forms, photo logs, data logs, analytical records) are downloaded, scanned, and/or entered into computer databases. Depending on the scope of the project and research design, various scientific analyses are carried out in controlled settings. Regardless of the scope and size of the lab, there will be policies and procedures established for handling the collections.

Field laboratory equipped with washing area and plenty of working and storage space. Photo by Patricia Clabaugh

Analysis and Interpretation

The relationship that artifacts have to each other and the circumstances in which they are recovered provide **archeological context**—the association of an artifact to other artifacts, features, or depositional units of sediments. All of the cultural and noncultural materials recorded or collected have a precisely defined location, documented *before* the material is removed from the location or context. When an artifact is removed from its original context without recording its precise location and other details, it usually has little or no scientific value. Contextual relationships can also be destroyed by erosion, natural disturbances such as animal burrows or tree tip ups, inadvertent ground disturbance from construction activities, or site looting and vandalism. The spatial relationship among artifacts and features in a disturbed site can never be restored.

Context is what allows archeologists to understand site dynamics. The very act of excavation destroys the contextual record, and only careful documentation (e.g., provenience, maps, plan and profile drawings, photographs, and field notes) allows archeologists to reconstruct and correctly interpret their findings. Following the scientific method, all recovered artifacts and site data are thoroughly analyzed before interpretations, conclusions, and recommendations are made.

Once all of the data are analyzed and interpreted, the results of the investigation are published in site reports, technical reports, monographs, books, and journals. Papers and poster sessions are often presented at professional meetings of organizations such as the Society for American Archaeology, Texas Archeological Society, and Council of Texas Archeologists to share findings and give details about archeological investigations. If an archaeological investigation is significant, popular summaries are also written and presentations are given to engage and educate the public, whose tax dollars are spent on much of the archaeology done in the United States today.

Curation

Archeological **curation** is the practice of "managing and preserving a collection according to professional museum and archival practices." This definition is from the US Department of the Interior's regulation Curation of Federally-Owned and Administered Archeological Collections (36 CFR 79.4[b]). The Texas equivalent is Texas Administrative Code, Title 13, Part 2, Chapter 29—Management and Care of Artifacts and Collections. These collections generally are from permitted archeological excavations and surveys on state, federal, or tribal lands or from public projects on private lands. At the end of the archeological excavation, the project collection (materials and records) is inventoried for transfer, in perpetuity, to a designated (certified) archeological repository. Most repositories will have curation guidelines for the archeologist to follow when preparing the collections for transfer. An agreement or contract to curate archeological collections will cover things like cost of curation, ownership, issues/details about the collection (e.g., types of materials, conservation assessments), and access and use.

Archeological Time

Chronology, or the sequencing of cultural and natural events, is fundamental to organizing and understanding the archeological record.

BC (Before Christ) and **AD** (Anno Domini, "the year of the Lord"); reference point is the birth of Christ.

CE (Current Era) and **BCE** (Before Current Era) are sometimes used in place of AD and BC as a way to express a date without referencing Christianity. The dates themselves are exactly the same dates expressed as AD or BC.

BP (Before Present) is the number of years before the present. Archeologists, by convention, use AD 1950 as a reference point.

Radiocarbon years or carbon-14 (^{14}C) years are used in a dating technique measuring the time required for radioactive ^{14}C in ancient organic material to have decayed to its present value relative to the carbon-12 (^{12}C) and carbon-13 (^{13}C) in the material. Ages are converted to calendar years BP (before 1950) to predate the atmospheric testing of the atom bomb, which significantly upset ^{12}C/^{14}C ratios after that time.

Calendar years are the 365 days that the earth orbits the sun.

"**ca.**" (or just "**c.**") stands for "circa" and means "about" or "approximately."

"**my**" or "**mya** stands for millions of years ago

Dating methods are either absolute (i.e., dendrochronology, carbon-14, archaeomagnetism) or relative (i.e., stratigraphy). Absolute dating relies on biological, chemical (radiometric), geological/electromagnetic sampling; relative dating relies on historical investigation to obtain the date range of a stratigraphic deposit.

Radiocarbon dating (also called carbon-14 [^{14}C] or carbon dating), measures the radioactive carbon content of organic materials. The age of any organic material can be calculated by measuring the ratio of

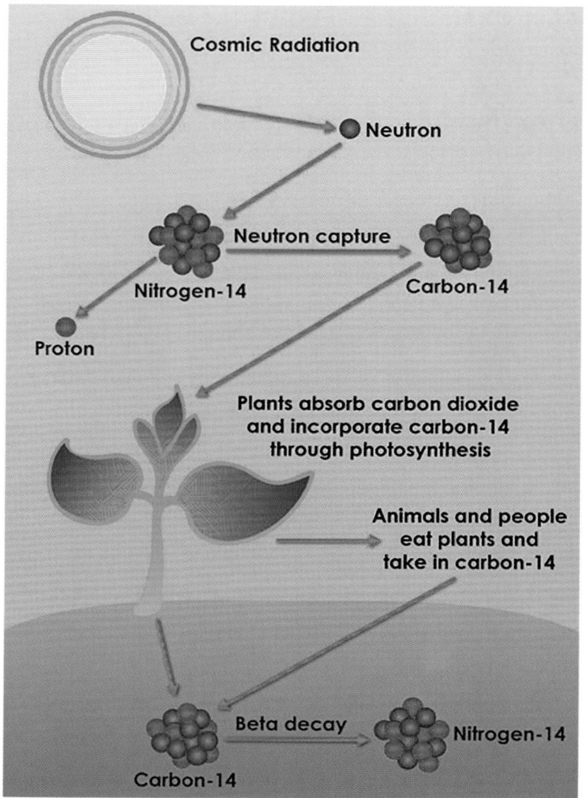

The earth's carbon cycle. Courtesy of Annenberg Learner

carbon-14 to carbon-12 (^{12}C). According to Beta Analytic, a professional radiocarbon dating laboratory, datable organic materials include "charcoal, wood, twigs, seeds, bones, shells, leather, peat, lake mud, soil, hair, pottery, pollen, wall paintings, corals, blood residues, fabrics, paper or parchment, resins, and water."

One radioactive form of carbon, carbon-14, is found within the bones and tissues of all living organisms in fairly uniform proportions relative to the amounts of the most common form of carbon, carbon-12. Because a living organism's tissues are constantly being reconstructed at the molecular level from materials taken into the body (e.g., air, food, water), this proportion is maintained at a fairly constant level within that organism as long as it is alive. When the organism dies and stops exchanging atoms and molecules with the surrounding environment, the proportion of carbon-12 to carbon-14 within that or-

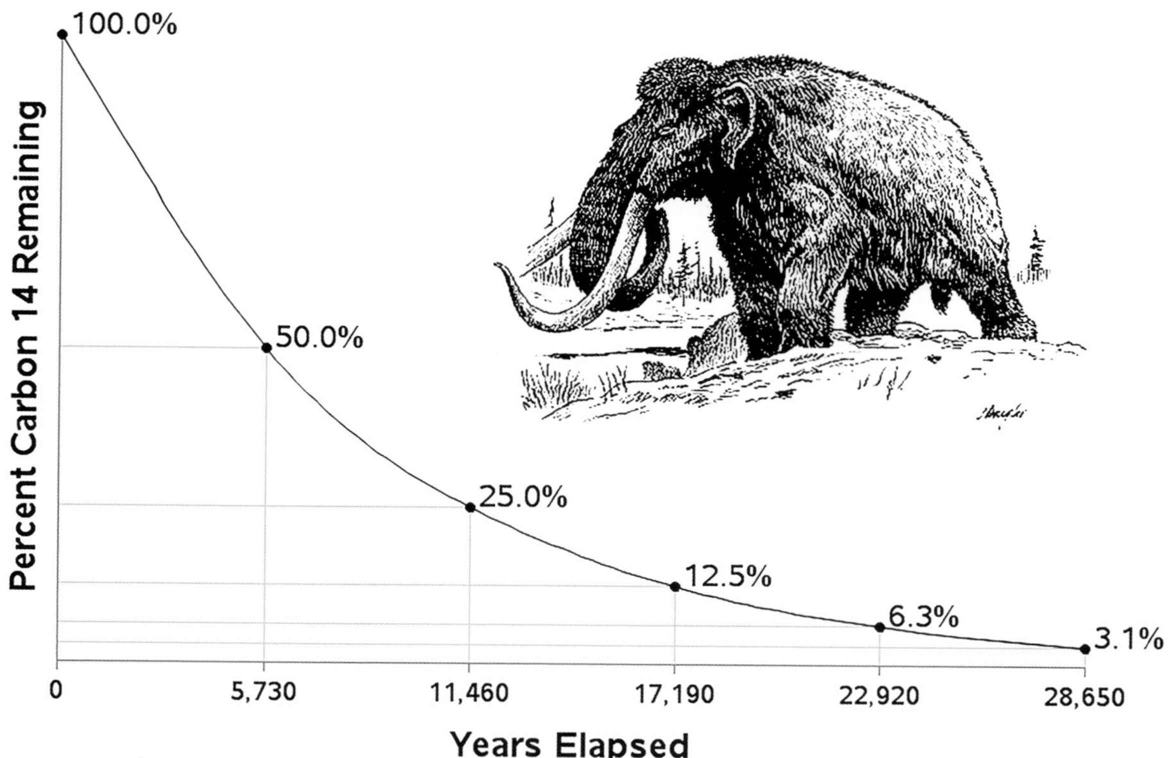

Rate of decay for carbon-14. Courtesy of Robert Allison

ganism's dead tissues begins to change at a constant rate that can be measured.

The rate of change is based on the radioactive half-life of carbon-14, which is approximately 5,730 years. This means that about 5,730 years after an organism dies, half of the original carbon-14 present in that organism at the time of death will have reverted or radioactively decayed into nitrogen-14. After the passage of about another 5,730 years, any remaining tissues of that organism will contain only one-fourth as much carbon-14 as when the organism died.

By measuring the proportions of carbon-14 to carbon-12 in a sample of animal or plant tissue, scientists can determine within a statistical range of a few percentage points when that animal or plant died in terms of years BP. About 50,000 years after the death of an organism, there is virtually no carbon-14 left in the tissues of that organism. Thus, the conventional carbon-14 method of radiometric dating that was initially developed in 1949 and widely used cannot accurately determine the death dates of organisms that died prior to about 40,000 to 50,000 years BP.

Accelerator mass spectrometric carbon-14 dating (AMS dating) is so precise that it has extended the early end of the range of accurate carbon-14 dating to about 100,000 BP. The AMS dating technique is becoming the preferred method of dating because a sample as small as 1 g can be dated accurately, whereas the conventional carbon-14 method requires a minimum of about 10 g or about one-fourth cup. The downside to this technique is that determining an AMS date costs two to three times that of a standard carbon-14 date.

Archaeology and Culture

Culture, in a very broad sense, is the means by which people adapt to their natural surroundings and to each other. Cultural learning is communicated through socially transmitted behaviors. A **cultural group** uses common rules and usually has common goals. As such, culture is both a set of guidelines for human behavior and the actual human behavior that results from the application of those guidelines (E. Hall 1977; Harris 1974; Peacock 1986). Information is conveyed from the various group elders and

Artists depiction of an Early Archaic Indian encampment in South Texas. Painting by Frank A. Weir, courtesy of texasbeyondhistory.net

leaders, family members, teachers, neighbors, friends, and acquaintances—society as a whole.

"Culture is communication, communication is culture."
—Anonymous

A **cultural stage** represents a technological level of development, but a **cultural period** is a time interval during which human groups in a particular area used a fundamental level of technology as a basic way of living. Related artifacts of a specific time or culture, especially from a single occupation or **component**, constitute an **assemblage**. Cultural innovations (new ideas or inventions) originate independently in many locations or may appear in only one location and the idea spreads or **diffuses** at variable rates across space and time.

Nonmaterial culture includes intangibles and abstractions such as thoughts, language, myths, cosmologies, ideologies, symbolism, religions, philosophies, and worldviews.

Culture Periods

The following discussion gives a brief outline of four main cultural periods. See also Perttula (2004), Turner and Hester (1993), Black (1989a, 1989b, 1989c), and Shafer (1986) for more site-specific discussions of these time periods.

- Paleoindian (12,000 to 8800 BP / 11,500–6500 BC)
- Archaic (8800 BP to 1250 BP / 6500 BC to AD 700)
- Late Prehistoric (1250 BP to 300 BP / AD 700–1700)
- Historic (after the arrival of the Spaniards in the 1500s)

Paleoindian

We know that people have been living in Texas for at least 12,000 years. In fact, there is some evidence that humans have been here for as long as 15,000 years or more (Waters and Jennings 2015). During the **Paleoindian** stage, small to moderate-sized extended family groups of about 15 to 25

Columbian Mammoth, *Mammuthus columbi*. Drawing by Robert Bruce Horsfall, courtesy of texasbeyondhistory.net

Paleoindian projectile point known as Clovis. Courtesy of the Center for the Study of First Americans

people traveled and camped together, collected wild plant foods, and hunted a wide range of game. These people are associated with the hunting of such large game animals as mammoths and mastodons, rarely camelids, and large, extinct forms of bison that lived during the last few thousand years of the **Pleistocene geological epoch**. The Pleistocene epoch is the latest in a series of ice ages that lasted from about 2 mya to 12,000 years ago. Several temporally sequential named cultures are recognized for this general stage of development, including Clovis, Folsom, Midland, and Plainview.

The archeological evidence gathered so far indicates that Late Pleistocene Texas hunter-gatherers had no permanent settlements, although recent discovery of rock pavements with square configurations in the marshy deposits at the Gault Site in northern Williamson County suggests that some form of temporary structures might have been erected. The Paleoindian people had no domesticated animals, with the possible exception of dogs. The tool assemblages of several different cultures attributed to the Paleoindian stage indicates that these peoples used large, shoulder-less stone points, often with ground stem edges and distinctive basal flutes or channels extending up each face. These points were often hafted to wooden or bone foreshafts that slotted into the ends of feathered darts, 1.2 to 1.8 m long, which were propelled by an **atlatl**, or throwing stick. The atlatl served to lengthen the thrower's forearm and allow the dart to be accurately thrown two times as far as one thrown without the use of the throwing stick. Other implements include a series of distinctive polyhedral cores, large bifacial cores, gravers and scrapers, bone foreshafts, bone needles, and bone awls. Flake debris from the manufacture and maintenance of points has been found to include distinctive flint types from quarry sources hundreds of miles apart, suggesting that most Paleoindian sites represent migrating groups ranging over great distances.

Very few Paleoindian sites have evidence of burned rocks, which suggests they had

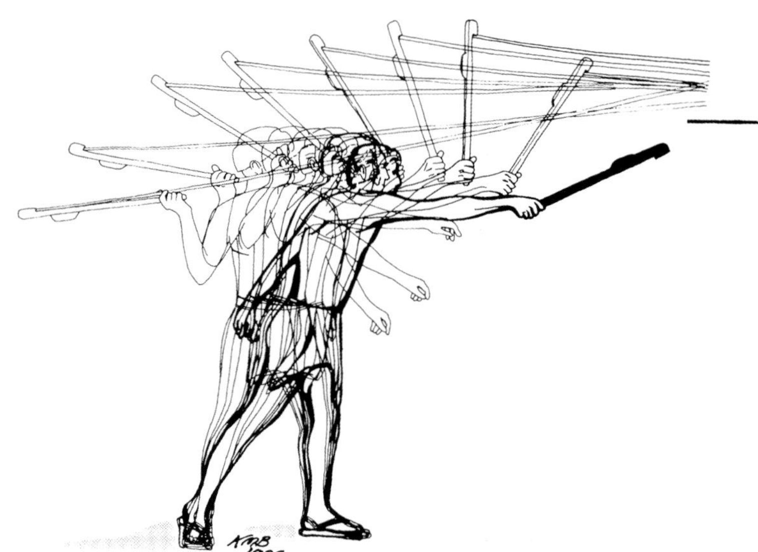

The hunter swings an atlatl, or spear-thrower, overhead. The atlatl has a hook at one end and a handle on the other end. The hook is angled so that when the arm is extended, the dart or spear is released and hurled forward to achieve great velocity. Drawing by Ken Brown, Texas Archaeological Research Laboratory

not yet developed a "hot-rock" cooking technology (Thoms 2009). These fire-cracked rocks would have been heated for baking in earth ovens, for griddle cooking, and for stone boiling. Recent investigations at the Gault Site in Central Texas are radically changing archeologist's thoughts about the Paleoindian adaptations; here, evidence of very dense remains suggests that groups were perhaps tethered to resources in this particular valley rather than far ranging, although a resident population has yet to be demonstrated.

Archaic

The **Archaic** stage in Texas corresponds to the onset of the modern **Holocene (recent) geological epoch**. The Archaic peoples continued to migrate in small family bands, searching for food, but were more confined to well-watered routes and areas than they had been previously. As populations increased during the period of the intense Altithermal drought, they developed what some archeologists have called the **broad-spectrum adaptation** in which all available types of edible plants and animals were consumed as an intensification of resource exploitation through the development of new technologies (Morgan 2015). To increase the digestibility of tubers and bulbs, they developed hot-rock cooking techniques, which eventually led to construction of large earth ovens resembling burned-rock mounds, sometimes measuring more than 1.8 m tall and more than 15.2 m in diameter (Thoms 2009). Another technological innovation involved the increased use of traps and snares for birds and small game. A ground-stone technology developed in which mortar holes with wooden or stone pestles, manos (hand stones), and metates (grinding slabs) were used for crushing seeds, pods, and wild grains.

The Archaic stage tool chest is marked by radically different kinds of dart-style projectile points distinguished by their large size. The points have corner or basal notches, resulting in multiple stemmed forms of stone projectile tips used with long spears/darts and atlatl throwing-stick devices. Other chipped-stone tools common to the Archaic stage in Texas are bifacial knives, scrapers, drills, gouges, and burins used for hunting and woodworking. Most Archaic peoples had a well-developed basketry and matting technology, resulting in lightweight, flexible products ideal for a mobile hunting-gathering lifestyle. They also developed ground-stone pipes, pendants, and in some areas such symbols of status differentiation as gorgets and exotic plumb-stones. So successful was the broad-spectrum adaptation that the sizes of the prehistoric groups increased, leading to increased competition with other Archaic groups for natural resources.

There is evidence of increasing **territorialism** among human groups in the Archaic stage, indicated by the presence of regional cemeteries; the placement and stashing of chert biface caches in areas with little chert

Excavation block exposing burned rock midden; note the black carbon-stained sediments in the soil. Courtesy of texasbeyondhistory.net

Early Archaic dart points from Hueco Tanks. Courtesy of Texas Parks and Wildlife Department

in order to "load the landscape" with this important stone-making material; intensification of settlements by the formation of semi-permanent and permanent structures; and the existence of widespread trade networks with neighboring and distant groups for such products as chert resources, marine shells, exotic items such as copper, and status items such as pipes.

In some parts of Texas the severe, prolonged droughts of the Altithermal may have eventually resulted in the concentration of many groups in certain restricted ecological **resource/refuge zones**, such as the Central Texas Hill Country, the Balcones Canyonlands, and the Sierra Madre of northern Mexico, while other zones, such as the South Texas Sand Sheet and the Southern High Plains, were probably only intermittently utilized.

"To archeologists, the human past is owned by no one. It represents the cultural heritage of everyone who has ever lived on Earth or will live on it in the future. Archaeology puts all human societies on an equal footing."
—Brian Fagan, British archeologist, 1996

Late Prehistoric

The **Late Prehistoric** stage is generally marked by the introduction of the bow and arrow and pottery technologies in many parts of Texas. These technological adoptions did not appear or spread simultaneously but were useful technological developments that appeared within a few hundred years of each other. In some places where game was no larger than white-tailed deer, the bow-and-arrow technology replaced the atlatl. But in other areas where bison or elk were abundant, the bow and arrow were used alongside atlatl dart hunting.

Because arrow shafts were smaller and lighter than atlatl dart shafts, there was a corresponding reduction in the size of stone

Deer were an important resource for prehistoric hunters and gatherers in Texas for much of the last 10,000 years. Courtesy of Texas Parks and Wildlife Department

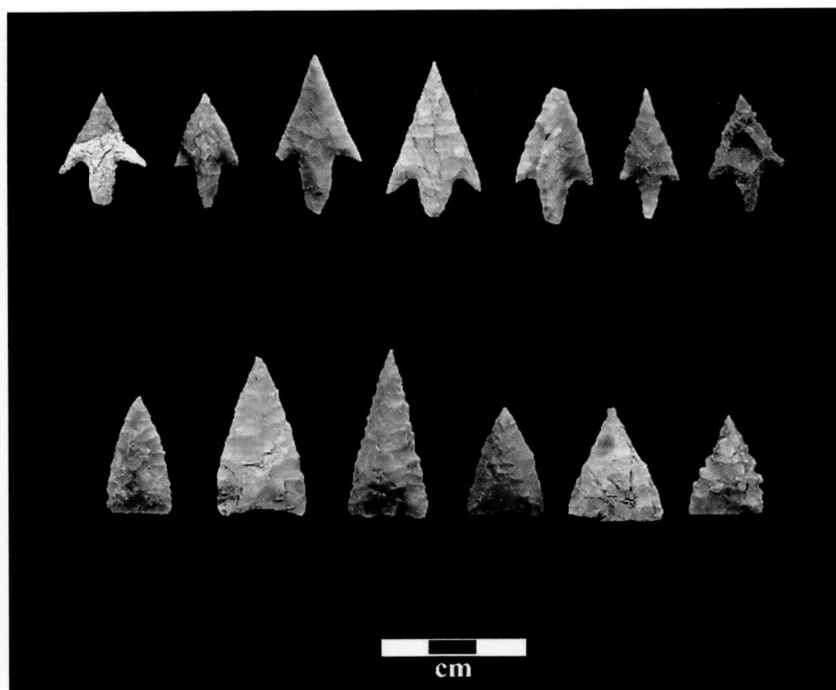

Late Prehistoric arrow points from the Texas coast. Photo by Robert Ricklis

projectile tips. Although much smaller than atlatl darts, arrow points can be just as effective at killing large game such as bison and elk. The small arrow stone tips are often referred to by collectors as "bird points," but they were effective at killing game of all sizes, including bison. However, the slow replacement of the atlatl/dart by bow and arrow may have been due to the time necessary for people who hunted disguised in skins of wolves or other nonthreatening animals to devise hunting strategies of stalking exceptionally large game.

Another significant change that marks the Late Prehistoric stage in some parts of Texas (mainly in the northeast, Panhandle, and far West Texas) involves the addition of horticultural practices. During the earliest part of the Late Prehistoric stage, the paleoenvironment was mesic or more favorable than the harsh drought conditions of the previous Altithermal. Throughout the latter part of the Archaic period, the groups residing in the northeastern woodlands and perhaps the tallgrass prairies of north-central Texas were growing domesticated forms of indigenous sunflowers, chenopodium, and marsh elder to obtain larger seeds than those of the wild varieties. But ca. AD 1100 these relatively locally domesticated species were supplemented, complemented, and eventually replaced by corn, beans, and squash that spread from western Mexico and the southwestern United States across northern Texas and into the northeastern United States.

American buffalo, Bison bison family. Drawing by Hal Story, courtesy of Texas Beyond History, Texas Archeological Research Laboratory

In many places horticulture provided a slight, relatively predicable edge for dependable food availability over the mere gathering of wild foods and grains, which allowed for increased sedentary lifestyles; the formation of semi-permanent homesteads, hamlets, and villages; and in some years, food surpluses. The sedentary existence and food surplus led to an increase in population, giving rise to the organization and development of chiefdoms and leaders who managed societies.

The four areas of Texas with Late Prehistoric semi-permanent horticulturalists were the eastern woodlands (Caddo Area), north-central Texas and the Texas Panhandle (adaptations to the tall- and short-grass prairies of the Plains Village Area), and far West Texas near El Paso (Mogollon Area). Settlements, pottery, and community organizations in each area were distinctively different. But in Central Texas and the Gulf Coastal and Rio Grande Plains areas, the nomadic hunter-gatherer lifestyles of the Archaic stage persisted, with the addition of the bow and arrow and sometimes, pottery, until Euro-American contact in the fifteenth century. The horticultural technology was often rather simple in southwestern and northeastern Texas; gardens and some fields were cleared, and simple dibble sticks and occasionally stone hoes were used for planting and weeding. In the upper Texas Panhandle and north-central Texas, where the roots of prairie grasses grew densely and held the soil, the horticulturalists developed a farming technology using bison tibias (lower leg bones) as digging-stick tips and perhaps bison scapulas (shoulder blades) as hoes. Undoubtedly the semi-sedentary lifestyle of horticulturalists led to the rise of a more specialized range of tool forms.

The chipped-stone tools of the Late Prehistoric stage consist of the smaller arrow points; moderately small end and side scrapers; drills in many forms; and in areas with bison, an ovate knife, which takes on a distinctive diamond shape during alternate edge resharpening. The Archaic ground-stone manos and metates used for seed grinding persisted and became more efficient by increasing the size of the mano grinding surfaces. The bone tools included awls for making baskets and deer hide clothing, bone shaft wrenches for straightening arrow shafts, bone rasps, and in some horticultural areas the bison tibia digging-stick tips and scapula hoes. Freshwater mussel shells were used as scrapers, as a means to shell corn kernels from cobs, and as pendants and inlays.

Wooden digging stick found in a dry cave in the Lower Pecos. Courtesy of Harry Shafer

Most of the horticultural Late Prehistoric groups also had fairly well-developed trade relations with distant groups from whom they received marine shell jewelry, painted pottery, turquoise, and other exotic items. Some of these nonlocal trade items might have served as token trade gifts to cement relationships with distant groups, especially after AD 1200 when intense droughts rendered local horticulture less predictable.

Pottery was generally adopted by both horticulturalists and hunting-gathering groups during the Late Prehistoric in most parts of Texas, except perhaps the Lower Pecos and South Texas regions. The delineation of Texas culture areas, as discussed here, is largely based on significant differences in ceramic technology. There are four main ways of forming pots: (1) freehand modeling vessel forms from lumps of clay; (2) building coiled vessels that are bonded

Decorated pottery sherds from East Texas. Photos by Timothy K. Perttula

by mashing coils together with a cord-wrapped paddle and anvil; (3) bonding clay coils with finger pressure, then smoothing and thinning the surfaces with wooden or gourd scrapers; or (4) making sheets of clay bonded along the edges. Utilitarian pottery vessels were often decorated using methods ranging from painting with pigments or asphalts, incising (wet clay scratches) and engraving (dry clay scratches), to modeled nodes, fillets, appliqués, or even the addition of effigy heads of animals or people.

Historic

The **Historic stage** refers to the period of cultural modifications of indigenous peoples by contact with Euro-American groups. Euro-Americans introduced many kinds of domesticated animals (horses, cattle, oxen mules, sheep, and goats), new technologies involving metal utilitarian implements (knives, files, chisels, guns, etc.), hardware (nails, etc.), and raw materials (barrel hoops, wagon and cart wheel rims, etc.), as well as glass, majolica-glazed pottery, and dyed fabrics. In areas where sufficient stable indigenous populations existed, such as along the Rio Grande in far West Texas, in far eastern Texas and Louisiana, and along major river crossings of the Camino Real (King's Highway) near the Balcones Escarpment, the Spaniards established a series of missions and presidios to pacify and convert the indigenous peoples.

Many indigenous hunter-gatherer groups were drawn to the missions to access Euro-American goods and to take advantage of the food redistribution systems established by the missions. Many of these named groups were listed in the various mission birth, death, baptism, and marriage records; however, some hunter-gatherer groups may have chosen to avoid the mission systems and remain unknown to the history of Texas. Euro-American contact brought exposure to new diseases that decimated indigenous populations and disrupted social organization. In addition, indigenous groups residing in and near established Euro-American settlements were subject to laws and religious teachings that disrupted local belief systems. Euro-Americans also condoned slave raiding of indigenous groups in Texas to obtain labor forces to work the silver mines of western Mexico. Furthermore, indigenous peoples were sometimes used as pawns in group interactions by societies aligned with French, Spanish, or American policies, military conflicts, and political disputes occurring among Euro-American empires. The social disruptions were so severe among declining populations that many groups with similar social systems could no longer effectively function and were forced to coalesce into confederacies to maintain their cultures.

Diorama showing Texas mission Indians. Courtesy of Texas Parks and Wildlife Department

The introduction of the horse by the Spanish dramatically changed transport and economics for Indian people. Painting by Nola Davis, Texas Parks and Wildlife Department

The capture and exchange of wild Spanish horses and other domesticated draft animals and the value of metal goods that proved to be more durable than stone implements attracted many non-mission groups to the Southern Plains from the Midwest, northeastern Plains, northwestern Plains, and the Great Basin. Some of these groups, such as the Athabascan-speaking Apache and Navajo from Canada, were already on their way south and arrived in northern Texas about the same time as the Spaniards around AD 1500. Others, such as the Comanche, arrived in Texas from the north during the early 1700s. Many of these people adopted an equestrian nomadic lifestyle, characteristic of the stereotypic image of the tepee-dwelling, bison-hunting, Plains Indians. As recent arrivals to the Southern Plains, they raided Euro-American and indigenous mission settlements across Texas.

The influx of the Euro-American trappers and settlers, along with numerous indigenous peoples from the north and west who were fleeing slave raid capture or were drawn to livestock wealth during the period when indigenous American Indian populations were in decline from diseases, raiding, and warfare, was creating considerable turmoil across the region. Following the Texas Revolution to gain its independence from Mexico (1835–36), and in response to the Apache and Comanche raiders seeking horses and food, President Mirabeau B. Lamar of the Republic of Texas instituted an Indian extermination policy against the non-missionized Indian groups. The republic also solicited foreigners and awarded land grants for colonies to settle north of the Spanish missions to serve as buffer settlements against Indian attacks.

Some parts of Texas, such as the Panhandle and Trans-Pecos regions, were under the control of equestrian Indians and were too hostile to attempt European settlement. The chaos persisted throughout the Mexican-American War (1846–48) and American Civil War (1861–65) and culminated in the Red River War (1874–75) in the Texas Panhandle. One military strategy used to subdue the equestrian nomads in the Texas Panhandle involved a program of horse and bison exterminating (the main Plains Indian food source). Following the termination of these hostilities, much of Texas was opened for settlement by cattlemen, sheepherders, and farmers. Steamships and railroads provided economic access to markets to encourage town sites and settlements. Historic archeologists have excavated a number of mission and non-mission sites and have contributed important information about the interactions of these diverse groups during the settlement of Texas (D. Fox 1983).

Culture History

The culture areas of Texas during the last few thousand years are distinguished by different artifact assemblages sometimes influenced by extensions of adjacent culture areas adapting to local ecoregions. The Texas culture areas reflect some stability, but the boundaries are not fixed or permanent through time due to climatic and technological changes that may cross-cut ecoregions. For example, the earliest recognized Paleoindian cultures in Texas tend to cross-cut regional distributions, as evidenced by their use of distinctive fluted points that demonstrated wide-ranging movements in sparsely occupied regions.

The timeframe for the first peopling of the New World is a subject of intense study. Until recently, most archeologists held that the earliest culture in North America was the Clovis culture from the Paleoindian period (about 11,200 BP) based on the widespread occurrence of distinctive large stone points. And many archeologists accept that the prehistoric era ended with the arrival of Columbus ca. AD 1492 in some parts the Americas, the beginning of the period after written records were produced. The subsequent interval when written descriptions and narratives are available to supplement the archeological materials is the historic era (generally AD 1492 to the present). In reality, however, written historical records by the earliest explorers were intermittent, often sparse to nonexistent for intervals between exploration expeditions, and occasionally provided biased observations depending on the intent and interests of the Crown/church/military/trading companies who financed the expedition. Realistically, the beginning of the historic era is a sliding date from one region to another depending on the frequency of visitation and the establishment and maintenance of copious records from sustained settlement.

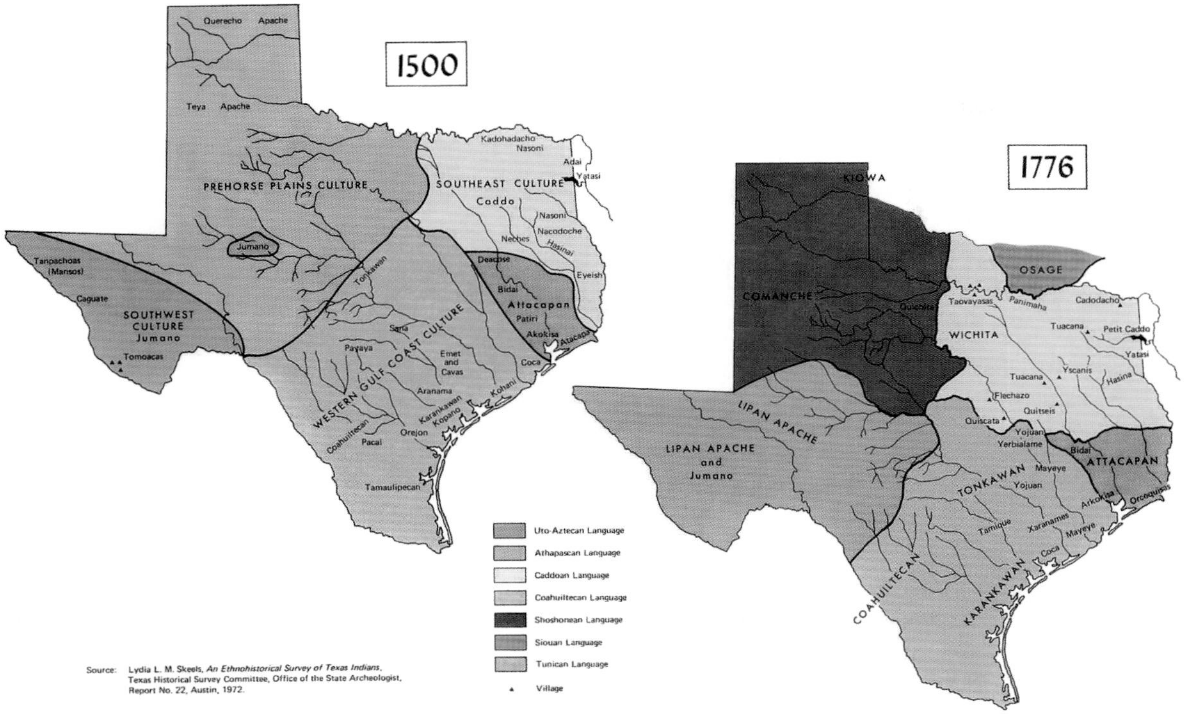

Source: Lydia L. M. Skeels, *An Ethnohistorical Survey of Texas Indians*, Texas Historical Survey Committee, Office of the State Archeologist, Report No. 22, Austin, 1972.

Approximate distribution of Indian groups in Texas, circa 1500 and 1776. From the Atlas of Texas, The University of Texas at Austin, 1976.

By careful systematic investigation during much of the twentieth century at literally thousands of prehistoric Indian sites, Spanish Colonial period sites, and later historic sites, archeologists have learned a great deal about the culture history of our state: the tool manufacturing and other production techniques of many prehistoric cultures, the distribution of cultures and the interaction and response of people within their environments, and the nature of interaction and exchange among diverse cultural groups. In many cases, archeologists have been able to separate fact from fiction about historic events. Archeologists have not just dug in the ground to discover these things. They have studied the journals and writings of the earliest Europeans in the New World; they have studied the public records stored in courthouses, title companies, archives, and libraries; and for purposes of making comparisons or replications, they have conducted oral interviews with indigenous peoples and studied the activities of living cultures today (Bousman et al. 1995; D. Fox 1983).

"Treat the Earth well. It was not given to you by your parents. It was loaned to you by your children."
—Kenyan proverb

Because of the dedication of several generations of Texas archeologists, we have a much better picture of our state's past. We distinguish four principal **stages** (general technology and settlement/subsistence strategies) or **periods** (time interval when the stage persisted) in Texas prehistory and numerous **cultural phases or cultural intervals** and their corresponding temporal subperiods and distinct human lifeways (known as **adaptations**). Environmental reconstructions associated with those periods are firmly established (Turner and Hester 1993; Black 1989a, 1989b, 1989c).

Such divisions of Texas prehistory and ancient human ecology add richness to our vision of the past and help dispel the erroneous notions that the earliest inhabitants of Texas lived in a sterile, monotonous world. They also help dispel misconceptions that indigenous peoples were fundamentally or radically different from us. They were not ignorant or perpetually bloodthirsty warriors and cannibals. Nor were they constantly at the mercy of things beyond their control; and they rarely if ever lived as "noble savages." The study of their cultures through archaeology has revealed that they were very practical, crafty, knowledgeable, and well adapted to their world at the technological level and lived successfully as hunters and gatherers for millennia (Bettinger 1991; Bicchieri 1972).

Levels of Adaptive Complexity

In this section we present a generalized range of human sociocultural stages of human adaptations. Note that the defined cultural adaptions do not constitute any notion of cultural "progress" or superiority. Instead, they constitute generalized human solutions made by various groups according to the size and complexity of the culture, the availability of natural resources, the capacity of groups to move and access resources within their territory, and even to some extent, the technological level groups had or could develop to meet their needs. While necessity is often said to be the mother of invention, the archeological record shows that people cannot always create new technological solutions to mitigate against dire situations. Some cultural responses proved to be successful to sustain a particular lifestyle; other, unsuccessful responses resulted in rapid cultural alterations, absorption by other cultures, or, rarely, mass cultural extinction.

In addition to studying both prehistoric and historic cultural resources, archaeology investigates the various **settlement/subsistence adaptations** or **lifeways** of human groups: hunter-gatherers, farmer-villagers, and urban dwellers (Black 1989a, 1989b, 1989c; Hester 1989; Wenke 1990).

"The history of the world is the record of a man in quest of his daily bread and butter."
—Hendrik van Loon, Dutch American historian

Hunter-Gatherers

Most prehistoric **hunter-gatherers** lived as small groups of people in band or tribal societies who briefly settled in one place from a few days to a few weeks but often moved to new places when the local resources were temporarily depleted. Such groups of usually about 25–100 people were often blood relatives, relatives by marriage, or adopted relatives. These hunting-gathering societies were maintained by peer or family hierarchical pressures or occasionally by the recognition of temporary leaders to achieve task-specific objectives. They usually had no long-term chiefs, rulers, or any other form of permanent central authority. Most bands or tribes often acted together spontaneously for the common good.

They spent most of their lives traveling to obtain food by hunting or trapping animals and gathering the edible portions of wild plants. Their life was not as hard as most of us urban people would imagine, because food procurement activities needed to be sufficient only to meet each day's needs. Usually sufficient food could be attained in a few hours' work, and the intensity of work involved far less effort than that used by horticulturalists and farmers in more complex cultures; occasionally, people would go a day or two with little food, but they generally relied on a broad spectrum of resources that included insects and bugs as well as plants and animals.

A mobile, wandering way of life generally precluded procurement of excess surplus food, as no storage facilities were available and the wandering lifeway limited the amount of goods that could be carried. Such groups occasionally assembled into much larger groups temporarily, usually for special reasons such as festivals, feasts, communal hunts, or trading events, and these events often coincided with the rapid ripening of select kinds of foods, such as nuts, berries, tubers, or cacti fruits. Hunter-gatherers were attuned to the diverse resources within their territorial range and the cycles of ripening plants.

Because North American tribes had no domesticated animals except dogs to serve as beasts of burden and followed nomadic settlement-subsistence patterns, they often maintained and carried few personal possessions and constructed temporary shelters. The tool kits consisted mostly of generalized chipped-stone tools used in multiple ways, an array of lightweight perishable artifacts (baskets, leather goods, etc.), and digging sticks. Some hunting-gathering groups in Texas occasionally made and transported pottery vessels. Thus, most hunting-gathering groups left relatively little evidence of their activities for archeologists to find, except when they made replacement chipped-stone tools or resharpened stone tools.

Sometimes the entire hunting-gathering group moved from one temporary camp to another in a generalized gathering mode. At other times they established centralized base camps of longer occupancy, and smaller task groups were sent to procure or forage for specific resources from the surrounding region. The small task groups set up logistical activity sites, from which their products were returned to the base camp. Most groups ranged freely within a familiar established territory to forage for food. Other mobility strategies involve regular cycles of movement within their territory on a seasonal basis; the entire mobility cycle might take a year or more to complete. Different cultural groups with different artifact assemblages might also simultaneously exploit a single territory with minimal to no conflict, provided that each group focused on different kinds of resources.

The principal types of sites that result from these alternative adaptive strategies include centralized base camps composed of temporary shelters, food-processing features and debris, and tool-manufacturing and maintenance activities. Short-term, temporary bivouac camps and logistical task stations were set up where specialized focal activities were conducted, such as cleaning and butchering of game, or where raw materials for tool making were obtained. Few hunter-gatherer groups exist today because this kind of lifestyle requires a low population density and great diversity of resources that exceeds the group's **carrying capacity** (the available resources exceeding the group's minimal needs).

With increased population numbers relative to available resources, territorial pressures forced most hunting-gathering groups to intensify food production, which requires a more complex social structure. Many hunter-gatherer groups became extinct or were assimilated by other cultures. With the advent of European technological changes, such as the introduction of metal tools and domesticated livestock (pigs, sheep, goats, etc.), and the population increase of settlers, hunting-gathering groups disappeared in Texas. Insufficient land and resources are available to permit modern people to practice the nomadic settlement-subsistence ways of their prehistoric hunting-gathering ancestors.

Farmer-Villagers

Farmer-villagers usually lived in semi-permanent to permanent homesteads, hamlet communities or towns composed of one or more families, or contemporaneous communities of hundreds of loosely related or unrelated people. They obtained food by hunting and gathering wild resources, growing cultivated crops or raising domesticated animals, and trading products with other groups. The semi-sedentary and full-time sedentary existence allowed for the accumulation of individual and communal property and wealth, landownership, and inheritance. Most horticultural societies operated as chiefdoms, with chiefs acting as a group leaders to arbitrate disputes over land and other property, plan for defense against enemies, and carry out other communal or civic projects.

The farmer-villager's yearly cycle was tied to seasonal crop production. Although cultivated crops could feed more people, considerable labor was involved in developing and maintaining field plots, planting, weeding, watering, protecting crops from deer and other animals, and harvesting. The agricultural cycle was punctuated with periods of slack time during growing seasons when groups could abandon their homesteads and communities and forage for game and wild plants, visit trade partners in distant communities, or attend festivals and feasts. However, considerable processing was needed for preserving and storing surplus food.

Specialized tools and other cultural adaptations were required to support these activities. Houses were generally constructed of more durable materials to last longer than those used by mobile hunter-gatherers. Since farmer-villagers lived for considerable lengths of time in a single location, they often left substantial amounts of physical evidence for archeologists to examine, such as house foundations, sometimes arranged around larger civic mounds or chiefs' houses; livestock pens; agricultural fields; granaries; or networks of irrigation canals. Such sites tend to have numerous storage pits, a wide range of locally or nonlocally made specialized tools, trade wares, and areas where copious amounts of manufacturing debris and food residue were discarded.

In Texas, farmer-villages developed during the past 1,000 years in predominantly three areas: (1) the Caddo occupations of northeastern and eastern Texas, which have ties to the mound-building cultures of the southeastern United States; (2) the Plains Village complexes in the river valleys of the Panhandle High Plains and adjacent Rolling Red-Bed Plains or north-central Texas; and (3) the eastern Mogollon groups in extreme far West Texas, which have ties to the southwestern Puebloan groups. Each region differs in its forms of houses, pottery, ways of life, and belief systems.

Urban Dwellers

Urban dwellers usually existed as groups of thousands or tens of thousands living together in a single central place, an urban center or a city. Such groups are marked by a complex (multiple-level) social organization sometimes with a ranked society led by people of an elite class, a strong centralized government, taxation and redistribution systems, some form of market economy, public architecture, and control or participation in an extensive trade network.

Ancient urban centers frequently had an inner core or perhaps several distinct zones of palaces, temples, commercial buildings, and markets surrounded by sizable residential areas. Numerous hamlets, or small, isolated farming villages beyond the outer fringes of the main residential zone, often supplied the urban centers with necessary goods to sustain them. In addition to many smaller residences occupied by commoners, early cities typically possessed several large monumental structures and palaces for rulers and smaller palaces and administrative buildings for key bureaucrats or nobles. None of the prehistoric people in Texas developed urban settlements, but these kinds of urban centers developed and existed in the Mississippi River basin in Mexico and Mesoamerica and in Peru and Ecuador of South America.

Some cultures developed recording systems consisting of knotted string mnemonic devices and/or a rudimentary form of writing with drawn symbols representing sounds. This level of recording marks a stage in social development of true civilizations. Urban dwellers often developed craft specialists or even guilds through which specialized workers could distribute goods. Most urban societies were also involved with long-distance trading for resources and exotic materials. The social and technological structures introduced by the Europeans to the New World allowed the development of urban centers and cities by Euro-American communities in Texas during the Historic period. An entirely separate branch of archaeology, known as **urban archaeology**, is devoted to the study of both ancient and modern cities.

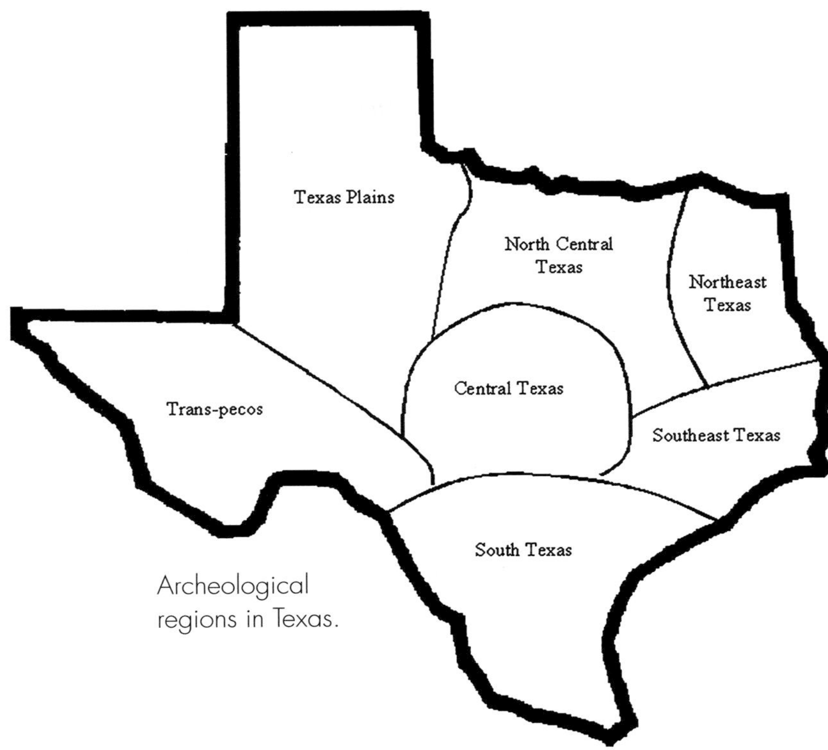

Archeological regions in Texas.

Regional Archaeology

The diversity of archeological ecoregions in Texas required prehistoric peoples to use different adaptive strategies. Seven such regions are discussed here.

Central and South Texas: Bexar County

Bexar County has more than 2,000 recorded archeological sites on record. Humans have passed through this region since at least the end of the last ice age about 12,000 years ago. Abundant plant and animal resources were available in the semi-desert, grassland, and forest zone ecosystems with abundant water found in the many springs, rivers, and streams in the area (Enquist 1987; Everitt and Drawe 1993; Kutac and Caran 1994; Riskind and Diamond 1986, 1988; Simpson 1988; Vines 1984). The county contains portions of two regional-scale landscape zones, the Coastal Plains and the Hill Country, which are divided by the Balcones Escarpment (Abbott and Woodruff 1986; Potter and Black 1995). The escarpment has been a major natural and cultural boundary throughout human prehistory and during the historic era (Palmer 1986). Because of these abundant resources and natural features Indian peoples frequented the area for millennia.

Most archeological sites occur along major drainages like Salado, Elm, Olmos, and Leon Creeks. Some scholars believe this pattern of distribution for Central Texas Archaic sites is due to the relatively warm Altithermal climatic episode that occurred during much of the Archaic period (Nance 1972). During such a time, proximity to water would have been a prime consideration in locating campsites. The Pavo Real archeological site is located on San Antonio's northwestern fringe. During the late 1970s, archeologists with the Texas Highway Department (now the Texas Department of Transportation, or TXDOT) discovered the site during highway expansion excavations. The site yielded chipped-stone tools and other evidence of occupation by Paleoindians as early as about 11,000 years ago. Paleoindian projectile points have been recovered in several localities in the Bexar County vicinity.

Archeological remains of the Paleoindian period were also unearthed along the banks of Salado Creek at the St. Mary's Hall school campus site. In the mid-1980s the Center for Archaeological Research at University of Texas at San Antonio (CAR-UTSA) excavated an ancient campsite containing Paleoindian projectile points from this site. They are parallel-sided lanceolate points with parallel oblique flake scara and a slightly concave base that are designated the St. Mary's Hall type. These points have sometimes been associated with the killing and butchering of extinct forms of bison, and at the Wilson-Leonard site in Williamson County, they have been radiometrically dated to ca. 10,000– 8700 BP.

By far the most common archeological sites recorded in Bexar County are from the Archaic period. Numerous extensive campsites, some covering many acres, are found in the northern portion of the county. Indeed, some are so large and were occupied for such lengthy periods that it is impossible to determine exactly where they begin and end. These Archaic period sites are primarily living surfaces and camps where dwellings, food preparation areas, and other activity areas were constructed and used (Black and McGraw 1985). The cultural evidence consists mainly of burned-rock features generated from various activities, from ancient cooking (hearths, cooking facilities, earth ovens) to tool manufacturing. These large **burned-rock middens** had multiple uses and often include discarded animal bones; fragments of stone, bone, and shell ornaments and tools; chipping debris from the manufacture of stone tools; stone grinding slabs (metates) and hand grinding stones (manos); and imported (exotic) materials and trade items. Many perishable materials used by the Indians, such as wooden tools, clothing, basketry, and other materials made of plant fibers, stalks, or leaves, often do not survive in the archeological record.

A: A pit is dug and filled with firewood and rocks, then burned; the result is a layer of red-hot rocks on the bottom and sides of the pit.

B: Moist, green plants or packing material is placed over the hot rocks; food is wrapped and placed on top of the plants then covered with more packing material. The mound is covered with a layer of soil and a fire is built on top of the mound.

C: When the food is cooked (up to 48 hours for some root foods), the layers of hot coals, soil, and packing materials are pulled back to expose the steam-cooked foods.

Ancient earth ovens were used to bake, smoke, or steam food. Courtesy of Alston Thoms

The Late Prehistoric stage sites in Bexar County were often located directly on top of the earlier Archaic living surfaces on the same landform. They are generally recognized by the presence of small arrow points and occasionally bone-tempered pottery. However, these people made no substantial changes in their hunting-gathering lifeways from the beginning of the Archaic period until the time of European contact. Virtually the only differences in cultural practices were the use of the bow and arrow (appearing ca. AD 500) and fired clay ceramics (appearing ca. AD 1200). Otherwise, the Late Prehistoric Indians continued the same hunting-and-gathering lifeway of their Archaic ancestors.

Historical excavations at the Alamo have identified deposits from the two Texas Revolutionary period sieges: the Siege of Béxar during October–December 1835, and the Battle of the Alamo between February 23 and March 6, 1836 (A. Fox 1992; Fox et al. 1976). In the Siege of Béxar, approximately 1,100 Mexican troops led by General Martin Perfecto de Cos (the brother-in-law of

Mexico's military dictator, President Antonio López de Santa Anna) were defeated by about 600 Texians under the command of General Edward Burleson and Colonel Benjamin Milam. The better-known 1836 Battle of the Alamo was waged between about 230 Texian defenders of the Alamo garrison led by Colonel William B. Travis and Colonel James Bowie and perhaps several thousand assaulting Mexican troops led by President Santa Anna.

Historic artifacts found in the deposits from these battles include cinders, bronze mortar round and cannonball fragments, lead musket and cannon shot balls, pieces of metal bayonets, flintlock rifle and pistol hardware, gun flints, and other scraps of metal. Some human remains attributed to these battles were also found. Several excavations conducted at the Alamo garrison by the CAR-UTSA in the 1970s and 1980s exposed remnants of fortification ditches and other earthworks from these battles (A. Fox 1992). Pick marks in the clay walls and floors of these ditches made in 1835 and 1836 were still visible during the twentieth-century archeological excavations.

Lower-Pecos

The Lower Pecos region is a fairly distinctive topographic region marked by a series of deeply incised, relatively closely spaced canyons with many large rock shelters and caves along the lower Pecos River, the Devils River, and the confluence with the Rio Grande. These shelters offer exceptional preservation of a rather distinctive cultural development in the hunting-gathering adaptive strategy. The vegetation variously consisted of grasslands on the uplands and ridges, and mesquite, acacia, yucca, and cacti covering valley walls and floors. Some of the nonperishable stone tools from the Lower Pecos region superficially resembled chipped-stone point types of the South and Central Texas regions; however, there are also many unique points that denote cultural differences, such as large contracting stemmed dart points with contracting bases.

The dryness of the Lower Pecos region and the frequent occupation of large caves and rock shelters has commonly permitted preservation of plant, cloth, wood, and fiber artifacts dating from the Early Archaic through recent times. These perishable artifacts, rarely found elsewhere in Texas, include basketry, matting, cordage, netting, sandals, throwing sticks/rabbit clubs, atlatls/darts, bows/arrows, cane and wooden cradles, small-game snares, rabbit fur blankets, tuber digging sticks, large cottonwood log mortars, and fire-starting drill sets (McGregor 1991, 1992).

The plant and animal food resources in the Lower Pecos region are from desert-adapted life-forms (Shafer 1986; Turpin 1991, 1995). Cooking features from small hearths to large burned-rock and earth ovens are common in open-air sites and inside large rock shelters for roasting sotol, yucca bulbs, onions, and various tubers. Bedrock mortar-hole sites (consisting of holes some 20 cm in diameter and 30 cm deep) and bedrock metate sites attest to the pounding and grinding of mesquite pods, seeds, and wild grains. The animal remains recovered from human coprolites (preserved feces) dating back 6,000 years inside rock shelters indicate that virtually anything that moved was considered fair game for consumption, including insects; rodents; birds; reptiles; fish; amphibians; small and medium-sized mammals such as rabbits, fox, coyote, bobcats, raccoons; and larger mammals such as deer, occasional mountain lions, bear, and bison. Features found inside rock shelters and caves commonly include bedding made of grass, singed cactus pads, and rabbit fur.

In addition to caves, rock shelters, and burned-rock ovens are groups of wickiup structures marked by a circular series of isolated stone foundations measuring 1.8–2.7 m in diameter. The deep canyons of the Lower Pecos also have a spectacular example of a bison jump used by Paleoindians

Pictographs or cave paintings are a remarkably well-preserved cultural record of the Lower Pecos. Photos by Alston Thoms

to kill herds of extinct forms of horse and bison. The bison jumps were also used in the Middle to Late Archaic period.

The Lower Pecos region is renowned for several styles of **pictographs** (cave and rock-shelter paintings) with motifs ranging from megascale figures several meters tall to clusters of miniature stick figures of people and mountain lions only a few centimeters tall. The diversity, detail, and concentration

of polychrome imagery, painted in red-orange, maroon, yellow, white and black, inside dry caves and rock shelters makes the Lower Pecos a world-class locale for rock art whose motifs are not found elsewhere in Texas. These images are not decorative art; they occur at sacred sites and reflect rich spiritual and religious experiences, portrayal of creation stories, and human interactions with powers needed to access and acquire game and other natural resources. An incredible range of imagery depicts humans, animals, plants, and spiritual icons.

The megascale human motifs are shown to have relatively large, rectangular bodies, sometimes with a white vertical stripe down the middle or a series of horizontal lines, perhaps reflecting skeletonized rib cages, with outstretched horizontal arms, relatively short legs, and small heads. They are often shown carrying wooden staffs/digging sticks or atlatls and darts, small bags, or pouches and wearing deer antler headdresses. Common animal motifs include deer (often impaled with atlatl darts), pumas/mountain lions, dogs/coyotes, water bugs/tadpoles, and such insects as grasshoppers and perhaps butterflies. The identified plants include mostly psychotropic peyote buttons (sometimes linked to deer) and datura pods.

The religious iconography includes images of people, or perhaps "flying" shaman drawn in oblique postures as if they are depicting during out-of-body or hallucinatory experiences; undulating arches/bridges separating the surface and sky realms from the underworld; occasionally amorphous caterpillar-like beasts or monsters; and perhaps self-imposed blood-letting and scarification sacrifices. Insofar as the motifs extend into northern Mexico, researchers have made important discoveries by interviewing the Huichol Indians for help in identifying and interpreting the motifs. The images appear to be visions obtained during a hallucinogenic altered state of reality resulting from the consumption of mescal beans from the mountain laurel bush, datura pods, and peyote buttons. The repetitive use of deer linked to peyote buttons and often impaled with atlatl darts, and occasional use of bugs related to water, suggests spiritual attempts to control access to game and water in a relatively dry environment.

It is a fairly common misconception that life was very austere for desert-dwelling people of the prehistoric Lower Pecos and for hunter-gatherers who lived in similar deserts elsewhere, but the archeological record indicates otherwise. Indeed, ancient desert dwellers apparently had considerable leisure time to create the beautiful and intricate personal adornments and fabulous rock-art murals found wherever they lived (Shafer 1986). Such human cultures are a profound testament to the variety of life-sustaining and life-enriching environments and the versatility and adaptability of the human species, as revealed through the studies of archaeology and anthropology.

Trans-Pecos and Far West Texas

West of the Lower Pecos Canyonlands is the Trans-Pecos region, a physiographically distinct area comprising dormant volcanoes, lofty mountains, and intervening valleys. The eastern Trans-Pecos near the Big Bend of the Rio Grande is characterized by numerous volcanic cones, dikes, and high grass-covered valleys and plains. The eastern Trans-Pecos contains diverse lithic materials available for making stone tools, including an abundance of rhyolites, basalts, jaspers, chalcedonies, and cherts. Prior to human occupation in the west, the Rio Grande flowed east of the Franklins through the Tularosa Basin and Hueco Bolson, transporting obsidian and chert cobbles from the northern Rio Grande to the desert region. The Trans-Pecos region is part of the Chihuahuan Desert and is variously covered with grasses, creosote, snakebrush, mesquite, paloverde, sotol, yucca, ocotillo, prickly pear, and other cacti in the lowlands and juniper and oak trees at higher elevations. Dominant large game consists of both mule and white-tailed deer, peccaries, mountain lions, mountain sheep/goats, and bear.

Most people in the Trans-Pecos through the Archaic practiced a broad-spectrum subsistence pattern, using small and large game mammals, reptiles, amphibians, and fish. The Trans-Pecos region has two cultural traditions: the Eastern Trans-Pecos/La Junta tradition and the Western Trans-Pecos/Jornada Mogollon tradition, which occurs mostly in El Paso County. Due to the intensity of urban and military developments around El Paso, the western region has twice as many recorded and far more excavated archeological sites than the eastern area. The Western Trans-Pecos/Jornada Mogollon tradition was followed by hunter-gatherers throughout much of the Early and Middle Archaic; however, around 2000 BC these Late Archaic people began to cultivate maize, which allowed them to become more sedentary. They lived in brush wickiups, semi-subterranean pit houses, and by AD 1000, contiguous-room adobe pueblos; they also produced pottery.

Before the introduction of pottery and horticulture, the people across the Trans-Pecos had a similar level of technology and tool kits to deal with their broad-spectrum adaptations, which through time tended to become restricted to smaller territories.

Nearly three dozen Paleoindian sites are recorded for the Trans-Pecos region; however, many are known primarily from surface finds of diagnostic points. Several Trans-Pecos Early Paleoindian sites have yielded evidence of Clovis and Folsom materials containing broken ground-stemmed, lanceolate projectile tips made of cherts outcropping in the Texas Panhandle and Chuska Mountains of northwestern New Mexico. The later Paleoindian Plano/Cody components are represented by Meserve, Golondrina, Angostura, Eden, and Scottsbluff points. The Archaic assemblages of the Eastern and Western Trans-Pecos are less well known than those of the Lower Pecos partly because of the relative scarcity of caves, thus a lack of perishable artifacts. The elaborately painted rock-art sites found in the Lower Pecos do not generally extend into the Trans-Pecos region, although in the West Texas region, different styles of elaborate painting attest to connections deep into Mexico.

One of the Archaic period hallmarks is the presence of burned-rock hearth features and ovens, which marks the invention of heat-transference cooking strategies. Radiocarbon dates from the Western Trans-Pecos region suggest that thermal rock features appear around 6000 BCE and persist in low frequencies throughout the Early and part of the Middle Archaic periods. The Archaic projectile-point forms of the Western Trans-Pecos region are unlike the stem-shaped points commonly found in the Central Texas region. They do, however, strongly resemble the sequence of dart points common to northern New Mexico, marked by the broad-bladed, shoulder-less points with long stems and either concave or straight bases (Bajada- and Jay-type dart points). The Middle Archaic dart points tend to have contracting stems, either with or without shoulders; a rather short, shouldered point form with broad concave bases; and an even-sided notched point form. Many dart-point specimens are extensively reworked, and the dart-point shapes reflect a broad range of sizes and forms depending on the extent and nature of the point reworking.

Around 3000 BCE, within the Middle Archaic period, the Eastern Trans-Pecos sites undergo drastic changes, marked by the appearance of small wickiup-like house structures, measuring about 1.8 m in diameter, that are associated with both ash basin hearths and burned-rock features. The occurrence of small brush structures also coincides with the increased use of rock shelters near El Paso. Overall, the nomadic movements seem to be sporadic. The adoption of maize cultivation supports a population increase, shifts in settlements and activities, and establishment of regional territories that differentiate the Eastern and Western Trans-Pecos.

Predominantly nomadic hunter-gatherers occupied the Eastern Trans-Pecos/La Junta area throughout most of prehistory. The Paleoindian and Archaic dart points of the Eastern Trans-Pecos resemble the styles and forms of darts made in the Lower Pecos. These people often lived in small (1.8–2.4 m in diameter) wickiup brush structures with stone foundations. They made large burned-rock earth ovens for processing sotol and mesquite. By 200 BC they started to rely more on corn from dryland cultivation and began making plain brownware pottery and living in larger semi-subterranean pithouses.

By AD 1000, the Jornada Mogollon were living in contiguous-room pueblos, manufacturing red-on-brown painted pottery, and trading through networks with distant groups to the south and north. Caves and rock shelters are not nearly as common as in the Lower Pecos, so the hunter-gatherers who exploited these areas constructed small, circular, probably dome-shaped wickiup structures with stone foundations. While some large burned-rock ovens are present, more often sites contain rock-lined hearth fields and cairns. Rock-art sites are much rarer in the Trans-Pecos region and consist mostly of pecked geometric designs rather than large painted motifs. Most of the extensive archeological excavations in the Trans-Pecos were conducted in the 1920s through 1940s.

• • • • • • • • • • • • • • •

NORTHEAST TEXAS

Todd McMakin, Archeological Consultant

The northeast region of Texas is the ancestral home of the Caddo Indians. Although the Caddo period really does not begin until after AD 800, there is significant evidence that later Caddo peoples were directly tied to earlier populations in the region. People have been living in northeast Texas for at least the last 10,000 years, evidenced by the presence of stone-tool forms associated with these early populations.

The lifestyles, subsistence practices, and cultural traditions of the Caddo probably developed from these earlier traditions. Although the link between the Caddo and previous cultures of their homeland has not yet been firmly established, similarities in tool-making traditions and pottery styles infer that the Caddo were indigenous to this region. Fortunately, many of the early Spanish and French expeditions into Texas encountered the Caddo during their forays. Accounts of such explorers apparently fill in many gaps in the archeological record about Caddo culture. However, they should probably be interpreted with at least a modicum of caution because of the possibility they are colored by ethnocentrism and other cultural biases. Many of those documents describe the types of plants the Caddo domesticated, the way they hunted, and the types of nondomesticated plants they consumed.

Most people assume that precontact American Indians were more in harmony with nature than people in the modern, industrialized world are today, which is probably true to a large extent. However, this does not mean that prehistoric and contact-period populations had *no* impact on the land around them. In fact, American Indians often had a considerable impact on their surroundings. We know through archeological data that American Indians effectively used fire for burning off large land areas. The practice was used to reduce understory growth and also to release fertile nutrients into the soil for agricultural purposes (Hudson 1976, 19). Of course, land was also disturbed through agricultural production and through thinning for domestic use. Paths and trails were cleared; some of these would be used into early historic times and then converted into the roads we use today.

In addition to impacts to vegetation, American Indians sometimes depleted animals, fish, and shellfish to very low numbers within a given region. In fact, there is substantial evidence that many large mammals alive at the beginning of the Pleistocene, called megafauna, were hunted to extinction by Indian groups.

Within east and northeast Texas, the Caddo Indians ranged from as far south as present-day Beaumont north into Oklahoma, from Louisiana west as far as Mexia, and possibly as far west as Killeen. This was a very large area but was only a small portion of the overall Caddo region. Caddo sites have been found in northeast Texas, northwest Louisiana, southwest Arkansas, and southeast Oklahoma (Perttula 1992, 56–62).

Artifacts associated with Caddo Indians in northeast Texas include pottery of many different shapes and colors, often decorated with raised nodes and fillets, intricate designs involving incisions and punctations in wet clay, and engraved lines in dry clay before firing. Also associated with these sites are stone tools used as knives and/or arrow or spear points. Many of the tools that people call "arrowheads" were actually too large to have been hafted onto an arrow and were most likely used as knives or spear points. Other types of stone tools include chipped-stone and ground-stone celts and hoes used for agriculture.

The Caddo Indians of historic times were divided into a number of different groups:

for example, Hasinai, Ais, Adai, Kichai, Tawakoni, Natchitoches, Cadohadocho, and Anardarko (Carter 1995, 182). As with all peoples, the Caddo left behind traces of their villages and campsites. Some of the largest sites are associated with the major river drainages of the Sabine, Red, and Neches Rivers. The Caddo were eventually driven out of Texas and settled in Oklahoma.

During the Historic period, northeast Texas would be settled by Euro-American populations seeking a better life "out west." The early settlers of the period left behind structural remains and small artifacts similar to those of today's farms and ranches. Houses were typically made of wood (sometimes logs) and often had a barn or other outbuildings in association. The fertile pastures were used for raising cattle, and some people grew agricultural products. The Civil War would have very little immediate effect on east Texas, although the war would certainly have some residual effects from the loss of east Texas men and from economic hardships. By the late nineteenth century, the timber industry had a strong hold on east Texas and resulted in the removal of millions of acres of timber to be shipped to the north and east.

• • • • • • • • • • • • • • •

SOUTHEAST TEXAS

Todd McMakin, Archeological Consultant

The prehistory of the southeast Texas region generally follows that of much of the rest of the state, with very early populations called Paleoindians following a highly mobile way of life. Paleoindians apparently relied for subsistence primarily on large, migratory mammals that ranged over much of North America during the Pleistocene, between 30,000 and 6000 BCE. After many years of being overhunted, the megafauna eventually became extinct (a variety of causes may have led to this, not just overhunting). However, humans are very adaptable creatures. As the megafauna died away, these early cultures started relying more and more on smaller game animals such as the white-tailed deer. It is at the extinction of the megafauna that the Archaic period begins. Although the Archaic was a time of change, the change was very gradual over the next 6,000 years. Minor variations in spear-point types were developed, and populations generally became less sedentary over this time. Eventually, by the end of the Late Archaic period, populations had become semi-sedentary, using one area for an extended time.

During the Archaic period, populations utilized local game species to supplement the plants that could be gathered for food. In fact, it is postulated that 70% or more of the calories consumed by Archaic populations were from plants. In addition, fish and shellfish were utilized extensively along the southeast Texas coast. Due to population increases throughout the Archaic period, sites become much more numerous and larger by the end of the Late Archaic (approximately AD 1). Shell midden sites are more numerous and probably represent a seasonal exploitation of these resources. Non-midden sites increase in numbers and in densities of artifacts.

Although northeast Texas cultures were undoubtedly influenced by cultures farther to the east, southeast Texas coastal cultures appear to have been influenced extensively by southeastern North American cultures. Late Prehistoric sites from southeast Texas have produced large numbers of Mississippian period Tchefuncte and Mandeville ceramics, which are typically found on sites from the Louisiana and Mississippi coasts. It could easily be argued that the exchange of technology would have been equaled in the exchange of ideas and social characteristics. In addition to interaction with people from the east, there is ample evidence that these populations had some contact with the Caddo to the north.

Although the cultures of the southeast

Texas coast had some limited interaction with early explorers, such as Cabeza de Vaca, not until the eighteenth century did prolonged contact take place. In the early part of the nineteenth century (1820s), many Anglo settlers made their way into southeast Texas, soon followed by many members of several eastern Indian groups, such as the Cherokee, Alabama, Coushatta, and Delaware. Such migrations had a significant impact on the life of the indigenous American Indians of southeast Texas.

By the mid-eighteenth century, large plantations were starting to spring up along the southeast Texas coast. In fact, the region was starting to resemble Louisiana both culturally and economically. The production of cotton became a major economic boom for southeast Texas. This agricultural lifestyle had long-lasting impacts on the natural communities in this area. In addition, the harvesting of pine timber significantly impacted the vegetation and overall ecology of the region.

• • • • • • • • • • • • • • • •

TEXAS PLAINS

Todd McMakin, Archeological Consultant

Unlike the Caddo populations to the east, native cultures of the High Plains relied heavily on buffalo hunting as a means of subsistence. In addition, by AD 1100, during the Late Ceramic period, corn, beans, and squash, the typical cultigens of Late Prehistoric American Indians, were farmed on the plains. These populations relied primarily on deer and smaller mammals. However, during the times bison herds made their way into this area, they became the primary staple of their diet.

As in other areas of Texas, the first populations on the plains were the Paleoindians. These early populations were highly mobile and left little evidence for archeologists to interpret their lifestyle. However, a few well-documented sites in the Panhandle have produced lithic tools that have been firmly dated through carbon-14 dating to at least 9000 BCE. Paleoindians typically hunted migratory megafauna, which consisted of the mammoth and a large form of bison, among others. By the end of the Paleoindian period, megafauna were extinct and populations adapted to the change by hunting smaller mammals such as the white-tailed deer. Since deer are not migratory animals, Paleoindian populations started settling down in larger camps. There is ample evidence for Archaic-period populations in the archeological record. In both the Paleoindian and Archaic periods, plants appear to have been a primary staple of the diet, with true domestication occurring ca. AD 1100.

As occurred in almost any region, there was considerable variety among Plains cultures. The following generalized discussion will fit most of these cultures. The Early Ceramic period begins around AD 200 and ends ca. AD 1100, when bison once again returned to the plains. The Early Ceramic period is characterized by the introduction of ceramics and the use of small arrows such as the Scallorn and Deadman points. There is evidence that cultures of this region were foragers with some ties to both the Mogollon groups to the southwest and Woodland-period groups to the north. Most of the sites are small campsites, in contrast to many of the large habitation sites found to the north and east.

As noted earlier, the primary meat source for Early Ceramic populations appears to have been deer and small game. This is probably an indication that bison were not readily available to these peoples. However, the bison would eventually return and would once again become a major factor in the subsistence of later cultures.

The Late Ceramic period began ca. AD 1100 with the return of bison to the plains. New types of arrow points, such as the unnotched Fresno and side-notched Washita, were highly represented in archeological site collections. There is some indication that these types of points were well suited to the hunting of bison because they were difficult to break and were relatively easy to make. During the Late Ceramic period, populations began to domesticate plants and relied heavily on horticulture to supplement bison hunting. Also, trade networks began to expand and included Puebloan groups from the west (Hughes 1991).

During the Historic period, the region was occupied intensively by the Apache, later by the Comanche, and then by Euro-Americans. The Apache relied heavily on bison and traded with Puebloan groups; most Apache residential sites contain Puebloan pottery. The Comanche were a horse culture that relied on bison. These groups moved in from the west and eventually pushed the Apache out of the Texas plains. These groups used goods received from Euro-Americans from the east, such as metal (including metal spear points), glass, and horses (Bagot and Hughes 1979, 30–44). By the late nineteenth century the bison had been hunted to near extinction, and the plains were being used primarily by Euro-American cattle herders. The Comanche had been pushed out of the plains by the US military by the late nineteenth century.

● ● ● ● ● ● ● ● ● ● ● ● ● ● ●

NORTH-CENTRAL TEXAS

Todd McMakin, Archeological Consultant

The region now encompassed within north-central Texas was occupied initially by Paleoindian populations dating back as far as 10,000 BCE. These populations subsisted primarily by hunting megafauna that seasonally migrated through this portion of Texas. It was necessary for these early populations to be extremely mobile to effectively utilize megafauna as a subsistence base.

As the megafauna eventually died out, these early populations turned to smaller game animals such as bison, deer, and turkey. Given the nature of these resources, it was not necessary for Archaic populations to be quite as mobile as the Paleoindians. Between 6000 BCE and AD 700, these populations appear to have stayed within limited ranges, occupying various locations on a seasonal basis to utilize plants and animals when they were most abundant. As populations eventually became less mobile, population pressure increased and eventually led to sedentary or semi-sedentary groups living in this area.

There seems to be very little evidence of the Late Prehistoric cultures of north-central Texas. The evidence that exists appears to indicate that groups retained a moderate level of mobility until ca. AD 1200–1300. At this time, the average site size appears to increase and there is evidence for long-term occupations. There is also evidence that Late Prehistoric groups may have used and relied heavily on corn, beans, and squash as domesticates. Game animals such as deer, turkey, and smaller mammals and reptiles would have supplemented their diet. Fish remains are also present on some sites.

Although historic documents for north-central Texas are sparse, surviving records point to the use of the region by groups from the north, east, south, and west. The Tonkawa, Wichita, Caddo, and Comanche appear to have used this area intermittently throughout the Early Historic period. Our lack of knowledge for this period also results from lack of excavations of sites with definable Early Historic components in the region. However, the information we have tends to indicate that none of the previously named Indian groups played a significant role in the region's history. Apparently such groups used the region as a travel corridor and spent very little time there.

By the late nineteenth century the eastern plains and Blackland Prairies of north-central Texas were being occupied rather extensively by Anglo populations, who used the plains for cattle grazing and the Blackland Prairies for cultivation and pasturage. Sites associated with these early settlers include house remains and outbuildings, such as barns and corrals.

Both the prehistoric and historic populations of north-central Texas had a significant impact on the environment. Overgrazing of livestock during the Historic period has resulted in reduced native species in many areas, and disturbances from land clearing and development have forever changed the landscape in the region.

● ● ● ● ● ● ● ● ● ● ● ● ● ● ● ●

Antiquities Laws

Federal and state laws make it illegal to collect artifacts or excavate sites on federal or state lands (public lands). Under any circumstance, artifact collecting should not be undertaken on public property unless a legal permit has been issued. Less than 5% of the surface area of Texas is in public ownership, so most archeological sites are on private property. In this case, only the landowner can give permission to visit, excavate, or collect.

The first federal law regarding cultural resources was the Antiquities Act of 1906, which authorized the president to designate historic and natural resources of national significance and to protect all historic and prehistoric ruins and objects of antiquity on federal lands. The federal government has passed more than a dozen laws stipulating that cultural resource studies shall consider effects on cultural resources when proposed projects occur on federal property, require a federal permit, or utilize federal funds, even when those projects occur on state or private lands.

Similarly, the State of Texas has an antiquities code that manages and protects significant cultural resources on publicly owned political subdivisions of Texas. The political subdivisions include property managed by state, county, and municipal agencies and even river authorities that were created by legislative actions.

- **Antiquities Act of 1906** (34 Stat. 225, 16 U.S.C. 431–433, as amended) prohibits the excavation or disturbance of "any object of antiquity" and all historic and prehistoric sites on lands owned or controlled by the federal government.
- **National Historic Preservation Act of 1966 (NHPA)** (54 USC 300101 et seq., as amended) ensures that the federal government consults with state and local parties to avoid, minimize, and mitigate any negative impacts to cultural and historic resources. The act was passed primarily to acknowledge the importance of protecting our nation's heritage from rampant federal development.
- **Archeological Resources Protection Act of 1979 (ARPA)** (Public Law 96–95, 16 U.S.C. 470aa–mm, as amended) states that collecting artifacts or excavating archeological sites is illegal without a permit. Only qualified professional archeologists are eligible to receive these permits.
- **Native American Graves Protection and Repatriation Act of 1990 (NAGPRA)** (Public Law 101–601, 25 U.S.C. 3001 et seq., as amended) includes provisions for intentional and inadvertent discoveries of American Indian cultural items on federal and tribal lands. Cultural items include, but are not limited to, American Indian human remains, funerary objects, sacred objects, and items of cultural patrimony.
- **Antiquities Code of Texas** (Natural Resources Code, Title 9, Chapter 191, as amended) forbids the collection or excavation of artifacts on state and political subdivision lands without a permit. Permits are issued only to qualified professional archeologists. This law also contains provisions for the protection of designated State Archeological Landmarks on private property.

The Texas antiquities code manages and protects significant cultural resources on publicly owned political subdivisions. These political subdivisions were created by legislative actions and include property managed by the state, counties, municipalities, and river authorities. The federal government and the State of Texas recognize the rights of private landownership; more than 95% of all lands in the state are privately owned. Even though private property can be taken with compensation under the policy of eminent domain for the development of projects for the public good (roads, pipelines, reservoirs, etc.), the taking of private lands due to the existence of a significant cultural resources for the public good is rare.

These records are currently maintained at the Texas Archeological Research Laboratory at the University of Texas, Austin. The recording and registration of archeological sites on private lands should not be threatening to private landowners. Due to the unique and fragile context of cultural resources, information about the locations of archeological sites is excluded from the general public and potential site vandals, even under requests through the Freedom of Information Act. Such documentation helps planners identify and consider impacts to cultural resources when they are designing alternative options for proposed projects crossing their property. The documentation also helps archeological researchers in identifying patterns of human settlements for specific cultures or time periods. Just because a site is listed in the state archeological site files does not allow anyone to trespass on private lands to visit these resources without landowner permission.

Resources

The Archaeological Conservancy
www.americanarchaeology.org/
A nonprofit organization dedicated to acquiring and preserving archeological sites discovered on private lands, including several in Texas.

Council of Texas Archeologists
www.counciloftexasarcheologists.org/
A nonprofit voluntary organization that promotes the goals of professional archaeology in the State of Texas. Site includes good information on guidelines and regulations for archeologists as well as extensive links to many archaeology-related sites.

National Park Service
http://www.nps.gov/archeology/
Learn about archaeology in the national parks, including Texas: http://www.nps.gov/state/tx/index.htm

The Portal to Texas History
http://texashistory.unt.edu/
From prehistory to the present day, explore exceptional history collections from Texas libraries, museums, archives, historical societies, genealogical societies, and private family collections.

Texas Archeological Society
www.txarch.org/
Nonprofit organization dedicated to promoting scientific studies and the preservation of cultural and historical resources in Texas.

Texas beyond History
http://www.texasbeyondhistory.net
A nationally award-winning virtual museum developed as an educational site to interpret and share the results of archeological and historical research on the cultural heritage of Texas with the citizens of Texas and the world.

Texas Indians
www.texasindians.com
Learn about individual Indian tribes with history in Texas.

Texas Parks and Wildlife Department
www.tpwd.state.tx.us/
Links to all parks and historic sites in Texas.

References

Abbott, P. L., and C. M. Woodruff Jr., eds. 1986. *The Balcones Escarpment: Geology, Hydrology, Ecology and Social Development in Central Texas*. Published for the Geological Society of America annual meeting, San Antonio, Texas, November. Santa Fe Springs, CA: Comet Reproduction Service.

Bagot, Joe T., and Jack T. Hughes. 1979. *Archaeological Inventory of a Portion of Caprock Canyons State Park in Briscoe County, Texas*. Canyon: Archaeological Research Laboratory, Killgore Research Center, West Texas State University.

Bettinger, R. L. 1991. *Hunter-Gatherers: Archaeological and Evolutionary Theory*. New York: Plenum Press.

Bicchieri, M. G., ed. 1972. *Hunters and Gatherers Today: A Socioeconomic Study of Eleven Such Cultures in the Twentieth Century*. Prospect Heights, IL: Waveland Press.

Black, S. L.1989a. Central Texas Plateau Prairie. In *From the Gulf to the Rio Grande: Human Adaptation in Central, South, and Lower Pecos Texas*, by Thomas R. Hester, Stephen L. Black, D. Gentry Steele, Ben W. Olive, Anne A. Fox, Karl J. Reinhard, and Leland C. Bement, 17–38. Arkansas Archaeological Survey Research Series 33. Final Report Submitted to the US Army Corps of Engineers, Southwestern Division. Study Unit 3 of the Southwestern Division Archaeological Overview. Prepared by the Center for Archaeological Research at the University of Texas at San Antonio, Texas A&M University, and the Arkansas Archaeological Survey. Wrightsville: Arkansas Department of Corrections.

———. 1989b. Environmental Setting. In *From the Gulf to the Rio Grande: Human Adaptation in Central, South, and Lower Pecos Texas*, by Thomas R. Hester, Stephen L. Black, D. Gentry Steele, Ben W. Olive, Anne A. Fox, Karl J. Reinhard, and Leland C. Bement, 5–16. Arkansas Archaeological Survey Research Series 33. Final Report Submitted to the US Army Corps of Engineers, Southwestern Division. Study Unit 3 of the Southwestern Division Archaeological Overview. Prepared by the Center for Archaeological Research at the University of Texas at San Antonio, Texas A&M University, and the Arkansas Archaeological Survey. Wrightsville: Arkansas Department of Corrections.

———. 1989c. South Texas Plains. In *From the Gulf to the Rio Grande: Human Adaptation in Central, South, and Lower Pecos Texas*, by Thomas R. Hester, Stephen L. Black, D. Gentry Steele, Ben W. Olive, Anne A. Fox, Karl J. Reinhard, and Leland C. Bement, 39–62. Arkansas Archaeological Survey Research Series 33. Final Report Submitted to the US Army Corps of Engineers, Southwestern Division. Study Unit 3 of the Southwestern Division Archaeological Overview. Prepared by the Center for Archaeological Research at the University of Texas at San Antonio, Texas A&M University, and the Arkansas Archaeological Survey. Wrightsville: Arkansas Department of Corrections.

Black, S. L., and A. J. McGraw. 1985. *The Panther Springs Creek Site: Cultural Change and Continuity within the Upper Salado Creek Watershed, South-Central Texas*. Archaeological Survey Report 100. San Antonio: Center for Archaeological Research, University of Texas at San Antonio.

Bousman, B., A. A. Fox, K. J. Gross, and I. W. Cox. 1995. *Historical Archaeology in Downtown San Antonio, Texas: An Evaluation of Properties at the Proposed VIA Downtown Park and Ride Facility*. Archaeological Survey Report 240. San Antonio: Center for Archaeological Research, University of Texas at San Antonio.

Carter, Cecile E. 1995 *Caddo Indians, Where We Come From*. Norman: University of Oklahoma Press.

Enquist, M. 1987. *Wildflowers of the Texas Hill Country*. Austin: Lone Star Botanical.

Everitt, J. H., and D. L. Drawe. 1993. *Trees, Shrubs, & Cacti of South Texas*. Lubbock: Texas Tech University Press.

Fox, A. A., ed. 1992. *Archaeological Investigations in Alamo Plaza, San Antonio, Bexar County, Texas: 1988 and 1989*. Archaeological Survey Report 205. San Antonio: Center for Archaeological Research, University of Texas at San Antonio.

Fox, A. A., F. A. Bass Jr., and T. R. Hester. 1976. *The Archaeology and History of Alamo Plaza*. Archaeological Survey Report 10. San Antonio: Center for Archaeological Research, University of Texas at San Antonio.

Fox, D. E. 1983. *Traces of Texas History: Archaeological Evidence of the Past 450 Years*. San Antonio: Corona Publishing.

Hall, E. T. 1977. *Beyond Culture*. Garden City, NY: Anchor Press/Doubleday.

Harris, M. 1974. *Cows, Pigs, Wars, and Witches: The Riddles of Culture*. New York: Random House.

Hester, T. R. 1989. Archaeological Synthesis. In *From the Gulf to the Rio Grande: Human Adaptation in Central, South, and Lower Pecos Texas*, by Thomas R. Hester, Stephen L. Black, D. Gentry Steele, Ben W. Olive, Anne A. Fox, Karl J. Reinhard, and Leland C. Bement, 5–16. Arkansas Archaeological Survey Research Series 33. Final Report Submitted to the US Army Corps of Engineers, Southwestern Division. Study Unit 3 of the Southwestern Division Archaeological Overview. Prepared by the Center for Archaeological Research at the University of Texas at San Antonio, Texas A&M University, and the Arkansas Archaeological Survey. Wrightsville: Arkansas Department of Corrections.

Hudson, Charles. 1976. *The Southeastern Indians*. Knoxville: University of Tennessee Press.

Hughes, Jack T. 1991. Prehistoric Cultural Developments on the Texas High Plains. *Bulletin of the Texas Archaeological Society* 60:1–55.

Kutac, E. A., and S. C. Caran. 1994. *Birds & Other Wildlife of South Central Texas*. Austin: University of Texas Press.

McGregor, R. 1991. Threaded and Twined Matting: A Late Introduction into the Lower Pecos. In *Papers on Lower Pecos Prehistory*, ed. S. A. Turpin, 141–48. Studies in Archaeology 8. Austin: Texas Archeological Research Laboratory, University of Texas at Austin.

———. 1992. *Prehistoric Basketry of the Lower Pecos, Texas*. Madison, WI: Prehistory Press.

Morgan, C. 2015. Is It Intensification Yet? Current Archaeological Perspectives on the Evolution of Hunter-Gatherer Economies. *Journal of Archaeological Research* 23 (2): 163–213.

Nance, R. C. 1972. Cultural Evidence for the Altithermal in Texas and Mexico. *Southwestern Journal of Anthropology* 28: 169–92.

Palmer, E. C. 1986. Land Use and Cultural Change along the Balcones Escarpment:

1718–1986. In *The Balcones Escarpment: Geology, Hydrology, Ecology, and Social Development in Central Texas*, ed. P. L. Abbott and C. M. Woodruff Jr., 153–61. Published for the Geological Society of America annual meeting, San Antonio, Texas, November. Santa Fe Springs, CA: Comet Reproduction Service.

Peacock, J. L. 1986. *The Anthropological Lens: Harsh Light, Soft Focus*. New York: Cambridge University Press.

Perttula, Timothy K. 1992. *The Caddo Nation, Archaeological and Ethnohistoric Perspectives*. Austin: University of Texas Press.

———, ed. 2004 *The Prehistory of Texas*. College Station: Texas A&M University Press.

Potter, D. R., and S. L. Black. 1995. Conceptual Framework. In *Archaeology along the Wurzbach Parkway: Module I Introduction, Conceptual Framework, and Contexts of Archaeological Investigations in Bexar County, South-Central Texas*, by D. R. Potter, S. L. Black, and K. Jolly. Studies in Archaeology 17. Austin: Texas Archeological Research Laboratory, University of Texas at Austin.

Riskind, D. H., and D. D. Diamond. 1986. Plant Communities of the Edwards Plateau of Texas: An Overview Emphasizing the Balcones Escarpment Zone between San Antonio and Austin with Special Attention to Landscape Contrasts and Natural Diversity. In *The Balcones Escarpment: Geology, Hydrology, Ecology, and Social Development in Central Texas*, ed. P. L. Abbott and C. M. Woodruff Jr., 21–32. Published for the Geological Society of America annual meeting, San Antonio, Texas, November. Santa Fe Springs, CA: Comet Reproduction Service.

———. 1988. An Introduction to Environments and Vegetation. In *Edwards Plateau Vegetation: Plant Ecological Studies in Central Texas*, ed. B. B. Amos and F. R. Gehlbach, 1–15. Waco, TX: Baylor University Press.

Scott, W. B. 1913. *A History of Land Mammals in the Western Hemisphere*. New York, The MacMillan Company.

Shafer, H. J. 1986. *Ancient Texans: Rock Art and Lifeways along the Lower Pecos*. Austin: Texas Monthly Press.

Simpson, B. J. 1988. *Field Guide to Texas Trees*. Texas Monthly Field Guide Series. Austin: Texas Monthly Press.

Thoms, A. V. 2009. Rocks of Ages: Propagation of Hot-Rock Cookery in Western North America. *Journal of Archaeological Science* 36 (3): 573–91.

Turner, S. E., and T. R. Hester. 1993. *A Field Guide to Stone Artifacts of Texas Indians*. 2nd ed. Austin: Texas Monthly Press.

Turpin, S. A., ed. 1991. *Papers on Lower Pecos Prehistory*. Studies in Archaeology 8. Austin: Texas Archeological Research Laboratory, University of Texas at Austin.

———. 1995. The Lower Pecos River Region of Texas and Northern Mexico. *Bulletin of the Texas Archaeological Society* 66: 541–60.

Vines, R. A. 1984 *Trees of Central Texas*. Austin: University of Texas Press.

Waters, M. R., and T. A. Jennings. 2015. *The Hogeye Clovis Cache*. College Station: Texas A&M University Press.

Wenke, R. J. 1990. *Patterns in Prehistory: Humankind's First Three Million Years*. 3rd ed. New York: Oxford University Press.

Ancient pictographs are found in rockshelters and caves throughout the Lower Pecos Canyonlands. Courtesy of Texas Parks and Wildlife Department

UNIT 3

Historical Naturalists of Texas

KRISTEN TYSON,
MARY PEARL MEUTH
Wildlife & Fisheries Extension Unit, Texas A&M AgriLife Extension Service

DAVID SCHMIDLY
President, University of New Mexico

Editorial Assistance: Valerie Taber, Rio Brazos Chapter, Texas Master Naturalist Program

Unit Goals

After completing this unit, volunteers should be able to

- understand the importance of expeditions and surveys in the natural history of Texas
- discuss the history of naturalists in Texas and their accomplishments
- identify the most significant naturalists of Texas

"Dedication to a cause is an apt descriptor for the pioneer Texas naturalist."
—Horace Burke, Texas A&M Professor Emeritus, 2003

This unit was compiled from essays written on the most significant naturalists in Texas as identified by the Texas Master Naturalist program. These essays were written by active Texas Master Naturalists from around the state, without whom this unit would not have been possible. While many other naturalists made significant and historically important contributions for the state of Texas, space limits the recognition and essays featured here. Also, we would like to acknowledge Horace Burke, Professor Emeritus, Texas A&M University, for his contribution to the Texas Master Naturalist Curriculum in its first 10 years of publication. His original unit, *Texas Naturalists prior to World War II* (2003), was a vital resource for the Texas Master Naturalists in their initial training.

Preface

David J Schmidly, Mammalogist and President, University of New Mexico

Texas is a place where major life zones intermingle. The fauna and flora include elements characteristic of the southeastern forests, the southern tropics, the southwestern deserts, the western mountains, and the northern Great Plains, as well as marine life associated with the extensive coast. For this reason, as well as its size and geographic location, Texas is the state with the greatest wildlife heritage in the United States (Schmidly 2002), which has attracted many important explorers and naturalists throughout its history to describe and study the state's natural history. The purpose of this unit is to explore the background, lives, and work of some of the most important naturalists whose extensive efforts provide not only a legacy of exploration but also the basis for understanding our modern fauna and flora. These individuals include explorers on some of the early expeditions and surveys to discover Texas, the state's early naturalists, university men (and several women) who represent the early academic naturalists, and a few modern-day naturalists. This is by no means an exhaustive list but a compendium of some of the most significant explorers and naturalists. Today, Texas has many outstanding amateur and professional naturalists associated with its universities, museums, state agencies, nature centers, and conservation organizations who continue the work of understanding and protecting our precious wildlife resources. We should be thankful to all these people for their legacy of dedication and insight to protect our invaluable natural resources.

Who Is a Naturalist?

The landscapes in Texas have seen dramatic change over the past couple of centuries, with change increasing in intensity over the recent decades. From a landscape of open ranges, large prairies, rolling hills, and scattered pine forests to the modern-day row-crop pasture, fragmented ranchlands, manicured urban areas, and patchwork of remnant natural habitats, humans have been there to both observe and influence these changes. Though the human influence has had a key role in the landscape up until this point, the observations made of these landscapes throughout this history will be the key to understanding Texas as we move forward in conservation.

This author's definition of a **naturalist** is anyone who studies and appreciates an object or organism in nature—studying it for a second while walking down a trail, for a minute while turning over a shell or leaf, or for a longer period of time to understand that part of the natural world. Can anyone be a naturalist as long as he or she has a moment of "observation and appreciation" with some element of the natural world (Buddle 2014)? A more refined definition of a naturalist provided on Buddle's website is, "*A naturalist studies the natural environment, generally with a broad range of interests, rather than with a particular specialty.*" However, some may contest that naturalists may begin their observations and studies by looking at the broad range of the natural environment but then become intrigued by the specific and decide to investigate further. Many of the early Texas naturalists did this on their expeditions and surveys, throughout their life span or as transient explorers in the state of Texas, becoming intrigued with the specifics. The role of Texas Master Naturalists is to begin their studies of the natural world found here in Texas and continue their study of nature by delving into these elements, all while keeping in mind the interconnectedness of the natural world.

"He instilled in me the mind and the values of a naturalist: to be open to all possibilities, to be a close and careful observer, to discipline my interpretation with facts, and to work hard at my passions so that they might bear fruit."
—Bernd Heinrich, The Snoring Bird

In historical context, many of the early naturalists were primarily collectors and observers—those who collected specimens intensely—while others made journals of observations on the behavior and ecology of their organisms of interest. All were involved in field-oriented activities (Burke 2003). In Samuel W. Geiser's "Men of Science, 1820–1880" (1958), he notes 1,060 individuals who contributed to the collections and observations of early Texas natural studies. Each of these contributors provided valuable records for the history of the state's changing landscape and its wildlife, but here we highlight the most significant naturalists in Texas history and provide a reflection on their personal interactions with the Texas landscapes, flora, and fauna. These early naturalists all date prior to the 1940s, before a large number of veterans from World War II entered colleges and universities. This marked a definite increase in natural history activities immediately following the war when these veterans, many of whom were continuing undergraduate education interrupted by the war, took advantage of the Servicemen's Readjustment Act of 1944 (better known as the GI Bill), to attend graduate schools (Burke 2003).

"He is the person who is inexhaustibly fascinated by biological diversity, and who does not view organisms merely as models, or vehicles for the theory but, rather, as the raison d'etre for biological investigation, as the Ding an sich, the thing in itself, that excites our admiration and our desire for knowledge, understanding and preservation."
—Douglas Futuyma, "Wherefore and Whither the Naturalist?"

Expeditions and Surveys

The pursuit of natural history in early Texas was not an easy task, and such activity was often hazardous to one's health, difficult, uncomfortable, and unappreciated (Peacock 1995). Many of these early naturalists spent only brief periods in Texas, as they collected alongside the paths of expeditions or surveys. Early settlers knew Texas to be a land of harsh habitats and lush resources. During the eighteenth century, the majority of the expeditions were carried out for Spanish mission building and converting the population to Christianity, with very little collection and notation made for biological data along the way. In the nineteenth century, the role of the expeditions expanded as settlers began to move into the region to set up homesteads and territory lines were drawn as a result of the newly signed Louisiana Purchase of 1803. These initial southern expeditions were financially backed by President Thomas Jefferson to mirror the success of the Lewis and Clark Expeditions in the north. Later in the 1820s, the expeditions were ordered by the Mexican Boundary Commission to help establish the boundary between the United States and Mexico. The next US Army expedition set off in 1849 at the command of the Mexican–United States Boundary Commission. These excursions were often accompanied by naturalists who provided the first organized collecting of flora and fauna, as well as reptiles and amphibians, along the border in Texas. The survey produced considerable biological information: 2,648 species of plants and a large number of animals collected during 1849–57 (Burke 2003).

Stephen Harriman Long (1784–1864)

Karen and Allen Ginnard, Gideon Lincecum Chapter, Texas Master Naturalist Program

Stephen Harriman Long was an explorer for the US Army and an engineer by education and training. His skill in engineering primarily encompassed the areas of topography and invention. Born in Hopkinton, New Hampshire, to Moses and Lucy (Harriman) Long, he received a bachelor of arts from Dartmouth College in 1809 and a master of arts degree from Dartmouth in 1812. In 1814, he was commissioned as a 2nd lieutenant in the US Army Corps of Engineers.

Major Stephen H. Long on the Rocky Mountain Expedition. Painting by Titian Peale, ca. 1835

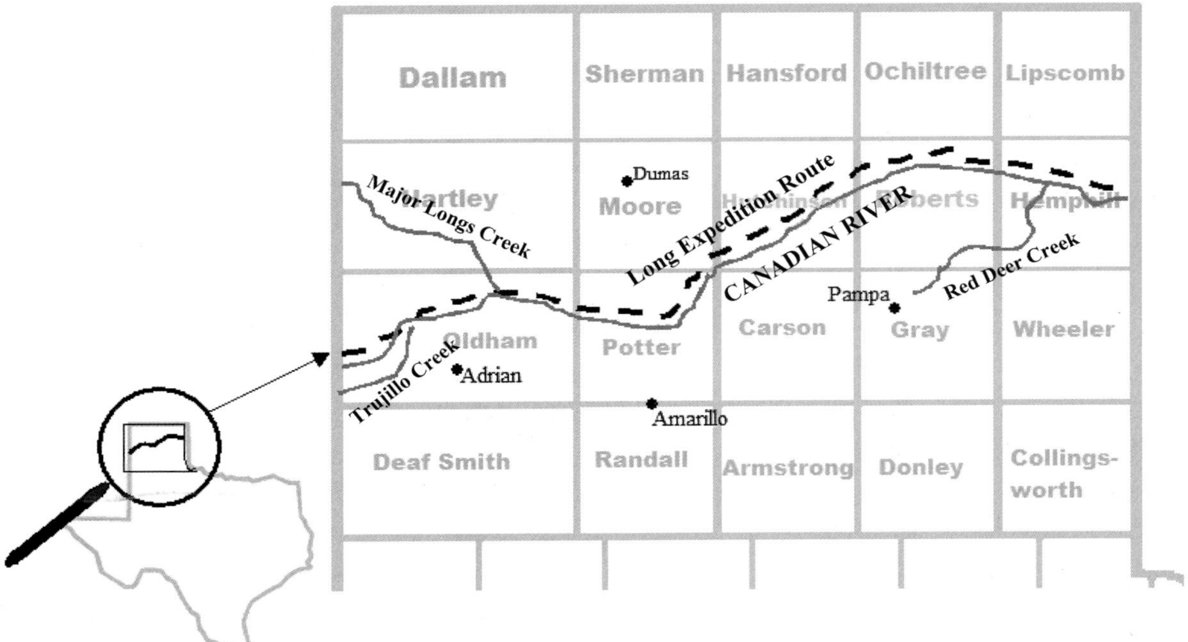

The route of the expedition taken by Stephen H. Long. Courtesy of Ashley Steinbach, intern, Texas A&M AgriLife Extension Service

Upon the reorganization of the army in 1816, he was appointed to the rank of major in April and assigned to the Southern Division under Maj. General Andrew Jackson as a topographical engineer (Anderson 2010).

In his capacity as explorer and topographical engineer for the US Army, Long, with his team of explorers, made his contribution to Texas natural history. His success can be attributed to assembling a talented team. On the expedition in Texas, the US Army planned to thoroughly explore the area that extended from the Red River north of Texas to the Platte, and west to the summit of the Rocky Mountains. Secretary of War J. C. Calhoun assigned Major Long to lead the June 1810 Long-Bell Expedition. The team included a military journalist, an assistant topographer, a zoologist, a botanist/mineralogist/surgeon, an assistant naturalist, a landscape painter, a guide/interpreter, hunters, a farrier, and various other service members who contributed to the overall safety or comfort of the expedition. Some of these men became famous in their own right for their part in the exploratory work. Edwin James, a botanist and geologist on the expedition, published the first comprehensive book on the expedition, *Expedition to the Rocky Mountains 1818–1819* (James 1823).

During the expedition, Long and his team found themselves short on food and supplies. Upon reaching the Arkansas River, Major Long decided to split the exploration team into two parties in the hope that one or both teams would find the necessary food and water needed to sustain the expedition. One team, under J. R. Bell, would proceed along the Arkansas River to Fort Smith. The other, led by Long, would head south to discover the source of the Red River. Long mistakenly thought the Canadian River was the Red River, so he did not find the springs that fed the tributaries as the source for the Red River (Nichols 1980). However, he and his party spent several weeks in the Texas Panhandle in August 1820, cataloging animal life, plants, minerals, and soil and noting prominent features across the Panhandle. The heat was intense, the insects were relentless, and food was scarce. The team sometimes went without water for 24 hours. The expedition was a difficult one, although rewarding. The contribution made by the expedition included the opportunity to briefly study and first record an encounter between Anglo-Americans and the Kiowa-Apache.

The spirit of these early naturalists was one of tremendous courage and fortitude. The conditions in which they worked were often hostile, uncomfortable, physically grueling, and harsh. Still, the desire to discover and catalog in the uncharted territories drove these men to continue their work even in the roughest conditions. The work they did benefited their current generation but also laid the foundation for future naturalists. Long covered roughly 26,000 miles during five exploration expeditions during his lifetime (Anonymous, n.d.). The Long Expedition that touched Texas land was the first scientific survey of the Panhandle region and dramatically increased the country's geographic knowledge of that region and the west.

Peter Custis (1781–1842)

Kristen Tyson, Texas A&M AgriLife Extension Service

When **Peter Custis** was asked to join the second major expedition initiated by President Thomas Jefferson, it is questionable whether he knew the political and historical importance before agreeing. For more than two years before the exploration of the Red River, the Jefferson White House struggled with two key issues, one being Spanish boundary claims over the true border of Louisiana. Second was the previous Lewis and Clark Expedition survey of the Missouri and Columbia Rivers that lacked a trained naturalist, which puzzled many in the scientific and natural history fields. This obvious exclusion, and the hiring of Meriwether Lewis, whose resume was not yet impressive enough to warrant such a large scientific expedition, left Jefferson with the need to settle Spanish unrest and attain an honest natural history review of the Red River Valley. Who would have known the Custis Expedition would help further the understanding of the fusion between government exploration and American nature study in its beginning years (Flores 1984)?

The proposed 15-month Red River expedition was meant to survey the mouth of the river, which was believed to rise in the mountains northeast of Santa Fe. In addition, Jefferson believed that Indian relations

The Late Prehistoric Caddo of East Texas were mound builders like many of the American Indian groups centered around the lower Mississippi Valley. Courtesy of Texas Parks and Wildlife Department

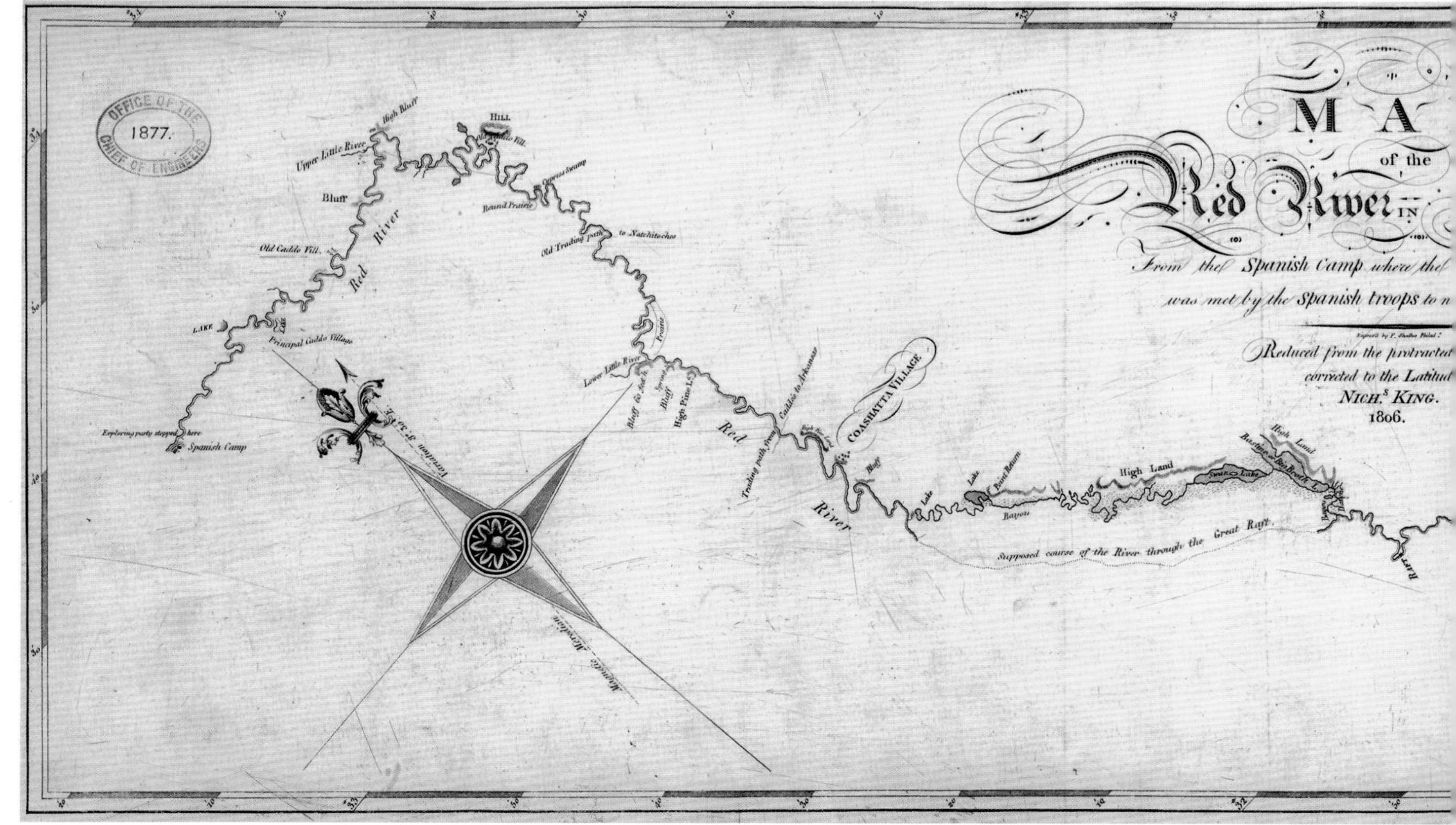

Peter Custis (1781–1842). Map of the Red River Expedition by Nicholas King (1771–1812). Courtesy of the Library of Congress, Geography and Map Division

could be fostered in the Southwest, and if reports were true, the natural bounty of minerals would provide the nation with endless commercial value. As if this expedition did not bear enough weight on its own, Jefferson secretly believed that scientific map work on the Red River would give the United States an undisputed claim to the river (Flores 1984). Members of the expedition were expected to record meteorological and topographical data, document flora and fauna, and note interactions with Indians and their unique characteristics, in addition to their survey work.

By 1805, a year after the first draft of the expedition, Thomas Freeman, an accomplished Irish American engineer, astronomer, and experienced Indian negotiator, was chosen as field leader (Flores 1984). It would take another year, despite intense efforts, before a naturalist was selected. Natural history professor Benjamin Smith Barton finally found the ideal candidate at the beginning of 1806: a young, unmarried naturalist who could handle the harsh terrain before him. Twenty-five-year-old medical student Peter Custis fit the requirements and would be available to travel that spring.

Prior to the fateful invitation to join the expedition, Peter Custis was only a year away from completing his doctorate from a Pennsylvania medical school. Originally from Virginia, Custis took his studies seriously and impressed his professor enough that, under Barton's tutelage, he had been educated in a diversified natural history curriculum (Flores 1984). Despite his remarkable classroom abilities, however, Custis did not seem to have any prior field experience.

The "Exploring Expedition of Red River" was now able to commence with the security of a naturalist, and Freeman and Custis began their journey, arriving in Mississippi in late April 1806. Throughout the journey, Custis was charged with keeping a meteorological chart three times daily and mapping

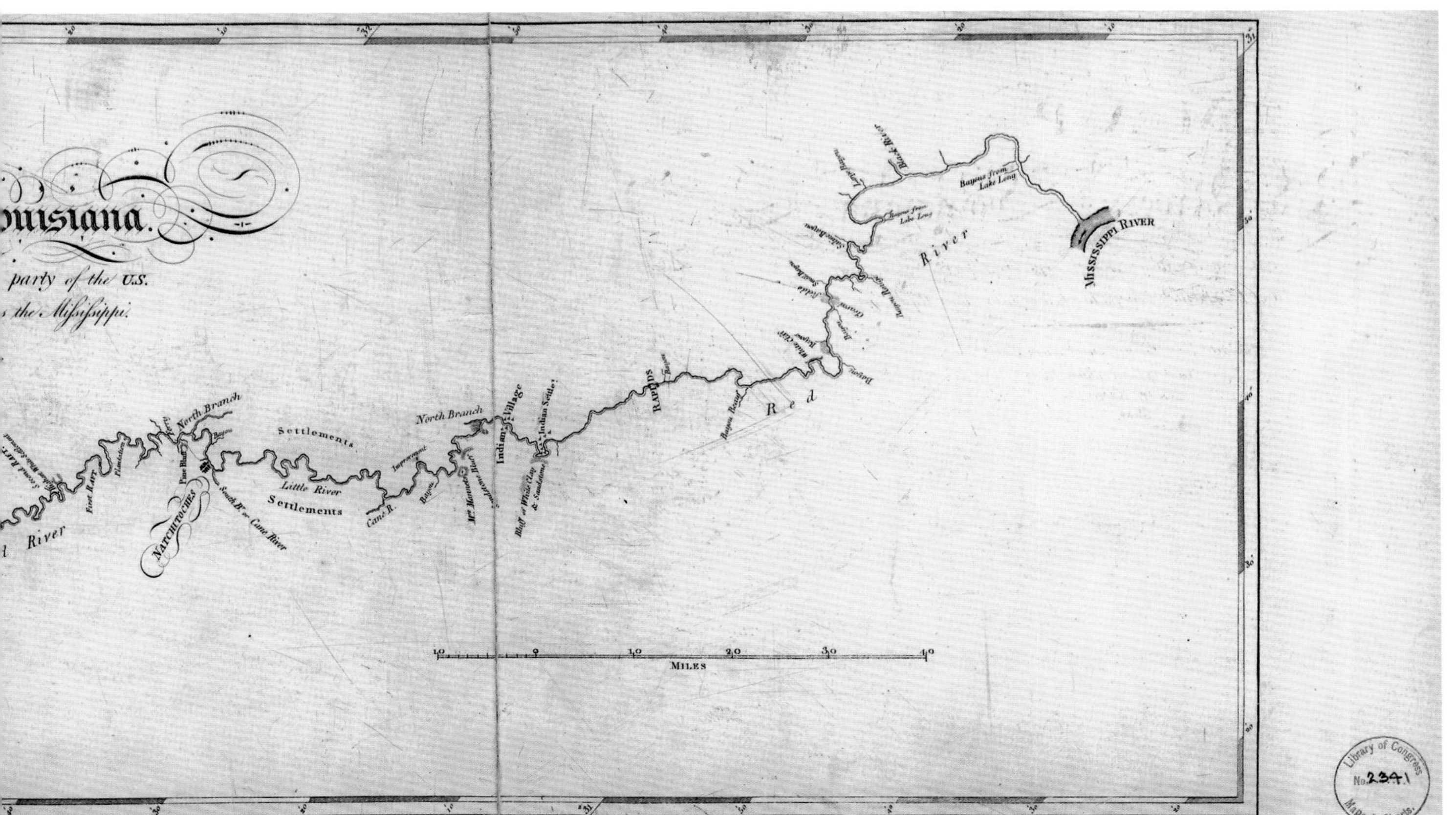

the river, thus he had "no time to make botanical excursions into the hinterland" (Custis 1806). However, he was able to take note of the natural history. Custis was given credit for his depiction of a Louisiana fox squirrel (*Sciurus niger ludovicianus* Custis) (Flores 1984). He named a siren-type creature the *Syren quadruped* and reported on numerous birds, including two currently extinct. Custis cataloged 50 vegetables and provided invaluable notes on trees indigenous to the area, including native pecans, white cedars, and bald cypress varieties. By June the explorers had traversed a massive swamp where Custis was able to add more than 40 entries to his botanical catalog. This month also marked the expedition's first interaction with native Caddo. This meeting gave Custis an opportunity to assemble ethnological data on the customs and mythology of one of the last remnants of the great Mississippian mound-building cultures of American antiquity. While among the Caddo, Custis documented big game, including black bears and white-tailed deer, 70 plants, and a mineral collection. Time was spent wisely on a botanical collection, which was among the first collected in the Trans-Mississippi West (Flores 1984).

In his spare time, Custis toured abandoned Indian villages and thanks to Caddo guides, viewed bison and peregrine falcons near a formerly prominent Caddo village. The expedition remained aware of nearby Spanish troops as they documented new and rare species along the river. Just as the expedition was reaching its apex in July, they were met by Spanish cavalry. In order to prevent a complete loss of valuable data, Jefferson ordered the men to conclude the expedition and return quickly.

Refreshed and rested in Pennsylvania, Custis began working on reports concerning the natural history he experienced over the short journey. He cataloged nearly 80 birds and animals and close to 190 plants in four months on the Red River, with three new discoveries credited to him alone. From the perspective of present-day naturalists, his catalogs are clearly one of the earliest detailed lists for a major North American river ecosystem (Flores 1984), and unfortunately they give evidence of how little of that landscape still exists today.

Perhaps because of political reasons, Jefferson chose not to broadcast the expedition, causing Custis to feel his contribution was in vain. This led Custis to complete his medical studies in Pennsylvania in 1807 and return to his native Virginia. He did continue to collect plants and eventually settled in as a physician in North Carolina, where he died on May 1, 1842.

Randolph Barnes Marcy (1812–1887)

Kristen Tyson, Texas A&M AgriLife Extension Service

Randolph Barnes Marcy is most notably known for his military history and guidebooks on border and frontier travels, but Texas naturalists appreciate him for other accomplishments. Born in Massachusetts, Marcy was career military from the beginning. He graduated from the United States Military Academy at West Point and served numerous tours in the war with Mexico. He then led an expedition looking for fort sites along the Texas frontier, surveying Indian villages along the way.

Randolph Barnes Marcy (1812–87). Courtesy of the Library of Congress, LC-B814-3790

Marcy wholeheartedly believed "there exists as wide as contrast as can be found" between the Indian and the Anglo-Saxon. He noted, however, that the habits of the prairie Indians assimilate very closely to each other in some respects (Marcy 1866). His assessment of the local Indians was often compared to the Spaniards' first contact with native peoples and to the similarities with Indians of New Mexico and the eastern states. Marcy enjoyed the pleasure of examining the native people he encountered so much that one of his books, *Thirty Years of Army Life on the Border*, dedicated more than four chapters (nearly 100 pages) to their way of life.

With a publication under his belt, Capt. R. B. Marcy received orders in 1852 to make an examination of the Red River and the country bordering it, from the mouth of Cache Creek to its sources. This was not Marcy's first exploration, as he had already toured the Canadian River in Arkansas, as well as the Trinity, Brazos, and Colorado Rivers in Texas (Marcy 1866). Marcy knew that a previous expedition had been sent in 1806, consisting of Freeman and Custis, and that they had great difficulty traversing the swampy rivers and encountered Spanish resistance before locating the source of the Red River. That same year Lt. Zebulon Pike was hired by the government to locate the same, but ended up traveling the Rio Grande. And the Long Expedition, using Pike's navigational notes, ended their journey along the Canadian River. To say that this venture was important is an understatement; to say it was fraught with hardship is truth, considering none of the travelers had yet reached the source of the Red River.

As the expedition made its way along the mouth of the Cache River, they were able to procure samples of black ore. Charles Upham Shepherd described it "as strongly resembling the black oxide of copper from the Lake Superior mines, for which I at first mistook it. It was partially coated by a thin layer of the rare and beautiful atacamite [muriate of copper]. This is the first instance in which this species has been detected in North America. . . . It affords me much pleasure to name it, in honor of the very enterprising and successful explorer to whom mineralogy is indebted for the discovery, *Marcylite*" (Marcy 1853, 155). (Marcylite was later identified as an impure atacamite [Merritt 1940].) Marcy noted that "the landscape here presented to the eye has a most charming diversity of scenery" (1866, 127) and found that the soil and timber were rich and vast. Less than a month into their travels they met friendly Indians whose accounts of the headwaters of the river discouraged the travelers because of its distance and difficulty. As they progressed, Marcy wrote of bears and deer, sour water and monotonous landscapes. Buffalo hunts and panther encounters kept the men engaged, but it was the arrival of desperately needed torrential rain in the wake of limited water that truly excited them.

On June 16, 1852, the party finally reached the North Fork of the Red River, which was only 25 miles from the Canadian River. With accurate longitude and latitude recorded, the company continued on for another 65 miles, facing a desperate lack of water for several weeks. Yet Marcy stated that "the magnificence of the views that presented themselves to our eyes as we approached the head of the river exceeded anything I had ever beheld" (1866, 150). After noting the geographic position of the headwaters, the men rested before turning back on July 4 toward home.

At the conclusion of this expedition, Marcy was chosen in 1854 "to go out into the unsettled parts of the state to locate and survey . . . any vacant lands, reservations for the exclusive use of the Indians" (Marcy 1866, 170). This would involve exploration of the sources of the Brazos and Big Wichita Rivers. Marcy continued to serve the army in several capacities, including supply runs and border patrols. With the Civil War erupting in 1861, Marcy saw more battle action and was provisionally promoted to the rank of brevetted brigadier general. This awarded him the title for commendable service but not the authority for which he hoped. (The US Senate did not confirm his wartime promotion before it expired.) When the war was over, he continued his US Army duties and published several more books on his life in the army and travels across the states. Marcy was finally awarded the rank of brigadier general when he was appointed inspector general of the US Army in 1878 and honorably retired in 1881. He died at his New Jersey home on November 22, 1887 (Cutrer 2010).

Charles Wright (1811–1885)

Kristen Tyson, Texas A&M AgriLife Extension Service

Although **Charles Wright** was not a Texan by birth, as the saying goes, he got here as fast as he could. Born in Connecticut in 1811 and graduated from Yale in 1835, Wright came to Texas to survey and teach school for a living. His survey work included the towns of Jasper, Angelina, Taylor, Newton, and Menard (Geiser 1937). He was a botanist by hobby, but after submitting a few specimens to Asa Gray of the Gray Herbarium of Harvard University in 1844, he began to seriously collect plants. In the meantime, he returned to the school system as principal of Rutersville College (in Fayette County) until 1845 and then relocated to Austin for further collecting.

Wright's fate changed around 1845 when Gray secured a botanical expedition for

Charles Wright (1811–85), an American botanist, ca. 1855.

Wright to travel with troops moving across the Rio Grande Valley to El Paso. This arduous journey of sleepless nights and constant storms depressed Wright. Despite the 673-mile walking journey, he was still able to send Gray over 1,400 specimens, albeit four years later (Geiser 1937). Perhaps due to the harsh conditions he endured in El Paso, Wright returned to his educational roots and taught school in New Braunfels, where he met botanist Ferdinand Lindheimer.

In 1851, Wright joined Col. J. D. Graham's survey of the Mexico–United States boundary and returned a year later with enough survey recordings to print in several notable publications and reports. From 1853 to 1855, he was the botanist for the US North Pacific Exploring Expedition, an international tour from Virginia to San Francisco, during which he kept an extensive journal and documented plants collected from the tropical habitats of Cape Verde, Japan, and the Bering Strait. Wright then collected in Nicara-

Collection areas of Charles Wright and goldenrod (*Solidago wrightii*), a species he collected. Courtesy of Yonassan Gershom

gua for a few months, and from 1856 to 1867 explored the botanical riches of Cuba. Upon his return, Wright served as acting director of the Gray Herbarium and librarian of Harvard's Bussey Institution (Geiser 1937). Before his death in 1885, Wright returned to live near his siblings at his native home in Connecticut.

Early Naturalists

"The psychological dangers of the frontier for the naturalist seem to be especially great when, as in Texas, the scientific frontier of exploration coincides with a geographical frontier. In Texas, as in the rest of the States, the early settler's suspicion of the scientist was a serious psychological obstacle."
—Samuel Wood Geiser, Naturalists of the Frontier, 1937

At the turn of the nineteenth century, many of the naturalists in Texas came as immigrants from Germany and England, and a few moved west from the established states on the eastern coast of America. These new naturalists were not in the state to make expeditions for collections only but came with a fascination for learning about the diversity of Texas' flora and fauna. Living conditions improved slightly after the Republic of Texas declared its independence in 1836, and there was a modest increase in the influx of naturalists into the state after Texas joined the United States in 1845. These explorers, some educated and some not, were interested in a wider range of flora and fauna, from Lindheimer, the "Father of Texas Botany" to John Allen Singley, who published the first list of mollusks for the state.

Gideon Lincecum (1793–1874)

Wallace Stapp, Capital Area Chapter, Texas Master Naturalist Program

Gideon Lincecum (1793–1874), a man of diverse interests, including natural history. He studied and wrote about the lives of ants and corresponded with Charles Darwin.

Gideon Lincecum is perhaps the first real frontier naturalist. He grew up in a family that lived on the edge of the frontier as it moved from Georgia to Mississippi. He was friends with the Muskogee and Choctaw in the area, and he became an expert with the bow and arrow and learned about the Choctaw culture (Burkhalter 2010). He had only five months of formal schooling at a primitive, temporary school on the Georgia frontier when, at age 14, he moved with his family to within a mile and a half of the school (Burkhalter 1965). His father paid seven dollars each for Gideon, his brother, and his sister to attend. It is said he learned a new lesson every 15 minutes: "At the end of five months [he] could read , . . . could write a pretty fair hand by copy . . . progressed in arithmetic to the double root of three, and had committed Webster's spelling book entirely to memory" (Geiser 1937). He later taught in a frontier school for a year and allowed the students to set and enforce the rules. In 1813, he married Sarah Bryan, and they settled in Columbus, Mississippi, for the next 30 years (Birch 2004). He studied with a famous Choctaw medicine man and compiled a herbarium with notes on more than 300 medicinal plants. This knowledge set him apart from other settlers, which allowed Lincecum to have a deeper understanding for the Indian traditions and beliefs (McGauch, n.d). The remnants of his collection eventually came to the University of Texas at Austin from his family. Benjamin Tharp reconstructed the herbarium and filled in the remaining labels, names, and uses of a substantial portion of the plants.

Lincecum had read everything he could find on medicine and became a doctor, hanging out his shingle in Columbus, Mississippi and for 20 years he was a successful doctor and pharmacist. In 1835, he led a group of 10 citizens of Columbus to the then-Mexican state of Texas. They saw the settled portions of Texas in about three months, and most of the delegation returned to Mississippi, but Lincecum stayed behind. He declared in his autobiography, "I cannot consent to return until I make myself able to make a satisfactory report . . . of this great country" (Geiser 1937). For four months in late 1835, he visited areas to the west in Indian-held lands. His descriptions of the land he visited and its wildlife are highlights of his autobiography. He was captured by Comanche, but he managed a remarkable escape by feigning a search to collect medicinal herbs. He almost joined the Texas Revolution in 1836 but was dissuaded by several prominent Texans because he had 10 dependent children.

In 1848, along with most of his family, he moved to Long Point, Texas, in Fayette County and began his naturalist career in earnest on 1,828 acres of fertile prairieland he had seen on his previous visit to Texas (Burkhalter 1965). The land was purchased for seventy-five cents per acre. Like author and naturalist Henry David Thoreau, Lincecum was capable of long, intense observations that he recorded in minute and astonishing detail. By 1860, he had composed 14 papers on natural history, including 3 dealing with the Choctaw as well as an autobiography. From 1860 to 1861 he corresponded with Charles Darwin, Louis Agassiz, and Alexander von Humboldt, among many others. His article on the agricultural ant was published in the *Journal of the Linnaean Society* and was sponsored and read by Charles Darwin. At that point, he became internationally known and recognized as a "thorough and respectable researcher, in spite of his lack of formal education" (McGauch, n.d.). He was elected a corresponding member of the Philadelphia Academy of Natural Sciences and contributed thousands of botanical specimens to world-class museums, including the Smithsonian Institution, the British Museum, and the Jardin des Plantes in Paris.

Lincecum was a southerner, and in 1867 he moved to Tuxpan, Mexico, to escape the Reconstruction period after the Civil War. Before he left, he sent all his collections of mammals, fossils, shells, birds, and insects to the Smithsonian Institution. In Mexico, he continued to collect and ship specimens abroad. A year before his death in 1874, he returned to his home and family in Long Point. When he was 17, a neighbor gave him a violin for Christmas, and every Christmas morning after that until his death he went outside and played a Scottish ballad. He is buried with his violin (Burkhalter 1965).

Jean Louis Berlandier (ca. 1805–1851)

Al McGraw, Archaeologist, Lindheimer Chapter

With contributions by Robert and Eva Fromme, Susan Flores Crissy, and Monica K. Flores

Jean Louis Berlandier was an early nineteenth-century European naturalist who explored northeastern Mexico and

Texas from 1826 to 1834. He was born around 1805 between Fort de l'Écluse, France, and Geneva, Switzerland. Berlandier studied botany in Geneva and was likely a pharmacist's apprentice before publishing several articles on plant species. He arrived in Mexico in 1826 as a botanist and zoologist to accompany a scientific commission for the exploration of northern Mexico and Texas (Hartman 2010).

Best known for his extensive identification of the region's botany and his faunal collections, Berlandier was also a prolific ethnographer who described the character and lifeways of the country. His memoirs included eyewitness and detailed descriptions of the natural setting, early settlers, towns (or *villas*), and native Texas Indians. Berlandier's journals are especially valuable because they were "acute and unbiased observations" (Hutchinson 1970). They were also written on the eve of the Texas Revolution, a poorly documented period of history when Texas was a politically unstable, rebellious state of the Mexican Republic.

A large part of Berlandier's zoological and botanical collections were made after 1827 when he became a member of the Comisión de Límites, or **Mexican Boundary Commission**, under the command of the Mexican general don José Manuel Rafael Simeón de Mier y Terán. The purpose of the multiyear expedition was both scientific and broadly political: to identify the region's natural resources, comment on the conditions of the region's inhabitants, assess the threat of political instability caused by American immigrants, and better determine the international boundary between the Sabine and Red Rivers.

Berlandier fish (*Pimelodus maculatus*). Courtesy of Record Unit 7052—Jean

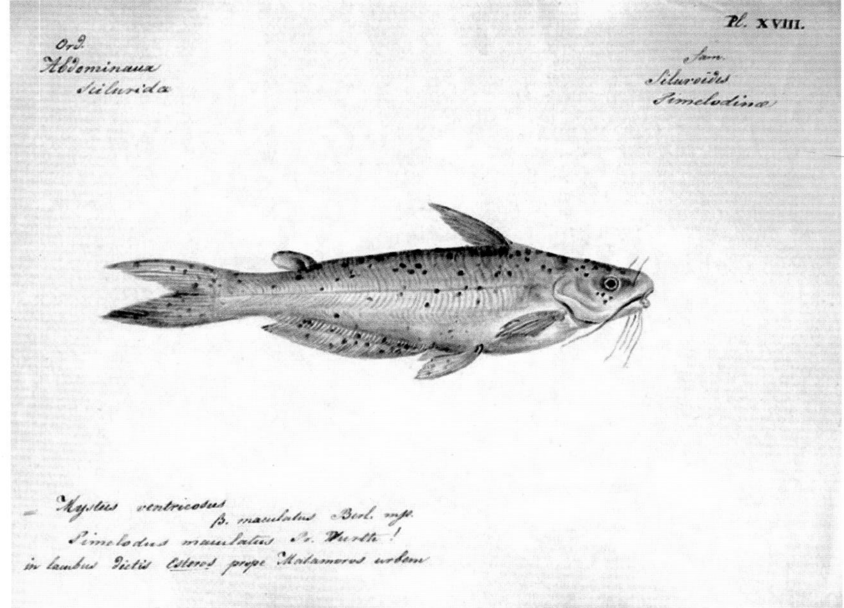

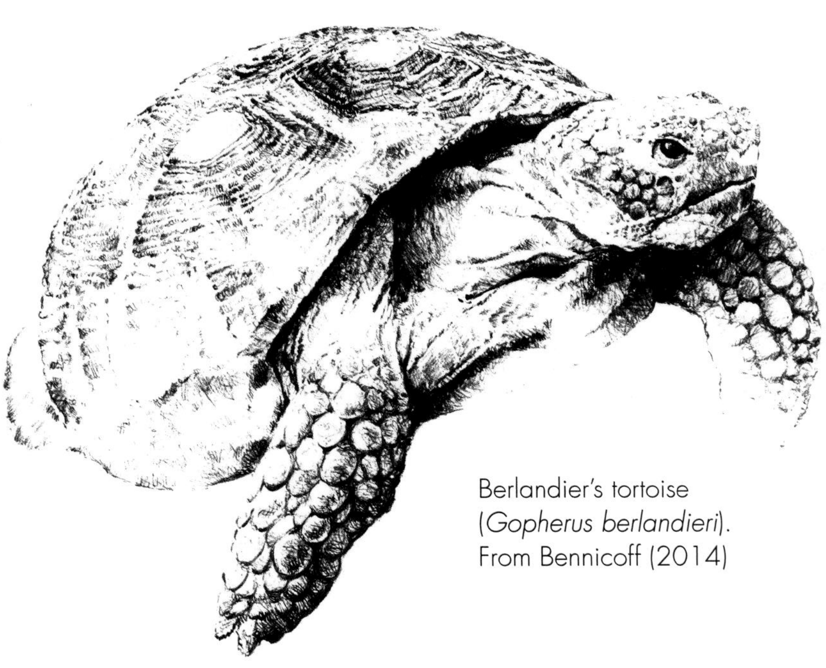

Berlandier's tortoise (*Gopherus berlandieri*). From Bennicoff (2014)

Berlandier texana, Texas greeneyes. Courtesy of Jeff McMillian, hosted by the USDA-NRCS PLANTS Database

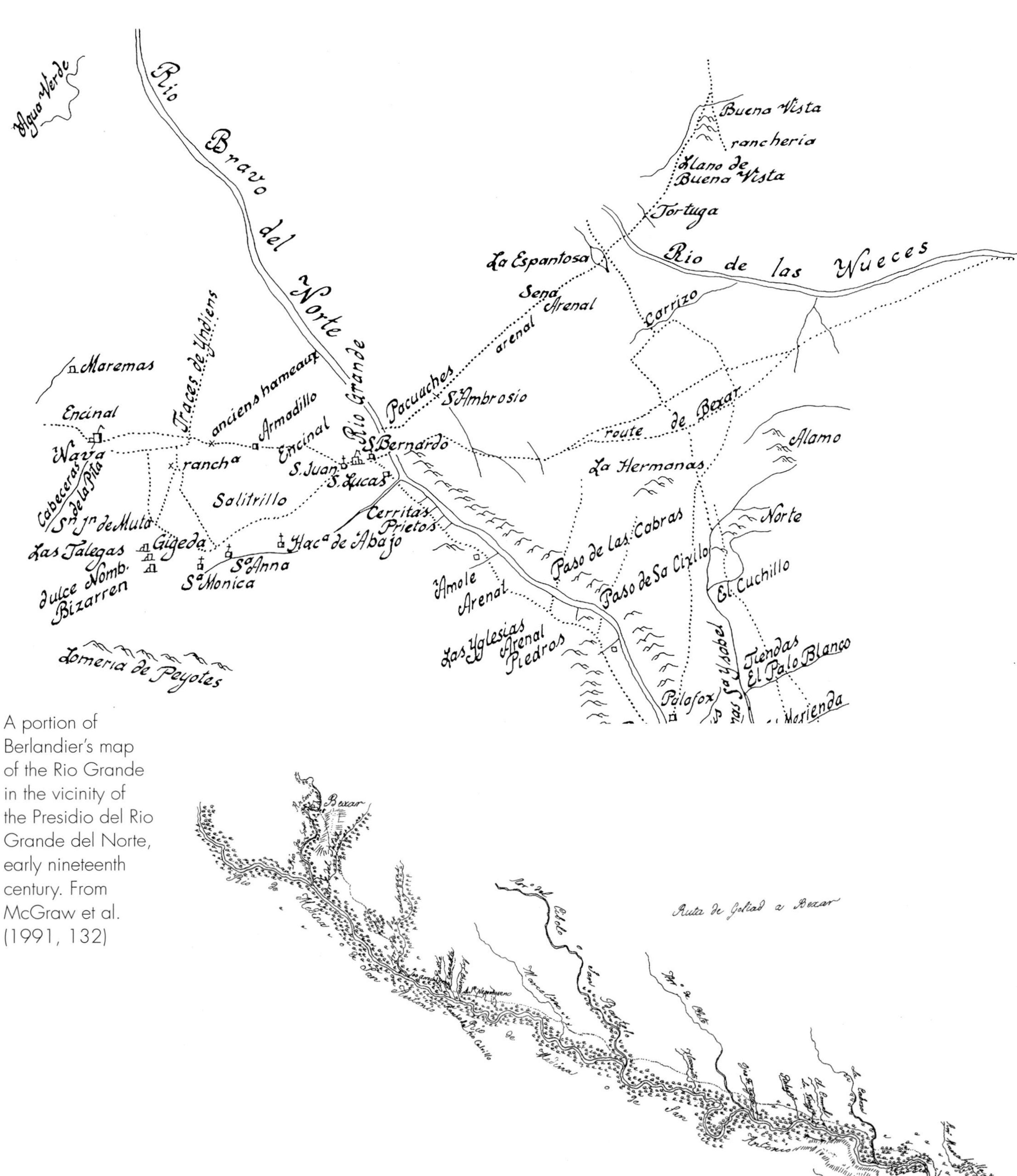

A portion of Berlandier's map of the Rio Grande in the vicinity of the Presidio del Rio Grande del Norte, early nineteenth century. From McGraw et al. (1991, 132)

Berlandier's map of a portion of the La Bahia Road between San Antonio and Cibolo Creek in the early nineteenth century. Partially redrawn from the original by A. McGraw, personal collection.

Berlandier's studies in natural history were broadly based. In addition to his interests in zoology and botany he compiled the earliest detailed multidecade meteorological and astronomical observations in northeastern Mexico and southern Texas. Berlandier's records also listed around 52,000 dried plant specimens that were shipped to his French sponsors for study between 1827 and 1831. His success was equivocal if not compromised because of the resulting dissatisfaction of his recipients (McGraw et al. 1991). Berlandier also compiled an impressive collection of watercolors of plant and animals, and his inventories resulted in a number of plant and animal species bearing his name.

Following the conclusion of the boundary survey commission in 1829–30, Berlandier settled in Mexico and independently continued to study and compile data on the region's plants and animals. He eventually became a pharmacist and doctor in Matamoros, and there is some indication he once was an *alcalde* (mayor/judge) of the town. Berlandier drowned in 1851 while trying to cross the flooded San Fernando River.

Berlandier's travels in Texas included most of the historical routes today known as the Camino Real de los Tejas National Historic Trail, Comanche trails north of San Antonio, and an excursion to the rumored San Saba silver mines. In 1834 he retraced some of his earlier regional routes to recollect specimens that were lost in earlier years. His journals along the Texas Camino Real and several trips between San Antonio and Goliad along La Bahia Road before 1834 have recently been reviewed from a historical archeological perspective (McGraw et al. 1991).

His records, although brief, described the abandonment of early ranchos at the turn of the nineteenth century, and his eyewitness account commented on their reestablishment and relocation in the 1820s. In addition to Jean Louis Berlandier's contributions as an important early Texas naturalist, the prolific information contained in his journals and papers continues to be of interest and of sometimes unexpected value to modern researchers in related multidisciplinary studies (Berlandier 1983).

Thomas Drummond (1790–1835)

Deborah Canterbury, Blackland Prairie Chapter, Texas Master Naturalist Program

"I could ask a thousand questions about my plants but I have no books to inform me."
—Thomas Drummond, *Naturalists of the Frontier*

Scottish-born **Thomas Drummond** was encouraged from an early age to pursue the field of botany by his older botanist brother and a circle of leading scientist friends. Little is known of his professional training, but his fieldwork brought him numerous accolades and appointments. His willingness to share and his gregarious personality won the respect of such botanists as Sir William Jackson Hooker and David Douglas. He was

Thomas Drummond (1790–1835).

Drummond's onion, wild garlic, or Drummond wild onion (*Allium drummondii* Regel), in the Lily family (Liliaceae). Synonyms: *A. helleri, A. nuttallii.* Courtesy of Lady Bird Johnson Wildflower Center

noted for his study of mosses, *Musci [americani] scotici* (Bird 1967), but many other plants bear his name, such as *Malvaviscus drummondii* (Turk's cap). Drummond's name is borne by about a dozen plant species (including *Potentilla drummondii* from the Rockies), the moss genus *Drummondia,* and one mammal, *Neotoma cinerea drummondii (pack rat),* assigned by John Richardson. He is one of five generations of naturalists/botanists (Lawley, n.d.).

During his first trips to America and Canada he survived snow blindness, loss of sled dogs from starvation, near–bear attacks, illness, and extreme isolation. Yet he still wanted to return to the Rockies and southern America after being inspired by William Hooker and those he met on previous trips to America. In 1831, funded by Hooker, he was able to travel once again to explore the southern states to collect specimens for his patron. Arriving in New York, Drummond traveled to Philadelphia, on to Baltimore, and then to Washington before setting out across the Alleghenies on foot, finding the terrain easier than that of the Rockies. He even took a steamboat down the Ohio River to St. Louis.

Drummond collected a vast number of plants in Louisiana before visiting Texas in 1833. It was recorded that he sent two tons of paper to New Orleans for preserving plants (Meikle 2005). He was also one of the first to gather good specimens in the area of Austin's Colony. In Texas, he was the earliest collector of insects for Thomas Kirby in Austin's Colony during 1833–34. Unfortunately, in Velasco, Texas, he and his companions were struck down by cholera, and he dosed himself with opium. Luckily, he survived, but many did not; he almost starved because no one was able to supply food. When exploring the Brazos River in early 1834, he again fell ill with a bilious fever and was smitten with boils from head to foot, which were so painful he could not lie down for seven nights (Mueller, n.d.).

Once he was healed, Drummond spent 21 months working the area between Galveston Island and the Edwards Plateau, especially along the Brazos, Colorado, and Guadalupe Rivers. His collections were the first made in Texas that were extensively distributed among the museums and scientific institutions of the world. He collected 750 species of plants and 150 specimens of birds. Drummond had hoped to make a complete botanical survey of Texas, but he died in Havana, Cuba, in 1835, while presumably making a collecting tour of that island. Hooker received a letter from the consul in Havana in March 1835 telling of Drummond's death. The details of his death were supposedly sent in another letter, which never arrived. None of the collection he had with him was returned (Lawley, n.d.).

Drummond was a quiet, intrepid, hardworking, and enthusiastic field naturalist, endowed, according to Richardson, with "an extreme quickness and acuteness of vision . . . [who] carried on under circumstances of domestic discomfort and difficulties, that would have quelled a meaner spirit" (Richardson 1829). Hooker asserted that he had "accomplished enough, by his zeal and researches, to secure to himself a lasting name throughout the botanical world" (Boynton 1918, 5). Drummond's collection of several thousand herbaceous plants from the prairies and Rocky Mountains, together with those of Douglas, Richardson, and Archibald Menzies, formed the basis for Hooker's *Flora Boreali-Americana* (1840).

The insects, 150 birds, and 50 mammals collected by Drummond were used by Richardson in *Fauna Boreali-Americana* (1829–37). Mount Drummond and the Drummond ice field in Banff Park, Alberta, are named after Drummond. His accomplishments led naturalists Ferdinand Jacob Lindheimer and Charles Wright to work in Texas to expand the discovery and classifications that he started.

Ferdinand Jacob Lindheimer (1801–1879)

Wallace Stapp, Capital Area Chapter, Texas Master Naturalist Program

"My bad mood during the first part of my being here [Galveston] obviously stemmed from the fact that I could not carry on my business of collecting [plants] during the windy and rainy weather. I probably should have rented myself a room right away, but I thought I would be staying here only four days. Now I am renting a little house by the week for one paper dollar (80c) a week. I find a new plant almost every day, one that I have never seen before. If only I can take other excursions I shall surely find much more that is of interest."
—Ferdinand Lindheimer to St. Louis botanist George Engelmann, April 29, 1843

Ferdinand Jacob Lindheimer was university educated in Germany and taught in a sec-

Ferdinand Jacob Lindheimer (1801–79), sometimes known as the "Father of Texas Botany." Courtesy of New Braunfels Conservation Society

The Texas prickly pear (*Opuntia lindheimeri*) is named after Frederick Lindheimer. Courtesy of Texas Parks and Wildlife Department

ondary school for seven years before joining many other German intellectuals who were escaping repression by immigrating to America in 1833. Once in America, Lindheimer joined a "Latin" farm community. In 1834, he and five other Germans went to New Orleans with plans to collect plants in Texas. (Of the historical naturalists who worked in Texas at different times, approximately one-fourth had attended a university in Germany.) After reports of Indian atrocities in Texas, Lindheimer and two friends went to Vera Cruz and then Jalapa, Mexico, where there was a German colony. In Jalapa, Lindheimer became manager of a distillery and pineapple and banana plantation. He also did some collecting of plants and insects. He wrote of the conditions in Mexico in the last months of 1835: "I recognized this was the moment to carry out my original plan of going to Texas, before the decisive battle. . . . My decision to go to Texas was already made"; he joined a group of Texas Volunteers who were posted to Galveston and missed the Battle of San Jacinto by one day (Geiser 1937). In 1842, Lindheimer was in St. Louis and met with George Engelmann to make a deal regarding collecting plants for Engelmann and Asa Gray of Harvard for eight dollars per 100 plants. He returned to Texas and began collecting around the existing German communities.

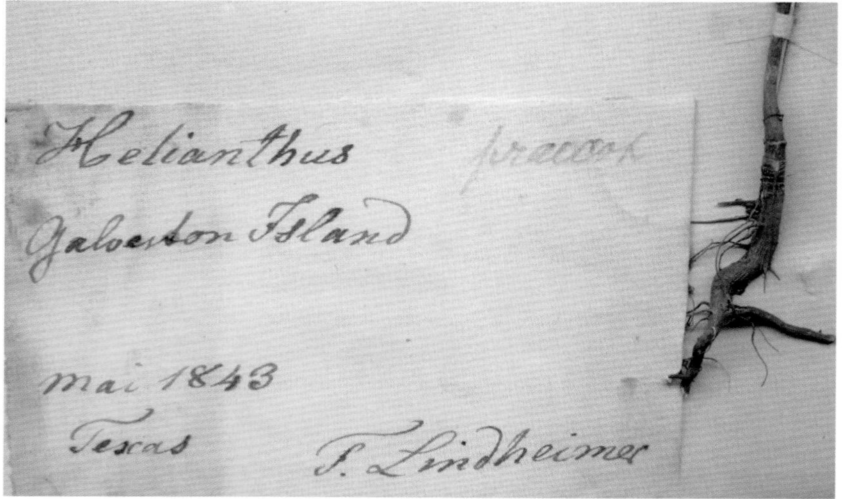

Texas yellowstar (*Lindheimera helianthus*). Courtesy of Botanical Research Institute of Texas

In 1844, he met Prince Solms of Braunfels and agreed to help the first group of immigrants find their way from Indianola to New Braunfels. He settled in New Braunfels on the Comal River, where he built a small cabin. For collecting, he bought a mule and a covered Mexican cart and provisioned it with pressing paper, flour and salt, two hunting dogs, and a shotgun. He collected around New Braunfels and Fredericksburg (in the middle of Indian territory) until his contract with Gray and Engelmann expired in 1852. In 1848, he led a utopian group,

"Bettina," to their site near Sisterdale and stayed with them for six months. For the next 20 years, collecting took a back seat to his job as publisher and editor of the respected *New Braunfels Zeitung* newspaper. He continued to collect until the end of his life; ultimately, 34 species and one genus were named after him (*Lindheimera*).

Because these specimens were sent to eminent botanists Gray and Engelmann, and eventually made their way to prominent museums worldwide, Texas flora was becoming widely known for its diversity and beauty through Lindheimer's descriptions. Lindheimer's name became synonymous with Texas botany, as he was the first permanent resident of the state to become a well-known naturalist, hence, his being called the "Father of Texas Botany" (Ragsdale 2010).

Carl Ferdinand von Roemer (1818–91), a German geologist who traveled extensively in Texas in 1845–46 to study the natural resources of the state. From Roemer (1995)

Carl Ferdinand von Roemer (1818–1891)

Karen and Allen Ginnard, Gideon Lincecum Chapter, Texas Master Naturalist Program

Carl Ferdinand von Roemer was a scientist born in Hildesheim, Hanover, Germany. He studied law at Göttingen from 1836 to 1839 upon the advice of a brother. However, his natural love was in the field of science. In *Dr. Ferdinand von Roemer, the Father of the Geology of Texas: His Life and Work*, the author explains Roemer's shift from law to science as follows:

> His future calling was, however, to be decided in favour of his natural bent. As he was about to present himself for examination in the higher legal course, for political reasons—although he himself was an innocent party—certain difficulties appeared and he withdrew. Thus science gained a brilliant scholar and geology a zealous investigator. (Simonds 1902, 131–32)

And with this fortunate turn of events, science did indeed gain a brilliant scholar and geology a zealous investigator when Ferdinand von Roemer received his PhD in paleontology in Berlin on May 10, 1842.

In 1845, Roemer came to Texas for both a scientific and practical visit. Just after the birth of the Republic of Texas in 1836, the German government was interested in exploring the then little-known Texas for the purpose of establishing German settlements. Roemer undertook the journey and spent a year and a half studying Texas' geology and paleontology. From November 1845 to May 1847, he explored from Galveston to Houston, as far west as New Braunfels and Fredericksburg, and as far north as Waco, studying the fauna, flora, and the geology of the country (Anonymous 2010, "Roemer").

His book *Texas* (1849), published in Bonn, Germany, and translated into English in 1935 by Oswald Mueller, describes

German immigration to Texas and the physical appearance of the state (Roemer 1849, 1935). Roemer was the author of the first monograph on Texas geology, *The Cretaceous Formations of Texas and Their Organic Inclusions*, published in Bonn in 1852. It was this work that won for him the epithet "Father of the Geology of Texas" (Simonds 1902). It should be noted, however, that this epithet is also used in connection with Robert Thomas Hill (1858–1941), an American geologist who contributed significantly to the understanding of geology and geography in Texas. Although Roemer's study was conducted earlier (1845 to 1847), his first publication in German (1849) was not translated to English until 1935. Robert Hill's study from roughly 1888 to 1903 was originally published in 1900 (Alexander 2010). Regardless, both men contributed significantly to the knowledge base of Texas geology, geography, and botany.

Roemer made a contribution to Texas that extends beyond the bounds of natural science. His observations about Texas culture and the anthropological environment opened the door for early German settlements, thus ensuring a history and tradition of integration of German influence in parts of Texas for years to come.

It seems often to be those journeys begun in academia that result in far-reaching impacts to culture, education, population, and diversity. The pioneering spirit in these early scientists cannot be overstated. They often worked in environments where inhabitants were either scarce or hostile or simply had not seen people of Anglo descent before. Roemer's exploration of Texas gave us some of the best information on early American Indian life in Texas, and for the most part, he found the Indians to be more "civilized" than the early settlers in Texas (Roemer 1935). His thorough scientific approach to the study of Texas ensured his place in Texas natural history, and his publications ensured future generations would benefit from his study and knowledge.

Gustav Wilhelm Belfrage (1834–1882), an entomologist.

Gustav Wilhelm Belfrage (1834–1882)

Deborah Canterbury, Blackland Prairie Chapter, Texas Master Naturalist Program

No accurate documentation exists concerning why the elusive descendant of nobility **Gustaf Wilhelm (G. W.) Belfrage** left his Swedish homeland to come to America, but had he not, a large, diverse collection of meticulously collected insects in Texas from the late 1800s would probably not be available today.

In a eulogy A. S. Packard stated, "If the insect fauna of Texas is, at the present time, better known than that of most of the Western States of this continent, it is largely due to the skill and industry of Belfrage and Jacob Boll" (1883, 424). Belfrage's care and dedication to collecting species was extraordinary and covered a variety of areas of the state. So respected was his care that several of his discoveries were named after him by some of our leading entomologists.

In a letter from 1861, Belfrage stated he left his home to live in the land of the "Yankees" and had apparently already sent a collection back to Sweden. In this particularly troubled time in America he found himself much in the same boat as many other Americans. He suffered from "that common disease called a lack of money" as the country was preparing for war. In an attempt to keep from starving, he sold off his collection of insects from Illinois (Geiser 1937, 233).

He received encouragement from leading entomologists to relocate to Texas, which turned out to be not only beneficial for his reputation but also lucrative, as he sold many of his finds to institutions and individuals. He arrived in Houston in 1867, and by 1869 he advertised an exchange-collection of 25,000 Texas insects. He exchanged a large collection with the Boston Society of Natural History and sent specimens to the Peabody Academy of Science in Harlem. In 1868–71, he sold large collections of insects to the Swedish Academy of Science in Stockholm and Harvard College (Geiser 1937). He did not just collect in Bosque and McLennan Counties; his travels took him to East, West, and deep South Texas.

Belfrage's plan to explore New Mexico in 1882 never came to fruition due to his untimely demise. At the time of his death, his collection comprised 36,881 pinned specimens, which was only a fraction of his life's work, a large portion of which was destroyed by fire. His collection is stored in the United States National Museum, which was placed under the charge of the Smithsonian Institution by an act of Congress in 1846 (United States National Museum 1875).

Ludolph Heiligbrodt (1847–1911)

Deborah Canterbury, Blackland Prairie Chapter, Texas Master Naturalist Program

The actual date that German-born **Ludolph Heiligbrodt** came to Texas is unknown, but after spending time at sea, he chose to become landlocked as a general store clerk in Lee County in the mid-1860s. His interest in insects piqued by the publications of

Ludolph Heiligbrodt (1847–1911). The Collection of Ludolph Heiligbrodt at the University of Texas. Courtesy of the University of Texas Biodiversity Collections

Hermann Burmeister, he started collecting specimens around Bastrop.

Heiligbrodt sent collections to the US Department of Agriculture and to the Smithsonian. Subsequently, he was asked to represent Texas by presenting his collections at the New Orleans Cotton Exposition in 1883–84. His collection was also used by Ezra Townsend Cresson in his publication *Hymenoptera Texana* (1872). A series of eight short papers on Lepidoptera and Hymenoptera of Bastrop County were published in the St. Louis journal *The Valley Naturalist.*

While collecting and publishing, he also served in the Bastrop school district for 40 years, first as a janitor and then as a teacher. Upon his death, Heiligbrodt's collection was donated to the University of Texas at Austin, where a portion of his work is still used today.

Julien Reverchon (1837–1905)

Charlie Grindstaff, Indian Trail Chapter, Texas Master Naturalist Program

Julien Reverchon showed signs of being a prominent botanist at a young age. By the time he was 14, he had already collected over 2,000 species of plants from his native France that he left in his brother's care (Perez 2010). In 1856, 19-year-old Reverchon emigrated with his father from France to Texas, "the Land of Promise," to join a utopian colony that had been established the prior year. The colony, La Réunion, lay across the Trinity River from the village of Dallas, population 400. La Réunion, while composed of approximately 350 cultivated French, Swiss, and Belgian musicians, artists, artisans, and intellects, had only two practical farmers. Not surprisingly, the venture failed in 1858. Maximilien Reverchon, Julien's father, foreseeing the doom, secured a small farm near Dallas (Geiser 1937). There Julien worked and studied the local plant and animal life for the next eight years.

Julien Reverchon (1837–1905). The Texas bluebell (*Campanula reverchonii*) was named for Julien Reverchon by Asa Gray. Courtesy of Carl Fabre, Capital Area

Reverchon married in 1864 and for the next five years his dairy farm and business interests occupied his time. His life during this period was almost devoid of scientific results. As he became more comfortable in Dallas, he began to enlarge his botanical collection and correspond with renowned botanists, such as Asa Gray, Sereno Watson, George Engelmann, and William Trelease, who encouraged him to widen his range of collection. Botanically speaking, the north-central region of Texas had barely been explored, while the west and northwest regions had not been explored at all. With the arrival of Jacob Boll in Dallas in 1869, Reverchon renewed his devotion to botany and began adding to his herbarium of local botanical specimens. In 1877, he discovered about a dozen new species of plants in Dallas County alone (Geiser 1937, 285). Additionally, he collected in 11 counties south and west of Dallas during a two-week trip to Brown County. In 1879, Reverchon and Boll traveled to Baylor County in northwest Texas to collect plants and fossils, respectively. It was on this trip that Reverchon found a spurge, for which Asa Gray named the genus *Reverchonia,* thus immortalizing the collector. Several other botanists also named plant species honoring him (Perez 2010).

In 1882, during his trip to Fort Concho in

West Texas, exploring Tom Green, Mitchell, Nolan, and Scurry Counties, his two sons died of typhoid fever at home in Dallas. In 1885, Reverchon and his wife traveled by wagon to Uvalde, approximately 350 miles to the southwest. It took them over a month to reach Uvalde because of almost constant rains along the way. He explored the basin of the Llano River and most of the Edwards Plateau region. He found the valley of the Llano and Sabinal Canyon to be "a paradise for the botanist" and did his most successful collecting there (Geiser 1937, 223).

Reverchon contributed to books by Gray and Sprague Sargent and wrote papers for several botanical and horticultural journals, including *Botanical Gazette*, *Garden and Forest*, and the *American Botanist*. Unlike most collectors of the time, Reverchon was a horticulturist, growing and studying the ecology of plants, as well as a botanist, collecting specimens. He freely contributed specimens to various institutions of science and learning, including the US Department of Agriculture and the Smithsonian Institution. During the last 10 years of his life he was professor of botany in the Baylor College of Medicine and Pharmacy at Dallas.

At the time of his death in 1905, his collection numbered over 20,000 specimens of 2,600 species of Texas flora, four of which are named after him (Houser 2013). This collection was considered the best collection of its kind in the world, which now resides at the Missouri Botanical Garden in St. Louis. Duplicates of his collections occur in many of the leading herbaria of the world, including the Botanical Research Institute of Texas in Fort Worth.

Charles S. Sargent of the Arnold Arboretum stated, "No one did more than Reverchon in exploring the flora of Texas. He made it possible for others to make known the remarkable richness of the Texas flora" (Charlton 1915, 213–14).William Trelease of the University of Illinois called Reverchon a "man of rare intelligence and enthusiasm whose work on the native plants of Texas and particularly of Dallas County, will long stand as the fullest and best" (Charlton 1915, 213–14). In 1914, the City of Dallas named Reverchon Park in his honor.

John Allen Singley (1850–1908)

Deborah Canterbury, Blackland Prairie Chapter, Texas Master Naturalist Program

John Allen Singley, a native of Pennsylvania, was known as a naturalist and ornithologist. A limited formal education did not deter him from teaching in a country school while studying medicine. Neither of these careers seemed to hold his interest and provide a life passion, however, and he began publications of his observations of natural history around 1884. He made a living by providing mail-order specimens of bird eggs and skins.

Singley was hired as an assistant geologist by the Geological Survey of Texas, and his survey results were published in

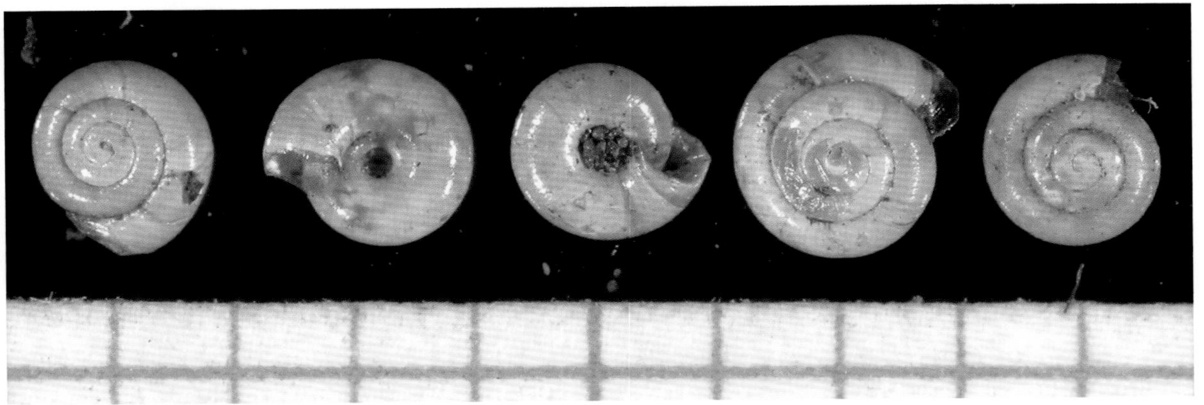

John Allen Singley (1850–1908). *Lucilla singleyana*, formerly known as *Zonites singleyanus*, was named for John Allen Singley. Courtesy of Francisco Welter Schultes

the *Fourth Annual Report of the Geological Survey of Texas* (Dumble 1892). Singley's two surveys appeared as "Preliminary Report on the Artesian Wells of the Gulf Coastal Slope" and "The Natural History of Texas" (part 1, "Texas Mollusca"; and part 2, "Texas Birds"). The mollusk collection consisted of an annotated list of 569 species, the first comprehensive list assembled in Texas. Singley was also reported to have an extensive collection of 6,000 specimens of 300 species collected from over 900 locales. These collections were sold to George Brackenridge and donated to the University of Texas (Casto 2010b).

His annotated bird species work was collected in Lee County, Galveston, the lower Rio Grande, and Corpus Christi. His works were the first from Lee County, and the Galveston work provided information about the ducks and shorebirds sold in markets in Galveston. Singley was a prolific writer with numerous articles published between 1884 and 1894. After 1894 he lost his passion for studying natural history and sold all of his large book collection. Singley died in Sonora, Mexico, in 1908 (Casto 2010b).

Henry Philemon Attwater (1854–1931)

Charlie Grindstaff, Indian Trail Chapter, Texas Master Naturalist Program

Henry Philemon Attwater (1854–1931). Courtesy of the Library of Congress, DEANE COLL—Attwater, Henry Philemon, 1854–1931

"One of the most important features of the great battle now being waged for conservation is the preservation of animal and plant life and the protection of it against the cruelty, the ignorance and the selfishness of its destroyers. After the most painstaking investigations by competent and impartial authorities, their testimony shows that many of the most useful birds are fast becoming extinct, valuable wild animals are on the verge of extermination, air and water are polluted, rivers and bayous are used as sewers and dumping grounds, forests are swept away, and fishes destroyed in the streams. This is not being done by savages and ignorant people but by men and women who boast of their civilization and education."

—Henry Philemon Attwater, speech to the General Session of the Farmers' Congress, July 28, 1913

Henry Philemon Attwater also noted in his speech to the Farmers' Congress that huge numbers of insect-eating birds are being killed, resulting in insect pests damaging crops to the extent of millions of dollars annually, which then required thousands of dollars being expended on spraying machinery and other devices for destroying those insects: "You are trying to do the work with sprayers that nature intended the birds to do."

Attwater, a conservationist and amateur naturalist who became an authority on Texas wildlife, was born in Brighton, England, in 1854. He immigrated to Ontario, Canada, in 1873, where he was a farmer and beekeeper. He became interested in natural history and the exhibition of collected specimens. In 1884 he and John A. Morden, a fellow Canadian naturalist, made a trip to Bexar County, Texas, to collect specimens. While there, Attwater met Gustave Toudouze, a naturalist and taxidermist, and the two of them were employed to prepare and exhibit natural history specimens in the Texas Pavilion at the New Orleans World's Fair in 1884 (Casto 2010a). Attwater opened a small museum in London, Ontario, to exhibit his collected specimens in 1886; however, it was not successful and closed the following year.

Attwater moved his family to San Antonio in 1889. During the 1890s he collected mammals and birds throughout the state. He also lectured and wrote on natural history and agricultural subjects and prepared exhibits of Texas natural products and wildlife for fairs and expositions (Casto 2010a). The ornithological collections he made in Bexar County in 1892 received a great deal of attention. He wrote three ornithological papers dealing "with the nesting habits of fifty species of birds in Bexar County, the occurrence of 242 species of birds in the vicinity of San Antonio, and the deaths of thousands of warblers during a blue norther in March 1892" (Casto 2010a). His field notes were published in the *Bulletin of the American Museum of Natural History*. Attwater was acquainted with zoologist and ornithologist J. A. Allen, whom he provided with hundreds of specimens of Texas mammals and his field notes, which Allen used as the basis for several papers, although Allen never visited Texas himself. Attwater contributed specimens to the Smithsonian Institution, collected birds for George B. Sennett, and provided notes for W. W. Cooke, Vernon Bailey, and others.

In 1900, he was appointed an agricultural and industrial agent of the Southern Pacific Railroad and relocated to Houston, where he lived the rest of his life (Meadows 2009). In this position, he continued to expand his collections and to promote the agricultural and business interests of the state, in addition to assisting the work of commercial clubs, fairs, and farmers' organizations.

Attwater's prairie chicken (*Tympanuchus cupido attwateri*). Courtesy of Texas Parks and Wildlife Department

Attwater was elected a director of the National Audubon Society in 1900 and served for 10 years. He was devoted to the protection of birds and other wildlife and became known for his conservation efforts. He was instrumental in the passage of the 1903 Model Game Law (Meadows 2009). After its passage, he "arranged for warning notices from the National Audubon Society to be distributed in railroad facilities throughout the state." Four years later he served on the game-law committee. He recommended hunters' licenses "be required for both resident and nonresident hunters and that the revenue from the licenses and fines be used solely for game protection and propagation" (Casto 2010a).

When he retired from the railroad in 1913, he immersed himself completely in the study of natural history. He was always eager to assist anyone who needed information or material that he could provide. The Attwater's greater prairie chicken (*Tympanuchus cupido attwateri*) and four small mammals are named in his honor, in recognition of his major contributions as a scientist and conservationist (Casto 2010a). As Henry Oberholser wrote in Attwater's obituary in the *Auk*, "He was always earnestly devoted to the protection of birds and other wild life, and his lectures and newspaper articles had an important influence on the movements for conservation in the State of Texas . . . for he was the first in the state to present the real facts concerning the importance of bird life in its relation to human welfare" (Oberholser et al. 1932).

Attwater sold his collection to the Witte Museum in San Antonio in 1922, and after his death in 1931, his papers were deposited in the Houston Public Library. Specimens that he collected are housed at the Smithsonian Institution, Field Museum, Dallas Museum of Natural History, Los Angeles County Museum, American Museum of Natural History, and the Houston Museum of Natural Science.

John Kern Strecker (1875–1933)

Karen and Allen Ginnard, Gideon Lincecum Chapter, Texas Master Naturalist Program

John Kern Strecker (1875–1933), a Baylor University naturalist who collected widely in Texas and wrote about many natural history subjects. Courtesy of Texas Collection, Baylor University

John Kern Strecker played an important part in advancing our knowledge of Texas birds, reptiles, amphibians, and mollusks. He rose from humble beginnings to become a recognized authority on Texas wildlife. Strecker , born at Waterloo, Illinois, on July 10, 1875, was a naturalist and civic leader. In November 1887 the Strecker family moved to Waco, Texas, from Fort Scott, Kansas. Strecker "had only a limited formal education and began his employment period as a stonecutter, his father's vocation" (Neck 2010).

At a young age Strecker began a lifelong interest in natural history. At 16, he published his first scientific paper, an article on local birds, in *National Bird Magazine*. He became a recognized authority on amphibians and reptiles of Texas and the Southwest from his scientific publications. Strecker began collecting snakes as a hobby in 1893, which led to a job as curator of the Baylor University Museum in 1903, and he directed its development until his death in 1933 (Neck 2010). Strecker's collections, field studies, and publications brought international contacts and exposure to the museum. Because of his efforts, the Baylor University Museum was renamed in his honor by university president Pat Neff in 1940 (Lintz 2010).

For his part in history, and most especially in the history of Baylor College, John Kern Strecker was honored in the Baylor University *1930 Roundup* with this inscription by its editor, Richard Wall:

> To a loyal friend of abiding good fellowship, whose unselfish service for Baylor University is reflected in the greater

> Baylor of today, and whose devotion to the University draws the admiration and gratitude of a host of friends . . . to John Kern Strecker, librarian and curator of the museum . . . the 1930 Round-Up is respectfully dedicated.

A series of literary productions and papers, including articles written and edited by John Kern Strecker, are housed in the Texas Collection at Baylor University in Waco. Strecker's life and works show how one person can rise to achieve status in his or her field by simply choosing a path that becomes a lifestyle rather than a vocation.

Vernon Orlando Bailey (1894–1942)

Kristen Tyson, Texas A&M AgriLife Extension Service

For **Vernon Orlando Bailey**, interest in wildlife and the outdoors started at a young age. He was born in 1864 in Manchester, Michigan, into a family where hunting and enjoying the outdoors was the norm. His father moved the family to Minnesota when he was six. Young Bailey spent his time "collecting birds, mammals, and reptiles, and he learned the art of taxidermy from a small book on the subject and had a great deal of experimentation" (Schmidly 2002, 23). As he developed into a young man, Bailey began to wonder about properly identifying the different species he was collecting. It was suggested that he contact C. H. Merriam, a naturalist by heart but a physician by career, who agreed to identify the animals Bailey collected. A warm friendship developed between the two men after that fateful 1884 exchange and led to young Vernon selling his collections to Merriam and abroad.

In 1887, Merriam hired Bailey and several other notable naturalists to collect specimens in the field, from the Great Plains to the Rocky Mountains (Zahniser 1942). Despite great success, Bailey chose to return home to Elk River after six months to be close to his family. The next year saw a more confident Bailey, and when he returned to fieldwork, he collected for the Bureau of Biological Survey, under Merriam, and the US National Museum (which in 1846 came under the charge of the Smithsonian Institution) for the next 45 years.

Part of the bureau's role was to create a nationwide biological survey, and Texas was one of the states chosen, thanks to its diverse ecoregions. Bailey came to Texas in 1889, focusing on the western landscape in Del Rio and the Trans-Pecos. Merriam named him chief field naturalist the next year, and Bailey was given the primary responsibility for training new field investigators and supervising the parties of field agents conducting biological survey work (Schmidly 2002). Each naturalist was tasked with collecting and recording the diverse flora and fauna across the state, rain or shine. Travel was mainly by foot, sometimes on horseback, sleeping in tents on the open

Vernon Orlando Bailey (1894–1942) during his work as field naturalist for the USDA Bureau of Biological Survey in 1898. Courtesy of the Smithsonian Institution Archives

plains. Field diaries revealed that the work was not for the fainthearted, but more often than not, the thrill of the chase was worth the pain and hardship. Upon completing fieldwork in the west, Bailey was sent to the Panhandle in 1892, and in 1899 he spent time along the coast. In total, Bailey spent 425 days surveying Texas before publishing his report in 1905 (Schmidly 2002).

Despite the punishing schedule and fieldwork, Bailey did slow down to enjoy the finer points of life. From 1893 to 1895 he took course work at the University of Michigan and George Washington University (Zahniser 1942). In 1899 he married Merriam's sister, Florence, who was recognized as an ornithologist. The Baileys traveled and worked well together in the field and enjoyed day trips surveying birds. With the conclusion of the Biological Survey of Texas in 1905, Vernon and Florence ventured on a 360-mile wagon trip from Texarkana to the Mexican line, near King Ranch (Schmidly 2002).

Before retiring from the bureau in 1933, Bailey contributed more than 13,000 mammal specimens to the survey collections, authored six publications, and was a proponent of more humane live traps, which he designed (Schmidly 2002). He also served as president of the American Society of Mammalogists and the Biological Society of Washington. He died April 20, 1942 (Zahniser 1942).

Florence Merriam Bailey (1863–1948)

Mary Ann Melton, Goodwater Chapter, Texas Master Naturalist Program

Florence Augusta Merriam Bailey was born in New York as the youngest of four children (her sister died at a young age). Her father and mother encouraged all of their children to study natural history and astronomy at an early age, as her father was specifically interested in scientific matters himself and had corresponded with John Muir, whom he had met in Yosemite prior to Bailey's birth (Oehser 1952).

Florence Merriam Bailey (1863–1948). Courtesy of Florence Merriam Bailey, Record Unit 7417—Florence Merriam Bailey Papers, 1865–1942, Smithsonian Institution Archives

Merriam Bailey began attending Smith College in 1882 as a special student, graduating with a certificate rather than degree in 1886. (She was later recognized with a degree in 1921.) While studying at Smith College, Merriam Bailey organized the Smith College Audubon Society on campus and wrote a series of articles to protest the harvest of birds for women's hats. At the time, most bird study was based on collections and skins; however, Merriam Bailey was more interested in studying living birds and their behavior in the field (Kofalk 1989). With the articles in the Audubon magazine, Merriam Bailey published her first book at the age of 26, *Birds through an Opera Glass.*

She encouraged the use of binoculars, and her simple purpose was to help "not only young observers but also laymen to know the common birds they see about them" (Oehser 1952, iv).

In 1885, Merriam Bailey was honored as the first woman associate member of the American Ornithologists' Union, which was founded by her brother, Clinton Hart Merriam. Through her brother's involvement as a chief of the US Biological Survey, Florence Merriam met Vernon Bailey, an avid naturalist, and as Paul Oehser put it in his memoriam of Merriam Bailey's life, "They were made for each other" (1952, 22). For the next 30 years, Florence Merriam Bailey spent time traveling back and forth between their Washington, D.C., home, the west coast, and states in between. She made field trips surveying birds while her husband collected and surveyed mammals, birds, reptiles, and plants. In 1898, she published *Birds of Village and Field*, which became one of the first popular American bird guides using simple field keys for identification and with illustrations by Ernest Thompson Seton, Louis Agassiz Fuertes, and John L. Ridgeway.

Through their travels in New Mexico, California, North Dakota, Oregon, and parts of Texas, Merriam Bailey published hundreds of articles in ornithological journals and two more books, *Birds of the Western United States* (1902) and *Birds of New Mexico* (1928). Her last major work was *Among the Birds in the Grand Canyon National Park*, published when she was past age 75.

Though not a robust woman, and as a girl threatened with tuberculosis, she developed a wonderful vitality, both physically and mentally. The rich experiences of the outdoors, especially in the great Southwest, which she loved, the companionship of her husband, and the stimulation of the work they were accomplishing—these were the rewards of the arduous life she chose to pursue.

University Men

In the late 1800s, the role of the naturalist changed from that of primarily an observer and collector to that of a researcher and professor. By the beginning of the 1900s, extensive collections had been made throughout much of the state, and although this material had been deposited in museums elsewhere, it provided merely a basis for inventory of Texas flora and fauna. At the turn of the century, attempts were made to provide vegetational analyses of Texas flora and to investigate its "ecology" (Burke 2003). Many young naturalists moved to Texas to take advantage of the establishment of the universities as places of research and education. Most notably, these "university" naturalists were anxious to put their mark on the research of the native flora and fauna, either in collections or in the field.

In 1876, the Agricultural and Mechanical College of Texas started classes with five professors and 50 students enrolled (US Department of Agriculture 1876). And in 1883, the University of Texas opened its doors to students on the original "Capitol Hill." A few notable naturalists who were involved in the establishment of early educational programs at these universities include William Bray, first professor of botany at the University of Texas in 1897; Frederick William Mally, first professor of entomology at the newly renamed Texas A&M College (TAMC) in 1899; and Mark Francis, who served as the first dean of the School of Veterinary Medicine of TAMC in 1888.

Joseph Daniel Mitchell (1848–1922)

Mary Pearl Meuth, Texas A&M AgriLife Extension Service

Born in 1848 to a Texas plantation owner, **Joseph Daniel Mitchell** was an "old-time naturalist" (Burke 2003, 23). His first education

Joseph Daniel Mitchell (1848–1922).

came on the grounds of his family's plantation in Calhoun County, Texas, in the Coastal Bend area, with a mother who nurtured his interests in nature and instilled in him a lifelong commitment to learning ("Mitchell Collection," n.d.). Mitchell's father, who was killed in a freak hunting accident when Mitchell was only five, was a leading ranchman in Calhoun County and inspired his son, whose first job was as a cowboy in the region. Roger Whitcomb, of the Victoria Historical Commission, which houses a large portion of J. D. Mitchell's collection, said that Mitchell was a good cowboy except he would sometimes interrupt his cowboying when he happened upon some specimen of natural history that would attract his attention (Whitcomb 1985).

In 1871, Mitchell was able to establish his own ranch in Calhoun County with his wife, Agnes Martha Wood, of Jackson County. Mitchell used the ranch as a showcase for the newest agricultural innovations, including some of the first blooded stock in the area, the first windmill west of the Colorado River for watering stock, and one of the first barbed-wire fences ("Mitchell Collection," n.d.). In 1887, he moved to Victoria with his family of 11 children (7 of whom lived to adulthood) and began divesting himself of his ranch holdings. He sold 13,500 acres to a colony of Swedish settlers in 1892 and virtually retired from ranching livestock. This move to town and movement out of the agricultural business allowed Mitchell to intensify his ongoing collection and study of natural history. He was a "gifted amateur student of Texas mollusks, insects, and reptiles" and an early expert along the Texas mid-coast. (Geiser 1937, 278).

Mitchell was also civic-minded. He became involved with the local Victoria schools and set the foundation for the establishment of the Victoria Independent School District. Mitchell Elementary School in Victoria is named for him. In addition to his school district functions, Mitchell served the Victoria community as a representative in the Texas State House in the 24th Legislative Session in 1893. During his term, the legislature established the Fish and Oyster Commission, a precursor to the Texas Game, Fish, and Oyster Commission, later named Texas Parks and Wildlife Department ("Mitchell Collection," n.d.).

Throughout his life, Mitchell continuously collected specimens in the mid-coast region of Texas. His collection included Indian relics, mineral specimens, insects, bird eggs, reptiles of Texas, and particularly shells. Mitchell continued correspondence with many well-known scientists and was often sought out as an expert on the natural resources in the coastal region of Texas. Later in life, Mitchell earned the moniker "bug man" as his interest in entomology expanded. He collected insect specimens in Victoria and vicinity and painstakingly arranged his collections with care, showing both his knowledge and love for the work for which he is most noted to this day.

The invasion of the boll weevil in the area and the subsequent establishment of a US Department of Agriculture (USDA) laboratory at Victoria in 1902 to study this pest opened up a new world for Mitchell (Burke 2003). He worked on several projects on the boll weevil, the cotton fleahopper ("cotton flea"), the cactus tick, and other agricultural pests. Mitchell became associated with the USDA Bureau of Entomology as a collaborator and continued to work with them for nearly 17 years.

Beyond his interest in collections of natural history, Mitchell published multiple papers on a diversity of species, including lists of Texas mollusks, as well as "The Poisonous Snakes of Texas, with Notes on Their Habitats" and other papers on reptiles and amphibians in Texas. Bryce Brown (1950) claims that Mitchell was the first citizen of Texas to specifically collect reptiles and amphibians. During his explorations, he discovered two previously unknown shells, which have been named in his honor—Mitchell's wentletrap (*Amaea mitchelli*) and Mitchell's macoma (*Macoma mitchelli*) ("Mitchell Collection," n.d.). Mitchell was a man who enjoyed sharing his knowledge and his writings, a great naturalist of his time, and a distinguished gentleman in his community.

Cotton boll weevil (*Anthonomus grandis*). This species entered Texas in the early 1890s, and its destructive habits were responsible for professional entomologists being sent to the state and the establishment of the Department of Entomology at Texas A&M University.

"Those who contemplate the beauty of earth find reserves of strength that will endure as long as life lasts."
—Rachel Carson, Silent Spring

William L. Bray (1865–1953)

Karen and Allen Ginnard, Gideon Lincecum Chapter, Texas Master Naturalist Program

William Bray was born in Burnside, Illinois, in September 1865 and was to become a botanist, forest ecologist. and teacher by his retirement in 1943. His education began at Cornell University (BS in 1891) and Indiana University (MS in 1893), culminating with his PhD thesis on the "Vegetation of Western Texas" earned from the University of Chicago in 1898. During this time, he spent a year (1896–97) working under Heinrich

William Bray (1865–1953), first head of the Botany Department at the University of Texas. Courtesy of Smithsonian Institution Archives, Image # SIA2008-0060

Gustav Adolf Engler at the Royal Botanical Garden in Berlin. Bray met Alice Weston while in Berlin, and they were married on December 28, 1899.

In 1897, Bray started his tenure as the first botanist on staff at the University of Texas at Austin and organized the Botany Department, eventually becoming its first head (Schmidly 2002). This new department was given the task to create a "Botanical Survey of the State for the purpose of studying the flora in its relation to the environmental factors of climate, rainfall, heat, geological structure and topography" (University of Texas 1898, 183). Within the *University Record*, Bray published "The Flora of Texas as a Field for Botanical Study."

Over his 10 years with the University of Texas, Bray published a number of papers on the ecological regions and vegetation of Texas. "A Forest Working Plan for the Long Leaf Pine Lands of Texas" (1903) was an attempt to balance his positions between exploitation and conservation (Durbin 1996). In 1903, he was appointed chief of the Division of Forestry for the World's Fair Commission of Texas. This gave him the chance to visit many parts of the state and collect wood specimens. Bray, in collaboration with W. F. Blair, displayed 130 of his collected specimens of Texas trees for the Louisiana Purchase Exposition in St. Louis in 1904. They "received the grand prize from the international jury. This exhibit later became the property of the University of Texas" (Saustrup 2010).

One of Bray's best-known works for and about Texas is *Forest Resources of Texas*, published in collaboration with the Bureau of Forestry in the US Department of Agriculture. In this work, Bray described the various ecoregions in Texas along with a study of the corresponding rain, nature of the soil and rock, temperature, sunlight, and winds—and how those factors impacted the trees in each area. The book included an explanation of the various types of trees in Texas and described in very practical detail the management tools necessary to ensure a sustainable forest in the state. The book outlined the benefits of, and need for, conservative lumbering in Texas and promoted private management and conservation of our natural forest resources.

In addition, Bray outlined a plan for how the State could support private foresters through legislation, education, police protection, and investigation of forest problems. Bray was particularly concerned that the State should step in with funding for a scientific investigation into "red heart," a fungus disease spreading rapidly through the Texas timber and generating economic losses for the state. Bray also called for a certain amount of timberlands to be retained by the State and managed for growth to prevent loss of native trees. His insight and understanding of the conservation issues that still challenge ecologists, environmentalists, and naturalists today contained astute observations for a publication written in 1903–4.

In 1907 he moved to Syracuse University in Syracuse, New York, as professor of botany, where he was so well regarded by the faculty and students of the College of Forestry that their first building was named Bray Hall in his honor. According to his obituary in the *Bulletin of the Torrey Botanical Club,* "his influence was far reaching in his inspirational teaching . . . his friendliness and leadership encouraged fellowship between students and . . . he enjoyed being 'Daddy Bray' to the plant scientists" (Faust, 298–300).

Isaac McKinney Lewis (1878–1943)

Karen and Allen Ginnard, Gideon Lincecum Chapter, Texas Master Naturalist Program

Isaac McKinney Lewis arrived at the University of Texas in September 1909, just two years after the first professor of botany

B83-415-2m

BULLETIN
OF THE
UNIVERSITY OF TEXAS

1915: No. 22

APRIL 15 1915

The Trees of Texas

An Illustrated Manual of the Native and Introduced Trees of the State

BY

Isaac M. Lewis, Ph. D.
Associate Professor of Botany
The University of Texas

Published by the University six times a month and entered as second class matter at the postoffice at
AUSTIN, TEXAS

Cover of *The Trees of Texas*, by Isaac McKinney Lewis.

there, William Bray, moved to Syracuse, New York. Bray's work influenced Lewis's work by laying a foundation on which Lewis could build and perhaps improve. The association of the two botanists is suggested by the use of some of Bray's illustrations, by permission, in Lewis's publication *The Trees of Texas*. In the preface to this book, Lewis mentions Bray by name (Lewis 1915).

Lewis, third son of Isaac R. Lewis and Margaret Jane (McKinney) Lewis, was born on a farm in Jasper County, near Rensselaer, Indiana. He had the misfortune never to know his father, who died in May preceding his birth. He was devoted to his mother throughout her lifetime. She had been a teacher, and to her he gave the credit for instilling in him the desire to secure an education (Williams 1943).

Lewis attended the country school near his home and finished eighth grade at the age of 14. By home study, while working on the farm, he prepared himself for a teacher's certificate and at the age of 17 began teaching in his home township of Barkley. In 1897 he entered the Indiana State Normal School. His work there was interrupted by trouble with his eyes following measles and by the necessity of earning his expenses, but he was able to finish in 1904 (Tharp 2000–2001).

He entered the University of Indiana in the fall of the same year and earned a BA in 1906, an MA in 1907, and a PhD in 1909. During 1908–9 he was instructor in botany at New Hampshire State College and assistant botanist in the experiment station. In September 1909 he came to the University of Texas to be an instructor in botany and to initiate work in bacteriology, later becoming a research professor there in 1938–39 (Tharp 2000–2001).

Although he made a name for himself as much for his work in bacteriology as for his work in botany, Lewis stayed true to his roots on the farm. He retained his love for botany and the soil. Having a keen analytical mind and a desire to solve problems served him well in his career and contributed to the thorough and concise publications he published.

One of Lewis's best-known works, *The Trees of Texas* (1915), was a guide to identification of some of the more common native and introduced trees in Texas written for nonscientists. Lewis attempted to stay away from technical terms, opting instead for a practical publication to be used by those not trained in botany. The book is a compilation of both original and published material, and full credit is given to the resources he used when preparing his publication. Bray's work is evident in several places, as well as in the photographic plates. With descriptions, pictures, and general information about distribution and soil, Lewis created perhaps the first easy-to-understand field guide that opened the world of botany to a broader audience.

Barton Warnock (1911–1998)

Mark Tyson, Texas A&M AgriLife Extension Service

A native Texan and legendary botanist, **Barton Holland Warnock** was a noted authority on the flora of West Texas. Warnock spent much of his life in the Trans-Pecos region, a 19 million–acre expanse of land laden with desert grasslands and ecologically diverse mountain ranges. This region lay close to his heart, and his passion for it was noted in the highly influential book *Wildflowers of the Big Bend Country, Texas*, where he stated that "this is the region of Texas best known to me and loved more each day as its fascinating ruggedness, its constant challenges, its glorious sunrises and sunsets, and its many wonderful people are encountered" (B. Warnock 1970, 6).

Sometime prior to 1934, Warnock accepted a scholarship and began attending Sul Ross State Teachers College in Alpine. He studied under the direction of Homer Sperry, father of the celebrity botanist Neil Sperry. When asked about choosing to major

Barton Warnock (1911–98). Courtesy of Archives of the Big Bend, Bryan Wildenthal Memorial Library, Sul Ross State University, Alpine, Texas

in botany, Warnock replied, "I wanted to chase around the desert" (K. Warnock, n.d.). It would not be long before Warnock was able to do just that. In 1937 he was selected to catalog plants on Ross Maxwell's campaign to catalog the flora and fauna of the land area that would become Big Bend National Park. Maxwell noted Warnock's fervor for collecting and recalled, "He wanted to collect plants. He would pester me every day to take him to a new spot that no one had seen yet" (K. Warnock, n.d.).

Warnock then set his sights on higher education, earning a master's degree from the University of Iowa in 1939 and a PhD in plant ecology from the University of Texas at Austin. In 1946 he accepted a faculty position in the biology department at his alma mater, where he was a student just 11 years earlier. During his tenure at Sul Ross, Warnock published a number of scientific journal articles, many of which focused on Trans-Pecos flora. Though important, his contributions to the scientific community were not Warnock's sole focus. Between 1970 and 1977, he published three separate books that focused on wildflowers of the Trans-Pecos region. In total, the books illustrated more than half of the vascular species of the region. Lamenting in one book, Warnock said, "It is somewhat unfortunate that most botanists write only for other botanists by using scientific and technical language" (B. Warnock 1974, 6). In releasing these three books, Warnock set out to assist the layperson who is primarily interested in identifying wildflowers without using all the difficult and detailed terms (B. Warnock 1974).

Warnock retired from Sul Ross in 1979 and for the next 19 years pursued his passion, a passion that resulted in his being called the "Botanist of the Big Bend." Warnock's legend lives on in the numerous plants that bear his name, such as the prairie brazosmint (*Warnockia scutellarioides*). Throughout his life, Warnock collected over 26,000 plant specimens, some of which were previously unidentified (Klepper 2012). His contributions to the Trans-Pecos and beyond are evidenced in those who had an opportunity to learn from him. Prominent botanists such as A. Michael Powell, John Averett, John Bacon Billie Turner, and Tom Watson are just some of Warnock's protégés (Turner 1998).

Walter Penn Taylor (1888–1972)

Mary Pearl Meuth, Texas A&M AgriLife Extension

"Mr. Taylor lived in an appropriate time when his interest, energy and skills could find an outlet when there was so much to be done. All that he did, he did well and his contributions were many and great."
—Gordon D. Alcorn, "In Memoriam"

In 1935, **Walter Penn Taylor** helped establish the Texas Cooperative Wildlife Research

Walter P. Taylor, 1888–1972. Courtesy of The American Society of Mammologists

Unit, part of the Texas A&M College system, and a precursor to the current Texas A&M AgriLife Wildlife & Fisheries Extension Unit. Born in 1888 near Elkhorn, Wisconsin, Taylor attended the University of California, Berkeley and earned his PhD in vertebrate zoology in 1914. His thesis was titled "The Status of the Beavers of Western North America, with Consideration of the Factors in Their Speciation" (*University of California Register* 1913–14, 35). He continued to work with the University of California, Berkeley's collections as the curator of mammals and the US Department of the Interior's (USDI) Fish and Wildlife Service as senior biologist for seven years (Alcorn 1972).

Taylor moved to College Station, Texas, in 1935, already a well-established and respected ecologist and wildlife conservationist (Burke 2003). He would also continue to hold his role as senior biologist with the USDI Fish and Wildlife Service until 1951. Over the course of his early career, he was involved with many conservation organizations, including the Ecological Society of America (1935); the Wildlife Society (1943–44); American Society of Mammalogists (1940–41); and the Texas Academy of Science (1944–45) (Lehmann 1972). Rollin H. Baker (1995), based on his firsthand knowledge of the program, considered establishment of the Texas Cooperative Wildlife Research Unit in 1935 to be the event that set the stage for modern wildlife conservation and management in Texas. This federally sponsored initiative was designed to encourage cooperating institutions to develop teaching and research programs to provide the trained wildlife specialists and the knowledge needed for the future (Burke 2003).

Texas A&M's Department of Fish and Game got its start under Taylor's leadership. He organized and staffed the department with educators, including William B. Davis, Randolph Peterson, Ben Ludeman, Dan Lay, Rollin H. Baker, and Henry Hahn. He also taught the first range ecology course and established the Department of Range Science for the college. Later in life, his teaching roles included lectures given at Oklahoma A&M University, La Vere College, Southern Illinois University, Murray State College, Claremont Graduate School, and the US Institute of Biological Sciences.

Taylor's role as a naturalist extended outside that as unit leader. As noted by Val Lehmann in his obituary of Taylor, "Taylor lived his thesis that the wildlife biologist was morally obligated to enter and operate in the marketplace" (1972, 1379). He was responsible for the state's first sportsman association, the Texas Wildlife Federation, and the Extension Unit's wildlife management program, Game Preserve Demonstrations. Working with the established Texas Game, Fish, and Oyster Commission, the precursor to the present Texas Parks and Wildlife Department, he promoted professional excellence and statewide conservation practices based on sound scientific research, including persuading the state to abandon the control of coyotes and bobcats on a bounty basis (Lehmann 1972).

Walter P. Taylor passed away in 1972 after finishing his career by working with Oklahoma A&M University and establishing a similar Cooperative Extension program there. He also became active in civic affairs in the city of Claremont, California, and served as a member of the city council from 1961 to 1964 and vice mayor from 1963 to 1964.

William Bennoni "Doc" Davis (1902–1995)

Mary Pearl Meuth, Texas A&M AgriLife Extension Service

William B. Davis, also "affectionately and respectfully referred to as 'Doc Davis,'" was a naturalist by his discipline and intensity studying the natural world, as well as by promoting high standards in every aspect of his professional and personal life (Schmidly and Dixon 1998, 1077). Davis was raised in Utah and Idaho as one of four children, and his early childhood was not an easy one. His father was killed in a sawmill accident when Davis was young, his mother was a cook, and his stepfather was an automobile dealer. He received no particular support or encouragement from his family to pursue education or study the natural world, but his interest in animals, especially birds, was lasting. By age 30, after obtaining a teaching certification and teaching for 13 years, Davis had published eight papers, mostly about woodpeckers, in three different journals.

William Bennoni "Doc" Davis (1902–95), a famed mammalogist who became the curator of the Texas Cooperative Wildlife Collection and head of the Wildlife and Fisheries Department at A&M.

Davis continued his education at Chico State College, finishing with a degree in education in 1932. In 1933, he worked with E. R. Hall of the University of California, Berkeley. This position led to his association with Joseph Grinnell, who agreed to chair Davis's graduate committee if he would switch his research to the field of mammalogy (Schmidly and Dixon 1998). In 1939, Davis finished his work at UC Berkley with a PhD. His dissertation, "The Recent Mammals of Idaho," was described by reviewer F. S. H. in *The Murrelet*:

> It is without exception one of the most valuable contributions on mammals that has been published in recent years. One hundred forty-one species of animals found in the State of Idaho are described. Each species is accompanied by its more acceptable common name, correct scientific name, geographic range, description of the animal, and records of occurrence based on all published information, as well as years of personal field investigation by the author. (1939, 24)

Davis then moved to College Station with his wife, Pearl, and their two children to begin a professorship with Texas A&M College's developing Department of Wildlife Science. He was appointed curator of the Texas Cooperative Wildlife Collections

(TCWC) in 1938 and held the position until his retirement in 1967. Over the course of his career at Texas A&M, Davis contributed more than 5,000 prepared specimens. Davis has been honored with patronyms for three taxa of mammals (*Uroderma bilobatum davisi, Dasypus novemcinctus davisi,* and *Tamias obscurus davisi*) and one reptile (*Phyllodactylus davisi*) (Schmidly and Dixon 1998).

Davis also served as head of the Wildlife and Fisheries Department at A&M from 1947 until his retirement. Under his tenure, the department became "one of the premier programs of its type in the country" (Schmidly and Dixon 1998, 1076). Davis's leadership instituted an "ologies"-based department focus, with classes on the biodiversity of mammalogy, herpetology, ichthyology, and ornithology. This division of the department was contrary to many popular game management traditional styles taught around the country at the time.

Davis stayed active in his research following his retirement, and his interest and enthusiasm for natural history remained strong. As his curriculum vitae described, his interests were the "ecology, differentiation and distribution of mammals, birds, reptiles, and amphibians in Mexico and the western United States" (Schmidly and Dixon 1998).

Valgene W. Lehmann (1913–1987)

Mary Pearl Meuth, Texas A&M AgriLife Extension Service

"Texan Val Lehmann has probably made a greater contribution to the future of conservation and wildlife than any man since Noah filled the Ark."
—*Southern Outdoors Magazine,* 1968

Valgene W. Lehmann (1913–87). Courtesy of Caesar Kleberg Wildlife Research Institute

In the "formative years" of the 1930s, another figure stepped to the front as a pioneer of wildlife management, Valgene W. Lehmann (Tewes 2014, 1). "Val" Lehmann was born in Brenham, Texas, in 1913 and began early making observations of bobwhite quail on his family's farmstead along the Brazos River tributaries. He even had early correspondence with other noteworthy naturalists, including Paul Errington and Herbert Stoddard, both considered to be intellectual giants in the founding of modern wildlife management (Tewes 2014).

After graduating from the University of Texas in 1934, Lehmann went to work with the Texas Game, Fish, and Oyster Commission as a field assistant and the US Biological Survey as a surveyor studying armadillos and bobwhite quail. With this experience and network of professional relationships built in both of those key organizations, Lehmann returned to school to complete his master's degree, studying fish and game, at Texas A&M University, and was awarded one of the first wildlife graduate degrees. His major advising professor at the time, Walter P. Taylor, approved his thesis, "Population

Studies of the Bobwhite in Colorado County, Texas," which included a brief study of the Attwater's prairie chicken in that region.

From 1939 to 1943, Lehmann joined the ranks of the Texas Game, Fish, and Oyster Commission as the regional director for 42 counties along the Texas coast. Lehmann set the foundation for working with landowners between the Coastal Prairies to the Rio Grande Plains to manage their properties for the benefit of native wildlife (Tewes 2014). In 1944 during World War II, Lehmann enlisted in the US Army, with a minor delay due to restrictive background checks on German descendants.

The highlight of Val Lehmann's career in wildlife management came in 1945 when he was hired by Caesar and Bob Kleberg to manage the nearly one million acres of the King Ranch for wildlife and other native game. This large range and the financial security of working with the King Ranch gave Lehmann the opportunity to experiment with a variety of ideas and to achieve many successes (Tewes 2014). One of his successful and continuing population management techniques included the systematic control of coyotes on the property through a full-time predator-control team, by trapping and poisoning, a solution to the overabundance of predators on the property at the time.

The King Ranch was also highly involved in game restoration programs around the state, providing captured deer, turkey, and quail to Texas Parks and Wildlife for restocking in troubled habitats. Lehmann stated, "Just about every county in Texas that can provide the range has gotten either deer or turkey from the ranch" (Tewes 2014, 3). Even President Lyndon B. Johnson received deer for his Central Texas ranch from the King Ranch stock. As the story goes, Lehmann was watching a television program and saw the president driving around his property near Stonewall, honking and scaring these deer. He was so upset that he drove to the Hill Country and demanded, with the Secret Service present, that President Johnson return the deer if he continued to chase them with his car (Tewes 2014).

After he retired in 1971 from his dream job with the King Ranch, Val Lehmann finally had the time to finish his book started earlier in his career, with many papers published on the species in between, *Bobwhites in the Rio Grande Plain of Texas* (1984). He also participated in many professional organizations, including the Texas Chapter of the Wildlife Society and Texas Nature Conservancy. Val Lehmann was a significant figure in the wildlife management, and as he put it, "[The King Ranch] blazed a trail for other ranchers, many of whom now consider a wildlife manager as essential as a livestock foreman" (Cortez 2001, 1).

Modern-Day Naturalists

There are also some modern-day naturalists of note that are rightfully significant within their local communities around the state of Texas. Two in particular that need highlighting are Elmer Kleb and Ned Fritz. These two gentlemen, both gentle giants by nature, were champions for the naturalists in East and North Texas, respectively.

Elmer Kleb (1907–1999)

Karen and Allen Ginnard, Gideon Lincecum Chapter, Texas Master Naturalist Program

As the concrete jungle advances and the sprawl of cities moves ever farther out into the countryside, there are those isolated protectors of the natural world that are to be commended for their often quiet, but effective, work. **Elmer Kleb** was one such man. He was not a trained naturalist. He had no formal education in any of the naturalist sciences and reportedly never completed fourth grade (Applebome 1988). What Kleb did have, however, was a 132-acre family farm, a desire to restore woodlands on his property, a love for birds, and a dream for sustaining his family's land in a natural state

Elmer Kleb (1907–99), a born naturalist who fought for the legacy of his family land near Houston. Courtesy of Harris County, Precinct 3, Kleb Woods Nature Center collection

by creating a nature reserve. In this effort, he was very successful.

The first Kleb family member came to the United States from Germany in 1846. In 1871, Conrad Kleb bought the first parcel of the family land near Hockley, Texas, now known as the Kleb Woods Nature Preserve. The land was originally cleared and farmed by Conrad and his son, Edward. Elmer was the only son of Edward and Minnie Kleb, and from the outset, he loved the land and animals more than people or farming (Applebome 1988).

After his parents died, Kleb began restoring the land to its natural state, ensuring the existence of plenty of feeders and nest boxes for many different species of birds and small animals. He loved all kinds of animals and stayed mostly on his land, rarely going into town. His plan was to create a nature reserve that he could donate to the Audubon Society. As he aged, he realized his dream through a grant from Texas Parks and Wildlife Department (Marshall 2004). The grant allowed him to fulfill his dream of donating his land and kept the government from claiming it for back taxes. Kleb was provided with living expenses and allowed to live out his final years on his land in order to carry on his restoration work.

Elmer Kleb loved the land, lived to restore it for the use of native species of plants and animals, and then left it as a legacy to teach generations to come about living in balance with the land. In all senses of the word, Elmer Kleb was a born naturalist.

Edward C. "Ned" Fritz (1916–2008)

Steve Houser, Texas Tree Trails, North Texas Master Naturalist

Edward C. "Ned" Fritz was an accomplished legal advocate for conservation. He was relentless, fearless, passionate, and persistent. Fritz fought hard for species and land protection—as a trial lawyer, an author, an activist, a lover of nature, and an inspiration to others. One of the greatest joys in life to those around him was working hard enough to receive an "atta boy" or "atta girl" from him (Houser, pers. comm.).

Ned was the first person to file a lawsuit under the National Environmental Policy Act. He founded the Texas Nature Conservancy, Texas League of Conservation Voters, and the Natural Area Preservation Association. Ned and his very supportive wife, Eugenie (or "Genie" to everyone she met), were founding members of the Dallas Historic Tree Coalition, which is now the Texas Historic Tree Coalition. He authored three books to educate the public and move Congress into action against clear-cutting our forests—*Sterile Forest, Realms of Beauty*, and *Clearcutting: A Crime against Nature*. Fritz won many battles and was rightfully called the "Father of Texas Conservation" (Holtcamp 2009). He was a personal hero and a true visionary leader who was many years ahead of his time.

One of Fritz's biggest land preservation

victories, the Big Thicket National Preserve (BTNP), outside Beaumont, which he is credited with saving, will allow future generations to share in his love of nature. The BTNP was the first of its kind in the National Park Service. This category was established primarily for the protection of certain resources. Activities like hunting and fishing or the extraction of minerals and fuels may be permitted if they do not jeopardize the natural values. In 1977, he led his group in a successful lawsuit, *Texas Committee on Natural Resources v. Bergland*, to stop and permanently ban the US Forest Service from clear-cutting on the 600,000 acres of national forests in Texas. This secured a landmark victory for environmentalists (Fritz Papers, 1950s–2008).

His passion was to "represent a normally unrepresented class, and that is Nature itself, which cannot speak verbally and has no ability to hire lawyers" (Todd 1977).

Conclusion

Thanks to the forethought and passions of collectors and professionals, the early natural history of Texas has been documented and preserved to such an extent that a well-rounded story of flora and fauna can be shared with generation after generation. Not only do these organisms offer a physical presence in our natural world, but the ecological lessons learned have provided invaluable details about the diversity of species and their original habitats. Were it not for meticulous field notes and journals by early Texas naturalists, the twentieth century would never have seen a more conservation-minded generation rise up to ardently study the native flora and fauna. The shift from collector to enlightened professor opened a new world for biologists. New laws were signed to protect endangered species, university programs were introduced to study and house the abundant collections, and changes for the better were on the way. Although the "old-time" naturalists are long gone, that does not mean that the study of the natural world is over. It simply means that we now have a library of resources to consult to better understand and learn about the native flora and fauna that make Texas unique.

Ned Fritz (1916–2008), a legal advocate for conservation, known as the "Father of Texas Wilderness." Courtesy of Texas Land Conservancy Louis Berlandier Papers, Box 12, Folder, 14, Smithsonian Institution Archives

References

Alcorn, Gordon D. 1972. In Memoriam: Walter Penn Taylor. *The Murrelet* 53 (3): 41.

Alexander, Nancy S. 2010. Hill, Robert Thomas. *Handbook of Texas Online, Texas State Historical Association. Accessed October 10, 2014.* http://www.tshaonline.org/handbook/online/articles/fhi26.

Anderson, H. Allen. 2010. Long, Stephen Harriman. *Handbook of Texas Online*, Texas State Historical Association. Accessed October 7, 2014. http://tshaonline.org/handbook/online/articles/flot3.

Anonymous. 2010. Roemer, Ferdinand von. *Handbook of Texas Online*, Texas State Historical Association. Accessed October 4, 2014. http://www.tshaonline.org/handbook/online/articles/fr055.

Anonymous. n.d. Other Explorers Follow Lewis and Clark: Stephen H. Long. NebraskaStudies.org. Accessed February 21, 2015. http://www.nebraskastudies.org/0400/frameset_reset.html?http://www.nebraskastudies.org/0400/stories/0401_0111.html.

Applebome, Peter. 1988. Tomball Journal; Rural Recluse Collides with an Unnatural World. *New York Times*, November 9. Accessed February 21, 2015. http://www.nytimes.com/1988/11/09/us/tomball-journal-rural-recluse-collides-with-an-unnatural-world.html.

Baker, R. H. 1995. Texas Wildlife Conservation-Historical Notes. *East Texas Historical Association* 33 (1): 59–72.

Bennicoff, Tad. 2014. Jean Berlandier, the Path from Geneva to Mexico. Smithsonian Institution Archives. Accessed February 21, 2015. http://siarchives.si.edu/blog/jean-louis-berlandier-path-geneva-mexico.

Berlandier, Jean Louis.1983. Papers of Jean Louis Berlandier, 1825–1855: A Guide. Gray Herbarium Library, Harvard University Library, Cambridge, MA. Accessed February 21, 2015. http://oasis.lib.harvard.edu/oasis/deliver/~gra00013.

Birch, Joanne Lemay. 2004. *The Gideon Lincecum Herbarium: A Floristic and Ethnobotanic Analysis*. Austin: University of Texas Press.

Bird, C. D. 1967. The Mosses Collected by Thomas Drummond in Western Canada, 1825–27. *The Bryologist* 70 (2): 262–66.

Boynton, Kenneth. 1918. Collecting Prickly Pear at Apalachicola. *Journal of the New York Botanical Garden* 19 (217): 5.

Bray, William L. 1904. *Forest Resources of Texas*. Washington, DC: Bureau of Forestry, United States Department of Agriculture.

Brown, B. C. 1950. *An Annotated Check List of the Reptiles and Amphibians of Texas*. Waco, TX: Baylor University Press .

Buddle, Christopher. 2014. *What Is a Naturalist?* SciLogs, Biodiversity, Natural History. Accessed February 21, 2015. http://www.scilogs.com/expiscor/what-is-a-naturalist/.

Burke, Horace. 2003. *Texas Naturalists prior to World War II*. Texas Master Naturalist Curriculum, Unit 3. Texas A&M AgriLife Extension/Texas Parks and Wildlife.

Burkhalter, Lois Wood. 1965. *Gideon Lincecum, 1793–1874: A Biography*. Austin: University of Texas Press.

———. 2010. Lincecum, Gideon. *Handbook of Texas Online. Accessed February 24, 2015.* http://www.tshaonline.org/handbook/online/articles/fli03.

Casto, Stanley D. 2010a. Attwater, Henry Philemon. *Handbook of Texas Online*, Texas State Historical Association. Accessed October 7, 2014. http://www.tshaonline.org/online/articles/fat07.

———. 2010b. Singley, John Allen. *Handbook of Texas Online. Accessed April 1, 2015.* http://www.tshaonline.org/handbook/online/articles/fsi33).

Charlton, O. C. 1915. Reverchon Park, Dallas, Texas. *Science* 42, n.s. (1076): 213–14.

Cortez, Oscar. 2001. Wildlife. King Ranch. Accessed April 1, 2015. www.king-ranch.com/stewardship-education/wildlife/. 1.

Custis, Peter. 1806. Letter to Dearborn, October 1, Letters Received, Unregistered Series, RG M221, National Archives, Washington, DC.

Cutrer, Thomas W. 2010. Marcy, Randolph Barnes. *Handbook of Texas Online*, Texas State Historical Association. Accessed October 14, 2014. http://www.tshaonline.org/handbook/online/articles/fma43.

Dumble, E. T. 1892. *Fourth Annual Report of the Geological Survey of Texas*. Austin: Ben C. Jones.

Durbin, John R. 1996. In Memoriam: William L. Bray. Documents of the General Faculty, University of Texas. http://www.utexas.edu/faculty/council/2000–2001/memorials/AMR/Bray/bray.html.

Edward C. Fritz Papers. 1950s–2008. Texas Archival Resources Online. DeGolyer Library, Southern Methodist University. Accessed April 14, 2015. http://www.lib.utexas.edu/taro/smu/00169/smu-00169.html.

Faust, M. 1955. William M. Bray. *Bulletin of the Torrey Botanical Club* 82 (4): 298–300.

Flores, D. L. 1984. The Ecology of the Red River in 1806: Peter Custis and Early Southwestern Natural History. *Southwestern Historical Quarterly* 88:1–42.

Futuyma, D. 1998. Wherefore and Whither the Naturalist? *American Naturalist* 151 (1): 1–6.

Geiser, S. W. [1937] 1948. *Naturalists of the Frontier*. Reprint, Dallas: Southern Methodist University Press.

———. 1958. *Men of Science in Texas, 1820–1880*. Dallas: Southern Methodist University Press.

———. 2010. Drummond, Thomas. *Handbook of Texas Online*. Accessed October 8, 2014. http://www.tshaonline.org/handbook/online/articles/fdr08.

Goyne, Minetta A. 1991. *Life among the Texas Flora: Ferdinand Lindheimer's Letters to George Engelmann*. College Station: Texas A&M University Press.

H. F. S. 1939. Review of *The Recent Mammals of Idaho*, by William B. Davis. *The Murrelet* 20 (1): 24.

Hartman, Clinton P. 2010. Berlandier, Jean Louis. *Handbook of Texas Online, Texas State Historical Association. Accessed October 9, 2014*. http://www.tshaonline.org/handbook/online/articles/fbe56.

Heinrich, B. 2007. *The Snoring Bird*. New York: HarperCollins.

Holtcamp, Wendee. 2009. Larger Than Life: The Inimitable Edward "Ned" Fritz Changed the Face of Texas Conservation. *Texas Parks & Wildlife Magazine*, August. Accessed April 14, 2015. http://www.tpwmagazine.com/archive/2009/aug/legend/.

Houser, Steve. 2013. The History of Reverchon Park and the Iris Bowl. *Irises, The Bulletin of the American Iris Society* 94 (3). Accessed February 15, 2015. http://www.arborilogical.com/uncategorized/the-history-of-reverchon-park-and-the-iris-bowl/.

Hutchinson, Alan. 1970. Review of *The Indians in Texas in 1830*, by Jean L. Berlandier. *Arizona and the West* 12 (4): 389–91.

James, Edwin. 1823. *Account of an Expedition from Pittsburgh to the Rocky Mountains, Performed in the Years 1819, 1820*. Vol. 1. London: Printed for Longman, Hurst, Rees, Orme, and Brown. Accessed February 21, 2015. www.americanjourneys.org/aj-144a/.

Klepper, E. D. 2012. Web Extra: Dr. Barton Warnock. *Texas Highways*, May. Accessed October 9, 2014. http://texashighways.com/people/item/2339-web-extra-dr-barton-warnock.

Kofalk, Harriet. 1989. *No Woman Tenderfoot: Florence Merriam Bailey, Pioneer Naturalist.* College Station: Texas A&M University Press.

Lawley, M. n.d. Thomas Drummond (1793–1835). *A Social and Biographical History of British and Irish Field-Bryologists.* Accessed February 21, 2015. http://rbg-web2.rbge.org.uk/bbs/learning/bryohistory/Bygone%20Bryologists/THOMAS%20DRUMMOND.pdf.

Lehmann, Valgene W. 1972. Walter P. Taylor, 1888–1972. *Journal of Wildlife Management* 36 (4): 1379–80.

Lewis, I. M. 1915. *The Trees of Texas: An Illustrated Manual of the Native and Introduced Trees of the State.* Bulletin of the University of Texas, No. 22. Austin: The University of Texas.

Lintz, David. Strecker Museum. *Handbook of Texas Online.* Accessed October 8, 2014. http://www.tshaonline.org/handbook/online/articles/lbs09.

Marcy, R. B. 1853. *Exploration of the Red River of Louisiana.* Washington, DC: Robert Armstrong Public Printer.

———. 1859. *The Prairie Traveler: A Hand-Book for Overland Expeditions.* The War Department. Accessed February 21, 2015. http://www.kancoll.org/books/marcy/.

———. 1866. *Thirty Years of Army Life on the Border.* New York: Harper and Brothers.

Marshall, Thom. 2004. Kleb Land Becomes Preserve, as Last Resident Wished. *Houston Chronicle*, June 5. Accessed February 21, 2015. http://www.chron.com/news/houston-texas/article/Kleb-land-becomes-preserve-as-last-resident-1955735.php.

McGauch, Anne. n.d. Gideon Lincecum–the Man: Washington County's Internationally Famous Botanist. Gideon Lincecum Chapter of the Texas Master Naturalist Program. Accessed April 1, 2015. http://txmn.org/glc/about/gideon-lincecum/.

McGraw, A. Joachim, John W. Clark Jr., and Elizabeth A. Robbins. 1991. *A Texas Legacy: The Old San Antonio Road and the Caminos Reales.* Austin: Texas State Department of Highways and Public Transportation.

Meadows, D. 2009. HMNS@100: Henry Attwater—Naturalist. Beyond Bones: Houston Museum of Natural Science. Accessed April 1, 2015. http://blog.hmns.org/tag/history-of-hmns/.

Meikle, L. H. R. 2005. Drummond of Forfar. *Scots Magazine*, Dundee, April, 362–67.

Merritt. C. A. 1940. Oklahoma Geological Survey, Mineral Report #8. *Copper in the "Red Beds" of Oklahoma.* Accessed April 1, 2015. http://www.ogs.ou.edu/pubsscanned/minreports/mr8.pdf.

Mitchell Collection. n.d. Victoria Regional History Center. Accessed October 2014. http://vrhc.uhv.edu/manuscripts/mitchell/home.htm.

Mueller, Cynthia. n.d. Thomas Drummond. Plant Answers.com. Accessed April 1, 2015. http://www. plantanswers.com.

Neck, Raymond W. 2010. Strecker, John Kern, Jr. *Handbook of Texas Online.* Accessed October 8, 2014. http://www.tshaonline.org/handbook/online/articles/fst88.

Nichols, Roger L. 1980. Long-Bell Expedition. Oklahoma Historical Society. Accessed February 24, 2015. http://digital.library.okstate.edu/encyclopenia/entries/L/L0010.html.

Oberholser, H. C., F. Kennard, A. Allen, and A. Foffin. 1932. Obituaries. *The Auk* 49 (1): 144–48.

Oehser, Paul H. 1952. In Memoriam: Florence Merriam Bailey. *The Auk* 69 (1): 19–26.

Packard, A. S., and E. D. Cope. 1883. *The American Naturalist: An Illustrated Magazine of Natural History*. Philadelphia: Press of McCalla and Stavely.

Peacock, H. 1995. Frontier Naturalists. *Texas Highways* 42 (5): 4–11.

Perez, Joan Jenkins. 2010. Reverchon, Julien. *Handbook of Texas Online*. Accessed October 6, 2014. http://www.tshaonline.org/handbook/online/articles/fre30.

Ragsdale, Crystal Sasse. 2010. Lindheimer, Ferdinand Jacob. *Handbook of Texas Online*. Accessed April 1, 2015. http://www.tshaonline.org/handbook/online/articles/fli04.

Richardson, John. 1829. *Fauna Boreali-Americana*. London: J. Murray.

Roemer, C. F. 1849. *Texas: Mit Besonderer Rücksicht Auf Deutsche Auswanderung Und Die Physischen Verhältnisse Des Landes*. Bonn, Germany: A. Marcus.

———. 1935. Texas: With Particular Attention to German Emigration and the Physical Conditions of the Country. Trans. Oswald Mueller. San Antonio: Standard Print Company.

———. 1995. *Roemer's Texas: 1845–1847 (With Particular Reference to German Immigration and the Physical Appearance of the Country: Described through Personal Observation)*. Trans. Oswald Mueller. Austin: Eakin Press.

Saustrup, Anders S. 2010. Bray, William L. *Handbook of Texas Online. Accessed October 8, 2014.* http://www.tshaonline.org/handbook/online/articles/fbrba.

Schmidly, D. J. 2002. *Texas Natural History: A Century of Change*. Lubbock: Texas Tech University Press.

Schmidly, David, and James Dixon. 1998. William B "Doc" Davis: 1902–1995. *Journal of Mammalogy* 79 (3): 1076–83.

Simonds, F. W. 1902. Dr. Ferdinand von Roemer, the Father of the Geology of Texas; His Life and Work. *American Geologist* 29 (March): 131–40.

Tewes, Christina. 2014. *Valgene Lehmann—Early Pioneer in Wildlife Management*. Caesar Kleberg Wildlife Research Institute No. 3. Kingsville.

Texas Committee on Natural Resources v. Bergland. 1977. Civ. A. No. TY-76–268-CA (433 F. Supp. 1235, 10 ERC 1326) (E.D. Tex. May 24, 1977). Accessed April 1, 2015. http://elr.info/sites/default/files/litigation/7.20720.htm.

Tharp, B. C. et al. 2000–2001. In Memoriam: Isaac McKinney Lewis. Accessed April 1, 2015. http://www.utexas.edu/faculty/council/2000–2001/memorials/SCANNED/lewis.pdf.

Todd, David. 1977. Interview with Ned Fritz, May 17. Dallas, TX. Accessed April 1, 2015. http://www.texaslegacy.org/bb/transcripts/fritznedtxt2.html.

Turner, B. 1998. In Memoriam: Barton H. Warnock, 1911–1998. Botany.org. Accessed

October 9, 2014. http://www.botany.org/bsa/psb/1998/ann098–3.html.

United States National Museum. 1875. Bulletin No. 1. Published under the direction of the Smithsonian Institution. Washington, DC: Government Printing Office.

University of California Register: 1913–14, with Announcements for 1914–15. 1913–14. Berkeley: University of California Press.

The University of Texas. 1898. *The University of Texas Record.* Vol. 1, no. 1. Austin: The University of Texas.

US Department of Agriculture. 1876. *Report of the Commissioner of Agriculture of the Operations of the Department for the Year of 1876. Texas.* Washington, DC: Government Printing Office. Accessed April 1, 2015. https://books.google.com/books?id=4CdTceqce-gC&lpg=PA357&ots=bqhs9FHYH0&dq=Report%20°f%20the%20Commissioner%20°f%20Agriculture%20Progress%20°f%20Industrial%20Education%201876&pg=PA357#v=onepage&q&f=false, 350–51.

Warnock, B. H. 1970. *Wildflowers of the Big Bend Country, Texas.* Alpine, TX: Sul Ross State University.

———. 1974. *Wildflowers of the Guadalupe Mountains and the Sand Dune Country, Texas.* Alpine, TX: Sul Ross State University.

Warnock, K. F. n.d. Dr. Barton H. Warnock. AggieHorticulture, Texas A&M AgriLife Extension. Accessed October 9, 2014. http://aggie-horticulture.tamu.edu/archives/parsons/heroes/warnock.html.

Whitcomb, Roger F. 1985. The Conchologist. Speech presented at 89th annual meeting of the Texas State Historical Association. Fort Worth, March 1.

Williams, O. B. 1943. Obituary, Isaac McKinney Lewis, 1878–1943. *Science* 97 (2526): 480–81. Accessed April 1, 2015. http://www.sciencemag.org/content/97/2526/480.citation.

Zahniser, H. 1942. Vernon Orlando Bailey, 1894–1942. *Science* 96:6–7.

Additional Resources

Allen, J. A. 1894. On the Mammals of Aransas County, Texas, with Descriptions of New Forms of *Lepus and Oryzomys. Bulletin of American Museum of Natural History* 7 (6): 165–98.

———. 1896. On Mammals Collected in Bexar County and Vicinity, Texas, with Field Notes by the Collector. *Bulletin of American Museum of Natural History* 8 (5): 47–80.

American National Biography. 1999. Vol. 1. New York: Oxford University Press.

Anonymous. 2010. Drummond, Thomas. *Handbook of Texas Online.* Accessed October 8, 2014. http://www.tshaonline.org/handbook/online/articles/fdr08.

Baker, Rollin H. 2000. Walter P. Taylor, Texas Renaissance Mammalogist. *Texas Society of Mammalogists Newsletter* 3–5.

BRIT Virtual Herbarium. Atrium Biodiversity Information System for the Botanical Research Institute of Texas. Accessed October 10, 2014. http://atrium.brit.org.

Casto, Stanley D. 1996. Texas Academy of Science Collection. Dolph Briscoe Center for American History, University of Texas at Austin.

Coats, A. M. 1969. *The Quest for Plants: A History of the Horticultural Explorers.* Ithaca, NY: Cornell University, Studio Vista Books.

Collins, Fred. 2009. Hotspots near You—Kleb Woods Nature Preserve, Hockley, Texas. *BirdWatching*, August 21. Accessed February 21, 2015. http://www.birdwatchingdaily.com/hotspots/76-kleb-woods-nature-preserve-hockley-texas/.

Drummond, T. 1830. Sketch of Journey to the Rocky Mountains and to the Columbia River in North America. *Hooker's Journal of Botany and Kew Garden Miscellany* 1:178–219. Accessed June 2013. http://www.biodiversitylibrary.org/bibliography/37944#/summary.

Friends of the Forfar Botanists, assisted by Alan Elliott. 2013. Thomas Drummond, 1793–1835. Accessed February 21, 2015. http://www.forfarbotanists.org/thomas_drummond_detail.pdf.

Hoeniger, Judith F. M. 1987. Drummond, Thomas. *Dictionary of Canadian Biography*, vol. 6. Accessed June 2013. http://www.biographi.ca/009004–119.01-e.php?BioId=36971.

Hooker, W. J. 1834–42. *Journal of Botany: Being a Second Series of the Botanical Miscellany.* Vols. 1, 3. London: Longman, Rees, Orme, Brown, Green.

Kleb Woods Nature Preserve: History. n.d. Harris County Precinct Three Commissioner Steve Radack. Accessed February 21, 2015. http://www.pct3.hctx.net/parks/KlebWoodsNaturePres.aspx?history.

Lawson, Russell M. 2012. *Frontier Naturalist: Jean Louis Berlandier and the Exploration of Northern Mexico and Texas.* Appendix 1. Albuquerque: University of New Mexico Press.

Lincecum, Jerry Bryan, and Edward Hake Phillips, eds. 1994. *Adventures of a Frontier Naturalist: The Life and Times of Dr. Gideon Lincecum.* College Station: Texas A&M University Press.

Nelson, E. C. 1990. James and Thomas Drummond: Their Scottish Origins and Curatorships in Irish Botanic Gardens. *Archives of Natural History* 17:49–65.

Oberholser, Harry Church. 1974. *The Bird Life of Texas.* 2 vols. Austin: University of Texas Press.

Rigg, John. 2012. Kleb Woods Nature Preserve. *Community Impact Newspaper* (Tomball-Magnolia), December 6. Accessed February 21, 2015. http://impactnews.com/houston-metro/tomball-magnolia/kleb-woods-nature-preserve/.

Shaw, Elizabeth A. 1987. *Charles Wright on the Boundary, 1849–52.* Westport, CT: Meckler.

Vanishing Wildlife. 1913. Texas Department of Agriculture Bulletins Nos. 31–34.

UNIT 4

Ecological Regions of Texas

DAVID H. RISKIND
Natural Resources Program, with contributions from additional Texas Parks and Wildlife Department Staff

Unit Goals

After completing this unit, volunteers should be able to

- identify and differentiate the features of Texas' ecological regions and subregions
- understand and communicate the use of different maps denoting various ecological regions of Texas
- explain some of the key the factors underpinning the ecological diversity in Texas

Introduction

It is human nature to organize what falls within identifiable boundaries. It is no different for the terrain and landscape called Texas. Because of geology, distinctive land features, soils, and climate, Texas, like all places on earth, has several readily identifiable regions. In turn, these regions have characteristic plant and animal communities, which are the result of interrelationships and interaction of long standing among abiotic and biotic elements. These patterns have been portrayed as maps and have been identified by a variety of terms, the most current of which is **ecoregion**.

The terms **natural region** and **bioregion** have been used as well. Both refer to the notion that the mapped unit reflects both plant and animal elements together with the other physical and climatic components. The terms natural region and **land resource area** are more generic, while **vegetational area/region** and **plant zone** simply refer to the emphasis on the dominant plant cover and structure. The brief discussion that follows provides some background on the construction of maps of natural, ecoregion, or vegetation regions, along with some special-purpose maps commonly used in Texas today available in published documents or on websites.

"For someone studying natural history, life can never be long enough."
—Miriam Rothschild, British entomologist

Are There Just *Ten*?

For the longest time, I recall hearing about "Gould's 10 Vegetational Areas of Texas" (1962); the words *Gould* and *ten* seem to have been particularly tightly linked. In 1962, the Texas Agricultural Experiment Station (TAES), Texas A&M University, published *Texas Plants—a Checklist and Ecological Summary*. For the first time, there was a publication that included a comprehensive checklist, with common and scientific names, of the plants of Texas. The booklet offered to the general public a very good, concise ecological summary of Texas and was distributed widely through the Texas A&M AgriLife Extension Service.

Looking closer, the 10 vegetational areas were contributed not by Frank Gould, the authority on Texas grasses at that time, but by Gerald W. Thomas, dean of the College of Agriculture, Texas Tech University, in *Texas*

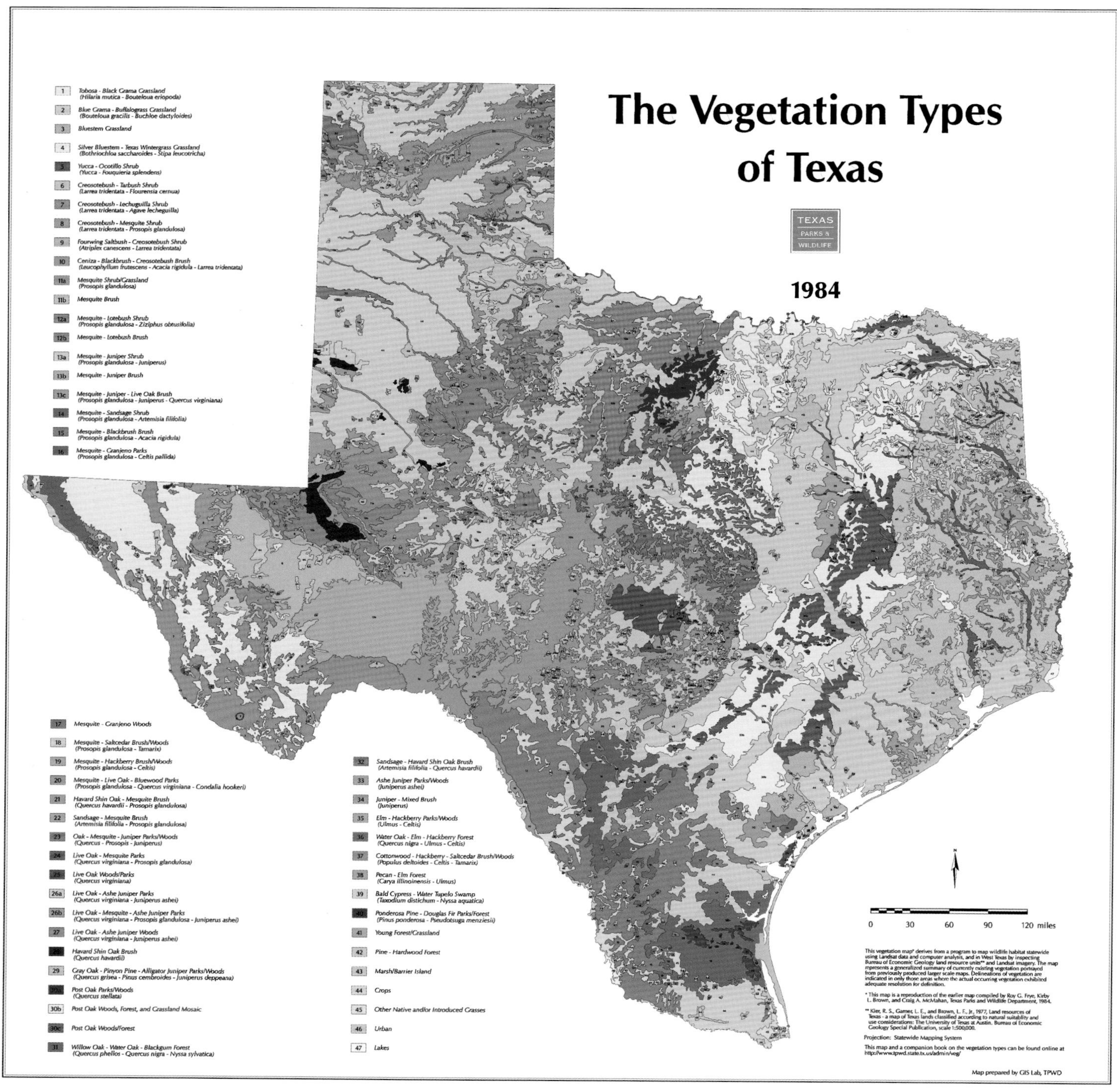

Vegetational types of Texas. Courtesy of Texas Parks and Wildlife Department

Plants: An Ecological Summary. The map was the cover of the checklist and was captioned "Vegetational Areas of Texas." Gould notes that the vegetational map is basically the same as that used in his *Texas Grasses, a Preliminary Checklist* (Gould 1957), a mimeographed document.

An updated version of this map, in collaboration with Thomas, is provided as the introduction to the *Manual of the Vascular Plants of Texas* (Correll and Johnston 1970). Here the 10 "Plant Zones" of Texas are briefly described much as in the previous versions but with some updated information and remarks on plant rarities and endemics. Interestingly, Thomas (1962) notes that the map is "basically and broadly" that mapped by Cory and Parks in their 1937 *Catalogue of the Flora of the State Texas.*

The most recent revision of the Texas A&M AgriLife Extension ecological summary was published in 1990; and J. L. Schuster and S. L. Hatch's 1990 *Ecological Summary* is a slightly expanded version of earlier treatments.

The *Texas Almanac, 2002–3* includes the same vegetation area map used in the 1990 TAES checklist; the abbreviated narrative is contributed by S. L. Hatch. The *Almanac* also includes a map showing the physical regions and subregions of Texas, the physiographic regions of the state, but these do not include any modern biotic factors. However, many of the subregions have familiar **toponyms**, a name based on a place or a place-name, especially one derived from a topographical feature, such as Blackland Belt, Post Oak Belt, Pine Belt, Coastal Prairies, Rio Grande Plain, or Edwards Plateau.

In just this short period, we have already seen that the terms "vegetational areas," "ecological summaries," and "plant zones" have been used to describe the natural regions of Texas. E. H. Johnston, an industrial geographer, published *The Natural Regions of Texas* in 1931, which laid out four major "physical" areas of Texas, but with 67 distinct subregions, which rely on physical features, substrate/soil, climate, and to a minor degree, plant cover. Few people ever refer to this work, but it is of historical interest and a good descriptive read.

B. C. Tharp, founder of the botany department at the University of Texas at Austin, published *The Vegetation of Texas* in 1939. He included a map of the vegetational regions, refined somewhat and reproduced in his *Texas Range Grasses* (1952, fig. 3), in which he described 18 regions and 22 subregions. This is still the most detailed overall vegetational map for Texas.

A more recent iteration of Tharp's map appears in *Preserving Texas' Natural Heritage* (1978, fig. 2). This effort was the result of a work session of experts on Texas flora and fauna and resulted in two maps showing 11 natural regions and 27 subregions. Sometime in the late 1990s, Texas Parks and Wildlife modified this map to include the Near-shore and Off-shore Marine Region, which is also used in the *Texas Environmental Almanac* (Reed and Sanger 2000).

A slightly different version of this map appears in *Unique Wildlife Ecosystems of Texas*, which, in my opinion, is the best and most concise overall description of the ecoregions of Texas. None of the contents were attributed, but the "Natural Regions" section was written by John E. Williams, then of the Natural Areas Survey Project, LBJ School of Public Affairs, University of Texas at Austin. It differs from the LBJ School version in that the Stockton Plateau is considered part of the Edwards Plateau rather than part of the Trans-Pecos. The US Fish and Wildlife Service map shows 8 major regions and 35 subregions for Texas. This scheme was adopted by the Texas Natural Heritage Program, now Texas Parks and Wildlife Department (TPWD) Wildlife Diversity, and recently republished in *Rare Plants of Texas* (Poole et al. 2007).

Just for the sake of confusion, there is a version of the LBJ School map as modified by Ray C. Telfair II (1999) in which he presents his version of refinement, with little explanation. Basically, several additional areas are split out of the East Texas forests, the Cross Timbers and Prairies are adjusted, and regions are renumbered. Telfair calls the Pineywoods (a.k.a. Piney Woods) region the East Texas Forest Region.

An element of this overall mélange of descriptive activity was an effort by TPWD to produce a map of Texas vegetation based on satellite imagery (McMahan et al. 1984). Forty-six cover types are presented and described. The map has been reproduced with brief text in a leaflet intended primarily for school groups. This map shows cover type rather than vegetation.

The geographer A. W. Kuchler (1964)

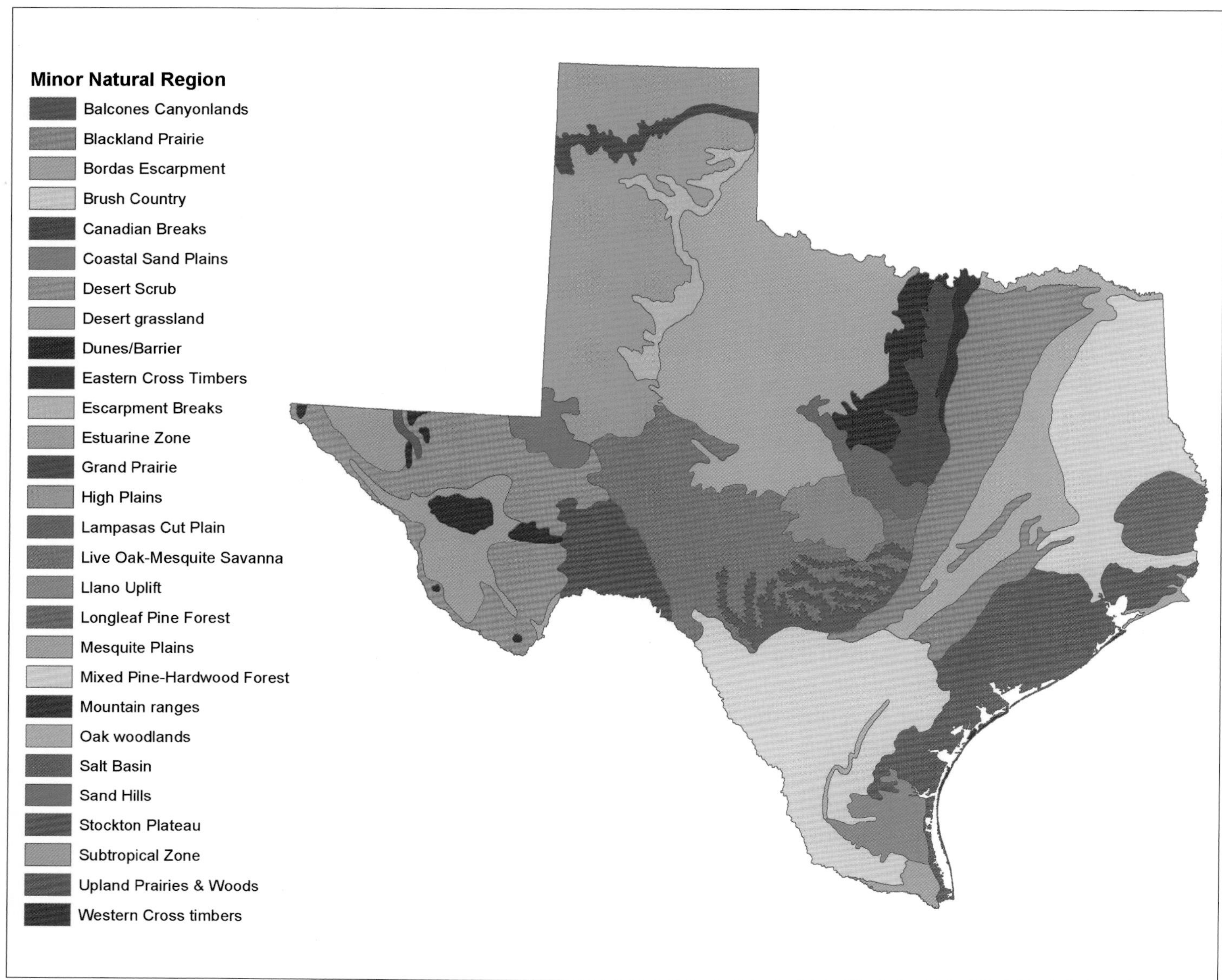

Minor natural regions of Texas.

published a map and a manual to accompany the map in *Potential Natural Vegetation of the Conterminous United States*. Texas is shown with 27 major types mapped, but this work endeavored to show the so-called climax or natural potential vegetation rather than the actual vegetation for Texas. It is little used today although it is an important work.

The USDA "Major Land Resource Areas" shows 25 resource areas in Texas, most of which spill over into adjacent states. Each link on the site shows the resource area, its extent, water, soils, land use, climate, potential natural vegetation, and other information. This scheme is weighted toward soils and climate but is a very useful tool for ecosystem management and land planning. The regional names are geographic and, to some degree, physiographic.

Why Are There So Many Different Treatments?

The answer is simple: scope, scale, and level of resolution, that is, coarse or fine, and the intended user for the product. And the truth is that many of the terms used are not clearly defined or perhaps even generally understood by most. How many people can be expected to understand the difference between plant regions, vegetation types, ecological regions, geographic regions, natural regions, biotic communities, ecoregions, bioregions, physiographic regions, biotic provinces, and land resource areas of Texas? Most mapping treatments rely on a combination of natural and physical features to delineate or map. The features used to delineate an area include geology, climate, soils, elevation, and plant cover or distinctive physiography (geological structure or landform). And frankly, some units are entirely artificial constructs; the "Trans-Pecos" is an example. Furthermore, most of these units have long-standing place-names or culturally derived labels as descriptors, which reflect a sense of place derived from and linked to the landscape features, such as geology, landform, soils, and plant cover—the vegetation.

In addition, Texas is a crossroads of a good part of North America's major structural elements—coastal plains, mid-continental high plains, desertic basins and ranges–as well as climatic zones (cold and warm temperate to subtropical) and biotic (plant and animal) communities, grasslands, forest, deserts, and subtropical communities. The Balcones Canyonlands is probably Texas' most distinctive, endemic "eco-type," although even this is sometimes simply considered an outlier of the Sierra Madrean communities of Mexico.

Special-Purpose Ecomaps

Yet another map to add to this already diverse mix is one in use by the hospitality industry and the Texas Department of Transportation (TxDOT) and TPWD, the originating agency. This map shows seven regions of Texas and is intended as a simplified informational piece for Texas' rapidly growing ecotourism industry. Its scale is coarser than many noted previously, and it conveys the essence of such diverse areas as the Big Bend Country, the Hill Country, the Piney Woods, and the Gulf Coast. Since many areas of east-central Texas are patchworks and interfingerings of mid- and tallgrass prairies and woodlands, it is a very simple matter to lump this into a new region called Prairies and Lakes for the ecotourists, or, on the slightly coarser scale, as Oak Woods and Prairies for the ecologists (see *Natural Regions of Texas* 1979). This map was used for the cover and as figure 1 in *Ecotourism and Conservation* (Holt et al. 2000). Regional boundaries for this map application are smoothed along county/political boundaries and, as a consequence, are rather coarse.

Another special-purpose map showing nine ecoregions is included in *Rare and Declining Birds of Texas* (Lockwood and Shackelford 2000). This ecoregional map looks like none of the others. It is intended to provide a framework for describing aspects of Texas' birdlife for the Partners in Flight program. The map is based on Bailey's (1978) Ecoregions of the United States. The coarser-scale map clearly reflects the fact that birds rely on much broader habitat/landscape features.

Griffith et al. (2004) published a map and descriptor in *Ecoregions of Texas*, an interagency collaboration, and defined these regions within context of a hierarchical continental spatial framework. This detailed effort maps and describes ecological regions based on traditional elements but also includes hydrologic factors. The regions and subregions are designated mostly by physiographic nomenclature—Chihuahuan Desert, Edwards Plateau, South Texas Plains, and so on. Ecoregion level III is roughly equivalent to the "Natural Regions of Texas," and level IV to the subregions. Level IV uses physiographic labels, such as Llano Uplift, but also includes some derived from the vegetation, such as Tamaulipan Thornscrub or Lost Pines. The primary sponsor of this mapping effort was the Environmental Protection Agency (EPA) with the purpose of providing a consistent continental mapping system for multiple agencies to use as an ecological framework for the nation and its constituent state subdivisions. In my opinion the map unit boundaries are quite accurate and could just as easily be used for the natural vegetation types contained therein.

Where Does This Leave Us?

Let me try to leave you with a bit of guidance on the use or application of any of the "natural" or "ecoregional" maps just discussed. First, whichever map you use, you need to clearly attribute, cite, or acknowledge the source. Second, if you modify any of these maps for your particular application or need, you should clearly describe what you have done and why. Third, if you choose to develop your own map to meet your particular project objective, fully describe your methods, paying particular attention to the boundaries you use and where you draw these boundaries; and be especially mindful of the scale at which you are working. If, for example, you use a soil or substrate boundary rather than a topographic boundary, then state that clearly. If you smooth boundaries along a watershed or topographic or political boundary, note your method.

Finally, be mindful that all of the maps we have discussed are composite maps. Physiographic maps combine landforms and geology; vegetation maps contain geology, soils,

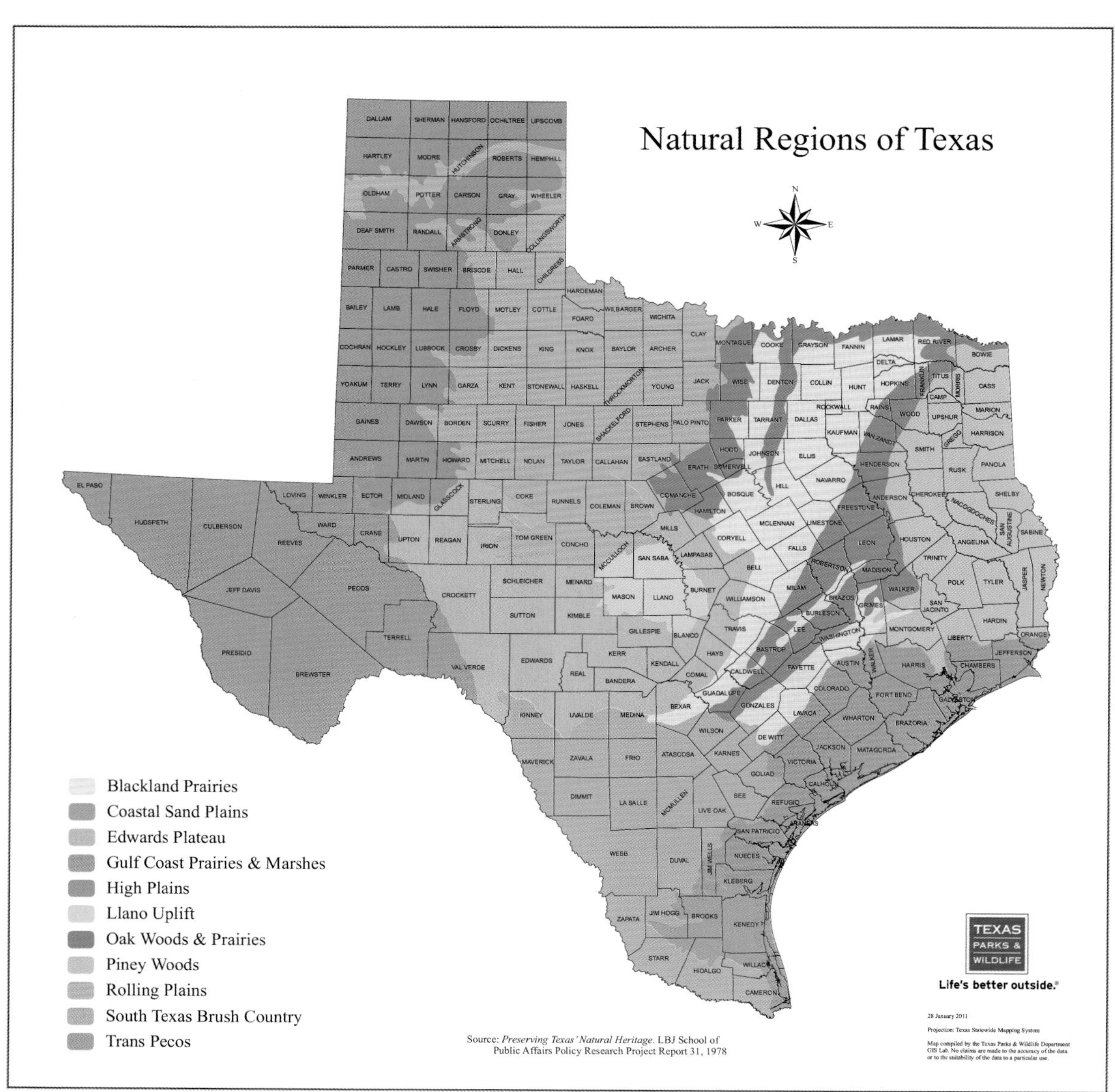

Natural regions of Texas.

and vegetation type and structure or potential natural vegetation; and natural region and ecoregion maps reflect the aforementioned elements plus at least some biotic or hydrologic factors. Thus, to an extent, most of the maps that have been used to graphically portray Texas' natural and physical diversity are, indeed, "ecoregional."

Texas Ecological Regions*

Texas is a large land area covering approximately 267,000 square miles. It is located at a geographic crossroads where many of the major regions of the United States come together: the coastal prairies, the southeastern pinewoods, the central hardwoods, the Great Plains, the southwestern deserts, and the southern extension of the Rocky Mountains. This accounts for the tremendous climatic and geographic diversity of the state. Texas has 10 climatic regions, 14 soil regions, and 11 distinct ecological regions. These ecological regions of the state represent differences in the soils, topography, geology, rainfall, and plant and animal communities. There are, however, several ways of classifying the natural environment, such as by river watershed basins, hydrologic subbasins, or vegetation systems.

Piney Woods

Overview

Located in eastern Texas, this gently rolling to hilly forested land covers 23,500 square miles. The soils of the region are characterized as deep loamy or sandy. Prior to European settlement, this area of Texas supported longleaf pine, shortleaf pine, loblolly pine, and oak-hickory forests. Today the region is composed of fragmented pine and pine-hardwood forests with some cropland and pastureland. The majority of national forests and other forestland located in Texas is found in this region, as is Texas' only natural lake, Caddo Lake. Dogwoods and red and white oaks are plentiful throughout the area. Though rapidly diminishing, the bottomland hardwood forests of oak-hickory, elm, sweetgum, sugarberry, and ash—the most diverse and richest wildlife habitats left in Texas—are located in the Piney Woods. The endangered red-cockaded woodpecker's habitat is in the pine forest. Rare plants found in the region include the southern lady's slipper orchid, golden glade cress, white bladderpod, and Texas trailing phlox. Rare plant communities include longleaf pine savannas and beech-magnolia forest. Swamps, bogs, and human-made lakes extend through the region, which has the state's highest rainfall. Lumber and cattle production are major industries in the area. Four national forests are located in the Piney Woods.

Location

The Piney Woods ecoregion covers approximately 15 million acres (actually part of a much larger area of pine-hardwood forests that extend into Louisiana, Arkansas, and Oklahoma) in northeastern Texas, extending from Bowie County in the north to Mont-

Natural Sites in the Piney Woods

- Angelina National Forest
- Atlanta State Park
- Big Thicket National Preserve
- Dangerfield State Park
- Davy Crockett National Forest
- Martin Dies, Jr. State Park
- Roy E. Larsen Sandyland Sanctuary (Texas Nature Conservancy)
- Sabine National Forest
- Sam Houston National Forest
- Tyler State Park
- White Oak Creek Wildlife Management Area

*Text (excluding sidebars) reprinted with permission from University of Texas Press. *Texas Environmental Almanac: Second Edition*, Texas Center for Policy Studies, compiled by Mary Sanger and Cyrus Reed, 2000, University of Texas Press, pp. 115–17.

Features of the ecological regions of Texas

Region	Size (sq mi)	Topography*	Annual rainfall (in)	Predominant vegetation	Rare plants and habitat	Rare animals and habitat
Piney Woods	23,500	Gently rolling to hilly forested	36–50	Pine, oak, and other hardwood forests	*Texas trailing phlox* Deep sandy soils of long-leaf pine woodlands *White bladderpod* Natural openings of pine-oak woodlands	*red-cockaded woodpecker* Pinewoods with widely-spaced, large, mature pine trees *bald eagle* *Breeding*: Along river systems or lakeshores with large, tall trees. Breeding populations occur in the eastern half of Texas. *Wintering: Mostly near large lakes and reservoirs. Wintering eagles occur in suitable habitat throughout Texas.*
Oak Woods and Prairies	19,000	Gently rolling to hilly	28–40	Oak and hickory woodlands; tallgrass prairies	*Large-fruited sand verbena* Openings within oak woodland on deep sands *Navasota ladies'-tresses* Openings and drainages in post oak woodlands	*Houston toad* Pine/oak woodland or savanna on deep, sandy soils
Blackland Prairie	23,500	Gently rolling to nearly level	28–40	Tallgrass prairies; mesquite, cedar elm, sugarberry	Tall-grass prairie plant community has become rare	
Gulf Coast Prairies and Marshes	21,000	Nearly level	30–50	Grasses; tallgrass prairies; live oak woodlands; some mesquite and acacias	*prairie dawn* Poorly drained, sparsely vegetated areas in open grasslands *slender rush-pea/South Texas ambrosia* Grasslands or mesquite-invaded grasslands	*Attwater's prairie chicken* Tallgrass coastal prairie *eastern brown pelican* Offshore islands, spoil islands, mud banks *Eskimo curlew* Migrates through the grasslands from the Arctic tundra to Pampas grasslands of Argentina, but some sources consider it extinct. *Houston toad* Deep, sandy soils *piping plover* Winters along Gulf Coast; tidal mudflats, sandflats, or algal flats *whooping crane* Winters on Texas Gulf Coast; marshes and sandflats of Aransas National Wildlife Refuge and nearby areas

Region	Size (sq mi)	Topography*	Annual rainfall (in)	Predominant vegetation	Rare plants and habitat	Rare animals and habitat
Coastal Sand Plains	4,000	Fairly level to undulating	24–28	Tallgrass prairie, live oak woodlands, mesquite savanna		black spotted newt (*Notophthalmus meridionalis*) black-striped snake (*Coniophanes imperialis*) South Texas siren (*Siren* spp.) Texas indigo snake (*Drymarchon corais erebennus*) Texas scarlet snake (*Cemophora coccinea lineri*) Texas tortoise (*Gopherus berlandieri*)
South Texas Brush Country	24,000	Level to rolling	20–32	Thorny brush including mesquite, acacia, prickly pear, and some grassland areas	*ashy dogweed* Mesquite grassland openings of thorny shrublands on deep, sandy soils *black lace cactus* Grasslands or mesquite-invaded grasslands *Johnston's frankenia* Rocky hillsides or saline clay loam flats within openings of thorny shrublands *star cactus* Openings of thorny shrublands on rocky, clay, loam soils *Texas ayenia* Subtropical woodlands on alluvial deposits on floodplains and terraces of the Rio Grande *Walker's manioc* Openings of thorny shrublands on sandy loam soils	*jaguarundi and ocelot* Dense, thorny, low brush *interior least tern* Bare sand, shell, and gravel beaches, bars, and islands associated with reservoirs along the Rio Grande Texas indigo snake (*Drymarchon corais erebennus*) Texas tortoise (*Gopherus berlandieri*)

(*continued*)

Region	Size (sq mi)	Topography*	Annual rainfall (in)	Predominant vegetation	Rare plants and habitat	Rare animals and habitat
Edwards Plateau	31,000	Flat to rolling to steep (referred to as Texas Hill Country)	15–34	Shortgrass grasslands, juniper shrubs and oak-juniper forest, mesquite	*Texas snowbells* Limestone edges or cliff faces along perennial streams *Texas wild-rice* San Marcos River; clear, constant temperature, spring-fed water *Tobusch fishhook cactus* Ashe juniper/oak rangelands on rocky, alkaline soils	*black-capped vireo* Semi-open rangelands with a diversity of low-growing shrubs *golden-cheeked warbler* Mature woodlands of oaks and Ashe juniper *Edwards Aquifer species* San Marcos salamander Texas blind salamander fountain darter (fish) Spring-fed waters of the San Marcos and Comal rivers in Central Texas *Clear Creek gambusia* Spring-fed headwaters of Clear Creek, a tributary of the San Saba River in Menard
Llano Uplift	5,000	Rolling to hilly	24–32	Oak-hickory woodlands; some mesquite and juniper brush and grasslands	*rock quillwort* Wet-weather pools on granite outcrops *basin bellflower* Gravelly or sandy soils	*black-capped vireo* Shrublands and open woodlands with vegetation reaching to ground level San Marcos gambusia (fish)
Rolling Plains	43,500	Gently rolling to rough and dissected	20–28	Originally midsized grasses, now mixed with other grasses; invaded by mesquite and junipers; hardwoods along and near streams	*Texas poppy-mallow* Within grasslands or open mesquite woodlands, usually on deep sands	*interior least tern* Along the Canadian and Red Rivers; bare sand and gravel beaches, sandbars *Concho water snake* Free-flowing streams over rocks, shallow riffles, and rocks or crevices along banks and shorelines
High Plains	34,500	Fairly level	15–22	Short grasses; mesquite and yucca in some areas, oak and juniper in others	Native shortgrass prairies and their associated plant and animal life have become rare	

Region	Size (sq mi)	Topography*	Annual rainfall (in)	Predominant vegetation	Rare plants and habitat	Rare animals and habitat
Trans-Pecos	38,000	Diverse, from valley floors to hills to plateaus to mountains	<12	Gradient from dry to wetter with increasing elevation; desert shrubland and succulent shrubland, grassland, oak-juniper-pinyon woodlands; evergreen forests	*bunched cory cactus* Rocky slopes, ledges, and flats in the Chihuahuan Desert on limestone *Chisos hedgehog cactus* Open shrublands on gravelly, flat, alluvial fan deposits *Davis green pitaya* Rocky hillsides of novaculite (a particular kind of rock) outcrops with sparse vegetation *Nellie cory cactus* Dry, rocky limestone outcrops on slopes in mountains of Chihuahuan Desert *Sneed pincushion cactus* Dry, rocky limestone outcrops on slopes in mountains of Chihuahuan Desert *Hinckley's oak* Found along arid limestone slopes at mid-elevations in Chihuahuan Desert *Little Aguja pondweed* Known to occur only within quiet seepage pools in Little Aguja Creek in the Davis Mountains *Lloyd's mariposa cactus* In full sun on limestone outcrops or rocky, alkaline soils on slopes or mesas *Terlingua Creek cat's-eye* Barren, dry, gypseous clay or chalky shales on low, rounded hills and slopes with sparse vegetation	*Mexican long-nosed bat* High-desert regions of Big Bend National Park *Mexican spotted owl* Canyon woodlands in mountain ranges of West Texas *Desert Spring fishes* Comanche Springs pupfish Leon Springs pupfish Pecos gambusia Big Bend gambusia Spring-fed desert wetlands and streams *Texas horned lizard* *mountain short-horned lizard*

*Although most of Texas is located on flat plains or rolling plains, there are substantial mountains in the Trans-Pecos region of far West Texas. The highest point in the state is Guadalupe Peak at 8,749 feet above sea level. Sea level is the lowest elevation in Texas and can be found in all coastal counties. Elevation naturally rises from east to west and south to north.

The classic example of the Piney Woods ecoregion can be found almost anywhere in East Texas. Courtesy of Texas Parks and Wildlife Department

gomery, Liberty, Hardin, and Orange Counties in the south.

Topography

Elevation in this rolling terrain ranges from 200–500 feet above sea level and includes pine, oak, and other hardwood forests.

Subregions

Longleaf Pine Forest
Mixed Pine-Hardwood Forest

Climate

Average annual precipitation is 36–50 inches. Average temperatures range from 45°F in the winter to 83°F in the summer, and humidity levels are usually high.

Soils

Upland soils are typically acidic, sandy loams and sands covering deeper sandy loams to clay subsoils. Soils in the bottomlands are characteristically acidic to calcareous, alluvial loams and clays. Acidic loamy soils are commonly found in the floodplains of streams (Hatch et al. 1990).

Geology

Geological outcrops are rare in the Piney Woods due to the abundant vegetation and deep soils covering the rocks. More important, this region of Texas has been slowly sinking over the last 60 million years, with very little uplift. The region's geological history is characterized chiefly by continual sedimentation (Spearing 1996).

Vegetation

Mixed pine-hardwood forests occur in the upland areas. Loblolly (*Pinus taeda*), shortleaf (*P. echinata*), and longleaf (*P. palustris*) are the native pines. Slash pine (*P. elliottii*) is an introduced species (from the southeastern United States) that has done quite well. Hardwood forests are more common along the rivers and streams.

HARDWOOD SPECIES

American beech (*Fagus grandifolia*)
ashes (*Fraxinus* spp.)
bald cypress (*Taxodium distichum*)
blackgum (*Nyssa sylvatica*)
cottonwoods (*Populus* spp.)
elms (*Ulmus* spp.)
hickories (*Carya* spp.)
magnolias (*Magnolia* spp.)
maples (*Acer* spp.)
oaks (*Quercus* spp.)
sweetgum (*Liquidambar styraciflua*)
walnuts (*Juglans* spp.)
water tupelo (*Nyssa aquatica*)

SHRUBS AND VINES

American beautyberry (*Callicarpa americana*)
blackhaws (*Viburnum* spp.)
blueberries (*Vaccinium* spp.)
dewberries (*Rubus* spp.)
dogwoods (*Cornus* spp.)
greenbriars (*Smilax* spp.)
hawthorns (*Crataegus* spp.)
poison ivy (*Rhus toxicodendron*)
redbud (*Cercis canadensis*)
southern wax-myrtle (*Myrica cerifera*)
trumpet honeysuckle (*Lonicera sempervirens*)
wild grapes (*Vitis* spp.)

Majestic pines grace the sky south of Dibol in Angelina County, Piney Woods ecoregion. Courtesy of Texas Parks and Wildlife Department

HERBACEOUS WILDFLOWERS

clovers (*Trifolium* spp.)
goldenrods (*Solidago* spp.)
milkpeas (*Galactica* spp.)
sennas (*Cassia* spp.)
several rare orchids (family Orchidaceae)
Texas trailing phlox (*Phlox nivalis* spp. *texensis*)*
tickclovers (*Desmodium* spp.)
vetches (*Vicia* spp.)
white bladderpod (*Lesquerella pallida*)*
wild indigos (*Baptista* spp.)

**Denotes an endangered species*

Ecosystem Change

In 1767, Nicolás de Lafora (a Spanish explorer) was crossing through present Houston County in the Piney Woods. He described the region as "hills covered with thick woods of Live Oak [*Quercus virginiana*], Common Oak [*Quercus* spp.], Walnut trees [*Juglans* spp.], and Pines [*Pinus* spp.], interlaced with many grape vines [*Vitis* spp.]." Forests still dominate the ecoregion, but timber production and human encroachment have modified and fragmented many of these once-pristine areas.

Wildlife: Birds

Only 2% of the red-cockaded woodpecker's former habitat remains. Populations are being helped by artificial cavity nests inserted in pines. The bald eagle is no longer endangered, and its status was reduced to threatened in 1995. It breeds in the eastern third of Texas, including the Piney Woods. The three most common warblers are listed here, but other warblers are found in the region.

- bald eagle (*Haliaeetus leucocephalus*)
- eastern wood pewee (*Contopus virens*)
- hooded warbler (*Wilsonia citrina*)
- indigo bunting (*Passerina cyanea*)
- magnolia warbler (*Dendrocia magnolia*)
- pileated woodpecker (*Dryocopus pileatus*)
- prairie warbler (*Dendrocia discolor*)
- red-cockaded woodpecker (*Picoides borealis*)
- wood duck (*Aix sponsa*)
- wood thrush (*Hylocichla mustelina*)

Wildlife: Mammals
Mammal species characteristic of the deciduous forests of the Piney Woods are typically those that reach the western limits of their US distribution in Texas (Davis and Schmidly 1997).

- Baird's pocket gopher (*Geomys breviceps*)
- cotton mouse (*Peromyscus gossypinus*)
- eastern flying squirrel (*Glaucomys volans*)
- eastern gray squirrel (*Sciurus carolinensis*)
- eastern harvest mouse (*Reithrodontomys humulis*)
- golden mouse (*Ochrotomys nuttalli*)
- northern river otter (*Lutra canadensis*)
- Rafinesque's big-eared bat (*Plecotus rafinesquii*)
- Seminole bat (*Lasiurus seminolus*)
- southeastern myotis (*Myotis austroriparius*)
- southern short-tailed shrew (*Blarina carolinensis*)
- swamp rabbit (*Sylvilagus aquaticus*)

Wildlife: Reptiles and Amphibians

- alligator snapping turtle (*Macroclemys temmincki*)
- broad-banded water snake (*Nerodia fasciata confluens*)
- dusky salamander (*Desmognathus fuscus*)
- eastern box turtle (*Terrapene carolina*)
- mud snake (*Farancia abacura*)
- pygmy rattlesnake (*Sistrurus miliarius*)
- southern leopard frog (*Rana sphenocephala*)
- spring peeper (*Hyla crucifer*)

Human Use and Development
Timber production is the ecoregion's leading land-use industry. The major commercial timber species are loblolly, shortleaf, longleaf, and slash pines. Cattle are the main livestock raised, but farms and ranches are typically smaller than the state average. Lakes and reservoirs provide ample outdoor recreation activities. Caddo Lake State Park houses the state's only naturally occurring lake, which covers 25,400 acres. Some of the lake has been dammed in a small section, so it is no longer completely natural. There are many beautiful cypress trees in the area, and major recreational activities include fishing, hiking, swimming, camping, and birding.

Oak Woods and Prairies

Overview
This area is divided into two parts, with one section to the east of the Blackland Prairie and the other to the west. Portions of the area to the west were called the Cross Timbers by early European settlers because the area once had post oak forests crossing strips of prairie grassland. The region is approximately 19,000 square miles of gently rolling to hilly landscape. The bottomland soils range from sandy loam to clay, while the prairie soils are sandy loam or sands. Flora includes post oaks, oak-hickory forest, plateau live oak, and tallgrass and midgrass prairies. Most of the flora and fauna have ranges that extend northward into the Great Plains or eastward into the forests. This area attracted early European settlers because the open grasslands and surrounding forest areas were ideal for settlement. Native Americans also were attracted by this unique combination of prairie and forestland.

Today, most of those grasslands have

been altered. Large concentrations of migrating geese and ducks winter in this region and can be observed in places like Hagerman National Wildlife Refuge on Lake Texoma. Cattle ranching is a major agricultural industry in parts of the region. The endangered Houston toad occurs in the eastern Post Oak Savannah ecoregion.

Natural Sites in the Oak Woods and Prairies

- Big Lake Bottom Wildlife Management Area
- Caddoan National Grasslands
- Cooper Lake State Park and Wildlife Management Area
- Gus Engling Wildlife Management Area
- Hagerman National Wildlife Refuge
- Purtis Creek State Park

Location

The Oak Woods and Prairies ecoregion covers approximately 12.5 million acres of land extending in irregular bands, running roughly north to south, through north-central and eastern Texas. This ecoregion is closely associated with the Blackland Prairie ecoregion, and the two ecoregions are often jointly referred to as the Greater Prairies and Lakes region.

Topography

Elevation ranges from 300 to 800 feet above sea level with gently rolling to hilly terrain (TPWD 2000a). This ecoregion is a transition zone between the Rolling and High Plains ecoregions and the Piney Woods of East Texas.

Subregions

- Western Cross Timbers
- Oak Woodlands (Post Oak Savannah)
- Eastern Cross Timbers

Climate

Average annual precipitation is 28–40 inches, with peaks around May or June. Average temperatures are fairly warm, ranging from 50°F in the winter to 88°F in the summer.

An example of the Oak Woods and Prairies ecoregion can be found just outside Tyler off Highway 7. Courtesy of Texas Parks and Wildlife Department

Tyler State Park offers many recreational activities for visitors to the Oak Woods and Prairies ecoregion. Courtesy of Texas Parks and Wildlife Department

Geology

Dinosaur Valley State Park is an area of very interesting geology found in the Oak Woods and Prairies ecoregion. Located just northwest of Glen Rose in Somervell County, it is a 1,524-acre scenic park along the Paluxy River. The park contains some of the best-preserved dinosaur tracks in the world in the riverbed of the Paluxy. Within the park, eastward-dipping limestones, sandstones, and mudstones can be seen. These were deposited approximately 113 million years ago along the shorelines of an ancient sea (TPWD 2001). For approximately the last million years, these layered formations have been dissected and carved by the Paluxy River, which in several places has cut them down to resistant beds, and sizable exposures of rock in the river bottom are now visible.

Soils

The upland soils are gray and slightly acidic sandy loams over firmer, clay subsoils. There are claypans found at varying depths, which restrict moisture percolation. The bottomland soils are reddish-brown to dark gray, slightly acidic to calcareous, alluvial loams and clays (Hatch et al. 1990).

Vegetation

The ecoregion can be characteristically described as an oak savanna, in which patches of oak woodland are interspersed within grasslands.

GRASSES

- beaked panicum (*Panicum anceps*)
- brownseed paspalum (*Paspalum plicatulum*)
- little bluestem (*Schizachyrium scoparium*)
- narrow leaf woodoats (*Chasmanthium sessiliflorum*)
- purpletop (*Tridens flavus*)
- silver bluestem (*Bothriochloa saccharoides*)
- switchgrass (*Panicum virgatum*)
- Texas wintergrass (*Stipa leucotricha*)
- yellow indiangrass (*Sorghastrum nutans*)

TREES AND SHRUBS

- blackjack oak (*Quercus marilandica*)
- elms (*Ulmus* spp.)
- hackberries (*Celtis* spp.)
- hickories (*Carya* spp.)
- junipers (*Juniperus* spp.)
- post oak (*Quercus stellata*)
- water oak (*Quercus nigra*)

FORBS

- crotons (*Croton* spp.)
- indigobush (*Amorpha fruticosa* var. *angustifolia*)
- large-fruited sand verbena (*Abronia macrocarpa*)*
- lespedezas (*Lespedeza* spp.)
- Navasota ladies'-tresses (*Spiranthes parksii*)*
- prairie clovers (*Petalostemon* spp.)
- sennas (*Senna* spp.)
- sneezeweeds (*Helenium* spp.)
- wild indigo (*Baptisia tinctoria*)

**Denotes an endangered species*

Ecosystem Change

Early settlers referred to this ecoregion as the Cross Timbers because they found belts of oak forest transecting strips of prairie grasslands. One Spanish explorer gave an account of this characteristic of the ecoregion in 1691 when he was crossing present-day Bastrop and Fayette Counties; he referred to this area as "pasture with timber on either side" (Weniger 1984, 12). The native prairies and oak savannas of the ecoregion were far-reaching, fertile areas of tall, productive grasses interspersed with various hardwoods. However, when the settlers arrived, much of this changed.

The once fairly open areas of prairies have since become "thicketized" due to suppression of natural wildfires, which once played an integral part in maintaining the unique ecological balance of the Oak Woods and Prairies ecoregion. The balance of the ecoregion has also been severely altered by the introduction of large herds of grazing cattle and horses and by the introduction of nonnative grass and forb species planted to provide forage for these voracious livestock grazers. Over the past centuries, humans have forever altered the once-pristine prairies of this ecoregion. Today, only small, scattered patches of true prairie remain.

Wildlife: Birds

BIRDS OF PREY AND SCAVENGER SPECIES

American kestrel (*Falco sparverius*)
black vulture (*Coragyps atratus*)
northern harrier (*Circus cyaneus*)
red-shouldered hawk (*Buteo lineatus*)
red-tailed hawk (*Buteo jamaicensis*)
turkey vulture (*Cathartes aura*)

PASSERINES AND WOODPECKERS

American robin (*Turdus migratorius*), primarily a winter resident
blue jay (*Cyanocitta cristata*)
brown thrasher (*Toxostoma rufum*)
brown-headed cowbird (*Molothrus ater*)
Carolina wren (*Thryothorus ludovicianus*)
downy woodpecker (*Picoides pubescens*)
eastern meadowlark (*Sturnella magna*)
European starling (*Sturnus vulgaris*)
great-tailed and common grackles (*Quiscalus* spp.)
loggerhead shrike (*Lanius ludovicianus*)
northern cardinal (*Cardinalis cardinalis*)
northern flicker (*Colaptes auratus*)
painted bunting (*Passerina ciris*), a beautiful songbird that is primarily a spring/summer resident
scissor-tailed flycatcher (*Tyrannus forficatus*), a spring/summer resident, a favorite of local birders
yellow-bellied sapsucker (*Sphyrapicus varius*)
yellow-billed cuckoo (*Coccyzus americanus*)
yellow-rumped warbler (*Dendrocia coronata*), primarily a winter resident

Wildlife: Mammals

LARGE MAMMALS

common gray fox (*Urocyon cinereoargenteus*)
coyote (*Canis latrans*)
eastern cottontail (*Sylvilagus floridanus*)
feral hog (*Sus scrofa*)
nine-banded armadillo (*Dasypus novemcinctus*)
nutria (*Myocastor coypus*), an introduced and potentially detrimental species (especially to populations of the native muskrat)
raccoon (*Procyon lotor*)
striped skunk (*Mephitis mephitis*)
Virginia opossum (*Didelphis virginiana*)
white-tailed deer (*Odocoileus virginianus*)

SMALL MAMMALS

eastern woodrat (*Neotoma floridana*)
fox squirrel (*Sciurus niger*)
fulvous harvest mouse (*Reithrodontomys fulvescens*)
gray squirrel (*Sciurus carolinensis*), less abundant than the fox squirrel
hispid cotton rat (*Sigmodon hispidus*)
northern pygmy mouse (*Baiomys talori*)
plains pocket gopher (*Geomys bursarius*)
white-footed mouse (*Peromyscus leucopus*)

Wildlife: Amphibians and Reptiles

copperhead (*Agkistrodon contortrix*)**
eastern box turtle (*Terrapene carolina*)

eastern coral snake (*Micrurus fulvius*)**
eastern hog-nosed snake (*Heterodon platirhinos*)
green treefrog (*Hyla cinerea*)
ground skink (*Scincella lateralis*)
Gulf Coast toad (*Bufo valliceps*)
Houston toad (*Bufo houstonensis*), endangered
red-eared slider (*Trachemys scripta*)
southern leopard frog (*Rana sphenocephala*)
water moccasin (*Agkistrodon piscivorus*)**
water snakes (*Nerodia* spp.)
western diamond-backed rattlesnake (*Crotalus atrox*)**
western hog-nosed snake (*Heterodon nasicus*)

***Denotes a poisonous species*

Human Use and Development

The Oak Woods and Prairies ecoregion is an area well suited for raising crops such as grains, vegetables, cotton, and fruit trees. It is also a prime area for ranching cattle, which is the principal agricultural industry (TPWD 2000a). This region was formerly used for extensive croplands through the 1940s, but since that time, much of the land has been converted back to native grasslands or pastures (Hatch et al. 1990). Native grasses and introduced species such as bermudagrass (*Cynodon dactylon*), bahiagrass (*Paspalum notatum*), weeping lovegrass (*Eragrostis curvula*), and clovers (*Fabaceae*) are used for grazing on these abundant pastures. The cow-calf-yearling operation is the major bovine enterprise, and these cattle can be found in many small herds on small landholdings (Hatch et al. 1990). Hunting is another common land-use enterprise in the ecoregion, with deer, quail, and squirrel being the primary game species (Hatch et al. 1990).

Blackland Prairie

Overview

The Blackland Prairie region is gently rolling and level land covering 23,500 square miles. It is named for the rich, deep, fertile black

Reintroduced Blackland Prairie on a farm near Temple. Courtesy of Texas Parks and Wildlife Department

soils that once supported the original tallgrass prairie communities and, due to land-use change, today support crop production and cattle ranching. Prior to the seventeenth century, this area in east-central Texas had 12 million acres of tallgrass prairie; now there are less than 5,000 acres. It is the grassland communities themselves—the big bluestem, little bluestem, switchgrass, and sideoats grama and associated herbaceous flora—that make these prairies unique. Agriculture and development have threatened the remaining grassland communities with extirpation from Texas. In portions of the region, farmland is threatened with extinction by urban sprawl and development.

Location
The Blackland Prairie ecoregion covers 11.5 million acres of land extending roughly northeast to south in uneven bands that run through north-central and Central Texas. This ecoregion is closely associated with the Oak Woods and Prairies ecoregion. The two ecoregions together are frequently referred to as the Greater Prairies and Lakes region. The Blackland Prairie represents the southernmost extension of the true prairies that extend from Canada to Texas.

Topography
The Blackland Prairie is gently rolling to nearly level, and elevation ranges from 300 to 800 feet. The lands are well dissected with river and stream systems that have rapid surface drainage.

Subregions
Blackland Prairies
Grand Prairie

Climate
Average annual precipitation is 28–40 inches, increasing from west to east. In the northern end of the region, May is the peak rainfall month, but the south-central area has a rather uniform distribution throughout the year. Average temperatures range from 47°F in the winter to 88°F in the summer.

Natural Sites of the Blackland Prairie
Aquilla Wildlife Management Area
Cedar Hill State Park
Dinosaur Valley State Park
Granger Wildlife Management Area
Mother Neff State Park

Geology
The Blackland Prairie ecoregion is defined by its deep, fertile black soils, which characterize the entire area. The alkaline parent materials of these soils were deposited roughly 100 million years ago when a shallow Cretaceous sea covered north-central Texas (Tuttle 2000). Deep, limy clay soils have formed over many years and have supported a rich growth of vegetation. Decaying organic matter deposited over thousands of years has given the ecoregion's soils their distinctive black color (Tuttle 2000).

Soils
Fairly homogeneous dark-colored, alkaline clays, often referred to as "black gumbo," mixed with some gray acidic sandy loams, characterizes the entire ecoregion. Soils in the upland regions are darker, calcareous clayey soils that change with increasing

Reintroduced Blackland Prairie on a farm near Temple. Courtesy of Texas Parks and Wildlife Department

depth into light marls and chalks (Hatch et al. 1990). In the bottomlands, soils are typically reddish-brown to dark gray in color, and they are slightly acidic to calcareous, alluvial loams and clays (Hatch et al. 1990).These Blackland soils are known for their high productivity and fertility, but continual cropping and erosion have caused many of the soils to lose productivity.

Vegetation

GRASSES

- big bluestem (*Andropogon gerardii*)
- buffalograss (*Buchloe dactyloides*)
- hairy grama (*Bouteloua hirsuta*)
- little bluestem (*Schizachyrium scoparium*)
- sideoats grama (*Bouteloua curtipendula*)
- silveus dropseed (*Sporobolus silveanus*)
- switchgrass (*Panicum virgatum*)
- tall dropseed (*Sporobolus asper* var. *asper*)
- Texas wintergrass (*Stipa leucotricha*)
- yellow indiangrass (*Sorghastrum nutans*)

TREES AND SHRUBS

- cottonwoods (*Populus* spp.)
- elms (*Ulmus* spp.)
- honey mesquite (*Prosopis glandulosa*)
- huisache (*Acacia farnesiana*)
- oaks (*Quercus* spp.)
- pecans (*Carya* spp.)

FORBS

- Asters (*Aster* spp.)
- late coneflower (*Rudbeckia serotina*)
- prairie bluet (*Hedyotis nigricans* var. *nigricans*)
- prairie clovers (*Dalea* spp.)
- snoutbeans (*Rhynchosia* spp.)
- vetches (*Vicia* spp.)

Ecosystem Change

The soils of the Blackland Prairie once supported a tallgrass prairie dominated by bluestems, sideoats grama, and switchgrass. However, much of this once-pristine prairie is gone, replaced by farmlands, pastures, and cities. Trees such as mesquite, blackjack oak, and post oak have invaded some of the more natural areas quite severely. The original prairie was both spectacular and expansive, as described by a Spanish explorer traveling through northeastern Travis County and southern Williamson County in 1721: "We set out through a country of beautiful plains with some very low hills at long intervals, all covered with abundant pasturage and a variety of flowers. . . . We proceeded toward the northeast. . . . The whole country is of low hills, without thickets or trees" (Weniger 1984, 28).

Wildlife: Birds

BIRDS OF PREY AND SCAVENGERS

- barn owl (*Tyto alba*)
- barred owl (*Strix varia*)
- black vulture (*Corgyps atratus*)
- Cooper's hawk (*Accipiter cooperii*)
- eastern screech-owl (*Megascops asio*)
- great horned owl (*Bubo virginianus*)
- red-shouldered hawk (*Buteo lineatus*)
- red-tailed hawk (*Buteo jamaicensis*)
- sharp-shinned hawk (*Accipiter striatus*)
- turkey vulture (*Cathartes aura*)

PASSERINES AND WOODPECKERS

- American robin (*Turdus migratorius*), primarily a winter resident
- blue jay (*Cyanocitta cristata*)
- brown thrasher (*Toxostoma rufum*)
- brown-headed cowbird (*Molothrus ater*)
- Carolina wren (*Thryothorus ludovicianus*)
- downy woodpecker (*Picoides pubescens*)
- eastern meadowlark (*Sturnella magna*)
- European starling (*Sturnus vulgaris*)
- great-tailed and common grackles (*Quiscalus* spp.)
- loggerhead shrike (*Lanius ludovicianus*)
- northern cardinal (*Cardinalis cardinalis*)
- northern flicker (*Colaptes auratus*)
- painted bunting (*Passerina ciris*), a beautiful songbird that is primarily a spring/summer resident
- scissor-tailed flycatcher (*Tyrannus forficatus*), a spring/summer resident, also a favorite of local birders

- yellow-bellied sapsucker (*Sphyrapicus varius*)
- yellow-billed cuckoo (*Coccyzus americanus*)
- yellow-rumped warbler (*Dendrocia coronata*), primarily a winter resident

Wildlife: Mammals

LARGE MAMMALS

- common gray fox (*Urocyon cinereoargenteus*)
- coyote (*Canis latrans*)
- eastern cottontail (*Sylvilagus floridanus*)
- feral hog (*Sus scrofa*)
- nine-banded armadillo (*Dasypus novemcinctus*)
- nutria (*Myocastor coypus*), an introduced and potentially detrimental species (especially to populations of the native muskrat)
- raccoon (*Procyon lotor*)
- striped skunk (*Mephitis mephitis*)
- Virginia opossum (*Didelphis virginiana*)
- white-tailed deer (*Odocoileus virginianus*)

SMALL MAMMALS

- American badger (*Taxidea taxus*)
- black-tailed prairie dog (*Cynomys ludovicianus*)
- eastern woodrat (*Neotoma floridana*)
- fox squirrel (*Sciurus niger*)
- fulvous harvest mouse (*Reithrodontomys fulvescens*)
- gray squirrel (*Sciurus carolinensis*), less abundant than the fox squirrel
- hispid cotton rat (*Sigmodon hispidus*)
- northern pygmy mouse (*Baiomys talori*)
- plains pocket gopher (*Geomys bursarius*)
- prairie vole (*Microtus ochrogaster*)
- Texas kangaroo rat (*Dipodymus elator*)
- Texas mouse (*Peromyscus attwateri*)
- white-footed mouse (*Peromyscus leucopus*)

Wildlife: Amphibians and Reptiles

- copperhead (*Agkistrodon contortrix*)**
- eastern box turtle (*Terrapene carolina*)
- eastern coral snake (*Micrurus fulvius*)**
- eastern hog-nosed snake (*Heterodon platirhinos*)
- green treefrog (*Hyla cinerea*)
- ground skink (*Scincella lateralis*)
- Gulf Coast toad (*Bufo valliceps*)
- red-eared slider (*Trachemys scripta*)
- southern leopard frog (*Rana sphenocephala*)
- water moccasin (*Agkistrodon piscivorus*)**
- water snakes (*Nerodia* spp.)
- western diamond-backed rattlesnake (*Crotalus atrox*)**
- western hog-nosed snake (*Heterodon nasicus*)

***Denotes a poisonous species*

Human Use and Development

The highly productive and fertile soils of the Blackland Prairie have actually played a role in the downfall of these prairie ecosystems. When settlers came to this area of Texas, they immediately began converting these native lands to farmlands because of the very suitable soils. Fortunately though, the European agricultural practice of preserving sections of land as hay meadows has helped protect sections of remnant Blackland Prairie. However, the more recent "urban explosions" around cities such as Dallas, San Antonio, and Waco have led to more prairie destruction. For this reason, less than 0.05% (5,000 acres) of virgin Blackland Prairie remains (Tuttle 2000). Today, crop production and cattle ranching are the two principal agricultural industries of the region.

Gulf Coast Prairies and Marshes

Overview

This nearly level plain area of 21,000 square miles borders the Gulf of Mexico from the Sabine River to Corpus Christi Bay. Prior to European settlement and twentieth-century development, this landscape included woodlands of sugarberry, pecan, elms, and live oaks and open prairies with native grasses. The soils of the area range from acidic sands to sandy loams, with clays

Natural Sites of the Gulf Coast Prairies and Marshes

- Aransas National Wildlife Refuge
- Attwater Prairie Chicken National Wildlife Refuge
- Brazoria National Wildlife Refuge
- Brazos Bend State Park
- Galveston Island State Park
- Goose Island State Park
- Laguna Atascosa National Wildlife Refuge
- Mad Island Wildlife Management Area
- Mustang Island State Park
- Padre Island National Seashore
- Texas City Preserve (Texas Nature Conservancy)
- Varner-Hogg State Park

occurring in the river bottoms. The flora includes tallgrass and midgrass prairies, cordgrass marshes, mesquite, and acacia. The region includes the barrier islands that protect the coastline from high winds and high ocean waves. The marshes along the bays and estuaries are important habitat for estuarine and marine species, including finfish and shellfish. Rare and near-extinct plants and animals include the slender rush-pea (South Texas ambrosia), prairie dawn, Attwater's prairie chicken, and the ocelot.

Location

The Gulf Coast Prairies and Marshes ecoregion occupies roughly 9.5 million acres of land along the eastern coast of Texas.

Topography

This region comprises nearly level plains, dissected by rivers and streams flowing into the Gulf of Mexico, and narrow bands of marsh bordering the coast. Elevations range from 250 feet in the Upland Prairies and Woods to sea level in the Dunes and Barrier Islands. Common vegetational areas of this ecoregion include barrier islands along the Gulf, salt grass marshes surrounding the bays and estuaries, tallgrass prairies, oak parklands and mottes, and a few tall woodlands around the river bottomlands.

The Padre Island National Seashore is a great example of the Gulf Coast Prairies and Marshes ecoregion. Courtesy of Texas Parks and Wildlife Department

An array of salt marsh grasses can be found along Padre Island National Seashore, Gulf Coast Prairies and Marshes ecoregion. Courtesy of Texas Parks and Wildlife Department

Subregions

Dunes and Barrier Islands Estuarine Zone
Upland Prairies and Woods

Climate

The Gulf Coast Prairies and Marshes is an area of high humidity and warm temperatures. Average annual rainfall varies from over 50 inches in the eastern portions of the region to less than 30 inches in the west. Average annual temperatures vary from 52°F in the winter to 85°F in the summer.

Geology

The Gulf Coast Prairies and Marshes region is a nearly level, slowly drained plain less than 150 feet in elevation, dissected by streams and rivers flowing into the Gulf of Mexico. The character of the coastline is shaped by the long and continuous confrontation with the sea, wind, and rain. Storms shape this ecoregion as a sculptor works clay, creating a tapestry of shallow bays, estuaries, salt marshes, dunes, and tidal flats. Soils of the marshy areas include acid sands, sandy loams, and clay. Soils of the Gulf Prairies contain more clay than the marsh areas and are very rich in nutrients.

Soils

The predominant soils in this ecoregion are acidic sands, sandy loams, and clays. These types of soils were formed through geological processes during the Quaternary period. They occur in bands of increasing age inland from the coastline. In general, the soils have slowly permeable profiles, and they show only slight textural variability with increasing depth. The soils of the more inland prairies and woodlands are neutral to slightly acidic dark clays and clay loams.

The clays were deposited as rivers meandered across the plain toward the Gulf in past years. Light neutral sands and darker sandy loams and clays characterize the coastal marsh soils. The coastal soils were deposited during the Holocene epoch and are continually modified by the Gulf of Mexico's waters. In the river bottomlands and deltaic plains, the soils are deep reddish-brown to gray and characterized by alluvial clays and loams. These soils are also primarily Holocene deposits.

Vegetation

Few areas of the Gulf Coast Prairies and Marshes remain in the pristine state of centuries ago. The vegetation composition has changed through the years, but the principal "climax" plants remain. Today, these native plants are joined by several invader and increaser species.

PLANTS OF THE UPLAND PRAIRIES AND WOODS SUBREGION

- big bluestem (*Andropogon gerardii*)
- brownseed paspalum (*Paspalum plicatulum*)
- little bluestem (*Schizachyrium scoparium*)
- live oak (*Quercus virginiana*)
- prairie dawn (*Hymenoxys texana*)
- slender rush-pea (South Texas ambrosia) (*Hoffmannseggia tenella*)
- sweetgum (*Liquidambar styraciflua*)
- water oak (*Quercus nigra*)
- yaupon (*Ilex vomitoria*)
- yellow indiangrass (*Sorghastrum nutans*)

INVADER AND INCREASER SPECIES

- acacias (*Acacia* spp.)
- mesquite (*Prosopis glandulosa*)
- threeawns (*Aristida* spp.)
- tumblegrass (*Schedonnardus paniculatus*)
- western ragweed (*Ambrosia psilostachya*)

WILDFLOWERS

- evening primroses (*Oenothera* spp.)
- Indian paintbrush (*Castilleja indivisa*)
- phlox (*Phlox* spp.)
- poppy mallows (*Callirhoe* spp.)

PLANTS OF THE DUNES AND BARRIER ISLANDS AND THE ESTUARINE ZONE

- bulrushes (*Scirpus* spp.)
- common reed (*Phragmites australis*)
- maidencane (*Panicum hemitomon*)
- marshmillet (*Zizaniopsis miliacea*)
- rushes (*Juncus* spp.)
- sedges (*Carex* spp. and *Cyperus* spp.)

Ecosystem Change

The Gulf Coast Prairies and Marshes have undergone dynamic ecosystem changes in the past centuries. In the Upland Prairies and Woodlands, the original vegetation types were tallgrass prairies and post oak savannas, but today these areas have become thicketized by the invasion of trees and shrubs such as mesquite (*Prosopis glandulosa*), acacia (*Acacia* spp.), and various species of oak (*Quercus* spp.). This increasing density of woody plants is primarily due to the suppression of natural wildfires. These natural wildfires are of key importance for maintaining the ecological balance of prairies and savannas by controlling the rate of woody growth. Much ecosystem change has also been caused by the introduction of nonnative grazing animals such as cattle and horses. Many of the marshes and coastal areas of the region have been converted to livestock grazing lands and farms in the last two centuries. However, in recent years, there has been increasing emphasis on preserving the remaining coastal and marsh ecosystems in their natural state. Today, many of the coast's marshes and beaches are protected as national preserves, refuges, and parks.

Wildlife

The Gulf Coast Prairies and Marshes ecoregion is home to a remarkable variety of wildlife species. This high species diversity is due to the Gulf Coast's vast array of habitats, temperate climate, and relative abundance of rainfall.

BIRDS

The habitats of this region provide prime nesting and feeding areas for a number of wild birds, including several endangered species. One such species, Attwater's prairie chicken (*Tympanuchus cupido attwateri*), has depended on the tallgrass prairies of this region as its sole habitat for centuries. Unfortunately, much of this once-pristine habitat has been converted to farmlands and urban areas. Thus, the Attwater's prairie chicken's numbers continue toward extinction.

Another of the Gulf Coast's most notable birds is the eastern brown pelican (*Pelecanus occidentalis*). This species is a great success story for conservation. The brown pelican's populations were near extinction by the early 1970s due to egg-shell thinning caused by the infamous DDT. Since the EPA banned DDT and other related organochlorine pesticides in 1972, the brown pelican's populations have skyrocketed, and today this unmistakable coastal resident can commonly be seen flying over the Gulf's waters.

The whooping crane (*Grus americana*) is another beautiful bird species that lives in the Gulf Coast Prairies and Marshes. In fact, there is only one natural population of migrating whooping cranes left in the wild, and these birds winter at Aransas National Wildlife Refuge within the Gulf Coast Prairies and Marshes ecoregion.

The piping plover (*Charadrius melodus*) winters along the Gulf Coast in tidal mudflats, sandflats, or algal flats.

Other noteworthy birds in the Gulf Coast Prairies and Marshes include

black skimmer (*Rynchops niger*)
laughing gull (*Larus atricilla*)
olivaceous cormorant (*Phalacrocorax olivaceous*)
piping plover (*Charadrius melodus*)
roseate spoonbill (*Ajaja ajaja*)

MAMMALS

One former resident of the Gulf Coast Prairies and Marshes was the red wolf (*Canis rufus*). This wolf was once fairly common in the southeastern United States, but by 1970 only a few wolves remained. These last few red wolves lived in the Gulf Prairies and Marshes in Texas and in a small area in southwestern Louisiana. Unfortunately, by 1980 this wolf was determined to be extinct in the wild due to habitat loss, hunting, and hybridization with the increasing coyote populations. Today, red wolves exist only through captive-breeding programs and in managed wildlife refuges. Noted mammals found in the Gulf Coast Prairies and Marshes include

Gulf Coast kangaroo rat (*Dipodomys compactus*)
marsh rice rat (*Oryzomys palustris*)
river otter (*Lutra canadensis*)

REPTILES AND AMPHIBIANS

The moist climate of the Gulf Coast Prairies and Marshes provides well-suited habitats for many reptiles and amphibians. The endangered Houston toad (*Bufo houstonensis*) is one of the amphibians found within the ecoregion. This toad has become increasingly rare due to habitat loss caused by rapid urbanization, and as a result, it has been protected by the Endangered Species Act since 1970. Other reptiles and amphibians native to the Gulf Coast Prairies and Marshes include

American alligator (*Alligator mississippiensis*)
Atlantic Ridley sea turtle (*Lepidochelys kempi*)
diamond back terrapin (*Malaclemys terrapin*)
Gulf Coast toad (*Bufo valliceps*)
loggerhead sea turtle (*Caretta caretta*)

Human Uses and Development

The lands of the Gulf Coast Prairies and Marshes provide a wide array of human uses. These include cattle ranching and farming for crops such as rice, sorghum, and corn. Much of the land is used for recreational purposes, including hunting, fishing, camping, and beachgoing. In addition, the Gulf Coast Prairies and Marshes region has been the site of the greatest industrial development since World War II and contains one of the largest urban areas in the United States—Houston. These increasing urban and industrial developments in the Gulf Coast Prairies and Marshes have caused drastic changes in the land, and today the individuals who call the Gulf Coast home are facing the task of balancing their uses of the land with environmental responsibility.

Natural Site of the Coastal Sand Plains
King Ranch (guided tours)

Coastal Sand Plains

Overview

This region occupies approximately 4,000 square miles. The vegetation of this area can be described as grasslands with coastal oak mottes, mesquite granjeno, and salt marshes. It is home to the King Ranch and other large cattle ranches. In the nineteenth century, wild horses roamed the area, and consequently the area has been known as the Wild Horse Prairie.

Location

The Coastal Sand Plains ecoregion is a fairly level region covering approximately 2.5 million acres of the southern coast of Texas. This region is bordered by the South Texas Brush Country and the Gulf Coastal Prairies and Marshes.

Topography

The elevations rise to less than 150 feet above sea level. The grasslands are being depleted by overgrazing and invasion of hardwoods. The King Ranch is located inside this ecoregion along with other large cattle ranches. The Coastal Sand Plains are also the home to the only coastal, hypersaline lagoon on the North American continent, Laguna Madre. It is one of three in the world. Most of the shrimp caught in the Gulf of Mexico breed and reside here (Texas Center for Policy Studies 2000).

Climate

Average annual precipitation is 24–28 inches (Campbell and Smith 1996). Average annual

Coastal Sand Plains ecoregion can be found along the Padre Island National Seashore. Courtesy of Texas Parks and Wildlife Department

temperature ranges from 70°F in the winter to 85°F during the summer.

Geology

The Coastal Sand Plains region is a remnant of the Holocene epoch, during which time a massive quantity of sand was transported from the coast to more than 50 miles inland. It is part of a belt of Late Cretaceous to Holocene deposits, extending from as far as New Jersey to Texas. These sedimentary rocks, deposited mostly in a marine environment, were later uplifted and now tilt seaward; part of them form the broad, submerged Atlantic Continental Shelf.

Soils

The Coastal Sand Plains soils are mostly windblown sands and dunes. Because it is part of the South Texas Plains and the Gulf Coastal Prairies, it has close to the same soil composition as these areas. Gray, clayey, saline, and sodic soils are found mixed in with the sands (Hatch et al. 1990). Soil color is typically brown to gray.

Vegetation

The region is primarily grassland with extensive mottes and salt marshes with small scattered areas of brush. The grassland areas have been decreased due to the extension of the oak scrub. Mesquite savanna and salt marshes are also present along with live oak woodlands. The lists of characteristic vegetation are from Hatch et al. (1990).

GRASSES

- big sandbur (*Cenchrus myosuroides*)
- bristlegrasses (*Setaria* spp.)
- paspalums (*Paspalum* spp.)
- seacoast bluestem (*Schizachyrium scoparium* var. *littoralis*)
- silver bluestem (*Bothriochloa laguroides*)
- tanglehead (*Heteropogon contortus*)
- windmillgrasses (*Chloris* spp.)

FORBS

- bush sunflowers (*Simsia* spp.)
- lazy daisies (*Aphanostephyus* spp.)
- orange zexmenia (*Zexmenia hispida*)
- prickly pear (*Opuntia humifusa*)
- tallowweeds (*Plantago* spp.)
- Texas croton (*Croton texensis*)
- velvet bundleflower (*Desmanthus velutinus*)
- western ragweed (*Ambrosia psilostachya*)

Ecosystem Change

Ecosystem change for the Coastal Sand Plains region is very similar to that of the South Texas Brush Country. The two regions combined have a history of the oldest land abuse in the state after three centuries of continuous grazing by livestock, suppression of prairie fires, and droughts. This area is an important cattle-producing area of Texas and supports several of the largest cattle ranches in the world (Telfair 1999).

Wildlife: Birds

About 80% of the 332 species of the long-distance North American migrant bird species travel through the Coastal Bend. The following common birds can be seen in the Coastal Sand Plains ecoregion, depending on season and location:

- altamira oriole (*Icterus gularis*)
- aplomado falcon (*Falco femoralis*)
- bobwhite quail (*Colinus virginianus*)
- Botteri's sparrow (*Aimophila botterii*)
- Bullock's oriole (*Icterus bullockii*)
- great kiskadee (*Pitangus sulphuratus*)
- green jay (*Cyanocorax yncas*)
- groove-billed ani (*Crotophaga sulcirostris*)
- olive sparrow (*Arremonops rufivirgatus*)
- painted bunting (*Passerina ciris*)
- peregrine falcon (*Falco peregrinus*)
- Rio Grande turkey (*Meleagris gallopavo*)
- vermilion flycatcher (*Pyrocephalus rubinus*)
- western kingbird (*Tyrannus verticalis*)
- white-tailed hawk (*Buteo albicaudatus*)

Coastal Sand Plains ecoregion can be found in the Padre Island National Seashore. Courtesy of Texas Parks and Wildlife Department

white-tipped dove (*Leptotila verreauxi*)
white-wing dove (*Zenaida asiatica*)

Wildlife: Mammals

Common mammals in the Coastal Sand Plains include the following species (Davis and Schmidly 1997):

- Attwater's pocket gopher (*Geomys attwateri*)
- common gray fox (*Urocyon cinereoargenteus*)
- deer mouse (*Peromyscus maniculatus*)
- eastern cottontail (*Sylvilagus floridanus*)
- eastern hog-nosed skunk (*Conepatus leuconotus*)
- eastern mole (*Scalopus aquaticus*)
- eastern spotted skunk (*Spilogale putorius*)
- eastern woodrat (*Neotoma floridana*)
- feral pig (*Sus scrofa*)
- fulvous harvest mouse (*Reithrodontomys fulvescens*)
- Gulf Coast kangaroo (*Dipodomys compactus*)
- hispid pocket mouse (*Chaetodipus hispidus*)
- Jones' pocket gopher (*Geomys knoxjonesi*)
- mountain lion (*Felis concolor*)
- nine-banded armadillo (*Dasypus novemcinctus*)
- northeastern grasshopper mouse (*Onychomys leucogaster*)
- ocelot (*Felis pardalis*)
- plains pocket gopher (*Geomys bursarius*)
- red wolf (*Canis rufus*)
- ringtail (*Bassariscus astutus*)
- Sirenia order (*Sirenia* spp.)
- southern plains woodrat (*Neotoma micropus*)
- spotted ground squirrel (*Spermophilus spilosoma*)
- Texas pocket gopher (*Geomys personatus*)
- Virginia possum (*Didelphis virginiana*)

Wildlife: Reptiles

- black spotted newt (*Notophthalmus meridionalis*)*
- black-striped snake (*Coniophanes imperialis*)*
- coral snake (*Micrurus fulvius*)
- horned lizard (*Phrynosoma hernandesi*)
- South Texas siren (*Siren* spp.)*
- Texas indigo snake (*Drymarchon corais erebennus*)*
- Texas scarlet snake (*Cemophora coccinea lineri*)*
- Texas tortoise (*Gopherus berlandieri*)*
- western coachwhip (*Masticophis flagellum testaceus*)

**Denotes an endangered species*

Human Use and Development

Human uses for the Coastal Sand Plains consist mostly of ranching. The region has been moderately to severely overgrazed by cattle. In the nineteenth century, large herds of feral horses roamed the land. The region has been called the "Wild Horse Prairie" for this reason. Though some crops are grown and harvested, the ranching industry outweighs farming heavily and crops are limited (Hatch et al. 1990).

South Texas Brush Country

Overview

This area encompasses approximately 24,000 square miles (USDA 2011). It was once covered with open grasslands and a scattering of trees. The original grasslands have become shrubland due to overgrazing. Today the area is characterized by thorny shrubs and patches of palms and subtropical woodlands. The area is home to many wild and rare species of plants and animals, including the ocelot and jaguarundi. The aplomado falcon was dependent upon these grasslands, and their loss has caused the falcon's demise. Urban development and agricultural use threaten the existing wildlife habitat. The natural resources of this region, the Gulf Coast Prairies, and the Coastal Sand Plains region contribute to the local economy of this area, where bird-watching and game hunting have become a source of revenue.

Location

The South Texas Brush Country is an area of level to rolling prairies in southern Texas. This ecoregion lies south of a line from Kinney County to Goliad County and is the western extension of the Gulf Coast Prairies and Marshes. It covers approximately 20 million acres of land.

Topography

Elevations range from 1,000 feet to sea level. The brush and mesquite prairies, dotted with deep lakes, characterize the entire ecoregion, which stretches down into the subtropical environment of the lower Rio Grande.

Subregions

Brush Country is characterized by mixtures of tall brush, including honey mesquite (*Prosopis glandulosa*) and spiny hackberry (*Celtis pallida*), on deep soils and shorter, dense brush species on the caliche soils.

Bordas Escarpment is an expansive mass of short brush, found on shallow caliche cuesta soils.

Subtropical Zone is a highly modified subregion on the southern tip of the South Texas Brush Country. Several

Natural Sites of the South Texas Brush Country

- Bentsen-Rio Grande Valley State Park
- Chaparral Wildlife Management Area
- Choke Canyon State Park
- Falcon State Recreation Area
- James E. Daughtrey Wildlife Management Area
- Las Palomas Wildlife Management Area
- Lower Rio Grande Valley Wildlife Refuge
- Park Falcon State Park
- Resaca de la Palma State Park
- Santa Ana National Wildlife Refuge

Chaparral Wildlife Management Area (WMA), located near Cotulla, South Texas Brush Country. Courtesy of Texas Parks and Wildlife Department

climatic factors, such as high rainfall, have allowed subtropical plant species to thrive here. Subtropical trees such as ebony (Ebenaceae) and anaqua (*Ehretia anacua*) dominate the remaining native plant communities (TPWD 1996).

Climate

Average annual precipitation varies from 20 to 32 inches . The average monthly rainfall is lowest in January and February and highest during May and June. Periodic droughts are common in this ecoregion. Average annual temperatures are relatively warm, ranging from 52°F in the winter to 87°F in the summer. Summer temperatures are high, with particularly high evaporation rates in the Laredo area.

Geology

The soil and rock formations in the region become progressively younger as you move from the western portions toward the coast. The ages of these formations range from upper Cretaceous deposits around Del Rio to Tertiary deposits around Laredo to recent Holocene deposits around Brownsville (Spearing 1996).

Soils

The predominant soils of the South Texas Brush Country are clays and clay loams. These soils vary from alkaline to slightly acidic (TPWD 1996). Dark, clayey soils, loams, and sandy loams are most common in the upland areas of the ecoregion. The bottomlands are composed of calcareous, silt loams and alluvial clays. The more coastal regions contain clay, saline, and sodic soils along with Galveston deep sands (Hatch et al. 1990).

Vegetation

The South Texas Brush Country is a truly unique ecoregion. It is known for its plains of thorny shrubs and trees and its scattered patches of palms and subtropical woodlands in the more southern Rio Grande Valley. The prairies were once much more extensive, dotted with "islands" of trees, as the early settlers described them (Hatch et al. 1990), and the valley woodlands were more widespread. Today, the characteristic vegetation consists of thorny brush such as honey mesquite, acacias (*Acacia* spp.), prickly pears (*Opuntia* spp.), and mimosa (*Albizia julibrissin*), mixed with areas of more open grassland. Shallow soils with efficient drainage generally support these plants. The list of grasses of clay soils and other characteristic plants are from Spearing (1996).

GRASSES OF THE SANDY LOAM SOILS

- big sandbur (*Cenchrus myosuroides*)
- chloris species (*Chloris* spp.)
- paspalum species (*Paspalum* spp.)
- plains bristlegrass (*Setaria leucopila*)
- seacoast bluestem (*Schizachyrium scoparium* var. *littoralis*)
- trichloris species (*Trichloris* spp.)

GRASSES OF THE CLAY SOILS

- Arizona cottontop (*Digitaria californica*)
- buffalograss (*Buchloe dactyloides*)
- common curly mesquite (*Hilaria belangeri*)
- pappophorum species (*Pappophorum* spp.)
- silver bluestem (*Bothriochloa saccharoides*)

OTHER PLANTS OF THE ECOREGION

- anaqua (*Ehretia anacua*)
- ashy dogweed (*Thymophylla tephroleuca*)*
- black lace cactus (*Echinocereus reichenbachii*)

The yellow flower of a prickly pear cactus (*Opuntia robusta*) is a welcome sign of spring at the Resaca De La Palma State Park in Brownsville, South Texas Brush Country. Courtesy of Texas Parks and Wildlife Department

desert yaupon (*Schaefferia cuneifolia*)
Johnston's frankenia (*Frankenia johnstonii*)*
southern live oak (*Quercus virginiana*)
star cactus (*Astrophytum myriostigma*)*
sugarberry (*Celtis laevigata*)
Texas ayenia (*Ayenia limitaris*)*
Texas wild olive (*Cordia boissieri*)
Walker's manioc (*Manihot walkerae*)*

**Denotes an endangered species*

Ecosystem Change

The original vegetation of the South Texas Brush Country was characterized by open grassland prairies along the coastal areas and increasingly brushy chaparral-prairies in the more upland areas. These chaparral-prairies were fairly extensive in the nineteenth century and earlier, as described by one settler who gave a portrait of them as they were in 1852: "Our town [Eagle Pass] lies on a sloping prairie, sprinkled with Mesquite trees like a vast and venerable orchard, and falling in successive platforms or terraces down to the river's edge" (TPWD 1996). Though this mesquite was part of the vegetation of the original prairies, it has become an ever-increasing presence in the South Texas ecoregion. It spreads as livestock graze on the tree's sweet pods and then disseminate the seeds. Now, because of this overgrazing, elimination of fires, and other factors, the plant communities have been altered to such a degree that ranches in the South Texas Brush Country face serious brush problems. In addition to mesquite, other woody plant species that have increased include acacia, whitebrush (*Aloysia gratissima*), Texas persimmon (*Diospyros texana*), lime pricklyash (*Zanthozylum fagara*), shrubby blue sage (*Salvia ballotiflora*), spiny hackberry (*Celtis pallida*), and lotebush (*Ziziphus obtusifolia*).

Wildlife

The South Texas Brush Country has a greater diversity of animal life than any other ecoregion in Texas (Hatch et al. 1990). This ecoregion is home to many near-tropical species whose ranges extend down into Mexico and Central America, numerous grassland species that range northward, and several desert species also commonly found in the Trans-Pecos.

BIRDS

The South Texas Brush Country is home to a remarkable variety of birds, a characteristic that attracts birders from all over the world year after year. Two major migration flyways, the Central and the Mississippi, converge here. The area is also the northernmost range for many rare tropical birds. Hence, South Texas offers some of the greatest birding opportunities in North America.

The plain chachalaca (*Ortalis vetula*) is a large, tropical bird that can be found in the extreme southern tip of Texas, especially in and around Bentsen-Rio Grande State Park. It is often heard more than seen because it lives rather elusively along the ground and in the trees, where it forages on insects, fruits, and leaves. The crested caracara (*Polyborus plancus*) is a raptor of open country, noted for its very distinct long, yellow legs. It feeds on both carrion and living prey. The green jay (*Cyanocorax morio*) is a South Texas Brush Country specialty, found nowhere else in the United States. This vivid, tenacious bird is numerous in woods and nearby towns along the lower Rio Grande.

Only six inches tall, the elf owl (*Micrathene whitneyi*), smallest of all North American owls, is found in desert lowlands where available nest cavities can be found in plants such as saguaro cactus (*Carnegiea gigantea*), oaks (*Quercus* spp.), and sycamore (*Platanus occidentalis*). The great kiskadee (*Pitangus sulphuratus*) can be confused with no other. Birders come from all over the world to see this dazzling, golden-bellied bird. The rose-throated becard (*Pachyramphus aglaiae*) is an extremely rare tropical bird that can be found in the lower Rio Grande Valley, also an esteemed prize for any birder's life list. The interior least tern (*Sterna antillarum*), a rare species, can be found on bare sand, shell, and gravel beaches, bars, and islands associated with reservoirs along the Rio Grande.

MAMMALS

The South Texas Brush Country supports 11 unique mammal species. Most of these are species characteristic of the tropical lowlands of northeastern Mexico, and they reach the northern distributional limits of their range in South Texas (TPWD 1996).

The collared peccary (*Tayassu tajacu*), also commonly referred to as the javelina, is the only member of the peccary family to occur in the United States. Although not unique to this area, it is a well-known resident of the South Texas Brush Country, feeding on the abundant mesquite and prickly pear fruits found here.

The ocelot (*Felis pardalis*) is a rare cat found in the remaining forests and brushy chaparrals of South Texas. Its range was once much larger, but due to habitat loss and overhunting, this feline is now a protected species. Sightings of this beautiful cat are most common around the Santa Ana National Wildlife Refuge, located along the Rio Grande in South Texas.

The even rarer jaguarundi (*Herpailurus yaguarondi*) is also a native to the South Texas Brush Country. It inhabits brushy thickets, forests, swampy areas, and habitats with cactus and mesquite. This small, elusive feline is now an endangered species due to habitat loss. A relative of the jaguarondi, the margay (*Felis wiedii*) once shared this habitat. It is known to have existed in Texas only on the basis of one specimen taken at Eagle Pass by Col. S. Cooper in the 1850s. Remains of this diminutive cat were found in Pleistocene deposits along the Sabine River in Orange County, indicating the margay ranged over a considerable portion of South Texas a few thousand years ago.

OTHER SOUTH TEXAS BRUSH COUNTRY MAMMALS

- Coues' rice rat (*Oryzomys couesi*)
- eastern hog-nosed skunk (*Conepatus leuconotus*)
- Gulf Coast kangaroo rat (*Dipodomys compactus*)
- Mexican long-tongued bat (*Choeronycteris mexicana*)
- Mexican spiny pocket mouse (*Liomys irroratus*)
- southern yellow bat (*Lasiurus ega*)
- Texas pocket gopher (*Geomys personatus*)
- white-nosed coati (*Nasua narica*)

REPTILES AND AMPHIBIANS

The South Texas Brush Country is truly a herpetologist's playground. An enormous assortment of reptiles and amphibians is found here.

The Texas tortoise (*Gopherus berlandieri*), a protected species, is exclusively found in South Texas. It feeds on prickly pear cactus, grasses, and even the droppings of other tortoises. Thousands of these tortoises have been collected for the pet trade in past years. This is one reason why the Texas tortoise is now protected (TPWD 1996).

The Texas indigo snake (*Drymarchon corais erebennus*), the largest snake in North America, is also a protected species. It owes its continual decline to habitat destruction, collection for the pet trade, and the practice of gassing tortoise burrows, a favored haven of the snake (TPWD 1996).

The mesquite lizard (*Sceloporus grammicus*) is well adapted to the habitat of the South Texas Brush Country. Its body is perfectly camouflaged to match the common honey mesquite tree here, one of its favored retreats (TPWD 1996).

OTHER NOTED "HERPTILIAN" RESIDENTS

- four-lined skink (*Eumeces tetragrammus*)
- keeled earless lizard (*Holbrookia propinqua*)
- Mediterranean gecko (*Hemidactylus turcicus*)

Mexican burrowing toad (*Rhinophrynus dorsalis*)
Mexican treefrog (*Smilisca baudinii*)
Rio Grande chirping frog (*Syrrhopus cystignathoides*)
rose-bellied lizard (*Sceloporus variabilis*)

Human Uses and Development

Historically, in the South Texas Brush Country, Mexican vaqueros developed the tools of the trade for herding wild Texas longhorns. This eventually gave birth to "that greatest of American heroes—the cowboy" (Hatch et al. 1990). It also brought about the cattle industry in South Texas, which is still one of the primary land uses in the South Texas Brush Country. Crops such as cotton, sorghum, flax, and other small grains are also grown here. Citrus orchards, sugarcane, and vegetable crops are all commonly planted in the more southern areas of the ecoregion because of the mild temperatures and highly favorable soils.

Edwards Plateau

Overview

The plateau encompasses approximately 31,000 square miles. Rivers, streams, and springs flow through the region. Two major aquifers underlie the area: the Edwards and the Trinity. It is dominated by limestone terrain but includes a wide variety of soil types, topography, and ecological conditions. Plateau live oak savanna and other oak woodlands and limestone glades occur throughout this region. It is home to one of the world's most diverse collections of aquifer fauna and endangered and rare species. Some of these plants and animals are found nowhere else on earth. The golden-cheeked warbler nests only in the Ashe juniper (a.k.a. cedar) of the area.

The springs and rivers of the region are home to the endangered San Marcos salamander and the endangered fountain darter. The rare plants of the region include the basin bellflowers and Texas snowbells. Ranching is the primary agricultural industry, but the natural beauty and opportunities for wildlife viewing and hunting have created a growing tourist industry in the region as well. The Balcones Escarpment—marked by a sharp topographic relief along the Balcones Fault Zone—borders the southeastern edge of the region and marks the transition zone between the plateau and the plains country on the south and east. The Balcones Escarpment runs from Del Rio to San Antonio and then northeast through Austin.

Location

The Edwards Plateau ecoregion encompasses approximately 24 million acres in west-central Texas. This region is often referred to as the Texas Hill Country. Visitors to the Edwards Plateau remember it for its stony hills, abundant springs, and steep canyons.

Topography

This ecoregion consists of rolling to very hilly terrain, and elevation ranges greatly from less than 100 feet to more than 3,000 feet (Smeins and Slack 1982). The Balcones Escarpment forms the ecoregion's border on its eastern and southern edges, but in the north and west, the Edwards Plateau blends into adjacent areas. The ecoregion's surface is typically rough and well drained because it is dissected by several river systems, including the Colorado, the Pedernales, and the Guadalupe.

Natural Sites of the Edwards Plateau

Balcones Canyonlands National Wildlife Area
Colorado Bend State Park
Devils River State Natural Area
Garner State Park
Government Canyon State Natural Area
Guadalupe River/Honey Creek State Natural Area
Kerr Wildlife Management Area
Kerrville-Schreiner State Park
Kickapoo Caverns State Natural Area

A full moon can be seen at a ranch outside Brady in the Edwards Plateau ecoregion. Courtesy of Texas Parks and Wildlife Department

Subregions

Balcones Canyonlands is characterized by its very rugged topography and exposed geological strata. Scarp woodlands dominated by oaks and mesquite with plentiful springs are typical.

Live Oak–Mesquite Savanna can be distinguished by its level to rolling grasslands interspersed with oak and mesquite wooded areas.

The Lampasas Cut Plain area is dominated by rolling grasslands with scattered mesquite woodlands. This entire subregion is also underlain by limestone deposits.

Climate

Average annual precipitation varies from15 inches in the west to 34 inches in the eastern portions of the ecoregion. However, more years have below-average than above-average annual rainfall, and droughts are fairly common in the ecoregion. To date, the most severe drought in the Edwards Plateau took place during the years 1950–58 (Smeins

A scenic view of the Edward Plateau ecoregion from Buck Hollow Ranch in Concan. Courtesy of Texas Parks and Wildlife Department

and Slack 1982). Typically, the highest average monthly rainfall occurs in May and June and again in September. Average temperatures range from 48°F in the winter to 87°F in the summer.

Geology

The Edwards Plateau is an ecoregion of diverse geology and beautiful scenery. Thousands of caves lie beneath the soils, and underground lakes of the Edwards Aquifer occur along the eastern edge of the ecoregion. This aquifer is an important source of water for surrounding cities, including Austin and San Antonio. It is also home to a variety of unusual and rare wildlife species.

Soils

Upland soils are mostly shallow, very stony or gravelly dark alkaline clays and clay loams underlain by limestone. Lighter-colored soils are on the steep side slopes, and deep, less stony soils are in the valleys. Bottomland soils are mostly deep, dark-gray or brown, alkaline loams and clays. The major soil management concerns are brush control, large stones, low fertility, excess lime, and limited soil moisture (Texas State Historical Association 1999).

Vegetation

GRASSES

- big bluestem (*Andropogon gerardii*)
- buffalograss (*Buchloe dactyloides*)
- cane bluestem (*Bothriochloa barbinodis* var. *barbinodis*)
- common curly mesquite (*Hilaria belangeri*)
- hairy grama (*Bouteloua hirsuta*)
- little bluestem (*Schizachyrium scoparium*)
- red grama (*Bouteloua trifida*)
- sideoats grama (*Bouteloua curtipendula*)
- switchgrass (*Panicum virgatum*)
- Texas cupgrass (*Eriochloa sericea*)
- Texas wild-rice (*Zizania texana*)*
- Texas wintergrass (*Stipa leucotricha*)
- tobosa (*Hilaria mutica*)
- tridens species (*Tridens* spp.)
- Wright's threeawn (*Aristida wrightii*)
- yellow indiangrass (*Sorghastrum nutans*)

**Denotes an endangered species*

TREES AND SHRUBS

- Ashe juniper (*Juniperus ashei*)
- honey mesquite (*Prosopis glandulosa* var. *glandulosa*)
- live oak (*Quercus virginiana*)
- post oak (*Quercus stellata*)
- redberry juniper (*Juniperus pinchotii*)
- Texas oak (*Quercus shumardii* var. *texana*)
- Texas snowbells (*Styrax texanus*)*
- Vasey shin oak (*Quercus pungens* var. *pungens*)

**Denotes an endangered species*

FORBS

- bitterweed (*Hymenoxys odorata*)
- broadleaf milkweed (*Asclepias latifolia*)
- broomweeds (*Amphiachyris* spp. and *Gutierrezia* spp.)
- bush sunflower (*Encelia californica*)
- Engelmann daisy (*Engelmannia pinnatifida*)
- mealycup sage (*Salvia farinacea* var. *farinacea*)

orange zexmenia (*Zexmenia hispida*)
prairie coneflower (*Ratibida columnifera*)
smallhead sneezeweed (*Helenium microcephalum*)
sneezeweed (*Helenium autmunale*)
western ragweed (*Ambrosia psilostachya*)

CACTUS

Tobusch fishhook cactus (*Sclerocactus brevihamatus* subsp. *tobuschii*), endangered

Ecosystem Change

The Edwards Plateau is characterized by grasslands, live oak–mesquite savannas, and juniper-oak woodlands. However, the open grasslands and savannas were much more common before settlers came to this area, and today midgrass and tallgrass communities have been replaced with shortgrass communities where grasses persist. In 1875, one settler described the Edwards Plateau as he remembered when he first found it in 1855: "The mountains [hills] are cedar bedecked; the valleys contain delightful prairies with occasional groves of trees of ten or twelve varieties of Oaks. The whole valley resembles a park, whose diversity and variety cannot be easily duplicated elsewhere" (Weniger 1984, 78). Overgrazing/overbrowsing by domestic livestock and wild herbivores and fire suppression are two factors that have contributed greatly to the ecosystem change of this area. The expansion of Ashe juniper has also had a tremendous impact on the ecosystem, causing a decrease in plant species diversity and an increase in soil erosion.

Wildlife: Birds

black-capped vireo (*Vireo atricapillus*)*
golden-cheeked warbler (*Dendroica chrysoparia*), highly endangered*
wild turkey (*Meleagris gallopavo*)

**Denotes an endangered species*

Wildlife: Mammals

The Edwards Plateau supports the largest white-tailed deer population in the United States (Hatch et al. 1990).

collared peccary, or javelina (*Pecari tajacu*)
nine-banded armadillo (*Dasypus novemcinctus*)
raccoon (*Procyon lotor*)
ringtail (*Bassariscus astutus*)
white-tailed deer (*Odocoileus virginianus*).

Wildlife: Reptiles and Amphibians

The very elusive and rare San Marcos salamander (*Eurycea nana*) is found only in Spring Lake and an adjacent downstream portion of the upper San Marcos River in the Edwards Plateau. The Texas blind salamander (*Eurycea* [*Typhlomolge*] *rathbuni*) has been listed as endangered since 1967. The primary reason for its endangerment is the pollution of the waters of the Edwards Aquifer. Other rare karst invertebrates are found in limestone caves, sinkholes, and fractures: Bee Creek Cave harvestman, Bone Cave harvestman, Tooth Cave harvestman, Tooth Cave spider, Tooth Cave ground beetle, Kretschmarr Cave mold beetle, and Coffin Cave mold beetle.

Human Use and Development

Ranching is the primary agricultural industry of the Edwards Plateau, with areas under cultivation largely confined to the valley bottoms and areas with deeper soils.

Llano Uplift

Overview

This area is characterized by large granite domes like Enchanted Rock in Gillespie County. The Llano Uplift is a unique geological formation—a granite mass that runs 70 miles across and is approximately 1,000 feet above sea level. The area encompasses approximately 5,000 square miles and is sur-

Natural Sites of the Llano Uplift

Canyon of the Eagles (Lower Colorado River Authority)
Enchanted Rock State Natural Area
Lost Maples State Natural Area
Inks Lake State Park
Mason Mountain Wildlife Management Area

rounded by the Edwards Plateau. The vegetation consists of oak-hickory, oak-juniper, mesquite, and grasslands. Ranching is the dominant agricultural industry, and tourism is emerging as an important economic activity for the region.

Location
The Llano Uplift, also known as the Central Mineral Region, is surrounded by the Edwards Plateau. Covering approximately 3.2 million acres, it has some of the oldest rocks in Texas and contains unique minerals and formations. Enchanted Rock, located near Fredericksburg, is one of the large granite domes characteristic of this region. The Llano Uplift is separated from the Blackland Prairies and South Texas Brushlands by the Balcones Escarpment on its southern and eastern sides. The High and Lower Plains lie to the north, while the Trans-Pecos region is to the west. The main counties in the region are Mason, Llano, Gillespie, and Burnet.

Topography
The entire region is a rolling to hilly landscape with an elevation from 825 to 2,250 feet above sea level.

Climate
Average annual precipitation is 24 to 32 inches, peaking in May or June and September. Average annual temperatures range from 64°F to 85°F.

Geology
The area is one of the most remarkable geological formations, as the earth here has been pushed up into a dome with salt some 1.35 billion years old.

A white swan on a pond in the Mason Mountain WMA in the Llano Uplift ecoregion. Courtesy of Texas Parks and Wildlife Department

Enchanted Rock is a monument of the Llano Uplift ecoregion. Courtesy of Texas Parks and Wildlife Department

Soils

The soils of the Llano Uplift are mostly coarse-textured sands that evolved from the weathering of granite rock over thousands of years. Upland soils are mostly shallow, reddish-brown to brown with gravelly, stony, sandy loams over granite and limestone bedrock. Large boulders exist on the soil surface in many areas.

Vegetation

The vegetation consists predominantly of oak savannas and woods and juniper breaks. There are 13 plant community types, three of which are endangered.

GRASSES

bluestem species (*Andropogon* spp.)
buffalograss (*Buchloe dactyloides*)
gramagrass (*Bouteloua* spp.)
indiangrass (*Sorghastrum* spp.)
switchgrass species (*Panicum* spp.)

SHRUBS AND HARDWOODS

common curly mesquite (*Hilaria belangeri*)
juniper (*Juniperus* spp.)
mesquite (*Prosopis* spp.)
shinnery oak (*Quercus havardii*)

FORBS

basin bellflower (*Campanula reverchonii*)*
rock quillwort (*Isoetes lithophila*)*

**Denotes an endangered species*

Ecosystem Change

The ecosystem change for the Llano Uplift region is very similar to that of the Edwards

Plateau region. Portions of this region support the highest deer density of the nation with one deer for every two to three acres. Several species of exotic ungulates also occur in this area, contributing to overgrazing. Brush control, large stones and limited soil moisture, and soil management are great concerns of this area.

Wildlife: Birds

black-capped vireo (*Vireo atricapillus*)*
golden-cheeked warbler (*Dendroica chyrsoparia*)*
mourning dove (*Zenaida macroura*)
northern bobwhite (*Colinus virginicus*)
northern mockingbird (*Mimus polyglottos*)
Rio Grande wild turkey (*Meleagris gallopavo intermedia*)

**Denotes an endangered species*

Wildlife: Mammals

black bear (*Ursus americanus*)
Brazilian free-tail bat (*Tadarida brasiliensis*)
eastern fox squirrel (*Sciurus niger*)
gray fox (*Urocyon cinereoargenteus*)
nine-banded armadillo (*Dasypus novemcinctus*)
raccoon (*Procyon lotor*)
ringtail (*Bassariscus astusus*)
striped skunk (*Mephitis mephitis*)
white-tailed deer (*Odocoileus virginianus*)

EXOTIC MAMMAL SPECIES

Many exotic species have been brought to this area.

axis deer (*Axis axis*)
blackbuck antelope (*Antilope cervicapra*)
European wild boar (*Sus scrofa*)
fallow deer (*Cervus dama*)
mouflon sheep (*Ovis ammon musimom*)
sika deer (*Cervus nippon*)

Wildlife: Amphibians

San Marcos salamander (*Eurycea nana*)
Texas blind salamander (*Eurycea rathbuni*)*

**Denotes an endangered species*

Wildlife: Fishes

fountain darter (*Etheostoma fonticola*)
Guadalupe bass (*Micropterus treculi*)
San Marcos gambusia (*Gambusia georgei*)

Human Use and Development

The main use for this region is ranching, not only cattle but sheep and goats as well. A few farms are located in the Llano Uplift. Deer leases and exotic big-game leases for hunting produce a major source of income. Most of the imported game is fenced in by private landowners in this area.

Rolling Plains

Overview

The Rolling Plains in north-central Texas cover 43,500 square miles. This area, along with the High Plains, is the southern end of the Great Plains of the central United States. Six Texas rivers run through the Rolling Plains: the Brazos, Canadian, Colorado, Concho, Red, and Wichita. The soils are soft prairie sands and clays, and flora includes juniper woodlands and prairie midgrasses. The Cap Rock Escarpment—a cliff that runs north-south—separates the High Plains and the Rolling Plains. Crop and livestock production are the major agricultural industries of this region.

Location

The Rolling Plains ecoregion lies east of the High Plains ecoregion and in some areas

Natural Sites of the Rolling Plains

Abilene State Park
Caprock Canyons State Park
Copper Breaks State Park
Gene Howe Wildlife Management Area
Matador Wildlife Management Area
San Angelo State Park

Rolling Plains ecoregion at the Anderson Ranch near Canadian. Courtesy of Texas Parks and Wildlife Department

overlaps the High Plains. It includes 28 million acres of gently rolling to rougher terrain, bordered on the west by the Oak Woods and Prairies and on the south by the Edwards Plateau. This ecoregion is actually part of the southernmost portion of the Great Plains of the central United States.

Topography
Elevation ranges from 800 to 3,000 feet above sea level. This area is dominated by grassland prairies and is dissected by many river systems flowing east to southeast, such as the Brazos and Wichita Rivers.

Subregions
Mesquite Plains
Escarpment Breaks
Canadian Breaks

Climate
Average annual precipitation is 20–28 inches, primarily from summer thunderstorms. The Rolling Plains ecoregion is characterized by semiarid climates in the western portions to more subhumid climates in the eastern areas. Summers are hot, with temperatures averaging from 75°F to 83°F. Winters are generally mild, ranging from 41°F to 55°F (TPWD 1999). The warm temperatures and dry winds also promote high evaporation rates in the area, which lessen the value of the precipitation.

Geology
Generally, soils here developed as streams depositing sediments into an inland sea that existed during the Triassic and Permian periods. In the last 12,000 years, erosion has greatly shaped the ecoregion's landscape,

The Anderson Ranch in Canadian features a diversity of range grasses and shrubs, Rolling Plains ecoregion. Courtesy of Texas Parks and Wildlife Department

both removing and covering Pleistocene and Holocene deposits. Outcrops of limestone, sandstone, mudstone, and shale can be found at various sites within the Rolling Plains. Caliche and gypsum deposits are also fairly common because of the region's small amounts of precipitation (TPWD 1999).

Soils

Upland soils are neutral to calcareous, sandy loams, clay loams, and clays. Saline soils and shallow and stony soils are also common here. In the bottomlands, reddish-brown alluvial, calcareous loams and clay soils can be found (Hatch et al. 1990).

Vegetation

GRASSES

- blue grama (*Bouteloua gracilis*)
- common curly mesquite (*Hilaria belangeri*)
- hairy grama (*Bouteloua hirsuta*)
- little bluestem (*Schizachyrium scoparium*)
- red grama (*Bouteloua trifida*)
- sand bluestem (*Andropogon hallii*)
- sand dropseed (*Sporobolus crytandrus*)
- sideoats grama (*Bouteloua curtipendula*)
- threeawn (*Aristida* spp.)
- western wheatgrass (*Agropyron smithii*)

TREES AND SHRUBS

- honey mesquite (*Prosopis glandulosa*)
- lotebush (*Ziziphus obtusifolia*)
- redberry juniper (*Juniperus pinchoti*)
- sand sagebrush (*Artemisia filifolia*)
- shinnery oak (*Quercus havardii*)

FORBS

- broadleaf milkweed (*Asclepias latifolia*)
- Lambert crazyweed (*Oxytropis lambertii*)
- prairie coneflower (*Ratibida columnifera*)
- slimleaf scurfpea (*Psoralia tenuiflora*)
- Texas poppy-mallow (*Callirhoe scabriuscula*)*
- western ragweed (*Ambrosia psilostachya*)
- western yarrow (*Achillea millefolium*)

**Denotes an endangered species*

Ecosystem Change

Rangeland, dryland, and irrigated cropland are major uses of this ecoregion. Poor management practices have increased mesquite, snakeweed, prickly pear, and sagebrush. Pinyon pines once occurred on bluffs and breaks but were cut down by early settlers. The area was once home to an abundance of American bison (Telfair 1999).

Wildlife: Birds

- burrowing owl (*Athene cunicularia*)
- greater roadrunner (*Geococcyx californianus*)
- interior least tern (*Sterna antillarum*), rare in the Rolling Plains
- snowy plover (*Charadrius alexandrinus*)
- Swainson's hawk (*Buteo swainsoni*)

Wildlife: Mammals

- American badger (*Taxidea taxus*)
- black-tailed prairie dog (*Cynomys ludovicianus*)
- plains pocket gopher (*Geomys bursarius*)
- plains pocket mouse (*Perognathus flavescens*)
- prairie vole (*Microtus ochrogaster*)
- Texas kangaroo rat (*Dipodymus elator*)

Texas mouse (*Peromyscus attwateri*)
thirteen-lined ground squirrel (*Spermophilus tridecemlineatus*)

Wildlife: Reptiles
Concho water snake (*Nerodia harteri paucimaculata*), a very rare species
plains hognose snake (*Heterodon nasicus nasicus*)
western diamondback rattlesnake (*Crotalus atrox*)

Human Use and Development
More than 75% of the land of the Rolling Plains is rangeland (Hatch et al. 1990). Crop and livestock production are the other major uses of land in the area. Ample wildlife habitats are created by the mixing of these varying croplands and rangelands. Thus, many wildlife species such as quail, mourning dove, white-tailed deer, and turkey live here, providing good recreational hunting opportunities.

High Plains

Overview
The High Plains region was called the Llano Estacado, or Staked Plains, by the early Spaniards. (The precise meaning of this designation is not certain.) This region occupies approximately 34,500 square miles. Like the Rolling Plains, the High Plains is the southern extension of the Great Plains of the central United States. The High Plains region has also been cited as the outwash sediments from the Rocky Mountains. The region was once home to herds of buffalo, pronghorn antelope, gray wolves, grizzly bear, and elk. It is now home to the sandhill crane, the kit fox, and the lesser prairie chicken, as well as prairie dogs and coyotes. The flora includes blue grama and buffalograss. Cottonwoods and willows are found along the rivers and tributaries. Mesquite, sandsage, and Havard shinoak also occur in this region. Each fall thousands of wintering waterfowl stop over to rest and feed at the playa (shallow lakes) that dot the region. The Ogallala Aquifer underlies the High Plains and the central United States. Cotton farming and cattle ranching are the major agricultural industries.

Natural Sites of the High Plains
Big Spring State Park
Gene Howe Wildlife Management Area
Palo Duro Canyon State Park
Playa Lakes Wildlife Management Areas
Rita Blanca National Grasslands
W. A. Murphy Unit Wildlife Management Area

Location
The High Plains, along with the Rolling Plains, is part of the Southern Great Plains of the central United States. The region encompasses approximately 20 million acres. The High Plains is a relatively high plateau separated from the Rolling Plains by the Llano Estacado Escarpment and is dissected by the Canadian River Breaks and the Caprock Escarpment in the northern portion of the Texas Panhandle.

Topography
The landscape is flat to rolling. Elevations range from 2,700 to more than 4,000 feet above sea level. Notable canyons include Tule and Palo Duro along the caprock. The unique ephemeral playas of this region are important for waterfowl, crop production, and recharge of the Ogallala Aquifer. Playas occupy some 340,000 acres in this region.

Climate
Average annual precipitation ranges from 15 to 22 inches. Rainfall is lowest in winter and midsummer and highest in April or May and September or October. Extended droughts have occurred several times throughout the past century. Average temperatures range from a low of 21°F in the winter to 92°F in the summer.

A flock of sandhill cranes (*Grus canadensis*) resting on a pond in Muleshoe National Wildlife Area in the High Plains ecoregion. Courtesy of Texas Parks and Wildlife Department

Geology

The High Plains is the largest level plain of its kind in the United States and rises from 2,700 feet on the east side to more than 4,000 feet in some areas along the New Mexico border. The area is covered with thick alluvial material. The Caprock Escarpment, caused mainly by surface erosion, divides the High Plains and the lower Rolling Plains. The escarpment rises abruptly in places nearly 1,000 feet above the plains. The area has few streams to cause local relief; however, several major rivers originate or cross the area. Topographically, the High Plains is an upland that overlies the great Permian Basin, a part of the Great Plains geosyncline, which has been folded under earth's crust due to downward warping.

Soils

Surface texture of soils ranges from clays on hardland sites in the north to sands in the southern portion of the region. Caliche generally underlies these surface soils at depths of two to five feet. Upland soils are mostly well drained, deep, neutral to alkaline clay loams and sandy loams in the southern portion. Many soils have large amounts of lime at various depths, while some are shallow over caliche.

Vegetation

Native vegetation of the High Plains is shortgrass prairie dominated by buffalograss. It is one of the most biologically diverse ecoregions of the United States and Canada, but it contains the fastest-declining bird populations on the continent. Although historically grassland, parts of the region have been invaded by mesquite, sand sagebrush, prickly pear, and yucca. Shinnery oak and sage are common invaders on sandy lands, and juniper has spread from the breaks to the plains in some areas. There are 11 plant community types in the region; two of them are unique to this region.

GRASSES

- blue grama (*Bouteloua gracilis*)
- buffalograss (*Buchloe dactyloides*)
- common curly mesquite (*Hilaria belangeri*)
- little bluestem (*Schizachyrium scoparium*)
- sand bluestem (*Andropogon gerardii* var. *hallii*)
- sand sagebrush (*Artemisia filifolia*)
- sideoats grama (*Bouteloua curtipendula*)
- switchgrass (*Panicum virgatum*)
- Texas wintergrass (*Stipa leucotricha*)

TREES

- cottonwood (*Populus deltoides*)
- French salt cedar (*Tamarix ramosissima*)
- mesquite (*Prosopis glandulosa*)
- Russian olive (*Elaeagnus angustifolia*)
- sugarberry (*Celtis laevigata*)
- western soapberry (*Sapindus drummondii*)
- willows (*Salix* spp.)

SHRUBS

- agarita (*Berberis trifoliolata*)
- buttonbush (*Cephalanthus occidentalis*)
- common chokeberry (*Prunus virginiana*)
- feather dalea (*Dalea farmosa*)
- fourwing saltbush (*Atriplex canescens*)
- Oklahoma plum (*Prunus gracilis*)
- prairie sagewort (*Artemisia frigida*)

Ecosystem Change

Fragmentation of native habitats, conversion to agriculture, and overgrazing continue to be major threats to this region, where immense herds of buffalo and pronghorn antelope once roamed the vast

A sunset view of playa lakes across the High Plains ecoregion. Courtesy of Texas Parks and Wildlife Department

prairies of blue grama and buffalograss. Today the plains are nearly 60% cropland (half of which is irrigated) and 40% rangeland. What little native vegetation is left now also includes more mesquite and juniper. Although much of the shortgrass prairie and the vast prairie dog towns are gone, large flocks of wintering waterfowl still come to the playa lakes of the region. The flat surface of the area encourages irrigation and mechanization. High winds, limited soil moisture, erosion, and irrigation water management are major concerns of this area.

Wildlife: Birds

- bald eagle (*Haliaeetus leucocephalus*)
- black-chinned hummingbird (*Archilochus alexandri*)
- canyon towhee (*Pipilo fuscus*)
- lark bunting (*Calamospiza melanocorys*)
- lesser prairie chicken (*Tympanuchus pallidicinctus*)
- mountain plover (*Charadrius montanus*)
- mourning dove (*Zenaida macroura*)
- northern bobwhite (*Colinus virginicus*)
- ring-necked pheasant (*Phasianus colchicus*)
- Rio Grande wild turkey (*Meleagris gallopavo intermedia*)
- sandhill crane (*Grus canadensis*)
- scaled quail (*Callipepla squamata*)

Wildlife: Mammals

- American badger (*Taxidea taxus*)
- Barbary (aoudad) sheep (*Ammotragus lervia*)
- bison (*Bos bison*)
- black-tailed jack rabbit (*Lepus californicus*)
- black-tailed prairie dog (*Cynomys ludovicianus*)
- coyote (*Canis latrans*)
- mule deer (*Odocoileus hemionus*)
- plains pocket mouse (*Perognathus flavescens*)
- pronghorn (*Antilocapra americana*)
- striped skunk (*Mephitis mephitis*)
- swift fox (*Vulpes velox*)
- thirteen-lined ground squirrel (*Spermophilus tridecemlineatus*)
- white-tailed deer (*Odocoileus virginianus*)

Wildlife: Amphibians and Reptiles

- dunes sagebrush lizard (*Sceloporus arenicolus*)
- Great Plains skink (*Eumeces obsoletus*)
- Great Plains toad (*Bufo cognatus*)
- New Mexico spadefoot (*Spea multiplicata*)
- Texas horned lizard (*Phrynosoma cornutum*)
- western hognose snake (*Heterodon nasicus*)
- western rattlesnake (*Crotalus viridis*)
- yellow mud turtle (*Kinosternon flavescens*)

Human Use and Development

The primary industries of the High Plains relate to agriculture, with irrigated cotton, wheat, grain, and sorghum the main crops. Ranching and petroleum developments are also abundant. Amarillo is the largest city of this area, but Lubbock, Plainview, and Borger are other important areas. This area leads the state in production of cotton, sorghum, and wheat.

Trans-Pecos

Overview

The Trans-Pecos ecoregion encompasses 38,000 square miles in the northern portion of the Chihuahuan Desert. Regarded as the most complex region of the state, it includes plateaus, desert valleys, and wooded mountains where many rare species are found. The only true mountain ranges in Texas are in the Trans-Pecos, and each has its own type of plants and animals. The flora of the region includes desert scrub, such as the creosotebush, desert grasslands, pinyon-oak juniper woodlands, yuccas, and agaves. The American peregrine falcon nests in this region. The Rio Grande creates the southern border, separating Texas from Mexico. Big Bend National Park is in the southern edge of the area in Brewster County, the largest county in Texas.

Location
The Trans-Pecos ecoregion covers approximately 19 million acres of land in far West Texas, extending east from the Pecos River (Smeins and Slack 1982). More specifically, the region extends eastward from the southwestern portions of Andrews County in the north to the western portions of Val Verde County in the south.

Topography
The region is perhaps the most ecologically complex ecoregion in Texas. Its contrasting habitats include mountains, desert valleys, and plateaus in the Chihuahuan Desert and extensive grasslands. Elevation of the region varies from 2,500 feet to 8,749 feet at Guadalupe Peak, the highest point in Texas (Smith and Campbell 1996).

Natural Sites of the Trans-Pecos
- Balmorhea State Park
- Big Bend National Park
- Big Bend Ranch State Park
- Black Gap Wildlife Management Area
- Elephant Mountain Wildlife Management Area
- Franklin Mountains State Park
- Hueco Tanks State Park
- Monahans Sandhills State Park
- Sierra Diablo Wildlife Management Area

Subregions
Mountain Ranges is characterized by higher rainfalls and the development of woody vegetation such as junipers, scrub oak, live oaks, pinyon pine, ponderosa pine, and Douglas-fir in the Chisos and Guadalupe Mountains.

Desert Grasslands is well described by its name. It occurs in the heart of the Trans-Pecos as a function of altitudes and soils, which are deeper and have higher clay content.

A scenic highway scene between Lajitas and Presidio in the Trans-Pecos ecoregion. Courtesy of Texas Parks and Wildlife Department

Desert Scrub is a subregion of low rainfall and rapid drainage. Creosotebushes, yucca, lechuguilla, and various small-leaved plants form the general vegetation.

Salt Basin is characterized by soils with high salt concentrations and gypsum dunes on a bolson area. Because the basin has no external drainage, there is a significant buildup of salts in its soils. Plants that grow here have a high degree of salt tolerance.

Sand Hills consists of shin oak and mesquite on windblown dunes and grasslands with some little bluestem grasses.

Stockton Plateau is made up of flat-topped mesas and plateaus intersected by steep-walled canyons and dry washes.

Climate

Average annual precipitation is usually less than 12 inches, but this is highly variable year to year (TPWD 2000c). Rainfall also increases at the higher elevations; for example, Mount Locke receives a reported 20 inches annually (Smeins and Slack 1982). High rainfall months for the ecoregion are generally July and August (Smeins and Slack 1982). Average annual temperatures range from 44°F in the winter to 82°F in the summer, with low humidity in most areas.

Geology

The Trans-Pecos ecoregion is a highly complex geological area. It is in great contrast to the rest of the state of Texas. While much of Texas is considered to be flat plains or rolling prairies, the Trans-Pecos is distinguished as an area of substantial mountain ranges, valleys, and deserts. Some of the chief mountain ranges of the region are the Davis, Chisos, Delaware, and Guadalupe. Interestingly, the oldest rocks in Texas are found in the Trans-Pecos, in the Franklin and Carrizo Mountains. These rocks consist of billion-year-old Precambrian igneous, metamorphic, and sedimentary deposits (Spearing 1996).

Some of the mountains in the region are characterized by volcanic rock; others, by limestone deposits. The mountains of Paleozoic age (250–600 million years old) are called the Marathon Uplift, and they are part of the ancient Ouachita Range. They were formed as the Ouachita Range emerged from the collision of two crustal plates during the formation of the supercontinent Pangaea, roughly 300 million years ago (Spearing 1996).

Almost all of the northwest-southwest-oriented ranges in West Texas were formed 60–120 million years ago (in the Mesozoic period) when North America separated from Eurasia. The mountains punched upward during this period as the North American Plate overrode the Pacific Plate (Spearing 1996).

Younger formations formed about 35 million years ago, as North America stretched in a relaxation period. As the crust stretched and cracked, downthrown basins and upthrown mountains were created. Igneous knobs and hills of lava were also formed during this time as volcanoes erupted and bubbles of lava rose to just below the sedimentary surface. These volcanic formations are visible parts of the scenery of Big Bend National Park. From 35 million years ago to today, erosion has been the primary force, affecting the dynamic landscape of the Trans-Pecos (Spearing 1996).

Soils

The soils of the Trans-Pecos have been formed mostly by mountain outwash materials. Textures and profile characteristics of the soils are varied, but most of the soils are generally alkaline (Smith and Campbell 1996). Caliche soils, rich in calcium carbonate precipitates, are widespread in the arid and semi-arid areas.

Vegetation

The Trans-Pecos is a region of diverse habitats and vegetation, shifting from desert

Caliche soils are widespread in the Trans-Pecos ecoregion. Courtesy of Texas Parks and Wildlife Department

valleys and plateaus to wooded mountain slopes and riverways. These varying habitats allow the ecoregion to support many different plant species. The primary plant communities are creosote desert scrub, desert grasslands, yucca and juniper savanna, and montane forests of pinyon pine and oak. Interestingly, the greatest abundance of rare plant species in Texas occurs in the Trans-Pecos ecoregion (Smith and Campbell 1996). Little Aguja pondweed (*Potamogeton clystocarpus*) occurs only within quiet seepage pools in Little Aguja Creek in the Davis Mountains. Terlingua Creek cat's-eye (*Cryptantha crassipes*) is found in barren, gypseous clay or chalky shales on slopes with sparse vegetation. Many cactus species are endangered because they have been gathered by collectors.

CACTI

- bunched cory cactus (*Coryphantha ramillosa*)
- Chisos hedgehog cactus (*Echinocereus chisoensis* var. *chisoensis*)
- Davis green pitaya (*Echinocereus viridiflorus* var. *davisii*)*
- Lloyd's mariposa cactus (*Neolloydia mariposensis*)
- Nellie cory cactus (*Coryphantha minima*)*
- prickly pear cactus (*Opuntia* spp.)
- Sneed pincushion cactus (*Coryphantha sneedii* var. *sneedii*)*

**Denotes an endangered species*

GRASSES

- buffalograss (*Buchloe dactyloides*)
- finestem needlegrass (*Stipa tenuissima*)

gramagrass (*Bouteloua* spp.)
plains bristlegrass (*Setaria leucopila*)
tanglehead (*Heteropogon contortus*)
Texas bluestem (*Schizachyrium cirratus*)
tobosa (*Hilaria mutica*)

WOODY SPECIES OF THE DESERTS

candelilla (*Euphorbia antisyphilitica*)
creosotebush (*Larrea divaricata*)
honey mesquite (*Prosopis glandulosa* var. *glandulosa*)
lechuguilla (*Agave lechuguilla*)
ocotillo (*Fouqueria splendens*)
sotol (*Dasylirion texanum*)
Spanish dagger (*Yucca torreyi*)
tarbush (*Flourensia cernua*)

WOODY SPECIES OF THE MOUNTAINS

alligator juniper (*Juniperus deppeana*)
Graves oak (*Quercus gravesii*)
gray oak (*Quercus grisea*)
Hinckley's oak (*Quercus hinckleyi*)*
limber pine (*Pinus strobiformis*)
oneseed juniper (*Juniperus monosperma*)
pinyon pine (*Pinus cembroides*)
ponderosa pine (*Pinus ponderosa*)
quaking aspen (*Pipulus tremuloides*)

**Denotes an endangered species*

WOODY SPECIES OF RIVERS AND STREAMS

honey mesquite (*Prosopis glandulosa* var. *glandulosa*)
Rio Grande cottonwood (*Pipulus wislizenii*)
salt cedar (*Tamarix gallica*)
willow (*Salix gooddingii*)

Ecosystem Change

Captain John Pope painted a general picture of the Trans-Pecos ecoregion as it was in 1854: "The country between the valleys of the Rio Grande and the Pecos consists of elevated table-lands [prairies] destitute of wood and water, except at particular points, but covered with a luxuriant growth of the richest and most nutritious grasses known to this continent. This region is intersected by three ranges of mountains, nearly parallel to each other. . . . The table-lands are covered with the Mesquite brush. . . . The Gramma grass, which extends in the most profuse abundance over the entire surface of these table-lands, is nutritious during the whole year, and the plains between the Rio Grande and the Pecos seem intended by nature for the maintenance of countless herds of cattle" (Weniger 1984, 28).

Interestingly, Captain Pope's prediction of the future use of the Trans-Pecos plains was fairly accurate because ranching is indeed the primary industry of the area today. Many of the original vegetative areas of the Trans-Pecos, including those described by Captain Pope, have been preserved in their natural state through the inception of several national and state parks. These include the beautiful Big Bend National Park, the Davis Mountains State Park, the Balmorhea State Park, and the Guadalupe Mountains National Park.

Wildlife

The Trans-Pecos supports a plethora of animal life. The varied and unique ecological areas, including deserts, plains, and mountains, provide these animals with many available homes. The region offers many rare species of wildlife their last remaining unspoiled habitats. In fact, more rare species of wildlife are found in the Trans-Pecos than in any other ecoregion in Texas.

BIRDS

The Trans-Pecos ecoregion has a larger variety of bird life than the entire state of New York (Peterson and Zimmer 1998). Birds here find homes in many habitats, including the mountains, grasslands, deserts, and forests. The mountains are of key importance because the natural layering of ecosystems that occurs at distinct altitudes as a result of varying environmental conditions (altitudinal zonation) provides for a greater number of available habitats and therefore a greater diversity of avian life.

Several species of jays are found in the Trans-Pecos. Steller's jay (*Cyanocitta stelleri*) is a common resident of the Guadalupe and Davis Mountains. Scrub jay (*Aphelocoma coerulescens*) is another common corvid resident of the Trans Pecos. Gray-breasted jay (*A. ultramarina*) is found only in Texas within the woodlands of the Chisos Mountains of Big Bend. Pinyon jay (*Gymnorhinus cyanoceohalus*) is found in West Texas, including the Trans-Pecos ecoregion.

The common black-hawk (*Buteogallus anthracinus*) is a very rare raptor that hunts along the streams and rivers of the southern portions of the ecoregion. Phainopepla (*Phainopepla nitens*) is a beautiful, tropical bird unique to the Trans-Pecos during its spring season spent in Texas. Colima warbler (*Vermivora crissalis*) is a Mexican bird whose entire US range is restricted to a few hundred acres of the Chisos Mountains in Big Bend National Park (Peterson and Zimmer 1998). Mexican spotted owl (*Strix occidentalis lucida*) has been listed as endangered since 1993. This very rare owl lives in the Guadalupe Mountains near the New Mexico border and in some areas of the Davis Mountains. It has never been found in any other mountains in Texas. Its declining populations are due to habitat loss. The following birds are also found in the Trans-Pecos region:

- acorn woodpecker (*Melanerpes formicivorus*)
- band-tailed Pigeon (*Columba fasciata*)
- canyon wren (*Catherpes mexicanus*)
- mountain chickadee (*Parus gambeli*)
- painted redstart (*Myioborus pictus*)
- pyrrhuloxia (*Cardinalis sinuatus*)
- scaled quail (*Callipepla squamata*)
- violet-green swallow (*Tachycineta thalassina*)
- western bluebird (*Sialia mexicana*)
- western screech-owl (*Megascops kennicottii*)

Wildlife: Mammals

The greatest number of unique species in the mammal fauna of Texas occur in the Trans-Pecos ecoregion. Approximately one-third of the 92 species of mammals that occur in the Trans-Pecos are primarily restricted in distribution to this region (Davis and Schmidly 1997). Most of these mammal species are characteristic of the Mexican plateaus and southwestern United States or the montane forests of the western United States.

BATS PRINCIPALLY OCCURRING IN THE TRANS-PECOS

The Mexican long-nosed bat (*Leptonycteris nivalis*) lives in the desert regions of Big Bend National Park, where it feeds on the nectar and pollen of many desert plants. Its long nose and tongue makes it well adapted for this type of feeding. These bats are endangered because they are often killed in southern Mexico by people wanting to control vampire bats, which are known to spread disease. Also, gave plants on which the bats often feed are being cleared for pasture and harvested to make liquor.

- California myotis (*Myotis californicus*)
- fringed myotis (*Myotis thysanodes*)
- long-legged myotis (*Myotis volans*)
- pocketed free-tailed bat (*Nyctinomops femorosacca*)
- spotted bat (*Euderma maculatum*)
- western mastiff bat (*Eumops perotis*)
- western red bat (*Lasiurus blossevillii*)
- Yuma myotis (*Myotis yumanensis*)

LARGE MAMMALS

Black bear (*Ursus americanus*) was formerly found in almost all of the ecoregions of our state, but due to overhunting and loss of habitat, it was practically nonexistent in Texas by the 1950s. However, a remarkable reestablishment of these bears has been occurring in the Trans-Pecos. Since the 1980s, bear sightings have become more frequent. Although the black bear is currently listed as a "state threatened species," effective recovery efforts and careful coexistence with this bear can lead to its continued reestablishment.

Fleet-footed pronghorn (*Antilocarpa americana*) is an animal of the West Texas plains. Among North American mammals, pronghorns are the fastest. Their top speed is estimated at 60 miles per hour, with sustaining speeds of 35 miles per hour for distances as great as twenty-seven miles (Hiller 1983).

Wapiti or elk (*Cervus elaphus*) exists in the wild in Texas in five small herds in the Guadalupe Mountains, Glass Mountains (Brewster County), Wylie Mountains (Culberson County), Davis Mountains (Jeff Davis County), and Eagle Mountains (Hudspeth County). This species of elk was introduced here in 1928 by Judge J. C. Hunter to replace the native elk (*C. merriami*) of the Trans-Pecos that went extinct near the turn of the century (Davis and Schmidly 1997).

Mountain sheep (*Ovis canadensis*) formerly ranged throughout many mountain ranges in the Trans-Pecos ecoregion; however, native populations are now extirpated. The last native sheep were seen in the Sierra Diablo in 1959, when the total population was estimated at just 14. Thanks to the Texas Parks and Wildlife Department, recent introductions of mountain sheep (or "bighorn sheep") in the Sierra Diablo, Van Horn Mountains, Elephant Mountain Wildlife Management Area, and Baylor Mountains have resulted in small, wild populations.

SMALL MAMMALS AND RODENTS

- banner-tailed kangaroo rat (*Dipodomys spectabilis*)
- black gray-footed chipmunk (*Tamias canipes*)
- brush mouse (*Peromyscus boylii*)
- cactus mouse (*Peromyscus eremicus*)
- desert pocket gopher (*Geomys arenarius*)
- desert pocket mouse (*Chaetodipus penicillatus*)
- hooded skunk (*Mephitis macroura*)
- Mearns' grasshopper mouse (*Onychomys arenicola*)
- Merriam's kangaroo rat (*Dipodomys merriami*)
- Mexican vole (*Microtus mexicanus*)
- Mexican woodrat (*Neotoma mexicana*)
- Nelson's pocket mouse (*Chaetodipus nelsoni*)
- rock pocket mouse (*Chaetodipus intermedius*)
- tawny-bellied cotton rat (*Sigmodon fulviventer*)
- Texas antelope squirrel (*Ammospermophilus interpres*)
- yellow-nosed cotton rat (*Sigmodon ochrognathus*)

Wildlife: Reptiles and Amphibians

The varying habitats of the Trans-Pecos provide homes for many unique and interesting reptiles and amphibians. There are three species of horned lizard in Texas, and all three can be found in the Trans-Pecos.

The famous Texas horned lizard (*Phrynosoma cornutum*) has been honored as the Texas State Reptile. It is listed as a threatened species. The mountain short-horned lizard (*P. douglassi hernandesi*) is also a threatened species. Its populations are much more restricted than the Texas horned lizard's. Habitat loss, collection for the pet trade (primarily for *P. cornutum*) , and the introduction of the red imported fire ant, which has displaced the native harvester ants, one of the horned lizard's chief food sources, are responsible for the decline of both lizards. The roundtail horned lizard (*P. modestum*) is the only one not currently protected under Texas law.

OTHER "HERPTILIAN" RESIDENTS

- Big Bend gecko (*Coleonyx reticulatus*)
- Big Bend patchnose snake (*Salvadora deserticola*)
- canyon treefrog (*Hyla arenicolor*)
- little striped whiptail (*Cnemidophorus inornatus*)

Mexican black-headed snake (*Tantilla atriceps*)
Mexican mud turtle (*Kinosternon hirtipes*)
New Mexico spadefoot (*Spea multiplicata*)
Texas lyre snake (*Trimorphodon biscutatus*)
Trans-Pecos blind snake (*Leoptotyphlops humilis*)
Trans-Pecos rat snake (*Elaphe subocularis*)

Human Uses and Development

Human populations within the Trans-Pecos ecoregion are sparse. The major cities of the region are Fort Stockton, El Paso, Fort Davis, Presidio, and Pecos. Ranching is the primary industry in this ecoregion. Some cropland is found in irrigated areas along the Rio Grande and the Pecos River. Land in this region is also being used for vineyards and the disposal of large volumes of municipal waste (Texas State Historical Association 1999).

References

Bailey, R. G. 1978. *Description of the Ecoregions of the United States* [The map, Ecoregions of the United States, was printed in 1976 at the scale of 1:7,500,000.]. Ogden, UT: USDA Forest Service, Intermountain Region.

Campbell, Linda, and Vickie Smith. 1996. *Exploring Texas Ecoregions*. Austin: Texas Parks and Wildlife Department.

Correll, D. S., and M. C. Johnston. 1970. *Manual of the Vascular Plants of Texas*. Renner: Texas Research Foundation.

Cory, V. L., and H. B. Parks. 1937. *Catalogue of the Flora of the State of Texas*. Bulletin No. 550. College Station: Texas Agricultural Experiment Station.

Davis, William B., and David J. Schmidly. 1997. *The Mammals of Texas: Online Edition*. Accessed February 23, 2015. http://www.nsrl.ttu.edu/tmot1/.

Dunlevy Smith, Vicki, and Linda S. Campbell. *Keep Texas Wild Video*. Texas Parks and Wildlife Department. Accessed March 30, 2015. http://www.youtube.com/playlist?list=PL6353227E5419A80D.

Gould, F. W. 1957. *Texas Grasses, a Preliminary Checklist*. Misc. Pub. MP-240. College Station: Texas Agricultural Experiment Station.

———. 1962. Texas Plants—a Checklist and Ecological Summary. Misc. Pub. MP-585. College Station: Texas Agricultural Experiment Station.

Griffith, G. E., S. A. Bryce, J. M. Omernik, J. A. Comstock, A. C. Rogers, B. Harrison, S. L. Hatch, and D. Bezanson. 2004. Ecoregions of Texas [color poster with map, descriptive text, and photographs]. Scale 1:2,500,000. Reston, VA: US Geological Survey.

Hatch, S. L., K. N. Gandhi, and L. E. Brown. 1990. *Checklist of the Vascular Plants of Texas*. Misc. Pub. 1655. College Station: Texas Agricultural Experiment Station.

Hatch, S. L., and J. L. Schuster. 1990. Texas Plants: An Ecological Summary. In *Checklist of the Vascular Plants of Texas*. College Station: Texas Agricultural Experiment Station. http://botany.csdl.tamu.edu/FLORA/taes/tracy/regeco.html.

Hiller, Ilo. 1983. Animal Speeds. In *Young Naturalist*, 32–24. Louise Lindsey Merrick Texas Environment Series, No. 6. College Station: Texas A&M University Press.

Holt, E. A., K. E. Allen, N. C. Parker, and R. J. Baker. 2000. *Ecotourism and Conserva-*

tion: Richness of Terrestrial Vertebrates across Texas. Occas. Pap. 201. Lubbock: Museum of Texas Tech University.

Johnston, E. H. 1931. *The Natural Regions of Texas*. University of Texas Bulletin 3113. Austin: University of Texas.

Kinnaird, Lawrence. 1958. *The Frontiers of New Spain: Nicolas De Lafora's Description, 1766–1768*. Berkeley, CA: The Quivira Society.

Kuchler, A. W. 1964. *Potential Natural Vegetation of the Coterminous United States*. New York: American Geographical Society.

Lockwood, M. W., and C. E. Shackelford. 2000. *Rare and Declining Birds of Texas: Conservation Needed*. 2nd ed. Austin: Texas Parks and Wildlife Department.

McMahan, C. A., R. G. Frye, and K. Brown. 1984. *The Vegetation Types of Texas including Croplands*. Austin: Texas Parks and Wildlife Department.

Natural Regions of Texas. 1979. Austin: Lyndon B. Johnson School of Public Affairs, University of Texas at Austin.

Peterson, Jim, and Barry R. Zimmer. 1998. *Birds of the Trans-Pecos*. Austin: University of Texas Press.

Poole, J. M., W. R. Carr, D. M. Price, and J. Singhurst. 2007. Natural Regions of Texas. In *Rare Plants of Texas*, by Poole et al., 3–26. College Station: Texas A&M University Press.

Preserving Texas' Natural Heritage. 1978. Policy Research Project Report Number 31. Austin: Lyndon B. Johnson School of Public Affairs, University of Texas at Austin.

Reed, Cyrus, and Mary Sanger. 2000. *Texas Environmental Almanac*. 2nd ed. Austin: Texas Center for Policy Studies, University of Texas Press.

Smeins, Fred E., and Douglas R. Slack. 1982. *Fundamentals of Ecology: Laboratory Manual*. Dubuque, IA: Kendall/Hunt Publishing.

Spearing, Darwin. 1996. *Roadside Geology of Texas*. Missoula, MT: Mountain Press Publishing.

Telfair, Ray C., II. 1999. *Texas Wildlife Resources and Land Uses*. Austin: University of Texas Press.

Texas Agricultural Experiment Station. 1962. *Texas Plants: A Checklist and Ecological Summary*. Misc. Pub. 585. College Station: Texas A&M University.

The Texas Almanac. 2002–3. *Dallas Morning News*, 54, 72.

Texas Center for Policy Studies. 2000. http://www.texascenter.org/publications.html.

Texas Parks and Wildlife Department. 1996. *Exploring Ecoregions of Texas*. Austin: Texas Parks and Wildlife Department.

———. 1999. *Exploring Texas: Rolling Prairies and Plains*. http://www.tpwd.state.tx.us/expltx/index.htm.

———. 2000a. *Exploring Texas: Features of the Prairies and Lakes Region*. http://www.tpwd.state.tx.us/expltx/p&lchart.htm. [no longer available]

———. 2000b. *Exploring Texas: The Trans Pecos*. http://www.tpwd.state.tx.us/expltx/bb/bb.htm. [no longer available]

———. 2000c. *Exploring the South Texas Plains*. http://www.tpwd.state.tx.us/expltx/index.htm. [no longer available]

———. 2001. *State Parks and Historical Sites. Dinosaur Valley State Park*. http://www.tpwd.state.tx.us/park/dinosaur/dinosaur.htm.

Texas State Historical Association. 1999. Soils of Texas. *Texas Almanac*. http://texasalmanac.com/topics/environment/soils-texas.

Tharp, B. C. 1939. *The Vegetation of Texas*. Edinburg: Texas Academy of Science.

———. 1952. *Texas Range Grasses*. Austin: University of Texas Press.

Thomas, G. W. 1962. *Texas Plants—an Ecological Summary*. Misc. Pub. MP-585. College Station: Texas Agricultural Experiment Station.

Todd, D., and D. Weisman. 2010. *The Texas Legacy Project: Stories of Courage & Conservation*. College Station: Texas A&M University Press.

Tuttle, Suzanne. 2000. The Prairie Systems of North Central Texas. Curriculum, chap. 3. Fort Worth Nature Center & Refuge.

Unique Wildlife Ecosystems of Texas. 1979. Albuquerque, NM: US Fish and Wildlife Service.

USDA, Farm Service Agency. 2011. *Final Programmatic Environmental Assessment for Voluntary Public Access Habitat Incentive Program State of Texas*. https://www.fsa.usda.gov/Internet/FSA_File/txpeafonsi.pdf.

USDA, Natural Resources Conservation Service. n.d. Major Land Resource Area (MLRA). Accessed February 23, 2015. http://www.nrcs.usda.gov/wps/portal/nrcs/detail/soils/survey/?cid=nrcs142p2_053624.

Vegetation/Cover Types of Texas. 2000. Austin: Bureau of Economic Geology, University of Texas at Austin.

Weniger, Del. 1984. *The Explorers' Texas: The Lands and Waters*. Austin: Eakin Press.

White, M. 2006. *Prairie Time: A Blackland Portrait*. College Station: Texas A&M University Press.

Additional Resources

Austin, M. E. 2006. Land Resource Regions and Major Land Resource Areas of the United States, the Caribbean Basin, and the Pacific Basin. *Agriculture Handbook* 296. Washington, DC: USDA Soil Conservation Service. Map and legend available at http://www.nrcs.usda.gov/Internet/FSE_DOCUMENTS/nrcs143_018672.pdf.

Bailey, R. G., P. E. Avers, T. King, and W. H. McNab, eds. 1994. Ecoregions and Subregions of the United States (map). USDA Forest Service, Washington, DC. [1:7,500,000. With supplementary table of map unit descriptions, compiled and edited by W. H. McNab and R. G. Bailey.] Map available at http://www.fs.fed.us/land/ecosysmgmt/ecoreg1_home.html. http://www.fs.fed.us/land/ecosysmgmt/index.html

Behler, John L., and F. Wayne King. 1988. *National Audubon Society Guide to North American Reptiles and Amphibians*. New York: Alfred A. Knopf.

Bezanson, D. 2000. Natural Vegetation Types of Texas and Their Representation in Conservation Areas. Master's thesis, University of Texas at Austin.

Blair, W. F. 1950. The Biotic Provinces of Texas. *Texas Journal of Science* 2:93–117. [Classic work giving the major faunal/vegetation/soil/climate provinces and districts of Texas.]

Brown, D. E., ed. 1982. *Biotic Communities of the American Southwest—United States and Mexico. Desert Plants.* Vol. 4, nos. 1–4. [An excellent community-based treatment for Texas west of 103 degrees.]

Doughty, R. W. 1983. *Wildlife and Man in Texas: Environmental Change and Conservation.* College Station: Texas A&M University Press.

Francaviglia, R. V. 2000. *The Cast Iron Forest: A Natural and Cultural History of the North American Cross Timbers.* Austin: University of Texas Press.

Fulbright, Timothy, and Fred Bryant. 2002. *The Last Great Habitat.* Kingsville: Caesar Kleberg Wildlife Research Institute, Texas A&M University.

Gould, F. W., G. O. Hoffman, and C. A. Rechenthin. *Vegetational Areas of Texas.* 1960. Austin: Center for American History, University of Texas at Austin.

Graham, G. L. 1992. *Texas Wildlife Viewing Guide.* Helena, MT: Falcon Press.

Gunter, A. Y., and M. Oelschlaeger. 1997. *Texas Land Ethics.* Austin: University of Texas Press.

Hauser, V. *Rivers of Texas.* College Station: Texas A&M University Press.

Hodge, Larry. 2000. *Official Guide to Texas Wildlife Management Areas.* Austin: Texas Parks and Wildlife Press.

Hunt, C. B. 1974. *Natural Regions of the United States and Canada.* San Francisco: W. H. Freeman. [Classic textbook describing the major landforms and geological and physiographic subdivisions of the continent.]

James, L. 2000. *Fragmented Lands: Changing Land Ownership in Texas.* The Agriculture Program, Agricultural Communications. College Station: Texas A&M University System. http://www.texas-wildlife.org/images/uploads/Fragemented_Land_study_IRNR.pdf.

Natural Resource Conservation Service. 2008. General Soil Map of Texas and Texas Soil Survey. Temple, TX: US Department of Agriculture. http://www.nrcs.usda.gov/wps/portal/nrcs/surveylist/soils/survey/state/?stateId=TX.

Omernik, J. M. 1987. Level II and IV Ecoregions of the Continental United States. Map (Scale 1:7,500,000). *Annals of the Association American Geographers* 77 (1): 118–25. Map revised November 2000. http://www.epa.gov/wed/pages/ecoregions/level_iii.htm. [This nationwide ecoregional framework, currently at level III, is an effort to provide a standardized basis for ecologically based planning and monitoring among federal and participating state and other governmental agencies.]

Parent, Laurence. 1997. *Official Guide to Texas State Parks.* Austin: Texas Parks and Wildlife Press.

Phelan, R., and J. Bones. 1996. *Texas Wild: The Land, Plants, and Animals of the Lone Star State.* New York: P. Dutton.

Preserving Texas' Natural Heritage. 1978. LBJ School of Public Affairs Policy Research Project Report 31. Austin: University of Texas at Austin.

Schmidly, D. J. 2002. *Texas Natural History: A Century of Change*. Lubbock: Texas Tech University Press.

Texas Parks and Wildlife Department. 1977. *Unique Wildlife Ecosystems of Texas*. Albuquerque, NM: US Fish and Wildlife Service.

———. 1999. *Exploring Texas: Features of the South Texas Plains Region*. http://www.tpwd.state.tx.us/expltx/sotx/sotxchart.htm. [no longer available]

———. 2002. *Region 5—Coastal Sand Plains*. http://www.tpwd.state.tx.us/nature/ecoreg/pages/cstsand.htm. [no longer available]

Texas State Historical Association. 2012. *Texas Almanac: 2012–2013*. Denton: University of North Texas.

Texas Threatened and Endangered Species. [Current list with ecoregion location(s) available from Texas Parks and Wildlife Department, Wildlife Diversity Branch, 1-800-792-1112.]

Truett, J. C., and D. W. Lay. 1984. *Land of Bears and Honey: A Natural History of East Texas*. Austin: University of Texas Press.

Wilkins, N., W. Grant, E. Gonzalez, A. Hays, M. Kjelland, D. Kubenka, J. Shackelford, and D. Steinbach. 2003. *Texas Rural Lands: Trends and Conservation Implications for the 21st Century*. College Station: Texas Cooperative Extension, Texas A&M University System; and San Marcos: American Farmland Trust.

Williams, John E. 1976. *Natural Areas Survey Project*. Austin: LBJ School of Public Affairs, University of Texas at Austin.

UNIT 5

Ecological Concepts

LOUIS VERNER (retired)
Texas Parks and Wildlife Department, with contributions from Antoinette Villarreal and Mark White

Unit Goals

After completing this unit, volunteers should be able to

- explain the ecological principles that apply to individual organisms, populations, communities, and ecosystems
- explain the balances that exist between ecosystems and the factors necessary to keep ecosystems in balance
- explain how different ecosystems are determined largely by different environmental factors
- describe the hydrologic cycle, the nitrogen cycle, and the carbon cycle
- explain succession and climax and list the factors responsible for each
- illustrate a food web and explain the importance of trophic relationships
- define biodiversity and understand the importance of managing for biodiversity
- identify ecological factors relevant to a threatened species
- understand the laws and procedures necessary for protecting species

"The Laws of Ecology:
Everything is connected.
Everything must go somewhere.
Nature knows best.
There is no such thing as a free lunch."
—Barry Commoner, 1971

"When we try to pick out anything by itself we find it hitched to everything else in the universe."
—John Muir, early naturalist and founder of Sierra Club

Defining Ecology

The term **ecology** is derived from the Greek word for house or household, *oikos*, and the English suffix, *-logy*, which denotes a field of study or academic discipline. First defined by the German zoologist Ernst Haeckel in 1866, it literally means the study of households (of nature). Haeckel wrote, "By ecology we mean the body of knowledge concerning the economy of nature—the investigation of the total relations of the animal both to its inorganic and its organic environment." A perusal of more recent texts reveals that Haeckel's basic definition persists to this day, with most focusing on the key importance of *relationships* and *interactions*. Examples include definitions by C. J. Krebs (2009), "Ecology is the scientific study of the interactions that determine the distribution and abundance of organisms," and R. Brewer (1988), "Ecology is the study of the relationships of organisms to their environment and to one another." A somewhat different definition offered by E. P. Odum (1963) stressed the then-emerging systems approach: "Ecology is the study of the structure and function of ecosystems."

"And what is the meaning of so tiny a being as the transparent wisp of protoplasm that is a sea lace, existing for some reason inscrutable to us—a reason that demands its presence by the trillion amid the rocks and weeds of the shore? The meaning haunts and ever eludes us, and in its very pursuit we approach the ultimate mystery of Life itself."
—Rachel Carson, Edge of the Sea

The definition of ecology as offered by the early English ecologist Charles Elton (1927, 1) is an especially appealing one to any Master Naturalist. He defined ecology as "scientific natural history." Natural history—particularly the observations and descriptions of plants and animals—as described by naturalists of the seventeenth, eighteenth, and nineteenth centuries, provided a good background for the emerging field of ecology in the twentieth century. What allowed for the transition to "scientific" natural history was Charles Darwin's theory of evolution. Specifically, his concept of natural selection provided a mechanism to explain how populations of organisms change, adapt, and evolve within an ever-changing environment. In the unifying framework of natural selection, ecologists go beyond merely describing the varied and amazing behaviors and adaptations of organisms to providing us with logical explanations of their evolutionary origins and purpose.

Levels of Biotic Organization

While early naturalists were most often interested in describing the adaptations of individual organisms, ecologists frequently investigate relationships and interactions at the following higher levels of **biotic organization** (note that these terms have very specific ecological meanings that differ from their common usage):

- **Population:** A group of organisms belonging to the same species occupying a particular area at the same time
- **Community:** An association of interacting populations usually associated with a given place in which they live, such as the riffle community of a freshwater stream

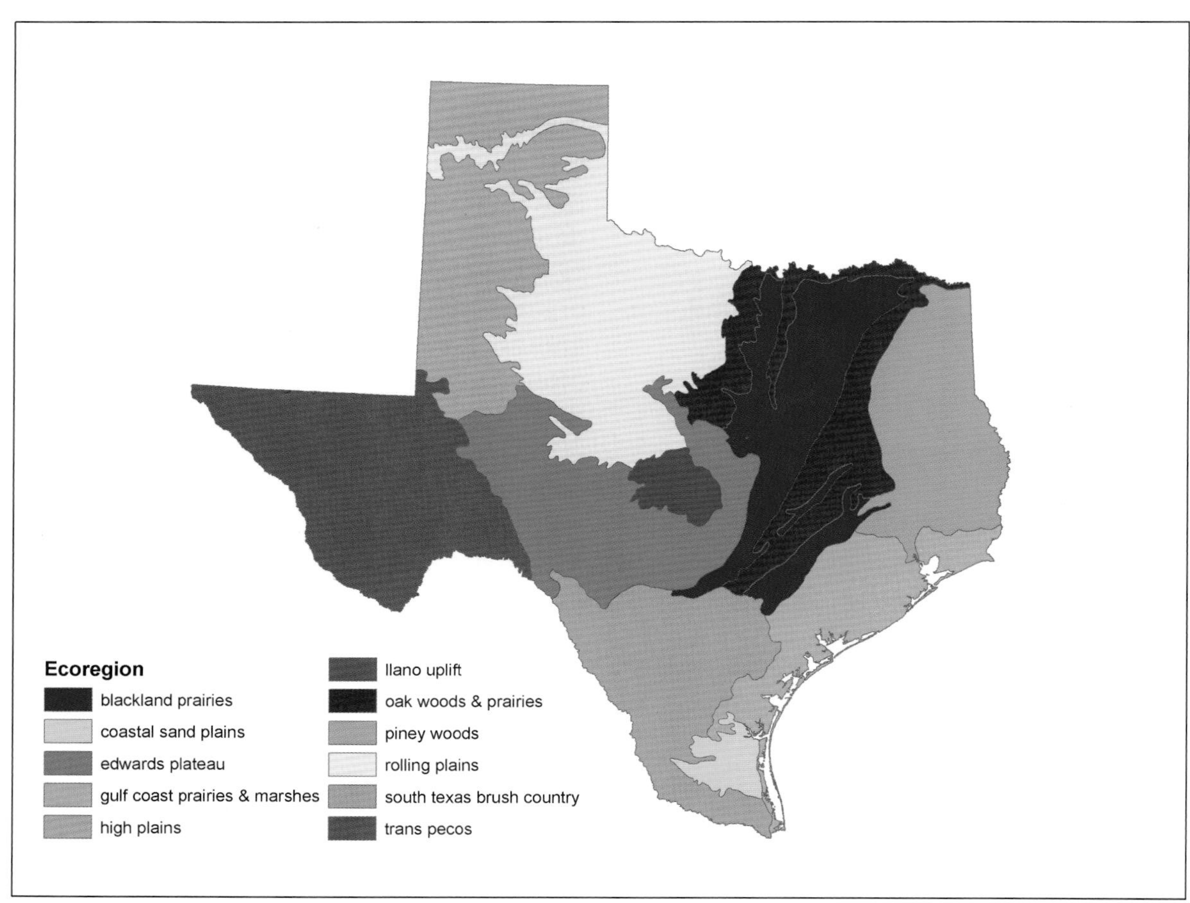

Ecoregions of Texas.

Major habitat types of the United States and Canada

- 1.1 Tropical Moist Broadleaf Forests
- 1.2 Tropical Dry Broadleaf Forests
- 2.1 Temperate Broadleaf and Mixed Forests
- 2.2 Temperate Coniferous Forests
- 3.1 Temperate Grasslands, Savannas, and Shrublands
- 3.2 Flooded Grasslands
- 4.1 Mediterranean Forests, Woodlands, Savanna, and Scrub
- 4.2 Deserts and Xeric Shrublands
- 6.1 Taiga and Boreal Forests
- 6.2 Tundra

Major habitat types of North America, a conservation assessment. From Ricketts et al. (1999)

Biosphere	That portion of the earth and its atmosphere in which life occurs and the physical-chemical environment in which it is surrounded.
Biome	Large areas with more or less the same type of abiotic and biotic factors create major ecosystems also called biomes.
Landscape	A mosaic of interacting ecosystems found over a relatively small geographic scale.
Ecosystem	An ecological system. The biological community of a given area and the physical environment with which it interacts.
Community	An association of interacting populations usually associated with a given place in which they live,
Population	A group of organisms belonging to the same species occupying a particular area at the same time.
Organism	An individual of a species.

Levels of ecological organization. Courtesy of Christine Kolbe

- **Ecosystem:** An ecological system; the biological community of a given area and the physical environment with which it interacts
- **Landscape:** A mosaic of interacting ecosystems found over a relatively small geographic scale
- **Biome:** A major, typical ecosystem composed of the same kinds of abiotic and biotic factors spread over a large area
- **Biosphere:** That portion of the earth and its atmosphere in which life occurs, along with the physical-chemical environment in which it is embedded

A cautionary note: These levels of biotic organization are often so ordered and imply a sense of increasing scale. Excluding the biosphere, which clearly does encompass the entire planet, any of the other terms may apply to any number of physical scales. Perhaps most familiar is the concept of an "ecosystem within a drop of pond water." While it is erroneous to think that the numerous organisms found in such a drop would be self-sustaining over any length of time, it is nevertheless true that functioning populations, communities, ecosystems, and even landscapes can be found within small confines, including individual organisms.

Ecosystem Characteristics

Master Naturalists will become better acquainted with the structure and functioning of the wide range of ecosystems across the state of Texas. But most important, they will also gain a greater understanding of the local ecosystem(s) where they live and will work as a Master Naturalist volunteer, including the ways in which each major component of the system interacts and depends on the rest to maintain the overall health of that system.

Climate

When any ecosystem is examined, it is clear that we can first organize it on the basis of its **biotic** (living) vs. **abiotic** (nonliving) components. Two important abiotic features common to all ecosystems are climate (regional patterns of temperature, precipitation, and wind) and nutrients (those chemical elements and compounds necessary to sustain life). We examine the role of

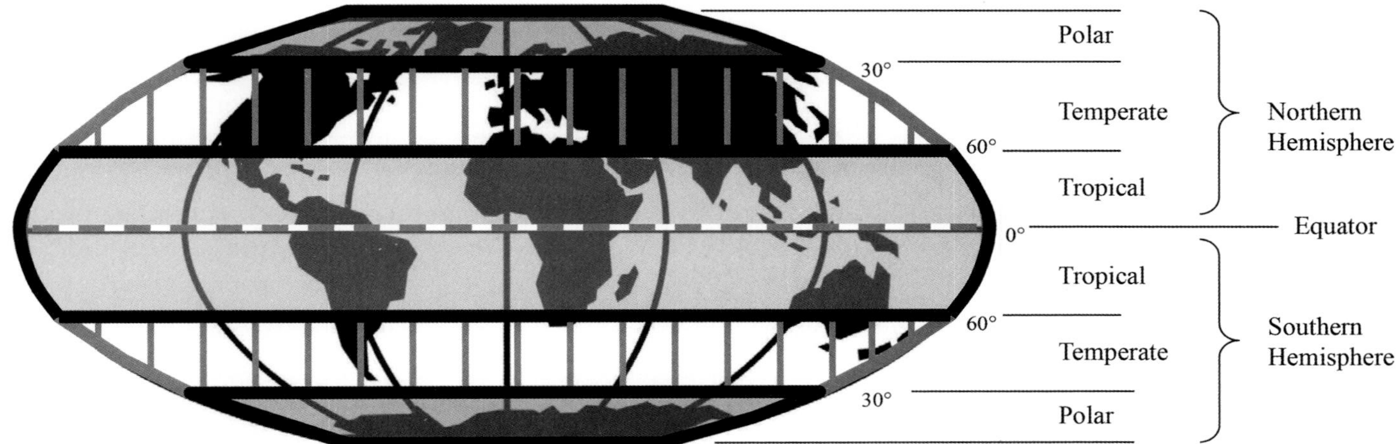

Map of the earth's climatic zones.

nutrients in a later section, but first we look at climate. On a large geographic scale, it is interesting to note that the world's major terrestrial ecosystems, often referred to as biomes, can be delineated almost entirely on the basis of mean annual temperature and precipitation. What role do you think these two climatological variables play in determining the 11 ecoregions of Texas?

Organisms of a given biome often exhibit unique adaptations reflective of their abiotic environment. For example, can you think of at least three features of desert plants (such as cacti) that have evolved in response to hot, arid conditions? How about desert animals, such as amphibians, reptiles, and small mammals? Organisms that are not closely related often exhibit similar adaptations to similar environmental conditions. This is known as **convergent evolution**. New and Old World rodents, and even the distantly related marsupials of Australia, look remarkably alike and share many of the same physiological and behavioral water-conserving adaptations in response to life in similar but widely separated desert habitats.

Trophic Relationships

To early twentieth-century ecologists, it became apparent that the most obvious functional relationship linking organisms together in any ecosystem was food based. Feeding or **trophic** relationships delineated who ate whom in order to obtain the energy and nutrients necessary for survival. Hence, any community of organisms could be organized on the basis of the following trophic levels:

- **Producers:** Those organisms capable of producing their own food, primarily by fixing energy from the sun via photosynthesis. These autotrophs (self-feeders),

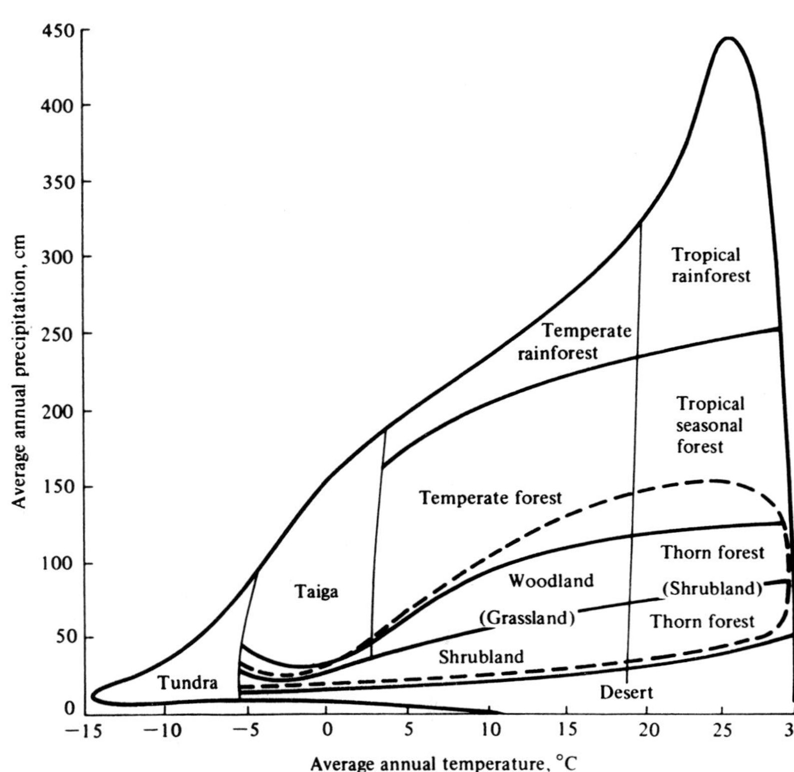

Precipitation and temperature gradients and relation to vegetation types. From Whittaker (1975)

including most plants as well as many bacteria and protists (single-celled organisms or eukaryotic microorganisms), then serve as the primary energy source for the rest of the biosphere.

- **Herbivores:** Those organisms obtaining their energy directly from autotrophs. They are also referred to as primary consumers.
- **Primary carnivores** (secondary consumers): Those organisms obtaining their energy from herbivores.
- **Secondary carnivores** (tertiary consumers): Those organisms obtaining their energy from other carnivores. While one could conceivably continue "stacking up" carnivores in this fashion indefinitely, we will soon find out why ecosystems rarely exceed four trophic levels.
- **Detritivores:** Also known as decomposers, these organisms obtain their energy from dead organisms. Through their actions, the building blocks of life are returned to the environment in their elemental form to be used over and over again. While often not considered a distinct trophic level, detritivores are indispensable members of the biotic community.

Food Chains and Food Webs

A sequence of organisms, each of which feeds on the trophic level preceding it, forms a **food chain**. A Texas example might be hackberry leaf–hackberry emperor caterpillar–eastern wood-pewee–sharp-shinned hawk. In most communities, dozens to hundreds of such food chains exist and are interconnected in such a way as to form a **food web**. Were all such trophic interactions to be included, the resultant food web would be too complex to actually draw, so most depict only a select group of organisms, such as that illustrated by Varley's simplified food web of an oak woodlot in England (Varley et al. 1973).

A simplified food chain with one consumer.

This food web (which is a mix of both specific and generic organisms) illustrates several complexities about trophic organization. First, not all organisms fit neatly into a single trophic level. Voles and mice, for example, are placed between the herbivore and primary carnivore trophic levels because they eat both plants and insects and like many other animals, including ourselves, are considered **omnivores**. Second, while detritivore food webs are often considered separately, in reality so-called herbivore food webs and detritivore food webs usually interweave in complex ways. Finally, such food webs do not tell us much about which species are the most "important" either in terms of energy flow or the stability of that particular community.

Varley, for instance, found that of all the species he identified, only the tiny parasitic fly, genus *Cyzenis*, was capable of effectively keeping outbreaks of the winter moth in check. In large numbers, winter moth caterpillars, like those of the gypsy moth, can cause widespread defoliation of hardwood trees, especially oaks, negatively impacting the entire forest community. Severe outbreaks of the winter moth became more common following widespread use of pesticides after World War II. While pesticide-resistant strains of the winter moth quickly emerged, the same did not hold true for its primary natural control agent, *Cyzenis*.

Pyramids of Numbers and Biomass

General patterns began to emerge from studies of community structure based on trophic relationships. The first of these was that in many habitats, there were usually many more producers (plants) than herbivores, more herbivores than primary carnivores, and seldom more than a few secondary, or top, carnivores per unit area. Representing the declining numbers of individuals in each succeeding trophic level graphically produced a **pyramid of numbers**. See the example of such a pyramid for numbers of individuals in a 0.1-hectare (roughly 0.25-acre) summer grassland community.

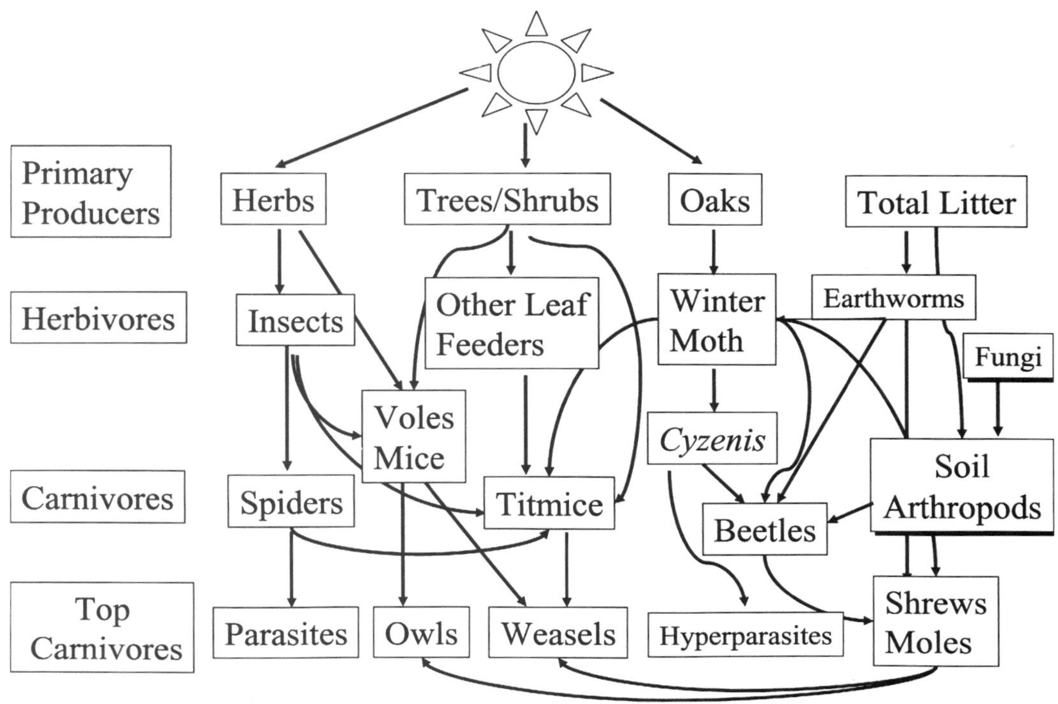

Simplified food web, Wytham Woods. From Varley et al. (1973)

It soon became obvious, however, that this pattern did not apply to all habitats. The following food web of Wytham Woods shows a partially inverted pyramid of numbers for a temperate forest. Forest communities are dominated by relatively small numbers of very large plants—trees. Each tree can support hundreds of herbivores, which in turn can collectively support thousands of primary carnivores. If one were to obtain the dry weight, or biomass, per unit area of each of these trophic levels, however, the resulting **pyramid of biomass** would assume its proper form, since the mass of a single tree clearly exceeds that of all the higher trophic levels it supports. The pyramid of biomass does seem to apply to most habitats, as seen in the following figures. However, data from some aquatic habitats indicated that even a pyramid of biomass could sometimes be inverted, with a smaller biomass of producers supporting a greater biomass of herbivores. How could this happen? It turns out that both the pyramid of numbers and of biomass are measuring static quantities; they are not taking time into account. In aquatic environments, primary produc-

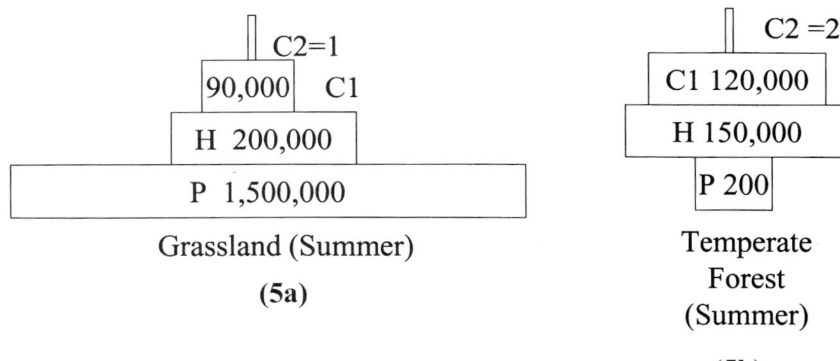

A pyramid of the numbers per trophic level of a 0.1-hectare habitat: A) grasslands in the summer months and B) temperate forest in the summer months.

A pyramid of the biomass per trophic level of a 0.1-hectare habitat for five different habitat types (C–G), expressed in grams of dry weight per square meter. Note the difference in biomass generated by the producers in the Wisconsin Lake habitat (96 g/m²) and that in the Panama Tropical Forest (40,000 g/m²).

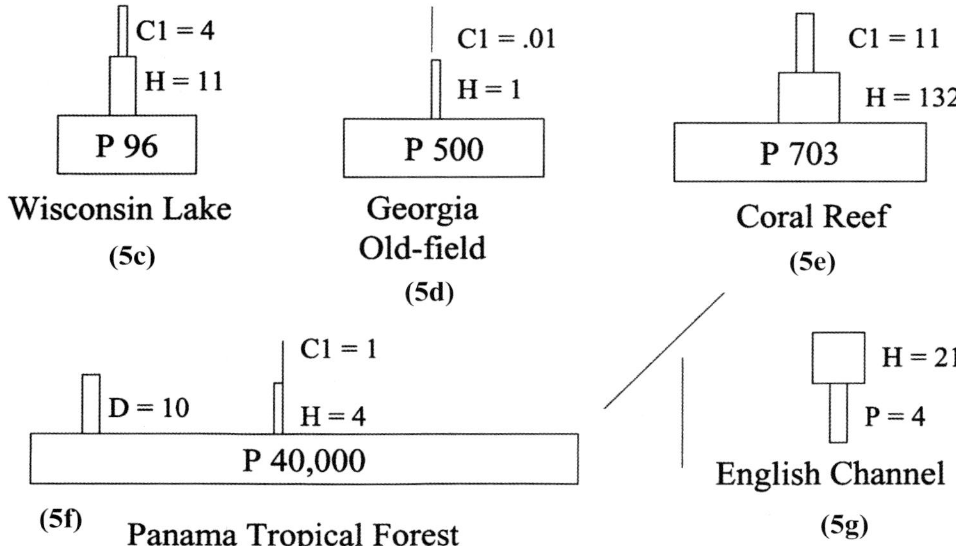

ers may be single-celled algal species that reproduce very rapidly, perhaps an order of magnitude more rapid than that of the herbivores. While their biomass at any point in time may be lower than that of the herbivores, over a given time period, say, a week or month, their total amount of biomass produced would in fact be much greater. An **energy pyramid**, showing the total amount of energy (biomass) fixed over time by each trophic level, would always show declining values at each higher level. This will become clear as we more closely examine the concepts of energy and energy flow through a community.

Energy Flow

For the sake of ecology, we are going to define **energy** as the capacity to do work. When you are "out of energy," your capacity to do work certainly feels limited. For all organisms, work includes not only doing something physical, such as running, flying, or vocalizing, but also maintaining basic life functions, such as cellular respiration, biochemical synthesis, and homeostasis (often lumped under the category of **metabolism**.) As long as they are alive, all organisms, from bacteria to plants to humans, must use stored energy to carry out these tasks and processes. Unless an organism can replenish the energy that is constantly being lost, it will die.

The original source of all energy utilized by organisms is the sun. Unfortunately, most organisms cannot use solar radiation, or light energy, directly to meet their energy needs. Only those organisms capable of photosynthesis, the process by which light energy is trapped and stored as chemical energy in the molecular bonds of carbohydrates (sugars), can accomplish this. Interestingly, less than 1% of the sun's light energy reaching the earth's atmosphere is converted into this available form of chemical energy by photosynthesis, yet it is responsible for all of the plant and animal productivity on the planet.

Unless this chemical energy stored in the cells of plants and animals enters long-term storage (this happened only once to any significant degree in the earth's history—during the Carboniferous period, some 330 million years ago, when all of our fossil fuels were formed), it is eventually oxidized (burned) in the process of respiration and degraded to heat, a low-grade form of energy no longer capable of performing biological work. For this reason we say that **energy flows** through an ecosystem. The daily influx of light energy from the sun that is fixed by the producers is roughly balanced by the daily outflow of heat produced by the myriad living, metabolizing organisms, ultimately radiating back into outer space.

Ecological Efficiencies

We can now go back and more closely examine the basic pattern we find in nature with regard to the pyramid of numbers and biomass. Why do most ecosystems support only 3 to 5 trophic levels—not 10, 20, or 100? Is that picture we have all seen of a tiny minnow being swallowed by a larger fish and that by a still larger fish, and so on until the last is swallowed by a great white shark false? In a word, yes! In order to see why, we need to follow a "packet" of energy as it makes its way from one trophic level to the next. As you will discover, the amount of energy produced at one trophic level is not transferred to the next trophic level with 100% efficiency. There are a number of ecological efficiencies that each play a role in reducing the amount of energy that makes it from one level to the next.

For purposes of illustration, we return to our 1,000 square meters (0.1 hectare) of grassland and assume that the amount of solar radiation captured by photosynthesizing plants is equal to 100,000 units per day. (Note: The standard unit of energy is the calorie; 1,000 calories equals a kilocalorie or kcal. Most ecological measurements of energy flow are in kcals, but for ease of calculation, actual unit values are not specified for this example.) In ecological terms, we would say that the plant community is fixing 100,000 units of energy per day. That amount is referred to as **gross primary production** (GPP). Is all of that energy available to the next trophic level, the herbivores? No. Plants must use some of that energy to meet their own metabolic needs. The amount of energy needed by plants for self-maintenance varies considerably—between 20% and 75% of what they produce. That leaves somewhere between 25% and 80% of the energy fixed in photosynthesis available for plant growth, or **net primary production**

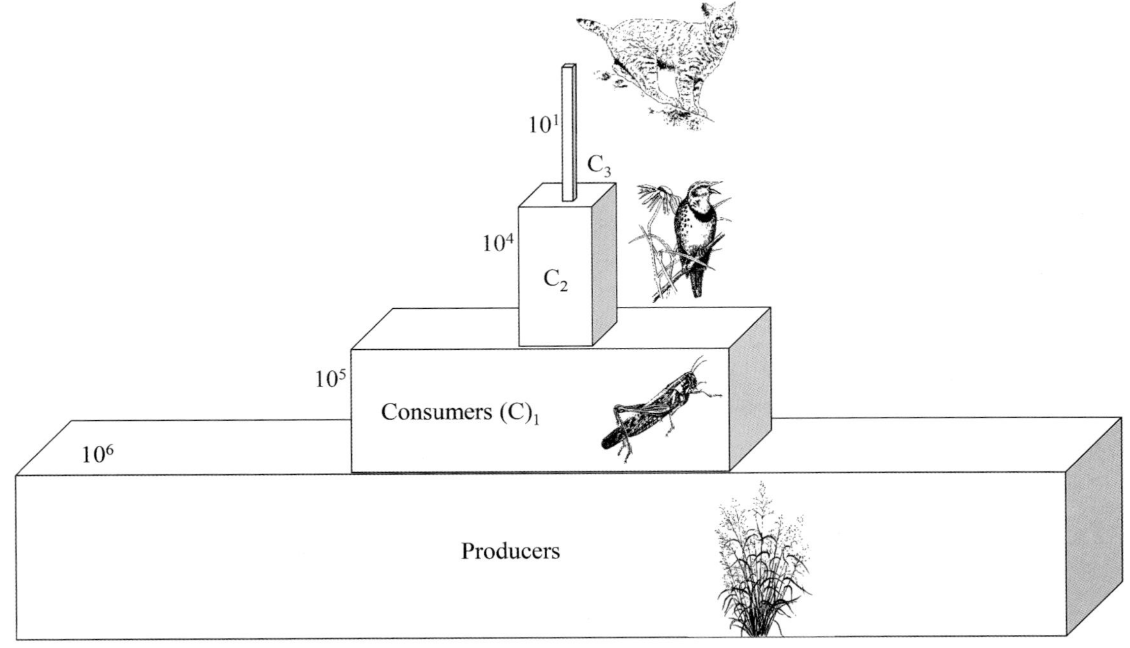

Pyramids of numbers and biomass. From Odum (1963)

(NPP). The ratio of net primary production to gross primary production is referred to as **net primary production efficiency**. Thus, the NPP efficiency for plants is between 25% and 80%. It is this reduced amount (somewhere between 25,000 and 80,000 units of energy), in the form of new plant biomass, that is potentially available for consumption by herbivores.

If we assume an NPP efficiency of 50% for our grassland example (actually typical for such ecosystems), the second tropic-level herbivores would have 50,000 units of energy available to them. But herbivores are not going to consume 100% of this daily plant production. The percentage of available plant material actually eaten is defined as **harvesting efficiency**. Harvesting efficiency of grassland herbivores varies between 5% and 30%. Let us assign a harvesting efficiency of 20% to our herbivores. That means they will eat (ingest) only 10,000 units of the NPP energy available (50,000 × 20% = 10,000). As you can see, we have already "lost" 90% of the energy we started with.

Let us continue to follow our packet of energy, now 10,000 units, as it proceeds through the herbivore trophic level. First, we have to be aware that consumers do not digest, or assimilate, everything they eat. Plant material, especially, has a lot of indigestible components, such as cell walls, so herbivores typically assimilate only about 30% to 60% of what they eat. This low **assimilation efficiency** means that the herbivores in our exercise will assimilate 3,000–6,000 units of energy. This value is also referred to as **gross secondary production** (GSP). What is the fate of the 4,000–7,000 units of energy that are not assimilated? They complete their passage through the digestive tract and are eliminated as fecal material, or **egestion**.

Not all of the energy assimilated by herbivores will result in growth (new animal tissue). Just as was the case for plants, a good deal of GSP must be used to meet the herbivore's basic metabolic needs. **Tissue growth efficiency** measures an organism's ability to convert GSP to **net secondary production** (NSP), or growth.

Here is where we see a significant difference between **ectotherms** and **endotherms**. You may know the former as "cold-blooded" and the latter as "warm-blooded" animals. Tissue growth efficiency is much higher for ectotherms (20%–50%) than for endotherms (1%–3%). Why are endotherms (birds and mammals) so inefficient? Maintaining an elevated body temperature turns out to be a metabolically expensive strategy for endotherms. It is a cost ectotherms do not have to worry about, so they can put this energy savings directly into growth.

If we apply the above tissue growth efficiencies to 5,000 units of herbivore GSP (recall that we calculated the value would be between 3,000 and 6,000 units), we can determine the amount of energy, in the form of new herbivore tissue, that will be available to the next trophic level, the primary carnivores. For ectothermic herbivores, like grasshoppers, that value will be 1,000–2,500 units of energy (5,000 × 20%–50%), while endothermic herbivores, like cottontail rabbits, will only produce 50–150 units of energy (5,000 × 1%–3%). You might want to reflect on these values when considering a diet for a hungry planet!

Some of you may have been rather incredulous that there are usually no more than three or four trophic levels in any ecosystem. A quick review of our energy flow calculations through just the first two trophic levels provides a pretty convincing rationale of why that is so. Starting with 100,000 units of energy photosynthesized by plants, we are left with only 50 to 2,500 units of energy in the form of herbivore biomass to feed a third trophic level of primary carnivores. That translates into a loss of somewhere between 97.5% and 99.95% of the original energy fixed by plants, hence the drastic reduction in both numbers and biomass observed in pyramids of numbers or biomass.

For the sake of completeness, we can calculate the amount of energy that might be available to a fourth and usually final trophic level of secondary carnivores. Let us generously assume that the primary carnivores are able to find and eat most all of the available herbivores, which we will further assume to be composed almost entirely of ectothermic insects. This allows us to assign a value of 2,000 units of energy ingested by these carnivores. Because animal tissue (meat) is more digestible than plant tissue (animal cells lack cell walls), carnivore assimilation efficiencies are higher, ranging between 60% and 90%. Taking the high value, we have 1,800 units of energy available for the carnivores' growth and metabolic needs. Employing the same tissue growth efficiencies as before, we end up with a production of 360–900 units of energy in the form of ectothermic primary carnivore tissue (1,800 × 20%–50%) and only 18–54 units of energy in the form endothermic primary carnivore tissue (1,800 × 1%–3%). How many secondary carnivores could be supported by this meager amount of primary carnivore tissue? Obviously, not many. So the fourth trophic level is usually drawn as a thin line, representing one or two individual secondary carnivores for an area of the size used in our illustration.

As a simplification, ecologists often employ the "10% rule" to illustrate the decline in available energy from one trophic level to the next. Doing the math, only one one-hundredth of 1% (0.01%) of the original amount of energy fixed by plants in a given area would be available to a possible fifth trophic (tertiary carnivores) level, which explains why one never sees them represented in energy flow diagrams. This low trophic level efficiency also accounts for the fact that "big, fierce animals," the top carnivores, are exceedingly rare. Since there is so little energy available per unit area, most top carnivores need to be highly mobile to cover the vast amount of territory needed to supply them with the energy needed to survive. Home ranges of wolves and mountain lions, for example, are on the order of 100–150 square miles. Their predatory activities often form energy links between neighboring ecosystems.

A mountain lion (*Puma concolor*), a carnivore and a consumer. Courtesy of Texas Parks and Wildlife Department

Nutrient Cycling

"For every atom lost to the sea, the prairie pulls another out of the decaying rocks. The only certain truth is that its creatures must suck hard, live fast, and die often, lest its losses exceed its gains."
—Aldo Leopold

The never-ending quest for energy is an important determinant of many of the unique and peculiar traits of organisms (e.g., weapons, armor, speed, poison, venom, mimicry, and camouflage). But life does not live on energy alone. In addition to the basic building blocks of oxygen, carbon, hydrogen, nitrogen, phosphorus, and calcium, which account for approximately 99% of living tissue, at least 20 other elements have been found to be essential to life. Many of these nutrients, including nitrogen and phosphorus, are in limited supply in the environment, and their availability may play a key role in determining ecosystem productivity.

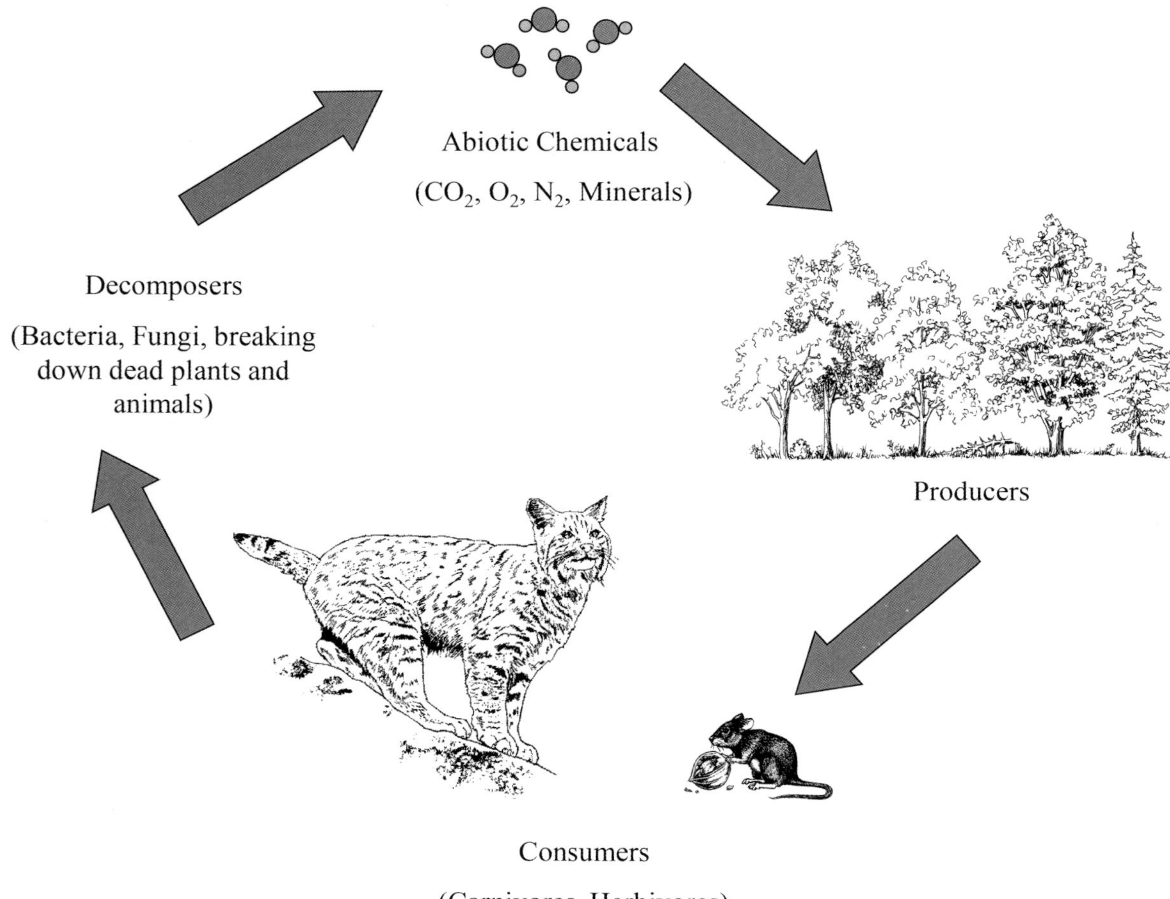

Nutrient cycling.

These elements move freely between the abiotic and biotic realms of an ecosystem. Plants take carbon dioxide from the air and water and nutrients from the soil to synthesize carbohydrates, proteins, and fats. Ingestion and assimilation by higher trophic levels incorporate these elements into the bodies of herbivores and carnivores. After death and decomposition, these nutrients are returned to their elemental form and again take up residency in the abiotic portion of the environment.

This continuous circulation of essential organic elements thus becomes a second important aspect of ecosystem function. Note that unlike energy, which flows through an ecosystem, organic elements are continually recycled. Some of the elements of which your body is currently (and temporarily) composed may well have resided in a dinosaur 100 million years ago or in the primordial bacteria that first colonized the planet over three billion years ago. Take these elements back further in time and we are all star dust!

Nutrient cycles are more formally referred to as **biogeochemical cycles**. This term emphasizes the fact that the biological (*bio*) realm and the geological (*geo*) realm are inextricably interconnected through the movement of these essential *chemical* elements. Of the many that exist, the most frequently detailed biogeochemical cycles are those of carbon, nitrogen, phosphorus, and sulfur, not surprisingly, given the magnitude of their importance to all organisms. Common to all is the presence of either a gaseous or sedimentary reservoir of the essential nutrient and a change in the chemical nature of the element as it passes through each step of the cycle. Sulfur and phosphorus are two important elements characterized by the fact that their main reservoir is found in sedimentary rock. Those wishing to learn more about these and other nutrient cycles are encouraged to do so by consulting any good ecology text or the Internet. For our example, we will now examine the details of the **nitrogen cycle**, a good representative of a gaseous cycle nutrient.

The Nitrogen Cycle

"The more flesh, the more worms."
—Hillel

Nitrogen is the fourth most common element in organisms, after oxygen, carbon, and hydrogen. With the exception of woody plants, proteins compose about 50% of the dry weight of organisms. Amino acids are the building blocks of proteins, and all (there are 20 common ones) include an amino group ($-NH_2$) as part of their basic structure. Nitrogen, however, does not exist freely in this form. In fact, outside biological processes, nitrogen exists almost entirely in its stable, very nonreactive gaseous form, N_2. The earth's atmosphere, which is 78% N_2, is the vast reservoir for this critical element. Even though terrestrial life is literally bathed in it, organisms cannot make use of this nitrogen unless it is first "fixed."

Nitrogen Fixation

Nitrogen fixation is the process of converting N_2 to either ammonia (NH_3) or nitrate (NO_3). Because N_2 is such a stable molecule, it takes a lot of energy to make this conversion. Lightning is good source for this high energy, and passing through the atmosphere, it can result in the electrical fixation of nitrogen with oxygen, forming nitrate. These nitrates are carried to the earth in rainwater and typically account for somewhere between 5% and 10% of the total amount of nitrogen fixed per unit area. Most nitrogen fixation is accomplished by a variety of terrestrial and aquatic microorganisms, especially by both free-living and symbiotic bacteria, a process known as **biological fixation**. These organisms convert N_2 to ammonia.

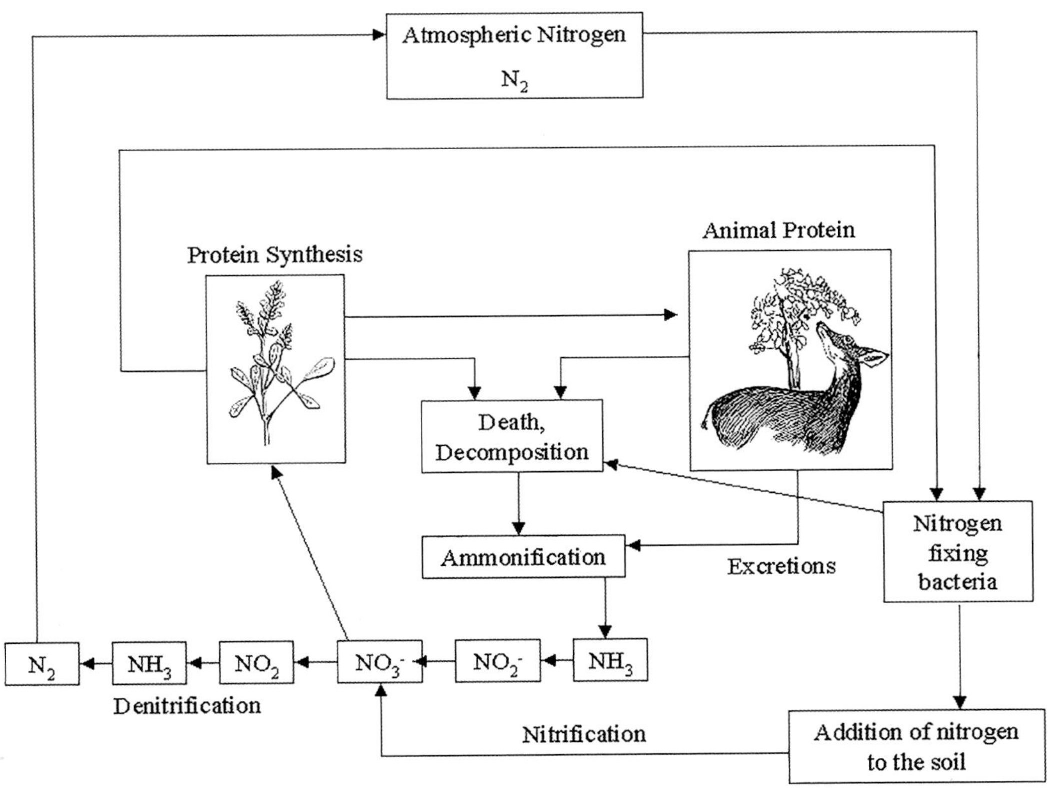

The nitrogen cycle. Courtesy of Christine Kolbe

In many terrestrial environments, legumes (members of the pea and bean family) are the primary plants that harbor symbiotic nitrogen-fixing bacteria in their root nodules. Both organisms benefit from this relationship. The bacteria, commonly of the genus *Rhizobium*, tap into the plant's stored food, acquiring the energy necessary to carry out fixation, while the legume benefits by having access to the excess ammonia produced beyond the needs of the bacteria. This explains why legumes are high in protein and why legumes like alfalfa, soybeans, clover, and vetch are planted as cover or rotational crops.

Not only does *Rhizobium* provide for its own nitrogen needs and that of the legume, but it may actually return as many as 250 pounds per acre of nitrogen compounds to the soil annually. These soil-based nitrogen compounds are available for uptake by the entire plant community, which will incorporate them into various nitrogenous plant structures (primarily proteins) and find their way to higher trophic levels through herbivory and carnivory.

Ammonification

Like fats and carbohydrates, animal proteins can be used as a source of biological fuel. When a protein's amino acids are catabolized (broken down for purposes of releasing energy), one of the products produced is ammonia. Because ammonia is toxic to the nervous system and its accumulation would rapidly lead to death, animals must excrete this waste product. It may be voided directly (fish), or it may first be converted to a less toxic form. Most mammals, including humans, convert it to urea, while most birds, reptiles, and invertebrates convert it to a more solid form, uric acid. Both of these compounds are the source of energy for another group of bacteria that convert them back to ammonia in a process known as **ammonification**. Upon death, this same process will similarly release ammonia as one of the breakdown products of protein catabolism. At this point in the biogeochemical cycle, nitrogen has left the organic realm and returned to an inorganic form.

Nitrification

While ammonification returns nitrogen once again to a form immediately usable by plants, ammonia is often further acted upon by two separate groups of soil-living bacteria (again as means of obtaining energy) before that can happen. The first group of bacteria converts ammonia to **nitrite** (NO_2), and the second group converts nitrite to **nitrate** (NO_3). Nitrate (in solution) is readily absorbed by a plant's roots and accounts for about 80% of a plant's nitrogen needs. This two-step process is known as **nitrification**. Because both of these compounds are negatively charged (**anions**), they readily bond to any number of positively charged **cations** present in the soil, such as potassium or magnesium, and precipitate out as various salts. These nitrogenous salts, such as potassium nitrate, are retained in the soil for a much longer time than ammonia and are therefore important components of a soil's fertility. Like table salt, nitrogenous salts readily dissociate in water, thus making the nitrate anion available for plant uptake after a rain.

Denitrification

Note that for the first time, nitrification results in compounds that pair nitrogen with oxygen. As you might expect, the bacteria responsible for these conversions must live in an **aerobic** environment—that is, there must be sufficient oxygen present in the soil's interstitial spaces for nitrification to proceed. Soils that have been compacted, waterlogged, or are otherwise **anaerobic**, often exhibit low plant productivity since production of nitrogenous salts is reduced or absent. Anaerobic conditions can set the stage for further depletion of soil productivity. Yet another group of bacteria, all anaerobes, obtain significant amounts of energy by converting nitrate or nitrite back to elemental nitrogen, N_2. While some may consider this process of **denitrification** "negative," or harmful in the sense that it lowers productivity, it does bring the nitrogen cycle full circle, thereby ensuring that atmospheric concentrations of nitrogen are maintained and that the system as a whole remains in balance.

The Hydrologic Cycle

While not considered a nutrient per se, water is a key constituent of life and the medium through which most nutrients are carried. The **hydrologic cycle** details the circulation of water between oceans, the atmosphere, and terrestrial ecosystems.

About five-sixths of the water that evaporates into the atmosphere comes from the earth's oceans, which cover 71% of its surface, but only three-fourths of global precipitation falls back on them. The difference, 8%–9%, is the precipitation that falls on land. In heavily vegetated areas, much of the precipitation is intercepted by plants and released back to the atmosphere as **evapotranspiration**. That which does not soaks into the ground or becomes surface runoff, creating our streams and rivers. Water that percolates through the soil may eventually reach an impermeable layer and reside there as **groundwater**. The upper surface of groundwater is referred to as the **water table**. Geological formations (permeable sand, gravel, or porous rock) that yield ground water in usable (in human terms) amounts are referred to as **aquifers**.

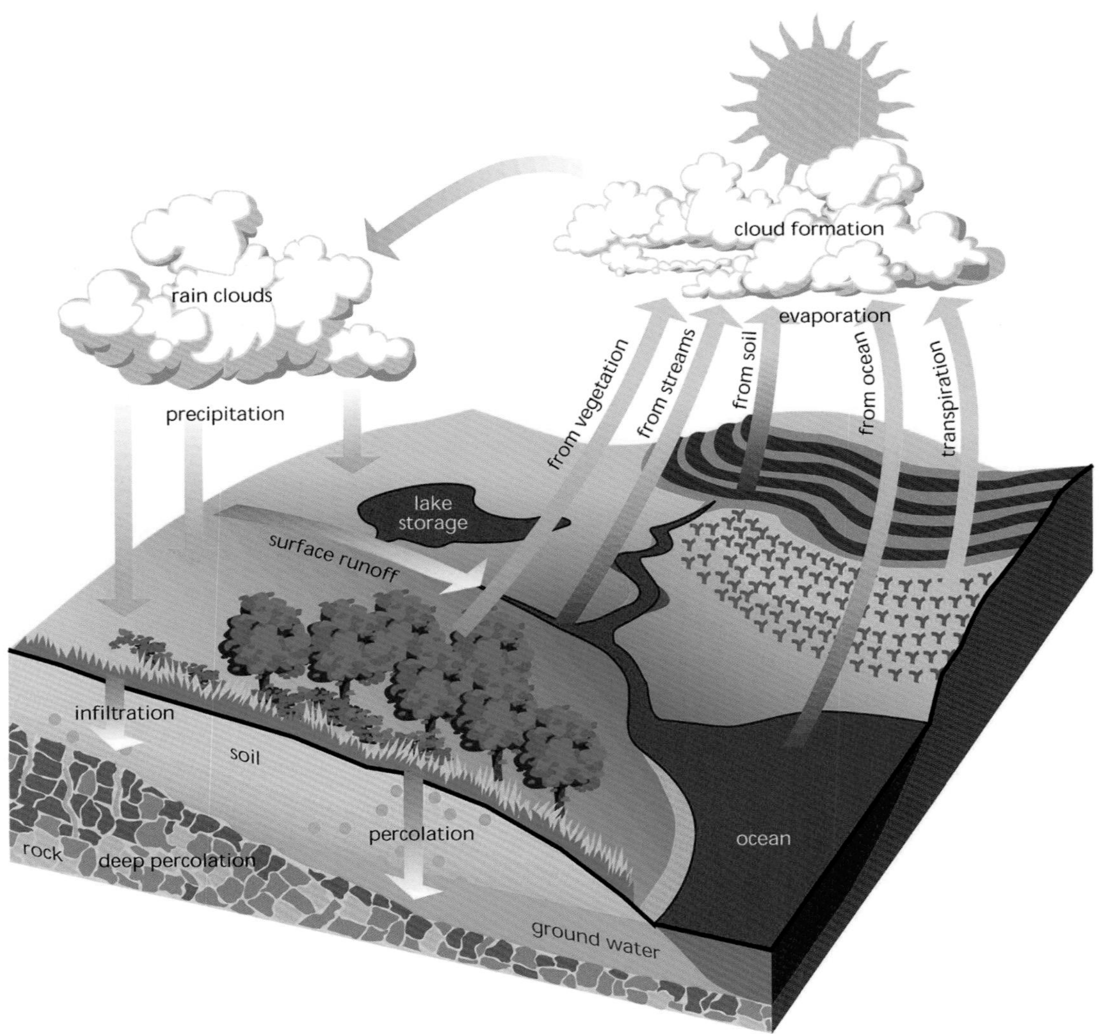

The hydrologic cycle. The transfer of water from precipitation to surface water and groundwater, to storage and runoff, and eventually back to the atmosphere is an ongoing cycle. Courtesy of US Department of Agriculture

The Ogallala Aquifer, the world's largest, stretches from southern South Dakota to northern Texas and is used to irrigate cropland responsible for a significant portion of the US agricultural and beef production. Current withdrawal rates greatly exceed the natural recharge rate, however, and this once great reservoir of essentially fossil water may become economically unavailable in the coming decades, thereby drastically altering this region's productivity. If not used along the way, all surface and groundwater eventually (over millions of years in the case of deep aquifers) makes its way back to the sea, thus completing the hydrologic cycle. Carried in solution will be many nutrients either leached from the soil or derived from the weathering of parental rock. These nutrients, such as phosphorus, will eventually be deposited in ocean sediments and will not enter a new biogeochemical cycle unless, and until, these deposits are again raised above sea level in a geological uplift.

The Carbon Cycle

Life-forms on earth are carbon based. Carbon is not only one of the major building blocks of all life (known to date), but it is inextricably bound to the way almost all organisms obtain their energy. For that reason the **carbon cycle** is sometimes referred to as the energy cycle. Plants take in carbon dioxide (CO_2) primarily from air and, when eaten, provide carbon to herbivores. Carnivores obtain their carbon from the animals that eat plants, and humans obtain their carbon from both plant and animal sources (omnivores). Decomposers obtain their carbon from the dead plants and animals they consume. Ultimately, all consumers and decomposers return most of the carbon back to the atmosphere.

In the process of burning our fossil fuels coal, oil, and gas, this carbon is now being returned to the environment as CO_2 at the rate of about seven billion tons per year. About half that amount seems to be accumulating in the atmosphere, and from this source of CO_2, an estimated one to two billion tons are used by plants in the process of photosynthesis to synthesize glucose, a simple carbohydrate or sugar. Simple sugars, the most basic form of food energy, can be further modified to form complex carbohydrates (starches) and various fats, oils, and proteins. Plants use some of these organic compounds for their own metabolic needs, thereby returning some carbon back to the environment as CO_2, but most is retained in the plant body. Herbivores (plant eaters) obtain their carbon (energy) from respiration, thus making it available once again to plants. That is the simple part of the cycle.

The more interesting part has to do with the amount of carbon that *is not* returned to the system as gaseous CO_2. Organic matter that escapes immediate decomposition may enter long-term storage as fossil carbon. This does not happen to any appreciable degree today, but vast quantities of carbon entered such long-term storage 285–350 million years ago in the oceans, and the remaining amount has most likely gone into increased plant biomass. The great majority of unoxidized carbon is not found in fossil fuels but in various carbonate rocks deposited as sediments on the bottom of lakes and oceans. Oceans are actually the single largest reservoir for CO_2, storing 60% more than the atmosphere.

When CO_2 dissolves in water, some of it forms carbonic acid that, in turn, may form various carbonates and bicarbonates. Because they are not very soluble, carbonates usually precipitate out and form sediments. One of the most common examples is calcium carbonate or limestone.

Implications for Management

Everyone has heard of the greenhouse effect and global warming. The **greenhouse effect** refers to the fact that gases (most prominently CO_2) in our upper atmosphere (troposphere) trap and hold radiant heat, much like the glass in a greenhouse. Increasing the

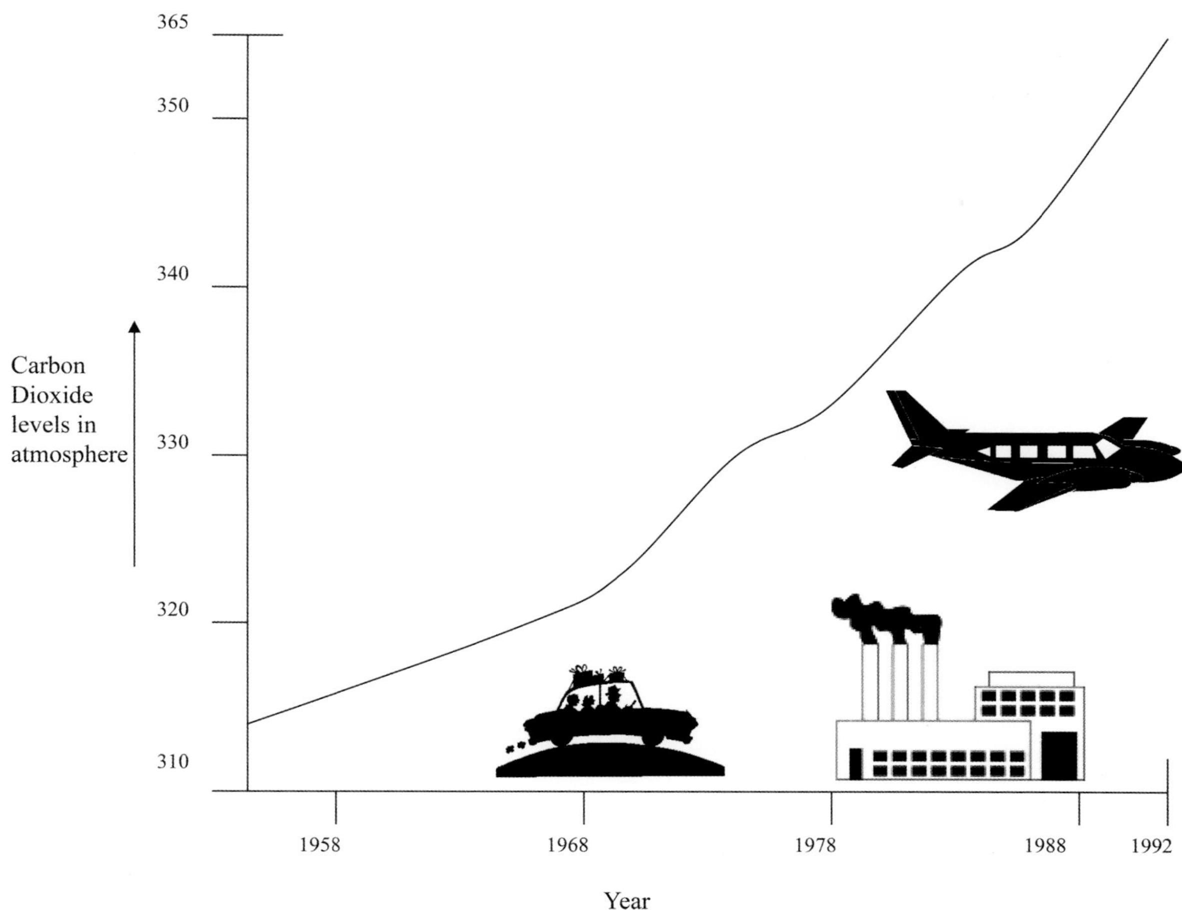

Increase in carbon dioxide in the environment.

concentration of greenhouse gases increases this heat retention. The vast majority of climatologists are now convinced that human activity, primarily the burning of fossil fuels, is directly responsible for the significant increases in greenhouse gas concentrations measured over the last 50 years (NASA 2015). If this trend continues, CO_2 levels could double by 2050, leading to a possible increase in global average temperature between 3.5°F and 9°F. The implications of such a temperature increase, at a rate 10–100 times faster than has occurred during the past 10,000 years, are profound. Hotter, drier conditions will negatively impact food production and water resources, increase the frequency and severity of storms and hurricanes, raise sea levels two to three feet (flooding coastal communities), and have a severe impact on most plant and animal communities.

If, for example, CO_2 levels do double by 2050, hardwood trees (and the entire assemblage of hardwood forest species) east of the Mississippi would have to shift 300 miles northward to find suitable climatological conditions. Plants and animals can, of course, shift their distributions in response to climate change, but following the retreat of the last ice age, northward movement of hardwood trees was only 12 miles per 100 years. The implication is that many members of those forest communities will simply not survive. In addition, there is concern that rising temperatures may set in motion a dangerous positive feedback or "runaway greenhouse" effect, causing a climate change that may not be possible to reverse.

The oceans serve as an important reservoir or sink for CO_2. However, as global temperatures rise, the ocean's ability to dissolve and hold CO_2 falls. Release of this oceanic

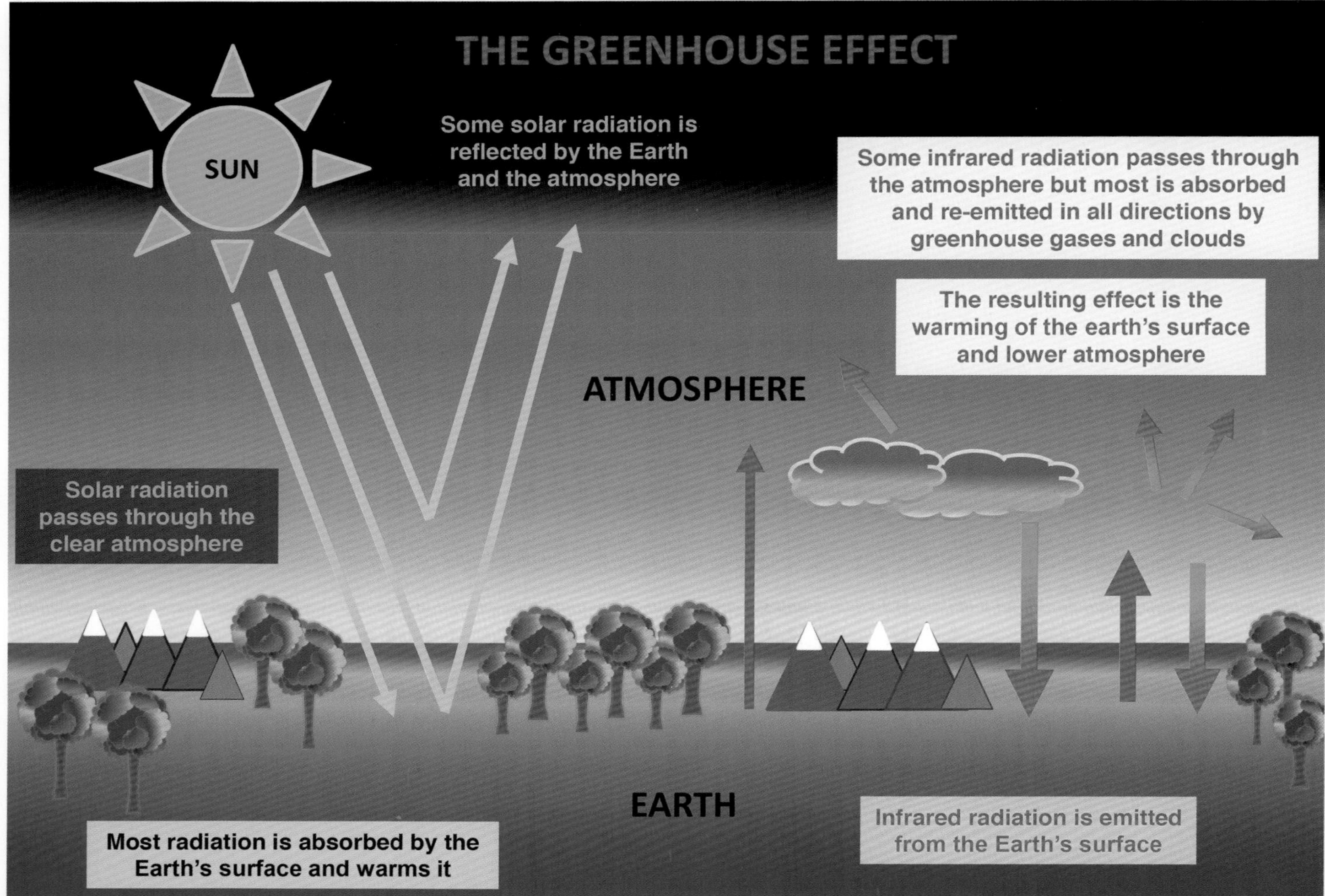

Greenhouse effect diagram. Courtesy of Christine Kolbe

CO_2 into the atmosphere will further accelerate the rate of change. Likewise, increasing temperatures on land will melt continental ice sheets, adding to rising ocean levels and exposing more dark, heat-absorbing landmass. It will also speed up decomposition rates, resulting in the release of even more CO_2. Finally, the continued destruction and burning of tropical forests exacerbates the problem twofold: deforestation directly contributes about one-fourth of the annual release of CO_2, and loss of these trees removes their ability to absorb excess CO_2. To at least partially offset rising CO_2 production, many countries have embarked on significant reforestation programs. Most experts agree, however, that significant reduction in the threat of global warming will not come without significant reduction in our use of fossil fuels.

Ecological Relationships

"A thing is right when it tends to preserve the integrity, stability, and beauty of the biotic community. It is wrong when it tends otherwise."
—Aldo Leopold

You have hopefully come to appreciate the importance of energy flow and nutrient cycling in providing a conceptual framework for the basic structure and function of ecosystems. But they alone do not explain the great diversity of life on the planet or the reasons for differences in the abundance and distribution of species. The remainder of this unit briefly examines **ecological relationships**, how interactions between and among individuals and species are equally critical to our understanding of ecology.

Niche versus Habitat

An organism's trophic relationships, its relative importance in the flow of energy, and the cycling of nutrients are important aspects of that species' role, or **niche**, in its biological community. Odum (1953) was careful to distinguish between the terms "niche" and "habitat." He equated the former to an organism's "profession" and the latter to its "address." Habitats are commonly referred to by the dominant vegetation in a given area, such as bottomland hardwood forest, desert scrub, or tallgrass prairie.

An example of niche is that the vegetation of a forest can support not only a large number of plant species as they occupy different niches—tall canopy trees, understory trees, shrubs, and grasses (because their heights vary, they differ in their requirements for sunlight and nutrients so survive together)—but also wildlife such as songbirds that occupy different elevations in the forest.

Ecologists more broadly define the niche of a species as the total of all its biotic and abiotic interactions within a given community, the range of conditions and resources within which any given species can persist.

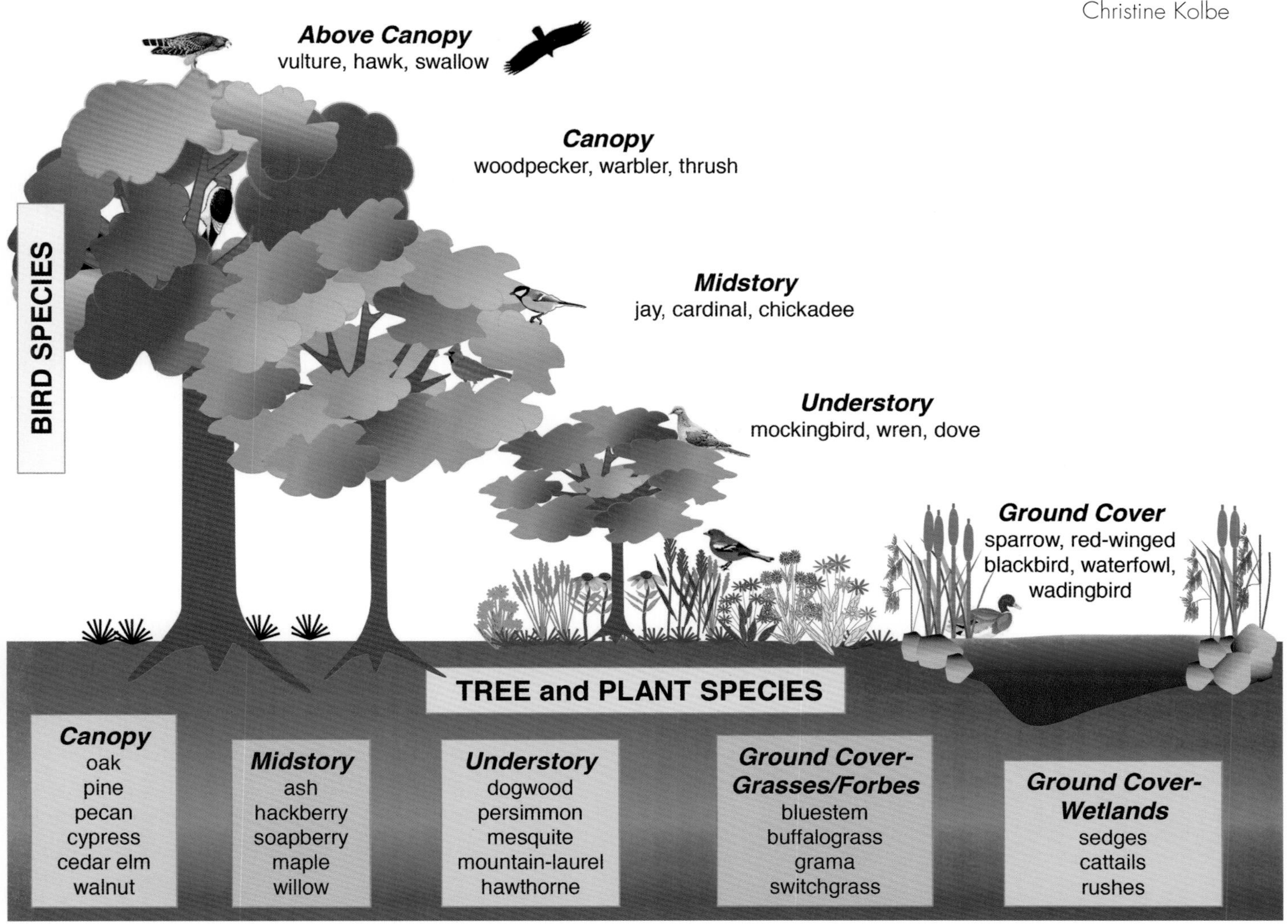

Species niches with birds. Courtesy of Christine Kolbe

When ecologists began to examine species' distributions within and between various habitats, they developed a number of niche-related hypotheses that seemed useful in describing the patterns they observed. The most basic and straightforward of these was first proposed by the Russian ecologist G. F. Gause (1934) and was often referred to as Gause's Rule or Gause's Principle. It states that two species cannot coexist on the same limiting resource. This concept was amplified by the American ecologist Garrett Hardin (1960, 1292), whose Competitive Exclusion Principle states that "complete competitors cannot coexist."

Species Interactions

What kinds of interactions exist among species? One way to answer this question is to determine what effect one species has on another's ability to survive and reproduce, how one species affects another's **fitness**. The table provides an exhaustive list of these possibilities.

For each described interaction, a zero (0) indicates that a species' fitness is neither increased nor decreased as a result of that interaction. A negative (–) indicates a decrease in that species' fitness as a result of interacting with the second, while a positive (+) indicates that a species' fitness increases as a result of the two-species interaction.

A coyote holding a cottontail. Courtesy of Texas Parks and Wildlife Department

Types of interactions and their effects

Interaction	Species	
	A	B
Neutralism	0	0
Competition	–	–
Amensalism	0	–
Predation	+	–
Commensalism	+	0
Protocooperation	+	+
Mutualism (obligatory)	+	+

Neutralism describes the case in which two species sharing the same habitat have no measurable effect on each other's fitness; a hawk and a soil invertebrate perhaps. This is assuredly a very common occurrence for many species sharing a given habitat but of little interest to those studying species interactions. **Competition** exists when two or more species (or individuals within a population) attempt to utilize a necessary resource in limited supply. Any use of a limited resource by one species means decreased availability to the other, and therefore competition is an interaction that always lowers the fitness of both species, hence the double negative.

Amensalism describes a two-species interaction in which the presence of one species negatively affects the other, but the first species neither gains nor loses fitness as a result. A herd of large animals walking over fragile plants would certainly reduce the plants' fitness without animals themselves being affected. **Predation** includes any interaction in which one species benefits by obtaining resources from another, to the latter's detriment. In addition to classic predator-prey interactions, it also includes herbivory and the many forms of parasitism.

A relationship wherein one species benefits from an interaction while the second remains unaffected is referred to as **commensalism**. One well-known example is the remora-shark relationship. Remora fish attach themselves to sharks (as well as other large oceanic predators) by means of a sucker on top of their head. They detach to feed on what the shark would otherwise leave behind during an act of predation and then reattach for a ride to their next meal. Cattle egrets similarly benefit by their close association with cattle, eating the various insects and small prey that are flushed by the cattle's movement.

Protocooperation and **mutualism** both describe interactions that benefit both species, with the latter being reserved for instances in which that relationship is obligatory. The coevolution of flowering plants and their pollinators is perhaps the most widespread and well-studied example of a whole class of plus-plus interactions, some of which are obligatory. The best-known example of mutualism is the symbiotic union of alga and fungus that forms lichens. Thanks to this association, lichens are able to flourish on bare rock and under extreme conditions intolerable to either the alga or fungus alone.

For years, the old dictum of "nature, red in tooth and claw" led many early ecologists to concentrate their attention on competition and predation as the two most important interactions shaping community structure. Examinations of both have indeed contributed extensively to our knowledge and understanding of community dynamics (see examples to follow), but ecologists have more recently begun to appreciate the degree to which win-win interactions (protocooperation and mutualism) also play a significant role in shaping communities.

Cascade Effects and Keystone Species

Interspecific interactions can affect the number of species present in a community and their relative abundance. **Cascade effects** may occur when the local extinction of one species significantly changes the population sizes of other species, potentially leading to other species losses. Such cascade effects are particularly likely when the lost species is a **keystone predator**, or a **keystone mutualist**. The following three examples illustrate this phenomenon.

In the rocky intertidal zone, the starfish, *Pisaster*, was shown to be a keystone predator (Paine 1974). When it was removed in a series of controlled experiments, the number of species in the community dropped from 15 to 8. In the absence of *Pisaster*, one of its favored prey species eliminated its inferior competitors and by doing so also brought about the demise of a second predator.

In the tropics, many plant-pollinator interactions are obligatory or mutualistic. There are over 900 species of figs (*Ficus* spp.) in the tropics, and each is pollinated by a single, unique species of wasp, so the loss of a fig species could wipe out one of the specialist wasps, or vice versa. But the following example illustrates that the loss of even one such keystone mutualist, such as the *Ficus* spp., could have far-ranging consequences. Manu National Park, located in southeastern Peru, is perhaps the planet's most biologically diverse World Heritage Site. A single tree of *F. pertusa* at Cocha Cashu in the

Ficus pertusa. Courtesy of Smithsonian Tropical Research Institute

Manu National Park had its figs eaten by 44 species of diurnal vertebrates over a 21-day period in a study done by Tello (2003).

On the other hand, an illustration of where the wasp could become the primary species in danger occurred in northern Borneo after the 1998 El Niño event caused severe droughts within the area. The local fig's production level plummeted. According the Tello, it took almost two years for the fig wasps in the area to recolonize into the affected regions, as they were locally extinct in some regions with the loss of fig trees.

Diversity of life in tropical coral reefs is among the highest recorded anywhere. Recent experimental studies indicate that the presence of so-called cleaner fish (wrasses), especially of the genus *Labroides*, may strongly influence that diversity. Common Pacific cleaner wrasses remain in specific locations within a reef (cleaning stations) and service a diverse number of larger fish, "clients." After advertising with a little "dance," a client fish will adopt a cleaning posture characteristic of that species. The cleaner wrasse will then go over the client, removing parasites, loose scales, and other debris. In small reefs where cleaner fishes were experimentally excluded for 18 months, overall fish species diversity declined 50%, and total abundance was reduced 75%. Removal of this one small (five to six inches), not very abundant fish resulted in a major breakdown of reef community structure, altering the movement patterns, habitat choice, and activity of a wide variety of reef fish species.

The lesson to be learned from these examples is that species interactions that appear inconsequential may end up being of profound importance in maintaining the diversity and stability of a given community. One could not have predicted any of the above outcomes solely on the basis of species abundance or energy flow. This is one reason why so many ecologists are worried about the continued worldwide decline in biodiversity. One never knows when the loss of a yet-to-be-identified keystone species may result in a cascade of effects that will further destabilize an ecosystem already at risk.

A cleaner wrasse (*Labroides dimidiatus*).

Population Dynamics

As illustrated in the preceding section, species interactions can have a profound effect on the number of individuals in a given population. **Demography** is the study of population dynamics. Clearly, many factors, both biotic and abiotic, can affect a population's size. Ultimately, though, we can track changes in **population density**, the number of individuals per unit area, by monitoring just four variables:

- **Natality:** the production of new individuals through either sexual or asexual reproduction
- **Mortality:** the loss of individuals through death
- **Immigration:** the movement of new individuals into a population
- **Emigration:** the movement of resident individuals out of a population

Even the more complex mathematical models for population growth (which we unfortunately must omit for the sake of brevity) are based on the following simple equation:

$$N_t + 1 = N_t + B + I - D - E$$

Verbally this reads: The number of individuals in a population at some unit of time in the future ($N_t + 1$) is equal to the current number of individuals (N_t) plus the number of new individuals recruited via reproduction (B) and immigration (I), minus the number lost to death (D) and emigration (E) over that unit of time.

If recruitment, "the process by which new individuals found a population or are added to an existing population" (Eriksson and Ehrlen 2008, 1), (B + I) exceeds loss (D + E), even by the smallest of margins over time, not only will the population grow, but it will grow exponentially (see discussion of population growth models that follows). If losses continue to exceed gains, a population will eventually go extinct. Population size will be stable only when B + I exactly equals D + E. The **growth rate** (*r*) of a population expresses the percent change of the initial population over some unit of time. Mathematically, $r = (B + I) \times (D + E) / N_t \times 100$. As an example, assume a population of 1,000 recruits 50 new individuals while losing 30 over the period of a year. This population's annual growth rate, *r*, would be 2%: (50 – 30) / 1,000 × 100 = 2.

Intrinsic versus Extrinsic Factors

In part, the job of population biologists and wildlife managers involves assigning values to each of these four variables to better predict population trends. Usually, this does not involve a direct count of individuals but rather an assessment of changes in rates—birth rates, death rates, and immigration and emigration rates. Some of the factors that influence these rates are **intrinsic** (internal) to the population itself, such as sex ratio, age distribution, age-specific survivorship and fecundity, and social structure. For example, a population comprising mostly young fertile individuals would be expected to grow much more rapidly in the future than a population with a high percentage of postreproductive individuals. For polygamous species, where a single male may mate with many females (white-tailed deer, for example), a population sex ratio skewed heavily toward males would have a much slower growth rate than one in which females outnumbered males.

There are numerous ways in which social structure may influence population growth. In some populations, as exemplified by certain species of salamanders, mating takes place in dense groups over a short one- or two-day period. This pattern, known as **explosive breeding**, requires a critical minimal number of individuals in order for successful mating to occur. A local population that slips below that threshold may be doomed to extinction, even though the remaining individuals are otherwise capable of reproducing. Territorial species, such as many of our songbirds, will behaviorally limit the number of breeding pairs allowed in a given habitat. Because territories are not compressible, the population will reach its upper limit when all available territories are occupied.

There are many **extrinsic** (external) factors that influence population size, including competition, predation, disease, pollution, hunting, and carrying capacity of the environment.

Carrying Capacity

Carrying capacity is a very important ecological concept. It is defined as the maximum number of individuals of a given species that a habitat can sustain indefinitely. When habitat quality improves, its carrying capacity increases. If it declines, so does the carrying capacity. This explains why both the quantity and quality of habitat are so critical to maintaining wildlife populations and why wildlife managers "manage" habitat as much as, or more than, they do wildlife.

What influences habitat quality? Habitat consists of the food, water, shelter, and spatial arrangement of resources needed by a given species for survival and reproduction. Because environments are dynamic rather

Cottontail with family. Courtesy of Texas Parks and Wildlife Department

than static, each of these habitat components is subject to constant change. When these changes are pronounced, they can dramatically affect population size. Note, however, that changes in a habitat's carrying capacity are species specific. Improving habitat quality for one species may lower the carrying capacity for other species in the same community.

A standardized measurement unit for animal consumption within their habitat can be calculated as an **animal unit** (AU). One AU is equal to the live weight of a cow and a calf, or 1,000 pounds (454 kilograms), under the assumption that animals of this weight consume a constant amount of forage (26 pounds of forage dry matter per day). The average weights of other various livestock and grazing animals can be compared to this standardized index. Using this index also allows managers to assess the balance between the number of animals consuming range vegetation and the ability of the vegetation to withstand foraging pressures. The limiting factor of using the animal unit as a stand-alone management tool is when comparing different target forage or browse species within one habitat, such as cattle and white tailed-deer. The AU equation fails to represent the potential carrying capacity of habitats where both animals forage for different vegetation (Bolen and Robinson 1995).

Population Growth Models

Across many taxa (numerous invertebrates, for example), populations frequently exhibit **exponential growth**. After a slow start, numbers begin to accelerate rapidly, essentially following a J-shaped curve upward.

As long as necessary resources are available, such populations will continue to expand until a change in environmental conditions brings about a cessation of growth, frequently followed by a crash to previously low densities. Growth of many insect populations continues in this manner throughout spring and summer until brought to a sudden halt by the first cold snap. Gause (1934), monitoring the growth rates of various laboratory protozoan populations, was one of the first to note the form of population growth—protozoan numbers would grow exponentially until a buildup of waste products became toxic, leading to a dramatic population collapse. Natural populations (not confined to artificial laboratory conditions as in Gause's experiments) that exhibit exponential growth are usually limited by factors that are not determined or affected by the population's density. These factors are therefore referred to as **density-independent**.

Populations of other species, exemplified by many long-lived vertebrates, may exhibit a **logistic growth** pattern, as shown in the graph. The S-shaped growth curve of these populations shows the effect of increasing **environmental resistance**. The greater the population size, the more the environment "pushes" against further growth. This is an example of a negative feedback loop. As density approaches the habitat's carrying capacity (K), growth slows, coming to a

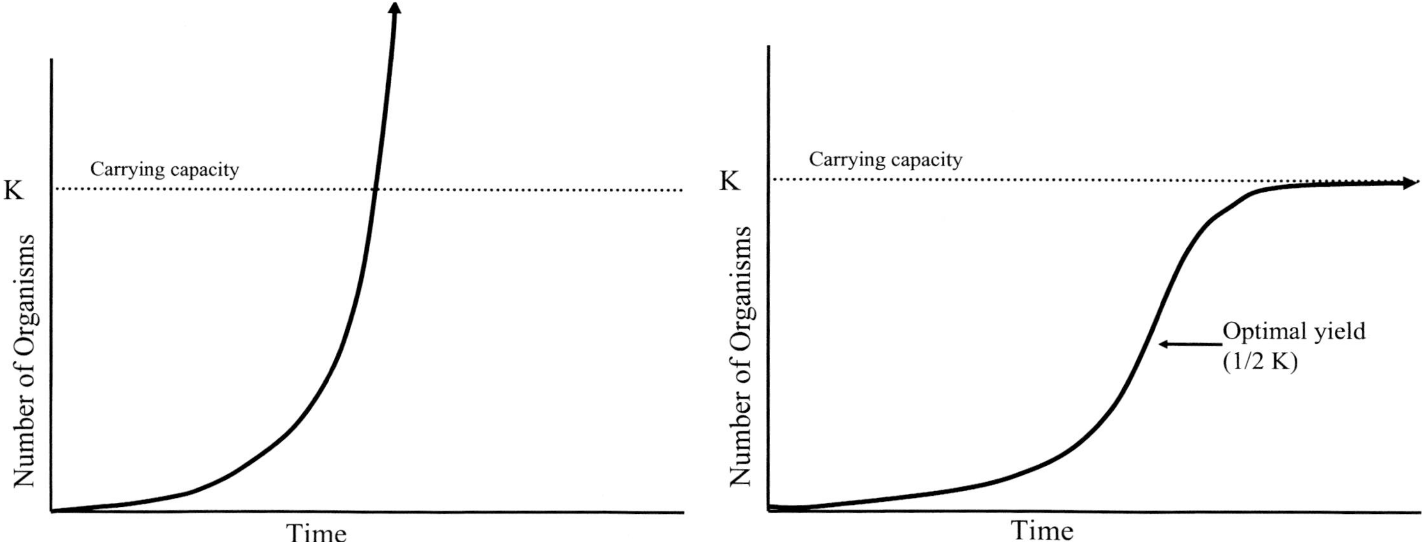

Two growth forms: exponential (first graph) and logistic (second graph). From Wilson and Bossert (1971)

complete stop when N = K. This model of population growth is said to be **density-dependent**; that is, the rate of growth is dependent on the population size.

Density-dependent growth can be the result of either intrinsic or extrinsic factors, or both. Studies across a wide spectrum of species have found that higher densities lead to greater social stress (agonistic behavior), which in turn negatively affects intrinsic factors such as natality and survivorship rates while increasing emigration rates, all leading to lower population size. Territoriality, especially as demonstrated by many songbirds, is a classic example of a density-dependent mechanism that results in logistic growth. Breeding pairs of songbirds defend an area that will provide them with the resources necessary to raise their young. There are only so many suitable territories in a given habitat, and they are not compressible. Hence, a local bird's population growth will depend on its density. The number of available territories sets the habitat's carrying capacity. When all available territories are filled, no further growth is possible.

Extrinsic factors, those external to the population such as predation and disease, may also limit population growth in a density-dependent fashion. Predators may become more efficient and specialize on prey when their numbers are high. Communicable diseases spread more rapidly in dense populations.

While natural (nonlaboratory) populations are unlikely to follow either of these models exactly, they are nonetheless useful in terms of assessing a population's likely response to change. Wildlife biologists make use of the logistic growth curve model to help them set bag limits for various game species. It turns out that the **optimal yield**, that is, the maximum number of animals that can be sustainably harvested, can be obtained by reducing the population to one-half K (see the graph). One-half K marks the inflection point of the logistic curve, the point at which the population exhibits its highest rate of growth. Harvests that drop a population below this point result in a longer recovery time for the population to recoup its losses.

Ecological Succession

Nature is dynamic. The natural world is undergoing constant change. One of the difficulties in predicting population size is that the carrying capacity of any given habitat rarely remains constant month to month, let alone year to year. These changes may be the result of short- or long-term weather patterns, human or natural disturbance, random events, or ecological succession.

Succession may be defined as the progression of community types at a given site through time until a relatively permanent, self-replacing **climax** community is established. Succession occurs in both aquatic and terrestrial environments. The former is referred to as **hydrarch** succession, and the latter, as **xerarch** (dry) succession. When this process begins in an environment lacking any organic matter, such as in a sterile body of water or on bare rock, it is called **primary succession**. **Secondary succession** occurs on sites that have recently lost an ecological community to some sort of disturbance but still retain organic matter and a readily available stock of organisms. Secondary succession can be observed on an area following a disturbance of some sort, such a forest fire, a flood, a tornado or hurricane, or on abandoned cropland, often referred to as old field succession.

Primary Succession

Primary succession may take hundreds or thousands of years before a climax community is established. The **pioneer community** is the first to occupy a barren site. It usually consists of a few species that have the capacity for long-distance dispersal and are hardy enough to persist in what are often extreme environmental conditions. Lichens, capable of growing on a bare rock face, are a good example of such pioneers. In such a case, the slow accumulation of organic matter over time may provide enough substrate for larger plants, perhaps mosses, to take root. These plants may literally overshadow the pioneers, eventually leading to their demise. Increasing deposition of organic matter provides enough resources for still larger plants to colonize. The plant communities that follow, known as **seres**, typically exhibit increased stratification, complexity, and species diversity. This process continues until the climax community is established. The figure shows an example of the plants that likely dominated the seral stages of primary succession following the retreat of New England's glaciers 12,000 years ago.

Unlike those found in earlier seres, climax community species are typically capable of self-replenishment. As long as the regional climate remains unchanged, and in the absence of widespread disturbance, climax communities achieve some level of steady-state stability. Examples of predominant climax communities in north-central Texas include the tallgrass prairie, post oak woodland, and post oak savanna.

While succession is often portrayed as an orderly progression from one predict-

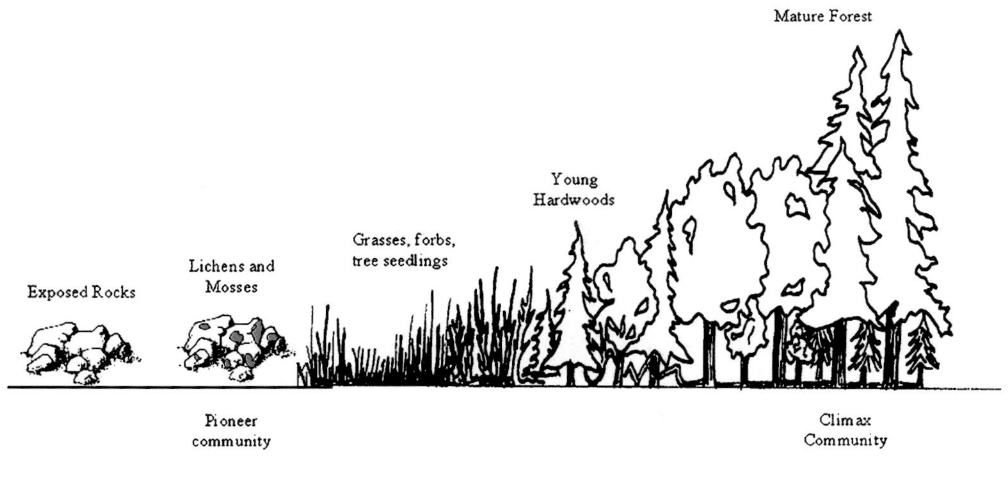

Primary succession. From Smith (1990)

The tallgrass prairie is an example of an endangered habitat.

able sere to another, evidence has shown that this view is overly simplistic. In reality, specific tolerances for light and moisture regimes, the ability of species to resist invasion, the frequency of disturbance, and the role of chance in the arrival of species are all important determinants in the appearance and longevity of any given sere.

Secondary Succession

While a local disturbance of some magnitude may result in the loss of many or all of the aboveground components of a community, the site's organic soil layer often escapes relatively unscathed. In addition to harboring the soil community's invertebrates, fungi, and microorganisms, this layer also serves as a seed bank, often containing viable seeds and spores from a number of previous communities. Without having to wait for early-succession species to arrive or for organic matter to accumulate, secondary succession usually proceeds much more rapidly than primary succession. While second-growth forests may not immediately share all the characteristics of a mature forest lost to disturbance, it is possible to see the return of most of the dominant species and a semblance of the climax community structure within 80–100 years.

One does not have to wait for a natural disaster to observe succession. When an old tree finally falls in a forest, perhaps taking several adjacent trees with it, the resulting hole in the canopy creates a light gap. The altered micro-climate at ground level (more light, reduced moisture) usually favors early-succession species that do best in those conditions. Over time, as the canopy again closes in, the more shade-tolerant species will eventually displace the light-gap pioneers. A number of ecologists now ascribe the great diversity one tends to see in mature forests at least in part to this dynamic process of light-gap succession.

A final observation to make about secondary succession is that the first plant species occupying a site following a disturbance often share an adaptive suite of life history characteristics. Like pioneer species, they are good at tolerating harsh conditions and are typically capable of long-distance dispersal. Unlike pioneers, however, which may live for hundreds of years, these early secondary-succession plants are usually short-lived and have a high reproductive capacity. Because of rapidly changing conditions associated with secondary succession, their winning strategy is to "find" a disturbed site quickly (thanks to large numbers of seeds or propagules capable of long-distance dispersal as well as the ability of their seeds to remain viable for extended periods in seed banks), grow and reproduce rapidly, and send out a voluminous number of offspring before they are replaced by superior competitors. These adaptations have earned them the name "fugitive species," as they are indeed always on the run. They are the same species we commonly call weeds. It will not surprise you that they are found in great abundance in human landscapes maintained in a perpetual state of disturbance or early succession.

Species Diversity

Species diversity, biological diversity, or biodiversity for short, is simply the number of species found in a given area. One of the more striking global patterns is the increase in species diversity observed as one proceeds from either pole to the equator. Greenland, for example, is home to 56 species of breeding birds; New York State has 105; Virginia, 212; Texas, 358; Guatemala, 469; while Colombia boasts 1,395. Many hypotheses have been proposed to explain this phenomenon: Decreasing latitude corresponds to increasing mean temperature and solar radiation, which results in greater plant productivity. Relatively unaffected by periods of glaciation, tropical systems are older (thereby allowing greater time for speciation), are more structurally complex (hence a greater number of potential niches), and have greater numbers of predators, thereby decreasing competition among prey species (recall the keystone predator effect of the starfish, *Pisaster*). It is, of course, likely that all of these, as well as other factors, contribute to the overall trend.

As noted in the previous section, biodiversity often increases along the time gradient of ecological succession (although the highest species diversity in temperate forests may occur in the pre-climax sere). In general, ecologists have observed that disturbed sites exhibit low species diversity, dominated by a few broadly adapted generalists, while undisturbed sites consist of a rich diversity of species, many of which are specialists occupying narrow niches.

Monocultures, communities dominated by a single plant species, as exemplified by our agricultural crops and suburban lawns, are inherently unstable. Our human constructs can be maintained only by high inputs of energy, chemicals, and constant management. Lacking both genetic and biological diversity, as well as normal community structure and feedback mechanisms, they are prone to outbreaks of "pest" and disease species. Large tracts of natural habitat are now threatened by introduced (nonnative) invasive species. Hundreds of invasives, such as phragmites, purple loose-

The starfish (*Pisaster ochraceus*) is a keystone species in the rocky intertidal zone. Courtesy of D. Gordon E. Robertson

strife, Japanese honeysuckle, privet, kudzu, chinaberry, and tree of heaven, are creating their own monocultures, resulting in a loss of species diversity and the creation of virtual biological deserts. Invasives have been recognized as the second leading cause of declining species diversity after habitat loss.

Many state agencies and conservation organizations, such as the Texas Master Naturalist Program, encourage homeowners to "wildscape" their property by replacing some or all of their lawns and nonnative trees and shrubs with native wildflowers, trees, and shrubs. These native plant landscapes provide important habitat for wildlife and reduce or eliminate the ecological damage done by the use of fertilizers, pesticides, and fossil fuels. It is one very important way that individuals can support and increase local biodiversity.

An invasive aquatic hyacinth. Courtesy of Texas A&M AgriLife Extension Service

Fragmentation and Edge Effects

As the human population continues to increase both locally and globally, the quantity and quality of remaining natural habitat continue to decline. If they are not lost completely, development significantly compromises the quality of the habitat that remains. Where once large contiguous tracts of habitat existed, only small, disjunct fragments, or habitat islands, remain. As fragment size shrinks, the ratio of an area's perimeter (edge) to its interior increases. Small habitat islands are subjected to larger fluctuations in light, temperature, moisture, and wind as well as a host of new biological stresses. Collectively, these negative factors associated with large perimeter-to-volume ratios are known as the **edge effect**.

Cutting holes in a forest to create more edge was once looked upon by wildlife managers as the premier technique for increasing the density of game species. Stature of this management technique was heightened by some ecologists touting its ability to increase overall species diversity. This was true, but only up to a point—the point at which interior forest specialists began to disappear as a result of the edge effect. In the case of forest habitats, the species added by increasing edge were those that frequented and preferred the interface between habitat types (forest and open fields), referred to as **ecotones**.

The species that literally like "living on the edge" are often **generalists**, species adaptable to a wide variety of conditions and capable of exploiting a large variety of resources. They are said to have a broad or wide niche. These traits have made them especially successful and common in our highly modified urban/suburban landscapes—white-tailed deer, squirrels, raccoons, rabbits, opossums, grackles, starlings, and house sparrows, to name but a few. While creating more edge did indeed increase densities of some game species and did initially increase overall species diversity by adding more generalists (already common), it did so at a cost—the decline and eventual loss of many interior forest specialists, most notably songbirds.

Unlike generalists, **specialist** species are so called because they are restricted to a narrow range of conditions, especially with regard to food and/or reproductive needs. They are said to have narrow niches. Recall that species diversity usually increases with ecological succession. With increasing structural diversity of the later seres comes increasingly complex community interaction, increased competition, and a resultant restriction of species' niche width. You can pack a lot more species into a habitat, thereby increasing species diversity, if each species is restricted to a narrow niche. It is not surprising, therefore, that a mature forest ecosystem would be home to many more specialists than early-succession edge habitat.

Increasing fragmentation (increasing edge) negatively affects interior specialist populations in one or both of the following ways:

- Many interior species avoid using the area for a few to many feet next to an edge. A road cut through the middle of a large tract thereby removes a considerably larger amount of habitat than the road itself from further use by these species.
- Reproductive success of interior species is often adversely and dramatically affected by increasing edge.

Many native and domestic predators enter forest habitats via edges. The smaller the habitat fragment, the greater the nest depredation rate by raccoons, rodents, opossums, skunks, snakes, and domestic cats. For interior forest birds, the brown-headed cowbird poses an especially serious threat. Primarily a grassland species, cowbirds were not common in the eastern half of the United States

Edge Effect – 100m buffer

- Minimum safe forest buffer given as 100 m (328 ft.).
- For a 50-acre parcel, only 30 acres of "interior" forest remains inside the edge.

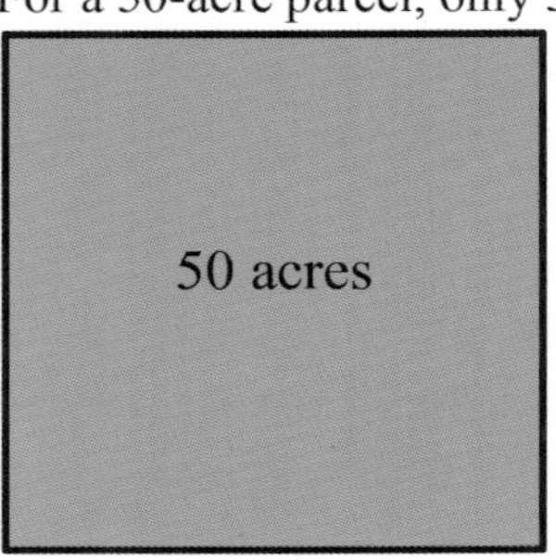

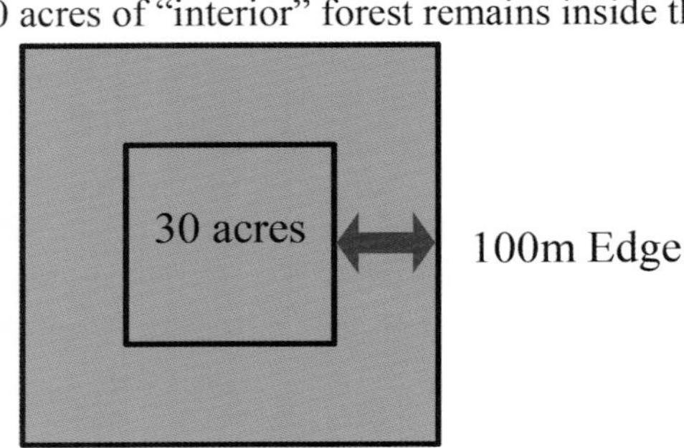

Edge Effect – 600m Buffer

- In areas of high cowbird density, edge effect may penetrate to 600m (1968 ft.).
- For a 100-acre parcel, only 10 acres of "interior" forest would remain.

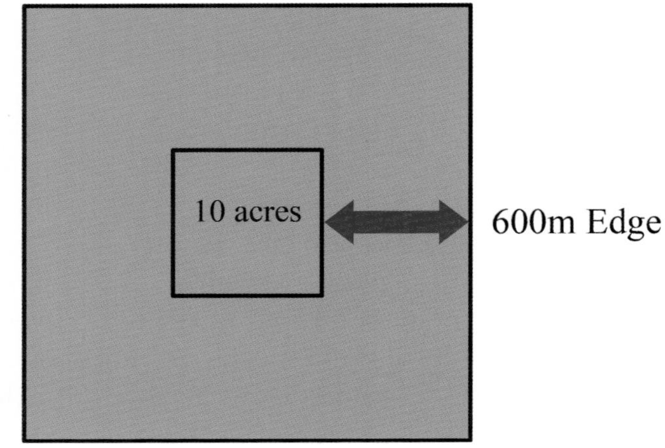

Edge effect, 100-meter buffer and 600-meter buffer. Courtesy of Lou Verner

until the East's forest-dominated landscape was altered to one more to its liking. Cowbirds are nest parasites, laying their eggs in the nests of other birds such as vireos and warblers. Their aggressive, fast-developing nestlings are usually the only ones to successfully fledge, thereby reducing the reproductive effort of the host parents to zero.

While adult cowbirds restrict themselves to the grass-dominated edges of a forest, they will commonly penetrate over 300 feet (100 meters) into a forest in search of a host's nest. This would result in a relatively small decline in the overall reproductive success of a species occupying a large contiguous block of forest, but it could be devastating to a population breeding in a smaller forest fragment. Consider the following scenarios: Assuming 328-foot (100-meter) penetration, a square 50-acre tract of forest would effectively be reduced to 30 acres of cowbird-free habitat, a 40% reduction of habitat. In areas of high cowbird density, these nest parasites have been known to penetrate almost 2,000 feet (600 meters) into a forest's interior. This would reduce the viable breeding habitat of a 100-acre tract to only 10 acres.

Note that both of these examples show the 50- and 100-acre tracts as squares, thereby minimizing the perimeter-to-volume ratio. If these tracts were long and narrow or irregularly shaped, it is likely that cowbirds and other nest predators would have access to the entire habitat, with the likely result being the total loss of breeding success of any interior specialists. For many interior forest species, highly fragmented forests may be **ecological traps**, providing birds with what appears to be suitable, attractive habitat, only to have their breeding attempts end in total failure. (Perversely, such forest fragments may be an ecological "mind" trap for us as well because we may be lulled into thinking we are preserving biodiversity by saving small habitat islands or "natural areas" in the midst of our growing sea of development, when, in actuality, we may not be.) While other factors are no doubt involved (deforestation in their tropical wintering grounds), loss of breeding habitat and habitat fragmentation have been identified as the primary reasons for the decline of many of North America's songbirds.

Black-capped vireo (*Vireo atricapilla*) an endangered species in Texas. Courtesy of Texas Parks and Wildlife Department

"Endangered species are sensitive indicators of how we are treating the planet, and we should be listening carefully to their message."
—Donald Falk, restoration ecologist

Endangered Species

Why do some species become rare and go extinct while others thrive? First, we must remember that extinction is a natural process. The species that exist today represent only a tiny fraction of all the species that have ever existed. Aside from geologically rare instances of mass extinction (such as the apparent asteroid impact that brought an end to the 140-million-year reign of the dinosaurs), extinction rates for any given group are usually low. For mammals, the fossil record indicates this rate was between 0.002 and 0.02 species per year. In the twentieth century, 25 mammals are known to have gone extinct, or 0.25 per year, or 12.5 to 125 times the "background" rate. In fact, given the current rate of loss of all species worldwide, we may be in the midst of one of the fastest extinction rates of all time. The primary cause of this sharp rise in extinction rates is, first and foremost, habitat loss. As already mentioned, our burgeoning human population continues to occupy, clear, and degrade more and more previously undisturbed land. Other factors, all related to human activity, include commercial hunting and fishing, predator and pest control, the exotic pet and plant trade, the introduction of alien species, and pollution.

Which species are we losing? Primarily those species at the top of food chains, primarily large carnivores for reasons we have already discussed, and a diverse group species that share the trait of being habitat specialists. Texas examples include the horned lizard, or "horny toad," which feeds almost exclusively on declining harvester ants; and the black-capped vireo, golden-cheeked warbler, and red-cockaded woodpecker, all of which have declined with the loss of their very specific nesting habitat requirements. In contrast, generalists, those species with broad diets and capable of surviving in a wide variety of habitats (especially those created by human activity), are common and often increase under conditions of disturbance.

So why should we care? What difference could it possibly make if we lose the horny toad or the black-capped vireo? There are three broad categories of arguments that are usually made to address such questions—aesthetic, practical, and moral or ethical (Brewer 1994).

The aesthetic argument is simply that the natural world has much to offer in terms of beauty, inspiration, and wonder. John Burroughs (1989) said, "I go to nature to be soothed and healed, and to have my senses put in tune once again." Destroying the natural world impoverishes us all. A 1993 survey by the US Fish and Wildlife service found that over 76 million Americans (39%) identify themselves as "wildlife watchers" and spent over $18 billion in pursuit of their hobbies. There are more active birders than golfers, and birding has become one of the country's fastest-growing outdoor activities. The state of Texas has 4 of the recognized top 12 birding sites in North America, and the Great Texas Coastal Birding Trail, which includes 308 sites and 100 participating local communities, attracts thousands of avid birders annually. Given its tremendous success, Texas Parks and Wildlife is working on creating additional birding and wildlife trails throughout the state.

On the practical side, all species are part of the web of life that sustains human life. There is no such thing as an "unnatural resource." Nature is the ultimate provider of all the goods and services that make our highly technological lives possible. Despite our ability to manufacture synthetic compounds, over 25% of all prescription drugs still rely on compounds derived directly from plants. A much higher percentage of drugs that have been developed to treat everything from cancer to HIV to malaria are modified derivatives of naturally occurring substances. An antiviral drug proven effective against a previously lethal form of herpes encephalitis was derived from an obscure Caribbean sponge and is now saving thousands of lives annually. When we lose any species, we lose forever the genetic information that is uniquely theirs and the opportunities to test them for potentially useful compounds. As far as services are concerned, there is simply no replacing the roles countless organisms and communities play in the maintenance of the atmosphere, biogeochemical cycling, soil formation, watershed management, pest control, and pollination.

Finally, there is a moral or ethical argument that can be made. Whether or not a species is deemed "beautiful" or "economically beneficial," the decision to destroy another species can be thought of as simply "not the right thing to do," in the same way that murdering another human is morally and/or ethically wrong. If we come to the understanding that humans are a part of nature, not apart from nature, we will appreciate the fact that all living things are members of one biotic community. In Aldo Leopold's words, "This new knowledge should have given us, by this time, a sense of kinship with fellow-creatures; a wish to live and let live; a sense of wonder over the magnitude and duration of the biotic enterprise" (1949, 109–10).

Threatened and Endangered Species Lists

The federal Endangered Species Act of 1973 committed the United States to preventing the extinction of plant and animal species. Most states, including Texas, have enacted their own legislation with similar provisions. **Endangered species** are those in imminent danger of extinction throughout their range. **Threatened species** are those likely to become endangered within the foreseeable future. Many states also include a third category, **rare** *species*, which recognizes species that, because of their low or declining numbers and the shrinking of critical habitat, need special attention.

At the federal level, the secretary of the Interior has the primary authority to list, delist, or change the status of any species. In Texas, the executive director of the Texas Parks and Wildlife Department (TPWD) determines which species are "threatened with statewide extinction," while the TPWD Commission determines those "likely to become endangered in the future."

Protection

Under both state and federal law, it is illegal to take, possess, transport, or sell any animal species designated as endangered or threatened without the issuance of a permit. State laws and regulations also prohibit commerce in threatened and endangered plants and the collection of listed plant species from public land without a permit issued by TPWD. Endangered species receive additional federal attention. Their essential habitats are also protected, and a recovery plan is supposed to be devised, based on knowledge of the ecology of the species. It outlines procedures designed to build up populations to a level where the chance of extinction is minimal, allowing the species to be delisted. Well-known success stories include the bald eagle, American alligator, and peregrine falcon.

Peregrine falcon (*Falco peregrinus*). Courtesy of Texas Parks and Wildlife Department

Summary

The great lesson of ecology is that everything truly is interconnected. An understanding of basic ecological concepts is crucial to understanding how the natural world works. It provides a framework for understanding how ecosystems are structured and how they function. Together with evolutionary theory, it provides us with insights into the myriad complex and fascinating behaviors, life histories and interactions of organisms, populations, and communities. It offers us a blueprint of how our own species might better and more harmoniously live within the constraints and limitations of this magnificent green and blue planet.

References

Bolen, E. G., and W. L. Robinson. 1995. *Wildlife Ecology and Management.* Upper Saddle River, NJ: Prentice Hall.

Brewer, R. 1988. *The Science of Ecology.* Philadelphia: Saunders College Publishing.

———. 1994. *The Science of Ecology.* 2nd ed. Philadelphia: W. B. Saunders.

Burroughs, John. 1989. *Gospel of Nature.* Carlisle, MA: Applewood Books.

Elton, C. 1927. *Animal Ecology.* London: Sidgwick and Jackson.

Eriksson, O., and J. Ehrlen. 2008. *Seedling Ecology and Evolution.* Cambridge: Cambridge University Press.

Gause. G. F. 1934. *The Struggle for Existence.* Baltimore: Williams and Wilkins.

Haeckel, Ernst. 1866. *Generelle morphologie der organismen* [General morphology of the organisms]. Berlin: G. Reimer. Accessed February 28, 2015. http://www.biodiversitylibrary.org/item/22319#page/11/mode/1up.

Hardin, G. 1960. The Competitive Exclusion Principle. *Science* 131 (3409): 1292–97.

Krebs, C. J. 1972. *Ecology.* New York: Harper and Row.

———. 2009. *Ecology: The Experimental Analysis of Distribution and Abundance.* 6th ed. San Francisco: Benjamin Cummings.

Leopold, Aldo. 1949. *A Sand County Almanac, and Sketches Here and There.* New York: Oxford University Press.

Major Habitat Types of the United States and Canada. 2010. Uploaded by Cephas, September 5. Terrestrial ecoregions USA CAN MEX.svg. In *Terrestrial Ecoregions of North America: A Conservation Assessment,* by Taylor H Ricketts et al. (Washington, DC: Island Press, 1999). Licensed under Creative Commons Attribution-Share Alike 3.0–2.5–2.0–1.0 via Wikimedia Commons. http://commons.wikimedia.org/wiki/File:Major_habitat_type_CAN_USA.svg#mediaviewer/File:Major_habitat_type_CAN_USA.svg.

Miller, G. T. 1992. *Living in the Environment.* 7th ed. Boston: Wadsworth Publishing.

NASA (National Aeronautics and Space Administration). 2015. Consensus: 97% of Climate Scientists Agree. Accessed April 14, 2015. http://climate.nasa.gov/scientific-consensus/.

Odum, E. P. 1953. *Fundamentals of Ecology.* 2nd ed. Philadelphia: W. B. Saunders.

———. 1963. *Ecology.* New York: Holt, Rinehart and Winston.

Paine, R. T. 1974. Intertidal Community Structure: Experimental Studies on the Relationship between a Dominant Competitor and Its Principal Predator. *Oecologia* 15:93–120.

Ricketts, Taylor H., Eric Dinerstein, David M. Olson, Colby J. Loucks, William Eichbaum, Dominick A. DellaSala, et al. 1999. *Terrestrial Ecoregions of North America: A Conservation Assessment*. Washington, DC: Island Press.

Smith, R. L. 1990. *Ecology and Field Biology*. 4th ed. New York: Harper and Row.

Tello, Jose G. 2003. Frugivores at a Fruiting *Ficus* in South-Eastern Peru. *Journal of Tropical Ecology* 19:717–21.

Varley, G. C., G. R. Gradwell, and M. P. Hassel. 1973. *Insect Population Ecology*. Oxford: Blackwell.

Whittaker, R. H. 1975. *Communities and Ecosystems*. 2nd ed. New York: Macmillan.

Wilson, E. O., and W. H. Bossert. 1971. *A Primer of Population Biology*. Sunderland, MA: Sinauer Associates Press.

Additional Resources

Barry, R. G., and R. J. Charley. 1970. *Atmosphere, Weather and Climate*. New York: Holt, Rinehart and Winston.

Hairston, N. G., F. E. Smith, and L. B. Slobodkin. 1960. Community Structure, Population Control, and Competition. *American Naturalist* 94:421–25.

UNIT 6

Ecosystems Concepts and Management

BARRON S. RECTOR
Associate Professor and Extension Range Specialist, Texas A&M University

Unit Goals

After completing this unit, volunteers should be able to

- understand and discuss the seven principles of ecology
- describe management, ecosystems, and ecosystem management
- identify the five ecological principles that can help assure the earth's ecosystems

"Harmony with land is like harmony with a friend; you cannot cherish his right hand and chop off his left. . . . The land is one organism."
—Aldo Leopold, Round River

Introduction

Today it is acknowledged that an important relationship exists between the management at a site-specific level (backyard, park, pasture, community, vegetation region, watershed, etc.) and the whole earth system. Management on a smaller scale can have impact at a larger scale. At a landscape level, it is recognized that things are interconnected. A term used today in the United States to describe this view is "ecosystem management." This phrase has become a popular buzzword in political arenas as well as with government agencies and private organizations. However, the term "ecosystem management" has numerous definitions and has resulted in some confusion on how ecosystem management should be conducted and accomplishments achieved. To understand current thinking and philosophy, we begin our study with the principles of ecology, definition of an ecosystem, and implications of management.

The confusion with the use of the term can be seen in the following illustration. The Bureau of Land Management (BLM) defines ecosystem management as "a process that considers the total environment. It requires the skillful use of ecological, economic, social and managerial principles to produce, restore or sustain ecosystem integrity and desired conditions, uses, products, values, and services over the long term. . . . Ecosystem management recognizes that people and their social and economic needs are an integral part of ecological systems" (*Federal Register* 1993, 43208–209). Despite this official definition, a report in the *High Country News* (Giller 1994, 2) referenced a Wyoming BLM public officer who stated that an offer was made to transfer an individual to a position in which he would be responsible for ecosystem management in the state of Utah and his technical skill would be of value, but he would not be in contact with the public. Are people to be included in the definition or not? This illustrates the first major problem resource managers will have as they try to implement ecosystem management. If ecosystem management is going to work,

The Llano River and the surrounding riparian landscape. Courtesy of Texas A&M AgriLife Extension Service

even at the lowest level, people must be able to tell each other what this kind of management means.

The movement to use ecosystem-style management has come about because of the need to recognize and deal with the "big picture." This includes dealing with larger scales in time, space, and social dimensions associated with natural resources. A second reason is the typical government approach to solving or improving resource problems. The ecosystem management approach now implies that something else is needed. We are currently struggling to determine what the most appropriate basis for action is and how we blend the technical and human aspects with management. "As humans, we have, like all other animals, an inherent bias toward our own interests. Our vision [management goal] must shift to an ecosystem perspective rather than a short term personal view of what's good for me is good for everyone and I can do with my land what I want because I own it!" (White 2001).

Principles of Ecology

How many times have we stopped to think about our land management practices and the effects these practices have on naturally occurring processes? This could be a monarch butterfly emerging from a chrysalis, clean water falling from the sky and flowing clear in a nearby creek, or a green grass-covered pasture turning to the yellow hue of broomweed by fall. Changes are occurring each day from natural processes, many of which we never notice or take the time to evaluate.

For many, our minds are lost in the narrow-sighted world of cause and effect related to outdoor recreation, lawn maintenance, protection of our property, and even agricultural processes, such as livestock weight gain, noxious plant kill or damage, and the amount of harvestable wildlife for the next hunting season. We too often forget that we are not in control of many things that happen to the land, plant communities, and animal resources around us. Many of these changes are described in the **Principles of Ecology**—principles or laws that we as land and resource managers should be working with and not against. An understanding of how our ecosystem functions may allow land managers to explain things that are observed and even allow us to predict some results of decisions and actions we make on the land. Knowledge of the ecosystem can help us understand the relationships among soil, water, plants, animals, and their environments. With knowledge of ecological principles, we can better accomplish our objectives.

Principle Number 1: **The plant or producer, the grazing animal or consumer, and the intrinsic value of a healthy ecosystem need to be looked at together, not separately.** Ecology is the field of study concerned with the mutual relationship of plants, animals, and microorganisms with their environment. Since range plants and animals are biological organisms, their interrelationships are ecological in nature. Range, forestry, and wildlife management is often looked at as applied ecology, since it consists of manipulating the environment in which both plants and animals live. Plants and animals often live together, and the welfare or future of each is dependent on the other. This is a fundamental concept of natural resource management.

Principle Number 2: **The natural resource manager should understand the change and know it has an influence on all management decisions.** The ecosystem is made up of living and nonliving things that are interconnected. An ecosystem includes all the organisms that live in an area and the physical environment with which those organisms interact. A change in any one of the components can invariably influence or cause a change in the relationship of all the other factors of the system. However, change is normal.

Principle Number 3: **For every action on the land, there are multiple reactions that can occur.** Humans often see only the target response to an action. Farmer Brown had a severe honey mesquite problem. He believed that the mesquite was using up all of the rainfall received, thus lowering his forage production and animal carrying capacity. Farmer Brown sprayed the mes-

Texas has seven herds of free-ranging desert bighorn sheep (*Ovis canadensis nelsoni*), which can primarily be found in the northern and western regions of the state. Courtesy of Texas Parks and Wildlife Department

The interface between humans and nature at a creekside crossing. Courtesy of Clinton J. Faas, cjfaas@gmail.com

High fences are a tool for managing foraging herd animals, such as white-tailed deer, and can be used to keep populations within or outside their boundaries. Courtesy of Clinton J. Faas, cjfaas@gmail.com

quite with a chemical to kill it. After a year, he visited the sprayed area to determine if the mesquite had died. He observed that much of the mesquite was dead, which was his target goal. His mistake was that he did not stop to observe the plants that had taken the place of the mesquite, a deciduous plant. Instead of a pasture dominated by cool-season perennial grasses that grew in the winter months when the mesquite had dropped all of its leaves, the land was open to full sunlight all year and now supported a complex of warm-season perennial grasses. Change had occurred through his actions and decisions.

Principle Number 4: **Nature abhors a void and provides plants through the processes of primary and secondary succession to fill the openness.** Management of lands has occurred through the introduction and manipulation of domestic livestock, high fencing for wildlife, and the planting of food plots for human-made objectives. Currently many areas do not have the carrying capacity of wildlife or domestic livestock once noted by our earlier managers and naturalists. Change occurred. As plant communities changed and responded to new uses or even excessive use, less forage was often available for consumption by domestic livestock and wildlife species. Less plant cover provided open, uncovered soils and an excellent opportunity for natural processes to respond. Lost beneficial plants were replaced with those less valuable to livestock or wildlife. Land managers must observe and evaluate the responses to their actions, or new plants and plant communities may not meet their goals, needs, or desired financial returns. A new plant community could lead to changing land uses, land value, livestock enterprises, and ownership goals. Recognizing and understanding the stages of soil, plant, and animal succession are key for the manager who is evaluating the effectiveness of management goals.

Principle Number 5: **Humans have found that nature knows best. Organisms that are suited and adapted to the change occupy the site.** With the loss of desirable, perennial plants, a decreased plant cover on the soil allows an increased loss of rainfall through increased evaporation from the soil surface, increased runoff, and increased use by newly established and often less efficient plants. Less water available in quantity or for a shorter period of time promotes plants that can live in a drier, more open soil environment. The new regime of plants does not provide the amount or same kind of biomass produced by previous occupants, and less litter or dead standing plant material is available for soil cover and for contribution to soil organic matter. Soil temperatures also rise. This new environment is conducive to many weeds and brush species.

Principle Number 6: **Everything must go somewhere.** Change does not always satisfy humans, who have sought to find the best plants, the miracle plants, and animals that eat brush and weeds to solve these problems. As an alternative, we plant non-native plant species that can survive on our changed, depleted, and otherwise mismanaged soils, only to find that nature is still in control. Native plants come up in planted coastal bermudagrass, alfalfa, and small grains. Thus, we look to new technology to keep these plants and natural processes out of our planted monocultures. We fertilize to give these plants a competitive edge, only to find out that excessive nutrients can accumulate or flow out of the system and cause damage on adjacent land and water resources, and we often unknowingly create the next problem. The ecosystem manager's job is to minimize the energy and nutrient drain on the ecosystem while ensuring ecosystem health.

Principle Number 7: **There is no such**

Prescribed burns are an excellent management tool for habitat enhancement. Courtesy of Natural Resources Conservation Service

thing as a free lunch. Before European settlers arrived, wildfires and fires set by the American Indians helped maintain much of our open natural prairies in Texas. The reduction of fire by the European settlers, as they worked to protect the environment, also created an environment that helped sustain many of the dense stands of woody plants we see as pests today. To push the ecosystem back to a natural state takes a lot of energy, human resources, and dollars. Every gain is won at some cost.

What Is Management?

Management is defined in *Merriam-Webster Online* as "the act or skill of controlling and making decisions about something." Management is the use of certain means to achieve desired results. Management clearly implies the influence and application of human manipulation. To some, the term "management" involves the concept of conquering nature, and they suggest that attempts to dominate nature contradict the ethic of sound natural resource management. It is true that traditional natural resource management has approached goal setting, problem solving, and planning from a technical basis alone, using assumptions about community values and objectives that may not be accurate. Today, however, management means planning, evaluating alternatives, establishing goals, implementing decisions, controlling resource flow and allocation to most effectively accomplish the goals, and then monitoring, adjusting, and replanning. Resource limitations and environmental constraints always affect management choices. The choice between short- and long-term goals (balance) requires forgoing some immediate benefits for long-term sustainability of natural resources. You cannot have it all now if you want the resource to be renewable and sustainable.

Drucker states, "Management always has to consider both the present and future—both the short run and the long run. A management problem is not solved if immediate profits are purchased by endangering the long-range health, perhaps even the survival, of the company. A management decision is irresponsible if it risks disaster this year for the sake of a grandiose future" (1974, 35). A decision is a judgment. It is a choice between alternatives. It is rarely a choice between right and wrong. One has to make a decision when a condition is likely to degenerate if nothing is done. The effective decision maker compares effort and risk of action to risk of inaction.

A management plan basically identifies where you are, where you want to go, and how you are going to get there. How many people do we know who planned to destroy their rangeland, bays, waterways, or forests? I have not met one yet. But if they did not plan to do this, then why did the plant and animal life in the Armand Bayou near Houston and the Oso Bay near Corpus Christi die? Management decisions resulted in this situation. There has been failure to understand how daily decisions affect long-term sustainability of natural resources. The decisions we make have implications for the future, and the future inherently involves the unknown. To reduce risk, we must understand our needs and the needs of the environment around us. And we must learn from our mistakes.

What Are Ecosystems?

Living organisms that interact with one another and with the nonliving or abiotic environment constitute an "ecosystem." The nonliving or abiotic factors of the environment include light, temperature, oxygen level, air circulation, precipitation, and soil type. The population of living organisms in a given area composes a unit known as a biotic community. The interrelationship of organisms can be viewed as a hierarchy.

The lowest level is a **population**, which is an interacting group of individuals of a single species. Populations of different species make up a **community**, and communities and their physical environments compose an **ecosystem**.

Organisms in an ecosystem may be grouped into trophic levels as determined by their mode of nutrition. Ideally, ecosystems can sustain themselves entirely by photosynthesis or chemosynthesis and the recycling of nutrients. **Autotrophic** organisms, called producers, either capture light energy and convert it, along with carbon dioxide and water, to energy-rich sugars, or they oxidize chemicals as a source of energy. **Heterotrophic** organisms such as herbivores (i.e., deer, antelope, and elk) eat only producers and are called primary consumers. Secondary consumers, such as **carnivores** (i.e., eagles, wolves, and owls), eat primary consumers. **Omnivores** such as bears may consume both plants and animals. **Decomposers** break down organic materials to forms that can be reassimilated as mineral components by the producers. The foremost composers in most ecosystems are bacteria and fungi.

In any ecosystem, the producers and consumers form food chains or connecting food webs that determine the flow of energy through the different trophic levels. Energy enters a food chain at the producer level and flows to subsequent levels of consumers and decomposers in an ecosystem. Only about 1% of the light energy striking a temperate-zone community is converted to organic material. This organic material and its energy pass to subsequent trophic levels, and as the organisms at each level respire, energy gradually dissipates as heat into the atmosphere. Some energy is stored in organisms that are not consumed and is released when they decompose.

Only a small portion of energy stored in one trophic level will flow to the next level. Most energy is lost as heat during growth, maintenance, and decomposition. About 10% of the energy stored in green plants that are eaten by cattle is converted to animal tissue; most of the remaining energy dissipates as heat. If 90% of the energy is lost as heat at each level of a food chain, then only about 0.1% of the original energy captured by the producers will be used in a typical food chain with three levels of consumers. Therefore, the longer the food chain, the greater the number of producers necessary to provide energy for the final consumer. In terms of the numbers of individuals and the total mass, there is a sharp reduction of usable energy at each level of the food chain. In a given part of the ocean, for example, billions of microscopic algal producers may support millions of tiny crustacean consumers, which, in turn, support thousands of small fish, which are finally eaten by one or two large fish. In other words, one large fish requires and depends on a billion tiny algae to meet its energy needs every day.

The interrelationships and interactions among the components of an ecosystem can be complex, but over the long term there is balance between producers and consumers. An increase in food made available by producers can increase the number of consumers. This increased number of consumers reduces the available food, which then inevitably reduces the number of consumers. The result is sustained self-maintenance of the ecosystem.

Ecosystems exhibit considerable variation in net productivity. **Net productivity** is defined as the energy produced by photosynthesis minus that lost in respiration. Productivity (in terms of biomass produced) is usually measured as grams per square meter of land per day: grasslands produce 0.5–3.0 grams, and deserts produce less than 0.5 gram.

Ecosystems are dynamic and under constant change. They undergo daily changes, seasonal changes, and changes that may take from 10 to hundreds of years. In the world of daily changes, photosynthesis occurs only during the daylight hours. Many

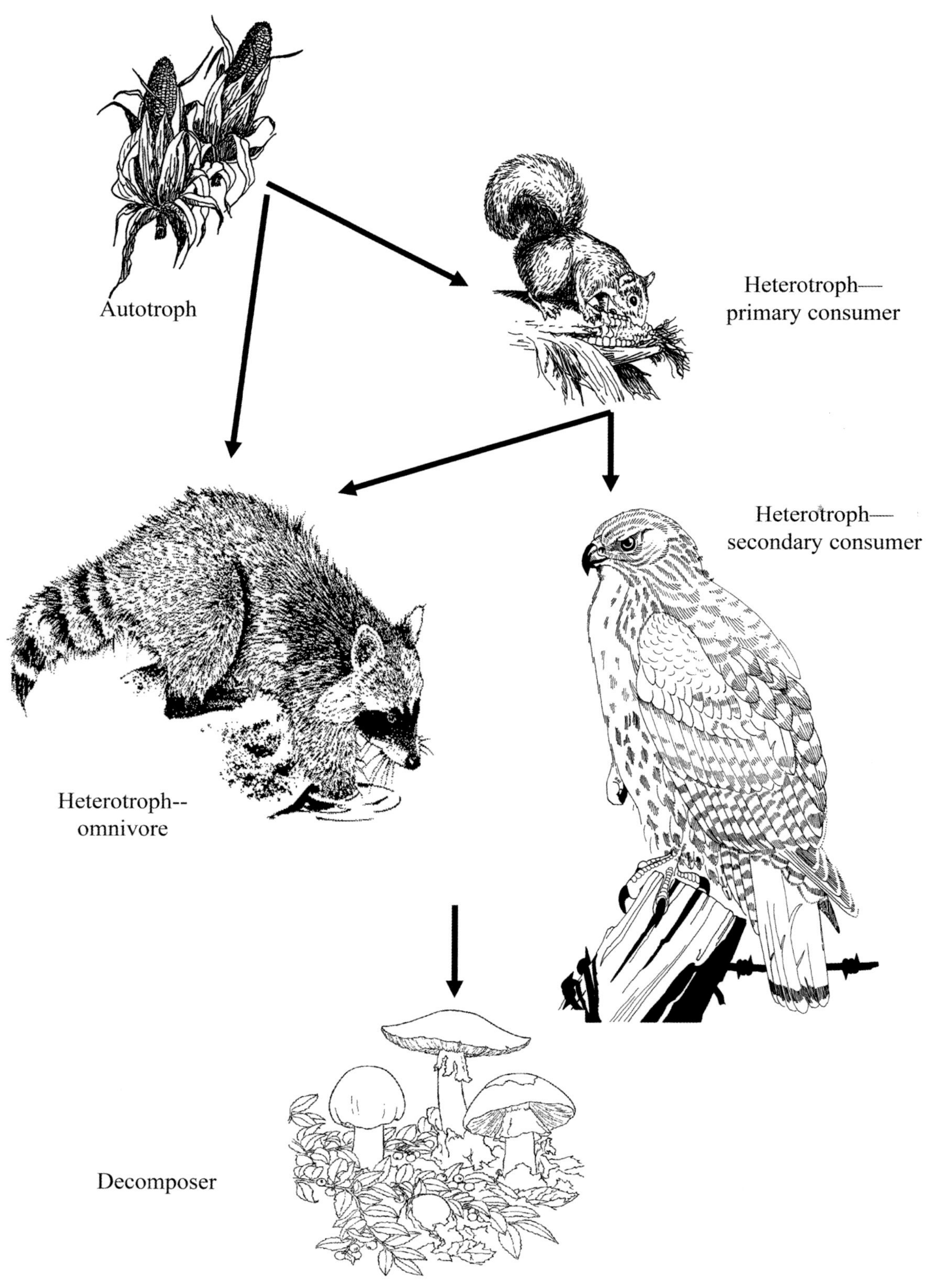

The trophic levels of an ecosystem.

animals in ecosystems are active during only daylight or nighttime hours, but not both. Plants can lose their leaves for part of the year. Seasonal periods of dormancy and rejuvenation are common in woody plants.

Each ecosystem includes a diversity of organisms distributed in specific patterns determined by the physical environment and by relationships with other organisms. A diverse growth form will exist in the organisms of an ecosystem. Species diversity depends on the number of species and number of individuals per species in an ecosystem. Species diversity is important in an ecosystem, as this increases the ecosystem's resilience.

Diverse ecosystems recover from stress such as drought or too much rain faster than do ecosystems with less diversity. Ecosystems can become saturated after a certain level of diversity is reached. Although diversity is valuable to a certain point, most ecosystems contain more diversity than is needed to reach peak productivity. The random loss of species does not impair the productivity of an ecosystem, for such extinctions leave behind a few species in each growth-form category, such as vines, canopy trees, and understory ferns. This raises the question, should we be concerned about the loss of biodiversity and extinctions that human activities are causing? Yes, we should, because these extinctions are not random. Human-driven extinctions probably have a greater impact on an ecosystem than do random extinctions.

What Is Ecosystem Management?

The word *ecosystem* comes from *eco*, which means "house"; *system* means that things are connected to form a whole; and *manage* means to conduct or direct or make decisions. Salwasser (1995) states, "**Ecosystem management** can be defined as the process of seeking to produce (i.e., restore, sustain or enhance) desired conditions, uses and values of complex communities or organisms that work together with their environment as integrated units. It seeks a broad focus on sustaining desired ecosystem conditions of diversity, long-term productivity and resilience, with yields of desired resources and uses being commensurate with the larger goal of sustaining these conditions." Since we are managing our local ecosystem, whatever we do affects the place we live and the future conditions we will live under. We cannot do just one thing. Everything is connected, and there are multiple responses to each action. Some responses are beneficial, and others are detrimental.

Ecosystem management requires communities and agencies to work together, using different means to achieve ends that are not defined by an agency in isolation from the community. This type of management requires both the community and agencies to develop "people skills" for effective implementation. Further, resource managers and agencies need to be clear about their role(s) in the process. Are they facilitators, leaders, providers of scientific knowledge and expertise, or the ground managers? The traditional approach has emphasized social and economic criteria with limited consideration of ecosystem processes. The ecosystem approach emphasizes ecosystem processes and long-term conditions in lieu of social and economic criteria.

As land ecosystem managers, we are managing the flow of energy and the cycling of nutrients in the ecosystem. We can make changes that work to our advantage as well as benefit the ecosystem. We successfully do this through an understanding and expectation of our actions. Natural processes do most of the work for free. A successful ecosystem manager utilizes a small fraction of the total energy budget and in return provides a service that aids the system in its function and continued survival.

In short, successful ecosystem managers time their interactions to the right moment and the right place, often becoming somewhat inconspicuous and seemingly unimportant. Planning and acting at larger-than-usual scales is implicit and a necessity in ecosystem management. There is importance of spatial scale when we recognize that differences exist between individual land enterprises and regional land-use objectives. Ecosystem management has often been interpreted to imply biophysical boundaries for the process. This may not always be appropriate or workable. In some instances the process may work better if boundaries are identified in social terms, as in naturally forming communities and groups.

Recently, the Ecological Society of America Committee on Land Use (Dale et al. 2000) identified five ecological principles that "can assure that fundamental processes of the earth's ecosystems are sustained":

1. Ecological processes occur within a temporal setting and change over time.
2. Individual species and networks of interacting species have strong and far-reaching effects on ecological processes.
3. Each site or region has a unique set of organisms and abiotic conditions influencing and constraining ecological processes.
4. Disturbances are important and ubiquitous ecological events whose effects may strongly influence population, community, and ecosystem dynamics.
5. The size, shape, and spatial relationships of habitat patches on the landscape affect the structure and function of ecosystems.

White (2001) states that these principles dictate several guidelines for land use. They

- examine impacts of local decisions in a regional context
- plan for long-term change and unexpected events
- preserve rare landscape elements and associated species
- avoid land uses that deplete natural resources
- minimize the introduction and spread of nonnative species
- avoid or compensate for the effects of development on ecological processes
- implement land-use and management practices that are compatible with the natural potential of the area

All ecosystems should be managed in an ecologically sustainable manner for current and future benefits. If this cannot be done with the proposed land-use or management practices, then management should select different goals or practices.

To meet the challenges of sustaining ecological systems and understanding our role as managers, we must first consider who was managing the lands of Texas before the European settlers began arriving in the 1820s. Even with the Indians present in Texas, much of this system was functioning through natural processes. Yes, they were living on the land, drinking the water, hunting game, and setting fires to the land. But the reason for management lies not in managing the "natural" but in managing the "not natural." The Spaniards introduced cattle to the Western Hemisphere in 1542. Cattle, sheep, goats, horses, donkeys, emus, and camels are not native to Texas. We have introduced foods, grains, pasture grasses, and other plants that are not native to the state. With all of the introduced, nonnative plants (about 1,500 species) and animals (about 96 species on Texas rangelands), humans must manage the land, soil, plants, and animals in order to keep what was natural healthy. Without management, the nonnative species will overtake our landscape, and the ensuing change will create an unhealthy, unsustainable environment. We must consider what humans are doing to the system. Consider the following actions and potential results:

- Planting bermudagrass or tall fescue in large acreages results in habitat fragmentation for deer.
- Large acreages of cotton, corn, and sorghum result in loss of cross-pollination of native plants.
- Overgrazing by cattle, sheep, and goats results in change from tallgrass to shortgrass prairie.
- Stopping all wildfires results in increased brush invasion.
- Promotion of planting monocultures results in suppression and loss of biodiversity.
- Laws and public policy such as Proposition 11, Qualification of Agricultural Land in Wildlife Management Use, can result in landowners incorporating wildlife management instead of solely using traditional agriculture.

The ecosystem management approach encompasses biological, environmental, and human factors, interactions, and impacts and responses. Ecosystem management is simply an ecologically based planning approach to integrate social, economic, and ecosystem-level considerations to improve sustainable benefits and integrity of the ecosystems we utilize. It involves all major stakeholders for the common solving of issues that transcend current management boundaries. This requires the development of a better understanding of relationships among land management activities, resource capabilities, social and economic demands, ecological health, and sustainability so that responsible management can be implemented by respective landowners (private, county, parish, state, federal, and even lessees).

To the US Fish and Wildlife Service, ecosystem management is an attitude, an approach and a philosophy that considers the whole environment within a geographic area. This means "protecting the function, structure and species composition of an ecosystem while providing for its sustainable socioeconomic use." The BLM (1994) considers that "the primary goal of ecosystem management is to develop management that conserves, restores and maintains the ecological integrity, productivity and biological diversity of public lands." Ranchers have become more environmentally pro-active in their management, for example, properly using animal health-care products, managing for lean meat by reducing animals' stress levels,

Overgrazing by cattle and other livestock herds is an important consideration when managing Texas rangelands. Courtesy of Texas A&M AgriLife Extension Service

One management tool that qualifies under Proposition 11, Qualification of Agricultural Land in Wildlife Management Use, is habitat control. Tractors can be useful tools in shredding pastures for grazing pressure on native pastures, disking strips for grasslands restoration, plowing ground to set up succession cycles, or shaping brush. Courtesy of Clinton J. Faas, cjfaas@gmail.com

managing habitat for wildlife, properly using herbicides, using proper stocking rates, and practicing conservation ethics. Planning for the future must include on- and off-ranch impacts and values. Ranchers will need to be active stakeholders in ecosystem planning along with all the various agencies and organizations, as well as ranch employees, neighboring ranches, nearby urban and suburban communities, and other stakeholders. Tools such as geographic information systems, remote sensing, aerial photography, and computer record keeping and analysis are invaluable to local ranchers, citizens, communities, and agencies for better planning, implementing, monitoring, and allocating resources to achieve solutions that sustain natural resource productivity for the future.

Summary

Ecosystem management is a "state of mind." It is a way to view things so that you consider what effects your actions may have on other organisms and parts of the natural ecosystem you are associated with and managing. The landowner, manager, or "steward" will have to make the right decisions and then seek the best methods to do the job right. We must understand the consequences of our actions in regard to the environment. Without understanding the principles of ecology and ongoing natural landscape processes, we could make the wrong decisions.

References

Bureau of Land Management. 1994. *Ecosystem Management in the BLM: From Concept to Commitment.* Gov. Pub. BLM/SC/Gi-94/005+1736. Washington, DC: Bureau of Land Management.

Dale, V. H., S. Brown, R. A. Haeuber, N. T. Hobbs, N. Huntly, R. J. Naiman, W. E. Riebsame, M. G. Turner, and T. J. Valone. 2000. Ecological Principles and Guidelines for Managing the Use of Land. *Ecological Applications* 10 (3): 639–70.

Drucker, P. F. 1974. *Management: Tasks, Responsibilities, Practices.* New York: Harper and Row.

Giller, C. 1994. Ranchers Blamed for Transfer of BLM Veteran. *High Country News* 26 (20): 2.

Salwasser, H. 1995. Ecosystem Management: Broadening Perspectives on Relationships among People, Land, and Resources. In *Starker Lectures,* comp. B. Shelby and S. Arbogast, 45–68. Corvallis: Oregon State University, College of Forestry.

US Department of the Interior. 1993. Grazing Administration Regulations, Proposed Rule. *Federal Register* 58 (155), 43208–231.

White, Larry D. 2001. Management of Range Ecosystems. Presentation notes at the Lost Pines Chapter, Texas Master Naturalist Training, April 23, Bastrop.

Additional Resources

Bailey, Robert G. 1996. *Ecosystem Geography.* New York: Springer.

Boyce, Mark S., and Alan Haney. 1997. *Ecosystem Management: Applications for Sustainable Forest and Wildlife Resources.* New Haven, CT: Yale University Press.

Burnside, Don, and Allen Rasmussen. 1997. Ecosystem Management: Can It Succeed? *Rangelands* 19 (2): 20–24.

Christensen, Norman L., Ann M. Bartuska, James H. Brown, Stephen Carpenter, Carla D'Antonio, Robert Francis, Jerry F. Franklin, James A. MacMahon, Reed F. Noss, David J. Parsons, Charles H. Peterson, Monica G. Turner, and Robert G. Woodmansee. 1996. The Report of the Ecological Society of America Committee on the Scientific Basis for Ecosystem Management. *Ecological Applications* 6 (3): 665–91.

Cortner, H., and Margaret Moote. 1999. *The Politics of Ecosystem Management.* Washington, DC: Island Press.

Daniels, Steven, and Gregg Walker. 1996. Collaborative Learning: Improving Public Deliberation in Ecosystem-Based Management. *Environmental Impact Assessment Review* 16:71–102.

Duane, T. 1997. Community Participation in Ecosystem Management. *Ecology Law Quarterly* 24 (4): 771–97.

Dyksterhuis, E. J. 1958. Ecological Principles in Range Evaluation. *Botanical Review* 24:253–72.

Ecological Stewardship: A Common Reference for Ecosystem Management. 1999. Ed. W. T. Sexton, A. J. Malk, R. C. Szaro, and

N. C. Johnson. 3 vols. Kidlington, Oxford, UK: Elsevier Science.

Gerlach, L., and D. Bengston. 1994. If Ecosystem Management Is the Solution, What's the Problem? *Journal of Forestry* 92:18–21.

Grumbine, R. Edward. 1994a. Reflections on "What Is Ecosystem Management?" *Conservation Biology* 11 (1): 41–47.

———. 1994b. What Is Ecosystem Management? *Conservation Biology* 8 (1): 27–38.

Hartig, John H., Richard L. Thomas, and Edward Iwachewski. 1996. Lessons from Practical Application of an Ecosystem Approach in Management of the Laurentian Great Lakes. *Lakes & Reservoirs: Research and Management* 2:137–45.

Lackey, Robert. 1998. Seven Pillars of Ecosystem Management. *Landscape and Urban Planning* 40:21–30.

Marsh, Lindell, and Peter Lallas. 1995. Focused, Special-Area Conservation Planning: An Approach to Reconciling Development and Environmental Protection. In *Collaborative Planning for Wetlands and Wildlife*, ed. Douglas Porter and David Salveson, 7–33. Washington, DC: Island Press.

McCormick, Frank. 1999. Principles of Ecosystem Management and Sustainable Development. In *Ecosystem Management and Sustainability*, ed. John Peine, 3–19. New York: Lewis Publishers.

Meffe, Gary K., Larry A. Nielsen, Richard L. Knight, and Dennis A. Schenborn. 2002. *Ecosystem Management: Adaptive, Community Based Conservation*. Washington, DC: Island Press.

National Research Council. 1998. *Forested Landscapes in Perspective: Prospects and Opportunities for Sustainable Management of America's Nonfederal Forests*. Washington, DC: National Academy Press.

Norwine, Jim, John R. Giardino, Gerald R. North, and Juan B. Valdes. 1995. *The Changing Climate of Texas: Predictability and Implications for the Future*. College Station: Geobooks, Texas A&M University.

Noss, Reed F. 1983. A Regional Landscape Approach to Maintain Diversity. *BioScience* 33:700–706.

Noss, Reed, and Allen Cooperrider. 1994. *Saving Nature's Legacy: Protecting and Restoring Biodiversity*. Washington, DC: Island Press.

Odum, Eugene P. 1993. *Ecology and Our Endangered Life-Support Systems*. 2nd ed. Sunderland, MA: Sinauer Associates.

Peck, Sheila. 1998. *Planning for Biodiversity: Issues and Examples*. Washington, DC: Island Press.

Peine, John D. 1999. *Ecosystem Management for Sustainability: Principles and Practices Illustrated by a Regional Biosphere Reserve Cooperative*. Boca Raton, FL: Lewis Publishers.

Rapport, David J., William L. Lasley, Dennis E. Rolston, N. Ole Nielsen, Calvin O. Qualset, and Ardeshir B. Damania. 2002. *Managing for Healthy Ecosystems*. Boca Raton, FL: Lewis Publishers.

Scott, J. M., B. Csuti, J. D. Jacobi, and J. Estes. 1987. Species Richness: A Geographic Approach to Protecting Future Biological Diversity. *BioScience* 37 (11): 782–88.

Sexton, William. 1998. Ecosystem Management: Expanding the Resources Management Tool Kit. *Landscape and Urban Planning* 40:103–12.

Smith, Robert Leo. 1972. *The Ecology of Man: An Ecosystem Approach*. New York: Harper and Row.

Spurr, Stephen H. 1969. The Natural Resource Ecosystem. In *The Ecosystem Concept in Natural Resource Management*, ed. George M. Van Dyne. New York: Academic Press.

Szaro, R., W. Sexton, and C. Malone. 1998. The Emergence of Ecosystem Management as a Tool for Meeting People's Needs and Sustaining Ecosystems. *Landscape and Urban Planning* 40:1–7.

Thomas, Stanley. 1995. Ecosystem Management and the Arrogance of Humanism. *Conservation Biology* 9 (2): 255–62.

UN Development Programme, UNEP, World Bank, World Resources Institute. *World Resources 2000–2001: People and Ecosystems, the Fraying Web of Life*. Washington DC: World Resources Institute.

Van Dyne, George M., ed. 1969. *The Ecosystem Concept in Natural Resource Management*. New York: Academic Press

Vogt, Kristiina A., John C. Gordon, John P. Wargo, and Daniel J. Vogt. 1997. *Ecosystems: Balancing Science with Management*. New York: Springer-Verlag.

Westley, Frances. 1995. Governing Design: The Management of Social Systems and Ecosystems Management. In *Barriers and Bridges to the Renewal of Ecosystems and Institutions*, ed. Lance Gunderson, C. S. Holling, and Stephen S. Light, 391–427. New York: Columbia University Press.

Wondolleck, Julia, and Steven Yaffee. 2000. *Making Collaboration Work: Lessons from Innovation in Natural Resource Management*. Washington, DC: Island Press.

Websites

Texas A&M AgriLife Extension Bookstore: http://agrilifebookstore.org [source of Extension Rangeland Ecology and Management publications]

Texas A&M AgriLife Extension: Texas Natural Resources Server: http://texnat.tamu.edu [source of information on range and wildlife management and water]

UNIT 7

Geology and Soils

CHRISTOPHER C. MATHEWSON
Regents Professor Emeritus of Geology, Texas A&M University, with contributions from the Natural Resources Conservation Service and William A. Foss

Unit Goals

After completing this unit, volunteers should be able to

- become aware of the basic geological processes of rock formation and the interactions that were instrumental in forming the geology of Texas
- trace the geological history of Texas
- describe the various landform regions of Texas
- describe the physical and chemical properties of soil
- discuss ways to prevent soil erosion
- become aware of and understand the basic geological processes of rock formation and interaction that were instrumental in forming the geology of Texas
- understand the geological composition and formation of aquifers and become familiar with those present in Texas

"Nature is an open book for those who care to read. Each grass-covered hillside is a page on which is written the history of the past, conditions of the present, and the predictions of the future."
—J. E. Weaver, American botanist and prairie ecologist

Introduction

The *American Heritage Dictionary* defines **geology** as "the scientific study of the origin, history, and structure of the earth." A liberal interpretation of the "history" in that definition could make geology quite literally the study of everything. However, in order to understand the effect of geology on the landscape and, consequently, on the habitat created on that landscape, it is really only necessary to have a basic understanding of geology and geological processes. As we learn about geology and study the effects of geological processes on habitat formation, it will become clear that the geology of a region is responsible for many of the ecological processes that influence the formation of habitat. For instance, the types of rocks underlying a region have a role in determining how high a mountain will rise if the land is uplifted by a geological process. A weak rock that is easily eroded will not allow the mountain to rise to a high elevation because the rock will be eroded by wind and rain as the land rises. Alternatively, a strong rock, resistant to erosion, can allow very high mountains to form because it will erode at a slower rate than the rate at which the land is uplifted. The height of mountains in a region will determine how much "rain shadow" exists on the leeward side of the mountains and how much rain will fall on the windward mountainsides, thereby shaping the ecologies that will form on each side of the mountain.

Thus, the geological processes that uplifted the mountains and the rocks that formed the mountains are directly responsible for what habitat was created. In order to understand Texas geology, first it is necessary to understand the basic terminology used to describe rocks. There are three basic types of rocks: igneous, sedimentary, and metamorphic.

Igneous Rocks

Igneous rocks are formed from crystallization of molten magma. **Magma** is simply

Flow-banded rhyolite. Courtesy of Michael C. Rygel

a collection of minerals heated by radiation in the earth's depth and pressure to the point that the minerals become liquid. Igneous rocks come in two types, intrusive and extrusive. **Intrusive** igneous rocks, such as granite, form large, visible crystals because the liquid cooled slowly as the molten magma "intruded" into other rocks around it. Because the other rocks insulated the magma, the cooling process was slow and large crystals were able to form in much the same way that sugar water when allowed to slowly evaporate will form large crystals of rock candy. **Extrusive** igneous rocks, such as basalt, form from magma or "lava" that extrudes onto the surface of the earth. The exposure to air causes the lava to cool quickly, making the crystals formed in extrusive rocks too small to see with the naked eye. Two igneous rocks may have exactly the same chemical composition but two different names and two different sets of physical properties based on whether they were intrusive or extrusive in origin. For example, granite (intrusive) and rhyolite (extrusive) have similar mineral compositions but have different crystal sizes. They, therefore, differ in physical properties such as resistance to weathering.

Sedimentary Rocks

Sedimentary rocks are formed by accumulation of pieces of other rocks. As other rocks, including other sedimentary rocks, are weathered and broken down into smaller and smaller pieces, they may be transported by wind, water, gravity, or biological activity to be redeposited at some distance from their original location. As they

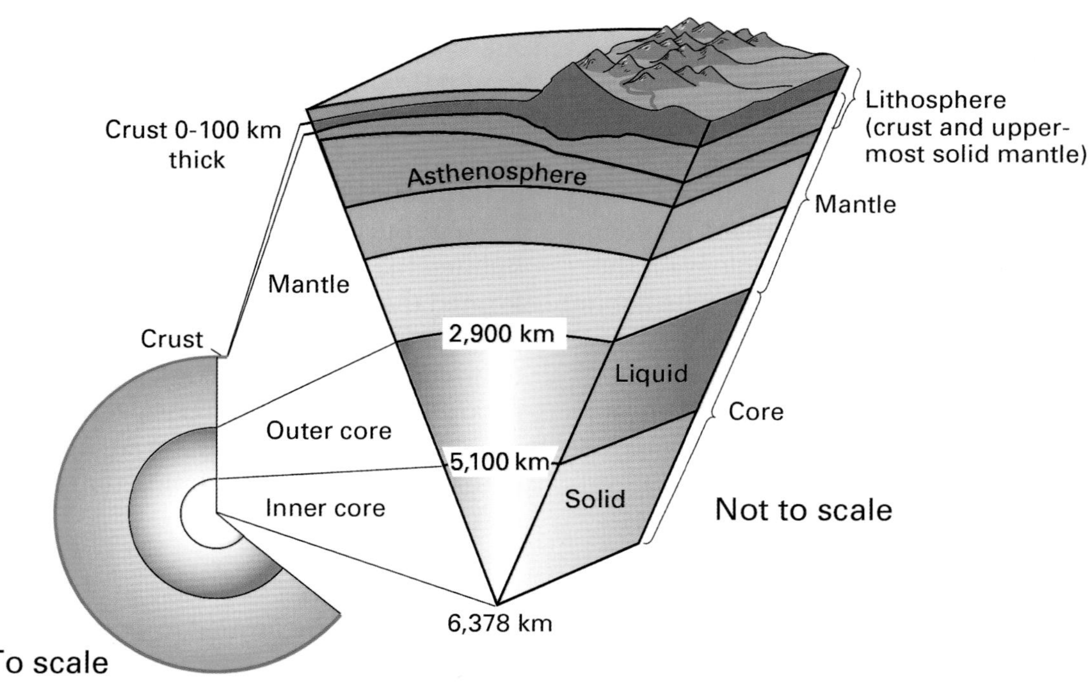

Divisions of the earth's interior.

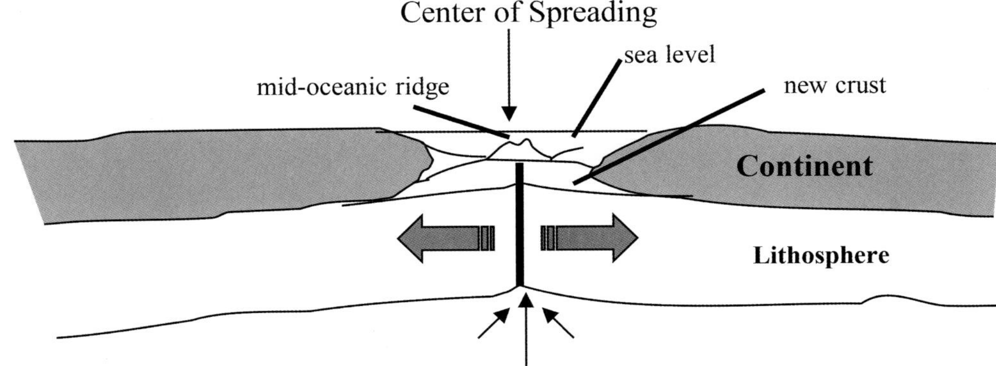

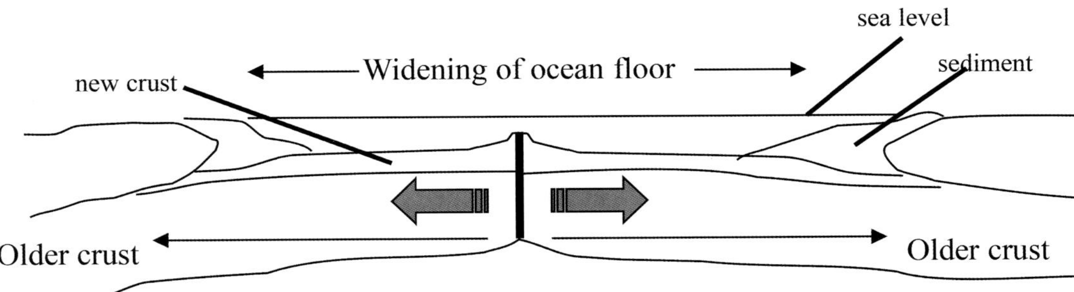

The seafloor spreading is an example of oceanic rifting.

are redeposited and compacted together by the weight of the material deposited on top of them, the pieces are recemented together into a new rock. Sedimentary rocks are named and described by the size of the individual pieces or **grains** that are cemented together. Sandstones are sedimentary rocks that contain large grains, which are visible to the naked eye. Siltstones, mudstones, and shales are all rocks formed of grains too small to be seen by the naked eye. The size of the grains also controls the amount of space between the grains and how easily air or water can flow through the rock. Rocks with smaller grains have more space between the grains and higher porosity, but the pores are not as well connected; therefore, water and air do not move easily through them. Rocks with connected pores allow water and air to flow through them more easily.

Sandstones make excellent aquifer materials because they have well-connected pores that allow water to flow through them easily. Shales make poor aquifers because the pores are not well connected. However, when shales break down into clay soils, the high porosity allows them to hold a large amount of water available for use by vegetation growing in the soil; sandstones generally break down into sandy soils that are well drained and do not hold large quantities of water. Sedimentary rocks can also form when minerals are dissolved in water and redeposited as the water evaporates. Large salt beds can be formed by evaporation of shallow bodies of salt water.

Metamorphic Rocks

Metamorphic rocks are formed when heat and pressure cause changes to the chemical or physical structure of a rock. For example, when a shale, which is relatively weak and easily eroded, is exposed to extremely high temperatures, the lighter minerals can melt and then recrystallize when the rock cools. This binds the rock together, creating a slate that is much stronger and more resistant to erosion. Metamorphic rocks can also form in areas where magma moves upward and creates high temperatures or at boundaries in the earth's crust where the movements of the plates can create intense pressures.

Plate Tectonics

Understanding what kinds of rocks exist is only part of learning geology. Learning how they are created is the second and much larger part. All geological processes are driven by heat radiating out from the core of the earth. Geologists believe the earth consists of three primary parts. The innermost **core** of the earth is believed to consist of molten metals such as iron and nickel. Solid metals may exist at the very center of the core, but most of the core is liquid. The **mantle** of the earth is believed to be semi-molten, with a wide variety of minerals present.

The **crust** is the solid outer "skin" of the earth and is much thinner than the mantle or core. The crust of the earth is separated into many large and small **plates**. Each plate interacts with those around it to form different features on the earth's surface. Two kinds of plates exist, thin but dense oceanic plates and thicker but less dense continental plates. The **oceanic plates** are created by magma extruded under the ocean that cools rapidly to form dense, heavy rock layers. Marine biological activity lays down layers of very small particles, forming thick shale units on the seafloor. **Continental plates** form through many different processes, but the result is a thicker, lighter plate. If you can imagine a bowl of melted cheese, the core is the runny, fully melted material at the bottom, while the mantle is the stringy material about halfway down, and the crust is the solid material that forms on the top of the cheese as it cools. Just as the skin of the cheese wrinkles when a chip is dipped into it, the crust of the earth deforms in areas where surficial plates interact with one another.

Many types of plate interactions can take place, and each creates different kinds of features on the earth's surface. A few types of plate interactions are (1) oceanic rifting, (2) transform faulting, (3) continent-continent collisions, (4) oceanic-continental subduction, and (5) midcontinent rifting. For information on the tectonic episodes in Texas, see appendix A.

Oceanic Rifting

In the middle of the Atlantic Ocean, the plates are moving away from one another. This **oceanic rifting** allows magma from the mantle to rise up and create new crustal material on the ocean floor.

Transform Faulting

In California, two plates are slowly sliding past each other. The plate under the Pacific Ocean is moving north-northwest, while the North American Plate is moving south-southeast. The area where the plates actually contact one another is creating **transform faulting** in the San Andreas Fault Zone, an area of intensely deformed rocks that are constantly being moved and twisted as the forces pushing the two plates past each other fracture and bend the rocks. Many of the hills and valleys along the California coast are formed by rocks being bent or broken upward or downward by the pressures exerted on the margins of the fault zone.

Continent-Continent Collisions

The Rocky Mountains are an area where an old continental plate impacted against the North American Plate and caused a large area of crust to be thrust upward in a **continent-continent collision**. The

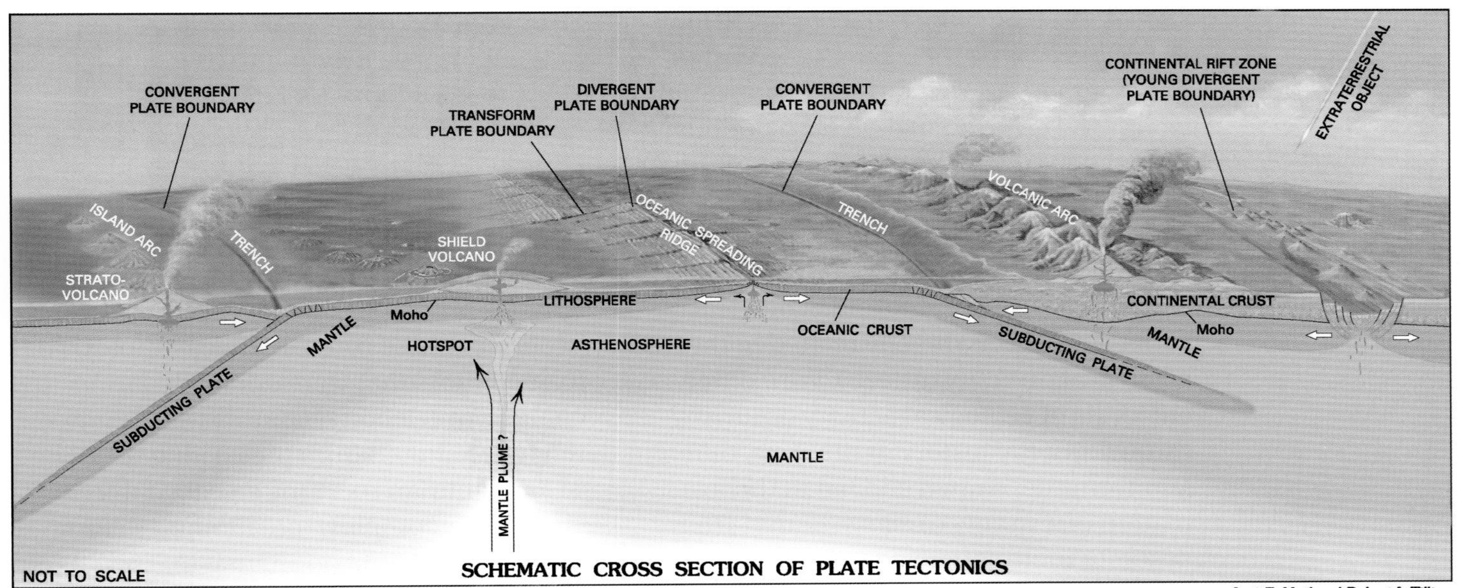

The origin of magma. From Simkin et al. (2006)

crust acted in much the same way as a car bumper would in a collision, bending and deforming upward as the plates were pushed into each other.

Oceanic-Continental Subduction

The Cascade Mountains in the Pacific Northwest are an example of the results of **oceanic-continental subduction**, an oceanic plate colliding with a continental plate and being subducted or driven under the continental plate. As the subducted oceanic plate is being pushed back down into the mantle, the temperature and pressure combine to melt the plate and turn it into magma. The magma boils up under the edge of the continental plate, uplifting the area as it moves upward. Portions of the magma will then erupt at the surface and form volcanoes, while the rest of the magma will stop below the surface and form intrusive igneous rock bodies. Thus, a mountain chain develops along the margin of the continent as a result of the uplifting magma.

Midcontinent Rifting

The Big Bend area of Texas is an example of **midcontinent rifting**. In some cases, a large continental plate will develop a weakness and magma from the mantle will begin to rise and cause the plate to separate or rift over the area where the magma is rising. As the continent begins to spread apart, large faults can develop, causing large areas of land to drop down as the land spreads apart.

Imagine a concrete decked highway bridge over a large river gorge being stretched at either end. As the bridge is stretched, the deck sections gradually pull apart and one by one lose contact with the footings supporting them and drop into the gorge. The same thing occurs when midcontinent rifting takes place. As the earth stretches out, large blocks of crust slowly drop down as they lose the support of the crust around them. The Big Bend area is a crustal block that was dropped down along two fault lines as a result of spreading along the Rio Grande Rift.

Now that you have a basic idea of how rocks form and how large plates made of rock interact, the history of Texas geology can be more easily understood. It is a complex story involving many changes in sea-level elevation due to glacial formation and melting, at least one continent-continent plate collision, magmatic uplift in Central Texas, and midcontinent rifting in far West Texas. Our state has undergone a series of depositional periods when layers of rock were created and erosional periods when rock layers were eroded and redeposited in new areas through the activity of wind, water, and gravity. Each of these periods brought about changes in what kinds of rocks were found at the surface in the areas affected and directly impacted how the landforms in the area developed.

All the physiographic and ecological variety in Texas is directly related to the geological diversity of Texas. With different kinds of geological activity occurring throughout the history of the state, different landforms developed and led to the formation of a variety of ecosystems—from desert to mountain to coastal plains. As you read the history of Texas geologically, look closely at the maps of the areas described and try to picture what kinds of landforms were present in relation to the geological activities occurring at the time. When you are finished reading the history, compare the geological map of Texas, which shows the kinds of rocks outcropping at the surface (and shows graphically the shape of the landforms created by the rocks outcropping) with the physiographic province (appendix B) and ecological region maps of Texas ("Ecological Regions" unit). The three maps are nearly identical and provide a perfect visual of what you will already know intuitively—the ecosystems, physiographic features, and habitat of Texas are undeniably linked directly to the composition of the rocks that are present and the geological processes that put them there.

Geological History of Texas

The story preserved in the rocks requires an understanding of the origin of the strata and how they have been deformed. **Stratigraphy** is the study of the composition, sequence, and origin of the rocks; what the rocks are made of; how they were formed; and the order in which the layers were formed. Structural geology reveals the architecture of the rocks: the locations of the mountains, volcanoes, sedimentary basins, and earthquake belts.

Precambrian Era

The geological history of Texas can be traced back more than 2 billion years when the igneous intrusions of the **Precambrian** occurred. These rocks include complexly deformed rocks that were originally formed by cooling from a liquid state as well as rocks that were altered from preexisting rocks.

Precambrian rocks, often called the "basement complex," are thought to form the foundation of continental masses. "Precambrian rocks underlie all of Texas" (*Texas Almanac* 1998–99, 65). These intrusions resulted in a number of granite bodies that are today exposed in the Llano Basin in Central Texas. Many of these granites are quarried as dimension (natural rock that is cut into blocks or slabs of a specific size) and monument stone. After the igneous activity ceased with the intrusion of the "Town Mountain Granite" near Marble Falls about 1.2 billion years ago, Texas was subjected to over 700 million years of erosion.

Paleozoic Era

During the Middle-Cambrian time, about 550 million years ago, Texas was covered by a shallow sea that deposited sandstone on the older crystalline rocks of the Precambrian. This was the beginning of a long period of time, the **Paleozoic era**, during which the landscape of Texas varied between shallow seas and lowlands. Texas was covered with sandstone, shale, and limestone. At the end of the **Pennsylvanian period**, about 280 million years ago, a major structural uplift occurred that lifted the land as much as 3,500 feet above its original low-lying position.

The Central Texas area became a series of mountains, related to similar uplifts in West Texas, Oklahoma, and Arkansas that were

Texas geological history

Millions of years before present	Era	Period	Epoch	Texas geological events
0.01	CENOZOIC	Quaternary	Holocene	Deposition of the sediments in the Texas river floodplains and along the Texas coast.
2.5			Pleistocene	Down-cutting of the Texas river valleys caused by a colder and wetter climate related to northern glaciations.
7		Tertiary	Pliocene	Deposition of sands and clays with some lignite beds in ancient river valleys and deltas that formed the Texas Coastal Plain. As the continent was uplifted, the modern Texas river systems formed and eroded their valleys into the Texas Hill Country.
26			Miocene	
38			Oligocene	
54			Eocene	
65			Paleocene	
136	MESOZOIC	Cretaceous		Deposition of limestone found throughout the Texas Hill Country. The Cretaceous ended with the uplifting of the North American continent and the formation of the Gulf of Mexico.
190		Jurassic		
225		Triassic		
280	PALEOZOIC	Permian		Formation of a great reef in a warm, shallow sea that existed in West Texas that today forms the Guadalupe Mountains and the highest point in Texas. Permian limestone also underlies part of the High Plains north of San Angelo.
325		Pennsylvanian		Deposition of limestone in shallow sea. Today it can be seen near Marble Falls and along the eastern edge of the High Plains. This limestone is mined near Marble Falls to manufacture white cement for architectural uses. The Pennsylvanian ended with a major tectonic uplift in Central Texas.
345		Mississippian		Deposition of limestone in a shallow sea. Most of this rock has been eroded away and is difficult to find today.
395		Devonian		Deposition of limestone in an equatorial sea. This rock is of limited extent throughout the Llano Basin area of Texas.
430		Silurian		Limited and isolated deposits of these sediments can be found in ancient cave features formed in the underlying Ordovician limestone in the Llano Basin.
500		Ordovician		Deposition of limestone and clayey-limestone (marls) in a shallow equatorial sea. Solution erosion of the limestone that could have started during the Silurian ultimately formed Longhorn Caverns.
570		Cambrian		The oldest sedimentary rocks in Texas were deposited in rivers and along the rocky coast composed of crystalline rocks.
4600	PRECAMBRIAN			The oldest rocks (gneiss and schist) that can be found in the Llano Basin. The uplift that occurred at the end of the Pennsylvanian brought these very old rocks near the surface so that they can be seen today. Texas is a major supplier of granite stone used throughout the world for monuments and buildings. The capital building in Austin was constructed of Precambrian granite from a quarry near Marble Falls.

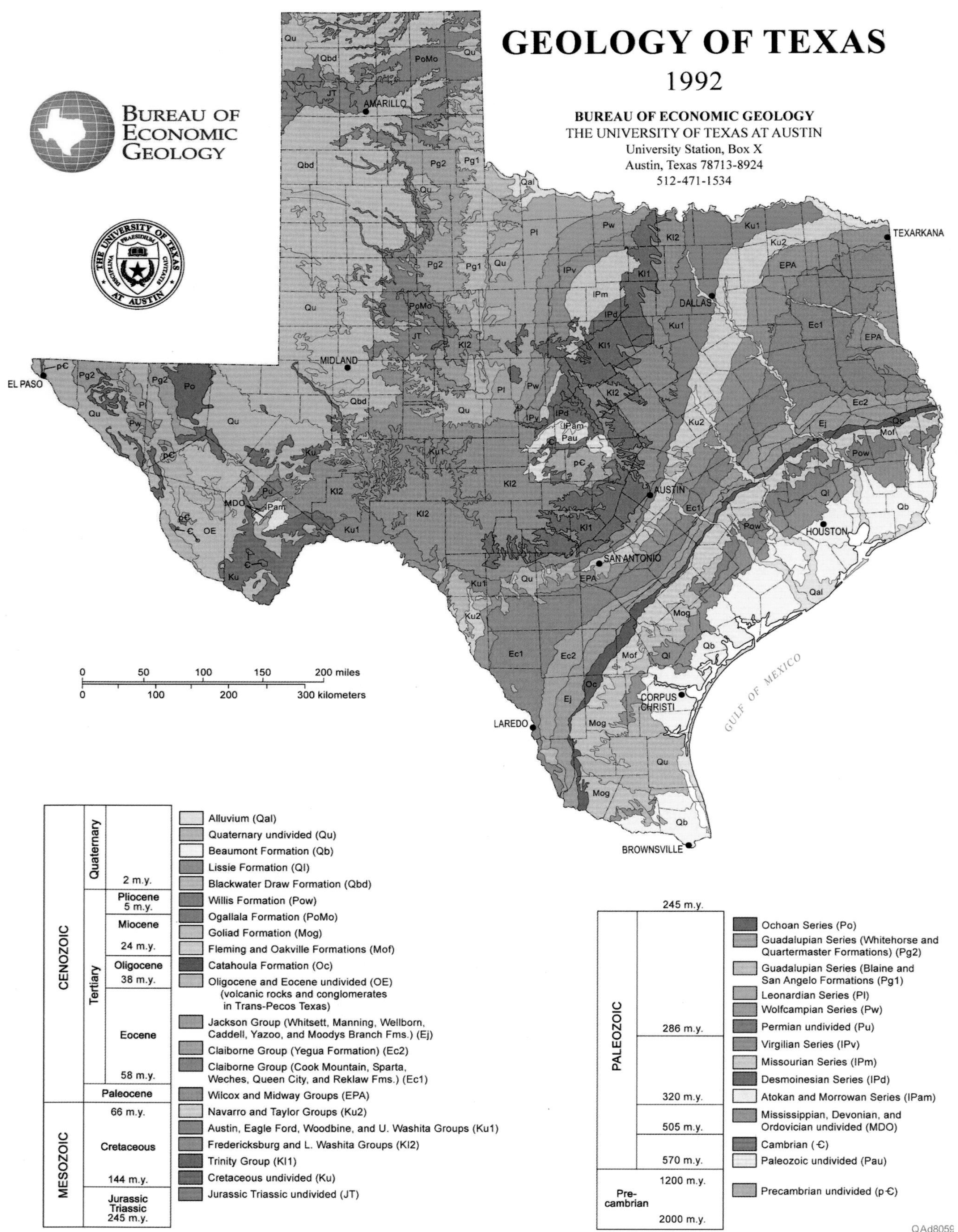

Geology of Texas. Courtesy of the Bureau of Economic Geology, the University of Texas at Austin

the formation of the ancestral Appalachian Mountains. The seas were displaced westward during the **Permian period**.

Great coastal reef systems developed around the shore of the Permian sea, where shallow basins and wide tidal floods of salt, gypsum, and red muds accumulated in the hot, arid land of the Panhandle, east to Wichita Falls, south to Concho County, and the Trans-Pecos (*Texas Almanac* 1998–99). Today we see the remains of these great reefs exposed in the Guadalupe Mountains, where the Capitan fossil reef complex, one of the largest in the world, is over 4,000 feet thick. Guadalupe Peak is the highest point in Texas, reaching to 8,751 feet above sea level.

El Capitan, Guadalupe Mountains National Park. Courtesy of Geoffrey J. King

Mesozoic Era

At the beginning of the **Mesozoic era**, about 200 million years ago, the Permian seas had filled with sediment and Texas was a low-lying desert environment. Very little rock evidence of the **Triassic** and **Jurassic periods** is exposed in Texas. Triassic sandstones and shales can be found along a relatively narrow band that stretches northward from east of Big Spring to Amarillo. These rocks are exposed along the erosional Caprock Escarpment and in the valley walls of the Canadian River northwest of Amarillo.

By about 135 million years ago, the North American continent began to subside below sea level again and a warm, shallow sea covered most of Texas. For over 70 million years, the sea deposited limestone, shale, and sandstone. The **Cretaceous** rocks in Texas are predominantly limestone, which range from thick beds deposited in open, shallow seas to thin beds deposited in tidal flats. As the Cretaceous came to a close, the North American continent rose again when the Gulf of Mexico began to form.

Earthquakes rocked the area that we know today as the Balcones Fault Zone, an arc-shaped zone that stretches from Uvalde on the southwest through San Antonio, Austin, and Dallas. To the west of this zone, the continent was rising, while to the east, the land was subsiding to eventually become the Texas coastal plain.

Cenozoic Era

During the past 65 million years, thick wedges of sandstone and shale have been carried from the rising mainland by eroding rivers to the ancestral Gulf of Mexico, where the sediment was spread along the shore by ancient coastal waves. Occasionally, swamps would form on the deltas of these ancient rivers. As the swamps slowly sank below sea level, the remains of great, forested wetlands were transformed into lignite and coal that we now mine to produce electric power.

While the coastal plain was slowly sinking, other more violent forces were active in far West Texas. The basin and range region of the western United States was developing. West Texas is situated at the southern end of this region. The land was disturbed by numerous faults that caused some areas to be uplifted while other areas were down-dropped. These tectonic changes resulted in a complex geological setting for far West Texas. Rocks of all ages, from Precambrian to modern, are exposed in this area. At the same time that West Texas was forming, the High Plains region of the Texas Panhandle was receiving thick deposits of sand that were being eroded eastward from the uplifting Rocky Mountains. These geological events formed the stage for erosional processes that developed the Texas landscape we know today.

During the latter part of the **Cenozoic era**, a great Ice Age descended upon the northern part of the North American continent. For more than 2 million years, there were successive advances and retreats of thick sheets of glacial ice. Four periods of extensive glaciations were separated by warmer interglacial periods. Although the glaciers never reached as far south as Texas, the state's climate and sea level underwent major changes with each period of glacial advance and retreat. Sea level during times of glacial advance was 300 to 450 feet lower than during the warmer interglacial periods because so much seawater was captured in the ice sheets. The climate was both more humid and cooler than today, and the major Texas rivers carried more water and more sand and gravel to the sea. These deposits underlie the outer 50 miles or more of the Gulf Coastal Plain.

"Leave it as it is. The ages have been at work on it and man can only mar it."
—President Theodore Roosevelt

Landforms of Texas

Just as the geological history of Texas established the framework upon which the various rocks were deposited, this framework also established the foundations for the current landscape of Texas. In general, one can divide the Texas landscape into five zones: Coastal Plain, Balcones Escarpment, Hill Country, High Plains, and West Texas Mountains.

Coastal Plain

Cenozoic-era rocks that are predominantly sandstones and shales underlie the Texas **Coastal Plain**. Because these sedimentary rocks have not been subjected to significant diagenetic processes of heat or pressure, they are generally weakly cemented and of low strength. As a result, they erode to form

The Coastal Sand Plains of South Texas are composed of grasslands and coastal oak mottes intermixed with mesquite, granjeno, and salt marshes. Unstable, windblown sand produces the characteristic dunes of this ecoregion. Courtesy of Texas Parks and Wildlife Department

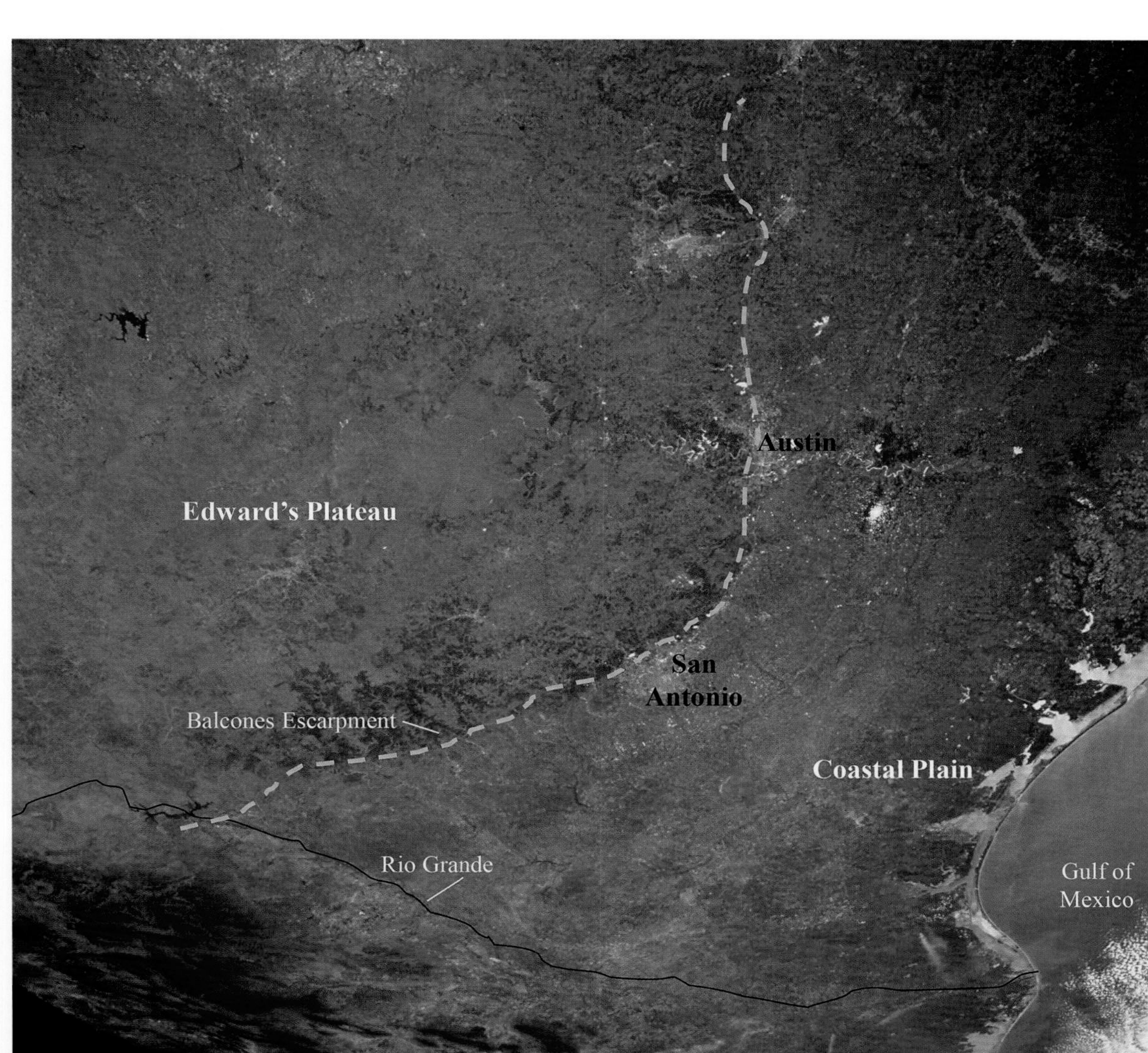

Aerial view of the Balcones Fault. Courtesy of National Aeronautics and Space Administration

a rolling surface. This pattern, however, reflects the orientation of the outcrop patterns of the underlying bedrock. Because the Coastal Plain bedrock was deposited as a series of wedges of sediment laid down during the development of the Gulf of Mexico, the outcrop patterns tend to parallel the Texas coast. The apparently disoriented rolling landscape of Texas actually has a distinctive orientation that is aligned with the Texas coast. The weakly cemented sandstone units are more erosion resistant than the shale units; thus, the Coastal Plain hills are predominantly sand-rich while the valleys are shale-rich. When one travels northwestward from the nearly flat-lying coast toward San Antonio, Austin, or Dallas, the rocks become progressively older and the hills become more pronounced. Thus, the general landform of the Coastal Plain is a series of northeast-southwest-oriented low ridges that are highest in the northwestern portion. These ridges control the orientation of many of the streams that flow across the Coastal Plain.

Balcones Escarpment

In contrast to the Coastal Plain, the **Balcones Escarpment** is a narrow zone characterized by rapidly changing to-

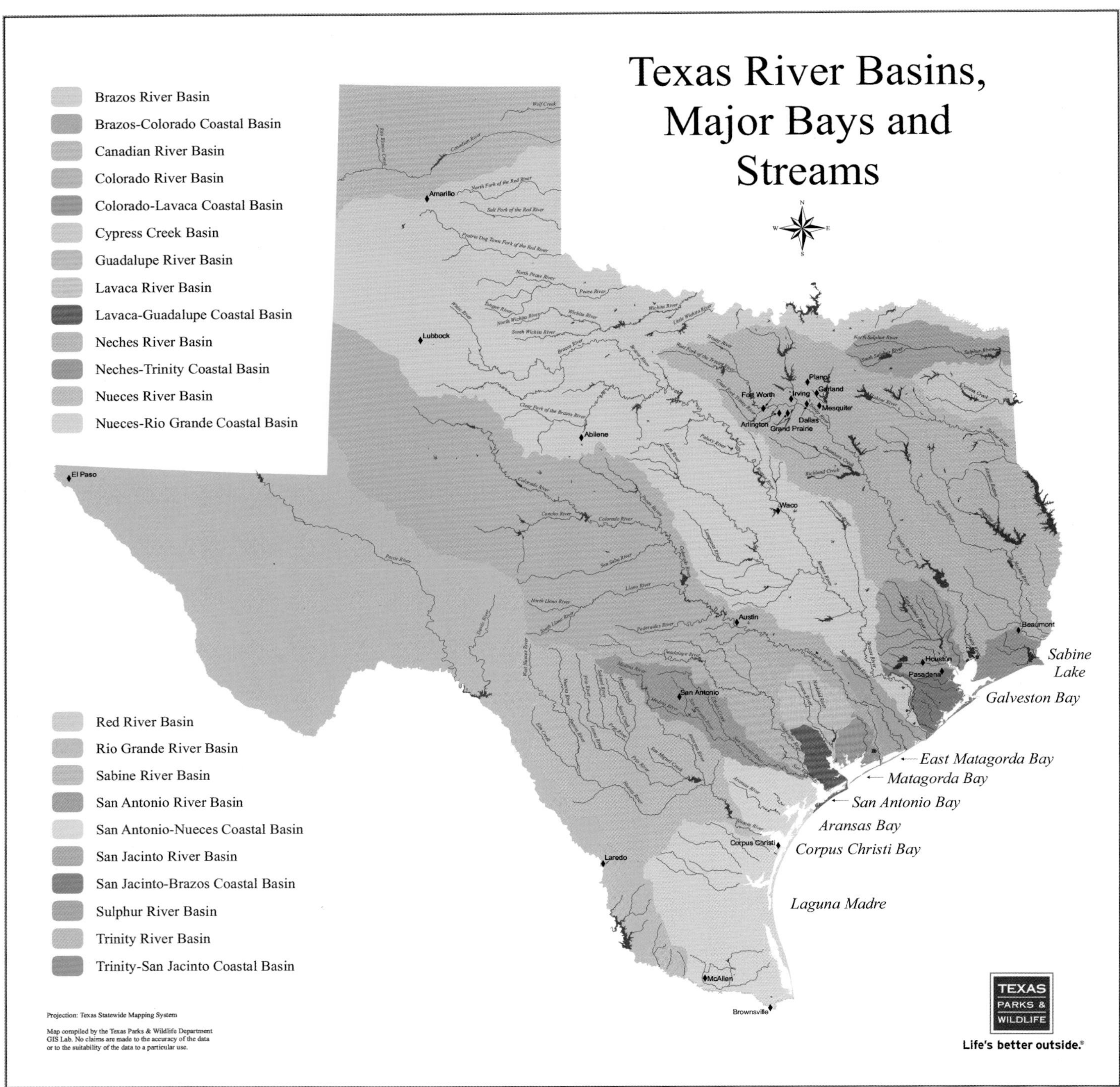

Map of major rivers showing the generally southeasterly flow of water in relation to the state's landforms. Courtesy of Texas Parks and Wildlife Department

pography. Faulting associated with the Post-Cretaceous continental uplift was concentrated in this narrow zone and produced a series of displaced bedrock blocks that are oriented parallel to the fault zone. The landform that marks the Balcones Escarpment today is the combined result of the northeastward-oriented fault blocks and the southeastward-oriented rivers that carry sediment to the Gulf of Mexico. As the land rose above sea level at the end of the Cretaceous, the Texas river system, composed of the Rio Grande, Colorado, Brazos, Trinity, Sabine, Red, and Canadian, started cutting downward across the fault blocks in the Balcones Fault Zone. Today, especially in the area between Waco and Del Rio, the Balcones Fault Zone is a noticeable northwestern boundary to the Texas Coastal Plain and a southeastern boundary to the Texas Hill Country.

Hill Country

West of the Balcones Escarpment and the Coastal Plain lies the Texas **Hill Country**. These hills are actually the result of valley erosion by the rivers that cut downward as the continent rose. The dominant character of this area is flat-topped hills and stair-step slopes into river valleys. This is best seen in the area along the Colorado River west of Austin. The pattern is visible but more subdued along the other rivers. The Colorado and its tributaries, the San Saba and Llano Rivers, have excavated a "hole" through the younger overlying rocks to expose the Precambrian crystalline igneous and metamorphic rocks in the Llano Basin. North of Waco, the Hill Country is subdued because the Trinity and Sabine Rivers have not eroded as far back as the rivers to the south. The western limit to the Hill Country is gradational because the erosive power of the river systems decreased as they approached their headwaters. To the south is the Edwards Plateau, a flat-lying landscape composed of Cretaceous limestone, while to the north lies the rolling terrain formed on Pennsylvanian and Permian sediments.

High Plains

The Texas **High Plains** are separated from the western Hill Country by the Caprock Escarpment, a noticeable band of steep slopes and cliffs. The Caprock Escarpment marks the northwestern edge of erosion by the Colorado, Brazos, and Red Rivers. Except for the canyon eroded by the Canadian River, the High Plains form a nearly flat landscape. South of the Caprock Escarpment, near Big

The Bamberger Ranch is an example of Hill Country landscape. Courtesy of Dawn Wenzel

The High Plains are found in the northern and western region of the state, a windswept, mesa-like geographic area with highly variable temperatures throughout the year. The natural vegetation of the High Plains region consists primarily of short grasses with considerable mesquite growth in the southern portion and agriculturally now primarily farmed with winter wheat, cotton, grain, and grain sorghums. Courtesy of Texas Parks and Wildlife Department

The Davis Mountains are a segment of the southern Rocky Mountains, found mainly in Jeff Davis County in western Texas and extending northward of Marfa for 45 miles. This range, also known as the Texas Alps, is host to dry scrublands, steep terrain, and a wide variety of range wildlife. Shown here is Mount Livermore. Courtesy of Mark Tyson

Spring, the High Plains region merges with the Edwards Plateau.

West Texas Mountains

Southwest of Fort Stockton and Pecos lies the **West Texas Mountains** area. Completely different geological processes produced the landform seen in this region. The topography is the result of tectonic uplift and volcanic eruptions combined with erosion by the Rio Grande and its tributaries. River erosion, however, is minimal because the region is arid. Thus, the landform takes on a sharp and angular appearance. The fault blocks provide the topographic relief, while physical weathering processes form the cliffs and talus slopes at the mountain base.

Soil

From rocks come soils. If not for the soil, life on earth would probably not exist at all. As one of the basic elements required to support plant life on the surface of this planet, soil provides habitat for thousands of plants and animals; and these plants and animals form part of the basic food chain that supplies nutrients to higher animal forms, including humans.

Soil properties and characteristics vary greatly depending on location, the corresponding climate, and the material from which the soil develops. These variations provide the great diversity of plants and animals throughout the world. Not only does the soil have an effect on plants and animals but it also affects people, and thus politics and human sociology.

Soil by its nature may be deep, shallow, fertile, infertile, productive, or nonproductive. Optimal agricultural production is possible in areas where nature has produced deep, fertile soils, conditioned by favorable climate. These regions are capable of producing high population densities of humans, animals, and plants. In areas where the soil is shallow and the climate less favorable, higher life-forms do not exist in such profusion.

Human society flourishes in regions where the soil has the capacity to produce more than adequate supplies of food and fiber. A nation with a good food supply has the potential to be a rich and powerful nation; a nation that cannot feed its people cannot be strong. The soil is the very basis of a healthy and prosperous society. A people who do not have to struggle to produce the minimum amount of food and fiber to survive have time to pursue other interests. This time and interest allow people to concern themselves with the arts, with other people, and with the plant and animal communities around them. Maintaining this environment requires a basic understanding of the soil.

What Is Soil?

Soil is a term used by many people, and it may have a different meaning to each of them. The farmer views soil as the material that produces his crops. To the engineer, soil supports the structures he or she designs. A housewife has an altogether different view of soil when she is doing her family's laundry. A soil scientist has an even different viewpoint. To a soil scientist, soil is a natural part of the earth's surface in which land plants grow, having properties caused by the integrated effects of climate and organisms acting upon parent material, as conditioned by relief over periods of time.

Soil as a Growth Medium

Soil supplies plants with elements required for their establishment, growth, and reproduction, including support, nutrients, water, and air.

Support: Unlike animals, most land plants are not mobile. Plants need a location in which to establish themselves. Soil supplies such a location and holds the plant roots in place while it supports the plant in an upright position so that it can take advantage of the sun.

Nutrients: The soil supplies the nutrients to complete the plant's life cycle. Decomposition of organic matter and the mineral parent material from which the soil is formed make these nutrients available to the plant.

Water: The soil acts as a temporary reservoir, storing water supplied by rain or irrigation. The soil's ability to store water allows the plant to use water on a constant basis without having to rely on daily rain or irrigation.

Air: Plant growth requires a supply of air to the roots. The voids within the soil store oxygen the roots need for respiration and growth.

Ideal Soil Concept

Some people think that there is an ideal soil condition. This is not the case. Different plants growing under different conditions have different needs. The soil properties and conditions optimum for one species of plant may not suit another. The loblolly pine cannot grow in the same soil pH conditions that the Ashe juniper thrives on. And wheat cannot survive in the same moisture conditions required to produce rice.

Generally speaking, a loam-textured soil containing 45% mineral matter, 5% organic matter, 25% water, and 25% air will supply the needs for a large majority of plants. Soil conditions are dynamic, and these components vary in proportion from time to time, place to place, and under changing cultural practices.

Soil put to the plow will usually experience a decrease in the amount of organic matter present. When it rains, the pores (voids) in the soil fill with water. Soon after the rain, the soil is saturated with water and the air is excluded from the soil. Gravity and capillary action draw the water down through the soil profile. As the water passes through the soil, air is drawn into the soil and fills the larger voids first. Mechanical and hoof traffic over the soil results in compaction of the soil. Compaction reduces the pore space. This, in turn, can reduce the ability of the soil to hold water, slow the infiltration of water, and slow the exchange of gases within the soil.

Virgin Soil Myth

Many think, falsely, that a pristine soil untouched by human hands is, by its very nature, fertile and productive. Soils age much like humans and animals: the very young are not nearly as productive or fertile as the mature, and the old are not as productive as the mature. Though not always the case, forests often grow on older soils. Frequently, these soils exhibit very low fertility. They may never have seen a plow, and when converted into farmland, they do not have the ability to produce a reasonable yield. This mistake has often been made in the past and is still being made today. Lands in the American Northeast and in the rain forests of Brazil have proven not to be able to withstand the strain of intensive agriculture.

Soil Formation

Soil is a living medium. Because it lives, it goes through stages of development. It begins as parent material and develops into a young, or immature, soil. Biotic and climatic processes change the character of this young soil, and it matures. In time, these processes carry on and add different properties and characteristics to the mature soil, and it becomes old.

The parent material that gives birth to the young soil may have its beginning as lava from a volcano or the material laid down by a glacier, a flood, or windblown deposits. The bottom of the ocean floor can be uplifted and drained, allowing the soil-building processes to begin. The parent material in its initial stages may not support vascular plant life. Primitive plants such as lichens and mosses can attach themselves to this material, and the life processes of these primitive plants, together with climatic conditions, produce weathering.

Weathering is the process of physical and chemical decomposition of parent material. Through weathering, parent materials continually reduce in size until the particles are small enough to retain and release the nutrients plants require to grow. Physical weathering is produced through abrasion, the wearing away of a surface that is rubbed or scraped against another surface. Abrasion reduces the size of soil particles. Wind and water carrying material such as sand and gravel that is harder than the parent material grind away at the parent material, setting free smaller and smaller particles.

Organisms living on the surface of the parent material produce acids that dissolve the minerals of the rock. They use these minerals as food. The dead and dying organisms produce organic matter that fills cracks and crevices. This organic matter, mixed with mineral matter, provides an environment favorable to higher life-forms and thus accelerates the weathering process.

Temperature fluctuations cause rock to expand and contract. These non-uniform expansions and contractions cause cracks and fractures in the rock. Water fills these cracks, and when the water freezes, the expansion of the freezing water causes the rock to break. Rain, as it passes through the atmosphere, picks up carbon dioxide. This produces a weak acid that has the ability to slowly dissolve rocks and minerals. Warm, moist conditions promote biotic activity and increase the rate of chemical reactions. Weathering progresses at a much faster rate in the tropics than in the temperate or arctic regions.

Slope, or relief, affects soil development. Soils developing on steep slopes are subject to more rapid erosion than soils on slight or level slopes. Many of the soil particles produced on the steep slopes may be washed away unless protected in some fashion. These particles are then deposited at the bottom of the slopes or wherever the grade break is sufficient for these particles to fall out of suspension. As a result, the soils at the bottom of the slope will be deeper and develop different characteristics from those of the soils on the steeper slopes.

Related to human time, this is an *incredibly slow* process. In some cases, it may take 6,000 years to develop one inch of soil from solid rock. In another instance, perhaps one inch of soil will develop in 500 years. In either case, one human generation of injudicious use of the land can result in a loss that may require hundreds of generations to recover.

While this weathering process is in action, developing soils produce soil layers called **horizons**. The three major horizons are A, B, and C. There are also O and R horizons. The combination of these horizons is known as the soil profile, and the horizons may have subdivisions:

- The **A horizon** includes the mineral layer lying on the surface or below an O horizon, characterized by an accumulation of organic matter and minerals weathered from the parent material. The A horizon may be divided into the Ap, Al, A2, and A3.
- The **B horizon**, characterized by the development of soil structure such as blocky, subangular blocky, prismatic, or columnar, depending upon existing soil conditions, may also accumulate calcium carbonates and clay particles leeched from the A horizon. We indicate or identify these horizons of accumulation by using lowercase letters following a capital "B": "w" (Bw) indicates accumulated calcium carbonate, and "t" (B2t) indicates clay accumulations. The B horizon may be divided into the BI, B2, Bk, Bw, B2t, and B3t.
- The **C horizon** is the layer that has not been subjected to extensive weathering. This is the parent material horizon from which the A and B horizons develop.
- The **O horizon** describes the surface layer of organic matter such as leaves, twigs, and dead animals in various stages of decomposition..
- The **R horizon** is consolidated rock material.

Soil development begins with the parent material, or the C horizon. As weathering progresses, different horizons develop. A very young soil may have only A and C horizons. With time and more weathering, divisions of the A and B horizons become evident.

Texas Soil Types

Soil is one of Texas' most important natural resources. The soils of Texas are complex because of the wide diversity of climate, vegetation, geology, and landscapes. More than 1,200 different kinds of soil are recognized in the state. Each soil has a specific set of properties that affects its use in some way. The location of each soil and information about

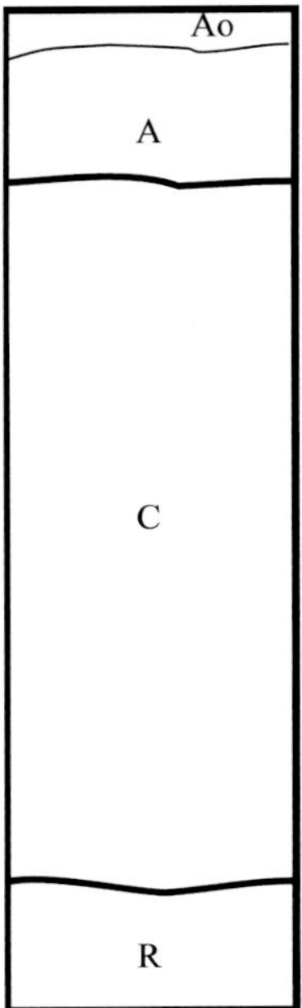

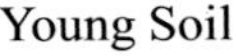

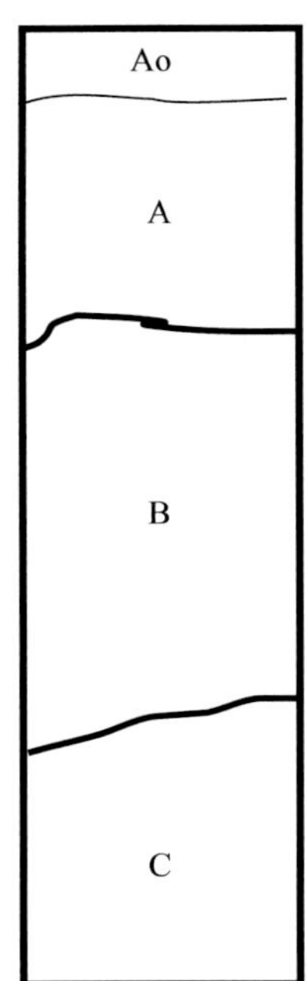

Intermediate Soil

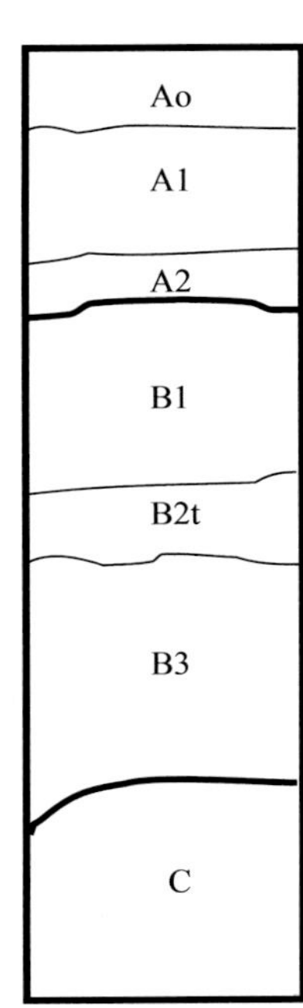

Mature Soil

Three major soil horizons.

its use appear in soil survey reports available for most counties. The soils of Texas reflect the interaction between the underlying geological units, the parent materials for the soils, and the climate and erosional processes acting on those parent materials. In areas where the climate is wet and warm, chemical weathering processes dominate, while in areas where it is dry, physical weathering processes dominate. Chemical weathering produces clay-rich soil, while physical weathering generally produces sandy soils.

Texas rainfall ranges from over 55 inches per year in Southeast Texas, near Port Arthur, to less than 10 inches per year in West Texas, near El Paso. The Texas rainfall pattern reflects the interaction of the maritime weather derived from the Gulf of Mexico (wet) and the continental weather (dry) derived from the arid Southwest. Lines of equal annual average rainfall tend to be oriented north-south across Texas. Average annual temperature is oriented east-west, with a maximum annual average temperature of over 70°F at Brownsville to less than 60°F north of Amarillo.

The Texas Coastal Plain, which was built southeastward from the Balcones Fault Zone by sediments deposited by the developing Texas river systems, is dominated by recently formed sedimentary rocks. These rocks were subjected to chemical weathering before they were deposited along the ancient Gulf of Mexico shoreline. As a result of this prior weathering, further chemical weathering during soil formation produces a series of soils that tend to parallel the Texas Coast. On the Coastal Plain, the soils that form on the clay-rich sediments, known as **vertisols**, are susceptible to shrink-swell processes.

In East Texas, where the climate is the wettest, deep weathering produces soils that have a clay-rich subsoil and are low in nutrients. The soils in East Texas are related to the soils of the southeastern United States. In Texas they are frequently covered in pine forests and, when cleared, must be fertilized if they are to be used for row crops. Soil scientists call these soils **ultisols** in recognition of their deep weathering and leached nature.

Farther westward and southward from East Texas, the climate becomes drier, and subhumid to semiarid climatic conditions are encountered. Alfisols and mollisols develop in these drier regions of Texas. **Alfisols** are commonly covered in hardwood trees and can support most crops after the land is cleared. The great grassland prairies of the central United States are found in areas where the climate is more semiarid and hardwood trees can no longer survive. These grasslands form on **mollisols**, which are nutrient-rich clayey soils. Mollisols are the dominant soil in Central Texas.

In the rugged, arid landscape of West Texas, the soils formed are **aridisols**, desert soils that are too dry to support most plants and without extensive irrigation cannot support agriculture except cattle and goat grazing. In parts of West Texas and in the Llano Basin no soils are formed, and the

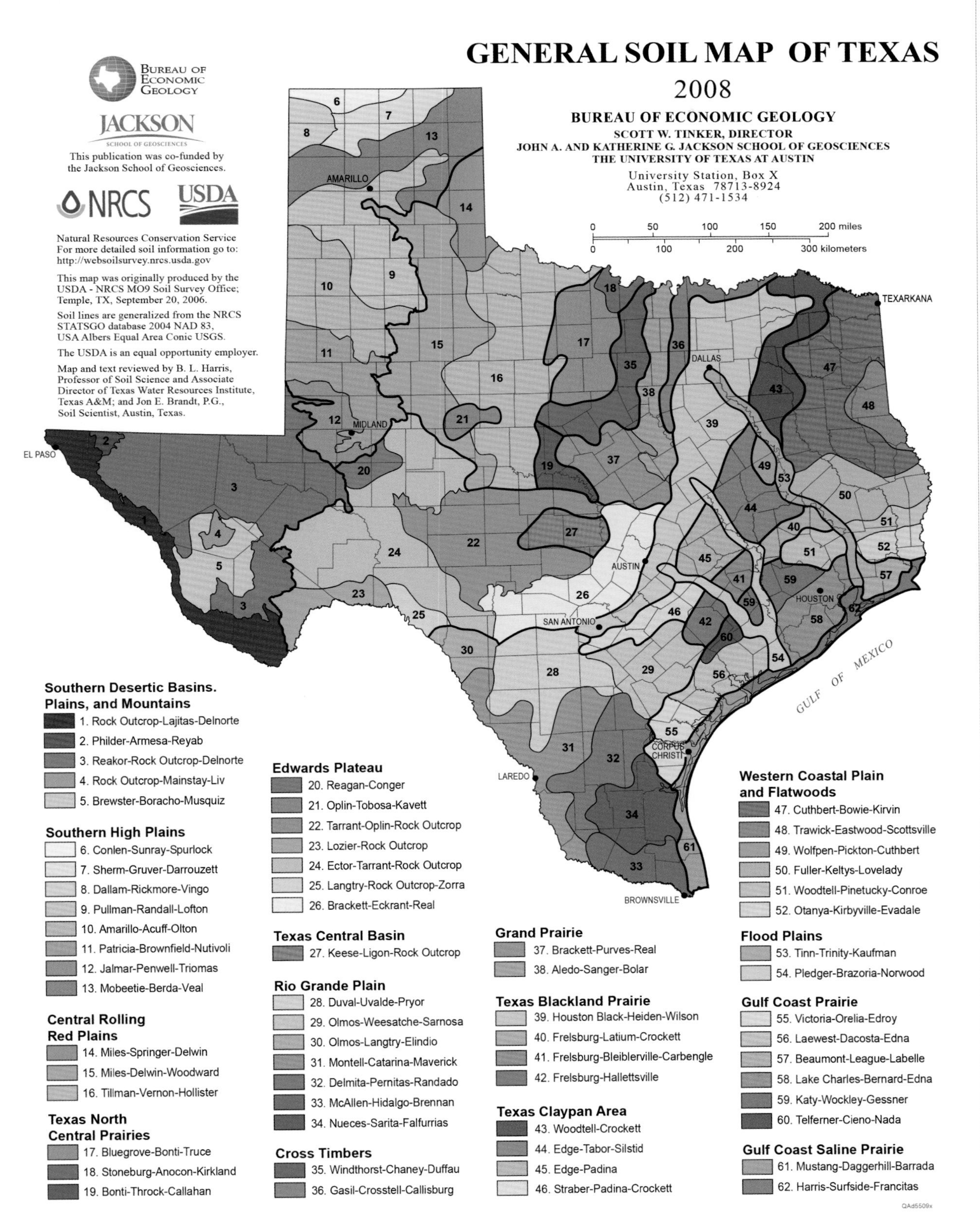

A general soils map for the state of Texas. Courtesy of the Bureau of Economic Geology, the University of Texas at Austin

bedrock is exposed at the surface. In Big Bend, the Guadalupe Mountains, and the Llano Basin, for example, soil formation has been limited to the chemical decay of the bedrock units. Soils formed from the early decomposition of the bedrock are known as **inceptisols** and **entisols**. See appendix C for a land-resources map of Texas and appendix D, "Common Rocks and Soils."

Soil Conservation

The vast expanse of Texas soils encouraged wasteful use of soil and water throughout much of the state's history. About 21% of all land area in Texas has been classified as "prime farmland." Settlers were attracted by these rich soils and the abundant water of the eastern half of the region. After using them to build an agriculture and agribusiness of vast proportions, they found their abuse had created critical problems.

In the 1930s, interest in soil and water conservation began to mount. In 1935, the Soil Conservation Service, now called the Natural Resources Conservation Service (NRCS), was created in the US Department of Agriculture (USDA). In 1939, the Texas Soil Conservation Law made it possible for landowners to organize local soil and water conservation districts.

As of 2014, the state had 216 soil and water conservation districts, which manage the conservation functions within the district. A subdivision of state government, each district is governed by a board of five elected landowners. Technical assistance in planning and applying conservation work is provided through the NRCS. State funds for districts are administered through the Texas State Soil and Water Conservation Board.

The 1997 National Resources Inventory showed that land use in Texas consisted of about 57% rangeland, 16% cropland, 9% pastureland, 6% forestland, 5% developed land, 2% federal land, 2% land in the conservation reserve program (CRP), 1% miscellaneous land, and 2% water.

Soil Subdivisions

Texas can be divided into major subdivisions, called Major Land Resource Areas (MLRAs), that have similar or related soils, vegetation, topography, climate, and land uses. Brief descriptions of these subdivisions follow.

Trans-Pecos Soils

The 18.7 million acres of the Trans-Pecos (southern desertic basins, palins, and mountains), mostly west of the Pecos River, are diverse plains and valleys intermixed with mountains. Surface drainage is slow to rapid. This arid region is used mainly as rangeland. A small amount of irrigated cropland exists on the more fertile soils along the Rio Grande and Pecos River. Vineyards and the disposal of large volumes of municipal wastes are two more recent uses of this land.

Upland soils are mostly well drained, light reddish-brown to brown clay loams, clays, and sands (some have a large amount of lime, and some have a large amount of gypsum or other salts). Many areas have shallow soils and rock outcrops, and sizable areas have deep sands. Bottomland soils are deep, well-drained, dark grayish-brown to reddish-brown silt loams, loams, clay loams, and clays. Lack of soil moisture and wind erosion are the major soil management concerns. Only irrigated crops can be grown on these soils, and most areas lack an adequate source of good water.

Upper Pecos and Canadian Valleys and Plains Soils

The Upper Pecos and Canadian Valleys and Plains area occupies a little over a half-million acres in the northwestern part of Texas near the Texas–New Mexico border. It is characterized by broad rolling plains

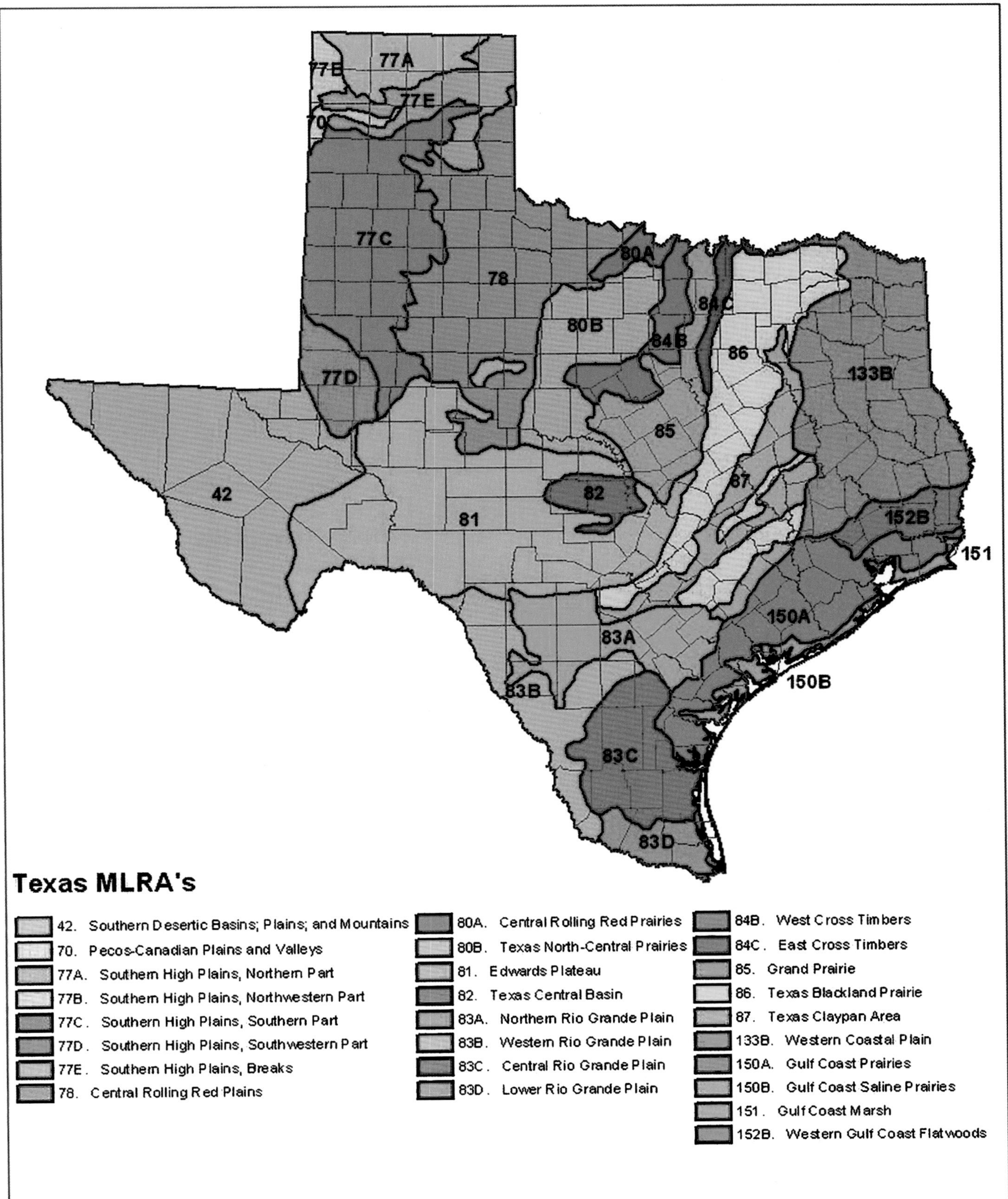

Texas Major Land Resource Areas (MLRAs). Courtesy of Natural Resources Conservation Service

and tablelands broken by drainageways and tributaries of the Canadian River. It includes the Canadian Breaks, which are rough, steep lands below the adjacent High Plains. The average annual precipitation is about 15 inches but fluctuates widely from year to year. Surface drainage is slow to rapid.

The soils are well drained and alkaline. They mostly formed in material weathered from sandstone and shale. The soils are generally reddish-brown clay loams and sandy loams, and depths range from shallow to very deep. The area is used mainly as rangeland and wildlife habitat. Native vegetation is mid- to shortgrass prairie species, such as hairy grama, sideoats grama, little bluestem, alkali sacaton, vine mesquite, and galleta in the plains and tablelands. Juniper and mesquite grow on the relatively higher breaks. Soil management concerns include low soil moisture and brush control.

High Plains Soils

The High Plains area (northern, northwestern, southern, and southwestern parts of Southern High Plains and the Southern High Plains Breaks) comprises the vast high plateau of more than 19.4 million acres in northwestern Texas. It lies in the southern part of the Great Plains province that includes large similar areas in Oklahoma and New Mexico. The flat, nearly level, treeless plain has few streams to cause local relief. However, several major rivers originate in the High Plains or cross the area. The largest is the Canadian River, which has cut a deep valley across the Panhandle section.

Playas, small intermittent lakes scattered throughout the area, lie up to 20 feet below the surrounding flat plains. A 1965 survey counted more than 19,000 playas in 44 counties, occupying approximately 340,000 acres. Most of the runoff from rainfall is collected in the playas, but only 10% to 40% of this water percolates back to the Ogallala Aquifer. The aquifer is virtually the only source of water in the area.

Upland soils are mostly well-drained, deep, neutral to alkaline clay loams and sandy loams in shades of brown or red. Sandy soils are in the southern part. Many soils have large amounts of lime at various depths, and some are shallow over caliche. Soils of bottomlands are minor in extent.

This area is used mostly for cropland, but significant areas of rangeland occur in the southwestern and extreme northern parts. Millions of cattle populate many large feedlots in the area. The soils are moderately productive, and the flat surface and underlying aquifer encourage irrigation and mechanization. Limited soil moisture, constant danger of wind erosion, and irrigation water management are the major soil management concerns; but the region is Texas' leading producer of three most important crops—cotton, grain sorghum, and wheat.

Rolling Plains Soils

The Rolling Plains include 21.7 million acres east of the High Plains in northwestern Texas. The area lies west of the North Central Prairies and extends from the edge of the Edwards Plateau in Tom Green County northward into Oklahoma. The landscape is nearly level to strongly rolling, and surface drainage is moderate to rapid. Outcrops of red beds of geological materials and associated reddish soils led to their sometimes being called Red Plains.

Limestone underlies the soils in the southeastern part. Some large areas of badlands are in the eastern part. Upland soils are mostly deep, pale brown through reddish-brown to dark grayish-brown, neutral to alkaline sandy loams, clay loams, and clays; some are deep sands. Many soils have a large amount of lime in the lower part, and a few others are saline; some are shallow and stony. Bottomland soils are mostly reddish-brown and sandy to clay; some are saline.

This area is used mostly for rangeland, but cotton, grain sorghum, and wheat are important crops. The major soil management concerns are brush control, wind erosion, low fertility, and lack of soil moisture. Salt spots are a concern in some areas.

North Central Prairie Soils

The North Central Prairie occupies about 7 million acres in north-central Texas. Adjacent to this area on the north is the rather small (less than 1 million acres) Rolling Red Prairies, which extends into Oklahoma and is included here because the soils and land use are similar. This area lies between the Western Cross Timbers and the Rolling Plains. It is predominantly grassland intermixed with small wooded areas. The landscape is undulating with slow to rapid surface drainage.

Upland soils are mostly deep, well-drained, brown or reddish-brown, slightly acidic loams over neutral to alkaline, clayey subsoils. Soils over shale bedrock units range from shallow to moderately deep, depending on the local soil-forming processes. Bottomland soils are mostly well-drained, dark brown or gray loams and clays. This area is used mostly as rangeland, but wheat, grain sorghum, and other crops are grown on the better soils. Brush control, wind and water erosion, and limited soil moisture are the major soil management concerns.

Edwards Plateau Soils

The 22.7 million acres of the Edwards Plateau are in southwestern Texas east of the Trans-Pecos and west of the Blackland Prairie. Uplands are nearly level to undulating except near large stream valleys, where the landscape is hilly with deep canyons and steep slopes. Surface drainage is rapid.

Upland soils are mostly shallow, very stony or gravelly, dark alkaline clays and clay loams underlain by limestone. Lighter-colored soils are on the steep side slopes and deep, less stony soils are in the valleys. Bottomland soils are mostly deep, dark gray or brown, alkaline loams and clays.

This is principally a ranching region. Raising beef cattle is the main enterprise, but it is also the center of one of the nation's major mohair- and wool-producing areas. This is a major deer habitat, and hunting leases provide a source of income. Cropland is mostly in the valleys on the deeper soils and is used mainly for growing forage crops and hay. The major soil management concerns are brush control, large stones, low fertility, excess lime, and limited soil moisture.

Central Basin Soils

The Central Basin, also known as the Llano Basin, occupies a relatively small area in Central Texas. It includes parts or all of Llano, Mason, Gillespie, and adjoining counties. The total area is about 1.6 million acres of undulating to hilly landscape.

Upland soils are mostly shallow, reddish-brown to brown, mostly gravelly and stony, neutral to slightly acidic sandy loams over granite, limestone, gneiss ,and schist bedrock. Large boulders are on the soil surface in some areas. Deeper, less stony, sandy loam soils are in the valleys. Bottomland soils are minor areas of deep, dark gray or brown loams and clays.

Ranching is the main enterprise, with some farms producing peaches, grain sorghum, and wheat. The area provides excellent deer habitat, and hunting leases are a major source of income. Brush control, large stones, and limited soil moisture are soil management concerns.

Northern Rio Grande Plain Soils

The Northern Rio Grande Plain comprises about 6.3 million acres in an area of southern Texas extending from Uvalde to Beeville. The landscape is nearly level to rolling, mostly brush-covered plains with slow to rapid surface drainage. The major upland soils are deep, reddish-brown or dark grayish-brown, neutral to alkaline loams and clays. Bottomland soils are mostly dark-colored loams.

The area is mostly rangeland with significant areas of cropland. Grain sorghum, cotton, corn, and small grains are the major crops. Crops are irrigated in the western part, especially in the Winter Garden area, where vegetables such as spinach, carrots, and cabbage are grown. Much of the area is good deer and dove habitat, and hunting leases are a major source of income. Brush control, soil fertility, and irrigation water management are the major soil management concerns.

Western Rio Grande Plain Soils

The Western Rio Grande Plain comprises about 5.3 million acres in an area of southwestern Texas from Del Rio to Rio Grande City. The landscape is nearly level to undulating except near the Rio Grande River, where it is hilly. Surface drainage is slow to rapid. The major soils are mostly deep, brown or gray, alkaline clays and loams. Some are saline.

Most of the soils are used for rangeland. Irrigated grain sorghum and vegetables are grown along the Rio Grande. The area provides good wildlife habitat, and hunting leases are a major source of income. Brush control and limited soil moisture are the major soil management concerns.

Central Rio Grande Plain Soils

The Central Rio Grande Plain comprises about 5.9 million acres in an area of southern Texas from Live Oak to Hidalgo County. It includes the South Texas Sand Sheet, an area of deep sandy soils and active sand dunes. The landscape is nearly level to gently undulating. Surface drainage is slow to rapid. Upland soils are mostly deep, light-colored, neutral to alkaline sands and loams. Many are saline or sodic. Bottomland soils are of minor extent.

Most of the area is used for raising beef cattle. A few areas, mostly in the northeastern part, are used for growing grain sorghum, cotton, and small grains. Much of the area provides good wildlife habitat, and hunting leases are a major source of income. Brush control is the major soil management concern on rangeland; wind erosion and limited soil moisture are the major concerns on cropland.

Lower Rio Grande Valley Soils

The Lower Rio Grande Valley comprises about 2.1 million acres in extreme southern Texas. The landscape is level to gently sloping with slow surface drainage. The upland soils are mostly deep, grayish-brown, neutral to alkaline loams, but coastal areas are mostly gray, silty clay loam and silty clay soils. Some are saline. Bottomland soils are minor in extent.

Most of the soils are used for growing irrigated vegetables and citrus, along with cotton, grain sorghum, and sugarcane. Some areas are rangeland used for growing beef cattle. Irrigation water management and wind erosion are the major soil management concerns on cropland, while brush control is the major concern on rangeland.

Western Cross Timbers Soils

The Western Cross Timbers comprises about 2.6 million acres. The area includes the wooded section west of the Grand Prairie and extends from the Red River southward to the northern edge of Brown County. The landscape is undulating and dissected by many drainageways, including the Brazos and Red Rivers. Surface drainage is rapid. The upland soils are mostly deep, grayish-brown, slightly acidic loams with loamy and clayey subsoils. Bottomland soils along the major rivers are deep, reddish-brown, neutral to alkaline silt loams and clays.

The area is used mostly for grazing beef and dairy cattle on native range and improved pastures. Crops are peanuts, grain sorghum, small grains, peaches, pecans, and vegetables. The major soil management concerns on grazing lands is brush control. Waste management on dairy farms is a more recent concern. Wind and water erosion are the major concerns on cropland.

Eastern Cross Timbers Soils

The Eastern Cross Timbers includes about 1 million acres in a long, narrow strip of wooded land that separates the northern parts of the Blackland Prairie and Grand

Prairie and extends from the Red River southward to the Hill County. The landscape is gently undulating to rolling and dissected by many streams, including the Red and Trinity Rivers. Sandstone-capped hills are prominent in some areas. Surface runoff is moderate to rapid.

The upland soils are mostly deep, light-colored, slightly acidic sandy loams and loamy sands with reddish loamy or clayey subsoils. Bottomland soils are reddish-brown to dark gray, slightly acidic to alkaline loams or gray clays. Grassland consisting of native range and improved pastures is the major land use. Crops of peanuts, grain sorghums, small grains, peaches, pecans, and vegetables are grown in some areas. Brush control, water erosion, and low fertility are the major concerns in soil management.

Grand Prairie Soils

The Grand Prairie consists of about 6.3 million acres in north-central Texas. It extends from the Red River to about the Colorado River. It lies between the East and West Cross Timbers in the northern part and just west of the Blackland Prairie in the southern part. The landscape is undulating to hilly and dissected by many streams, including the Red, Trinity, and Brazos Rivers. Surface drainage is rapid.

The upland soils are mostly dark gray, alkaline clays; some are shallow over limestone, and some are stony. Some areas have light-colored loamy soils over chalky limestone. Bottomland soils along the Red and Brazos Rivers are reddish silt loams and clays. Other bottomlands have dark gray loams and clays. Land use is a mixture of rangeland, pastureland, and cropland. The area is mainly used for growing beef cattle. Some small grain, grain sorghum, corn, and hay are grown. Brush control and water erosion are the major management concerns.

Blackland Prairie Soils

The Blackland Prairie consists of about 12.6 million acres of east-central Texas extending southwesterly from the Red River to Bexar County. There are smaller areas to the southeast. The landscape is undulating with a few scattered wooded areas that are mostly in the bottomlands. Surface drainage is moderate to rapid.

Both upland and bottomland soils are deep, dark gray to black alkaline clays. Some soils in the western part are shallow to moderately deep over chalk. Some soils on the eastern edge (sometimes called graylands) are neutral to slightly acidic grayish clays and loams over mottled clay subsoils. Blackland soils are known as "cracking clays" because of the large, deep cracks that form in dry weather. This high shrink-swell property can cause serious damage to foundations, highways, and other structures and is a safety hazard in pits and trenches.

Land use is divided about equally between cropland and grassland. Crops grown are cotton, grain sorghum, corn, wheat, oats, and hay. Grassland is mostly improved pastures with native range on the shallower and steeper soils. Water erosion, cotton root rot, brush control, and soil tilth (the general suitability of the soil to support plant growth) are the major management concerns.

Claypan Area Soils

The Claypan Area consists of about 6.1 million acres in east-central Texas just east of the Blackland Prairie. The landscape is a gently undulating to rolling, moderately dissected woodland also known as the Post Oak Belt or Post Oak Savannah. Surface drainage is moderate. Upland soils commonly have a thin, light-colored, acidic sandy loam surface layer over dense, mottled red, yellow, and gray claypan subsoils. Some deep, sandy soils with less clayey subsoils are present. Bottomlands are deep, highly fertile, reddish-brown to dark gray loamy to clayey soils.

Land use is mainly rangeland. Some areas are in improved pastures. Most cropland is in bottomlands that are protected from flooding. Major crops are cotton, grain sorghum, corn, hay, and forage crops, most of which are irrigated and grown in protected floodplains. Brush control is a major management concern on rangeland; irrigation water management on cropland is a major management concern; water erosion is a serious concern on the highly erosive claypan soils, especially where they are overgrazed.

East Texas Timberlands Soils

The East Texas Timberlands consists of about 16.1 million acres of the forested eastern part of the state. The landscape is gently undulating to hilly and well dissected by many streams. Surface drainage is moderate to rapid. This large area has many kinds of upland soils, but most are deep, light-colored, acidic sands and loams over loamy and clayey subsoils. Deep sands are in scattered areas, and red clays are in areas of "redlands." Bottomland soils are mostly brown to dark gray, acidic loams and some clays.

The land is used mostly for growing commercial pine timber and for woodland grazing. Improved pastures are scattered throughout and are used for grazing beef and dairy cattle and for hay production. Some commercial hardwoods are in the bottomlands. Woodland management concerns include seedling survival, invasion of hardwoods in pine stands, effects of logging on water quality, and control of the southern pine beetle. Lime and fertilizers are necessary for productive cropland and pastures.

Coast Prairie Soils

The Coast Prairie includes about 8.7 million acres near the Gulf Coast in Southeast Texas. It ranges from 30 to 80 miles in width and parallels the coast from the Sabine River in Orange County to Baffin Bay in Kleberg County. The landscape is level to gently undulating with slow surface drainage. Upland soils are mostly deep, dark gray, neutral to slightly acidic clay loams and clays. Lighter-colored and more sandy soils are in a strip on the northwestern edge, and some soils in the southern part are alkaline. Some soils are saline and sodic. Bottomland soils are mostly deep, dark-colored clays and loams along the small streams but are greatly varied along the rivers.

Land use is mainly grazing lands and cropland. Some hardwood timber is found in the bottomlands. Many areas are also managed for wetland wildlife habitat. The nearly level topography and productive soils encourage farming. Rice, grain sorghum, cotton, corn, and hay are the main crops. Brush management on grasslands and removal of excess water on cropland are the major management concerns.

Coast Saline Prairies Soils

The Coast Saline Prairies region consists of about 3.2 million acres along a narrow strip of wet lowlands adjacent to the coast. It includes the barrier islands that extend from Mexico to Louisiana. The surface is at sea level or just a few feet above sea level and includes many areas of saltwater marsh. Surface drainage is very slow.

The soils are mostly deep, dark-colored clays and loams; many are saline and sodic. Light-colored sandy soils are found on the barrier islands. The water table is at or near the surface of most soils. Cattle grazing is the chief economic use of the various salt-tolerant cordgrasses and sedges. Many areas are managed for wetland wildlife. Recreation is popular on the barrier islands of the Texas Coast. Providing fresh water and access to grazing areas are the major management concerns.

Gulf Coast Marsh Soils

The Gulf Coast Marsh is a 150,000-acre area in the extreme southeastern corner of Texas. The area can be subdivided into four parts: freshwater, intermediate, brackish, and saline (saltwater) marsh. The degree of salinity of this system grades landward from saltwater marshes along the coast to freshwater marshes inland. Surface drainage is very slow. This area contains many lakes, bayous, tidal channels, and human-made canals. About one-half of the marsh is fresh, and one-half is salty. Most of the area is susceptible to flooding either by fresh water drained from lands adjacent to the marsh or by salt water from the Gulf of Mexico.

Most of the soils are very poorly drained, saturated continuously, and soft and can carry little weight. In general, the organic soils have a thick layer of dark gray, relatively undecomposed organic material over a gray, clayey subsoil. The mineral soils have a surface of dark gray, highly decomposed organic material over a gray, clayey subsoil.

Most of the almost treeless and uninhabited area is in marsh vegetation, such as grasses, sedges, and rushes. It is used mainly for wildlife habitat. It is part of the fertile and productive estuarine complex that supports marine life of the Gulf of Mexico, providing wintering ground for waterfowl and habitat for many fur-bearing animals and alligators. A significant acreage is firm enough to support livestock and is used for winter grazing of cattle. The major management concerns are providing fresh water and access to grazing areas.

Flatwoods Soils

The Flatwoods area includes about 2.5 million acres of woodland in humid Southeast Texas just north of the Coast Prairie and extending into Louisiana. The landscape is level to gently undulating. Surface drainage is slow. Upland soils are mostly deep, light-colored, acidic loams with gray, loamy, or clayey subsoils. Bottomland soils are deep, dark-colored, acidic clays and loams. The water table is near the surface at least part of the year.

The land is mainly used for forest, but cattle are grazed in some areas. Woodland management concerns include seedling survival, invasion of hardwoods in pine stands, effects of logging on water quality, and control of the southern pine beetle.

Physical Properties of Soil

Soil has certain physical characteristics: color, texture, pore space, and structure.

Color

Color is a characteristic of soil affected by organic matter, moisture, and to some extent mineralogy. Most minerals, if crushed, give soil a gray color, unless the minerals have gone through some chemical change. The red and yellow color of some soils is caused by the oxidation and hydration of soil minerals. Organic matter has the effect of darkening the mineral matter of the soil matrix to a brown or dark brown color.

Some soils are considered black, but in reality they are not black but very dark brown. Poor drainage and low organic matter create a gray color. Soils high in organic matter are characteristically dark brown. Moisture also changes the color of the soil. Not all soil colors are affected equally by moisture. Some markedly darken when wet, while others change only slightly.

Texture

The **texture**, or feel of soil, is affected by the relative proportions of the three soil separates. **Soil separate** is a size classification of the individual soil particle. These separates are classified as sand, silt, or clay.

Sand feels gritty to the touch. Of the soil separates, sand particles are the largest. They range in size from 0.05 mm to 2.0 mm and have a rounded shape. Sand is not chemically very active, but it is important to the makeup of the soil because it supplies bulk. Because of the relatively large size of sand particles, they do not pack closely together. The space between the sand grains provides room for air, water, and smaller soil particles. Sand permits easy penetration of plant roots, facilitates the infiltration of water, and allows the exchange of gases between the atmosphere and the soil.

Silt particles are intermediate-sized particles ranging between 0.002 mm and 0.05 mm. Silt is somewhere between sand and clay in size. Silt particles express some of the properties of both sand and clay. Because they are larger than clay particles, they are not as chemically active, but they are more active than sand particles. The space between silt particles is smaller than those of sand. This allows silt to retain water against the effect of gravity better than sand. The silt in soil makes more water available to plants. Silt feels slick compared to the gritty feel of sand.

Clay is the smallest of the soil separates and feels sticky. Clay particles are less than 0.002 mm in effective diameter. **Effective diameter** describes how a sphere of a given diameter would react to gravity in an aqueous solution. Clay particles are not necessarily round in shape. Their shape varies, but for the most part they are ribbon-shaped. Clay particles are the most chemically active of all the soil separates. These particles are so small that they are only a few molecules thick, which allows the electrochemical properties of these molecules to affect soil fertility. The individual molecules that the plant requires are loosely held on the surface of the clay particles. Clay reacts much like a magnet. It has a weak electrical charge that holds charged ions. These ions are constantly being replaced by the same or different ions in the soil solution.

The **soil solution** is the soup of soil life. The soil solution is aqueous in nature and is made up of many ingredients, including minerals and salts produced by the decomposition of the soil. Bacteria, insects, fungi, and decaying organic matter float about in this mixture. The concentration of these ingredients constantly fluctuates with the alternate wetting and drying of the soil.

Pore Space

Pore space is the space in the soil not filled by the organic or mineral portion of the soil. In a productive average soil, about 45% of the soil is pore space, which is divided into macro pores and micro pores. The **macro pores** are the larger voids that, under field-capacity conditions, are filled with air. The **micro pores**, at field capacity, are filled with water. A soil is at field capacity when gravity has removed the free soil moisture into the drier soil below.

Soils with well-proportioned macro and micro pore space provide good conditions for plant growth. If the soil is too open and the large macro pores are disproportionate to the micro pores, the soil lacks the ability to hold sufficient water for plants during periods of dry weather, and the soil is droughty. Plants become moisture stressed rapidly. This condition is typical of sandy soils.

Soils with higher clay content tend to have a greater proportion of micro pores. These soils hold more water than do sandy soils, but gas exchange is slower because of the small size of the pores. Water moves into and through these soils much more slowly. These soils can become waterlogged more easily, and plants will suffer from oxygen deficiency more rapidly.

Loamy soils have approximately equal proportions of sand, silt, and clay. This textural class exhibits the best characteristics of both the sandy and clayey soils. The relative proportions of sand, silt, and clay in the soil are not the only determiners of amount and type of pore space present. Soil structure has a major effect on pore space and also affects the density of the soil.

Soil Structure

Soil structure describes the arrangement of individual soil separates (sand, silt, and clay) into aggregates (clusters, or peds) that are reasonably stable. There are seven types of soil structure:

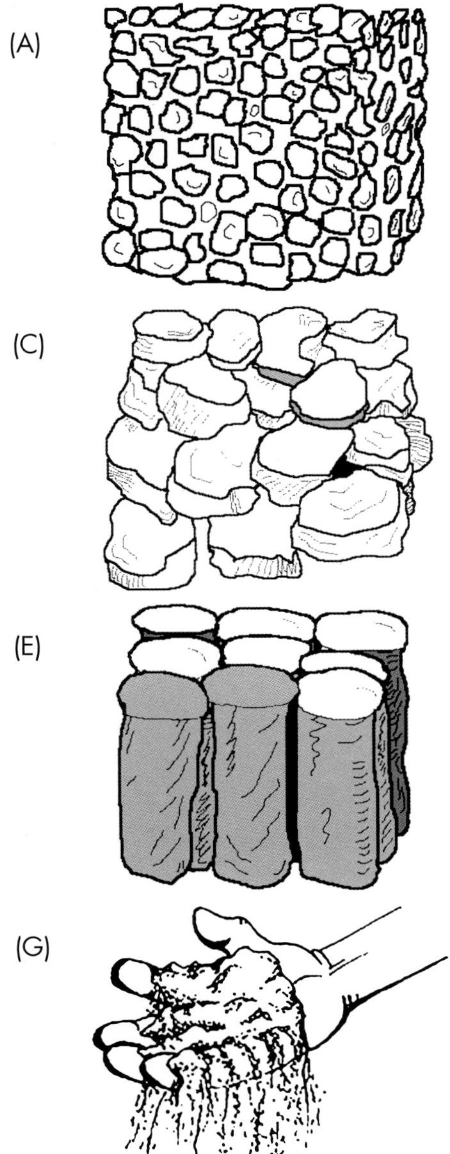

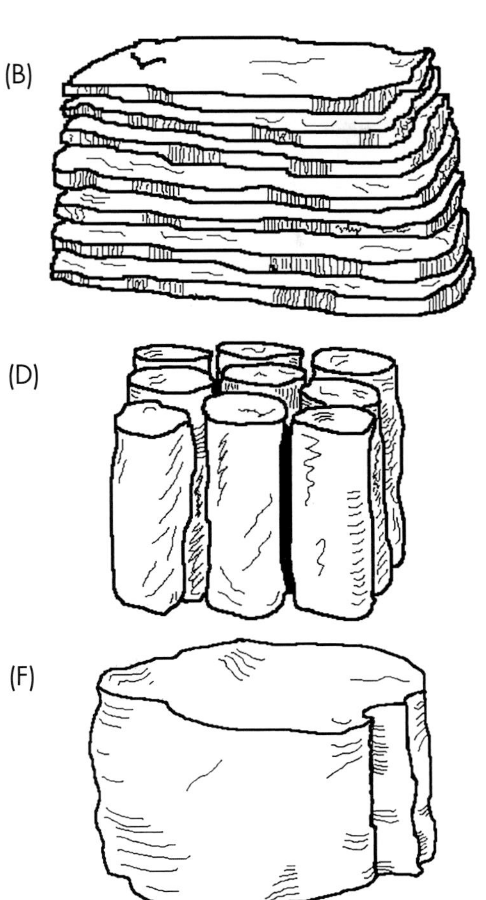

Types of soil structure: (A) granular, (B) platy, (C) blocky, (D) prismatic, (E) columnar, (F) massive, and (G) single-grained. Courtesy of National Aeronautics and Space Administration

1. **Granular:** relatively nonporous small spheroidal clusters not fitting into adjoining aggregates
2. **Crumb:** similar to granular aggregates though relatively more porous
3. **Platy:** platelike, where the plates overlap as roof shingles do, with a tendency to impair permeability
4. **Blocky:** blocklike peds with angular faces that fit into the angular faces of the adjoining peds
5. **Subangular blocky:** similar to blocky, though ped faces are more rounded and fit into adjoining aggregates
6. **Prismatic:** similar to blocky, though more columnlike; the aggregate longer than wide, with angular faces forming the face of the adjacent ped
7. **Columnar:** peds are similar to the prismatic, but the top is rounded compared to the angular top of the prismatic structure; peculiar to soils with high exchangeable sodium in the B horizon

There are two other soil grades—single-grained and massive. **Single-grained** comprises loose grains, not aggregates. This is the condition found in sands. **Massive** is the condition found in finer-textured soils in which the soil structure has been broken down because of traffic or other conditions when the soil is wet, for example, the condition of the soil after an automobile has gotten stuck in the mud and the mud has dried. The consistency of the soil is bricklike.

The aggregation of the sand, silt, and clay modifies the effects of the normal soil texture. Blackland soil with clay percentages in the range of 60% would normally be very impervious to air and water if not for the effects of soil structure and aggregation. The soil structure and aggregation make the many small, individual particles act as larger particles, resulting in increased pore space as compared to a single-grain situation. With the increase in pore space, water and air can enter the soil easier and at a faster rate. Roots easily penetrate the soil where the faces of the peds meet.

Structure develops from single-grained soil particles. These single particles are brought together and bound by cementing agents. Several factors are involved in the process of aggregation, and structure formation is most apparent in soils with colloidal clay and organic matter. It is thought that a part of the process of aggregation is the result of the electrical charge associated with the clay. Drying of the soil removes the water held around the clay particle and draws the particles closer to one another until the electrical charge of each particle can influence the adjacent particle and cause them to bind together, even if loosely.

Aggregation is also affected by the growth of plant roots. As the growing roots and root hairs expand between the soil particles, the resulting pressure forces the particles together. When the root dies, it leaves a line of weakness between the soil clusters that tends to keep the clusters separate. Roots may also produce chemicals that act as cementing agents, adding stability to the aggregates formed. Grass roots, because they are so extensive compared to those of other plants, contact more of the soil and thus seem to produce more aggregation than do other plants.

Not only higher vascular plants but also microorganisms and fungi affect aggregate formation. The extensive mycelial growth of fungi binds the soil particles together. Organic gums and waxes produced by soil microorganisms form cementing agents that assist structure formation, binding soil particles together into aggregates and eventually peds.

The alternate wetting and drying of the soil is also a mechanism of aggregate formation. Soil with high, expansive clay content tends to expand when wetted. This swelling forces soil particles and clusters of soil particles together, forming them into soil structure or peds. The non-uniform drying of the soil caused by roots extracting moisture from different points in the soil causes the soil to begin to shrink; lines of weakness form in these areas, thus defining the soil aggregate.

Not all aggregates are held together by equal forces. Some are stable; however, some are held together by much weaker forces. Aggregate formation is a continuing dynamic process with aggregates constantly being formed and destroyed. Wetting of the soil also has a tendency to break down the soil aggregates. As the soil is wetted, the air within the soil is forced to the center of the aggregate. With the advance of the wetting front, the air pressure within the aggregate increases until it causes the aggregate to explode.

Soil aggregates are destroyed by other mechanical means as well. Animal traffic and trailing will break down the structure of the soil, as will the effects of the plow of modern agriculture. The beating effect of raindrops on the surface of the soil also breaks down soil aggregates. Light animal traffic and raindrop impacts affect the surface; however, the plow affects the soil at a greater depth.

In certain soils the plow can improve the structure of the soil by breaking up structure that impedes the growth of plant roots at specific depths. Though it may improve the soil temporarily, it also exposes the soil to the damaging effects of falling raindrops. If the granular structure of the soil surface is broken down into individual particles, these particles tend to fill the voids created by the granules and impede the infiltration of water into the soil. It also restricts the flow and exchange of gases within the soil.

Soil structure can best be maintained by protecting it from excessive traffic and by maintaining a protective cover to prevent the deleterious effect of raindrop impact. Maintaining high organic levels in the soil will improve soil structure. Addition of organic materials proves helpful in the short term, but conditions need to be maintained to create an environment where soil can sustain its own adequate natural levels. **Vegetative cover** is the single best way to protect the soil structure. Adequate vegetative cover protects the soil from falling raindrops; and the vegetation, by natural processes, returns the necessary organic matter to the soil on a continuing basis.

Soil Reaction

Soil reaction refers to the relative acidity or alkalinity of the soil. Soil can be **acidic**, **alkaline**, or **neutral**. Soil reaction is measured as **pH**. A pH value of 7 is neutral. Values less than 7 are acidic, and values greater than 7 are alkaline. The acidity of the soil is related to the colloidal fraction of the soil. There may be active acidity in the liquid portion of the soil, but the potential acidity is contained on the surfaces of the clay and organic particles in the soil. The **potential acidity** of the soil may be 50,000 times greater than the **active acidity**.

Soil acidity is a function of the hydrogen ion (H) concentration of the soil solution immediately surrounding the organic or inorganic colloidal particle. When the hydrogen ion concentration is equal to the hydroxyl (OH) concentration, the solution is neutral. When the number of H ions exceeds the number of OH ions in the soil solution, the soil is acid. If the OH ions exceed the number of H ions, the soil is alkaline.

High-rainfall climates promote acidic soils. Soils in humid regions are more thoroughly leached of the soil bases such as calcium and magnesium. Arid regions do not receive the leaching; thus, they generally retain more of their bases, counteracting the effect of the hydrogen and maintaining the soil in a more alkaline condition.

Inorganic soils with a pH value of 3.5 are rare, and a value of 4.0 is considered very strongly acidic. In arid regions pH values may reach alkalinity levels of 10 to 11. This, however, requires a presence of high-sodium salts in the soil.

pH	Examples of solutions
0	Battery acid, strong hydrofluoric acid
1	Hydrochloric acid secreted by stomach lining
2	Lemon juice, gastric acid, vinegar
3	Grapefruit juice, orange juice, soda
4	Tomato juice, acid rain
5	Soft drinking water, black coffee
6	Urine, saliva
7	"Pure" water
8	Sea water
9	Baking soda
10	Great Salt Lake, milk of magnesia
11	Ammonia solution
12	Soapy water
13	Bleach, oven cleaner
14	Liquid drain cleaner

The pH scale.

Soil reaction is an important characteristic of soils. The relative acidity or alkalinity of the soil determines the solubility and availability of certain elements that plants require for optimum growth. Plant nutrient levels are optimal in the pH range of 6.0 to 7.5 for most plants. This range adequately provides most of the nutrients plants need to grow. If the pH dips below 6.0, the availability of the major plant food elements such as phosphorus, potassium, calcium, magnesium, and sulfur is considerably reduced. Plant food elements such as copper, zinc, iron, and manganese become much less available when the pH levels increase above 7.5. Note that these conditions exist for most agriculturally produced crops *and* nonagricultural plants that grow under similar conditions; but some plants have adapted to the extremes and would not produce well in any conditions except the extreme.

Soil Fertility

Soil fertility is the condition of the soil to supply to the plant the mineral elements in proper amounts and proportion as needed for the establishment, development, and reproduction of the plant species. The **colloidal fraction** of the soil, comprising the mineral clay portion and the finely divided organic material, supplies the majority of the fertility to the soil.

Sand and silt may have some cation-exchange capacity, but it is so small it is not generally taken into consideration when discussing soil fertility. **Cation-exchange capacity** (CEC), the property of the colloidal material that gives fertility to the soil, comprises the negative electrically charged sites along the colloidal material surfaces that allow it to act as a magnet attracting positively charged cations. Some of the elements that make up these cations are the nutrients the plant extracts in order to grow and reproduce.

The CEC differs according to individual soils and the kinds of clay minerals in the soil. Young soils with newly weathered clays such as montmorillonite possess a higher CEC than do the older illite clays in which the clays have been extensively weathered. Organic matter has approximately four times the CEC of the mineral fraction of the colloidal complex of the soil.

Addition of commercial or organic fertilizers can change the amount and proportion of components absorbed at the soil colloid-exchange sites. Soil-amending chemicals, such as fertilizer or lime, have a greater effect on soils with low CEC than on soils with high CEC because soils with high CEC are buffered more. Because of the many sites of exchange, greater portions of amendments must be applied to drastically change the proportions of elements absorbed on the soil colloid. Thus, a greater response would be expected from a fertilizer application on a sandy soil than on a clay soil high in organic matter. But the response would be short lived, because with fewer exchange sites the soil cannot hold as many fertilizer elements. Increasing the natural fertility of a soil that has been disturbed by plowing, mining, erosion, or other means is best accomplished through the application of fertilizer, either commercial or organic. Fertilizer dramatically increases the amount of organic matter present in the soil.

Fertilizer applied in proper amounts and proportions will not only supply nutrients for higher plants but will also supply nutrients to the soil microorganisms such as bacteria, fungi, and *Actinomyces*. With this proliferation of organic matter there is an accompanying increase in the CEC. Note that with the increase in organic matter there will also be an increase in the rate at which the organic matter decomposes. At some point in time a dynamic equilibrium will be reached and the nature of the soil and the climate will maintain a somewhat steady level of organic matter in the soil.

Soil Erosion

Erosion is the wearing away of a substance. In the case of soil, it is the wearing away of the earth's surface. There are two types of soil erosion: geological and accelerated erosion. **Geological erosion** is the slow method by which nature's forces try to bring all surfaces into one plane. **Accelerated erosion** occurs because of the effects of humans and occurs at a much faster rate.

Erosion rates on undisturbed land in a humid or subhumid climate may amount to perhaps 0.002 tons of soil lost per acre per year. Under cultivation with mismanagement and dramatic climatic conditions, erosion rates could reach 4–50 tons per acre per year. Soil erosion is a scourge of society because it reduces the productivity of the land. When the soil is eroded, we cannot produce the amount of food and fiber needed to sustain an ever-growing population.

Reduced productivity puts marginal soils that were once considered not worth cultivating into cultivation. This puts wildlife land into cultivated agriculture and deprives wildlife of adequate habitat. Allowing erosion to continue ensures a lower standard of living for all, as it costs more to produce less. The losses to erosion are not only to the soil itself. Erosion reduces the productivity of the land, and sediments resulting from this erosion create their own problems. Waterways and lakes become silted and cease to function properly. To maintain them properly requires a great expense to the nation for dredging and other forms of silt removal. Silt-burdened lakes and rivers become turbid, and the aquatic life in these habitats begins to suffer.

There is also the loss of water. Soil has the capacity to temporarily act as a reservoir of rainfall. Land that has been eroded cannot hold excess rainfall, so the rainwater is lost to overland flow and rapidly ends up in the drainageways and rivers. This uncontrolled water often causes damage from flooding, another expense to the public. This lost water could have been stored in the soil until it could percolate slowly through the soil to be stored in aquifers and drawn out at a later date. Erosion can also result in the formation of gullies that are at best unsightly, scarring the landscape. These gullies impede the travel of machinery, animals, and humans alike.

We need to understand the processes that result in erosion. For erosion to occur, the soil particles or groups of soil particles must be dislodged and transported somewhere else. Wind and water both have the means to dislodge and move soil.

Four Principles to Prevent Soil Erosion

Principle 1: Protect the surface of the soil from the impact of falling raindrops. Raindrops possess kinetic energy, which dissipates when raindrops strike the soil. Raindrops hitting the soil surface hammer apart the soil granules. The individual soil particles that make up the granule are then dislodged and thrown up into the air. Once dislodged, they are subject to being transported away. These particles can be thrown as much as two feet into the air, depending on the size of the raindrop and the intensity of the rainfall. On a flat slope the particles

An eroded slope. Courtesy of Natural Resources Conservation Service

The impact of a raindrop. Courtesy of National Oceanic and Atmospheric Administration

are tossed up and fall back much in the same place. As the slope of the land increases, they are moved farther and farther down the slope.

Any protective covering will reduce the damage caused by raindrops. A permanent sod cover is best; however, any cover will help. When the raindrops hit the canopy of grass over the soil, the energy of the rain dissipates on the leaf of the plant. Most of the kinetic energy is lost here, and the water runs harmlessly down the stem until it contacts the soil surface. In the absence of growing plants, mulch such as dead leaves and crop residue, or even gravel, will act to dissipate this energy. The greater the percentage of cover over the soil, the more the erosion is reduced.

In humid climates more rain falls than in arid ones, but erosion rates may be higher in the arid regions. Often arid regions experience a greater intensity of rainfall, and because rain is infrequent, the soil is covered less by vegetation; as a result, erosion rates can be very high. An area of the American West can lose more soil in one rainfall event than an area in the American East will lose in 10 years.

Principle 2: Prevent the water from concentrating. Water, as it moves across a slope, will seek out the lowest point and concentrate there. As the water concentrates, it gains mass. Gravity moving this mass downhill increases water's energy. The greater the mass, the more energy it carries with it. This energy gives the water the ability to trans-

An eroded riverbank. Courtesy of Texas Parks and Wildlife Department

port more and larger soil particles. These particles, rolling and tumbling against the soil surface, scour and dislodge more and larger particles, thus increasing the rate of erosion. Paths and trails are points where water tends to concentrate, and because traffic has destroyed the vegetation, the soil is very susceptible to erosion.

Principle 3: Reduce the velocity of the water as it moves downslope. Higher velocities mean higher energy levels, thus greater erosion potential. Long slopes result in increased velocities, just as an automobile continuously increases in velocity as it coasts down a long slope. Unlike the automobile, the water picks up more water, it gains mass, and the energy at the end of the slope is much greater than it was at the top or even halfway down the slope. Any structure that reduces the slope or the slope length will reduce the velocity. Structures placed across the slope that will safely drop the water to a lower level will reduce the velocity on that slope. Another means is to divert the water so that it follows a gentler slope on a graded contour. The length of the slope is important to the velocity. There is less erosion potential on a short, steep slope than on a long, lesser slope.

Principle 4: Get more water into the soil. Anything that will get more water into the soil will reduce erosion. The cover protects the bare soil from raindrop splash and prevents the resulting fine particles from blocking the pores so that the water can be channeled into the soil. Obstructions across the slope of the land, such as plant stems and residue, increase the friction of the water, slowing it down, thus giving it more time to soak in.

The first principle of water erosion prevention is the same for wind erosion. Cover is the method used to protect soil from blowing winds. The principle that causes an airplane to fly is the same principle that causes soil to blow. Wind velocities blowing over the surface decrease as they approach the surface. Soil particles lying on the soil surface experience an attraction to the surface. If the soil particle or group of particles is the proper size, it will extend above the surface of the ground to a certain degree. To the degree that the wind blowing over the surface of the individual particle has sufficient velocity, the air pressure above the soil grain is reduced enough to overcome the particle's attraction force to the ground.

When this occurs, the soil grain pops free of the surface and may rise as high as two feet. At this point it is blown forward by the force of the wind and comes back to earth, knocking loose other particles, which are then raised from the soil surface. The larger particles bounce along the soil surface as **surface creep**; the smaller particles are held in suspension by the wind and blown away. This problem is most prevalent in sands because fine sand has the proper aerodynamic properties to blow. But it can occur in other soils if the aggregates possess similar properties. Because the organic matter is lighter than the mineral portion, it is blown farthest away, leaving behind infertile, droughty sand.

Wind erosion prevention consists of any practice that will reduce the wind velocities at the surface of the soil. This may be accomplished by residues, windbreaks (vegetative obstructions planted perpendicular to the erosive wind), roughening the surface, or plowing up stable soil aggregates too large to be blown.

Responsibility for Soil Erosion

Farmers bear the brunt of the blame for erosion, but there are others equally responsible. Miners denude the landscape when mining ore or mining topsoil to use in landscaping for urban development. Home developers, industry, and road builders take up valuable farmland, forcing farmers to cultivate marginal land. Even parks create erosion with paths caused by the traffic of park visitors. The problem of soil erosion is not the problem of any one group; it is a problem of the people.

If farmers and ranchers want to maintain their standards of living, they must conserve their goose that lays the golden egg. Absentee landowners, who have removed themselves from the land because off-the-farm jobs are easier and financially more stable need to accept the responsibility and help put something back into the land they own but do not operate.

"The history of every nation is eventually written by the way in which it cares for its soil."
—Franklin D. Roosevelt

"Why is it we never think about rationing until we see the bottom of the barrel?"
—Abraham Lincoln

Social planners must recognize that productive farmland covered by homes, lawns, asphalt, and concrete is as gone as if it had washed away. It will not produce again. Consumers who purchase the cheapest food in the world need to know where this food comes from, and they need to accept their share of the responsibility to keep it coming. The cost of conservation is high, and this burden should not be laid on one group alone. Our soil is a limited resource. We must maintain it and keep it productive. This is not a situation of "pay me now or pay me later." When it's gone, it's gone.

Groundwater

Water moves underground through pores, cracks, and holes that are often seen in rocks on the earth's surface. These cracks and holes develop through the process of weathering, as well as through faulting and fracturing during tectonic events. In addition, natural pore space exists between the grains of the rock.

Sandstone is one of the principal types of rock through which water can move underground. Sandstone is formed by physical and chemical weathering of rock where the weather-resistant minerals are concentrated as sand-sized grains. The processes of erosion, transport, and deposition concentrate these sand-sized grains into porous deposits that are capable of transmitting groundwater. The sand grains along with gravel and other coarse materials form what is known as clastic aquifer, characteristic of the groundwater systems of the Texas Gulf Coast.

Limestone is formed when plant and animal skeletons, made up of calcium carbonate, settle to the bottom of ancient oceans. This carbonate mud accumulated and was subsequently buried under overlying sediments. Limestone generally has less pore space between individual rock grains. However, it is also brittle and tends to crack and fracture. Limestone is also soluble and forms caves and underground conduits, characteristic of the Edwards Aquifer in San Antonio.

During the earth's history, many episodes of fracturing and faulting have occurred in most areas. These processes formed cracks and faults in the limestone through which water could move. This water, which fell onto the earth's surface as rain, dissolved some of the calcium carbonate and carried it away in solution. This chemical process, through geological time, creates holes and caverns that continue to expand as more water moves through. These holes, cracks, caverns, and faults provide channels that both store and transmit water.

An **aquifer** is a rock or soil that contains and transmits water in quantities sufficient for appropriate uses. Aquifers can be made up of many types of soil or rocks, such as sandstone and limestone. Water is stored both between the grains of the rock and also in cracks, holes, fractures, and caverns that have developed within the rock. There are nine major aquifers in Texas: Trinity, Trinity Edwards, Ogallala, Gulf Coast, Edwards, Seymour, Hueco-Mesilla Bolson, Cenozoic Pecos Alluvium, and Carrizo-Wilcox. Sixteen

Major Aquifers of Texas

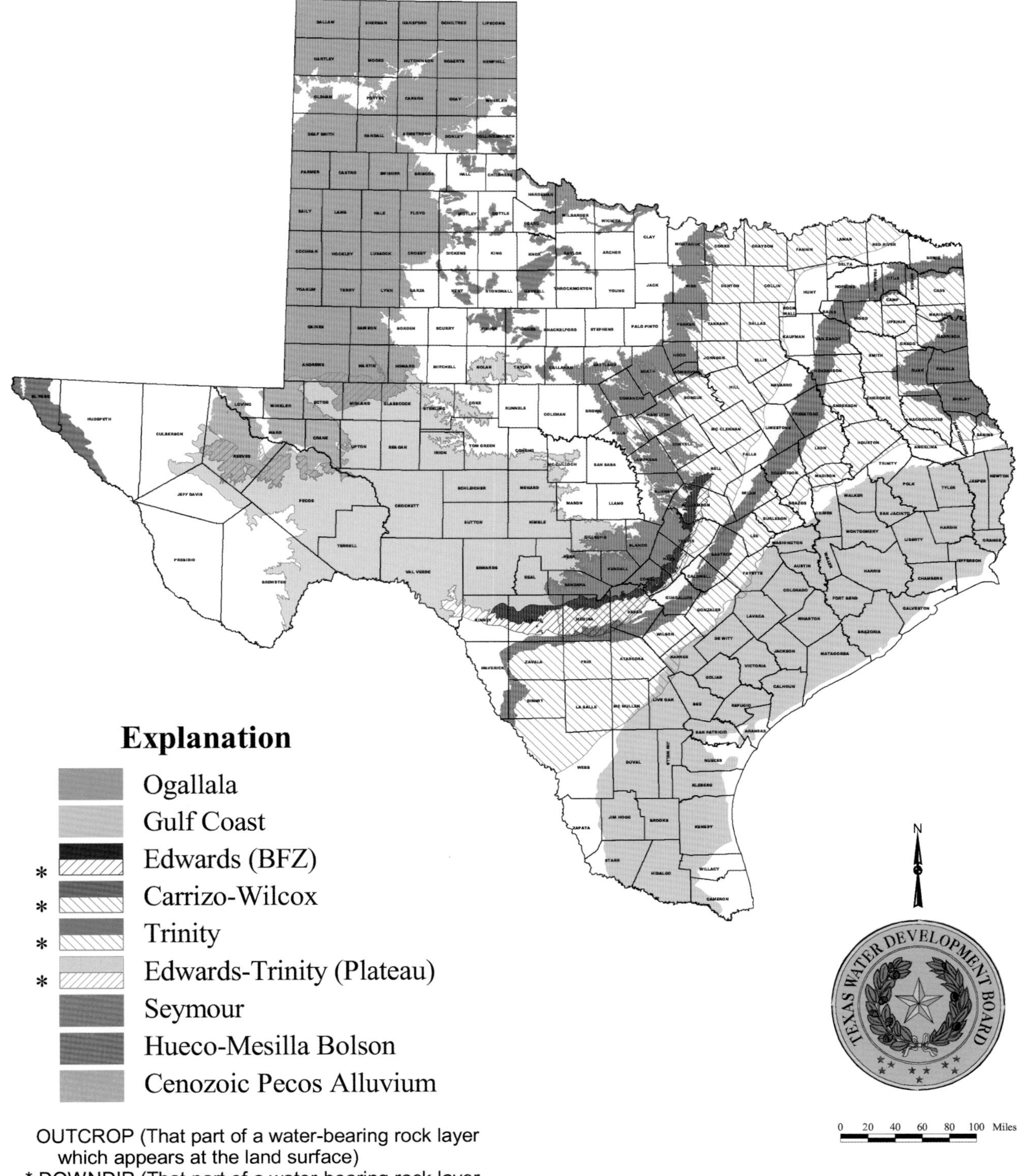

Major aquifers of Texas. Courtesy of the Texas Water Development Board

minor aquifers exist as well. Aquifers cover approximately 76% of the area of Texas.

Recharge is the process in which precipitation and streamflow enter the subsurface and move into an aquifer. Some aquifers, such as the Edwards, recharge through fractures, faults, and solution openings (such as sinkholes and caves) in the exposed limestones. Others, such as the Carrizo-Wilcox Aquifer, recharge through infiltration of rainfall and streamflow directly into the porous sandstone aquifer.

Discharge is the flow of groundwater from rock to the surface. This can occur through natural as well as human processes. Natural discharge occurs through springs and through seeps in swamps or beds and banks of streams. Discharge areas are lower than recharge areas, and water moves through aquifers by the force of gravity. Wells act as human-made discharge points from aquifers.

The flows from the springs and discharges from some wells enter nearby streams and rivers and become surface water, which then flows into downstream lakes and eventually to the Gulf of Mexico. Along its journey to the Gulf, the water that originated as discharge from the aquifers is used for many purposes by municipalities, industries, and agriculture and for sustaining wildlife.

In the mid- to late 1980s, 11 million acre-feet of groundwater was withdrawn for use in Texas; only 5.3 million acre-feet recharged the aquifers during that time. Water is the major limitation of population growth in Texas. As the population grows, our groundwater supply will become more stressed and limited. Thus, we must conserve our groundwater resources by using this limited resource wisely and finding alternative methods for meeting water needs.

"Water is the driving force of all nature."
—Leonardo da Vinci

Resources

County Soil Surveys. The soils in most Texas counties have been surveyed by the US Department of Agriculture and Texas A&M AgriLife Extension Service. The best source of a local soil survey for a specific county is the county agricultural agent.

Geologic Atlas of Texas. Geological maps of the state at a scale of 1:250,000 are available from the Bureau of Economic Geology, University of Texas at Austin.

Geological Field Trip Guidebooks. Many local geological societies and university faculty lead geology field trips and print guidebooks. Check with your local university Geology Department for more information.

Simkin, Tom, Robert Tilling, Peter Vogt, Stephen Kirby, Paul Kimberly, and David Stewart. 2006. *This Dynamic Planet: World Map of Volcanoes, Earthquakes, Impact Craters, and Plate Tectonics*. 3rd ed. Washington, DC: US Geological Survey.

Texas Almanac 1998–99. http://texashistory.unt.edu/ark:/67531/metapth162515/.

Texas Environmental Almanac. 2000. Texas Environmental Profiles. 2nd ed. Texas Center for Policy Studies and Environmental Defense. Austin: University of Texas Press. http://www.texascenter.org/almanac/TXENVALMANAC.HTML.

APPENDIX A

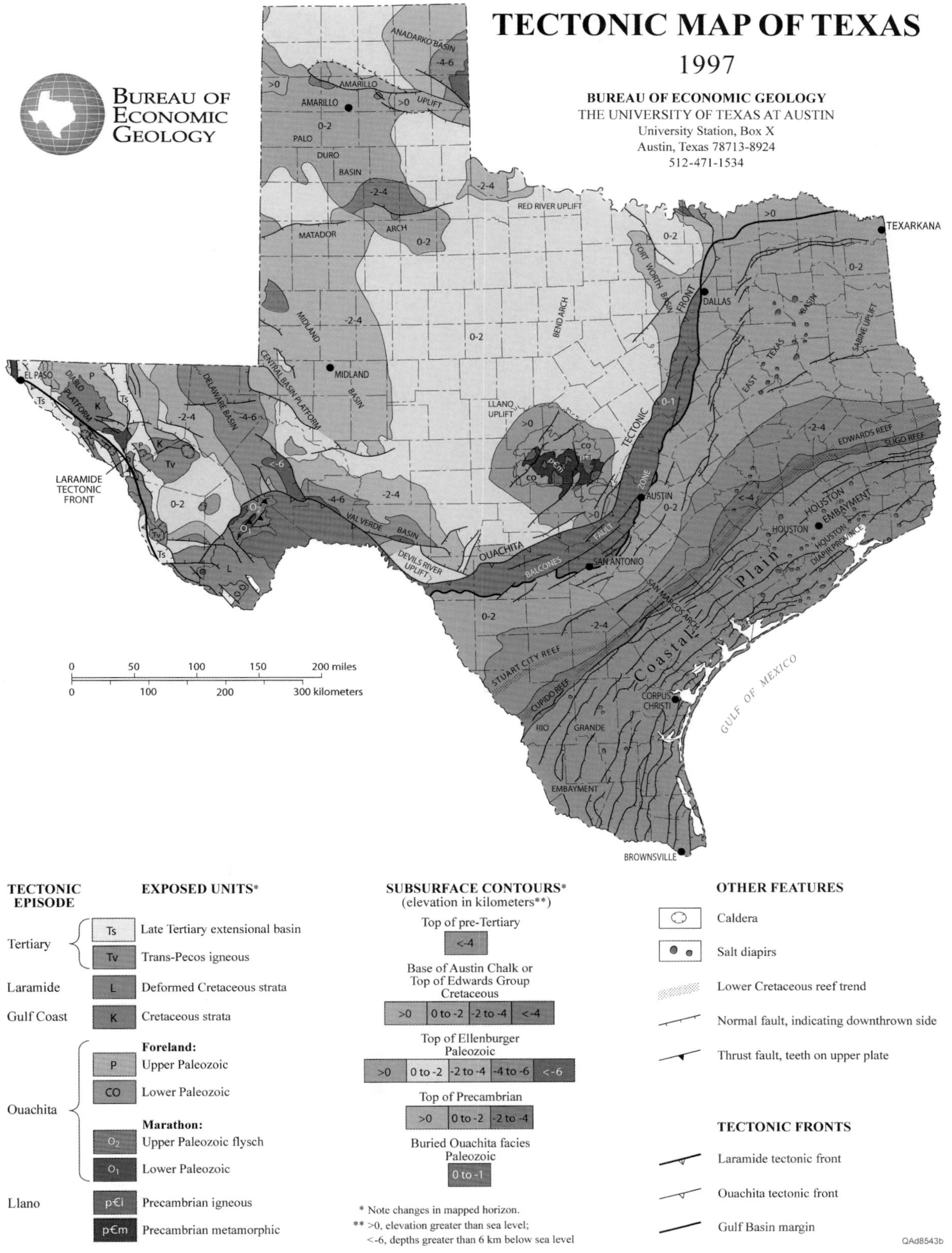

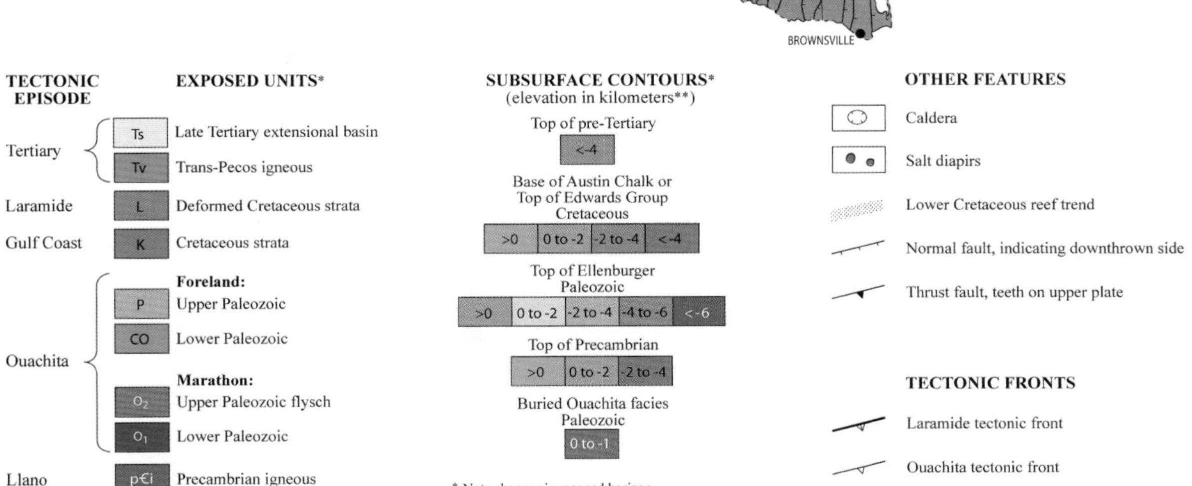

Tectonic map of Texas. Courtesy of the Bureau of Economic Geology, the University of Texas at Austin

APPENDIX B

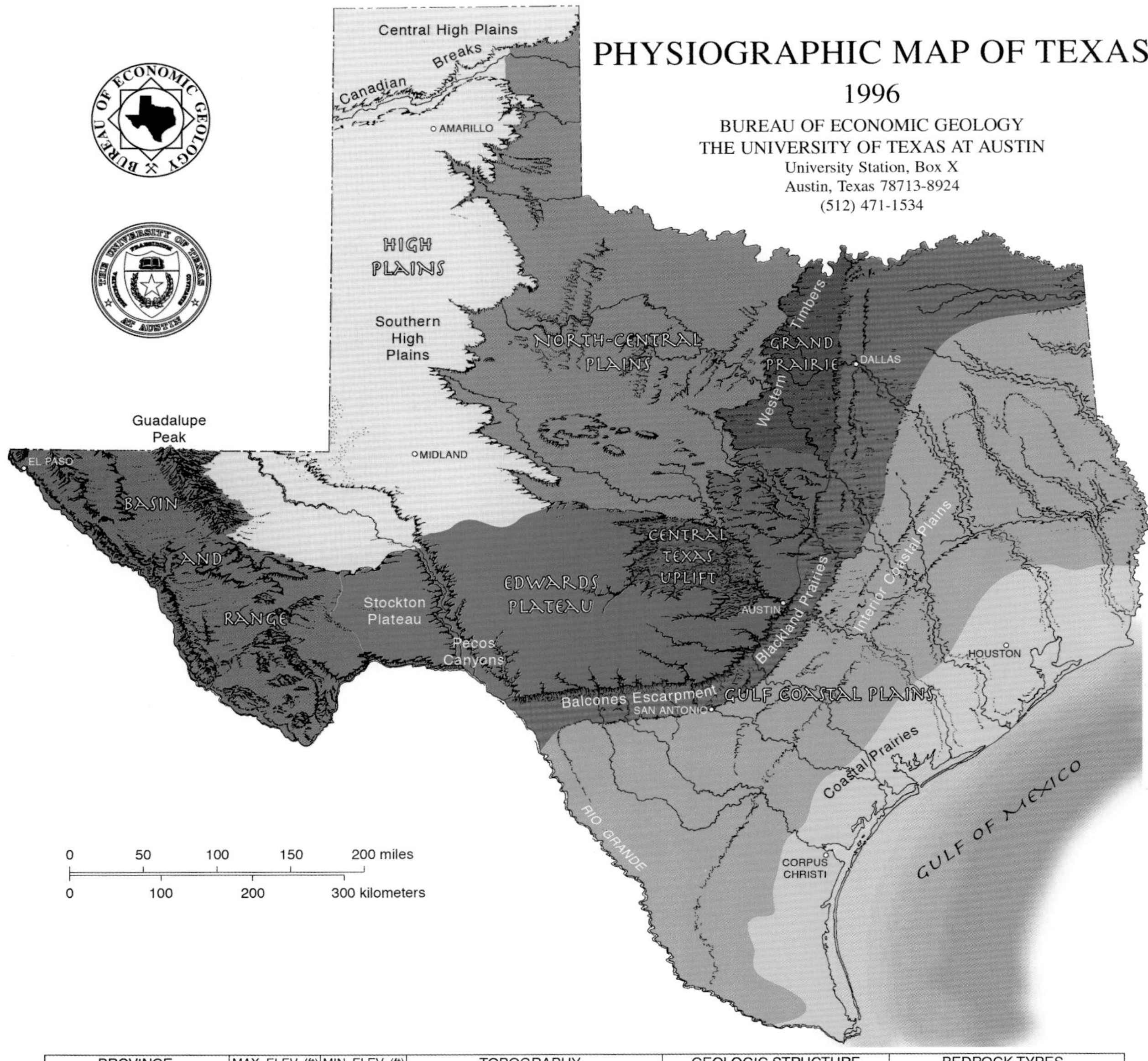

PROVINCE	MAX. ELEV. (ft)	MIN. ELEV. (ft)	TOPOGRAPHY	GEOLOGIC STRUCTURE	BEDROCK TYPES
Gulf Coastal Plains					
Coastal Prairies	300	0	Nearly flat prairie, <1 ft/mi to Gulf	Nearly flat strata	Deltaic sands and muds
Interior Coastal Plains	800	300	Parallel ridges (questas) and valleys	Beds tilted toward Gulf	Unconsolidated sands and muds
Blackland Prairies	1000	450	Low rolling terrain	Beds tilted south and east	Chalks and marls
Grand Prairie	1250	450	Low stairstep hills west; plains east	Strata dip east	Calcareous east; sandy west
Edwards Plateau					
Principal	3000	450	Flat upper surface with box canyons	Beds dip south; normal faulted	Limestones and dolomites
Pecos Canyons	2000	1200	Steep-walled canyons		Limestones and dolomites
Stockton Plateau	4200	1700	Mesa-formed terrain; highs to west	Unfaulted, near-horizontal beds	Carbonates and alluvial sediments
Central Texas Uplift	2000	800	Knobby plain; surrounded by questas	Centripetal dips, strongly faulted	Granites; metamorphics; sediments
North-Central Plains	3000	900	Low north-south ridges (questas)	West dip; minor faults	Limestones; sandstones; shales
High Plains					
Central	4750	2900	Flat prairies slope east and south	Slight dips east and south	Eolian silts and fine sands
Canadian Breaks	3800	2350	Highly dissected; local solution valleys		
Southern	3800	2200	Flat; many playas; local dune fields		
Basin and Range	8750	1700	North-south mountains and basins	Some complex folding and faulting	Igneous; metamorphics; sediments

Physiographic map of Texas. Courtesy of the Bureau of Economic Geology, the University of Texas at Austin

APPENDIX C

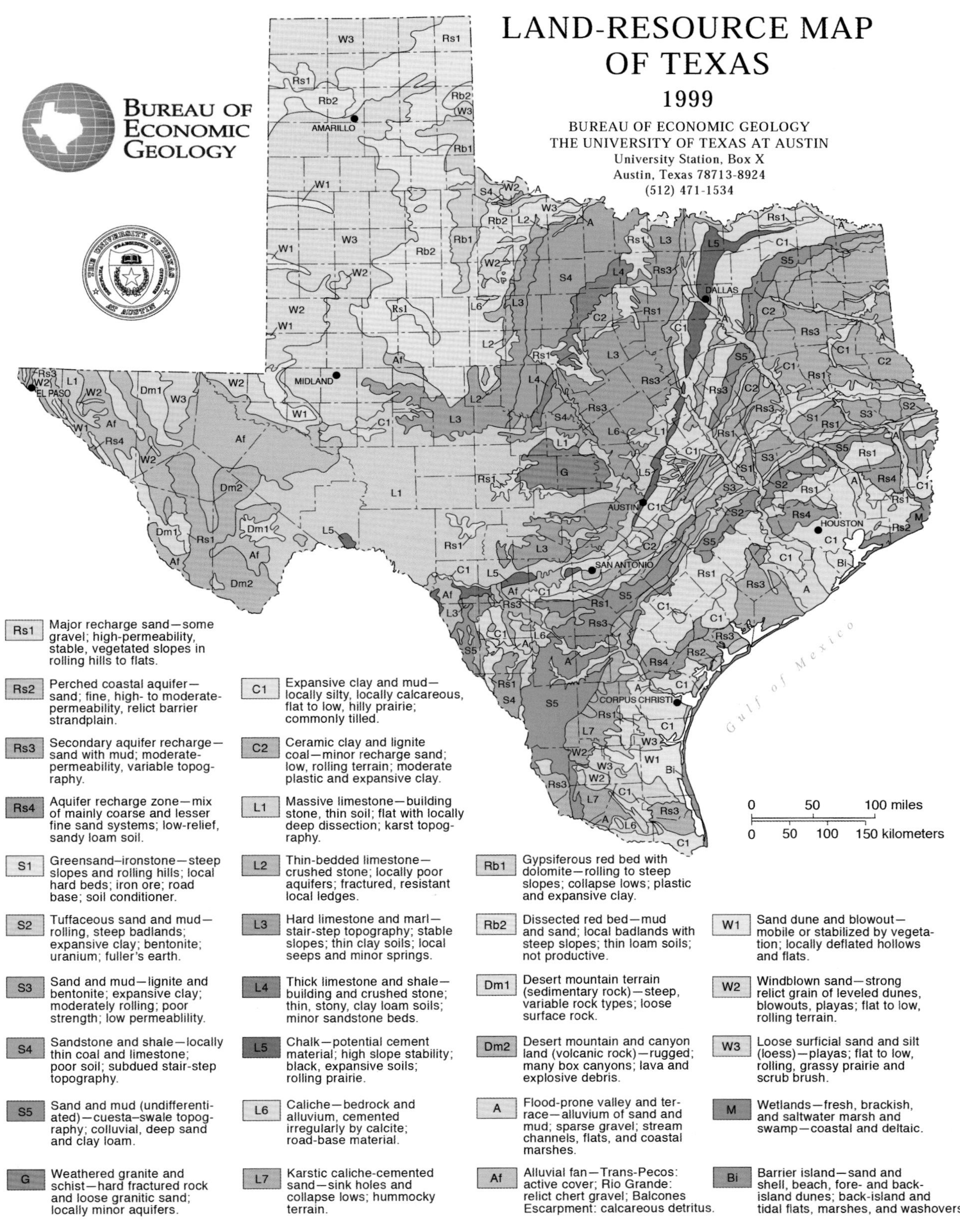

Land-resource map of Texas. Courtesy of the Bureau of Economic Geology, the University of Texas at Austin

APPENDIX D

Common Rocks and Soils

The Rock Cycle

All rocks are related through the rock cycle, which is controlled by the natural physical and chemical processes active in and on the earth. There are three basic rock types: igneous, derived from fire and the cooling of molten earth materials; sedimentary, derived by the settling out of rock particles that have been weathered and transported; and metamorphic, derived by the alteration of rock materials by high pressure and temperature.

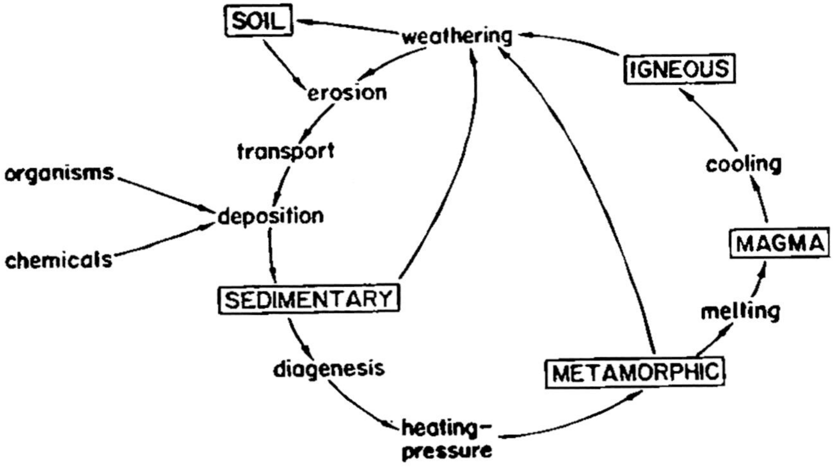

GEOLOGIC ROCK CYCLE

Follow the rock cycle: If we start with molten earth material (MAGMA) and allow it to cool, IGNEOUS rocks are formed. If they are exposed to the surface of the earth and weathered, eroded, and transported to a new depositional site, they form SEDIMENTARY rocks. When they are buried and subjected to high pressure and temperature, sedimentary rocks are altered into METAMORPHIC rock. SOIL is formed through the in-place weathering of an earth material.

Intrusive Igneous Rocks

Evidence for internal earth heat related to the cooling of a magma source is demonstrated by the geysers and hot springs in Yellowstone National Park, Wyoming.

Intrusive igneous rocks exposed at the surface following erosion of the overlying rocks intruded by the magma. Note the rounded, smooth surface of the landscape, reflecting the large mass and uniformity of the rock body.

Coarse crystals indicate slow cooling of an intrusive igneous rock.

Lava flow on the "Big" Island of Hawaii that entered the Pacific Ocean. Note the black sand beach created by wave erosion of the lava.

Extrusive Igneous Rocks

Extrusive igneous rocks are volcanoes. On the left is a continental volcano dominated by ash deposits, rich in silica and aluminum minerals that make up the volcanic mountain. Continental volcanoes are explosive volcanoes, as occurred at Mount St. Helens. On the right is an oceanic volcano, rich in iron and magnesium, erupting on Hawaii. This volcano is not an explosive event but dominated by volcanic fountains and lava flows that cool and harden on the earth's surface.

Diamond Head on Oahu Island, Hawaii. Note the crater in the center and the volcanic deposits around the edge.

Identification of Intrusive Igneous Rocks

Granite: Light-colored rock, quartz and feldspar rich, clearly visible minerals, some dark minerals.

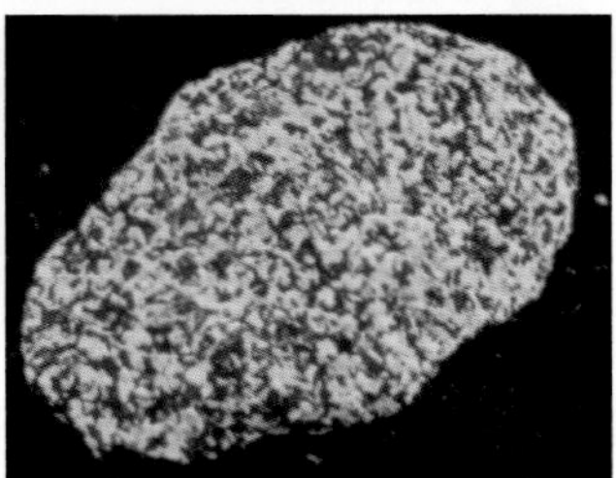

Diorite: Gray-colored rock caused by an increased concentration of iron and magnesium.

Gabbro: Black color caused by a high concentration of iron and magnesium and a minimum amount of quartz.

Identification of Extrusive Igneous Rocks

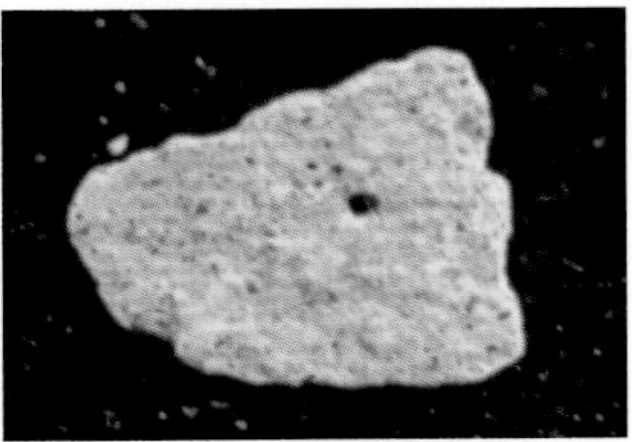

Rhyolite: Light-colored, very fine, crystal-sized rock with similar mineralogy of granite; often associated with continental volcanoes.

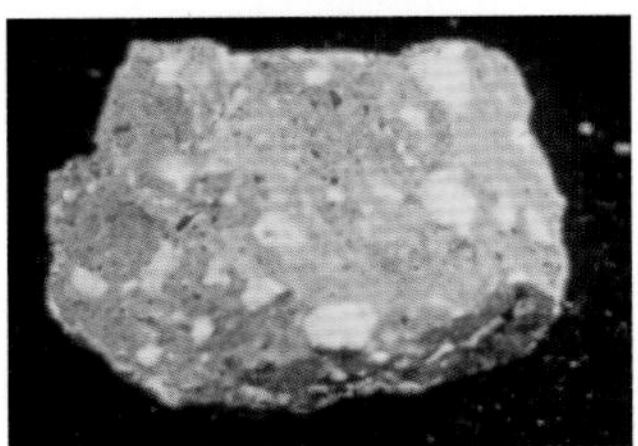

Andesite: Very fine, crystal-sized rock with the mineralogy of a diorite; often associated with deep-earth source materials.

Basalt: Black, very fine, crystalline rock with the mineralogy of a gabbro; often associated with oceanic environments.

Rock Decay

Weathering: The decay of rock materials by physical and chemical processes active on or near the earth's surface that result in the degradation and breakdown of the rock.

Physical weathering: Breakdown of an intact rock mass into smaller particles by the expansion of water as it freezes, expansion of tree roots growing in fractures, and the breakage of rocks as they fall.

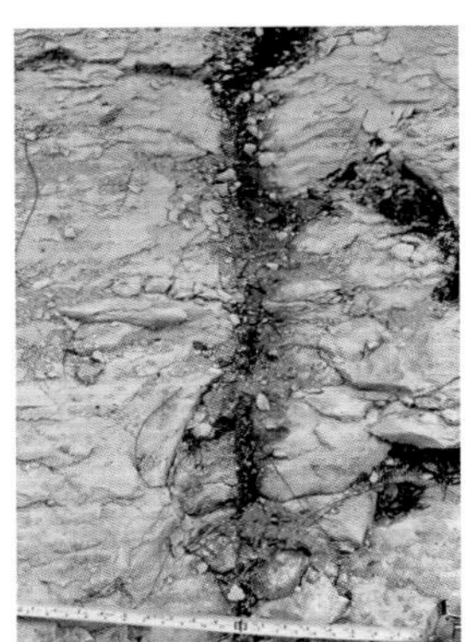

Chemical weathering: Breakdown of the minerals in the rock material through chemical reactions with water—the most significant chemical process—biochemical reactions with plants, and the direct chemical reaction with oxygen, water, and other elements like iron.

Erosion and transport: Earth forces pick up, erode, and transport weathered materials to new locations to create sedimentary rocks. The size of the particle eroded and transported is directly related to the amount of energy in the erosion/transport process.

Erosion also produces the interesting landforms on the earth's surface; without erosion the earth's landscape would be boring.

Clastic Sedimentary Rocks

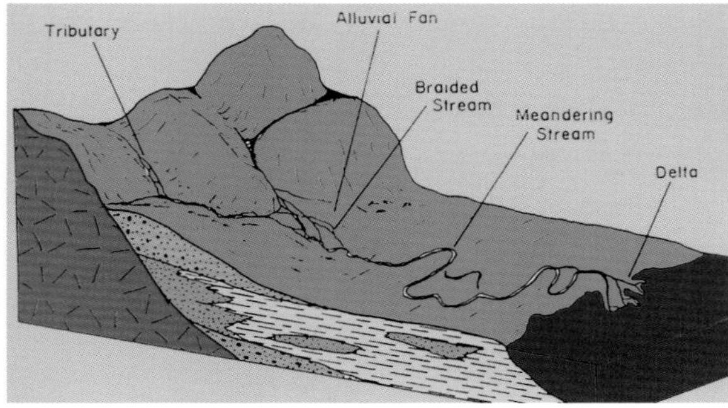

Clastic sedimentary rocks are formed through the transport and deposition of weathered earth materials. The transport distance and energy influence the particle size and shape from poorly sorted, large, and angular to well sorted, fine, and rounded. The three-dimensional characteristics of a sedimentary rock deposit are controlled by the physical conditions of the environment of formation.

Talus: Poorly sorted mixture of rock particles derived from a nearby location, often at the base of a steep slope or cliff; particles generally angular or poorly rounded.

River deposits: Moderately sorted mixture of gravel- to sand-sized particles generally becoming finer in size and more rounded in a downstream direction; characteristically show a fining upward grain-size trend that reflects the decreasing energy in the river as the river water levels or possibly floodwaters recede.

Delta: Sands are predominantly fine to very-fine grained and show a general coarsening upward trend that reflects the filling of the waterbody as the delta advances. As the water level shallows, the river's ability to transport sediment decreases and the coarser sediments are deposited. These delta front sand deposits rest on a fine clay bed, prodelta muds, deposited below and in front of the advancing delta sands. Once the river has effectively filled the area, the sediments that get deposited on top of the delta sands are delta plain muds deposited during river floods.

Floodplain: Very fine-grained clayey particles; very low-energy environment; often forms wetland areas and settings.

Windblown: Aeolian, very well-sorted, very fine-grained sands, fine clays, and silts removed by the winds; occurs as sand dunes.

Organic Sedimentary Rocks

Limestone: Calcium carbonate–rich rock derived from coral and other marine animal shells; often is calcium-rich algae accumulation.

Coal: Accumulation of plant matter preserved in an oxygen-deprived anaerobic environment in which all plant cells and components have been altered into carbon.

Chemical Sedimentary Rocks

Evaporites: Salt concentrated through the evaporation of saline waters in an arid climate; gypsum also formed through the evaporation process.

Chemical replacement: Petrified wood is produced by the chemical replacement of plant cells by inorganic chemicals that ultimately produce a solid rock.

Sedimentary Rock Identification

Classification of clastic rocks is based entirely upon the grain size of the sedimentary particles that make up the rock. Additional descriptors, such as color, grain size, sorting, degree of cementation, mineralogy of the grains, fossils, and sedimentary structures, enhance the complete description of the sedimentary rock.

Organic and chemically derived sedimentary rocks are classified by the dominant chemical that makes up the rock sample. Limestone is composed of calcium carbonate derived from corals and other carbonate marine animals, while coal is derived from the decay of plant materials. Rock salt is composed of salt concentrated through the evaporation of saline to brine waters.

Mountain: Composed of clastic, horizontal sedimentary rocks that are sandstones.

Conglomerate: Very coarse-grained and poorly sorted deposit generally close to the source area of the particles.

Sandstone: Fine, sand-sized particles showing sedimentary structures (cross-beds) that reflect deposition in a river.

Shale, mudstone: Very fine clay- and silt-sized particles deposited in a low-energy environment; often react with water to become "mud."

Limestone: Composed of lime (calcium carbonate) derived from marine organisms or chemical concentration.

Rock salt: Salt or halite; chemically precipitated salt in an arid environment where marine salt water evaporates and results in salt formation.

Metamorphic Rocks

Once a sedimentary particle is deposited, it undergoes a sequence of gradual changes that begin with the process of diagenesis, during which the water is forced out of the pore spaces and the rock mass compacts in response to the overburden loads. Expulsion of the water is followed with cementation and compaction that convert the loose sedimentary particles into a sedimentary rock. With continued burial and increased temperature the pore voids are filled with cement derived from the sedimentary rock. This leads to the formation of an altered, metamorphosed rock that is massive and has high strength but the same mineralogy and chemistry of the original sedimentary rock—a low-grade metamorphic rock. Continued burial and high temperatures combined with the introduction of hot fluids from within the earth lead to the formation of new minerals and a new rock fabric—a high-grade metamorphic rock.

Low-Grade Metamorphic Rocks

Quartzite: Derived from the alteration of quartz sandstone to produce a massive quartz rock with very high strength and erosion resistance.

Slate: Derived from shale that has been altered to a thin-bedded hard rock that looks like a shale but is harder and more massive.

Marble: Formed by the cementation of limestone with calcium carbonate cement that forms a hard, weather-resistant rock material.

High-Grade Metamorphic Rocks

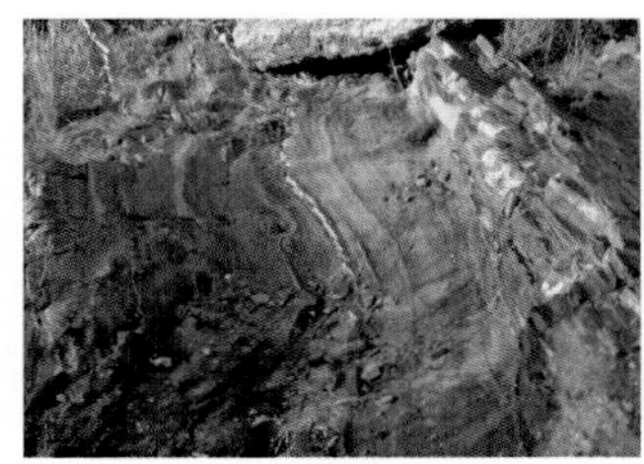

Schist: Complete alteration and recrystallization of a clay-rich shale to form a rock composed of orientated mica minerals.

Gneiss: Coarse, crystalline, altered rock that often looks like a banded granite. Note the parallel bands of gray minerals in the pink rock mass (*upper*). Sample of gneiss showing the amount of deformation caused during the maximum level of heating and pressure (*lower*).

Texas Soils

Soil Formation

Soils are the result of in-place weathering, both physical and chemical processes. Five major factors establish the general characteristics of soil: parent material, climate, topography, organisms, and time. The parent material is the original earth material subjected to weathering and impacts the rate of soil formation, properties of the soil, and soil-profile thickness. Climate, on both the regional and local scales, impacts the freeze-thaw cycles and the amount of available moisture for chemical weathering. The topography of the site impacts the erosion rate, drainage of runoff, and deposition of eroded materials. Organisms, including plants, insects, and animals, add or remove chemicals and mix and aerate the soil. Time controls the amount of soil development by establishing how long the soil remains in place before being eroded or covered by other sediments.

Soils of Texas

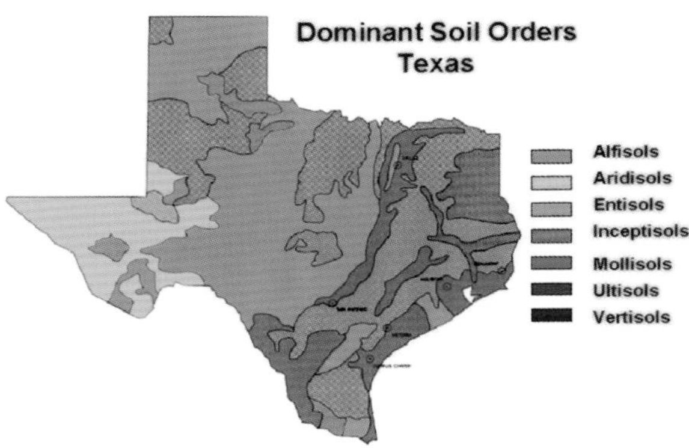

Dominant Soil Orders of Texas. Courtesy of TAMU Soil Characterization Laboratory. http://soildata.tamu.edu

Alfisols: Excellent agricultural soils that have a gray to brown surface horizon and a well-developed clay subsurface horizon; moderately weathered.

Aridisols: Soils formed in a desert environment that frequently have a gravel surface caused by wind erosion, often have cemented horizons with calcium carbonate and iron oxide, and are salty.

Entisols: Recent weathered materials that do not have developed horizons commonly form in young, active landscape areas.

Inceptisols: Young soils that show weathering of the parent materials without severe alteration of the bedrock.

Mollisols: Grassland soils that have a thick, dark, organic-rich, upper horizon; excellent for grain crops.

Ultisols: Deeply weathered soils that form in a moist climate where chemical weathering dominates; often red in color from iron oxide staining (rust).

Vertisols: Clay-rich soils highly susceptible to shrink-swell cycles depending on the rainfall conditions; a very costly natural hazard to homes and roads because of shrink-swell damage to structures.

Histisols: Mature soils developed in a wetland environment, organic-rich, saturated, and a chemically reducing environment with little available oxygen.

Rocks, Soils, and Society

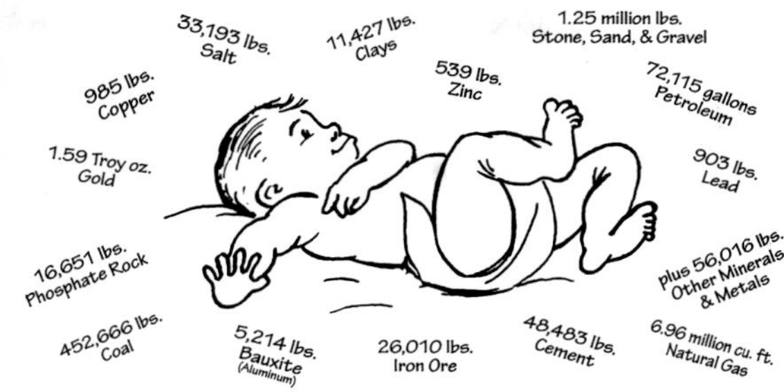

Each year, new minerals must be mined to support our lives and lifestyles. The 2015 Mineral Baby shows examples of the 3.11 million pounds of minerals, metals, and fuels the average American will need in his or her lifetime. Courtesy of Minerals Education Coalition, Society for Mining, Metallurgy and Exploration Foundation (http://www.mineralseducationcoalition.org/sites/default/files/uploads/baby_2013.pdf)

Each of us will need 31,779 pounds of salt, 14,530 pounds of iron ore, and 1.11 million pounds of stone, sand, and gravel in our lifetime. Where will these resources come from? Modern society obtains the resources required for modern life through either agricultural or mining processes.

The agricultural industry provides many of our critical resources, such as food, timber for lumber, clothing fibers such as cotton and wool, leather, and pharmaceuticals. We also benefit from other things that are grown, such as flowers and landscaping, national forests, wetlands, and grasslands.

The mining and minerals industry provides the remaining critical resources that maintain modern society, such as metals like iron, copper, aluminum, and lead; construction materials like sand and gravel for roads and concrete for structures; gemstones such as diamonds and rubies; industrial minerals like abrasives for polishing and grinding; and pharmaceuticals such as the minerals in vitamins and medicines.

UNIT 8

Weather and Climate

JOHN NIELSEN-GAMMON
Texas A&M University Regents Professor of Atmospheric Sciences, Texas State Climatologist

Unit Goals

After completing this unit, volunteers should be able to

- discuss what processes affect the daytime and nighttime temperatures
- describe the main processes driving Texas weather and climate
- identify cloud formations and the weather and climate they can predict or represent
- understand the short-term and long-term relevance of climate variability and change to Texas ecology
- describe a typical year of weather in Texas

"For me, a landscape does not exist in its own right, since its appearance changes at every moment; but the surrounding atmosphere brings it to life—the light and the air vary continually. For me, it's only the surrounding atmosphere which subjects their true value."
—Claude Monet

Introduction

The atmosphere of Earth is quite unlike that of the nearby planets Venus and Mars. The atmospheres of both Venus and Mars have large concentrations of carbon dioxide, but on Earth, most of the carbon dioxide is now underground in the form of calcium carbonate rock and coal or dissolved in the ocean. Nitrogen, which is not highly soluble in water, became the dominant constituent, presently composing 78% of the atmosphere.

Oxygen was almost completely absent from the atmosphere during the earth's first two billion years. As it evolved, life has become increasingly able to utilize carbon dioxide in ways that produce oxygen as a byproduct. Photosynthesis is such a process. The subsequent decay of plant life takes up oxygen and returns carbon dioxide to the atmosphere to complete the cycle, but if plant material gets buried without decaying, the cycle is broken and oxygen builds up in the atmosphere at the expense of carbon dioxide.

When oxygen grew to 1% of the atmosphere, about 700 million years ago, respiration became possible. About 400 million years ago, oxygen reached 10%, high enough to support an **ozone layer** in the stratosphere that would protect the earth's surface from lethal levels of ultraviolet radiation. Each ozone molecule consists of three oxygen atoms.

With the ultraviolet shield in place, life on dry land became commonplace. As plant life spread, oxygen levels rose still further. Finally, by 300 million years ago, creatures with lungs appeared, requiring oxygen concentrations similar to those found today (21%). Without the plants leading the way, the atmosphere would not be able to support animal (including human) life.

Temperature is most easily defined as how hot a substance (such as air) feels. At the atomic level, air temperature goes up with the kinetic energy of the air molecules (mostly nitrogen and oxygen) as they vibrate, spin, and move around randomly. At **absolute zero** (0 K [kelvin], or –273°C, or –454°F), the molecules would be still.

One of the gases in the air—indeed, the one with the most widely varying concentration—is **water vapor**, the invisible, gaseous

A cloud photographed from an airplane window. Courtesy of Ron Pieket

form of water. It is what the water in a glass turns into if you leave it sitting out for a few days and let it evaporate (literally, “become vapor”). Steam, like a cloud, is composed of many tiny drops of liquid water and has a whitish appearance. Note that what you see are tiny particles of water, not water vapor gas.

If you cover the glass, the water will not evaporate much because the water vapor is trapped inside the glass, so eventually equilibrium is reached: the rate at which the gaseous water molecules randomly run into the surface of the liquid (and get absorbed) soon equals the rate at which the water is trying to evaporate. When this happens, the air is said to be **saturated** with respect to water.

For any given amount of water vapor in air, there is a particular temperature at which that air would be saturated. Any colder, and some of the water vapor would condense into liquid. Any warmer, and any liquid water lying around would evaporate. The temperature at which the air is exactly saturated is called the **dew point**. The name comes from the fact that often at night the temperature at the ground will drop to the point that any additional cooling causes water to condense as dew (liquid) on the ground and on vegetation. If it is cold enough for ice to form, the corresponding temperature is called the **frost point**.

Another common measure of humidity is **relative humidity**, the amount of water in the air divided by the amount in the air if it were saturated. So when the temperature

All the water seen here is in liquid form, whether as puddles on the ground, dense droplets in the clouds, or scattered droplets in the layer of haze. The water vapor, which is water in its gas phase, is invisible. Courtesy of John Nielsen-Gammon

equals the dew point, the relative humidity equals 100%.

A Typical Day of Weather

The main processes that drive weather and climate may be found in one day's worth of observations of temperature and humidity. On a typical sunny day, the temperature is lowest shortly after sunrise. The temperature then rises rapidly, reaching a maximum in midafternoon. The temperature falls rapidly around sunset before falling slowly the rest of the night.

The dew point never exceeds the temperature. Indeed, the relative humidity almost never gets more than a few tenths of a percent above 100%, depending on how fast the extra water vapor can condense into liquid form. Typically, the highest humidity occurs in the morning. During midday, the dew point drops, reaching its lowest point by midafternoon. A rapid rise in dew point takes place around nightfall, with the moisture in the air fairly steady through most of the night.

Solar Energy

The source of energy for the morning rise in temperature is the sun. The atmosphere absorbs about one-third of the solar energy, much of which is ultraviolet light absorbed in the stratosphere. The bulk of the radiation, which is in the visible part of the electromagnetic spectrum, passes right through the atmosphere and reaches the ground. Good thing, too; if light did not pass through the air, we would have a hard time seeing anything. Air, by itself, can absorb only enough solar radiation in a day to heat up a degree or two. You notice much absorption or scattering of visible radiation only when the air is especially dusty or hazy or when the sun is so low on the horizon that there is a lot of atmosphere between you and the sun.

A sunset with the orb of the sun visible.

"The sun, with all the planets revolving around it and dependent on it, can still ripen a bunch of grapes as if it had nothing else in the universe to do."
—Galileo

When the light finally hits something, it can either be reflected away or absorbed. You can tell just by looking—the lighter-colored an object is, the more light is bouncing off and reaching your eye. Black objects absorb almost all the visible radiation that hits them. And when an object absorbs electromagnetic energy, it heats up; black objects, which absorb the most, consequently heat up the most. The air that touches the hot object becomes hot itself, and winds and turbulence then distribute this heat through the air, often as high as a mile up into the atmosphere. So the air temperature rises in the morning not because the sun heats the air but because the sun heats the ground and the ground heats the air next to it.

Infrared Radiation and the Greenhouse Effect

If that were the end of the radiation story, the earth would have been heating up for the past four billion years and would be quite toasty by now. But all objects, not just the sun, emit electromagnetic radiation.

Both the intensity of the radiation and its wavelength depend on the temperature of the object; the very hot sun emits a lot of mostly visible radiation; the earth emits a smaller amount of mostly infrared (atmospheric scientists also call it **longwave**) radiation. You cannot see infrared radiation, but special sensors can pick it up; thus, we can "see" clouds at night in infrared (IR) satellite images.

Although air does not absorb or emit much visible radiation, certain gases in the air (especially molecules with a more complex atomic structure than nitrogen or oxygen, most notably water vapor and carbon dioxide) can absorb and emit infrared radiation. The IR satellite images utilize a small range of wavelengths in which no commonly occurring atmospheric gases absorb or emit radiation, so about all we see is radiation emitted by the ground and by the liquid and frozen water droplets in clouds. So the ground not only absorbs solar radiation during the day but also emits infrared radiation all the time. It emits the most radiation when temperatures are hottest. In simplest terms, the ground heats up when the incoming solar radiation is more intense than the outgoing (emitted) longwave radiation, and the ground cools off when the outgoing longwave radiation exceeds the incoming solar radiation (which happens especially at night, when the visible radiation from space is nearly zero).

An infrared satellite image of Hurricane Andrew as it approached the Florida coast in August 1992. Courtesy of National Oceanic and Atmospheric Administration

As seen from space, the earth is always gaining energy from the sun and radiating away a nearly identical amount. At any particular wavelength, the amount of energy radiated away depends on the temperature and the atmospheric composition. A warmer object radiates more energy. If you add gases to the atmosphere that can radiate energy away, that radiation tends to escape from higher up in the atmosphere where it is colder. Thus, the radiation loss decreases, and the earth warms up until it is back to radiating what it did before. This increased temperature caused by radiatively active atmospheric gases is called the **greenhouse effect**.

Conduction, Convection, and Latent Heat

So far we have considered the two main processes affecting the temperature of the ground surface and the atmosphere: absorption of incoming solar radiation and emission of outgoing infrared radiation. But a few other things are going on at the same time.

Conduction describes the transfer of heat from the ground to the air when the ground is warmer than the air when they come in contact. **Convection** describes vertical wind currents carrying the resulting hot air up away from the ground. If instead the ground is colder than the air, as often happens at night, the ground would gain heat from the air. Since cold air sinks, the air that cools by contact with the cold ground stays near the surface, producing a shallow layer of cold air known as a nocturnal inversion. This explains why the air is usually windy and gusty during the day but often becomes calm near the ground at night.

The processes of **evaporation** and **condensation** also affect the temperature. You have experienced that evaporation makes things cooler when you step out of a tub or shower and feel cold until you dry off. On a molecular level, the fastest molecules are the ones that escape from liquid into the air, leaving behind slower-moving molecules and reducing the average temperature. The extra energy stored in the water vapor molecules is ready to be converted into heat again as soon as the vapor condenses into liquid form. This energy is called **latent heat**. On a typical day, depending on the dampness of the soil and vegetation, as much or more energy can be lost from the ground to the air through evaporation as through conduction.

As a general rule, the higher you go in the atmosphere, the proportion of air that is water vapor decreases, so vertical mixing tends to carry water vapor away from the ground. Thus, the dew point is usually lowest during midafternoon when mixing is strongest, and the dew point is usually highest just after sunrise when the dew has evaporated but the turbulence is low.

The Seasons

The only significant external source of energy for the earth is the sun. The daily rotation of the earth on its axis brings parts of the earth into sun and parts into shadow, with the resulting differences between daytime and nighttime temperatures. Similarly, the year it takes the earth to complete one orbit around the sun involves changes in solar radiation that cause the seasons.

A common misconception is that summer is the warmest season because the earth is closest to the sun then. The earth's orbit is so nearly circular that this effect has little direct impact, and in fact it helps moderate the Northern Hemisphere winter since the earth is closest to the sun in January. Instead, the seasons are caused by the tilt of the earth on its axis. In January, the Southern Hemisphere is pointed somewhat toward the sun, so it receives most of the solar radiation that hits the earth; in July, the Northern Hemisphere is pointed somewhat toward the sun, so it gets more than its share of solar radiation. The tropics receive about the same amount of solar radiation year-round, so temperatures do not change much throughout the year.

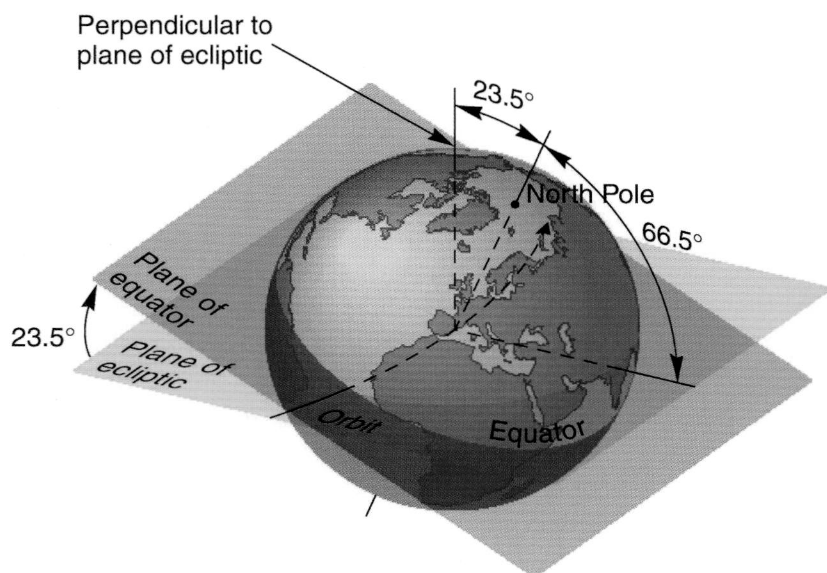

Diagram showing the earth's tilt toward and away from the sun during summer and winter.

The same principles explain why there is less sunlight in winter than summer and less sunlight in midafternoon than noontime: sunlight from a sun that is not directly overhead has to pass through more of the atmosphere, and when it reaches the ground, the sun's rays are spread out over a larger surface area. The shorter days help make winter cooler too.

Winds and Forces

The winds in the atmosphere are driven by air pressure gradients: differences in air pressure from one place to the next. Atmospheric **air pressure** is almost completely caused by the force of gravity, so the air pressure at a given location is almost exactly equal to the total weight of air above that location. Air is heavier than you might think: there are about 14 pounds of air over every square inch of ground, producing an air pressure of 14 pounds per square inch. If you climb a mountain or ascend in an elevator, the air pressure decreases because there is now less air above you.

At similar pressures, hot air is less dense than cold air. As a result, the weight of a warm column of air is less than the weight of a cold column of air, and the air pressure beneath the warm column of air is also less. Thus, differences in temperature from one place to another give rise to pressure differences, leading to horizontal winds. Ultimately, all the winds in the atmosphere exist because the sun does not heat the earth evenly, instead producing warm and cold air.

Global Winds

In the **tropics**, deep and strong thunderstorms are common. Air ascends within these thunderstorms, exits their tops 10 to 15 miles up, and spreads out horizontally. Much of this air ultimately descends gradually back toward the surface in the **subtropics**, forming vast deserts such as the Sahara and the Arabian Peninsula. On average, then, equatorial regions are warm and moist, while subtropical regions are warm and dry. This pattern is altered by the presence of continents and oceans and the march of the seasons. For example, vast numbers of thunderstorms take place over India in summertime but not wintertime, a phenomenon known as the **monsoon**. A weak version of a monsoon takes place over northern Mexico, Arizona, New Mexico, and extreme West Texas in summertime, as the land heats up and moist air flows in from the south.

In midlatitudes, the warm tropical and subtropical air meets the cooler air from temperate and polar regions. The air masses do not exactly "clash," but the large variations in temperature imply large variations in density and pressure, and the strong pressure gradients imply strong winds. The strongest winds are found about 10 miles above the ground, in a band of wind that circles the globe from west to east called the **jet stream**. The strong winds, and the temperature gradients associated with them, are unstable and break down into massive northward and southward excursions of the jet stream that can extend halfway between the pole and equator. At the ground, the instability takes the form of the traveling high- and low-pressure centers and cold and warm fronts so common during the fall, winter, and spring. During the summer in the Northern Hemisphere, the jet stream moves north and cold fronts rarely reach Texas.

There is a paradox here: If wind is caused by air moving from high pressure to low pressure, how can the jet stream circle the globe? The air cannot possibly be always moving toward lower pressure, because if you follow the jet stream on a map, you eventually make a complete circle and end up at the same place (and pressure) where you started.

The rotation of the earth causes the wind to be deflected to the right of what pressure alone would produce, so the jet stream actually blows "sideways." If you imagine yourself in the middle of the jet stream and facing downstream, low pressure will be to your left and high pressure will be to your right in the Northern Hemisphere; the deflection is to the left in the Southern Hemisphere and is near zero in the tropics. Near the ground, friction reduces the deflection of the wind, so the wind is blowing almost directly toward low pressure.

"Forget not that the earth delights to feel your bare feet and the winds long to play with your hair."
—Khalil Gibran, Lebanese poet and author of *The Prophet*, 1923

Sea Breezes, Fronts, and Dry Lines

The 24-hour cycle of sunlight produces temperature and pressure patterns that change with the time of day. For example, the temperature of large bodies of water barely changes at all during a 24-hour period, while land surfaces heat up during the day and cool off at night. The pressure gradient these temperature differences produce drives the sea breeze during the day and the land breeze at night. The **sea breeze** is an onshore (blowing from sea to land) wind caused by high temperatures and low pressures over land during the day. The sea breeze effect adds to whatever large-scale winds are already present, but when the large-scale winds are light or blowing weakly toward water, the onset of the sea breeze in late morning or early afternoon is very noticeable. The leading edge of the sea breeze can take the form of a front, or sharp temperature and wind contrast, that progresses inland (sometimes hundreds of miles) during the afternoon and evening, often accompanied by a line of clouds or **thunderstorms**.

Meanwhile, the earth's rotation gradually causes the sea breeze winds to curve to the right, or **veer** (change direction in a clockwise manner), so that by the middle of the night they may be blowing parallel to the coast. A little more veering, and the winds become a **land breeze**, blowing from land to sea around dawn.

The sea breeze front is just one example of an atmospheric front. Larger-scale weather systems, such as wintertime low-pressure systems, almost always involve a cold front and usually a warm front as well. A **cold front** is a moving, narrow zone of strong temperature contrast in which the cold air is replacing the warm air at the surface; a **warm front** is the opposite. Cartoon pictures of fronts usually depict them as thin boundaries, but such discontinuities are rare. More often the frontal position marks the warm edge of the strong temperature gradient, which may extend for a few hundred miles into the colder air.

Warm fronts in spring and fall in Texas are often associated with heavy rains. If the warm front is slow to move, warm air reaches the front from the south and ascends over the layer of cold air, producing clouds and rainfall over a particular area for a long period of time, as long as the supply of air from the south continues. In winter, warm fronts often cause **freezing rain**, when the low-level cold air north of the warm front is below freezing and the air above the front is above freezing. If the raindrops do not freeze (and turn into **sleet**) on the way down, they freeze when they come in contact with the cold ground and form a dangerous layer of ice.

Texas gets its share of cold fronts too. Some of the strongest cold fronts in the United States, known as **blue northers**, strike Texas. A blue norther is triggered when a cold front moves south from Canada. The cold air behind the front, unable to move southwest across the Rocky Mountains, piles up along the eastern side of the mountains and is deflected southward across the Great Plains into Texas. Strong northerly winds and a sudden drop of 10°–25°F herald the arrival of a blue norther. While they are rarely accompanied by much precipitation, they usually bring the coldest weather of the year. During a drought, they can also cause serious dust storms in West Texas.

Ice from a freezing rain.

Dust kicked up by a squall line during a drought colors the sunset. Courtesy of John Neilson-Gammon

Another type of atmospheric boundary is more common in Texas than anywhere else in the world. A **dry line** is formed when warm, moist air, originating from the Gulf of Mexico, moves northwest and comes in contact with hot, dry air moving northeast from higher elevations in the interior of Mexico and New Mexico. The confluence of these airstreams is aided by the formation of a **lee trough**, or line of low pressure, east of the mountains as air sinks and warms after passing over the Rockies. Temperatures do not differ much on either side of the dry line, but the amount of moisture in the air can differ by a factor of 4 or more. When springtime severe weather develops, the first thunderstorms usually form along the dry line and move northeast.

Clouds, Precipitation, and Severe Weather

Clouds are composed of tiny drops of liquid water or tiny ice crystals. Each individual cloud droplet is so small that you could fit about 200,000 of them on one fingernail. Clouds are given Latin names according to their altitude and structure. Names of midlevel clouds (about 3–7 miles up) carry the prefix alto- (from *altus*, "high"), while names of higher clouds are prefixed with cirro- (from *cirrus*, "a lock of hair," referring to their typically wispy appearance). The two basic structure categories are **stratus** (meaning "stretched out"), a broad, flat cloud typically covering most or all of the sky, and **cumulus** (meaning "heap"), an upright, lumpy cloud with a flat base. Stratus clouds form when large areas of the atmosphere are lifted uniformly, while cu-

Stratus clouds. A stratus deck starts to break up over California's San Joaquin Valley. Courtesy of John Nielsen-Gammon

Cumulus clouds. Courtesy of National Oceanic and Atmospheric Administration

mulus clouds form from individual buoyant updrafts. A final cloud descriptor, **nimbus**, lacks the imagination of the others; in Latin, it literally means "a dark rain cloud."

"The heavens declare the glory of God; the skies proclaim the work of His hand."
—Psalm 19:1

Clouds form when ascending air cools so much that the air becomes saturated, and further ascent causes some of the water vapor to condense into liquid water or ice particles, depending on the temperature and the types of particles already present in the air. A related phenomenon, **fog**, is like a cloud touching the ground, except the cooling of the air normally takes place through means other than ascent.

Just as Texas weather goes through seasonal cycles, so do clouds and the weather they represent. In the wintertime, high cirrus clouds are common and often indicate nothing more than that Texas is south of the core of the upper-level jet stream. In late spring, the sudden approach of thick cirrus clouds can mean that a squall line or other organized convective system has developed to the west and is heading your way. In summer, cirrus usually indicate the presence of thunderstorm activity, and in early fall, if the cirrus edge forms a broad curve across the sky, a tropical storm or hurricane may be nearby.

Low-level clouds are common in the morning when the air is moist. Often the clouds are oriented in long bands with gaps in between, and it only takes about three bands to fill the sky. This banding indicates the presence of wind above the ground.

A cumulonimbus cloud. Courtesy of National Oceanic and Atmospheric Administration

Eventually, by midmorning, the winds aloft will have been brought to the ground as the ground heats up and stirs the air. Before that happens, winds at ground level may be light and variable, but you can predict the wind direction later that morning just from looking at how the clouds are lined up. Later in the day, that structure breaks down and the clouds evolve into boundary-layer cumulus clouds.

Rain and Snow

Cloud droplets are so small that they basically float in the air. Raindrops are a million times heavier. So how does the atmosphere turn clouds into rain? There are two main mechanisms. First, if the air is warm enough and there is enough water vapor being converted into cloud droplets, the droplets will grow in size as they run into each other and stick together (technically, collide and coalesce). Once a few big droplets form, they start slowly falling, which allows them to run into more cloud droplets, which causes them to get even larger so they fall faster.

Second, there are very few particles floating around in the atmosphere that will allow ice to form on them at temperatures only slightly below freezing, and water vapor will condense onto ice more readily than it will condense onto liquid water. Thus, once a few ice particles form, they rapidly extract water vapor from the air. Meanwhile, water starts evaporating from the remaining liquid water droplets to make up the difference for the cloud water droplet to gain in size. Eventually, there are a few large snowflakes where before there were a lot of tiny water droplets. The snow falls toward the ground, melts as its temperature rises above freezing, and reaches the ground as rain. This mechanism can work only if the cloud extends high enough into the atmosphere that its top is well below freezing.

A raindrop hitting a puddle. Courtesy of US Department of Agriculture

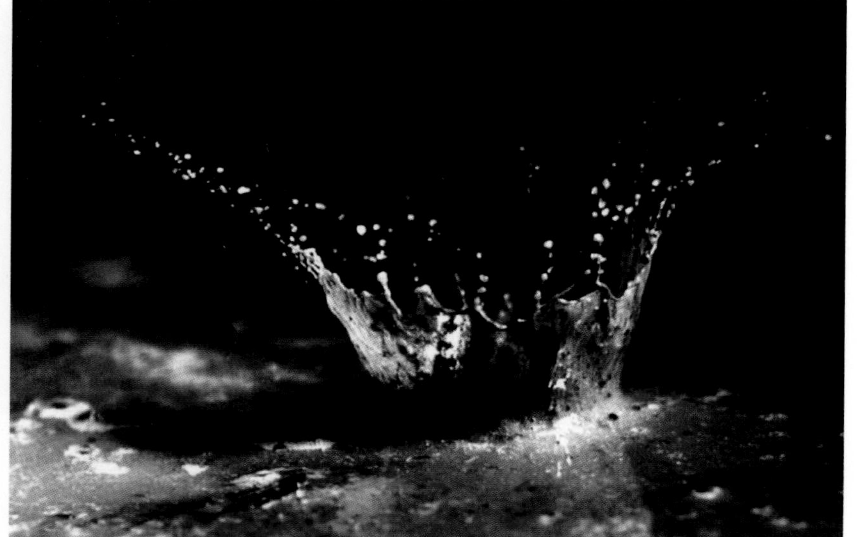

Tornadoes

Tornadoes are one of the most dramatic forms of severe weather. Texas is located at the southern end of "Tornado Alley," which also extends through Oklahoma and Kansas and is where tornadoes are most common in the world. Tornadoes are most frequent in springtime, with a secondary peak in the fall.

Tornadoes are a product of instability and wind shear. **Convective instability** refers to a situation in which the water vapor condensing into liquid or ice droplets in an ascending column of air releases enough latent heat to keep the column warmer than its surroundings and keep the air ascending. In spring and fall, moist low-level air from the Gulf of Mexico often flows northward beneath still-cool air aloft, creating a situation of instability. In the summertime, the air aloft is rarely cool enough to produce vigorous instability (although garden-variety thunderstorms are common then), and in the wintertime, the Gulf of Mexico is usually too cool to act as a good source of warm, moist air.

Vertical wind shear refers to a situation in which winds at one level of the atmosphere are blowing in a different direction or at a different speed than winds at another, nearby level of the atmosphere. For example, it is not unusual in a severe weather situation for surface winds to be blowing strongly from the southeast and winds at a

A close-up of a tornado. Courtesy of National Oceanic and Atmospheric Administration

A full view of a low-precipitation supercell thunderstorm. Courtesy of National Oceanic and Atmospheric Administration

height of two miles to be blowing strongly from the southwest. These large variations in wind can be tilted into a vortex by a strong convective updraft, and an updraft also enhances any swirling of the winds already present beneath it. The result can be a **rotating updraft** that persists for up to several hours and forms the core of a **supercell thunderstorm**. Most strong tornadoes originate at the base of supercell thunderstorms.

The final trigger for a tornado is thought to be the sharp low-level contrasts in temperature found beneath many thunderstorms, as cool downdraft air comes in contact with the warm, moist air feeding the updraft. The temperature differences cause the air to tumble, and if it is then ingested into the updraft of a strong thunderstorm, the tumbling can be amplified into the strong vortex called a tornado.

Damage from a tornado is categorized using the **enhanced Fujita scale**, ranging from EF0 (minimal damage) to EF5 (strong enough to sweep a foundation clean and rip up asphalt from a road). Strong tornadoes (from EF2 to EF5) are rare, but they tend to last longer and cause the most fatalities.

A tornado that occurs over a body of water is known as a **waterspout**. While the base of a tornado is often visible only because of the dust and debris it stirs up, a waterspout appears as a tube of cloud extending all the way to the water. Some waterspouts are not true tornadoes but simply rapidly rotating updrafts in an environment of weak wind shear beneath ordinary convective clouds. Over land, vortices known as **dust devils** can form even when there are no clouds. In a dust devil, the superheated ground provides the buoyancy for a very strong updraft when the sun is bright and the winds are light. In the hot, dusty valleys of West Texas in sum-

Damage from a tornado at Kellerville, Texas, on June 8, 1995. Courtesy of National Oceanic and Atmospheric Administration

A dust devil. Courtesy of West Texas Mesonet, Texas Tech University

mertime, dust devils can last for over an hour and grow to thousands of feet tall.

Hail

Hail is created when liquid water in an updraft does not have time to freeze in midair before it comes in contact with particles of solid ice within the cloud. If the ice becomes large enough, it can fall all the way to the ground before melting. Most supercell thunderstorms produce hail, but hail can also be produced in any strong thunderstorm. A strong updraft allows the ice to remain suspended in the updraft where it can grow to large sizes. Dry air aloft is also favorable to hail because it allows the hailstones to remain cool through evaporation as they fall to the ground.

Lightning

Lightning is the visible manifestation of an electrical discharge taking place within a thunderstorm, among thunderstorms, or between a thunderstorm and the ground. The exact cause of the electrical fields that produce lightning is not known, but they are believed to be caused by massive numbers of collisions between solid ice particles within the cloud and other ice particles covered by a thin film of water.

Thunder, the audible consequence of lightning, is caused by the rapid expansion of the air as it heats to several thousands of degrees within the lightning channel. While the speed of light is amazingly fast, the speed of sound is comparatively slow, and this fact can be used to estimate the distance to any audible lightning flash. Just count the number of seconds between the visible flash and the sound of the thunder and divide by 5 to get the approximate distance in miles.

Lightning kills many more people every

Large chunks of hail. Courtesy of National Oceanic and Atmospheric Administration

Nighttime exposure of lightning. Courtesy of National Oceanic and Atmospheric Administration

year than tornadoes. The safest places to be to avoid lightning are indoors or in a car. It is difficult for lightning to penetrate a space partially enclosed by metal, such as a car interior. If indoors, avoid touching metal objects connected to the ground outside. This includes telephones with cords and bathtubs filled with water. If stuck outdoors, avoid standing beneath a tree and instead crouch low to the ground, discarding any large metal objects such as umbrellas and golf clubs.

Hurricanes

A **hurricane** is a roughly circular storm, about 100–500 miles across, that forms over warm water in the tropics and has peak surface winds of at least 74 miles per hour. The same storms are known as **typhoons** in the western Pacific and **cyclones** in the Indian Ocean. This is especially confusing since another name for tornado in the United States is cyclone.

In the Atlantic, the official hurricane season runs from June through November, but most hurricanes form in August or September. A hurricane forms when a mass of tropical convection generates enough heat and low pressure that air converges into the convective area at low levels, amplifying any rotation already present. If the winds become strong enough, the air is able to extract heat and moisture from the ocean faster than the thunderstorms are able to dissipate it, and the storm intensifies rapidly into a hurricane.

Tropical disturbances are the main source of rainfall for most of Texas during late summer and early fall, but there are many dangerous aspects to a hurricane. The most obvious cause of damage is the strong winds, which are felt near the area of landfall. Another potential cause of damage is the **storm surge**, the rise in sea level (as much as 20–30 feet in extreme cases) that accompanies the low pressure and strong winds of the hurricanes. Some hurricanes produce numerous tornadoes, causing more damage than the hurricane winds themselves. Finally, and most important, even after a hurricane has moved onshore and died, large amounts of very moist, unstable air remain. These hurricane remnants can produce torrential rains, especially if they are lifted by hills or interact with a larger-scale weather system. Indeed, flooding from rainfall is the leading cause of death from hurricanes.

Hurricane Ike approaching the Texas coast, September 12, 2008. Courtesy of National Oceanic and Atmospheric Administration

Texas Climate and Climate Change

There is no single Texas climate. The wide range of climates, combined with a wide range of soils, produces an impressive diversity of plants and animals. Indeed, the primary categorization of the world's climates is based on vegetation variations. Most of Texas occupies one of two global climate categories—**humid subtropical** (eastern Texas) and **midlatitude steppe** (western Texas)—the exception being mountainous elevations in West Texas. The humid subtropical climate in Texas is a variant that features year-round precipitation, so there is no true, typical dry season. In the steppe (or short grassland) of Texas, there is less precipitation overall, and most precipitation falls during the warmer months of the year.

The cause of these rainfall differences is geography, particularly the latitude of Texas and the land and sea beyond its southern border. The mountains to the west prevent most Pacific moisture from reaching Texas, so most rainfall comes from moisture-laden air from the Gulf of Mexico and points farther south and east. This air enters Texas along the Gulf Coast and across the Texas-Mexico border between Laredo and Brownsville; the border west of Laredo is closed to moisture by the formidable obstacle of the Mexican Plateau. During the summer, low pressure over the southwestern United States allows moist air to move northwestward into West Texas, producing frequent summertime thunderstorms. During wintertime, that low pressure is absent, and traveling weather disturbances tend to carry the moisture northward, frequently missing western Texas entirely.

The same winds give Texas fairly uniform temperatures during the summertime. Daytime temperatures are coolest along the coast, before the air has had a chance to be heated by much land surface, and at higher elevations and mountains in West Texas. In winter, temperatures are more variable because cold and warm fronts frequently pass through and bring different air masses to the state. Wintertime temperatures are warmest to the south, particularly in the Rio Grande Valley, and coldest to the north, particularly in the Texas Panhandle.

"Sunshine is delicious, rain is refreshing, wind braces us up, snow is exhilarating; there is really no such thing as bad weather, only different kinds of good weather."
—John Ruskin, English writer, 1819–1900

A Typical Year of Weather

Wintertime is marked by rapidly changing weather patterns. While the Panhandle receives relatively little precipitation during the winter, a large fraction of it falls as snow. Farther south, snow is progressively more unusual, so that the southeastern third of the state may typically make it through an entire year without a snowflake. Similarly, the temperature drops below freezing al-

Snowfall at Caprock Canyon State Park in the Texas Panhandle. Courtesy of Texas Parks and Wildlife Department

most every day in the Panhandle and almost never in the Rio Grande Valley. Many annual plants and wildflowers are actively growing during the wintertime, but the growth is mainly underground. Because temperatures are low, not much evaporation takes place and the ground tends to stay moist. Plants use this time to develop their root systems so that they have access to deep, wet soil if surface moisture becomes scarce later in the year.

In springtime, the weather changes a bit more slowly, and thunderstorms start taking over as the primary source of rain. From April to June, the dry line is especially active in western Texas. Springtime thunderstorm activity reaches a peak in May, which is reliably one of the wettest months of the year throughout Texas. In midafternoon of a typical active day, isolated thunderstorms will first develop along the dry line. The first thunderstorms will trigger other thunderstorms, until eventually a line of thunderstorms, called a **squall line**, is marching southeastward across Texas. The squall line, if it survives long enough, does not reach eastern Texas until after midnight. During summer, thunderstorms are more widespread and less likely to be severe. For plants, the relatively large amount of precipitation during the summer is counteracted by the high temperatures, which cause large amounts of evaporation and force plants to use more water. Plants can respond by closing their stomata so that they no longer exchange gases with the atmosphere, when not enough water is available to their root systems.

Tropical disturbances, including hurricanes, become more common during August and (especially) September. Average rainfall reaches a peak in September in the Gulf Coast region and West Texas. The Gulf Coast maximum is caused by occasional tropical storms striking the coastline. Hurricanes are rare—two years in three no hurricanes strike Texas—but even tropical depressions, if they are slow moving, can produce large amounts of precipitation. This precipitation is not reliable, and the climatological mean rainfall totals are strongly affected by the occasional tropical flood. In West Texas, the extra September rains come from remnants of hurricanes that form in the eastern Pacific off the Mexican coast, travel northward, and come ashore near Baja California.

A roll cloud over Kyle Field in College Station, Texas. Courtesy of John Nielsen-Gammon

Autumn does not seem particularly intimidating compared to the freezes of winter, the tornadoes of spring, the heat waves of summer, and the hurricanes of September. Actually, a wide variety of severe weather can take place in autumn. In October, the Gulf of Mexico is still warm, so tropical air masses can reach Texas without passing over cooler water and losing their strength. When the tropical air is ingested into a cool-season weather disturbance, the result can be torrential rain and massive flooding. In November, southeastern parts of Texas experience a second severe-weather season, with one or two tornado outbreaks happening most years. Finally, December is not too early for very cold air to spill deep into Texas from the north. This time of year is also the wettest season for extreme northeastern Texas.

Drought

The simplest definition of **drought** is perhaps the best: a period of time that is too dry. Texas precipitation is irregular; even the most humid parts of Texas can go a month or longer without any rainfall. Plants native to Texas, by virtue of the fact that they live here, have demonstrated that they (or their progeny) can survive even the extended dry spells that we call drought. Indeed, if we did not have droughts, the plants common to our natural environment would eventually be crowded out by more vigorous, water-loving plants that have not developed drought tolerance.

Droughts are a problem primarily because of our need for a regular water supply. Farms without irrigation require rainfall at the right times and the right amounts; ranches need enough rain to provide for each season's growth of grasses. Irrigated farms as well as towns and cities obtain their water from wells or reservoirs; during drought the water supply decreases both because of the lack of natural rainfall and the increased watering and irrigation to make up for it. Fires, more common during droughts, are a part of the natural environment but are a serious problem when they strike areas where people live.

A few months of significantly below-normal rainfall is enough to cause a drought in Texas, especially during the summertime when water evaporates quickly from the soil. Periods of drought can last for several years, as they did during the early and mid-1950s. Drought feeds on itself: with less moisture in the ground, there is less moisture to evaporate into the air, so thunderstorms are less likely and air temperatures are higher.

As of this writing, the second-worst drought on record began in October 2010. During the first 12 months of the drought, Texas received only 40% of its normal rainfall statewide. At first, the largest impacts were agricultural, with several billion dollars in losses from major crops. Fire also caused devastating, localized damage. As the drought continued, year after year, the largest impacts shifted to water supplies, both human and natural, as stream flows remained low and coastal estuaries became more and more saline.

El Niño

Scientists are gradually beginning to discover how changes in certain parts of the ocean-atmosphere system can cause large changes in climate in other parts of the globe. By far the most dramatic and most well-studied local change is El Niño. The term **El Niño** refers to unusually warm water temperatures in the equatorial eastern Pacific Ocean; the corresponding term for unusually cold temperatures is **La Niña**.

El Niño and La Niña affect the global weather patterns, including those over Texas, by altering the distribution of thunderstorm activity along the equator. During El Niño, the warm waters play host to a lot of thunderstorm activity over the eastern Pacific, while during La Niña, the cold sea-surface temperatures suppress thunderstorm activity. The thunderstorms, in turn, drive the global wind patterns, and if the thunderstorms change position or intensity, so do the global winds.

The largest impact on Texas weather is on wintertime precipitation in the eastern half of the state. An El Niño winter normally brings above-normal rainfall to eastern Texas, particularly along the Gulf Coast, while a La Niña winter often is accompanied by wintertime drought. The first few months of the drought that started in 2010–11 were caused (or at least strongly influenced) by a moderately strong La Niña.

"Nature, to be commanded, must be obeyed."
—Francis Bacon, Novum Organum, 1620

Plants and trees dropping their leaves during the Texas drought of 2011. Photo taken in September 2011 in East Texas. Courtesy of John Nielsen-Gammon

A dry stock tank during a drought. Courtesy of John Nielsen-Gammon

An Alphabet Soup of Natural Variability

El Niño is one of the most important modes of natural variability that affects our climate, but there are several others. Some, particularly those modes that involve changes to the atmosphere alone, are difficult to predict and come and go fairly quickly.

One such atmospheric mode is the North Atlantic Oscillation (NOA). As the name implies, most of the action takes place over the North Atlantic, although most of the Northern Hemisphere is affected. In its positive phase, the jet stream is farther north than usual over the Atlantic. For eastern North America, even as far from the North Atlantic as Texas, this tends to mean warmer-than-normal conditions during the wintertime. In its negative phase, the jet stream is farther south and eastern North America is cool. Once developed, an NAO pattern can be locked into place for weeks to months.

An important mode felt primarily in the ocean is the Atlantic Multidecadal Oscillation (AMO). Because the ocean is heavily involved, a particular phase lasts longer, as its name implies—two to four decades. In a positive AMO, most of the Atlantic Ocean north of the equator is warmer than normal. In the summertime, this enhances thunderstorm activity over the ocean, at the expense of thunderstorm activity over land. Thus, even as tropical activity is enhanced over water, it is suppressed over land in places that include the southern and central United States. Conversely, a negative AMO favors increased summertime rainfall over the southern United States.

Over the North Pacific, the strongest atmospheric mode is the Pacific-North America (PNA) pattern. This jet stream pattern consists of a broad trough (southward dip) in the jet stream over the central North Pacific, a ridge (northward excursion) in the jet stream over the West Coast of North America, and a second trough over the central United States and Canada. This pattern can be locked into place from two to four weeks. A strong positive PNA pattern is associated with very cold weather across the central United States, with arctic air plunging southward all the way to Texas and beyond.

The dominant long-term oceanic pattern in the Pacific is called the Pacific Decadal Oscillation (PDO). It has the same erratic multidecade time scale as the AMO, though why the AMO merits a "multi" in its name and the PDO does not is hard to understand. The positive PDO is essentially a slow version of El Niño, but with larger temperature changes at higher latitudes. The positive phase corresponds to warm tropics but cooler sea-surface temperatures in the midlatitudes. A positive PDO has a similar effect on Texas climate as does an El Niño: cool and wet during the wintertime.

Texas is somewhat unusual compared to other parts of the globe in that it is strongly influenced by temperature patterns in both the Atlantic and Pacific Oceans. This causes a greater amount of long-term climate variability than in most other places. For example, the period 2005–14 was characterized by frequent and intense droughts in Texas. During that period, the AMO favored dry summers and the PDO favored dry winters, so it is no surprise that average rainfall ended up below normal.

Global and Local Warming

Besides the year-to-year and decade-to-decade climate changes that accompany phenomena such as El Niño and the AMO, there are much larger and longer-lasting climate changes as well. Perhaps the most prominent are the ice ages, the last of which ended a little more than 10,000 years ago. There is now concern that humankind may be causing its own significant climate changes on a global scale, through the generation of carbon dioxide and other gases that absorb and emit infrared radiation. These gases produce the greenhouse effect, making the earth warmer than it would be otherwise. The fear is that human-made increases in the amounts of these gases in the atmosphere will lead to even warmer surface temperatures (global warming) and a whole host of related problems such as increased drought and sea-level rise, although there will doubtless be benefits to the warmer temperatures and increased carbon dioxide as well.

The logic is simple, but the climate system is complex, involving interactions among the atmosphere, the oceans, the plants, and snow and ice. Computer simulations of the possibly changing climate are almost impossible to verify without waiting another 50 years, and much depends on what actually gets added to the atmosphere in the interim. The best estimates of actual temperature changes over the past century indicate that the temperature of the earth is rising at an unusually rapid rate, and natural process can only account for a small fraction of that warming. What we do about the problem depends on whether we are willing to let our descendants live with the possible consequences of not doing anything.

Warmer temperatures are probably the most likely for the future. Models also predict precipitation changes, but those

30-yr Normal Precipitation: Annual
Period: 1981-2010

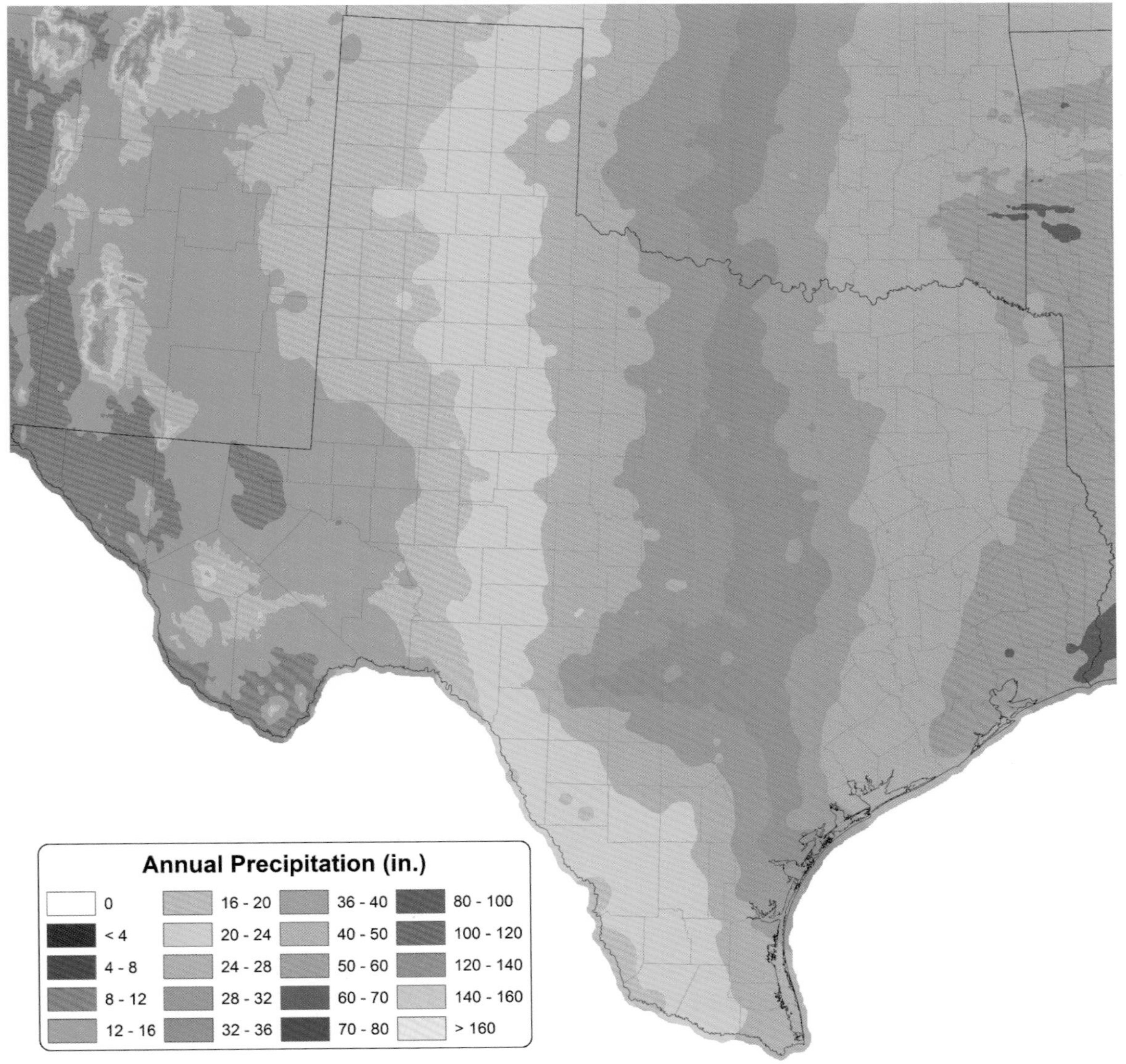

Average annual precipitation. Copyright © 2014, PRISM Climate Group, Oregon State University, http://prism.oregonstate.edu, map created December 9, 2014

are small compared to the natural variability Texans live with already. Even if rainfall stays the same, though, temperatures will affect water by causing greater evaporation, reduced stream flow, and larger water demand. The natural systems likely to feel the strongest effects are those at the end of the natural water delivery systems: the inhabitants of bays and estuaries along the Texas Gulf Coast. Reduced stream flow means reduced freshwater inflows, and this will change the chemistry and ecosystems of the Texas coasts.

Also, warmer temperatures imply a greater carrying capacity of water vapor in the atmosphere. That means that a given storm will be able to produce more rainfall. Texas already holds the US record for great-

30-yr Normal Mean Temperature: Annual
Period: 1981-2010

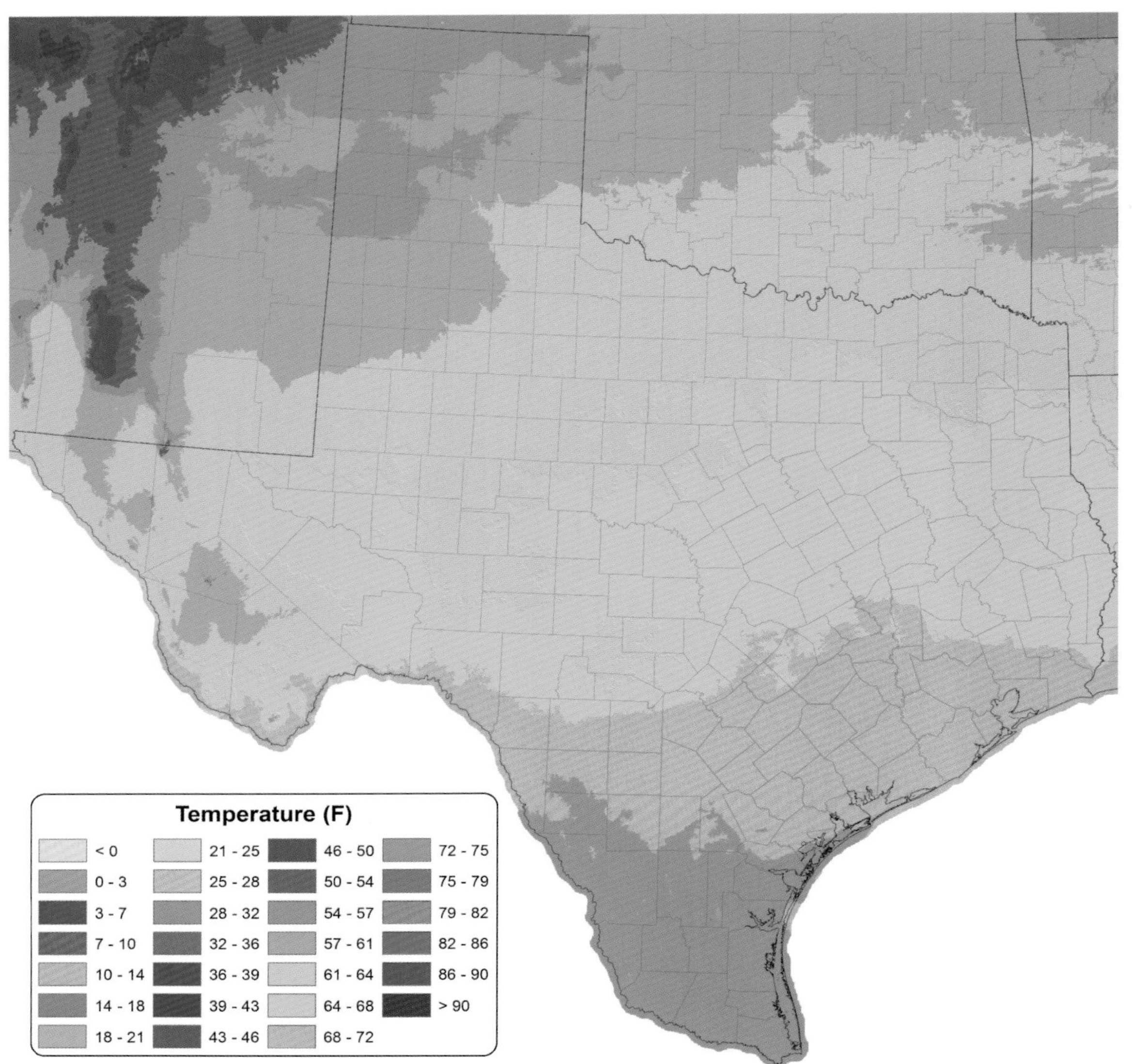

Average annual temperatures. Copyright © 2013, PRISM Climate Group, Oregon State University, http://prism.oregonstate.edu, map created December 9, 2014

est 24-hour rainfall amount (a whopping 43 inches in Alvin in 1979), and flooding will be a growing problem unless our infrastructure keeps up. Alas, this means that Texas is one of those places that will probably see both worse droughts and worse flooding. Texas weather is never normal, and we can look forward to it being even less so.

Severe weather will probably change, too, but whether it will get better or worse is mostly unknown and probably depends on the particular type of severe weather. For example, the evidence on hurricanes points to an overall decrease of hurricane frequency but an increase in the upper limit of hurricane intensity. A lot will depend on the details of how wind patterns change, both along the ground and aloft.

Meanwhile, we alter the local environment all the time, such as by constructing roads and buildings and by planting gardens. Particularly in large cities, the net effect of urbanization is to cause surface temperatures to rise by as much as several degrees. This change, which could have been called local warming but is actually known as the **urban heat island**, does not have the same global implications, but it certainly makes life less bearable in Texas cities during the summertime. Other alterations to the environment take the form of air and water pollution and can also be more important than global warming at the particular locations that are affected.

Climate Forecasting

While scientists really have no way of knowing if their forecasts of the climate 100 years from now are getting better, skill in forecasting the climate six months or a year from now is beginning to improve markedly, primarily because of the rapidly developing ability to simulate the atmosphere and the ocean simultaneously. As ocean temperatures and currents gradually change, the climate conditions at various points on the earth change with them. El Niño is a good example of this; a good fraction of our ability to forecast climate comes from our ability to forecast El Niño.

There is a difference between the ability to forecast climate a year from now and the ability to forecast weather a year from now. There is good reason to believe it is impossible to be able to say (with accuracy) that it will rain on Friday a year from now but not on Saturday. Even most climate forecasts do not say categorically that a particular

A hazy day in Texas City. Courtesy of Texas Parks and Wildlife Department

location will be above or below normal. Instead, about all that can be forecasted is the probability of certain weather outcomes, such as whether temperatures will be above or below normal.

Weather Forecasting

Weather forecasting also relies on computer simulations of the atmosphere. The big difference is that in weather forecasting, it is crucial to get the exact current conditions of the atmosphere right. If a model's representation of the present is bad, the future will only get worse. Taking the previous computer forecast as a first guess of the current state of the atmosphere, the computer takes all the recent observations of the atmosphere and tries to come up with a complete three-dimensional picture of the atmosphere that is consistent with the observations, the laws of physics, and previous observations as reflected in the previous forecast. The computer then simulates how that atmospheric state will evolve over the next few hours, few days, or few weeks.

The accuracy of weather forecasts has improved steadily and substantially over the past few decades for most forecast parameters. A five-day forecast in 2010 was about as accurate as a two-day forecast in 1980. Of the common forecast parameters, the most difficult to forecast remains summertime precipitation over the southern United States, including Texas. It is quite common to hear many days of forecasts of "20% chance of rain," and if it rains one day out of five, the forecast was correct. However, it would be much more useful to know which day it was going to rain.

Despite the improvements in computer forecasts of the weather, it remains true that a skilled human, using and interpreting the computer's forecast, can on average produce a forecast that is better than the computer's forecast. Since the computer will never know the exact state of the atmosphere or be able to simulate its evolution perfectly accurately, there will always be room for a human in weather forecasting, and there will always be someone hearing the forecast who is upset the forecast was not correct.

"Nature is painting for us, day after day, pictures of infinite beauty if only we have the eyes to see them."
—John Ruskin, English writer, 1819–1900

Texas' unique weather patterns will continue to be difficult to accurately forecast as our earth's climate evolves.

Resources

Books

Bomar, G. W. 1995. *Texas Weather*. 2nd ed. Austin: University of Texas Press.

Bonan, G. B. 2008. *Ecological Climatology: Concepts and Applications*. 2nd ed. Cambridge: Cambridge University Press.

Lutgens, F. K., and E. J. Tarbuck. 2013. *The Atmosphere: An Introduction to Meteorology*. 12th ed. Upper Saddle River, NJ: Prentice Hall.

Neelin, J. D. 2011. *Climate Change and Climate Modeling*. Cambridge: Cambridge University Press.

Nese, J. M., and L. M. Grenci. 1998. *A World of Weather: Fundamentals of Meteorology*. 2nd ed. Dubuque, IA: Kendall/Hunt.

Websites

ATMO Class Tutorials: http://atmo.tamu.edu/courses/wflm/tutorials.html [An online short course on the basics of meteorology and weather]

Intergovernmental Panel on Climate Change (IPCC): http://ipcc.ch [Comprehensive discussions of the science behind climate change]

National Weather Service: http://www.weather.gov [Real-time weather data and weather and climate forecasts]

National Climatic Data Center: http://www.ncdc.noaa.gov [Historical climate data]

National Weather Service Climate Prediction Center: http://www.cpc.ncep.noaa.gov/products/precip/CWlink/MJO/enso.shtml [Do your own El Niño tracking.]

Office of the Texas State Climatologist: http://climatexas.tamu.edu [Access to historic climate data and reports]

UNIT 9

Texas Water Resources

TEXAS A&M AGRILIFE EXTENSION

TEXAS WATER RESOURCES INSTITUTE

Kevin Wagner, Associate Director
Nikki Dictson, Extension Program Specialist III
Lucas Gregory, Project Specialist
Clare Entwistle, Research Assistant
Kirstin Hein, Student Technician
Allen Berthold, Research Scientist
Chelsea Hawkins, Student Technician
Aubry Wolff, Student Technician
Brian Jonescu, Research Assistant
Drew Gholson, Extension Program Specialist
Diane Boellstorff, Assistant Professor and Extension Water Resource Specialist

Unit Goals

After completing this unit, volunteers should be able to

- understand the water cycle and identify water resources of Texas
- be aware of the importance of water conservation and protection of both surface and groundwater sources
- understand the management of water resources in Texas, including water rights and ownership
- be familiar with state water planning and groundwater management
- understand water availability models, drought contingency plans, and water conservation plans
- become familiar with the Texas Parks and Wildlife Department's Land and Water Strategic Plan
- understand how water quality is assessed and managed and how the planning process is being used to improve water quality
- be familiar with state and federal agencies and water resources institutes that work with the public on issues concerning water quality
- become familiar with emergent water policies and issues
- understand the benefits that rainwater harvesting and other conservation practices can provide

Water Resources in Texas

Texas possesses tremendous water resources both above (surface water) and below (groundwater) ground. The rivers, creeks, lakes and reservoirs, springs, wetlands, estuaries and bays, and Gulf of Mexico making up the **surface water** of the state are our lifeblood, providing drinking water and recreation, supporting renowned fisheries, and fueling industry, energy production, and economic growth.

Texas ranks fifth in the United States in miles of coastline, contains 4 of the 15 longest rivers in the United States (Rio Grande, Red, Brazos, and Pecos), and enjoys 1.26 million acres of lakes, 2.1 million acres of saltwater bays, and more miles of rivers and streams than any other state in the nation. Six of the 20 largest reservoirs in the United States in terms of surface area are in Texas (Toledo Bend, Wright Patman, Sam Rayburn, Livingston, Texoma, and Falcon). In addition, Texas boasts significant **groundwater** resources, including numerous major and minor aquifers that cover the majority of the state. The most significant of these is the Ogallala Aquifer, which is one of the largest groundwater aquifers in the world and underlies the Texas Panhandle as well as parts of seven other states.

All of these waters provide many valuable ecosystems services as well as water supplies for the citizens, landscape, and wildlife of Texas. Surface water accounts for 40% of water used in Texas, with groundwater supplying the remaining 60%. Only California exceeds Texas in annual groundwater use. However, these critical water sources face several challenges in the coming years, including sedimentation of aging reservoirs, lack of viable sites for new reservoirs, loss of wetland and riparian wetlands across the state, aquifer drawdown, and reduced flows in springs and rivers that results in lower freshwater inflows to estuaries and bays.

Surface Water

Texas has an extensive and diverse system of surface waters, including rivers and streams, lakes and reservoirs, springs and wetlands, bays and estuaries, and the Gulf of Mexico. Its 191,000 miles of streams and rivers are dispersed across 23 river basins, including 15 major river basins and 8 coastal basins, which generally flow from west to east to the bays and Gulf of Mexico.

The amount of surface water available is dependent on the amount of precipitation (which includes rain, ice, sleet, and snow), evaporation, evapotranspiration by plants, and infiltration into the ground—the basic principles of the water cycle. The water cycle, or **hydrologic cycle**, is defined by a continuous movement of water. As water heats up, it evaporates, changing from a liquid to a gas vapor. For example, water evaporates from oceans, lakes, and rivers and enters the atmosphere. **Transpiration** is the process by which plants lose water vapor through their leaves, and **evapotranspiration** is the sum of transpired and evaporated water. Water vapor in the atmosphere cools and condenses, forming clouds, and changes back to a liquid or solid that then falls back to the ground as **precipitation**—rain, sleet, and snow. This precipitation then soaks into the ground to be used by plants, reaches shallow groundwater and deeper aquifers through **percolation** through the soil, or runs off via the surface or underground to streams, rivers, lakes, and the ocean, where it evaporates and begins again its journey through the hydrologic cycle. The fate of rainfall is determined by the vegetation, soils, topography, climate, geology, and land management. The interactions between the water cycle, watershed, and soils define the hydrology or natural water flow of any stream and lake.

Surface water, an important source of water for Texas, is growing in significance. In 2008, it accounted for almost 6.5 million acre-feet of water used in Texas (TWDB 2012). In the future, surface water will become more important as development of new surface water sources begin to supply more than half of the "new" water needed to meet Texas' growing needs.

Hydrologic cycle. Courtesy of Nikki Dictson, Texas Water Resources Institute

Rivers and Creeks

Rivers, creeks, and streams are all characterized by channelized flow confined within a bed and stream banks. The main function of a **river** or **creek** is to transport water and sediment downstream. A small creek will flow downhill and eventually join with another creek or larger river. A **watershed** or river basin is an area of land that contributes or drains water from precipitation to a particular creek or river. As the land area increases and connects with more creeks, the flow will continue to increase. Watersheds can be determined at many different scales, including the initial small creek, all the way up to a scale as large as a river basin, which

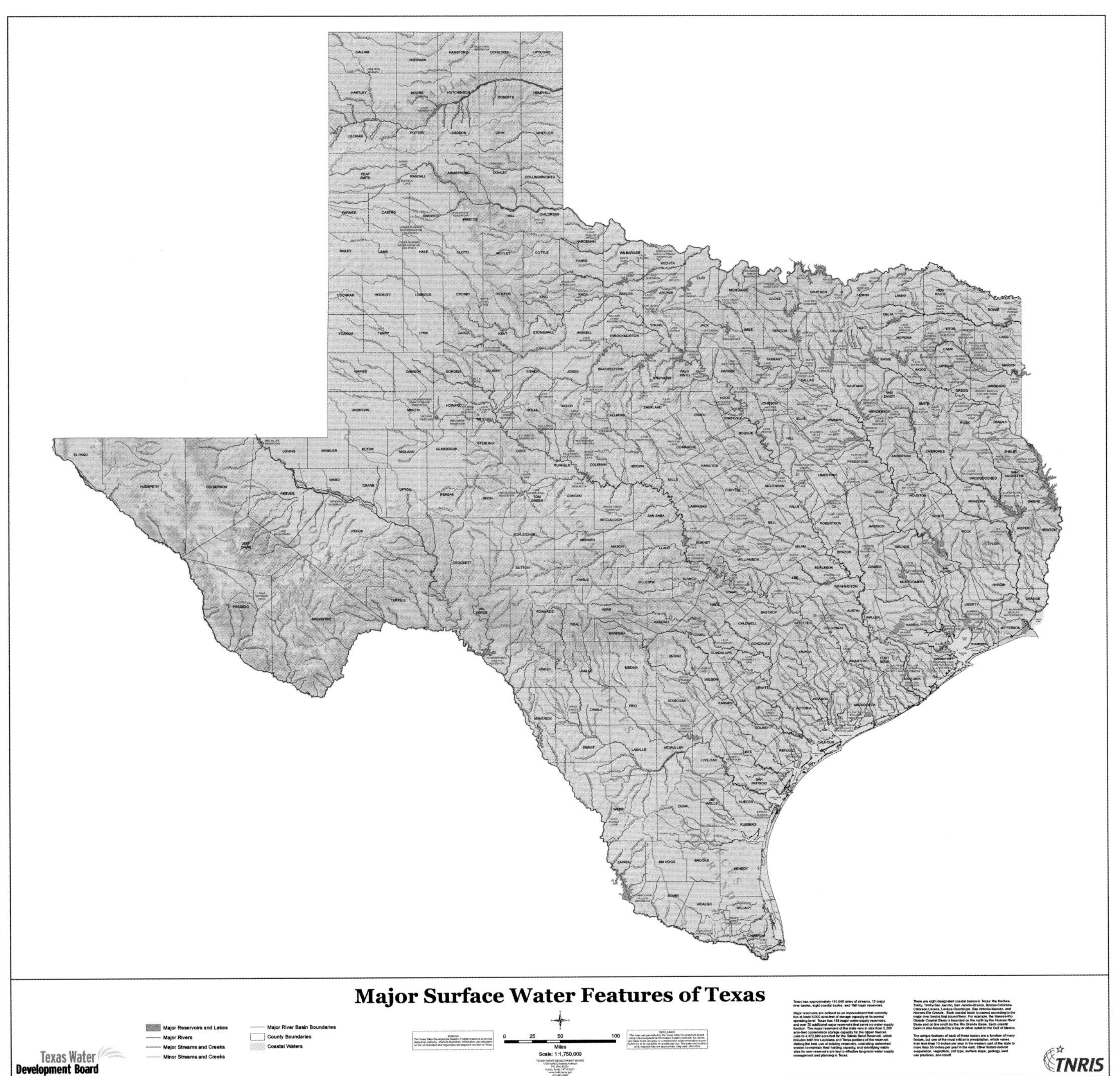

Major rivers in Texas. Courtesy of Texas Water Development Board

is a collection of many different watersheds. Watersheds are separated by elevation high-points (the highest point of an area of land, such as the top of a hill or mountain) called **divides**, as the rain will flow to a different point depending on which side of the divide it falls.

A **perennial stream** is a stream or creek that flows continuously throughout the year; such streams may be fed by springs or a groundwater discharge area. An **intermittent stream** flows only at certain times of the year when it receives water from springs or surface water but generally flows continuously for at least one month or more. **Ephemeral streams** are those that flow only in direct response to precipitation; they have no spring or continuous surface water source.

River Basins and Coastal Basins

The 15 major river basins in Texas are the Brazos, Canadian, Colorado, Cypress, Guadalupe, Lavaca, Neches, Nueces, Red, Rio Grande, Sabine, San Antonio, San Jacinto, Sulphur, and Trinity.

The 8 designated coastal basins in Texas are the Neches-Trinity, Trinity–San Jacinto, San Jacinto–Brazos, Brazos-Colorado, Colorado-Lavaca, Lavaca-Guadalupe, San Antonio–Nueces, and Nueces–Rio Grande. Each coastal basin is named according to the major river basins that bound it. For example, the Nueces–Rio Grande Coastal Basin is bounded on the north by the Nueces River Basin and on the south by the Rio Grande Basin. Each coastal basin is also bounded by a bay or other outlet to the Gulf of Mexico.

Lakes and Reservoirs

Texas has only one natural **lake**, or natural topographic depression collecting a body of surface water at least 20 acres in size—Caddo Lake, situated on the border of Texas and Louisiana. The remaining lakes are human-made reservoirs where a river has been dammed to impound water. A major **reservoir** is defined as an impoundment that currently has at least 5,000 acre-feet of storage capacity at its normal operating level (an acre-foot of water is equivalent to the volume of water required to cover one acre to a depth of one foot, or 325,851 gallons). There are more than 188 major water-supply reservoirs and 20 more that serve no current water-supply function. Reservoirs provide important water supplies, especially in Texas, with variable stream flow. They capture and store floodwaters for use during times of drought and when rivers are low or dry. Many of the major reservoirs were constructed during the 1960s and 1970s for the primary purpose of flood control, with water supply being a secondary benefit. There has been little construction of reservoirs since that time.

The major reservoirs of the state vary in size from 5,200 acre-feet conservation storage capacity for Upper Nueces Lake to 4,472,900 acre-feet for Toledo Bend Reservoir, which lies on the border of Louisiana and Texas. Currently, more than half of the available surface water in the state is supplied by reservoirs. During the state water-planning processes, reservoirs have been proposed to meet future water-supply needs, but the numbers proposed have varied between each five-year water plan. The 1984 state water plan proposed 44 reservoirs, the 2002 version included 8 major and 10 minor reservoirs, and the 2007 plan included recommendations for 14 major and 2 minor reservoirs. The current 2012 plan includes 26 new major reservoirs to meet the needs, producing an additional 1.5 million acre-feet per year in 2060 (TWDB 2012). Most of these are proposed to be east of Interstate Highway 35, where rainfall and runoff are more plentiful and evaporation rates are less. There are challenges to constructing new reservoirs: few viable

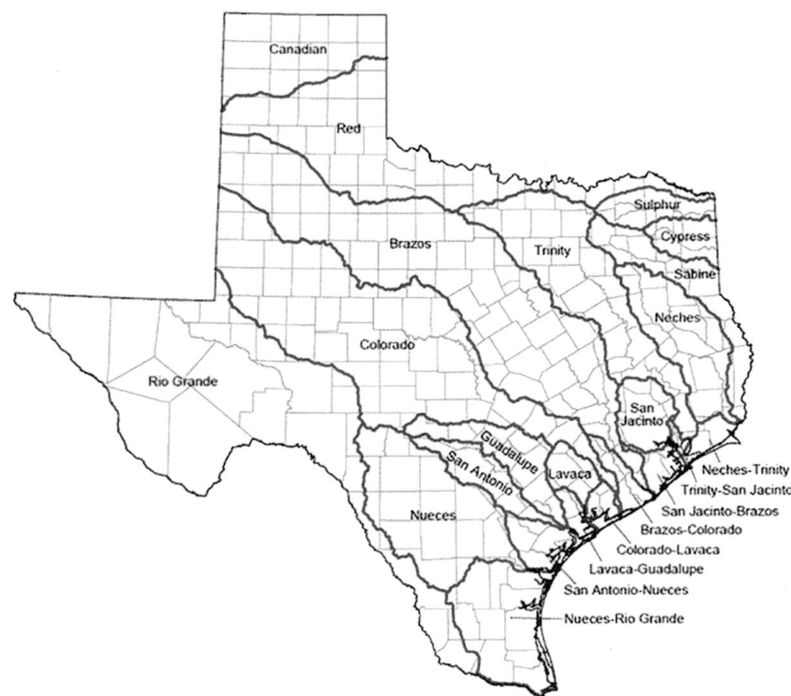

Major river basins in Texas. Courtesy of Texas Water Development Board

sites remain, permits are much more difficult to obtain due mainly to environmental concerns, and the cost of construction has increased faster than the inflation rate.

Proper management includes making the best use of existing reservoirs, controlling watershed erosion to maintain their holding capacity, and identifying viable sites for new reservoirs. These are all key measures to effective long-term water-supply management and planning in Texas.

Wetlands

Wetlands are lands that are either permanently or seasonally saturated or inundated by water and support water-tolerant vegetation. These transitional places between the water and the land are frequently referred to as marshes, swamps, or bogs. They are complicated ecosystems that provide many ecosystem services, such as reducing pollution by trapping, naturally breaking down, and absorbing pollutants (Stephenson et al. 2003). Coastal wetlands are salt water or a combination of salt water and fresh water along coastal shorelines, shallow bays and inlets, swamps, marshes, mudflats, bayous, and deltas. Freshwater wetlands receive water from rainfall, springs, rivers, and other sources that have plants adapted for fluctuating water levels. These wetlands include riparian areas along riverbanks and streamsides, as well as wetlands along lakeshores, floodplains, bottomlands, marshes, seeps, ponds, and swamps.

Wetlands and riparian areas capture and hold water, allowing it to slowly infiltrate into the ground to aquifers, thus recharging groundwater. Protecting wetlands saves up to $30 billion a year in flood-related repair costs in the United States (Stephenson et al. 2003). Wetlands provide habitat for thousands of species of fish, birds, reptiles, amphibians, insects, and mammals, as well as opportunities for recreation and enjoying natural beauty while hunting, fishing, birding, boating, hiking, wildlife watching, and photographing. Many natural products depend on wetlands, including fish, shrimp, crops, and trees, and wetland-related businesses generate hundreds of millions of dollars each year.

Wetlands, however, are in jeopardy due to historic draining and conversion. It has been estimated that between the 1780s and 1980s, Texas lost more than 50% of its original wetlands (Mitsch and Gosselink 1993),

Caddo Lake on the border of Texas and Louisiana. Photo by Lucas Gregory, Texas Water Resources Institute

San Bernard River. Photo by Nikki Dictson, Texas Water Resources Institute

or more than seven million wetland acres, an area approximately the size of Dallas, Fort Worth, Houston, and San Antonio combined.

Riparian Areas

Riparian areas are specialized wetlands found along the banks of creeks, rivers, and bayous. These green vegetation zones create the key connection between the upland grasslands and forests and the rivers and streams. The specialized vegetation along flowing waterways has unique root systems and characteristics that stabilize banks and can tolerate both dry and very wet soil conditions (or wetland situations).

Properly functioning riparian areas are excellent buffer zones that provide a variety of ecosystem services:

- high-quality habitat for both aquatic and terrestrial species
- dissipation of flood energy and reduced downstream flood intensity and frequency
- higher, longer-lasting, and less variable baseflow between storm events
- deposition of sediment in the floodplain, stabilizing it and maintaining downstream reservoir capacity longer
- use and filtering of debris and nutrients to improve water quality and dissolved oxygen levels in the aquatic system
- shade over streams from riparian vegetation canopies, which reduces temperatures, providing lasting habitat and a food base for aquatic and riparian animals
- fewer exotic undesirable plant species
- higher biodiversity than found in terrestrial uplands
- stable banks, which reduce erosion and protect ownership boundaries
- increased economic value through wildlife, livestock, timber, and recreational enterprises
- improved rural land aesthetics and real estate values

Riparian area with healthy diverse riparian vegetation zones consisting of aquatic plants, grasses, forbs, shrubs, understory trees, and large trees in North Texas. Photo by Nikki Dictson, Texas Water Resources Institute

Healthy riparian vegetation zones should have diverse vegetation consisting of aquatic plants, grasses, forbs, shrubs, understory trees/brush, and large trees. Mature plants and seedlings should also be present. Riparian vegetation slows down overland flow; captures sediment, nutrients, and other pollutants and organic matter; and increases infiltration in the floodplain/riparian area. These areas act as sponges, holding high amounts of water and nutrients in the soils, slowly releasing water back into the creek that sustains baseflows, and reducing peak flows. By reducing the level of runoff, they decrease the chances for pesticides, fertilizers, and fecal matter to reach streams and worsen water quality.

Management of the land, streams, and riparian zones affects not only individual landowners but also livestock, wildlife, aquatic life, and everyone downstream. By understanding the processes, key indicators, and impacts of disturbances (activities that hinder recovery), landowners and other citizen stakeholders can evaluate these systems and improve their management to restore healthy stream conditions. Riparian ecosystems play an important role in providing water for Texans today and in the future.

Springs

Springs are areas where groundwater discharges to the surface. Historically, springs were very important, serving as critical stops along stagecoach routes and providing power for mills and supplying water for medicinal treatment, drinking, and recreational areas and parks. A Texas Water Development Board (TWDB) report on significant springs of Texas in 1975 assessed and reviewed 281 major and historical springs previously identified in the state. The report found, at that time, that 65 of those springs no longer existed or had been inundated by reservoirs. The TWDB report speculated that the decline of spring flows began after Spanish colonization, as clearing of forests and heavy grazing reduced infiltration and recharge of the aquifers supplying them. Moreover, as more wells were dug, artesian pressure was reduced, decreasing spring flows further. In 1975 the total flows from springs was estimated to be more than three million acre-feet per year. The Edwards (Balcones Fault Zone) and the Edwards-Trinity Aquifers account for 139 of the springs in Texas. The two largest are the Comal and the San Marcos, both located in south-central Texas and prized for their beauty and recreation opportunities. Springs show the intricate and complex connection between groundwater and surface water (Brune 1975).

Estuaries and Bays

An **estuary** is the area where the fresh water from a river flows to the salty water of the ocean. Estuaries are called many names: bays, sounds, harbors, and lagoons. While they may have different names, they all represent the transitional zone from river to sea. **Bays**, while oftentimes are estuaries, are more specifically defined as a body of water partially enclosed by land but having a wide outlet to the sea.

The mixing of fresh water and salt water makes estuaries a unique environment. Thousands of species of birds, mammals, fish, and other marine species rely on these habitats to survive. Estuaries are known as the "nurseries of the sea" because their waters are more enclosed than the open ocean, making them a more protected area for species to reproduce and raise their young. It is estimated that 95% of the Gulf's recreationally and commercially important fish and other marine species rely on estuaries at some point during their life cycle (TWDB 2015a). The organisms living in and around estuaries provide important services to the environment and surrounding coastal cities. Water filtration, nutrient regulation, shoreline stabilization, and flood protection are a few of the vital functions that these diverse ecosystems provide.

Estuaries hold tremendous commercial value as well. Tourism, fisheries, and recreational activities thrive in these coastal regions and greatly benefit our state's economy. Due to their location between the ocean and rivers, estuaries also serve as harbors and ports used for shipping and transportation. The combined ecological and commercial services that estuaries provide is estimated to contribute billions of dollars in revenue to the state (TWDB 2015a).

Texas has 367 miles of coastline. There are seven major and five minor estuaries along the coast of Texas, which vary in size, salinity, and ecology. Together they span 2.6 million acres of the Texas Gulf Coast (TWDB 2015a).

Major Estuaries

The seven major estuaries are the Sabine-Neches, Trinity–San Jacinto, Colorado-Lavaca, Guadalupe, Mission-Aransas, Nueces, and Laguna Madre.

The Sabine-Neches Estuary consists of Sabine Lake. This estuary is the smallest one along the Texas coast and contains the freshest water of all the other major estuaries. Texas' largest estuary, and the seventh largest in the United States, is the Trinity–San Jacinto, which includes Trinity Bay,

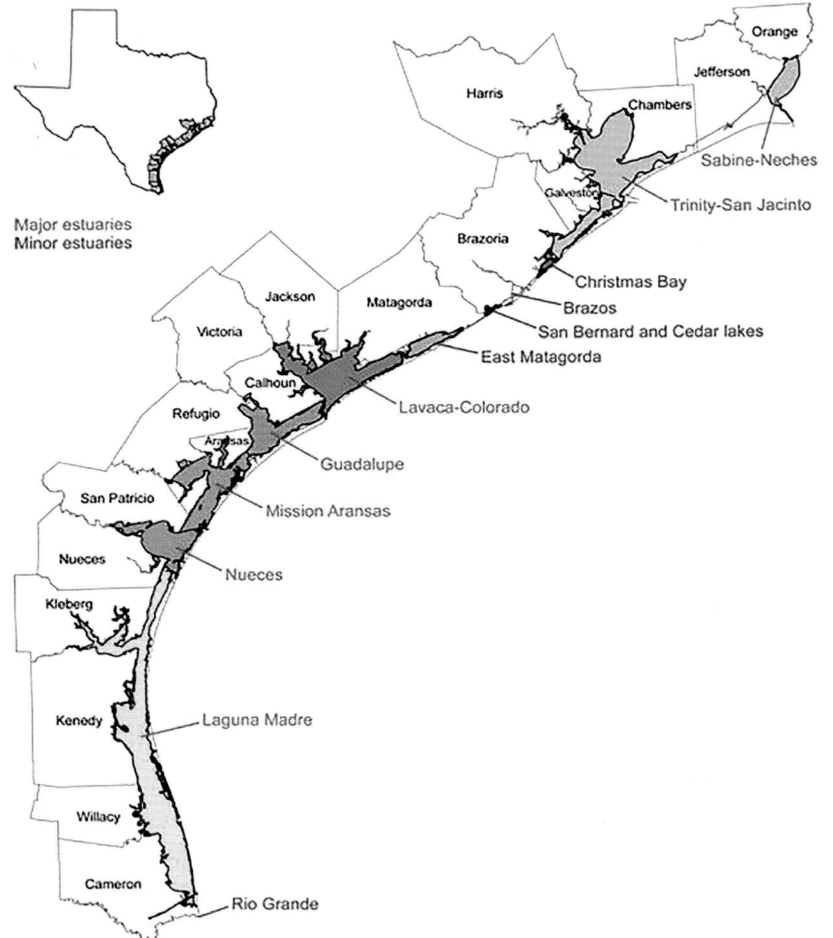

Major and minor estuaries in Texas. Courtesy of Texas Water Development Board

Galveston Bay, East Bay, and West Bay. Both the Guadalupe and San Antonio Rivers flow into the Guadalupe Estuary. San Antonio Bay, Mission Lake, Hynes Bay, Espiritu Santo Bay, and Mesquite Bay are all encompassed in the Guadalupe Estuary, which typically does not have a direct outlet into the Gulf of Mexico because it is blocked by Matagorda Island. The Nueces Estuary, which includes Nueces Bay, Corpus Christi Bay, and Oso Bay, also does not connect with the Gulf. This estuary is separated from the Gulf by Mustang Island.

The Colorado-Lavaca Estuary has freshwater inputs from the Colorado River, Lavaca River, and Tres Palacios River. These rivers terminate in Matagorda Bay, Lavaca Bay, and several other smaller bays. The Mission-Aransas Estuary contains Aransas Bay, Copano Bay, and several smaller bays. It receives its fresh water from the Aransas and Mission Rivers. The Laguna Madre Estuary, which stretches from Corpus Christi to the US border with Mexico, is the only hypersaline lagoon in the nation. This estuary is divided by the Saltillo Flats into the Upper Laguna, which includes Baffin Bay, and the Lower Laguna, which includes South Bay.

Minor Estuaries

There are also five minor estuaries: Christmas Bay, Brazos River Estuary, San Bernard Estuary, East Matagorda Bay, and the Rio Grande Estuary. Minor does not mean that these estuaries play a less important role. They are just smaller and less complex than the major estuaries. All the minor estuaries lie in between the major estuaries along the Texas coast. East Matagorda Bay is unique in that there is no direct source of fresh water into the estuary. The bay receives its fresh water from runoff from the surrounding watersheds and precipitation. Christmas Bay is the estuary farthest north, and the Rio Grande Estuary is the farthest south, located along the tip of Texas bordering Mexico.

Threats to Bays and Estuaries

Texas has one of the fastest-growing populations in the United States. As more people choose to make Texas their home, the demand for water will continue to rise. The demand on our surface water will be great, and it is projected that all water will be fully appropriated. This pressure on our freshwater systems could cause significantly reduced critical freshwater inflows to our estuaries, especially during droughts (National Wildlife Federation 2004). Without the mixing of fresh water and salt water, the entire ecological processes of estuaries are at risk. Many species that depend on estuaries to reproduce and grow would no longer have those sheltered waters. Water quality would also decline. All the organisms that live and thrive in estuarine environments depend on the mixture of fresh water and saline water.

The quality, quantity, and timing of freshwater inflow from rivers is important to maintain the natural salinity, nutrient, and sediment loading regimes that support the unique biological communities of each estuary and also to ensure healthy ecosystem function. To continue to benefit commercially and ecologically from estuaries as part of our state's water resources, we need to ensure that sufficient and timely flows continue to be supplied from our rivers to our estuaries.

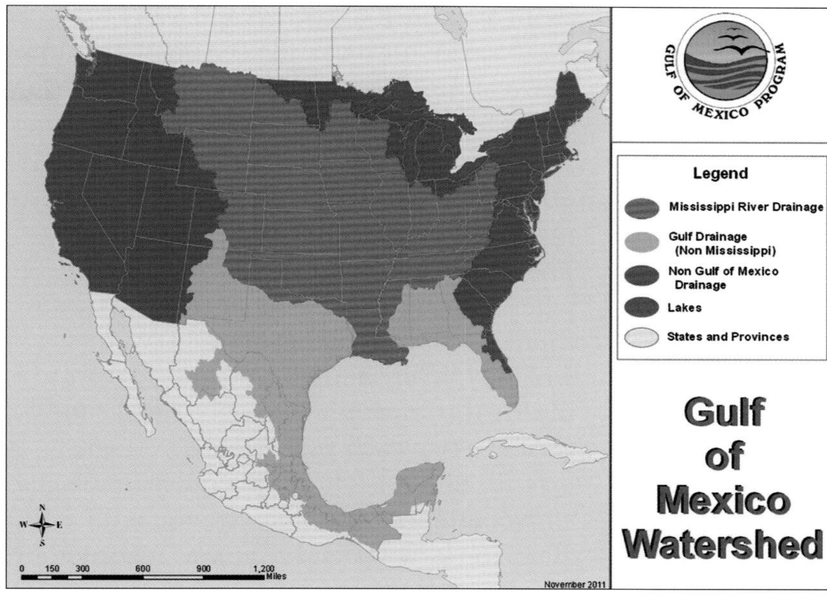

The Gulf of Mexico's watersheds. Courtesy of Environmental Protection Agency

Gulf of Mexico

A **gulf** is defined as a large body of ocean or sea that is partly surrounded by land. Although very similar to a bay, a gulf is much larger than a bay. The Gulf of Mexico borders Texas, as well as Alabama, Florida, Louisiana, and Mississippi. It also has port connections in six Mexican states: Tamaulipas, Vera Cruz, Tabasco, Campeche, Yucatán, and Quintana Roo. Both the United States and Mexico form the Gulf Coast, which spans more than 4,000 miles. The Gulf opens up to connect with the Caribbean Sea through the Yucatán Channel and the Atlantic Ocean through the Straits of Florida, making it important for transport and shipping. It is the ninth-largest body of water in the world, covering about 600,000 square miles, and is one of the top eight fishing ports in the world due to the many fisheries that make the Gulf their home (Gulf of Mexico Foundation 2015).

The Gulf's Dead Zone

Dead zones are known to occur in oceans and the Great Lakes where there is not enough oxygen to support aquatic life. These areas are known as hypoxic zones, zones where there are low oxygen levels. These areas are often caused by excess nitrogen and phosphorus. About 60% of the continental United States drains into the Gulf of Mexico through 33 major river systems, including the Mississippi River, and 207 estuaries. Even though that fresh water is important for ecological processes in and around the Gulf, it also means that pollution and runoff from inland can terminate in the Gulf of Mexico. Most of the excess nitrogen and phosphorus comes from sources such as sewage treatment plants and fertilizers used on agricultural fields, recreation areas like golf courses, and lawns in residential areas.

This buildup of nutrients causes large algal blooms. Eventually the algae die and start to sink. Bacteria begin decomposing the dead algae as it sinks, using up the available oxygen. Fish and other sea life that can

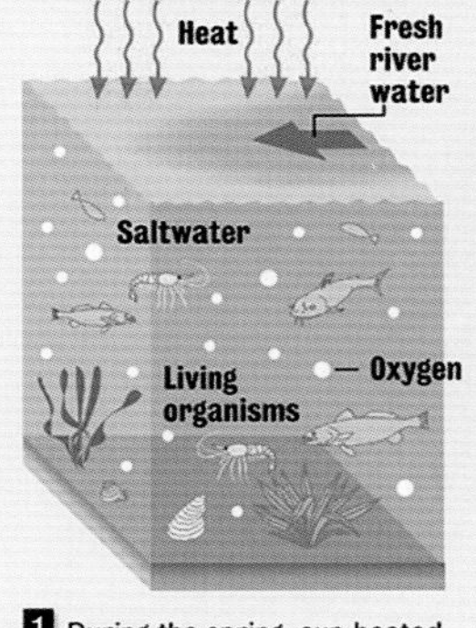

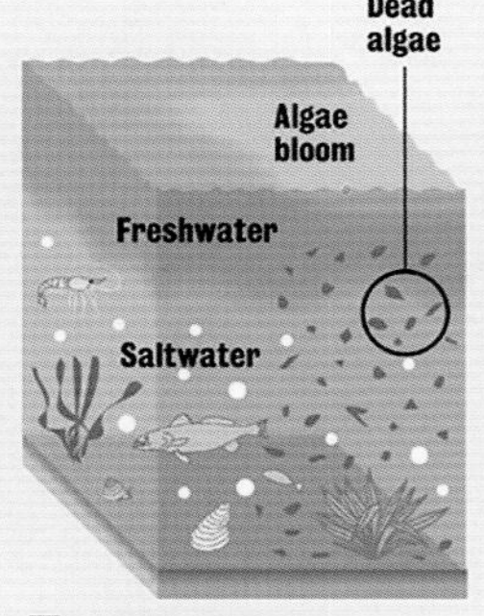

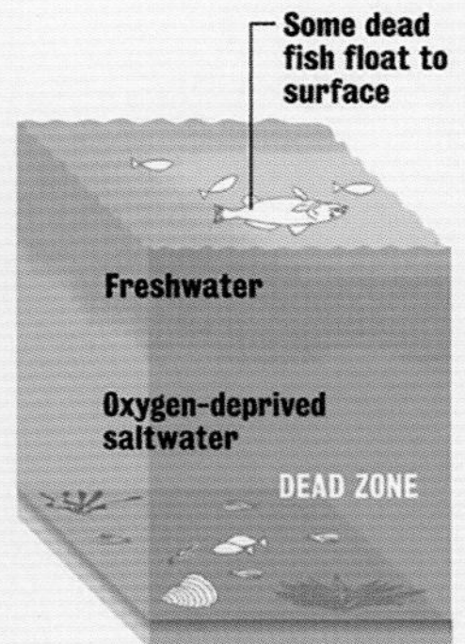

How a dead zone forms and an environment becomes hypoxic. From Swenson (2007)

swim are able to move up and away from these areas; however, the sea life that cannot move or moves too slowly, such as worms, clams, and crabs, die in these hypoxic zones.

The Gulf of Mexico's dead zone was first documented in 1972. It is located in the north off the coast of Texas and Louisiana. The zone can last for several months, appearing over the summer and lasting until there is a strong mixing of ocean waters, which typically happens from cold fronts during the fall and winter. The dead zone varies in size each year, but on average, it extends about 5,300 square miles (Louisiana Universities Marine Consortium, n.d.). In 2002, the largest dead zone was recorded to be around 8,481 square miles.

Brine Pools

A **brine pool** is a craterlike depression along the seafloor where the salinity is three to five times greater than that of the surrounding ocean. This dense, saltier water creates a small lake on the ocean floor that contains its own surface and shoreline. The water, because of its density, does not mix with the outside ocean water. Submarines that submerge into the Gulf of Mexico can land on these lakes and float on their surface.

Brine pools are located in other parts of the world, but they are not a common occurrence, so the presence of them in the Gulf of Mexico is fairly unique. The lakes in the Gulf of Mexico can be as little as 1 foot wide and as big as 12 miles long (Carney 2002).

The high concentration of salt in these areas is due to the Louann Salt Layer that is partially located under the Gulf. The plates move and shift under the Gulf, eventually causing some of the salt tectonics to fracture, which allows the salt layer to seep out from under the surface. These fractures cause the pools and other ridges along the

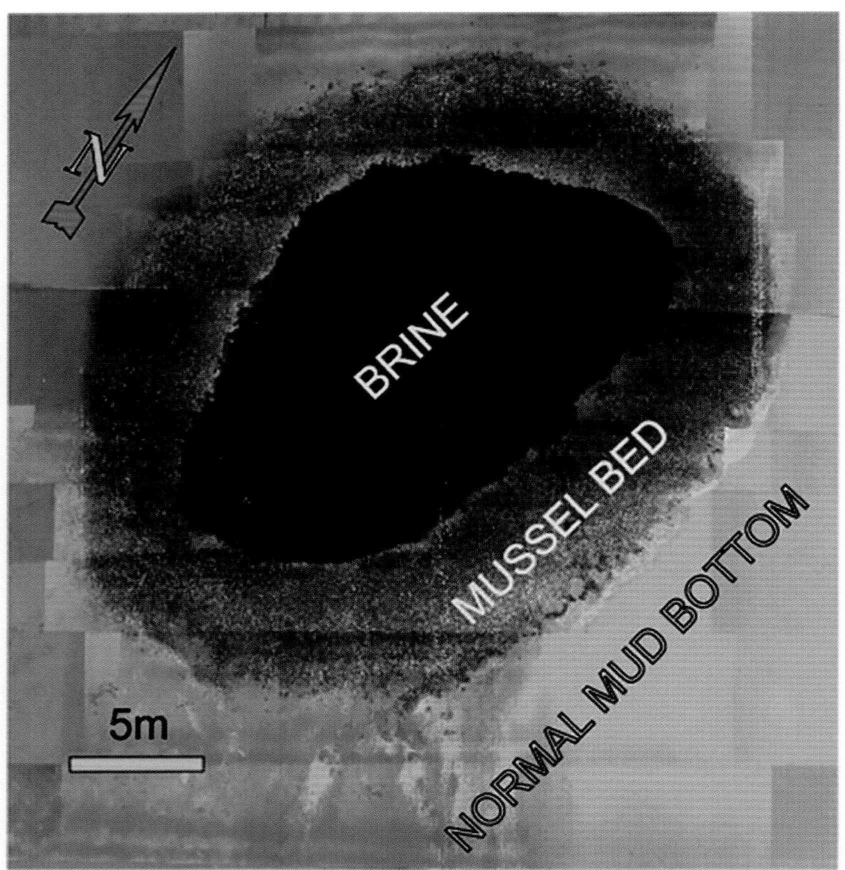

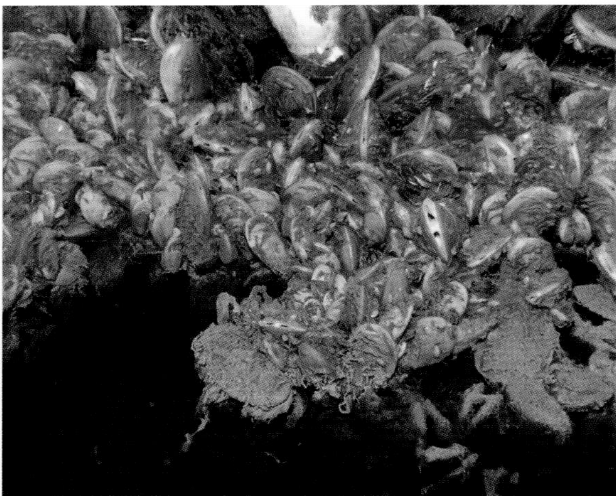

(*Above*) Mussels at the edge of a brine pool. Courtesy of Bob Waters, National Geographic

(*Left*) The Brine Pool is a craterlike depression on the seafloor filled with very concentrated brines coming from the Luann Salt Layer. The brine contains a high concentration of methane gas that supports a surrounding dense mussel bed. Image based on a mosaic created by Ian McDonald, Texas A&M University. Courtesy of Gulf of Mexico 2002, National Oceanic and Atmospheric Administration/ Office of Exploration and Research

ocean floor. The brine also contains high levels of methane, which supports the mussel beds that form around the lakes.

Groundwater

Water moves underground through pores, cracks, and holes, which are often seen in rocks on the earth's surface. These cracks and holes develop through the process of weathering, as well as through faulting and fracturing during tectonic events. In addition, natural pore space exists between the grains of the rock.

Aquifers

An **aquifer** is a rock or soil that contains and transmits water in quantities sufficient for appropriate uses. Aquifers can be composed of many types of soil or rocks, such as sandstone and limestone. Water is stored both between the grains of the rock and in cracks, holes, fractures, and caverns that have developed within the rock.

There are nine major aquifers in Texas: Trinity, Trinity Edwards, Ogallala, Gulf Coast, Edwards, Seymour, Hueco–Mesilla Bolson, Cenozoic Pecos Alluvium, and Carrizo-Wilcox (see map). Sixteen minor aquifers exist as well. Aquifers cover approximately 76% of the area of Texas. The main use for groundwater is irrigation. In 2000, 86% of all irrigation water used in Texas came from groundwater. More groundwater is used for irrigation in Texas than for all other uses combined.

Recharge is the process in which precipitation and stream flow enter the subsurface and move into an aquifer. Some aquifers, such as the Edwards, recharge through fractures, faults, and solution openings (such as sinkholes and caves) in the exposed limestone. Others, such as the Carrizo-Wilcox, recharge through direct infiltration of rainfall and stream flow into the porous sandstone aquifer.

Discharge is the flow of groundwater from rock to the surface. This can occur through natural as well as human processes. Natural discharge occurs through springs and seeps in swamps or beds and banks of streams. Discharge areas are lower than recharge areas, and water moves through aquifers by the force of gravity. Wells act as human-made discharge points from aquifers.

The flows from the springs and discharge from some wells enter nearby streams and rivers and become surface water, which then flows into downstream lakes and eventually to the Gulf of Mexico. Along its journey to the Gulf, the water that originated as discharge from the aquifers is used for many purposes by municipalities, industries, and agriculture and to sustain wildlife.

• • • • • • • • • • • • • • •

MAJOR AQUIFERS

Texas Water Development Board

The Ogallala is the largest aquifer, containing 90% of the total water in Texas aquifers. The Edwards Aquifer provides the sole source of drinking water to over 1.5 million people in South Texas.

Ogallala Aquifer

The Ogallala Aquifer extends under 46 counties of the Texas Panhandle and is the southernmost extension of the largest aquifer (High Plains Aquifer) in North America. The Ogallala Formation of late Miocene to early Pliocene age consists of heterogeneous sequences of coarse-grained sand and gravel in the lower part, grading upward into clay, silt, and fine sand. In Texas, the Panhandle is the most extensive region irrigated with groundwater. Water-level declines are occurring in part of the region because of extensive pumping that far exceeds the recharge. Water conservation measures by both agricultural and municipal users are being promoted in the area.

Gulf Coast Aquifer

The Gulf Coast Aquifer forms an irregularly shaped belt that parallels the Texas coastline

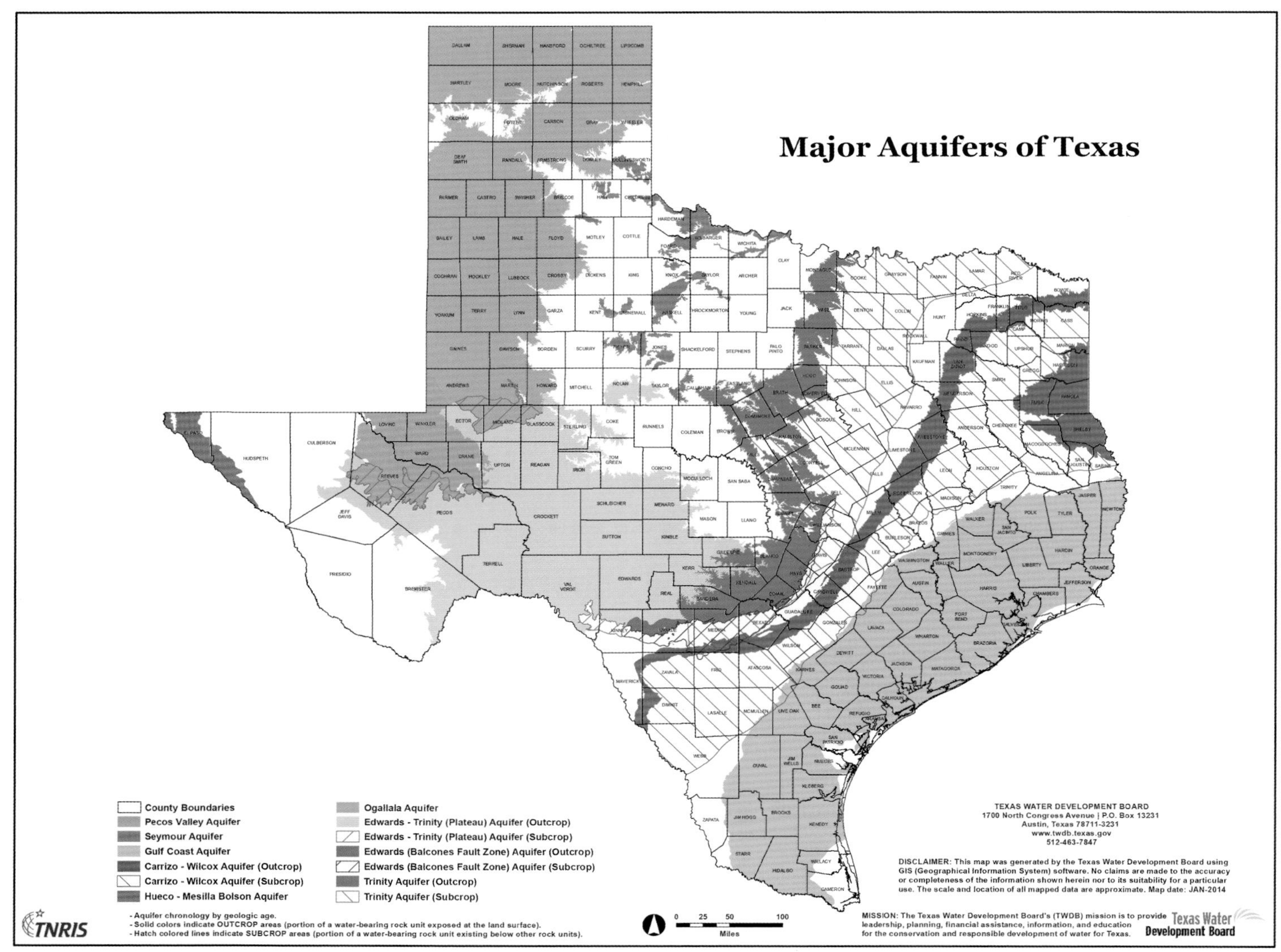

Major aquifers of Texas. Courtesy of Texas Water Development Board

and extends through 54 counties from the Rio Grande northeastward to the Louisiana border. The aquifer system is composed of the water-bearing units of the Catahoula, Oakville, Fleming, Goliad, Willis, Lissie, Bentley, Montgomery, and Beaumont Formations. This system has been divided into three major water-producing components referred to as the Chicot, Evangeline, and Jasper Aquifers. Municipal uses account for about 51%, and irrigation accounts for about 36% of the total pumpage from the aquifer.

Water quality is generally good northeast of the San Antonio River Basin but deteriorates to the southwest. Years of heavy pumpage have caused significant water-level declines in portions of the aquifer. Some of these declines have resulted in significant land-surface subsidence, particularly in the Houston-Galveston area.

Edwards (Balcones Fault Zone) Aquifer
The Edwards (BFZ) Aquifer forms a narrow belt extending through nine counties from a groundwater divide in Kinney County through the San Antonio area northeastward to the Leon River in Bell County. A poorly defined groundwater divide in Hays County hydrologically separates the aquifer into the San Antonio and Austin regions. Water in the aquifer occurs in fractures, honeycomb zones, and solution channels in the Edwards and is associated with limestone forma-

tions of Cretaceous age. More than 50% of aquifer pumpage is for municipal use, while irrigation is the principal use in the western segment.

San Antonio is one of the largest cities in the world that relies solely on a single groundwater source for its municipal supply. The aquifer also feeds several well-known recreational springs and underlies some of the most environmentally sensitive areas in the state. In 1993, the Texas legislature created the Edwards Aquifer Authority (EAA) to regulate aquifer pumpage for the benefit of all users: agricultural, municipal, and environmental. The EAA has an active program to educate the public on water conservation and operates several active groundwater recharge sites. The San Antonio River Authority also has a number of flood-control structures that effectively recharge the aquifer. Furthermore, conservation districts are promoting the use of more efficient irrigation techniques, and market-based, voluntary transfers of unused agricultural water rights to municipal uses are becoming more common.

"Take a good course in water and air; and in the eternal youth of Nature, you may renew your own."
—John Muir, early naturalist and advocate for the preservation of the US wilderness

Carrizo-Wilcox Aquifer

Extending from the Rio Grande in South Texas northeastward into Arkansas and Louisiana, the Carrizo-Wilcox Aquifer provides water to all or parts of 60 counties. The Wilcox Group and overlying Carrizo Sand form a hydrologically connected system of sand locally interbedded with clay, silt, lignite, and gravel. Throughout most of its extent in Texas, the aquifer yields fresh to slightly saline water, which is primarily used for irrigation in the Winter Garden District of South Texas and for public supply and industrial use in Central and Northeast Texas. Because of excessive pumping, the water level in the aquifer has been significantly lowered, particularly in the artesian portion of the Winter Garden District of Atascosa, Frio, and Zavala Counties and in municipal and industrial areas in Angelina and Smith Counties.

Trinity Group Aquifer

The Trinity Group Aquifer consists of basal Cretaceous-age Trinity Group Formations that extend from the Red River in North Texas to the Hill Country of Central Texas. Formations comprising the aquifer include the Twin Mountains, Glen Rose, and Paluxy. Where the Glen Rose thins or is absent, the Twin Mountains and Paluxy Formations coalesce to form the Antlers Formation. In the southern extent, the Trinity includes the Glen Rose and underlying Travis Peak Formations. Water from the Antlers portion of the Trinity is used mainly for irrigation in the outcrop area of North and Central Texas. Elsewhere, water from the Trinity is used primarily for municipal and domestic supply. Extensive development of the Trinity Aquifer in the Dallas–Fort Worth and Waco areas has historically resulted in water-level declines of several hundred feet.

Edwards-Trinity (Plateau) Aquifer

The Edwards-Trinity Aquifer underlies the Edwards Plateau, extending from the Hill Country of Central Texas westward to the Trans-Pecos region. The aquifer consists of sandstone and limestone formations of the Trinity Group Formations and limestones and dolomites of the Edwards and associated limestone formations. Groundwater movement in the aquifer is generally toward the southeast. Near the edge of the plateau, flow is toward the main streams, where the water issues from springs. Irrigation, mainly in the northwestern portion of the region, accounts for more than two-thirds of the total aquifer use and has resulted in significant water-level declines in Glasscock and Reagan Counties. Elsewhere, the aquifer supplies fresh, but hard, water for municipal, domestic, and livestock use.

Seymour Aquifer

The Seymour Aquifer consists of isolated areas of alluvium (deposits left by flowing streams) found in parts of 22 north-central and Panhandle counties in the upper Red River and Brazos River Basins. Eastward-flowing streams during the Quaternary period deposited discontinuous beds of poorly sorted gravel, silt, sand, and clay that were later dissected by erosion, resulting in the isolated remnants of the formation. Individual accumulations vary greatly in thickness, but most of the Seymour is less than 100 feet. The lower, more permeable part of the aquifer produces the greatest amount of groundwater. Irrigation pumpage accounts for more than 96% of the total use from the aquifer. Water quality general ranges from fresh to slightly saline. However, the salinity has increased in many heavily pumped areas to the point where the water has become unsuitable for domestic and municipal use. Natural salt pollution in the upper reaches of the Red and Brazos River Basins precludes the full utilization of these water resources.

Hueco–Mesilla Bolson Aquifers

These aquifers are located in El Paso and Hudspeth Counties in far western Texas. They occur in Quaternary basin-fill deposits that extend northward into New Mexico and westward into Mexico. The Hueco Bolson, located on the eastern side of the Franklin Mountains, consists of up to 9,000 feet of clay, silt, sand, and gravel and is the principal source of drinking water for both El Paso and Juarez. Located west of the Franklin Mountains, the Mesilla Bolson reaches up to 2,000 feet in thickness and contains three separate water-producing zones.

Groundwater depletion of the Hueco Bolson has become a serious problem. Historically, large-scale groundwater withdrawals, especially for the municipal uses of El Paso and Juarez, have caused major water-level declines and significantly changed the direction of flow, resulting in a deterioration of the chemical quality of the groundwater in the aquifer.

Cenozoic Pecos Alluvium Aquifer

Located in the upper Pecos River Valley of West Texas, the Cenozoic Pecos Alluvium Aquifer is the principal source of water for irrigation in Reeves and northwestern Pecos Counties and for industrial uses, power supply, and municipal use elsewhere. Consisting of up to 1,500 feet of alluvial fill, the aquifer occupies two hydrologically separate basins: the Pecos Trough in the west and the Monument Draw Trough in the east. Water from the aquifer is generally hard and contains dissolved solids concentrations ranging from less than 300 to more than 5,000 parts per million. Water-level declines in excess of 200 feet have historically occurred in Reeves and Pecos Counties but have moderated since the mid-1970s with the decrease in irrigation pumpage.

Source: Texas Center for Policy Studies, *Texas Environmental Almanac*

● ● ● ● ● ● ● ● ● ● ● ● ● ● ● ●

Management of Texas Water Supplies

Texas water resources—surface water and groundwater—are managed by different entities and rules in Texas. The state owns surface water and manages it by appropriating water rights. The Texas Commission on Environmental Quality (TCEQ) is the primary agency that administers surface water rights. Groundwater is recognized by state statute to be a landowner's property right subject to reasonable regulation and management by local groundwater conservation districts (GCDs).The TWDB reviews and approves groundwater management plans developed by GCDs and participates in the establishment of desired future conditions for aquifers in groundwater management areas.

Texas develops a state water plan based

on a 50-year planning period and updates it every five years using 16 regional water-planning groups. The plan is designed to meet the state's needs for water during times of drought with combinations of both surface water and groundwater. Groundwater and water availability models are tools used to assess the effect of pumping and droughts on groundwater availability and to predict the amount of water available in reservoirs, rivers, and streams under differing conditions. Drought contingency plans are required for all public water systems to be prepared for drought and other water shortages.

Surface Water Rights

The State of Texas owns surface water and manages it by appropriating water rights. It grants permission to different groups and individuals to use its water. Texas recognizes two basic doctrines of surface water rights: the riparian doctrine and the prior appropriation doctrine. Under the **riparian doctrine**, landowners whose property is adjacent to a river or stream are allowed to divert and use up to 200 acre-feet of water per year for domestic and livestock purposes.

The **prior appropriation doctrine**, adopted by Texas in 1895, has evolved into the modern system used today. With only a few exceptions, water users today need a permit for an appropriated water right from TCEQ. The prior appropriation system recognizes the "doctrine of priority," which gives superior rights to those who first used the water, often known as "first in time, first in right." In most of Texas, water rights are prioritized only by the date assigned to them and not by the purpose for which the water will be used. Only water stored in Falcon and Amistad Reservoirs in the middle and lower Rio Grande Basin is prioritized by the purpose of its use, with municipal and industrial rights having priority over irrigation rights during times of drought.

When issuing a new water right, TCEQ assigns a priority date, specifies the volume of water that can be used each year, and may allow users to divert or impound the water. Water rights do not guarantee that water will be available, but they are considered property interests that may be bought, sold, or leased. The water rights system works hand in hand with the regional water-planning process. The agency may not issue a new water right unless it addresses a water-supply need that is consistent with the regional water plans and the state water plan.

Texas relies on the honor system in most parts of the state to protect water rights during times of drought. However, TCEQ has appointed **watermasters** in four parts of the state to oversee and continuously monitor stream flows, reservoir levels, and water use. The Rio Grande Watermaster coordinates releases from the Amistad and Falcon reservoir system. The South Texas Watermaster serves the Nueces, San Antonio, Guadalupe, and Lavaca river and coastal basins and also serves as the Concho Watermaster for the Concho River and its tributaries in the Colorado River Basin. The Brazos Watermaster Program, initiated in 2014, has jurisdiction over the lower Brazos River Basin, including and below Possum Kingdom Lake (TCEQ 2015a).

Texas has very little water remaining for appropriation to new users. In some river basins, water is overappropriated, meaning that the rights already in place amount to more water than is typically available during drought. This lack of "new" surface water makes the work of water planners all the more important. Now more than ever, regional water plans must make efficient use of the water that is available during times of drought.

Groundwater Rule of Capture

Landowners in Texas own the water below their property. Historically, Texas has followed the English common law rule that landowners have the right to capture or remove all of the water that can be captured from beneath their land. This **rule of**

capture doctrine was adopted by the Texas Supreme Court in its 1904 decision *Houston & T. C. Railway Co. v. East.*

In part, the rule was adopted because the science of quantifying and tracking the movement of groundwater was so poorly developed at the time that it would have been practically impossible to administer any set of legal rules to govern its use. The *East* case and later court rulings established that landowners, with a few limitations, may pump as much water as they may beneficially use even if the withdrawal causes neighboring wells to go dry.

Limitations to the rule of capture include five common law exceptions. A landowner may not

- "maliciously take water for the sole purpose of injuring his neighbor"
- "wantonly and willfully waste" groundwater
- negligently drill or pump from a well in a manner that causes subsidence on a neighbor's property
- pump from a contaminated well
- trespass onto another's land in order to pump groundwater (Dowell 2014)

Because local GCDs are the state's preferred method of groundwater management, these districts are able to enact rules and regulations on groundwater withdrawal limitations. Today, Texas is the only western state that continues to follow the rule of capture.

Projected water demand and existing supplies, 2010–60. From TWDB (2012)

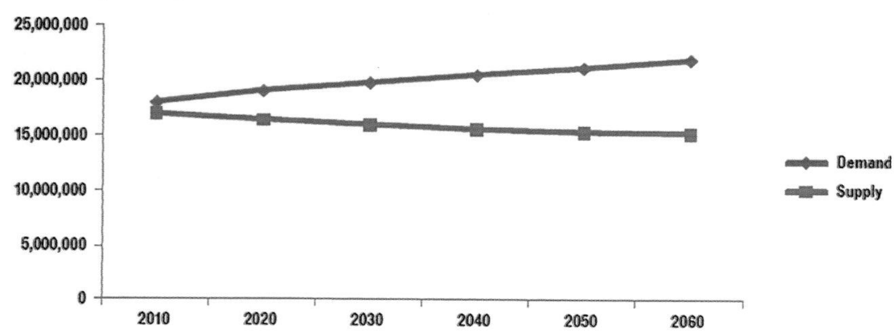

State and Regional Water Planning

Responding to the drought of the 1950s and recognizing the need to plan for Texas water in the future, the Texas legislature created the Texas Water Development Board in 1957 to develop water supplies and prepare state water plans to meet the state's future water needs. The state water plan, based on a 50-year planning period, is designed to meet the state's water needs during times of drought. The plan includes all categories of water use: municipal, manufacturing, irrigation, mining, livestock, and steam-electric power.

In the mid-1990s, Texas suffered an intense 10-month drought during which reservoir and aquifer levels declined and widespread crop failures led to economic losses in the billions. In 1997 the Texas legislature established a new regional water-planning process based on a "bottom-up," consensus-driven approach in which the state was broken into 16 regional planning groups (see regional planning map). The 16 planning groups, each made up of about 20 members, represent a variety of interests, including agriculture, industry, environment, public, municipalities, business, water districts, river authorities, water utilities, counties, groundwater management areas (GMAs), and power generation.

The current 2012 state water plan estimates, based on the state's population growth at 82% during the 50 years between 2010 and 2060 to 46.3 million people, that water demand will increase by 22%, from about 18 million acre-feet per year in 2010 to 22 million acre-feet in 2060 (TWDB 2012).

Existing water supplies are expected to decrease by 10% during that time primarily as a result of the depletion of the Ogallala Aquifer and depletion and reduced reliance on the Gulf Coast Aquifer. It is estimated that by 2060 the state will need an additional 8.3 million acre-feet of water. The regional planning groups recommended 562 unique water-supply projects designed to meet these additional needs with total capital costs of $53 billion to design, construct, and implement the strategies, which include development of new groundwater and surface water supplies, conservation, reuse, and desalination (TWDB 2012).

These 16 regional water-planning groups identify water needs and recommend water management strategies to meet these needs at the regional scale. The planning groups conduct all functions during open meetings in an open and participatory manner. They hold special public meetings when they develop their scope of work and hold hearings before adopting their regional water plans. This public involvement helps direct the planning and determine which water management strategies to recommend. Consensus building within the planning groups is crucial to ensure sufficient support for adopting the plan. Planning group members adopt plans by vote at open meetings in accordance with each group's respective bylaws.

The ongoing work of the regional water-planning process consists of 10 tasks:

- describing the regional water-planning area
- quantifying current and projected population and water demand over a 50-year planning horizon
- evaluating and quantifying current water supplies
- identifying surpluses and needs
- evaluating water management strategies and preparing plans to meet the needs

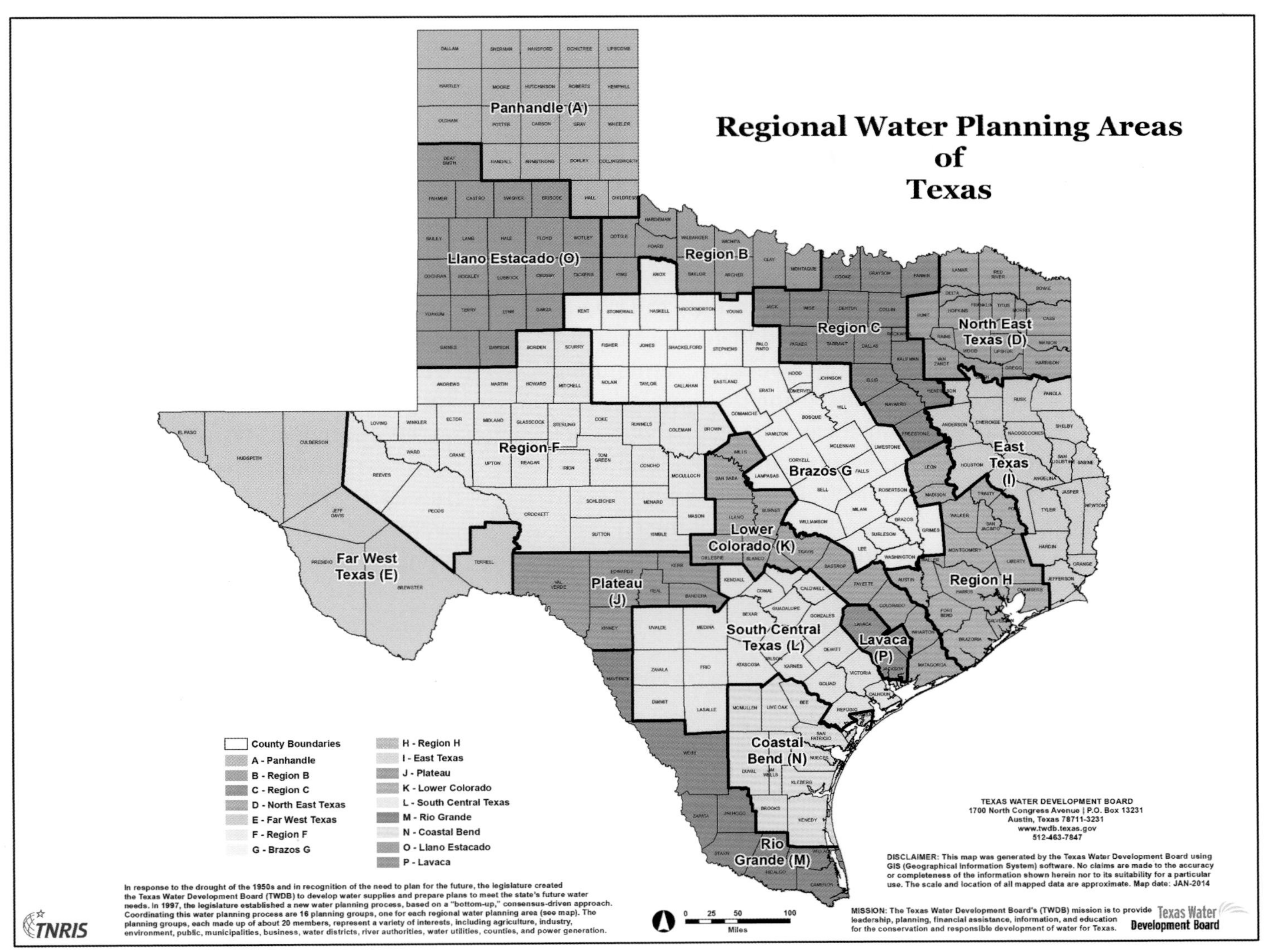

Regional water-planning groups. Courtesy of Texas Water Development Board

- evaluating impacts of water management strategies on water quality
- describing how the plan is consistent with long-term protection of the state's water, agricultural, and natural resources
- recommending regulatory, administrative, and legislative changes
- describing how sponsors of water management strategies will finance projects
- adopting the plan, including the required level of public participation

Once each planning group adopts its regional water plan, the plan is sent to the TWDB for approval. TWDB then compiles information from the approved regional water plans and other sources to develop the state water plan. The final plan is then submitted to the lieutenant governor, governor, and the legislature (TWDB 2013).

The latest state water plan, Water for Texas 2012, is the ninth and summarizes the efforts of about 450 planning group members, numerous technical experts, the public, and several state agencies (TWDB, Texas Parks and Wildlife Department, Texas Department of Agriculture, and TCEQ) between 2007 and 2012. According to TWDB, this process has resulted in greater public participation, public education, and public awareness, underscoring the benefits of directly involving local and regional decision makers and the public in water planning. Planning for the 2017 state water plan is currently under way. For details of the current plan, see TWDB (2012).

• • • • • • • • • • • • • • •

GROUNDWATER CONSERVATION DISTRICTS (GCDS)

Texas Groundwater Protection Committee

Local GCDs are the state's preferred method of groundwater management. As of 2014, there are 99 confirmed districts in Texas. GCDs are created by either the Texas legislature or the Texas Commission on Environmental Quality through a local petition process. GCDs are in charge of managing groundwater. Within their jurisdictions, GCDs provide resources for the conservation, preservation, protection, recharge, and prevention of wasting groundwater resources.

GCDs have three primary legislatively mandated duties:

1. Permitting nonexempt water wells
2. Developing a comprehensive groundwater management plan
3. Adopting the necessary rules to implement the management plan

Permits may be required by a GCD for all water wells except

- wells specifically exempted by a GCD
- statutorily exempt wells:
    - water wells used solely for domestic use or for providing water for livestock or poultry on a tract of land greater than 10 acres and constructed, equipped, or drilled so they are incapable of producing more than 25,000 gallons of groundwater per day
    - water wells used solely to supply water for a rig actively engaged in drilling or exploration operations for an oil or gas well permitted by the Railroad Commission of Texas (RRC)
    - water wells authorized by the RRC for mining activities

A GCD's principal power for preventing waste of groundwater is requiring that all water wells, with certain exceptions, be registered and permitted. Water wells that require permits are subject to GCD rules governing spacing, production, drilling, equipping, and completion or alteration. Even exempt water wells are subject to GCD rules governing spacing, tract size, and well construction standards to pre-

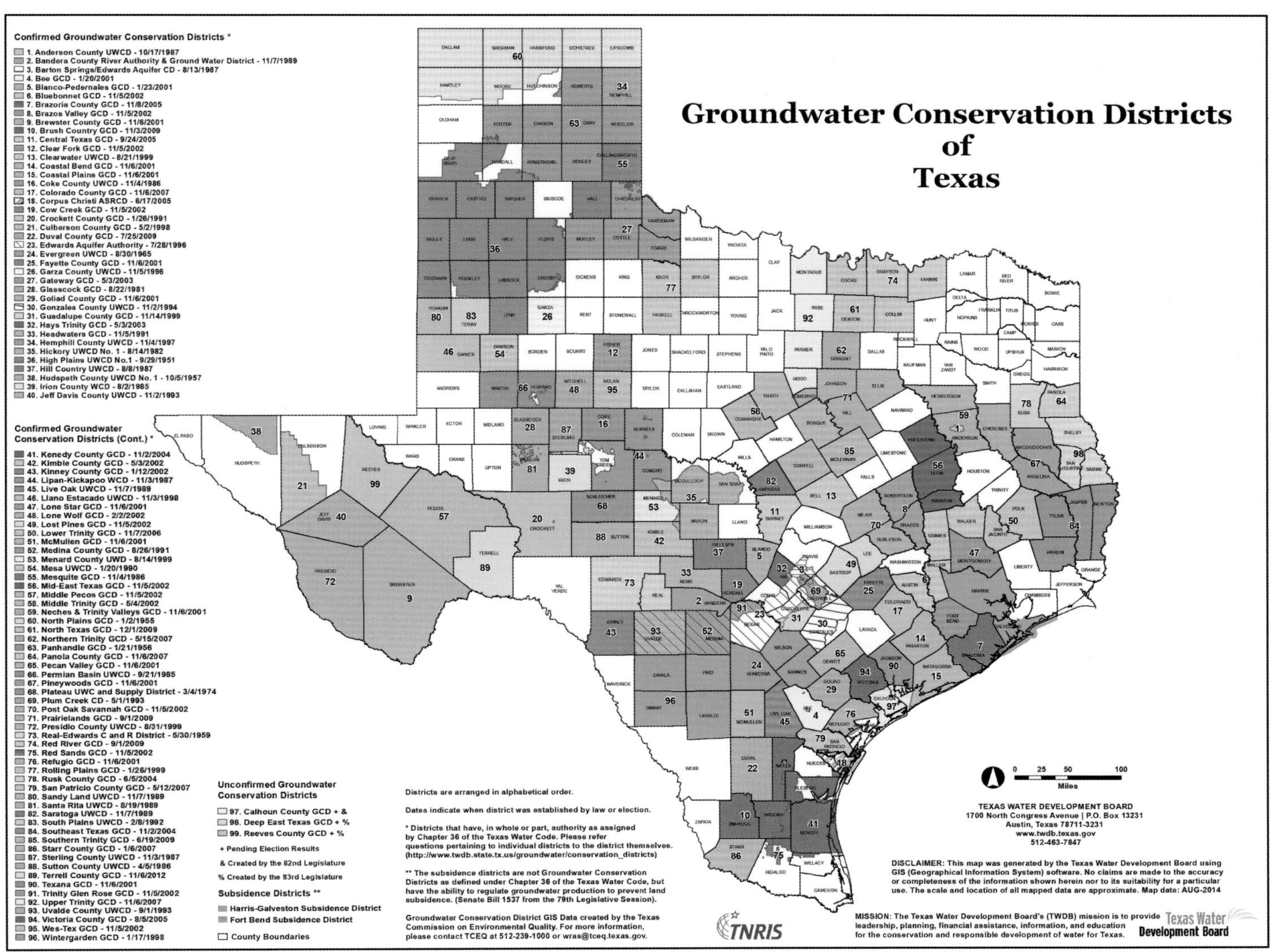

Groundwater conservation districts of Texas. Courtesy of Texas Water Development Board

vent unnecessary discharge or pollution of groundwater.

Source: Texas Groundwater Protection Committee (n.d.a)

• • • • • • • • • • • • • • • • •

GROUNDWATER MANAGEMENT AREAS (GMAS) AND DESIRED FUTURE CONDITIONS (DFCS)

Texas Groundwater Protection Committee

The TWDB designated GMA boundaries in response to legislation passed in 2001 by the Texas legislature. The GMAs were to encompass all major and minor aquifers in the state. The objective was to define areas considered suitable for managing groundwater resources. Ideally, a GMA coincides with the boundaries of a groundwater reservoir or a subdivision of a groundwater reservoir. However, GMAs may be defined by other factors, including the boundaries of political subdivisions. In December 2002, the TWDB designated 16 GMAs, covering the entire state. Only one area, Groundwater Management Area 5, does not include any GCDs.

Originally, the GMAs determined which GCDs needed to coordinate joint planning by sharing their management plans. In 2005, the legislature changed the direction of

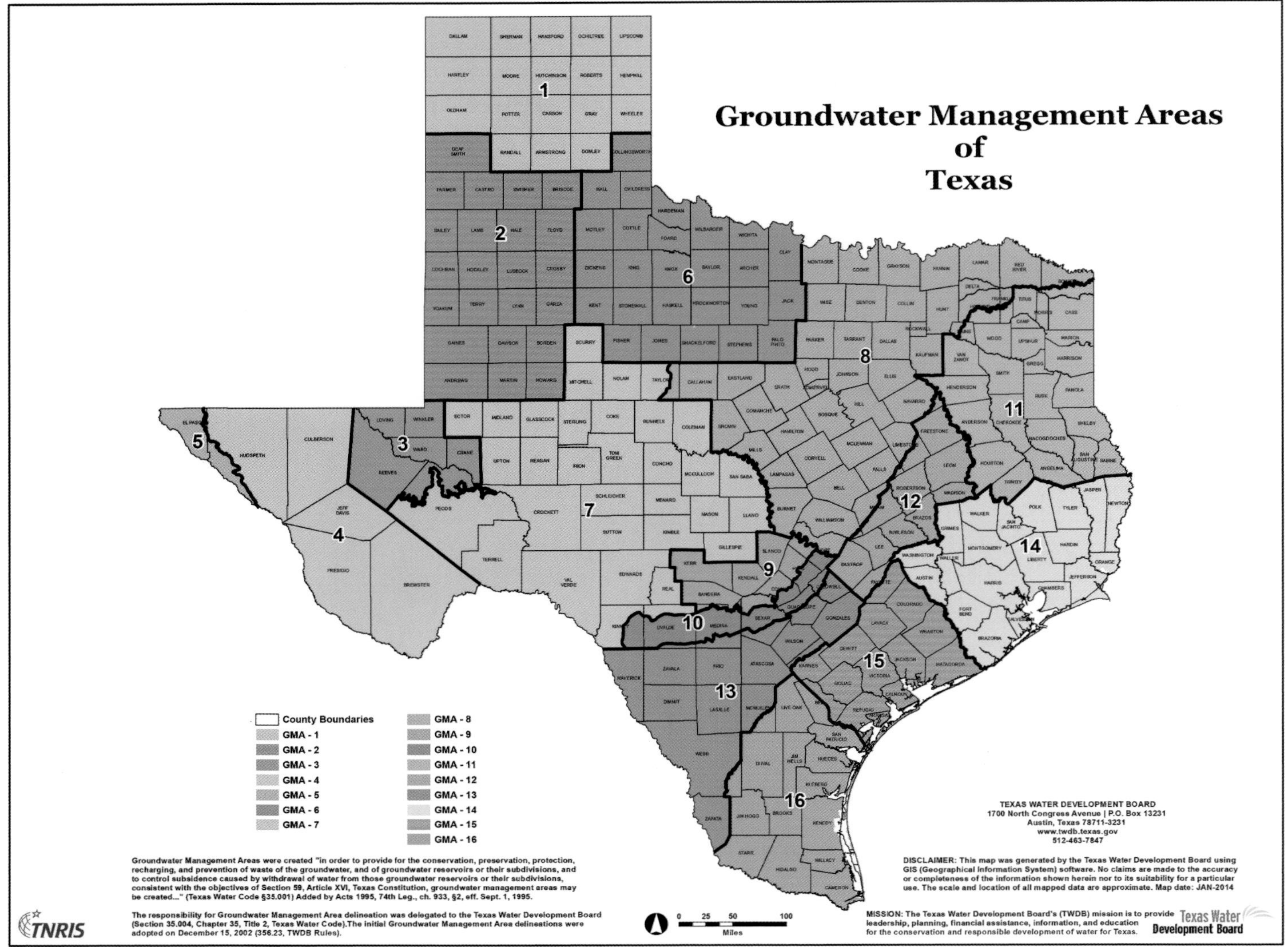

Groundwater management areas of Texas. Courtesy of Texas Water Development Board

groundwater management. The new requirements required joint planning in GMAs among GCDs.

> The district representatives shall meet at least annually to conduct joint planning with the other districts in the management area and to review the management plans, the accomplishments of the management area, and proposals to adopt new or amend existing desired future conditions. (Texas Water Code Sec. 36.108[c])

What this change means is that rather than individual GCDs determining the amount of available groundwater, the GCDs managing shared aquifer(s) would meet, at least annually, to decide desired future conditions (DFCs) for such aquifer(s). DFCs are the desired, quantified conditions of groundwater resources, such as water levels, spring flows, or volumes, at a specified time or times in the future or in perpetuity. DFCs form the basis for quantifying the groundwater volume available for use, known as modeled available groundwater. The DFC must be adopted by a two-thirds vote of the GCD representatives present at a GMA meeting where at least two-thirds of the GCDs are present. Both TCEQ and the TWDB have developed processes and rules to appeal DFCs, the joint planning process, and a district's actions.

The TWDB is responsible for providing each GCD and regional water-planning group, located wholly or partly in the GMA, with modeled available groundwater quantities. Groundwater availability models (GAMs) and other data help establish modeled available groundwater for the relevant aquifers within the GMA. Once the modeled available groundwater is determined, GCDs use it, along with other criteria, to issue groundwater withdrawal permits consistent with the DFC of the aquifer. These permits and associated monitoring help the districts track the withdrawals to help achieve DFCs.

Source: Texas Groundwater Protection Committee (n.d.b)

• • • • • • • • • • • • • • •

GROUNDWATER AVAILABILITY MODELS (GAMS)

Texas Water Development Board

Groundwater is difficult to observe and measure because it is below the land surface and responds to rainfall much more slowly than rivers and lakes do. Aquifer systems are complex because of groundwater flowing into and out of an aquifer, the interaction between surface water and groundwater, and the uncertainty of aquifer properties. Because of groundwater's complexity, computer models are excellent tools for assessing the effect of pumping and droughts on groundwater availability. Groundwater availability modeling is the process of developing and using computer programs to estimate future trends for water available in an aquifer. The modeling is based on hydrogeologic principles, actual aquifer measurements, and stakeholder guidance.

GAMs include comprehensive information on each aquifer, such as recharge (amount of water entering the aquifer); geology; rivers, lakes, and springs; water levels; aquifer properties (hydraulic conductivity, storativity, specific yield, and porosity); and pumping. Each model is calibrated to ensure that the models can reasonably reproduce past water levels and groundwater flows.

Completed models have proven valuable in water planning. Texas law requires GCDs and regional water-planning groups to use modeled available groundwater in their management and regional water plans. This is based on the DFCs of aquifers determined for the 16 GMAs. GAMs have been and will continue to be used to estimate the modeled available groundwater for each aquifer in each GCD, as appropriate.

Source: Texas Water Development Board, "Groundwater Models"

• • • • • • • • • • • • • • •

Water Availability Models (WAMs)

Since Texas surface water law follows the rule of prior appropriations, there is a need to evaluate if new or amended water rights can be permitted and to determine when that water is allocated. TCEQ uses computer simulations known as water availability models (WAMs) to predict the amount of water available in a river or stream under specific conditions. More specifically, WAMs are used "to determine whether water would be available for a newly requested water right, amendment or whether a water right amendment can affect other water rights" (TCEQ 2014b).

WAMs are based on historical hydrology where geospatial data (drainage area, connectivity, evaporation, etc.) and water rights data (location, diversion amount, priority data, use, etc.) are input in the model. Within the model, TCEQ evaluates two scenarios to determine whether to recommend to grant or deny an application:

- The Full Authorization simulation evaluates maximum use of all appropriated amounts of water of all existing water rights and water levels to evaluate recommendations for perpetual water rights and amendment applications.

- The Current Conditions simulation includes current conditions and return flows to evaluate applications for term water rights and amendments (TCEQ 2014b).

Model results provide insight regarding unappropriated flows, reliability of water rights, naturalized and regulated flows, and instream flow frequency. With these results, water rights management strategies that meet the various demands such as environmental flows and agricultural and municipal demands can be identified, and TCEQ can determine how much water can be allocated to permits.

Drought Contingency and Water Conservation Plans

Public water systems are required to have a contingency plan to conserve water in times of drought and emergency. Drought contingency plans define drought stages and identify measures to be implemented at each stage. Increasingly severe measures are implemented with each subsequent drought stage. These plans are designed for short-term response to severe hydrologic drought conditions. Wholesale public water suppliers, irrigation districts, and retail public water suppliers with 3,300 or more connections must submit drought contingency plans to TCEQ and revise them at least every five years. Retail public water suppliers, serving fewer than 3,300 connections, are not required to submit plans to TCEQ but are obligated to prepare and adopt a drought contingency plan and make the plan available to TCEQ when requested (TCEQ 2014a).

Additionally, TCEQ and TWDB both require water providers and other entities to develop water conservation plans and revise them at least every five years. These plans outline the long-term strategies that water providers will implement to reduce water consumption and water loss, increase water recycling and reuse, and improve overall water use efficiency. TCEQ receives plans from entities applying for a new or amending an existing water right, nonagricultural water rights holders of 1,000 acre-feet or more annually, and agricultural water rights holders of 10,000 acre-feet or more annually. TWDB receives plans from entities applying for or receiving more than $500,000 in financial assistance and retail public utilities that provide potable water service to 3,300 or more connections (TCEQ 2015b).

Texas Parks and Wildlife Department Land and Water Strategic Plan

The Texas Parks and Wildlife Department's (TPWD) Land and Water Strategic Plan, first developed in 2002 and last updated in 2010, is a guiding document describing how TPWD will conserve the natural and cultural resources of Texas for future generations. TPWD bases its decisions regarding the state's conservation and recreation needs on the criteria developed in this plan. The plan promotes stewardship on public and private lands and waters; protection of the state's unique natural and cultural resources; partnerships with all stakeholders; use of science as the backbone of decision making; participation in the outdoors; appreciation of nature in citizens, young and old; and business approaches that leverage industry standards and best practices to support the department's mission (TPWD 2013) .

Management of Texas Water Quality

Water quality management in Texas is based on the federal Clean Water Act (CWA) administered by the US Environmental Protection Agency (EPA). The CWA requires states to establish and implement water quality standards. These standards serve as the basis for water quality management in all states and define designated uses for water bodies, establish water quality criteria to protect these waters, and define antidegradation polices intended to keep clean waters clean. In Texas, TCEQ is charged with implementing the CWA and managing water quality. In this role, TCEQ defines water bodies and water quality standards, measures water quality, assesses water quality in relation to established water quality standards, identifies causes and sources of water quality problems, and works to protect and restore water quality (TCEQ 2010).

Water Quality Standards

Water quality standards are established based on the designated use(s) that the water body should support. The state has established five water body–use categories:

- Aquatic Life: Protects plants and animals living in and around the water
- Contact Recreation: Ensures that water is safe for contact recreation such as swimming
- Public Water Supply: Gauges water suitability for public consumption
- Fish Consumption: Sets maximum pollutant levels in waters where fish that are harvested are consumed
- General Uses: Defines general conditions that water bodies should meet to support a variety of uses such as navigation and irrigation water supply

Water quality criteria, which define the instream conditions that support the designated use, can be either narrative or numeric. Narrative criteria are often related to aesthetics and prohibit a defined condition in the water body, such as foam on the water's surface or excessive odors. Numeric criteria establish pollutant limits that should not be exceeded in the water body (TCEQ 2010). For example, *E. coli* levels should not exceed a geometric mean of 126 colony-forming units per 100 milliliters of water to protect water bodies for swimming (Wagner et al., forthcoming). These standards establish water body–specific goals, which subsequently influence allowable discharge permit limits and water quality monitoring data evaluations.

Most large- and medium-sized water bodies are assigned specific uses. The uses of smaller water bodies often adhere to the designated uses of the larger downstream water body they flow into; however, this is not always the case, as the stream's flow type is also considered. Water quality standards are applied to three flow types in Texas: perennial streams, intermittent streams with pools, and intermittent streams. Perennial streams maintain flow year-round under normal flow conditions; intermittent streams with pools are those that stop flowing but maintain persistent pools; and intermittent streams are those that flow for only a portion of the year. These and all water quality standards are defined in the Texas Administrative Code (Title 30, Part 1, Chapter 307), along with water body–specific designated uses.

Water Quality Monitoring and Assessments

Monitoring is conducted statewide to collect water quality data used to determine if water bodies are supporting their designated uses. Data collected often include biological, chemical, hydrologic, and physical characteristics of the water body. TCEQ, partners in TCEQ's Clean Rivers Program, and other third-party organizations such as universities, private entities, and volunteers participate in water quality data collection activities, following standardized monitoring and data management procedures to ensure data quality (Wagner et al., forthcoming).

During routine monitoring the same group of stations is monitored according to a defined schedule. This approach allows long-term trends in water quality to be readily determined. Monitoring typically occurs quarterly with one sampling event planned during each season. Other types of monitoring are also used, including systematic or targeted monitoring, permit-support monitoring, and effectiveness monitoring. These three types of monitoring are respectively used to evaluate specific water body concerns, collect additional water quality data where water discharge permits have been requested, and determine the effectiveness of water quality management strategies (TCEQ 2010).

TCEQ conducts a water body assessment every two years. Not all monitored water bodies are included in this assessment, as insufficient levels of data may prevent an accurate assessment. This assessment evaluates water quality monitoring data collected over the most recent seven-year period and requires a minimum of 10 samples for most parameters to evaluate standards attainment and at least 20 bacteria samples to evaluate for contact recreation use. While this data set may seem small, it provides a sufficient level of certainty while maximizing limited monitoring resources. Assessment results are compared to established water quality standards to determine whether they are meeting or exceeding the allowable limits (Wagner et al., forthcoming).

The 305(b) Report and 303(d) List

As a part of the state's biennial water quality assessment, TCEQ is required to develop and submit separate reports to the EPA that describe the state's water quality and the extent to which the water bodies meet applicable standards. These reports are referred to as the 305(b) Report and 303(d) List, collectively known as Texas Integrated Report of Surface Water Quality. The 305(b) Report presents the results of the water quality assessment, while the 303(d) List identifies waters that do not meet at least one of their designated uses and applicable water quality standards.

Within the 305(b) Report, water bodies are aggregated into five use attainment categories, according to how well water bodies attain applied water quality standards and support their designated use:

Category 1: Attaining the water quality standard and no use is threatened

Category 2: Attaining some of the designated uses, no use is threatened, and insufficient information (or none) is available to determine if

Measuring flow for water quality monitoring. Courtesy of Texas Water Resources Institute

the remaining uses are attained or threatened

Category 3: Insufficient information (or none) is available to determine if any designated use is attained

Category 4: Standard is not supported or is threatened for one or more designated uses but does not require the development of a total maximum daily load (TMDL):

- A TMDL has been completed and approved by EPA.
- Other pollution-control requirements are reasonably expected to result in the attainment of the water quality standard in the near future.
- Nonsupport of the water quality standard is not caused by a pollutant.

Category 5: Water quality standards not being met or being threatened for one or more designated uses by one or more pollutants:

- A TMDL is under way, scheduled, or will be scheduled.
- Water quality standards will be reviewed before a TMDL is scheduled.
- Additional data and information will be collected before a TMDL or review of the water quality standard is scheduled.

These categories are essentially a report card on water quality provided for each assessed water body. The categories also inform the public about how the state plans to address noted water quality issues. Waters falling into Category 1 currently meet all of their designated uses and require only routine water quality monitoring, while those in higher categories require additional effort to improve water quality management. These categorical assessments are applied to each designated water body use and the individual parameters that determine the support of that use. For example, the Contact Recreation use category is supported by bacterial parameters such as *E. coli*. If *E. coli* levels are found to be higher than the allowable limit, then that water body is considered to have an impaired contact recreation use. Multiple designated uses are applied to water bodies, and they are supported by multiple parameters. As a result, more than one use attainment category may be applicable for that water body, and multiple impairments may exist (TCEQ 2010; Wagner et al., forthcoming).

Pollution and Pollution Management

Water pollution can occur for a variety of reasons and be caused by natural sources or human influences. Specifically, sources can include agriculture, urban development, industry, and naturally occurring mineral deposits or wildlife. These sources are categorized as either point or nonpoint sources of pollution. **Point sources** are those that can be traced to a defined point such as a wastewater discharge. **Nonpoint sources** are diffuse in nature and cannot be traced to a specific point. Instead, they occur widely and are often carried to the water body via rainfall runoff. Nonpoint sources can include runoff of fertilizers from farms or lawns, manure from livestock or wildlife, and sediment from the landscape or construction sites. Management of these two source types is quite different due to the nature of the pollutant source (TCEQ 2010).

Texas Pollutant Discharge Elimination System (TPDES)

Point sources of pollution are regulated by TCEQ through the TPDES, an extension of the National Pollutant Discharge Elimination System and a requirement of the CWA. Discharges regulated under this program include wastewaters from industry, municipalities, some agricultural operations, and urban stormwater. These permits define the type of discharge and type of treatment used, establish discharge volume limits, and set maximum pollutant discharge levels. Monitoring and reporting requirements are also included in TPDES permits. These requirements control the discharge of wastewaters into the state's surface waters. Collectively, these permit requirements set the level of wastewater treatment required to adhere to the permitted limits (TCEQ 2010).

Nonpoint Source Pollution Management

Nonpoint sources of pollution in Texas are managed jointly by TCEQ and the Texas State Soil and Water Conservation Board (TSSWCB) through the Texas NPS program. This program outlines the state's comprehensive strategy to address nonpoint source pollution issues, which include water quality management programs paired with regulatory, voluntary, financial, and technical assistance approaches. Water quality assessments, planning, implementation, and education are cornerstones of this management process.

Implementation of the Texas NPS program is carried out through partnerships with numerous local, regional, state, and federal organizations. In all cases, a watershed approach is used to geographically focus management efforts based on hydrology, establish reasonable water quality goals for the watershed, coordinate priorities across the watershed, and establish well-integrated yet diverse partnerships that adequately and appropriately reflect the constituents of the watershed.

TSSWCB primarily focuses its efforts on watersheds that are rural in nature and have significant agricultural and forestry operations that may contribute to the overall pollutant load. Urban watersheds and those that contain a significant amount of point source pollution contributions are primarily dealt with by TCEQ. Regardless of the water quality issues a watershed is experiencing, two primary tools are used to address these issues: TMDLs and watershed protection plans (WPPs) (TSSWCB 2015).

Total Maximum Daily Loads (TMDLs)

At their core, **total maximum daily loads** are defined as the maximum amount of a specific pollutant that a water body can carry and still meet applicable water quality standards. Further, they identify a water body's dominant sources of pollution, allocate the water body's allowable loading between point and nonpoint sources, and establish a pollution reduction goal for the water body to meet its water quality standards. TMDLs are also conservative because they incorporate margins of safety to allow for inherent variations in water quality, seasonal factors, and future growth in the watershed. Typically, TMDLs are developed for single pollutants; thus, water bodies with multiple impairments may have multiple TMDLs.

Section 303(d) of the CWA requires that TMDLs be developed to address impaired waters generally within 13 years of the water body's initial listing as impaired. Once developed, TMDLs are submitted to the EPA for review and approval. Upon completion, TMDL **Implementation Plans (I-Plans)** are developed to outline strategies necessary to meet the pollutant reduction goals set forth in the TMDL. I-Plans commonly include regulatory measures to address pollutant loading from permitted point source dischargers and voluntary management measures to address nonpoint source pollutants. These can include more restrictive discharge permit limits for regulated entities and items such as enhanced education and outreach programs or voluntary management practice implementation for nonpoint sources. I-Plans also provide assurances that TMDL goals will be carried out by identifying responsible parties and funding sources. I-Plans define measures of success and describe water quality targets expected to be met and narrative goals that show plan implementation progress. Ultimately, the goal of the TMDL and its accompanying I-Plan is to restore water quality such that it achieves its designated water quality standards (Wagner et al., forthcoming).

Watershed Protection Plans (WPPs)

Watershed protection plans are the other primary strategy employed by the state to address water quality issues. They are built upon the watershed planning concept, which uses a local, stakeholder-driven, voluntary planning process to address complex water quality issues. WPPs can be developed to protect unimpaired waters from future pollution or to restore impaired waters. Once developed, WPPs outline a suite of prioritized management strategies focused on meeting the plan's defined environmental objectives.

WPPs are similar to TMDLs but take a more holistic approach to water quality management by considering all potential causes and sources of pollution and water body impairments. In fact, the state encourages WPPs to address threats to both surface water and groundwater within watersheds. Measuring implementation success and progress toward water quality goals is also a critical component of a WPP, which serves as a report card for water quality restoration efforts and informs stakeholders of the need for adaptations to the plan.

To ensure that WPPs successfully meet their water quality goal, the EPA has developed a set of guidelines that WPPs should include. Beyond these guidelines, WPPs can include a variety of items and should be tailored to fit the watershed (TSSWCB 2014).

Agencies and Entities Engaged in Texas Water

Numerous state and federal agencies and other organizations are involved in provid-

The Arroyo Colorado was one of the first watersheds in Texas with a Watershed Protection Plan. Courtesy of Texas Water Resources Institute

ing information on water resources, conducting research in water-related areas, and helping protect water quality.

State Agencies

Texas A&M AgriLife Extension Service

The Texas A&M AgriLife Extension Service provides high-quality, practical educational resources to Texans based on university research through its statewide network of county extension agents and professional educators. AgriLife Extension's focus is to respond to local needs with pertinent and timely solutions. Water is the focus of many of its programs and covers diverse topics from rainwater harvesting to on-site wastewater treatment and agricultural and landscape irrigation technologies.

Texas A&M AgriLife Research

Texas A&M AgriLife Research works to conduct research related to agriculture, natural resources, and life sciences. Water is a primary focus of many projects. AgriLife Research scientists commonly develop and evaluate wastewater treatment technologies, establish on-farm practice standards to reduce adverse water quality impacts, and work to improve the efficiency of irrigation technologies. AgriLife Research scientists have also made strides in water quality management by developing computer-based management tools that predict and represent real-world conditions and aid in the development of water quality restoration plans.

Texas A&M Forest Service

The mission of the Texas A&M Forest Service is to protect and sustain the trees, forests, and related natural resources, as well as the water quality, in Texas. Forests are critical to water resources because they prevent erosion and serve as a natural filter to remove pollutants. Texas A&M Forest Service programs enable sustainable forest utilization and associated water resource protection. Its programs promote proper forest management and demonstrate best management practice effectiveness. Texas A&M Forest Service employees provide technical assistance to landowners, further protecting the state's forest resources.

Texas Commission on Environmental Quality (TCEQ)

As the environmental agency for the state, TCEQ's goal is to protect the state's public health and natural resources. TCEQ administers drinking water, water use and availability (i.e., water rights and others), and water quality programs. TCEQ is largely responsible for permitting and regulating natural resources, including water quantity and quality, and enforcing several federal environmental regulations within the state. It also distributes monetary support and facilitates research to enhance information on water resources. TCEQ oversees many watershed programs, including the TMDL program, a portion of the state's nonpoint source program, monitoring, and assessment of waters, pollutant discharge permitting, and allotment of the state's surface waters for beneficial uses. TCEQ also administers and financially supports the Clean Rivers Program, a partnership between the commission and regional water authorities that coordinates and conducts water quality monitoring, assessments, and stakeholder participation in the water quality management process.

Texas Department of Agriculture (TDA)

TDA is primarily a regulatory agency that supports water management in Texas through the licensing and training of agricultural professionals engaged in practices that may affect water quality, specifically herbicide and pesticide application. TDA regulates pesticides through label compliance, training and licensing users, registering products, and assessing possible environmental impacts of pesticides. It also manages training and licensing of prescribed burn managers.

Texas Department of State Health Services
The primary role of the Texas Department of State Health Services involves protection, promotion, and improvement of the health of the people of Texas. Its primary role related to water quality is monitoring and issuing fish and shellfish consumption advisories. Local agents of the state Health Services Department, such as county health departments, may also regulate permitting, design, installation, operation, and maintenance of on-site sewage facilities.

Texas General Land Office (GLO)
As the historical administration of state lands and resources, the GLO has grown to include several other projects and regulation responsibilities, including caring for the Texas coast through the Texas Coastal Management Program and the Coastal Impact Assistance Program. GLO also directs the Coastal Oil Spill Prevention and Response Program, Local Government Wetland Plans, Coastal Nonpoint Source Program, Texas Beach Watch Program, Coastal Texas 2020, Adopt-A-Beach Program, and Small Spill Prevention Program.

Texas Parks and Wildlife Department (TPWD)
TPWD is charged with conserving the state's fish and wildlife, their habitat, and cultural and historical sites across Texas. Managing the state's fisheries equates to managing water quality and quantity. TPWD is actively engaged in water quality monitoring programs, pollution investigations, habitat assessments, and plans for the future of aquatic species in Texas. TPWD provides countless technical resources to Texans and financial assistance, where possible, to protect critical habitats and species.

Texas State Soil and Water Conservation Board (TSSWCB)
The TSSWCB administers Texas soil and water conservation law and coordinates conservation and nonpoint source water pollution abatement programs. It provides technical assistance to landowners through a statewide network of soil and water conservation districts. TSSWCB is the lead agency in Texas charged with planning, managing, and abating agricultural- and forestry-related nonpoint source water pollution. TSSWCB also administers several programs aimed at improving water resources in the state, such as the Water Quality Management Program, the CWA Section 319(h) grant program, and flood-control programs.

Texas Water Development Board (TWDB)
TWDB provides information and support for planning, financial assistance, and outreach for the conservation and development of Texas water. Although water quantity is its primary focus; it does maintain an immense database of groundwater resources that include ample groundwater quality data. Additionally, TWDB oversees the statewide water-planning process and administers multiple funding programs for water infrastructure and conservation projects.

The Railroad Commission of Texas (RRC)
The RRC maintains regulatory authority over oil and gas production activities. This includes waste management and minimization efforts for oil and gas industry operations, well permitting, and enforcement for environmental violations. The RRC also administers the state's well-plugging program, which often addresses wells that are directly impacting surface water quality.

Federal Agencies

US Section, International Boundary and Water Commission (IBWC)
The IBWC was formed to apply the boundary and water treaties established between the United States and Mexico and work to resolve any differences arising between the nations. In Texas, this specifically applies to the Rio Grande, which forms our southern border. The IBWC commonly deals with water deliveries between nations but is also engaged in water quality management. The

US Section of IBWC serves as a Clean Rivers Program partner and conducts water quality monitoring on the Rio Grande and Pecos River in Texas.

National Oceanic and Atmospheric Administration (NOAA)
NOAA collects climate data, which helps improve the understanding and stewardship of the environment. It also conducts weather monitoring, charts seas and skies, guides use and protection of ocean and coastal resources, and conducts research to help understand these resources.

Natural Resources Conservation Service (NRCS)
The NRCS is part of the US Department of Agriculture (USDA) and works to improve and protect soil, water, and other natural resources for the United States. In most counties agency staff are located at USDA Service Centers and provide technical assistance to landowners by meeting with them on their property and providing management planning to meet landowner goals and conserve natural resources. A number of financial assistance programs are also available to qualifying landowners.

United States Army Corps of Engineers (USACE)
The USACE is a public engineering design and construction management agency that provides engineering services, environmental restoration, and construction support for civil and military projects. Projects typically include constructing and managing large reservoirs, controlling floods through levees, dredging rivers and canals, and maintaining shipping channels. In addition, USACE is charged with regulating waterways, restoring degraded ecosystems, managing natural resources, constructing sustainable facilities, and cleaning up old military installations.

United States Environmental Protection Agency (EPA)
The EPA is the national regulatory agency responsible for implementing environmental laws. This includes the CWA, which requires water quality standards to be established and implemented, monitoring and assessment of waters to be completed, and remedial actions to be taken as needed. EPA also has jurisdiction over the quality of drinking water, groundwater quality, and discharge permitting. However, EPA has often delegated this authority to the states. In Texas, TCEQ has assumed these roles and is responsible for implementing EPA regulations.

United States Geological Survey (USGS)
The USGS provides impartial, scientific information on the health and productivity of ecosystems, environments, natural resources, climate, and land use. Within these roles, USGS operates numerous stream gaging stations, which provide critical information on stream flow, including historical flow records that are widely used in water resources management and planning. The USGS also conducts numerous special studies to investigate water resources.

US Bureau of Reclamation (Reclamation)
The role of Reclamation is to manage, develop, and protect water and related resources. In Texas, Reclamation provides municipal, industrial, and irrigation water through its management of Choke Canyon, Meredith, Texana, and Twin Buttes Reservoirs.

Water Resources Institutes

Several Texas universities have established water resources institutes or centers to conduct research, provide education and outreach, and/or promote effective policies for water. The institutes have various focus areas and goals.

The Meadows Center for Water and the Environment
Established by Texas State University, the Meadows Center for Water and the Environment coordinates and expands the universi-

ty's efforts in aquatic resource management. Through its programs, the center promotes a holistic approach to the management of natural systems with a focus on sustainability and equitable use. The Meadows Center developed the Texas Stream Team program to expand water quality data collection through a network of trained citizen-scientists and partners. The center also conducts water quality assessments and characterization of watersheds, watershed planning and implementation, education, and outreach.

Texas Institute for Applied Environmental Research (TIAER)

The TIAER, part of Tarleton State University, conducts research, economic investigations, and institutional, statutory, and regulatory analyses to help solve environmental problems at the state and national levels. This includes water quality monitoring, recreational use and attainability analysis, lab analysis, economic and environmental modeling, public policy, and planning.

Texas Sea Grant

Texas Sea Grant's mission is to improve the understanding, use, and stewardship of Texas coastal and marine resources by providing education and outreach to citizens and governments along the coast. This includes educational demonstrations to show impacts of land use on watershed health and water quality. To better facilitate this goal, Texas Sea Grant developed the Texas Coastal Watershed Program, which includes several smaller groups, each with a specific focus, such as development, wet-smart landscapes, stormwater management, and wetland remediation as well as planning for specific coastal watersheds.

Texas Water Resources Institute (TWRI)

First established in 1952 as the Water Research and Information Center, TWRI was designated as the state's water resources research institute in 1964 by the Texas legislature and governor. It brings together research scientists, students, county agents, program specialists, agency partners, and others to address complex natural resource issues holistically. TWRI uses sound and timely research, effective policies, and extension and outreach activities. It accomplishes these objectives by focusing on three key program areas: water quality improvement, water sustainability and security, and water resources outreach and training. TWRI also serves as a repository for numerous educational resources available to citizens and professionals alike.

Local Entities and Committees

Throughout the state, there are various entities and committees whose purpose is to manage, develop, and/or protect Texas water and other natural resources.

River Authorities

River authorities are political subdivisions of the state charged with managing, developing, and protecting the state's surface waters. River authorities vary in their scope, size, and services provided. Some produce electricity, own and sell water, provide water and wastewater treatment services, and oversee the health and well-being of water resources in their jurisdiction. Others are small entities that do not provide services or sell water or power. Many river authorities serve as partners in TCEQ's Clean Rivers Program and either conduct or support water quality monitoring in their basins. Current authorities in Texas include

- Angelina and Neches River Authority
- Brazos River Authority
- Canadian River Municipal Water Authority
- Guadalupe–Blanco River Authority
- Lavaca–Navidad River Authority
- Lower Colorado River Authority
- Lower Neches Valley Authority
- Northeast Texas Municipal Water District
- Nueces River Authority

- Red River Authority of Texas
- Rio Grande Regional Water Authority
- Sabine River Authority of Texas
- San Antonio River Authority
- San Jacinto River Authority
- Sulphur River Basin Authority
- Trinity River Authority
- Upper Colorado River Authority

Soil and Water Conservation Districts (SWCDs)

SWCDs are a subdivision of state government consisting of a board of directors elected from and by landowners who live and operate within the district. Each district develops a plan outlining the district's natural resources, natural resource concerns, and conservation needs. SWCDs are advised and coordinated by the TSSWCB and are typically co-located with USDA-NRCS, which also provides technical support for conservation planning. This enables SWCDs to provide relevant conservation planning to qualifying landowners.

Emerging Policies and Issues

Many of the recommended strategies in the state water plan have pros and cons, which are controversial at times. However, all the strategies are needed to meet future water demands.

Reservoir Construction

Surface water reservoirs have played a major role in supplying water for Texas since the 1950s. To meet future needs, 26 new reservoirs have been proposed that would generate an estimated 1.5 million acre-feet per year by 2060. This is almost 17% of projected future water needs in Texas.

However, construction of new reservoirs will be challenging due to potential adverse environmental impacts, land requirements, and high costs. Water losses from evaporation and long-term siltation are also undesirable features of reservoirs. Nevertheless, this strategy is critical to meeting future water-supply demands in the state.

Interbasin Transfers

Diversions of water from one river basin to another, known as interbasin transfers, are a key strategy in the state water plan. There are currently more than 150 active interbasin transfers in Texas with an additional 15 planned. Interbasin transfers are often controversial due to concerns over potential environmental impacts to both the basins involved and economic and future water-supply impacts to the basin of origin. For this reason, transfers are subject to special requirements to ensure that the basin of origin is protected and the benefits of the diversion outweigh the detriments to the originating basin. Since 1997, few interbasin transfers have been permitted because of provisions implemented that year. These provisions impart junior water rights status on interbasin transfers, thus placing a major disincentive on this water management strategy. Many groups are calling for the removal of these provisions. It should be noted that groundwater transfers are not subject to these rules.

Aquifer Storage and Recovery (ASR)

ASR is underground storage of water in a suitable aquifer during times when water is available and the recovery of that water from the same aquifer during times of need. ASR is expected to meet only 0.9% of new water demand; however, this approach is being viewed favorably because it eliminates high evaporative losses experienced at surface reservoirs in Texas. Currently, San Antonio, Kerrville, and El Paso are using ASR for water storage. However, there has not yet been widespread adoption in Texas due to concerns over the ability to recover stored water, quality of the recovered water, cost-effectiveness, and potential for other pumpers to capture stored water. An improved legal/public policy framework is needed to

Recomended New Major Reservoirs

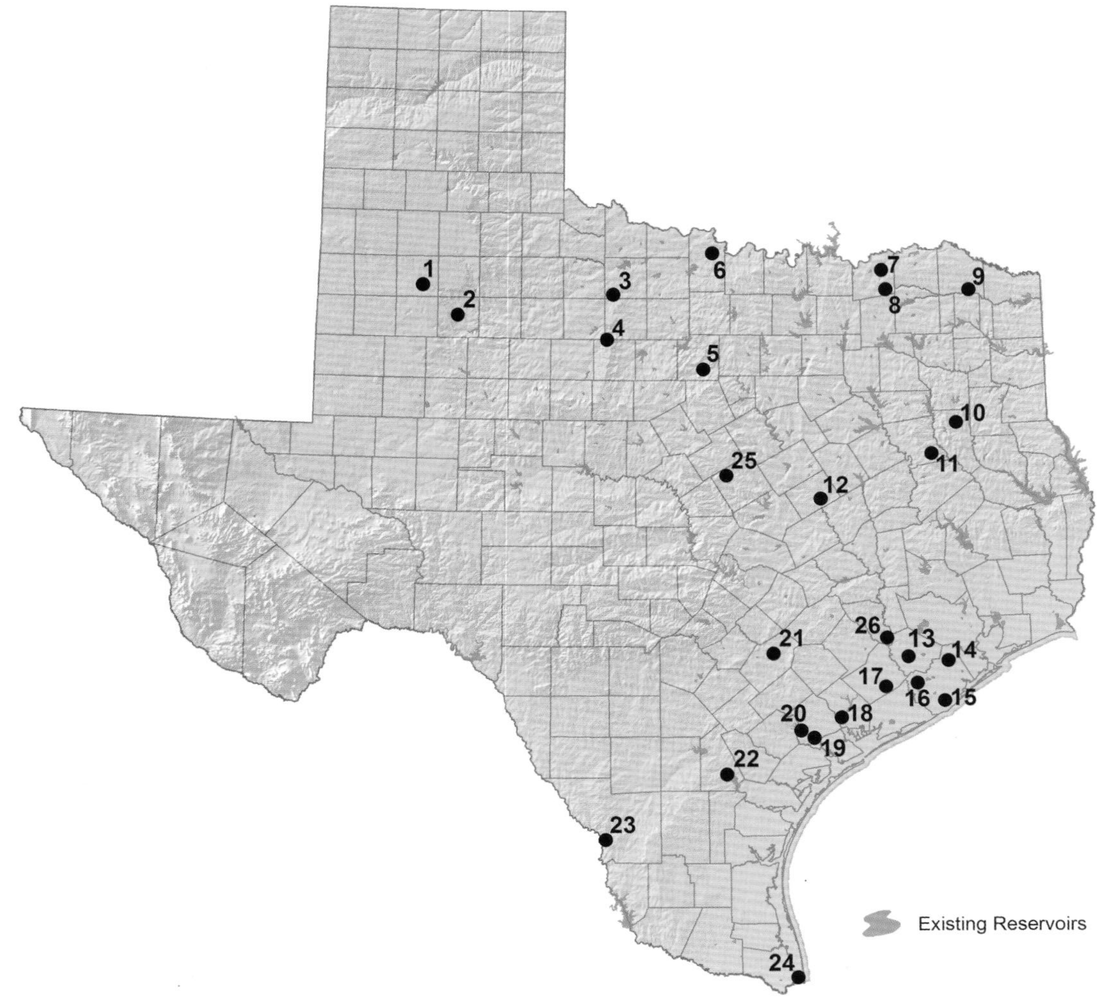

1 Jim Bertram Lake 07
2 Post Reservoir
3 Millers Creek River Augmentation
4 Cedar Ridge Reservoir
5 Turkey Peak Reservoir
6 Lake Ringgold
7 Lower Bois d'Arc Reservoir
8 Lake Ralph Hall
9 Marvin Nichols Reservoir
10 Lake Columbia
11 Fastrill-Replacement Project (Off Channel
12 Brushy Creek Reservoir
13 Fort Bend Off-Channel Reservoir
14 Brazoria Off-Channel Reservoir
15 Dow Off-Channel Reservoir
16 Gulf Coast Water Authority Off-Channel Reservoir
17 LCRA San Antonio Water System Project (Off Channel)
18 Lavaca Off-Channel Reservoir
19 GBRA New Appropriation (Lower Basin, Off-Channel)
20 GBRA Exelon Project
21 GBRA Mid Basin Project (Off-Channel)
22 Nueces Off-Channel Reservoir
23 Laredo Low Water Weir
24 Brownsville Weir
25 Coryell County Reservoir (Off-Channel)
26 Allens Creek Reservoir

Proposed new reservoirs in Texas. Adapted from the Texas Water Development Board's draft *Water for Texas 2012* by Texas Water Resources Institute

enhance adoption of ASR in Texas (TWDB 2011).

Reuse

Aside from municipal water conservation, reuse is one of the most cost-effective water-supply strategies. It is expected to provide more than 915,000 acre-feet annually, which is 10% of future water supply for the state, by 2060 (TWDB 2012). Water reuse refers to the process of using treated wastewater for a beneficial purpose. It is frequently used for irrigating golf courses and public parks and for manufacturing and cooling purposes.

San Antonio Water System Twin Oaks Aquifer and Storage Recovery Plant. Courtesy of Leslie Lee, Texas Water Resources Institute

San Antonio Water System Dos Rios Water Recycling Center. Courtesy of Leslie Lee, Texas Water Resources Institute

However, it is also being used for drinking water. San Antonio and El Paso use treated wastewater in conjunction with ASR to provide future water supplies. Big Spring and Wichita Falls are using it for drinking water. This trend is expected to continue with Brownwood and other communities considering using treated wastewater to meet drinking water demands. A major challenge for any community considering directly reusing treated wastewater for drinking water is overcoming the "yuck factor." In many cases, however, the quality of the treated wastewater is much higher than that of traditional water supplies, as it must meet TCEQ water quality standards.

A majority of the stream flow in many streams and rivers across Texas originates from, or is heavily augmented by, wastewater discharges. As towns and cities have grown and increased the amount of water discharged to rivers and streams, the hydrology of these rivers and streams has changed. Some streams that were historically dry have become perennial from the year-round discharges. Many downstream water rights are also dependent on these discharges. Further, in some cases, the quality of water discharged from wastewater treatment plants exceeds that of the receiving stream, thus improving its overall water quality. As reuse increases across the state, care must be taken to avoid potential negative impacts on downstream water quality, water users, and stream flows.

Annual average unit costs (dollars per acre-foot) according to water-supply strategy. Courtesy of Texas Water Development Board

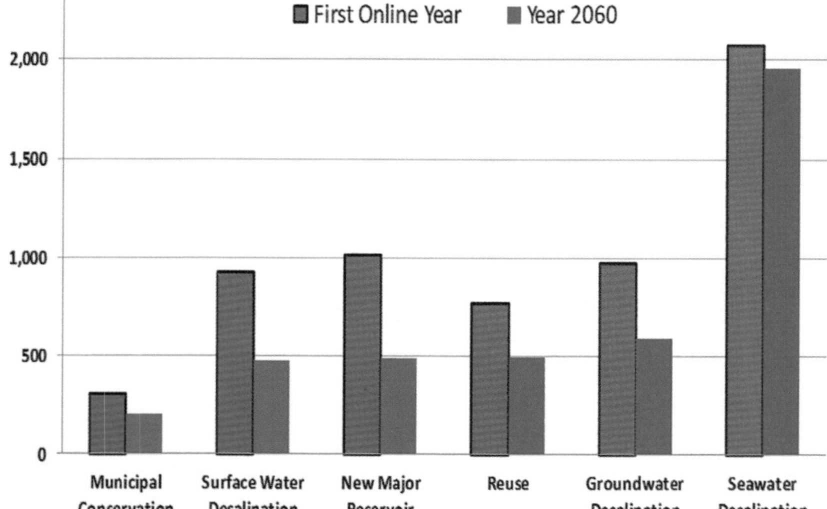

Desalination

Desalination is expected to provide almost 310,000 acre-feet annually (3.4% of total water demand) by 2060, the majority from brackish groundwater desalination (TWDB 2012). Because seawater desalination is so expensive, it is not an attractive alternative yet. Brackish groundwater is abundant in many regions of the state. As of 2012, there were almost 100 desalination plants in use in Texas. However, issues with disposal of brine and questions regarding potential impacts of brackish groundwater withdrawals on fresh groundwater exist. Concentrate, or brine, management can become one of the most important factors in determining the feasibility of a plant. Concentrate produced during seawater desalination is disposed of through deep-well injection or returned to the ocean, while brackish groundwater facilities dispose of brines through deep-well injection, surface water bodies, evaporation ponds, wastewater treatment plants, or industrial process use. These disposal methods can be costly and raise environmental concerns. Concerns abound regarding whether pumping an aquifer's brackish water layers may cause mixing of brackish water with fresh water in the aquifers. In some areas, no geological formations divide brackish and fresh groundwater, and the fresh water simply sits atop the heavier salty water. More research is needed to assess this potential and how it can be mitigated.

Groundwater/Surface Water Interaction

Surface water and groundwater resources are often hydrologically connected. Many surface water streams originate from springs, which are discharge points for groundwater aquifers. Conversely, stream flows frequently recharge underground aquifers. Nevertheless, surface water and groundwater are managed differently. The State of Texas owns surface water and manages it by appropriating water rights. Groundwater is recognized by state statute as a landowner's property right subject to reasonable regulation and management by local groundwater conservation districts.

Because most surface water in Texas is already fully appropriated, many water suppliers are turning to groundwater to meet growing demands. In regions of the state where surface water flows are highly dependent on spring flows, impacts from increased groundwater usage may soon be seen in reduced stream flows and impacts on water rights. An example of these impacts is the lawsuit between Texas and New Mexico regarding pumping along the Rio Grande, which has reduced flows in the river, impacting downstream users.

Southmost Regional Water Authority regional desalination plant near Brownsville. Courtesy of Danielle Kalisek, Texas Water Resources Institute

However, developing and implementing a planning and management approach that adequately accounts for groundwater/surface water interaction will be controversial because of the different legal principles governing their management and the potential implications on property rights and local control. Any approach taken must acknowledge and address these legal differences and implications.

Financing Infrastructure

The passage of Proposition 6 and subsequent creation of the two-billion-dollar State Water Implementation Fund for Texas (SWIFT) established an enhanced process for financing water infrastructure projects. However, questions remain regarding how to best assist small, disadvantaged communities and fund needed education programs. Funding education and outreach is needed to achieve goals of water conservation, which is expected to provide 24% of future water demands. Sufficient support and resources have not been provided to achieve this goal. Further, SWIFT loan programs may not be a suitable program for assisting small, disadvantaged communities. Other options (e.g., grant programs) may be needed to help assist these at-risk communities.

Freshwater mussels from the San Saba River. Courtesy of Charles Randklev, Texas A&M Institute of Renewable Natural Resources

Endangered Species Act and Water Management

More than 90 species in Texas are listed as federally threatened or endangered by the US Fish and Wildlife Service, with an additional 30 species listed as candidate species and over 50 species recently petitioned or proposed for listing. Many of these are water-dependent species. Providing suitable habitat and flows for these species will be critical to their survival but also has potentially significant implications on water management in the state. For example, a 2009 lawsuit claimed TCEQ violated the Endangered Species Act by allowing too much water to be withdrawn from the San Antonio and Guadalupe River Basins, disrupting inflow into the estuaries and leading to a decrease in species used as food by the endangered whooping crane. This allegedly resulted in the loss of two dozen whooping cranes. Although the Fifth Circuit Court of Appeals in Louisiana ruled in favor of TCEQ, until the endangered species' water needs are adequately addressed, this will continue to be an issue.

Providing for Environmental Flows

Providing sufficient flows within streams and rivers, as well as inflows to bays and estuaries along the coast, is critical to maintain aquatic species. Regional water-planning groups are beginning to recognize environmental flows in the planning process. Planning groups are required to follow the TCEQ environmental flow standards and rules, use site-specific studies when available, and apply the 1997 Consensus Criteria for Environmental Flow Needs when evaluating water management strategies involving surface water development and permitting. Currently, environmental flow needs are not formally acknowledged as a category of water need to be planned for and met. Without this formal acknowledgment, some anticipate that environmental flow needs will not be met.

Nutrient Water Quality Standards

The EPA is requiring all states to develop water quality standards for nutrients, including nitrogen and phosphorus. In response, in June 2010 TCEQ adopted nutrient standards for 75 lakes and procedures for applying nutrient limits to wastewater permits that require most wastewater plants to remove nutrients, particularly phosphorus, from their wastewater. The TCEQ is now conducting studies and evaluations to develop nutrient standards for streams, rivers, and estuaries. As nutrient standards are implemented across the state, increased efforts will be required to reduce nutrient runoff from fertilizer application and nutrient discharges from wastewater plants.

What You Can Do

We all make an impact on our water supplies, and conserving water is the best way for you to make a positive impact on existing and future water resources. Water conservation is expected to meet 24% of the state's future water needs. Following are just a few ways to start conserving water and improving water quality.

Harvest Rainwater

Rainwater harvesting, which captures, diverts, and stores rainwater for later use, is an alternative water-supply approach anyone can use. Rainwater harvesting reduces demand on existing water supplies while reducing runoff, erosion, and contamination of surface water. Harvested rainwater can be used for nearly any purpose, including landscape irrigation, stormwater control, wildlife and livestock watering, in-home use, and fire protection. Rainwater harvesting systems can range in size and complexity. Information on constructing these systems is available from the Texas A&M AgriLife Extension Service and other online resources.

Rainwater harvesting tank at the WaterSense-labeled home in Dallas. Courtesy of Leslie Lee, Texas Water Resources Institute

Provide Voluntary Land Stewardship

As former president and native Texan Lyndon B. Johnson said in 1947, "Saving the water and the soil must start where the first raindrop falls." This holds true to this day. The health of the land is manifested in the quality and quantity of surface water and groundwater. As such, land stewardship is the key to providing plentiful, clean water for future generations. Take advantage of education opportunities and resources provided by the AgriLife Extension to learn more about what you can do to improve your land and water. In many cases, technical and financial assistance is also available through your local soil and water conservation district. Contact your local district and USDA-NRCS field office about a conservation plan and cost-share funding that may be available.

Practice Nutrient Management

A good fertilization program provides essential nutrients to lawns, landscapes, and crops. To improve water quality and proactively prepare for coming nutrient water quality standards, use nutrient management and erosion control best management practices. Apply fertilizers (organic and conventional) according to soil tests and reasonable yield estimates. Also, implement practices to reduce erosion and filter runoff (e.g., leave filter strips and buffers along streams and waterways).

Take Control of Your Irrigation System

To save water, one of the best things you can do is take control of your irrigation system. Whether you irrigate a tenth of an acre or thousands of acres, improving the scheduling and management of your irrigation can make a big difference. Studies estimated that 9.5 million acre-feet of water are used to irrigate crops and another 2.3 million acre-feet to irrigate lawns, landscapes, and golf courses (Cabrera et al. 2013). Altogether, irrigation accounts for 11.8 million acre-feet, or two-thirds, of water use in the state, so improvements in this area have the potential to provide the greatest impacts.

Many people are content with allowing preset irrigation schedules to dictate watering. This often leads to watering during times when irrigation is unnecessary (e.g., during or immediately following rainfall). Both cropland and lawn/landscape irrigation can benefit from proper irrigation scheduling. Higher cropland yields and reduced water usage have resulted from improved scheduling. Several technologies are available to help properly schedule irrigation. Using evapotranspiration (ET) estimates, soil moisture sensors, and/or plant stress sensors can help improve irrigation scheduling and prevent watering when it is not needed.

Routinely checking your irrigation system to ensure it is working properly is also important, and routine maintenance is essential. Just one broken sprinkler head in your lawn irrigation system can waste 300 gallons per hour.

Drought-tolerant plants conserve water. Courtesy of Leslie Lee, Texas Water Resources Institute

Select Drought-Tolerant Plants

Planting drought-tolerant crops, turf, and landscapes can significantly impact water use and conservation. Using the appropriate crop, grass, and/or landscape species can not only conserve water but also make water management easier and less expensive. Plant species and crop varieties differ significantly in their water needs and drought resistance. Contact your local county extension agent for more information on drought-tolerant species.

Fix Leaks

According to the EPA, the average household loses more than 10,000 gallons each year as a result of leaks that could be easily fixed. Nationally, leaks waste more than one trillion gallons each year. Some 10% of homes have leaks that waste over 90 gallons per day. Common leaks include worn toilet flappers, dripping faucets, and other leaking valves. Fixing these easily corrected leaks can save homeowners nearly 10% on their water bills.

Install Water-Conserving Fixtures and Appliances in Your Home

A few simple actions can save you water, electricity, and money. Installing high-efficiency appliances, water-conserving faucets and showerheads, and high-efficiency toilets can significantly reduce water and energy use, particularly for older homes. Showering accounts for about 17% of residential indoor water use. Replacing standard showerheads, which use about 2.5 gpm (gallons per minute), with performance showerheads, which use about 1.75 gpm, can reduce water use for showering by 30%.

Toilets are the largest water user in the home, accounting for nearly 30% of residential indoor water consumption. More than 40% of homes still have older toilets that use about 3.5 gpf (gallons per flush). Installing a high-efficiency toilet, which uses less than 1.3 gpf, can save more than 60% of water per flush. Faucets account for more than 15% of indoor household water use. Installing WaterSense-labeled bathroom sink faucets and accessories can reduce a sink's water flow by 30%. If you are not in the market for a new faucet, you can still conserve by replacing the aerator in your older faucet with a more efficient one.

The average washing machine uses about 41 gallons of water per load, making it the second-largest water user in the average home. When it is time to replace your clothes washer or dishwasher, consider buying an efficient, water-saving Energy Star washer. High-efficiency washing machines use 35% to 50% less water and 50% less energy. Finally, consider installing other water-conserving measures, such as a pressure-reducing valve on your main water line or recirculation system for your hot water (EPA 2014).

WaterSense faucet. Courtesy of Leslie Lee, Texas Water Resources Institute

Get Involved

Finally, get involved. Participate in regional water-planning efforts. Encourage others, including neighbors and decision makers, to conserve water and support needed infrastructure improvements. Together, we can make a difference.

Conclusion

Texas possesses tremendous surface water and groundwater resources. However, increasing demands driven by our growing population, along with frequent droughts, are stressing these resources. Without significant intervention, our continued economic prosperity, our quality of life, and our precious water resources and the ecosystems that depend on them will be jeopardized. Fortunately, carefully planned measures and programs are in place to ensure Texas has sufficient water supplies and healthy ecosystems. Through strategic planning at the state, regional, and local levels, measures have been identified in conjunction with local stakeholders to address our state's water resource concerns and are now being implemented. However, we all have a part to play in conserving our waters and preserving their quality. The best-laid plans cannot be successful without everyone's help. Through judicious management of our personal water usage, involvement in planning efforts, and encouraging and educating others, we can all make a difference.

References

Brune, G. 1975. *Major and Historical Springs of Texas*. Texas Water Development Board Report 189.

Cabrera, R., K. Wagner, and B. Wherley. 2013. An Evaluation of Urban Landscape Water Use in Texas. *Texas Water Journal* 4 (2): 14–27.

Carney, B. 2002. Lakes within Oceans. National Oceanic and Atmospheric Administration. Accessed September 28, 2014. http://oceanexplorer.noaa.gov/explorations/02mexico/background/brinepool/brinepool.html (revised June 25, 2010).

Dowell, T. 2014. Did You Know? Q&A with Tiffany Dowell. *txH$_2$O* 10 (1): 28–29. Accessed February 28, 2015. http://twri.tamu.edu/publications/txh2o/summer-2014/did-you-know/.

EPA (Environmental Protection Agency). 2014. Conserving Water. Accessed February 28, 2015. http://www.epa.gov/greenhomes/ConserveWater.htm (updated April 24, 2014).

Gulf of Mexico Foundation. 2015. Gulf of Mexico Facts. Accessed September 28, 2014. http://www.gulfmex.org/about-the-gulf/gulf-of-mexico-facts/.

Louisiana Universities Marine Consortium. n.d. Hypoxia in the Northern Gulf of Mexico. Accessed September 28, 2014. http://www.gulfhypoxia.net/overview/.

Mitsch, W. J., and J. G. Gosselink. 1993. *Wetlands*. 2nd ed. New York: John Wiley.

National Wildlife Federation. 2004. Bays in Peril: A Forecast for Freshwater Flows to Texas Estuaries. Accessed September 28, 2014. http://texaslivingwaters.org/wp-content/uploads/2004/10/bays-in-peril_report_summary.pdf.

Stephenson, Karen, Ann Miller, and Nancy Herron. 2003. Texas Treasures: Wetlands. Texas Parks and Wildlife Department. http://www.tpwd.state.tx.us/publications/pwdpubs/media/pwd_bk_k0700_0908.pdf.

Swenson, Dan. 2007. How the Dead Zone Forms. *Times Picayune*, June 9.

TCEQ (Texas Commission on Environmental Quality). 2010. *Preserving & Improving Water Quality: The Programs of the Texas Commission on Environmental Quality for Managing the Quality of Surface Waters*. TCEQ No. GI-351. Austin.

———. 2014a. Drought Contingency Plans. Accessed March 5, 2015. https://www.tceq.texas.gov/permitting/water_rights/contingency.html (last modified February 10, 2015).

———. 2014b. Water Availability Models. Accessed March 5, 2015. https://www.tceq.texas.gov/permitting/water_rights/wam.html (last modified October 23, 2014).

———. 2015a. Brazos Watermaster. Accessed March 5, 2015. https://www.tceq.texas.gov/permitting/water_rights/wmaster/brazos-river-watermaster (last modified February 6, 2015).

———. 2015b. TCEQ Water Conservation Programs. Accessed March 5, 2015. https://www.tceq.texas.gov/permitting

/water_rights/conserve.html/#plans (last modified February 10, 2015).

Texas Center for Policy Studies. 2000. *Texas Environmental Almanac*. 2nd ed. Austin: University of Texas Press.

Texas Groundwater Protection Committee. n.d.a. What Is a Groundwater Conservation District (GCD)? Accessed April 2, 2015. http://tgpc.state.tx.us/POE/FAQs/GCDs_FAQ.pdf.

———. n.d.b. What Is a Groundwater Management Area (GMA)? Accessed April 2, 2015. http://tgpc.state.tx.us/POE/FAQs/GMAs_FAQ.pdf.

Texas Water Code. 2005. Sec. 36.108(c). Accessed April 2, 2015. http://www.statutes.legis.state.tx.us/Docs/WA/htm/WA.36.htm.

TPWD (Texas Parks and Wildlife Department). 2013. *Land and Water Resources and Conservation Recreation Plan*. Accessed February 28, 2015. http://www.tpwd.state.tx.us/publications/pwdpubs/media/pwd_pl_e0100_0687_2013.pdf.

TSSWCB (Texas State Soil and Water Conservation Board). 2014. Watershed Protection Plan Program. Accessed August 20, 2014. http://www.tsswcb.texas.gov/en/wpp.

———. 2015. Texas Nonpoint Source Management Program. Accessed March 6, 2015. http://www.tsswcb.texas.gov/managementprogram.

TWDB (Texas Water Development Board). 2011. *An Assessment of Aquifer Storage and Recovery in Texas*. Texas Water Development Board Report 0904830940. Austin.

———. 2012. 2012 State Water Plan. Accessed February 28, 2015. http://www.twdb.state.tx.us/waterplanning/swp/2012/index.asp.

———. 2013. Water for Texas: Regional Water Planning in Texas. Accessed March 5, 2015. http://www.twdb.texas.gov/publications/shells/RegionalWaterPlanning.pdf.

———. 2015a. Bays & Estuaries. Accessed February 28, 2015. http://www.twdb.texas.gov/surfacewater/bays/index.asp.

———. 2015b. Groundwater Models. Accessed February 28, 2015. https://www.twdb.texas.gov/groundwater/models/index.asp.

Wagner, K., L. Gregory, and T.A. Berthold. Forthcoming. Water Quality Management. In *Water Sustainability: Global Issues and Technology/Management Advancements*, ed. D. Chen. Boca Raton, FL: CRC Press.

UNIT 10

The Nature of Naming

BARRON S. RECTOR
Associate Professor and Extension Range Specialist, Texas A&M University

MATTHEW R. McCLURE
Professor of Biology, Lamar State College–Orange

Unit Goals

After completing this unit, volunteers should be able to

- discuss the uses and importance of the classification system
- identify the main parts of a scientific name
- understand why the binomial classification system is important
- discuss the pitfalls of using common names
- demonstrate their ability to classify local plants

"The world is a beautiful book, but little use to who cannot read it."
—Carlo Goldoni, Italian playwright and poet, 1707–93

Introduction

Knowledge of the earth and its plants and animals is of great importance, as humans act as their stewards. Our existence and life on earth are controlled by many factors, such as the air we breathe and the animals and plants we depend on as our constant associates. It is true that through the process of becoming civilized, we have acquired a wide variety of skills that enable us to modify our environment in a limited way and to use our environment to meet our needs and ambitions. Regardless, we still must foster the connection to these organic beginnings and resources for our continued survival.

From birth, we begin to explore our surroundings and make associations with people, food, objects, noise, or anything that crosses our path. As a child, I would take walks at my grandparents' place and name the plants and animals that I did not know. Not because I knew I would become a naturalist by trade or because I felt the need to catalogue each one through taxonomic classification, but merely out of the curiosity and imagination of a child. Plants with thorns would become "pointy plants," birds that were red would become "red birds," and snakes that made noise with their tails would become "rattling snakes." This innocent naming of those things observed would be any ancient naturalists' initial way of talking about the natural objects found along their path—descriptive and identifying.

The story of an animal or plant is told with its name, both common and scientific. By naming these organic objects around us, we are able to see the changes in the environment and get a better understanding of the constant dynamics of change occurring on the landscape. Naming also allows us to communicate with other people about those organic objects that we see and appreciate. This method of communication is visual. When referencing the "red bird," you automatically have a picture in mind of what this "red bird" could look like, what season it generally shows up in your backyard, how

Ruby-throated hummingbird (*Archilochus colubris*) nectaring on larkspur, Lake Lewisville Environmental Learning Area, April 28, 2014. Courtesy of Larry Brennan, Elm Fork Chapter

it sounds, and even possibly what its nest looks like. This is the story of this animal told through its name.

However, within the scientific community, this led to problems with naming objects merely on their descriptions, because a "red bird" could identify a multitude of species that we know today. This could be a northern cardinal, a scarlet tanager, a red-headed woodpecker, or even a vermilion flycatcher. The need for formal systems of naming and classification became apparent from these initial observational and descriptive names, which eventually spurred the taxonomic classification system put into place today for all natural objects.

"Look deep into nature and then you will understand everything better."
—Albert Einstein

Why Do We Classify?

Our earth environment is rich with living things. There are about two million different, known types of living things. Just as humans have found it necessary to place various screws, nails, bolts, nuts, washers, and the like into different groups, it is also necessary to classify organisms into groups. To **classify** something means to arrange it into groups.

A good classification system helps in at least two ways. It provides an easier means to deal with living things by dividing them into groups of similar organisms, and it makes information about specific organisms easier to organize and find. For example, it is often convenient to talk about large groups such as birds or smaller groups such as ducks, songbirds, or owls. Information about specific organisms, such as where screech-owls live, what mallard ducks eat, or how long it takes robin eggs to hatch, can be found more easily if a good classification system is used.

Just as there are many different ways to group screws, nails, nuts, bolts, and washers, so there are many different ways to classify living things. One method is to classify

A black swallowtail caterpillar (*Papilio polyxenes*) munches on Queen Anne's lace at Helton Nature Park, Floresville. Courtesy of Kayla Gasker, Alamo Area Chapter

them according to where they normally live. In this method, we would have groups of saltwater organisms, pond organisms, wetland organisms, stream organisms, meadow organisms, shortgrass prairie organisms, high-desert grassland organisms, desert organisms, tropical forest organisms, pine forest organisms, under-a-rock organisms, and so on. Although this method might be useful, it would present many problems, since many organisms live in several different places and some move from place to place as they pass through various stages of their life cycles.

Another method to classify living things could be in the ways that they move—fly, walk, slither, hop, run—or the foods that they eat—plants, meat, insects, nectar. However, this too would cause confusion and misclassification of creatures who move in different ways throughout their habitats (ducks that swim and fly) or of creatures that switch foods seasonally (white-tailed deer foraging on more woody browse plants in the winter than in the summer). The classification system in use today places organisms into groups based on physical characteristics, which are more consistent across the range of time and location. If it were not for a good classification system, most information about the organisms would be lost in a hodgepodge of facts.

Who Developed the Classification System?

Although various systems of classification have been proposed and even used, the system used today was proposed more than 200 years ago. History shows that the Greek scientist and philosopher Aristotle attempted the first recorded classification of organisms. Prior to Aristotle and his work in the fourth century BC, records of biological discoveries were either too fragmentary to be of use or the records have been lost. Aristotle wrote several scientific essays, primarily about animals. All of Aristotle's essays about plants have been lost. Theophrastus of Eresos, a brilliant student of Aristotle, is credited with giving us the first known classification system for living organisms. He described the parts, uses, and habitats of plants and arranged them primarily by the different forms of their leaves and grouped them as trees, shrubs, or herbs. Theophratus classified nearly 500 species of plants. After Theophratus, other Greek and Roman scholars prepared and wrote many new classifications.

Beginning in the fifteenth century, classification became more complicated. European explorers returned to Europe with new plants from other parts of the world that had never been seen before. Current systems had dwelled on the classification of medicinal plants, but botanists began to turn their efforts to classifying and cataloguing all types of plants. These new systems employed the description of a plant to include a few unique characters. By 1623, the Swiss botanist Gaspard Bauhin had used this classification method to describe about 6,000 species of plants. All of this occurred 100 years before the Swedish botanist Carolus Linnaeus introduced the binomial system of nomenclature used today.

Early attempts at building a classification system had employed a utilitarian approach to classification for predominantly medicinal and useful plants. Thousands of new plants were being found and classified in a system of just a few unique characteristics, so John Ray, an English naturalist, in the seventeenth century developed the first system of classification based on multiple features and the natural relationship that existed among plants. In 1686, he published *Historia Plantarun* and was the first to give a biological definition of the species (Mayr 1982).

The use of physical characteristics of organisms led to problems and the system left much to be desired. In the mid-1700s, Carolus Linnaeus, a Swedish naturalist, set forth a new classification system in his works *Species Plantarum* and *Systema Naturae.*

Carolus Linnaeus, father of modern taxonomy. Line engraving by Felice Zuliani after Tramontini after Alexander Roslin, 1775. Courtesy of Wellcome Images, UK

Scholars readily accepted and adopted his system. The Linnaean system had more flexibility than previously used or proposed systems. Linnaeus tried to do more than simply publish long lists of plants and animals with Latin binomials. He organized plants into 24 classes, based primarily on the features of stamens, including the number of stamens per flower, whether or not they were fused together, and whether or not they occurred on the same flower as the pistils.

Taxonomy is the study of naming organisms but is also described as the science of discovering, describing, naming, and classifying organisms. Taxonomists use a classification hierarchy or an arrangement of graded levels. The system currently has eight major levels: **domain, kingdom, phylum, class, order, family, genus,** and **species**. The original system of Linnaeus did not use the domain level, which was added above the kingdom level by taxonomists in the 1990s.

What Is a Species?

The word **species**, which generally means "kind," was first used in 1686 by John Ray, who recognized that species were biological units based on reproduction. More recently, Ernst Mayr defined species as "groups of actually or potentially interbreeding natural populations, which are reproductively isolated from other such groups" (1942, 120). This means that members of a species have the potential to interbreed in nature but are generally incapable of interbreeding successfully with members of a different species. Such interbreeding cannot occur because there are habitat or courtship differences or the interbreeding may result in a hybrid that could be frail, reproductively

Taxonomic classification levels

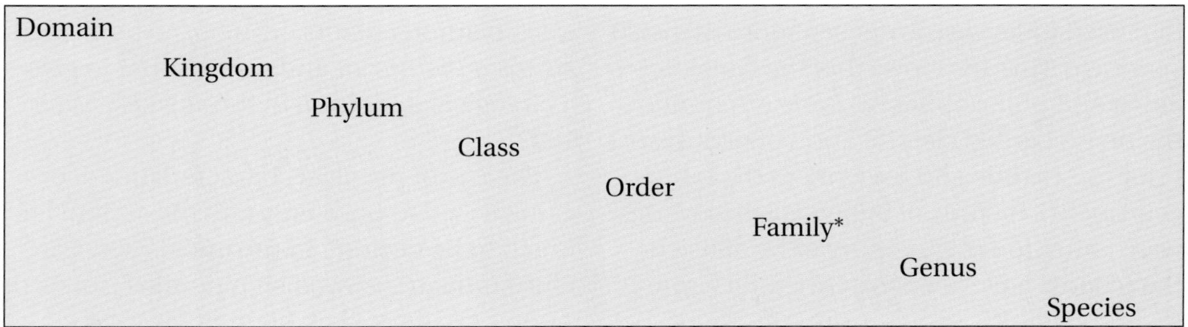

*Family names for animals end with the letters "idae." Family names for plants end with "aceae."

sterile, or produce offspring that cannot reproduce.

"Taxonomy (the science of classification) is often undervalued as a glorified form of filing—with each species in its folder, like a stamp in its prescribed place in an album; but taxonomy is a fundamental and dynamic science, dedicated to exploring the causes of relationships and similarities among organisms. Classifications are theories about the basis of natural order, not dull catalogues compiled only to avoid chaos."
—Stephen Jay Gould, from *Wonderful Life* (1989)

How Are Species Named?

Linnaeus proposed and used a system of **binomial nomenclature** to name species. *Binomial* means "two-name," and *nomenclature* means "naming." Our system for naming people is binomial. Linnaeus needed to choose a language for his system of naming organisms. Latin was used because no one spoke Latin as a native language. Most worldly scholars knew Latin and would be able to understand the scientific name of the organism. Latin is also a descriptive language and suited the purposes of Linnaeus well. If Linnaeus had picked his native language to name organisms, his life's work would have become out-of-date as the meanings of the descriptive words he chose to describe an organism changed. For example, we know the word *charity* to mean "the giving of money or service," but in the 1600s, *charity* meant simply "love." If all languages had been acceptable for naming organisms, then scientists or taxonomists would have had to become linguists just to be sure that they were talking about the same organism that others were discussing.

A scientific species name is made up of a **generic name** and a **specific epithet**. The generic name is the same as its genus and is

White-tailed deer (*Odocoileus virginianus*). Courtesy TPWD

always capitalized. The specific epithet, or specific name, that follows is never capitalized.

Both generic name and specific epithet are italicized (or underlined when written out by hand). The complete scientific name of plants or animals also includes the initials or name of the person or persons who first described the species. The scientific names of plants that were first described by Linnaeus still bear an "L." after the binomial. The authors name is not italisized.

Using the white tailed deer as an example, the scientific name, *Odocoileus virginianus* Z., can be broken down like this: *Odocoileus* (the genus name) *virginianus* (the species name), Zimmerman (the zoologist who coined the name, often abbreviated or even omitted). If the object of classification is a subspecies, such as the key deer, the subspecies name is included: *Odocoileus virginianus clavium*.

Bouteloua curtipendula (Michx.) Torr. Courtesy of the USDA/NRCS Plants Database

To make things more detailed, if there are two authors who worked on naming that species, both of their names are included after the specific epithet, along with secondary authors if the species is reclassified later. Additional key abbreviations can also be included to distinguish varieties (var.), subspecies (ssp.), a variety of species under one genus (spp.), or one specific species unknown within a genus (sp.). These abbreviations are not italicized.

Consider Drummond's red maple, for example, correctly identified as *Acer rubrum* L. var. *drummondii* (Hook. and Arn. ex Nutt.) Sargent. The original red maple tree was described by Linnaeus. The variety of this red maple was named for Thomas Drummond, who described it while on a trip to Velasco, Texas, in 1833. William Jackson Hooker and George Walker Arnott coined it in *The Botany of Captain Beechey's Voyage* in 1841. It was finally reclassified by Charles Sprague Sargent in his *Report on the Forests of North America* in 1884.

The grama grasses are all in the genus *Bouteloua*; the plant commonly named sideoats grama, has a scientific name of *Bouteloua curtipendula* (Michx.) Torr. In many cases, well-defined but less important characteristics of a plant have been used to define a variety status of plant species. Sideoats grama has been recognized to have two forms, one with underground rhizomes and one without rhizomes. These have been named *Bouteloua curtipendula* (Michx.) Torr. var. *caespitosa* Gould & Kapadia and *Bouteloua curtipendula* (Michx.) Torr. var. *curtipendula*, respectively. These very specific varietal names become important in the seed-trade world: for example, *Andropogon gerardii* var. *gerardii* is big bluestem, and *Andropogon gerardii* var. *paucipilus* is sand bluestem. Likewise, Plains bluestem, Ganada bluestem, Spar bluestem, and Ironmaster bluestem are all *Bothriochloa ischaemum* var. *ischaemum*. The grasses are

Master Naturalist Volunteer Discovers New Plant

Botanical Research Institute of Texas Identifies Plant New to Science

Tom Harvey, Texas Parks and Wildlife Department

Fort Worth. With more than 5,000 flowering plants native to Texas, the odds of anyone discovering a new species are slim to none. Texas Master Naturalist Volunteer Jeff Quayle of Fort Worth beat those odds in April 2000 when he discovered a plant new to science at Lake Mineral Wells State Park.

Quayle, a self-taught botanist, was hiking in the park when he found a plant that was unfamiliar. He recognized it was from the genus *Senecio* but knew nothing else about the mysterious wildflower, described as a short-lived annual in the sunflower family that grows up to waist high and produces yellow flowers in spring.

Quayle took a sample back to the Botanical Research Institute of Texas (BRIT) in Fort Worth. There it was examined by Dr. Ted Barkley, a BRIT research associate and professor emeritus of botany at Kansas State University. Barkley sent sample copies to experts around the world, including the Smithsonian Institution and the Royal Botanic Gardens in Kew, England, but no matches for the plant were found.

After considerable study, the plant was designated as *Senecio quaylei* T. M. Barkley. The scientific name has three elements: *Senecio* is the genus name, *quaylei* is the species name (after the discoverer), and "T. M. Barkley" is the name of the person who first described the new species. There is no common name for this plant, but Barkley says "Quayle's ragwort" would be appropriate. It is a member of the sunflower family, the largest family of flowering plants, including sunflowers, goldenrods, sagebrushes, and ragweeds. The formal publication of the new species occurred December 19, 2000, in the botanical journal *SIDA* (now called *Journal of Botanical Research Institute of Texas*), a scientific publication of BRIT.

Barkley says there are several reasons why the *Senecio quaylei* discovery is important. From a botanical science view, it shows subtle interactions among naturally occurring plant species that should be better understood if people are to manage our biological endowment wisely. For example, the fact that the plant produces only infertile seeds raises questions on whether it has pollinators (such as insects) that are only active during part of the year or whether the lack of pollinators reflects a broader environmental problem. If the plant is just a remnant of a once widespread species, that may also indicate broader problems. Barkley says any discovery that adds hard data to the botanical knowledge base could potentially help develop new pharmaceuticals, aid genetic research into high-tech plant breeding, yield horticultural (gardening) uses, act as an indicator species to warn of environmental problems, or provide other benefits.

Senecio quaylei T. M. Barkley ("Quayle's ragwort").

"The discovery of a new species in a region close to home captivates the imagination," said Barkley. "North Central Texas has been settled by European mankind for a century and a half, and it has been easy to assume that all of the plants growing spontaneously here are either recorded in the herbaria and the botanical literature, or else they are adventive weeds of recent introduction. A new species such as *Senecio quaylei* reminds us that the flora and fauna are dynamic things of endless fascination. It also underscores the value of citizen volunteers for scientific efforts."

all the same species and variety, but their common names reflect human-determined selections for taller plants, larger leaves, better palatability, or growth on specific soils, or they have some other specific trait that separates them out in the market and use on the landscape. Which one is better? It all depends on what types of soils they will be planted in, how much rainfall occurs, and how that specific grass would meet the needs of the landowner.

Animal species names, when written in full, contain the generic name, specific epithet, author's last name, and year of publication. For example, the full scientific name for humans is *Homo sapiens* Linnaeus, 1758. In most literature, however, this may be written simply as *Homo sapiens*, or abbreviated as *H. sapiens* when the full name has already been provided within the written work. If the author's name and year are in parentheses, it means there was a change in the genus name since the original publication of the species. For example, the Atlantic deer cowrie is *Macrocypraea cervis* (Linnaeus, 1771) but was originally published as *Cypraea cervis* Linnaeus, 1771. Animal subspecies names are written as a trinomial with the subspecific name following the binomial species name. The two subspecies of the Texas flat snail, *Polygyra texasiana*, are *Polygyra texasiana texasiana* and *Polygyra texasiana texasensis*.

What Are the Pitfalls of Using Common Names?

The names used to identify plants or animals in everyday conversation are common names, which have various origins. The approximately 5,000 species of plants known to occur in Texas have been named by people just like you and me—including early European settlers, American Indians, traveling naturalists, and others. Plants were named from characteristics such as their smell, color, or beauty; if they hurt, bite, or scratch; and the general appearance that reminded the namer of something he or she already knew. Many plants were named by early naturalists or travelers after similar or look-alike plants they already knew in Europe. Often, when you see a plant at the same stage of growth seen by the person who named it, you can see why the name was given.

Hearing a plant's common name may produce a visual picture. Sometimes this visual picture will not match the plant when the plant is a seedling or in winter growth. Some plants have been named after people as a way of formally recognizing them for their work or some special contribution. For example, Texas Master Naturalist volunteer Jeff Quayle had a plant named after him when he discovered a new species. Plant common names have usually been based on some physical-visual character of the plant—the plant is spiny, thorny, hairy, colorful, large flowered, or odiferous, or it grows in a particular season or in a discrete area.

There are two major problems you should be aware of when using common names. First, common names often include more than one species. An example is grama grasses. The name "grama" is the common name for all grasses in the genus *Bouteloua*. Grama grasses in Central Texas may refer to sideoats grama, tall grama, red grama, hairy grama, Texas grama, and others. Although these grasses are related, they are independent plant species that grow in different situations, respond to management differently, are encouraged or suppressed under a natural fire regime, produce different amounts of forage on particular soils and range sites, and may even represent different stages of plant succession, soil moisture regime, and land health. Quite often in the animal kingdom, a common name may apply to several different organisms. The name "gopher" has been used to refer to a salamander, a turtle, a frog, one of several snakes, or any of about 50 different types of rodents. The name "speckled trout" can refer to either a saltwater member of the drumfish family (Sciaenidae) or a freshwater member of the trout family (Salmonidae).

The second problem is that a single species often has more than one common name. Depending on where you grew up or where you went to college, you may refer to the plant *Clematis drummondii* as Drummond clematis, Texas virgins-bower, old-man's beard, graybeard, grandad or grandpa's beard, love in the mist, goat beard, barbas de chivato, or hierba de los averos. Common names will differ from community to community, across the state, from state to state, and from country to country. Some native plants in Texas have up to 36 common names. This fact may make life confusing and stresses why we use scientific names in training, science, government documents, and industry literature. Several authors, societies, and agencies have accepted specific common names, but there is still much inconsistency throughout the world and in publications when referring to plants or animals by their common names. To help alleviate this problem, taxonomists spend their careers determining the scientific names of plants and animals and studying the relationships between species. At times even the taxonomists themselves have muddied the water on the names of plants or animals.

Consider the common plant name "thistle." Because thistles usually have thorns and are harmful to the touch, many people will call any bristly-thorny, upright plant a thistle. After examining the use of this common name, it has been found that in Texas, 66 species of plants have the name "thistle" as part of a common name. Most of these plants are in the sunflower family, Asteraceae. They include plants such as Texas thistle, bull thistle, sow thistle, yellow starthistle, and musk thistle. These thistles occur in the genera *Cirsium*, *Sonchus*, *Centaurea*, and *Carduus*, respectively. Consider "Russian thistle." It is not a member of Asteraceae, the sunflower family, but is in Chenopodiaceae, the goosefoot family. This plant is also named "tumbleweed." Also consider the confusion that exists with names like "blue-eye grass." Plants with this name are in the genus *Sisyrinchium* in Iridaceae, the iris family. These plants are not grasses at all, but their leaves or early growth resembles a grass leaf or leaves. The Mexican poppy, *Kallstroemia grandiflora* Gray, is a member of Zygophyllaceae, the caltrop family, not Papaveraceae, the poppy family.

Grass spikelet of bitter panicgrass (*Panicum amarum*), found on sand dunes of Quintana Beach County Park in Brazoria County on September 20, 2014. *P. amarum* is important for stabilizing sand dunes. Courtesy of Peggy Romfh, Cradle of Texas Chapter

What Is the Future of Systematic Biology?

By the turn of the eighteenth century, botanists had begun to oppose the artificial system of Linnaeus because his system often placed unrelated plants together. Until the latter half of the nineteenth century, virtually all classification systems were based on the belief that living organisms had not changed since their creation and would not change in the future. Currently, the definition of *species* that most scientists agree on is "a group of similar organisms."

Carolus Linnaeus thought that the number of species was established at the biblical creation. All of the classification systems based on this theory fell into disfavor when the ideas of Charles Darwin and Alfred Wallace spread, and the classification system began to be based on evolutionary relationships. Classification systems that try to reflect evolution are said to be **phylogenetic**. Taxonomists consider phylogenetic systems to be superior to previous systems

Kingdoms and their characteristics

Kingdom	Monera (10,000 species)	Protista (250,000 species)	Fungi (100,000 species)	Plantae (250,000 species)	Animalia (1,000,000 species)
Cells	One-celled or colony of cells	One-celled (most), multi-celled (some)	One-celled (some), multi-celled (some	Multi-celled	Multi-celled
Cell structure	No nucleus, no organelles, cell membrane, cell wall (some)	Nucleus, organelles, vacuole, cell membrane, cell wall (some)	Nucleus, organelles, cell membrane, cell wall	Nucleus, organelles, cell membrane, cell wall, vacuoles	Nucleus, organelles, cell membrane, vacuoles
Method of obtaining food	Photosynthesis, decomposer, parasite	Absorption, trap or engulf, flagella, pseudopodium, cilia, photosynthesis	Decomposer, parasite, absorption, partnership	Mostly photosynthesis	Parasite, prey
Movement method	In water, in host	Pseudopodium, flagella, cilia	Lives on host	Grows toward light source	Muscular movement, in water, in air, in soil
Reproduction method	Conjugation, fission	Conjugation, fission, asexual, sexual	Spores, asexual budding	Propagation (grafting, budding, cutting, layering)	Asexual, sexual
Environmental function	Producer (some), consumer (some)	Plantlike producer, animal-like consumer	Consumer	Mostly producer	Consumer (herbivores, carnivores, omnivores)
Environmental importance	Decomposition, food chain, produces nitrogen/vitamins/antibiotics, in human/animal intestines	Ocean/pond food chain, human food source, produce oxygen	Decomposition, produce antibiotics, use in making bread, used in fermentation	Food source, medicines, dyes	Food source, labor, recreation
Examples	Bacteria, cyanobacteria	Plankton, algae, amoeba, volvox, paramecium, diatoms	Mushrooms, molds, mildews, yeasts	Angiosperms, gymnosperms, mosses, ferns, liverworts, horsetails	Sponges, worms, mollusks, insects, fish, mammals, amphibians, birds, reptiles

but cannot agree on which phylogenetic system is best. Their opinions differ on the basic assumptions about the features of an organism that best reflects the phylogeny of organisms.

Systematists are now developing new approaches to phylogenetic classifications. Keep in mind though, that ultimately all classifications are human artifacts and that there is no "universal truth" to be found. The newer systems are more explicit in their assumptions and are more testable scientifically. One of the most widely adopted systems of the past two decades is called **cladistics**, generally defined as a set of concepts and methods for determining cladograms. Cladograms express hypotheses about evolutionary relationships among organisms. The goal of cladistics is to evaluate and improve classifications.

Several of the newer classification systems being evaluated depend on techniques of molecular biology. These newer approaches challenge the more traditional systems and ask if molecular data are now more important than traditional data from leaf shape and flower morphology. At present, biologists classify all organisms into five kingdoms: Monera, Protista, Fungi, Plantae, and Animalia. This system was suggested by Robert H. Whittaker in 1969. Today the methods of cladistics in particular as they apply to molecular data (e.g., DNA, RNA, proteins) provide phylogenies that show the five-kingdom system to be inadequate for making a classification system for all living things.

Why Learn Scientific Names?

Unlike common names, scientific names provide a global standard for naming species. The scientific name of a species is the same in every country, regardless of spoken language or regional dialect. For example, the species name for the blue crab that lives in the Gulf of Mexico and the Atlantic Ocean is *Callinectes sapidus*. Whereas the common name "blue crab" may refer to other species in other parts of the world, the binomial scientific name *Callinectes sapidus* refers only to this species.

References

Hooker, Sir William Jackson, and G. A. Walker Arnott. *The Botany of Captain Beechey's Voyage*. London: Glasgow University Press.

Mayr, E. 1942. *Systematics and the Origin of Species from the Viewpoint of a Zoologist*. New York: Columbia University Press.

Sargent, Charles S. 1884. *Forests of North America: Exclusive of Mexico*. Washington, DC: US Department of the Interior.

Whittaker, Robert H. 1969. New Concepts of Kingdoms of Organisms. *Science* 163: 150–60.

Additional Resources

Barkley, T. M., ed. 1977. *Atlas of the Flora of the Great Plains*. Ames: Iowa State University Press.

Campbell, N. A., J. B. Reece, L. A. Urry, M. L. Cain, S. A. Wasserman, P. V. Minorsky, and R. B. Jackson. 2011. *Biology*. 9th ed. San Francisco: Benjamin Cummings.

Chase, Agnes. 1922. *First Book of Grasses*. Rural Text-Book Series. New York: Macmillan.

Cheatum, E. P., and R. W. Fullington. 1971. *The Aquatic and Land Mollusca of Texas. Part One: The Recent and Pleistocene Members of the Gastropod Family Polygyridae in Texas*. Bulletin 1, pp. 1–74. Dallas: Dallas Museum of Natural History.

Correll, D. S., and H. B. Correll. 1972. *Aquatic and Wetland Plants of the Southwestern United States*. Washington, DC: Environmental Protection Agency.

Correll, D. S., and M. C. Johnston. 1970. *Manual of the Vascular Plants of Texas*. Renner: Texas Research Foundation.

Cronquist, A. 1988. *The Evolution and Classification of Flowering Plants*. 2nd ed. Bronx: New York Botanical Garden.

Cronquist, A., and F. F. Thorne. 1994. Nomenclatural and Taxonomic History. In *Caryophyllates: Evolution and Systematics,* ed. H. D. Behnke and T. J. Mabry, pp. 5–25. New York: Springer-Verlag.

Gandhi, K. N., and R. D. Thomas. 1989. Asteraceae of Louisiana. *Sida Miscellany* no. 4:1–202.

Gould, Frank W., and R. B. Shaw. 1983. *Grass Systematics*. 2nd ed. College Station: Texas A&M University Press.

Hitchcock, A. S. 1951. *Manual of the Grasses of the United States*. Rev. Agnes Chase. Miscellaneous Publication 200. Washington, DC: US Department of Agriculture.

Jones, S. D., and A. E. Luchsinger. 1986. *Plant Systematics*. 2nd ed. New York: McGraw-Hill.

Kartsez, J. T., and R. Kartsez. 1980. *A Synonymized Checklist of the Vascular Flora of the United States, Canada and Greenland.* Vol. 2, *The Biota of North America*. Chapel Hill: University of North Carolina Press.

Mayr, E. 1982. *The Growth of Biological Thought*. Cambridge, MA: Harvard University Press.

Moore, Randy, W. Dennis Clark, and Darrell S. Vodopich. 1998. *Botany*. 2nd ed. New York: WCB/McGraw-Hill.

Radford, Albert E., William C. Dickison, Jimmy R. Massey, and C. Ritchie Bell. 1974. *Vascular Plant Systematics*. New York: Harper & Row.

Texas Forest Service. 1963. *Forest Trees of Texas*. College Station: Texas Forest Service.

Tunnell, J. W., Jr., J. Andrews, N. C. Barrera, and F. Moretzsohn. 2010. *Encyclopedia of Texas Seashells*. College Station: Texas A&M University Press.

USDA, NRCS. 2002. The PLANTS Database, Version 3.5. http://plants.usda.gov.

van Welzen, P. C. 1997. Paraphyletic Groups or What Should a Classification Entail. *Taxon* 46:99–103.

Weniger, D. 1984. *Cacti of Texas and Neighboring States*. Austin: University of Texas Press.

Woese, C. R., O. Kandler, and M. L. Wheelis. 1990. Towards a Natural System of Organisms: Proposal for the Domains Archaea, Bacteria, and Eucarya. *Proceedings of the National Academy of Science* 87:4576–79.

Plant Reference Websites

Aggie Horticulture: http://aggie-horticulture.tamu.edu/

International Oak Society: www.internationaloaksociety.org

Lady Bird Johnson Wildflower Center: www.wildflower.org [A searchable database of

7,000+ native plants by scientific or common name]

Native Plant Society of Texas: http://www.npsot.org

NatureServe Explorer: explorer.natureserve.org [A full vascular flora of the United States and Canada, including a searchable database for more than 70,000 plants, animals, and ecological communities]

Neil Sperry's Gardens: http://www.neilsperry.com

Texas Master Gardeners Association: www.txmg.org

Tree Care Industry Association: www.tcia.org

UNIT 11

Plants

BARRON S. RECTOR
Associate Professor and Extension Range Specialist, Texas A&M University

JASON SINGHURST
Plant Ecologist, Texas Parks & Wildlife Department

Unit Goals

After completing this unit, volunteers should be able to

- explain why it is important to be familiar with plant names
- describe the classes of plants
- become familiar with and describe the parts of a plant
- compare and contrast the four classes of plants
- become familiar with leaf and flower types, placement, and arrangements to identify plants
- explain what an invasive plant is and give some examples

Why Study the Natural History of Plants?

"Till now man has been up against nature, from now on he will be up against his own nature."
—Dennis Gabor, Hungarian-British inventor of holography

For many centuries, humans have relied on plants for survival and pleasure. Today plants still have great influence on our lives, either directly or indirectly. The plant is the foundation of the range, forest, and aquatic ecosystems and the primary producer of foodstuffs for consumers, including range livestock and wildlife. For a natural resource manager, knowledge of plants, soils, and climatic conditions forms the basis for the fundamental principles of natural resource management and successful land management. Plants provide a tool for monitoring the effects of environmental change and the effects of various management strategies.

The United States has extreme variation in environmental conditions. This variation has provided growing conditions for about 5,000 named flowering plant species in Texas. Texas is well known for its plant diversity, as it is the only state in the union to have both oaks and pines of the eastern and western United States. Some 326 plant species are **endemic** to or grow only in Texas. Because of the variability in weather, past management on the landscape, and different goals of land ownership and use, no two properties are exactly alike, have exactly the same plant species or densities of plants, or have exactly the same capability for the production of plants. For many reasons, each landowner or land manager needs to have some idea of the names of the plants growing on the land and their value and meaning in a management sense. The plant species growing on the land can often indicate the success or failure of the land manager. We have found that plants respond to the management we impose on the land.

Wildlife, livestock, and plants belong together. Their marriage, so to speak, though sometimes a little rocky, has passed the test of time. However, animals and plants do not necessarily exist for each other's convenience. In fact, it appears that plants will try anything to avoid being eaten. Plants

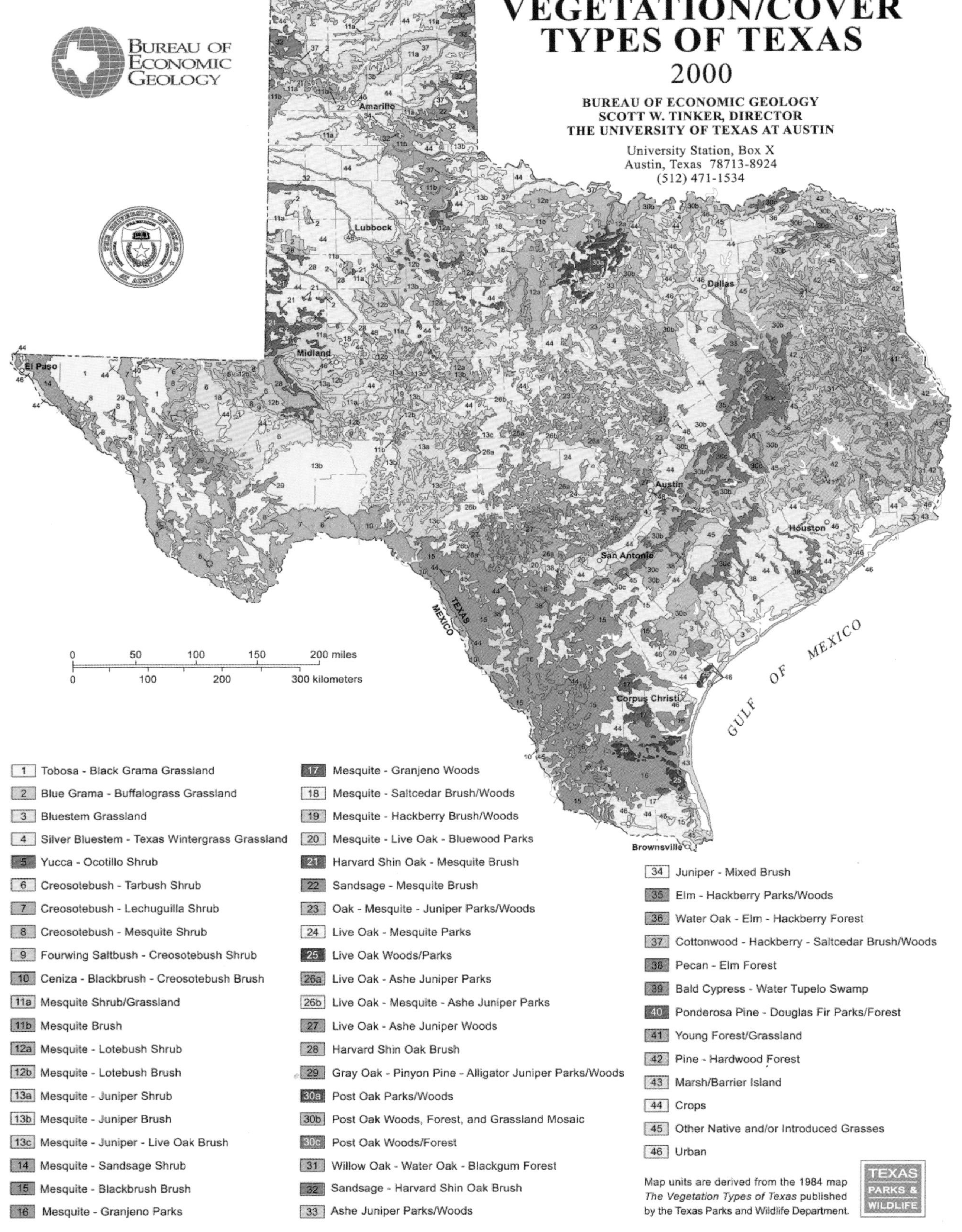

Vegetation cover types of Texas. Courtesy of the Bureau of Economic Geology, the University of Texas at Austin

will crawl under rocks, grow thorns, give off obnoxious odors, grow inaccessibly high in the air or low to the ground, become unpalatable, change from high-nutrient quality to low, and even produce toxic chemicals.

Why Know the Names of Plants?

Some people know plants by sight or general appearance. Many people have lived close to plants for a long time and have come to recognize, consciously or unconsciously, the many characteristics that make plant species different from each other. Others have learned the value of a plant through experience with that plant. Needless to say, some plants are easier to distinguish than others. Anyone can learn to identify a good number of things, whether they are people, cow breeds, or plants. A human characteristic is to name things and arrange them in some orderly fashion in order to communicate knowledge.

Farmer Brown was watching "ole Bessy" the cow eat one day; she took a bite of a plant and started to chew it. After about 30 seconds of chewing, "ole Bessy" became very sick and died right there in front of him. Farmer Brown raced up to the house, called his local veterinarian, and explained what had happened. The vet asked for the name of the plant to look it up in a book describing poisonous plants. At this question, Farmer Brown scratched his head and ultimately admitted that he did not know the name of the plant. Then the vet asked what the plant looked like. Farmer Brown told the vet that the plant was green, about a foot tall, and had a yellow flower. The vet laughed and stated that farmer Brown had just given the description of about 500 species of plants in Texas. Thus, the moral of the story. We name plants because the plant name is the communication medium to which all information about the plant is tied or attached. Without knowing the plant's name, we cannot look it up in a book and find all information that others have written about it. Without the name and the attached information, we can learn about plants only through experience, which could be a costly problem.

If Farmer Brown had known the name of this particular plant, the veterinarian or another resource person could have helped him with knowledge about its poisonous aspects. He could learn about methods to avoid the problem or prevent it from occurring again. If he had known that this particular plant was toxic to grazing cattle, he might have changed his management and even controlled this plant species before a problem occurred. New plants are always arriving to various properties through mud on tires, through weeds baled in hay purchased from another area, by wind from adjoining properties, and even in the fur of wildlife that crosses property lines.

There are many reasons for knowing names of plants. We can use this knowledge to

- determine the plant composition, which will lead to determining range condition/land health
- determine which plants in a pasture are forage plants for livestock/wildlife
- determine noxious or invasive plants that have a control measure associated with them
- determine potentially poisonous plants present or those already causing a problem
- understand the nutritive differences that exist among different classes of plants
- aid in determining the proper kind and class of livestock or wildlife best suited for the land
- recognize plants that may have characteristics suitable for genetic selection/engineering
- determine the kind and quality of forage available, which helps in estimating a stocking rate
- determine when a particular pasture

should be grazed from the kinds of plants growing there
- determine when to rest a pasture or apply other maintenance practices
- know how to treat a child who has eaten a plant in your home and become violently ill
- know what to say to a neighbor who has a new weed and declares the plant originated on your property
- be pro-active for finding foreign invasive plants that alter natural ecosystem properties

Where Do I Get Help with Identification of a Plant?

Many popular books and publications are available today to assist with the identification of flowering plants and may be for sale in your local bookstores. These include edible wild plants, native plants for landscaping, wildflowers, and poisonous plants. All of the plants we need to know may not be pictured. County agents with Texas A&M AgriLife Extension Service should be able to provide a good identification or recommend that your specimen be sent to an extension specialist in an appropriate agricultural/natural resource department at the state's land grant university. Other resources are available in most communities: personnel with state fish and game agencies, the USDA Natural Resources Conservation Service, State Forest Service, US Forest Service, the Native Plant Society and its members, professors in biology or associated departments at universities and junior colleges, teachers at local public and private schools, private and not-for-profit organizations, and various Internet sites.

Classes of Plants

Many different kinds of plants grow in pastures, on roadsides, in vacant lots, and in our parks and yards. Some we may classify as "weeds," "brush," "trees," or "grasses." These are broad categories generally describing the growth form of a plant or what it looks like. Another way to classify plants is based on physical structure, which includes four major classes:

1. Grasses (native and introduced)
2. Grasslike plants (look like grasses and include sedges, bulrushes, and rushes)
3. Forbs (herbaceous flowering plants other than grasses and grasslike plants)
4. Woody plants (such as shrubs and trees)

It will not be possible to learn the names of all plants in each of the four classes. You should first become familiar with species that furnish important signs of change and land health, forage for livestock and wildlife on your pastures, or plants potentially poisonous to grazing animals such as cattle, horses, and donkeys. Usually there will be 20 to 40 plant species in a range area, site, or pasture that are recognizable as highly palatable to livestock or wildlife, have a large forage production potential, are a potential major pest or invader, or may serve as a key plant species to be observed for making ranch management decisions.

Grasses

Grasses have jointed stems, which are usually hollow, except at the nodes or joints, and are branched. Leaves appear in two rows on the stem and are usually flattened. Leaf veins are parallel. Grasses are our most important range plants when considering the livestock industry. They may be divided into native and introduced categories based on the origin of the grass species. Both groups have the same general appearance, but native grasses occur naturally in North America (and in this case, Texas), while introduced species occur naturally outside this area. Introduced grass species are imported or brought into this country.

Grasses are members of the Poeaceae, or

IMPORTANT RANGE PLANT GROUPS

	GRASSES	GRASSLIKE		FORBS	SHRUBS (Browse)
		Sedges	Rushes		
STEMS	Jointed Hollow or Pithy	Solid Not Jointed		Solid	growth rings Woody Solid
LEAVES	Parallel Veins stem leaf Leaves on 2 sides of stem	stem leaf Leaves on 3 sides of stem	stem leaf Leaves on 2 sides of stem; rounded	"Veins" are usually netlike	
FLOWERS	(floret)	stamen ovary male female (may be combined)		Often showy	
EXAMPLE	Western Wheatgrass	Threadleaf Sedge	Wire Rush	Western Yarrow	Big Sagebrush (twig)

Important groups of plants on the range. Courtesy of Texas A&M AgriLife Extension Service

grass family. Variety of grasses in the vegetation or flora of Texas far exceeds that of any other state, with about 181 genera and 723 species of native, introduced, or exotic grasses (Shaw 2012). Grasses are typical but highly specialized **monocots**, meaning that they have one "seed leaf" or one embryonic leaf in their seeds from which they sprout. The earliest grasses probably grew in mesic or somewhat moist habitats under tropical or subtropical climatic conditions. Modern grasses that inhabit the warmer regions of the earth are extremely diverse both in respect to vegetation and reproductive characteristics.

Grasslike Plants

Grasslike plants look similar to grasses and are sometimes confused with them. Sedges and rushes are the most common plants in this category. Both have parallel leaf veins, but neither has nodes on the stems as grasses do. Sedges often have solid stems that are triangular in cross section. Sedge leaves, usually flattened, appear in three rows on the stem. Rush stems are either hollow or pithy, usually rounded, and unbranched below the floral (flower) parts. Leaves are mostly near the base of the plant and may be either round or flattened.

Forbs

Forbs are broad-leaved plants with annual stems. Leaves may have either parallel or net veins, although net veins are more common. Forbs are often incorrectly referred to as weeds. Many of them, such as alfalfa, are beneficial and provide valuable livestock and wildlife forage and seeds. The term "weed" is used when the plant is considered a pest. A general weed definition states that "weeds are plants whose virtues have yet to be discovered."

Woody Plants, Subshrubs, Shrubs, and Trees

Shrubs are plants with woody stems that live from one year to the next, meaning that they are perennials. Usually the stems branch out from near the base of the plant. **Trees** are like shrubs in growth form but usually have a definite trunk with branches well elevated above the ground. This plant class may often be referred to as browse or brush plants. The term "brush" may also note a grouping of woody plants where the various species living together are not identified. Trees can be identified by leaves, bark, twigs, fruit, flower, and overall tree form. Identification keys can also be helpful. When identifying trees by leaves, there are several leaf shapes, forms, and arrangements that will help narrow the search.

Plant Parts

Plants are like people; each is an individual. Some may look alike; others do not. Each plant species has some part or parts that are different from parts of all other plants. Similar plants have some characteristics by which you can recognize them as members of a particular species.

Grasses

Roots: Roots typically have no joints, no leaves, and no flowers. The growing part of each root is in the tip. Grasses have a fibrous root system composed of numerous branched roots all approximately the same size. The main functions of roots are to carry water and minerals from soil to stems, store food, and anchor plants.

Stems: Stems of grasses are made up of nodes (joints) and internodes (length of stem between nodes). Stems are usually hollow except at the nodes but sometimes have pith in the center similar to corn stems. The stem's main function is to transport water and minerals from roots to leaves and manufactured food from leaves to roots.

Rhizomes: Rhizomes are actually creeping, underground stems with joints and leaflike scales. Rhizomes store food that is manufactured in leaves and also vegetatively produce new plants.

Stolons: Stolons are aboveground prostrate stems. Runners of strawberry plants and bermudagrass are stolons. Stolons vegetatively produce new plants and store food. Buffalograss has stolons. Stolons may bear normal leaves, or the leaves may be highly reduced.

Vegetative parts: Aboveground vegetative parts include stems and leaves. At each node on the stem there is a bud that may produce a branch or may remain dormant. Leaves also arise from buds at nodes on the stem. The leaf is made up of two parts: the sheath, which fits tightly around the stem, and the blade, which is the flattened, expanded portion. These two parts are joined together at the collar. Sometimes, on the inside of the collar next to the stem is a small projection known as the ligule. The ligule, sometimes small and inconspicuous, may be a membranelike structure or a tuft of hairs. Some grasses have earlike tips or projections arising from the collar and clasping the stem. These tips are called auricles.

The growing parts of grass leaves are at the collar and the base of the sheath. If a grass leaf is grazed before it is fully developed, it will continue to grow. If it is fully developed when grazed, it will not continue to grow. The terminal bud or growing point of the grass plant is close to the ground surface. Seldom do livestock remove the growing point by grazing. If they do, the stem will no longer grow. Buds at the stem will begin to develop new stems to replace the original ones.

Flowering parts: The reproductive (flowering) parts of a grass plant are called the inflorescence, which is made up of smaller units known as the spikelets. At the base of each spikelet are two chafflike bracts called glumes. A single grass flower is a floret. There may be one or more florets in each spikelet. When there is more than one, each floret is supported by a stem known as the rachilla. Each fertile floret at maturity produces a caryopsis (seed).

The grass inflorescence is highly variable in number and size of spikelets and the deposition of the spikelets on the main axis or on branches. The inflorescence is delimited at the base by the uppermost culm leaf, which often is characterized by an enlarged sheath and a short, greatly reduced blade. Grass inflorescences are classified as spikes, racemes, or panicles:

Spike: All spikelets are sessile (without a stalk or stem) on the main inflorescence axis.

Raceme: All spikelets are borne on individual flower stalks (pedicels) developed directly from the main axis, as in wheat, or with some spikelets sessile and some pediceled on the main axis, as in little barley or little bluestem.

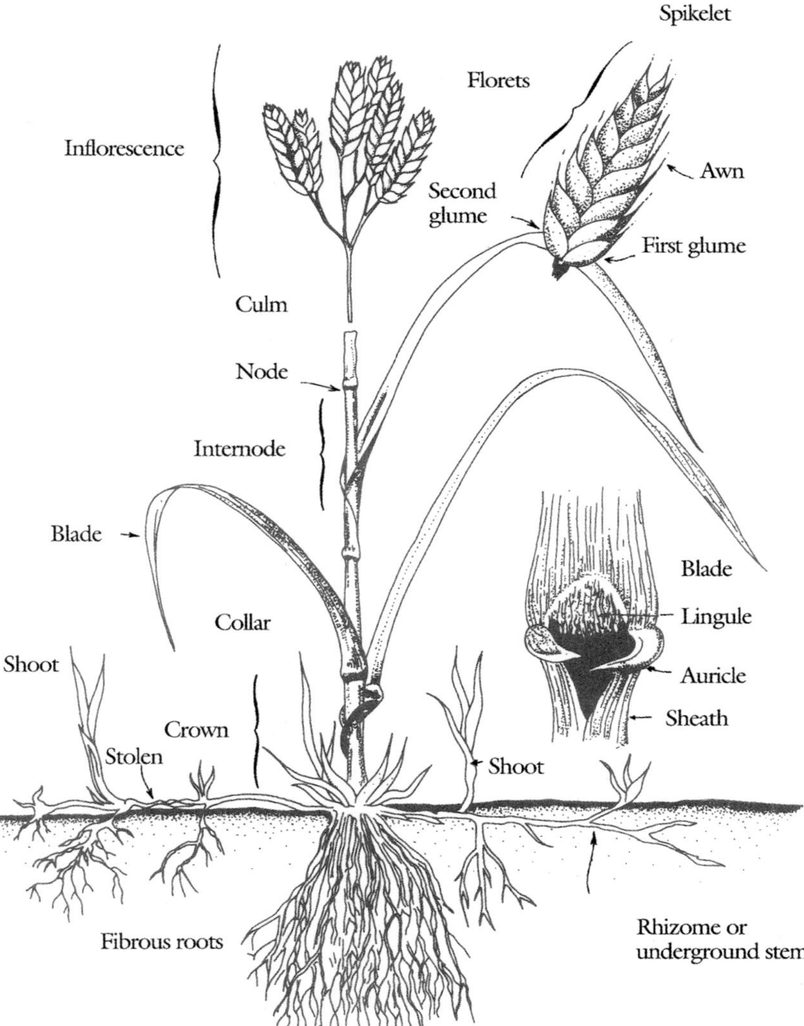

The parts of grass plants. Courtesy of Texas A&M AgriLife Extension Service

(A) rhizome (underground stem), fibrous roots, shoots

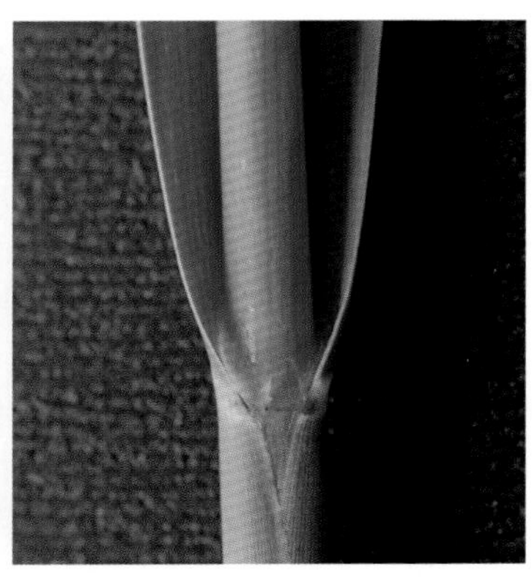

(B) blade, ligule, auricle, sheath

(C) inflorescence

(D) individual florets, 1st glume, 2nd glume

Parts of a grass plant, bitter panicgrass (*Panicum amarum*), found in the Quintana Beach Park in Brazoria County. The images are close-ups of featured grass plant parts. Courtesy of Peggy Romfh, Cradle of Texas Chapter

Panicle: Spikelets are all or in part on rebranched branches, with some having all spikelets sessile or short pediceled on unbranched primary inflorescence branches.

Forbs

Forbs vary more than grasses because the forb classification includes many different plant families, while all grasses belong to the grass family. Forbs, like grasses, have leaves, stems, roots, and flowers. Differences in plant parts are usually distinct enough to distinguish grasses from forbs, but it may be difficult to tell one forb from another.

Floral parts: Floral parts are usually used to identify forbs. The floral base is the receptacle, the expanded part of the stem to which the other floral parts are attached. The sepals, collectively known as the calyx, are usually green and make up the outer row of floral bracts. The petals, collectively known as the corolla, are usually showy or brightly colored. They are the floral bracts just inside the sepals. The stamens are located inside the floral bracts; each consists of a filament (slender stalk) and an anther

Firewheel (*Gaillardia pulchella*) at Jackson Nature Park, Stockdale. Courtesy of Kayla Gasker, Alamo Area Chapter

(pollen sac) attached to the end of the filament.

The innermost floral part is the pistil, composed of stigma, style, and ovary. The stigma is the tip of the pistil, where pollen grains are received and germinate. The style is the slender central portion of the pistil that connects the stigma with the ovary. The ovary is the basal portion of the pistil and contains one or more ovules, which mature into seeds.

Leaves: Leaves of forbs may vary and commonly have three main parts: the blade, or expanded part of the leaf; the petiole, a stalk connecting the blade to the stem; and the stipules, a pair of small appendages situated at the base of the petiole. Often the stipules are absent, and occasionally other leaf parts are missing. Leaves are classified as either simple or compound. Simple leaves are those with a single blade and petiole, while compound leaves have several blades or leaflets (as on a Texas bluebonnet). Compound leaves are either pinnately or palmately compound. Pinnately lobed leaves can be distinguished from palmately lobed leaves by examining the veins. In a pinnately lobed leaf, the veins will arise from several points along a central axis. A palmately lobed leaf has veins that arise at the same point at the base of the leaf.

Stems: Stems of forbs, like grasses, have nodes (joints) and internodes (the distance between each node). Branches of stems and

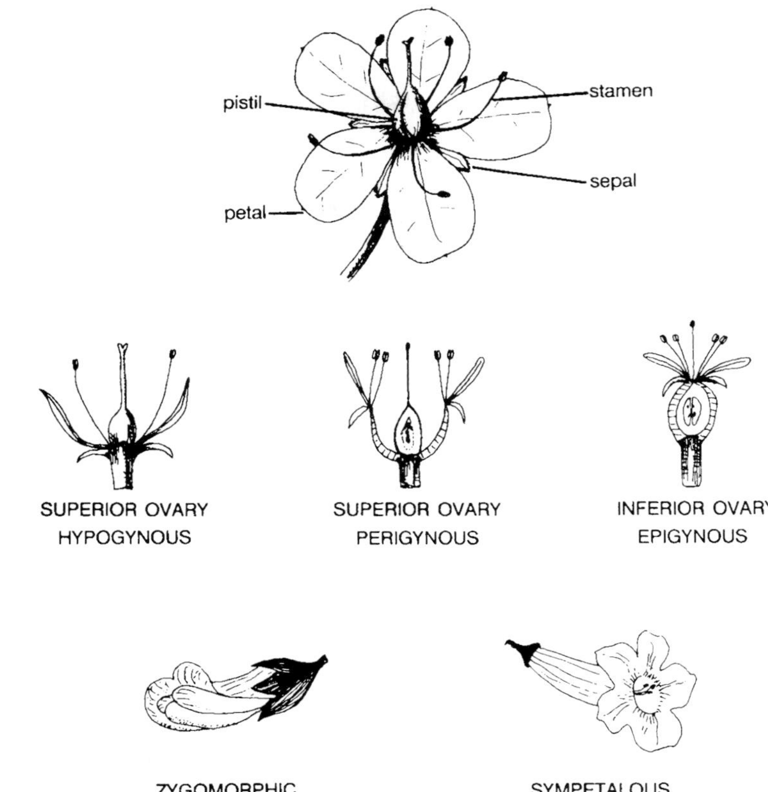

Parts of a flower. Courtesy of Texas A&M AgriLife Extension Service

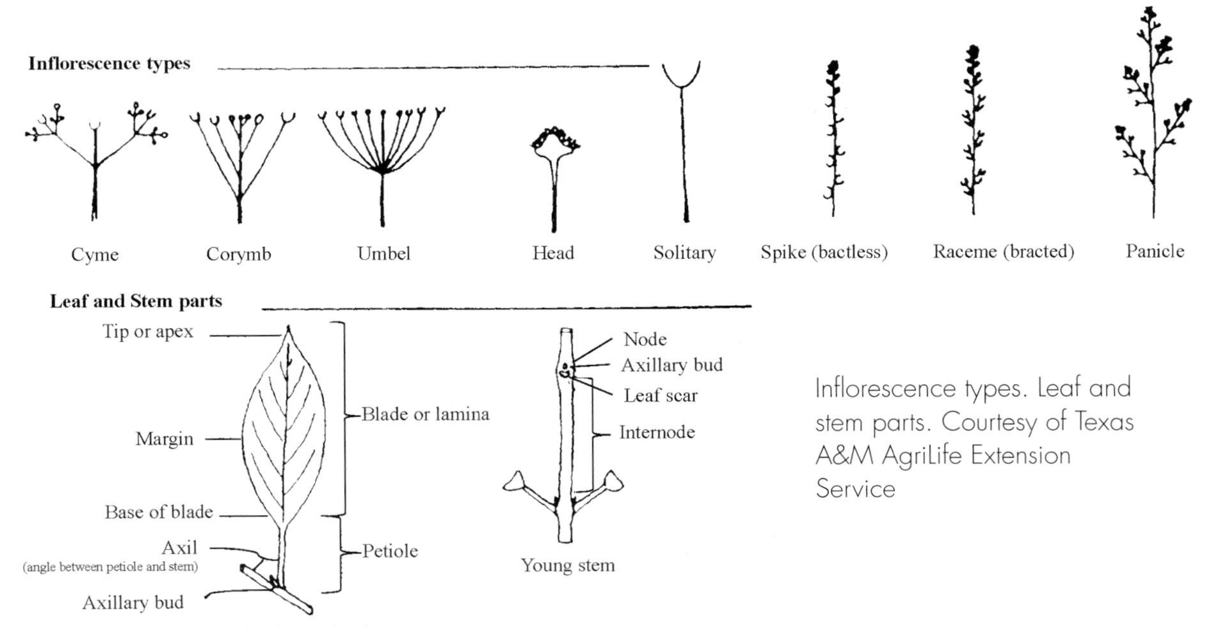

Inflorescence types. Leaf and stem parts. Courtesy of Texas A&M AgriLife Extension Service

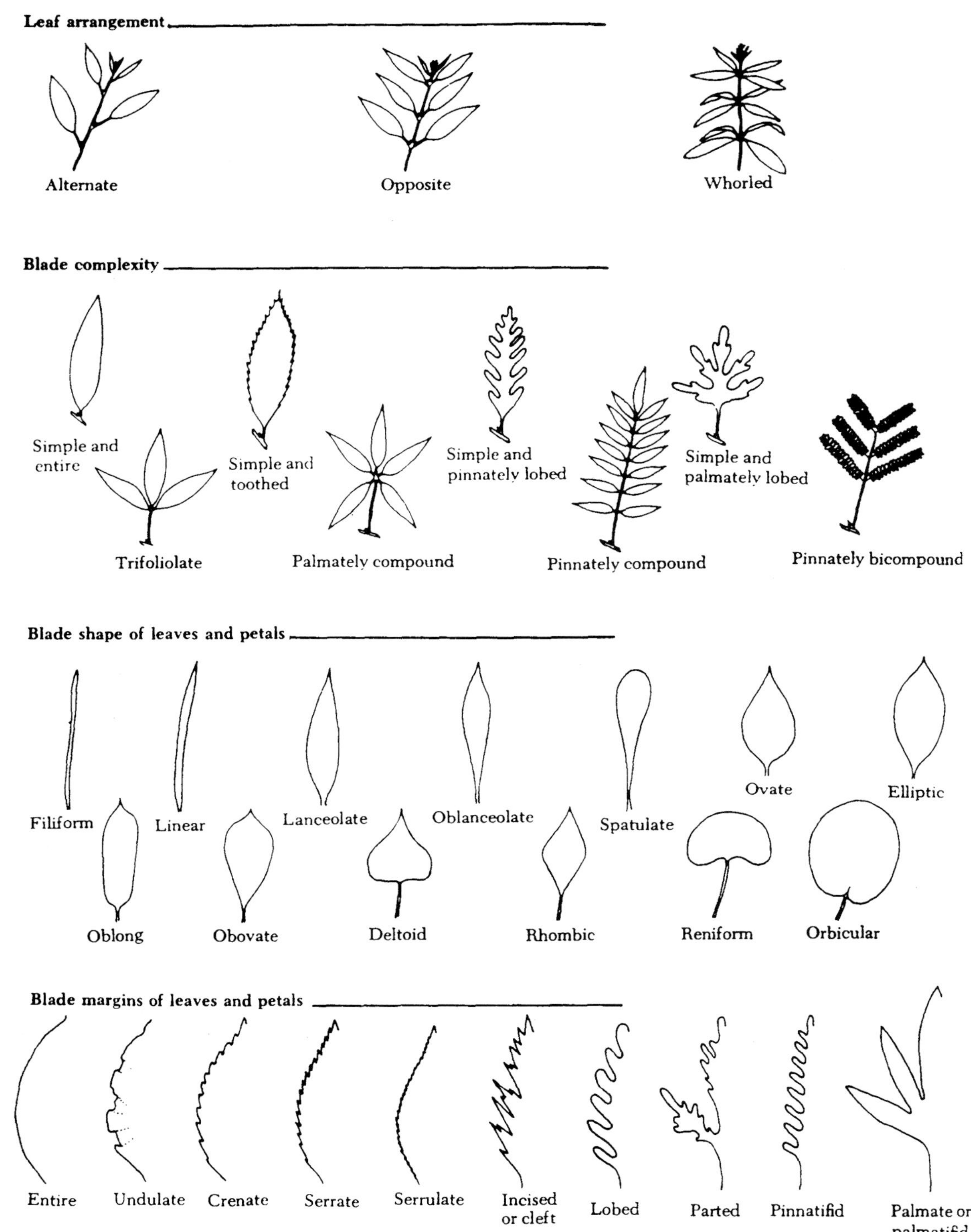

Leaf identification. Courtesy of Texas A&M AgriLife Extension Service

new leaves arise from buds at the nodes of the stems. Stems are classified as prostrate (spreading on the ground), erect, or climbing. Many species of forbs, such as the common dandelion, produce stems so short they are unnoticed. Such plants are called acaulescent or stemless. The flower stalk of a dandelion is not a stem but a scape that supports the flower.

Roots: Roots often are not fully appreciated by those who study plants. Roots are underground and go unnoticed, but they are as important as the showy aboveground parts. Roots make up more than 50% of a plant's dry weight. Carrots and turnips are specialized, enlarged fleshy roots that store large amounts of reserve food and water in their tissues. Some roots are fibrous, meaning they are made up of many long, slender, branched roots of the same diameter. This type of root system is typical of grasses. Most forbs have root systems that develop from a prominent structure called the primary root. Offshoots from the primary root are called secondary roots. If the primary root remains prominent during the growing season, as occurs in beets and carrots, it is known as a tap root.

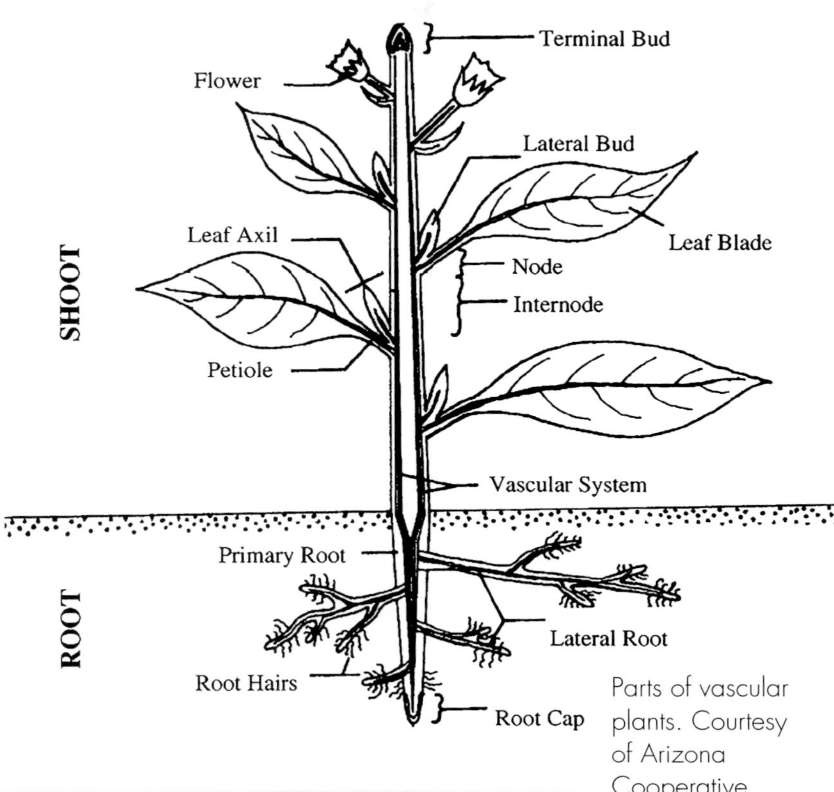

Parts of vascular plants. Courtesy of Arizona Cooperative Extension Service

Range Plant Classification by Season

Like other plants, range and pasture plants have different growing seasons. We can classify range plants into two main categories by growing season. Cool-season plants grow mainly during the cool weather of fall, winter, and spring. Examples of range and pasture cool-season plants include Texas wintergrass, rescuegrass, ryegrass, Canada wildrye, Texas bluebonnet, and Engelmann daisy. Warm-season plants grow mostly in the frost-free months of spring, summer, and fall. Examples of range and pasture warm-season plants include little bluestem, Kleingrass, sideoats grama, western

Little barley (*Hordeum pusillum*) is an example of a cool-season grass. Courtesy of Matt Lavin

Little bluestem (*Schizachyrium scoparium*) is a an example of a warm-season grass. Courtesy of the USDA-NRCS Plants Database

ragweed, bermudagrass, partridge pea, and silverleaf nightshade.

Evergreen plants have green leaf material in all seasons. Examples are live oak, junipers, yaupon, algerita, yucca, and ephedra. Deciduous plants lose their leaves in the fall and include honey mesquite, shinoak, flameleaf sumac, prickly ash, eastern persimmon, and pecan.

Classification by Life Cycle

Range and pasture plants live for different periods of time. An individual plant may live for one, two, or several years. **Annual** plants emerge, grow to their maximum size, reproduce, and die all in one growing season. These kinds of plants are propagated by seeds and live less than one year. Examples include common broomweed, giant ragweed, oldfield threeawn, bitter sneezeweed, Texas bluebonnet, and woolly croton or dove weed.

Biennial plants emerge, reproduce, and die over a two-year period. They emerge the first year but do not flower until the second year and then die. There are very few biennials of major importance on Texas rangelands and pastures. However, thistles are biennials and cover much of the state. Additionally, purple scabiosa, or pincushion, is another introduced biennial invading much of the area of the state north and east of Dallas to Kansas.

Perennial plants live more than two years, start from seed, or sprout back each year from rootstocks, crown buds, or branches. This type includes all trees, most shrubs, and plants such as sideoats grama, Mexican sagewort, yellow indiangrass, King Ranch bluestem, and trumpet creeper.

Classification by Succession and Climax

With respect to succession and climax, range plants normally fall into one of three categories: plants that decrease in abundance with grazing pressure (decreasers), plants that first increase in abundance when grazed and then decrease with continued grazing pressure (increasers), and plants that invade the range when the first two categories are removed by overgrazing (invaders).

Invasive and Nonendemic Plants

Livestock grazing has been one of the most important management tools for our natural grasslands and established pastures in Texas, but throughout time, a number of exotic, invasive plant species have gained a foothold on Texas grazing lands and all other associated landforms and riparian and aquatic systems. Much consideration is given to the impact of foreign and invasive plants. Are these plants detrimental to the natural system? Are naturally occurring processes negatively affected? Can society and humans survive in a human-created environment without the use of invasive plants? Can the goals and progress humans state as important be reached with invasive plants present?

The word *invasive* is usually defined as meaning "intrusive, invading, and offensive." To be invasive may imply that the organism has never occurred on a specific site or niche prior to its first introduction. Invasive plants are those that have a tendency to spread and invade healthy landscapes, ultimately causing some kind of negative impact. Invasive plants are often best defined as "plants that do not stay where they are planted." Invasive plants occur all over the state of Texas and today are recognized as a serious environmental threat. An "invasive species" is defined by Presidential Executive Order 13112 as a species that is (1) nonnative (or alien) to the ecosystem under consideration and (2) whose introduction causes or is likely to cause economic or environmental harm or harm to human health.

When we consider which plants are invasive, we think of plants such as honey mesquite, common broomweed, ragweed, huisache, dewberry, greenbriar, persimmon, and prickly pear. These plants will increase on the land and are looked at as pests that reduce livestock carrying capacity of the land and may contribute to economic decline of a farm or ranch. In reality they are plants that are native to Texas and are actually responding to human management and/or changes in the prevailing climate. Problems with these plants may be most adequately tackled by changing the land management that created a suitable environment or place for them to grow. From an ecological perspective, these native plants, often named "weeds" or "brush," are classified as "invaders." As part of the natural ecology and change in the landscape, however, they are supposed to be here, albeit not in the abundance we often observe.

Macartney rose (*Rosa bracteata*). Courtesy of the USDA-NRCS Plants Database

Invasive plants are those that are and have been introduced to Texas from foreign countries. Plants that have been moved from their native habitat to a new location (such as a different country) are typically referred to as "nonnative," "nonindigenous," "exotic," or "introduced" to the new environment. Exotic plants that are invasive plants in Texas include Chinese tallow tree, musk thistle, Macartney rose, Scotch thistle, yellow star thistle, Malta star thistle, blessed milk thistle, jointed goatgrass, Christ-thorn, camel thorn, Japanese honeysuckle, Japanese and Chinese privet, and Jerusalem cherry. (Only two of these are listed on the TDA Noxious Weeds list: Chinese tallow tree and musk thistle.) Although there are exceptions, these invasive plants thrive in disturbed niches and get a foothold on sites where naturally occurring processes have been weakened or eliminated.

"The invasion of noxious weeds has created a level of destruction to America's environment and economy that is matched only by the damage caused by floods, earthquakes, wildfire, hurricanes, and mudslides."
—Bruce Babbitt, former secretary of the Interior, 1998

Invasive species have been introduced into Texas in a variety of ways, but little is currently known about how most made their way into the state. Many times the knowledge of who brought the plant into the state or why is now lost and forgotten. Initially, these kinds of plants could have come from seeds stuck on the clothing of early pioneers; or they could have been contaminants in feedstuffs brought from Europe, Asia, or Africa. This type of introduction occurred long before we had USDA Animal Plant and Health Inspection Service ports of entry inspectors, the Texas Seed Trade Law, or the Federal Noxious Weed List, or even before there was any concern about what effect foreign plants could have in Texas. Many times, plants were introduced intentionally for beneficial purposes but later turned out to be invasive and did not stay where they were planted. Humans seldom knew the biology of an introduced plant, nor did they speculate on what the plant might do in the future or in the environment once established. Who would have guessed that Macartney rose from Japan, introduced in the 1850s as the "living fence," would now be a major invasive plant of pastures in the eastern half of Texas? Or that wonderful introduced livestock forage grass named "Johnsongrass" would cost Texas taxpayers $53 million in 1998 for chemical control on Texas roadsides alone? Or that King Ranch bluestem, a noted grass useful in the recovery and protection of played-out farmland, would be the number-one weed on roadsides in Central Texas today? It is estimated that 100 million acres in the United States are infested with invasive plants and that every year, the invasion accounts for an additional 3 million acres infested.

Humans consider that "the value of a plant is in the eye of the beholder." A potentially invasive plant such as Jerusalem cherry is pretty and a suitable potted plant or ornamental in the house or on the patio at Christmastime and during the winter months. What we fail to recognize is the "potential" for any exotic plant to be invasive if it is introduced to a suitable surrounding niche or environment. Those folks who thought the Jerusalem cherry plant growing in a nice clay pot was dead threw it over the backyard fence into another niche. They did not know that the seed in the mature fruit on the dead plant would germinate, create surviving and reproducing offspring, and cause a future invasion.

What Should Be Done with Invasive Plants in Texas?

To be successful in land management and to maintain a healthy functioning ecosystem in the twenty-first century, it is paramount that managers of Texas rangelands and pasturelands (both natural and modified or disturbed lands), parks, refuges, lands waiting to be developed, and urban complexes understand the impact of their decisions about what is planted on the land. Any new foreign or introduced plant must be heavily scrutinized for what it will do after planting and establishment. You must ask, "Will the plant stay where it is planted?" An introduced plant species might be useful in an agricultural or land restoration sense but could be devastating to the health and ecosystem functions of Texas natural lands or streams and rivers. What we do in land management and the impact of our decisions must also be considered in the light of the larger landscape or ecosystem. The hardest impact to predict is the influence of invasive plants on natural processes.

What Is the Impact of Invasive Plants in Texas?

One of the major problems with invasive plants in our established native pastures is that the landowner cannot identify a new species of plant when it shows up. If the landowner sees a new plant in a pasture and cannot name it, most often the plant is ignored. There is a certain amount of risk in ignoring the plant or believing that it is not a problem and will just go away. The decision to not seek out the name of the new plant can lead to future problems. It is only through the correct name of a plant that we can look it up in a book, talk to an authority, verify its value on the landscape, or seek methods of management that would control or eliminate the plant. Just one plant left to flower and set viable seed can lead to hundreds or thousands of plants present in a few short years. This is especially true for exotic thistles such as musk thistle, a native of Europe, which may have from 300 to 600 seeds per flowering head. We must also monitor roadsides and rights-of-way where any and every invasive plant can get started and survive. Once many of these plants set and shatter seed, the problem may not go away or be solved for years, as we have seen on continually disturbed soils. Several years of good seed production will lead to an abundance of seed in the soil bank. Plants such as distaff thistle, a native to Italy and the Mediterranean region, are noted to have viable seed in the soil for up to 19 years.

"If we do not permit the Earth to produce beauty and joy, it will in the end not produce food either"
—Joseph Woodkrutch, American naturalist

Most weedy species do not germinate all of the previous year's seed in one year, as do many of our domestic or row-crop species. This is a survival mechanism to spread the germination of seed out over a longer period of time. Even the native Texas bluebonnet will germinate only 10% to 15% of seed in any one year. Plants continue to come up for many seasons. Managers who begin to work on control of a new plant some years after the initial invasion may have to address a larger problem than when the plant first showed up. The management cost is increased, and the potential for further spread encouraged.

Each land manager or owner is the steward of the land managed, whether 1 acre or 50,000 acres. There is a certain amount of complacency that exists in Texas because land managers, owners, and lessees are working only with short-term goals, concerns for what can be gained today or the profit that can be made today. To maintain healthy Texas lands that will be productive for years to come, all land managers must assume the role of stewardship and not think that the next owner or manager can or will solve the problems that exist today. In many cases, it may be more expensive to solve today's problem tomorrow.

New and present owners are constantly seeking to find the magic plant that will solve all grazing problems, grow every day of the year, and produce premium cattle. Homeowners seek to find the most unusual and aesthetically pleasing plants for their landscapes, often trying to outdo their neighbors. This search reflects the fact that we still do not understand how to manage the plants that already occur on the land, or it is an excuse to hide the results of years and generations of mismanagement. For example, kudzu was introduced into the United States as a forage legume for cattle. Cattle were observed to eat the leguminous vines readily, and it was nutritious. But we had no expectation of how or what this foreign plant could do here. The vines ultimately grew up into trees and out of the reach of grazing cattle. The kudzu did not remain short, in the grazing profile, or where it was planted but has become the number-one exotic invasive plant of the Mississippi River watershed. Now it covers trees and invades the landscapes of many urban regions in the area. It is known to an invasive, serious pest, but now kudzu occurs in Tarrant, Grayson, Colorado, and several East Texas counties. Invasive plants like kudzu are not sterile and are not suitable forage alternatives when the negative impacts on the environment are reviewed. They produce viable seeds, and because they are not native and act like weeds, they can spread rapidly.

Kudzu (*Pueraria* spp.). Courtesy of US Fish and Wildlife Service

How Did Invasive Plants Get Here?

Many invasive plant species are introduced unintentionally. For example, during the drought of 1996, hay was bringing a premium price in the livestock industry. Many bales of hay were sold that contained just about anything that grew in the hay pasture or meadow. Goosegrass (*Eleusine indica*), an introduced annual grass with no forage value, occurred in some of these hay fields and was cut and baled. Unsuspecting buyers who just needed hay to get by bought the contaminated bales and introduced goosegrass as feed into their pastures that had large areas of open bare ground conducive for a new weed to survive. This grass helped fill the weed niche after the next rain but also lowered the grazing value of the pasture. It is advisable to know your hay producer and what is growing in his or her hay fields. Successful invasive plants have strategies for survival or self-preservation. Exotic invasive plants are also successful on Texas lands because the biological or ecological factors and mechanisms that kept these plants under control in their native land are not present in Texas (disease, insects, biological predators, exact nutrient requirements and soils, prevailing weather conditions, etc.).

Goosegrass (*Eleusine indica*). Courtesy of the USDA-NRCS Plants Database

Changes in landownership in Texas are now becoming a further problem with invasive plants. A plant once planted by a previous landowner may now be looked at by a new landowner as a problem. Some new landowners may not know the name of an introduced plant and think it is native and natural. The previous landowner may not have left records of what was planted on the land during the previous 50 years. Many times cultivars are hard to distinguish when they are all the same genus and species. Because a cultivar is named does not mean that a taxonomic difference exists between it and another named cultivar.

Cultivars are human-selected plants that have characteristics meeting a human vision or desired need. These characteristics include leaf length, time of flowering, size of seeds, temperature adaptability, time of maturation, period of green-up, and the growth cycle. Most exotic plant cultivars are not selected because they will not become invasive. Generally ease of establishment, fast growth, and ability to set a large amount of viable seed are desirable qualities. Just what an invasive plant needs to be successful!

Are Common Bermudagrass and Chinese Tallow Trees Invasive Plant Species?

Common bermudagrass (*Cynodon dactylon*) is one of the most successful invasive plants in Texas. In some situations it has great value to the landowner, such as in a lawn or grazing pasture. Common bermudagrass spreads through stolons, rhizomes, and production of viable seeds. Some landowners have tried to establish other grass species or cultivars only to end up with common bermudagrass because the seed of this grass is now in the soil over most of the state. In this situation, a valuable agricultural and landscaping grass can be considered an

Bermudagrass (*Cynodon dactylon*). Courtesy of Matt Lavin

invasive plant. Common bermudagrass, a warm-season perennial native to Africa, is a prolific seed producer. It is also a weed of ditches, vacant lots, roadsides, and gardens and grows along streams, lakes, and marshy swales. Is it of value in these situations or an invasive plant? The value is tied to the expectations that a person has for a given piece of land. Again, value is in the eye of the beholder. A safe exotic plant may be best described as one that has sterile flowers, produces no seed, has no means of vegetative reproduction, and stays where it is planted. But what if the soil is bulldozed and carried or transported to a new site with this plant growing in the soil? It is difficult to find an exotic plant or example where the potential for spreading would absolutely not occur.

Invasive plants can have a negative impact on Texas wildlife. Most invasive plants do not provide food or much value to native wildlife in Texas. Wildlife species are tied to a certain group of native plants that can serve as food, a source of water, and shelter. Most native plants are also associated with a native animal or group of animals as part of their natural ecology. The planting of many foreign plants or invasive plants in large landscape patches can further the current problems seen in Texas concerning wildlife and plant habitat fragmentation. Numerous examples abound. Some invasive species can threaten the existence of native plants and animals and may even serve to cause human-related problems. The Chinese tallow tree (*Triadica sebifera*), first introduced as an ornamental for landscaping, is now invading much of the area in Southeast Texas, from pastureland to vacant lots.

Tallow trees are changing the coastal grassland prairie into a wooded thicket of limited value. Although the leaves, flowers, and stems of this plant are not eaten by any known wildlife species, some individuals declare that the flowers are a valuable food source for bees. When this is examined further, we find that, yes; the introduced European honeybee visits the flowers of the Chinese tallow tree. It must be remembered, however, that the European honeybee was introduced into this hemisphere to pollinate most of the food plants brought from Europe and Asia. Remarkably, the only native plants of Texas available every day in our supermarkets to feed the human population are pecans and prickly pear pads in the form of nopalitos. Most other plants available for eating have been introduced.

Chinese tallow tree (*Triadica sebifera*). Courtesy of USDA-NRCS Plants Database

What Is Executive Order 13112?

Invasive plant species cause a combination of economic, environmental, and human health threats. Typically, studies that document the harm from invasive species conclude that the United States needs to strengthen its legal authorities and existing programs. Determining whether a nonnative plant is invasive requires a context-specific analysis. A plant species may cause harm in one type of ecosystem but not in others. Ecosystems are dynamic and ever changing, and their vulnerability changes over time as well. Therefore, it is practically impossible to create a definitive list of invasive plants. The benefits of introducing an invasive species must be weighed against the potential harm caused by that species. This is the focus of the new national invasive species management plan set forth in Executive Order 13112. The management plan is focused on those nonnative species that cause or may cause significant negative impacts and do not provide an equivalent benefit to society. To examine this document, finalized in 2001, visit http://www.invasivespeciesinfo.gov/laws/execorder.shtml.

Resources

Ajilvsgi, Geyata. 1984. *Wildflowers of Texas.* Bryan, TX: Shearer Publishing.

Barkley, T. M., ed. 1977. *Atlas of the Flora of the Great Plains.* Ames: Iowa State University Press.

Benson, Lyman. 1979. *Plant Classification.* 2nd ed. Lexington, MA: D. C. Heath.

Carr, William R. 2009. An Annotated List of Plant Taxa Endemic to the Lone Star State. Incomplete working draft. Nature Conservancy of Texas.

Chase, Agnes. 1922. *First Book of Grasses.* Rural Text-Book Series. New York: Macmillan.

Correll, D. S., and H. B. Correll. 1972. *Aquatic and Wetland Plants of the Southwestern United States.* Washington, DC: Environmental Protection Agency.

Correll, D. S., and M.C. Johnston. 1970. *Manual of the Vascular Plants of Texas.* Renner: Texas Research Foundation.

Cox, Paul W., and Patty Leslie. 1991. *Texas Trees: A Friendly Guide.* San Antonio: Corona Publishing.

Diggs, G. M., Jr., B. L. Lipscomb, and R. J. O'Kennon. 1999. *Shinners and Mahler's Illustrated Flora of North Central Texas.* Fort Worth: Botanical Research Institute of Texas.

Diggs, G. M., Jr., B. L. Lipscomb, M. D. Reed, and R. J. O'Kennon. 2006. *Illustrated Flora of East Texas.* Vol. 1, *Introduction, Pteridophytes, Gymnosperms, and Monocotyledons.* Fort Worth: Botanical Research Institute of Texas.

Dumroiese, R. K., ed. 2003. *Native Plants Materials Directory: 2003–2004.* Moscow: University of Idaho Press.

Enquist, Marshall. 1987. *Wildflowers of the Texas Hill Country.* Austin: Lone Star Botanical.

Fountain, M. S., L. C. Jones, and B. Cunningham. 2008. *Winter Key to Deciduous Plants of East Texas.* Nacogdoches, TX: Tree Book Publications & Posters.

Gandhi, K. N., and R. D. Thomas. 1989. Asteraceae of Louisiana. *Sida Miscellany* no. 4:1–202.

Gould, Frank W. 1975. *The Grasses of Texas.* College Station: Texas A&M University Press.

———. 1978. *Common Grasses of Texas*. College Station: Texas A&M University Press.

Gould, Frank W., and R. B. Shaw. 1983. *Grass Systematics*. 2nd ed. College Station: Texas A&M University Press.

Harper-Lore, B., and M. Wilson, eds. 2000. *Roadside Use of Native Plants: United States* [arranged alphabetically by state]. Washington, DC: Island Press.

Hart, Charles R., Tam Garland, A. Catherine Barr, Bruce B. Carpenter, and John C. Reagor. 2000. *Toxic Plants of Texas: Integrated Management Strategies to Prevent Livestock Losses*. Texas A&M AgriLife Extension Publication B-6105. College Station: Texas A&M University.

Hart, C. R., B. Rector, C. W. Hanselka, R. K. Lyons, and A. McGinty. 2008. *Brush & Weeds of Texas Rangelands*. College Station: Texas A&M AgriLife Extension.

Hatch, S. L., N. K. N. Gandi, and L. E. Brown. 1990. *Checklist of the Vascular Plants of Texas*. Texas Agricultural Experiment Station M-7–90. College Station: Texas A&M University.

Hatch, Stephan L., and Jennifer Pluhar. 1993. *Texas Range Plants*. College Station: Texas A&M University Press.

Haukos, D. A., and L. M. Smith. 1997. *Common Flora of the Playa Lakes*. Lubbock: Texas Tech University Press.

Hitchcock, A. S. 1951. *Manual of the Grasses of the United States*. Rev. Agnes Chase. Miscellaneous Publication 200. Washington, DC: United States Department of Agriculture.

Kingsbury, John M. 1964. *Poisonous Plants of the United States and Canada*. Englewood Cliffs, NJ: Prentice Hall.

Loughmiller, C., and L. Loughmiller. 2006. *Texas Wildflowers*. 2nd ed. Austin: University of Texas Press.

Metzler, S., and V. Metzler. 1992. *Texas Mushrooms*. Austin: University of Texas Press.

Miller, J. H. 2003. *Nonnative Invasive Plants of Southern Forests: A Field Guide to Identification and Control*. General Technical Report SRS-62. Asheville, NC: United States Department of Agriculture, Forest Service, Southern Experiment Station.

Miller, J. H., and K. V. Miller. 1999. *Forest Plants of the Southeast and Their Wildlife Uses*. Auburn, AL: Southern Weed Science Society.

Nebraska Department of Agriculture. 1979. *Nebraska Weeds*. Rev. ed. Lincoln: Nebraska Department of Agriculture Bureau of Plant Industry.

Niehaus, T. F., C. L. Ripper, and V. Savage. 1984. *A Field Guide to Southwestern and Texas Wildflowers*. Boston: Houghton Mifflin.

Nixon, E. S. 2010. *Gymnosperms of the United States and Canada*. Illus. B. Cunningham. Nacogdoches, TX: Tree Book Publications & Posters .

———. 2012. *Trees, Shrubs, & Woody Vines of East Texas*. 3rd ed. Illus. B. L. Cunningham. Nacogdoches, TX: Tree Book Publications & Posters.

Nixon, E. S., and J. G. Kell. 1993. *Ferns and Herbaceous Flowering Plants of East Texas*. Nacogdoches, TX: Self-published.

Nokes, J. 1986. *How to Grow Native Plants of Texas and the Southwest*. Austin: Texas Monthly Press.

Phillips, George R., Frank J. Gibbs, and Wilbur R. Mattoon. 1975. *Forest Trees of Oklahoma: How to Know Them*. Oklahoma State Board of Agriculture Forestry Division and USDA Forest Service Publication No. 1, rev. ed. No. 11.

Poole, J. M, W. R. Carr, D. M. Price, and J. R. Singhurst. 2007. *Rare Plants of Texas*. College Station: Texas A&M University.

Richardson, Alfred. 2002. *Wildflowers and Other Plants of Texas Beaches and Islands*. Austin: University of Texas Press.

Schmutz, Ervin M., and Lucretia Breazelae Hamilton. 1979. *Plants That Poison*. Flagstaff, AZ: Northland Press.

Shaw, R. B. 2012. *Guide to Texas Grasses*. College Station: Texas A&M University Press.

Shaw, R. B., B. S. Rector, and A. M. Dube. 2011. *Distribution of Texas Grasses*. Fort Worth: Botanical Research Institute of Texas.

Simpson, B. J. 1988. *A Field Guide to Texas Trees*. Austin: Texas Monthly Press.

Stein, J., D. Binion, and R. Acclavatti. 2003. *Field Guide to Native Oak Species of Eastern North America*. FHTET-2003–01. Morgantown, WV: US Department of Agriculture, Forest Service.

Stutzenbaker, C. D. 1999. *Aquatic and Wetland Plants of the Western Gulf Coast*. Austin: Texas Parks and Wildlife Press.

Texas Forest Service. 1963. *Forest Trees of Texas*. College Station: Texas Forest Service.

Texas Parks and Wildlife Department. 2004. Texas Natural Diversity Database. https://tpwd.texas.gov/huntwild/wild/wildlife_diversity/txndd/.

Tull, D. 1999. *Edible and Useful Plants of Texas and the Southwest*. Austin: University of Texas Press.

Tull, D., and G. O. Miller. 1991. *A Field Guide to Wildflowers, Trees, & Shrubs of Texas*. Houston: Gulf Publishing.

Turner, B. L., H. Nichols, G. Denny, and O. Doran. 2003. *Atlas of the Vascular Plants of Texas*. Vol. 1, *Dicots*. Vol. 2, *Ferns, Gymnosperms, Monocots*. Fort Worth: Botanical Research Institute of Texas Press.

Turner, M. W. 2009. *Remarkable Plants of Texas: Uncommon Accounts of Our Common Natives*. Austin: University of Texas Press.

USDA-NRCS. 2002. The Plants Database, Version 3.5. http://plants.usda.gov.

Vines, Robert A. 1960. *The Trees, Shrubs and Woody Vines of the Southwest*. Austin: University of Texas Press.

Warnock, Barton H. 1970. *Wildflowers of the Big Bend Country, Texas*. Alpine, TX: Sul Ross State University.

Weathers, Shirley A. 1998. *Field Guide to Plants Poisonous to Livestock*. Fruitland, UT: Western US Rosebud Press.

Weniger, D. 1984. *Cacti of Texas and Neighboring States*. Austin: University of Texas Press.

Western Society of Weed Science. 1992. *Weeds of the West*. Las Cruces, NM: Western Society of Weed Science.

Wilbur, Robert L. 1963. *The Leguminous Plants of North Carolina*. North Carolina Agricultural Experiment Station, Technical Bulletin No. 151.

Wills, Mary Motz. 1961. *Roadside Flowers of Texas*. Austin: University of Texas Press.

Weed and Invasive Plant Websites

Bureau of Land Management Invasives and Noxious Weeds: http://www.blm.gov/wo/st/en/prog/more/weeds.html

Federal Interagency Committee for the Management of Noxious and Exotic Weeds (FICMNEW): http://www.fs.fed.us/ficmnew/

Invaders Database System, University of Montana–Missoula: http://invader.dbs.umt.edu/

National Invasive Species Council, US Department of the Interior: http://www.invasivespecies.gov/

National Park Service, Weeds Gone Wild: http://www.nps.gov/plants/alien/

North American Invasive Species Management Association: http://www.naisma.org/

Texas A&M Forest Service: http://txforest service.tamu.edu

The Nature Conservancy, Global Invasive Species Team: http://tncinvasives.ucdavis.edu/

Trees of Texas: http://texastreeid.tamu.edu/

USDA-APHIS Weeds: http://www.aphis.usda.gov/wps/portal/aphis/home or http://www.aphis.usda.gov/plant_health/plant_pest_info/weeds/downloads/weedlist.pdf

USDA-ARS, Noxious Weeds in the US and Canada: http://invader.dbs.umt.edu/Noxious_Weeds/

USDA Introduced, Invasive, and Noxious Plants: https://plants.usda.gov/java/noxiousDriver

Weed Science Society of America: http://wssa.net/

Western Society of Weed Science: http://www.wsweedscience.org/

Plant Reference Websites

Aggie Horticulture: http://aggie-horticulture.tamu.edu/

International Oak Society: www.internationaloaksociety.org

Lady Bird Johnson Wildflower Center: www.wildflower.org [A searchable database of 7,000+ native plants by scientific or common name]

Native Plant Society of Texas: http://www.npsot.org

NatureServe Explorer: explorer.natureserve.org [A full vascular flora of the United States and Canada, including a searchable database for more than 70,000 plants, animals, and ecological communities]

Neil Sperry's Gardens: http://www.neilsperry.com

Texas Master Gardeners Association: www.txmg.org

Tree Care Industry Association: www.tcia.org

UNIT 12

Ornithology

CHARLES JACK RANDEL III
Texas A&M University

NOVA J. SILVY
Regents Professor, Texas A&M University

Editorial Assistance: Mark Lockwood, Texas Parks and Wildlife **and** **Mary Anne Weber,** Education Director, Houston Audubon Society

Unit Goals

After completing this unit, volunteers should be able to

- understand the causes for bird diversity
- understand and discuss the habits of bird migration
- identify the primary flyways of North America and Texas
- explain bird behavioral characteristics in relation to environments and environmental changes
- become aware of and communicate conservation concerns for birds
- identify and communicate how birds function within ecosystems
- develop an awareness of how bird populations are monitored and managed

"The woods would be silent if no birds sang there except those that sang best."
—Henry Van Dyke, American author, educator, and clergyman

Why Study the Natural History of Birds?

Throughout the course of history, birds have been a favorite natural wonder for humans. From many of the earliest civilizations such as Egypt and Rome, we have descriptions of birds, partly because of the ease with which they can be observed in a natural setting. Observation of birds has been used, for example, by sailors looking for land and American Indians locating the direction to water. Birds also have been used throughout history both as a means of obtaining food (falconry) and as a major food source (eggs, young, and adults). Birds have been sought out for their feathers to decorate costumes and headwear and as pets for their bright colorations, singing ability, and/or ability to mimic human speech. The most notable are the parrots, but other less known species of birds such as the Common Hill Myna (*Gracula religiosa*) of India and the Black-billed Magpie (*Pica hudsonia*) of North America are kept as pets. It is, however, illegal to keep native species as pets nowadays. In more recent times, humans have begun to use birdwatching and feeding as a leisure activity.

All common names of birds are capitalized by the standards set by the International Ornithological Committee (IOC). More information on this standard can be found at http://www.worldbirdnames.org/english-names/spelling-rules/capitalization/.

From singing in the early mornings and evening to nesting in the backyard, birds appear less concerned about human activity than some other groups of animals. With this in mind, it is not hard to understand why there are many books dedicated to the study of birds: field identification guides, photo journals, and works on the natural histories of a group such as hummingbirds. Guides and photo journals are made to

A Northern Cardinal (*Cardinalis cardinalis*) spotted in Washington County, Texas, shows leucistic traits with patches of white feathers. Courtesy of Dave Redden, Gideon Lincecum Chapter

enhance the enjoyment of people who enjoy viewing birds by actively searching them out on birding vacations or by just viewing them on a feeder from the kitchen window.

Natural histories give a more intimate look at the lives of birds and often include descriptions of nests, eggs, and preferred habitat types. This information provides a better understanding of each bird and its life requirements. Knowledge of migration patterns, breeding behavior, life span, and potential mortality factors aid in predicting year-to-year changes in population abundance. Declining bird abundance has led to recent concern in the United States for grassland birds such as the Dickcissel (*Spiza americana*) and Grasshopper Sparrow (*Ammodramus savannarum*). Texas in particular has several birds recognized by the US Fish and Wildlife Service as threatened or endangered, such as the Golden-cheeked Warbler (*Setophaga chrysoparia*), Black-capped Vireo (*Vireo atricapilla*), Whooping Crane (*Grus americana*), Attwater's Prairie Chicken (*Tympanuchus cupido attwaterii*), and the Lesser Prairie Chicken (*T. pallidicinctus*). With the understanding of the natural histories of these birds, changes in land management practices have greatly improved the chances of bringing these species back from the brink of extinction.

A pair of Whooping Cranes (*Grus americana*), including one that is wearing a tracking monitor, wade in the tidal marshes of Aransas National Wildlife Refuge, March 5, 2013. Courtesy of Peggy Romfh, Cradle of Texas Chapter

The continued study of the natural history of bird species will give greater insight into how anthropogenic changes affect birds. An important change is the increase in urban areas, which has caused dramatic changes in the populations of some bird species. White-winged Dove (*Zenadia asiatica*) formerly resided only in the southern portion of Texas; however, these birds can now be seen as far north as Oklahoma City. It is important to understand how the change in distribution is affecting other dove species (Mourning Dove, *Z. macroura*; and Inca Dove, *Columbina inca*) due to displacement and competition.

Diversity of Birds

Birds are an amazingly diverse group of animals. Worldwide, ornithologists estimate that there are nearly 10,000 species of birds. Birds (class Aves) are separated into 29 major taxonomic groups, or orders. The birds in each order are a lineage of related species. The diversity of birds reflects their evolutionary adaptation to a great variety of habitats and modes of life.

Birds occupy forests, fields, deserts, shorelines, and nearly every habitat in-between. A diversity of bill sizes and shapes, legs, feet, wings, modes of locomotion, diets, behaviors, and physiologies lend to the many ecological opportunities for birds. Due to its size, latitude (generally, locations closer to the tropics have greater species diversity), and varied habitats, Texas has a tremendous amount of avian diversity.

California is host to more species of birds—about 657—than any other state or province in North America. Texas follows in second place with 639, followed by Florida (516). Some species seen in Texas (e.g., Green Jay, *Cyanocorax yncas*; Plain Chachalaca, *Ortalis vetula*) cannot be found anywhere else in the United States. For these reasons, Texas attracts ornithologists and bird-watchers from across the nation.

To examine bird diversity, we can use a number of categories to group birds, for example, five categories based on their lifestyles and habitat:

1. Land birds (terrestrial species such as hawks, quail, woodpeckers, doves, and songbirds)
2. Freshwater species (e.g., some ducks, rail, and herons)
3. Seabirds (e.g., frigatebirds, boobies, pelicans)
4. Flightless land birds (e.g., ostrich and emus)
5. Underwater flyers (e.g., penguins, cormorants, and anhingas)

Or we can separate birds into 12 groups based on their body shape and lifestyle:

1. Long-legged waders (herons, egrets, storks, spoonbills, flamingos, bitterns, limpkins, ibises, cranes)
2. Ducklike (surface-feeding ducks, diving ducks, stiff-tailed ducks, mergansers, coots, whistling-ducks, geese, swans, pelicans, grebes, loons)
3. Perching (sparrows, kingfishers, cuckoos, bulbuls, crows, flycatchers, parrots, mockingbirds, blackbirds, ravens, starlings, jays, magpies, shrikes, buntings)
4. Fowl-like (chicken, turkey, rails, gallinules, jacanas)
5. Hawklike (hawks, kites, eagles, ospreys, harriers, caracaras, falcons, vultures)
6. Owls (true owls, barn owls)
7. Upland ground (woodcocks, quails, peacocks, partridges, pheasants, grouse, turkeys, roadrunners, chachalacas, nightjars)
8. Hummingbirds
9. Tree-clinging (woodpeckers, nuthatches, creepers)
10. Upright-perching waterbirds (auks, murres, puffins, cormorants, anhingas)
11. Gull-like (gulls, fulmars, shearwaters, albatrosses, terns, skimmers, gannets, boobies, storm-petrels, frigatebirds, skuas, jaegers, tropicbirds)
12. Pigeonlike (pigeons, doves)

Similarly, we can separate birds into categories based on their food habits. Birds

Mallards (*Anas platyrynchos*). Courtesy of Kayla Gasker, Alamo Area Chapter

Plain Chachalaca (*Ortalis vetula*). Courtesy of Texas Parks and Wildlife Department

Red-cockaded Woodpecker (*Picoides borealis*) in W G Jones State Forest near Conroe. Courtesy of Michael Long and Texas A&M Forest Service

can be plant eaters and eat flowers, pollen, and nectar. Other plant eaters feed on fruits and seeds, while others eat fibrous plant materials, including leaves and stems. Species that eat animals may be insectivorous, eating insects and/or small invertebrates. Animal eaters may also be strictly piscivorous and feed on fish, amphibians, and larger aquatic invertebrates. Some animal eaters are carnivorous and feed on warm-blooded prey. Birds can be either scavengers or omnivores. Within a taxa (order, family, or genus), however, food habits differ greatly. Although the previous two methods of separating groups of birds are artificial and not based on taxonomic relationships, they help us understand the diversity of birds and their habitats.

Why Do Different Birds Live in Different Places?

Birds occupy habitats that meet their needs for various resources—food, water, space, and nesting locations and materials. Generally, different birds match, or correspond to, different environments. They "fit" into a particular environment due to past conditions of the environment and the characteristics passed on through generations of that bird species. They inhabit environments having favorable conditions for life. For example, the Red-cockaded Woodpecker (*Picoides borealis*), an endangered species suffering from habitat loss, is dependent upon mature southern pine forests. These dwindling pine forests have the necessary resources for the woodpeckers: mature, live cavity trees for roosting and nesting, a suitable stand of pine trees with minimal hardwood midstory as a colony site, and adequate foraging trees.

Species select environments that meet their habitat requirements. Shorebirds such as American Avocets (*Recurvirostra americana*) are found along marshes and on flats or beaches of the Gulf where they forage for aquatic invertebrates. Swallows such as Purple Martins (*Progne subis*) spend large amounts of time in the open rural areas and savannas of Texas where they forage on insects. Purple Martins historically nested in cavities of hollow trees but today nest exclusively in human-made houses and gourds. They are the only bird in North America that wholly depends on human-made structures for nesting. The more commonly found structure is the condominium-type martin houses. The number of specific examples is nearly endless, as each species fits a particular portion or type of environment.

Migration

Although birds have specific adaptations for a particular environment, they also must tolerate the changes their environment experiences—seasonal changes, long-term directional changes, and erratic changes. More than any other group of animals, birds deal with seasonal changes of environments by extraordinary feats of long-distance migration. Migration is closely timed to the patterns of seasonal changes and is a yearly cycle. Birds migrate to escape unfavorable climates and exploit favorable conditions in other climates. Neotropical migrants nest (breed) in the temperate climates of Canada and the United States and migrate to Central and South America and the Caribbean during the winter.

Other species relocate to the Gulf Coast states of the southern United States. Flying south allows these birds to escape the physiological stresses of winter, taking advantage of better food supplies and the milder climate of the southern regions during winter

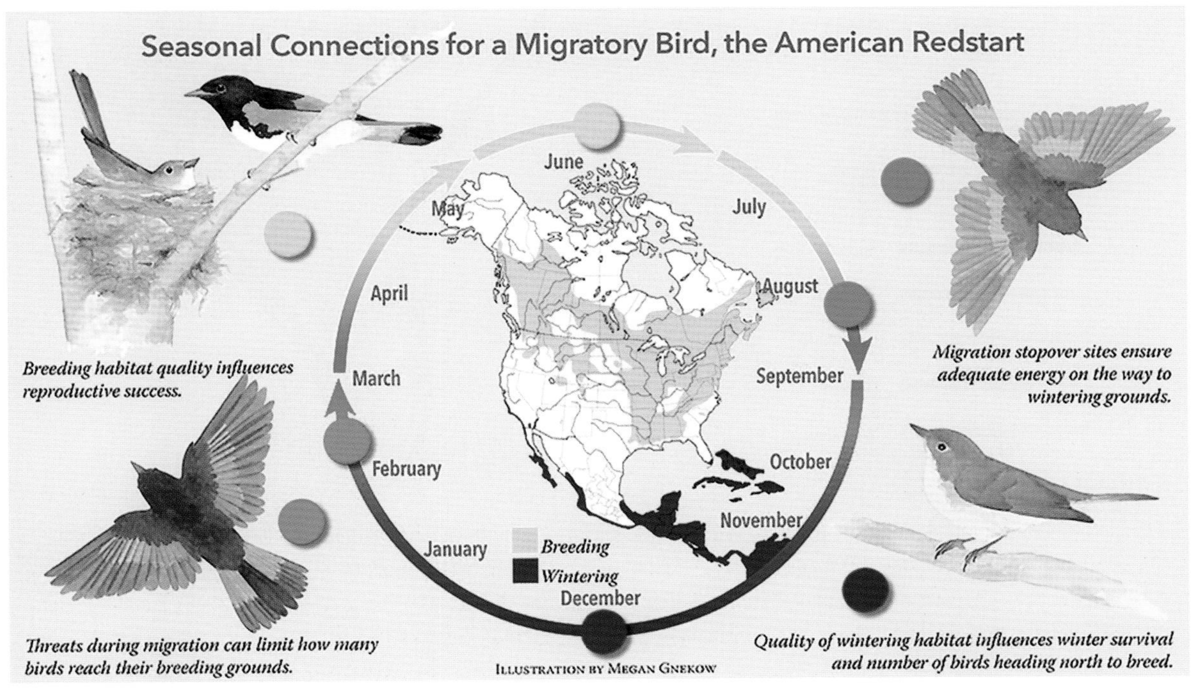

The migration cycle. Megan Gnekow © 2010 Cornell Laboratory of Ornithology

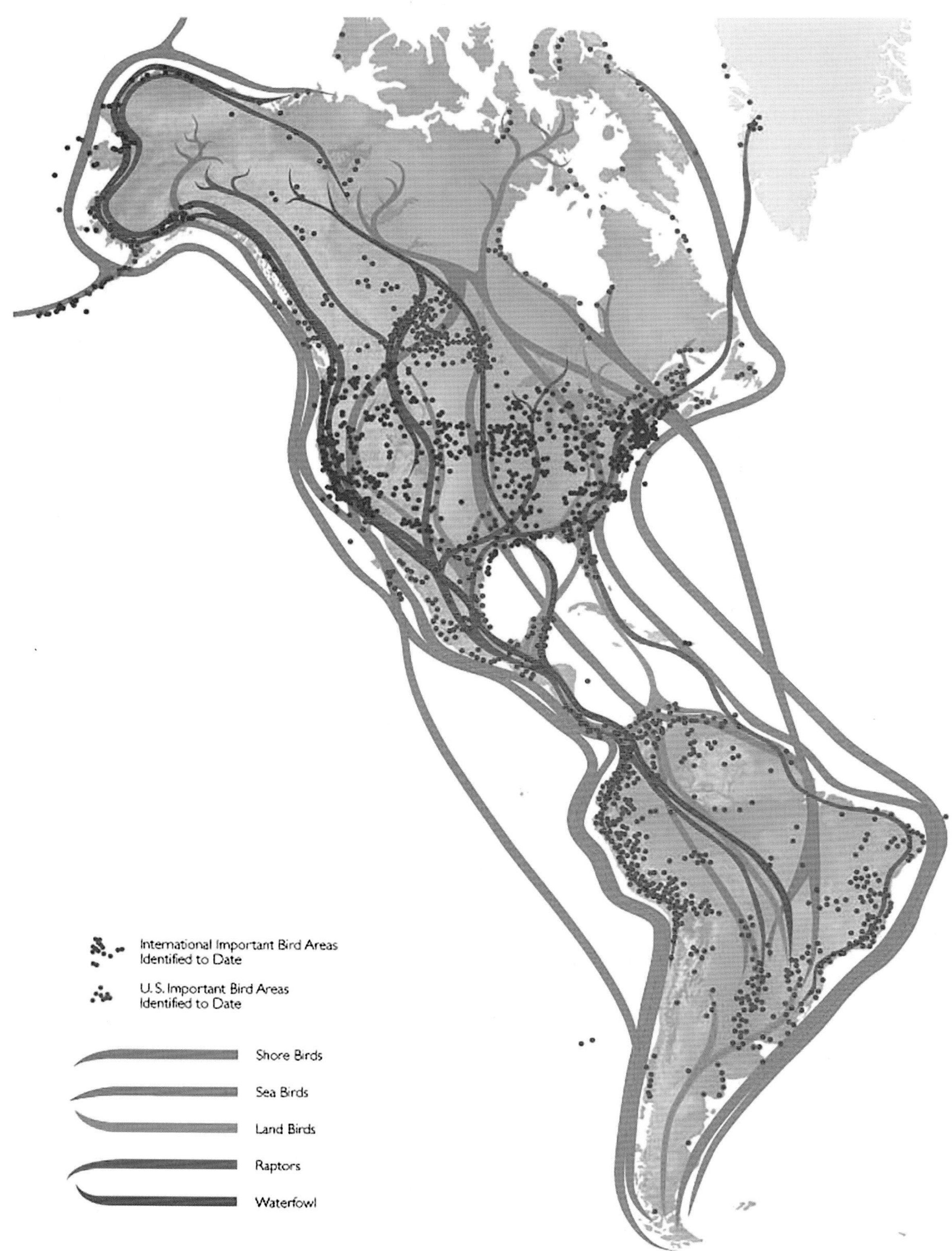

North American migration flyways. Courtesy of National Audubon Society

months. The migrants return north in the spring to exploit the productive temperate regions' abundant food supplies, longer daylight hours of the northern latitudes, and less competition for nesting space. Some migrants travel greater distances than others to reach their wintering or nesting grounds—from just a few miles to thousands of miles.

Most Texas birds are not year-round residents and are considered to be seasonal residents or passersby during migration. More than half of the birds recorded in Texas are migrants. This gives Texans the unique advantage of being situated in the path of two flyways, or principal routes used by North American birds—the **Mississippi Flyway** and the **Central Flyway**. Occasionally birds usually associated with the Atlantic Flyway or Pacific Flyway may get funneled down into Texas. This means that Texas is very important to the species migrating along these routes. Of the North American species listed as Neotropical migrants, 333 of the 338 are documented for Texas.

Texas provides important wintering habitat for migrants from the north, including loons, grebes, geese, ducks, shorebirds, gulls, and hawks, as well as thrushes, warblers, and sparrows. On the other hand, some species from the south find valuable summer nesting habitat in Texas, including some flycatchers, swallows, warblers, and orioles. These lists are in no way complete. Many other species are year-round residents or are seen during brief periods of the year when migration is in progress (late March to mid-May and September to November).

The upper Texas coast is critically important habitat for migrating birds. Birds use the uplands, wetlands, beaches, and marshes as feeding, resting, and nesting sites. The Houston Audubon Bolivar Flats Shorebird Sanctuary is a great spot for shorebird habitat. Sandpipers, plovers, terns, gulls, and herons populate the mudflats. Wintering flocks of American Avocets are an impressive sight, too. Aransas National Wildlife Refuge supports hundreds of thousands of migrating birds each year.

Other important locations include Houston Audubon High Island Bird Sanctuary, Anahuac National Wildlife Refuge, Attwater Prairie-Chicken National Wildlife Refuge, Brazoria National Wildlife Refuge, the Gulf Coast Bird Observatory Quintana Neotropical Bird Sanctuary, and state parks along the Gulf Coast. Some of the coastal areas are thought of as "migrant traps" that provide shelter for spring migrants following a "fallout" episode. When northward-migrating birds encounter spring storms or strong headwinds, they stop their migration abruptly at the shore and seek shelter in the Gulf mottes and woodlands, appearing to "fall out" of the sky.

How Do Birds Cope with Changes in Their Ecosystem?

Organisms operate in their environment under specific ecological constraints. Bird populations are limited by four factors: habitat, climate, food and water, and disease and parasites. Organisms, by nature, change the ecosystem in which they live. An ecosystem consists of both the physical environment and the biological communities. Organisms affect their ecosystem by altering conditions, adding or subtracting resources, and interacting with other individuals. The physical environment itself may change due to abiotic factors. For example, climatic variations may affect temperature and food availability. Within bird communities a number of species interactions are at work to establish community structure, including competition and predation. We will examine how birds deal with these and other "pressures" within their environment.

Competition

Competition occurs when the use or defense of a resource by one individual reduces its availability to other individuals.

This may be the single most important factor responsible for determining community structure. Competition can be acted out as aggression toward other individuals so that one individual or species is excluded, or more commonly as "exploitation competition" where one individual or species suffers from reduced resources.

Birds compete for a number of different resources, including food supplies, nest sites, nest materials, mates, and territories. The territories usually contain one or more of the other resources. To cope with competition for food supplies, some species participate in **resource partitioning**. Different species either feed in different parts of their shared habitat (as do many warblers having similar habitat preferences) or take food of different sizes. However, if individuals do not share overlapping resources, they **defend territories** as a strategy for reducing competition. Some types of territories are simple and defended for a single resource, such as the feeding territories of hummingbirds. However, many breeding territories include food, mates, and nest sites. Territory size depends on population density and the availability of resources. Territories can be very small, such as the nest and a small area around it in gull colonies, or quite extensive, such as the territories of Bald Eagles (*Haliaeetus leucocephalus*).

Competitive encounters elicit antagonistic behavior. However, most birds will go through much effort to avoid physical contact with another individual. The encounters involve displays of threat or submission. In defending territories, birds advertise their presence vocally.

"The proof of evolution lies in those adaptations that arise from improbable foundations."
—Steven J. Gould, American evolutionary biologist

Predation

Many strategies such as mobbing, calls and displays, flocking, selection for small clutches, and cavity and colonial nesting exist as strategies to deter predators. **Mobbing** is one of the most obvious displays of antipredator aggression. Small groups of songbirds can be seen chasing and calling around a hawk or owl. This behavior is most common around breeding grounds. The purpose of this behavior is to divert the predator away from nesting areas or simply to confuse the predator and urge it on its way. **Alarm calls** associated with mobbing function to alert other individuals of the same and other species of the presence of a predator. Other birds may join in the mobbing or are protected by being put on alert. Why the predators do not turn on the mobbing birds and attack is not known. It may be that these predators rely on surprise as an integral part of their hunting strategy.

Another conspicuous antipredator strategy is the exaggerated **injury display**. For example, instead of remaining quiet on the nest, an adult Killdeer (*Charadrius vociferus*) will feign a broken wing or tail while fluttering away from the nest with the intent of diverting the predator from the nest or young. Similarly, some birds will assume a "crouching" position and dart back and forth across the ground in a "rodent-run" maneuver to distract the predator.

Single species and multispecies **flocks** have distinct advantages when predators pose a threat. Birds in flocks can focus on feeding and relax. Because many individuals are present, flocks have better predator detection than individuals. Birds within a flock also communicate with each other. Alarm calls alert others and remove the possibility of a surprise attack by the predator. Large flocks also cause predator confusion upon flushing.

Another strategy to avoid predation is **cavity nesting**. One-half of all orders of birds build nests inside cavities or holes. Cavity nests are safer from predators than open nests or those constructed on the ground. Nest placement and construction are important, as predation is the greatest cause

An example of mobbing with a Northern Mockingbird agitated by a Swainson's Hawk. Courtesy of John English, Big Country Chapter, www.johnenglishphoto.com

of nesting failure by birds. Clutch size also seems to be related to the type of nest built by a particular species. Species that nest in holes or cavities tend to have a greater number of eggs per clutch. Some research has suggested that over time increased predation has selected for smaller clutch sizes. Birds that lay small clutches require less time for egg laying—a period when they are particularly vulnerable. Smaller

An adult Killdeer (*Charadrius vociferus*) on eggs placed in a gravel bar. Courtesy of Elisa Lewis, www.twoshutterbirds.com

A Northern Cardinal's (*Cardinalis cardinalis*) nest and eggs.

clutches are less noisy and conspicuous to predators. Also, laying a small clutch allows birds to risk fewer eggs at a time to predation and keeps available the possibility of renesting. Antipredator behavior associated with nesting includes the adults removing eggshells from the nest. Clean nests are less likely to attract predators.

Like birds in large flocks, **colonial nesting** birds have an advantage in predator detection. It appears that some birds form colonies in response to food sources, while other species are colonial nesters due to the predator protection afforded by the lifestyle. Yet some colonies expose the birds to an even greater predation risk. Colonial nesting is a widespread habit among the various taxonomic groups of birds. Seagulls, House Sparrows (*Passer domesticus*), penguins, and blackbirds participate in this behavior. Colonial nesters can detect predators more easily and can form larger mobs to threaten advancing predators. Predation is heavier on the nests at the outer edges of a colony than those on the interior. Usually, more experienced, older birds acquire central nesting sites. "Predator saturation" may occur with colonial breeders. Eggs and young birds represent a significant food resource to predators. When so many nestlings are available for such a brief time, predators may be unable to build their populations to a large enough size to completely benefit from this overwhelming food source.

Parasitism and Disease

Birds are host to a large variety of **parasites** and **microscopic pathogens** like bacteria and viruses. Common bird parasite residents include chewing lice that live on dandruff, blood, or other fluids; fleas; louse flies; relatives of bed bugs; ticks; and mites. Internal worms and flukes also are common. Although little is known about the impact of such organisms on most bird populations, ectoparasites (those living externally on a bird) can increase nestling mortality in birds living in large colonies. Such is the case with Cliff Swallow (*Petrochelidon pyrrhonota*) nestlings where bedbuglike parasites infest the nests and feed on fledglings.

To combat parasites and pathogens, some birds practice **nest sanitation** by removing fecal packets produced by nestlings. Other species carefully select nest materials that are known for their ability to inhibit bacteria and ectoparasites. For example, European Starlings (*Sturnus vulgaris*) select green plants, such as yarrow, as nest lining. The sprigs of green plants are added to the nest before hatching and continue to have fumigant effects. Starlings also remove fecal packets of their young, but only very early in the life of the nestlings. This species is particularly hardy and can withstand large populations of nest mites.

Some species reuse old nests, while others build new nests rather than risk the threat of parasites. In large colonies, where parasites are a greater problem than in small colonies, Cliff Swallows prefer to construct new nests. Swallows also may move the entire colony to a new site to escape the threat of parasites.

Birds that frequent backyard bird feeders may be susceptible to some diseases that are spread through shared food or by conditions that encourage disease (damp, contaminated food or fecal droppings). Four common diseases are salmonellosis, trichomoniasis, aspergillosis, and avian pox

Salmonellosis is caused by a group of bacteria that can spread throughout the body, causing abscesses that form on the lining of the esophagus as part of the infection process. The bacteria are passed from the infected bird through fecal droppings. This is a problem at bird feeders where droppings can easily contaminate food. Salmonellosis is seen more frequently than any other bird feeder disease.

Trichomoniasis comes from a group of protozoan parasites that afflict pigeons and doves. The Mourning Dove is very susceptible. Trichomoniasis typically causes sores in the mouth and throat. Unable to swallow, the bird drops the contaminated food or water, leaving it for other birds to consume, thus spreading the disease.

Aspergillosis is a fungus that grows on damp feed and in the debris beneath the feeder. The bird inhales the fungal spores, and the fungus spreads through the lungs and air sacs, causing pneumonia and bronchitis.

Avian pox is more noticeable than other diseases due to the wartlike growths on the featherless surfaces of a bird's face, wings, legs, and feet. Direct contact with infected birds spreads the virus. Shed viruses are picked up by healthy birds from food or feeders or by insects that mechanically carry the virus on their body.

Disease cannot be overlooked as a complication of backyard bird feeding. Sick birds are less alert and less active. They feed less

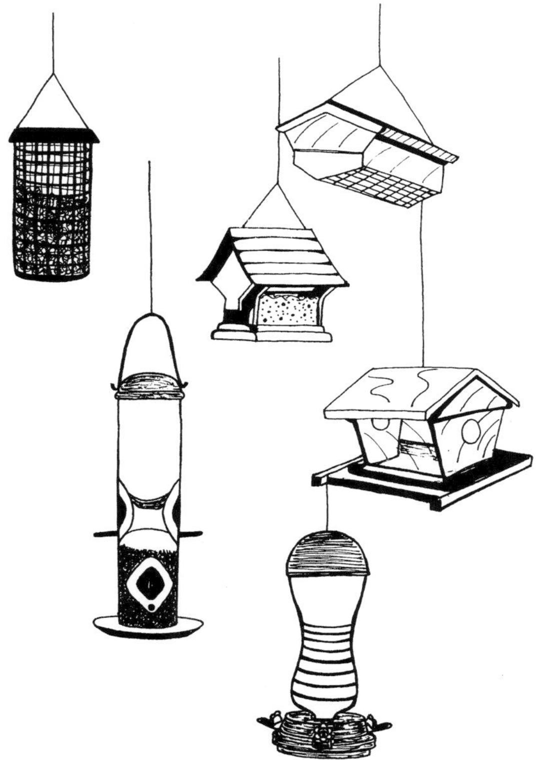

Keep your bird feeders and baths clean. Disinfect feeders by scrubbing with a weak bleach solution of ¼ cup bleach to 2 gallons of warm water every few weeks and more often in summer or rainy periods. Rinse and allow feeders to dry before refilling.

An avian pox outbreak was reported in Duval County, Texas, in 2000 and was seen on birds such as the Wild Turkey (*Meleagris gallopavo*). Courtesy of Jason Hardin, Texas Parks and Wildlife Department

and may cower on a feeder and be hesitant to fly. To reduce the risk of spreading disease at feeders, it is important to provide adequate space around feeders, clean waste and prevent contamination by droppings, clean the feeders regularly, and use fresh, dry stored food.

Habitat Alteration

Habitat alteration is currently one of the most contentious issues related to many bird species today. Declining numbers of many species of birds is due in part to the changes occurring in their given habitat, including loss of preferred nesting areas and decrease or increase in resources. Numerous alterations in habitat have negatively affected bird populations.

However, in the case of some species, changes in habitat have increased numbers. One example is the Lesser Snow Goose (*Chen caerulescens*), whose numbers have dramatically increased in the past 20 years. Even so, there is growing concern about how the species is affecting its own summer/breeding habitat and what effect this might be having on other species sharing the summer/breeding range.

An example of habitat fragmentation.

Habitat alteration is also being used in management practices to restore areas to what is thought to be historical habitat. This manipulation of habitat is an attempt to recovery many grassland birds, such as the reintroduction of fire into ecosystem management of grasslands. Prescribed fire removes invasive woody plant species such as Ashe juniper (cedar) in Central Texas and reduces the encroachment of McCartney rose in South Texas.

One habitat alteration that causes concern is urbanization. Increases in urban acreage have led to fragmented habitat, which in many cases is detrimental to bird populations. Many birds, including grassland and woodland species, need to have large, continuous tracts of land. Fragmentation of habitat leads to what is called edge effect. For some wildlife species, increased edge provides more accessibility to resources, but for birds these edges become predator corridors, which leads to increased mortality and in many cases decreased nest success, both of which affect the overall population numbers of birds.

"The major problems in the world today are the result of the difference between the way nature works and the way people think."
—Gregory Bateson, English anthropologist

Food Availability

A bird's food supply is not a constant, unchanging resource. Food supplies—whether plant or animal—change from season to season and year to year with changes in weather. Population size and the growth of a population are limited by the quantity and quality of available food. Abundant food supplies do not present a problem. However, birds may engage in particular behaviors to deal with food shortages or anticipated food shortages.

In preparation for winter, Acorn Woodpeckers (*Melanerpes formicivorus*) hoard food in granary trees. Acorns that are pounded into existing holes, or those chiseled out for this purpose, serve as emergency rations for winter. Granary trees are used year after year by these birds. Other birds also save food for later. The Loggerhead Shrike (*Lanius ludovicianus*), known for impaling prey on cactuses and barbed wire, will do the same to prey items intended for later meals. Birds in the families Sittidae, Paridae, and Corvidae commonly create seed caches. They take advantage of temporary food surpluses by accumulating "leftovers" for times of food shortage. Instead of gathering food, some species disperse in great numbers over long distances to escape widespread food shortage.

Species that defend territories for food resources may alter the territory size depending on food availability. In cases of food shortage or low-quality food, birds may expand their feeding territory. In species with extended family units, the birds may be engaged in cooperative feeding of the young when food is limited or of poor quality for a given season. If food is insufficient, parents may not be able to adequately nourish their chicks. The smallest chicks of a brood may starve when older, larger nest mates outcompete them for food.

Environmental conditions, like food supply, can affect the timing of reproduction in birds. When food is not adequate, females can delay egg production, thereby limiting clutch size. From a different perspective, however, evidence of abundant food very early in the spring can trigger early reproduction. Year-round availability of high-quality food allows many tropical species to engage in two breeding seasons annually.

Some species may take advantage of abundant food resources. Sufficient, predictable food supplies may cause individuals in some populations of a species, but not others, to mate with multiple females. Generally, food resources that are either clumped and/or defended in a territory lead to multiple mates.

Little Blue Heron (Egretta caerulea) with green treefrog (Hyla cinerea), Pilant Lake, Brazos Bend State Park. Courtesy of Chris Cunningham, www.twoshutterbirds.com

Temperature Changes

Birds are **endothermic**. They are able to maintain relatively high body temperatures throughout a wide range of air temperatures. This ability allows birds to inhabit environments with extremes in climate—tropics, temperate, and polar zones. Birds regulate their body temperature (**thermoregulation**) when ambient temperatures are outside their thermoneutral range—when temperatures are either too warm or too cool. Mechanisms must be in place to aid in heat loss, and birds must take in sufficient energy (food) for metabolic heat production. Birds use both behavioral and physiological means for thermoregulation.

Birds can be susceptible to heat stress. To facilitate heat loss, birds use panting and evaporative cooling. Sweat glands are not present in birds, so ridding the body of water by sweating is not an option. It is also likely the apteria (areas of the body from which feathers do not grow) and other unfeathered surfaces (legs) aid in heat loss.

Birds may engage in a variety of behaviors to stay warm. Many birds select microclimates that provide warmth or shelter

Two cold Inca Doves (*Columbina inca*) sitting on a pine tree branch. Courtesy of Texas Parks and Wildlife Department

from the elements. Some nest sites, holes, and burrows protect birds from the cooling effects of the wind. Small birds having a higher body surface area to mass ratio may be particularly vulnerable to heat loss and therefore seek protection. Other birds may seek the warmth and protection provided by other individuals. Northern Bobwhite (*Colinus virginianus*) are known to huddle together.

How Do Birds Function in Ecosystems?

Nothing in nature stands alone. Birds, like all other organisms, are connected in some way to individuals of the same and other species. The presence of a particular bird in an ecosystem will affect the diversity of the whole bird community—which other species can coexist in the same area. Birds affect the vegetation, the invertebrate populations, and the vertebrate populations of an ecosystem. On a smaller scale, organisms like fungi and microbes also are important to the ecosystem dynamics. Birds, due to their great diversity, have many roles within an ecosystem. They are foragers, predators, and prey. Additionally, they have evolved special relationships with other species. Some birds are plant pollinators, and some are hosts to parasites and brood parasites.

Predators

The role of birds as **predators** is one that helps keep populations of prey species from becoming too abundant. In an extreme case, overpopulation could cause starvation of the prey species. Predators also help improve the overall health of a species by removing sick, old, and injured animals from the population. By removing these individuals from the population, those that remain can more easily obtain resources that ensure the "most fit" prey animals are able to reproduce. Predators are a vital component of ecosystems.

Raptors, such as hawks, owls, and eagles,

American Kestrel (*Falco sparverius*). Courtesy of Texas Parks and Wildlife Department

An Osprey (*Pandion haliaetus*) with a fish in its talons is an example of a predator. Courtesy of John English, Big Country Chapter, www.johnenglishphoto.com

Wild Turkey (*Meleagris gallopavo*). Courtesy of Larry Brennan, Elm Fork Chapter

Eastern Blue Bird (*Sialia sialis*). Courtesy of John English, Big Country Chapter, www.johnenglishphoto.com

with their large talons and sharp beaks, are readily identified as predators. Raptors prey on many types of organisms, from insects (American Kestrel, *Falco sparverius*), to birds (Peregrine Falcon, *F. peregrinus*) and fish, (Osprey, *Pandion haliaetus*) to animals as large as pronghorn antelope (*Antilocapra americana*) fawns (Golden Eagle, *Aquila chrysaetos*). Several other bird predators are not as easily recognized, for example, the Common Merganser (*Mergus merganser*), which feeds on fish, and Black-chinned Hummingbird (*Archilochus alexandri*), which feeds insects to its young.

Prey

Prey species are those that serve as a food source for other species in a given ecosystem. Many species of birds are considered prey species, which may include having eggs taken and eaten from nests and adults serving as a food source for larger predators, such as reptiles, mammals, and other birds (Red-tailed Hawk, *Buteo jamaicensis*).

Most predation on birds occurs in the early stages of life as either an egg or nestling. Humans seek out some of the better-known adult prey species as a food source. Collectively known as game birds, this group includes but is not limited to Ring-necked Pheasant (*Phasianus colchicus*), Mourning Dove, Northern Bobwhite, and Wild Turkey (*Meleagris gallopavo*).

A female Lucifer Hummingbird (*Calothorax lucifer*) feeding off an agave flower in Chisos Mountains, Big Bend National Park. Courtesy of Cynthia McKaughan

Seed Dispersal

Birds also function in the role of **seed dispersers** at all levels of the ecosystem. Generally birds that have thick bills, such as finches, grosbeaks, and sparrows, specifically exploit seeds as a food source. Most cannot process all the seeds consumed and pass them out their system, often within sight of the plant they consumed, but just as often several hundred miles away during migration. Some corvids, such as Blue Jays (*Cyanocitta cristata*) and Pinyon Jays (*Gymnorhinus cyanocephalus*), actually store seeds in the ground for a winter food source. Even with exceptional spatial memories, birds, like squirrels, cannot consume all of the seeds that they store over the course of the winter; thus, they unknowingly plant seeds from multiple plant species.

Pollinators

The role of birds as **pollinators** in an ecosystem has been well documented. Hummingbirds and orioles both rely on nectar as a primary food source. While feeding, they collect pollen on their heads or backs and disperse this to other flowers. This exchange of pollen ensures that plants produce viable offspring, which includes fruits, nuts, and seeds. All of these plant offspring are then used by other organisms, including birds, as a food source later in the year.

How Are Birds Monitored?

Birds are most often monitored through survey methods such as point counts, transects, and observation, each of which can be easily conducted.

Point Counts

Point counts are conducted from a set of predetermined points by a surveyor. While at these points, the surveyor counts the number of birds of each species observed and heard within a given area. These counts are then used to determine which species are present and within what types of habitats the birds are found. Point counts also are used to determine population trends and local bird densities of the survey area. Many point counts are conducted on an annual basis to better understand how bird numbers and diversity change on a year-to-year basis.

Transects

Transects are used to count the number of birds and number of bird species along a survey line. Transects are generally linear with set limits on the distance for which birds are to be counted. Dimensions of a transect are set prior to conducting the survey. Length can range from under 100 yards to several miles; the width also varies but is generally from 15 to 20 meters on either side of the center line of a transect. How the birds are counted depends on the goal of the person conducting the census. If the goal is to determine which species are present in the area, both songs and visual identification count toward the number of bird species on that particular line. Some transects are used to count only those birds that appear to be using the particular habitat and may count only the number of visually identified birds within the set boundaries that are performing activities such as perching and feeding.

Some transects are conducted annually to see if there are fluctuations in the number of birds and bird species from year to year. This method is commonly employed in areas where there is concern about specific bird species. Transects are also used by the Texas Parks and Wildlife Department to estimate concentrations of game species (Northern Bobwhite and Mourning Dove) to help set hunting limits and compare data from year to year.

A male Northern Bobwhite Quail (*Colinus virginianus*) perched on a mesquite calling perch. Photo Courtesy of Becky Ruzicka, Texas A&M AgriLife Extension Service

The Scissor-tailed Flycatcher (*Tyrannus forficatus*) is a summer herald migrating through Texas each year. This one was found in McMullen County. Courtesy of Clinton J. Faas, cjfaas@gmail.com

"Living wild species are like a library of books still unread. Our heedless destruction of them is akin to burning the library without ever having read its books."
—Representative John Dingell of Michigan

Rare-Bird Reports

Rare-bird reports are used to document the occurrence of birds outside what is thought to be their accepted range. Details of rare-bird sightings are often requested by local Audubon societies or more formally by the Texas Bird Records Committee to collect data about the occurrence of the species in the local area or state and to archive documentation of their occurrence. After a rare-bird sighting, many people, anxious to add a particular bird to their life list, will drive several hundred miles for a chance to see the bird.

Public Involvement

Several other survey methods are conducted annually throughout the United States: for example, the Audubon Society's Christmas Bird Count, the Breeding Bird Survey, and the Great Backyard Bird Count. All of these surveys rely on the participation of the general public and would make a great Master Naturalist volunteer project. Volunteers are asked to survey birds in their area and note the number of species and individuals of each species observed in a given time period or along a given route. These surveys monitor population trends of bird species at a given time of the year to determine if bird species are increasing or declining over time.

Resources

Books

Arnold, K. A., and G. Kennedy. 2007. *Birds of Texas*. Auburn, WA: Lone Pine Publishing International.

Baicich, P. J., and C. J. O. Harrison. 2005. *Nests, Eggs, and Nestlings of North American Birds*. 2nd ed. Princeton, NJ: Princeton University Press.

Benson, K. L. P., and K. A. Arnold. 2001. *The Texas Breeding Bird Atlas*. College Station and Corpus Christi: Texas A&M University System. http://txtbba.tamu.edu/.

Elbrock, M., E. Marks, and C. D. Boretos. 2001. *Bird Tracks & Sign: A Guide to North American Species*. Mechanicsburg, PA: Stackpole Books.

Lockwood, M. W., and B. Freeman. 2014. *The Texas Ornithological Society Handbook of Texas Birds*. 2nd ed. College Station: Texas A&M University Press.

Scott, S. D., and C. McFarland. 2010. *Bird Feathers: A Guide to North American Species*. Mechanicsburg, PA: Stackpole Books.

Travis, N. T., K. A. Arnold, and C. R. Smith. 1997. *Birds of Texas*. 4 vols. Austin: Texas System of Natural Laboratories.

Websites

All about Birds: www.allaboutbirds.org [an online bird guide with over 596 native North American bird species indexed, including bird and nest cams, educational materials, and bird-watching information]

American Birding Association: http://aba.org/

Birds of the Upper Texas Coast: http://www.texasbirding.net/ [offers numerous links to birding-interest websites throughout Texas, North America, and abroad]

Cornell Lab of Ornithology: http://www.birds.cornell.edu/

Houston Audubon Society: www.houstonaudubon.org [an educational and conversation group very active in the eastern parts of the state]

National Audubon Society: http://www.audubon.org/

Texas Parks and Wildlife Department: http://tpwd.texas.gov/state-parks/parks/things-to-do/birding-in-state-parks [information and check lists, habitat projects, birding activities and programs]

Professional Ornithological Societies

American Ornithologists Union and Cooper Ornithological Society: http://www.aou.org/

Association of Field Ornithologists: http://www.afonet.org/index.html

Raptor Research Project: www.raptorresource.org

Texas Ornithological Society: www.texasbirds.org

Wilson Ornithological Society: www.wilsonsociety.org

UNIT 13

Entomology

WILLIAM GODWIN
Adjunct Professor of Biology,
Jarvis Christian College

CHARLES ALLEN
Extension Entomology Program Leader,
Texas A&M Agrilife Extension Service

MOLLY KECK
Extension Entomologist,
Texas A&M Agrilife Extension Service

WIZZIE BROWN
Extension Entomologist,
Texas A&M Agrilife Extension Service

MIKE MERCHANT
Extension Entomologist,
Texas A&M Agrilife Extension Service

BRYANT MCDOWELL
Entomology Intern,
Texas A&M Agrilife Extension Service

Unit Goals

After completing this unit, volunteers should be able to

- demonstrate an appreciation for insects and an interest in entomology
- discuss why insects are so biologically diverse, why this diversity is threatened, and why the conservation of insect biodiversity is important
- understand the systematic relationships among various insect groups
- discuss basic principles of insect behavior and ecology and relate these to environmental adaptations
- understand the role that insects play in local ecosystems and various other ecosystems in Texas
- demonstrate knowledge of methods for collecting insects
- demonstrate familiarity with the insect fauna of Texas

"We should preserve every scrap of biodiversity as priceless while we learn to use it and come to understand what it means to humanity."
—E. O. Wilson

Introduction

Insects make up about 80% of the world's described animal species and are believed to compose a biomass larger than that of any other group of terrestrial animals. There are about 1 million described species, but estimates suggest the total number of insect species is 2.5 million to 10 million. Insects continually demonstrate their capacity to adapt and survive. In this unit you will receive a brief introduction to the incredibly broad subject of entomology. From an anthropocentric point of view, some insects are pests of our food, homes, and landscapes; some bite or sting; and some transmit human diseases. Many have beneficial functions such as pollination, production of food or fiber, and recycling of dead organic matter. But the majority of insects have no impact on the human population (other than stirring intellectual curiosity). Here we provide a starting point, some principles, a few basic techniques, and hopefully inspiration.

This unit of the curriculum is broad by necessity. It seeks to relate insects to the nat-

A dragonfly (Odonata: Aeshnidae). Courtesy of Texas Parks and Wildlife Department

ural history of all regions of Texas. It is meant to be used statewide, and this may seem to be a hindrance to your progress. If you can reasonably expect to find 5,000 insect species in your closest natural area, then how can you afford the brainpower to learn about other areas? But remember, knowing the names of insects does not make you a naturalist. A Master Naturalist is able to make connections. Many times a little knowledge about some other region will trigger you to connect things going on at home.

"The last word in ignorance is the man who says of an animal or plant: What good is it? . . . If biotic, in the course of aeons has built something that we like but do not understand, then who but a fool would discard seemingly useless parts? To keep every cog and wheel is the first precaution of intelligent tinkering."
—Aldo Leopold

For example, you may read about some arachnid typical of the western deserts like solfugids (sunspiders or windscorpions). If you live in the eastern forests, you could think to yourself that they are more important to others than to you. You might find yourself wishing that you had a naturalist book exclusively devoted to your area. However, it is possible to think about this in another way; if solfugids are common in the western deserts, they will be of less concern to easterners. When you find them in the farkleberry barrens of the Big Thicket, you should be surprised. Environments undergo change over time. The distribution and biology of organisms can also change in response to the changing environment. Knowledge of other regions will equip you to know what is remarkable in your own and allow you to make connections.

What Is Entomology?

Entomology is both a basic and an applied science that deals with the study of insects and their relatives. Entomologists are at the cutting edge of scientific research in such areas as biotechnology, systematics, genetics, molecular biology, physiology, biological control, and integrated pest management. Applied entomology develops and transfers knowledge to those who use it to benefit society (protecting food, homes, and human health). Employers include universities, government agencies, and private industry. There are ample opportunities to work with people.

Because of its diversity, entomology provides many choices and opportunities for those interested in nature and sciences. Some entomologists work in the field, others work in the laboratory or classroom, and still others find a niche in regulatory entomology or international activities. If you are interested in genetics, molecular biology, or biotechnology, you can learn to apply modern tools and experimental methods in the study of insect diversity and the improvement of plant and animal resistance to insect attack. If you enjoy chemistry or physiology, you can conduct research on insect development, behavior, or reproduction. If you like to work with computers, you can develop software to aid farmers, foresters, and others predicting and managing pest outbreaks.

Edward S. Ross's Brief Entomological Explorations in Texas

Progress in the study of Texas natural history was fairly well derailed by events of World War II. The staff of colleges and museums shrank to skeleton crews as people were called away. Everything from paper to tires, ink, and gasoline became scarce. One sidelight though, was the arrival of a young army lieutenant from California, Edward S. Ross.

While war was breaking out around the world in 1939 and 1940, Ross was occupied in studies at Berkeley and the California Academy of Sciences (CAS). He had been interested in the insects associated with animal burrows since high school and had described a new genus of histerid beetle found only in the burrows of kangaroo rats. While working at the CAS, Ross described several more new species of histerids that had been collected by C. C. Goff in the burrows of Florida pocket gophers. Goff had died early in 1939, leaving a mass of unpublished data and undescribed species. Young Ross was called on to help complete Goff 's work. On the day following the Japanese attack on Pearl Harbor, Ross applied for a commission as entomologist in the Army Sanitary Corps. His first assignment was with the 8th Service Command Medical Laboratory at Fort Sam Houston in San Antonio.

Ross came to Texas aware of the remarkable discoveries that Goff and others had made in the burrows of Florida pocket gophers. He also knew that Texas had several other species of pocket gophers whose burrows had never been investigated. Ross was about to be the first to do so. While stationed at Fort Sam Houston, Ross had his own car, which allowed him to devote time off to exploring his new local environment. Soon he became acquainted with Ellen Quillen, who had been the museum director at San Antonio's Witte Museum for fifteen years. Quillen's greatest contribution to Texas natural history had been convincing Alfred Witte to fund the establishment of a museum at Brackenridge Park in 1926. She was very much interested in botany and knew that pocket gophers were abundant in the sandy hills south of San Antonio.

Quillen introduced Ross to A. J. Kirn of Somerset, Texas. Kirn's amateur studies of nature were made possible by the revenues from several small oil wells on his land in the sandy outcrop of the Carrizo Formation. In the winter of 1942–43 Kirn and Ross set about trapping gophers and placing subterranean pitfall traps in the vacated burrows. They also excavated burrows to reach the insect inhabitants of nest and storage chambers. Many times their excavations extended six feet square and four feet deep. Occasionally they were assisted by another army lieutenant named H. Radcliffe Roberts, who later became director of Philadelphia's Academy of Sciences.

These pioneer studies by Ross and Kirn resulted in the description of one new histerid beetle, named *Onthophilus kirni* in honor of Kirn. They also found another histerid named *Spilodiscus gloveri*, which had been described in 1870 from a single specimen collected at Fort Cobb, Indian Territory. Ross and Kirn collected several specimens of *S. gloveri* and finally pinned down its specific habitat 73 years after its discovery. O. L. Cartwright described six new species of scarab beetles from the Ross/Kirn collections in 1944. One of these was named *Aphodius rossi* in honor of its collector. Many other arthropods were collected and sent to specialists.

Before leaving for service in New Guinea and the Philippines, Lieutenant Ross concluded his 1944 paper "Arthropod Collecting in the Burrows of a Texas Pocket Gopher" by encouraging entomologists everywhere to excavate animal burrows of all kinds in search of exciting and rare discoveries. Such discoveries are ongoing nearly 60 years later. Many kinds of burrows are still unexplored, and new species await discovery. So now if you run across *A. rossi* or *O. kirni* in your Texas beetle collecting, they will hopefully be more than obscure scientific names and you will notice that a little study can make you aware of the exciting stories that lie behind many of the scientific names that fill insect catalogs.

Why Study Insects?

Pioneer entomologists in the eighteenth century would have been relatively confident that many of the insects they discovered were unknown to science at the time. For example, the beetles discovered by Thomas Say in the Great Plains during 1823 were probably previously undiscovered. Today, and for many decades past, that conclusion has been exclusively the privilege of specialists with years of training and access to collections and rare papers. This condition has been a growing impediment to the contribution of amateurs. Often, it takes years of study to reach a point where you can recognize new discoveries. Simply identifying an insect to family level (let alone genus and species) requires experience and good dichotomous keys to the group you are studying. How could you ever get the critical mass of knowledge necessary to know that some fact is new or to begin to relate things? Birds are much friendlier in this respect, given that one may see only just over 600 bird species in Texas. With checklists and identification guides you can quickly reach the point of recognizing a rare bird or even a new state record. Insects can be more difficult to discover because their numbers are so immense and they are not always readily visible to the eye.

A zebra longwing (*Heliconius chorithonia*). Courtesy of Texas Parks and Wildlife Department

A major trend in biology is emerging, which is making information about what is known more readily available than ever before. This trend is called bioinformatics. It will allow people to develop a level of expertise in some aspect of natural history that was attainable only with some difficulty in the past.

Being able to determine new information is what makes an expert. As you read this, data from specimens in insect collections across the country are being entered into databases that are available online. Some automatically generate distribution maps with county records and regional checklists. Identification guides with keys and pictures are more accessible than ever. In recent years, the tide of information has turned dramatically, making scientific information available to more than just the academic community.

If you like insects, from dragonflies to dung beetles to ants, you can use the Internet to find lists of the species known from Texas. You can also locate high-quality pictures of identified specimens and county-level distribution maps. You can collect your own specimens and more rapidly than ever make lists for your own area and identify new county or even state records. You may want to e-mail the professionals who often do not have the time to go out and collect the most basic information on behavior, life cycles, or distribution. They will be happy to hear your news. If enough naturalists recognize this opportunity, it will be the beginning of a renaissance of the contributing amateur entomologist. When you are able to sit at your home computer and see that the dragonfly you caught over your cattle tank is not pictured in the list of Texas species, then a simple and powerful change will have occurred.

An insect fossil (Palaeodictyoptera: Spilapteridae) from the upper Carboniferous period to Permian period in Kansas.

What Is Diversity?

The word *diversity* is used a lot these days. What does it mean? It may refer to the number of different taxa (species, genera, families, etc.). It may refer to diversity of form or the variety of habitats and foods utilized. Some may have used it to refer to large numbers of individuals, though this seems like an entomological stretch. Usually when diversity is referenced, what is really being discussed is richness. Diversity in an ecological context has two components—richness and evenness. There is far more to the concept of biodiversity than just short species lists versus long species lists. But to avoid getting into a discussion of theoretical ecology, we may just say that insects are diverse in all the possible meanings of the word.

Insects are the most speciose group of organisms. Four out of five animals are insects. Their physical forms vary from primitive generalist morphologies that have not appreciably changed for millions of years, to specialized parasites and casts in social species. They are found in almost every nonpolar terrestrial and freshwater habitat. Some water striders or gerrids even inhabit the ocean surface.

There is an insect adapted to feed upon almost every natural concentration of organic matter, including horns, hair , dung, fungus, carrion, petroleum, wood, blood, pollen, nectar, bones, seeds, and even wax.

Insect species richness can be attributed to many qualities. These include their ancient origin, high rate of reproduction, ability to adapt to change, powers of chemical adaptation, small size, powers of dispersal, ability to aestivate or diapause, and metamorphosis.

Ancient Origin

The earliest fossils of insects are from the Devonian period. They have been around for perhaps 400 million years. They have survived many of the major extinction events of the past but not without some changes. The extinction event at the end of the Permian period, about 250 million years ago, was the end for many ancient orders. The rise of flowering plants during the Cretaceous period undoubtedly influenced the rise of many groups.

Rate of Reproduction

Ecologists have described two strategies for reproduction: R-strategy and K-strategy. **K-strategists** produce very few young but invest a large amount of time and care in them. Humans are an example of K-strategists. **R-strategists** produce a large

K-strategist.

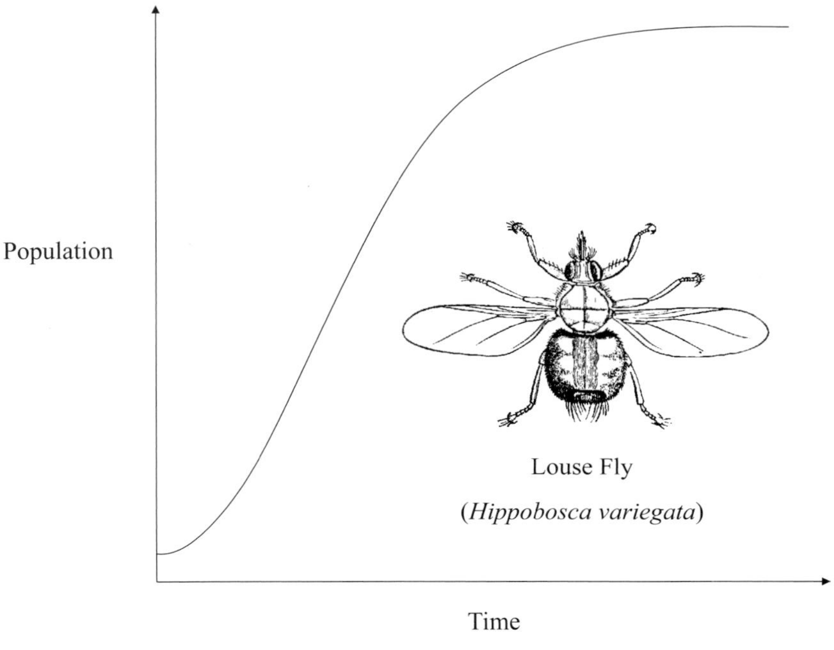

Population

Louse Fly

(*Hippobosca variegata*)

Time

Population

Spider
(Araneae)

Time

R-strategist.

amount of offspring but invest very little time and care in them in the hopes that a few will survive to reproductive age. Most insects are R-strategists, and this is one of the major reasons for their success. R-strategy is especially successful in insects because of their small size, rapid maturation, and wide dispersal.

Ability to Adapt to Change

Having small body size allows for more individuals to coexist in a habitat, and abundant offspring allow for more variation in the population. Combine this with excellent powers of dispersal, and you have a good recipe for adaptation. When some drastic change occurs in the environment, a species with many individuals that have varying traits will have some individuals that survive and pass on their successful genes.

Powers of Chemical Adaptation

Adaptations are not limited to physical aspects of the body. There is a long history of chemical co-adaptation between plants and plant-eating insects. During the Carboniferous period, insects fed on primitive forests. Insects were abundant when the gymnosperms became the dominant plant life on land in the Permian period. Some scientists have associated the radiation of the flowering plants during and after the Cretaceous period with insects. For hundreds of millions of years insects have been eating plants and plants have been developing new chemical defenses. This long history of co-evolution may be one reason why we see such varied plant chemicals (some that are deadly poisonous and some that we use) and such speciose plant-eating groups such as the weevils. The weevils (family Curculionidae) have often responded with a new species each time the host plant speciates, a trait that has allowed family Curculionidae to grow to one of the largest families in the

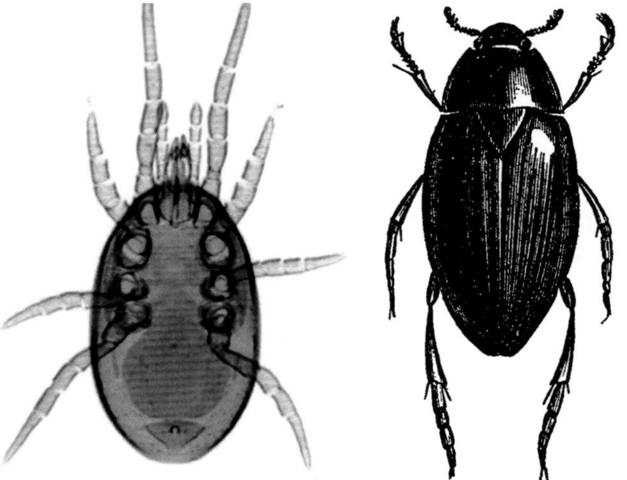

(*Left*) A boll weevil, *Anthronomus gradis* (Coleoptera: Curculionidae). Courtesy of Clemson University–USDA Cooperative Extension, Bugwood.org

(*Center*) A mite (Acarina). Courtesy of Alex Mangini, USDA Forest Service, Bugwood.org.

(*Right*) Water scavenger beetle, *Hydrophilus triangularis* (Coleoptera: Hydrophilidae).

order Insecta, with over 40,000 described species.

Size

Small size reduces the requirements for life and generally allows for more individuals to live in a location, thus varying the genetic pool. Natural selection may proceed more rapidly in such a situation. There are also more possible adaptive niches for small animals. It would not be unusual to find an insect species adapted to feed on the seeds of one particular plant, but this would be very unlikely among larger vertebrate animals. The smaller you are, the greater your potential resources.

Powers of Dispersal (Flight)

Small size and the power of flight combine to give insects excellent powers of dispersal. They may accidentally travel distances great enough to colonize oceanic islands like Hawaii. By colonizing new habitats in this way, some insects have been able to undergo speciation. Aquatic insects are typically good dispersers because they must be capable of moving between relatively small, isolated habitats. Some insects use their powers of dispersal to migrate long distances.

Some migrations like that of the monarch butterfly are well known. Others are not. People on the Gulf Coast have observed migrations of dragonflies in the fall. Weather radar has been used to track migrating masses of moths and aphids. Ability to survive inhospitable weather by waiting it out in a resting stage, aestivation or diapause, allows insects to survive in harsh climates.

Ability to Aestivate or Diapause

Insects may aestivate (normally during the summer) during unfavorable periods of heat or drought. Several species of lady beetles go through a summer aestivation in areas where summer temperatures are extreme. **Diapause** is another form of waiting out unfavorable conditions. Diapause is a resting period of suspended animation that normally occurs during winter. Eggs, larvae, pupae, or adults may diapause. Adult boll weevils diapause during winter. Prior to going into diapause, they cease reproduction and store food energy as body fat. Once in diapause, they leave the field and search out shelter in leaf litter or other cover. Their cellular respiration slows, allowing them to burn less of their stored energy; and their reproductive organs atrophy.

Metamorphosis

Metamorphosis is a change in form during development. Insects go through metamorphosis as they grow from egg to adult. There are four types of metamorphosis: ametabolous (no metamorphosis), hemimetabolous (incomplete metamorphosis), paurometabolous (gradual metamorphosis), and holometabolous (complete metamorphosis).

The most recognized type of metamorphosis is the complete life cycle or holometabolous, which includes egg, larva, pupa, and adult. This type of metamorphosis is most advantageous and has contributed to the success of insects because it helps insects avoid competition between life stages, usually because there are different hosts for the larval and adult stages. In some cases, the mouthparts are completely different in larvae and adults; therefore, competition for the same food is impossible. For example, a caterpillar eating leaves is not in competition with the adult that feeds on nectar, whereas an aphid is in direct competition with its offspring for the same plant material.

Additional advantage is conferred by the egg and pupal stages that are well adapted for passing unfavorable times like winter or drought. The ability to use seasonal food sources expands the possibilities for specialization. Avoiding competition for resources between adults and larvae allows for greater population numbers. Both

(A) egg

(B) larva (caterpillar)

(C) pupa (chrysalis)

The life cycle of a monarch butterfly, *Danus plexippus* (Lepidoptera: Nymphalidae) with stages of (A) egg, (B) larva (caterpillar), (C) pupa (chrysalis), (D, E) and adult. Monarch development from egg to adult is completed in about 30 days. Courtesy of Cathy Downs, Hill Country Chapter

(D) newly emerged adult

(E) adult

specialization and greater numbers are favorable for the increase of species richness, which is dependent on the diversity of resources and the ability to subdivide their use. Metamorphosis is one way that insects are able to subdivide the use of resources and pack more species into a habitat.

Diversity of Higher Categories

Species diversity is more than just a species list for a location. Since species are arranged in a hierarchy of genera, families, and orders, any list may be more or less remarkable based on its spread of higher categories. Eventually you should be able to see that the many layers of any list's species-level diversity may be thought of as the shallowest layer. Ordinal-level diversity is based more on body plan and food source. It is possible to characterize orders by habits or gross food type. Superordinal-level diversity is very ancient and is based on the most fundamental adaptations that insects made hundreds of millions of years ago. When we classify animals, it seems logical to say there are birds, mammals, reptiles, amphibians, fish, insects, and then a bunch of other invertebrate kinds. This

A collembola (Poduromorpha). Courtesy of Tom Murray

view is pervasive. Look at how we assign the professions. There are ornithologists, mammalogists, herpetologists, ichthyologists, entomologists, and invertebrate zoologists. Of all these disciplines only invertebrate zoology shares the wide spread of superordinal diversity that entomology has.

Be aware when you are in the field that this deep diversity exposes a long history of development all around you. It is possible to find some closely related species that are thought to have diverged from a common ancestor since the last ice age. Or possibly even because of it. You may find some butterflies or bees or ants that are thought to have originated in the end of the Cretaceous period when dinosaurs were last living. When you see wingless collembola, dragonflies with wings that do not fold, and beetles with collapsible wings, you should have a feeling for their age. They are developments that were as old to the dinosaurs as the dinosaurs are to us.

Why Does It Remain Important to Study Insects?

People who describe themselves as entomologists are not really telling you much more than that they work with insects. Insects impinge upon so many areas that a great variety of people could be called entomologists, and often their work is so distantly related that they would find little in common to talk about. If we list several subdisciplines of entomology, then you will get a good understanding of the spread of the field and why the study of insects is important.

Taxonomy

Taxonomists study insect variety. They seek to name the species and classify them into groups based on evolutionary relationships. Some taxonomists prefer to be called systematists. Taxonomy means study of names, while systematics implies an all-out effort to determine true evolutionary relationships based on similarity of species. It is possible to be a taxonomist without concerning yourself with evolution. Systematists always have evolution on their mind.

Medical Entomology

Medical entomologists specialize in the control of insects and other arthropods that afflict human health either directly or indirectly. Several insects can be vectors, or carriers of disease. Medical entomologists seek to reduce disease-vectoring insects and/or their ability to vector the diseases. Examples include fleas (bubonic plague), mosquitoes (malaria, yellow fever, dengue), biting flies (tularemia, leishmaniasis), mites, ticks (Lyme disease, Rocky Mountain spotted fever), lice (typhus), and some biting Hemiptera (Chagas disease). If you meet a military entomologist, you are probably talking to a medical entomologist. Many mosquito-prone counties like Harris County employ medical entomologists.

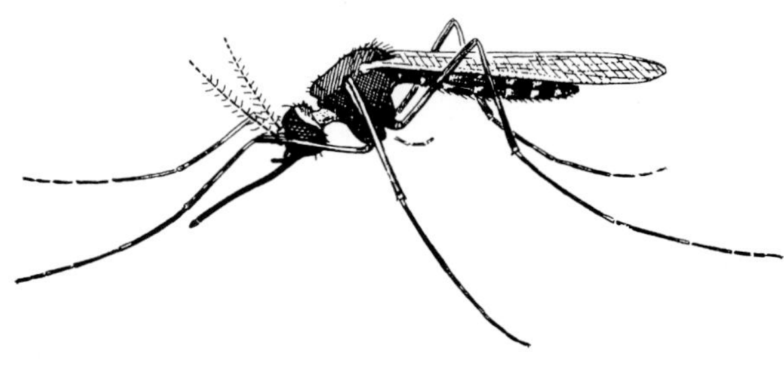

A mosquito (Diptera: Culicidae).

Veterinary Entomology

Pests of livestock that take blood include horse flies, stable flies, horn flies, black flies, or buffalo gnats, various sucking lice, horse stomach bots, ticks, cattle grubs, and sheep kids. Various types of mange are caused by mites. Until the mid-1970s, animals in the United States were susceptible to screwworms, which would enlarge wounds and feed on tissue. Screwworms were eradicated from the United States and Mexico by sterile male release. They have been pushed back to Central America thus far. Screwworm eradication has been worth millions of dollars to ranchers and has also benefited wildlife such as deer.

Forestry Entomology

Trees grown for timber, shade, or use in landscapes commonly have insect pest problems. Pine plantations of East Texas are susceptible to bark beetle infestations that can kill acres of trees by eating their vascular cambium. Numerous borer species damage and kill trees, especially those stressed by drought or other factors. Defoliators can impair the growth of trees or kill by repeated defoliations. Some tree-feeding insects have been implicated in the transmission of deadly tree diseases like Dutch elm disease and oak wilt. Others, like aphids, just make a mess by releasing sticky honeydew (droppings).

Forensics

Insects may be used as evidence in criminal investigations. Insect evidence in a homicide may be used to determine time of death, cause of death, or movement of the body. Detailed studies have been made to determine what happens to a body over time under different circumstances. Many major law enforcement agencies have forensic entomologists on staff or hire them as consultants or expert witnesses. Forensics also may be used to answer questions of contraband trafficking or movement of suspects or materials across the country.

An example of entomology through forensics. Courtesy of William Godwin

Urban Entomology

Insect pests of human habitations and other structures have been a constant problem throughout history. Problem insects include cockroaches, ants, termites, mites, carpet beetles, silverfish, bed bugs, spiders, fleas, clothes moths, powder post beetles, and house flies. These problems are common and diverse enough to employ the urban entomologist full-time on many staffs.

Other Disciplines

Specializations for entomologists go on and on. Apiculturalists raise bees for honey and pollination. Archeologists have used entomology to study ancient civilizations. Insect physiologists and molecular biologists pick apart the chemical reactions in an attempt to discover new ways to control pests and new applications of insect-based systems that have value to humans.

What Does the Future Hold for the Study of Insects?

For professional entomologists, the work ahead is abundant and promising. Work may be categorized as solving insect problems, using insects to solve other problems, and studying insects as part of the natural environment. Solving insect problems will remain the most crucial part of entomology. With luck, we will remain one step ahead of pests as they challenge us by developing resistance to insecticides or are introduced

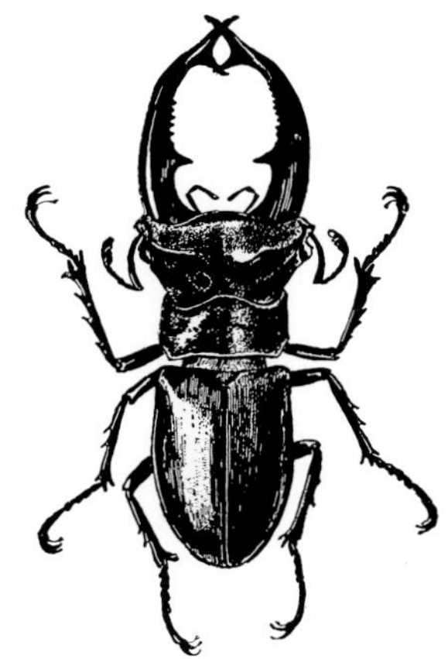

A stag beetle, *Lucanus elaphus* (Coleoptera: Lucanidae).

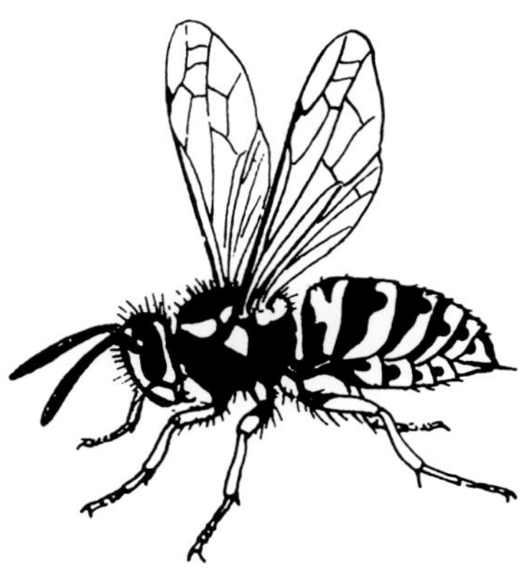

A yellow jacket, *Vespula* sp. (Hymenoptera: Vespidae).

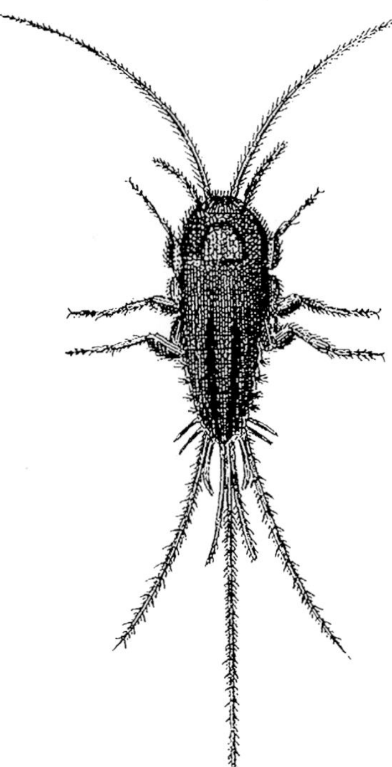

A silverfish (Thysanura).

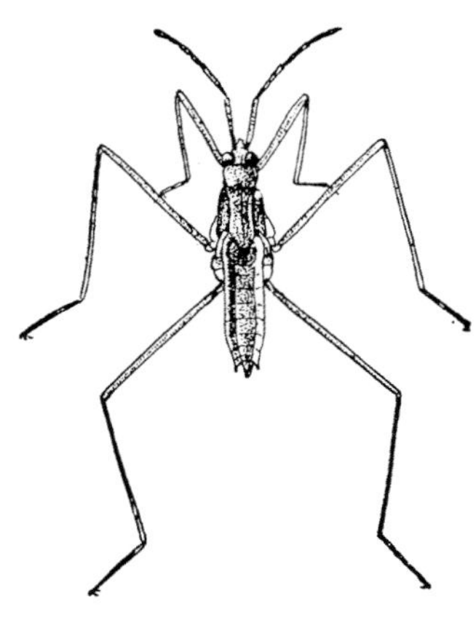

A water strider (Hemiptera: Cerridae).

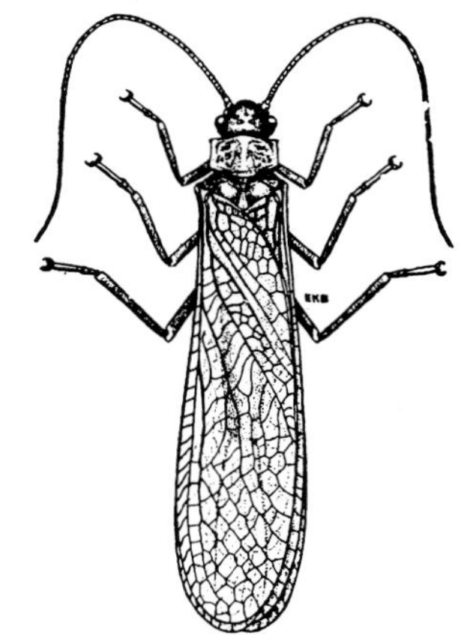

A stonefly (Plecoptera: Perlidae).

to new areas. Some clever scientists will continue to find ways to use insects as solutions to other problems. Forensic entomologists will continue to refine their detective ability. Molecular biologists work toward using insects to produce useful products. Effective ways to use insects as indicators of the health of terrestrial ecosystems will be perfected. New biocontrol agents for invasive weeds or pests will be introduced. Taxonomists will steadily close the large gaps in our knowledge of the insect fauna by describing new species and documenting distribution. Ecologists will continue to tell us how insect species behave and interact within ecosystems. Bioinformatics people will increasingly make our knowledge more easily available and, by doing so, uncover what is left to be done.

Crop Protection

For thousands of years humans have struggled to produce crops for food and fiber, and insect pests competed for the resources. Crop failures due to insect pests, crop diseases, droughts, and floods led to human starvation. Early farmers learned that certain production practices (cultural practices), use of certain crop cultivars, and reliance on pests' natural enemies improved their ability to reliably produce crops and avoid starvation. Over time human populations grew and developed treatments to control pests. Initially, pesticides were used effectively, but overreliance on them brought about contamination issues, environmental damage, and effects on human health. Integrated pest management strategies were developed that combined the use of cultural practices, resistant crop cultivars, biological control, and pesticides to deliver science-based, low-pesticide-use strategies for crop production. New technologies were developed to speed up and improve the development of pest resistance in crop plants. As the earth's human population continues to grow, food and fiber demand will intensify. And the struggle to increase production from declining farmland and water resources, and to protect crops from pests, will intensify.

Protection of Human Health

Insects transmit disease organisms to humans, domesticated animals, and wildlife. In Europe, 75 to 200 million people (30% to 60% of the population) were killed by bubonic plague, transmitted from rats to humans by flea bites between 1346 and 1353. Even today over one million people die from mosquito-borne diseases each year. Worldwide, malaria is the biggest concern. The advent of modern pesticides and improved standards of living (air conditioners, window screens, and public health interventions) have saved millions of lives and largely limited malaria and many other mosquito-borne diseases to tropical areas. However, some 40% of the population of the world remains vulnerable to malaria. As recently as 2012, 1,868 cases of human West Nile virus were reported to the Texas Department of State Health Services (TxDSHS), and the disease caused the deaths of 89 Texans. The threat to human health from malaria, chikungunya, West Nile virus, Rift Valley fever, eastern equine encephalitis, St. Louis encephalitis, LaCrosse encephalitis, western equine encephalitis, and other mosquito-borne diseases continues. In addition, the Center for Disease Control lists 14 important tick-borne diseases in the United States. TxDSHS reports Lyme disease is the most prevalent, but ehrlichiosis, relapsing fever, and Rocky Mountain spotted fever also cause human disease in Texas.

Biocontrol

Beneficial insects have been recognized for thousands of years. The practice of introducing or augmenting beneficial insects is a large part of biocontrol. Insects may be introduced to control harmful insects, weeds, or even the detrimental effects of useful animals. For example, the red imported fire ant is familiar to everyone. Efforts were under way in 2001 to introduce a tiny phorid fly that parasitizes the ants. It is not expected to dramatically affect the fire ant, but it is hoped that the fly will be one of many factors limiting fire ant success.

A classic weed biocontrol story is that of prickly pear cactus in Australia. It was planted as hedges there in the nineteenth century. By the 1920s it had become a serious problem covering 50 million acres. A South American cactus moth (*Cactoblastis cactorum*) was introduced, and within 10 years the cactus was reduced by 90%. Today the US Department of Agriculture (USDA) is investigating biocontrol of 52 invasive plants using insects as the biological control agent.

Biocontrol of invasive plants is helping to manage and restrict the growth of salt cedar along waterways in West Texas and giant salvinia in East Texas lakes. Biocontrol of nonliving problems is also sometimes possible. In the mid 1970s, Texas A&M entomologists introduced the dung beetle (*Onthophagus gazella*) to Texas from Africa. This resulted from a search for dung beetles that were more efficient at their job than native beetles. Each cow pie covers a certain amount of ground, and all these pieces add up to cover thousands of acres. If the cow pies are removed, plant productivity increases. This also reduces breeding places for horn flies and stable flies and increases soil fertility when dung beetles bury manure. But remember, biocontrol must be done with extreme caution to avoid unwanted effects. New candidates are studied exhaustively in quarantine. Even with extreme study, biocontrol is still controversial.

How Are Insects Classified?

Insects as a group are subdivided many ways. Usually the divisions are based on structural or developmental similarities. The category of order is most familiar to people. There are about 31 orders of insects depending on the reference.

Most orders end in the Greek word for wing, *ptera*. Beetles are in the order Coleoptera. Butterflies and moths are in the order Lepidoptera. Wingless orders may also have *ptera* in the order name; however, it is usually preceded by *a*: *aptera*, meaning "no wing." Siphonaptera are fleas and wingless insects. Some orders do not end in *ptera*. Odonata and Thysanura are two examples. Any entomology textbook will have good accounts of the orders of insects. As a naturalist, you should recognize on sight some of the more abundant orders like Coleoptera, Hymenoptera, Heteroptera, and Lepidoptera. There will always be some obscure or rare orders that you will have difficulty finding. For example, Mecoptera, Zoraptera, and Plecoptera are always a prize. Grylloblatodea is the only insect order that is not known from Texas.

Entomology textbooks and reliable sources on the Internet will provide you with much detailed information on the biology and distribution of various orders. However, it may sometimes be difficult for you to find information related to Texas. For example, Plecoptera are much more abundant and diverse in mountainous areas of the North and West than in Texas. Consequently, an account of them in a general text may present them as being less rare or special than they actually are in Texas. The appendix lists accounts tailored when possible to help Master Naturalists understand orders as they relate to Texas. Also included is brief information on collection and curation.

Defining the term "insect" is a task that appears simpler than it actually is. Students realize that as we learn more, our interpretation of nature changes. Older literature often used words that now have different meanings. Not many years ago, Insecta was the class of six-legged arthropods that have body segments arranged into three regions. Today it is widely accepted that the six-legged arthropods should be placed together in the class Hexapoda. The most up-to-date concept of insects includes those arthropods that have three body regions, six legs, and external mouthparts.

The terms "Insecta" and "Hexapoda" may seem confusing. Even entomologists have argued their precise applications. The problem arises from interpretation of three odd orders that are usually considered to be the most primitive insects. Collembola, Protura, and Diplura are three orders that have their mouthparts somewhat internalized and were traditionally classified as insects. Some authorities now place them in three separate classes, concluding that the characteristics of the Hexapoda evolved independently at least four times. This group is primitively wingless and has enclosed spermatophores in a pouchlike structure, giving rise to the

Characteristics of Insecta

Class	Antennae (no.)	Body regions (no.)	Legs (no.)
Arachnida	0	2	8
Chilopoda (centipede)	2	2	1 pair per body segment
Crustacea	4	2	10+
Diplopoda (millipede)	2	2	2 pairs per body segment
Hexapoda	2	3	6

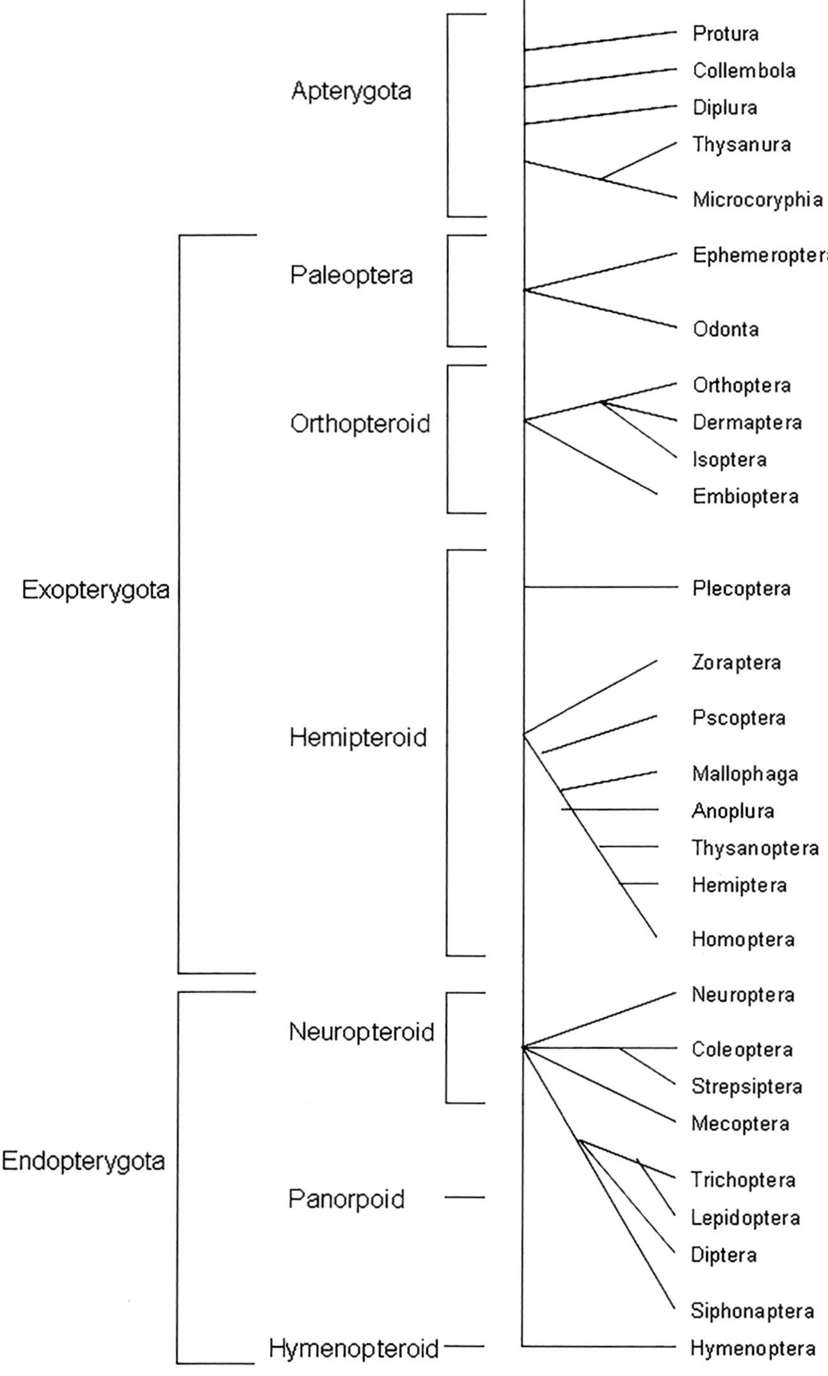

Family tree of the Hexapoda.

taxon sometimes used to contain the three orders—the subclass Entognatha. Other insects have distinctly external mouthparts. Currently, the prevailing trend among taxonomists is to place the Collembola, Protura, and Diplura in the subclass Entognatha and include the other 28 orders in subclass Insecta. Some consider Hexapoda a superclass containing the classes Entognatha and Insecta. Just remember that if someone refers to class Hexapoda, the reference is to all 31 orders of six-legged arthropods. Someone using the term "Insecta" may be including all 31 orders or just the 27 that have external mouthparts. You may see references to class Entognatha or subclass Entognatha. The general term "insect" still refers to all 31 orders.

Wings are very useful features for classification. Exclusive of the Entognatha, the Insecta includes the wingless orders (subclass Apterygota), orders with primitive nonfolding wings (division Paleoptera or subclass Pterygota), and orders with folding wings (division Neoptera). The presence or absence of wings as a characteristic can be confusing because some groups have lost their wings while others never developed them. Primitively wingless orders that are believed to have never had wings include Collembola, Diplura, Protura, Thysanura, and Microcoryphia. Other wingless insects like lice and fleas had winged ancestors. Most winged orders have some wingless representatives.

Insects in the division Paleoptera are characterized by membranous wings that do not fold horizontally over the abdomen. Several orders of Paleoptera lived in the Permian, but today only Odonata (dragonflies) and Ephemeroptera (mayflies) survive.

Neopterous insects such as walkingsticks, mantids, earwigs, cockroaches, termites, grasshoppers, termites, sucking bugs, thrips, book lice, lice, beetles, lacewings, wasps/bees/ants, moths/butterflies, fleas, scorpion flies, and flies have the ability to fold the wings in various ways such that they are held flat over the abdomen. The majority of the insects you will encounter belong to the Neoptera.

Mode of development is another way to subdivide the orders. As mentioned before, there are four types of metamorphosis. Insects with no metamorphosis are **ametabolous**. Young of ametabolous insects resemble the adults but are generally smaller in size. Ametabolous insects are all primitively wingless.

In those insects with simple metamorphosis, the wings (if present) develop externally during the immature stages and there is no quiescent stage preceding the last molt. Two forms of simple metamorphosis are recognized. **Hemimetabolous** insects are those with incomplete metamorphosis. Their aquatic young are called naiads, which look very different from the adult stages. Examples include Odonata, Ephemeroptera, and Plecoptera. **Paurometabolous** insects have terrestrial young called nymphs. Nymphs live in a habitat that is similar to that of the adult, and they are very similar in appearance to the adults. Examples include Heteroptera, Blattodea, and Orthoptera.

Holometabolous insects are those with a complete metamorphosis and four distinct life stages of an egg, larva, pupa, and adult. The larva stage actively feeds, growing and molting as it does. It will then enter the pupal stage, which is commonly called a resting stage, and although it may not be mobile, many changes are happening. Mouthparts may be changing, wings and mature genitalia are forming, and the overall appearance of the insect may be completely different. Once the pupal stage is complete, the adult will emerge.

The terms **endopterygota** and **exopterygota** refer to the mode of wing development. Insects that undergo simple metamorphosis have wings that develop outside the body. These are the exopterygote insects. Insects that have complete metamorphosis with egg, larva, pupa, and adult are all endopterygote. Their wings develop internally in the pupal stage.

What are the comparative virtues of common names and scientific names? Common names may seem more familiar, easier to remember, and more descriptive, which all are comforting. But they fail miserably on the important point of communication. Different people have different common names for things. They vary by region, ethnicity, and even age of the person. For example, the American cockroach goes by many common names: in Texas we call them roaches, in Florida they are palmetto bugs, in the Southwest they are water bugs, in Mexico they are cucarachas, and universally they are often called by shouting expletives!

As we learn more, even scientific names can change over time. There is a system to keep track and continue to recognize those people who have contributed in the past to naming an animal. For example, Carl Linnaeus named the monarch butterfly *Papilio plexippus* in 1758, grouping it with other butterfly genera of swallowtails. It was cited like this: "*Papilio plexippus* Linnaeus 1758." Later Jan Kluk decided that the monarch was unlike the swallowtails and put it in the genus *Danaus*. It became *Danaus plexippus* (Linnaeus 1758). We put parentheses around Linnaeus's name so everybody will know that it was described in one genus but moved to another because someone showed that it fit better there.

Suppose another person today caught some monarchs and thought they were a new species? He could describe them and give them a name, but since Linnaeus did it first, the older name has priority. The new name is called a junior synonym and cataloged. If interested, there is much more to this line of discussion. See Winston (1999).

Why Do Different Insects Live in Different Places?

If you encounter insects and wonder why they are out, consider what it is they are doing. The time and place of insect activity are generally an adaptation to some requirement for living. Timing is everything, and insect presence in a place may coincide with food, mates, or places to oviposit or spend the winter.

Seasonal abundance may be synchronized with some favorable condition. Many beetles are more active in early spring because the leaves they feed on are just budding out. Later in the season, the tender leaves will be tougher and protected with tannins. While it may seem that most insects are active during spring months, many are active during colder, winter months. Dung beetles that specialize on deer pellets are active all winter because deer pellets dry too rapidly in hot, dry weather. In fact, the greatest diversity of leaf litter fauna in Texas occurs during the cool, damp winter for the same reason.

A hemimetabolous dragonfly (Odonata).

Emergence may also be synchronized for mating purposes. Sometimes males emerge sooner than females to be ready for mating. Conspicuous masses of insects that you see may be related to mating and oviposition (depositing of eggs). Mayflies sometimes emerge in tremendous numbers to briefly mate and lay eggs. Other insect masses may disperse randomly; for example, large numbers of water beetles have been known to rain down on parking lots because, while dispersing, they mistake the glinting windshields and chrome for a body of water. Insects on true migrations sometimes astound us with their numbers. Gulf Coast residents are familiar with large masses of migrating dragonflies that show up in the fall. And the monarch butterfly is well known for its migratory behavior and will arrive in amazing numbers in Mexico. Insects preparing for winter can catch our attention as well, such as masses of an introduced ladybird beetle that spends the winter in houses and barns.

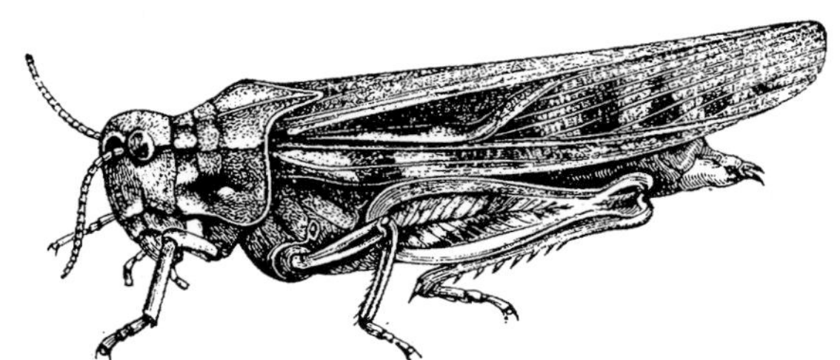

A paurometabolous grasshopper (Orthoptera: Acrididae).

Some insects may occur in specific habitats because they are avoiding competition or filling special niches for which they are uniquely adapted. Such insects are often described as relictual. Relicts are persistent remnants of formerly more widespread organisms. They may be primitive species that are holding on by adapting to marginal habitats or remnants of formerly more extensive habitats. A few places where relict species

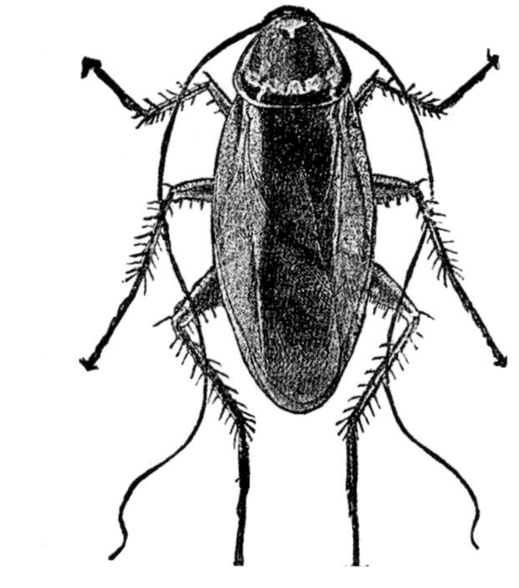

A roach is an exopterygote (Blattodea).

A monarch migration. Courtesy of Texas Parks and Wildlife Department

may occur are sand dunes, mountaintops, caves, and springs.

How Do Insects Adapt to Environmental Changes?

Insects encounter both natural and human-made changes in the environment. Usually responses involve high fecundity and dispersal, although it is possible to identify examples of low reproductive rate and isolationism. A natural change like long-term drought will cause changes in the environment. You might think of drought as causing the spread of arid-adapted western forms toward the east. This will occur in a blotchy pattern as a result of differences in soil moisture capacity, aquifers, and weather. Imagine western and eastern forms seesawing back and forth across the state as climate fluctuates over hundreds or thousands of years. Insects that produce a large number of offspring and disperse over miles of territory are adapted to take advantage of new habitats as they occur.

On a shorter time scale we make drastic changes to the environment. Any change we make will benefit some species and hurt others. We have built highways with grassy medians that allow prairie species to spread into forests. We plant crops in monocultures, like cotton or pine trees, allowing insects that are adapted to eat those plants to flourish. Then we spray those populations with insecticides or expose them to transgenic insecticidal compounds and worry that the pests may be developing resistance to the pesticides. Understanding how resistance develops will help you understand how insects evolve in response to environmental changes.

When we spray a field that is infested with a pest, we do not kill 100% of the insects. Some will survive. Often these survivors have some innate quality that allows them to resist the control. Survivors will breed with other survivors and then pass on the genes that are preadapted for survival. After several generations have passed, we have bred a "super bug" that is resistant to the pesticide. We are forced to change pesticides or use strategies of combined methods of control.

Fertilization of crops can affect insect populations. One of the challenges for herbivorous insects is to acquire enough protein. Plants with an excess of nitrates may build up quantities of amino acids in their tissues. One of the qualities producers use to select pasture grasses is protein content. Hay contests award prizes to producers of hay that tests highest for protein content. Just as high-protein hay is detected, preferred, and selected by grazing livestock, it is detected, preferred, and selected by insect herbivores. Highly productive forages (cultivars selected for high protein/digestibility, highly fertilized, irrigated) are often more vulnerable to damage from outbreaks of insect herbivores such as armyworms.

Other possible responses to changes humans make in the environment include host plant switching and flourishing with introduction into these modified habitats. The boll weevil's initial switch from trees in the cotton family to cultivated cotton occurred in Mexico. Its subsequent movement across the US-Mexican border and spread across the South represented the invasion of a Mexican species through a landscape unnaturally populated with its host plant. Another example is the Colorado potato beetle, which lived unobtrusively on wild plants of the *Solanum* genus in the Rocky Mountains until farmers planted potatoes along the lines of settlement. After the beetle became adapted to feeding on potatoes, continuous potato production created a potato beetle highway to the east, and by 1874 potato beetles had spread across the United States. In both cases human agricultural industries were severely damaged.

Less common strategies involve the loss of dispersal ability or fecundity (reproductive rate). Many insects have lost the ability

Fall armyworms (Lepidoptera: Noctuidae). Courtesy of Texas A&M AgriLife Extension Service

to fly. This may be a response to disuse in habitats where dispersal is not beneficial or flight may be actively selected against. Selection against something means that the individuals with that trait are eventually eliminated from the population. Over time selection against some trait will tend to eliminate the trait. An example is the bed bug, which is related to other true bugs like stink bugs and giant water bugs.

It is possible to imagine several circumstances in which dispersal ability would be selected again; for example, species on islands may encounter selection against dispersal. On a small island, far out at sea, the traits encouraging dispersal are quickly weeded out because those individuals flying away are lost at sea. Nonflying individuals survive and reproduce. Islands do not necessarily need to be surrounded by ocean. An island can be any habitat type surrounded by an immense area of another type. Islands include mountaintops in West Texas, fields of dunes, isolated soil types, or geological formations, or they can be based on cryptic things like shallow groundwater or micronutrients in the soil.

Some insects that are adapted to niches with limited resources or special circumstances may have excessive reproductive capacity (R-strategy) selected against. The alternative, K-strategy, involves production of few young, which receive much parental care. Passalid beetles invest much work constructing galleries in logs. There is also intense competition for this resource in the forest. Passalids or Bess beetles have adapted to this situation by having fewer offspring and taking better care of them.

Bess beetle, *Odontotaenius disjunctus* (Coleoptera: Passalidae). Courtesy of Gerald J. Lenhard, Louisiana State University, Bugwood.org

How Do Insects Function in Ecosystems?

A short list of functions includes pollination, carrion removal, dung removal, disease transmission, erosion, predation, parasitism, herbivory, and phoresy. Insects affect the composition of the atmosphere, build the soil, influence the vertebrate communities, and affect what our woods and prairies look like.

Naturalists Making Associations

Knowing a lot of information about insects or nature in general is admirable, though observing nature and making associations distinguish the naturalist. You might buy thousands of beautiful butterfly specimens from all over the world and memorize the names of everything in your fabulous collection, but that will not make you a naturalist. You might go a step further and use your collection to write scientific papers on the relationships of different groups. Do a good job and you can become a renowned scientist, but you will not be a naturalist. Only when you begin to make associations between your insects and their environment will you be a naturalist. Recognizing relationships is the most satisfying part of being a naturalist.

Imagine knowing what to expect in some new situation or figuring out where to look for some new species. Consider cave insects: Collectors have been able to predict the occurrence of new beetle species based on the pattern of cave distribution. At first, some caves were explored and some remarkable beetles discovered; then other caves were surveyed. Some contained the same beetles, and others contained slightly different ones.

What was going on? A little study of geology maps showed that caves occurred only in certain rock formations, and these were separated sometimes by non-cave-containing formations. Once this was discovered, it was simple to look at the map and see other isolated cave-containing rock formations and look there for additional undiscovered species of cave beetles. What a wonderful feeling it must have been to find the predicted beetle.

There are ways to increase your chance of making associations. Relictual or highly host-specific insects will have tighter patterns of association. Pick insect groups with easily identifiable limiting factors. Examples of these include flightlessness, blindness, host specificity, or substrate specificity. Flightlessness and blindness often evolve in insects that are tied to a particular small habitat. Host specificity may occur in some herbivores that have adapted to deal with noxious, plant-produced chemicals. Many parasites of vertebrate animals are host-specific to some degree. Examples of substrate specificity include insects associated with sand dunes, springs, rock outcrops, or clay formations. Some brief accounts of insect associations may start you thinking.

Vertebrate Associations

Birds and mammals have many insect associations. Pocket gophers are subterranean rodents that live in areas of loamy or sandy soil. Their closed burrows can be up to 500 feet long and support a community of insects, many of which occur nowhere else. These burrows may include flies, histerid beetles that eat fly larvae, dung beetles, moths, cave crickets, and carabid beetles adapted to eat crickets. Woodrats (*Neotoma* spp.) build large middens of sticks and debris. These are habitat for many specially adapted insects like the flower scarab (*Euphoria devulsa*). Prairie dog burrows provide habitat for several insects. One dung beetle is known only from these burrows. A beetle in the genus *Ataenius* is associated with squirrel nests in trees. *Omorgus howelli* is a beetle adapted to live in the refuse of owl nests. Cliff swallow nests are inhabited by hemipterans in the family Cimicidae (cliff swallow bugs, *Oeciacus vicarius*) that feed on blood. Human bed bug (*Cimex lectularis*) is a related species with a similar blood-feeding biology. The bat bug (*C. adjunctus*) is another cimicid that is very rare in Texas but common in areas of the Midwest. If its bat hosts are removed from houses, bat bugs will feed on humans. A family of beetles (Platypsyllidae) inhabit the pelts and nests of beavers. Deer feces support a number of tiny winter-active dung beetles (*Aphodius* spp.). The association of mosquitoes and ticks with mammals and birds is well known. Blood meals are required for development in ticks and to support reproduction in both ticks and mosquitoes.

Insect Associations

Some insects are associated with other insects. Nests of leaf-cutting ants (*Atta* spp.) are inhabited by many associates, including a beetle (*Euparixia moseri*) and a cockroach (*Attaphila fungicola*). Harvester ant nests support populations of tenebrionid beetles. Army ant columns (*Neivamyrmex* spp.) are infiltrated with ant-mimic staphylinid beetles. Larvae of certain butterflies in the family Lycaenidae live with ants. Native fire ants have beetles (*Euparia castanea*) that live with them (myrmecophiles), and the red imported fire ant has its own myrmecophile, a type of beetle (*Martineziella dutertrei*). Some ants raise aphids like a rancher raises cattle. They protect them from parasitic wasps and predaceous insects and in return collect the sugary honeydew produced by the aphids.

Plant Associations

Insect-plant associations are not unusual, but some are more striking than others.

A sphinx moth caterpillar (Lepidoptera: Sphingidae). Courtesy of Max Traweek

The yucca moth (Prodoxidae) is associated with only yucca plants, which are solely pollinated by these moths. The female moth collects pollen from the yucca plant with her mouthparts and inserts her egg into the ovary of the yucca flower. After she lays her eggs, she will then take the pollen she has collected and place it on the stigma of the flower where she has just laid her eggs, guaranteeing that her larvae will have a seed to feed on. This is just one example, but the list of herbivores and specific hosts is enormous.

Special Habitat Associations

Some insects are associated with special physical habitats. The naiads of primitive dragonflies in the family Petaluridae dig burrows in areas of seeping aquifers in East Texas. Caves of the Edwards Plateau have a well-documented fauna, and Monahans Sand Dunes, west of Odessa, have endemic beetles. The dunes of the Wild Horse Desert in South Texas have many endemics, including a bee (*Colletes saritensis*) that is named after the town of Sarita. *Fossocarus creoleorum* is a Pleistocene beetle relic that lives only in the sandy land of the southern Big Thicket region and flies to lights during cold winter rainstorms. These are examples of some of the variety of associations you may discover.

"That which is not good for the beehive cannot be good for the bees."
—Marcus Aurelius, *Meditations*

What Are Some Conservation Concerns for Insects?

Invertebrate conservation is a broad topic. Endangered species usually come to mind first. We may become alarmed at the disappearance of a particular cave beetle or rare butterfly because that represents a further decay of our environment. However, there is much more to think about. Extinction is a process that has occurred for millions of years. It is a natural part of life. The discussion and concerns in recent years are that human activity is increasing the number of species being lost. Invasive pests (introduced by humans) and habitat loss are major causes of some of the extinctions we are experiencing.

Food for Wildlife

Decline in raw numbers of insects may also be a concern because of their value as food for other animals such as fish, quail, turkeys, or songbirds. Sometimes the absence of a well-liked vertebrate can be related to insect disappearance. For example, our sadness over decline of the horned lizard or horny toad is probably due in part to the decline in population of their main food source, the harvester ant (*Pogonomyrmex* spp.), which was displaced by the more territorial and aggressive red imported fire ant (*Solenopsis invicta*).

Disappearing Populations

Many times the disappearance of charismatic insects like fireflies, butterflies, or dragonflies becomes a topic of discussion. When people notice that a familiar insect is gone, they wonder what it means. Every entomologist will face the question sometime: "Why don't I see as many of insect X as

I did when I was a kid?" It may be because that person has outgrown running around in creeks and fields all summer, or there may be other reasons. For example, fire ants are thought to have affected populations of fireflies. Corn pollen contains a Lepidoptera-toxic protein that in high doses is toxic to butterfly larvae. The presence of the protein toxin has created concern among conservationists about the impact of the technology on nontarget insects such as monarch butterflies. Although it was initially a concern, scientific studies and risk assessments have shown that Bt pollen drift onto host plants poses minimal risk to butterfly populations. Changing pastures from grazing lands to monoculture hayfields reduces butterfly numbers by removing larval food plants and flowers that provide blooms and nectar sources for adults. Short- and long-term droughts also impact populations of butterflies by reducing available nectar sources. Urbanization and land fragmentation reduce habitats of various insects and can affect their population sizes and the likelihood one will come in contact with them.

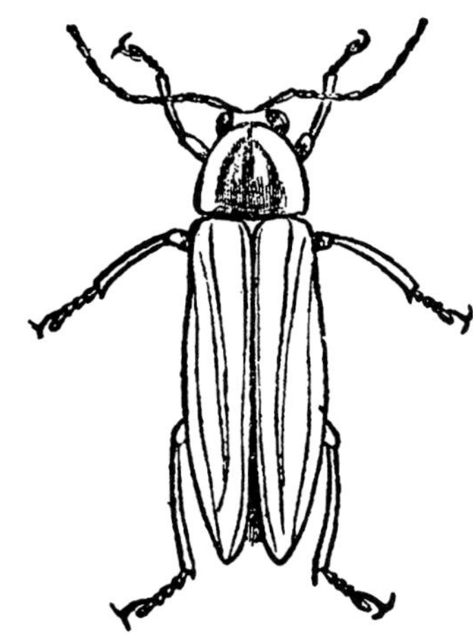

A firefly (Coleoptera: Lampyridae).

Texas threatened and endangered insects

Common name	Scientific name
Insects	
A ground beetle	*Rhadine exilis*
A ground beetle	*Rhadine infernalis*
American burying beetle	*Nicrophorus americanus*
Coffin Cave mold beetle	*Batrisodes texanus*
Comal Springs dryopid beetle	*Stygoparnus comalensis*
Comal Springs riffle beetle	*Heterelmis comalensis*
Helotes mold beetle	*Batrisodes venyivi*
Kretschmarr Cave mold beetle	*Texamaurops reddelli*
Tooth Cave ground beetle	*Rhadine persephone*
Spiders and relatives	
Bee Creek Cave harvestman	*Texella reddelli*
Bone Cave harvestman	*Texella reyesi*
Government Canyon cave spider	*Neoleptoneta microps*
Madla's Cave spider	*Cicurina madla*
Robber Baron Cave harvestman	*Texella cokendolpheri*
Robber Baron Cave spider	*Cicurina baronia*

Source: TPWD (2015).

All are listed as federally endangered.

Hugging the Border

Many animals that may be common elsewhere are rare in Texas because their geographic range barely crosses our border. Species shared with Mexico probably first come to mind, but Texas also impinges on Louisiana swamps, and our border passes close by the Ozarks and Wichita Mountains. High Plains species may be found in national grasslands of the Panhandle. The Guadalupe and Franklin Mountains are the eastern edge of the western basin and range province. If you set out to do it, you could find new state records of border-hugging species in any of these areas.

Threatened and Endangered

There are several lists of species that are thought to be in danger of extinction. Some agencies like the World Wildlife Fund and the International Union for the Conservation of Nature develop lists that may help you determine what people think is rare or endangered. The only official endangered species lists are those of the federal and state governments.

Endangered invertebrates can be split into two groups—those that were probably rare when the first settlers arrived and those insects that were formerly more common but have been detrimentally affected by changes we have made to the environment. There are probably many insects that are in as much or more peril than those on the federally endangered species list but just have not received federal or state protection.

Other insects that are vulnerable to extinction or threatened probably occur in your corner of the state. Refer to the list in Drees and Jackman (1998). Look at the lists of neighboring states, and you will see that they have different opinions about what is rare and endangered. Other insects are associated with endangered vertebrates and plants. Consider the endangered Tobusch fishhook cactus (*Sclerocactus brevihamatus* subsp. *tobuschii*). This cactus hosts a species of weevil in the genus *Gerstaekeria* that is probably an undescribed species. If this weevil lives only on the Tobusch fishhook cactus, then should it be considered endangered as well? If the weevil is eating the endangered cactus, should it be managed? Is it possible that the weevil has some beneficial effect on the cactus? These are all important questions. Texas lists just over 30 other threatened or endangered plants. Do they have similar insect associates?

A species' strategy for adaptation to change should be the first consideration of conservationists. R-strategists may be able to persist in a mosaic of different habitat types and adapt to our changes by continually moving. K-strategists may be more at risk for extinction, but some may be better adapted for existence on small reserves.

How Are Insects Monitored?

If you are seriously interested in monitoring techniques for insects, refer to *Insect Conservation Biology* by M. Samways (1994) and *Invertebrate Surveys for Conservation* by T. R. New (1998). Presented here is a brief account of things to consider.

An insect survey is a project that sounds simple enough at first but tends to become rapidly complicated. It is a lot like the Master Naturalist program in that it is an interesting pursuit that renders much knowledge and pleasure but will never be finished. The best plan for the naturalists of an area is one of gradual accumulation with the intention of developing a database that will allow for comparisons over time. If it is very important that you produce some kind of insect survey rapidly, then given the abundance and diversity, you must reduce your search. The first thing cut is usually the number of taxa. You may limit your survey to an order like Lepidoptera or Hymenoptera. Since these are still large groups, you may further want to limit your survey by resource group: for example, survey the insects of rotten logs or streams.

Think about your area and what makes it special. If you are surveying old-growth woods, consider groups that rely on dead wood or tree holes. If you are surveying a prairie, plant eaters like chrysomelid beetles or plant hoppers will be abundant. If you have no idea, then just go collecting in your area and see what groups are diverse enough to provide some information. Think about your goals. Do you want to compare one place with others? Do you want to gather evidence for the success or failure of some management technique? Do you just want a list of rare or special insects of a place?

Standard Samples

If the goal of your survey is to document species richness, trapping and collecting in any form is useful. Generally, the more collecting methods, the more species. However, if you ever plan to compare results in any way, you will need standardization. Why? If you want to compare your area to another, you should spend equal amounts of effort in both areas, or at least be able to say what the difference in effort was. Bias in sampling may make one area appear different than it really is. It is a good idea to build in standardization practices regardless of your goals, in the event that others will want to compare their data to yours someday.

You may standardize in many easy ways. When using a trap, trap days or hours are a good unit. You may say, "We collected 75 species in three trap days at our prairie but only 25 in an equal amount of time at the city park." This indicates a greater diversity of species in the prairie habitat than the city park. Other ideas for standard units are sweep net sweeps, volume of litter sifted, number of trees beat, or length of transect walked. Just about every collecting method may be standardized in some way.

Morphospecies

You do not have to let your inability to identify a group of insects hold you back. You may resort to the concept of morphospecies. Just determine the different kinds of insects in your sample and give them numbers. Label a set of representatives as morphospecies 1, 2, 3, and so on. Then you can proceed with your project, and later when you get real identifications, you can replace the morphospecies with names.

Accelerating Your List

If you are in love with one particular place and want to spend years learning about it, you might decide to start keeping a total insect list. You will not live to see it done, but you can go faster by trapping, putting out a request for specimen donations, and inviting collections to be compiled with yours.

Trapping

There are simple insect traps that can run, or continuously collect, for weeks or months. They will provide you with big samples and catch rare things that you would never see in years of walking and observing. They can produce quarts of insects for you. For more information on how to trap, refer to "How Can Insects Be Trapped?" in this unit.

Donation

You may contact the curator of a large, well-run insect collection to arrange donation

An insect collection.

of samples. They may be tickled to get your samples from areas where their staff have never collected. Once your specimens are in a major collection, they are in the direct path of specialists. Over years, the experts in various fields may use and identify your specimens. Curators are usually happy to meet seriously interested people. You do not even have to stay in Texas; museums in other states have collectors in Texas.

When to Quit

How do you know when you have documented the insect fauna of an area? The simplest answer is when your list stops growing. Of course, it will probably never stop growing entirely, but it will level off. Colwell and Coddington (1994) called this the species **accumulation curve**. The first sample you take from your study will be composed of species that are new to you. The second sample will have some species that you have seen before and some new ones. If you graph the accumulation of species new to you on paper, then over time you should see a steep line that gradually levels off. When this happens, you have evidence that your study is nearing completion. This is just one more reason for standardizing your samples.

How Can Insects Be Trapped?

This list of insect traps is not exhaustive. There are special traps and techniques for all kinds of insects. Entomology journals often have notes on new ones.

Pitfall Traps

Pitfall traps are small cups that are buried with their rim level with the soil surface. Passing insects walk over the edge and fall in. Placing fluid in the traps will prevent escape. If traps are being placed out for a day or less, use soapy water. For more than a day you must consider preservation. Alcohol with a little glycol to prevent evaporation will work. Straight ethylene glycol in the form of antifreeze is an excellent preservative but must be used with extreme caution to prevent poisoning of animals. Propylene glycol is a more environmentally friendly option that will not be as attractive to animals but should still be used with caution. Covers of chicken wire can protect vertebrates and admit insects.

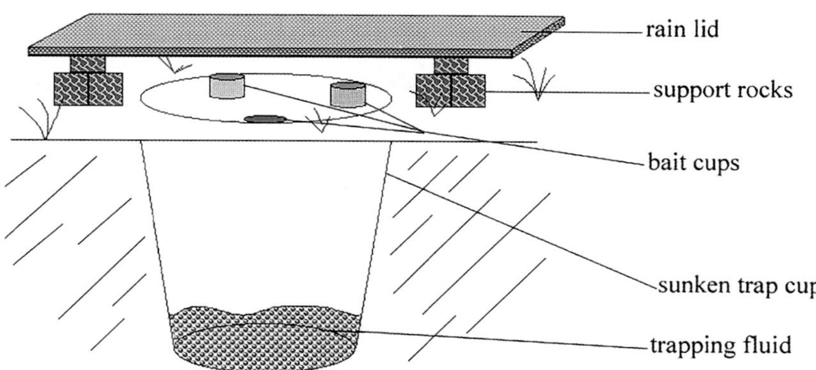

A pitfall trap. Courtesy of Dawn Wenzel

Pitfalls should be covered with a rain lid if you are worried about them filling. Disposable plates work well. Support them with sticks driven through at an angle and into the soil. Another idea is to cover with a heavy board or flat rock supported by three to four small rocks.

The addition of bait placed near a pitfall trap can increase the number of insects collected. It is convenient to have some small bait cups such as bottle tops or condiment cups. These can be paper-clipped to the side of your pitfall or suspended by wire. Your bait depends on what you are attempting to collect. Carrion, dung, and butyric acid are all examples of baits that can be used.

Malaise Traps and Flight Intercept Panels

Malaise traps collect small, flying insects. They are usually tentlike structures made of mesh fabric. They have a vertical panel with a rooflike lid to keep insects from passing over. In some models the top is inclined so that one end is higher. Malaise traps are placed across a fly zone, such as a break in a forested area, to capture insects flying out of or into trees. Insects become disoriented in the Malaise trap and travel to the highest point, which is equipped with a collection jar, usually filled with alcohol. Malaise traps can be expensive to purchase, but a clever person can make one after seeing a picture.

Flight intercept traps or **windowpane traps** collect the insects that drop when encountering an obstacle. These traps consist of a vertical panel with fluid-filled pans below to catch the insects. For a panel, use an old window screen, a salvaged window, or even some screen wire stretched between two trees. Any kind of long, narrow pan will also work. For fluids, follow the recommendations for pitfall traps. Flight intercept traps should also be placed in natural flyways.

A Malaise trap. Courtesy of William Godwin

Flight interception trap. Courtesy of William Godwin

Berlese Traps

Rich leaf litter and soil often contain dense populations of insects. Most of these are tiny, but they are interesting and important parts of the ecosystem. A **Berlese device** allows you to collect clean samples of soil insects into alcohol. A Berlese funnel is a container for leaf litter that has a screen wire bottom. As the material in the funnel dries, the insects seek refuge deeper in the soil.

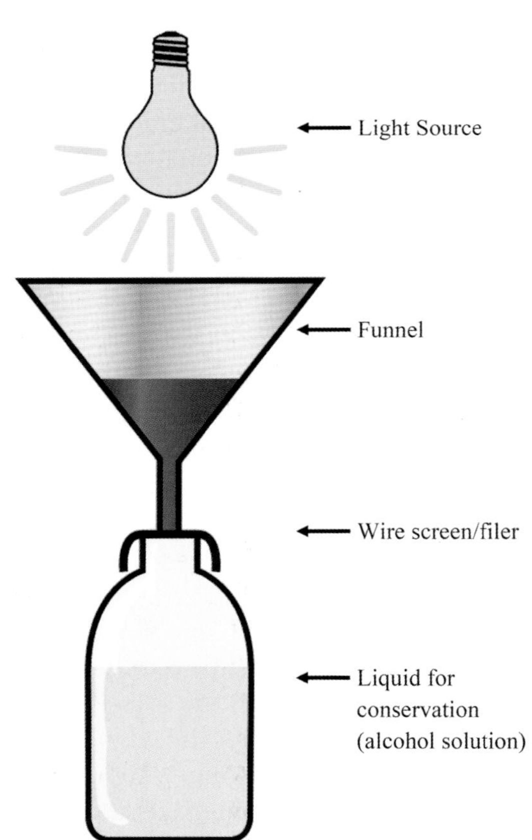

Berlese funnel. Courtesy of Mary Pearl Meuth, Texas A&M AgriLife Extension Service

Soon they fall through the screen into your bottle or pan of alcohol below.

Be careful not to pack soil so deep in the Berlese that it will not dry quickly. Suspend a light bulb over the soil to dry it faster. Placing the soil in a conical pile or piling it up around the edges of the Berlese will also hasten drying.

Berlese funnels have been made from two-liter plastic bottles, milk jugs, trashcans, and canvas water buckets from army surplus stores. Serious Berlese users often field-sift their litter to concentrate it. You can buy or make field sifters that are similar to a windsock with half-inch screen wire sewn in about eight inches from the top. A wire hoop supports the screen and provides a handle for you. Another wire hoop and handle are sewn in the rim. Leaf mold is placed in the top and shaken. The insects fall through the wire into your bag with other debris. Sticks and large trash are left out. The end of the sifter bag is tied shut until you are ready to dump your concentrated sample into the Berlese.

Hanging Bait Trap

Many insects are attracted to rotting fruit or vegetable matter, which can be used in a **hanging bait trap**. Cut windows in the sides of a plastic milk jug, leaving a two-inch pan in the bottom. Fill the pan with a fluid of rotten bananas, sugar water, beer, or anything handy that will make a smelly, fermenting liquid. Suspend these in trees and check them every day. You will be surprised at the large, beautiful beetles that are attracted and drown in your trap. Pull them out and rinse them off in soapy water or alcohol. Check these traps often enough that your specimens do not decay; once a day should be fine.

Yellow Pan Traps

Yellow pan traps, bright yellow pans or bowls filled with a little soapy water, are often used to catch many insects that are attracted to colorful displays. You will need a fine aquarium fishnet when you check these traps. Pour the trap water through the net, and go on to the next trap and wash the net out in a white pan of alcohol to examine your catch. Blue bowls are used sometimes and may catch different insects, but yellow pans are the most successful.

Bottle Trapping

Most people are familiar with the design of minnow or fish traps that have an inward-pointing funnel. **Bottle trapping** is the same idea used to trap actively swimming aquatic insects. A canning jar with a plastic funnel attached will collect large samples of water beetles when it is sunk in the edge of a pond or stream. Be sure to point the funnel parallel to the bank.

Light Traps

Light trapping is probably the most loved technique for entomology classes and field trips. It is exciting because of the tremendous variety of insects that may be attracted. Another advantage is the ability to watch them alive on the sheet in front of you. You may pick and choose the specimens you want to collect, thus avoiding the problem of sorting through dense samples.

Insects are attracted to the blue end of the spectrum of visible light and to ultraviolet. Collectors have taken advantage of this for years by using fluorescent lights that

A light trap. Courtesy of Michael Merchant

put out blue and ultraviolet light. Mercury vapor lights will also attract insects but can be hard to find. Do not try to use a yellow sodium vapor bulb; these are designed to not attract insects.

There are many ways to set up your light. The most common is a clothesline style. Hang a white sheet with clothespins on a rope that is taut between trees or hang the white sheet over a fence or other object. Allow the bottom two feet of the sheet to drape on the ground. Put a second or third sheet on the ground to catch more insects. Adjust your light so that it shines on the sheet, forming a reflector and surface for the insects to land on.

Lindgren Funnel

Some forest insects are visually attracted to standing tree trunks. The **Lindgren funnel** is a device that mimics tree trunks. It is a nested stack of black plastic funnels that are all one or two inches apart and hung in the forest with the narrow part pointed down. A fluid-filled collecting jar is attached at the bottom. Insects fly to the vertical black object, expecting to land on a tree trunk. Instead, they are funneled down to the waiting jar.

Sweeping

A heavy muslin or canvas butterfly net is often used to **sweep** through vegetation. The passing net knocks off insects, and they fall into the net with some weedy debris. After 8 to 10 sweeps the collector stops to dump the contents into a jar or perhaps pick and choose specimens as they emerge from the net.

Beating

Suspend a square meter of white cloth between two crossed sticks, and hold this horizontally under a tree branch or bush; these are commonly referred to as **beating sheets**. Placing a sheet on the ground and beating the vegetation above the sheet is another version of beating. With a stout stick, knock the branches around and see what falls onto your sheet. Beating at night will produce insects that are not active during daylight. Try beating different plants to see what associations there are.

Seining and Aquatic Nets

Aquatic insects are often collected with water nets. If you are sampling a stream, you may hold a fine screen vertically in the water and have someone upstream kick around to stir things up. Insects will drift down to be caught in your **seine**. **Aquatic, or D nets**, are designed specifically for collecting aquatic insects. While they can be costly, they are excellent if you are interested in collecting in streams and other running-water sources.

Emergence Traps

Emergence traps are constructed by inverting a screen-wire pyramid over a habitat and fastening a collecting bottle upside down at the top of the pyramid to measure the process of insect emergence from that habitat.

(*Left*) A sweeping net. Courtesy of Michael Merchant

(*Right*) A beating sheet trap. Courtesy of Michael Merchant

If you are interested in collecting emerging aquatic insects, float the collector over water by attaching Styrofoam floats.

Rearing

You will learn more about species by raising or rearing them. When collecting immature insects, be sure to collect them with their food source. This is usually the object, plant, or other host where you collected the immature. Provide water and humidity, especially if your insect pupates, as it needs moisture to emerge from the pupal case.

Other Techniques

The list of techniques could go on interminably. You can look more up in entomology books or on the Internet. A few you might investigate are subterranean pitfall traps, canopy flight intercept traps, pheromone traps, butterfly traps, and sugar baiting.

How Can Insects be Identified?

Identification of insects is no small task. You should be proud if you can identify insects to their family. If you want to identify insects to genus and species, you will need some specialized literature, including keys, figures, and checklists. If you get interested in identification to genus and species, then it is recommended that you specialize in a particular order or family, depending on the size and complexity of the group. The following is a guide to how to identify insects (see the appendix for accounts of the orders and brief information on collection and curation).

Equipment

Three necessities to properly identify insects are a good book, magnification source, and light. The book should be a college-level entomology textbook with keys and figures. The most widely used is *An Introduction to the Study of Insects* (Borror et al. 1989). This book has good keys to orders and families and includes figures. It will allow you to identify most insects found in Texas to family. If you are identifying aquatic insects, *An Introduction to the Aquatic Insects of North America* (Merritt and Cummins 1984) will help you make identifications to genus.

Dichotomous Keys

Dichotomous keys are crucial to identification. A dichotomous key is a series of couplets that lead you to an identification. At each couplet, you answer questions about characteristics of your insect, which will lead you to another couplet, eventually narrowing down the characteristics to provide an identification. The best way to start is to use a dichotomous key to insect order. Once you have determined the order of the insect, you can use family, subfamily, and/or species keys for further identification. Once you have utilized your order keys, you will find you may be able to recognize the major orders on sight and go directly to the family key.

Magnification

Your ideal source of magnification will be a binocular dissecting microscope of 30× to 40× magnification, although it may be difficult to find or expensive to purchase. You

An *Actias luna* female raised on American sweetgum. Courtesy of Shawn Hanrahan

may be able to arrange to use one at your local high school, college, or museum. Many identifications can be made with a 10× hand lens or loupe if you do not have access to a microscope. Some people have adapted old compound microscopes that were built for looking at glass slides. A jeweler's loupe held up to a light may also work.

Light

Magnification will be useless without the proper light. The ideal light is one that uses a powerful halogen bulb like those in slide projectors with a fiber-optic light delivery that you can point at your specimen. If you are clever, this kind of light is not hard to build yourself. You just need a bright light source, a lens to focus it, and a piece of fiber-optic cable to conduct the light. An old slide projector from the thrift store might be adapted. You can do well with other lights; just remember that brighter is better. If you are lucky enough to have a fiber-optic light or other intense, directed light, you will want to make yourself a light diffuser. Figure out how to pass your light through a piece of Mylar film before it hits your specimen and see the great difference it makes. If you cannot acquire Mylar, use opaque Scotch tape.

Literature

Your need for special papers and books will depend on your depth of study. Most Master Naturalists will never need more than a college text with keys to family. To attempt generic and species identifications on your own, you will need to find special publications. Learning about a group of insects is much easier when you can read what others have learned before you. This is all contained in the body of scientific literature. The scientific name of an insect will be your key to all the information ever printed on it.

Through the use of the Internet, interlibrary loan, and some patience, you will be able to obtain any literature you need. Short descriptions of new species will be found in journals and bulletins. They will attempt to give enough information to identify the species and differentiate it from similar species. Revisions are longer papers that attempt to cover all the species of a particular group at once and bring everybody up to date.

Monographs are attempts to round up all the information on bigger groups like families. Catalogs and checklists attempt to list all the names for insects of a particular group in an area like North America or Texas. Useful maps for insect study include Geologic Atlas of Texas, county soil maps, plats, topographic maps, survey maps, Blair's biotic regions, and vegetational regions of Texas.

Extension

Texas A&M AgriLife Extension has various excellent resources that can assist you in identification of insect pests or problems. Every county in Texas has one or more county agents, but not every county has an entomologist. Many of these agents have had basic entomology courses and can identify common problem insects. Some counties also have integrated pest management (IPM) agents who have a degree or extensive education in entomology or IPM program specialists with degree(s) in entomology. In addition, extension entomologists hold a doctorate degree in entomology and can be found in a handful of counties.

Where Are Insect Collections?

Collections will be useful when learning taxa or making identifications. It would be difficult to list all the collections in Texas, because the list would soon be outdated. It is better to tell you how to find collections in your area. Most universities and colleges have at least a small collection. Texas A&M University has the largest insect reference collection in the Southwest. Larger towns and cities often have municipal museums.

Correctly mounted insects prepared by US Navy medical entomologists assigned to the Navy Environmental and Preventive Medicine Division at Pearl Harbor. Courtesy of US Navy

A spider in a garden, *Argiope* sp. (Aranoea: Araneidae).

Collections of insects can be found at municipal museums in Dallas, Houston, Waco, Fort Worth, El Paso, and San Antonio. Many state and federal agencies maintain insect reference collections. They can often be found at headquarters of state and national parks. Many private individuals have fine insect collections.

How Can Land Be Managed for Insect Diversity?

This practice is very rare. Apart from a few places managed to encourage butterflies, most other land that is managed in a way that increases insect diversity is actually managed for some other reason. Most collectors recognize this little serendipity. People manage land for various natural purposes. These include native prairies, forests, wildlife, hunting, bird sanctuaries, and wetlands. There are many things you can do that will affect insect species richness and general numbers.

Leave dead wood. Standing dead trees and fallen logs are habitat for many insects. Mature forests have plenty of fallen logs, standing dead wood, tree holes, and stumps. Each type of dead wood may have different insects. For example, *Phileurus* is a genus of black, shiny scarabs that have a preference for standing dead wood.

Encourage diversity of native plants. Look around your area to identify plants that might have once occurred there and replace them.

Encourage habitat-building animals. These include burrowing mammals, midden-building pack rats, pond-building beavers, deer, owls, and leaf-cutter ant nests. Any animal that moves soil or builds nests creates microhabitat. For example, *Stephanucha annae* is an endemic Texas beetle that lays eggs in the compost layer under push-ups formed by pocket gophers. The tunnels created by the gopher provide habitat for many more species. Beaver lodges and pack rat middens have their own specially adapted species. Deer support a community of dung beetle species that would otherwise not occur. Owls produce habitat for beetle species that live in owl pellet accumulations.

Allow leaf litter to build up. Rather than rake or burn leaves, you can let them form a humus layer. Experience from Berlese collecting will show you that healthy layers of decomposing leaves support many insects, as the brown thrasher has learned in searching for food.

A mature forest with snags and deadfall. Courtesy of Texas Parks and Wildlife Department

Build compost piles. Anyone who ever turned over the compost knows there are many insects at work in there.

Do not "improve" natural features like springs and streams. Subtle changes to aquatic environments can drastically affect aquatic insects. For instance, cordulegasterids are rare dragonflies that inhabit shallow, sandy streams. The female inserts her abdomen into the water to the sandy bottom to deposit her eggs. Damming the stream would raise the water level and eliminate the cordulegasterids.

Leave or add cover, such as logs and rocks, for insects. Turning over rocks should give you an idea of the insects that are taking advantage of them.

Use target-specific pesticides and identify pest species correctly. Identifying insects before applying pesticides is extremely important. What you may think is a pest may actually be a beneficial insect or causing no damage, and the use of pesticides without cause may decrease your insect diversity. Once you have identified your pest, the use of target-specific pesticides will ensure that you are targeting only the pest. Broad-spectrum pesticides, used when the pest is not present, too often, or at too high an application rate will result in resistance and reduction of insect diversity.

How Can You Make a Contribution?

The study of insects has many advantages that may be attractive to you. You will find them easily and in sufficient abundance. Insect life cycles are generally rapid enough that you can study their development in a short time. Many are easily raised in terrariums where you can study them. Others can be observed in their natural habitat. Studies of the insects associated with particular plants like oaks, prickly pears, or nightshades have been performed through observational science. If you are attracted to water, you might consider studying the insects of springs, creeks, rivers, marshes or swamps, or other bodies of water. Habitats with specialized insects are all around you. A partial list to get you thinking includes caves, tree holes, sand dunes, tree bark, rotten logs, mushroom meadows, riparian areas, and concentrations of specific plants, dead animals, and ant nests.

Perhaps the greatest incentive for you to study insects is the existence of great gaps in our knowledge. Just like empty spaces on maps were opportunities for great explorers, the unknown in entomology is your opportunity for the satisfaction of original discovery.

What is the logical result of your studies? Once you have gathered some information on distribution or life history, how do you know if it is remarkable? If it is, then how do you report it? This is where amateurs benefit from association with professionals and libraries. Get to know a professional entomologist who is interested in the same group you are. He or she will have a good idea of where the gaps in knowledge are. Also use libraries. If you know the scientific name of an insect, you have access to all the information ever published on it. This is especially true now that electronic key word searches are available. You might read up on the butterfly that you have reared and find that nothing is published about its biology. Once you have determined this, the only step remaining is to publish the information.

Most scientific journals publish scientific notes. These are often short, nontechnical accounts of observations by amateurs. A little library or Internet searching may turn up a journal, bulletin, or newsletter dedicated to your group of interest. Pick one out and see what the published notes look like. A few examples are the *Coleopterists' Bulletin*, *Southwestern Entomologist*, *Flea News*, and *Tachinid Times*.

What Are the Insects of Interest in Texas?

In Texas, special attention is given to four specific insects or groups of insects because of their large-scale impact, their need for conservation, or their aesthetic value for Texas residents: honeybees, red imported fire ants, monarch butterflies, and dragonflies.

Honeybees

Honeybees (*Apis mellifera*) are not native to the Americas. European honeybees (*A. m. mellifera*) were brought to North America by early settlers in the early to mid-1600s. Honeybees have become an important part of human-dominated ecosystems, with the need for the pollination of large, monoculture crops. African honeybees (*A. m. scutellata*) were brought to Brazil in 1956 in the hopes of developing a hybrid more suitable for honey production in tropical and subtropical climates. Africanized honeybees, hybrids between European and African bees, quickly became established in the local, feral population, rapidly spreading through South and Central America and Mexico and reaching Texas in 1990.

Behavioral differences, related to the predictability of resources, exist between Africanized and European honeybees. Africanized bees are characterized by accentuated defensive behavior, high rates of brood production, and frequent swarming and absconding, all beneficial for surviving in an unpredictable environment. Swarming, or colony fission, is the means by which honeybee colonies reproduce. Most of the workers of the established colony leave with the old queen, forming a new, founder colony, leaving behind additional workers that raise a new queen and remain in the original hive location. Absconding refers to the abandonment of a nest site by the entire colony, typically caused by a disturbance or seasonal changes in resources. These traits are incompatible with current beekeeping practices, making managed colonies difficult to handle.

The defensive behavior of Africanized honeybees involves faster response times, increased numbers of alerted bees, and more stinging activity compared to European bees, posing potential hazards to human and livestock health. All counties in Texas today have reported Africanized honeybees. Therefore, all feral bees are believed to be Africanized honeybees or have the Africanized honeybee gene. We no longer test for Africanized honeybees, because all feral bees will test positive for this gene.

Colony collapse disorder (CCD) was first described in the United States in 2006. It is characterized by the rapid loss of the colony's adult bee population. The involvement of pathogens is supported by the transmissibility of the disorder through the reuse of equipment from CCD colonies. Although

A bumblebee, *Bombus* sp. (Hymenoptera: Apidae), on a cactus flower. Courtesy of Clinton J. Faas, cjfaas@gmail.com

many contributing factors are cited, recent studies indicate a close association between CCD and the varroa mite (an exotic honeybee parasite). The mite transmits a number of viruses, including Israeli acute paralysis virus and tobacco ringspot virus, which have both been associated with CCD. Other CCD-associated stressors include moving colonies for pollination, pesticides (particularly neonicotinoids), nutritional deficiencies (lack of nectar-producing plants), diseases/predators/parasites, and honeybee genetics (low disease/parasite removal in domestic strains).

Red Imported Fire Ant

Ants provide many important ecological functions in natural ecosystems. However, invasive species, such as the red imported fire ant (*Solenopsis invicta*), create many problems in native habitats and human-dominated areas. The red imported fire ant was accidentally introduced into the United States in the 1930s around Mobile, Alabama, probably in ship ballast soil, and arrived in Texas by 1953. Red imported fire ants now occur in the eastern two-thirds of the state, as well as some urban areas in western Texas. They are adapted to exploit disturbed habitats, surviving under a wide variety of environmental conditions.

They have a high reproductive potential, with the ability to produce thousands of reproductive adults each year. In their location of origin, South America, populations are regulated by different predators and pathogens, as well as competition with other species. However, only a few of these regulating mechanisms occur in the United States, allowing densities much greater than in South America. Red imported fire ants create a variety of problems, such as damage to electrical equipment; injury to humans, livestock, and pets; and damage to agricultural crops. There is also concern about the impact of red imported fire ants on wildlife species, such as the northern bobwhite quail (*Colinus virginianus*), Texas horned lizard (*Phrynosoma cornutum*), and white-tailed deer (*Odocoileus virginianus*).

Fire ants spread naturally through mating flights and colony movement, as well as by anthropogenic means, such as automobiles and the transport of infested materials (potted plants, hay, turfgrass, etc.). A number of chemical baits have been developed to control these ants. However, none of these provide complete control, except in small, localized areas, which require continued treatment.

Monarch Butterflies

Monarch butterflies (*Danaus plexippus*) were given the genus name *Danaus* in 1802 by the entomologist Jan Kluk. Some place them in the family Danaidae. Others consider the danaids to be a subfamily of the Nymphalidae. The name Danaidae is apropos. The original Danaids were 49 daughters of Danaus who were condemned to spend eternity carrying urns of water to a leaking cistern for the crime of murdering their husbands. The lepidopteran danaids are similarly cursed to carry their offspring north to the milkweed meadows of North America every spring. The fall generation must fly back to Mexico each fall.

Monarch butterflies are perhaps the best example of a well-known and loved arthropod. We have studied monarch migration, biological adaptations, and their relatedness to other butterflies. Through monarchs, millions of school children have learned about metamorphosis, migration, and mimicry.

Despite their popularity, the destination of migrating monarchs remained a mystery until 1976. Many other important questions still remain. How do the butterflies navigate? What are migration routes, and what affects them? What are the origins of the migration phenomenon? Monarch Watch is an organization formed in 1991 to study monarchs and promote conservation.

Every fall the shortening days trigger emergence of a generation of monarchs that postpone mating and reproduction in response to an urge to fly south. Monarchs from all over the eastern United States make a remarkable trip south to a few mountain refuges in central Mexico, where they spend the winter. Populations living on the western side of the Rocky Mountains have winter roosting sites in California. They spend the winter in clumps on trees and then spread north, depositing eggs on milkweed plants in spring. Migrating monarchs can fly up to 33,000 miles. Migrations can go wrong sometimes. Groups arrived in Britain in the fall of 1876, 1933, 1968, 1981, 1983, and 1995. It is possible to determine that trans-Atlantic monarchs originated in North America by analysis of the cardenolid chemicals that they accumulated while feeding on toxic milkweed plants as larvae. Different

Red imported fire ants, *Solenopsis invicta* (Hymenoptera: Formicidae). Courtesy of Texas Parks and Wildlife Department

species of milkweed have slightly different cardenolides.

Monarchs have long been known to be distasteful to predators because of the chemicals that accumulate in their bodies. Their bright orange and black colors serve in part to advertise distastefulness. This is called aposematic coloring. The viceroy butterfly is another species that closely resembles the monarch. For many years, the viceroy was cited as an example of Batesian mimicry in which one tasty butterfly takes advantage of another's acrid defenses by mimicking it. It has since been determined that the viceroy, too, has distasteful defense, and both species reinforce each other's reputations by sharing warning colors. This is known as Müllerian mimicry.

Threats to monarch populations include deforestation of roosts in Mexico and California and habitat loss of their host plant, the milkweed. Pollen from corn engineered to contain the insect toxin from the bacterium *Bacillus thuringiensis* (Bt) has been shown to be toxic to monarch larvae, but studies and risk assessments suggest the threat to monarch populations from Bt corn pollen in the environment is minimal. Predation by wasps has also been blamed for monarch decline. Some butterfly gardeners have reported paper-nest-building wasps to be preying on their pet monarch larvae. Predation by wasps will certainly be augmented by our construction of favorable wasp habitats like sheds, porches, and eaves. Protozoan parasites of monarchs have also been discovered. In 1966 *Ophryocystis elektroscirrha* were found to infest monarchs. Spores on leaves are eaten by larvae, and the parasite may kill larvae and disrupt adult emergence or vitality.

To contact Monarch Watch, visit http://www.monarchwatch.org. You can find information about monarch biogeography, trans-Atlantic migrations, and much more by entering key words on any Internet search engine, such as "monarch," "Danaidae," or "*Danaus plexippus*."

Dragonflies

Dragonflies have begun to give the butterflies some competition for the attention of amateur naturalists. They are appreciated for their species diversity, color, beauty, and abundance. And they are useful as indicators of the health of aquatic habitats. The dragonflies are perfect examples of insects that have gained popularity through the medium of the Internet. Forrest Mitchell of Texas A&M AgriLife Research in Stephenville, Texas, encouraged this interest by placing chilled dragonflies on his flatbed scanner to make beautiful, high-quality digital images. Before this technique was used, students of dragonflies were limited to killing and preserving specimens that typically lost some degree of coloration when dead.

Dragonflies and damselflies are in the order Odonata. They have aquatic larvae called naiads, which are typically predators on other aquatic invertebrates. Consequently, adult dragonflies will be commonly found around bodies of water. Many, however, will leave the water's edge and hunt insect prey in fields and fencerows. You will find that differences in habitat are important in determining dragonfly species. Rivers will support different species than ponds and lakes do. Some rare species will be found only in microhabitats like boggy seeps or clean, sandy woodland streams. A wide variety of habitat requirements and tolerance levels for pollution or disturbance allows the Odonata to be useful as bioindicators.

Some dragonflies, like the large colorful *Anax junius*, migrate in masses to the coastal regions of Texas each fall and fill the residents' yards on some fall days. For more information, search the Internet using key words such as "dragonflies" (in Texas) and "damselflies" (in Houston), "Dr. John Abbott," "Richard Orr," "Bob Honig," and "Robert Behrstock."

APPENDIX

The following accounts of the orders of insects are tailored when possible to help Texas Master Naturalists understand different orders as they relate to our state. Also included is brief information on collection and curation.

Blattodea: Common name: cockroaches. Contains many more interesting species than just the familiar household pests. Many species that inhabit leaf litter, soil, rotten logs, or animal nests are never pests. Some species are important components of forest ecosystems. Some roaches are actually pretty. The Cuban roach is pale green. Sand roaches in the family Polyphagidae are mottled brown like the pattern on some bird eggs. Some have interesting biologies, such as the polyphagid that lives only in the colonies of leaf-cutter ants. Pin and dry roaches like Orthoptera. Some people spread left wings. See Stidham and Stidham (2001) for the most up-to-date list. 4 Texas families.

Coleoptera: Common name: beetles. The words *most*, *biggest*, and *greatest* are often used in association with Coleoptera. About 40% of the insects are beetles; 25% of animals are beetles. Two of the largest families, Staphylinidae and Curculionidae (weevils), are larger than most orders. It is difficult to convey the spread of beetles through the environment in one paragraph. Nearly every source of large organic molecules in nature serves as food for some beetle. These include wood, bone, hair, fungus, insects, all plant parts, carrion, manure, algae, and humus. Coleoptera are present in every habitat type except the marine and coldest polar regions. The number of collectors and enthusiasts is rivaled only by the lepidopterists. Coleopterists usually specialize in one or a few families. If you become interested in Coleoptera, get a field guide to the Coleoptera. There are several, but due to the large size of the order they always leave out more than they include. *American Beetles* by Arnett and Thomas (2001) has been updated and reprinted, listing 131 families in North America and is the best single reference. It includes keys and references you need to get started. Most beetles should be pinned. Some soft-bodied forms can be collected in alcohol, though some may be distorted by alcohol. The most current authorities are Lawrence and Newton (1995), who list 166 families worldwide. No list of families occurring in Texas is available, but a checklist of Texas beetles is in preparation by Edward Riley of the Texas A&M Department of Entomology. He serves as the contact for an informal group of beetle collectors that meets every winter.

Collembola: Common name: springtails. Tiny, widespread, less common as habitats dry; present by and on water, in moist soil, and sometimes in vegetation. They jump by means of a ventral appendage. Collect into alcohol with aspirator. Abundant in Berlese samples of soil. Float a narrow jar lid containing alcohol by the edge of a pond or stream, and collect them as they jump in. Common in lawns. Preserve in alcohol. Mount on glass microscope slides. 7 Texas families.

Dermaptera: Common name: earwigs. Common under rocks and other debris, in crevices and rotten logs. Present in nearly all types of habitats but less common as conditions become colder and drier. Collect by turning rocks and logs, in pitfalls, and in Berlese of leaf litter. Pin and dry specimens. 4 Texas families.

Diplura: Common name: two-pronged bristletails. Tiny, usually less than 10 mm long, pale, elongate, rare in collections. Found in rich, moist soil and leaf litter, animal burrows, caves. Collect by Berlese.

Diplura are a prize whenever collected. Store in alcohol. 2 Texas families.

Diptera: Common name: flies. Although the name "fly" is attached to many other orders of insects, true flies belong only to order Diptera. The order of true flies is characterized by having only two wings. Entomologists recognize this distinction by making the common name a single word for non-Diptera (scorpionfly) and two words for Diptera (horn fly). Diptera is one of the larger and more difficult orders to identify. Like the beetles they are spread throughout the environment and occupy almost every imaginable niche. As larvae, many feed on decaying organic matter, some are aquatic, and some are parasitic on mammals. Diptera will be a major component of Malaise, flight intercept, and yellow pan traps. No list of Texas families available.

Embiidina: Common name: webspinners. Length 4–10 mm. Tiny elongate insects that construct and inhabit networks of silk tunnels in soil, crevices of rocks, and tree bark. Collect by searching out silk tunnels. Winged males rarely come to light. Females are wingless. Males are needed for identification. Embiidina are rare in collections but may be abundant in the environment. A semitropical group that occurs north as far as South Carolina or Utah. All three North American families known from Texas. E. S. Ross is the world authority on Embiidina. See Ross (2000) for an introduction to the order.

Ephemeroptera: Common name: mayflies. Naiads are aquatic predators and detritivores. Adults emerge and fly. Look for them on vegetation near water. Sometimes found at lights many miles from water. Collected best at lights, also by sweeping waterside vegetation or by rearing the naiads collected in the water. This is the first highly speciose order. Many families have special habitat requirements. Some burrow in riverbanks. Some used as indicators of water quality. Store in alcohol. Many people study Ephemeroptera because of their value as indicators of water quality. Search for the USGS web page on mayflies of Texas where 11 families are cited for the state.

Grylloblatodea: Common name: rock crawlers. These insects live in high mountains near glaciers. They are not found in Texas.

Hemiptera: Common names: true bugs, cicadas, hoppers, psyllids, whiteflies, aphids, scale insects. The order Hemiptera is divided into the suborder Heteroptera, the true bugs; the suborder Auchenorrhyncha, the cicadas and hoppers; and the Sternorrhyncha, the jumping plant lice (psyllids), whiteflies, aphids, coccids, mealybugs, and scales. These insects have piercing, sucking mouthparts, and most feed on plants. A few are predators of insects and other small animals, and some feed on mammals, including humans. Bed bugs and kissing bugs are examples of Hemiptera that feed on humans, other mammals, and birds. Generally Hemiptera can be collected from plants. Heteroptera and Auchenorrhyncha can be pinned or pointed and pinned. Sternorryncha can be preserved in vials in alcohol. No list of Texas families available.

Hymenoptera: Common names: ants, bees, wasps, sawflies. This is another gigantic order like Coleoptera and Diptera. Collectors and scientists divide it into more workable groups, including ants, bees, symphyta, aculeata, and parasitica. Symphyta is the primitive suborder of Hymenoptera characterized by a broadly attached abdomen. Most of these are herbivorous. The rest of the Hymenoptera belong to suborder Apocrita and are often subdivided into artificial groups for convenience. One of these groups is referred to as the aculeata, the group of Hymenoptera (excluding ants) with a sting. Aculeata may be thought of as the big wasps. Parasitica generally refers to the tiny wasps that parasitize other insects. Some people specialize within these groups and rarely study other Hymenoptera. Texas A&M University is known for work on parasitica and ants. Other ant specialists are at Sam Houston State University, and St. Edwards University has workers in aculeates and bees. No students of Texas Symphyta are known. The Central Texas Mellitological Institute is available for those interested in bees.

Most hymenopterists collect specimens with Malaise traps. Symphyta and aculeates are mostly collected by netting. Yellow pan traps collect some aculeates. Some Symphyta are attracted to blue pan traps. Parasitica are collected mostly by sweeping and Malaise. Yellow pan traps were invented for this group, and some workers use them exclusively. Rearing of parasitic Hymenoptera from their insect hosts can be very interesting. They can be reared by bottling insect eggs, larvae pupae, or adults to see what may emerge. Put stems and leaves bearing scale insects into containers and see what tiny parasitic wasps emerge. Certain bees dig tunnels into soil or wood and pack them with pollen. Mud daubers are bee relatives that pack chambers with stung insects or spiders. Other bee relatives dig nests in the ground and provision them. Ant collectors use pitfall traps, Berlese, and tree beating.

Isoptera: Common name: termites. Most people familiar with termites would not imagine collecting them, but several have interesting shape and biology. All four North American families have representatives in Texas. Species in the family Odotermitidae known from far West Texas may get up to 20 mm long. The family Termitidae contains species with nozzle-headed soldiers called nasutes that squirt noxious secretions from their head. In dry areas of the state desert termites build delicate coral-like mud tubes over grass and other plants. The most significant pests belong to family Rhinotermitidae. These require contact with the soil.

Kalotermitidae are known as dry wood termites and do not require soil contact. Different casts include workers, soldiers, and reproductives called alates. Often mass emergences of alates in spring will fill the air and provide great feasts for wildlife. Only soldiers and alates are identifiable. Collect by chopping into wood or digging into colonies. Preserve in alcohol. 4 Texas families.

Lepidoptera: Common names: butterflies, moths, skippers. Perhaps the most popular order of insects. In recent years, efforts to promote butterfly watching in the style of bird-watching have been successful. They have also been the most successful order at attracting the attention of collectors. A quick search in your library or on the Internet will turn up several good guides. These universally treat the colorful and easy-to-identify butterflies and skippers. It is ironic that moths make up the majority of the Lepidoptera and receive less attention from collectors. Most people are familiar with the leaf-eating larvae of many butterflies. Less well known are those lepidopteran larvae that bore into stems, mine the inside of leaves, tunnel into fruits and nuts, and eat submerged aquatic plants, dried grain, beeswax, fungi, lichens, or wool. Rarely, a few lepidopteran larvae parasitize or prey on insects, eat dried meat and cheese, or take blood meals.

Butterflies and skippers are typically netted while flying. One kind of butterfly trap consists of a wooden platform with a cylinder of meshlike fabric that is open on one end suspended in the air over the platform, with about one inch of space between the board and the mesh. Bait, like rotten fruit or fish, is placed in the center of the board. Butterflies are attracted and land on the board. Once they walk to the bait in the center, they are directly under the mesh bag. When they fly away, they go up into the bag and accumulate. Moths are mostly collected at lights at night.

Lepidoptera are pinned with their wings spread on special boards for drying. Lepidopterists are notoriously precise about mounting. Standard mounting places the wings horizontally perpendicular to the body with the hind margins of the front wings at right angles to the body. The hind wings are brought up to a point where the gap between fore and hind wing forms an equilateral triangle.

When collecting large numbers of Lepidoptera at a light or trap, collectors often field-pin specimens. First specimens are killed a few at a time in a clean, powerful kill jar. Then specimens are pinned through the thorax, unspread in rows in boxes. Later the pinned specimens are placed in a humid relaxing chamber made of an airtight container with wet paper towels and a little vinegar or Listerine until they soften enough to be mounted properly. This way collectors can maximize their time in the field.

Many Lepidoptera are too tiny to pin and spread. These microlepidoptera often are abundant and have fascinating biologies. These can be pinned using special minuten needles, fine forceps, and very fine foam. Using a razor blade, cut very shallow trenches into a piece of the finest foam pinning bottom available for lining the bottom of drawers and boxes. Plastazote foam is best. Then with fine forceps, pin the microlepidopteran through the thorax with a minuten needle. Rub the pinning material vigorously with the steel forceps on the surface where the little wings are expected to be spread. This builds up a charge of static electricity. If the specimen is fresh and dry, then its wings will magically be spread by the electricity when you stick the pinned specimen onto the pinning material so that its body fits into the groove you cut.

A complete and up-to-date checklist for Lepidoptera of Texas is not available, but some promising developments are occurring. Charles Bordelon and Ed Knudson of the Texas Lepidoptera Survey (TLS) are producing extremely useful guides to Texas Lepidoptera. Bordelon and Knudson (1999) published *Lepidoptera of the Big Thicket National Preserve* and *A Checklist of Lepidoptera of the Audubon Sabal Palm Sanctuary in Cameron Co., Texas* (1998) through TLS. The survey has also published a 12-volume *Texas Lepidoptera Atlas* (Knudson and Bordelon (2010). Search the Internet for Texas Lepidoptera Survey or Texas butterfly and moth information.

An excellent online resource for lepidopterists is Paul Oppler's US Geological Survey *Butterflies and Moths of North America*, which presents state- and county-level distribution maps for species and is designed to gradually accumulate information. See "Butterflies of North America" at http://www.butterfliesandmoths.org/.

Mantodea: Common names: mantids, praying mantis. Only one family (Mantidae) occurs in North America. Familiar predators of other insects in gardens and yards. Collect by beating or hand-picking from vegetation. Occasionally they come to lights. Pin and dry like Orthoptera. See Stidham and Stidham (2001) and Rondón et al. (2007) for up-to-date lists. 2 Texas Families.

Mecoptera: Common name: scorpionflies. These insects are uncommon enough that you should be delighted whenever they are found. They inhabit wooded areas. Some are found along the margins of woods. Others are only found deep in old-growth forest. Larvae crawl through soil and leaf litter, feeding on dead or dying insects. Family Panorpidae contains bright orange and black scorpionflies that are the most commonly encountered mecopterans. They are named for the males' abdominal claspers, which resemble a scorpion's stinger. In fall look for the brightly colored insects along the edge of woods. Smaller, pale panorpids may be found in deep East Texas woods. Family Bittacidae contains the hanging craneflies. These superficially resemble the craneflies common in early spring. They have four wings, not two like the Diptera. Bittacids are rare. They are found most often in old-growth forest along rivers in the eastern part of the state. The family Meropeidae includes the earwig scorpionflies or forcepsflies. These extremely uncommon insects seem to be tied to the deepest, most undisturbed beech/magnolia forest of East Texas. Presence of any Mecoptera usually indicates a healthy old-growth forest. Collect most Mecoptera by netting them as they fly. Rare scorpionflies will sometimes turn up in Malaise traps. Meropeidae have been collected in yellow pan traps. Pin mecoptera and spread their wings. Search the Internet for Mecoptera in Texas. 3 Texas families.

Microcoryphia: Common name: jumping bristletails. Length 10–12 mm, elongate with three tails, cylindrical in cross section, jumping behavior. Uncommon in collections. Not uncommon in moist woodlands. Some inhabit dry areas, living in crevices and under rocks. Collect by Berlese, pitfall, beating vegetation, searching ground with flashlight. Store in alcohol. 2 Texas families.

Neuroptera: Common names: lacewings, mantidflies, antlions, owlflies, spongilla flies. Many people become familiar with this order through the pit-building antlions (Myrmeleontidae) that live in dry, sandy soil. However, few make the association between the subterranean larvae and winged adult. Adult antlions remotely resemble dragonflies but have visible antennae and fly weakly. All other Neuroptera are predators. Food sources for various kinds include aphids, beetle and moth larvae, spider eggs, freshwater sponges, scale insects, and mites. Some have aquatic larvae that are general predators. Others have larvae that prey on insects on or under tree bark. Neuroptera are the most primitive of the holometabolous orders. They are the first group for which we may use the term "larva." All families are attracted to light. Many are weak fliers so lights should be placed close to habitats. Look in places with deep, sandy soil for Ascalaphidae and Myrmeleontidae. Place lights in old-growth forests to find other unusual families like Dilaridae. Beat juniper trees in spring on the Edwards Plateau to get Raphidiidae. Corydalidae come to light from large streams. Sialidae do so from ponds and lakes. Other families show up at lights sporadically. 12 Texas families.

Odonata: Common names: dragonflies, damselflies. Naiads are aquatic predators. Adult dragonflies hunt insect prey over water or sometimes in fields and fencerows far from water. The most common family, Libellulidae, found generally distributed by ponds and streams. Chances are good that any dragonfly around a pond or in a field is a Libellulid or Aeshnid. Along large streams and rivers Gomphidae and Corduliidae are more common. Rarities include Cordulegasteridae, found only by small, sandy woodland streams in the east. Still rarer are Petaluridae, which inhabit miry seeps deep in East Texas woods. Damselflies are smaller Odonata that fly weakly by the side of ponds and streams. Three families of damselflies are widespread. Protoneuridae is a tropical insect that barely reaches the valley of the Rio Grande. Collect Odonata with a net as they fly. Some collectors pin and spread them, but they are subject to greasing up and losing colors. Some collectors place specimens in small envelopes and drop them into wide-mouth bottles of acetone. Museums place specimens in clear plastic envelopes with labels and store them in shoeboxlike containers. 10 Texas families.

Orthoptera: Common names: grasshoppers, locusts, crickets, katydids, lubbers, cave crickets, mole crickets. Found in many other habitats besides grassy meadows. Tridactylidae and Tetrigidae are adapted for semi-aquatic life. Gryllacrididae inhabit caves and burrows. Katydids in the Tettigoniidae are difficult to get out of the canopy of East Texas forests. Lubbers swarm over Gulf Coast marshes and West Texas deserts. Gryllotalpidae tunnel through moist soil. Toothpick grasshoppers in the Acrididae inhabit pitcherplant bogs. Collect by sweeping or netting during flight or in pitfalls. Some are attracted to light. Specimens should be pinned and dried. Usually the left wings are spread. See Stidham and Stidham (2001) for a checklist of Texas Orthoptera. 8 Texas families.

Phasmida: Common name: walkingsticks. Length 10–100 mm. Sticklike herbivorous insects that are more common in the South. California and Florida have families that do not occur in Texas. Heteronemiidae and Pseudophasmatidae occur in Texas. Collect by beating trees or sweeping vegetation. Heteroneiids may occur in mass emergences and defoliate trees. Mated pairs of pseudophasmids mass under bark of dead trees in East Texas in the fall. Pin and dry specimens. Support them while they are drying. See Stidham and Stidham (2001), Otte and Brock (2005), and Arment (2006) for up-to-date lists of Texas Phasmida. 2 Texas families.

Phthiraptera: Common names: chewing or biting lice, sucking lice. Small parasites of birds and mammals. Chewing or biting lice (formerly Mallophaga; now Rynchophthirina, Amblycera, and Ischnocera) may bite hosts, causing skin irritation. Infected animals appear run down and emaciated and if not killed by the lice, are at high risk to contract diseases. Hosts include elephants, African pigs, guinea pigs, chinchillas, marsupials, dogs, and birds. Sucking lice feed on the blood of their hosts and can transmit diseases such as endemic typhus in humans. They parasitize many kinds of mammals, including seals, sea lions, otters, squirrels, ungulates (cattle, deer, pigs, horses), rodents, canids (dogs, foxes, coyotes), peccaries, and humans. Phthiraptera can be collected from bird nests and the bodies of animals. Stored in alcohol vials. No list of Texas families available.

Plecoptera: Common name: stoneflies. Aquatic naiads are predators or detritivores. Plecoptera are less common in Texas than in most other states because they generally require cool, clean waters. Their occurrence here is generally cause for greater surprise than it is elsewhere. Summer stoneflies (Perlodidae, Perlidae) emerge as adults in the summer and are the more common kinds. They are mostly predators. Less common winter stoneflies (Taeniopterygidae, Capniidae, Nemouridae, Leuctridae) emerge in early spring here but can be delayed by water temperature in places like cold springs. Winter stoneflies often fill the detritivore niche of ephemeropterans in some streams. Collect by light or by sweeping vegetation along very clean streams or near springs. Some species may emerge in abundance from unpolluted, but muddy rivers in East Texas. Store in alcohol. Plecoptera are rare enough that all specimens should be saved. Search for Plecoptera of Texas on the Internet to learn who studies them here. 6 Texas families.

Protura: Common name: coneheads. Verging on microscopic, rare in collections, probably more widespread than is currently thought, associated with fungus in moist soil habitats. Collect by Berlese. Protura are so uncommon that all specimens should be saved. Store in alcohol. Slide-mount for identification. 2 Texas families.

Psocoptera: Common names: booklice, barklice. Many people have had their only experience with this order of insects while reading dusty old books or magazines. Any books stored in a dusty barn or house without air conditioning will support colonies of these tiny, nearly transparent insects. They feed on starchy glue in bindings and are pests of stored grain and dry pet foods. Psocoptera is a diverse and speciose order. Collect by beating tree branches, Berlese of leaf mold, bird or mammal nests, turning of rocks and logs, and examination of lichen-covered rocks. Free-living species are often winged. Aspirate them or pick up with a fine, damp paintbrush. Store in alcohol. Difficult identifications will require technical literature, slide-mounted specimens, and a good microscope. Psocopteran identification to family is a difficult task. To help in identification, search for Texas Psocoptera on the Internet. 24 families in North America. No list of Texas families available.

Siphonaptera: Common name: fleas. Fleas are considered to be close relatives of the Diptera and Mecoptera. They are all parasitic blood feeders. Caterpillar-like larvae live in the nests of animals and feed on dandruff and dried blood. Most are associated with mammals, and a few are bird parasites. The fleas that most people are familiar with belong to the family Pulicidae, which includes the cat flea, dog flea, stick-tight flea of poultry, and the oriental rat flea. These fleas are interesting because of their detrimental effects, but there are several other families that have a degree of host specificity and are interesting to collectors. Charles Rothschild and his daughter, Miriam, are two well-known flea collectors. A quick literature search will turn up many popular articles on their collections. Being a southern state, Texas is a good place to see flea diversity. The chigoe flea is uncommon in South Texas. These burrow into the skin around people's toes and form pea-sized sores. Carnivore fleas (Vermipsyllidae) attack bears, wolves, and foxes. Ischnopsyllidae are bat parasites. The greatest variety are found on various rodents. Always exercise caution with fleas and rodents. If you are exposed to any flea, rodent, or rodent nest and develop the slightest illness or cold, see your doctor and mention that you have been collecting fleas. Several human cases of bubonic plague are reported each year from West Texas. These originate commonly from exposure to prairie dogs and their fleas. Collect fleas by examining hosts or their nests. Collect them into alcohol and mount on glass slides for identification. Search the Internet for checklists of fleas and other flea news. 7 families in North America. No list of Texas families available.

Strepsiptera: Common name: twisted-wing parasites. Debate over the position of these strange insects continues today. They have been placed in the Coleoptera by some and in their own order by others. Still others have speculated that they are relatives of the Diptera. Our species are parasitic on other insects, that is, the hosts have been stylopized (parasitized by a strepsipteran). Only the males look anything like an insect. They are sometimes collected in Malaise traps. Females are typically wormlike parasites inside other insects. They commonly attack certain Orthoptera, Homoptera, and Hymenoptera. They may also be reared from captive parasitized hosts. Look for insects with strange bumps that spread the plates of the abdomen. This is often the only evidence of the parasite. Paper wasps (*Polistes*) are commonly stylopized in the fall. One species attacks fire ants. Parasitism impels the host to climb to the top of a blade of grass and await emergence of the parasite. Strepsiptera are uncommon. Specimens should be collected whenever possible. 4 families in North America. No list of Texas species is available.

Thysanoptera: Common name: thrips. Tiny insects are often found in flowers. Some wingless. Others with distinctive fringed wings that resemble feathers. Most easily collected by beating flowers against white paper. Look for tiny elongate insects crawling among the pollen. Other kinds will come from Berlese of leaf mold. A few species found in tree bark or random vegetation. Many suck plant juices. A few of these are pests. Others are beneficial predators. Collect into alcohol with a fine paintbrush dipped in alcohol. Mount on glass slides for identification. Search Texas Thysanoptera on the Internet to help in identification. No list of Texas families available.

Thysanura: Common names: silverfish, firebrats. Length 2–20 mm, elongate with three tails, flattened or convex, not cylindrical, not jumping. Common in soil, leaf litter, under bark, occasional household pest of pantries and barns. One kind inhabits fire ant nests. Collect by Berlese, pitfall, under rocks and debris, in dirty/dusty feed rooms or pantries. Store in alcohol. 2 Texas families.

Trichoptera: Common name: caddisflies. These small mothlike flying insects are better known for their case-building aquatic larvae than the adults. Any book on aquatic insects will devote a portion to the larvae. They are often identifiable to family based on the structure of the case. Cases are built of sand, gravel, vegetation, or other detritus joined together by silk. They are often used as indicator species for water quality. Different kinds of water bodies will contain different families. Springs and clean streams are inhabited by rare kinds, while muddy or polluted rivers will hold more common kinds. Adults are collected most commonly at lights near water, also by sweeping and beating streamside vegetation. Preserve adults and larvae in alcohol. See Moulton and Stewart (1997) for a checklist of Texas Trichoptera. 9 Texas families.

Zoraptera: Common name: zorapterans. These tiny insects were not discovered until 1913. They inhabit rotten logs and sometimes sawdust piles in the eastern forests of Texas. Aspirate them quickly before they run deep into crevices. They will appear most like smaller, faster termites. Males and females may or may not be winged. The order is composed of one family (Zorotypidae) with one genus (*Zorotypus*) and two species. If you want to become a world expert on an order of insects quickly, study the Zoraptera. Store specimens in alcohol. Zoraptera are so rarely collected that they should always be taken.

References

Arment, Chad, ed. 2006. Stick Insects of the Continental United States and Canada: Species and Early Studies. Landisville, PA: Coachwhip Publications.

Arnett, R. H., Jr., and M. C. Thomas. 2001. *American Beetles*. 2 vols. Boca Raton, FL: CRC Press.

Blair, W. F. 1950. The Biotic Provinces of Texas. *Texas Journal of Science* 2 (1): 93–117.

Bordelon, C. W., and E. C. Knudson. 1998. *A Checklist of Lepidoptera of the Audubon Sabal Palm Sanctuary in Cameron Co., Texas*. Houston: Texas Lepidoptera Survey.

———. 1999. *Lepidoptera of the Big Thicket National Preserve*. Houston: Texas Lepidoptera Survey.

Borror, D. J., C. A. Triplehorn, and N. F. Johnson. 1989. *An Introduction to the Study of Insects*. 6th ed. Philadelphia: Saunders.

Colwell, R. K., and J. A. Coddington. 1994. Estimating the Extent of Terrestrial Biodiversity through Extrapolation. *Philosophical Transactions of the Royal Society London* B 345:101–18.

Drees, B. M., and J. Jackman. 1998. *Field Guide to Common Texas Insects*. Houston: Gulf Publishing.

Knudson, E., and C. Bordelon. 2010. *The Texas Lepidoptera Atlas*. Vol. 12, *Sesioidea*. Texas Lepidoptera Survey: Privately printed.

Lawrence, J. F., and A. F. Newton Jr. 1995. Families and Subfamilies of Coleoptera (with Selected Genera, Notes, References and Data on Family Group Names). In *Biology, Phylogeny, and Classification of Coleoptera*, ed. J. Pakaluk and S. Slipinski, 779–1006. Warsaw, Poland: Warszawska Drukarnia Naukowa.

Merritt, R. W., and K. W. Cummins. 1996. *An Introduction to the Aquatic Insects of North America*. 3rd ed. Dubuque, IA: Kendall/Hunt Publishing.

Moulton, S. R., II, and K. W. Stewart. 1997. A Preliminary Checklist of Texas Caddisflies (Trichoptera). In *Proceedings of the 8th International Symposium on Trichoptera*, ed. R. W. Holzenthal and O. S. Flint Jr., 349–53. Columbus: Ohio Biological Survey.

New, T. R. 1998. *Invertebrate Surveys for Conservation*. New York: Oxford University Press.

Otte, D., and P. D. Brock. 2005. *Phasmida Species File: Catalog of Stick and Leaf Insects of the World*. 2nd ed. Philadelphia: The Insect Diversity Association and the Academy of Natural Sciences, Cafe Press.

Rondón, A. A. A., Francesco Lombardo, and Lauro José Jantch. 2007. *Checklist of the Neotropical Mantids (Insecta, Dictyoptera, Montodea)*. *Biota Colombiana* 8 (2): 105–58.

Ross, E. S. 2000. Embia: Contributions to the Biosystematics of the Insect Order Embiidina. *Occasional Papers of the California Academy of Sciences* 149:1–53.

Samways, M. J. 1994. *Insect Conservation Biology*. London: Chapman and Hall.

Stidham, J. A., and T. A. Stidham. 2001. Preliminary Checklist of the Orthopteroid Insects (Blattoidea, Mantoidea, Phasmatoidea, Orthoptera) of Texas. *Insecta Mundi* 15 (1): 35–44.

TPWD (Texas Parks and Wildlife Department). 2015. Nongame and Rare Species Program: Federal and State Listed Species. Accessed April 14, 2015. https://tpwd.texas.gov/huntwild/wild/wildlife_diversity/nongame/listed-species.

Winston, J. E. 1999. *Describing Species: Practical Taxonomic Procedures for Biologists*. New York: Columbia University Press.

Additional Resources

Abbott, J. C., K. W. Stewart, and S. R. Moulton II. 1997. Aquatic Insects of the Big Thicket Region of East Texas. Supplement, *Texas Journal of Science* 49 (3): 35–50.

Arnett, R. H., Jr. 2000. *American Insects: A Handbook of the Insects of America North of Mexico*. 2nd ed. Boca Raton, FL: CRC Press.

Baumgardner, D. E., J. H. Kennedy, and B. C. Henry. 1997. New and Additional Records of Texas Mayflies (Insecta: Ephemeroptera). *Transactions of the American Entomological Society* 123:55–69.

Burke, H. R. 1963. Coleoptera Associated with Three Species of *Solanum* in Texas. *Southwestern Naturalist* 8 (1): 53–60.

Burke, H. R., A. F. Amos, and R. D. Parker. 1991. Beach Drift Insects on Padre Island National Seashore, Texas. *Southwestern Entomologist* 16 (3): 199–203.

Castner, J. L. 2000. *Photographic Atlas of Entomology and Guide to Insect Identification*. Gainesville, FL: Feline Press.

Feynman, R. P. 1999. *The Pleasure of Finding Things Out*. Cambridge, MA: Perseus Books.

Goulet, H., and J. T. Huber, eds. 1993. *Hymenoptera of the World: An Identification Guide to Families*. Publication 1894. East Ottawa: Centre for Land and Biological Resources Research, Research Branch, Agriculture Canada.

Holldobler, B., and E. O. Wilson. 1990. *The Ants*. Cambridge, MA: Belknap Press of Harvard University Press.

Lugo-Ortiz, C. R., and W. P. McCafferty. 1995. The Mayflies (Ephemeroptera) of Texas and Their Biogeographic Affinities. In *Current Directions in Research on Ephemeroptera*, ed. L. Corkum and J. Cibrowski,151–69. Toronto: Canadian Scholars Press.

McCafferty, W. P. 1983. *Aquatic Entomology: The Fisherman's and Ecologist's Illustrated Guide to Insects and Their Relatives*. Boston: Jones and Bartlett Publishers.

Neck, R. 1996. *A Field Guide to Butterflies of Texas*. Houston: Gulf Publishing.

Reddell, J. R. 1970. A Checklist of the Cave Fauna of Texas. V. Additional Records of Insecta. *Texas Journal of Science* 22 (1): 47–65.

Szczytko, S. W., and K. W. Stewart. 1977. The Stoneflies (Plecoptera) of Texas. *Transactions of the American Entomological Society* 103:327–78.

Tinbergen, N. 1958. *Curious Naturalists*. The Natural History Library. Garden City, NY: Anchor Books, Doubleday.

Triplehorn, C. A., and N. F. Johnson. 2005. *Borrer and Delong's Introduction to the Study of Insects*. 7th ed. Belmont, CA: Thomson Brooks/Cole.

Wiersema, N. A. 1998. Newly Reported and Little Known Mayflies (Ephemeroptera) of Texas. *Entomological News* 109:27–32.

Website Resources

Aggie Horticulture: http://aggie-horticulture.tamu.edu [Combined horticulture information resources of the teaching, research, and extension program at Texas A&M University]

Agricultural and Environmental Safety: http://www-aes.tamu.edu/ [Agricultural chemicals and environmental safety information from the Texas Agricultural Extension Service]

Biological Control of Weeds in Texas: http://bc4weeds.tamu.edu/ [Overview and latest news on identification and management of tough Texas weeds with biological control]

BugGuide.net: http://bugguide.net/node/view/15740 [An online community of naturalists who enjoy learning about and sharing observations of insects, spiders, and other related creatures]

Center for the Study of Digital Libraries: http://www.csdl.tamu.edu/ [Texas A&M Engineering Experiment Station site provides a focal point for digital libraries and research technology for the state of Texas]

Department of Entomology, Texas A&M University: http://entomology.tamu.edu

Digital Dragonflies: http://agrilife.org/dragonfly/ [Great photos on this site about dragonflies and damselflies and how they relate to water quality issues]

Field Guide to Common Texas Insects: http://texasinsects.tamu.edu/ [Extensive, useful information about the most common insects of Texas]

Insect Image Gallery: http://entomology.tamu.edu/image_gallery/ [View special insect image collections or search database of agricultural pest images]

Insects in the City: http://citybugs.tamu.edu

Insects in the Classroom: http://iitc.tamu.edu [Collaborative site for educating students about insects; lesson plans and other resources available for study and use by teachers and the public]

Texas A&M AgriLife Extension Bookstore: https://agrilifebookstore.org/ [Award-winning communications support unit of the Texas A&M University System Agricultural Program]

Texas Imported Fire Ant Research and Management Project: http://fireant.tamu.edu [Provides information about the fire ant in Texas: current activity, management solutions, latest research news, and other issues]

USDA Agricultural Research Service: http://www.ars.usda.gov/ [Scientific research organization]

Integrated Pest Management

Hort IPM: http://hortipm.tamu.edu/ [Educational information on integrated pest management for commercial nursery and floral crop producers. Extensive database of pesticide information]

Pecan Kernel: http://pecankernel.tamu.edu/ [Information on integrated pest management for pecan growers across Texas]

Texas IPM Program: http://ipm.tamu.edu/ [The Extension IPM program in Texas is operated in partnership with the Texas Pest Management Association, the Texas Department of Agriculture, Texas AgriLife Research, CSREES, USDA and the citizens of Texas; research-based information provided by scientists in partnering agencies and Texas A&M AgriLife Extension Service scientists is extended to growers through County Extension Agents and Extension Specialists]

Society Sites

Entomological Society of America: http://www.entsoc.org

Society of Southwestern Entomologists: http://sswe.tamu.edu

UNIT 14

Ichthyology

JOHN MCEACHRAN
Professor Emeritus and Curator Emeritus of Fishes, Biodiversity Research, and Teaching Collections, Department of Wildlife and Fisheries Sciences, Texas A&M University

KEVIN CONWAY
Assistant Professor and Curator of Fishes, Biodiversity Research and Teaching Collections, Department of Wildlife and Fisheries Sciences, Texas A&M University

Unit Goals

After completing this unit, volunteers should be able to

- demonstrate an appreciation for fishes and an interest in ichthyology
- discuss the diversity of fishes in Texas and demonstrate familiarity with the different groups of fishes
- understand the relationships among various groups of fishes
- demonstrate knowledge about the general characteristics of the major groups of fishes
- discuss basic principles of fish behavior, physiology, and ecology and relate these principles to environmental adaptations
- discuss the habitat needs of various groups of fishes

Why Study Fishes?

There are a host of reasons for studying the natural history of fishes, ranging from the joy of knowledge for its own sake to the more practical applications. Let us start with knowledge for its own sake and work toward how fishes directly impact humans. Human beings are endowed with very inquisitive minds. Much of our education is concerned with understanding the basic principles that underlie the functioning of life on earth, far beyond what we need to survive as a species. In other words, humans have a basic desire to learn about the world around us. One must also bear in mind these ideal investigations occasionally lead to practical solutions to problems that appear to be totally unrelated to the initial investigation.

So how do fishes fit into this mind-set? Organisms that we classify as fishes are more numerous in number of species, have a greater variety of body shapes, occupy a greater number of habitats, feed on a greater range of prey with a greater variety of feeding mechanisms, and have a larger number of modes of reproduction than the other groups of vertebrates (amphibians, reptiles, birds, and mammals). In fact, some of the things that fishes do in their life pursuits are mind-boggling. In addition, fishes have now been dated back to the dawn of life in the fossil record. Fishes gave rise to the other vertebrate groups, including humans, so the study of fishes may reveal much about the other groups of vertebrates as well. Recent fossil jawless fishes from China date to the Early Cambrian (535 million years ago), when most of the phyla of organisms first appear in the fossil record. These early fishes gave rise to the remainder of the vertebrates, and a relative of the lungfishes gave rise to the tetrapods (amphibians, reptiles, birds, and mammals) in the Devonian (about 390 million years ago).

Historically, why were fishes studied and why does it remain important? From the mid-eighteenth to the early twentieth century, natural history was a major scientific field that was investigated to further

Jean Louis Rodolphe Agassiz: Influential American Naturalist

The naturalist who played the largest role in establishment of natural history research in the United States never set foot in Texas. However, most of the naturalists that followed were either of his educational lineage or of an educational lineage significantly affected by him.

Jean Louis Rodolphe Agassiz (1807–73) was a Swiss naturalist and museum builder who arrived in the United States in 1846. A year later he was awarded a professorship at Harvard College and proceeded to build a world-class museum and educational program in natural history. He attracted students from across the United States and made Harvard the center for the study of natural history in the New World. His students continued his research and teaching efforts and established natural history museums throughout the United States. A colleague, Charles Frederic Girard (1822–95), published the section on fishes in the first natural history study of Texas (Mexican Boundary and Pacific Railroad surveys). Agassiz's most distinguished student, David Starr Jordan (1851–1931), carried on Agassiz's tradition, first at Indiana University and later at Stanford University (which he founded). Jordan and his students surveyed and described the majority of the fish fauna of North America before describing many of the marine fishes of Hawaii, Samoa, and Japan. They collected widely in the freshwater and coastal waters of Texas. Of the 13,000 species of fishes known in 1922, Jordan and his students described more than 2,500 (about 20% of the total). Most of the scientists who studied and taught vertebrate natural history in the United States in the mid- to late twentieth century are academic descendants of David Starr Jordan, such as Carl L. Hubbs (1894–1979) and George S. Myers (1905–85). Carl Hubbs collected widely in Texas and published many papers on Texas fishes during his 70-year career. His son, Clark Hubbs (1921–2008), was the leading ichthyologist in Texas during the latter half of the twentieth century and early twenty-first century.

Clark Hubbs. Courtesy of University of Texas

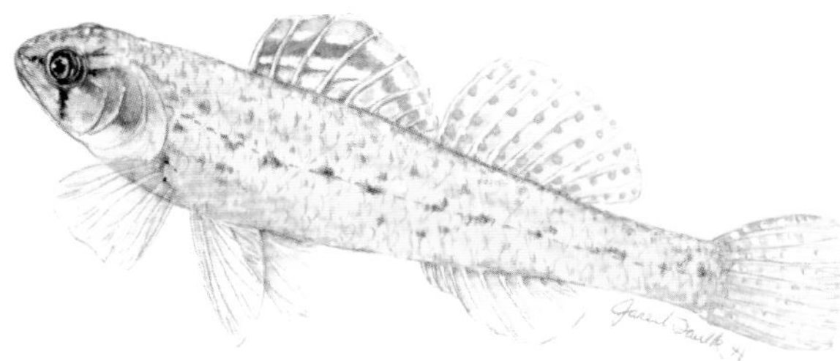
A fountain darter (*Etheostoma fonticola*). Courtesy of Texas Parks and Wildlife Department

our knowledge. However, some of the major expeditions led by the military or by other representatives of the federal government had geopolitical or economic goals, such as the Lewis and Clark Expedition to the West Coast (1803–6) and the Long Expedition to the Rocky Mountains (1819–20, 1823). By the late nineteenth and early twentieth centuries the government was conducting fisheries surveys both in fresh and marine waters to assess fishery resources. At about this time, government fishery labs and hatcheries were also raising fishes to stock streams and lakes across the United States. Fishery surveys and stocking programs continue to the present day to assess and increase our fishery resources.

Diversity of Fishes

Fishes also defy identification. They are defined mostly by what they are not rather than what they are. They are vertebrates that, for the most part, live in the water and lack limbs (forelimbs and hind limbs). In other words fishes are vertebrates other than tetrapods. As is often the case, when a group of animals cannot be defined, it generally means that they do not form a natural group, and such is the case with fishes. A natural group of animals is derived from a single ancestor and includes all of the descendants of that ancestor. As tetrapods are derived from fishes, it is the separation of tetrapods from fishes that renders the latter as an unnatural grouping. Though collectively fishes do not represent a natural group, ichthyologists consider several smaller subgroupings of fishes to represent natural groups, including the hagfishes, lampreys, cartilaginous fishes, ray-finned fishes, and lobe-finned fishes (including the tetrapods).

Hagfishes are the most primitive vertebrates and are defined by lacking mandibular jaws and paired fins, clearly defined vertebrae, and functional eyes. They are entirely marine and live largely buried in soft sediments, where they feed on soft-bodied invertebrates and carrion. There are about 77 species worldwide, only one of which occurs off the Texas coast.

Lampreys also lack mandibular jaws and paired fins, but they have true vertebrae and eyes. Their mouth consists of an oval sucking disc that enables them to attach to other fishes and feed on their flesh. They occur in both fresh and marine waters, but all species reproduce in fresh waters. There are 46 living species, two of which live in the fresh waters of East Texas.

Cartilaginous fishes have mandibular jaws and true vertebrae and are distinguished from the ray-finned fishes in possessing cartilaginous skeletons, tooth-like scales with an enamel-like covering, and horny fin rays (ceratotrichia) that are unsegmented and unpaired. They are commonly known as the chimaeroids, sharks, skates, and rays and, for the most part, are found only in marine waters. There are about 1,000 living species, and about 78 species occur off the Texas coast. A few of these enter Texas estuaries and bays.

Ray-finned fishes possess mandibular jaws, bony skeletons, thin scales lacking an enamel-like covering (though there are some exceptions), and segmented and paired fin rays (lepidotrichia). Ray-finned fishes occur in all habitats where fishes occur. There are more than 32,000 species.

Lobe-finned fishes possess lobed pelvic and pectoral fins that articulate with the body via a single bone (the humerus) and typically possess a well-developed lung.

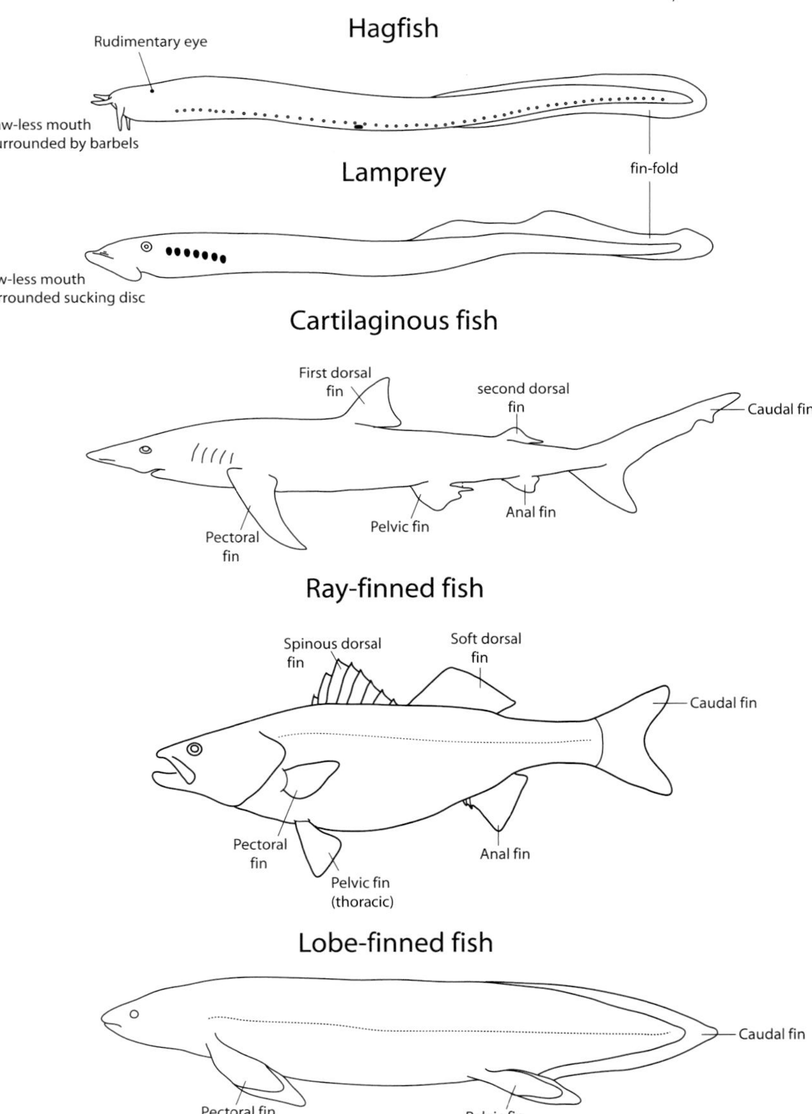

Body types of fishes. Courtesy of Kevin Conway

Like the ray-finned fishes, lobe-finned fishes also possess segmented and paired fin rays (lepidotrichia). There are approximately 25,000 species of lobe-finned fishes, yet only two living groups (representing 8 species) are considered typical "fishes." This includes the lungfishes (6 species of freshwater fishes found in South America, Africa, and Australia) and the coelacanths (2 species of marine fishes found in deeper coastal regions throughout the Indo-Pacific Ocean). The remainder of the lobe-finned fishes are tetrapods (i.e., fishes that left the water) and are covered in other units on amphibians, reptiles, birds, and mammals.

Fishes now number over 33,000 species; there are approximately 25,000 species of other vertebrates (tetrapods). An additional 100 to 200 species of fishes are described every year with no end in sight. Only a relatively small number (approximately 30) new species of amphibians and reptiles are described each year, and even fewer birds and mammals. It is estimated that when all aquatic areas of the earth are thoroughly surveyed, there will be about 50,000 species of fishes, almost twice the number of the other vertebrates combined. The bulk of the new species will come from the tropical waters of the western Pacific and Indian Oceans and the fresh waters of tropical South America, Africa, and Southeast Asia, but new species of fishes are still being discovered and described from US waters.

Fishes of Texas

Texas has a diverse fish fauna in both its fresh and marine waters. There are about 243 species of fishes that live in the many rivers, artificial lakes, and ponds (tanks) of the state. The majority of the species are in the families Cyprinidae (minnows), Catostomidae (suckers), Ictaluridae (catfishes), Cyprinododontidae (killifishes), Fundulidae (topminnows), Percidae (darters), and Centrarchidae (sunfishes and basses).

The state is divided into four distinct faunal areas: an eastern area extending from Louisiana to the Trinity River, a central area including the Brazos and Colorado Rivers, a northern area including the drainage system of the Red River in the Panhandle, and a southwestern area extending from the Guadalupe River system westward to New Mexico and southward to Mexico.

The eastern area receives abundant precipitation, and streams are permanent and moderately clear with sandy bottoms. Fishes are typical of the Mississippi River Valley and include lampreys, sturgeons, and pickerels and many species of minnows, darters, and sunfishes.

The central area is semiarid, and its two main rivers vary in several respects. The Brazos is muddy and slow moving, and the Colorado is clear and fast flowing. The fish fauna is less diverse than the eastern area and includes minnows, darters, and sunfishes, some of which are endemic to the area.

The northern area is characterized by turbid water and dominated by fishes of the northern plains that reach their southern limit in the area. This includes minnows, darters, and sunfishes, some of which are endemic to the area.

The southeastern area is semiarid with some streams drying during part of the year and others maintained by springs. Many of

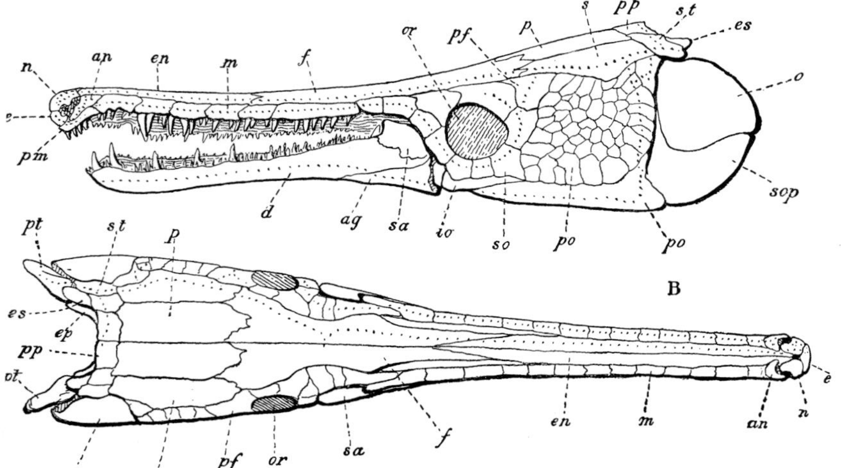

Skull of the alligator gar (*Atractosteus spatula*) (top) and longnose gar (*Lepisosteus osseus*) (bottom). From Goodrich (1909)

the fishes are known exclusively from this area. This includes minnows, killifishes, and livebearers, in addition to a tetra (Characidae) and a cichlid (Cichlidae) that are widespread in northern Mexico and are the only members of their respective families in the United States.

The marine fish fauna off the Texas coast is diverse, with the species composition varying with depth distance from shore and substrate. Members of the Sciaenidae (drums), Ariidae (marine catfishes), Clupeidae (herrings), and Engraulidae (anchovies) are the dominant fishes in estuaries, bays, and inshore areas. Nearly all of these fishes use the estuaries as nursery grounds. Most of the benthic habitats on the Texas continental shelf are sand to muddy silt; however, salt domes and other substrates support coral reef assemblies in a few areas. **Benthic fishes** are those that live and feed on or near the bottom of seas or lakes. **Pelagic fishes** are those that live and feed away from the bottom in the open water column.

Benthic fishes that live on the midcontinental shelf include members of the Sparidae (porgies), Triglidae (searobins), and Bothidae (lefteye flounders). These fishes produce pelagic eggs and larvae, and the larvae develop independent of estuaries. Benthic fishes of the outer continental shelf include members of the Lutjanidae (snappers), Phycidae (hake), and Scorpaenidae (scorpionfishes). Fishes associated with the hard reefs include typical coral reef fishes, including members of the Pomacentridae (damselfishes), Chaetodontidae (butterflyfishes), and Labridae (wrasses).

The pelagic fish fauna of the Texas continental shelf is also diverse. On the inner half of the continental shelf, there are numerous species of Clupeidae (herring) and Engraulidae (anchovies) feeding on plankton and Carangidae (jacks) feeding on smaller fishes. Pelagic fishes of the outer continental shelf include various members of the Carcharhinidae (requiem sharks) and Scombridae (tuna and mackerels).

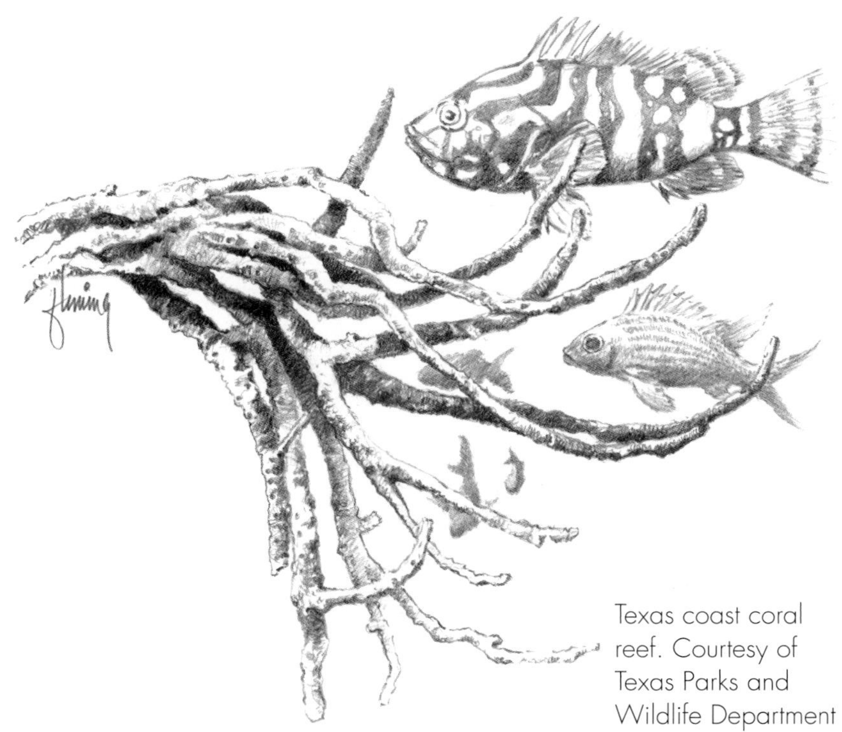

Texas coast coral reef. Courtesy of Texas Parks and Wildlife Department

Shapes of Fishes

Most people have a mental image of a fish as a spindle-shaped animal that resembles a minnow or salmon, with a terminal mouth, single dorsal fin centered at about midlength, a forked-shaped tail or caudal fin, pelvic fins located on the belly, and an anal fin along the ventral surface of the body slightly posterior to the dorsal fin. Fishes do, however, exhibit a vast repertory of shapes. The typical fish shape just described fits those pelagic fishes that actively swim in the water column.

There are only a few shapes that are acceptable for an active life in the water column because of the negative effects of density and viscosity of water on locomotion. Fishes must expend considerable energy to overcome the thickness and stickiness of water. The shape just described minimizes the impedance of water to locomotion. Thus, fishes that actively move through water tend to be similar in shape. The most active and fastest swimmers are the most constrained in shape because resistance of water increases with speed. Thus,

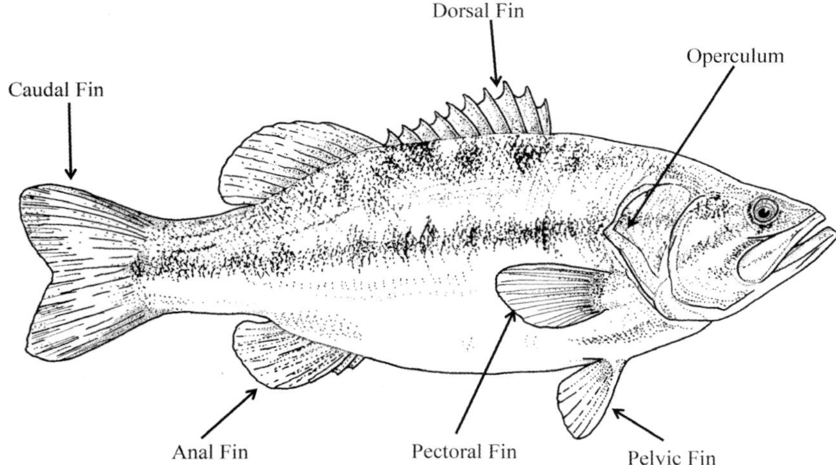

Anatomy details of a Guadalupe bass (*Micropterus treculii*). Courtesy of Texas Parks and Wildlife Department

fishes that pursue such a life have to be of similar shape. These fishes are shaped like mackerels, tunas, and white sharks. Note that porpoises, dolphins, and whales resemble these fishes because they have had to overcome the same constraints.

Fishes that are suspended in water but swim slowly are less constrained and assume a greater variety of shapes. Shapes range from long and eel-like fishes to short and globular or box-shaped. Rather than optimized for speed, these fishes are optimized for energy conservation. They are, however, constrained in regard to their density. They must be the same density as the water in which they swim in order to stay afloat. If they are heavier than water, they will have to expend energy to remain afloat. Density is reduced by storing low-density oils in the flesh, gastrointestinal tract, or bones or by possessing a swim bladder. Swim bladders are outgrowths of the intestinal tract and are found only in ray-finned fishes.

Fishes that live around coral reefs have another kind of constraint related to intricacies of the reef habitat. These fishes are specialized for maneuverability. For this reason, they tend to be short, compressed, and deep bodied, with the paired fins an-

Fish Body Shape Types

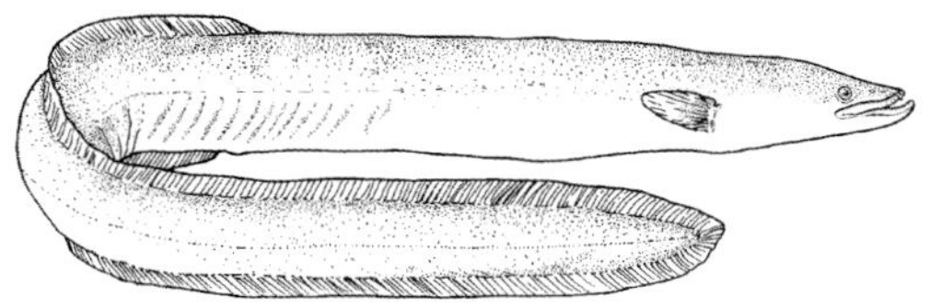

American Eel - Anguilliform

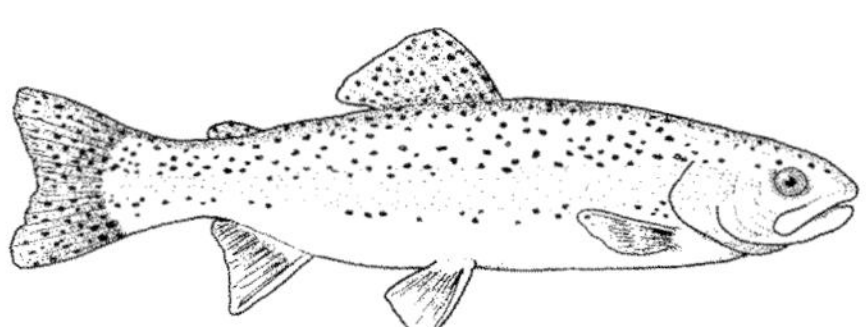

Rainbow Trout - Fusiform

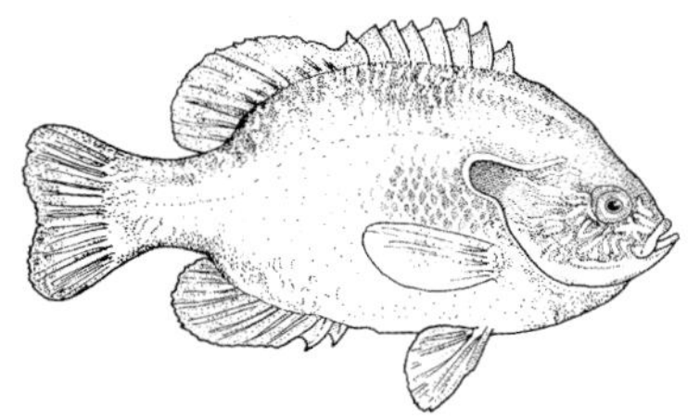

Longear Sunfish - Compressiform

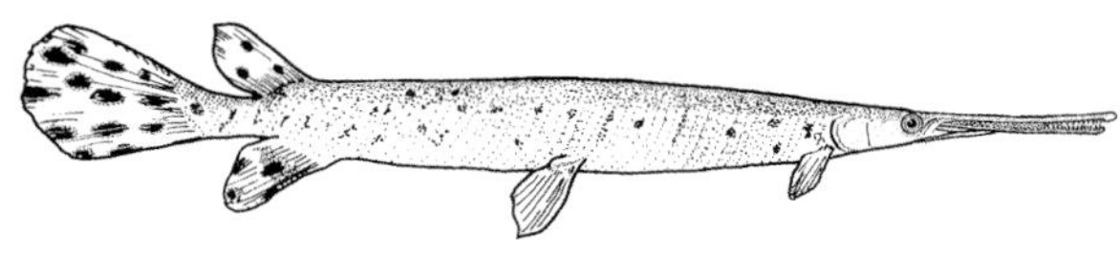

Alligator Gar - Sagittiform

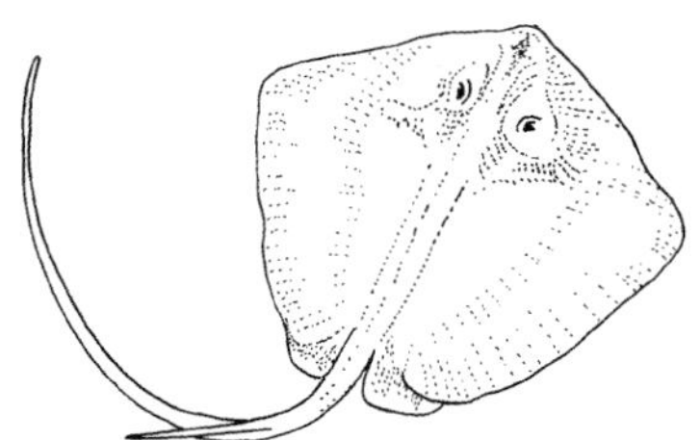

Atlantic Stingray - Depressiform

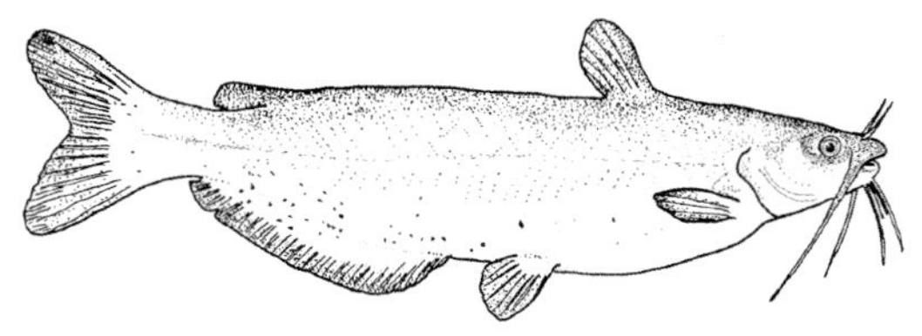

Channel Catfish – Intermediate (Combination of Shapes)

The body shape of a fish can give a quick assessment of the fish's way of life. Courtesy of Mary Pearl Meuth, Texas A&M AgriLife Extension Service

teriorly arranged one above the other. The paired fins function as rudders and braking devices and are most efficient when placed anteriorly one above the other. As do the slow-moving pelagic fishes, they need to be neutrally buoyant to remain suspended in the water column with minimum effort; thus, they typically possess a swim bladder. Fishes that spend the majority of their life on the bottom (benthic fishes) are less constrained in their shapes. For a number of reasons, it is often advantageous to blend in with the background. Camouflage can protect benthic fishes from predators and/or allow them to ambush their prey. Benthic fishes tend to be elongated and depressed. Some, like scorpionfishes, resemble rocks or coral heads covered with algae.

In summary, the shape of fishes is related to a number of factors in their particular habitat. The ultimate shape is a compromise among a host of factors concerned with locomotion, feeding, and staying alive. With a basic idea of the constraints of different environments, it is possible to examine the shape of a fish and to predict where it lives.

The shape is also determined by the genetic potential of the fish species. If the fish species does not have the genetic blueprint for a particular shape, the shape will not happen. For instance, ray-finned fishes are, for the most part, not depressed or flattened, but there is apparently a need for the flattened shape in benthic habitats. To compensate, flatfishes have become compressed and then lie on their side to approximate a depressed shape. Flatfishes include flounders, halibuts, and soles. They start out life very much compressed, but during development one of their eyes migrates to the other side of the head, and they assume a benthic existence by lying on either their right

Longear sunfish (*Lepomis megalotis*), a common sunfish (Centrarchidae) found in rivers and lakes from Canada to Mexico. Courtesy of Kevin Conway

Blacktail shiner (*Cyprinella venusta*), a common minnow (Cyprinidae) with a typical fusiform body shape. Courtesy of Kevin Conway

Hogchoker (*Trinectes maculatus*), a common flatfish found in the lower parts of estuaries along the Gulf Coast. Courtesy of Kevin Conway

or left side. These fishes are truly unique among the vertebrates in being asymmetrical. Much can be learned by examining the shape of fishes and predicting their habitats. It is important to realize that evolution does not always follow the simplest path. The path followed is related to the genetic potential of the particular fish group.

Diversity of Habitat

Although fishes are, for the most part, restricted to aquatic habitats, some fishes can, for extended periods of time, live out of the water. There are very few regions of the aquatic world that lack fishes. In fresh water, fishes are found from anaerobic swamps and temporary bodies of water to torrential streams and lakes of the Andes of South America at 3,812 meters (15,507 feet) and the headwater streams of the Himalayas in Asia at 5,600 meters (18,373 feet). Some freshwater fishes occur in highly saline waters, and others live in low-pH acidic rivers such as the Rio Negro in South America or the peat swamp forests of Southeast Asia.

Fishes that live in anaerobic waters obtain their oxygen by means of lungs or other richly vascularized tissue that is brought into contact with the air. Fishes that live in temporary ponds resemble insects in

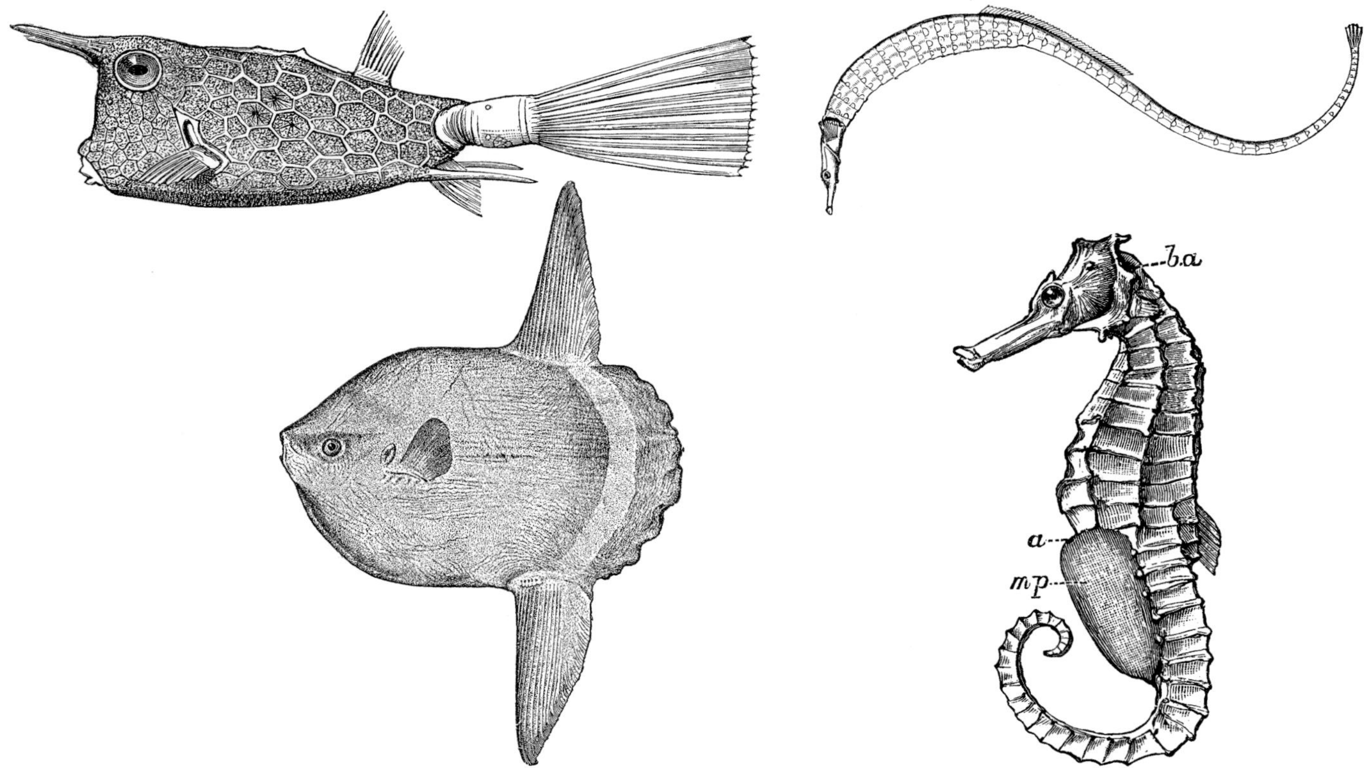

The body shapes of many fishes are difficult to classify, including those of the longhorn cowfish (*Lactoria cornuta*), the ocean sunfish (*Mola mola*), and the seahorses and pipefishes. From Harmer et al. (1910)

that they grow and reproduce during rainy periods but assume an inanimate state during dry periods. As the water dries up, fertilized eggs laid in the mud at the bottom of the pool go into an arrested development (referred to as **diapause**) until the rains return. As the water rises, they undergo rapid development, mature, and spawn before the next drought.

Fishes that live in torrential mountain streams have flattened bodies, suckerlike mouths, and suckerlike fins that enable them to resist the water currents and to feed on the algae (or invertebrates inhabiting the algae) growing on the rocky bottoms. Fishes living in low-pH waters have special hemoglobin that enables them to capture oxygen from the acidic water. Texas does not challenge fishes with such extreme habitats, but there is considerable chemical and physical variation in aquatic habitats across the state that are correlated with amount of precipitation and amount of stream flow. The distribution of fish species reflect these factors.

In marine waters, fishes live from exposed tidal flats to depths of 8,000 meters (approx. 26,250 feet), and from the tropics to polar latitudes with temperatures below –2°C. Fishes that spend much time above the water on the mudflats (mudskippers) obtain oxygen through vascularized organs, have thick integument that resists desiccation, and have eyes adapted for sight on land. They gather their food on land and go into the water only to avoid desiccation or terrestrial predators. Fishes that inhabit great depths live in almost complete darkness, under extreme pressure, and in a very food-poor environment. In most cases, such deep-sea fishes have reduced eyes, lack swim bladders, and have poorly calcified skeletons. Eyes are metabolically expensive and are greatly reduced or totally lost in environments in which they are not needed. On the other hand, these fishes have very acute senses of smell and touch. Because of the great pressure, fishes are unable to keep gas in their swim bladders, and there is little available calcium for skeletal structures. Fishes that live in super-cooled waters of the north and south polar regions have an antifreeze system in their blood that prevents them from freezing. The antifreeze is a protein that lowers the freezing point of the tissue below that of the water in which these fishes live.

Again, the marine waters off Texas lack these extreme habitats, but habitat varies with distance from shore, substrate, salinity, and temperature, and fish species are distributed according to their habitat requirements.

How Have Fishes Adapted to Their Environment?

Fishes have adapted to their environment in various ways, including how they obtain food and how they reproduce.

How Fishes Feed

The other groups of vertebrates display a wide variety of modes of feeding, but none rival the fishes. Fishes range from carnivores, omnivores, herbivores, to parasites, and the variety of feeding modes within each of these categories is truly amazing. There are straightforward carnivores that swim down their prey. Others, however, are lie-and-wait predators that lurk in the shadows or weed beds or lie buried in the sand and ambush unsuspecting prey. Many of the ambush predators are aided with powerful suctorial mouths to engulf prey or electric organs to stun their prey. Another group of fishes is endowed with a dorsal fin spine

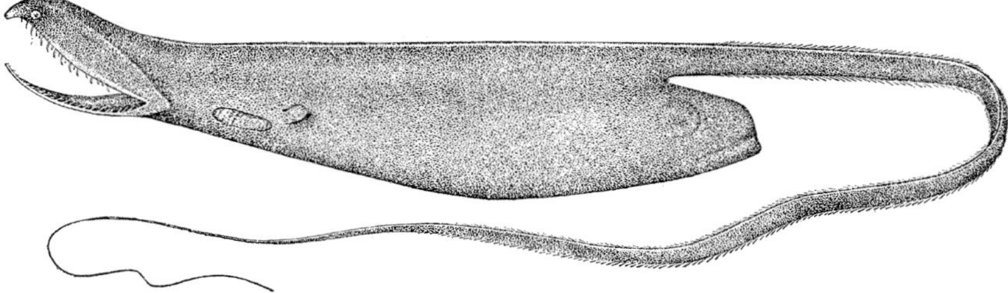

Deep-sea gulper eel (*Saccopharynx ampullaceus*), a highly predatory deep-sea fish capable of swallowing large prey items, aided by a massive mouth and highly distensible stomach. From Harmer et al. (1910)

modified into a fishing pole and a lure to entice their prey within range of their mouth. The relative size of prey varies greatly. Some of the largest fishes such as the manta rays, basking sharks, and whale sharks feed on minute zooplankton that is filtered out of the water.

Deep-sea viperfishes are able to disarticulate their jaws (like snakes) and have greatly distensible stomachs and engulf fishes larger than themselves. Many pelagic sharks and piranhas have cutting teeth and are able to take bites out of their prey. Pipefishes and sea horses have syringelike mouths that suck individual zooplankton out of the water column. The archerfish dislodges terrestrial insects from plants above the surface by spitting drops of water.

A large number of fishes, including some of the most derived, are herbivorous. Most consume algae because much of it is easier to break up and digest than vascular plants. Few, if any, fishes are able to digest cellulose or have resident bacteria in their guts that can break down cellulose. Most herbivores simply graze and browse algae off substrates.

Some of these herbivores (parrotfishes, filefishes, and triggerfishes) have beaklike teeth for cutting the algae; others (loaches, armored catfishes, and some cichlids) have lips and jaw teeth that resemble scrub brushes that scour rocks and other hard substrates of algae. Damselfishes are special in that they can be considered farmers that cultivate stands of algae growing on coral heads. These fishes are territorial and stake out manageable substrates on coral heads and keep all other herbivores out. With little grazing pressure, algae grow on the coral substrates, and the damselfishes weed out types of algae that are inedible.

"It is not the strongest of the species that survives, not the most intelligent, but the one most responsive to change."
—attributed to Charles Darwin

Parasitic fishes are not that uncommon, and they have a wide variety of means of obtaining nutrients from their hosts. A majority of the lampreys attach themselves

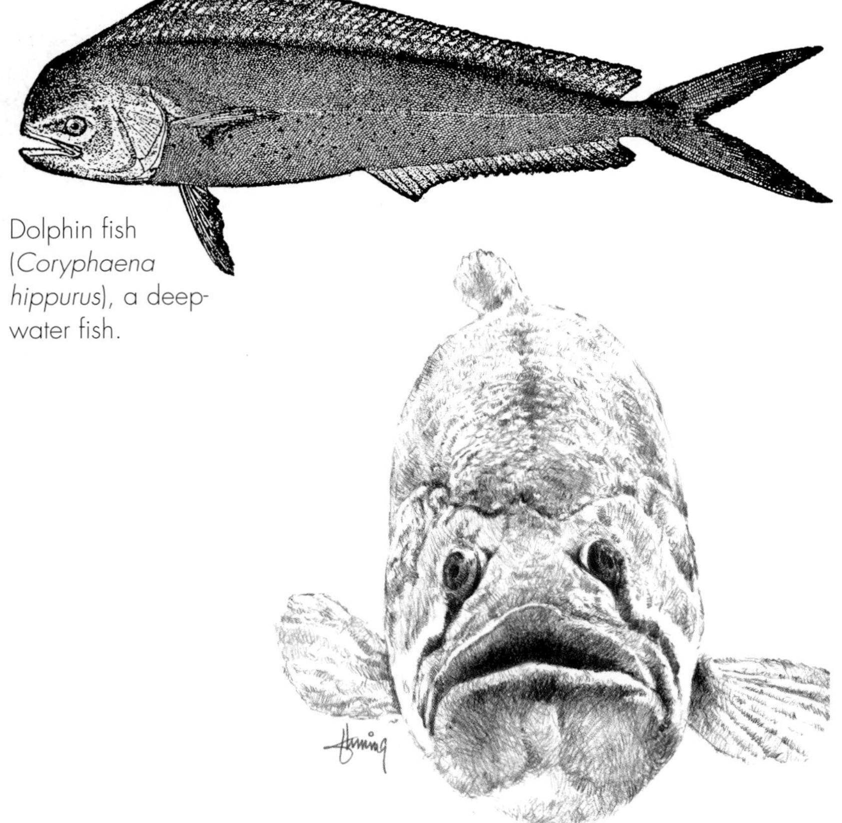

Dolphin fish (*Coryphaena hippurus*), a deep-water fish.

Grouper (Epinephelinae), a carnivorous fish.
Courtesy of Texas Parks and Wildlife Department

Tilapia (Cichlidae), an herbivorous fish.

to other fishes by means of their suctorial discs, rasp holes in the sides of their host, and live on the body fluids. Hagfishes, the other jawless fishes, use their rasping jaws to burrow into dead and dying fishes and consume their hosts from the inside. A deep-sea eel feeds in a similar manner but, unlike the hagfish, has mandibular jaws. There are a number of fishes in tropical fresh waters that live on the scales removed from their hosts. Some of the cichlid fishes from the great lakes of Africa make their living by parasitizing the scales, flesh, or young of mouth brooding fishes. In some cases, the parasitic fishes closely resemble their host fishes, thus enabling them to approach to within striking distance. Aggressive mimicry is also practiced by a blenny that resembles the cleaning wrasses that set up cleaning stations on coral reefs. The blenny, however, removes pieces of flesh and scales rather than parasites from its hosts.

How Fishes Reproduce

All life on earth prospers because parents are successful in replacing themselves. In other words, on average, each parent replaces itself with a reproductive adult during its lifetime. Each parent, on average, produces a single reproductive offspring.

Fishes have evolved a wealth of modes of reproduction and rival the rest of the vertebrates in the variety. The vast majority of fishes are single sexed (either males or females) and broadcast their sperm or buoyant eggs into the water. The sperm fertilizes the eggs, and the fertilized eggs float off and are on their own. The parents end their parental involvement with the spawning act. This type of reproduction is very chancy in that the fertilized eggs have a very small probability of survival. The floating fertilized eggs are consumed by a host of predators. Thus, fish species that practice broadcast spawning produce millions of eggs, and of these millions relatively few will survive to reproduce.

Other species invest less energy in producing gametes and more energy into ensuring that their fertilized eggs have a reasonable chance of survival. A number of fishes produce large, sticky eggs that are fertilized and deposited in places relatively free of predators. Eggs may be deposited on aquatic plants and shells or buried in the bottom. A subset of fishes that deposit fertilized eggs in safe areas will remain with the eggs until the eggs hatch and thus invest additional energy in their offspring. Some, such as the Siamese fighting fish, build bubble nests and defend the nest and newly hatched young until they can defend themselves. The freshwater angelfish deposits fertilized eggs on leaves of aquatic vegetation, fan the eggs to ensure they get enough oxygen, and defend the newly hatched young from predation.

The ultimate in egg depositors are those fishes that carry their young either in their mouths or on their bodies. A number of the cichlid fishes scoop up the fertilized eggs after spawning and mouthbrood them until the young are fairly accomplished swimmers. Male sea horses and pipefishes brood their young in belly pouches. A number of different groups of fishes have gone the route of mammals in brooding their young internally. This is the case in the majority of the sharks and rays and in a number of the ray-finned fishes. Generally, fishes that practice internal brooding produce a very large egg that has a large supply of yolk to nourish the young. However, some fishes with internal development supply nourishment to the young through uterine milk, unfertilized eggs, or a placental attachment. In one unique case in a species of shark, the first embryo to descend into the uterus consumes all subsequent embryos.

In addition to the great diversity of reproductive modes, fishes are diverse in their sexual orientation. Most fishes are either male or female and remain so throughout their lives. However, some, such as the sea basses, start out life and first function as females and later change to and function as males. Other fishes such as parrotfishes have primary males and females, but some of the females change into secondary males that are very different in coloration from the primary males. There are a few fishes that are bisexual and actually fertilize themselves.

How Do Fishes Function in Ecosystems?

Although fishes are generally considered to be near the top of the food chain, they occupy a number of trophic levels from herbivores to top carnivores and tend to dominate a number of aquatic habitats. They dominate their habitats through a combination of consumption and being consumed. In most habitats fishes are more diverse in number of species than all of the other multicellular animals. They also have a decided effect on the other multicellular organisms through predation.

Fish in the Great Lakes parasitized by lamprey eels (Petromyzontiformes). Courtesy of US Geological Survey

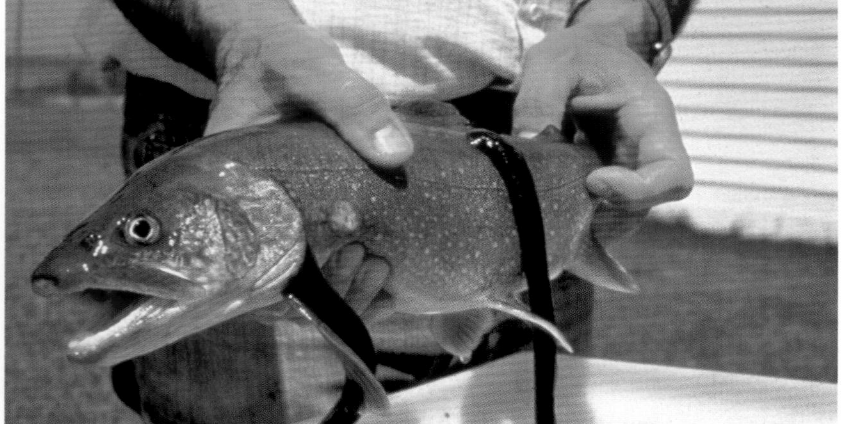

Texas ShareLunker black bass (*Micropterus* spp.) eggs. They are typically deposited in an area of slow-moving water and guarded by the males until they hatch. Courtesy of Texas Parks and Wildlife Department

Planktivores play an important role in the food chain. Many of these fishes form vast schools that filter the water for microscopic zooplankton and, in turn, are consumed by larger predators such as larger fishes, birds, or marine mammals. For instance, small lantern fishes, ranging from 4 to 13 centimeters in length, consume zooplankton and, in turn, are eaten by a variety of larger fishes, dolphins, and porpoises. Thus, fishes play a role that is critical to the well-being of the upper end of the food chain.

A number of freshwater and brackish-water fishes consume larvae of terrestrial insects such as mosquitoes. Mosquitoes are often vectors for diseases such as malaria. Thus, the fishes that consume mosquitoes (mosquito fishes) are often important in the control of malaria and other mosquito-transported diseases. They have been transported worldwide to perform this function.

Anadromous fishes that undergo a migration between marine and fresh water at some stage in their life cycle, such as the salmon, are very instrumental in the transfer of nutrients. The Pacific salmon are born in freshwater streams, in some cases over a thousand miles from the ocean. After an initial period in these waters, the young migrate downstream to the ocean and spend their juvenile life at sea, where they do most of their growing. They migrate back to their natal streams to spawn, die, and fertilize these waters with their bodies. Their progeny and all other organisms in the streams benefit from their ultimate sacrifice. The migrating salmon also serve as an important food for bears and humans.

The role of fishes in a particular habitat is crucial but often very subtle. Coral reefs are occupied by a diverse group of herbivorous fishes that keep algae closely cropped. Without the herbivorous fishes the algae

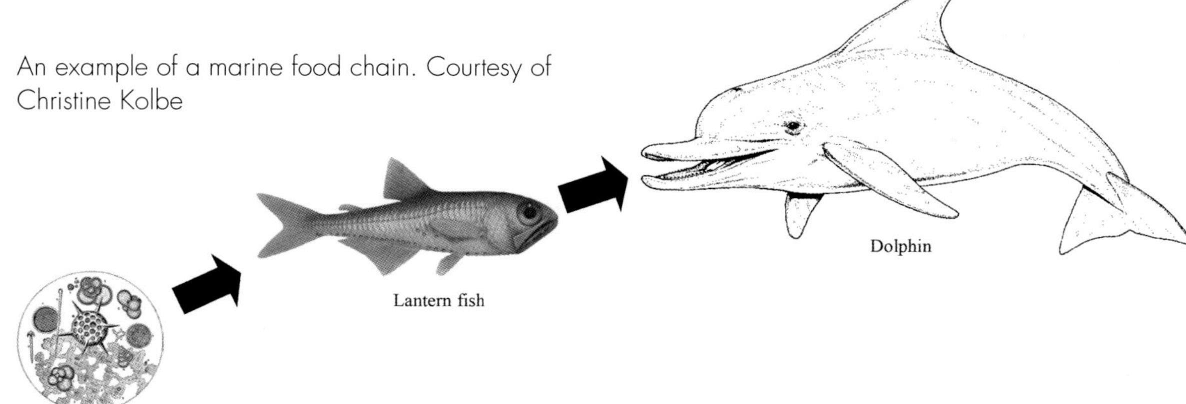

An example of a marine food chain. Courtesy of Christine Kolbe

would bloom and destroy the reef-building coral, because the coral polyp lives symbiotically with an algae. The algae need light to photosynthesize. A dense covering of algae will inhibit photosynthesis and result in the death of the coral polyp. If the reef-building coral dies, the reefs will erode away, and the whole ecosystem will be lost. Thus, the herbivorous fishes enable the reef-building coral to control the algae. The significance of these fishes can be judged by building a barrier on the reef that excludes these fishes. Within a short time the algae forms a dense mat that kills the underlying reef-building coral.

Some fishes can be considered "keystone species" in that they influence the diversity of the remainder of the community. Damselfishes are territorial herbivores on coral reefs. A fish stakes out a hexagonal piece of territory on a reef substrate and cultivates the algae that grow within its territory. The fish selectively "weeds" the patch to remove algal forms that are less desirable and aggressively defends the patch from other herbivores. The result is that the patch develops into a stand of algae that may serve as a refuge to a wide variety of invertebrate organisms. The algal mat has a negative effect on the underlying coral polyps and leads to their death. However, localized death of the reef structure leads to a greater diversity of organisms and to the overall health of the ecosystem. This situation is similar to the effects of a large tree dying and falling in a tropical rain forest. The fallen tree creates an open space that simulates the regeneration of life in the forest. Fishes in other habitats play similar roles but are less well documented.

All of these activities can have profound but, in some cases, subtle effects on humans. Fishes also have more direct effects on humans. They are a major food source for humans, serve as important recreational activities, and are objects of a very large pet industry. The worldwide harvest of fishes is 100 million metric tons. This total is thought to be at or slightly above the maximum sustainable level. In other words, the world catch cannot be further expanded without negatively affecting the populations of the exploited species. It is often thought that aquaculture and mariculture will enable humans to expand their take of fishery resources. However, intensive production of

Striped bass (*Morone saxatilis*) are an example of anadromous fishes that can be found spawning in Texas streams. Courtesy of US Fish and Wildlife Service

Cocoa damselfish (*Stegastes variabilis*) are keystone species in coral reefs along Texas' Gulf Coast. Courtesy of Texas Parks and Wildlife Department

fishery resources can have negative effects on the environment and negatively affect artisanal fisheries.

"The civilized people of today look back with horror at their medieval ancestors who wantonly destroyed great works of art or sat slothfully by while they were destroyed. We have passed this stage. . . . Here in the US we turn our rivers and streams into sewers and dumping grounds, we pollute the air, we destroy our forests and exterminate fishes, birds, and mammals not to speak of vulgarizing charming landscapes with hideous advertisements. But at best it looks as if our people were awakening."
—Theodore Roosevelt, June 25, 1913

Some Conservation Concerns for Fishes

Like other groups of organisms, fishes have been negatively impacted by humans and will be increasingly impacted as human populations expand and compete for resources. The history of fisheries is a long story of overexploitation. Through technology, humans have greatly increased the efficiency of harvesting fishes, and greater efficiency leads to overexploitation of the resources. In many cases, fish species that were exceedingly abundant prior to exploitation have not returned to their former abundance decades after the collapse of the fishery. Several species, such as some of the whitefishes of the Great Lakes in the midwestern United States, have gone extinct due, at least in part, to overfishing. The problem with the management of fishery resources is that it is more or less trial and error. The initial population size and structure of exploited stocks are often not known, and management measures are not put in place until the resource is in decline.

Humankind exerts many subtle effects on fishes that may go unnoticed until the fishes, and often the entire ecosystem, are in decline. Dams have had a less subtle effect on anadromous fishes. They often prevent the adults from reaching their natal spawning grounds. Dams have negatively impacted the Atlantic and Pacific species of salmon and a number of species of sturgeons. Dams also affect large riverine fishes that migrate long distances within a single river. Dams on the Colorado River of Colorado are responsible for the decline of many of the fishes that were formerly abundant, such as the Colorado squawfish, humpback chub, and razorback sucker. Dams also have major effects on habitats. They change a habitat dominated by stream flow to a lake environment. Fishes adapted to flowing water may not thrive in a lake environment. Also, fishery managers often introduce fishes into these artificial lakes from other areas. The introduced species may further negatively impact the native fishes and may lead to their extinction.

In Texas, dams have negatively affected the flow of nutrients into estuaries, the replenishment of sediments along the coasts, and the amount of water reaching the estuaries. Estuaries are highly productive environments that are nourished by nutrients

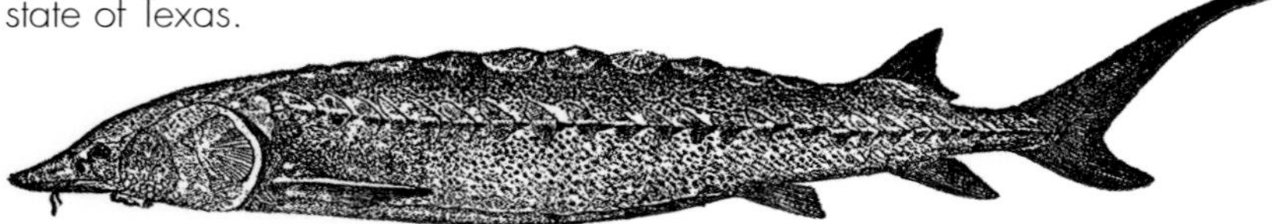

Short-nosed sturgeon (*Acipenser brevirostrum*), an anadromous fish that spawns along coastal rivers and has been extirpated from the Gulf and state of Texas.

flowing into tributaries within the drainage system. Beaches along the coast depend on sediments eroding from lands within the drainage system to replace the sediments removed by wave action. Much of the plant and animal life in estuaries requires a low-salinity habitat. If dams restrict too much water, the salinity of estuaries may increase, much to the detriment of the plants and animals.

Any human activity that modifies the aquatic environment can negatively impact aquatic organisms. Dredging, bulkheading, and draining of wetland areas remove or alter aquatic habitats and often interfere with life cycles of aquatic organisms. Deforestation near a stream can alter the habitat by increasing water temperatures and siltation. These changes can make the stream habitat unfit for the aquatic organisms. Agriculture, industries, and municipalities negatively impact fishes through chemical and biological pollution. Pesticides, herbicides, and fertilizers applied to agricultural lands often run into streams, rivers, and coastal areas. These products can either directly kill aquatic organisms or negatively impact their habitat. Fertilizers can cause plankton blooms that use up the dissolved oxygen and lead to fish kills. Every summer a large area of the continental shelf off Louisiana and eastern Texas becomes anaerobic presumably because of the application of fertilizers to agricultural land adjoining the Mississippi River in the Midwest.

References

Goodrich, E. S. 1909. *A Treatise on Zoology*. Ed. Sir Ray Lankester. Part IX, *Vertebrata Craniata (First Fascicle: Cyclostomes and Fishes)*. 8 vols. London: A. & C. Black.

Harmer, S. F., W. A. Herdman, T. W. Bridge, and G. A. Boulenger. 1910. *Fishes, Ascidians etc*. London: Macmillan.

Additional Resources

Helfman, Gene S., Bruce B. Collette, Douglas E. Facey, and Brian W. Bowen. 2009. *The Diversity of Fishes: Biology, Evolution, and Ecology*. 2nd ed. Malden, MA: Wiley-Blackwell Science.

Hoese, H. D., and R. H. Moore. 1977. *Fishes of the Gulf of Mexico: Texas, Louisiana, and Adjacent Waters*. College Station: Texas A&M University Press.

Hubbs, C., R. J. Edwards, and G. P. Garrett. 2008. *An Annotated Checklist of the Freshwater Fishes of Texas, with Keys to Identification of Species*. Texas Academy of Science. http://www.texasacademyofscience.org/assets/GeneralFiles/hubbs_et_al_2008_checklist.pdf.

McEachran, John D., and Janice D. Fechhelm. 1998. *Fishes of the Gulf of Mexico*. Vol. 1, *Myxiniformes to Gasterosteiformes*. Austin: University of Texas Press.

Moyle, Peter B., and Joseph J. Cech. 2000. *Fishes: An Introduction to Ichthyology*. 4th ed. Upper Saddle River, NJ: Prentice Hall.

Paxton, John R., and William N. Eschmeyer. 1994. *Encyclopedia of Fishes*. New York: Academic Press.

Thomas, C., T. H. Bonner, and B. G. Whiteside. 2007. *Freshwater Fishes of Texas*. College Station: Texas A&M University Press.

Travis, N. T., C. Hubbs, J. D. McEachran, and C. R. Smith. 1994. *Freshwater and Marine Fishes of Texas and the Northwestern Gulf of Mexico*. Austin: Texas System of Natural Laboratories.

UNIT 15

Herpetology

LEE A. FITZGERALD
Professor and Curator of Amphibians and Reptiles, Biodiversity Research and Teaching Collections, Department of Wildlife and Fisheries Sciences, Texas A&M University

TOBY HIBBITTS
Curator of Herpetology, Biodiversity Research and Teaching Collections, Department of Wildlife and Fisheries Sciences, Institute of Renewable Natural Resources, Texas A&M University

Unit Goals

After completing this unit, volunteers should be able to

- communicate the characteristics of amphibians and reptiles and how they differ from other vertebrates
- understand the relationships among the major groups of amphibians and reptiles and how they are related to fish, mammals, and birds
- demonstrate basic knowledge of ecology and life history of amphibians and reptiles in Texas
- outline and communicate the challenges confronting conservation of amphibians and reptiles in Texas

The naturalist in Texas will find it relatively easy to explore our state's diversity of amphibians and reptiles. Because of the state's large size and geographic complexity, Texas is home to 231 native and exotic species of amphibians and reptiles, more than any other US state. Amphibians and reptiles together are known as **herps** or **herptiles**, and the regional or local diversity of amphibians and reptile species is referred to as **herpetofauna**. Amphibians and reptiles are studied together more for convenience and tradition than for their biological affinity. Naturalists tend to be genuinely interested in both groups, perhaps because the techniques for finding and capturing both groups are the same, they are often found in the same places, and they are cared for in the same way in museums. Essentially all prominent Texas herpetologists have studied both amphibians and reptiles.

Several recent monographs and field guides, which include distribution maps and details about the natural history of specific species, will aid in field identifications. This unit is designed to serve as a general introduction to herpetology for the naturalist in Texas. The origin of amphibians and reptiles will be covered to place herps in proper evolutionary context. Sections on amphibian and reptile diversity focus on broad patterns and concepts central to the natural lives of herps and the processes that have resulted in the diversity of herps in Texas. Amphibians and reptiles together encompass enormous diversity, and not surprisingly, the processes that drive the diversity of salamanders, frogs, squamates (lizards and snakes), turtles, and crocodilians are different. A number of books and Internet resources are listed at the end of this unit, so the herpetological naturalist can use this unit as a guide for study of individual species as well as higher taxonomic groups and herpetological communities.

Also covered is an overview of herpetological conservation topics especially relevant to Texas. The principal causes of all biodiversity loss, such as habitat alteration, invasive exotic species, commercial exploitation, and pollution, affect herpetofauna as well as other flora and fauna; some case studies of particular interest are reviewed. The section on finding herps in Texas points out the

Texas horned lizard (*Phrynosoma cornutum*). Courtesy of Lee Fitzgerald

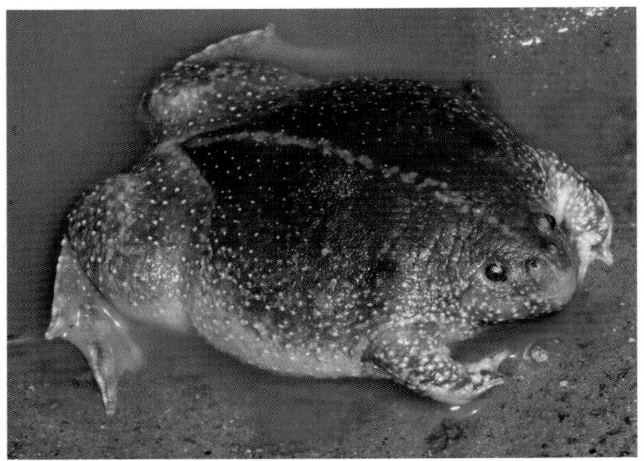
Mexican burrowing toad (*Rhinophrynus dorsalis*). Courtesy of Toby Hibbitts

American alligator (*Alligator mississippiensis*) in marsh grass at Anahuac National Wildlife Refuge, April 26, 2011. Courtesy of Pete Romfh, Cradle of Texas Chapter

basics for getting started, some mistakes to avoid, and common techniques for catching herps and studying herpetological communities.

A Brief History of Herpetology and the Texas Herpetological Society

Early naturalist explorers such as Jean Louis Berlandier, John Bartlett, and William Emory made the first collections of herps from Texas. Several naturalists of historic importance, including Edward Drinker Cope, for whom the journal *Copeia* is named, studied those collections in the late 1800s. John Strecker was based at Baylor University and became known as the "Father of Texas Herpetology." He published 60 articles on Texas herpetofauna, including the first checklist of Texas herps in 1915. An impressive list of noted herpetologists, including W. Frank Blair, Roger Conant, William B. Davis, James R. Dixon, Howard Gloyd, Karl P. Schmidt, Hobart Smith, Edward Taylor, John Werler, and Alan Wright, worked with Texas herps after Strecker's career. Today, several of these great herpetologists' students are practicing the science of herpetology at universities and museums around the world. In *Texas Snakes*, Werler and Dixon (2000; see also Dixon 2013) give a more complete history of herpetology in Texas, including the development of literature on Texas herpetofauna.

The advancement of herpetology in Texas is intertwined with the story of the Texas Herpetological Society (THS). The THS stands out as a unique group effort among amateur herpetologists, academicians, and students that has provided a systematic inventory of the herps of Texas spanning 60 years. Indeed, the list of past presidents of THS is a who's who of prominent herpetologists. The THS was conceived in 1938 at a meeting of the Texas Academy of Science,

Amphibian and reptile species richness in Texas

Taxon group	Families	Species	Notes
Amphibians	15	72	
Frogs	9	42	Tipton et al. (2012) list 4 species of frogs that may possibly occur in Texas.
Salamanders	6	30	Tipton et al. (2012) list 2 species of salamanders that may possibly occur in Texas.
Reptiles	21	159	
Crocodilians	1	1	
Turtles	7	31	1 exotic species, *Pseudemys nelsoni*
Squamates	13	127	
Lizards	9	51	Exotic species: 4 geckos, 1 *Ctenosaura*, 1 *Anolis*
Snakes	4	76	1 exotic species, *Rhamphotyphlops braminus*; 1 exotic subspecies, *Nerodia fasciata pictiventris*
Totals	36	231	

Source: Dixon 2013; Tipton et al. 2012; Hibbitts and Hibbitts 2015.

and the first meeting was held April 15–16, 1939. In the early 1940s, a constitution was drafted, the first THS newsletters were published, and several field meets were held. After a hiatus during World War II, the society was reorganized in 1946, and Bryce Brown became president. Brown, Hobart Smith, working at Texas A&M at the time, and Frank Blair at University of Texas began building the society in earnest. Since that time, THS has held annual field meets during a long weekend in April or May almost without fail.

The THS field meets are an impressive gathering of amateur and professional herpetologists from all over Texas, often with a sampling of visitors from around the world. Field meets are designed to provide an inventory of herpetofauna in a particular county in Texas and are usually located on a large ranch, state park, or wildlife management area. The organizing committee purposely chooses understudied areas of the state, and field meets provide important information on the distribution of herps around the state. It is not surprising to find as many as 100 herp enthusiasts at the field meets. Besides its regular members, the THS welcomes university herpetology classes,

Ring-necked snake (*Diadophis punctatus*) found at the Katy Prairie Conservancy in Waller. Courtesy of Toby Hibbitts

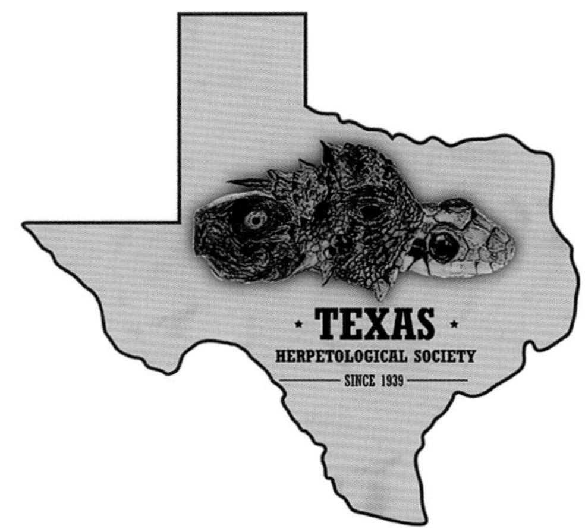

Texas Herpetology Society Symbol. Courtesy of THS website

Herpetologist searching for reptiles. Courtesy of Toby Hibbitts

high school biology classes, and anyone interested in finding and learning about herps in the field. The field meet is a time for old friends to camp and hunt herps together and learn about their natural history.

When so many experienced herpetologists converge on an area, it is impressive how many herps are found. As a result of THS field meets, a number of species of herps have been added to the state checklist, and dozens of species have been found in counties for the first time. Participation in THS field meets would be a good activity for Texas Master Naturalist chapters whose members are interested in field herpetology. The THS also holds a fall meeting and banquet, usually including a research symposium and keynote speaker. The THS and other regional herpetological societies in Texas support herpetological research and other ventures that benefit education and research on the natural history of herps in Texas and around the world (See "Resources for Herpetological Naturalists in Texas" at the end of this unit).

Jacobsen's organ. Courtesy of Morgan Osborn, intern, Texas A&M AgriLife Extension Service

Common Characteristics of Amphibians and Reptiles

Amphibians and reptiles are not closely related, but they do share a few common characteristics. Both amphibians and reptiles possess **Jacobsen's organ**, a specialized olfactory organ in the roof of the mouth. Jacobsen's organ is highly developed in the lizards and snakes (squamates) that rely heavily on olfaction to sense their surroundings. The tongue-flicking behavior we notice in snakes and some lizards is how they sense their surroundings by sampling molecules in the air or on the ground with their tongue and inserting it into Jacobsen's organ.

Both amphibians and reptiles have a common opening to the digestive, reproductive, and urinary tracts called the **cloaca**.

Large alligator snapping turtle (*Macrochelys temminckii*). Courtesy of Toby Hibbitts

Texas earless lizard (*Cophosaurus texanus*). Courtesy of Toby Hibbitts

Amphibians and reptiles can both excrete nitrogenous waste in the form of either urea or uric acid. Most amphibians excrete urea, which leaves the body in abundant dilute urine, but two species of tropical frogs that live in dry environments are known to produce uric acid. Uric acid is insoluble and can be excreted with little water. Production of uric acid is therefore an important means of conserving water. Turtles and crocodilians can excrete either urea or uric acid, depending on water balance. All herps are **ectotherms**, meaning their temperature regulation depends on the environment, not metabolism (cold-blooded). Almost all other organisms (e.g., fish and insects) are also ectotherms, so this feature alone does not really unite amphibians and reptiles in the evolutionary sense.

Being cold-blooded was once considered a lower form of life, but modern ecologists realized that ectothermy actually has its own set of advantages over the warm-blooded (endothermic) mammals and birds. Because of the low energy requirements of ectothermy, amphibians and reptiles can simply wait it out when times are tough, such as when food is scarce or the climate is too cold, hot, or dry. Ectothermy may also explain why there are so many small-bodied and elongated species of herps compared to mammals and birds. The high metabolic cost of endothermy is the reason there are few long-bodied mammals like weasels and ferrets and none smaller than shrews. Our large Texas herps such as the alligator snapping turtle, American alligator, leatherback turtle, and bullsnake are impressive because of their formidable size, but equally impressive are the tiny hatchling ground skinks, blind snakes, and toadlets. How can they be so tiny? The answer is that their ectothermic metabolism does not constrain the evolution of small body size or the evolution of the elongated body forms that are so common in snakes and lizards.

Bullsnake (*Pituophis catenifer sayi*).

Some herps possess various physiological adaptations and complex behaviors to absorb and dissipate heat from the environment by taking advantage of direct and indirect solar and infrared radiation, conduction, convection, and evaporation of water from their lungs and bodies. Large reptiles such as turtles and crocodilians have circulatory systems that allow blood to be shunted away from the lungs to aid

Traditional classifications of families of amphibians and reptiles in Texas

	Common name
Class Amphibia	
Subclass Lissamphibia	
Order Caudata	salamanders and newts
Suborder Sirenoidea	
Sirenidae	sirens
Suborder Salamandroidea	
Amphiumidae	amphiumas
Plethodontidae	lungless salamanders
Proteidae	mudpuppies, waterdogs, and the olm
Salamandridae	salamandrids
Ambystomatidae	mole salamanders
Order Anura	frogs and toads
Scaphiopodidae	spadefoots
Bufonidae	toads
Craugastoridae	northern rain frogs
Eleutherodactylidae	robber frogs
Leptodactylidae	Neotropical grass frogs
Hylidae	hylid treefrogs
Microhylidae	narrowmouth toads
Ranidae	true frogs
Rhinophrynidae	burrowing toads
Class Reptilia	reptiles
Order Testudinata	turtles, terrapins, and tortoises
Suborder Cryptodira	hidden-necked turtles
Chelydridae	snapping turtles
Cheloniidae	sea turtles
Kinosternidae	mud and musk turtles
Trionychidae	softshell turtles
Emydidae	New World pond turtles and terrapins
Testudinidae	tortoises
Order Squamata	squamates
Suborder Iguania	iguanas, chameleons
Iguanidae	iguanid lizards
Crotaphytidae	collared and leopard lizards
Phrynosomatidae	scaly, sand, and horned lizards
Polychrotinae	anoloid lizards
Suborder Scleroglossa	
Gekkonidae	geckos
Eublepharidae	eyelash geckos
Scincidae	skinks
Teiidae	whiptails
Anguidae	glass and alligator lizards
Suborder Serpentes	
Leptotyphlopidae	blind snakes and threadsnakes
Colubridae	harmless and rear-fanged snakes
Elapidae	coralsnakes, cobras, kraits, seasnakes
Viperidae	vipers and adders
Crotalinae	pitvipers
Order Crocodylia	
Alligatoridae	crocodilians
	alligators

heat retention and maximize the amount of oxygen taken out of the blood when they are not breathing. Blood can also be shunted toward the extremities to help absorb heat while basking or to dissipate heat while cooling. Along with its advantages, being cold-blooded can also be a disadvantage in some ways; for example, herps may find themselves more vulnerable to predators and accidents when they are cold, time periods for foraging and mate seeking are restricted by weather, and the global distribution of herps is limited to relatively warm regions.

The Relationships of Amphibians and Reptiles to Other Vertebrates

The fundamental common feature of amphibians and reptiles, and the one they share with other terrestrial vertebrates, is their tetrapod origin. The characteristic of four limbs arose with the common ancestor of all terrestrial vertebrates, and along with mammals and birds, amphibians and reptiles are classified as **tetrapods**. Even snakes, and some lizards and salamanders, are "limbless tetrapods" because loss of limbs in these groups is a condition derived from their fully limbed ancestors. A good example of a limbless lizard in Texas is the slender glass lizard (*Ophisaurus attenuatus*).

The relationships among tetrapods are visualized in a branching diagram of their genealogical relationships, referred to as a "phylogenetic tree." The phylogenetic tree of tetrapods depicts the evolutionary relationships of amphibians and reptiles to other groups. The amphibians and all their descendants form a cohesive group known as the tetrapods. Such arrangements that include ancestors and all their descendants are called **monophyletic groups**. Systematic biologists elucidate the makeup of monophyletic groups by identifying characteristics that were derived from common ancestors (evolutionary novelties) and how they are shared among descendants.

Taxonomy then follows the branching pattern in the phylogenetic tree. The names we use for taxon groups—for example, class, family, genus, species—refer to the nested hierarchies in the phylogeny. For Harry Greene, a well-known naturalist and herpetologist with Texas roots, and many others, herpetology is the study of all tetrapods because it is impossible to talk about the placement of reptiles in evolution without including birds (which are part of the reptile branch), and it is impossible to discuss relationships between reptiles and amphibians without mentioning the branch that includes the ancestors of all mammals.

Traditional classifications are good for listing names of taxa but may not reflect well the relationships among groups of organisms. Hierarchical, or phylogenetic, classifications (shown in the table on hierarchical classifications) show more clearly the placement of groups (i.e., amphibians and reptiles) and are increasingly used in textbooks, including new herpetology texts. Each level of indentation corresponds to sister taxa on an evolutionary tree. In the hierarchical classification, the Tetrapoda consists of Amphibia + Amniota; these are each other's closest relatives. Similarly, mammals are the sister group to reptiles, snakes are within the branch that includes autarchoglossan lizards, which is sister to the gekkotan lizards, and so on.

Birds are part of an archosaurian lin-

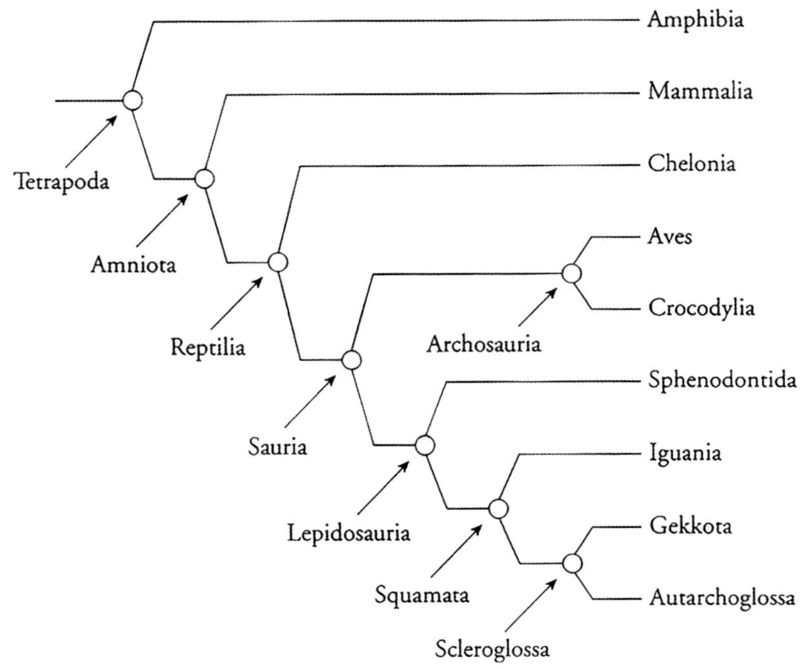

Tetrapod phylogeny.

Archeopteryx, long considered the iconic first bird. The fossil found in Germany in the 1860s has led to the discussion of evolution and the relationships between birds and reptiles. Courtesy of National Geographic

Hierarchical classification of extant tetrapods in Texas

Tetrapoda
- Amphibia
  - Caudata
  - Anura
- Amniota
  - Mammalia
  - Reptilia
    - Testudinata
    - Sauria
      - Archosauria
        - Crocodylia
        - Aves
      - Lepidosauria
        - Squamata

Hierarchical classifications such as this one reveal the relationships among groups. Each level of indentation corresponds to branches in the evolutionary tree, or phylogeny.

eage that is most closely related to either dinosaurs or crocodilians and therefore are part of the same evolutionary branch that includes all other reptiles: turtles, crocodilians, birds, the sphenodon, and lizards + snakes + amphisbaenians. By tradition, we elevate birds to the level of class, but by doing so we obscure their close relationships to crocodilians. When herpetologists and ornithologists get together, we joke that birds are "glorified reptiles" or lizards and snakes are "lower birds." The lineages of reptiles, including birds, are much more closely related to each other than to the amphibians, with which they have not shared a common ancestor in 300 million years.

Systematics and Natural History of Amphibians and Reptiles

Naturalists are interested in the characteristics used to identify herps and how these traits help explain the way species fit their environment. A phylogeny consisting of species, genera, and families into phylogenetic relationships is like the periodic table of elements for chemists. The natural hierarchy of monophyletic groupings depicted in a phylogenetic tree is a handy tool, because the patterns of shared, derived characteristics at various levels in the phylogeny help us understand the big picture of how adaptations, convergent evolution, and inherited similarities have resulted in the diversity of amphibians and reptiles. In our overviews of amphibians and reptiles of Texas, we will see how the characteristics that distinguish genera and families of herps in Texas go a long way toward explaining their similarities and differences in their natural history.

Working through an example helps us appreciate how traits define groups of herps and relate to their natural history. Consider our state's 11 species of venomous snakes: Texas coralsnake, copperhead, cottonmouth, and 8 species of rattlesnakes in two genera. The pygmy rattlesnake and massasauga share many characteristics derived from their common ancestor, including large platelike scales on the head. This genus *Sistrurus* is sister to the genus *Crotalus*, which includes 30 species of rattlesnakes as well as the 6 *Crotalus* species found in Texas. Together, *Crotalus* + *Sistrurus* form a branch of the tree based on the fact they share the rattle and share it with no other group. The rattlesnake's rattle evolved only once in all of snakedom.

As we back farther down the hierarchy,

Southern copperhead (*Agkistrodon contortrix*). Courtesy of Toby Hibbitts

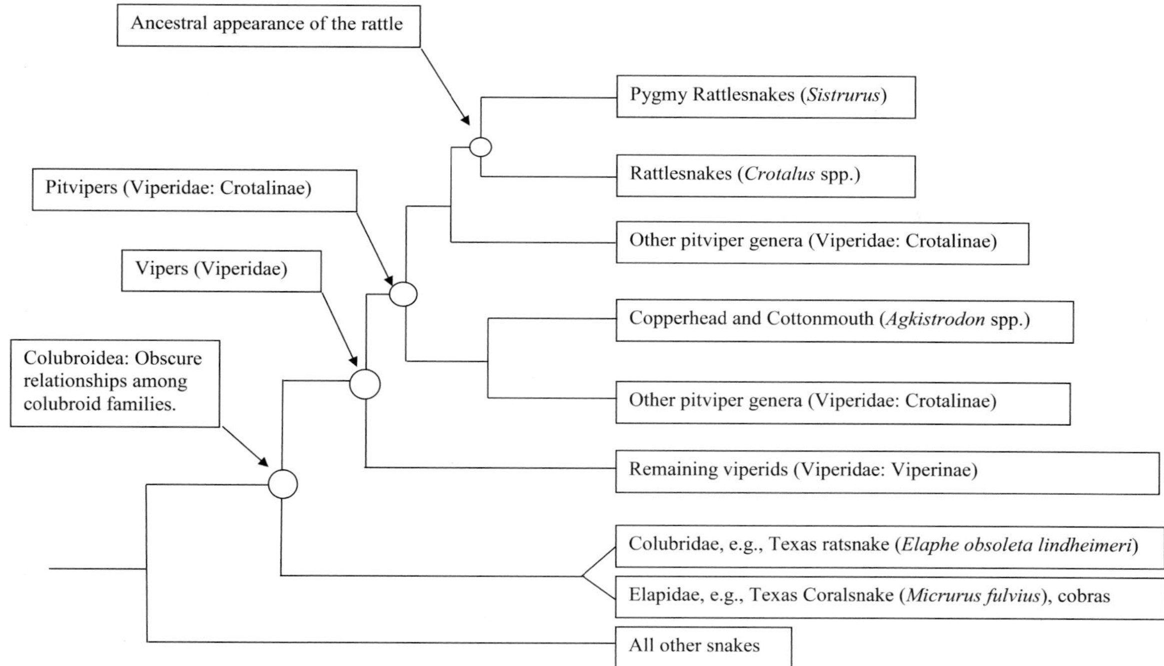

This phylogeny (tree of life) of the venomous snakes of Texas shows that rattlesnakes, cottonmouth, and copperhead are not especially closely related to the Texas coralsnake. Each is more closely related to other pitvipers, of which there are 16 genera around the world. Nodes between the branches indicate ancestor relationships. These genealogical relationships therefore allow the naturalist to visualize how the venomous snakes of Texas belong to several very different groups of snakes. It is apparent the rattle evolved once, but venom probably evolved multiple times, long before there were pitvipers and coralsnakes.

the rattlesnakes (*Crotalus* + *Sistrurus*) share many characteristics with all other pitvipers, so named for the infrared-sensing pits between eye and nostril. The pitviper branch includes our cottonmouth and copperhead, which are members of the same genus, *Agkistrodon*, but we see that genus is more closely related to other genera of pitvipers that are distributed on various continents. Likewise, the rattlesnakes are more closely related to other pitviper genera than they are to the relatives of cottonmouths and copperheads. The Texas coralsnake belongs to a lineage embedded in the family Elapidae, which includes cobras and their allies. Although the Texas coralsnake is one of our venomous species, it is actually more closely related to the Texas ratsnake and other nonvenomous snakes in the family Colubridae in our state than to the Viperidae, which contains all of our pitvipers.

The hierarchical phylogeny of snakes permits us to disentangle the similarities and differences among them and serves as an example of using systematics to understand natural history. By understanding relatedness among pitvipers and other snakes, it is readily apparent that evolution of venom happened a long time ago, before the appearance of species of rattlesnakes and coralsnakes we know today. Additionally, because Texas coralsnakes and rattlesnakes are both venomous, yet not closely related, we can see that having venom is not particularly useful in understanding the relationships among our state's venomous species.

Natural History and the Diversity of Amphibians

There are more than 7,000 known species of extant amphibians in 3 orders: salamanders (Caudata), frogs (Anura), and caecilians

(Apoda). Caecilians are wormlike amphibians that inhabit tropical regions of the world; there are none in Texas. Amphibians as a class share a few common features, such as **metamorphosis** from larval form to adult form and relatively **permeable skin** with **mucous and granular glands** that secrete mucus and toxins. Development of granular glands varies among groups, but most amphibians are capable of producing at least some **toxic skin secretions**. In some groups, such as newts and toads, toxins are very poisonous. It is clear that in combination with defensive behaviors, toxic skin secretions serve to deter predators.

Amphibians also have a stronger dependence on moist microhabitats than do other terrestrial vertebrate classes. Amphibians do not have claws, true nails, or scales. Gas exchange may occur via lungs, gills, or the skin. Lungs are completely absent in salamanders of the family Plethodontidae, of which there many interesting species in Texas. Among the plethodontid species that live on land gas exchange takes place entirely through the skin. The skin of amphibians is also important for water absorption. Many frogs and toads, for example, have patches on their lower abdomen that are used to imbibe water. Amphibians have a

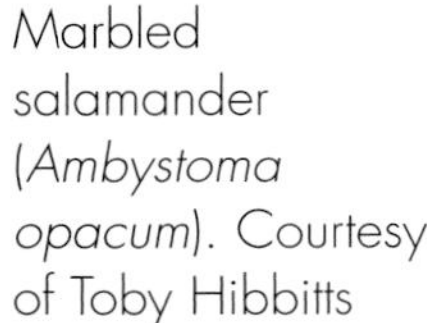
Marbled salamander (*Ambystoma opacum*). Courtesy of Toby Hibbitts

Crawfish frog (*Rana areolata*) in a defensive position, found in Waller. Courtesy of Toby Hibbitts

tympanum and **columella** (a bone in the ear that conducts sound from the tympanum) that allows hearing in the air, and a well-developed **olfactory epithelium** that permits them to detect odors. When the naturalist observes a frog or toad sitting quietly on the mud or in shallow water, there is actually a lot going on. It is simultaneously regulating water balance and temperature and taking in many stimuli from its surroundings.

Being an amphibian has apparently not constrained the diversification of the group. Because of many recent discoveries of frogs, especially in the tropics, and refined understanding of systematics and taxonomy, the number of amphibian species has skyrocketed in recent years. The number of amphibian species surpassed that of mammals by the mid-1990s, and the number of species has almost doubled since the 1980s. Nor have amphibian features constrained the places where amphibians may live. Amphibians occur everywhere except Antarctica; extreme northern parts of Europe, Asia, and North America; and most oceanic islands. In Texas, amphibians occur statewide in virtually all habitats, even the driest and hottest parts of the Chihuahuan Desert, where amphibians have developed fascinating adaptations to live in extremely dry and unpredictable environments.

Diversity of Amphibian Lifestyles

Overarching natural history patterns help explain the diversity of amphibians: variations in amphibian life cycles, the ecology of amphibian larvae, patterns of development from egg to adult, and species isolating mechanisms.

Life History Strategies

Amphibian life cycles can be thought of as a game with a few key pieces that can be tinkered with to accomplish different **life history strategies**. Strategy refers to the traits species possess that keep their populations going as these traits are continually fine-tuned by environmental selection pressures. Key components of the amphibian life history game are **larval period** (time spent as a tadpole or salamander larva), **terrestrial period** (time spent living on land), and **egg laying** (when, where, and how many eggs are laid).

Individuals play their own life history game, in an evolutionary sense, to maximize chances for survival and reproduction in the environments where they live. The result is that each species—and sometimes populations within a particular species—ends up with a characteristic life history. Amphibian life histories are varied and sometimes amazing. Depending on the species, amphibians in Texas can remain buried underground for years without eating or breeding, are found only in caves, protect their young, skip the tadpole stage entirely, and exist in the most numerous populations of animals in a hardwood forest. It is not surprising that the life cycles of amphibians are often the principal point of interest for naturalists.

Although the life cycle characterized as egg-larva-adult is considered typical for amphibians, the life history game has been played so many different ways that there is actually a complete gradient in amphibian life histories. In fact, only 20% to 25% of salamander species have this “typical” life cycle. Instead, most salamanders deposit a few eggs in moist microhabitats, they care for them, and the eggs hatch into fully formed juveniles. Most frog species lay large numbers of eggs in water, and aquatic tadpoles metamorphose into adults. The length of time spent in the tadpole stage is highly variable, however. In some environments, it pays to devote time and energy to the larval stage and less time to living and growing as a terrestrial frog. In other circumstances, the aquatic environment may be undependable or risky, in which case it pays to shorten the tadpole stage and get on with life as a frog.

Variations on this theme characterize the different salamander and frog families, which is not surprising since life history traits are inherited among groups of related species. True frogs (Ranidae) have highly aquatic tadpoles that take from several months to more than a year before metamorphosing into juveniles. Toads (Bufonidae) and treefrogs (Hylidae) have much shorter larval periods, usually metamorphosing within a few weeks to several months. In contrast are the spadefoots (Pelobatidae), known for their explosive breeding aggregations and extremely short larval period.

In the Big Bend and Trans-Pecos regions, Couch’s spadefoot (*Scaphiopus couchii*) may **aestivate** (analogous to hibernation) underground for more than a year, waiting for rains. When sufficient rain falls, the Couch’s spadefoots emerge and breed during one or two nights. Their superactive tadpoles

Fern Banks salamander (*Eurycea pterophila*). Courtesy of Toby Hibbitts

Green treefrog (*Hyla cinerea*). Courtesy of Toby Hibbitts

Metamorphosing southern leopard frog (*Lithobates sphenocephalus*). Courtesy of Toby Hibbitts

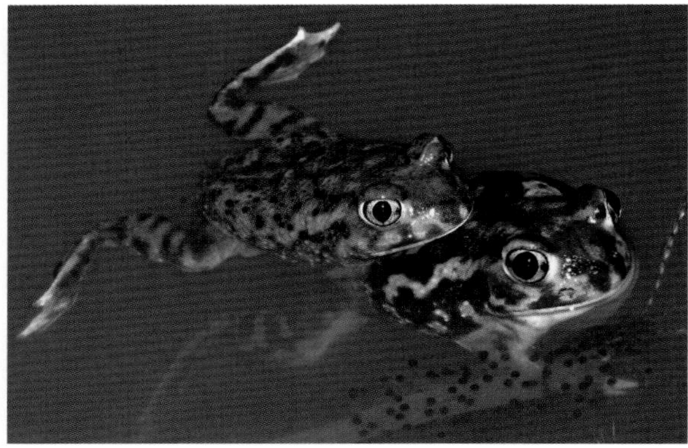

Couch's spadefoot (*Scaphiopus couchii*). Courtesy of Toby Hibbitts

grow and achieve metamorphosis in as few as 10 days. The New Mexico spadefoot (*Spea multiplicata*) has added another twist to its life history strategy. The first cohort of tadpoles in a pool are fairly typical herbivorous spadefoot tads. But if a second cohort is produced in the same pond, these may develop enlarged mouths and modified mouthparts for carnivory. They then cannibalize their unlucky predecessors.

Barking frogs (Eleutherodactylidae, *Craugastor augusti*) have arrived at the extreme end of the aquatic-terrestrial gradient. Like other members of their genus, they completely bypass the tadpole stage. Their eggs are laid in humid microhabitats and develop directly into miniature barking froglets. The adaptation of direct development frees barking frogs from dependence on standing water for reproduction and aids their existence in dry climates. Probably because of the innovation of direct development and their uncanny ability to colonize islands, frogs in this family have radiated into more species than any other vertebrate genus.

Salamanders also have highly evolved life history strategies. Newts (Salamandridae), represented in Texas by the red-spotted newt and the black-spotted newt, are aquatic as adults and courtship occurs in the water. Their larvae either metamorphose into **efts** (terrestrial juveniles), which lead a terrestrial life for up to several years, or they may skip the eft stage and metamorphose into aquatic adults. Depending on environmental circumstances, there are trade-offs to spending time as an eft or larva, so the life history is fine-tuned to meet local environmental challenges. The changes that occur during metamorphosis from larva to terrestrial eft and again into aquatic adults are truly amazing. The forest-dwelling efts have relatively thick granular skin, eyes that see well in air, defensive behaviors, and foraging modes suited for life on the forest floor. During transformation to aquatic adults, equally dramatic changes occur in skin, color, eyes, feet, and shape of the tail that fit life in the water. Males in the breeding ponds develop fancy adornments used for courtship.

Herpetology texts, basic zoology texts, and other sources thoroughly review the anatomy of amphibian eggs and larvae and amphibian metamorphosis. Field guides and monographs such as *Texas Amphibians* (Tipton et al. 2012) provide specific details of life histories of all the amphibians native to Texas. While only introduced here, these topics are the zoological underpinnings of amphibian natural history, and readers may wish to review these resources as their interest in herpetological natural history expands.

Larval Ecology

A significant portion of the lives of many frogs and salamanders is spent as aquatic larvae. In the last several decades, ecologists have realized that tadpoles and salamander larvae have complicated and interesting ecologies. The life of an amphibian larva can be as distinct from that of the adult as a caterpillar's is from the life of the butterfly it will become. Amphibian larvae live in ecological communities, interacting with each other and predators. The aquatic stage of many frog species is probably more significant to the maintenance of their species than any other stage, an observation that

Black-spotted newt (*Notophthalmus meridionalis*). Courtesy of Toby Hibbitts

Barred tiger salamander larvae (*Ambystoma mavortium*). Courtesy of Toby Hibbitts

Red-spotted toad (*Bufo punctatus*). Courtesy of Toby Hibbitts

Austin blind salamander (*Eurycea waterlooensis*). Courtesy of Toby Hibbitts

inspired tadpole ecologist Richard Wassersug to proclaim that frogs are merely packages used to transport the species' genes from pond to pond.

Frog tadpoles come in several basic types that show various modifications, depending on the species. They all have gills inside a branchial chamber that exits via a spiracle. The most common type of tadpole has a well-developed fleshy oral disc lined with papillae, a keratinized beak, several rows of keratinized teeth, and a spiracle on the left side of the body. All Texas frogs that produce tadpoles have this type of tadpole except the family that includes the narrowmouth toads and sheep frog, Microhylidae. Microhylids have filter-feeding tadpoles with well-developed oral discs, no keratinized mouthparts, and a single midventral spiracle. Regardless of the morphological type, tadpoles are primarily herbivorous, using various means to scrape or filter small bits of plant material and algae. Tadpoles in later stages of development tend to become opportunistic feeders and more omnivorous. Salamander larvae have external gills. They are opportunistic predators, feeding on a variety of prey, including insects, crustaceans, and worms.

Amphibian larvae of different species forage in different places in a pond—in the water column, on standing aquatic vegetation, and on the bottom. Hence, there are a variety of ecological niches that are occupied by different frog and salamander larvae. Many possess feeding and swimming morphologies well suited to their lifestyles. Amphibian larval ecology is dominated by two determining factors: whether or not they inhabit permanent or ephemeral water bodies and the presence of predators. The common predators of amphibian larvae include predaceous beetle larvae, some true bugs, dragonfly larvae, and fish. Mud turtles, chicken turtles, and garter snakes are also important predators on larvae.

There are strong feedbacks (for example, the interactions between life span, maturity, growth rate, number and size of eggs) among the life history strategies just described: risks of predation and water permanency. Tadpoles in temporary pools are generally very active, eat a lot, grow fast, have short larval periods, and metamorphose into relatively small froglets and toadlets. This suite of traits lets them reach metamorphosis before the pond dries up, but these characteristics also make them particularly vulnerable to predators. At the other end of the spectrum, permanent pools maintain a stock of predators that breeding amphibians must continually face. Tadpoles inhabiting permanent water bodies usually take longer to reach metamorphosis, are less active, and are more cryptic than their counterparts in temporary pools. Tadpoles in permanent water also grow to a larger size, such as tadpoles of bullfrogs and other true frogs. Many are toxic, and it is known that toad tadpoles secrete toxins that are noxious to fish and other aquatic predators.

Together, these interactions between predator-prey, life history strategy, and the environment paint the picture of amphibian natural history. A good case study is one concerning the frog community in the Big Bend region. Gage Dayton found that in Big Bend National Park, Couch's spadefoots are very active and outcompete other tadpoles, but they are extremely susceptible to predators. Great Plains narrowmouth toads, Texas toads, and red-spotted toads are less competitive than Couch's spadefoots but are much better at living with predators. Couch's spadefoots also have the shortest larval period and live in the most ephemeral pools, whereas the other species take about a month to reach metamorphosis and are therefore relegated to pools that last at least that long. The tadpoles' interactions with each other, their susceptibility to predators, and the ephemeral nature of pools determine where species live and whether they live alone or together. Across the Big Bend landscape, the patterns of occurrence of these frogs results from a complex interaction between frog breeding events, water permanency, tadpole ecology, and predators.

Development and Species Divergence in Salamanders

Texas has a relatively high diversity of salamanders, with 29 species in six families. Salamanders are a group of vertebrates that exhibit patterns of morphological divergence caused by the timing of their development as they grow from small larvae and metamorphose to the adult form. Changes in the timing of development of morphological features is called **heterochrony** (*hetero* = change, *chron* = time). During growth from embryo to adult, different features develop at different times, and some features grow faster than others.

As a group, salamanders show a propensity for arrested development, that is, for truncating the development of features such as parts of the head or limbs. As adults, salamanders that retain characteristics from the larval stage are usually referred to as **paedomorphic** or **neotenic**. The development of head shape, mouthparts, and absorption of gill filaments, for example, may stop at an early stage of development while the animal continues to grow and reach sexual maturity. The result is a salamander that retains larval characteristics in the adult form. In many cases, we know that truncated development has produced new kinds of salamanders that are very different from their ancestors.

Even entire families of salamanders are characterized by their larva-like characteristics. Sirens, for example, have external gills, poorly developed limbs, and undeveloped mouthparts. These are all juvenile characteristics that have become fixed. Similarly, Proteidae, the family containing Gulf Coast waterdogs (*Necturus beyeri*), the amphiumas, and species of lungless salamanders and mole salamanders, are also paedomorphic, exhibiting larval characteristics that are explained by truncated development of the ancestral condition. The various spring and cave salamanders of the Balcones Escarpment, such as the Texas blind salamander (*Eurycea rathbuni*), are all good examples of paedomorphic salamanders.

Courtship and Species Divergence in Salamanders

Among salamander families, there is an interesting trend of increasing complexity in courtship and transfer of sperm from male to female. The most ancestral salamander families, Cryptobranchidae and Hynobiidae, have external fertilization. Those families do not occur in Texas. Although two species of sirens are well known in Texas, courtship in these species has never been observed anywhere. Their anatomy suggests they also have external fertilization. All other salamanders have internal fertilization. Males produce a waxy structure with a cap of sperm called a **spermatophore** that is either introduced into the cloaca of a female or deposited on the substrate and picked up by the female. Males produce chemical cues that stimulate females to breed, and individuals respond to the chemical cues of their own species. Females have structures called **spermatheca** inside the cloaca that receive the spermatophore. Each species has distinctive spermatophores that match the spermatheca.

In the Salamandridae (newts) native to Texas, males pursue and capture females with their hind limbs and rub the female's face with glands on their head to apply chemical stimulants. The spermatophore is then deposited and the female picks it up, or the male may place it directly into her cloaca. The Texas species of mole salamanders (Ambystomatidae) also court in the water, except the marbled salamanders (*Ambystoma maculatum*). Male mole salamanders lead females on a walk, fanning chemicals onto her snout with their tails. The female nudges the male, causing him to deposit a spermatophore that she then picks up.

In the highly derived and speciose lung-

Ambystoma sp. spermatophore containing salamander sperm. Courtesy of Morgan Osborn, intern, Texas A&M AgriLife Extension Service

less salamanders (Plethodontidae), courtship is even more elaborate. Males lead females on a tail-straddling walk, where the female straddles the male's tail while resting her chin on his tail. This behavior is unique to the family. When the male deposits a spermatophore, he turns and blocks the walking female so that her cloaca is positioned precisely over the spermatophore that she then picks up. These movements are very precisely matched for body size among species and even populations; a mismatch in size reduces the efficacy of mating. This implies that the mating system of these salamanders may not only keep salamanders of different species from hybridizing but may also be a factor driving the morphological divergence between populations, eventually leading to speciation. The courtship behaviors and mating systems of salamanders have clearly been important in generating and maintaining diversity in salamanders.

Spotted dusky salamander (*Desmognathus conanti*). Courtesy of Toby Hibbitts

Frog Vocalizations

Everyone has heard frogs croak, and naturalists quickly learn to identify frog species based on their calls. It does not take much experience to realize, however, that the natural history of frog vocalizations is exceedingly complex. In the cacophony of frog calls on a rainy night in eastern Texas, how do the dozen or so species even hear each other, much less distinguish individuals of their own species and find mates? Do males call only to attract females, or do their calls have other purposes?

Most male frogs worldwide, and all those in Texas, have a vocal sac that, when distended, functions as a resonator. Sound is produced when air passes over the vocal chords. When the nostrils are closed and the vocal sac inflated, air is oscillated back and forth between the lungs and vocal sac, producing the various long croaks, rapid trills, and chirps. There are different types of vocal sacs depending on the species: a single large sac under the chin (median subgular), paired sacs under the chin (paired subgular), paired lateral sacs that distend on either side of the head, or internal vocal sacs. Most native Texas frogs have median subgular sacs, with the exception of leopard frogs, which have paired lateral sacs, and other ranids and hylids that have single or paired internal sacs. The size of the frog and shape of the vocal sac influence the qualities of the call, whereas temperature, substrate, and vegetation affect how well the call is transmitted.

In a few species, females give a call in response to the male's call, but females

Texas toad calling (*Anaxyrus speciosus*). Courtesy of Toby Hibbitts

Gray treefrog calling (*Hyla versicolor*). Courtesy of Toby Hibbitts

Snake eating a fish. Courtesy of Toby Hibbitts

of most species do not have mating calls. The larynx is undeveloped in female frogs, and they lack the vocal sac. However, both females and males of many species will produce a loud distress call when grasped by a predator. Distress calls are a last line of defense for a frog under attack, as in "the enemy of my enemy is my friend." For example, skunks or foxes may investigate a distress call and interrupt the feeding event of a snake or other frog predator. We know this works in some cases—frog distress calls are known to get the attention of herpetological naturalists, who will drop whatever they are doing to find the distressed frog as well as the snake that may be eating it.

Each species of frog has a distinct set of calls. A large number of field and laboratory studies have revealed that males use courtship calls to attract females and other types of calls to defend territories and communicate with other males. Males in a breeding chorus continually assess their situation and vary their calls according to circumstances in order to save energy or increase their competitiveness against other males. Predators cue on frog calls; hence, males are faced with the trade-off of producing calls that are most attractive to females or least noticeable to predators. Elegantly designed playback experiments, some accomplished in natural field conditions, indicate that chorusing frogs make these complicated decisions all the time. Males can assess the intensity of other males' calls and judge the distance between them. They can also gauge the body size of other calling males—an important piece of information, since large males usually win contests. It has even been shown that bullfrogs can identify other males individually.

Other experiments have shown that females generally prefer complex calls, but males may not expend the energy to produce the most attractive call unless motivated to do so by competing males. In isolation, male gray treefrogs and other hylid species, members of the family Hylidae, give a simple call, but when the density of males in the chorus increases, so does the complexity of their calls. When multiple males are advertising for females, they reduce overlap in their calls to avoid acoustic interference. This is the reason frogs commonly sing duets, alternating calls between individuals or even between species. Males can very rapidly adjust the timing of components of their calls and instantly seize a moment of silence to insert a call into the chorus. All the while, females are choosing who they mate with, and not surprisingly, it makes a big difference. Research in some species has revealed a direct link between call characteristics that are attractive to females and the vitality of their progeny.

Natural History and the Diversity of Reptiles

There are more than 9,000 species of turtles (Testudinata), crocodilians (Crocodylia), lizards and snakes (Squamata), and tuataras (Rhyncocephalia, endemic to New Zealand) that make up the reptiles studied by herpetologists. Lizards and snakes are closely related and belong to the same major branch of reptiles that we call the **Squamatas**. As a group, squamates share many features, including a transverse cloacal slit, regular skin shedding, and paired copulatory organs in males, **hemipenes**. Reptiles produce **amniote** eggs that, unlike amphibian eggs, have a set of three membranes surrounding the embryo that serve to collect waste (allantois), exchange gases with the environment (chorion), and cushion the embryo and prevent dehydration (amnion). A calcareous shell that can be either hard or leathery typically completes the package. Amniote eggs come in various forms, and many species of squamates in Texas are live bearers, meaning they retain eggs inside their bodies and give birth to live young. In these instances, eggs are not encased with a shell.

All reptiles, with the exception of crocodilians and birds, have a three-chambered heart with a single ventricle. Crocodilians, like birds and mammals, have a septum dividing the ventricle into two chambers, resulting in a four-chambered heart. The

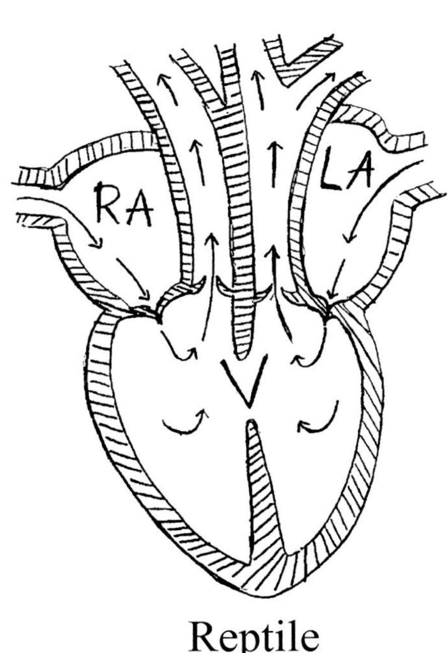

Reptiles have a three-chambered heart. Courtesy of Morgan Osborn, intern, Texas A&M AgriLife Extension Service

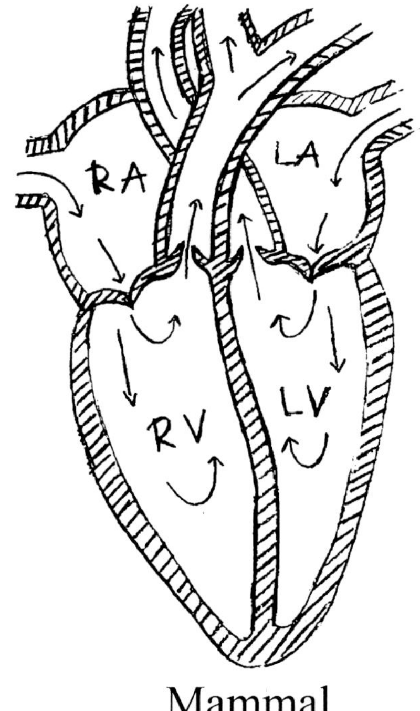

Mammals have a four-chambered heart. Courtesy of Morgan Osborn, intern, Texas A&M AgriLife Extension Service

outer skin of reptiles is thickened to form scales, and crocodilians and skinks have bones below the surface of the skin called **osteoderms**. Osteoderms are particularly well developed in crocodilians. The knobs running down the back of the American alligator, for example, are osteoderms lying under the surface of the skin. Stiff scales are not always present in reptiles, as in softshell turtles and the leatherback sea turtle, which have a flexible covering of skin on their shells instead of hard scales.

The basic tetrapod skeletal structure typical of most lizards has been variously modified in different groups of reptiles, allowing them to function well in different aquatic and terrestrial habitats. Limb loss is a recurring pattern in squamates. Several lizard families, including members of the Scincidae and Anguidae found in Texas, exhibit varying degrees of reduced limbs or lack of limbs depending on the species. All snakes in Texas are completely limbless, but ancestral snakes with origins deep in the squamate branch, such as the Texas blindsnake (Leptotyphlopidae), retain vestiges of the pelvic girdle.

Turtles are instantly recognizable because of their shell; they have had much the same appearance since long before the age of dinosaurs. The turtle shell, with all its obvious advantages of protection and conservation of water, deserves special mention because it constrains almost every aspect of turtle life history and biology. The top part of the shell (**carapace**) consists of the vertebral column, ribs, and pelvic and pectoral girdles that are fused with dermal bone. The vertebral column is fused to the top of the plastron, and the bones of the carapace are flat, expanded former ribs that encase the body. The **plastron** (bottom shell), derives from abdominal ribs called gastralia. The whole shell is covered with thin scutes (modified scales) made from keratin.

It is easy to examine these unique features of a turtle's shell when a naturalist finds a turtle skeleton on a nature walk. Consider the placement of your pelvic and pectoral girdles, well outside your rib cage. In turtles, both the pelvic and pectoral girdles are situated within the rib cage. No other vertebrates are like this. One consequence of the turtle shell is that it constrains the size of eggs that females produce. Eggs that are too large would not pass through the opening in the shell. This adds an important variable to the life history game, in terms of the size of eggs and how many are produced by turtles. Another consequence of the shell is that when turtles pull their head and limbs into the shell their shell, they do not breathe. Turtles breathe only when "out of their shell." In turtles, a unique arrangement of membranes attaches the lungs to the viscera, and abdominal muscles and movements of the limb girdles move the viscera and force air in and out of the lungs. Box turtles, including the two species that occur in Texas, are somewhat unique in that they fill and empty their lungs via movements of their limbs while they are walking. Sea turtles, on the other hand cannot breathe when they are crawling on land, which explains why we see them stop to breathe when they emerge onto nesting beaches.

Texas tortoise (*Gopherus berlandieri*) found in Hidalgo. Courtesy of Toby Hibbitts

The internal organs of reptiles are typical of other vertebrates and also show modifications depending on the group. All rep-

Spiny softshell turtle (*Apalone spinifera*). Courtesy of Toby Hibbitts

tiles have lungs and breathe air, and some aquatic turtles are also very good at aquatic respiration. Softshell turtles, including the two species in Texas, are particularly good at aquatic respiration, possessing specialized skin structures in the buccal cavity (mouth) that aid gas exchange as they pump water in and out of the throat. Reptiles do not have a diaphragm to aid in filling the lungs as mammals do. Squamates and crocodilians pump air in and out of the lungs by expanding and contracting the sides of their bodies. Internal organs of snakes are modified to accommodate their elongate body form and dietary habits. Only the right lung is developed in most snakes (the left lung is vestigial), and they have a long, well-developed stomach to accommodate their huge meals.

An interesting feature of most turtle species, all crocodilians, and several lizard species is their system of sex determination. In these reptiles, sex is not determined by genotype but by the temperature at which eggs are incubated. Temperature-dependent sex determination occurs after the first few weeks of incubation. In most turtles and lizards, high temperatures produce females, and low temperatures, males. In most crocodilians, high temperatures produce males. In the American alligator and some turtles, males are produced at intermediate temperatures and females at more extreme high and low temperatures. Hence, the nesting environment and weather are the determining factors in producing males and females. Conservation biologists have taken advantage of temperature-dependent sex determination to propagate large numbers of female sea turtles and tortoises for restocking programs.

Reptiles are a large and diverse group and, like amphibians, are found almost everywhere. Texas is a great place for appreciating and studying reptiles, and they can easily be found during any warm month of the year in virtually every corner of the state. Beyond the general commonalities just outlined, turtles, crocodilians, and squamates are each very different. References and other resources listed at the end of this unit will enable Master Naturalists to get a good start in learning about the natural history of each group and species of interest. Much information is available on the American alligator, and various sources are available that give natural history details on turtles. Recent

Loggerhead sea turtle (*Caretta caretta*) eggs in a nesting cavity. Courtesy of Steve Hillebrand

field guides on Texas snakes and lizards are up-to-date resources with good photographs of the species.

Diversity of Lifestyles among Lizards and Snakes

Some principal factors have overwhelmingly influenced the natural lives of the squamates: thermal biology, foraging mode, locomotion, and reproductive mode.

Thermal Biology

Thermal biology refers to the role of temperature in the lives of organisms. As previously mentioned, all amphibians and reptiles are ectotherms, and temperature is a central factor in the lives of most herps. Thermal biology is strongly linked to water balance, and interested readers may want to refer to sections in the references that deal specifically with water balance and adaptations for water conservation. The physiological systems of different lineages of herps are tuned to fit their environments, and some groups operate at relatively low or relatively high temperatures.

Amphibians in the field have body temperatures that generally fall between 50°F (10°C) and 80.5°F (27°C), whereas lizard body temperatures are higher, ranging between 68°F (20°C) and 106°F (41°C). Species that live in cool environments, stream salamanders or nocturnal geckos, for example, tend to have lower body temperatures in the field than species that live in hot places. Some desert-dwelling whiptails are regularly active at temperatures higher than normal human body temperature, 98.6°F (37°C). It is not unusual to find whiptails active with body temperatures of 104°F (40°C). Metabolism increases with body temperature up to a point, above which metabolic systems are compromised and metabolic rate begins to crash. For most lizards, body temperatures above 108°F (42°C) are lethal after a few minutes.

The role of thermal biology is particularly evident among the squamates, and it is easy for the naturalist to observe behaviors related to regulation of body temperature. Most naturalists have seen lizards and snakes basking on rocks and trees to warm themselves in the sun. The more patient observer will notice lizards changing posture, exposing themselves to wind, and shuttling between sun and shade—these "shuttling ectotherms" use behavior to regulate their body temperature. Physiological mechanisms that affect body temperature include shunting blood to or away from extremities to aid in heating or cooling, especially in large species. Changing colors affects absorption of heat, and it is common to see lizards that are particularly dark when they are cool.

Squamates can also pant to get rid of heat-laden moisture from the lungs. Absorbing direct solar radiation is only one means of elevating body temperatures. Reflected solar radiation, infrared radiation, and conduction of heat from the substrate all contribute energy that can raise body temperature. Evaporation, convection (carrying heat away in the wind), and heat radiated from the animal's body itself are ways that heat energy is lost. Behavior and physiology give squamates a lot of control over their temperature and metabolism. They readily achieve body temperatures that are higher or lower than the temperature of the surrounding environment. Hence, a basking lizard arrives at a momentary, delicate balance of all of these factors to achieve its body temperature. Environmental conditions change continuously with passing sun, clouds, and breezes, and so does the equation that determines body temperature.

Species in the families Teiidae, Phrynosomatidae, and Crotaphytidae are examples of lizards that thermoregulate to maintain relatively stable body temperatures when they are active, regardless of the temperature of surrounding environmental temperature (**thermoregulators**). Geckos and

A bullsnake (*Pituophis catenifer sayi*) basking in the sun near Crockett. Courtesy of Toby Hibbitts

many snakes show more variable patterns of body temperature that tend to conform to surrounding environmental temperatures (**thermoconformers**).

Despite the controls that shuttling ectotherms can exert over environmental conditions, environmental temperatures do limit daily activity patterns of lizards and snakes. In hot environments, diurnal lizards typically bask early to achieve their preferred temperature, are active in the morning, retreat into burrows or other shelter during the extreme hot parts of the day, and resume activity in late afternoon.

Because temperature exerts strong influence on metabolic rate, the ability of squamates to perform various functions varies with their body temperature. Temperature affects practically everything lizards and snakes (and all herps) do, including how well they run and jump, digest their food, hear, see, and defend themselves and how long they may remain active. Lizards are able to run faster when their body temperature is close to their preferred temperature. Running speed and stamina are much reduced at temperatures outside this range. Garter snakes and other snakes shift their defensive behavior from fleeing at optimal body temperatures, to bluffing, striking, and biting at lower body temperatures. Such behavioral shifts presumably occur because at low body temperatures, the snake's locomotion is impaired to the extent that it has a better chance of defending itself by standing its ground.

The greater earless lizard (*Cophosaurus texanus*) basking in the sun near Terrell. Courtesy of Toby Hibbitts

Foraging Modes among Lizards

There are two extremes of foraging mode that squamates can use to obtain prey: actively seeking their prey or waiting in ambush. Herpetologists have classified these two extremes as sit-and-wait versus active foraging. Because finding food is central to the lives of organisms, foraging mode carries with it consequences for almost everything else—energetics, morphology, behavior, predator avoidance, and even aspects of thermal biology. These two foraging modes are strongly tied to the major lineages of lizards.

In Texas, the sit-and-wait mode is characteristic of the iguanian families (Phrynosomatidae, Polychrotidae, and Crotaphytidae), whereas the autarchoglossan families Teiidae and Scincidae are active foragers. Typically, sit-and-wait foragers like spiny lizards (*Sceloporus* spp., Phrynosomatidae) and the green anole (*Anolis carolinensis*, Polychrotidae) wait in ambush for insect prey and then dash out to seize it. Sit-and-wait foragers are visually oriented predators. They are good at sprinting for relatively short distances and generally do not have as much stamina as active foragers. Sit-and-wait foragers, which

Fence lizard (*Sceloporus undulatus*). Courtesy of Toby Hibbitts

Texas spotted whiptail (*Cnemidophorus gularis*). Courtesy of Toby Hibbitts

Roundtail horned lizard (*Phrynosoma modestum*). Courtesy of Toby Hibbitts

rely more on cryptic coloration to avoid detection than active foragers that flee predators, have striped or mottled patterns that are confusing when in motion.

The classic active foragers are the whiptails (*Aspidoscelis* spp., Teiidae). Whiptails move quickly from patch to patch searching under leaf litter, poking into nooks and crannies, or chasing down prey. In general, whiptails have higher preferred body temperatures than sit-and-wait foragers. It should not be surprising then, that actively foraging whiptails have a higher metabolic capacity than their sit-and-wait counterparts. Whiptails also eat more prey to fulfill their energy budgets. Active foraging lizards use both vision and olfaction to find prey, and the lineages that are characterized by active foraging species have much more developed chemosensory abilities. Teiids have long, protrusible tongues used to sample chemical cues in the environment, much like those of snakes. Conversely, iguanians do not have as well-developed olfactory systems and rely less on chemical cues to find prey.

In biology, there are exceptions to every generality, and the foraging dichotomy in lizards is no different. In reality, there probably is a rough gradient in foraging modes among various genera and families. Individuals also alter their foraging behavior depending on circumstances, such as when prey is extremely abundant or patchy. The three species of horned lizards in Texas are examples of lizards that do not neatly fit the foraging dichotomy. Horned lizards have a tanklike body form that seems to go along with their dietary specialization on ants. An individual of our state reptile's home range includes several harvester ant mounds that it visits to obtain its meals. Despite the exceptions, considering lizards and snakes as sit-and-wait rather than active foragers is a convenient way to gain insight into their lifestyle and ecology.

Foraging Modes among Snakes

The features that define snakes are intimately entwined with their modes of foraging and locomotion. Of course, the most salient feature of a snake is its long, thin body form. The elongate shape of snakes, coupled with lack of limbs, presents certain obstacles as well as opportunities for foraging. Limblessness keeps snakes very much in contact with the substrate, whether on the ground or in trees, and snakes are especially good at obtaining chemical cues from the substrate. They possess very well-developed chemosensory abilities and use their forked tongues and Jacobsen's organ to constantly sample their surroundings. Chemical cues orient snakes to the trails used by prey, as well as trails of potential mates or competitors.

One constraint of snake body form is that a small head goes along with a thin body. How have the problems of having a small head and not having limbs to manipulate prey been reconciled in snakes? The answer is that snakes have evolved specializations to eat very large prey and to eat infrequently. It is well known that snakes engulf large prey whole, but other limbless reptiles do not generally engulf their prey. Limbless lizards such as the slender glass lizard, eat many small prey. Some snakes also eat many small prey, particularly the blind snakes (Leptotyphlopidae and Typhlopidae).

Snakes have very specialized heads to deal with eating large prey. They have very loosely constructed skulls that permit flexibility and movement. Skull elements are reduced, although the floor of the braincase is strong. The lower mandibles are not fused, and the glottis can be shifted around so the snake can breathe when its mouth is full. Snakes typically engulf prey by taking advantage of the loose configuration of upper and lower jaws and "walking" their heads around the prey with side-to-side movements. It is a myth that snakes "unhinge" their jaws from the skulls. The skull of a snake has a number of movable joints that allow flexibility, but the mandibles do remain hinged to the cranium at all times. The sharp, curved teeth hold the jaw in place while the other side is moved forward. These adaptations allow both large and small species of snakes to eat amazingly large prey for their body size. It is not uncommon for pitvipers to eat prey heavier than they are and larger in diameter than their own heads. Vipers are especially good at eating large prey quickly.

Western diamondback rattlesnake (*Crotalus atrox*) coiled, waiting for a meal. Courtesy of Toby Hibbitts

Slender glass lizard (*Ophisaurus attenuatus*). Courtesy of Toby Hibbitts

A cottonmouth snake (*Agkistrodon piscivorus*) flicking its tongue. Courtesy of Toby Hibbitts

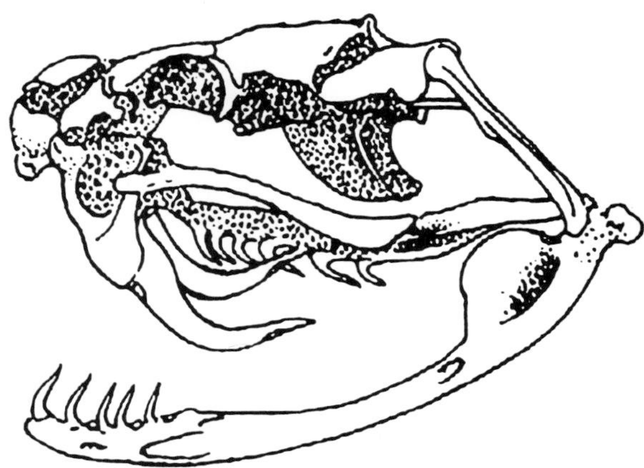

An example of solenoglyphous dentition. Courtesy of Morgan Osborn, intern, Texas A&M AgriLife Extension Service

Cottonmouth (*Agkistrodon piscivorus*) found at Cook's Branch Conservancy, Montgomery County, showing the white lining of its mouth during its characteristic defensive display. Courtesy of Toby Hibbitts

The dentition of snakes is classified into four categories. Many colubrid snakes in Texas have undifferentiated teeth, and are called **aglyphous**. Snakes with enlarged fangs at the rear of the mouth are called rear-fanged snakes, or **opisthoglyphous**. Although some rear-fanged snakes in Africa are extremely dangerous, there are no deadly rear-fanged snakes in North America. In Texas, hognose snakes, Texas lyre snake, black-striped snake, and night snakes are examples of colubrids with opisthoglyphous dentition. The pitvipers have **solenoglyphous** dentition, with hollow front fangs that rotate on the maxilla bone of the upper jaw. The Texas coralsnake, an elapid, has hollow fangs, but they are fixed on the end of a nonrotating maxilla. The pitvipers and coralsnakes inject venom in a manner analogous to the workings of a hypodermic syringe. Muscles in the head squeeze venom glands, forcing venom through ducts that lead into the hollow fangs.

Constricting, Swallowing, and Envenomation

All snakes are carnivores; there are no herbivorous snakes. Snakes subdue their prey in three basic ways that more or less correspond to evolutionary lineages of snakes. Subduing prey by constriction is used by several genera of snakes in Texas, including ratsnakes, kingsnakes, and their allies. Constrictors immobilize and often suffocate their prey by constricting it as they begin to swallow it. Other snakes, including garter snakes and watersnakes, simply subdue their prey by swallowing it alive.

The third method of subduing prey, used by pitvipers and coralsnakes, is envenomation. Taking large prey can be dangerous, and numerous scars on large snakes attest to confrontations they have had with prey. Pitvipers usually strike and release, then track the prey after it is incapacitated. Envenomation as a foraging mode is thought to have allowed pitvipers to take very large prey at less risk to themselves. Additionally, proteolytic properties of pitviper venoms break down tissues inside the prey, presumably aiding digestion of large prey items.

Most herpetologists agree that snake venoms and envenomation evolved as an adaptation for prey capture that was later co-opted for defense. A great deal of research has been done on the form and function of pitvipers, the heat-sensing pit organ, and the functional morphology of how snakes engulf their prey. Additional resources at the end of this unit provide excellent summaries of these interesting topics.

Locomotion in Snakes

In the case of squamates, having no limbs has certain advantages for locomotion. A long, thin body enables snakes to negotiate narrow openings and move through complex difficult terrain, such as tall grass, where limbs might hinder more than help. It is thought limblessness has evolved many times among lizards and snakes. All snakes have at least 120 vertebrae in front of the tail, and some as many as 400. Each vertebra has projections that strengthen connections between them, and complex muscular arrangements connect overlapping sets of vertebrae. Snakes have the same number of ventral scales as vertebrae, and the ribs from each vertebra are connected to the ventral scales. This system allows snakes to precisely control movements along their entire body.

Snakes locomote in several ways, including the familiar **lateral undulation**. Snakes moving this way generate force against objects in the environment and move forward in a wavelike motion from point to point. Coachwhips, racers, and whipsnakes can move surprisingly fast with lateral undulation, which is well suited for negotiating complex habitats such as tall grass, debris piles, and rock piles. Snakes also move with **rectilinear locomotion**, reminiscent of a caterpillar crawl with the snake's body stretched out. Snakes moving by rectilinear locomotion push their ventral scales onto the ground in several places, pull themselves forward, and then anchor the ventral scales in a forward position. It is not uncommon to find large rattlesnakes traveling by rectilinear locomotion. Once disturbed, however, they will usually switch to lateral undulation to retreat faster.

In **concertina locomotion**, the snake's crawl is reminiscent of a concertina musical instrument. The snake moves from point to point by pushing itself onto the ground, lifting and scrunching its body, then stretching forward. **Sidewinding** is an efficient mode of locomotion used by some snakes that live in soft, sandy habitats. There are no sidewinders in Texas, but sidewinding arose independently in several species of pitvipers that live in deserts around the world.

Snake skeletons. Courtesy of Lee Fitzgerald

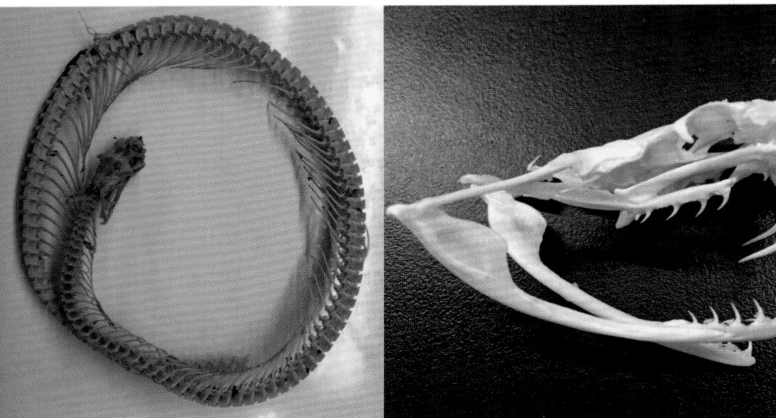

Reproductive Modes

Snake and lizards reproduce in various ways: live bearing, laying eggs, and parthogenesis.

The Oviparity-Viviparity Continuum

The herpetological naturalist quickly learns that some snakes, including all the pitvipers, watersnakes, and garter snakes, give birth to their young alive (**viviparity**), whereas many others lay eggs (**oviparity**). Shops around Texas sometimes sell fake rattlesnake eggs as curios, which is a completely inaccurate portrayal of their fascinating reproductive strategy. All rattlesnakes give birth to litters of pups, and in species that have been studied, the female attends the newborns until they disperse after their first shed. Many lizards in Texas, including the mountain short-horned lizard, rosebelly lizard, mesquite lizard, crevice spiny lizard, and blue spiny lizard, are also live bearers. Embryos of viviparous squamates are nourished from yolk. The calcareous shell is not added to the eggs of viviparous species, as babies are born in a sac of extraembryonic membranes they promptly rupture. In general, mothers provide little or no nourishment to retained eggs, but females of a few species of viviparous skinks in the Neotropics are known to provide nourishment to embryos via a placenta-like structure.

There are pros and cons to viviparity and oviparity. Once eggs are laid, oviparous females are no longer burdened with carrying a clutch of eggs. Eggs can be laid in places favorable to hatchling survival and growth, even if such places are outside the usual habitat of females. Many fence lizards in the genus *Sceloporus* make nesting migrations outside their home range to lay their eggs. Presumably this aids their young by giving them a start on dispersal outside the female's range. Viviparous females, on the other hand, avoid problems that can befall eggs, such as nest predation, disease, and poor conditions for incubation (e.g., too cold, hot, or dry). Live-bearing snakes and lizards can take advantage of behavioral thermoregulation to control their body temperatures and hence the incubation temperature of eggs retained inside their bodies. Therefore, it makes sense that viviparity in lizards is common in cold climates, whether at high latitudes or high elevations. Some skinks and other lizards protect their nests.

Many families, genera, and species of squamates have independently evolved to live bearing from their egg-laying ancestors. A survey of viviparity across the phylogenetic tree of squamates shows live bearing evolved at least 45 different times in lizards and more than 30 times in snakes. In reality, there is an oviparity-viviparity continuum in squamates that ranges from eggs laid with embryos only beginning to develop, to fully developed babies at birth.

In most oviparous lizards, about half of embryonic development occurs before the eggs are laid. Depending on the species and population, eggs may be retained for varying periods of time as the embryos develop. Therefore, retention of eggs inside the female's body can be thought of as an extension of parental care of eggs. The flexibility that eggs may be retained for short or long periods allows squamates to tinker with the oviparity-viviparity continuum, in the evolutionary sense, to achieve a life history that balances the benefits of laying eggs versus retaining them. But as with all life history strategies, there are trade-offs. Carrying developing eggs, the gravid condition of reproductive females, is costly. When gravid, females have worse locomotory performance and consequently are at greater risk of predation.

Snake eggs hatching. Courtesy of Terry Hibbitts

Parthenogenesis

Six of the 11 species of whiptails (*Cnemidophorus* spp., Teiidae) in Texas reproduce asexually. There are no males or sperm, and mothers produce identical daughters—true genetic clones. This type of reproduction is called **parthenogenesis** and is known worldwide in seven lineages of lizards and one snake. Parthenogenesis is a complex subject involving several different mechanisms. Details of exactly how parthenogenesis works are given in herpetology texts and other books.

In the most common form, exhibited by all-female whiptail species in Texas, **parthenogenetic species** or **parthenoforms** arose when two different sexually reproducing species mated and produced fertile hybrid female offspring. It is known, for example, that *Aspidoscelis uniparens* originated from hybridization events between *A. gularis*

Checkered whiptail (*Cnemidophorus tesselatus*), a parthenogenetic lizard. Courtesy of Toby Hibbitts

and *A. inornatus*. Hybridization events could easily have happened multiple times; hence, there may be various "complexes" of parthenoforms, as in the *A. laredoensis* complex. Some parthenogens have the typical condition of two sets of chromosomes (diploid), whereas others have three sets (triploid).

Why do these all-female species persist without the overarching advantage of sexual reproduction—increasing genetic variation so offspring can adapt to changing environments? In a sexually reproducing species, each individual leaves, on average, one descendant copy of each gene. The advantage of clonal, asexual reproduction is every gene in the parthenoforms doubles in frequency in each descendant generation. Additionally, because all the individuals are reproducing females, populations grow more rapidly than those sexual species. Parthenogens like the exotic snake species in Texas, *Rhamphotyphlops braminus* (Typhlopidae), are also well suited for dispersal. Theoretically, one individual can found a new population because she has no need for a mate.

Conservation of Texas Herpetofauna

Amphibians and reptiles in Texas have been affected by the same factors that are causing loss of biodiversity all over the planet: habitat loss and fragmentation, harmful invasive species, environmental contamination, and commercial exploitation. Although no species we know of have been deliberately extirpated in Texas, there are unfortunate examples of how each of these factors has affected Texas' herpetofauna. For example, the western smooth greensnake, an inhabitant of the coastal prairies, has not been found in Texas in more than 35 years.

The known range of a number of salamanders, frogs, lizards, snakes, and turtles is in severe decline. The good news is that herps have been granted the legal status of other wildlife, and the public today appreciates them more than ever. Several species of amphibians and reptiles in Texas are listed as threatened or endangered by the State of Texas and the US Fish and Wildlife Service. Status of species changes over time, and naturalists need to keep informed of current lists. For example, the American alligator is no longer a federally endangered species, and our endemic Concho watersnake was listed, then delisted, and its conservation status is currently being reassessed. Federally listed species include the five species of sea turtles, San Marcos salamander, Texas blind salamander, Barton Springs salamander, Jollyville Plateau salamander, Georgetown salamander, Salado salamander, Austin blind salamander, and Houston toad. These species plus 26 other amphibians and

Houston toad (*Bufo houstonensis*). Courtesy of Toby Hibbitts

San Marcos salamander (*Eurycea nana*). Courtesy of Toby Hibbitts

reptiles are listed as threatened by Texas Parks and Wildlife Department.

Habitat

Amphibians and reptiles as a group tend to persist, but the ever-increasing number of roads, increasingly fragmented habitats, and altered wetlands negatively affect local populations. Herpetological conservation is a relatively new endeavor, and there are not many detailed studies on the effects of habitat change on persistence of populations. Forestry practices and range management affect herpetological communities mostly by altering the mosaic of forested and open habitats. Different species respond in their own way to these kinds of changes, and detailed studies of the effects of land-use practices are becoming more common. In some instances, altered habitats favor sun-loving reptiles, but at the detriment of other species.

By and large, however, alteration of habitats and fragmenting habitat tend to cause disappearance of the most ecologically specialized species and changes in the makeup of ecological communities. Several species and groups of herps in Texas do have relatively stringent habitat requirements. A prime example is how fragmentation by roads and destruction of sand dunes in the Monahans Sandhills in West Texas impacts populations of the dunes sagebrush lizard. This species has a very small geographic range occurring only in shinnery oak dune complexes of the Monahans Sandhills in the vicinity of Monahans and the adjoining Mescalero Sands in southeastern New Mexico. Dunes sagebrush lizards live only in association with dune blowout formations in this small ecosystem, and when the dunes are disturbed, the dunes sagebrush lizard populations plummet.

The neotenic *Eurycea* salamanders of the Balcones Escarpment, for example, require clean and permanent water in the spring systems associated with the Edwards Aquifer. The black-spotted newt has a relatively small range in southern Texas and northeastern Mexico and has apparently been affected by agricultural practices. Alligator snapping turtles, map turtles, and cooters are most abundant in relatively clean and unaltered streams and rivers. Habitat for our endemic Concho watersnake and Harter's watersnake consists of riffle-and-pool reaches of the upper Brazos and Colorado River drainages, and these snakes are increasingly difficult to find in areas where they were once common. Drought, altered streams, siltation, and altered water flows are likely culprits in their decline. Perhaps one the rarest and least-known snakes in the world is found in Texas, the Louisiana pinesnake. Biologists have learned that Louisiana pinesnakes are

Habitat alterations, such as water impoundments like the US Army Corps of Engineers' Canyon Lake Dam, have had profound impacts on herpetological species. Courtesy of US Army Corps of Engineers

tightly associated with longleaf pine forests, which are dependent on fire and have mostly disappeared. It almost goes without saying to the concerned naturalist that conservation of wetlands, large blocks of forest, desert, and grassland habitat types is paramount for the conservation of many amphibians and reptiles as well as other types of biodiversity.

Harmful Invasive Species

The state reptile, the Texas horned lizard, is now considered rare east of Interstate Highway 35 in areas where it was very common 40 years ago. Horned lizards are also ecological specialists, fine-tuned by natural selection to be specialized ant feeders. Although there is no smoking gun to explain the frustrating decline of Texas horned lizards, it makes intuitive sense that the expansion of red imported fire ants and the concomitant decline of native ants had a lot to do with it (horned lizards cannot live on a diet of fire ants). It is completely unknown to what extent fire ants may be affecting other herp species, especially diminutive ground- and soil-dwelling snakes and lizards. There are published reports of fire ants swarming

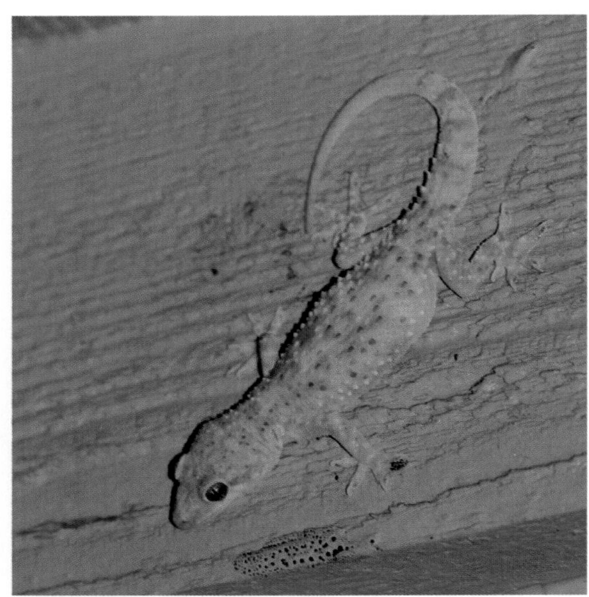

Mediterranean gecko (*Hemidactylus turcicus*). Courtesy of Toby Hibbitts

Texas horned lizard (*Phrynosoma cornutum*). Courtesy of Toby Hibbitts

nesting turtles, causing them to abandon nesting sites.

At least six lizards, one snake, and one turtle have been introduced into Texas. To date there are no serious environmental consequences of these introductions, but the brown anole is thought to be competitive with native green anoles. Although they are not harmful, Mediterranean geckos can become abundant on houses and other structures, and some people consider them a nuisance. The ranges of these exotic herps in Texas will probably expand, and we can likely expect more species to be introduced over time. In fact, a brown treesnake, the same species that wreaked environmental havoc on Guam, was found alive in Corpus Christi on May 12, 1993, after spending at least seven months inside sealed cargo in transit from Guam to Texas.

The commercial trade in pet reptiles and amphibians is a constant source of potential invasive species. There are at least 36 known invasive species recently in commercial trade that occur in Texas, including 3 species that are already established in Texas. Resource managers, Master Naturalists, and the public need to be vigilant about preventing the introduction and spread of invasive species.

Environmental Contamination

Contamination from pesticides, runoff, and other kinds of pollution does affect herps.

Several studies in Texas and elsewhere show that various species of herps accumulate contaminants, but the population-level effects are not easy to document. There is one excellent case study, conducted in Texas, that should serve as a warning for the future. In the 1970s, evidence was uncovered that was resoundingly similar to the DDT pesticide crisis that caused eggshell thinning in birds. During his research, Robert Fleet found high levels of pesticides in a snake community in southern Texas. A very disturbing result was the snake species that reproduced by laying eggs (oviparous) were all but absent from the community, whereas live bearers (viviparous) remained.

Current research is investigating even more insidious effects of contaminants on herptiles, such as disruption of the endocrine system that can lead to reproductive failure and other problems. A compelling and highly controversial line of research led by Tyrone Hayes has demonstrated that some of the most common agricultural chemicals disrupt the endocrine systems of frogs, causing chemical castration and hermaphroditism, where male frogs have ovaries and testes. This is far from normal and clearly a cause of concern for society as well as for frogs.

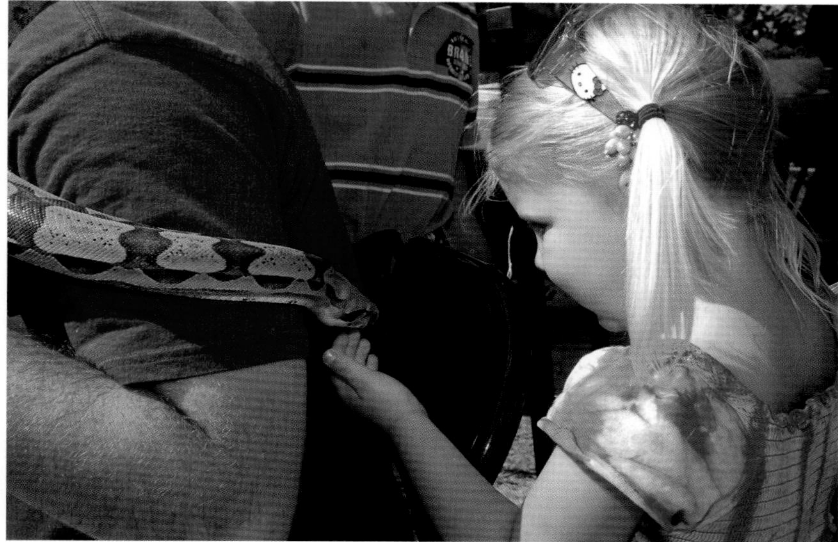

Child admiring a pet boa constrictor. Courtesy of Texas Parks and Wildlife Department

Smooth softshell turtle (*Apalone mutica*). Courtesy of Toby Hibbitts

Commercial Exploitation

More people than ever before appreciate herps, and their appreciation motivates many to keep herps as pets. It is not uncommon for boys and girls, or even adults, to catch a frog, lizard, snake, or turtle and want to keep it. Except for endangered species, this type of use is probably not a problem for conservation of herps. Wildlife laws in Texas are not designed to control individual experiences with small numbers of amphibians and reptiles but rather to monitor the commercial use of wild herps that could be unsustainable.

Surprisingly large numbers of amphibians and reptiles are collected from the wild in Texas each year to be sold as pets or for skins, meat, and curios. In 1999 Texas Parks and Wildlife Department began collecting data on the collection of nongame species. Some patterns in the trade are apparent. Most collection in the wild is concentrated in a few areas of the state, and surprisingly few collectors are responsible for the majority of herps collected. In 1999, more than 45,000 herps were reported collected in the wild in Texas.

Although about 100 species (depending on taxonomy used) were collected, 12 species accounted for 90% of the total. In decreasing order they were spiny softshell, western diamondback rattlesnake, collared lizard, sideblotched lizard, red-eared slider, tiger salamander, Couch's spadefoot, yellow mud turtle, marbled whiptail, ornate box turtle, and green toad. The commercial trade in freshwater turtles is of worldwide concern, and 16,110 native turtles were collected in Texas in 1999. Spiny softshells, pond sliders, yellow mud turtles, and ornate box turtles together accounted for 98% of all the turtles collected.

Texas' famous rattlesnake roundups carry with them important implications for conservation, environmental education, and the way society views rattlesnakes. Many people have heard of rattlesnake roundups, where a fair or carnival is organized over a three-day weekend to celebrate the collection of rattlesnakes. Fewer people realize, however, that rattlesnakes are traded year-round outside public roundups and the rattlesnakes are destined for the commercial trade in meat, skins, gall bladders, and curios (see appendix A). Rattlesnake commercialization is a complex issue, and Texas Parks and Wildlife Department and rattlesnake roundup organizers have worked together to monitor rattlesnake roundups since research published in 2000 highlighted the need for proper management of rattlesnakes. The three professional academic herpetological societies in North America published a factual and informed position statement in 2006 that decries wanton destruction of rattlesnakes for roundups and recommends ending destructive rattlesnake roundups and replacing them with festivals that celebrate the role of rattlesnakes in nature.

Rattlesnake roundups carry with them important implications for conservation, environmental education, and the way society views rattlesnakes. Overcrowding in pits is a common example of mistreatment of rattlesnakes. Improper holding and transport were the primary causes of injury to rattlesnakes at roundups. Courtesy of Lee Fitzgerald

Amphibian Decline and Amphibian Monitoring Transects

Throughout the 1990s, conservation biologists became aware of what seemed to be a mysterious decline in amphibians throughout the world. The current view is that although many populations of amphibians are in decline, there is not one single cause. Ultraviolet radiation, contaminants, global climate change, and amphibian diseases, particularly chytrid skin fungus, are all implicated in amphibian population declines. Recent attention to the problem has resulted in programs to obtain long-term data on amphibian communities. The Texas Amphibian Watch program is a monitoring effort organized by Texas Parks and Wildlife Department (TPWD). The program includes several activities aimed at amphibian identification, monitoring, and conservation. Members of the Master Naturalist chapters may be interested in participating in some of the advanced activities, particularly establishing a long-term nocturnal road transect for monitoring frog calls (aural transect) and reporting standardized amphibian monitoring data to TPWD through the Texas Nature Trackers Program.

Identifying Amphibians and Reptiles

There is a great amount of information available to help students of amphibian and reptile natural history in Texas. Several up-to-date monographic treatises, field guides, and websites include accurate and sometimes extensive natural history information, keys to identification, drawings, and photographs. In particular, Texas naturalists should consult the recent field guides *Texas Snakes* (Werler and Dixon 2005), *Texas Amphibians* (Tipton et al. 2012), *Texas Lizards* (Hibbitts and Hibbitts 2015), and the comprehensive *Amphibians and Reptiles of Texas* (Dixon 2013). Other resources for the herpetological naturalist in Texas are also listed at the end of this unit.

Amphibian and reptile houses at several zoos in Texas present excellent educational opportunities for naturalists. Several internationally recognized natural history collections, the Biodiversity Research and Teaching Collections at Texas A&M University, the Texas Memorial Museum at University of Texas at Austin, and the collections at University of Texas at Arlington, serve as repositories of preserved specimens for scientific study and teaching. These collections, painstakingly assembled and curated since the 1930s, provide the scientific basis for all literature on Texas' amphibians and reptiles and are the scientifically defensible record of how amphibian and reptile diversity has changed in Texas during the twentieth century. Information from natural history collections is increasingly available online, and naturalists will want to take advantage of searchable databases available through these collections' websites.

Finding Herps

It is necessary to catch most herps in order to see and identify them (see appendix B for suggested field trips). Many herpetologists want to keep specimens temporarily to photograph them or show them to other members of the group. Individuals studying natural history of herps in the wild, therefore, need to be fully aware of TPWD regulations about nongame wildlife. Almost all herps are classified as nongame, and collection of nongame in the wild requires a Texas hunting license or a collection permit. Road cruising, especially at night, is one of the most productive techniques for finding snakes. However, it is illegal to collect wildlife from a vehicle in Texas, and recent regulations require wearing reflective vests while outside the vehicle. It is the naturalist's responsibility to be aware of private land boundaries and avoid trespassing.

At the time of this writing, regulations limit individuals to possession of 10 specimens of a species and 25 total individuals without a commercial or dealer permit or herp stamp on the hunting license. The possession limit of 10 specimens per species, 25 total specimens was created as an enforcement mechanism for the nongame regulations. If an individual possesses more than the limit, it may be assumed the individual is involved in some type of commercial activity. The possession limit was not designed to manage populations or constrain current levels of use (see the TPWD website, https://tpwd.texas.gov/, and use the search field at the top of the page). Regulations and the lists of permitted and prohibited species change over time. It is paramount to refer to TPWD regulations before collecting herptiles.

Searching on Foot

Most herps are found simply by walking through suitable habitat and actively searching for individuals that are active or in their refugia. On a typical outing, the accomplished herpetological field collector is equipped with a few plastic bags for amphibians and very small reptiles, one or two cloth bags for snakes and lizards, a notebook and pen, a camera, and often a tool for turning rocks and logs. A potato rake is an efficient tool for searching through leaf litter and turning and breaking apart rotting logs. If aquatic habitats are present, a dip net is very useful for sampling tadpoles and salamander larvae. Many herpetologists carry a noose pole for catching active lizards. Noose poles can be made from old fishing poles, with a noose tied from dental floss, monofilament line, or cotton thread. Some of the

Finding and catching a snake that was hidden inside a rotten log. Courtesy of Toby Hibbitts

websites listed in "Resources for Herpetological Naturalists in Texas" at the end of this unit maintain links to businesses that cater to herpetologists and sell specialized hooks, nets, and tongs.

While searching for herps on foot, keep an eye out for active lizards and snakes, and look under suitable cover where herps may be hiding. Many species take refuge under rocks, underneath and inside fallen logs, and under the bark of standing snags. The hook or rake is useful for turning rocks and tearing apart rotten logs. Microhabitats are disturbed when searching for herps, and it is important to put logs and rocks back in their original positions. Piles of boards, sheet metal, junk piles, and fallen-down buildings are excellent places to search for herps because of the abundance of refugia and the ease with which the habitat can be taken apart and thoroughly searched.

Never try to catch a venomous snake without a compelling reason. Naturalists usually do not have a compelling reason, and it simply is not worth the risk of snakebite to catch and handle pitvipers on a naturalists' outing. Venomous snakes are easy to identify without capture. Pitvipers can often be photographed in situ, and if found undisturbed will often stay put long enough for others in the group to arrive and observe them.

The number of herps found is basically a function of the time spent in the field and the intensity of the search. The best collectors tend to stay out the longest, be very active, walk long distances, and have a good feel for what kinds of microhabitats are likely to be productive. In the Peterson Field Guide, *Amphibians and Reptiles of Eastern/Central North America*, Conant and Collins (1991) give a classic overview of herp-catching and herp-handling techniques, illustrations of how to hold live herps, and the common tools used by herp-oriented naturalists. It takes a lot of practice to catch herps by hand, and there is no formula for instant success. Most herps are caught by hand grabbing, though be advised that the reptiles may bite. Some nonvenomous snakes will bite hard and draw blood. Learn to be quick.

Time-Constrained Searches

Herps are more abundant or more active in some places than others, and herpetologists and naturalists are often interested in monitoring differences in herptile activity among sites and through time. Time-constrained searches keep track of person-hours spent searching for herps so that the number of animals encountered during different searches can be compared. The starting and ending time for a search is noted, along with how many individuals of each species are found for each observer. For example, three observers searching for two hours would total six person-hours of search time. In our example, if 12 animals were encountered, the yield would be 2 animals per person per person-hour for that search. This result can be compared to other searches at the same place on different days or to different sites. The method does have its limitations. Time-constrained searches are subject to variability among observers and to the vagaries of weather that affect herp activity during a particular search. Still, the method is easy to put into practice and allows comparisons of herp species and their numbers over time and at different places.

Coverboards and PVC Pipe Traps

Coverboards and PVC pipe traps function by creating artificial refugia that are attractive to herps. Coverboards are simply sheets of plywood or other material that are laid out in suitable habitat. Lengths of PVC pipe driven into the ground in wetlands retain water and provide a good refugium for frogs, especially treefrogs. These traps work well in many situations and have the great advantage that herps do not remain trapped. They do not have to be checked daily, and maintenance is very low compared to that for pitfall traps. Coverboards and pipe traps can be configured in grids for standardized sampling.

Trapping

There may be occasions when naturalists want to use simple trapping methods for catching reptiles and amphibians that are otherwise hard to observe or when conducting an organized inventory or study. Before trapping or sampling, one should have a clear answer to the question, "How am I going to handle, transport, and care for trapped animals?" If the decision is made to embark on a herpetological inventory that includes trapping, it is very important to have permits, a complete plan of operations, and all the materials necessary to manage a large number of captive herps.

Herpetologists routinely adapt and modify techniques to the particular situation. Prior knowledge of species' natural history gives clues about the microhabitats they may be using, and it takes ingenuity to invent ways to lure them from hiding or extract them from their refugia. Following are some common trapping techniques that apply to many situations, but as with all field methods, resourcefulness is the key to success.

Minnow Traps, Hoop Nets, and Seining

Commercially available minnow traps can be purchased at sporting goods stores and bait shops and are excellent traps for watersnakes, sirens, amphiumas, and waterdogs. Minnow traps are secured to the shore or a branch with care taken to leave part of the trap above water so that captured animals can breathe. Watersnakes enter traps on their own, especially after minnows have become trapped. The funnel entrance holes may need to be enlarged so large snakes can enter. Minnow traps can be baited with dog food, lunch meat, or catfish bait when trapping amphiumas and sirens.

Hoop nets, large funnel traps made for catching fish, are commercially available and are the preferred method for turtle trapping. Make sure to have a permit for using hoop nets. Hoop nets can be baited with fish or a punctured can of sardines to trap sliders and snapping turtles. Bait with melon rinds or cabbage if trapping herbivorous cooters. Again, it is important to anchor hoop traps, leaving part of the trap exposed so turtles can breathe. It is not uncommon for alligators and gar to get caught in large hoop traps. Turtle trappers should be prepared for this exciting occurrence when trapping in the rivers and lakes of East Texas.

Seining and dip netting are excellent methods for sampling tadpoles and sala-

Using a dip net to sample a wetland for aquatic amphibians and reptiles. Courtesy of Terry Hibbitts

mander larvae. A six-foot seine with one-fourth- or one-eighth-inch mesh and a dip net should be standard gear for a herp-collecting trip. Small, sturdy seines can be fashioned from mosquito screen and work well when seining through water with dense vegetation. Seining can also be used for sirens and amphiumas in the right conditions, as well as for turtles in shallow habitats. Dip nets of various sizes, ranging from aquarium nets to long-handled dip nets with small mesh, are useful for sampling tadpoles and salamander larvae in small pools and along undercut banks of streams and pools.

Pitfall and Funnel Traps and Array Trapping

A pitfall trap is a can or bucket buried flush with the surface of the ground. Animals simply fall into them and cannot escape. Five-gallon buckets make excellent pitfall traps. Two #10 cans stacked together also work well. Buckets nest within each other, making transport easier. It is best to cover pitfall traps with a coverboard elevated slightly off the surface. Plywood squares 16 × 16 inches make an excellent shade cover for five-gallon bucket traps. The cover provides shade for trapped animals and an enticing entrance for herps.

Pitfall traps are commonly connected together with a low drift fence, usually about 18 to 24 inches high and buried about 6 inches in the ground. Pitfall traps can be interconnected with drift fences in various configurations but are always most effective if they are longer than 25 feet. Drift fences work by intercepting a wandering herp that may follow the fence to a waiting pitfall or funnel trap. Materials used for drift fences are aluminum or galvanized flashing, hardware cloth, mosquito screen, plastic sheeting, or silt screen. The choice of fencing material depends on how long the fences need to last, ease of installation, and economics.

Funnel traps placed along drift fences also increase capture rates, especially for snakes. The same minnow traps mentioned previously work well for this purpose, or funnel traps can be made from mosquito screen or hardware cloth.

A drift fence. Courtesy of Chip Ruthven, Texas Parks and Wildlife Department

Checking a drift fence. Courtesy of Chip Ruthven, Texas Parks and Wildlife Department

Drift fence configurations can vary depending on circumstances. Sometimes long fences can be positioned haphazardly in suitable habitat if the objective is simply to sample a particular group or species. Two types of standardized drift fence arrays are commonly used in many herpetological field studies. Standardized arrays provide good coverage and can be deployed at randomly chosen locations within the sampling area for herpetological studies that require a statistical design. One type of standardized herp array consists of four drift fences, minimum 25 feet (approximately 8 meters) in length, with a five-gallon bucket on each end and funnel trap on each side of the fence. These four fences are configured in an open + shape, with 25 feet separating the arms of the +.

An alternative configuration is a Y-shaped design, with a five-gallon bucket in the middle of the Y, funnels on either side of the fences, and five-gallon buckets on the terminal ends of the fences. The arms of the Y are arranged at 120°. This design also uses minimum 25-foot-long drift fences. The Y arrays have the advantage of saving materials and labor for installation. We have also used Y arrays with only one bucket in the middle and three funnels at the terminal ends of the fences. These arrays use far fewer materials and are relatively quick to install.

Pitfall traps and drift fences are very productive means for catching many kinds of herps and may be worth the trouble if a group is committed to continued sampling of an area. Be advised, however, that arrays are hard to install and maintain, and capture rates will be low unless a large number of arrays are deployed and checked regularly. The traps need to be checked at least every other day without fail. The edge where pitfalls are buried in the soil needs to be maintained, and water that accumulates in pitfalls after rain must be promptly removed.

These tasks become quite tedious, and the workload increases exponentially as more arrays are deployed. We have found that deploying fewer than six arrays and opening them on occasional weekends is hardly worth the trouble. It is more productive to run time-constrained searches. Conversely, large array systems that are in operation for 7- to 10-day sampling periods will yield large samples of herps. Finally, it is crucial to securely close pitfall traps between sampling periods and leave funnel traps inoperable.

APPENDIX A

Conservation of Commercially Exploited Rattlesnakes

Although most people in Texas have heard of rattlesnake roundups, the fact that rattlesnakes from roundups end up as commercially traded wildlife is largely unknown. Rattlesnakes are traded to supply an international trade in skins, meat, gall bladders, and curios. Five species are used in eight states: western diamondback rattlesnakes (*Crotalus atrox*) in Texas, Oklahoma, and New Mexico; eastern diamondback rattlesnakes (*C. adamanteus*) in Alabama, Florida, and Georgia; prairie rattlesnakes (*C. viridis*) in Kansas, Texas, Oklahoma, and New Mexico; and timber rattlesnakes (*C. horridus*) in Pennsylvania, Georgia, Alabama, and Florida. Blacktail rattlesnakes (*C. molossus*) occasionally appear in the trade in New Mexico and Texas. The issues surrounding exploitation and conservation of rattlesnakes are complicated and a source of concern for wildlife professionals.

Rattlesnake roundups are a standing tradition for several Texas towns that hold these events during a weekend in the spring. As many as 26 towns in Texas have held rattlesnake roundups in the past, and 14 rattlesnake roundups were held in Texas in 1993. Organized rattlesnake hunts have continued in Oklahoma since they originated in Okeene in 1939, and the state has been home to five traditional rattlesnake roundups. The roundups themselves and the trade in rattlesnakes are economically and socially important to the towns where they are held. The forty-third annual Sweetwater Rattlesnake Roundup was held in Sweetwater, Texas, in 2001 and generated tens of thousands of dollars for civic projects, with substantial amounts of money spent in the community by tourists. More than 70,000 paying customers attended the 1993 Freer, Texas, Rattlesnake Roundup.

Timber rattlesnake (*Crotalus horridus*). Courtesy of Toby Hibbitts

The commercial trade in rattlesnakes occurs throughout the year independent of roundups, although it is practically impossible to quantify because it is unregulated. The best estimates are that 15% of western diamondback and eastern diamondback rattlesnakes entering the trade originate from roundups. In the 1990s, probably fewer than 125,000 rattlesnakes of all species entered the trade yearly in the entire United States. Western diamondback rattlesnakes from Texas probably account for 75% of the total. The number of rattlesnakes collected varies enormously according to demand for skins and meat. The take was high in the mid-1980s and declined in the 1990s.

Although rattlesnake ecology and population biology remain poorly understood, lack of data has not precluded both proponents and opponents of rattlesnake commercialization from drawing hard conclusions. A general belief among proponents of rattlesnake commercialization is that rattlesnake populations cannot be extirpated. Those favoring unrestricted harvest claim their mission as a public service to rid the countryside of dangerous vermin or to maintain the balance of nature. Ironically, if rattlesnakes were eliminated, an important cultural feature of the towns supporting rattlesnake roundups and the millions of dollars in revenue generated by the roundups and the trade would be lost. In contrast to proponents' claims, professional biologists have expressed concern that removal of thousands of rattlesnakes per year might adversely affect rattlesnake populations.

Depending on the region and season, western diamondback rattlesnakes are taken by road collecting and den hunting. At the Freer roundup, held in late spring, practically all western diamondback rattlesnakes were collected by road cruising or by walking fence lines. In northern Texas and Oklahoma, western diamondback rattlesnakes are hunted in early spring as they emerge from wintering sites. In these areas, it is common to spray gasoline fumes deep into dens, forcing the snakes to emerge. Not surprisingly, experiments have shown that gasoline fumes harmed rattlesnakes and co-inhabitants of snake dens, such as box turtles, other snakes, and invertebrates. Interestingly, few hunters collect the majority of the take. Depending on the year, the top two hunting teams collected between 25% and 85% of all the rattlesnakes at rattlesnake roundups. Most hunters or teams collect only a few snakes.

Analysis of the take of western diamondback rattlesnakes from 1959 to 1997 at the roundup at Sweetwater showed no long-term trends but was characterized by extreme variability. Body size and sex ratios of hunted western diamondbacks vary significantly by region and through time, but these differences were probably due more to geographic and temporal variation than from effects of hunting. More male rattlesnakes are collected than females, because males are more active and range over larger areas. Males are therefore more likely to be encountered by hunters.

Prairie rattlesnake (*Crotalus viridis*). Courtesy of Toby Hibbitts

The western diamondback rattlesnake is a mascot for several Texas towns, signaling the unique cultural value of rattlesnakes. Several towns elect beauty queens in honor of their rattlesnake roundup, and a giant statue of a western diamondback rattlesnake stands outside the Freer Chamber of Commerce. It is therefore ironic that rattlesnakes are often mistreated. A controversial activity at some rattlesnake roundups is killing snakes by decapitation and butchering them in public, sometimes by beauty pageant contestants or celebrities. We are not aware of any other instance in North America where killing of wildlife is used as entertainment for spectators. "Education" shows stress the risk of snakebite, to the exclusion of accurate natural history information. Meanwhile, handlers perform daredevil tricks with hundreds of rattlesnakes in a pit, sending an unclear message to the public about rattlesnakes that has little to do with the natural lives of these secretive, solitary predators.

It is obvious that rattlesnakes have high economic and cultural value, but the im-

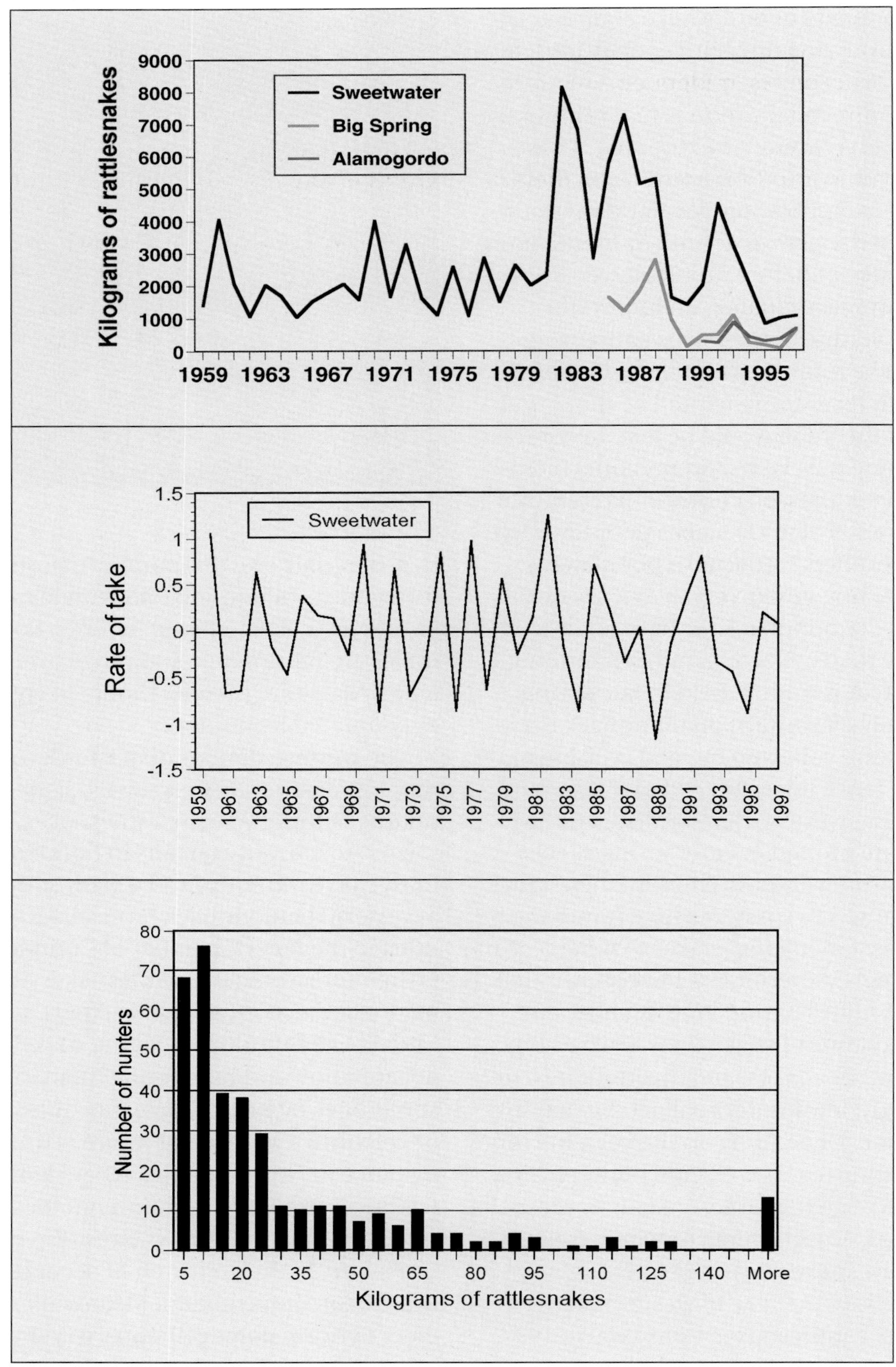

Top: Kilograms of western diamondback rattlesnakes brought to rattlesnake roundups. *Middle:* Although the number of rattlesnakes in a given year at Sweetwater was sometimes very large (e.g., 1982, 1986), harvest rate over 39 years (1959–97) was close to zero (–0.007). *Bottom:* Most hunters contributed small numbers of rattlesnakes to the overall harvest. The top two hunters combined contributed 25% to 85% of all rattlesnakes harvested.

portance of ensuring that rattlesnakes remain available from the wild seems lost on roundup organizers, traders, and most state fish and game commissions. The cornerstone of North American wildlife conservation, tightly controlling commercial uses of wildlife and appreciating wildlife through its use, has so far not applied to rattlesnakes. Recommendations for management of hunted rattlesnakes are obvious and have been made repeatedly.

Management programs for exploited rattlesnakes should include licensing of commercial traders, organizers of rattlesnake harvest events, and hunters so that the true magnitude of trade can be measured. Information also is needed on local versus regional impacts of hunting. It is critical to gather data on the portion of the commercial trade in rattlesnakes originating outside the roundups. Recent regulations in Texas, Kansas, and Oklahoma are examples of positive steps in this direction.

Another priority for conservation programs of harvested rattlesnakes is the incorporation of rules for proper hunting practices and treatment of live rattlesnakes and putting an end to making a spectacle of live rattlesnakes in public. The bottom line is that making fun of wildlife and mistreating live animals does not fit into a wildlife conservation model any more than unregulated commercialization. There are positive signs that public education at some rattlesnake roundups may be changing. Organizers and snake handlers at all rattlesnake roundups are enthusiastic about changing their shows and incorporating accurate information.

APPENDIX B

Field Trips for the Herp-Oriented Naturalist

A herpetologist's favorite place to be is in the field looking for animals on a warm spring day. Texas is one of the best states in the nation to look for amphibians and reptiles due to the great diversity of species and habitats. Knowledge of natural history of the amphibians and reptiles, and their habitat affinities in specific regions, is vital for the successful observation of herps. For example, the Texas lyre snake is found only at night on rocky hillsides in far western Texas. Without this information, it would be very unlikely for a well-intentioned naturalist to ever see this interesting snake. A good starting point before any field trip is to compile a list of species that may potentially be encountered by referring to field guides and by checking localities on online databases from the Biodiversity Research and Teaching Collections, Texas A&M, and other natural history collections.

It is very important to remember, when looking for amphibians and reptiles, that all logs and rocks should be left in their original positions. The environments under logs and rocks are very important for a wide variety of animals and should be disturbed as little as possible. There are many places throughout Texas to look for amphibians and reptiles, but it is the naturalist's responsibility to have proper permits, be aware of land ownership, and respect landowners' rights. Several places are recommended for field trip to search for amphibians and reptiles.

Sabine National Forest. Courtesy of Terry Hibbitts

Sabine National Forest

The Sabine National Forest in far eastern Texas is an excellent place to conduct herpetology field trips. Habitat types include uplands dominated by loblolly pine and bottomland forests dominated by oaks and sweetgum. Amphibians and reptiles are best found in these areas by searching on foot, turning logs, and encountering herps that are active. On warm spring and summer nights, calling frogs can be observed around almost any body of water. Some of the species expected to be found in the Sabine National Forest are marbled salamander, dwarf salamander, southern leopard frog, bronze frog, gray treefrog, red-eared slider, three-toed box turtle, ground skink, five-lined skink, green anole, ribbon snake, yellow-bellied watersnake, Texas ratsnake, and southern copperhead. Many other species may also be found but are much less common, for example, the spotted salamander, pickerel frog, and timber rattlesnake.

LBJ National Grassland. Courtesy of Grasslands Bed and Barn website

LBJ National Grassland

The LBJ National Grassland near Decatur is another very good spot to find amphibians and reptiles. This area is situated in the Cross Timbers ecoregion. The creeks and lakes are surrounded by post oak woodlands, and the hills are covered in prairie grasses with rock outcrops. Amphibians and reptiles are most commonly encountered under rocks or logs. Common species of the area include cricket frog, Great Plains narrowmouth toad, ornate box turtle, red-eared slider, Texas spiny lizard, prairie skink, six-lined racerunner, lined snake, ringneck snake, Great Plains ratsnake, and broad-banded copperhead. Some other, less common species that can be encountered by the lucky naturalist include the green toad, eastern fence lizard, and pygmy rattlesnake.

Amistad National Recreational Area. Courtesy of Terry Hibbitts

Amistad National Recreation Area

The Amistad National Recreation Area, located around Lake Amistad near Del Rio, is situated along the edge of the Trans-Pecos ecoregion. The area is made up of rocky limestone hills bisected by deep canyons. Mesquite is one of the dominant woody plants, especially in the canyons and lower areas. The hillsides are covered with many cactus species and arid land plants such as yucca and acacia. The amphibians and reptiles of this area are usually encountered when they are active. One can, however, have some success finding them by overturning rocks and yucca stalks. Road cruising is productive in this area, and many nocturnal amphibian and reptile species can be found on the roads. Some of the more common species include Couch's spadefoot, Texas toad, Texas spotted whiptail, marbled whiptail, tree lizard, greater earless lizard, coachwhip, bullsnake, night snake, and western diamondback rattlesnake. Some possible species to be encountered are the barking frog, Texas banded gecko, and gray-banded kingsnake.

References

Conant R., and J. T. Collins. 1991. *Reptiles and Amphibians of Eastern/Central North America*. 3rd ed. Peterson Field Guides. Boston: Houghton Mifflin.

Dixon, J. R. 2013. *Amphibians and Reptiles of Texas*. 3rd ed. College Station: Texas A&M University Press.

Hibbitts, T.D, and Hibbitts, T.J. 2015. *Texas Lizards: A Field Guide*. Austin: University of Texas Press.

Tipton, B., T. Hibbitts, T. J. Hibbitts, T. D. Hibbitts, and T. LaDuc. 2012. *Texas Amphibians: A Field Guide*. Austin: University of Texas Press.

Werler, J., and J. R. Dixon. 2000. *Texas Snakes*. Austin: University of Texas Press.

Additional Resources

Adams, C. E., J. K. Thomas, K. J. Strnadel, and S. L. Jester. 1994. Texas Rattlesnake Roundups: Implications of Unregulated Commercial Use of Wildlife. *Wildlife Society Bulletin* 22:324–30.

Axtell, R. W. *Interpretive Atlas of Texas Lizards*. Edwardsville, IL: Privately printed.

Berish, J. 1998. Characterization of Rattlesnake Harvest in Florida. *Journal of Herpetology* 32:551– 57.

Brown, W. S. 1993. Biology, Status and Management of the Timber Rattlesnake (*Crotalus horridus*): A Guide for Conservation. *SSAR Herpetological Circular* 22:1–78.

Campbell, J. A., D. R. Formanowicz Jr., and E. D. Brodie Jr. 1989. Potential Impact of Rattlesnake Roundups on Natural Populations. *Texas Journal of Science* 41:301–17.

Chippindale, P. T., A. H. Price, J. J. Weins, and D. M. Hillis. 2000. Phylogenetic Relationships and Systematic Revision of Central Texas Hemidactyliine Plethodontid Salamanders. *Herpetological Monographs* 14:1–80.

Cogger, H. G., and R. G. Zweifer, eds. 1998. *Encyclopedia of Reptiles and Amphibians, a Comprehensive Illustrated Guide by International Experts*. 2nd ed. San Diego, CA: Academic Press.

Crother, B. I. 2000. Scientific and Standard English Names of Amphibians and Reptiles North of Mexico, with Comments regarding Confidence in Our Understanding. *SSAR Herpetological Circular* 29.

Dixon, J. R. 2000. *Amphibians and Reptiles of Texas*. 2nd ed. College Station: Texas A&M University Press.

Dixon, J. R., and J. E. Werler. 2005. *Texas Snakes: A Field Guide*. Austin: University of Texas Press.

Fitzgerald, L. A., and C. W. Painter. 2000. Rattlesnake Commercialization: Long-Term Trends, Issues, and Implications for Conservation. *Wildlife Society Bulletin* 28:235–53.

Greene, H. W. 1997. *Snakes: The Evolution of Mystery in Nature.* With photographs by Michael and Patricia Fogden. Berkeley: University of California Press.

Heyer, W. R., M. A. Donnelly, R. W. McDiarmid, L. C. Hayek, and M. S. Foster, eds. *Measuring and Monitoring Biological Diversity: Standard Methods for Amphibians.* Washington, DC: Smithsonian Institution Press.

Pough, F. H., R. M. Andrews, J. E. Cadle, M. L. Crump, A. H. Savitzky, and K. D. Wells. 1998. *Herpetology*. Upper Saddle River, NJ: Prentice Hall.

Price, A. H. 2009. *Venomous Snakes of Texas: A Field Guide*. Austin: University of Texas Press.

Tennant, A. 2006. *Texas Snakes*. 3rd ed. Lone Star Field Guide. Lanham, MD: Taylor Trade Publishing.

Travis, N. T., J. R. Dixon, and C. R. Smith. 1999. *Amphibians and Reptiles of Texas:*

Taxonomic and Distributional Inventory with Bibliography. Austin: Texas System of Natural Laboratories.

Weir, J. 1992. The Sweetwater Rattlesnake Round-Up: A Case Study in Environmental Ethics. *Conservation Biology* 6 (1): 116–27.

Zug, G. R., L. J. Vitt, and J. L. Caldwell. 2001. *Herpetology: An Introductory Biology of Amphibians and Reptiles*. 2nd ed. New York: Academic Press.

National and Regional Herpetological Societies

American Society of Ichthyologists and Herpetologists (ASIH): http://www.asih.org/. [Publishes *Copeia*]

Austin Herpetological Society: https://www.facebook.com/AustinHerpetologicalSociety

Dallas-Fort Worth Herpetological Society: http://www.dfwherp.org/

East Texas Regional Herpetological Society: http://eths.org/

Herpetologists' League (HL): http://www.herpetologistsleague.org/en/index.php. [Publishes *Herpetologica* and *Herpetological Monographs*]

Society for the Study of Amphibians and Reptiles (SSAR): http://ssarherps.org/. [Publishes *Journal of Herpetology, Herpetological Review, Herpetological Circulars, Contributions to Herpetology and Facsimile Reprints in Herpetology, Catalogue of American Amphibians and Reptiles, Herpetological Conservation*]

Texas Herpetological Society: http://www.texasherpsociety.org/

West Texas Herpetological Society: http://www.westtexasherpsociety.org/

Website Resources

Biodiversity Research and Teaching Collections: http://brtc.tamu.edu

Herps of Texas: http://www.herpsoftexas.org/

Society for the Study of Amphibians and Reptiles. *Catalogue of American Amphibians and Reptiles*. http://ssarherps.org/publications/caar/. [Includes individual species accounts contributed by many authors. Each account cites all published literature about a particular species and provides updated distribution maps and a summary of the species' biology.]

Texas Natural History Collections, Texas Memorial Museum: http://integrativebio.utexas.edu/biodiversity-collections

Tree of Life: Terrestrial Vertebrates: http://tolweb.org. [A project containing information about the diversity of organisms on earth, their history, and characteristics. The information is linked together in the form of the evolutionary tree that connects all organisms to each other.]

Vert-Net: http://vertnet.org. [A comprehensive database for vertebrate specimen information, including herps.]

UNIT 16

Mammalogy

JOHN YOUNG
Mammalogist, Wildlife Division, Texas Parks and Wildlife Department (former)

KEVIN HERRIMAN
Northeast Texas Ecosystem Project Leader, Wildlife Division, Texas Parks and Wildlife Department

JONAH EVANS
Mammalogist, Wildlife Division, Texas Parks and Wildlife Department

Unit Goals

After completing this unit, volunteers should be able to

- become familiar with the common, native Texas mammals in your ecoregion
- demonstrate knowledge about the general characteristics of the 3 major (subclasses) of mammals
- discuss basic principles of mammal behavior, physiology, and ecology and relate these principles to environmental adaptations
- demonstrate familiarity with the 10 orders of mammals found in the state
- discuss the diversity and distribution of mammals in Texas and an understanding of the role of mammals in Texas ecosystems
- demonstrate knowledge of estimating/measuring mammal populations
- demonstrate knowledge of methods for trapping, marking, monitoring, and observing mammal populations
- understand threats to mammals in Texas

"Our task must be to free answers by widening our circle of compassion to embrace all living creatures and the whole of nature and its beauty."
—Albert Einstein

Introduction

Mammals were originally four-footed terrestrial animals, and most living forms retain this basic structure. Over the past millennia, this class of animals has diversified to fill a great number of niches. Mammals now encompass a wide variety of different species. Most are terrestrial, but there are about 1,000 winged species, all bats, and 80 aquatic species, mostly whales and dolphins. While not a large group—approximately 5,400 species compared with nearly 10,000 species of birds, 33,000 fishes, and a million insects—mammals provide humans with food, clothing, recreation, crop protection, and insect control; provide occasional nuisance problems; and serve as religious, spiritual, and cultural symbols.

"Plans to protect air and water, wilderness and wildlife are in fact plans to protect man."
—Stuart Udall, US secretary of the Interior, 1961–69

Wildlife professionals study mammals to identify problems and to promote conservation and management based on sound science. Many professionals and conservation-minded individuals believe we have an ethical responsibility to protect all species from extinction. Some nature enthusiasts enjoy wildlife watching and identifying tracks, hair, skulls, or other animal signs

The ocelot (*Leopardus pardalis*) is listed as an endangered species in Texas.

as a way to be more aware of their environment. As William B. Davis wrote, "Mammals and birds, insects and spiders, plants, soil and climate are all bound together in a great interrelated system of material and energy. We cannot get along without the wild animals. It will help if we pay some attention to them and try to read the fascinating life story of each" (Davis and Schmidly 1994). Whatever your reasons for studying mammals, learning about their characteristics, habits, and identifying features can provide a lifetime of enjoyment.

Note that this unit of the Master Naturalist curricula provides only a broad overview of mammals. Entire books have been written covering single species, families, or orders. Lengthy physical descriptions, lists of habitats, gestation periods, and other factual data are readily available in scientific works, in encyclopedias, and on the Internet. One good reference that provides detail on specific animals is *Mammals of Texas* (Schmidly 2004).

Pronghorn (*Antilocapra americana*). Courtesy of Texas Parks and Wildlife Department

Major Characteristics of Class Mammalia

Mammals are an advanced group in the animal kingdom that share unique features not found in other animals. Distinguishing features of mammals include the following:

- body covered with hair, which is reduced in some mammals such as whales and armadillos
- integument (skin) with sweat, scent, sebaceous (skin glands that open into hair follicles that produce and secrete sebum, a light yellow, oily fluid), and mammary glands
- mouth with teeth (also reduced in some species such as armadillos)
- movable eyelids and fleshy external ears
- four limbs in most and adapted for many modes of locomotion

- four-chambered heart
- respiratory system with lungs, larynx, and muscular diaphragm
- highly developed brain
- endothermic (produces heat internally) and homoeothermic (maintains stable body temperature)
- internal fertilization; eggs develop in a uterus with placental attachment except in monotremes, primitive mammals that lay eggs: echidnas (spiny anteaters) and duck-billed platypus
- young nourished by milk from mammary glands, including the monotremes

The key characteristics unique to mammals are hair and mammary glands. The mammary glands produce milk that nourishes the young, and the hair helps insulate the body and maintain a relatively high, constant body temperature. Also, the skin serves as a protective barrier, a layer of epidermis over a layer of fat.

A coyote in the snow. Courtesy of Yathin S. Krishnappa

Classification of Mammals

The class Mammalia is divided taxonomically into three major groups (subclasses) by their mode of reproduction and embryonic development: monotremes (subclass Prototheria), marsupials (subclass Metatheria, formerly Marsupialia), and placentals (subclass Eutheria).

Monotremes are mammals that lay eggs. The eggs are incubated in a subterranean nest. After the eggs hatch, the young feed on the milk secreted by the mother. Females possess no teats, and the milk oozes along special hairs. Only five monotreme species still exist, the duck-billed platypus and four species of echidna. All five are found only in Australia or New Guinea.

Marsupials are born tiny, very immature in comparison to other mammals, and must climb into the mother's pouch, called a marsupium. Once in the pouch they grab hold of a teat and do not leave until they are well developed. The most-recognized example of a marsupial is the kangaroo. The Virginia opossum is the only marsupial native to the United States and Texas.

Placental mammals are the most common types of mammal in all but Australia. Placental mammals are those whose young develop over a long period of time in the female's uterus. Over 95% of mammals worldwide are placentals, including humans.

In addition to being classified by mode of reproduction, mammals are often separated into groups based on diet. The common types include herbivores, carnivores, omnivores, insectivores, and granivores. **Herbivores** eat only plants, and most common are rabbits and hares, manatees, and rodents such as nutria and muskrats. **Omnivores**, such as opossums, coyotes, and foxes, are like humans in that they eat a combination of plants and meat. **Carnivores**, such as the mountain lion or river otter, eat almost entirely meat. **Insectivores**, such as bats and shrews, eat insects, while **granivores**, such as squirrels, eat seeds and nuts. There are also a few other specialized feeders: frugivores (fruit), piscivores (fish), sanguinivores (blood), and nectarivores (nectar).

Embryonic Development

Eutherians, like their closest relatives the marsupials, give birth to live young. In eutherians, however, the young are nurtured within and from the body of the mother by the placenta, which allows nutrients to pass from the blood of the mother into the embryo's bloodstream. The placental system is slightly more efficient at delivering nutrients than that of the marsupials.

Marsupial young are born hairless and virtually helpless; they must crawl to a special pouch where they continue development. Some eutherian mammals, such as the rodents and some carnivores, are not very different from the marsupials—the young are born hairless and blind and must be nurtured by their mother for a time before they can begin to live on their own. The primary difference is that the young are not raised in a special pouch, as in marsupials.

The degree of development at birth varies greatly among different eutherian groups. Some young ungulates (hoofed species) can walk within minutes of being born, while human children may take years to accomplish this. The length of parental care following birth also varies greatly, from about a month to several years.

A Virginia opossum (*Didelphis virginiana*) carries its offspring on its back once they leave the marsupial pouch.

Undeveloped red wolf pups (eutherian). Red wolves (*Canis rufus*) were once found in Texas and have been listed as extirpated from the state of Texas. Adult wolf (*inset*). Courtesy of US Fish & Wildlife Service and Texas Parks and Wildlife Department

An ungulate young fawn. Courtesy of Texas Parks and Wildlife Department

Reproductive Strategies and Advantages

One of the primary advantages of sexual reproduction is comparatively greater genetic variation among offspring. Genetic variation provides populations the potential ability to meet environmental changes by adaptation. Mammals can be divided into two groups based on the degree of development at birth: those that bear **altricial** young (virtually helpless) and those that bear **precocial** young (relatively well developed). Each mode is typically associated with a different life history strategy.

Mammals with altricial young live under generally unstable conditions with seasonal or unpredictable food resources. They are small in size and subject to heavy predation. Normally litters are large (>7), the young are born in a nest, and the gestation and suckling periods are short. The young reach sexual maturity rapidly and have short life spans. Under favorable conditions breeding may occur throughout the year. High reproductive rates allow these mammals to take advantage of even brief periods of food abundance. Such opportunism results in high population turnover and population densities that are unstable seasonally and annually. A variety of smaller mammals and many rodent species exhibit this pattern of reproduction, including rabbits and shrews. On the other end of the altricial spectrum are many of the predators such as coyotes, foxes, and bobcats, whose young are born helpless and depend on parental care to survive.

Mammals with precocial young include the ungulates, some rodents, and cetaceans, which typically live in a stable environment with a predictable food base. These animals are often large, reach sexual maturity late, and have a prolonged gestation period. Although these mammals have a slow reproductive rate, the survival rate of young is high because of the extended parental care. Population stability, a low reproductive rate, low population turnover, and dependence on a stable environment make these animals more vulnerable to habitat alteration.

Excellent examples of the advantages and disadvantages of this type of reproduction are typified by white-tailed deer and black bear in Texas. Black bears, once historically abundant in Texas, were extirpated (deliberately exterminated) and are now slowly repopulating the Trans-Pecos from Mexico. Black bears have taken decades to reestablish even a limited presence in Texas. On the other hand, white-tailed deer have responded favorably to landscape changes and, due to high survival rates and lack of natural predators, are now creating overpopulation problems in some areas.

Identification Techniques

The mammals of North America are a diverse and fascinating group. However, because most mammals are nocturnal, secretive, and quiet, they tend to be elusive. For instance, on a walk through the woods, you might expect to see only five or six species of mammals—perhaps an armadillo, a cottontail rabbit, a squirrel, and maybe a white-tailed deer. But the woods contain other kinds of mammals that are not as easily discovered. Because many mammals are secretive, you must pay close attention to the evidence they have left behind. Some of the signs that can be used for identification purposes include trails and paths, track and tail trails, droppings (or scat), burrows, nests, dens, and hair remains.

Identifying Tracks

When outdoors, look closely at the mud along streams, ponds, and dusty roads, and you will often find an abundance of mammal tracks. Examine the forest floor, and you will probably see rabbit and deer droppings and might find **scat** (feces) from a carnivore made up of pieces of bone and hair. A good field guide for identifying animal tracks is an important tool for a mammologist. Mark

Elbroch's (2003) *Mammal Tracks & Sign: A Guide to North American Species* is an excellent resource. Another is James Halfpenny's (1986) *Field Guide to Mammal Tracking in North America*. The appendix contains prints of some common mammal tracks.

Identification by Hairs

Entire books have been developed on how to identify mammals by their hair. However, systematic identification by hair characteristics is generally not a useful field technique since you need a microscope to view hair scales and other key features. However, it is possible to learn how to identify hair from species with unique hair such as rabbits and deer. A thorough examination of field identification of mammal hair can be found in reference guides and online.

Identification by Skull and Teeth

One of the most common and important methods for identifying mammals is examining variations in skulls and teeth. The latter are often the most important characteristic for identification. Mammals have four main types of teeth, each of which has a different purpose. Some mammals have all four, while some have only two or three types. Herbivores like white-tailed deer have tall molars with ridged, flat upper surfaces for grinding coarse vegetation. Rabbits have well-developed incisors for clipping vegetation and ridged molars for grinding grasses. Wide molars with low, bumpy crowns are found on omnivores like coyotes and javelinas.

The eastern cottontail (*Sylvilagus floridanus*). Courtesy of Max Traweek

Carnivores such as bobcats have sharp canine teeth to grab and stab their prey. In addition, carnivores have carnassials, specialized teeth used for shearing meat. In adult carnivores, the **carnassials** are the last upper premolar and the first lower molar. If you articulate the mandible and skull (put the two together at the joint) and open and close the jaw, it is easy to see which pair of teeth would shear meat. This helps in distinguishing between premolars and molars. The only carnivorous Texas species that does not have well-developed canines is the raccoon. Even so, the raccoon's skull still looks like that of a carnivore and should not be difficult to recognize.

The coyote skull figure provides an overview of the key features of a skull and teeth that may be used in identifying mammals. Again, vast amounts of minute details on skull features have been collected and published in a variety of texts.

As you become familiar with mammals, you will find that the skulls of mammals from different orders look very different. Soon you will be able to tell the skull of an insectivore from that of a carnivore. The skulls of species in different orders are very distinctive, but learning to identify mammals at the familial or generic level gets more complicated. Keys to identifying mammals by their skulls and teeth are available, for example, *A Manual of Mammalogy: With Keys to Families of the World* (Martin et al. 2011). However, some distinguishing features for certain groups are presented here.

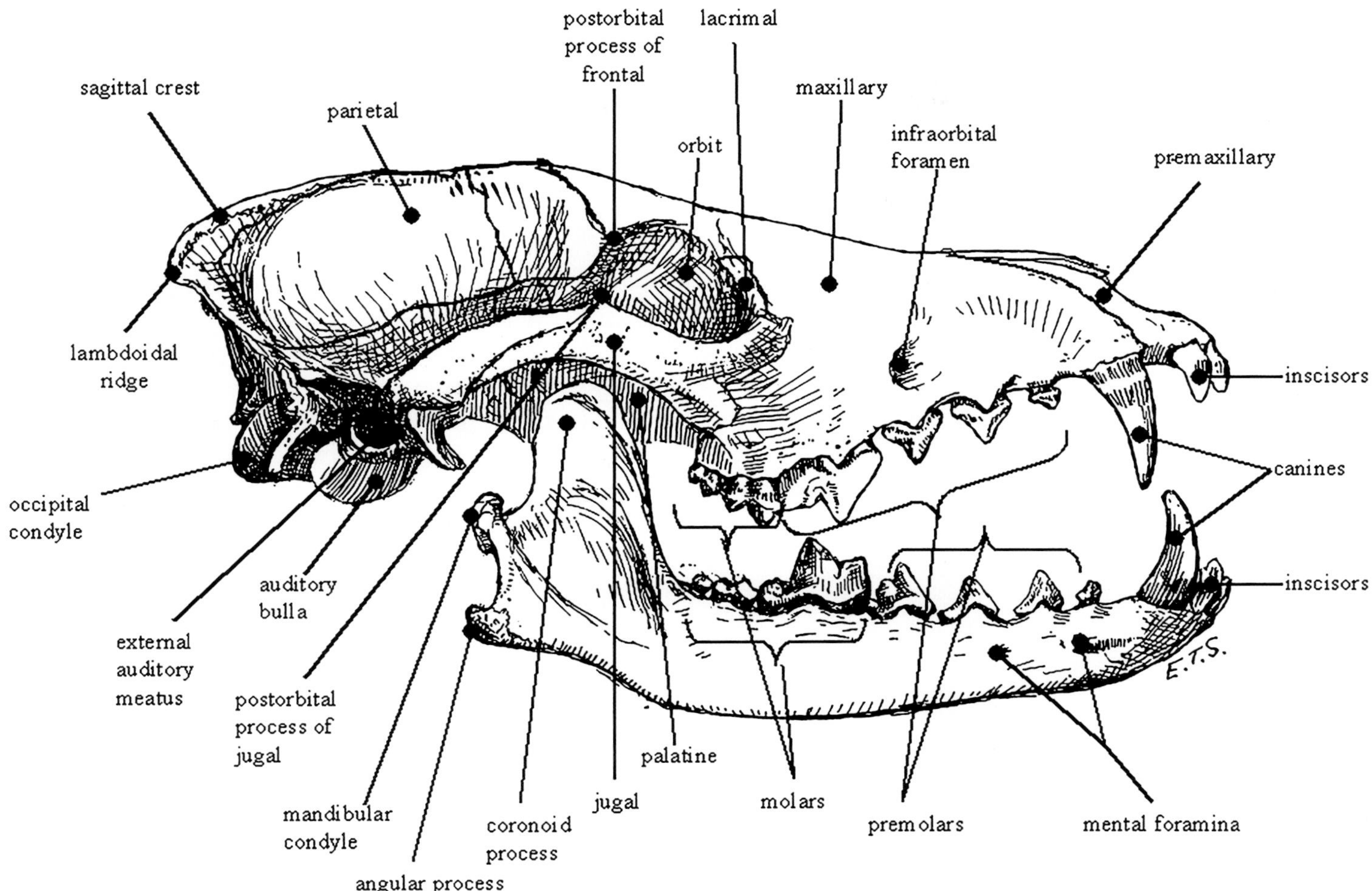

Skull key for a coyote (*Canis latrans*) skull.

Tooth formula is one of the easiest ways to identify mammals at the generic level. In many cases, the tooth formula is a distinguishing trait by itself. Tooth formulas are expressed, for example, as I 2/1, C 1/1, PM 3/4, and M 3/3. This means that the mammal with this tooth formula has

- 2 incisors in each half of the upper jaw/1 incisor in each half of the lower jaw
- 1 canine in each half of the upper and lower jaws (i.e., one canine/quadrant)
- 3 premolars in each half of the upper jaw/4 premolars in each half of the lower jaw
- 3 molars in each quadrant of the jaw (3 in each upper half, 3 in each lower half)

Marsupials (opossum) have the following skull characteristics. Although the first two traits are diagnostic, it is probably easier to remember to check for the inflected angular process:

- an inflected (turned inward) angular process on the dentary
- a primitive state of dentition:
  - a tooth formula of I 5/4, C 1/1, PM 3/3, M 4/4 in contrast to I 3/3, C 1/1, PM 4/4, and M 3/3 for placentals
  - the molars primitive in shape and triangular (**tribosphenic**) rather than square
- a relatively small braincase

Insectivores are characterized by red pigmented teeth. Any time you encounter a tiny mammal skull with red-tipped teeth, you should know right away that it is a shrew and in order Insectivora.

Mammal genera and species in Texas

Group	Order	Characteristic species (including exotics)	Species in Texas (no.)
Marsupial	Didelphimorphia	Opossum	1
Placental	Chiroptera	Bats	33
	Xenarthra	Armadillo	1
	Lagomorpha	Hares and rabbits	5
	Rodentia	Rodents	69
	Carnivora	Carnivores	28
	Artiodactyla	Even-toed ungulates	14
	Insectivora	Moles and shrews	5
	Sirenia	Manatee	1
	Cetacea	Whales and dolphins	27

Members of the Rodentia family use their large incisors for gnawing at their food, typically seeds or other plant material, such as this ground squirrel with grass seeds. Courtesy of John English, Big Country Chapter, www.johnenglishphoto.com

North American rodents have the following skull characteristics:

- one incisor per quadrant of the jaws
- a large **diastema** (gap between teeth) and no canines
- yellow enamel on the incisors

Mammals in Texas

Texas, with its wide variety of soils, climate, vegetation, topography, and extensive coastline, is home to 184 species of mammals. Only 10 orders of Mammalia are currently found in Texas. Some of the species are not common to Texas but are known from a few sightings or beachings, in the case of whales and dolphins. Over the years, many large exotic ungulates have been brought into the state, and tens of thousands now roam wild. Because they are not native to the state, they are not included here.

Characteristics of the Major Groups of Mammals in Texas

The following information provides a brief description of the characteristics of each of the mammalian orders along with the number of species in Texas.

Order Didelphimorphia

Didelphimorphia are among the oldest and most primitive of mammals. The chief characteristic of species in this order is a marsupium, or pouch, on the abdomen of females. Young are born after only partial development and conclude their development in the marsupium.

Order Chiroptera

This order contains the bats, the only mammals capable of true flight; the others are gliders. Chiroptera is the second-largest order worldwide with approximately 1,000 species. Only the rodents outnumber bats in number of species. As a group, bats are crepuscular or nocturnal, and many are

Mexican free-tailed bat (*Tadarida brasiliensis*), a member of the order Chiroptera. Courtesy of US Fish and Wildlife Service

specialized to use ultrasound for navigation and to locate prey. Most species feed entirely on insects. Some species hibernate, while others, such as the Mexican free-tailed bat, migrate seasonally.

Order Xenarthra

This group evolved in South America. Texas has only one representative that just recently invaded the state. This order includes armadillos, sloths, and anteaters. Considered the most primitive placentals of the New World, the order contains 30 species worldwide. Members are highly specialized in structure and habits.

The nine-banded armadillo (*Dasypus novemcinctus*) is an example of a species from the order Xenarthra.

Order Lagomorpha

Lagomorphs include rabbits, hares, and pikas. Worldwide there are 90 species. Lagomorphs are distinguished from rodents by an extra pair of upper incisors and premolars 2/2 or 3/2, while rodents have 2/1 or 0/0 premolars. Food is almost entirely vegetable matter.

Order Rodentia

Rodentia is the largest of all mammalian orders with approximately 1,700 species worldwide. The main distinguishing feature of rodents is their incisors, which grow continuously throughout their life. Most rodents eat plant material, but many consume insects, and some, like the grasshopper mouse, are carnivorous. Most rodents do not hibernate, but some, such as ground squirrels, do. Sixty-nine species of native rodents occupy Texas, making this the most diverse group of mammals in our state.

A "predatory" mouse, the northern grasshopper mouse (*Onychomys leucogaster*) is known to eat insects, scorpions, small mice, and a variety of plants. Courtesy of Texas Parks and Wildlife Department

Order Carnivora

Generally defined as flesh-eating mammals, there are 280 species worldwide in the order. Although all members of the group eat flesh, some, such as the raccoon or coyote, feed almost exclusively on vegetation in spring and summer months. Texas had 28 native carnivores representing five different families within the order, but 6 of these have been extirpated. The red fox, although common throughout much of the state, is not native to Texas.

Order Artiodactyla

The artiodactyls have either two or four (usually) hooves on each foot, with the exception of the peccary, which has four hoofed toes on each forefoot but only three on the hind. This order includes our most economically important domestic animals along with the majority of the large mammals in the world, some 220 species worldwide. Artiodactyls are further divided into suborders by gastrointestinal features. Those with a two- or three-chambered nonruminating stomach include the families Suidae (two chambers), Tayassuida (two chambers), and Hippopotamidae (three chambers). The Camelidae and Tragulidae have three-chambered ruminating stomachs, while Antilocapridae, Bovidae, and Cervidae have four-chambered ruminating stomachs.

Fourteen species of artiodactyls are native to Texas, although three of these—the mountain sheep, bison, and American elk—have been extirpated. Bison and elk have been reintroduced but are mostly on ranches behind high fences.

Bison (*Bos bison*) from the family Bovidae. Courtesy of John English, Big Country Chapter, www.johnenglishphoto.com

Order Insectivora

The Insectivora includes a hodgepodge of primitive placental mammals encompassing 373 species worldwide. Most are small and nocturnal and feed extensively on insects and other invertebrates, playing a large role in controlling insect pests. One species of mole and four species of shrew occur in Texas.

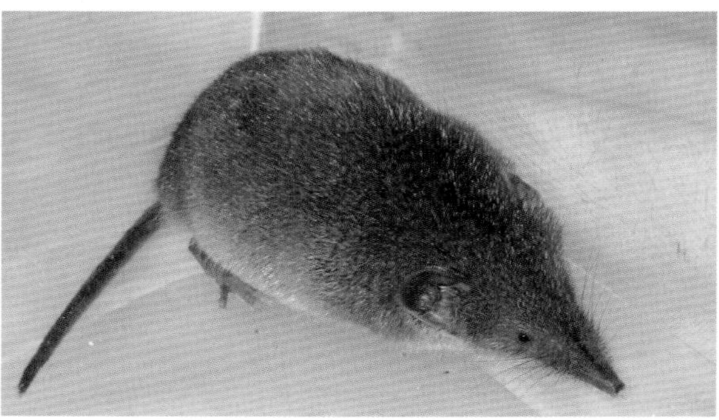

An example of a shrew from the order Insectivora.

Order Sirenia

Worldwide there are only four species in the order Sirenia. The West Indian manatee is the only species that occurs in Texas. Its key identifying characteristics are rounded tail flukes and split upper lips.

Order Cetacea

Cetacea are fish-shaped mammals adapted to a strictly aquatic habitat. There are 90 species worldwide encompassing whales, dolphins, and porpoises. Cetacea have their front limbs modified into flippers or fins with no hind limbs and have nostrils that open on top of the head through a single or double blowhole. Cetacea lack vocal cords. The largest of all known mammals living or extinct were contained within the order Cetacea. Twenty-seven species of Cetacea have been recorded in Texas, although many of these are from single beachings or sightings decades old.

Bottlenose dolphins (*Tursiops truncatus*), marine mammals found in the Gulf of Mexico, leap through the water near Port Aransas ahead of a large ship on November 22, 2011. A dolphin is an example of a cetacean. Courtesy of Pete Romfh, Cradle of Texas Chapter

Distribution of Mammals in Texas

The geography of Texas and its large landmass are key factors in the diversity of animals and plant life found within the state. Wide variations in soil, climate, and topography make the vegetation and animal life of Texas unusually rich. In fact, within the United States the diversity of animal life found in Texas is only exceeded in California and New Mexico.

Texas encompasses 11 unique vegetation areas ranging from the Pineywoods, typical of the southeastern United States; the Trans-Pecos mountains, indicative of southwestern deserts; to the South Texas Plains, similar to some tropical habitats and in close proximity to Mexico. The map shows the vegetation types of Texas and where these types occur across the state.

The distribution of mammals throughout the state is often a result of the vegetative habitat that the animal prefers. In addition, due to its location and broad range of ecological areas, many mammals reach their distributional limits within Texas. For example, before jaguars were extirpated from Texas, it was the only state where they occurred in the United States. The distribution of plants and animals throughout Texas is of more than academic interest. Landowners, managers, and state agencies use these data to manage natural resources for recreation (hunting, fishing, and bird-watching), commercial harvest, and conservation.

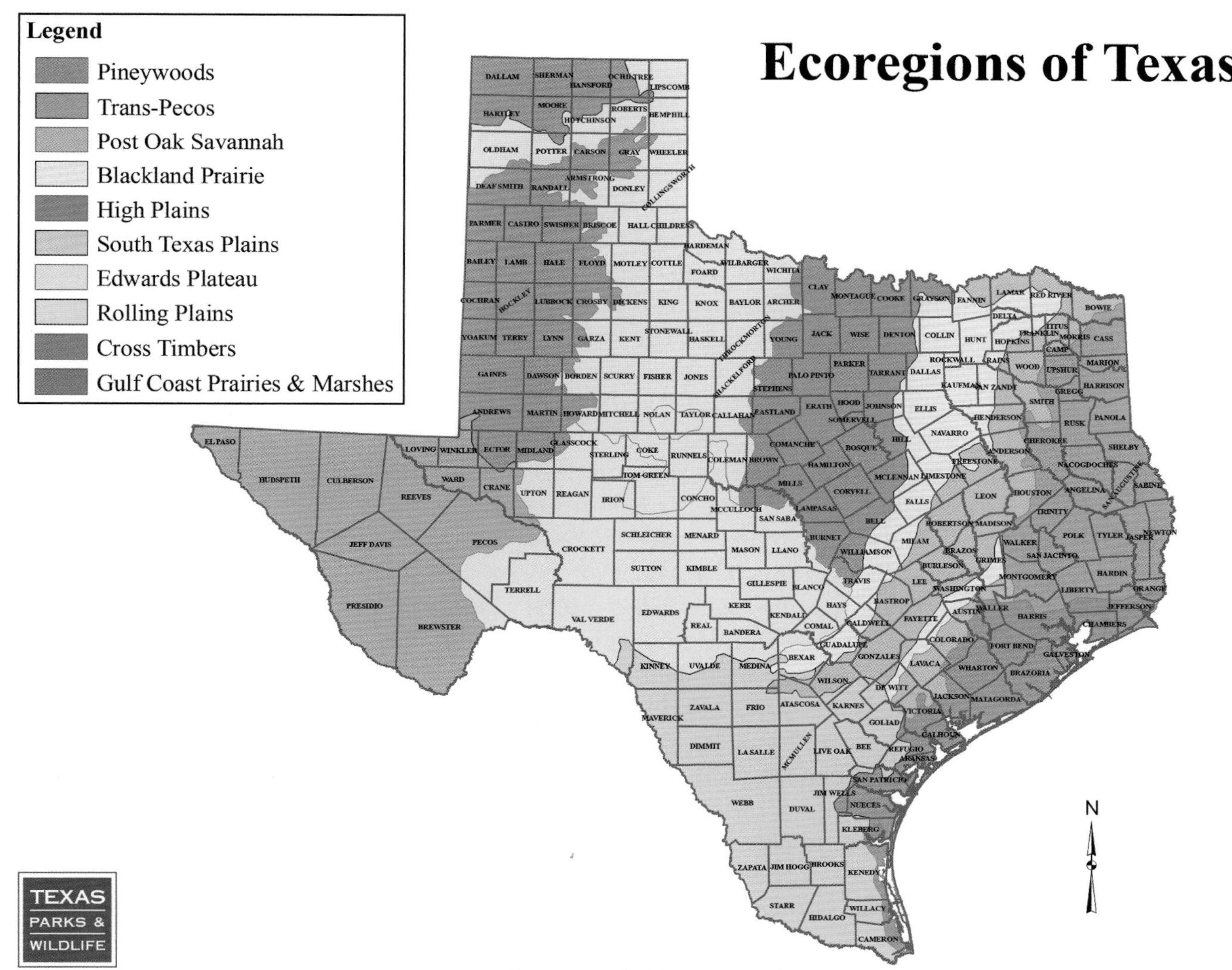

Natural regions of Texas.

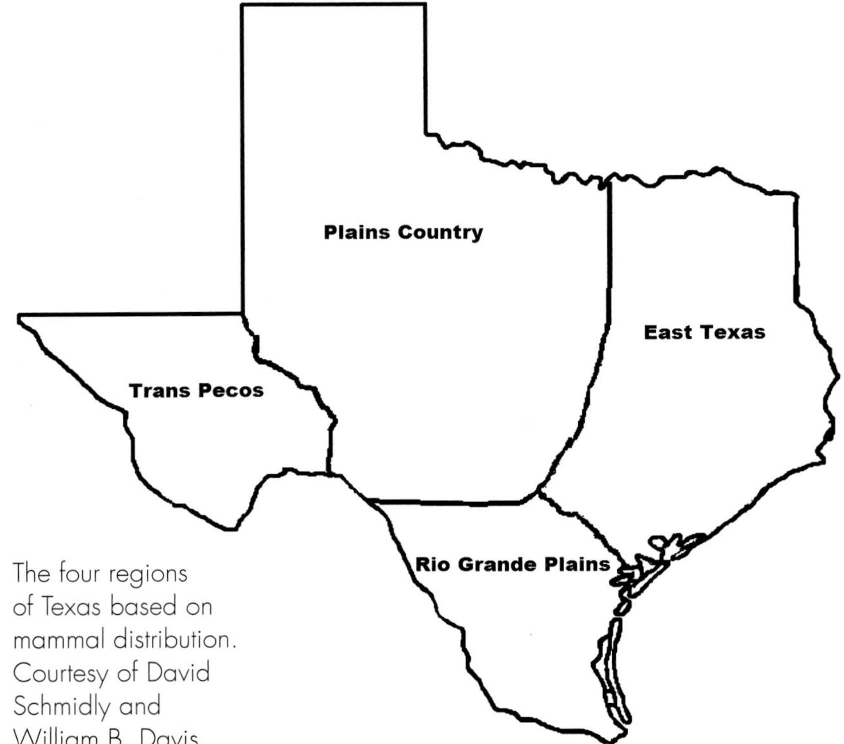

The four regions of Texas based on mammal distribution. Courtesy of David Schmidly and William B. Davis

For convenience, Davis and Schmidly (1994) arranged Texas into four regions based on the ecological distribution of mammals: Plains, Trans-Pecos, East Texas, and Rio Grande Plains. The Trans-Pecos region includes the mountain and basin country west of the Pecos River. The Plains Country includes the High Plains, Rolling Plains, Cross Timbers, and the Edwards Plateau. The Pineywoods, Central Texas Woodlands, Blackland Prairies, and Coastal Prairies and Marshes make up the East Texas region, while the Rio Grande Plains region encompasses South Texas. The Balcones Escarpment serves as the major geographic barrier separating the Plains Country from East Texas and the Rio Grande Plains. Geographic barriers play a large role in distribution of mammals and plants by creating physical barriers to movement and dispersal and sometimes creating isolated populations that may eventually result in formation of a subspecies of a particular species.

Some mammals, called ubiquitous species, are found throughout the state. Other animals are principally found in one of the four regions just described. The table (from Davis and Schmidly 1997) shows distribution of mammals in Texas. All animals listed as extinct in Texas were removed from this table. As a Master Naturalist it is not necessary for you to be familiar with all the species within Texas, only those that occur in your area.

Estimating the Number of Mammals in Wild Populations

The goals of managing animal populations are mostly expressed in terms of population size. For example, when dealing with endangered or rare species, managers often try to increase population size. When dealing with pest species or in specific cases when a species reaches high populations and may cause damage to habitat for itself and/or other species, managers may try to reduce population size. Population size is the measure by which the success of various management programs are judged, so estimating populations is critical to modern wildlife management.

Various methods are used to estimate populations. The accuracy of each method is affected by factors such as weather, time of day, observer variability, limited time and money, observability of the animal (i.e., is it easily visible and readily recognizable), seasonal time of year, and abundance and distribution of the animal. In addition, a single estimate of population size at one point in space and time is usually of limited value and provides little information on population status.

The terms “census” and “population estimate” are used in relation to population estimation. A **census** is commonly aimed less at determining the actual numbers of individuals in a population than at estimating an index of abundance from a certain sampling size (Overton 1971).

Distribution of mammals within Texas

Mammals generally distributed throughout the state		
Virginia opossum	*Didelphis virginiana*	(absent from portions of the Trans-Pecos)
silver-haired bat	*Lasionycteris noctivagans*	
big brown bat	*Eptesicus fuscus*	(not in Rio Grande Plains)
eastern red bat	*Lasiurus borealis*	
hoary bat	*Lasiurus cinereus*	
Brazilian free-tailed bat	*Tadarida brasiliensis*	
eastern cottontail	*Sylvilagus floridanus*	
black-tailed jackrabbit	*Lepus californicus*	(not in the Big Thicket of East Texas)
hispid pocket mouse	*Chaetodipus hispidus*	(not in the Big Thicket of East Texas)
American beaver	*Castor canadensis*	
fulvous harvest mouse	*Reithrodontomys fulvescens*	(not on the High Plains)
white-footed mouse	*Peromyscus leucopus*	
deer mouse	*Peromyscus maniculatus*	
hispid cotton rat	*Sigmodon hispidus*	
coyote	*Canis latrans*	
common gray fox	*Urocyon cinereoargenteus*	
black bear	*Ursus americanus*	(now extinct except for remnant populations in the Trans-Pecos)
ringtail	*Bassariscus astutus*	
common raccoon	*Procyon lotor*	
long-tailed weasel	*Mustela frenata*	
striped skunk	*Mephitis mephitis*	
mountain lion	*Felis concolor*	(now gone from much of the range except South Texas and the Trans-Pecos)
bobcat	*Lynx rufus*	
white-tailed deer	*Odocoileus virginianus*	
bison	*Bos bison*	(now extinct in the wild in Texas)
Mammals occurring principally in the Trans-Pecos		
Mexican long-nosed bat	*Leptonycteris nivalis*	
California myotis	*Myotis californicus*	(disjunct record from Rolling Plains)
fringed myotis	*Myotis thysanodes*	(disjunct record from Rolling Plains)
long-legged myotis	*Myotis volans*	(disjunct record from Rolling Plains)
Yuma myotis	*Myotis yumanensis*	
western red bat	*Lasiurus blossevillii*	
spotted bat	*Euderma maculatum*	
pocketed free-tailed bat	*Nyctinomops femorosacca*	
western mastiff bat	*Eumops perotis*	
gray-footed chipmunk	*Tamias canipes*	
Texas antelope squirrel	*Ammospermophilus interpres*	(also in western part of Edwards Plateau)

(*continued*)

desert pocket gopher	*Geomys arenarius*	
rock pocket mouse	*Chaetodipus intermedius*	
Nelson's pocket mouse	*Chaetodipus nelsoni*	
desert pocket mouse	*Chaetodipus penicillatus*	
Merriam's kangaroo rat	*Dipodomys merriami*	
banner-tailed kangaroo rat	*Dipodomys spectabilis*	(also in southern part of High Plains)
brush mouse	*Peromyscus boylii*	(also on escarpment breaks of Rolling Plains)
northern rock mouse	*Peromyscus nasutus*	
cactus mouse	*Peromyscus eremicus*	(also in extreme western part of Rio Grande Plain)
Mearns' grasshopper mouse	*Onychomys arenicola*	
tawny-bellied cotton rat	*Sigmodon fulviventer*	
yellow-nosed cotton rat	*Sigmodon ochrognathus*	
Mexican woodrat	*Neotoma mexicana*	
Mexican vole	*Microtus mexicanus*	
hooded skunk	*Mephitis macroura*	
wapiti or elk	*Cervus elaphus*	(native population extinct; reintroduced into Guadalupe Mountains)
mountain sheep	*Ovis canadensis*	(native population extinct; reintroduced into several mountain ranges)
Mammals occurring principally in the Plains Country		
thirteen-lined ground squirrel	*Spermophilus tridecemlineatus*	(also in a narrow strip through Central Texas from the Red River and Dallas region south to Corpus Christi and east to Colorado County)
plains pocket gopher	*Geomys bursarius*	
Jones' pocket gopher	*Geomys knoxjonesi*	
Llano pocket gopher	*Geomys texensis*	
plains pocket mouse	*Perognathus flavescens*	(also in El Paso County)
Texas kangaroo rat	*Dipodomys elator*	
Texas mouse	*Peromyscus attwateri*	
prairie vole	*Microtus ochrogaster*	(subspecies haydeni)
black-footed ferret	*Mustela nigripes*	(now extinct in Texas)
Mammals occurring principally in the Rio Grande Plains		
Mexican long-tongued bat	*Choeronycteris mexicana*	
southern yellow bat	*Lasiurus ega*	
Texas pocket gopher	*Geomys personatus*	
Gulf Coast kangaroo rat	*Dipodomys compactus*	
Mexican spiny pocket mouse	*Liomys irroratus*	
Coues' rice rat	*Oryzomys couesi*	
white-nosed coati	*Nasua narica*	(also in Big Bend region of the Trans-Pecos)
eastern hog-nosed skunk	*Conepatus leuconotus*	
ocelot	*Felis pardalis*	(formerly more widely distributed)

(*continued*)

margay	*Felis wiedii*	(now extinct in Texas)
jaguarundi	*Felis yagouaroundi*	
Mammals occurring principally in East Texas		
southern short-tailed shrew	*Blarina carolinensis*	
southeastern myotis	*Myotis austroriparius*	
Seminole bat	*Lasiurus seminolus*	
Rafinesque's big-eared bat	*Plecotus rafinesquii*	
swamp rabbit	*Sylvilagus aquaticus*	
eastern gray squirrel	*Sciurus carolinensis*	
eastern flying squirrel	*Glaucomys volans*	(barely enters the Cross Timbers area of the Plains Country)
Attwater's pocket gopher	*Geomys attwateri*	
Baird's pocket gopher	*Geomys breviceps*	
marsh rice rat	*Oryzomys palustris*	(also in coastal region of Rio Grande Plain)
eastern harvest mouse	*Reithrodontomys humulis*	
cotton mouse	*Peromyscus gossypinus*	
golden mouse	*Ochrotomys nuttalli*	
prairie vole	*Microtus ochrogaster*	(subspecies ludovicianus)
river otter	*Lutra canadensis*	
Mammals occurring principally in West Texas (Plains Region and Trans-Pecos)		
western small-footed myotis	*Myotis ciliolabrum*	
western pipistrelle	*Pipistrellus hesperus*	
Townsend's big-eared bat	*Plecotus townsendii*	
rock squirrel	*Spermophilus variegatus*	
black-tailed prairie dog	*Cynomys ludovicianus*	
Botta's pocket gopher	*Thomomys bottae*	
yellow-faced pocket gopher	*Cratogeomys castanops*	
western harvest mouse	*Reithrodontomys megalotis*	
plains harvest mouse	*Reithrodontomys montanus*	(also in the Blackland Prairies of East Texas)
silky pocket mouse	*Perognathus flavus*	
white-ankled mouse	*Peromyscus pectoralis*	
piñon mouse	*Peromyscus truei*	
white-throated woodrat	*Neotoma albigula*	
porcupine	*Erethizon dorsatum*	
swift or kit fox	*Vulpes velox*	
grizzly or brown bear	*Ursus arctos*	(now extinct)
mule deer	*Odocoileus hemionus*	
Mammals occurring principally in western Texas (Trans-Pecos and Plains region) and Rio Grande Plains		
desert shrew	*Notiosorex crawfordi*	
ghost-faced bat	*Mormoops megalophylla*	

(*continued*)

cave myotis	*Myotis velifer*	
pallid bat	*Antrozous pallidus*	
big free-tailed bat	*Nyctinomops macrotis*	(two records from East Texas)
desert cottontail	*Sylvilagus audubonii*	
Mexican ground squirrel	*Spermophilus mexicanus*	
spotted ground squirrel	*Spermophilus spilosoma*	
Merriam's pocket mouse	*Perognathus merriami*	
Ord's kangaroo rat	*Dipodomys ordii*	
northern grasshopper mouse	*Onychomys leucogaster*	
southern plains woodrat	*Neotoma micropus*	
gray wolf	*Canis lupus*	(now extinct in Texas)
American badger	*Taxidea taxus*	
western spotted skunk	*Spilogale gracilis*	
common hog-nosed skunk	*Conepatus mesoleucus*	(relict population in the Big Thicket probably extinct)
collared peccary	*Tayassu tajacu*	
pronghorn	*Antilocapra americana*	(now extinct in Rio Grande Plains)
Mammals occurring principally east of the 100th meridian		
Elliot's short-tailed shrew	*Blarina hylophaga*	
least shrew	*Cryptotis parva*	
eastern mole	*Scalopus aquaticus*	
eastern pipistrelle	*Pipistrellus subflavus*	
northern yellow bat	*Lasiurus intermedius*	
evening bat	*Nycticeius humeralis*	
nine-banded armadillo	*Dasypus novemcinctus*	
eastern fox squirrel	*Sciurus niger*	
northern pygmy mouse	*Baiomys taylori*	(has spread to Plains regions)
eastern woodrat	*Neotoma floridana*	
woodland vole	*Microtus pinetorum*	
common muskrat	*Ondatra zibethicus*	(also in Canadian, Pecos, and Rio Grande drainages)
red wolf	*Canis rufus*	(now extinct in Texas)
mink	*Mustela vison*	
eastern spotted skunk	*Spilogale putorius*	
jaguar	*Panthera onca*	(now extinct in Texas)
Species unique to Texas (most of geographic range confined to mainland part of state)		
Gulf Coast kangaroo rat	*Dipodomys compactus*	
Texas kangaroo rat	*Dipodomys elator*	
Attwater's pocket gopher	*Geomys attwateri*	
Texas pocket gopher	*Geomys personatus*	
Llano pocket gopher	*Geomys texensis*	

Source: From Davis and Schmidly (1997).

Population estimate is an approximation of the true population size based on some sampling method.

Methods for estimating populations include roadside counts, capture-recapture studies, line-transect analysis, sampling, and a myriad of other techniques. Texas Parks and Wildlife uses roadside surveys for estimating population trends in many species of mammals and is the only technique discussed here. For details on other population estimation methods, refer to *Research and Management Techniques for Wildlife and Habitats* (Bookhout 1996).

During roadside counts rural roads are driven at a designated speed (for example, 20 miles per hour), time of day, and season. The number of individuals of the species observed is related to the distance traveled (Overton 1971). This technique can be easily applied to large areas and provides good comparisons between years and long-term population trends (Kline 1965). To yield best results, standardize the time of year and procedure used for each species you wish to monitor. The best results occur when the species is at its most stable range and thus likely to be viewed. For white-tailed deer this will be anytime from July to October; for rabbits, summer counts during July and August are best. Surveys should not be conducted during rains. Binoculars can be used, when needed, if you are interested in determining the sex or age class of the mammal observed. If necessary, a vehicle can be stopped long enough to make a conclusion on sex and/or age. Take these factors into account when conducting a roadside survey:

- Avoid roads that double back.
- Cover different habitat types.
- Conduct counts two or three times within the same week and average them for a total count.
- Have two to three people conducting the count for best results.
- Use a standardized data sheet and re-

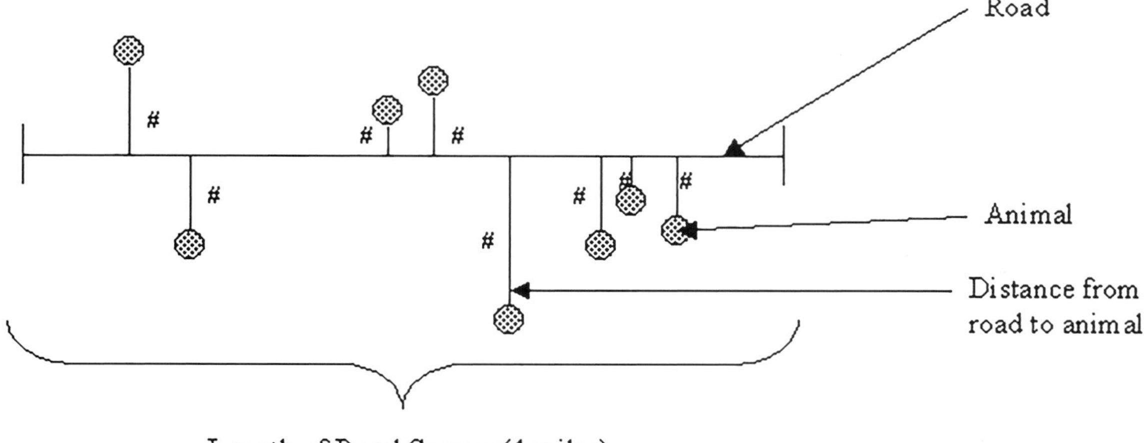

Spotlight count calculation.

Average # (ft) *2 = width of sample area (ft)

Distance traveled (4 mi) *5280 ft/mi = length of sample area (21120 ft)

Width of sample * length of sample = total sample area (ft^2)

Total sample area (ft^2)/ 43,560 ft^2/acre = acreage of sample

Acreage of sample/number of animals seen (8) = density (acres/animal)

Texas Parks and Wildlife Department Fur-Bearing Animal Regulations include the following: No person may take a fur-bearing animal on privately owned land or body of water without the consent of the owner of the land or water or the owner's agent. Taking of fur-bearing animals on statutory wildlife sanctuaries, public roads and highways, or their rights-of-way is prohibited. Landowners or their agents may take nuisance fur-bearing animals in any number by any means at any time on that person's land without the need for a hunting or trapping license. However, fur-bearing animals or their pelts taken for these purposes may not be retained or possessed by anyone at any time except licensed trappers during the lawful open season and possession periods. Nuisance fur-bearing animals may be captured and relocated if the person has received authorization from the department and the owner of the property where the release will occur.

cord path or road number, starting time, distance traveled, and number of animals seen by age, sex, or as an unknown.

Counting the number of animals seen over one mile will provide a ratio of that species per mile in the area sampled. To determine density, start by averaging the distances in feet that the animals were seen from the vehicle or by observers. Multiply this number by 2 to account for both sides of the path or road. This number is now the width of the sample area. Multiply the distance traveled (miles) by 5,280 to determine the length of the sample area in feet. Multiplying the total length of the sample area by the width of the sample area gives you the total area sampled in square feet. Dividing this number by 43,560 (number of square feet per acre) gives the acreage sampled. Dividing this number by the number of animals seen gives the density in terms of animals per acre. For example, if 50 acres are sampled and 5 rabbits are seen, then the density of the area is one rabbit for every 10 acres.

Use caution when making conclusions on populations based on roadside surveys. Counts should be compared to other counts only in the same months and looked at over a period of several years. A low count in one year may not indicate a decrease in population size; however, low counts or decreasing counts in successive years may indicate a decreasing population.

Capturing Mammals

Mammals are captured for food, research, fur, and/or when they are creating a nuisance problem for individual or groups of landowners. A variety of capture methods exist and can be used to capture and release an animal unharmed or to capture and kill the animal for harvest. There are five categories of traps: live traps, leg-hold traps, body-gripping traps, snap traps, and snares.

Live traps capture mammals unharmed. Live traps are effectively used in residential areas or in situations where the animal creating a problem may be transplanted to another area. For example, Bailey and Hancock live traps resemble an open suitcase and half-open suitcase, respectively, and are used to trap and relocate an individual beaver. They are not effective for intensive trapping efforts.

Leg-hold traps are manufactured in several sizes and are available with padded and unpadded jaws. Properly used, leg-hold traps are an effective and economical way of trapping animals. However, the possibility of trapping nontarget species may limit the application of leg-hold traps. They are used extensively for beaver, muskrat, nutria, coyote, and raccoon. Traps are set in travel lanes or near burrow openings with or without bait.

Body-gripping traps, most commonly the Conibear, are used chiefly in water for muskrat, beaver, and nutria. Conibears do not allow for release of the animal, ideally resulting in a quick kill. These traps are typically placed at the entrances of burrows or lodges and in runs or slides. Most states prohibit use of Conibear traps on dry land.

Snap traps are used to control mice and

Small javelinas, also known as collard peccaries (*Tayassu tajac*), in a live trap. Courtesy of Max Traweek

rats and have the advantage of providing little danger to nontarget species. Typical baits used include peanut butter, oatmeal, and apple. Snap traps can be used outdoors to capture rodents when only a few animals are involved or to capture animals for identification or population indexing purposes.

Snares are made of a light wire or cable looped through a locking device or a small nylon cord tied so it will tighten as the animal pushes against the snare. Many states strictly regulate their use, so check state regulations before setting any snares. Snares are very effective on a wide variety of animals. They are placed on well-defined trails or at a specific entrance such as a hole in a fence. Recent bear research has relied heavily on the use of snares to capture bears and allow researchers to immobilize them for fitting with radio collars.

Other methods for capturing and/or controlling mammals include using dogs (mountain lion), fumigants (prairie dog control), exclusionary devices (fences for deer), drop nets, rocket nets, and toxicants. Due primarily to pressure from the public, in recent years habitat modifications have become a tool of the wildlife manager to reduce animal damage complaints. Habitat modification involves manipulating an area to make it less attractive to a species or modifying an adjacent area to make it more attractive.

(*Top*) A corral trap with two guillotine-style gates. Courtesy of Mark Tyson, Texas A&M AgriLife Extension Service

(*Bottom*) Another form of trap useful for capturing feral hogs (*Sus scrofa*) is a box trap. Courtesy of Mark Tyson, Texas A&M AgriLife Extension Service

Mammal Marking Techniques

Although the live-capture techniques just described are often used to control animal populations, they are also effective in capturing animals for study. Once an animal is captured for study, however, it needs to be marked for monitoring and possible recapture at a later date. Animals are typically marked to track problem individuals (e.g., bears), to estimate population densities in mark-recapture studies (e.g., rodents), to collect data on migration patterns, to monitor specific individuals over time (e.g., white-tailed deer), to obtain life history information on certain species, and to answer other research questions. Marking animals takes some expertise to prevent injury or inhibiting an animal's movement and should not be conducted without expert assistance. Many states and the federal government may require individuals to obtain a license or permit to band animals.

Mammals can be marked with special tags made from metal or plastic in a variety of shapes and colors. Tags are designed to be attached to the mammal based on the species so that the tag does not interfere with that mammal's day-to-day activities. **Ear tags** are usually designed to be interlocking, self-locking, or a rivet design that cannot be easily pried apart. Tags should be placed in the lower inner region of the ear where there is heavier cartilage to reduce tearing of the ear or losing the tag. Tags should be loose enough not to interfere with blood circulation. Puncture holes in the animal's ear should be treated appropriately to prevent infection. Tags have also been designed to mark foot webs and interdigital webbing of the hind and fore flippers. Tags have been used on a variety of terrestrial and marine mammals and are very effective for marking animals.

A white-tailed deer (*Odocoileus virginianus*) with an ear tag. Courtesy of Michelle Haggerty

Neck collars and bands have been designed for field identification of free-ranging animals. Collars are expansible to allow for growth and are highly visible. However, their longevity depends on the manufacturing material, climate, and behavior and sex of the animal collared. Collars are typically used on ungulates but have been used effectively on birds, bats, and marine mammals.

Armbands placed on the forearms of bats have been the most widely used technique for marking these flying mammals. Several different band types are available, including serially numbered bands, numbered and unnumbered plastic bands, and celluloid rings. What type of armband is utilized depends largely on the bat size and species.

Branding is an inexpensive, permanent, and visible means of marking animals. While branding is usually associated with the conventional hot-branding utilized on cattle farms, hot branding plays no role in modern wildlife management and has been replaced by freeze-branding or cryo-branding. Branding irons are supercooled in a mixture of dry ice and methanol or liquid nitrogen and placed on a shaved or washed area of skin. The epidermis is temporarily frozen and destroys the pigment produced in the hair follicles, causing regrowth of white instead of colored hair. Freeze-branding has particular value for permanently marking long-lived animals.

Toe clipping is a widely used technique to individually mark small mammals, particularly rodents. The nail and first joint of the toe are removed with sterile scissors. The technique is rapid, inexpensive, and permanent, but sometimes clipped toes cannot be distinguished from toes lost in a trap. No direct adverse effects of toe clipping were reported for small mammals in some studies (Kumar 1979; Korn 1987). However, toe clipping indirectly lowered the life span of male meadow voles (Pavone and Boonstra 1985). While toe clipping is not recommended for use on bats, it has been used on coyotes, hares, and fur seal pups.

Tattoos provide a simple, efficient means of permanently marking a wide range of mammals. Best results are achieved by tattooing any lightly pigmented area that is clean and essentially hairless. Standard pliers or an electric tattooing pencil can be used with a contrasting dye applied liberally. Tattoos add no weight to an animal and are inconspicuous to predators but cannot be read without having the animal in hand. Tattooing has been successfully used on rabbits, white-tailed deer, bats, and bears.

A more modern technique of permanently marking individuals is the use of **PIT tags**. Each PIT tag has a microchip that emits a specific signal or number when scanned, similar to a bar code on an item from a grocery store. PIT tags are inserted under a mammal's skin with a syringe. Marking mammals with PIT tags is more expensive than most other marking methods, and PIT tags may wander under an animal's skin, especially on large mammals. But for long-term identification of individuals, PIT tags may be more reliable than other methods.

In addition to these methods, dyes and paints have been used as temporary external markers to identify polar bears at a distance, fluorescent pigments for monitoring movements of small rodents at night, and radioactive isotopes as inert implants. External attachments, such as streamers, and metabolizable radionucleotides have also been used to monitor movements of various mammals (Silvy et al. 2012).

How Mammals Function in Ecosystems

Some mammals exert a substantial force within ecosystems, especially those at the top of the food chain (e.g., mountain lion). Mammals present on a landscape that can dramatically change the habitat are known as keystone species (e.g., prairie dog and beaver). Actions at either end of a food web send ripples throughout the web. For example, removing a top predator such as a mountain lion will have an effect right down to the soil organisms. Certain herbivores and/or granivores will be more or less numerous than they would be were the lion present, and that will affect the dynamics and specifics of plant recruitment and survival and the survival of other predators.

Small mammals influence the structure and function of grassland ecosystems as consumers of plants and arthropods, as movers of soil and soil nutrients, and as the primary prey of raptors, snakes, and carnivorous mammals. Herbivorous and granivorous mammals may affect vegetation structure and diversity directly by consuming taller grasses and shrubs, or indirectly, through differential seed predation and dispersal. Finally, burrow systems created by prairie dogs and other rodents may provide critical refuges for other small animals in a grassland with little vegetative cover. Over 200 species of animals have been documented as using prairie dog burrows, including burrowing owls, making the prairie dog a keystone species in the prairie ecosystem.

The entire hydrology of North America has been affected by beavers, and a wide variety of plants and animals are dependent on the wetlands created by beavers. Porcupines, deer, moose, elk, and other herbivores have dramatically affected plant communities across North America. As you can see, patterns in the distribution and abundance

Mountain lions, reclusive by nature, have home ranges of 50,000 to 80,000 acres. As human encroachment reaches further into their habitat, mountain lions have been recorded occurring in every county of Texas except for the northernmost counties of the Panhandle, human interactions with this large mammalian predator will continue. Public awareness and conservation education will be the biggest tool for this species to continue in the state. Courtesy of Louis A. Harveson, Borderlands Research Institute for Natural Resource Management, Sul Ross State University

of mammals may simultaneously reflect and affect the stability of an ecosystem.

Conservation Concerns

Chief among the number of conservation concerns for mammals and all wildlife species is the destruction of habitat, particularly native prairie, bottomland hardwood forest, longleaf pine forest, and large blocks of natural habitat. Humans compete directly and indirectly for all the same resources that other mammals need. Constructing a new home may result in habitat fragmentation, blockages and isolation of mammal movements and populations, and reduced habitat suitability for certain species.

Many of the larger mammals require vast tracts of land to be able to roam, breed, and rear young successfully. The more fragmented a landscape becomes, the harder it is for some animals to disperse, creating isolated populations that result in inbreeding and decreased genetic diversity that may affect the ability of the species to survive over time. In addition to reducing a population's genetic diversity, landscape fragmentation can result in increased mortality from crossing highways.

The second challenge to mammalian conservation is public intolerance to medium-sized and large mammalian predators like the coyote and mountain lion. While mountain lions rarely attack humans, people are generally uncomfortable when a mountain lion occupies land in or around their residence. Concerns about personal safety and livestock depredation will usually result in an effort by individuals to remove the offending animal.

APPENDIX A

Key to the Major Groups (Orders) of Mammals In Texas

This dichotomous key is a useful tool to distinguish individuals from the 10 Orders of mammals native to Texas. This key is courtesy of The Mammals of Texas, Schmidly 2004.

1. • Body covered dorsally, and tail completely, by bands of bony plates; snout tapering and lacking teeth anteriorly; eight peglike teeth on each side of upper and lower jaws: Order Xenarthra (armadillos, sloths, and allies).
   • Not as above: go to 2
2. • Body torpedo-shaped; hind legs absent; front limbs developed into paddles; hairless or nearly so; live in ocean or coastal waters: go to 3
   • Not as above: go to 4
3. • Body ending in a broad, horizontally flattened, rounded fluke; no dorsal fin; muzzle squarish, covered with stout bristles; short bristlelike hairs scattered sparingly over rest of body; nostrils terminal; length 2.5 to 4.5 m: Order Sirenia (manatee and allies).
   • Body ending in horizontal, expanded (not rounded) flukes; blowhole (nostrils) on top of head; most Texas forms with dorsal fin; length 2.5 to 30 m: Order Cetacea (whales, porpoises, and dolphins).
4. • Hand and arm developed into leathery wing: Order Chiroptera (bats).
   • Hand and arm normal, not developed into a wing: go to 5
5. • Hoofed mammals; two or four toes on each foot: Order Artiodactyla (even-toed ungulates).
   • Toes usually armed with claws, not hoofs: go to 6
6. • Total of 10 upper incisors; big toe of hind foot without claw; tail prehensile: Order Didelphimorphia (opossums).
   • Total of six or less upper incisors; all toes armed with claws; tail not prehensile: go to 7
7. • Snout highly flexible and protruding conspicuously beyond mouth; eyes very small or hidden; length of head and body usually less than 150 mm: Order Insectivora (shrews and moles).
   • Snout normal, or if protruding conspicuously then length of head and body much more than 150 mm; eyes normal: go to 8
8. • Total of two incisors in lower jaw, one on each side: go to 9
   • Total of four or more incisors in lower jaw (two or three on each side): go to 10
9. • Total of two incisors in the upper jaw, one on each side so that incisor formula is 1/1: Order Rodentia (rodents).
   • Total of four incisors in the upper jaw, two on each side, one in front of the other in tandem; incisor formula 2/1: Order Lagomorpha (hares and rabbits).
10. • Marine dwellers, fore and hind limbs developed into flippers; tail normal or vestigial, never developed into flukes: Order Pinnipedia (seals and walruses).
    • Mainly land dwellers, limbs never developed into flippers, but hind feet may have webs between the toes: Order Carnivora (carnivores).

APPENDIX B

Common Texas Mammal Tracks

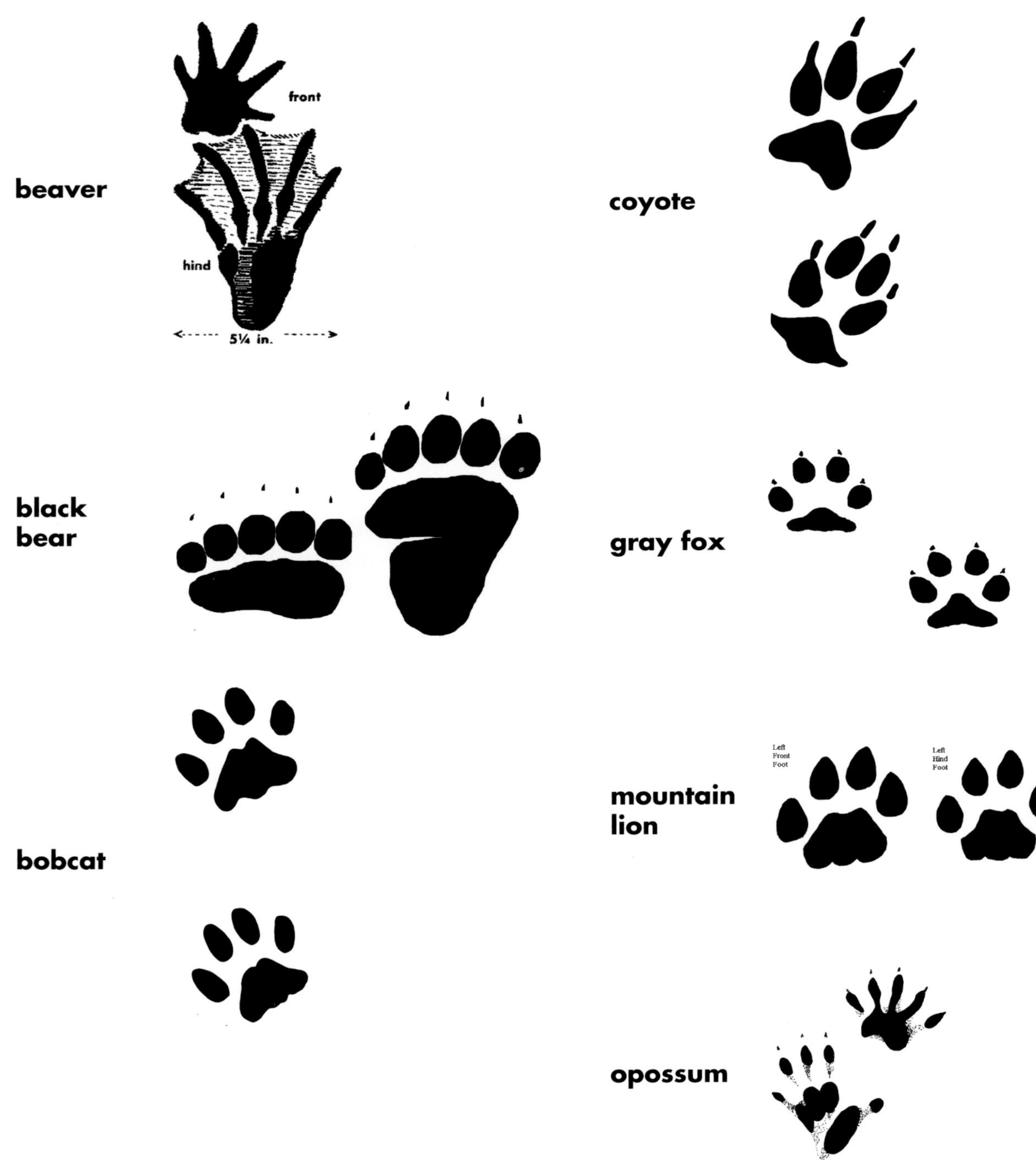

porcupine

rabbit

raccoon

ringtail

river otter

spotted skunk

striped skunk

white-tailed deer

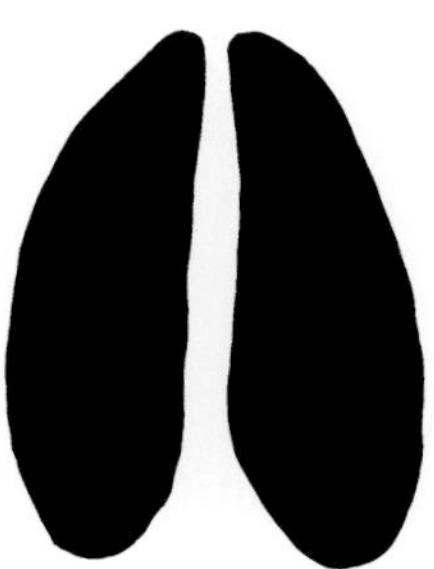

References

Bookhout, T. A. 1996. *Research and Management Techniques for Wildlife Habitats*. Lawrence, KS: Allen Press.

Davis, W. B., and D. J. Schmidly. 1994. *Mammals of Texas*. Austin: Texas Parks and Wildlife Press. http://www.nsrl.ttu.edu/tmot1/.

———. 1997. *The Mammals of Texas—Online Edition*. Lubbock: Texas Tech University . Accessed April 1, 2015. http://www.nsrl.ttu.edu/tmot1/distribu.htm.

Elbroch, M. 2003. *Mammal Tracks & Sign: A Guide to North American Species*. Mechanicsburg, PA: Stackpole Books.

Halfpenny, J. 1986. *A Field Guide to Mammal Tracking in North America*. Boulder, CO: Johnson Books.

Kline, P. D. 1695. Factors Influencing Roadside Counts of Cottontails. *Journal of Wildlife Management* 29:665–71.

Korn, H. 1987. Effects of Live-Trapping and Toe-Clipping on the Weights of European and African Rodent Species. *Oecologia* 71:597–600.

Kumar, R. K. 1979. Toe-Clippings Procedure for Individual Identification of Rodents. *Laboratory Animal Science* 19:679–80.

Overton, W. S. 1971. Estimating the Numbers of Animals in Wildlife Populations. In *Wildlife Management Techniques*, ed. K. H. Giles, 403–55. Washington, DC: Wildlife Society.

Pavone, L. V., and R. Boonstra. 1985. The Effects of Toe Clipping on the Survival of the Meadow Vole (*Microtus pennsylvanicus*). *Canadian Journal of Zoology* 63:499–501.

Schmidly, D. J. 2004. *The Mammals of Texas*. 6th ed. Austin: University of Texas Press.

Silvy, Novy J., Roel R. Lopez, and Markus J. Peterson. 2012. Techniques for Marking Wildlife. In *The Wildlife Techniques Manual: Research*, 230–57. Baltimore: Johns Hopkins University Press. Accessed April 1, 2015. http://www.researchgate.net/publication/230771189_Techniques_for_marking_wildlife.

Additional Resources

Ammerman, L. K., C. L. Hice, D. J. Schmidly, and C. Brown Schmidly. 2012. *Bats of Texas*. College Station: Texas A&M University Press.

Brown, Tom. 1983. *Tom Brown's Field Guide to Nature Observation*. Berkeley, NY: Tom Brown and Brandt Morgan.

Burt, W., and R. Grossenheider. 1976. *Peterson Field Guides: Mammals*. Boston: Houghton Mifflin.

Campbell, L. 1995. *Endangered and Threatened Animals of Texas*. Austin: Texas Parks and Wildlife Press.

Elbroch, M. 2006. *Animal Skulls: A Guide to North American Species*. Mechanicsburg, PA: Stackpole Books.

Headstrom, Richard. 1971. *Identifying Animal Tracks, Mammals, Birds and Other Animals of the Eastern United States*. New York: Dover Publications.

Jones, J., Jr., and Clyde Jones. 1992. Revised Checklist of Recent Land Mammals of Texas, with Annotations. *Texas Journal of Science* 44 (1): 53–74.

Jones, J., Jr., and R. Manning. 1992. *Illustrated Key to Skulls of Genera of North*

American Land Mammals. Lubbock: Texas Tech University Press.

Kays, R. W., and D. E. Wilson. 2009. *Mammals of North America*. 2nd ed. Princeton, NJ: Princeton University Press.

Martin, R. E., R. H. Pine, and A. F. DeBlase. 2011. *A Manual of Mammalogy: With Keys to Families of the World*. 3rd ed. Long Grove, IL: Waveland Press.

McKinney, B. P. 1996. *A Field Guide to Texas Mountain Lions*. Texas Parks and Wildlife Department Bulletin PWD BK W7100–274.

Murie, Olaus J. 1974. *A Field Guide to Animal Tracks*. Peterson Field Guide Series. Boston: Houghton Mifflin.

Pittman, M. T., B. P. McKinney, and G. Guzman. 1995. Ecology of the Mountain Lion on Big Bend Ranch State Park in Trans-Pecos Texas. *Proceedings of the Annual Conference of Southeastern Association of Fish and Wildlife Agencies* 49:552–59.

Roth, C. 1982. *The Wildlife Observers Guidebook*. Englewood, NJ: Prentice Hall.

Schraer, W. D., and H. J. Stoltze. 1987. *Biology: The Study of Life*. Newton, MA: Allyn and Bacon.

Stokes, Donald, and Lillian Stokes. 1987. *A Guide to Animal Tracking and Behavior*. Boston: Little, Brown.

Vaughan, T. A. 1986. *Mammalogy*. 3rd ed. Philadelphia: CBS College Publishing.

Wallace, R. A., J. L. King, and G. P. Sanders. 1981. *Biology: The Science of Life*. Glenview, IL: Scott Foresman.

Wilson, D. E., and S. Ruff, eds. 1999. *The Smithsonian Book of North American Mammals*. Washington, DC: Smithsonian Institution Press.

Wilson, Don E., and DeeAnn M. Reeder. 1993. *Mammal Species of the World, a Taxonomic and Geographic Reference*. 2nd ed. Washington, DC: Smithsonian Institution Press.

UNIT 17

Forest Ecology and Management

ORIGINAL AUTHOR
KATHY FLANNERY
Texas A&M Forest Service

REVISIONS COMPILED BY
JOHN WARNER
Urban District Forester, Texas A&M Forest Service

With contributions from staff at Texas A&M Forest Service:
Leslie Kessner, Conservation Education Coordinator, College Station
Mark Kroeze, CA, Staff Forester II, San Antonio
Michael Merritt, CA, Staff Forester III, Houston
Oscar Mestas, CA, Staff Forester III, El Paso
Gretchen Riley, CA, Staff Forester II, College Station
Donna Work, Biologist, Lufkin

Unit Goals

After completing this unit, volunteers should be able to

- identify the major forested regions of Texas
- understand the diversity of forests found in Texas
- compare and contrast forest and urban forest ecology
- understand and describe the stages of succession in natural and forested ecosystems
- understand the benefits and ecosystem services forests provide
- know the important role fire plays in ecological restoration of healthy forests
- be familiar with traditional forestry management
- list and describe the benefits and ecosystem services trees provide in an urban environment

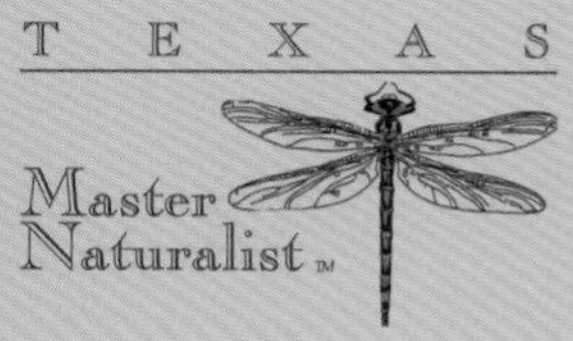

"A nation that destroys its soils destroys itself. Forests are the lungs of our land, purifying the air and giving fresh strength to our people."
—President Franklin Roosevelt

The mission of the Texas A&M Forest Service is to provide statewide leadership to assure that Texas' trees, forests, and related natural resources are wisely used, protected, enhanced, and perpetuated for the benefit of all. For more information, visit http://tfsweb.tamu.edu.

TEXAS A&M FOREST SERVICE

Introduction

Forest ecology is the study of the forest as a biological community, with the interrelationships between the various trees and other organisms constituting the community, and of the interrelationships between these organisms and the physical environment in which they exist (Spurr 1980). Many different types of forests can be found in Texas, ranging from the urban forest to the deep East Texas pine forest. More than half of the 1,100 species of native trees in the United States are found in the South. Of these species, between 255 and 281 species and varieties are native to Texas. In addition, many exotic species have been introduced and now grow in various parts of the state. Of the 13 ecoregions in Texas, 4 are major forested regions: (1) the southern pine forest, (2) the central hardwoods, (3) the subtropical forest of the Rio Grande Valley, and (4) mountain forest areas.

Forested Regions of Texas

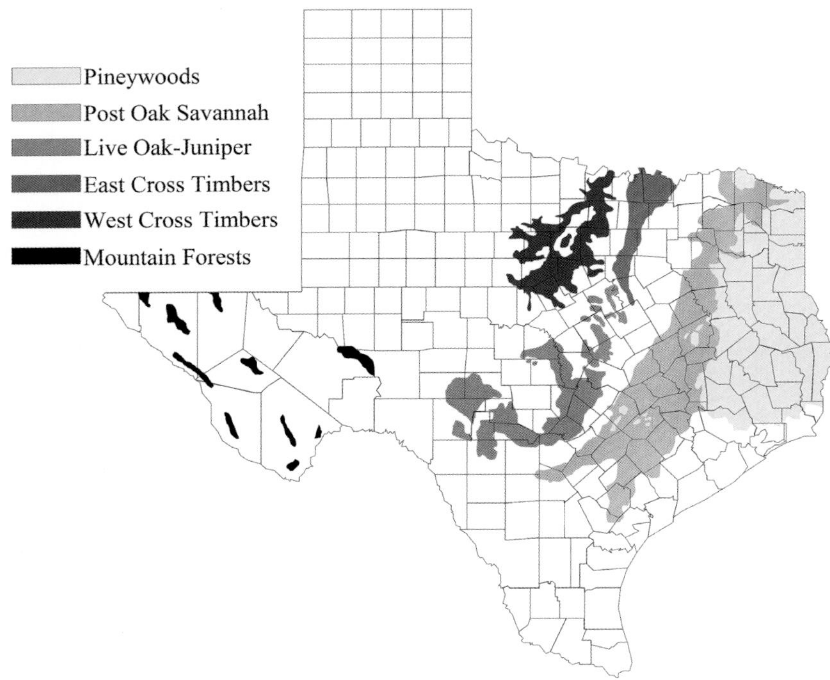

The forested regions of Texas. Courtesy of Texas A&M Forest Service

In East Texas, the southern pine-hardwood forests comprise 12.1 million acres in all or parts of 43 counties. The rich timberlands contain not only commercially desirable southern pine—loblolly, shortleaf, and longleaf—but a diverse mixture of upland and bottomland hardwoods common to the South. Principal hardwoods present in the region include oaks, hickory, and maple.

Farther west, the oak woodlands of east-central and north-central Texas cover over 8 million acres. These post oak–dominated forests range from open post oak savanna to dense Cross Timbers brush and include other hardwoods such as elm, hickory, live oak, and blackjack oak. An abundance of tallgrass species thrive in the understory. The term "Cross Timbers" is said to originate with the early settlers who, in their travels from east to west, crossed alternating patches of forests and prairies and affixed the name to these forests.

"In his travels to the western frontier in the early 1830s, American writer Washington Irving characterized the Cross Timbers as 'forests of cast iron.' Irving used this colorful metaphor to emphasize the toughness of the vegetation that he encountered—a nearly impenetrable forest of stunted oak trees."
—Richard V. Francaviglia, *The Cast Iron Forest*

Just southwest of the post oak forests is the Edwards Plateau. This region is the meeting ground for many plant communities, including the western pocket for dwarf palmetto, the eastern limit for piñon pine, the southern reaches for walnuts and elms, and the northern edge for many woody legumes. Approximately 60 species of native trees are found here, including the rare canyon mock orange and Texas mock orange and the federally listed Texas snowbells, species now reduced to remnant populations on steep bluffs.

The general cover type of this region is classified as a live oak–Ashe juniper park, where the open grasslands are interspersed with live oak mottes. Dense "cedar breaks" of Ashe juniper, a common sight over much of the region today, were documented by early explorers as limited to rocky slopes and deep canyons. Nearly impenetrable thickets of white oak—called **shinneries**—

Southern pine forest. Courtesy of Texas A&M Forest Service

Central hardwoods. Courtesy of Texas A&M Forest Service

provide habitat for the endangered black-capped vireo. Some of the shinnery oaks are among the smallest in America. In places, fully mature trees are not over knee high and resemble pygmy forests, while in other areas the same species may grow 20 to 30 feet tall to form almost impenetrable thickets. The riparian zones of the Edwards Plateau are dominated by pecan, sycamore, and bald cypress, descendants of giants logged by the first settlers for shingles and other construction components.

At the southernmost tip of Texas, in the Rio Grande Valley, remnant subtropical forest is found. Once a species-rich and resilient ecosystem, the Tamaulipan thornscrub has been fragmented over the years by agriculture and urbanization. Remnant forest islands are composed mainly of riparian gallery forests sporadically connected to upland thorn that is dominated by mesquite, granjeno, Texas ebony, and anaqua.

The westernmost forested region of Texas falls in the arid mountains west of the Pecos River. These mountain forests are a continuation of the Rocky Mountain forest cover types. At lower elevations, piñon-juniper woodlands are intermixed with oaks such as netleaf, Graves, and Emory. Pockets of ponderosa pine and Rocky Mountain Douglas-fir can be found at higher elevations where it is as much as 10 degrees cooler than below. These forests are home to small populations of elk, black bear, mountain lion, and other animals.

Ponderosa pines in the Davis Mountains. Courtesy of Texas A&M Forest Service

"Trees clean our air, water and soil. They add greatly to our health, our sense of well being, our ecology, and the quality of our lives as well as our economic future in a great many ways."
—Steve Houser, Certified Arborist

Tree Facts

You do not have to stand in the middle of the woods to be surrounded by the forest. Your house, food you eat, clothes you wear, and books you read may contain wood from the trees growing in Texas. Forests provide shelter for animals like birds and deer. They give people a nice place to relax and play. They even help clean the water we drink and the air we breathe. It does not matter where you are—the forest is with you. Texas trees deserve our attention. They contribute to our health, our economy, and the character of our state.

- Texas forests cover over 60 million acres—more than a third of the area of the entire state and about the size of Louisiana and Mississippi combined. Texas is only second to Alaska in the most forested land in the United States.
- There are 4.9 billion trees in Texas, a tree-to-Texan ratio of nearly 200 to 1.
- Two trees found in the Rio Grande Valley, guaiacum and ebony, produce the hardest wood in the United States. The tree with the lightest wood, corkwood, grows near the mouth of the Brazos River. Drooping or weeping juniper, so named for the drooping characteristic of its branches, grows in the Big Bend area but has not been reported to be native elsewhere in this country.
- Texas also claims the world's largest contiguous oak forest. Found in West Texas, Havard shin oak is a low-growing tree and can be seen off I-10 in the Sandhills of Monahans.
- This natural, renewable resource helps reduce energy costs, produce clean water, and provide habitats for wildlife and recreational opportunities for Texans. It also enables a healthy, vibrant economy. Forests contribute over $23 billion annually to the Texas economy. Major industries are
  forestry and logging: $1.1 billion
  lumber and panels: $1.7 billion
  furniture/flooring/windows/cabinets: $5.0 billion
  paperboard: $2.5 billion
  bags: $6.1 billion

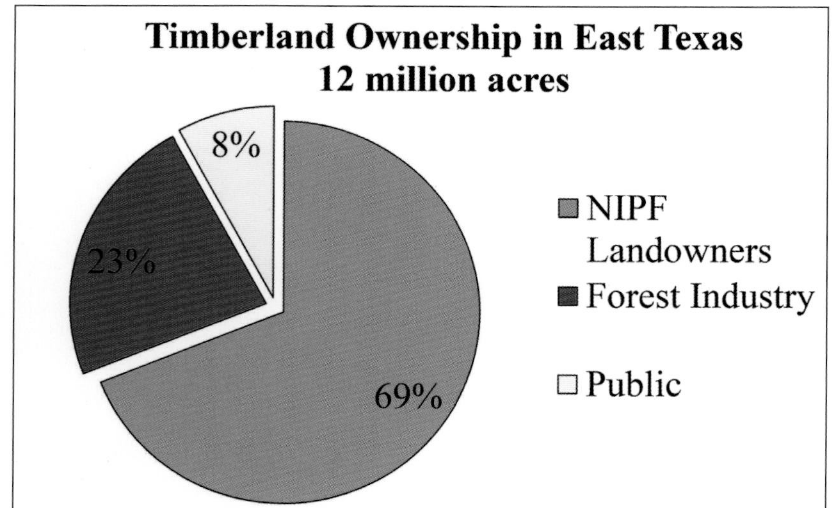

Timberland ownership in East Texas. Courtesy of Texas A&M Forest Service

Forests provide a multitude of things that we as humans utilize every day of our lives. Humans in turn play an important role in forest ecosystems. The interconnectedness of plants, animals, and humans is evident. Balancing the needs of plants and animals, while providing for our own needs, is the key to the overall health and well-being of the forest community.

Forest Ownership in East Texas

According to the most recent Texas Statewide Assessment of Forest Resources published by Texas A&M Forest Service, East Texas' 43 counties consist of 12.1 million acres of forest and 9.4 million acres of non-forest land. Approximately 8.2 million acres (69%) is considered family forest ownership or privately owned by non-industry. A declining forest industry and increasing timber investment group ownerships combine to own nearly 2.7 million acres (23%), followed by public lands such as national forest with over 970,000 acres (8%). Statewide, landownership is held by private individuals, partnerships, or corporations, who own 55.9 million acres (94%). Of the 211 counties, not including those in East Texas, 48.1 million acres (40%) meet the USDA Forest Service definition of forestland.

Ecology: How Do Forest Ecosystems Work?

Forest ecosystems change through the processes of succession, disturbance, and recovery.

Succession

Succession is the replacement of one plant community in an area with another of a different plant composition over time. In theory, a forest naturally progresses through a series of successional stages, of distinct plant communities also known as sere communities. Within each **sere** is a unique shift of plant communities and its parallel animal population. A simple explanation of the different stages may be described as grasses, shrubs, seedling trees, sapling trees, young forest, and mature forest.

Succession is divided into two categories: primary and secondary. **Primary succession** begins when plant communities establish in unoccupied spaces, such as a newly formed volcanic island or sandbar, where there has never been a plant community before. Succession that follows the disturbance of an existing community, such as hurricane, flood, or wildfire, is termed **secondary succession**. We mostly see and encounter secondary succession in our lives daily.

Early stages of succession are characterized by shade-intolerant plant species that quickly colonize and establish on-site. These plants, known as **pioneer species**, can include forbs, grasses, wildflowers, small

1st Year	2nd Year	3rd to 18th Year	19th to 30th Year	30th to 70th Year	70th to 100th Year	100th Year surplus
Horseweed dominant; crabgrass, pigweed	Asters dominant; crabgrass	Grass scrub community; broomsedge grass; pines coming in during this stage.	Young pine forest	Mature Pine forest; understory of young hardwoods	Pine to hardwood transition	Climax oak-hickory forest

Primary succession timeline. Drawing courtesy of Texas A&M Forest; table courtesy of Duke University

woody shrubs, and vines that are fast growing and usually germinate from an existing seed bank in the soil where they have been lying dormant, waiting for the right conditions to return in order to grow. Pioneer species are poor competitors and need full sunlight to thrive. As pioneer species take root, they provide foraging areas for many game birds, migratory birds, hawks, rats, mice, reptiles, amphibians, and other small fauna.

The next stage of succession follows as new seeds, which are often introduced and dispersed by wildlife and wind, are brought into the area; thickets are formed with small woody shrubs, perennial weeds, and grasses, followed by the introduction of shade-intolerant tree species such as pine, cedar, and hackberry. These trees are faster growing and shorter lived. They can also tolerate some shade as they germinate and start to sprout. As these trees grow and mature, they tower over and shade out the original pioneer species. Larger fauna like squirrels, opossum, and raccoon move in. The foraging animals will bring in acorns, hickory nuts, and seeds of other shade-tolerant tree species, some of which are slower growing but live longer. The longer-lived shade-tolerant trees will begin to grow and over time will replace the pine and other shorter-lived species. Eventually a mature forest stand condition is created.

The last stage of succession is termed the **climax** and in theory is the final stable, self-maintaining, and self-reproducing state of forest development. However, as the forest ages, trees die from various causes and fall to the ground. Openings in the overhead canopy provide sunlight to the forest floor. This enables **gap phase succession** to occur and new plants to establish. A climax forest can quickly be returned to a secondary successional stage as a result of insect or disease attacks, wildfire, tornadoes, and other disturbances.

It is easy to imagine succession as a naturally progressing step-by-step process from one community to the next and ultimately ending in a climax forest. However, it is more like a mosaic: a dynamic, complex, and constantly changing ecosystem that fluctuates forward and back among different seres caused by many external factors and disturbances. This constant state of change creates a large amount of diversity across the landscape, which meets the equally diverse habitat requirements for various plant and animal species.

Disturbance

While the process of succession is driven by the maturation of plant communities, **disturbances** caused by external factors can alter the process. The disturbance type and scope determine the impact, both positive and negative, on the site's existing and future plant communities. Natural and human-caused disturbances can include tornadoes, hurricanes, insects, disease, wildfire, ice, hail, drought, strong winds, land-use changes, urban sprawl, and forest management.

Disturbance alters the progression of succession by moving the community to either an earlier or later stage. For example, a wildfire disturbance may lengthen a pioneer stage by killing back the hardwoods, which creates openings where young pines can seed in. On the other hand, an infestation of southern pine beetles in a mature pine forest may hasten the onset of a hardwood forest by prematurely killing the existing pines.

The growth of cities and suburbs continues to convert many acres of productive forest into subdivisions, industrial parks, and other types of urban growth. Many local and state governments are now more closely monitoring and managing this "urban sprawl." Cooperation between the various government entities and adherence to principles of development excellence can slow this trend. However, the unalterable fact is that this growth will continue.

For example, according to the North Texas

Council of Governments, regional population around the Dallas–Fort Worth metroplex is expected to double from 6 million to 12 million people by 2050. Planners at Vision North Texas state the area is headed for traffic nightmares, poor air quality, increased urban heat island effect (energy demand), and other negative effects if development continues as it has in the past. Vision North Texas is a public, private, and academic partnership created to serve as a forum for dialogue and action on these important issues. The three partners are the North Texas Council of Governments, the Urban Land Institute (professionals involved with land development and building), and the University of Texas at Arlington.

"God has cared for these trees, saved them from drought, disease, avalanches and a thousand tempests and floods. But He cannot save them from fools."
—John Muir, *Our National Parks*

Recovery

The natural process of succession is the reason vegetative communities recover after disturbances in the environment. No matter what type of disturbance occurs, there is always a plant community equipped to establish itself on the site. Depending on the desired result, management tools and techniques can aid in a speedy recovery for the site. For example, if a tornado occurs on state or federal forested lands that are highly utilized by recreation enthusiasts, management may be required to improve both the aesthetic quality and the safety of the site. In addition, if a landowner is growing trees commercially and an ice storm impacts the property, a decision will need to be made on the course of action to take to salvage damaged trees and regenerate the affected site.

Damage caused by ice storm. Courtesy of Dale E. Martin

Texas Forest Values and Management

According to the Texas Statewide Assessment of Ecosystem Services, Texas' forests provide the following services:

- There are 581,400 acres located in urban areas of Texas.
- Texas forests provide numerous ecosystem services valued at $92.9 billion annually:
  watershed regulating = $13.2 billion/year
  climate regulating = $4.2 billion/year
  biodiversity services = $14.8 billion/year
  cultural services = $60.4 billion/year
  air quality services = $190.3 million/year
  Watershed regulating services were assessed as three primary functions:
  water capture = $489.7 million/year
  water filtration = $4.2 billion/year
  water regulation = $8.5 billion/year
  Climate-regulating services were assessed through the forest's capacity to store and accumulate carbon:
  carbon storage = $3.1 billion/year
  carbon accumulation = $1.2 billion/year
  Biodiversity services were assessed through a base value provided by all forests as well as additional value for ecologically important areas (hotspots):
  biodiversity base = $14.5 billion/year

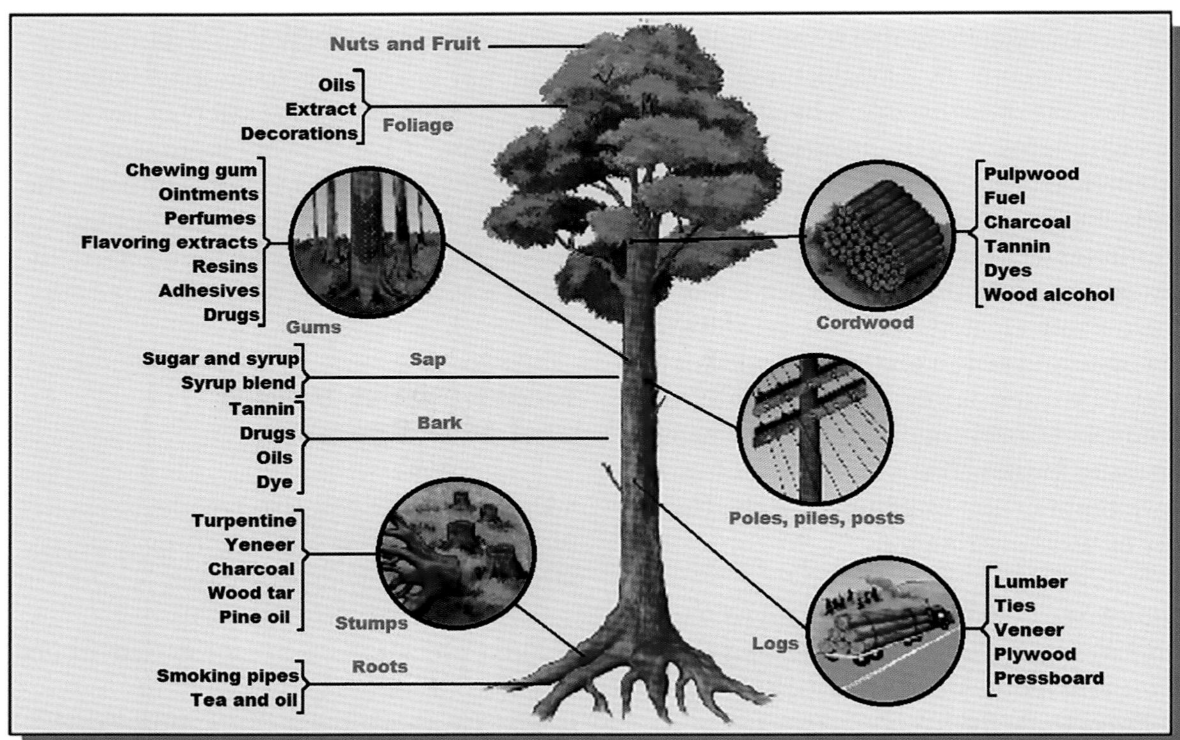

Useful products from trees. Courtesy of Texas A&M Forest Service

biodiversity hotspot = $326.1 million/ year

Humans mimic natural disturbances in the forest ecosystem to obtain desired results—whether for beautiful places, recreational opportunities, wood and paper products, financial investments, or change in species composition. Forests have always provided essential natural resources for society. Even today, forest products are found in everything from lumber to oils, lipstick, toothpaste, and copy paper. The list of products is almost endless.

There are also numerous, less commercial goods and services that forests offer. Forests promote clean sources of water and provide habitat for wildlife as well as multiple opportunities for recreation. There are many aesthetic benefits both in rural and urban settings that forests provide, enhancing our quality of life. The demand on forests increases along with human population growth. Fortunately, trees are a renewable resource and, if managed properly, can provide multiple benefits forever. How we choose to manage the forest depends largely on who owns the land.

Forest Management Tools

Forestry is an art and a science and involves managing the natural resources that are associated with forestland. A forest can be managed for multiple benefits, including wildlife habitat, protection of water quality, range, wilderness, timber production, and recreation. Management tools used to mimic natural processes include, but are not limited to, prescribed burning, thinning, harvesting, mechanical and chemical site preparation, and reforestation. Management for commercial pine, upland hardwood, or bottomland forests occurs primarily in East Texas; thus, the tools mentioned are reflective of that region. The landowner's objective for the land determines the type and extent of management operations. Visit the Texas A&M Forest Service website at http://tfsweb.tamu.edu/FMIS for information on a wide range of commonly asked questions and problems facing new as well as expert landowners in Texas.

Federal Forests

As with anything of value, beauty, and human benefit, the debate over how to manage public forestland goes back many years. In the early 1900s, two different philosophical approaches to forest management led to the creation of the National Park Service, which manages national parks such as Big Bend National Park, the Big Thicket National Preserve, Guadalupe Mountains National Park, and Padre Island National Seashore; and the US Forest Service, which manages national forestlands such as the Caddo-LBJ National Grasslands and Davy Crockett and Sam Houston National Forests.

The National Park Service management developed around John Muir's concept of preservation. Parks were set aside for the primary purpose of remaining in their natural state and allowing nature to take its course. The USDA Forest Service philosophy developed under the conservation or multiple-use ideology, referred to by Gifford Pinchot, known as the "Father of Forestry," as "the greatest good, for the greatest number, in the long run" (1947, xvii). Under the Multiple-Use Sustained-Yield Act of 1960, Congress directed that the national forests be managed for recreation, range, timber, watershed, and wildlife. Both management philosophies have their place in society and should be understood. Unfortunately, the terms "preservation" and "conservation" tend to be used interchangeably, which results in confusion.

Maintaining a Healthy Forest Ecosystem through Best Management Practices

By using best management practices (BMPs), loggers, foresters, and landowners protect water bodies from pollution during and after forestry operations. BMPs are management tools that include leaving trees and other vegetation along streams (streamside management zones, SMZs) to stabilize stream banks, filter runoff, and shade the water, as well as aid infiltration of rainfall. These SMZs also serve as wildlife habitat and travel corridors.

Properly built and rehabilitated roads during forestry operations reduce runoff and siltation that can degrade water quality. Properly installed waterbars and wing ditches are some of the techniques used to protect soil and water during and after forestry operations. Reseeding skidder trails,

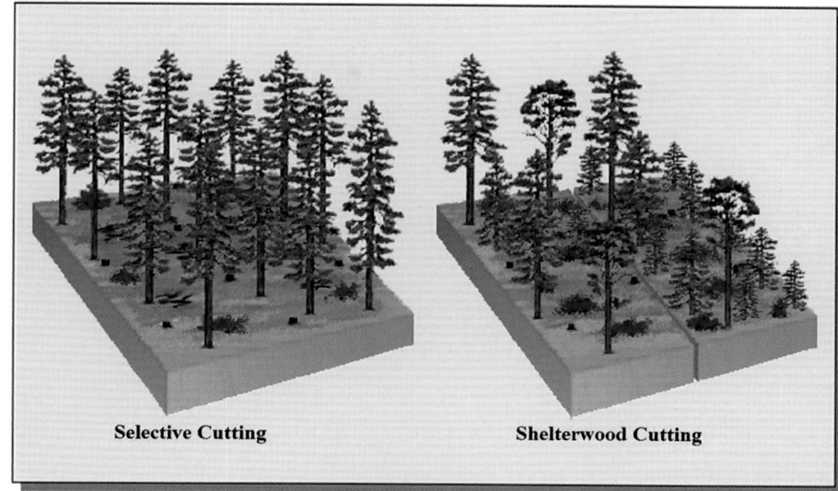

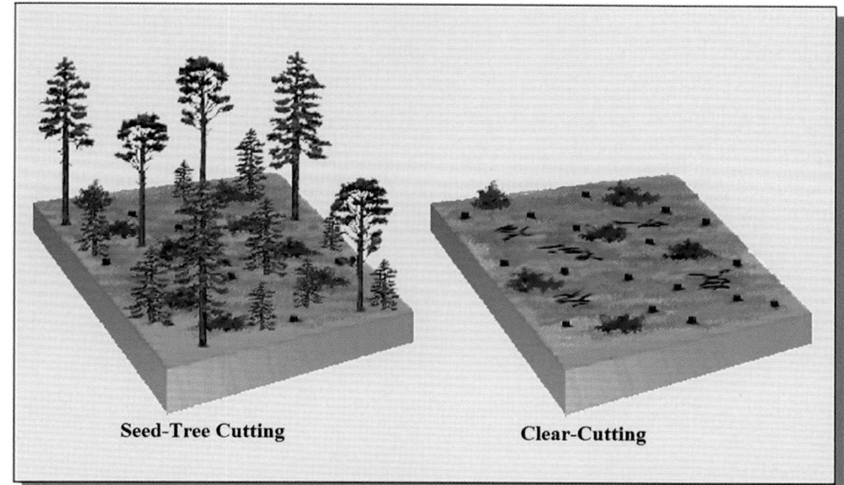

(*Top*): Tree harvesting method I: shelterwood cutting and selective cutting. Courtesy of Texas A&M Forest Service

(*Bottom*): Tree harvesting method II: seed-tree cutting and clear-cutting. Courtesy of Texas A&M Forest Service

A streamside management zone (SMZ) that has been cleared upland of the riparian zone (*inset*). Courtesy of Texas A&M Forest Service

Waterbar and wing ditch. Courtesy of Texas A&M Forest Service

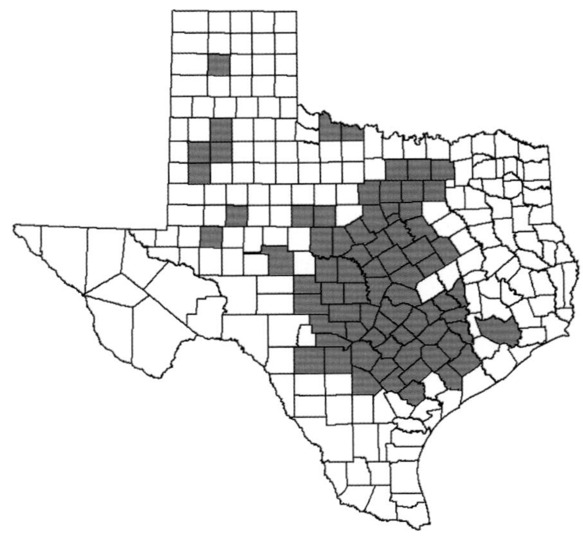

Oak wilt counties. Courtesy of Texas A&M Forest Service

Oak wilt leaves. Courtesy of Texas A&M Forest Service

logging decks, and other bare ground after the operation is complete are also good practices and provide more wildlife food.

Streams and other natural water systems supply cities with the resources they need to meet the water demands of their citizens. This includes water to drink, wash clothes, and irrigate gardens. Cleaner water is a direct result of using forestry BMPs.

Forest Health Issues

Another example of managing a healthy forest involves knowledge of forest insects and disease. Millions of different insects and fungi live in the forest. Some provide benefits such as pollination or aid in decomposing and recycling dead wood. Fortunately, in East Texas, serious fungal-caused diseases associated with forest trees are not common, but there are two tree diseases of concern—fusiform rust and annosus root rot. Neither disease kills large numbers of trees. However, in Central Texas, the tree disease known as **oak wilt** is killing thousands of oak trees in about 60 Texas counties.

Aerial view of an oak wilt spread in Central Texas. Courtesy of Texas A&M Forest Service

Fungal mats are most commonly formed on standing trees, but they also can develop on logs, stumps, and fresh firewood cut from diseased red oaks. Courtesy of Texas A&M Forest Service

Measures can be taken to break root connections between live oaks or dense groups of red oaks to reduce or stop root transmission of the oak wilt fungus. The most common technique is to sever roots by trenching at least four feet deep with trenching machines, rock saws, or ripper bars. Trenches more than four feet deep may be needed to assure control in deeper soils. Courtesy of Texas A&M Forest Service

Propiconazole (Alamo) is the only fungicide scientifically tested and proven effective (when properly applied prior to infection) for use as a preventive treatment to protect live oaks from oak wilt. Courtesy of Texas A&M Forest Service

Fungal mats, which are reliable indicators for diagnosis of oak wilt, can be found by looking for inconspicuous narrow cracks in the bark of dying red oaks leading to hollow areas between the bark and wood. Courtesy of Texas A&M Forest Service

The oak wilt fungus can be transmitted from one tree to another through root connections when oak trees grow closely together, called mottes. Infection centers among live oaks in Texas expand at an average rate of 75 feet per year, varying from no spread to 150 feet in any one direction. Courtesy of Texas A&M Forest Service

Oak Wilt Facts

- The causal agent is the fungus *Ceratocystis fagacearum.*
- It exists solely in the vascular system of the tree except when a red oak is producing a fungal spore mat that allows spores to exist outside the tree.
- It can potentially affect all oak species, but red and live oaks are more likely to express symptoms because of their vascular structure.
- Local spread (tree to tree) occurs by root connections/grafts among oak trees.
- Longer-distance spread can occur by the sap-feeding nitidulid beetle, contaminated with *C. fagacearum* from feeding on a fresh wound of an oak tree.
- Fungal spore mats, the only source of inoculum for *C. fagacearum* spores, occur only on red oaks.
- Nitidulids are attracted to fresh wounds as a food source on healthy oak trees.
- Management techniques consist of trenching, injecting the fungicide propiconazole, and painting fresh wounds on live or green tissue.
- Trenching is done to disrupt the root connections and reduce the potential future spread. However, current research finds that trenching is not as effective as previously thought.
- Injections of fungicide preserve the tree from the effects of the fungus for around two years when done correctly. However, the fungicide does not prevent the infection; it only suppresses the symptoms.
- Painting fresh wounds with tree wound paint prevents attraction and feeding of the nitidulid beetles.
- The Texas A&M Forest Service has several foresters in Central Texas whose primary job responsibility is oak wilt management. When dealing with a deadly pathogen such as oak wilt, it is wise to check with an experienced consulting arborist who is also a degreed plant pathologist for recommendations relating to your area. The effects of the disease can vary according to the tree species and the particular forest stand involved (the number of trees and urban versus rural forests) and your location in the state.

Pine Bark Beetles

In the commercial forests of East Texas, pine bark beetles are the insects of concern. There are five species that attack and kill pine trees. Three species of engraver beetles and the black turpentine beetle typically kill only scattered trees. Their impact on the forest resource is seldom serious. However, the **southern pine beetle** (*Dendroctonus frontalis*) can cause catastrophic timber losses. This is the only pine bark beetle capable of killing trees over large areas resulting in

Southern pine beetle infestation. Courtesy of Texas A&M Forest Service

The life cycle of a southern pine beetle. Courtesy of Texas A&M Forest Service

Damage by a southern pine beetle. Courtesy of Texas A&M Forest Service

Demonstration of the cut-and-leave practice of management for southern pine beetle infestation. Courtesy of Texas A&M Forest Service

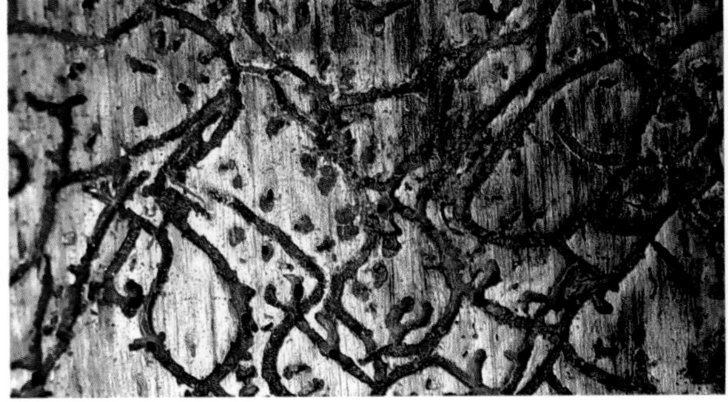

Damage done by a southern pine beetle in East Texas. Courtesy of Texas A&M Forest Service

The larvae (or grub) will feed between the bark and the wood for a period of time and then bore into the sapwood of the tree. On a still, warm day, it is not uncommon to hear a rhythmic chewing or crunching sound made by the larvae of the sawyer as they feed. Courtesy of Texas A&M Forest Service

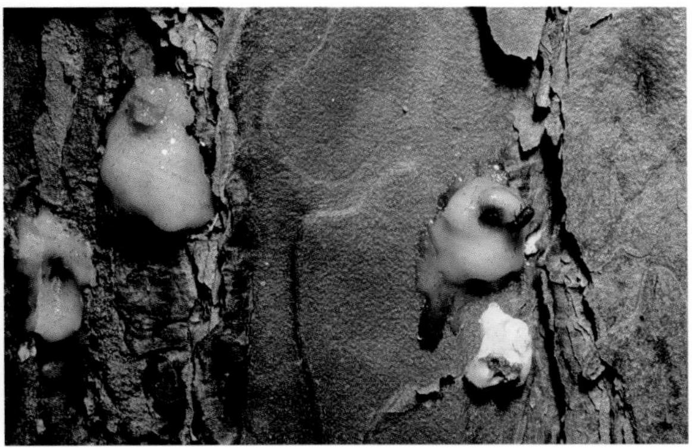

The attacks of the southern pine beetle are usually limited to the bottom six to eight feet of the trunk of the pine tree, and a large mass of pitch or resin will usually form where they attack. Pitch tubes are a sure sign of attack. Courtesy of Texas A&M Forest Service

Mature larvae may reach a length of two inches. Courtesy of Texas A&M Forest Service

severe timber losses. When direct management is applied to spreading/expanding southern pine beetle infestations, timber losses are minimized. When management is delayed or not applied, serious losses can occur.

Infestations of the southern pine beetle (SPB) in East Texas can be managed by a method known as "cut-and-leave" to reduce losses from spot (infestation area) growth and proliferation. The Texas A&M Forest Service recommends application of the cut-and-leave procedure in situations where prompt salvage or other control alternatives are not feasible. The method is designed to disrupt spot growth in small to medium-sized spots by dispersing attacking beetles. Also, survival of developing broods in felled trees may be reduced. The management technique is simple and inexpensive and requires a minimum of labor, equipment, and training.

How to Apply

1. Identify the active trees within the spot. The most recently attacked trees in an active infestation will still have green foliage, along with "pitch tubes" and/or early signs of boring dust.
2. Fell all active trees toward the center of the spot.
3. Fell a horseshoe-shaped buffer of green, uninfected trees around the active head of the spot and leave them lying on the ground with crowns pointed toward the center of the spot. The buffer should be as wide as the average height of the trees in the spot (40–60 feet wide).
4. Old dead trees with no bark beetles remaining should be left standing to allow development of parasites and predators that help control beetle populations.
5. If possible, check the treated spot after two weeks for reinfestations (breakouts) around the boundary. Re-treat all breakouts.
6. The buffer strip of green trees must be included to assure effective control, particularly for spots treated during warm months.

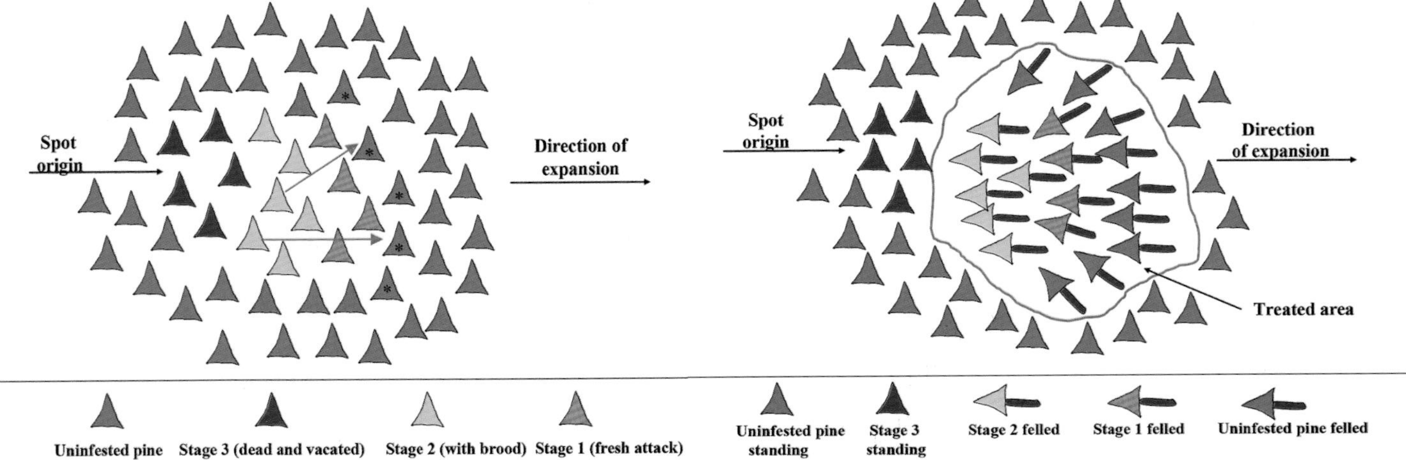

(A) Untreated area infested by southern pine beetle, and (B) treated area infested by southern pine beetle. Courtesy of Texas A&M Forest Service

When to Apply
Cut-and-leave treatment can be applied at any time of the year. However, the treatment appears most successful during the summer months to spots with 10–100 active trees. Prompt treatment after detection is recommended because experience has shown that large spots (100+ active trees) are difficult to control regardless of the treatment applied. However, spots with fewer than 10 active trees are often soon abandoned by the beetles and may require no treatment.

Challenges to Our Forests

The following is from Texas A&M Forest Service's "Texas Statewide Assessment of Forest Resources: A Comprehensive Analysis of Forest-Related Conditions, Trends, Threats and Opportunities" (September 2008).

Stakeholder Issues
The following six forest resource issues were identified as being most critical to the conservation, protection, and enhancement of forest resources in Texas:

***Issue 1:* Population Growth and Urbanization**
Texas communities are growing at an alarming rate. Community leaders need proactive management tools and technical support systems to help prepare for the effects of "high velocity" growth on forest resources before it happens—not after.

***Issue 2:* Central Texas Woodlands Conservation**
The woodlands of Central and West Texas are valuable resources for shade, recreation, wildlife, environmental, and watershed protection. Yet, these resources are coming under increasing pressure from an exploding population, land fragmentation, wildfires, invasive plants, oak wilt, and other pests. Cooperation and partnerships to protect and conserve these critical resources are essential if the high quality of life residents have come to expect in these regions of the state is to continue.

***Issue 3:* Sustainability of Forest Resources in East Texas**
For more than a century, the forests of East Texas have provided a number of economic and societal advantages such as manufacturing, employment, recreation, and environmental protection. Today, pressure on this resource has never been greater. East Texas is experiencing unprecedented change in the management and use of the Pineywoods. Population growth, ownership changes and parcelization, residential development, and nonconsumptive demands will impact the forested landscape for decades to come.

***Issue 4:* Water Quality and Quantity**
In Texas, most freshwater resources originate in the eastern portion of the state, making forestland a critical factor in meeting our water needs since they provide the cleanest water of any land use. In the rest of the state, where water supplies are limited, controlling non-native and invasive vegetation may produce higher water yields. With Texans already placing high demands on water resources, and the state's population exploding, it is imperative to continue to focus on this critical issue to ensure the quality of life that we Texans expect.

***Issue 5:* Wildfire and Public Safety**
Since its inception in 1915, Texas A&M Forest Service has been tasked with the responsibility of wildfire suppression, defending both the property and lives of Texas citizens. This is a growing issue for Texas. Since 1996, the state has seen significant fire seasons in 8 of the past 12 years. Once primarily a rural concern,

wildfires are now clearly a statewide threat. In recent years, wildfires have threatened and, in some cases, burned through small towns and large cities alike, destroying hundreds of homes. Three primary factors are combining to create these intense fire seasons—population growth, changing land use, and increasing drought frequency.

***Issue 6:* Urban Forest Sustainability**
With the addition of nearly 7 million residents since 1990, rapid urbanization is creating intense pressure on the sustainability of the trees and forests in Texas communities. Trees provide economic, health, and environmental benefits that are important to the quality of life in Texas communities. It is critical to plant, care for, and conserve the trees in communities where Texans live, work, and play.

Wildfires

According to Texas A&M Forest Service, Texas wildfires destroyed almost 3,000 homes in 2011, but more than 10 times that number were saved due to firefighting efforts and preplanning by local communities. Communities where people live, work, and play in areas adjoining forests, greenbelts, and other natural areas are termed the "**wildland urban interface**" (WUI). Wildfires will occur where people live—not if, but when—and if a community has not prepared, the economic, social, and environmental consequences can be far-reaching. Fire-adapted communities take the right steps in advance to minimize damage to homes and property, increase public safety, protect infrastructure and businesses, save millions of dollars, and ensure future tourism and local recreation opportunities.

Fire plays a major role in the health of the forest. It can be beneficial or destructive depending on the time of year, location, size, and intensity. Wildfires, the majority of which are human caused, constitute a serious threat to the forest resource, particularly newly planted plantations and young forest stands. In addition, as Texas forests become more fragmented, wildfires increasingly threaten lives, homes, and other property.

East Texas wildfire. Courtesy of Texas A&M Forest Service

Professional foresters and land managers use prescribed burning as a restoration ecological management tool to help maintain a healthy fire-adaptive ecosystem, such as conifer forests, prairies, native grasslands and rangelands, and estuaries, by reducing understory, vegetation density, and fuel (vegetation) load, thereby lessening the risk of disastrous wildfires. Many plant species within these areas are fire dependent, requiring fire to germinate, become established, or reproduce. Benefits of prescribed burning include removing competing vegetation; changing species composition to help control invasive species; rejuvenating wildlife habitat by improving the quantity and quality of forage; increasing soil nutrients; and improving recreational opportunities, such as hiking and camping.

Texas Invasive Species

An **invasive species** is nonnative to the ecosystem and has the likelihood to cause economic or environmental harm or harm to human health. Visit www.texasinvasives.org for more information. Each of the key Texas ecoregions has an invasive plant or pest species causing environmental damage. Texas Master Naturalists are part of the citizen-scientists making up the Invaders of Texas Program, which trains and equips volunteers to detect invasive species and network with local and regional teams continuously seek out and report these species.

Urban Forests: Where Texans Live, Work, and Play

"The time has come for urban communities to stop seeing the trees and start looking at the forest.
—John P. Rousakis, mayor of Savannah, Georgia, National Urban Forestry Conference, 1978

Eight of the top 15 fastest-growing large cities in the United States are in Texas, and Texas is second in the nation behind California in population (World Population Review 2014). The **urban forest** can be defined as the tree and plant community that occurs within an urban or community area, including parks, schools, residential areas, commercial districts, and areas along roads. Urban areas are generally associated with mixed-use development, vast human-made structures, and high population density. The year 2009 marked the first time in human history that more people lived in urban areas than rural areas, and this trend has continued. In Texas, the trend toward urbanization or rural flight follows the worldwide norm. The estimate of the urban population in 1950 was 62%, and in 2005 was 86% (Combs 2008).

What benefits does the urban forest provide? They can be economically quantified through environmental services like air quality, energy conservation, stormwater reductions, and noise attenuation. Additionally, social scientists have demonstrated that interactions with plants in urban settings provide numerous psychological and social benefits, including reduced stress and anxiety, improved medical recovery and convalescence, greater job satisfaction and productivity, and enhanced quality of life (Wolf 2003).

Due to increasing urbanization, the discipline of urban ecology has sought to better explain the relationship between living organisms within the setting of an urban area. One urban ecology issue is the relationship between native trees and insect diversity. A research study in South Texas identified native trees as having significantly larger total insect populations and species diversity than those of a nonnative tree planted in the urban forest (Van Driesche et al. 2010).

The overdevelopment of an area with an excessive amount of "hardscapes" (brick, glass, concrete, etc.) and a shortage of trees has the following consequences:

- Heat is greatly increased in the summertime up to 13°F or more (known as the urban heat island effect), which has a negative effect on air quality and increases energy consumption.

- Vehicles parked in parking lots in the full sun without the shade of trees creates evaporative emissions from fuel tanks, which has a negative effect on air quality.
- Stormwater runoff and the potential for flooding downstream increase. Rainfall quickly runs off hardscapes, but trees intercept and hold rainwater, which slowly filters into the ground and helps recharge underground aquifers.
- There is a direct and negative effect on wildlife, which need trees and forests for habitat or food. It also reduces or prevents the connectivity of natural areas that some wildlife need for survival.
- Benefits offered by trees and forests are limited. Given the many benefits of trees just in regard to improved air quality, urban forests are considered to be the very lungs of a community.

The primary manager of the urban forest on public lands is typically the local municipal government. It is common for the urban forestry program to be housed within either parks and recreation or in the public works departments. The person who manages the urban forestry department will often have the job title city forester or urban forester. Typically, the city forester plans and directs the daily work tasks of the city to fulfill the goals set forth in the urban forest master plan. Some cities will also utilize a city arborist to manage tree permits, oversee development plans, or manage private tree maintenance activities.

The urban forest master plan is a long-range plan that incorporates the views of the community in how the urban forest functions. This document is created with input from a diverse group of stakeholders and identifies the current status of the urban forest, goals, and issues that will affect the urban forest both positively and negatively. Stakeholders at the municipal level can include chambers of commerce, utility boards, independent school districts, universities, home owner associations, local forestry and tree groups, arborists, Friends of the Park organizations, city urban forest advisory groups, Master Naturalist groups, Master Gardener groups, and local scouting organizations.

As urban forests are mostly under the influence of human management, one challenge is the inherent perceptions and lack of advanced tree knowledge by the general population in the community. For example, without increased education opportunities available to the municipal staff or residents, the improper selection and planting of trees may lead to increased tree mortality and less citywide canopy cover, since planted trees make up a large portion of many urban forests, especially in residential areas. Additionally, irreparable damage can be done with just one incorrect pruning cut on an established tree; therefore, a well-trained workforce completing tree maintenance activities is also crucial for the long-term success of the urban forest.

Growth and development have a positive effect on a local economy and can keep it viable. However, haphazard urbanization can negatively affect the urban ecology and quality of life. By using smart, ecological approaches to planning and by following best management practices, urban growth can maintain and support the urban forest. Trees are an important component of the urban landscape, providing many benefits besides beauty and shade. The benefits of trees can be grouped into social, communal, environmental, and economic categories.

Several Texas cities are good examples of urban forests. Fort Worth holds the distinction of being the first city in Texas to become a Tree City USA by meeting the criteria of having a tree board or urban forestry department, establishing a tree care ordinance, having a forestry budget of at least two dollars per capita, and observing Arbor Day by proclamation of the city council. In 2013, American Forests selected the City of Austin as one of the top urban forests in the United States by virtue of its civic engagement in maintaining the urban forest, having a management plan and activities, and making the urban forest and green space accessible to the public, among other criteria.

According to the International Society of Arboriculture (2011), these are some of the benefits of trees:

> **Social Benefits**
>
> The calming effect of nearby trees and urban greening can significantly reduce workplace stress levels and fatigue, calm traffic, and even decrease the recovery time needed after surgery. Trees can also reduce crime. Apartment buildings with high levels of greenspace have lower crime rates than nearby apartments without trees. . . .
>
> **Communal Benefits**
>
> Even when located on a private lot, the benefits provided by trees reach well out into the surrounding community. Likewise, large-growing trees can come in conflict with utilities, views, and structures that are beyond the bounds of the owner's property. . . .
>
> **Environmental Benefits**
>
> Trees alter the environment in which we live by moderating climate, improving air quality, reducing stormwater runoff, and harboring wildlife. Local climates are moderated from extreme sun, wind, and rain. . . .
>
> **Economic Benefits**
>
> Property values of landscaped homes are 5 to 20 percent higher than those of non-landscaped homes. . . .
>
> **Trees Require an Investment**
>
> An informed home owner can be responsible for many tree maintenance practices . . . [but] may require the services of a professional arborist. Arborists have the knowledge and equipment needed to prune, treat, fertilize, and otherwise maintain a large tree. Your garden center owner, university extension agent, community forester, or consulting arborist can answer questions about tree maintenance, suggest treatments, or recommend qualified arborists.

The public has developed a desire for more parks, wilderness areas, and other "green space" areas to offset the negative psychological and social effects of urban sprawl. While these areas usually cannot be managed for forest products, they can be beneficial to a community or region in other ways: increase in property values, recreational opportunities and health benefits, stormwater retention and cleaning, heat island reduction, air pollution mitigation, and community cohesion. With an ever-shrinking land base, both society and land managers face tough challenges regarding managing our forests to meet everyone's needs.

Heritage Trees

Trees are a part of Texas' heritage and are documented and celebrated by the Texas Forest Service in two ways: Famous Trees of Texas and the Texas Big Tree Registry. The Texas Forest Service (2012) first published

(*Top*) This Famous Tree of Texas is the live oak under which Gen. Sam Houston set up an encampment in March 1836, following the fall of the Alamo, to strategize a plan to defeat Mexican general Santa Anna. Courtesy of Texas A&M Forest Service

(*Bottom*) This Famous Tree of Texas is the revered live oak anchor of the Comanche County courthouse square. Courtesy of Texas A&M Forest Service

This Famous Tree of Texas is also on the Texas Big Tree Registry. A champion in 1965, it is believed to be one of the largest baldcypress in the state. Courtesy of Texas A&M Forest Service

Edward C. "Ned" Fritz

Ned Fritz was well known as the "Father of Texas Conservation." Fritz received his law degree from Southern Methodist University. He was a very passionate person legendary for his courage and dogged persistence, as well as his relentless efforts to preserve wilderness and halt clear-cutting in national forests. He enjoyed the dedicated support of his wife, Eugenie (or Genie to everyone she met), who helped him immensely in organizing files and data as well as assisted in keeping him on track.

Fritz founded the Texas Committee on Natural Resources (now the Texas Conservation Alliance), a group that petitioned the USDA Forest Service to stop clear-cutting. Numerous lawsuits were filed over many years to ensure his message was heard. He was also involved in the passage of the 1969 National Environmental Policy Act and the 1976 National Forest Management act as well as the Texas Wilderness Act. The Wilderness Act effectively preserved five wilderness areas in the national forests of East Texas.

He authored two books on the subject: *Clearcutting: A Crime against Nature* and *Sterile Forest: The Case against Clearcutting*. The following quote from *Clearcutting* summarizes his concerns:

> Clearcutting is a very questionable practice on public lands. Unquestionably, clearcutting has large impacts on the other multiple uses and resources of the forest. A clearcut is the epitome of a single use excluding other uses for some time. Its impacts extend well beyond the area affected. Frequently clearcuts and the accompanying roads pollute streams and destroy valuable fisheries. Clearcuts are ugly. In mountainous terrain clearcuts ruin scenic beauty for miles. A most critical concern is the effect that clearcutting may have on biological diversity. I personally consider the loss of biological diversity the most important problem facing the planet. . . . A clearcut looks like a war zone. It is the radical surgery of the timber business. The soil washes off like blood. (9, 31)

(*continued*)

Fritz did not fear controversy, and he constantly educated others about better stewardship of our land. He also founded the Natural Area Preservation Association (now Texas Land Conservancy), was a founding member of the Texas Historic Tree Coalition, and cofounder of the Texas Chapter of the Nature Conservancy.

Janice Bezanson, a close friend of Ned and Genie Fritz, as well as the longtime executive director for Texas Conservation Alliance and founding member of the Texas Historic Tree Coalition, said that "I lost count of the things Ned accomplished that people said couldn't be done. He was the most persistent person on the face of the earth. He had a marvelous sense of humor, very deadpan. His motivation and personal relationships were very affectionate. His family and his daughters adored him. He was very musical and wrote songs, and he's written some wonderful poetry" (Holtcamp 2009).

An example of his literary skills can be found in *Realms of Beauty: A Guide to the Wilderness Areas of East Texas*: "The freer a forest is from the manipulations of human beings, the more clearly the spirit of earth and sky is manifested in the marvelous processes that we sense. Let our eyes and minds now drink the beauty and sing the praises of seven areas where, by the grace of humankind, East Texas plant communities may survive and evolve as long as life endures in this verdant region."

Ned Fritz was an inspiration to all those around him and a true Texas pioneer in many ways. He is a perfect example of what one individual with a strong desire can do to make a difference.

"Famous Trees of Texas" in 1970 to "memorialize those trees which have been witness to some of the exciting periods and events in Texas 'frontier history.'" The purpose of the Texas Big Tree Registry is

- to locate and recognize the largest known species of its kind that grow in the state of Texas;
- to obtain the cooperation of the tree owners to encourage the protection and preservation of these specimens as landmarks for future generations to enjoy;
- to stimulate interest in and a greater appreciation of trees—their worth as a natural resource and as individual specimens.

Texas Tree Trails is a cooperative effort between Texas A&M Forest Service, Texas Historic Tree Coalition, and Cross Timbers and Blackland Prairie Urban Forestry Councils. More information about this unique collaborative partnership can be found by visiting www.texastreetrails.org. Texas Tree Trails recognizes the distinctiveness trees offer to places people live, work, and play. The interactive website and phone app are able to showcase the importance of trees and make trees relevant to a twenty-first-century technology-driven audience and demographic.

"We cannot preserve significant trees that we fail to publicly recognize as important assets."
—Steve Houser, Certified Arborist

References

Combs, Susan. 2008. Texas in Focus: A Statewide View: Demographics. Accessed April 1, 2015. http://comptroller.texas.gov/specialrpt/tif/03_Demographics.pdf.

Francaviglia, Richard V. 2000. *The Cast Iron Forest: A Natural History of the North American Cross Timbers*. Austin: University of Texas Press.

Holtcamp, Wendee. Larger Than Life. *Texas Parks and Wildlife*, August 2009. http://www.tpwmagazine.com/archive/2009/aug/legend/.

International Society of Arboriculture. 2011. Benefits of Trees. Accessed April 1, 2015. http://www.treesaregood.com/treecare/resources/benefits_trees.pdf.

Pinchot, Gifford. 1947. *Breaking Ground.* New York: Harcourt Brace.

Spurr, Stephen Hopkins. 1980. *Forest Ecology*. 3rd ed. New York: John Wiley & Sons.

Van Driesche, R. G., R. I. Carruthers, T. D. Center, M. Hoddle, J. Hough-Goldstein, L. Morin, L. Smith, D. L. Wagner, R. W. Fuester, J. Goolsby, R. W. Pemberton, P. D. Pratt, M. B. Rayamajhi, P. W. Tipping, et al. 2010. Classical Biological Control for the Protection of Natural Ecosystems. *Biological Control* 54 (Suppl. 1): S2–S33.

Wolf, K. L. 2003. Ergonomics of the City: Green Infrastructure and Social Benefits. In *Engineering Green: Proceedings of the 11th National Urban Forest Conference*, ed. C. Kollin. Washington DC: American Forests. http://www.naturewithin.info/UF/AmForErg.pdf.

World Population Review. 2014. Texas Population 2014. Accessed April 1, 2015. http://worldpopulationreview.com/states/texas-population/.

Website Resources

Alamo Forest Partnership: www.alamoforestpartnership.org

Alliance for Community Trees: http://actrees.org

American Forest & Paper Association: www.afandpa.org

American Forest Foundation: www.forestfoundation.org

American Forest Foundation, Project Learning Tree: https://www.plt.org/

American Forests: www.americanforests.org

Arbor Day Foundation: www.arborday.org

Association for the Pulp and Paper Industry (TAPPI): www.tappi.org

Association of Consulting Foresters: http://www.acf-foresters.org

Benny Simpson's Texas Native Shrubs: https://aggie-horticulture.tamu.edu/ornamentals/nativeshrubs/

Famous Trees of Texas: http://tfsweb.tamu.edu/websites/famoustreesoftexas

Forest History Society: www.foresthistory.org

Forest Inventory and Analysis National Program: www.fia.fs.fed.us

Forest Landowners: www.forestlandowners.com

Forest Resources Association: www.forestresources.org

InterfaceSouth: www.interfacesouth.org

International Society of Arboriculture: www.isa-arbor.org

i-Tree: www.itreetools.org

National Association of State Foresters: www.stateforesters.org

The National Map (USGS): http://nationalmap.gov

National Tree Benefit Calculator: www.treebenefits.com/calculator

The Nature Conservancy: http://www.tnc.org

Official Smokey Bear Website: www.smokeybear.com

Society of American Foresters: www.safnet.org

Southern Forest Products Association: www.sfpa.org

Stephen F. Austin State University, Arthur Temple College of Forestry and Agriculture: http://forestry.sfasu.edu

Texas A&M Department of Ecosystem Science and Management: http://essm.tamu.edu

Texas A&M Forest Service: http://tfsweb.tamu.edu

Texas A&M Forest Service, Texas Forest Information Portal: http://texasforestinfo.tamu.edu

Texas A&M Forest Service, Texas Tree Planting Guide: http://texastreeplanting.tamu.edu

Texas A&M Forest Service, Trees of Texas, How to ID: http://texastreeid.tamu.edu

Texas Commission on Environmental Quality: www.tceq.texas.gov

Texas Forestry Association: www.texasforestry.org

Texas Forestry Museum: www.treetexas.com

Texas Historic Tree Coalition: www.txhtc.org

Texas Invasives: www.texasinvasives.org

Texas Project Learning Tree: www.plttexas.org

Tree Trust: http://treetrust.org

Trees Are Good: http://www.treesaregood.org

Urban Forestry South: www.urbanforestrysouth.org

USDA Forest Service: www.fs.fed.us

USDA Natural Resources Conservation Service: www.nrcs.usda.gov

US Geological Survey: www.usgs.gov

Web Soil Survey: http://websoilsurvey.sc.egov.usda.gov/App/HomePage.htm

World Forestry Center: http://www.worldforestry.org

Additional Resources

Dana, S. T., and S. K. Fairfax. 1980. *Forest and Range Policy: Its Development in the United States*. 2nd ed. New York: McGraw-Hill.

Duff, Mark L. 1998. *Opportunities for Forest and Range Restoration in the Texas Hill Country*. Texas A&M Forest Service, Kerrville Office. Accessed April 1, 2015. http://www.texasoakwilt.org/Documents/Stewardship/HillCountry.pdf.

Foster, Steven. 1995. *Forest Pharmacy: Medicinal Plants in American Forests*. Durham, NC: Forest History Society.

Fredrickson, L. H., S. L. King, and R. M. Kaminski, eds. 2005. *Ecology and Management of Bottomland Hardwood Systems*. Gaylord Memorial Laboratory Special Publication No. 10. Puxico: University of Missouri–Columbia.

MacCleery, Douglas W. 1993. *American Forest of Resiliency and Recovery*. Darby, PA: Diane Publishing.

Maxwell, Robert S., and Robert D. Baker. 2000. *Sawdust Empire: The Texas Lumber Industry, 1830–1940*. College Station: Texas A&M University Press.

McWilliams, William H., and Roger G. Lord. 1988. *Forest Resources of East Texas*. New Orleans, LA: USDA Southern Forest Experiment Station.

Miller, J. H. 2003. *Nonnative Invasive Plants of Southern Forests: A Field Guide to Identification and Control*. General Technical Report SRS-62. Asheville, NC: USDA Forest Service, Southern Experiment Station.

Nixon, Elroy, and Bruce L. Cunningham. 2012. *Trees, Shrubs, & Woody Vines of East Texas*. 3rd ed. Forester-Artist.com.

Powell, Michael A. 1998. *Trees and Shrubs of the Trans-Pecos and Adjacent Areas*. Rev. ed. Austin: University of Texas Press.

Smith, David. 1986. *The Practice of Silviculture*. 4th ed. New York: John Wiley & Sons.

South Carolina Forestry Commission. 1990. *Benefits of Urban Trees*. USDA Forestry Report R8-FR17. http://www.state.sc.us/forest/urbben.htm.

Texas A&M Forest Service. 1963. *Forest Trees of Texas: How to Know Them*. Bulletin 20. 8th ed. College Station: Texas A&M Forest Service.

———. 2010. *Environmental Credit Marketing Survey Report*. http://texasforestservice.tamu.edu/uploadedFiles/FRD/Ecosystem_Services/ECMSurveyReport.pdf.

———. 2012. *Texas Forest Action Plan*. Texas Statewide Assessment of Forest Resources. http://txforestservice.tamu.edu/uploadedFiles/Sustainable/assessment/Texas%20Forest%20Resource%20Strategy.pdf.

Williston, Hamlin L., William E. Balmer, and Daniel H. Sims. 1992. *Managing the Family Forest in the South*. Management Bulletin R8-MB1. Atlanta: USDA Forest Service, Southern Region.

Yahner, R. H., C. G. Mahan, and A. D. Rodewald. 2012. Managing Forests for Wildlife. In *The Wildlife Techniques Manual*, ed. N. J. Silvy, 2:55–73. Baltimore: Johns Hopkins University Press.

Young, Raymond A., and Ronald Giese. 1990. *Introduction to Forest Science*. 2nd ed. Madison, WI: John Wiley & Sons.

UNIT 18

Aquatic Systems Ecology and Management

MICHAEL P. MASSER
Professor and Department Head, Wildlife and Fisheries Science, Texas A&M University

TODD D. SINK
Assistant Professor and Fisheries Extension Specialist, Texas A&M University AgriLife Extension Service

Unit Goals

After completing this unit, volunteers should be able to

- describe the characteristics of water
- communicate the characteristics and properties of aquatic systems
- understand and communicate how aquatic systems function
- be familiar with management techniques for aquatic systems
- understand and communicate threats to aquatic systems

Introduction

Life on earth evolved in an aquatic system. Aquatic systems are extremely diverse, ranging from marine to fresh, static to flowing, basic to acidic, and cold to hot. While all aquatic systems are dependent on water, not all have a constant water level or continuous water supply. Water more than any other element or compound makes life possible on earth. In this unit we explore the properties of water, aquatic ecology, and basic management of aquatic systems.

"There is magic on this planet; it is contained in water."
—Loren Eisley, *The Immense Journey*

Characteristics of Water

Water is one of the most abundant compounds or molecules on earth. The reason water makes life possible on earth lies within its unique properties, which include its surface tension, specific heat, density, and ability to dissolve other substances. Also important is that water at moderate earth temperatures is in a liquid state, so it forms our oceans, rivers, wetlands, and lakes. Water is an extremely stable compound, meaning that it does not readily break down or interact in chemical reactions. The H_2O formula for water indicates that each molecule consists of two atoms of hydrogen and one atom of oxygen. However, water has a most interesting and unique structure, in that the hydrogen atoms do not oppose each other at a 180° angle to the oxygen but instead cluster to one side, at a 104.5° angle to the oxygen atom. This angle gives the water molecule a "bipolar" structure—the hydrogen side being positively charged and the oxygen side being negatively charged. These unequal charges make water molecules attract each other, forming clusters in which each water molecule bonds to three others (forming what is called a **tetrahedral** structure of four water molecules). This structure gives water the unique abilities to

- develop surface tension
- be a solid, liquid, or gas over a relatively small temperature range

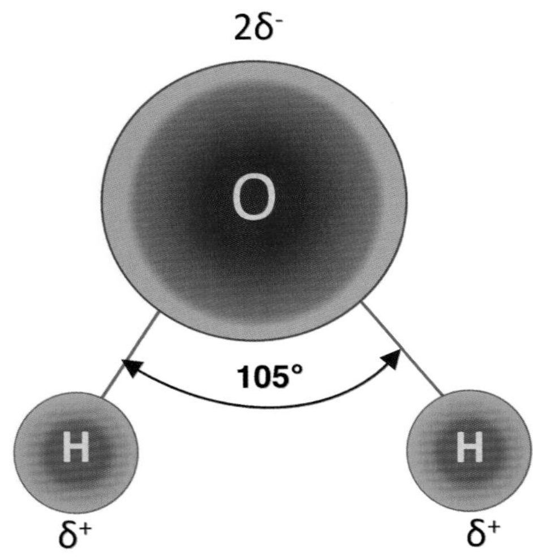

A water molecule, H_2O. Courtesy of Christine Kolbe

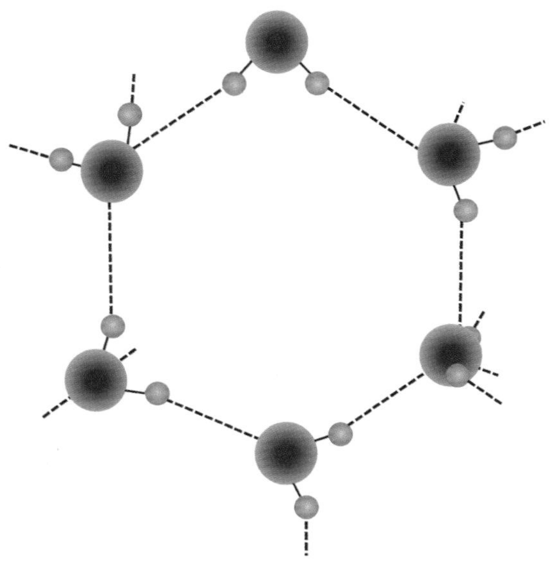
Water molecules are close together at 39°F and are structured far apart when freezing. Courtesy of Christine Kolbe

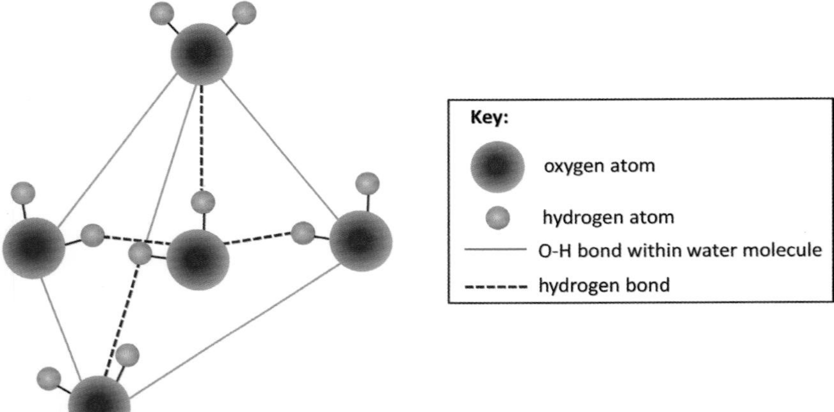

Water molecules in a tetrahedral shape. Courtesy of Christine Kolbe

- become less dense in its solid state
- have a high specific heat
- dissolve other substances

The **surface tension** of water gives it a strong, elastic exterior and enables water to form droplets, move through minute openings in soils and living tissues, and allow some creatures to inhabit its surface.

The bonds water forms with surrounding water molecules and other molecules are called **hydrogen bonds**. These weak hydrogen bonds between water and molecules are constantly breaking and re-forming, depending on temperature and pressure. As temperature increases (and pressure decreases), this molecular activity increases and some water molecules are lost from the surface to become **water vapor** (water vapor comprises single molecules of water in a gaseous state). As water vapor (i.e., clouds) cools, it re-forms or condenses to liquid water (i.e., forms raindrops). A unique property of water is that its solid state is less dense than its liquid state. As liquid water cools, its structure becomes most dense at 39°F (4°C). Because of its tetrahedral structure, water cooled below this temperature becomes less dense, traps more gases, and therefore freezes, or becomes a solid at the surface. This surface freezing traps warmer water (usually 39°F) below and makes it difficult for large bodies of water to freeze solid. The fact that water freezes at the surface, but not uniformly (as a solid block), makes life possible under the ice.

A substance's **specific heat** is its capacity to absorb heat (or thermal energy) in relation to temperature at a constant volume. Water has an extremely high specific heat, which means it absorbs or releases heat slowly and therefore stores large quantities of thermal energy. This allows all bodies of water (particularly the oceans) to store enormous quantities of solar energy in the form of heat, which is one of the issues concerning climate change and global weather patterns. This stored energy is transferred to the atmosphere and drives global weather patterns, with increasing thermal energy creating more volatile weather events. This specific heat means even small water bodies warm and cool slowly compared to the atmosphere, making aquatic systems very stable environments for aquatic organisms.

Finally, water is considered the **universal solvent** because of its ability to dissolve so many other elements and compounds. Substances dissolved in water (minerals, nutrients, gases, etc.) then move freely, or diffuse, within the water body, making them available to aquatic organisms. These physical characteristics of water make it the medium of life on earth, and life as we know it cannot exist without water.

Water Cycle

The water or **hydrologic cycle** is basic to life on the earth. It is a continuous process involving the exchange or circulation of water between the oceans, the atmosphere, and the land. The energy forces that drive the hydrologic cycle are solar radiation (radiant energy emitted by the sun) and gravity. It is estimated that 1.1×10^{15} acre-feet, or 325,520,833 cubic miles, of water exist on the earth. Over 97% of this water is

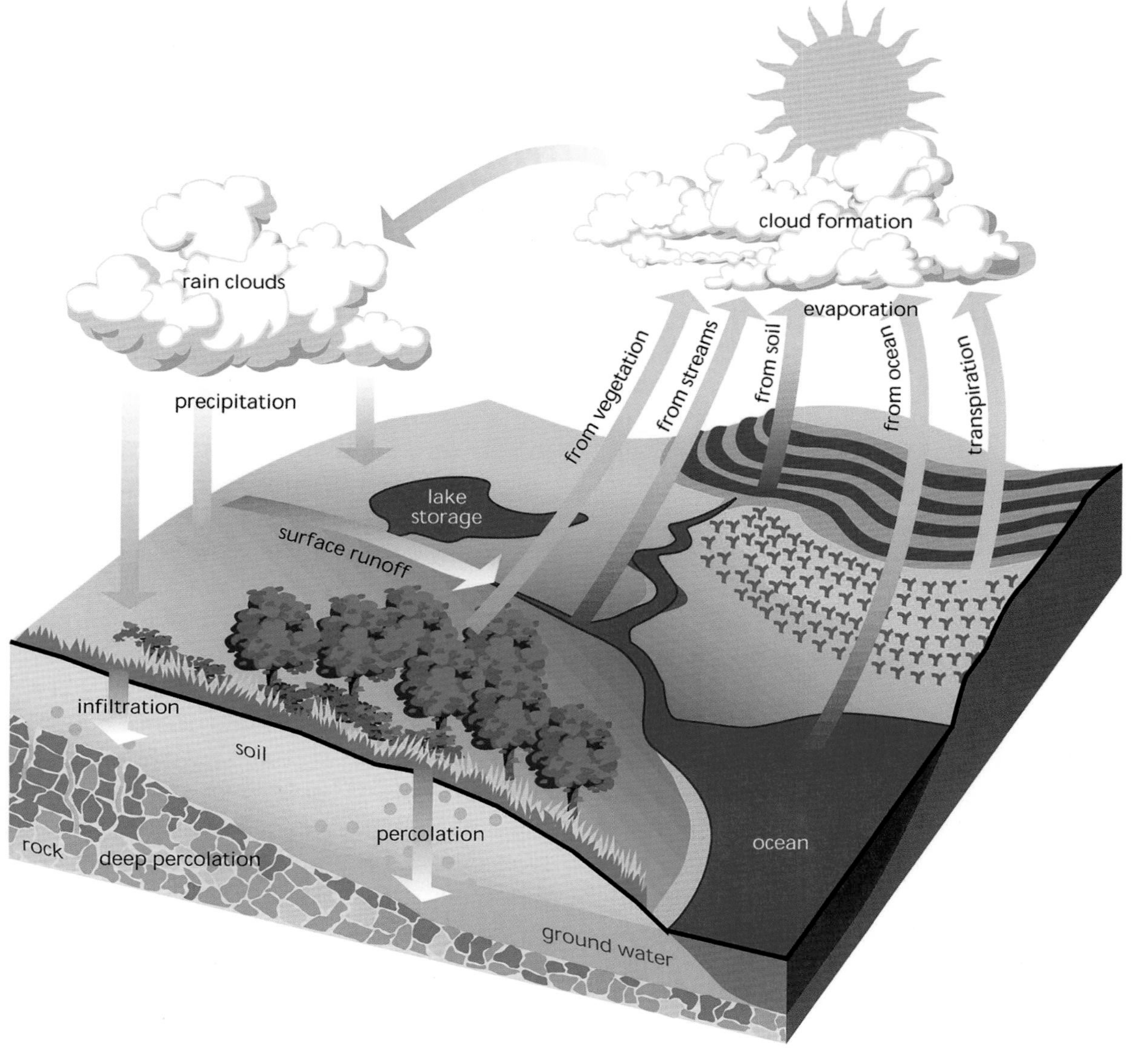

The hydrologic cycle. The transfer of water from precipitation to surface water and groundwater, to storage and runoff, and eventually back to the atmosphere is an ongoing cycle. From *Stream Corridor Restoration: Principles, Processes, and Practices* (10/98), Interagency Stream Restoration Working Group (FISRWG) (15 federal agencies)

in the oceans. The remainder is in ice (glaciers, snow, etc.), 2%; groundwater, 0.58%; lakes and rivers, 0.02%; or the atmosphere, 0.001%. The amount of fresh water is only 2.9×10^{13} acre-feet. Living organisms utilize only 0.000078% of the total water on the earth. Evaporation (mostly from the oceans) and transpiration (from plants) release water vapor to the atmosphere. Atmospheric water falls back to the earth as rain or snow precipitation. Water falling as precipitation can

- evaporate back into the atmosphere
- collect to form fresh surface waters (rivers, lakes, etc.)
- be frozen within glaciers
- percolate into the ground
- be incorporated into living organisms

Fresh surface waters can evaporate into the atmosphere, percolate into the ground, be absorbed by organisms, or flow back to the oceans. Groundwater can flow back into surface waters, be absorbed by plants, be stored in "aquifers," or flow back to the oceans. It is estimated that the recycling or renewal times for water are 37,000 years for oceans, 16,000 years for ice, 300 years for groundwater, 1 to 100 years for lakes, 280 days for soil moisture, 12–20 days for rivers, and 9 days for atmospheric moisture. Thus, fresh water at the surface is very transient and rapidly recycles.

Characterizing Aquatic Systems

Aquatic systems can be divided into lentic or lotic systems. **Lentic systems** are standing or nonflowing waters, and **lotic systems** are flowing water systems. Obviously, this classification is overly simplistic, and both systems have many common characteristics as well as some distinct differences. Wetlands, reservoirs, and aquifers are examples of aquatic systems that have both lentic and lotic characteristics.

Watersheds

A **watershed** is the land area from which water drains into a common watercourse. All land is part of a watershed, and we all live within a watershed. As water moves along the surface, through the soil, or through rock layers, it dissolves and transports sediment and minerals. There are 15 major watersheds or river systems identified in Texas with a total of 191,000 river/stream miles. Five of these start in other states or Mexico. Therefore, Texas receives/shares much of its water with its surrounding states and Mexico.

Lotic Systems

Streams, creeks, and rivers are lotic systems or environments. In Texas, some 11,247 streams have been named. Streams in a watershed are classified based on size and hierarchy in the watershed. The smallest streams in a watershed have no tributaries or feeder streams and are classified **first-order streams**. First-order streams run together to form a second-order stream, second-order streams run together to form a third-order stream, and so forth up to tenth-order streams.

First-, second-, and third-order streams are generally called **headwater streams**; fourth- through sixth-order streams are called **midsized streams**; and seventh- through tenth-order streams are **large streams or rivers**. The Rio Grande and Red River are examples of tenth-order streams.

Streams or rivers such as the Rio Grande (900 river miles long), Red (860 river miles long), Colorado (600 river miles long) and Brazos (840 river miles long) drain watersheds encompassing thousands of square miles in Texas, Mexico, and many surrounding states. Rivers like the San Jacinto (39 river miles long) and the Sulfur (90 river miles long) have relatively small watersheds. Obviously, rivers that drain directly into other larger rivers are, in actuality, part of the larger watershed and have been arbitrarily subdivided for analytical or political reasons.

Watersheds in Texas. Courtesy of Texas Parks and Wildlife Department

Streams in upland areas generally have higher or steeper gradients/slopes and are cooler and faster flowing than streams in lowland areas. Rainfall, stream gradient, vegetation, and soil/substrate generally determine stream flow characteristics. Streams that flow constantly are called **perennial streams**, while those that flow only occasionally are called **intermittent streams**. Many first- and second-order streams are intermittent streams.

Flow rate or velocity varies widely within a stream or lotic system. Streams are usually characterized by pools, riffles, and meanders (bends). **Pools** are deeper, slower-moving water sections, while **riffles** are shallow, faster-moving water sections of a stream. **Meanders** change the flow patterns of streams by focusing currents into specific areas, thus creating pools or riffles. Rainfall in the watershed increases flow in the streams. High flow velocities scour streambeds, moving stones, gravel, and silt and cutting new channels and banks. Flowing waters transport nutrients, sediments, and aquatic organisms. Aquatic organisms that live in these lotic environments must adapt to withstand these flow changes, find sheltered areas, or be transported downstream.

The primary energy source in lotic envi-

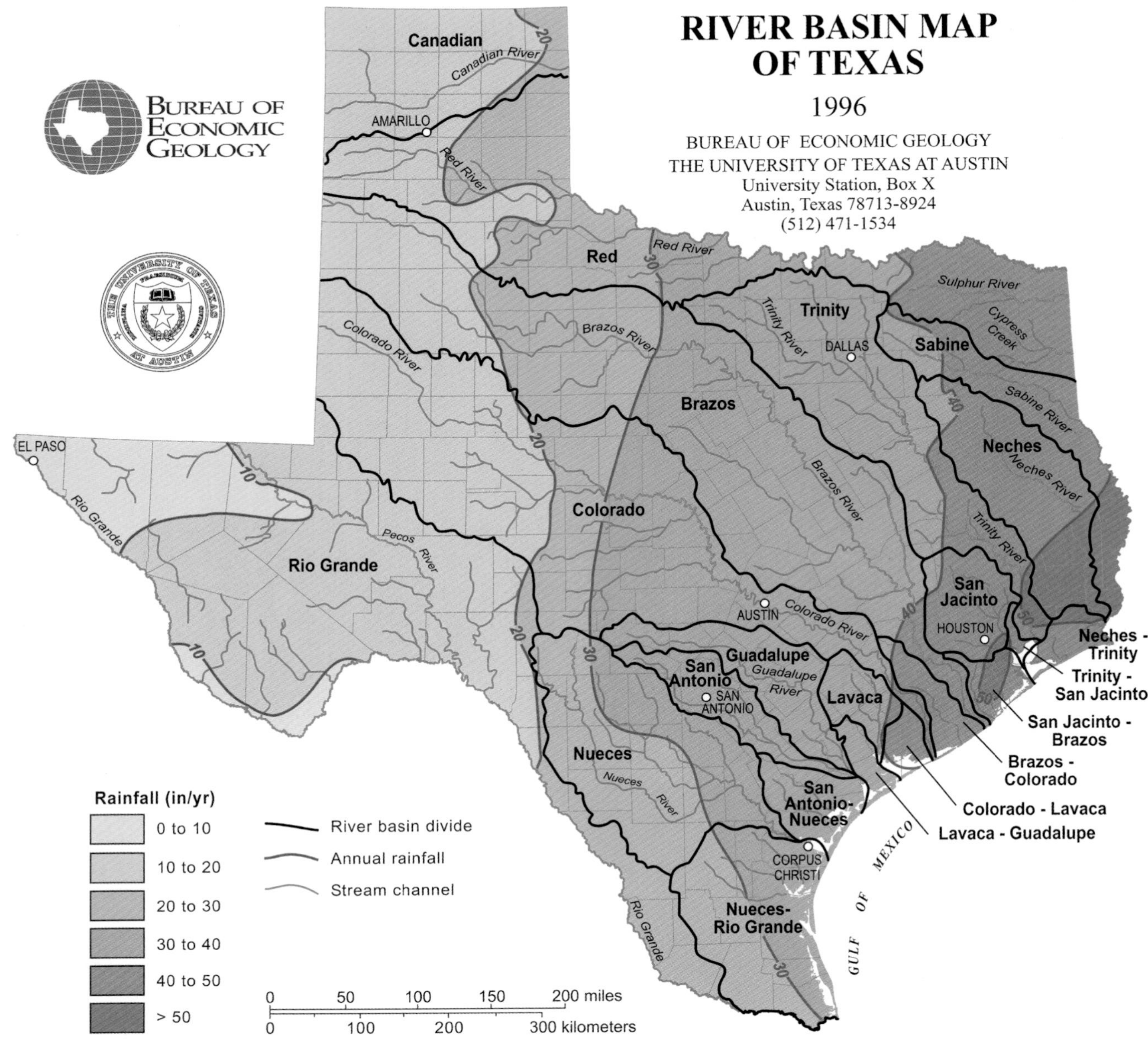

River basins	Texas length (miles)	Texas area (sq mi)	Number of major reservoirs*	Conservation storage (acre ft)*	Storage (acre ft/sq mi)
Brazos	840	42,800	19	3,322,880	75
Canadian	200	12,700	2	560,900	44
Colorado	600	39,893	11	3,803,900	95
Guadalupe	250	6,070	2	420,000	70
Lavaca	74	2,309	1	157,900	68
Neches	416	10,011	4	3,455,500	345
Nueces	315	16,950	2	931,640	60
Red	680	30,823	7	4,593,460	149
Rio Grande	1,250	48,259	3	3,772,000	78
Sabine	360	7,426	2	6,041,300	814
San Jacinto	70	5,600	2	570,400	102
Trinity	550	17,696	14	6,969,710	388

**Data from Texas Water Development Board.*

Texas major river basins, coastal basins, and major bays. Courtesy of Texas Parks and Wildlife Department

The Rio Grande. Courtesy of Texas Parks and Wildlife Department

ronments is exogenous (from the outside). Organic material and nutrients from the surrounding environment or watershed supply energy for bacteria and other microorganisms, macroinvertebrates, and fish. Some photosynthetic production does occur from algae and rooted vegetation but is minor compared to influx of organic matter from the outside.

Lentic Systems

Lakes, ponds, and ephemeral pools are lentic systems. However, all are part of a watershed and receive water from rainfall events. Most lakes and ponds overflow during heavy rainfall events and thus have some characteristics similar to those of lotic systems. Ponds and lakes accumulate exogenous nutrients and sediment over time, becoming nutrient rich and shallower with less volume. This accumulation and its associated changes are part of the natural successional cycle. Lakes tend to accumulate sediments near the shoreline and thus slowly become shallower and smaller in volume from the edges inward. The expected life of a pond is only from 25 to 100 years before it is filled in to the point that it becomes a swamp or wetland. Watershed characteristics above the pond or lake will determine the life of the water body. These characteristics include soil, slope, vegetation type, and land-use patterns. Agricultural practices like row cropping and livestock grazing, mining, and

This East Texas pond is a lentic system, meaning the water is still. Courtesy of Texas A&M AgriLife Extension Service

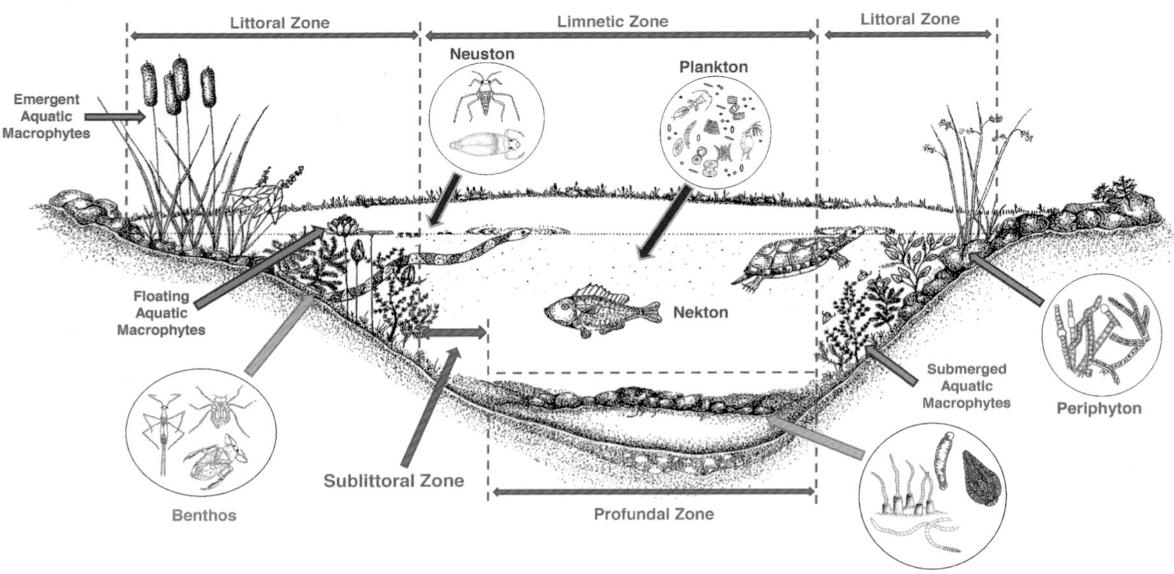

Horizontal lake zones. Courtesy of Christine Kolbe

certain industrial practices in the immediate watershed increase nutrient and sediment accumulation in ponds and lakes.

Light penetration drives lentic systems probably more than any other single factor. The littoral zone and limnetic zones of a lentic system are where light penetrates. Only in these areas can plants grow or photosynthesize. Turbidity in the water also affects the depth of these zones. The **littoral zone** comprises areas near shore, underwater humps, or islands where light penetrates to the bottom. This region tends to be highly diverse and productive in plant and demersal (close to shore) animal life. While exogenous material dominates the food chain of lotic systems, lentic systems produce most of their own food (endogenous) through photosynthesis of plants within the system.

The **limnetic zone** is the open water away from shore where light penetrates. Free-floating and microscopic plants (phytoplankton or algae), microscopic animals (zooplankton), and pelagic (meaning open water, away from the shore) animals inhabit this zone. Light does not penetrate into the **profundal zone** below the limnetic zone. This zone can be inhabited by animal life but is dependent on temperature, dissolved oxygen, and other water quality factors. This zone can become anaerobic (depleted of oxygen) at times and may not be inhabitable by life-forms other than anaerobic microorganisms (e.g., bacteria).

The **benthic zone** is the bottom and consists of organic and mineral sediments. Much of the benthic zone can be anaerobic, particularly below the profundal zone. However, where oxygen is present, this zone is highly productive and inhabited by invertebrates that consume detritus (decaying material).

Lotic environments are often more productive (i.e., greater biomass per area) than lentic environments because constant influx of organic matter and nutrients, more stable dissolved oxygen levels, and their shallowness increase plant life and recycling of nutrients.

Water and Temperature Quality Parameters

Temperature, driven by solar energy, is the primary physical parameter in aquatic environments. Most aquatic organisms are **poikilothermic**, or cold-blooded, meaning that they assume the temperature of their environment. Thus, environmental temperature affects their metabolism and controls feeding, reproduction, and behavior. Many microorganisms survive and thrive only over specific temperature ranges and are dormant outside that temperature range. While most fish survive throughout a broad range of temperatures due to their cold-blooded or poikilothermic method of body temperature regulation, they are often classified as cold-water, cool-water, warm-water, or tropical/subtropical.

Cold-water and tropical/subtropical classifications are determined by upper and lower, respectively, lethal temperature tolerance, while cool-water and warm-water classifications are determined by the optimum temperature for growth. Cold-water fish are typically restricted to very deep or far northern ocean areas around the Arctic and Antarctic. There are a few freshwater, cold-water species in North America, such as the arctic char, which has a preferred temperature range of less than 50°F (10°C) and undergoes larval development at 41°F to 44.6°F (5°C to 7°C). Temperatures greater than 57°F (14°C) can be lethal for arctic char.

There are no cold-water fish species in Texas. Rainbow trout, for example, are cool-water fish and cannot survive at temperatures above 68°F (20°C). One defining characteristic of cool-water fish is that the optimal temperature for growth is typically between 55°F and 68°F (13°C and 20°C). Rainbow trout are not native to Texas, although they have been stocked during winter months in some lakes and the cool tailwaters of a few very deep reservoirs. Trout do not survive the summer months in Texas, with the only year-round fishery being the tailwater section directly behind Canyon Lake Dam. Texas has no native species that can truly be considered cool-water species.

Warm-water fish make up the most abundant class of fish in Texas. These are species with arguably the widest temperature tolerance. Most tolerate from 39°F to 100°F (4°C to 38°C), meaning that they are typically widespread throughout Texas and the United States, and include familiar species such as largemouth bass, Guadalupe bass, bluegill, redear sunfish, and channel catfish. However, the main characteristic of this group that denotes them as warm-water species is that the best growth occurs in the 74°F to 85°F (23°C to 29°C) range. Many tropical/subtropical species cannot survive temperatures below 55°F (13°C).

There are very few freshwater species native to Texas that could be classified as tropical/subtropical. The best example of a subtropical species in Texas is the Rio Grande cichlid, which has a minimum temperature tolerance of 57°F (14°C) that limits its northward spread from its native range of Mexico and South Texas. Tilapia species from Africa, which have been widely introduced in Texas as forage fish and for aquatic vegetation control, are likely the most common tropical/subtropical species encountered in Texas.

Temperature differences are ecologically very important and determine species composition, food chain diversity, and

Guadalupe River. Courtesy of Texas Parks and Wildlife Department

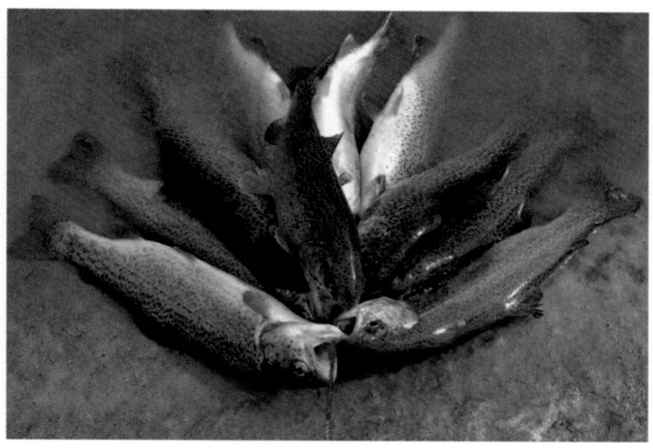

Rainbow trout, a cool-water fish. Courtesy of Texas Parks and Wildlife Department

Tilapia. Courtesy of Texas Parks and Wildlife Department

nutrient recycling. Shallow water changes temperature more rapidly than deep water, and water surfaces exposed to sunlight warm faster and stay warmer than shaded waters (i.e., streams with tree canopies). In general, water changes temperature slowly enough that it never gets as cold or warm as the air. As water warms, evaporation tends to release heat and slow the warming effect of solar energy. As water cools, the warmer water sinks and the cooler water rises (at 39°F), freezing at the surface.

Turbidity

Chemically, water is a clear, colorless liquid. **Turbidity** is the cloudiness or haziness of water, which is caused by individual particles in suspension that are generally invisible to the naked eye. Another way to think about turbidity is the degree of transparency of water. Suspended sediments, dissolved substances, and microorganisms increase turbidity and thus decrease the water's transparency. Turbidity caused by suspended solids (muddy water) can be an indication of erosion problems within the watershed or a clay layer within the water body. Lowland streams tend to have turbid water because of the constant influx of sediments after rainfall, especially in disturbed watersheds, and the redistribution of sediments in the stream itself. Highland streams tend to be less turbid.

Turbidity caused by a population growth of microorganisms ("bloom"), usually microscopic algae, indicates the presence of nutrients. Algal turbidity is an indication of primary productivity but can also become too dense, indicating high (excessive) nutrient inflows from the watershed. Productivity in aquatic systems refers to the amount of carbon that is fixed per unit of area. While water is essential for life, carbon is also essential because it harnesses the fuel needed for life in the form of sugars (i.e., glucose, $C_6H_{12}O_6$) and as structural building blocks for organisms. Productivity is an indirect measure of the amount of biomass supported in a fixed area. An area with 30 moles of carbon fixed per cubic meter per year indicates much more carbon fixation in the form of sugars than an area with 10 moles of carbon fixed per cubic meter per year, meaning that area can sustain a greater animal biomass and therefore is more productive.

Clear water is not necessarily good, as it may indicate low primary productivity or that nutrients are tied up in rooted vegetation and not cycling efficiently through the food chain. A water clarity level of 18 to 24 inches is usually sufficient for phytoplankton populations and sight-feeding predators (e.g., largemouth bass). Turbidity is typically measured by using a Secchi disk. Productivity limits the carrying capacity of the water,

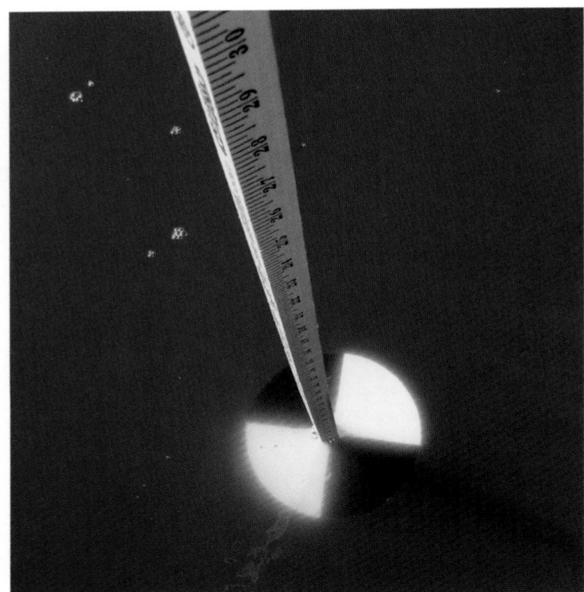
Secchi disk. Courtesy of Michael Masser

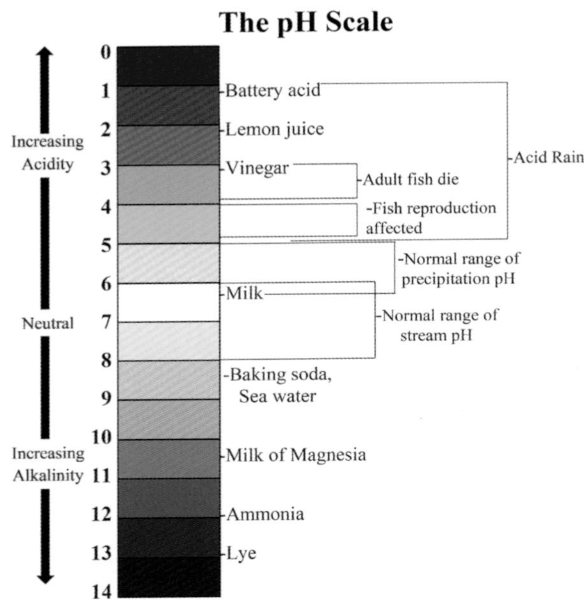

pH scale. Courtesy of Ashley Steinbach, intern, Texas A&M AgriLife Extension Service

which is the biomass of the organisms it can sustain. High-productivity waters have greater carrying capacities because they can sustain a greater mass of organisms.

pH

The **pH** is measured on a scale from 0 to 14, which measures acidity (hydrogen ions) and alkalinity (hydroxide ions) of water. A pH of 7 is neutral (balanced in H+ and OH– ions), above 7 is alkaline (or basic), and below 7 is acidic. The pH scale is logarithmic, which means that a pH change of 1 point is a 10-fold increase or decrease in acidity or alkalinity. The pH is equal to $-\log_{10}c$, where c is the hydrogen ion concentration in moles per liter. Fresh waters generally have a pH between 6 and 10. The pH of water is not static and changes or cycles daily. Changes in the pH of a body of water occur during a 24-hour cycle because of respiration and photosynthesis. Carbon dioxide from respiration (particularly at night) reacts with water to form carbonic acid (releases H+). Carbonic acid drives pH downward, making the water more acidic. During the daytime, pH tends to move upward (the water becomes more alkaline) because the carbon dioxide is removed by plants for photosynthesis and the oxygen produced by the plants again bonds with the free hydrogen ions to form water.

The pH of the water is strongly influenced by the pH of the rocks and soils in the watershed and the accumulation of organic matter in the mud. Water bodies in areas with certain mining activities (e.g., coal) can receive acidic drainage, causing the water to have a very low pH. Often pH influenced by mine drainage can be in the range of 4 to 6. In areas with very thin and acidic soils, acid rain can lower pH in water bodies in a similar way to mine drainage. The pH of a body of water can be modified by adding lime, gypsum, alum, bicarbonate, and certain other chemicals, as discussed later.

Alkalinity and Hardness

Alkalinity is a measure of bases in water. These bases include hydroxides (OH–), carbonates ($C03^{-2}$), and bicarbonates ($HC03^{-}$). Alkalinity is related to, but not the same as, pH. Alkaline bases act as buffers to absorb hydrogen ions and resist or stabilize pH changes. **Hardness** is a measure of divalent (+2) ions, mostly calcium and magnesium.

In chemical tests, both alkalinity and hardness are measured in parts per million (ppm) of calcium carbonate equivalence, which leads many people to think that they are the same. If alkalinity and hardness are both derived from limestone soils, then they usually have similar values. It is possible, however, to have water that is high in alkalinity and low in hardness, and vice versa.

Primary productivity can be enhanced if the alkalinity and hardness are maintained above 20 ppm. Alkalinity can be increased by adding agricultural limestone, hydrated lime, quick lime, sodium bicarbonate, or sodium hydroxide. Generally, agricultural lime is the least expensive and most predictable chemical to adjust alkalinity.

Hardness can also be increased by the addition of agricultural limestone, hydrated lime, quick lime, gypsum, or calcium chloride. For ponds low in hardness but high in alkalinity (typical of Texas ponds filled or supplemented with well water from the Wilcox strata), gypsum can be added to balance the difference. Calcium is an essential element in muscle and nerve physiology, development of cell membranes and bones, and many other important metabolic functions. Low hardness (<20 ppm) can hinder egg development, causing fish eggs to die after spawning.

More information on these water quality factors can be found in Southern Regional Aquaculture Center (SRAC) and Texas Agricultural Extension Service (TAEX) publications (Wurts and Durborow 1992; Masser and Jensen 1991; Stone et al. 2013; Lock and Davis 1986).

Fish eggs. Courtesy of Todd Sink

Dissolved Oxygen

Dissolved oxygen is probably the single most important water quality factor. Low dissolved oxygen is by far the most common cause of fish kills. Water obtains oxygen from two sources: diffusion from the air and photosynthesis by aquatic plants and algae. Atmospheric oxygen diffuses into water from the air. Diffusion is a slow process but can be aided by the action of wind or some type of agitation that mixes air and water together (e.g., waterfalls, riffles, and aerators).

Oxygen dissolves in water at very low concentrations. Our atmosphere is 20% oxygen, or 200,000 ppm (or milligrams per liter [mg/L]). However, seldom will a body of water have more than 10 ppm dissolved oxygen. Oxygen simply does not dissolve well in water. Dissolved oxygen concentrations below 3 ppm stress most warm-water species of fish (5 ppm for cold-water species), and concentrations below 2 ppm for prolonged periods will kill many species and larger fish. Also, many fish that have been stressed

Waterfalls agitate water to speed up diffusion of atmospheric oxygen into the water. Courtesy of Todd Sink

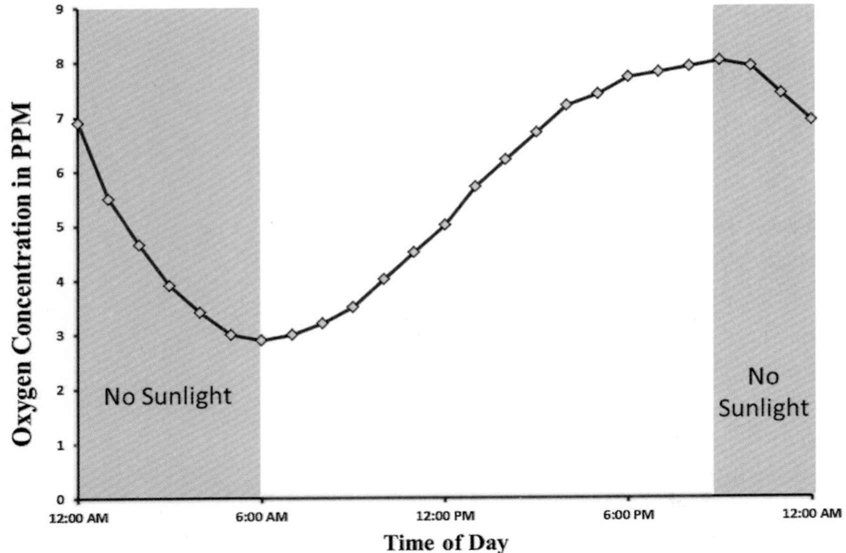

Dissolved 03 daily cycle for ponds during warm weather.

by low dissolved oxygen concentrations will become susceptible to diseases. Dissolved oxygen in the range of 1 to 2 ppm will kill many, if not all, large fish, depending on the duration.

The primary source of oxygen for lentic water bodies is microscopic algae or phytoplankton. Submerged rooted plants also produce oxygen, but not in the high quantities that phytoplankton produces. In the presence of sunlight, algae and submerged plants produce oxygen through photosynthesis and release this oxygen into the water. At night and on very cloudy days, algae consume oxygen from the water for respiration. In lotic or stream environments, oxygen concentrations are more stable because the moving water is constantly mixing and dissolving oxygen from the atmosphere.

At night, no oxygen is produced through photosynthesis, and the respiration of the algae, higher plants (macrophytes), fish, and the decomposers (bacteria and other microorganisms) consumes oxygen from the water. Thus, dissolved oxygen cycles up and down daily with photosynthesis and respiration. This explains why the oxygen concentration in a lotic system is lowest just prior to dawn and why most low dissolved-oxygen fish kills occur between 4:00 a.m. and 7:00 a.m. Under normal conditions, more oxygen is produced by photosynthesis than is removed by respiration. The figure shows a general oxygen cycle for ponds during warm-weather conditions.

Cold water holds, or will dissolve, more oxygen than warm water. Therefore, as temperature increases, less oxygen will dissolve and is present in the water. The amount of oxygen that water will dissolve at different temperatures (saturation) and sea-level atmospheric pressure varies from 14.6 ppm at 32°F (0°C) to 10.0 ppm at 80°F (27°C), and 6.93 ppm at 95°F (35°C). Water bodies can supersaturate with oxygen on sunny days when algal populations are very dense (heavy bloom). Very high concentrations of oxygen (twice saturation) during the day indicate that an oxygen depletion might occur that night.

Critically low dissolved-oxygen concentrations can usually be predicted. Low dissolved-oxygen levels occur because of one of the following reasons:

- too many pounds of fish present
- seasonal variation: higher water temperatures result in the water holding less oxygen
- extremely high oxygen demands caused by high nighttime respiration as a result of dense algal blooms or dense stands of submerged vegetation plus fish and waste decomposition
- excessive decomposition from algae bloom or aquatic macrophyte die-offs, sometimes associated with aquatic weed control efforts
- turnovers related to weather changes such as rain, wind, and cold air (lotic environments only)
- reduced oxygen production from photosynthesis because of reduced sunlight from cloud cover, fog, or haze
- lack of agitation from wind or waves

Most low-oxygen problems occur during the summer when temperatures are warm, algae blooms or submerged macrophytes

Algal bloom. Courtesy of Todd Sink

are dense, and aquatic organisms' metabolic rates are high. All of these conditions can cause more oxygen to be removed from the water body at night than is produced during the day. Also, still and overcast days may reduce the amount of dissolved oxygen absorbed by wave action or produced by photosynthesis. This condition may promote an oxygen depletion. Fish kills from oxygen depletions can range from "partial" to "total." In a partial kill, the dissolved-oxygen concentration gets low enough to suffocate sensitive species and larger fish, but many small fish and hardy species survive. Most oxygen depletions cause partial fish kills. Total fish kills are relatively rare.

Nitrogen Wastes

All animals produce nitrogenous wastes from the digestion and metabolism of proteins in their diet. Ammonia is the principal nitrogen waste product of aquatic animals. It is excreted directly into the water from the gills and kidneys of fish or other aquatic organisms. Ammonia is toxic at high concentrations to most aquatic organisms. Ammonia is also produced from bacterial decomposition of the proteins from dead animal or plant matter, including algae.

Algae, macrophytes, or bacteria quickly absorb ammonia once it is released into the water. Algae and certain bacteria use ammonia as a nutrient for growth and reproduction. Certain aerobic (oxygen-requiring) bacteria use ammonia as a food source in a process called **nitrification**, an important process by which toxic nitrogenous wastes are decomposed.

Nitrification

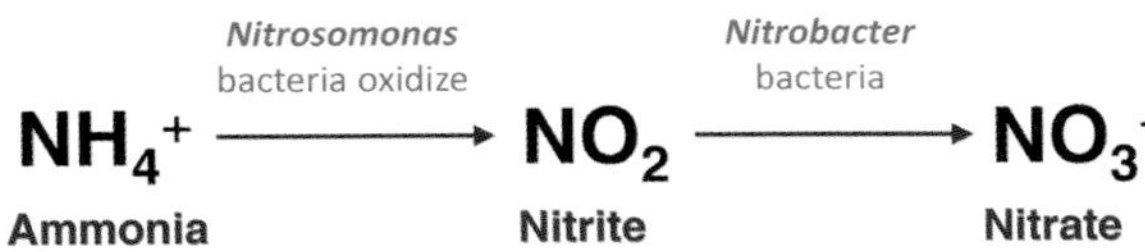

Nitrification diagram. Courtesy of Christine Kolbe

During nitrification, bacteria of the genus *Nitrosomonas* convert (oxidize) ammonia to nitrite, and bacteria of the genus *Nitrobacter* convert nitrite to nitrate. Ammonia and nitrite are both toxic to some species of fish; nitrate is not. Ammonia in water dissolves into two compounds: ionized (NH_4 +) ammonium and un-ionized (NH_3) ammonia. Un-ionized ammonia is extremely toxic to fish and most other aquatic organisms, while ionized ammonia is relatively nontoxic. Un-ionized ammonia levels as low as 0.4 ppm can cause death of small fish. Reduced growth and tissue damage can occur at as little as 0.06 ppm.

The ratio of the total ammonia nitrogen (TAN) in the un-ionized form depends on temperature and pH. The amount of toxic un-ionized ammonia increases as temperature and pH increase. Under good water quality conditions, ammonia is seldom a problem. Ammonia can become a serious problem, however, if

- overfeeding or overfertilizing is common
- a sudden algal/phytoplankton or macrophyte die-off occurs
- excessive amounts of manure from livestock washes into the water body
- a high afternoon pH drives the un-ionized ammonia concentration to a toxic level

High ammonia levels can occur at any time of the year, but they are most likely during the summer because of higher metabolic rates. Managing high ammonia levels is difficult to impossible.

Nitrite is also toxic to some species of fish and other aquatic organisms. Under normal conditions, nitrite does not accumulate to toxic levels because it is rapidly absorbed by algae bacteria, or macrophytes. Nitrite can reach toxic levels if bacterial decomposition (nitrification) is disrupted in small impoundments, especially those with high feeding or manure inputs. Most nitrite problems occur during fall and winter when sudden changes in water temperatures disrupt normal bacterial conversion. Nitrite poisoning is also referred to as "brown blood disease" since the blood of infected fish is a brownish rather than reddish color.

Temperature, dissolved oxygen, and chloride ions affect nitrite toxicity. A nitrite concentration as low as 0.5 ppm can cause stress in some species of fish. Nitrite toxicity is reduced in waters with chloride ion concentrations of greater than 30 ppm. This chloride level is fairly common in many Texas waters because of the marine-based geology of the rocks and soils. In low-chloride waters experiencing high nitrite levels, non-iodized stock salt can be added to increase chloride levels to reduce the effects of nitrites.

Salinity

Salinity is typically measured in parts per thousand (ppt). Full-strength seawater is 35 ppt salt. In Texas many wells, streams, and rivers suffer from salt intrusion. Again, this salt is a remnant of rocks and soils derived from marine sediments when much of Texas was a seabed. Salinity below 2 ppt can be tolerated by most species of freshwater fish and invertebrates. Some freshwater fish species can tolerate 15 to 20 ppt salinity. Low salinity levels (0.5 to 3.0 ppt) actually reduce osmotic stress in freshwater fish. Many aquatic plants can also tolerate low levels of salinity (<2 ppt), but not all. Salinity can be managed only by introducing fresh water to the water body, which may not be practical.

Phosphorus

Phosphorus is an essential element for plant growth. The amount of phosphorus often regulates primary productivity in a body of water. Some phosphorus enters bodies of water in runoff from the watershed and in groundwater from the dissolution of phosphorus in rocks. Phosphorus can exist in several chemical forms, but the soluble orthophosphate is most available to aquatic plants. Concentrations of total phosphorus are usually very low in water bodies and seldom exceed 0.1 ppm. The fate of most phosphorus is to end up in the mud.

Phosphorus precipitates out of the water column and is absorbed by aerobic muds. The rate of this absorption depends on acidity and/or calcium carbonate content. As pH and calcium carbonate concentrations increase, so does the rate of phosphorus absorption. Again, much of Texas has soil derived from limestone, which has high calcium carbonate concentrations and relatively high pH. Some phosphorus redissolves into the water but usually is insufficient to maintain algal blooms. Rooted aquatic macrophytes can absorb phosphorus directly from the water or from the mud. Research has shown that primary productivity can be increased through the addition of phosphate fertilizers. Many private impoundment managers use high-phosphorus fertilizers to increase primary productivity and thus fish biomass.

Ecology: How Do Aquatic Ecosystems Work?

Lentic systems are often classified based on nutrient inputs and cycling. The process of change from nutrient poor to nutrient rich is called **eutrophication**. Nutrient-poor lakes are classified as **oligotrophic**. Typically these lakes have low input of nutrients from their watersheds (particularly phosphorus), inorganic sediments, a small surface-to-volume ratio (i.e., deep), and low productivity. Oligotrophic lakes are generally clear, blue-water lakes with low dissolved-oxygen demands, low rates of decomposition, and low total biomass or numbers of organisms. Typically, oligotrophic lakes are found in areas dominated by primary rocks (e.g., igneous). Today no reservoir in Texas is considered oligotrophic. As nutrients increase, particularly phosphorus, lakes are classified as mesotrophic. **Mesotrophic** lakes tend to have moderate inputs of nutrients from their watersheds, some organic buildup in the sediments, and moderate productivity. Texas Hill Country reservoirs such as Travis, Canyon, and Medina are considered mesotrophic.

As nutrients increase further, lakes become eutrophic. **Eutrophic** lakes tend to be shallow and have high nutrients, high organic sediments, and green water (high phytoplankton content). Eutrophic lakes have high dissolved-oxygen demands, high rates of decomposition, and high total biomass of aquatic organisms. Rita Blanca, Mitchell, and Texana are eutrophic reservoirs in Texas.

Most private impoundments in Texas are classified as mesotrophic or eutrophic because of their relatively shallow and nutrient-enriched nature. Again, some reservoirs in the Hill Country that are relatively deep, are low in organic sediments, and receive moderate nutrient input are considered mesotrophic.

All lentic systems undergo eutrophication as part of natural succession. Eventually, all reservoirs and ponds fill with sediment, becoming wetlands and eventually dry land. The natural process of eutrophication is accelerated by human activities like mining, farming, and urban development. The moving water of lotic systems strongly influences the characteristics of their ecology. Lotic systems fluctuate widely and rapidly in volume of stream flow and input of nutrients because of substrate and inflow differences. Flooding and drought strongly influence stream flow rates and nutrient inputs, as do cultural uses of the watershed. The slope or grade of a stream influences its erosion and siltation characteristics.

Streams with steep slopes have high flow rates, are relatively straight with rapids and waterfalls, and tend to erode banks and cut deeper, but narrower channels. As stream slope moderates, flow rates are reduced, heavier sediments drop out or are deposited, and the stream forms bends or meanders. Often these meanders are cut off from the main stream because of flooding and deposition and form **oxbow** lakes.

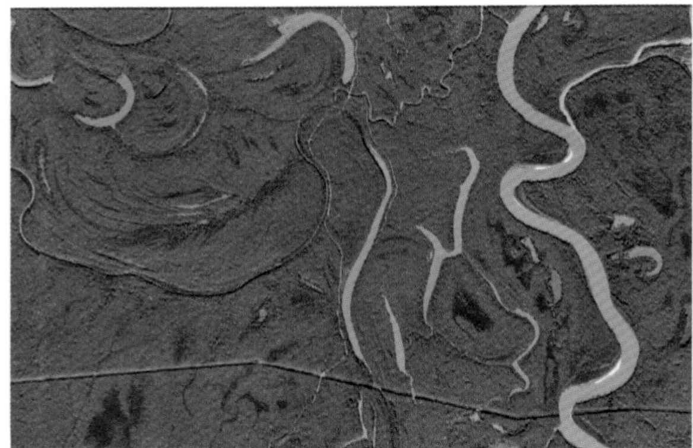

Oxbow lakes. Courtesy of Todd Sink

When the stream/river reaches relatively flat slopes, its velocity is greatly reduced; it spreads out and deposits much of its sediment. Flood events cause the stream to overflow its banks and deposit sediment in the **floodplain**. People have extensively utilized floodplains for agriculture and settlement because of their deep, nutrient-rich soils. When a stream flows into a lake or the ocean, the remaining sediment drops out, forming a fan-shaped **delta**. Most Texas reservoirs are constructed on stream or river courses and therefore trap large amounts of sediments from the upstream watershed. This sediment not only reduces the volume of the reservoir but also introduces nutrients, which accelerate eutrophication.

A hydroelectric generator on Chickamauga Dam in Tennessee. Courtesy of Todd Sink

As a result of the constant input of nutrients from the watershed and their transportation downstream along with some organisms, particularly during floods, streams are highly dynamic systems. Stream temperatures tend to be moderate, and dissolved oxygen and carbon dioxide concentrations tend to be relatively stable and high, except in very deep pools during low flow or because of pollution. Deep water can go stagnant in low flows and have low dissolved-oxygen problems (i.e., depletions). Pollution (e.g., organics) decomposing in a deep pool can also cause dissolved-oxygen depletions during low flows. These conditions increase productivity to the point that most streams are 6 to 30 times more productive than lentic waters.

In Texas there are 212 major reservoirs. Most were impounded for water supply, electrical generation, or flood control. Impounding streams dramatically alters their ecology and hydrology. Reservoirs trap nutrients and sediments that were previously transported downstream and alter flow patterns. Basically, impoundments replace a lotic system with one more lentic in nature. Most aquatic organisms adapted to lotic environments cannot tolerate static water conditions and are eliminated or severely reduced in reservoirs. Downstream of reservoirs water flows can fluctuate radically from high flows during peak hydroelectric generation, or high releases during flood events, to little or no flow during off-peak hours or drought conditions. These abnormal flow patterns adversely impact many lotic fish and invertebrate species. For this reason, today many reservoirs are operated to provide a minimum stream flow at all times in an effort to provide critical habitat conditions for lotic organisms.

Aquatic Flora

Aquatic flora includes a wide variety of plants from microscopic algae to large trees

Well-flowing stream. Courtesy of Todd Sink

(e.g., cypress). Generally, aquatic plants are divided into four groups: algae, floating, submerged, and emergent. **Algae** are primitive plants that do not flower or produce seeds but reproduce asexually or through spore production. Most other aquatic plants are angiosperms (flowering plants). **Floating** aquatic plants include only those that completely float (roots and all). **Submerged** plants have flaccid stems and are usually rooted to the bottom. **Emergent** or shoreline plants have relatively rigid stems. Most submerged and all emergent plants inhabit only the littoral zone, while planktonic algae, true floating plants, and some submerged plants such as hydrilla and Eurasian watermilfoil can inhabit the limnetic zone.

Some aquatic plants have mechanisms that allow them to transport oxygen from the atmosphere throughout the plant and thus survive anaerobic water or soil conditions. Many aquatic plants have no cuticle, as terrestrial plants do, and thus can easily absorb gases and nutrients directly from the water. Many rooted aquatic macrophytes are perennials and have rhizomes, tubers, or stolons (underground stem/root systems), which store food reserves and resprout or root to form new plants. Most floating aquatic plants have waxy surfaces to shed water and keep their stomata open (open-

A cattail is an emergent plant.

Water hyacinth (*Eichhornia crassipes*), an invasive species. Courtesy of Todd Sink

Giant salvinia (*Salvinia molesta*), an invasive species. Courtesy of Michael Masser

Hydrilla (*Hydrilla* spp.), an invasive species. Courtesy of Texas Parks and Wildlife Department

ings in the leaves for gas exchange with the atmosphere). Often floating and emergent aquatic plants transpire large amounts of water to the atmosphere and can contribute to increased water loss from rivers, ponds, and reservoirs.

In small private impoundments (which number well over one million in Texas alone), with their relatively shallow depths and usually high nutrient inputs, native aquatic plants can take over large areas, reducing access and impacting fishing, swimming, and other activities. However, in large public water bodies it is usually nonnative (i.e., exotic) plants that are problematic. These nonnative species have been released into or have invaded our environment without any of their native diseases, herbivores, or other controlling factors. Without any natural checks and balances, these plants can invade and infest large areas, restricting navigation, recreation, irrigation, and other societal uses.

Nonnative aquatic plants that are currently a problem in Texas include hydrilla, water hyacinth, salvinia (giant and common), giant reed, and Eurasian watermilfoil. In 2001, a Texas Parks and Wildlife survey showed that 90 public rivers and reservoirs were infested with hydrilla, 30 with water hyacinth, 19 with Eurasian watermilfoil, and 9 with salvinia. Certain plants such as golden algae produce toxins that can lead to fish kills. Golden algae blooms typically occur during the cooler months in higher-pH and more saline public and private freshwater impoundments of the state. Certain blue-green algae (cyanobacteria) can also produce toxins that may be toxic to wildlife and livestock that drink from impoundments with heavy blooms during the summer months. For more information on aquatic plants, visit the AQUAPLANT website at http://aquaplant.tamu.edu.

Aquatic Fauna

Aquatic ecosystems also support a large and diverse group of animals (fauna), including microscopic zooplankton, worms, fish, reptiles, birds, and mammals. Like aquatic flora, most aquatic fauna have special mechanisms to survive in aquatic environments, such as mechanisms for reproduction, respiration, movement, food gathering, and many other vital functions. Because water is dense, aquatic animals use more energy to move through water than land animals use to move through the atmosphere. Therefore, most aquatic animals are streamlined and have surfaces that reduce friction or repel water (e.g., ducks). Also, because of the aquatic environment, internal fertilization is unnecessary, and most aquatic animals simply release sperm and eggs into the water, where fertilization and incubation occur (excluding aquatic reptiles, birds, and mammals).

Stream invertebrates often have adaptations for clinging to the surface of rocks or vegetation or for burrowing into the sediment. Fish that must swim fast to chase prey (e.g., pelagic predators like white bass) or fight strong currents (e.g., trout) must be more streamlined than fish that inhabit slow-moving or stagnant waters (e.g., sunfish). Mammals and birds that inhabit aquatic environments often have webbed feet and specialized organs for capturing prey (e.g., beaks of cormorants). Again, not all aquatic fauna are native. Nonnative species problematic in Texas waters include zebra mussels, nutria, common carp, tilapia, and apple snails. These species often outcompete, replace, or alter the environment of native species.

Zebra mussel, an invasive species. Courtesy of Texas Parks and Wildlife Department

Aquatic Food Chains

Basically, all food chains, whether terrestrial or aquatic, begin with plants. Plants and a few chemosynthetic bacteria capture energy from sunlight and manufacture food. A **food chain** is the transfer of this food energy, starting with plants, through a series of organisms (bacteria to animals) eating one another. In ecological terms, green plants and chemosynthetic bacteria are called **primary producers**.

All other life forms are **consumers**. Consumers are subdivided into groups such as **primary consumers** or herbivores, which consume plants directly; **secondary consumers** or carnivores, which consume animals (which eat plants); **omnivores**, which consume both plant and animal matter; **parasites**, which consume tissues of another living creature (usually without killing it); and **detritivores**, which consume dead or decaying organic matter. Food chains can have secondary carnivores that consume other carnivores. Many species of fish are secondary carnivores (e.g., largemouth bass and pike).

Generally, food chains are no longer than four or five sequential steps or links. The shorter the food chain, or the nearer the organism is to the start of it, the greater the amount of overall energy available. Available energy is converted into biomass or living tissue. So, increased energy means increased biomass. Herbivores are closer to the start of the food chain and therefore have more available energy and greater biomass than carnivores. Often animals near the start of the food chain are said to feed "low on the food chain." In general terms, as one animal consumes another, about 10% of the energy is converted to biomass and 90% is lost or used in metabolism. For example, a fish such as a largemouth bass must consume 8 to 10 pounds of prey to

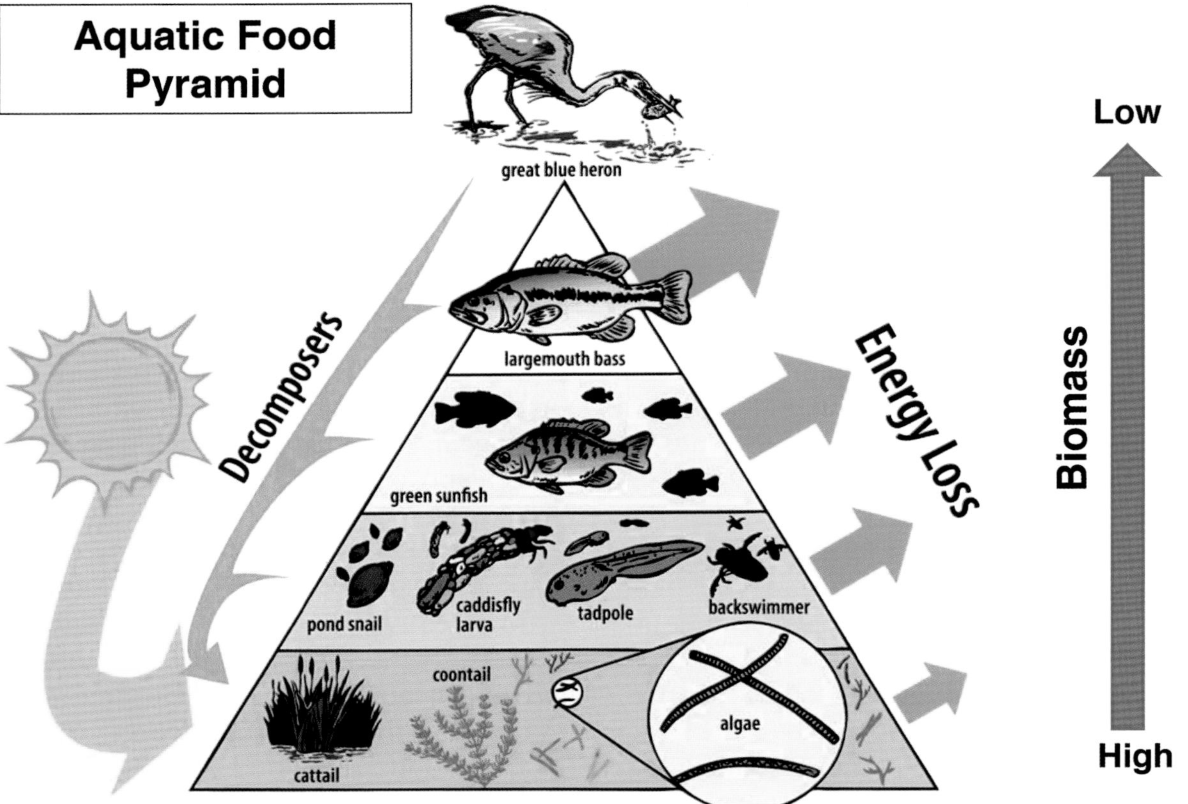

Aquatic food pyramid. Graphic with modifications courtesy of Texas Aquatic Science partners: Texas Parks and Wildlife Department, The Meadows Center for Water and the Environment, and the Harte Research Institute for Gulf of Mexico Studies. Courtesy of Christine Kolbe

gain one pound. Food chains are not independent of each other but form an interconnected **food web**. Food webs are usually extremely complex, involving a multitude of organisms.

In fresh water, all food chains start with algae, chemosynthetic bacteria, or higher vascular plants. Algae are by far the most important primary producers in aquatic food chains. Aquatic herbivores are generally either free-floating near microscopic animals (e.g., zooplankton), or insects, crustaceans, mollusks, or worms. Zooplankton, insects, and crustaceans are by far the most important primary consumers in aquatic food chains. A few native North American fish are omnivorous, but none are strictly herbivorous. In fresh water, the major food chain is detrital based: little direct herbivory takes place; the major energy pathway is from detritus. The primary consumers of detritus are bacteria, fungi, protozoans, worms (annelids and nematodes), mollusks, insects, crustaceans, and some species of fish (e.g., common carp and buffalo).

The Chickamauga Dam on the Tennessee River. Courtesy of Todd Sink

Management: How Do We Mimic Natural Processes in Aquatic Systems?

First, it is important to remember that most Texas rivers and streams have been modified (dammed) for cultural purposes, which can include water supply (human, animal, and irrigation), navigation, hydroelectric power, flood control, pollution abatement, recreation, or fish and wildlife habitat. Most impoundments, whether public or private, have more than one purpose, and management must reflect the desired uses. Therefore, possibly the most important question is, What are we managing for?

Watershed Management

It should be obvious from the previous discussions that siltation, water quality, and other critical factors are influenced by the watershed, whether it is a lentic or lotic system. Therefore, any aquatic management strategy must include watershed management, including the following strategies:

- establishing better vegetation cover
- reducing nutrient inputs
- reducing livestock and agricultural impacts
- creating a riparian buffer

Often clay turbidity or muddiness is caused by exposed soils in the watershed. Establishing vegetation in the watershed to cover exposed soils can reduce or eliminate clay turbidity and reduce erosion and siltation. Usually native turfgrass establishment is the simplest way to reduce erosion in areas with full sun conditions. The size or width of turf needed to stop turbidity depends on conditions of watershed size, slope, and rainfall events. A minimum 50-

Erosion damage caused by livestock can be seen around ponds like this one throughout Texas when water access is poorly managed. Courtesy of Kay Ledbetter, Texas A&M AgriLife Extension Service

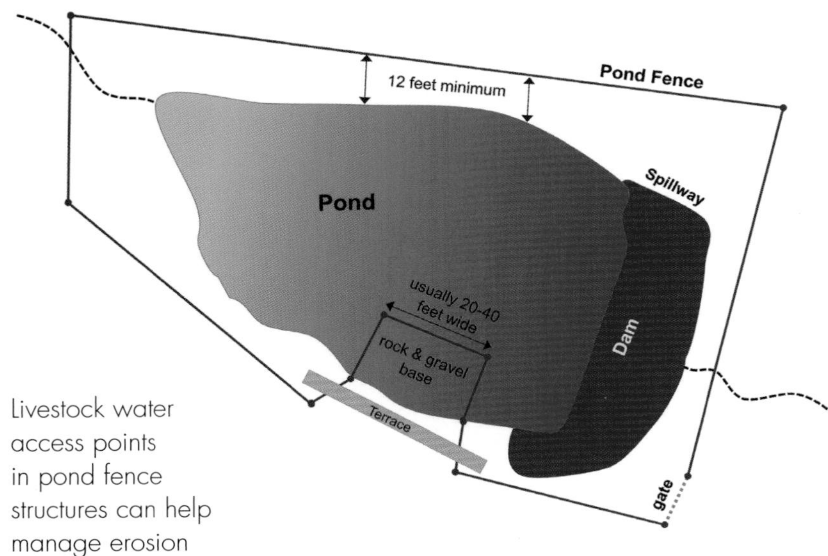

Livestock water access points in pond fence structures can help manage erosion along the pond banks. Courtesy of Christine Kolbe

foot buffer strip of turf is sufficient for most small impoundments in relatively small watersheds with gentle slopes. As the slope or size of a watershed increases, larger buffer strips of turf would be needed. In heavily wooded watersheds it may not be possible to establish turf or other ground vegetation to reduce erosion and consequent turbidity.

Turf buffers can also reduce nutrients entering ponds or streams from the watershed. Again, larger turf buffers are needed for greater slopes and larger runoff areas. In general, the larger the turf buffer, the greater the nutrient absorption. Nutrients can also be reduced by not applying fertilizers or manures within 30 feet of ponds or streams (a greater distance with increased slope).

Livestock trample turf around ponds or streams, leading to devegetation and erosion, which tends to produce shallow areas and turbidity. Shallow shorelines can encourage the invasion of unwanted aquatic vegetation. Livestock should be fenced from ponds and streams and provided with water troughs that are away from ponds or sensitive riparian areas. Where water troughs are not possible, livestock should be fenced from all but a small section of the pond or stream. The area selected for livestock access should have a gentle slope where runoff is limited. Access should not be on a pond dam. Often adding gravel to the access area will reduce livestock impacts.

Riparian buffers are usually associated with rivers or streams. They are simply

A riparian forest. Streamside forest cover serves many important functions, such as stabilizing stream banks and moderating diurnal stream temperatures. Courtesy of Todd Sink

zones along the borders of streams that are left intact with native vegetation adapted to riparian conditions. Again, these act as filters for nutrients, reduce erosion and siltation, and serve as wildlife habitat and migration corridors. A minimum width for a riparian buffer is 50 feet; wider ones are needed in areas of steep slopes or highly erodible soils. Where riparian buffers have been destroyed, native turfgrasses can be established to stop erosion and siltation. Over time, native woody and herbaceous riparian species may reestablish within this zone.

In order for the aquatic food chain to develop, some degree of water clarity is necessary for phytoplankton populations (the base of the food chain) to receive sunlight for photosynthesis. Ponds that are managed for sight-feeding fish species such as largemouth bass and bluegill should have 18 to 24 inches of visibility throughout most of the year to facilitate this process. Turbidity in ponds caused by suspended clay particles may require treatment with agricultural limestone, aluminum sulfate, or calcium sulfate to break their negative charges, which allows them to settle to the pond bottom.

Management of Private Impoundments

The following ingredients are essential for successful pond management for fishing and other recreational activities:

- pond construction and watershed management
- species selection and stocking
- elimination of unwanted and reduction of overpopulated species
- liming and possibly fertilization
- harvesting and record keeping
- maintenance of species balance
- management of aquatic vegetation

Many of these topics are beyond the scope of this discussion, but additional information on managing private impoundments for fishing can be found in Lock (1993) and Masser et al. (1999) and other publications on the Texas A&M AgriLife Extension Aquaculture, Fisheries, and Pond Management website.

Stocking

Species for **stocking** into private impoundments have been selected based on research. Ponds larger than one acre can be successfully managed for largemouth bass and sunfish. Ponds smaller than one acre should be managed for species that readily accept a pelleted ration and can be reared at high density, like channel or blue catfish, hybrid striped bass, and hybrid bluegill. Research has shown that bluegill sunfish can provide adequate forage (i.e., prey) for largemouth bass with no other species necessary. Bluegill are multiple spawners, providing adequate year-round forage for the bass. Bluegill feed low on the food chain and thus do not compete directly with bass for food. Catfish and redear sunfish also can be stocked along with bass and bluegill if desired. Most other species have some negative effects on bass fishing in the long term.

Liming

Liming (addition of powdered agricultural limestone) is necessary where soils are acidic (mostly East Texas) to increase nutrient release and thereby increase primary productivity. Ponds with a total alkalinity of less than 20 ppm will benefit from liming.

Fertilization

Fertilization can increase primary productivity where more fish production is desired and can increase fish production by four- to sixfold. Some ponds in nutrient-rich watersheds do not need fertilization. The purpose of fertilization is to stimulate planktonic algae and thus increase food through the natural food chain to the fish. Fertilization should not be initiated if an aquatic weed problem exists, as it will stimulate further weed growth. An added benefit of fertilization is to cloud the water, shading the bot-

A triploid grass carp, used as a biological control on submerged aquatic plants. Courtesy of Texas Parks and Wildlife Department

tom, which suppresses the establishment of rooted aquatic vegetation, if the fertilization program can be initiated prior to weed growth or immediately after chemical weed treatment. Muddy ponds, ponds with a total alkalinity of less than 20 ppm, and ponds with a constant water flow exiting the pond should not be fertilized. Supplemental feeding of forage fish with a pelleted ration will increase their growth and reproduction and indirectly benefit the largemouth bass population by providing a greater biomass of forage.

Harvesting and Record Keeping

Harvesting and **record keeping** are extremely important in pond management. Most ponds are not properly harvested (if at all) because of the perception that small fish will continue to grow. Fish do not grow unless they have adequate food. The presence of many small fish, particularly bass, means that they do not have enough to eat. This situation, called "crowding" or "stunting," is very common. Usually, bass stunt between 8 and 13 inches in length. When large numbers of bass this size are encountered, harvesting is critical to bass population recovery if the goal is to produce larger bass. Otherwise, stunted bass populations produce plentiful fishing action and can also result in very large sunfish, which are highly desired by many anglers. Generally, about 10 pounds of bass can be removed per acre per year in unfertilized ponds, and 25 to 35 pounds per acre per year in well-fertilized ponds; note that the majority of harvested bass should be in the 8- to 13-inch range.

Therefore, pond owners can have a direct impact on the desired bass population size structure. For a trophy bass fishery, considerable fishing pressure may be needed to reduce the population of largemouth bass less than 12, 14, or even 16 inches. Over time, this practice results in fewer but larger bass, provided good water quality and adequate forage are present.

Bluegill can also stunt, usually in the 3- to 4-inch size range. Stunted bluegill usually indicate the absence of largemouth bass, which can consume only bluegill that are less than one-third of their total length (e.g., 15-inch largemouth bass can consume bluegills up to 5 inches long). The addition of larger, 8- to 14-inch, largemouth bass usually corrects the problem. If stocked at sizes smaller than this, the small bass also have to compete with the bluegill for food rather than eat the bluegill and their offspring directly, and growth will be inhibited, resulting in delayed correction of the problem. If unwanted species (e.g., crappie, common carp, or bullheads) are present, then removal of all fish using the registered pesticide rotenone is necessary. After removal of the entire fish population, the pond should be restocked with appropriate fish species.

Aquatic Vegetation

Finally, the most common problem encountered in private impoundments is unwanted or nuisance **aquatic vegetation**. Most ponds are relatively shallow and accumulate nutrients over time. This is the ideal situation for aquatic vegetation, which often takes over the pond, rendering it unusable for its desired purposes. Aquatic vegetation can be controlled through mechanical, biological, or chemical (herbicides) means. Mechanical control tends to be extremely time consuming, laborious, tedious, and a repetitious endeavor and rarely, if ever, leads to a lasting control of the vegetation.

Therefore, most pond owners are unwilling to practice mechanical control. Biological control of submerged aquatic plants can be accomplished in Texas using triploid grass carp. A permit from the Texas Parks and Wildlife Department is necessary before these fish can be purchased from a certified triploid grass carp provider with an exotic species permit and stocked into private Texas waters.

Federal and state laws closely regulate chemical or herbicide application. Only a handful of herbicides are registered by the US Environmental Protection Agency for use in aquatic vegetation control. Correct identification of the aquatic plant and selection and application of the registered herbicide are critical for chemical control to be successful. In addition, the Texas Commission on Environmental Quality (TCEQ) also has regulations regarding the use of certain herbicides and the area to be treated in private aquatic environments. For additional information on identification and control of aquatic plants, visit the AQUAPLANT website at http://aquaplant.tamu.edu.

Management of Rivers and Streams

Most streams, unless intermittent, are considered public waters and therefore cannot be altered without permission of state or national regulatory agencies. However, riparian areas around streams can be managed to entrain nutrients, reduce erosion and stabilize banks, and encourage wildlife. As previously discussed, maintaining a riparian buffer at least 50 feet wide and encouraging native riparian vegetation are good management practices along stream corridors.

There are methods to assess stream quality by analyzing water quality and macroinvertebrate populations. **Macroinvertebrates** (insects, mollusks, crustaceans, and worms) can be barometers of stream health. Macroinvertebrates like stonefly larvae, mayfly larvae, caddisfly larvae, and certain snail species are indicators of unpolluted streams. Crayfish, dragonfly larvae, blackfly larvae, cranefly larvae, and hellgrammites are organisms that tolerate a wide variety of conditions and endure some pollution. Macroinvertebrates such as midge larvae and tubifex worms generally tolerate polluted conditions. So by collecting, classifying, and establishing relative abundance of various species of macroinvertebrates, stream quality can be determined. The US EPA has developed protocols for sampling macroinvertebrates to determine stream health (http://water.epa.gov/scitech/monitoring/rsl/bioassessment/ch07main.cfm).

Threats to Aquatic Systems

Human activities are the main threats to aquatic systems. As the human population continues to increase, the increased demand for natural resources, particularly water, will affect aquatic systems. As previously discussed, human impacts include removal

A mayfly larva, and indicator of an unpolluted stream. Courtesy of Michael Masser

and transfer of water, pollution (both point and nonpoint source), erosion, siltation, and introduction of nonnative, noxious species. Nutrient pollution, erosion, and siltation are particularly acute in public waters because of current land-use patterns.

"Unfortunately, our affluent society has also been an effluent society."
—Hubert Humphrey, speech at Gannon College,1966

Conclusion

People have little or no natural intuition about the aquatic environment. We have the perception that water should be clear because we want to see into it. Yet clear water in ponds and reservoirs usually indicates low primary productivity and therefore supports fewer numbers of aquatic organisms. While native aquatic plants can benefit many species of aquatic invertebrates, amphibians, reptiles, fish, birds, and mammals, they can infest at such high densities that they become detrimental to many of these aquatic organisms, especially in private ponds. This is particularly true of invasive, nonnative, aquatic weed species. So, the aquatic environment is not always what we perceive and must be studied carefully to be understood. This unit has been an attempt to lay a foundation for an understanding of aquatic ecology. This foundation can be expanded through further examination of extension and scientific literature.

References

Lock, Joe T. 1993. *Management of Recreational Fish Ponds in Texas.* Texas Agricultural Extension Service Publication B-213. College Station, TX. http://www.agrilifebookstore.org/Management-of-Recreational-Fish-Ponds-in-Texas-p/b-213.htm

Lock, Joe, and James Davis. 1986. *Liming Farm Fish Ponds in East Texas.* TAEX Publication L-864. http://wildlife.tamu.edu/files/2010/04/4_Liming_Farm_Fish_Ponds.pdf.

Masser, Michael P., and John W. Jensen. 1991. *Calculating Treatments for Ponds and Tanks.* SRAC Publication No. 410. https://srac.tamu.edu/index.cfm/event/getFactSheet/whichfactsheet/83/.

Masser, Michael, Don Steinbach, and Billy Higginbotham. 1999. *Catfish Ponds for Recreation.* Texas Agricultural Extension Service Publication B-1319. http://2kjj1d3°dhc3296c07jhe511.wpengine.netdna-cdn.com/files/2013/10/Catfish-Ponds-for-Recreation.pdf.

Stone, Nathan, Jay Shelton, Brian Haggard, and Hugh Thomforde. 2013. *Interpretation of Water Analysis Reports for Fish Culture.* SRAC Publication No. 4606. https://srac.tamu.edu/index.cfm/event/getFactSheet/whichfactsheet/262/.

Wurts, William A., and Robert M. Durborow. 1992. *Interactions of pH, Carbon Dioxide, Alkalinity, and Hardness in Fish Ponds.* SRAC Publication No 464. https://srac.tamu.edu/index.cfm/event/getFactSheet/whichfactsheet/112/.

Additional Resources

Barnes, R. S. K., and K . H. Mann. 2009. *Fundamentals of Aquatic Ecology.* 2nd ed. Oxford: Blackwell Scientific Publications.

Dobson, M., and C. Frid. 2008. *Ecology of Aquatic Systems.* 2nd ed. Oxford: Oxford University Press.

Dodds, W. K., and M. R. Whiles. 2010. *Freshwater Ecology: Concepts and Environmental Applications of Limnology*. 2nd ed. New York: Academic Press.

Mays, L. W. 2012. *Ground and Surface Water Hydrology*. New York: Wiley Publications.

Thorp, J. H., and A. P. Covich. 2014. *Freshwater Invertebrates: Ecology and General Biology*. New York: Academic Press.

Wetzel, R. G. 2001. *Limnology*. 3rd ed. New York: Academic Press.

Website Resources

AQUAPLANT: http://aquaplant.tamu.edu

EPA Benthic Macroinvertebrate Protocols: http://water.epa.gov/scitech/monitoring/rsl/bioassessment/ch07main.cfm

Southern Regional Aquaculture Center: https://srac.tamu.edu/

Texas A&M AgriLife Extension Aquaculture, Fisheries, and Pond Management: http://fisheries.tamu.edu/

UNIT 19

Wetland Ecology and Management

JEFF RAASCH
State Wetland and Joint Venture Program Leader

With contributions from Texas Parks and Wildlife Department staff:
Anne Rogers, Water Quality Program Leader
Beth Bendik, Conservation Ecologist
Ryan McGillicuddy, Conservation Ecologist, Inland Fisheries Division
Matthew Symmank, Wildlife Biologist, Richland Creek WMA
Tom Hegar, Watershed Conservation Team Leader

Unit Goals

After completing this unit, volunteers should be able to

- explain what a wetland is
- know the types of wetlands
- describe the types of wetlands in Texas
- be familiar with the state and federal regulations affecting and governing wetlands conservation in Texas

Texas Wetlands: A Vanishing Resource

Wetlands are one of Texas' most valuable natural resources. Bottomland hardwood forests (river swamps), riparian corridors, coastal wetlands, and playa lakes are vital to maintaining our unequaled fish and wildlife resources. Wetlands provide flood protection, improve water quality, and provide the basis for other economic benefits totaling billions of dollars nationwide each year. It is estimated that Texas has lost over half of its original wetlands. Much of this loss has been in response to meeting our needs for food, fiber, housing, and industrial development, all of which are vital to maintaining the economic health of Texas. If we are to assure that same economic vitality and quality of life for the future, the citizens of Texas must work together now to conserve our remaining wetlands.

What Is a Wetland?

To know what to protect, we must first know what a wetland is. Wetlands are among the most important ecosystems on earth. They not only provide numerous products for human use and consumption but are invaluable as the "kidneys of the landscape" for their ability to purify polluted rivers, prevent and minimize flooding, protect shorelines, and replenish groundwater sources. Wetlands also provide valuable habitat to numerous species of fish and wildlife.

But what is a wetland? **Wetlands** are defined by the State of Texas as areas "including swamp, marsh, bog, prairie pothole, or similar area, having a predominance of hydric soils that are inundated or saturated by surface or groundwater at a frequency and duration sufficient to support, and that under normal circumstances do support, the growth and regeneration of hydrophytic vegetation" (Texas Administrative Code, n.d.). Simply stated, wetlands contain (1) water or saturated soils for at least part of the year,

(2) plants that have adapted to life in wet environments (hydrophytic vegetation), and (3) special soils that develop under depleted oxygen conditions (hydric soils).

Wetlands can be swamps, bottomland hardwood forests, marshes, bogs, springs, resacas (oxbow lakes), playa lakes, and saline (alkaline) lakes. Wetlands are found along rivers, streams, lakes, ponds, and coastlines; in upland depressions where surface water collects; and at points of groundwater discharge such as springs or seeps. They are found in both saltwater and freshwater systems, on every continent except Antarctica, and in every climate from the tropics to the tundra. As their name indicates, they are "wet land," since they are located in the transition zone between upland and open water. Both aquatic and upland plant and animal species may

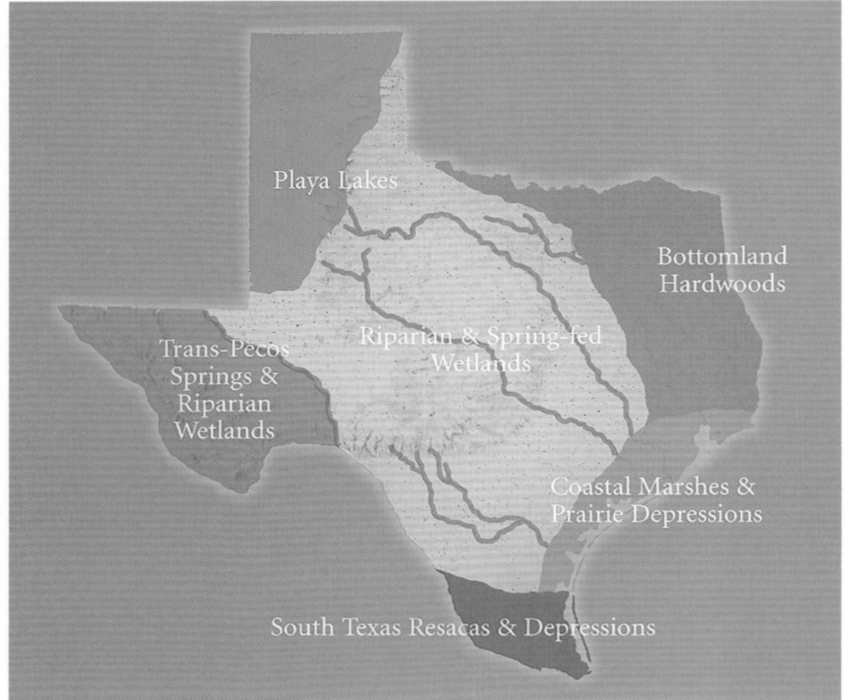

Wetland regions of Texas. Courtesy of Texas Parks and Wildlife Department

Bald cypress (*Taxodium distichum*), like this one in Caddo Lake, can be found in freshwater swamps and riparian areas in Central and East Texas. Courtesy of Texas Parks and Wildlife Department

Pitcher plant bogs in East Texas are considered a special management area for the US Forest Service, as the diversity of vegetation in these wetland bogs is high. Courtesy of Texas Parks and Wildlife Department

therefore depend on wetlands for their survival.

"Three parameters are used to define wetlands:
- *Hydrology*
- *Soils*
- *Vegetation"*

—Jeff Raasch, Robert Spain, Larry D. McKinney, and Andrew D. Sansom, *Wetlands Assistance Guide for Landowners*

"Coastal wetlands in Texas provide some of the most important wintering and migration areas in North America for waterfowl using the Central and Mississippi flyways"
—Jeff Raasch, Robert Spain, Larry D. McKinney, and Andrew D. Sansom, *Wetlands Assistance Guide for Landowners*

Brown pelican (*Pelecanus occidentalis*) is a common migratory bird that frequents Texas coastal wetlands during the warm months of the year. Courtesy of Texas Parks and Wildlife Department

Why Are Wetlands Important?

It is now widely recognized that wetlands provide a variety of ecological functions beneficial both to the natural ecosystem and to humans. The functions that benefit humans are also known as ecosystem services, which are typically protected through regulation under legislation such as the Clean Water Act and protect the resource for both humans and wildlife. Some ecosystem services provided by wetlands include

- flood control
- erosion control
- groundwater recharge or discharge
- removal of sediment and toxicants/water quality improvement
- removal or transformation of nutrients
- commercial uses (e.g., shellfishing or timber)
- fish and wildlife habitat
- outdoor recreation/education

Not all wetlands provide all functions and services, and each wetland is unique. Several of these ecosystem services are particularly important in Texas.

Flood Control

Rivers, streams, and other wetlands form natural floodplain systems that play an invaluable role in offsetting flood damage by regulating and maintaining the hydrology in rivers and streams during flood events. The dense wetland vegetation reduces the velocity of floodwaters that travel through the system, which allows water to percolate into and be stored in the underlying soils. Over time, the floodwaters are slowly released back into the river or stream, the atmosphere, and the groundwater. By reducing the rate and amount of stormwater entering the river or stream, wetlands lessen the destructiveness of the flood. In Wisconsin, a study demonstrated that a watershed composed of at least 30% wetlands could reduce floodwater levels by 60% to 80% compared to watersheds containing no wetlands (Sather and Smith 1984).

Erosion Control

Erosion of soils can be caused by increases in water velocities from upstream construction sites, unvegetated ground, or agricultural fields. Wetland vegetation provides an important buffer to adjacent bodies of water by filtering and holding sediments that would otherwise enter lakes and streams and eventually fill them.

An example of a diverted stream's erosion damage after the Bastrop State Park fires. Courtesy of Texas Parks and Wildlife Department

Groundwater Recharge

Many people depend on aquifers (underground reservoirs) for their water. In certain cases, wetlands help recharge or refill these groundwater supplies by allowing water to stand and be absorbed back underground. Riparian wetlands also help recharge shallow alluvial aquifers adjacent to streams, which slowly release water and sustain the baseflow of streams in drier portions of the year.

Socioeconomic Values

Wetlands are economically valuable because of the number of species that depend on them. We receive many economic benefits from maintaining our wetland areas. Some of these are directly measurable, such as the jobs created through commercial fishing, harvesting of fur-bearing animals, and forestry interests. Other values are not measured as easily. Tourist dollars associated with the ever-growing nature-tourism industry are continually increasing. Wetlands will continue to be used as important recreation areas for people to connect with each other as well as with nature.

Recreational fishermen on Caddo Lake, an example of values provided by wetlands. Courtesy of Texas Parks and Wildlife Department

Reduction of Water Pollution

Wetlands absorb and filter a variety of sediments, nutrients, and other natural and human-made pollutants that would otherwise degrade rivers, streams, and lakes. Water flowing from uplands into water bodies often passes through wetlands, which maintain and improve water quality by filtering out nutrients and sediments before they reach the river or stream. Wetlands lessen the effects of nonpoint source runoff into water bodies by reducing flow velocities and by acting as a sediment, nutrient, and heavy-metal trap. One study found that nitrogen and phosphorus retention in riparian forests were 89% and 80%, respectively, compared to 8% and 40% in cropland (Lowrance et al. 1997). Additionally, forested areas adjacent to rivers lower the water temperature in hot summer months, which reduces undesirable algal blooms that decrease water quality and can kill aquatic organisms. In estuaries, sediment can harm filter feeders such as oysters and also impedes sight-dependent feeders such as trout.

Wildlife Habitat

Wetlands provide essential nesting, migratory, and wintering areas for more than 50% of the country's migratory bird species. Texas is one of the most important waterfowl wintering areas in the Central Flyway and provides habitat for three to five million birds each year. The Central Flyway is a bird migration route that generally follows the Great Plains in the United States and Canada. Wetlands provide habitat for one-third of the federally listed endangered and threatened plant and animal species. Additional benefits include supplying important nursery and spawning habitat for 60% to 90% of the commercial fish species (Lellis-Dibble et al. 2008).

Recreation

Many recreational activities take place in and around wetlands, including hiking, waterfowl hunting, fishing, observing nature, and canoeing. Wetlands provide a multi-billion-dollar fishing, hunting, and outdoor recreation industry nationwide.

Mallards (*Anas platyrhynchos*) taking off from a lake along the Texas coast are year-round residents in certain areas. Courtesy of Texas Parks and Wildlife Department

Texas Wetland Types

What kinds of wetlands do we have in Texas? Wetlands in Texas are generally divided into two groups: coastal wetlands and freshwater wetlands. Coastal wetlands occur along coastal shorelines, shallow bays, swamps, marshes, mudflats, and deltas. They support plants and animals that have adapted to changes in salinity. Freshwater wetlands are dependent on rainfall, springs, rivers, and other water sources. Because many Texas freshwater wetlands become drier during our hot summers, plants and animals that can survive fluctuating water conditions do best here.

Riverbanks, streamsides, lakeshores, floodplains, bottomlands, marshes, ponds, and swamps make up freshwater wetlands. The state is divided into wetland regions according to climate. Described here are some of the more common types of wetlands in Texas.

East Texas

East Texas is dominated by **bottomland hardwood forest** ecosystems. These forests are characterized by broad-leaved (e.g., oak, elm, ash) and needle-leaved (e.g., cypress) deciduous plants that typically grow in creek and river floodplains. Not all bottomland hardwoods meet the wetland definition. Ridges, mounds, and terraces within the bottomland hardwood ecosystem are often located at a landscape position too high to remain flooded, ponded, or saturated long enough to meet wetland criteria. These higher areas typically support a very diverse forest with a mix of cherrybark oak, swamp chestnut oak, Shumard oak, water oak, sweetgum, sweet pecan, American elm, eastern red cedar, and loblolly pine.

Some areas of bottomland hardwood forests are too high in elevation and therefore do not receive the required flooding to support the types of plants that make up typical bottomland hardwood wetlands. A slight drop in landscape elevation will result in changes in species diversity in favor of those species that can tolerate longer periods of inundation and wetter soils. Typically, these transitional areas support willow oak, laurel oak, green ash, and cedar elm but are often dominated by one or two species. These transitional areas often meet the definition of wetlands. Another drop in landscape elevation and tree species diversity is reduced even more. These areas pond or flood for long durations and typically support water-tolerant species in monocultures of overcup oak, red maple, water elm (planar tree), or bald cypress, depending on site conditions.

Bottomland hardwood forest ecosystems contain a great variety of trees, shrubs, and vines that grow together in different vegetation assemblages, depending on soil type, water depth, velocity, and flood duration. Bottomland hardwood forests in Texas support over 180 species of trees. Characteristic herbaceous species include sedges, arrowheads, smartweed, spider lilies, and bladderwort. Common animals found in these forests include waterfowl, eastern wild turkey, swamp rabbit, furbearers, and gray and fox squirrels.

Conversion of floodplain forests to other land uses places bottomland hardwood forest ecosystems among the most severely altered ecosystems in the United States. Loss of these forests has been caused by many activities, including water-control structures, agriculture, logging, mining, petroleum extraction, development, and pollution.

In far Southeast Texas, large clay flats meet the wetland definition because of very high rainfall averages (50–55 inches per year), flat topography, and clayey soils. These prairie wetland systems are seldom ponded but for a few days and remain saturated throughout much of the late winter and early spring. Many of these areas are used for rice production and are valuable waterfowl habitat. When not farmed, these areas support herbaceous wetland plants such as flatsedge, annual sumpweed, smartweed, switchgrass, broomsedge bluestem, and rattlebox. If not controlled, the highly invasive exotic tree Chinese tallow will completely dominate many of these areas, converting these valuable historic prairie wetlands to scrub/shrub wetland with little or no understory.

The Gulf Coast

The Gulf Coast contains a diversity of saline, brackish, intermediate, and fresh marsh wetlands, including wet prairies, forested wetlands, barrier islands, mudflats, estuarine bays, bayous, and rivers. Saline and brackish marshes are most widely distributed south of Galveston Bay, while intermediate and fresh marshes are the most extensive marsh type east of the bay. The existence and extent of specific plant species within these different wetland types depend on their specific tolerances to salt concentrations and variability in water depth. Some overlap of species can be found within the different wetland types on the Gulf Coast.

Coastal wetlands in Texas provide one of the most important wintering and migration areas in North America for waterfowl using the Central and Mississippi Flyways. The bald eagle, peregrine falcon, brown pelican, and whooping crane all depend on the marshes and estuaries for food, as do otter, alligator, and swamp rabbit. Coastal development poses a severe threat to coastal wetlands through conversion to other habitats, saltwater intrusion, subsidence, groundwater withdrawal, erosion, sedimentation, decreased water quality, and impacts to wildlife and waterfowl.

On the Texas coast, several important habitats occur along the transition from open water to marshland. **Seagrass beds** are submerged wetlands that are inundated by seawater most of the time. These beds are vegetated by a number of grasslike plant species that can tolerate short-term aerial exposure but generally prefer prolonged/permanent shallow inundation. These areas are extremely important in the life cycle of many marine species as they serve as nurseries for many fish and invertebrates.

The brown pelican (*Pelecanus occidentalis*) and the whooping crane (*Grus americana*) are two federally listed endangered species that benefit from wetlands enhancement programs. Courtesy of Texas Parks and Wildlife Department

Tidal/mudflats are unvegetated mud or sandy sediments that are alternately flooded and exposed with the changing tides. In some cases, these areas can become covered in algae and are then considered "algal flats." They provide important foraging areas to many species of shorebirds.

Saline marshes are wetland areas dominated by the influence of full-strength or nearly full-strength seawater and tidal action along the Texas coast. Seawater has a salinity of 36 grams (g) of salt/L of H_2O. Salt- and flood-tolerant grasses and herbs such as smooth cordgrass, blackrush, saline marsh aster, saltwort, glasswort, and sea-lavender are the predominant plant species present.

Brackish marsh (mesohaline) communities, the most extensive communities in most systems, are transitional between saline and intermediate marshes. They are tidal wetlands subject to salinities generally between 5 and 20–25 g/L. Areas are vegetated with grasses and herbs capable of tolerating variable salinity and flooding conditions, such as marshhay cordgrass, saltgrass, saltmarsh bulrush, marsh hemp, and hairypod cowpea.

Intermediate marshes (oligohaline) reflect greater plant diversity than the saline or brackish marsh assemblages. They are tidal wetlands subject to salinities between 0.5 and 5.0 g/L. Areas are vegetated by flood-tolerant grass and herb species, which are also capable of tolerating some variability in salinity. Some of these plants include seashore paspalum, marshhay cordgrass, Olney bulrush, Colorado River hemp, common reedgrass, coastal water-hyssop, bearded sprangletop, and cattail.

Fresh marshes support the greatest diversity in plant species of all marsh types and are tidal or nontidal wetlands subject to salinities of less than 0.5 g/L. Dominant vegetation includes giant cutgrass, American lotus, white water-lily, smartweed, marsh millet, arrowhead, seedbox, cattail, and alligator weed.

South Texas

South Texas **freshwater** or **brackish wetlands** include small, isolated depressions and resacas (oxbows), which are relic meanders of the Rio Grande. Coastal depressions are formed when clay soils, exposed by wind action, trap and hold water. They often supply the only fresh water for resident wildlife in an area generally devoid of creeks and rivers.

Interdunal swales are **depressional wetlands** located between beach dunes along the coastline. Areas can range in salinity from fresh to saline, depending on the time of year, proximity to the coastline, storm events, and other factors. Vegetation is usually dominated by brackish to fresh grasses and other herbaceous species.

Mangrove swamps are **saline wetlands** located in far South Texas that are dominated by salt and tidally adapted tree species (mangroves). These wetlands replace salt marshes as the dominant coastal wetland type in tidal saline environments as climates transition from temperate to subtropical and tropical latitudes (i.e., moving toward the equator).

The High Plains and Rolling Plains of the Panhandle

The High Plains and Rolling Plains of the Panhandle support wetlands predominantly in playa lakes and saline lakes (High Plains), and in water-table-influenced basins and riparian habitats (Rolling Plains). **Playas** are ephemeral wetlands characterized by Randall or Ness clay soils and are very similar to potholes but have a different geological origin. **Saline lakes** are generally larger than playas, very saline, and influenced by groundwater. A few playas and playalike basins with connections to groundwater occur in the Rolling Plains. **Riparian wetlands** include main channels of creeks and rivers and associated wet meadow, bog, and beaver pond habitats.

Many playas provide important wetland habitat for Panhandle wildlife, including pheasants, shorebirds, sandhill cranes, and waterfowl. Courtesy of Kevin Kraai, Texas Parks and Wildlife Department

The playa lakes region of the United States includes portions of Colorado, Kansas, New Mexico, Oklahoma, and northwestern Texas. Texas alone has over 19,000 playas, which are the wintering and breeding area for several million ducks, geese, and other migratory birds. Several threatened and endangered species use wetland habitat in the playa lakes region, including the once-listed and still-protected bald eagle. Many Neotropical migrant birds use playas as well, including the long-billed curlew, American avocet, killdeer, Mississippi kite, mountain plover, lark bunting, and American kestrel.

Because playa lakes are fed by rainwater, many may be dry for extended periods of time. The 86 plant species living in playas have adapted to this unpredictable, rapidly changing environment. The most common plants found in the playa lakes include spikerush, curly dock, bulrush, cattail, pink and willow smartweed, pondweed, woollyleaf bursage, and barnyardgrass. Woody species in riparian habitats include plains cottonwood, buttonbush, net-leaf hackberry, native plum, western dogwood, and persimmon.

Few playa lakes have escaped alteration by humans. Many have been altered for irrigation, grazing and crop purposes. Others provide important wetland habitat for Panhandle wildlife, including pheasants, shorebirds, sandhill cranes, and waterfowl.

Riparian Wetlands

Riparian systems and associated woodland areas are thought to be the most widespread wetland type found in Texas. These systems are found from the High Plains of the Panhandle to the South Texas Brushlands and to the Pineywoods of East Texas. Riparian habitats are the interface or transitional area located between a stream or lake and the surrounding uplands. Plant species and community types found in riparian systems are generally hydrophilic (preferring the presence of water) and are greatly influenced by climate, physical geography and topography, soils, hydrology, and land use.

Riparian habitats are especially important in the western portions of the state. These areas are critical components of healthy stream systems, providing a number of benefits to people, water, fish, and wildlife, including improved water quality as a result of absorption and runoff filtration; bank stability due to the dense root masses provided by riparian plants; forage and habitat for wildlife; improved aquatic habitat resulting from cooler shaded water, instream structure provided by woody debris, and nutrient contributions from leaf litter; reduced downstream flooding as a result of slower velocities and absorption; increased aesthetic value; and improved aquifer recharge associated with slower velocities. Additionally, these ecosystems provide protective pathways of migration for animals such as birds, deer, and small mammals, as well as habitat for a large number of animal species.

Freshwater Springs and Headwaters

Freshwater springs emanating from subterranean caves found throughout the limestone formations of the Edwards Plateau in Central Texas are an important link to wetland systems in both Central and Southwest Texas. In West Texas they are often the only wooded areas with trees and shrubs to provide protection for wildlife, shade for streams, and food sources for waterfowl and fish-eating birds. While these spring systems are habitat for significant numbers of unusual plants and animals, they are also highly vulnerable to water pollution and overutilization by nearby cities and agricultural projects. This overutilization of aquifer waters causes springs to cease their flow. Many springs in the Edwards Plateau and the Trans-Pecos region that supported threatened and endangered species have disappeared.

"To waste, to destroy our natural resources, to skin and exhaust the land instead of using its usefulness, will result in undermining the days of our children, the very property which we ought by right to hand down to them amplified and developed."
—Theodore Roosevelt

"We abuse the land because we regard it as a commodity belonging to us. When we see land as a community to which we belong, we may begin to use it with love and respect."
—Aldo Leopold

Loss of Wetlands

Historically, wetlands were not widely recognized as valuable or appreciated. In fact, wetlands were often regarded as "wastelands" and breeding grounds for insects, pests, and disease and were considered impediments to development and progress. As a result, wetlands have been readily converted to other land uses.

According to a 2009 survey performed by the US Fish and Wildlife Service, approximately 392 million acres of wetlands existed in 1780 in lands that now form the United States (Dahl 1990). Of that, 221 million acres were found in the lower 48 states. Since that time, humankind has caused a significant reduction in wetlands. Currently, the lower 48 states support only an estimated 110.1 million acres, or 28% of the original wetland acreage (Dahl 2011). An estimated 95% of all wetlands were fresh water, and 5% were in the marine or estuarine (saltwater) systems. Estuarine emergent (salt marsh) wetland was the most prevalent type of estuarine and marine intertidal wetland. Salt marsh made up an estimated 66.7% of all estuarine and marine wetland area. Forested wetlands made up the single largest category (49.5%) of wetland in the freshwater system (Stedman and Dahl 2013). Freshwater emergents made up an estimated 26.3%; shrub wetlands, 17.8%; and freshwater ponds, 6.4% by area.

Urbanization is a major cause of wetland loss in Texas and the United States. Courtesy of Texas Parks and Wildlife Department

The difference in the national estimates of wetland acreage between 2004 and 2009 was not statistically significant, but wetland area declined by an estimated 62,300 acres (25,200 hectares) between 2004 and 2009. The reasons are complex and potentially reflect economic conditions, land-use trends, changing wetland regulation and enforcement measures, and climatic changes. In Texas, much of those losses can be attributed to construction of reservoirs in East Texas. Proposed construction of new reservoirs in this region continues to threaten many thousands of acres of bottomland hardwood forest.

Certain types of wetland exhibited declines while others increased in area. Factors contributing to this decline in the loss rate include increased public awareness and support for conservation, expansion of public- and private-sector restoration programs, enactment of Swampbuster measures in the Farm Bill since 1985, Clean Water Act Section 404 implementation, requiring mitigation efforts if wetlands are destroyed, and a decline in converting wetlands due to the tax reform of 1986.

Texas has experienced an estimated 56%

loss of wetlands in the past 200 years (TPWD 1997). Impacts from various land uses in the watershed, such as urbanization, grazing, farming, and industrial development, contribute to the loss. Human physical activities that contribute to wetland loss include filling, draining, excavation, water diversion, clearing, and flooding of the wetland areas.

Wetlands Creation, Enhancement, and Restoration

Wetland **restoration** is the rehabilitation of a degraded wetland or hydric soil area that was previously a naturally functioning wetland. Wetland **enhancement** is the improvement, maintenance, and management of existing wetlands for a particular function or service, possibly at the expense of others. Wetland **creation** is the conversion of a non-wetland area into a wetland where one never existed before. **Constructed** wetlands are specifically designed to treat both nonpoint and point sources of water pollution.

An important term used in development is **mitigation** of wetlands, referring to a wetland lost as the result of a construction project where the developer has to create a similar wetland providing the same services as the lost wetland. The big problem is that the created wetlands rarely function as the natural wetland did.

Common Wetland Management Practices

Much of the following information has been adapted from Neilson and Benson (2000). Depending on the goals of the landowner, active management of wetlands may sometimes be appropriate. Decisions to alter characteristics of wetlands through management activities should include consideration of potential effects on the fish, wildlife, and plant communities supported by the wetland. Landowners should also be aware that some activities in wetlands may require local, state, or federal permits. Manipulation of wetlands can have beneficial and/or destructive consequences. For example, removing vegetation, adding livestock, logging, or water-control structures can lead to erosion; increasing the inundation period can promote waterfowl or fish but eliminate some amphibian or invertebrate communities.

Wetlands can be managed through the application of a wide variety of manipulated tools such as prescribed fire, grazing, water-level control, diking, herbicides, small mammal management, and disking. Most of these practices are used to manage wetlands for wildlife and to control succession, therefore conserving wetlands. Management of wetlands will also depend on the goals and objectives of the landowner and the wetland type and location. Although the basic concepts and techniques are relatively simple, managers should recognize that only site-specific assessments and subsequent management programs can achieve objectives successfully. Whenever possible, the expertise of professionals should be consulted for recommendations and ultimate formulation of plans. Wetlands are dynamic systems often having subtleties that may complicate management actions. Following are some common and general practices for the management of wetlands.

Shredding/Mowing

This usually involves mowing dense vegetation or shrubs with a large rotary mower mounted behind a tractor. This practice is useful for increasing interspersion of vegetative types by reducing thick vegetative cover and reverts succession from shrub vegetation to shallow water, emergent vegetation, grass, and/or other vegetation types.

"The reasons that wetlands are legally protected have to do with their value to society, not with abstruse ecological processes that occur in wetlands."
—W. J. Mitsch and J. G. Gosselink, *Wetlands*

Controlled (Prescribed) Burning

Burning maintains vegetation and improves water and cover interspersion. Burning is best conducted under cool, moist, low-wind conditions. Spring is generally the best time to burn, if wetlands are dry enough. Results of burning vary with the vegetation being burned, burning conditions, time of year, and the frequency of burning. Burning allows the soil to release nutrients, reduces the amount of shrubs and dead vegetation, therefore improving the vigor and quality of forbs and grasses, and allows new seeds to reach the soil to germinate. Burning also opens up areas to improve wildlife access.

Fish and Wildlife Harvesting and Wildlife Damage Management

Fishing or hunting of species in and around wetlands can improve fish and wildlife populations and health as well as the quality of the wetland. If specific individuals are a nuisance, wildlife damage management may also be recommended in addition to increasing creel and bag limits. Professional wildlife biologists often have to exclude, trap, relocate, euthanize, repel, poison, shoot, or frighten these individual animals to reduce or eliminate damaging behaviors or health hazards. Direct control techniques like relocation, trapping or toxicants, and selectively shooting only problem animals are commonly used and effective. Nonlethal methods of predator control include livestock confinement or exclusion fences. Methods of controlling herbivores (deer, rabbits, etc.) include exclusion fences, taste and area repellents, scare tactics, and decoys of other predators.

Livestock Grazing

Livestock grazing management is a practice for managing the use of vegetation by livestock. This tool can also be used to manipulate successional stages to benefit various wildlife, wetland and water health, and vegetation interspersion. This practice also includes excluding livestock when necessary. When using grazing as a management tool, careful consideration should be given to proper grazing use, timing, intensity, rotation, and tools such as fencing.

Brush Piles

Brush piles within and near wetlands provide wildlife cover and food. Brush piles can be made from saplings or tree branches and should be loosely piled 3 to 5 feet high and 15 feet in diameter.

Nest Boxes/Platforms

Some wildlife species require nesting cavities. If natural cavities are not present, artificial cavities can be used. The particular design and placement of nest boxes often determine which species will utilize the structure. Many individual species prefer particular cavities (diameter of hole, depth, area, etc.), certain locations (field, woods, water, etc.), and certain nest box or platform heights.

Liming

Water pH ranges near 7.0 (neutral) support most living species in a wetland. When water quality tests show low pH levels (below 7.0), the level can be adjusted to 7 to 8 by using agricultural lime. Some wetland types and some areas of the state do not naturally fall within the pH range of 7 to 8 and should not be adjusted without considering the need and the potential impacts to fish, wildlife, and plant communities. Liming is an exceptional tool for exceptional circumstances. It should not be promoted except to reverse an artificial change to a natural pH range, such as acidification from anthropogenic sources. Liming a naturally acidic East Texas pitcher plant wetland, for example, would be harmful.

Plantings (Trees, Shrubs, Grasses, and Other Aquatic Plants)

Plantings should provide diversity of plant species, food and cover sources for fish and wildlife, and increased water quality. Planting trees or shrubs provides perching and nesting sites for mammals and waterfowl and can improve or restore riparian areas.

Timber Harvest/Selective Cutting

With this management tool, selected trees are cut a few at a time. This type of thinning can release nutrients for remaining trees, thereby allowing increased mast production (fruits and seeds of shrubs, woody vines, trees, cacti, and other nonherbaceous vegetation available for animal consumption; Forage Information System 1991) or growth stimulation of other mast-producing and surrounding trees. This practice benefits wildlife species feeding in flooded mature oak woodlands. At least three to four den (old mature) and large dead (snag) trees per acre should be maintained.

Water-Control Structures

Various structures made out of concrete, pipes, wood, or other material are useful to control the water levels in wetlands or ponds. These structures are usually combined with dams and shallow dikes for water control and are recommended only when inadequate structures are present in an existing dam or dike. Water-control structures allow for the management of water levels, which increase or decrease the amount of and types of aquatic vegetation, depending on the water level. This method can also be used to manage the quality of water in a pond or wetland and for the control of unwanted fish. It is also useful for creating a desirable interspersion of open water and vegetation.

Facts and Fiction: Wetlands Conservation on Private Lands

Much of the following information is from Raasch et al. (2000). Throughout Texas, many landowners are interested in habitat conservation on their property. However, two common concerns prevent them from restoring or enhancing habitat: (1) fear of any ensuing regulations and (2) a lack of funds to defray restoration costs. These obstacles to wetlands conservation on private lands could best be overcome by offering landowners incentives to conserve their wetlands. Incentives, rather than regulations, foster pride and land stewardship since landowners are integrally involved in decision making and planning throughout the duration of the project.

The elimination of incentives to wetland conservation would encourage landowners to consider initiating conservation activities on their property. While some disincentives do exist that may limit certain activities in wetlands, many are misperceptions; in other words, they are simply untrue or have limited application. As a general rule, incentive programs do not prohibit common land-use practices (e.g., grazing, hunting); however, those activities may be managed to prevent adverse impacts to the wetland project.

Most economic incentives to landowners are offered through specific wetlands programs. Because wetlands incentive programs are voluntary, landowners assist in determining the terms of their own conservation agreement. Each program offers different incentives; therefore, landowners should select a program that best suits their individual needs and interests. Following are some of the most common perceptions concerning disincentives to wetland conservation and the relevant facts.

Perception 1: Creating, restoring, or enhancing wetlands subjects landowners to wetlands regulations.

Fact: Several scenarios exist for landowners who have created, restored, or enhanced wetlands:

1. Created, restored, or enhanced wetlands that are maintained as part of an ongoing agricultural operation are exempt from Clean Water Act regulations.
2. Agricultural fields flooded during the

winter for waterfowl will not be impacted by Clean Water Act regulations unless discharges of dredged or fill material occur.

3. Landowners who enhance, restore, or create nontidal wetlands but who think they may later want to return them to their condition prior to the conservation activity can, with some advanced planning, be authorized to do so under Clean Water Act Nationwide Permit 27. This permit authorizes reversion of restored, enhanced, or created nontidal wetlands and riparian areas back to their prior condition if certain conditions are met. Interested landowners should contact the US Army Corps of Engineers for details.

Perception 2: Having or managing habitat that encourages endangered species eliminates future land-use options.

Fact: Landowners are responsible for existing endangered species habitat already present on their property. However, landowners can avoid liability for endangered species or even species under consideration for listing (i.e., a candidate species) that may be attracted to any new habitat by entering into a "Safe Harbor" agreement. Under this initiative, a landowner who intends to manage habitat in a way that attracts or benefits a listed species may enter into a cooperative agreement with the US Fish and Wildlife Service or a state agency that protects the landowner from any additional responsibility under the Endangered Species Act, beyond those that existed at the time a landowner enters into the agreement. While landowners are required to protect the habitat of any species present at the time the agreement was signed (their baseline responsibilities), they are under no obligation to protect additional suitable habitat that may have developed or any additional individuals or species that may have been attracted by the habitat improvements. Landowners not participating in a Safe Harbor or Candidate Conservation Agreement will be responsible for any new individuals residing on the property.

Perception 3: Hunting is not allowed under wetland agreements.

Fact: Habitat incentive programs generally do not restrict hunting by owners or lessees. Hunting is normally limited only by federal and state regulations.

Perception 4: Pest treatment on crops is regulated under wetland agreements.

Fact: Pesticide or herbicide treatment of adjacent cropland is generally not regulated by wetland agreements.

Perception 5: Grazing, haying, or mowing is not allowed.

Fact: Managed grazing, haying, or mowing is permitted in most situations when it does not adversely impact the restoration project. The request must be made in advance and written into the easement.

Perception 6: Timber harvest is not allowed.

Fact: Limited timber removal is permitted in most situations when it does not adversely impact the restoration project. The request must be made in advance and written into the easement.

Perception 7: My land will become open to the public.

Fact: Public access is not a condition of wetland agreements. The incentive program contact may check on the project's success throughout the contract period but will notify the landowner in advance.

Choosing the Best Option or Options for the Landowner

The future of our wetlands is closely linked to land-use decisions made by the stewards of the wetlands resource. Approximately 95% of Texas' lands are privately owned. Therefore, the role of the private landowner in wetlands conservation is crucial. As understanding and appreciation for wetlands increase, several voluntary programs have been created to help landowners act as stewards of their land by conserving and restoring wetlands. To help landowners become more effective stewards, they should be provided with a broad array of voluntary conservation and management options from which to choose a stewardship strategy. With a firm understanding of the landowner's objectives, property, and potential problems and opportunities, it is possible to proceed toward choosing the option or options best suited for the landowner.

Federal Regulations That Affect Wetland Conservation

A summary of important regulations that directly affect wetland conservation has been compiled here, including the Clean Water Act, Rivers and Harbors Act, Endangered Species Act, and the Food, Agriculture, Conservation and Trade Act. Additional information about each regulation, its permitting process, its restrictions, and involved agencies can be found through the responsible governing agency for the regulation.

Clean Water Act: Section 404 (33 US Code § 1344 [1986 & Supp. 1991])

The US Congress enacted the Clean Water Act (the Act) to "restore and maintain the chemical, physical, and biological integrity of the Nation's waters." Section 404 regulates the placement of dredged and fill material into waters of the United States, including wetlands. The Act authorizes the issuance of permits for such discharges as long as the proposed activity complies with environmental requirements specified in Section 404(b)(1) of the Act. Section 404 is the primary federal program regulating activities in wetlands. The Section 404 program is administered by both the US Army Corps of Engineers (Corps) and the US Environmental Protection Agency (EPA), while the US Fish and Wildlife Service (USFWS), National Marine Fisheries Service (NMFS), and several state agencies play important advisory roles.

The Corps has primary responsibility for the permit program and is authorized, after notice and opportunity for a public hearing, to issue Section 404 permits. EPA is responsible for reviewing and commenting on permit applications being evaluated by the Corps. The environmental guidelines used to evaluate Section 404 permits generally prohibit discharges of dredged or fill material into US waters unless the following conditions apply:

- There is no available, practicable alternative with fewer adverse effects on the aquatic ecosystem.
- Dischargers will neither violate other applicable regulations or laws (e.g., state water quality standards, toxic effluent standards, Endangered Species Act), nor significantly degrade the waters into which they discharge.
- All appropriate and practicable steps have been taken to avoid, minimize, and otherwise mitigate impacts on the aquatic ecosystem.
- The activity is water dependent.

In determining waters that are within the scope of the Clean Water Act, Congress intended to assert federal jurisdiction to the broadest extent permissible under the commerce clause of the Constitution. One factor that establishes a commerce connection is the use or potential use of waters for navigation. Other factors include (but are not limited to) use of wetland (or other water) by federally listed endangered species or for recreation by interstate visitors.

As defined in Section 404 program regulations, wetlands are "those areas that are inundated or saturated with surface or groundwater at a frequency and duration sufficient to support, and that under normal circumstances do support, a prevalence of vegetation typically adapted for life in saturated soil conditions." In applying this definition in the field, government agency scientists use indicators of vegetation that has adapted to life in wet environments (hydrophytic vegetation), hydric (anaerobic) soils, and hydrology to identify wetlands and to establish their boundaries.

Section 404 regulates only the discharge of dredge or fill material into "waters of the United States." Discharges of dredged and fill material are commonly associated with activities such as port development, channel construction and maintenance, fills to create development sites, transportation improvements, and water resource projects (such as dams, jetties, and levees). Anyone in violation of the Section 404 program, either by conducting an unauthorized activity or by violating permit conditions, is subject to civil or criminal action or both.

Clean Water Act: Section 401 Water Quality Certification (33 US Code § 1341 [1986])

Section 401 of the Clean Water Act, the State Water Quality Certification program, requires that states certify compliance of federal permits or licenses with state water quality requirements and other applicable state laws. Under Section 401, states have authority to review any federal permit or license that may result in a discharge to wetlands and other waters under state jurisdiction to ensure that the actions would be consistent with the state's water quality requirements.

Federal permits that do not meet these requirements will not receive a State Water Quality Certification and thus cannot be issued. This certification process is routinely delegated in whole or in part to the state agency with the authority to regulate the quality of state waters. In Texas, the Texas Commission on Environmental Quality (TCEQ) provides a Section 401 certification to the Corps, indicating that the proposed activity will comply with the applicable sections of the Clean Water Act pursuant to the Section 404 permitting program and that such activity will not adversely affect the quality of state waters. Texas oil and gas activities covered by Section 404 are certified by the Railroad Commission of Texas.

The US Environmental Protection Agency encourages states to define protection of water quality broadly to include protection of aquatic life, wildlife, aquatic habitat, vegetation, and hydrology required to maintain the aquatic system. Currently, Texas addresses only aquatic life. Certification is based on whether a proposed activity would meet requirements for conventional and nonconventional pollutants, water quality standards, new source performance standards, and requirements for toxic pollutants (and any more stringent, relevant state law or regulation). Certification can address physical, chemical, and biological impacts, depending on how a state designs and applies its water quality standards and other appropriate requirements of state law. Currently, Texas does not address biological criteria.

Clean Water Act Nationwide Permit 27

Nationwide Permit 27 of the Clean Water Act allows lands that have been converted to nontidal wetlands, through landowner agreements between the USFWS or the NRCS, to be reverted to prior condition and used within five years without requirement of an individual Section 404 permit or review by the Army Corps of Engineers. "Prior condition" is the condition as of the initial effective date of the agreement as it is documented by either the USFWS representative and/or the NRCS representative.

Section 10, Rivers and Harbors Act of 1899, United States Army Corps of Engineers

Section 10 of the Rivers and Harbors Act of 1899 requires a permit for dredging or the placement of fill or structures in navigable waters of the United States. "Navigable waters" have been defined by the US Army Corps of Engineers (USACE) as "those waters that are subject to the ebb and flow of the tide and/or are presently used, or have been used in the past, or may be susceptible for use to transport interstate or foreign commerce." This includes the ability to float a water body and/or use by migratory birds. Section 10 is similar to Section 404 of the Clean Water Act; however, Section 404 covers all waters of the United States without regard to their navigability and is therefore much broader in scope than Section 10.

In the state of Texas, which has four USACE districts—the Galveston District,* Fort Worth District, Tulsa District, and Albuquerque District—navigable waters include the following rivers:

- **Angelina River**: From Sam Rayburn Dam in Jasper County upstream to US Highway 59 in Nacogdoches and Angelina Counties and all USACE lands associated with B.A. Steinhagen Lake in Jasper and Tyler Counties, Texas
- **Big Cypress Bayou**: From the Texas-Louisiana state line in Marion County, Texas, upstream to Ellison Creek Reservoir in Morris County, Texas
- **Brazos River**: From the point of intersection of Grimes, Waller, and Washington Counties upstream to Whitney Dam in Hill and Bosque Counties, Texas
- **Colorado River**: From the Bastrop-Fayette County line upstream to Longhorn Dam in Travis County, Texas
- **Neches River**: USACE lands associated with B.A. Steinhagen Lake in Jasper and Tyler Counties, Texas
- **Red River**: From the US Highway 71 bridge at the Texas-Arkansas state line upstream to the Oklahoma-Arkansas state line and from Denison Dam on Lake Texoma upstream to Warrens Bend, approximately 7.25 miles north-northeast of Marysville, in Cooke County, Texas
- **Rio Grande**: Frata-Webb County line upstream to the point of intersection of the Texas-New Mexico state line and Mexico
- **Sabine River**: From the point of intersection of the Sabine-Vernon Parish line in Louisiana with Newton County, Texas, upstream to the Sabine River–Big Sandy Creek confluence in Upshur County, Texas
- **Sulphur River**: From the Texas-Arkansas state line upstream to Wright Patman Dam in Cass and Bowie Counties, Texas
- **Trinity River**: From the point of intersection of Houston, Madison, and Walker Counties upstream to Riverside Drive in Fort Worth, Tarrant County, Texas

* Navigable waters in the Galveston District are determined on a case-by-case basis and, therefore, are not included in this list.

Classified as a "navigable waterway," the Rio Grande near Presidio. Courtesy of Whitney Root, Big Country Chapter

Endangered Species Act, US Fish and Wildlife Service

The Endangered Species Act requires federal agencies to conserve endangered and threatened species. It prohibits any person from "taking" endangered or threatened animal or plant species. "Taking" is interpreted broadly to include killing, harassing, or harming a protected species. The definition of "harm" includes modifying or degrading a species' habitat such that the change would significantly impair breeding, feeding, or shelter and would result in injury to the species. Under Section 7, all federal agencies must ensure that their actions are not likely to jeopardize the continued existence of any endangered or threatened species or adversely modify or destroy any of their habitat. These requirements apply to all activities carried out, funded, or regulated by a federal agency, including activities in wetlands.

A state can propose or support the listing of wetlands-dependent species, thereby bringing the act's protection to bear on its wetlands. Listing, however, is based on the status of the species and is not simply an attempt to protect wetlands. States can identify potential species, conduct the research necessary to determine status, and, if needed, petition the federal government to include these species. States may also seek to engage landowners in conservation agreements that may preclude the need for listing.

The federal government is also supposed to designate "critical habitat" for a species at the time it is listed. As noted, federal agencies are not authorized to modify adversely or destroy critical habitat. For listed species, the US Fish and Wildlife Service is required to prepare "recovery plans" that outline a strategy to conserve and recover the species. Recovery plans should outline habitat protection and other steps necessary for the conservation of the species.

Long-term habitat conservation plans (HCPs) must be developed as part of the permit application process. States may wish to initiate or participate in the preparation of HCPs and to advocate for wetlands protection as part of the plans. However, HCPs may be of limited use for wetlands protection because they require the presence of a federally listed endangered or threatened species.

Food, Agriculture, Conservation and Trade Act of 1990 (Swampbuster Provisions), United States Department of Agriculture (USDA)

The Swampbuster Provisions are part of the amended 1990 Food, Agriculture, Conservation and Trade Act (1990 Farm Bill). Swampbuster withholds USDA benefits to farmers who convert wetlands into croplands after December 23, 1985. Swampbuster reduces the incentives to convert wetlands to croplands by denying eligibility for almost all farm program benefits on all acres operated by a grower who either converts a wetland or plants on a converted wetland.

When applying for federal farm program benefits, landowners indicate whether they plan to manipulate any "wet" areas. If so, the USDA must determine if these "wet" areas are wetlands. Conversion of wetlands may result in Swampbuster violations. For violations, USDA must conduct a site visit before reducing program benefits. A violator can regain eligibility for future farm program benefits by restoring the converted wetland to its original condition. Landowners may, however, prepare a mitigation plan that allows them to produce an agricultural commodity on converted wetlands that were either frequently cropped, or converted between 1985 and 1990, in exchange for restoring prior converted cropland on their property. Mitigation plans must be approved prior to conversion of the wetlands.

State Programs and Regulations for Wetlands in Texas

Texas A&M Forest Service Best Management Practices Project

With cooperative funding from the Environmental Protection Agency and the Texas State Soil and Water Conservation Board, the Texas A&M Forest Service implemented an educational project encouraging forest landowners, loggers, and foresters to voluntarily implement forestry best management practices (BMPs). Texas forestry BMPs protect water quality and address planning, road construction and maintenance, harvesting, site preparation and planting, prescribed burning, silvicultural chemicals, and streamside management zones (SMZs).

Major educational components of the BMP Project currently include a program on continuing education for logging professionals on best management practices. A Texas Forestry BMP guide is revised and published every few years, most recently in 2014. BMP demonstration forests are located on state lands in East Texas and are available for loggers, landowners, or land managers to see side-by-side demonstrations of various BMPs. To accommodate those who are unable to visit a state forest, virtual tours of these demonstration areas (along with additional information about the BMPs) can be found on the Texas A&M Forest Service Water Resources at http://tfsweb.tamu.edu/water.

Recognizing that unpaved county roads can have a major water quality impact, the BMP Project has provided water quality awareness training to county road crews and county commissioners. This newly formed relationship is expected to be mutually beneficial due to the natural linkages between forest industry and county roads. Landowner workshops have been conducted in areas of the state where there are no county landowner associations. These workshops provide informational resources for landowners on water quality and other stewardship issues like tree planting, wildlife, and sustainable forestry.

Texas General Land Office Texas Coastal Management Program

The Texas Coastal Management Program (CMP) was developed to more effectively and efficiently manage coastal natural resource areas and the uses that affect them. The CMP is a tool for balancing protection of coastal natural resources with encouragement of economic growth. The Coastal Coordination Council, comprising state, local, and public representatives, was formed to coordinate the current coastal programs, statutes, and rules administered by federal, state, and local agencies. The council's rules establishing CMP goals and policies are based on existing local, state, and federal law and regulations. A major role of the Coastal Coordination Council is to review agency actions for consistency with the goals and policies.

Landowners can receive financial assistance for water-control structures such as this one found on the Richland Creek WMA to manage water levels in their wetlands. Courtesy of Texas Parks and Wildlife Department

Texas Commission on Environmental Quality Water Diversion under the Texas Water Code (Section 11.121)

The Texas Water Code states that individuals cannot appropriate state water, or begin construction of any work designed for the storage, taking, or diversion of water, without first obtaining a permit from the TCEQ for the appropriation. However, persons wishing to construct for personal use on their own property a dam or reservoir to impound or contain no more than 200 acre-feet of water for domestic and livestock purposes, including wildlife habitat, are exempt from this permit requirement.

Roles of Federal and State Agencies in Wetlands

Many government agencies within Texas are involved in varying aspects of wetland management, regulation, and technical and financial assistance. Appendix A lists agency names and web addresses for additional information.

Texas A&M AgriLife Extension Service works hand in hand with its Texas A&M System partners, the state legislature, and the communities it serves. Its mission to provide community-based education has remained unchanged for almost a century. With a vast network of 250 county extension offices and 900 professional educators, the expertise provided by the extension service is available to every Texan. Since extension educators are well aware that a program offered in Dallas might not be relevant in the Rio Grande Valley, the Extension Service custom-designs its programs to the different areas of the state, significantly depending on residents for input and program delivery.

The mission of the Texas A&M AgriLife Extension Service is a seemingly simple one: to improve the lives of people, business, and communities across Texas and beyond through high-quality, relevant education. Carrying out this mission, however, is a massive undertaking, one that requires the commitment of each and every one of the agency's employees. Through the programs these employees provide, Texans are better prepared to

- eat well, stay healthy, manage money, and raise their children to be successful adults
- efficiently help themselves through preventing problems and using tools for economic stability and security
- improve stewardship of the environment and of the state's natural resources.

Today Texas A&M AgriLife Extension Service is known for its leadership, dedication, expertise, responsiveness, and trustworthiness. Texans turn to the AgriLife Extension service for solutions, and its agents and specialists respond not only with answers but with a significant return on investment to boost the Texas economy.

The Justin Hurst WMA, located in Brazoria County, is part of the Central Coast Wetlands Ecosystem Project (CCWEP). The CCWEP's mission is to provide for sound biological conservation of all wildlife resources within the central coast of Texas for the public's common benefit. Courtesy of Texas Parks and Wildlife Department

Texas A&M Forest Service (TFS) is involved in wetlands primarily in an advisory capacity to private landowners. The TFS provides management assistance to owners of forestlands, many of which are in wetland areas. Present policies accept or encourage timber harvest in wetlands.

Texas General Land Office (GLO) is the state agency responsible for the management of state-owned public lands not specifically purchased by or deeded to other agencies. These lands include coastal wetlands inland to the line of mean high tide and up rivers to the limit of tidal influence, as well as the beds of state-owned rivers. The GLO is a proprietary and not a regulatory state agency. Users of state-owned lands who wish to engage in mineral extraction, occupancy, or encumbrance of public lands must obtain leases or easements and pay a fee. The GLO is also the state's lead agency for coordinating the Coastal Management Plan designed to preserve public beach access, protect coastal wetlands and other coastal natural resources, and respond to beach erosion along the Texas coast.

Texas Commission on Environmental Quality (TCEQ) implements many sections of the Texas Water Code and the federal

Clean Water Act and Safe Drinking Water Act. The TCEQ develops water quality requirements designed to protect attainable uses and to maintain the quality of waters in the state. These standards are the basis for permits issued by the TCEQ that authorize discharges into or next to waters in the state. TCEQ also reviews applications for Clean Water Act Section 404 permits, which require a state water quality certification under Section 401 of the Clean Water Act. TCEQ administers wastewater and water rights permit and enforcement programs.

Texas Parks and Wildlife Department (TPWD) has primary responsibility for protecting the state's fish and wildlife resources. TPWD acquires, manages, and protects wildlife and its habitat and acquires and manages parklands and historic areas. Additionally, TPWD biologists offer technical guidance to landowners and communities seeking to protect, manage, and conserve natural resources.

TPWD has programs to protect or manage wetlands. The state park system, which provides attractive and educational areas for public recreation, also features many aquatic and wetland habitats. Master plans are prepared for each park prior to development to ensure that important natural areas such as wetlands are protected.

TPWD has acquired lands in virtually every part of the state for the conservation, management, and study of wildlife species. Wildlife management areas typically include wetlands and open water for use by resident and migratory wildlife. Wildlife management areas specifically managed for waterfowl have been purchased with federal funding and by funds generated by the state waterfowl stamp required of all waterfowl hunters. In addition, TPWD conducts research to help determine management practices for waters and wetlands necessary to promote and sustain fisheries.

Texas Soil and Water Conservation Board (TSWCB), working in conjunction with Texas' 216 soil and water conservation districts, encourages the wise and productive use of the state's soil and water resources through technical assistance programs and conservation activities. The state board is the lead agency responsible for planning and management of nonpoint source pollution control relating to agriculture and silviculture. Field staff located throughout the state consult with local soil and water districts and landowners to ensure that appropriate land and water conservation methods are applied.

Texas Water Development Board (TWDB) administers state and federal financing programs for water-related projects and forecasts and plans for long-term water needs with associated data-collecting and resource studies. The board prepares the State Water Plan, which outlines current and future needs for water and wastewater treatment projects in Texas for the next 50 years. In response to increasing competition for water, escalating infrastructure costs and statewide drought conditions, the 75th Texas Legislature passed Senate Bill 1, the Brown-Lewis Water Plan. Senate Bill 1 directs 16 Regional Water Planning Groups (RWPGs) to plan for a region's 30- and 50-year water needs by identifying the most cost-effective and environmentally sound water-management strategies. The TWDB will develop a statewide water plan using the regional plans.

United States Army Corps of Engineers (Corps) provides design and engineering services and construction support for a variety of military and civilian projects worldwide. One civil duty includes protecting the integrity of the navigable waters of the United States, wetland resources, and the nation's water resources. These responsibilities are carried out through the issuance or denial of Clean Water Act Section 404 and other permits authorizing certain activities in wetlands and other waters of the United States. The Corps' duties also include maintaining navigation and shipping channels, providing emergency response to natural disasters, regulating discharges of dredged or fill material, operating and maintaining flood control reservoirs, and regulating activities in wetlands.

United States Environmental Protection Agency (EPA) is responsible for implementing federal laws designed to protect the nation's natural resources. This is done primarily through regulation, but EPA has also developed a wide variety of funding, planning, and education programs. EPA has the authority to regulate wetlands under Section 404 of the Clean Water Act. The EPA offers a Wetlands Helpline that responds to questions and provides materials on a variety of wetlands topics. The helpline can be reached Monday through Friday from 8:30 a.m. to 5:30 p.m. EST, at (800) 832–7828.

United States Fish and Wildlife Service (USFWS) is the principal federal agency responsible for conserving, protecting, and enhancing certain fish and wildlife and their habitats, in particular migratory species, including waterfowl, shorebirds and songbirds, and federally listed threatened and endangered species. Among other roles, the USFWS administers the federal Endangered Species Act and establishes and maintains a system of over 500 national wildlife refuges nationwide. The USFWS also manages the taking of migratory waterfowl and conducts research and monitoring programs to inventory and record changes in populations of fish and wildlife and in habitats.

USDA Farm Service Agency (FSA) was formed to administer commodity price and income support programs, farm operating loans, the federal crop insurance program, and conservation cost-share programs. The agency was formed from part of three other agencies: the Agricultural Stabilization and Conservation Service (ASCS), the Farmers Home Administration, and the Federal Crop Insurance Corporation.

USDA Natural Resources Conservation Service (NRCS) provides technical and financial assistance to landowners in development and implementation of resource management systems that conserve soil, air, water, plant, and animal resources. This agency employs soil scientists, plant scientists, and engineers that can provide assistance in identifying, restoring, enhancing, and creating wetlands. The NRCS is the lead agency for identifying and delineating wetlands on both grazing and agricultural lands in the United States.

Wetland Conservation Initiatives in Texas

"A true conservationist is a man who knows that the world is not given by his fathers but borrowed from his children."
—John James Audubon

The Texas Wetlands Conservation Plan

The Texas Parks and Wildlife Department's Wetlands Assistance Guide is one component of the Texas State Wetlands Conservation Plan (SWCP). TPWD, in a statewide cooperative effort, completed the Texas Wetlands Conservation Plan in 1997. It focuses on nonregulatory, voluntary approaches to conserving Texas' wetlands, including

- enhancing landowner's access to new and existing incentive programs and other land-use options through outreach and assistance
- developing and encouraging land management options that provide an economic incentive for conserving existing wetlands or restoring former ones
- coordinating regional wetlands conservation efforts

Over the course of a year (1995–96), three Regional Advisory Groups (East Texas, the coast, and the Panhandle) periodically met to identify regional and statewide issues associated with conserving Texas wetlands.

Through these meetings, landowners and representatives from agriculture, industry, business, conservation, and government developed recommendations and proposals for action to address the identified wetland issues. These results form the core of the Texas Wetlands Conservation Plan. The Texas Parks and Wildlife Commission approved a resolution on April 17, 1997, supporting the Texas Wetlands Conservation Plan, and the governor signed it in July 1997.

Lone Star Land Steward Awards

Since 1995, TPWD has recognized and honored private landowners for their accomplishments in habitat management and wildlife conservation through the Lone Star Land Steward Awards. The program recognizes landowners in all habitat types within the 10 ecological areas of Texas, from timberlands to native prairies and from marshes to mountain ranges. One landowner is recognized from each of the 10 ecological regions. In addition, a wildlife management association and a corporation or foundations are recognized in two special categories. Landowners can apply or be nominated by any individual or organization. Ranchers, farmers, foresters, and other land managers and cooperatives may participate. Applications for nominations are available at http://www.tpwd.state.tx.us/landwater/land/private/lone_star_land_steward/.

Land Trusts Offer Long-Term Land Protection

A land trust is a local, regional, or national nonprofit organization that protects land for its natural, recreational, scenic, or productive value. Land trusts have varying conservation objectives; some work in specific geographic areas or concentrate on protecting different natural or cultural features. Generally, land trusts manage purchased or donated land and easements for conservation purposes. For information on Texas' land trusts, see http://www.texaslandtrustcouncil.org/.

Texas Prairie Wetland Project

In 1991, Ducks Unlimited, TPWD, US Fish and Wildlife Service, and USDA NRCS partnered to create the Texas Prairie Wetlands Project (TPWP). The partnership was established to help deliver the habitat objectives set forth by the Gulf Coast Joint Venture (GCJV), with the primary goal of providing habitat for wintering waterfowl that would improve survival rates and body conditions before spring migration. TPWP works with private landowners to restore, enhance, and create shallow-water wetlands through a 28-county focus area along the Gulf.

TPWP projects focus on harvested croplands, moist-soil areas, emergent wetlands, and other created wetlands to increase biodiversity for waterfowl and other wetland-dependent species. In return, landowners sign a minimum 10-year wetland development agreement and commit to managing and maintaining the wetlands. TPWP works closely with rice producers to improve fields and infrastructure for water conservation, production, and habitat management.

• • • • • • • • • • • • • • • •

UTILIZING WETLANDS TO SUPPLY WATER: A MODEL FOR THE FUTURE OF TEXAS

Matthew Symmank, Richland Creek WMA, TPWD

Richland Creek Wildlife Management Area (RCWMA) is located along the Trinity River in Freestone and Navarro Counties, approximately 80 miles downstream of the Dallas–Fort Worth (DFW) metroplex. The goal of this TPWD-owned property is to conserve and enhance 14,238 acres of remaining Trinity River bottomland for wildlife habitat and provide for public recreation. Bottomland hardwood areas, such as RCWMA, are critical because of their importance in flood control, water filtration, and wildlife habitat. Texas has lost most of its beneficial river bottomlands because of agricultural land conversion and reservoir projects over the past few decades. With water demand rapidly increasing, some of the last remaining bottomland hardwood stands along the Trinity are threatened with development.

Projections from water planners at the Texas Water Development Board expect water demand in the DFW region to nearly double by 2060. In addition, due to an increase in demand for clean water, wastewater discharge from the DFW metroplex is also increasing because of population growth. During low-flow periods as much as 95% of Trinity River water south of Dallas is wastewater discharge from the DFW metroplex. Trinity River water contains high concentrations of nutrients such as nitrogen and phosphorus (from wastewater treatment facilities and urban runoff), making the river a challenging water-supply source.

Texans are faced with the problem of supplying water to a growing population while avoiding adverse impacts to remaining bottomland hardwood habitat throughout the state. As a solution to the problem, TPWD partnered with Tarrant Regional Water District (TRWD) on a project designed to provide a reliable water supply to the

Richland Creek WMA wetlands. Courtesy of Matthew Symmank, Texas Parks and Wildlife Department

DFW metroplex without construction of a new reservoir. The George W. Shannon Wetlands Water Recycling Project on RCWMA will eventually supply 90 million gallons of water every day to the Fort Worth region by cleaning nutrient-rich Trinity River water using the natural filtering process of wetlands. This project harnesses the ecological function of wetlands for the benefit of humans by helping meet our needs for clean water. Not only is this project an innovative, environmentally friendly method of water supply; it is also cost effective. An economic analysis by TRWD shows that the development of wetlands for water filtration costs half as much as new reservoir construction.

The process begins when water is pumped from the Trinity River into one of five sediment basins totaling 120 acres. From there, the water flows through 20 shallow wetland cells, totaling 1,740 acres. The wetland cells are thick with native wetland vegetation beneficial to migratory waterfowl and shorebirds, as well as wading birds and a variety of mammal species. The wetland vegetation utilizes the nutrients in the water, efficiently removing approximately 95% of river sediment, 55% of nitrogen, and 40% of phosphorus during much of the year. After filtering, the water is pumped into Richland-Chambers Reservoir adjacent to RCWMA. The water from Richland-Chambers is utilized as a water-supply source for TRWD customers, including the cities of Fort Worth, Mansfield, and Arlington and the Trinity River Authority. The water eventually returns to the Trinity River by way of wastewater treatment plants, where the recycling process begins again.

These wetland cells are highly productive emergent marshes ideal for waterfowl, wading birds, and shorebirds. The shallow water depths create an excellent environment for highly preferred waterfowl plant species such as smartweed, barnyardgrass, and wild millet. Waterfowl also feed on the abundant invertebrates throughout the marshes. Wading birds consume the plentiful fish and frogs, while shorebirds utilize mudflats to forage for invertebrates. TPWD can actively use moist-soil management practices to maximize available food for migratory birds. The entire project area is open to public waterfowl hunting during season and year-round to birding.

The wetland water recycling project on RCWMA is a model for the future water-supply needs of Texans because it provides additional water without the need of a new reservoir. TPWD is proud to be a partner with TRWD on an innovative use of wetlands as an alternative to reservoir construction. Everyone benefits from increasing our water supply through water recycling while at the same time creating high-quality wildlife habitat on public lands for the benefit and enjoyment of all Texans.

• • • • • • • • • • • • • • •

APPENDIX A

Websites for Key Federal and State Agencies and Other Organizations

The following list of agencies and organizations is a starting point for anyone's Internet investigation into the realm of wetlands. Many of the links go to the home page of the organization, so please investigate each website to find many good sources of information about wetlands.

State Agencies

Texas A&M AgriLife Extension Service: http://agrilifeextension.tamu.edu/

Texas A&M Forest Service: http://txforestservice.tamu.edu/

Texas Commission on Environmental Quality: http://www.tceq.texas.gov/

Texas General Land Office: http://www.glo.texas.gov/

Texas Parks and Wildlife Department: http://www.tpwd.state.tx.us/

Texas Water Development Board: http://www.twdb.state.tx.us/

Federal Agencies

United States Army Corps of Engineers-Regulatory Program: http://www.usace.army.mil/Missions/CivilWorks/RegulatoryProgramandPermits.aspx

United States Department of Agriculture: http://www.usda.gov/wps/portal/usda/usdahome

United States Environmental Protection Agency: http://www.epa.gov/

United States Fish and Wildlife Service: http://www.fws.gov/

United States Geological Survey: http://www.usgs.gov/

USDA Farm Services Agency: http://www.fsa.usda.gov/FSA/

USDA Natural Resources Conservation Service: http://www.nrcs.usda.gov/wps/portal/nrcs/ site/national/home/

USFWS Region 2: http://www.fws.gov/southwest/

Nongovernmental Organizations

Ducks Unlimited–Texas: http://www.ducks.org/texas

The Nature Conservancy–Texas: http://www.nature.org/ourinitiatives/regions/northamerica/unitedstates/texas/index.htm

Society of Wetland Scientists: http://www.sws.org/

APPENDIX B

Wetland Resource Books

Compiled by Zoe Ann Stinchcomb,
Texas Freshwater Fisheries Center

Cox, Donald D. 2002. *A Naturalist's Guide to Wetland Plants: An Ecology for Eastern North America*. Illustrated by Shirley A. Peron. Syracuse, NY: Syracuse University Press.

Keddy, Paul A. 2010. *Wetland Ecology: Principles and Conservation*. 2nd ed. Cambridge: Cambridge University Press.

McPherson, Steward. 2006. *Pitcher Plants of the Americas*. Granville, OH: McDonald and Woodward Publishing.

Redington, Charles B. 1994. *Plants in Wetlands*. Illustrated by Pamela H. See. Redington Field Guides to Biological Interactions. Dubuque, IA: Kendall Hunt Publishing.

APPENDIX C

Additional Resources

Texas Parks and Wildlife Resources

Aquatic WILD is a pre-kindergarten through grade 12 environmental and conservation education program focused on aquatic wildlife and habitats, including wetlands. The curriculum is available through attendance at hands-on workshops for formal and informal educators: http://www.tpwd.state.tx.us/learning/project_wild/aquatic_wild.phtml.

Texas Aquatic Science is an online curriculum for students grades 6–12. This comprehensive guide explores water "from molecules to ecosystem, and headwaters to ocean." Each of the 14 chapters has an overview video and connections to aquatic resource careers. The teacher's guide is full of hands-on activities. Texas Aquatic Science is a cooperative education project sponsored by Texas Parks and Wildlife, the Harte Research Institute for Gulf of Mexico Studies at Texas A&M University–Corpus Christi, and the Meadows Center for Water and the Environment at Texas State University. Student guide: http://texasaquaticscience.org/; and teacher guide: http://www.tpwd.state.tx.us/publications/learning/aquaticscience/.

Texas Treasures: Wetlands is a TPWD booklet about wetlands in Texas:http://www.tpwd.state.tx.us/publications/pwdpubs/media/pwd_bk_k0700_0908.pdf.

TPWD Wetland Posters: Coastal Wetland Poster and Fact Sheets, West Texas Cienega: http://www.texasthestateofwater.org/screening/html/factsheets_posters.htm.

Loaner Trunks

Coastal Ecosystem Treasures Trunk is available to any educator in Texas. The trunk includes posters, videos, curriculum, activities, interactive CD-ROMS, and games: https://tpwd.texas.gov/education/resources/resources/loaner-trunks.

Texas Wetlands Discovery Trunks are available for loan in several urban areas across the state. The trunk contains lesson plans, books, posters, videos, Texas Amphibian Watch materials (including a frog and toad calls CD-ROM), and field equipment to guide students in their investigations of wetland habitats. The trunks emphasize hands-on learning both in the classroom and in the field: https://tpwd.texas.gov/education/resources/resources/loaner-trunks.

Texas Parks and Wildlife Magazine

The State of Wetlands, July 2006. The entire issue examines Texas' wetlands: http://www.tpwmagazine.com/archive/2006/jul/.

"Pollution Solution," by Bill Dawson, September 2003: http://www.tpwmagazine.com/archive/2003/sept/scout1/.

"Washing the Water," by Wendee Holtcamp, July 2006: http://www.tpwmagazine.com/archive/2006/jul/ed_7/index.phtml.

"Pollution Solution" and "Washing the Water" highlight Richland Creek Wildlife Management Area wetlands, the nation's first water recycling wetland. This constructed wetland, located 80 miles southeast of Dallas–Fort Worth, pulls water from the Trinity River and cycles it through the wetland, removing pollutants and sediment efficiently and cheaply. Ultimately, the cleaned water is used to supplement the Fort Worth water supply. The wetland is a haven for wildlife and managed to maximize benefits to wildlife.

Additional Wetland Information on the TPWD Website

Find links to wetland ecology, conservation, regulations, landowner assistance, and the Texas Wetlands Conservation Plan: http://www.tpwd.state.tx.us/landwater/water/habitats/wetland/ecology/index.phtml.

Non-TPWD Websites and Resources

American Wetlands Month occurs each May and is hosted by the EPA and partners. Local groups can add their event to the online event calendar. Support materials for events is available at http://water.epa.gov/type/wetlands/outreach/index.cfm.

Caddo Lake Institute is a nonprofit organization founded to protect Caddo Lake. In 1993, Caddo Lake was designated a "Wetland of International Importance" under the Ramsar Convention. It is the only site to hold that designation and was the thirteenth site listed in the world: http://www.caddolakeinstitute.us/index.html.

The **Environmental Protection Agency (EPA)** website contains a composite of links to activities, curriculum, programs, tools, and videos all related to wetlands: http://water.epa.gov/type/wetlands/outreach/education_index.cfm.

Estuaries 101 is an NOAA resource designed to be used by teachers in grades 6–12. The Estuaries 101 curriculum deepens students' understanding about estuaries and how estuaries affect their daily lives: http://estuaries.noaa.gov/Teachers/Home.aspx.

Project WET (Water Education For Teachers) is a water education curriculum for teachers to explain water resources to youth. Workshops are provided by partner organizations in several Texas cities. Online training is also available. Numerous supplementary publications are available, including student books, maps, posters, and guide for conducting water festivals: www.projectwet.org.

Texas A&M Aquaplant, a pond manager diagnostic tool presented by Texas A&M Wildlife and Fisheries Science Extension Unit, helps in identification of aquatic plants: http://aquaplant.tamu.edu/plant-Identification/.

Texas A&M Extension AgriLife and Sea Grant provide information about wetland types, values, events, and news related to Texas wetlands: http://texaswetlands.org/.

Texas Living Waters Project is co-hosted by National Wildlife Federation and Sierra Club. It is not specific to wetlands but provides up-to-date information on water issues in Texas: http://texaslivingwaters.org/.

Trib+Water is an online freshwater news wrap-up and analysis, co-published by the *Texas Tribune* and the Meadows Center for Water and the Environment. Sign up for the newsletter: http://www.texastribune.org/plus/water/.

USDA Natural Resources Conservation Service has information on wetlands: http://www.nrcs.usda.gov/wps/portal/nrcs/main/national/water/wetlands/. See its video on how Florida farmers are using NRCS conservation programs to convert their marginal farmland back into wetlands. This helps create wildlife habitat, improves water quality, and prevents flooding: https://www.youtube.com/watch?v=MUlE4-WTONU.

US Fish & Wildlife Service National Wetlands Inventory is a website devoted to wetlands, including a national inventory: http://www.fws.gov/wetlands/_index.html.

USGS National Wetlands Research Center addresses emerging issues related to wetland ecosystems: http://www.nwrc.usgs.gov/index.html.

World Wetlands Day, February 2, is hosted by the Ramsar Convention on Wetlands. Each year the organization produces a packet that includes an educational leaflet, posters, and stickers. The website has a wealth of additional information: http://archive.ramsar.org/cda/en/ramsar-activities-wwds-world-wetlands-day-2/main/ramsar/1–63–78%5E21729_4000_0__.

WOW! The Wonders of Wetlands is an instructional guide for educators that provides a resourceful and creative collection of wetland activities, information, and ideas. The book can be purchased online, but courses are also offered. A Spanish version of the book is available. Environmental Concern, the owner of the WOW! The Wonders of Wetlands website, has numerous additional resources on its site: http://www.wetland.org/education_wow.htm.

References

Dahl , T. E. 1990. *Wetlands Losses in the United States 1780s to 1980s*. Washington, DC: US Department of the Interior, Fish and Wildlife Service.

———. 2011. *Status and Trends of Wetlands in the Conterminous United States: 2004 to 2009*. Washington, DC: US Fish and Wildlife Service. Accessed April 14, 2015. http://www.fws.gov/wetlands/Documents/Status-and-Trends-of-Wetlands-in-the-Conterminous-United-States-2004-to-2009.pdf.

Forage Information System, Oregon State University. 1991.Terminology for Grazing Lands and Grazing Animals. Accessed April 14, 2015. http://forages.oregonstate.edu/fi/topics/pasturesandgrazing/grazingsystemdesign/grazingterminology.

Lellis-Dibble, K. A., K. E. McGlynn, and T. E. Bigford. 2008. *Estuarine Fish and Shellfish Species in U.S. Commercial and Recreational Fisheries: Economic Value as an Incentive to Protect and Restore Estuarine Habitat*. US Department of Commerce, NOAA Tech. Memo, NMFSF/SPO-90. Washington, DC: US Department of Commerce. Accessed April 14, 2015. http://www.habitat.noaa.gov/pdf/publications_general_estuarinefishshellfish.pdf.

Lowrance, R., L. Altier, J. D. Newbold, R. R. Schnabel, P. M. Groffman, J. M. Denver, D. I. Correll, J. W. Gilliam. J. L. Robinson, R. B. Brinsfield, K. W. Staver, W. Lucas, and A. Todd. 1997. Water Quality Functions of Riparian Forest Buffers in Chesapeake Bay Watersheds. *Environmental Management* 21 (5): 687–712. Accessed April 14, 2015. http://www.esf.edu/efb/mitchell/Lowrance%20et%20al%201997.pdf.

Mitsch, W. J., and J. G. Gosselink. 1993. *Wetlands*. 2nd ed. New York: John Wiley.

Neilson, E. L., and D. E. Benson. 2000. *Wildlife Habitat Evaluation Program National Manual*. Stillwater, OK: Adaptive Concepts.

Raasch, Jeff, Robert Spain, Larry D. McKinney, and Andrew D. Sansom. 2000. *Wetlands Assistance Guide for Landowners*. Austin: Texas Parks and Wildlife Department. Accessed April 14, 2015. https://tpwd.texas.gov/publications/pwdpubs/media/pwd_bk_r0400_0020_11_00.pdf.

Sather, J. H., and R. D. Smith. 1984. *An Overview of Major Wetland Functions and Values*. US Fish and Wildlife Service FWS/OBS-84/18. Washington, DC: USFWS.

Stedman, S., and T. E. Dahl. 2013. *Status and Trends of Wetlands in the Coastal Watersheds of the Conterminous United States: 2004 to 2009*. Washington, DC: National Oceanic and Atmospheric Administration, National Marine Fisheries Service, and US Department of the Interior, Fish and Wildlife Service.

Texas Administrative Code. n.d. Title 30: Environmental Quality. Part 1: TCEQ. Chapter 307: Texas Surface Water Quality Standards. Rule 307.3 Definitions and Abbreviations, sec. (84). Accessed April 14, 2015. http://texreg.sos.state.tx.us/public/readtac$ext.TacPage?sl=T&app=9&p_dir=F&p_rloc=166377&p_tloc=14748&p_ploc=1&pg=4&p_tac=&ti=30&pt=1&ch=307&rl=5.

TPWD (Texas Parks and Wildlife Department). 1997. *Texas Wetlands Conservation Plan*. Austin: TPWD. Accessed April 14, 2015. https://tpwd.texas.gov/publications/pwdpubs/media/pwd_pl_r2000_0005.pdf.

UNIT 20

Rangeland Ecology and Management

BARRON S. RECTOR
Associate Professor and Extension Range Specialist, Texas A&M University

Unit Goals

After completing this unit, volunteers should be able to

- define and describe rangeland
- define rangeland management
- describe why rangeland management is different from an agricultural vocation
- list the basic component categories of rangeland management
- list and describe the four founding principles of grazing management
- understand and be able to communicate the importance of land management goals
- describe how native grasses grow
- describe, compare, and contrast rangeland management tools
- develop an awareness of grazing, brush, and weed issues and management on Texas rangelands

Introduction

One generally envisions a range as vast grassland somewhere "out West" grazed by large herds of roaming bison, while others see lands grazed by herds of cattle, sheep, and native animals. This notion is restrictive when rangelands are viewed at their true level of diversity and complexity. **Rangeland** is defined as "land on which the indigenous vegetation (climax or sub-climax) is predominately grasses, grass-like plants, forbs or shrubs that are grazed or have the potential to be grazed, and which is used as a natural ecosystem for the production of grazing livestock and wildlife" (Allen et al. 2011, 5). Rangelands occupy about 47% of the world's land area and about 36% in the United States (Casper 2007). Today some 90 million acres, or approximately 60% of the lands in Texas, are classified as rangeland. Rangeland includes prairies, grasslands, shrublands, deserts, wetlands, riparian areas, and tundra.

When the Europeans came to Texas in the 1820s, settlers found that 90.6% of the lands in Texas were rangeland. Texas rangelands have now been converted to croplands or farmlands, urban and suburban development, highways, sites for industry, parks, and open spaces for recreation. Some have become reservoirs. Rangelands still remain the state's largest natural resource.

What Is a Rangeland?

For many, rangelands bring to mind scenic vistas, grazing animals, and room to roam. Thad Box, former dean of the College of Natural Resources at USO, wrote that "America's rangelands were always grazed. Although our virgin rangelands did not have cattle on them, they had plant-eating animals for as long as we have evidence. Rangeland evolved with grazing." He further states, "Pre-history teases us with tidbits. We know there were plant-eating dinosaurs. Pollen tells us what kinds of plants. The fossil record gets better after the last ice age. We know there were little horses and giant bison in abun-

Rangelands can be defined in different ways, but the definition generally pertains to grazing livestock. Courtesy of Natural Resources Conservation Service

Cattle herds on an idealistic view of rangelands. Courtesy of Robert Lyons, Texas A&M AgriLife Extension Service

dance. And, that many grasses and shrubs were similar to the ones we have today" (2001c, 22).

Our first recorded history of American rangelands is in journals of early explorers, usually adventurers and soldiers with little scientific training. The medical officers often become the interpreters of natural history. There is nothing written by ecologists or range managers; such people did not exist. The main information recorded was the land's ability to provide forage for expedition horses and wild animals for human survival.

Rangeland is a classification of land, a natural land that is not plowed, fertilized, or irrigated. It is a recognized home of native plants and animals. No single characteristic differentiates rangelands from croplands or forestlands. Stoddart et al. state, "Rangelands are those areas of the world, which by reason of physical limitations—low precipitation, rough topography, poor drainage, or cold temperatures—are unsuited to cultivation and which are a source of forage for free-ranging native and domestic animals, as well as a source of wood products, water and wildlife" (1975, 2–3).

Slightly more than 70% of Texas' non-federal lands are grazing lands, including range, pasture, and forest. **Range** consists of grasslands, shrublands, marsh areas, riparian areas, deserts, and woodlands that do not support commercial timber production. **Forestlands** support tree cover used for commercial timber production but may be grazed at times. **Pastures** support introduced forage plants and receive periodic cultural treatments such as fertilization, herbicides, and shredding. At the world level, rangelands also include steppes, savannas, and even the arctic tundra.

Rangelands produce forage for livestock and many species of wildlife. Texas is the leading producer of natural fibers (wool and mohair) and red meat (beef, lamb, venison, and cabrito). Texas rangelands support the nation's largest white-tailed deer population and significant numbers of other big-game

In Texas, water is the most valuable commodity for any rangeland or land manager.

Texas' rapid growing population and expanded development of urban areas into historically agriculturally producing lands have implications for both land conservation and the resource conservation of commodities such as water.

animals, both native and exotic. In addition, habitat is provided for large and diverse populations of nongame wildlife species.

As a critical issue today, rangelands are most important for the valuable commodity, water, which is necessary for sustaining life and the well-being of both people and animals. The future of Texas depends on this one commodity. The state's rapid population growth is creating a need for more water. Most of Texas waterways have their headwaters on and are filtered by rangelands.

"The major problems of the world are the result of the difference between the way nature works and the way people think."
—Gregory Bateson, British anthropologist and social scientist

Although there are fewer ranching operations in Texas today, another rapidly increasing use of rangeland is for nonproduction purposes. People want to own land as a hedge against inflation, a place to pursue a certain rural kind of lifestyle, or as a place to retire or recreate. In many areas of Texas the demand for white-faced steers has been replaced with an interest in white-tailed deer, and bobwhite quail in lieu of black-baldy cattle. Well-managed rangelands have a great visual appeal: wildflowers in the spring, autumn colors, birdsong, and glimpses of flourishing native wildlife and grazing livestock.

Rangelands set aside as open space provide for much outdoor recreation, particularly for those who enjoy the sport of hunting. Texas has a rich land heritage. Both the land and its flora developed under the influence of the bison and other grazing animals. One of the first uses of Texas' rangelands was for ranching. They have affected "western" movies, country-western music and poetry, clothes, and even athletic events, such as rodeos.

An ever-increasing population with ever-increasing demands on the state's natural resources must still be fed and clothed. Conversion of rangeland to other uses (home sites, highways, intensive crop production, urbanization, and industrial development) is accelerating. Conflicts of use, lower production from misuse, accelerated soil erosion and loss, and inefficient use of rainfall all indicate the need for proper use and management of rangelands. Stewardship of rangelands starts with humans on the land but goes much further, having social and economic value for landowners and all of the state's citizens.

"As we approached the valley of the Pecos, an entire change took place in the scene. On the 31st of May we arrived at a plain covered with grass and flowers, and surrounded by regularly formed table mountains. The grass and flowers were so thick and high, that our horses had difficulty in making their way through, and the sweetest perfume, principally of the American centaurea [probably a star thistle or basketflower], filled the atmosphere."
—Julius Fröbel, *Seven Years' Travel in Central America, Northern Mexico, and the Far West of the United States*

Development of Rangeland Management

Rangeland management is the "manipulation of rangeland components to obtain the optimum combination of goods and services for society on a sustained basis" (Allen 1991). Even though rangeland management has focused on the manipulation of livestock grazing intensity, timing, and frequency to maintain or improve the range resource, rangeland management is complex and involves more than just grazing management components. The discipline of rangeland management provides the knowledge and principles that can be used to manage for rangeland sustainability. The concept of rangeland sustainability represents a philosophical balance between the needs of society and the needs of the resource. The welfare of the range resource is critically linked to the welfare of society. Rangeland management exists today because people have abused the land in the past.

The introduction of grazing livestock to the North American continent is still controversial; however, horses were included in Hernán Cortés's exploration of Mexico in 1515 and Hernando de Soto's expedition in Florida in 1539. The considerable stock of 1,000 horses, 500 cows, and 5,000 sheep brought by Francisco Vázquez de Coronado in 1540 is considered the "first record of importation of cattle into the territory properly part of the United States." From these herds, escaped and abandoned animals began stocking the range area. Additional herds brought by successive Spanish and European settlers represented a "motley array of kinds, shape, and breeds" from European countries (Stoddart et al. 1975, 82).

The range-livestock industry can trace its origin to the settlers moving west to the Mississippi Valley in 1830s, merging their herds with the feral livestock, and moving northward from Texas. As Stoddart explains, "Broad expanses of grassland gave impetus to the livestock industry, and though for some years there was a lack of transportation and market facilities, there began a general increase in the Western livestock population" (Stoddart et al. 1975, 82).

Driven by demand for production during the Civil War, the availability of land resources from passage of the Homestead Act in 1862, and federal policies on land sales, the number of cattle and other grazers built up to alarming proportions in West Texas. The grass resource was considered to be almost limitless in its capacity. H. L. Bentley of Abilene, Texas, wrote of the cattle business boom in the 1860s:

> Men of every rank were eager to get into the cow business. In a short time every acre of grass was stocked beyond

> its fullest capacity. Thousands of cattle and sheep were crowded on the ranges when half the number was too many. The grasses were entirely consumed; their very roots were trampled into the dust and destroyed. In their eagerness to get something for nothing, speculators did not hesitate at the permanent injury, if not the total ruin of the finest grazing country in America. (Bentley 1898, 72)

From the beginning, ranches were overstocked. To increase profit, absentee owners bought more stock. By the early 1880s cattle owners knew the range was deteriorating. The infamous "die-up," beginning in 1884, confirmed their worst suspicions. Don Biggers described it well: "In the winter of 1884 began a series of the most disastrous years ever known in the cattle history. . . . When a blizzard would sweep over the country, the cattle would drift before it, and it was then no uncommon sight to see great herds of cattle rolling southward, nothing to eat, nothing to drink, pelted by sleet and covered with snow; while around them the pitiless blizzard seemed to howl in fiendish glee" (Biggers and Connor 2003, 121). This was repeated in 1886, 1887, and 1894. Depending on the areas, between 30% and 90% of the cattle on plains rangelands died in a 20-year period. High rollers were losing money on their investment.

After the 1886 die-up, USDA botanist George Vasey visited the ranches affected and made collections of plants. Then again in 1894, USDA agrostologist (one who studies grasses) J. G. Smith collected and reported the deterioration of lands from overgrazing and recommended bringing stocking rates more in line with **carrying capacity**—the number of animals a piece of land will support—along with the need for research. In the following year, a series of range experiment stations were established by C. C. Georgeson—with one in Abilene and one in Channing—to report on the "fallacy of overstocking and demonstrating range improvement practices." Georgeson, with the help of H. L. Bentley, brought ranchers that were involved in these experiments together and held a "meeting of stockmen." They worked to describe common terms of land management, such as carrying capacity, land capability, and the basis for stocking rates, with very little agreement from the general livestock and ranching community statewide. "One stockman offered a resolution: 'Resolved, that none of us know, or care to know, anything about grasses, native or otherwise, outside the fact that for the present there are lots of them, the best on record, and we are after getting the most out of them while they last.'"

Besides this initial establishment of rangeland management practices by these stockmen, the profession of range manager itself had not established until at the earliest

When the Land Belonged to God, by C. M. Russell, oil. Courtesy of Montana Historical Society, MacKay Collection, Helena, Montana

The winter of 1886 was extremely harsh and had devastating consequences on the livestock industry.

1910. Up until this point, with the botanical collections and scientific explorations of the region's ecology, a concern developed for the "deteriorating land productivity." And as Thad Box wrote, "In the next decade [1910–1919] range management, as we know it, came into its own" (2001b, 46). One of the first technical ranch analysis surveys was done by James Jardine during this time. Arthur Sampson, a plant ecologist and later professor of rangeland management, made the connection between ecological theory and practical management. During this time frame across the country, several universities opened classes in rangeland management and began to address the types of usage of lands, which gave birth to the rangeland management profession.

World War I national policy was to raise more livestock, and ranchers were encouraged to overstock. When the war ended, with the added pressure put on the land for war production, many ranchers found the land degraded by decades of chronic misuse. However, a new age of rangeland management began to grow from this depression and degradation, from seeds sown prior to the war. As Thad Box reported, "The seeds of scientific land care had been sown in the dust. A fledgling science sprouted. Its growth depended on making the sordid conditions of the western rangelands an important issue in the minds of the general public. Responsibility for land needed to become a spiritual issue" (2001c, 46). A series of rangeland conservation acts were passed shortly thereafter, including the Taylor Grazing Act of 1934, which brought regulation to the public domain.

"Do we not already sing our love and obligation to the land of the free and the home of the brave? Yes, but just what and whom do we love? Certainly not the soil, which we are sending helterskelter downriver. . . . Certainly not the plant, of which we exterminate whole communities without batting an eye. Certainly not the animals, of which we have already extirpated many of the largest and most beautiful species. A land ethic of course cannot prevent alteration, management, and use of these 'resources,' but it does affirm their right to continued existence, and, at least in spots, their continued existence in a natural state."
—Aldo Leopold, "The Land Ethic"

What Is Rangeland Management?

Mort Kothmann recorded the shift in rangeland management as started by Maj. John Wesley Powell in 1869 with a survey through the western United States after the Civil War. Powell "recognized that the lands of the west were 'a different kind of land' that was not suitable for cultivated agriculture, but was suitable for production of grazing animals." The USDA in Texas recognized the need to control and manage grazing in order to restore rangeland vegetation along with the development of sustainable production principles. Kothmann stated that by this time, "the need for 'range management' was widely recognized by a significant group of scientists, educators, and practicing professionals and the American Society of Range Management was organized in 1948," an organization that was to bring together landowners and range managers with a "strong natural resources conservation ethic." In the 1960s, the discipline of ecology had a noticeable shift "from land conservation and management to science and research" (2001, 47).

Stoddart et al. described rangeland management as "the science and art of optimizing the returns from rangelands in those combinations most desired by and suitable to society through the manipulation of range ecosystems. . . . [It is] biological because it deals with the response of vegetation to cropping and the response to the animals which harvest the crop; physical because climatic, topographic and

In 1935 Congress passed Public Law 74–46, in which it recognized that "the wastage of soil and moisture resources on farm, grazing, and forest lands . . . is a menace to the national welfare" and established the Soil Conservation Service (SCS) as a permanent agency in the USDA. In 1994, SCS's name was changed to the Natural Resources Conservation Service to better reflect the broadened scope of the agency's concerns. To this day, the agency continues to provide range managers and landowners resources for conservation and education.

hydrological factors determine the kind and degree of use that can be made of range; and social because the needs of society determine the uses to which range resources are put" (1975, 26).

Holechek et al. defined rangeland management as "the manipulation of rangeland components to obtain the optimum combination of goods and services for society on a sustained basis" (2001, 5). They describe it as having two basic components: (1) protection and enhancement of the soil and vegetation complex and (2) maintenance or improvement of the output of consumable range products, such as red meat, fiber, wood, water, and wildlife. Of paramount importance to rangeland management is the principle that the management of livestock, wildlife, and other natural resources conserves the integrity of the rangeland ecosystem without permanent damage.

"We abuse land because we regard it as a commodity belonging to us. When we see land as a community to which we belong, we may begin to use it with love and respect."
—Aldo Leopold

The rangeland management profession is unique among agricultural vocations in that it deals with the plant and animal interface rather than with plants or animals in isolation. The distinguishing feature of rangeland management is that it deals with manipulating the grazing activities by large herbivores so that both plant and animal production will be maintained or improved (Holechek et al. 2001).

Early rangeland management practices concerned manipulation of livestock grazing intensity, timing, and frequency to ameliorate adverse grazing impacts on the soil and vegetation. More recently, rangeland management has broadened to include manipulation of many components of rangeland ecosystems other than livestock, such as fire, wildlife, and human activities. Rangeland management is distinct from other disciplines in that it integrates knowledge from several disciplines into a unified system. The basic components of rangeland management can be categorized into biological, physical, and anthropological factors.

Initially, range managers were concerned primarily with the biological component, particularly plants. They studied responses of plant communities to grazing because plant communities are the primary producers of food for grazing animals (from elk and antelope to grasshoppers). However, they soon recognized that a plant community's responses to grazing could not be understood without knowledge of individual plant physiological processes. Because plant productivity depends on the interaction between climate and soils as well as grazing influences, the additional need to understand the physical environment became apparent.

Since rangeland management is geared toward producing products usable to humans, social, economic, cultural, and technological considerations are a critical part of the rangeland management equation. Holechek et al. (2001) explained further: "As an example, range management on some private lands in the US is becoming increasingly oriented to the production of harvestable wildlife. In the US, food costs are low, much of the human population has considerable time for recreational pursuits, growth in the human population is relatively low, and the country is characterized by a high level of affluence. In contrast, most countries of Africa have rapidly expanding human populations and low levels of affluence, and food costs account for a major portion of the per capita income. In such countries, maximization of livestock production is the primary orientation of range management" (2001, 7–8).

Holechek et al. added that "ecology, defined as the study of the relationship between an organism or group of organisms and their environment, has been and will continue to be the foundation for range management" (2001, 8). The 1990s was a transition period for the rangeland management profession. Kennedy et al. (1995) stated that it was characterized as a period in which the commodity production goal-oriented approaches of the past gave way to new approaches that center around sustainability, diversity, holism, and integrated natural resource planning.

Grazing Management for Native Pastures

Grazing management has been defined as "manipulation of grazing in pursuit of a defined objective" (Allen 1991, 12). Texas ranchers have long used grazing management as a tool to make a profit in the livestock industry, whether they realized it or not. Grazing is a natural animal function and a complex interaction between the plant and the animal. Grazing management becomes the means by which the ranch owner or manager supervises the cost of producing and harvesting raw materials while keeping and sustaining the productivity of the land resource. Thus, grazing management in this sense is controlling to achieve profit but also includes goals related to land, plant, animal, water, recreational, and society that the landowner has established. Grazing management on rangeland has been founded on four ecological principles: proper use, proper season of use, proper distribution, and proper kinds and classes of animals.

- **Proper use** is closely tied to "stocking rate." There is a proper amount of plant tissue that can be removed through grazing that allows the plant to continue to grow and remain in high vigor. Overstocking is the number-one factor causing rangeland degradation today.
- **Proper season of use** is closely tied to the season of growth: cool-season forages are grazed in the cooler months of the year, and warm-season forages are grazed predominantly in the summer growing season. Dormant-season grazing is also highly accommodating to wildlife needs during the hard winter months.
- **Proper distribution** of animals was particularly important in early ranching when ranch pastures were large in size. Proper distribution looked at more uniform grazing across a pasture. Distribution could be affected by distance to water, time of the year, grazing obstacles such as cliffs or ridges, and size of pastures.
- **Proper kinds and classes of animals** are related to the need to recognize the important diet components for grazing animals. The kinds of plants growing on rangeland must be considered to adequately match the forage available to the kind of animal that will consume what is growing. In this case, cattle prefer grass but will eat shrubs and forbs as secondary items. Sheep prefer forbs, and white-tailed deer and goats primarily use browse.

In its most practical sense, ranchers use grazing management as a tool to impact plant succession, soil erosion, and animal production. How animals are stocked can impact or directly change the rangeland native plant communities. Ranchers and land managers must recognize that certain grazing practices can cause a dynamic change in the plant composition and health of a pasture, a change that can be positive or negative. A change in plant composition can affect the performance of grazing animals and alter the productivity and profitability of the entire ranch enterprise. Grazing management strategies should be designed with plant, soil, and animal performance in mind.

"Plans are dreams of the wise."
—German proverb

Livestock grazing management is a tool for all range managers. Courtesy of Natural Resources Conservation Service

Native grazing wildlife, such as the white-tailed deer, must be considered in grazing and habitat management plans when considering the range system as a whole. Courtesy of Larry Brennan, Elm Fork Chapter

Maintaining an optimum balance between plant and animal requirements should be the primary grazing management goal. Maintenance of adequate organic matter or litter cover on the soil is important. This can be a challenge but is directly linked to the loss or improvement in the livestock carrying capacity of the ranch and the invasion of unwanted weeds and brush. Without adequate grazing, the desirable plants may be reduced and the undesirable plants increased.

The rules and outcomes of grazing rangeland are different from those on agronomic ("tame" or "improved") pastures that rely on exotic (introduced) grasses and fertilizer inputs. The decision maker will often have to disregard practices used in annual grazing programs for livestock (such as oats, wheat, or forage sorghums) and grazing exotic grass pasture such as bermudagrass, dallisgrass, or bahiagrass. In a rangeland system, grazing management is the key to maintaining a healthy productive range ecosystem because this system is totally dependent on the availability of resources, either introduced or native, and the ecological processes that regulate growth.

Goals of Landownership

There are many reasons why anyone owns or operates a ranch. Generally these reasons are related to landowner goals, and if the goals are known, decisions about the use of land and other resources can be made (thus management). The ranch or land base operation must have planned goals and determine how the goals are going to be achieved. The goal of resource management should be either to improve or to maintain. Grazing management should be designed to satisfy both the enterprise goals and resource goals.

Goals can be grouped in many ways: long term–short term, personal-financial, general-specific, or operational-nonbusiness, and so on. However, the most important and useful grouping should be based on order of importance; that is, which are those goals of the resource owners (the landowner and livestock owner)? If all of these resources are owned by the ranch firm, then the goal-setting task is easier because there are less likely to be conflicting goals. However, if the resource owner(s) does not clearly identify and communicate his or her goals, then other people in the business are less effective in helping achieve the goals.

In the planning process, knowing the goals of the landowner is important. Too often, the ranch manager is more concerned with operational goals, such as when to spray and when to move livestock. These goals relate to day-to day-operations and decisions. Long-term goals spell out those associated with economic and resource stability: where the landowner wants to be in future years, how much grass to grow, who to give inheritance, and total development of the ranch.

Short-term goals usually cover actions and decisions within a year. These goals outline the decisions and the actions needed to accomplish them. Once goals are set and accepted, every action can be evaluated. Goals probably should not be set in concrete but be adaptive and allowed to evolve and mature through time and as conditions change. Goals should be made known to all involved with the ranch operation. The chief decision maker needs to prioritize goals and be willing to compromise. The rancher may not be able to achieve two goals simultaneously, that is, maximize revenue from wildlife and minimize contact with people, or chemically spray for weed control and have the best food supply for wildlife/livestock production. Some goals may actually serve as constraints and should be identified as such.

How Do Native Grasses Grow?

To grow and reproduce, grass leaves capture sunlight and carbon dioxide, while roots acquire water and nutrients. If highly productive and healthy perennial grasses are to

Big bluestem (*Andropogon gerardii*), a warm-season native perennial, is often referred to as "ice-cream" grass because of the high nutrition and palatability. Courtesy of Natural Resources Conservation Service

live from year to year, they must be allowed to manufacture and store sufficient energy to develop buds that are vigorous enough to survive the winter and begin growing next spring.

The basic building block of a grass plant is a **phytomer**. Each phytomer has a leaf blade, a sheath that supports the blade, and a node where the sheath is connected to the stem (a culm). The part of the culm between two nodes is an internode. The node contains up to four root buds and one shoot bud. Near the base of a shoot, grasses produce several nodes with little or no elongation of the internodes. This region of the grass tiller (shoot) is the crown. The growing point is the region on the top of a tiller where cell division is occurring and new phytomers are being produced. Roots and new shoots grow from buds that are on nodes. Nodes elevated above the ground cannot produce roots. The crown is the region with several nodes that are near the soil surface, providing the opportunity for growth of new roots and new tillers. The leaves of grasses may live only 30–90 days. Roots and crowns may live one to three years. Thus, regular replacement of these plant parts is required to keep them alive.

All grass tillers begin growth with a growing point developing from a dormant bud or below ground level until it is elevated and/or triggered to become reproductive. As long as the tiller is vegetative, it has the potential to produce an indefinite number of leaves. When the tiller is triggered to elevate or become reproductive, there is no further potential for new leaf initiation. When first elongated, a tiller appears to be vegetative since no seed head is evident. In some grasses, tillers remain as elongated

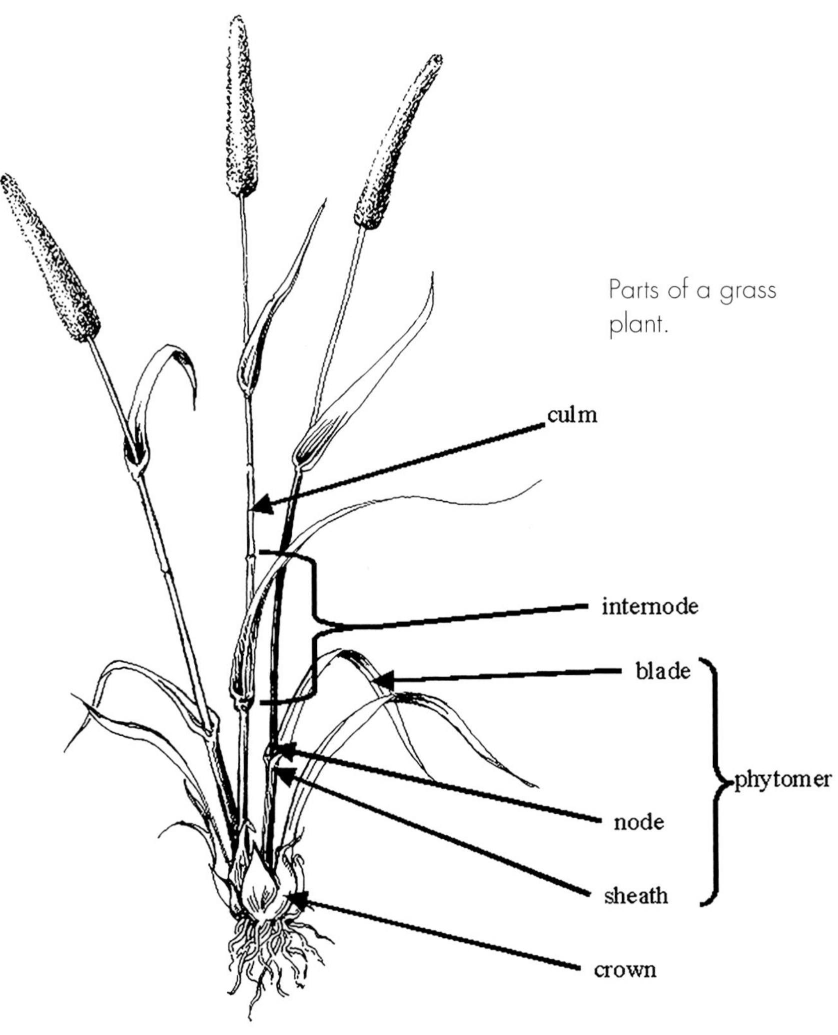

Parts of a grass plant.

vegetative tillers because the seed head either never develops or dies at an early stage of growth. In many situations, elongation is a transitional stage between the vegetative and reproductive stages of grass growth. If the tiller has become reproductive, a seed head will emerge.

Removal of the growing point of an elongated tiller breaks the dormancy of the buds associated with the tiller. New growth potentially could occur by the development of three different kinds of tillers from dormant buds. The most rapid growth occurs from an intact growing point of the defoliated tiller. The timing of stem elongation is very important due to the subsequent exposure of the growing point to grazing. Some grasses have no stem elongation until about the time the growing point enters the reproductive phase. Such grasses maintain their growing point below or at ground level throughout most of the growing season and are resistant to continuous or close grazing. Some grasses, such as switchgrass, elevate their growing point early in their development because of elongation of internodes or stem.

Early in the season, all grasses have their growing points close to or at ground level. Since grazing livestock cannot physically graze any closer than about an inch from the soil surface, there is less danger of removing the growing point at this time. Although the plants may be grazed, each grazed tiller can continue to produce new leaf material. However, if internode elongation has occurred and the growing point is removed, new leaf material must come from dormant buds.

Since a grass bud that is developing into a new tiller has no leaves, it must depend on energy provided by either residual leaf material or energy from carbohydrate storage organs. If severe defoliation has occurred through overgrazing and repeated grazing of the grass, the only source of energy for new tillers is stored carbohydrates. If severe defoliation does not occur and some residual leaf material remains, new tiller growth can receive energy manufactured by the remaining leaf material, and there is no depletion of carbohydrate reserves. As the new tiller develops, it draws upon the carbohydrate reserves. If sufficient time is allowed for new leaf material to develop and become adult leaves, they can replenish the carbohydrate reserves and no harm is done. However, if severe defoliation is repeated before the new tiller has an opportunity to achieve an age of returning carbohydrates to the reserve storage, the grass will be stressed beyond possible regrowth. So we must remember that when grasses elevate their growing point early in the growth cycle, these grasses must be managed differently than grasses that elevate their growing point late in the growth cycle.

Grasses such as switchgrass are well suited to rotational grazing. This type of grazing is designed to remove the growing point but must be followed by a period of rest (non-use) to allow the development of new tillers that can be grazed in the future. For switchgrass, the non-use period is around 45 days. Rangeland pastures usually have a mixture of grasses with different growth habits. Specific management for specific grasses is relatively easy in a monoculture, but in a range situation with mixed grasses, the rancher must identify key grasses or those he or she would like to manage and develop a grazing program based on ranch goals.

Grass Growth: Implications for Management

The main forage plants for cattle on Texas native rangeland pastures are grasses, both warm and cool season, annuals and perennials. These grasses evolved over hundreds of years under conditions characterized by grazing, periodic fires, and variable and often extreme weather patterns (drought to flood). Grasses can tolerate livestock grazing but are not immune to impacts from overstocking. Native grasses are growing on

Switchgrass (*Panicum virgatum*) is a perennial warm-season grass that does well with rotational grazing.

a nutrient base that is provided by a particular kind of soil. Unlike the management of exotic pasture (such as bermudagrass), nutrients are not added to this system through fertilization. Nor is it irrigated to promote greater production. Native grass pastures should be managed through livestock grazing to take only approximately 15% to 25% of the year's current growth. This means that only one out of four leaves produced this year will be harvested. The remaining forage is harvested by other grazers such as grasshoppers and serves to protect the soil surface, provide nesting cover for ground-nesting birds (e.g., bobwhite quail) and promote future plant growth.

With a 15% to 25% harvest efficiency on native grass pastures, research has shown that it is not economical to fertilize native grasses for greater production. In a proper grazing situation, enough grass just cannot be eaten to make it possible to get the investment back. In fact, fertilization of native grass pasture often decreases the amount of desirable grasses and will allow invasive species such as weeds to establish.

Good grazing management on native grass pastures will leave enough green leaves of desirable forage grasses ungrazed so that they can carry on photosynthesis, maintain the health of the plant, and provide grazeable leaves sooner, a situation in which young leaves will continue to elongate and grow. In the native grass system, ungrazed grass becomes litter when it dies. Litter and plant cover protect the site from future erosion and help sustain a healthy water and nutrient cycle, thus promoting a healthy and productive pasture in the future. In a livestock operation on native grasses, the only nutrients removed from the pasture system are those that are sold and taken off the land through the calf. The amount of nutrients removed from the pasture system is greater in a haying operation.

Another example of poor grazing management of native grass pastures is stocking more animals on the land than the land can sustain. This is the number-one factor causing rangeland degradation. Too many animals can remove too many leaves from a plant and leave no plant growth for litter or soil cover. Without adequate leaves for photosynthesis, root growth and production are severely limited, the plant can decline in vigor, and next year's production can be lowered. A grass plant tries to compensate for excessive top-growth removal by producing more tillers (shoots) than can be supported by the available root system. As the root mass decreases, this ultimately leads to disappearance of the grass plant. When this happens, the forage base and its production decline, and the level of animal performance and numbers that can be stocked will decline.

Past grazing history affects the kinds and

A managed pasture in Pin Oak, Texas. Courtesy of Mary Pearl Meuth, Texas A&M AgriLife Extension Service

An overgrazed field in North Texas. Courtesy of Dale Rollins, Texas A&M AgriLife Extension Service

quantity of plants that will grow in a native pasture. Overgrazing the amount of forage produced does not leave adequate dormant forage to serve as litter or a plant that can recover over time. With bare ground increasing and soil erosion accelerating under this type of management, the opportunity for weed and brush invasions or even the increase of poisonous plants can occur. Increasing bare ground is also directly tied to reduced water infiltration rates into the soil during future rainfall events. With greater rainfall runoff and less water infiltration, pasture productivity drops, soil erosion increases, and water quality decreases.

What Does Grazing Management Control?

Efficient management works to maintain the proper balance between the grazing animal's demand for forage and the amount of forage produced. There are several controlling factors. First, the rancher is running a certain kind and class of livestock. If the livestock are a small breed of cattle such as Longhorns, the forage demand per animal is lower than for a breed such as Beefmaster, Brangus, or a larger frame-breed. Forage intake is directly related to animal size. The breed selected determines, to a certain extent, the amount of forage that has to be grown to meet individual animal demand. Second, the rancher selects a cow/calf, stocker, or replacement animal program. The kinds of animals raised, from young animals to older animals, determines the nutritive value and quantity of forage to be produced.

The kind of animal to be grazed must then be matched with the forage production capability of the ranch. If stockers are to be run in the fall, winter, and early spring, will the dormant standing crop in a warm-season perennial grass pasture meet this demand? Dry-matter production may meet the quantity requirement, but will the nutritive value of dormant grass meet the needs of a growing animal at this time of year? Animal performance may be improved in this case by supplementing limiting elements such as nitrogen or phosphorus and sometimes energy. Dormant-season grass harvesting may be more pragmatic using a grazing program with a cow/calf operation where calves are born toward the end of the dormant period.

What Is the Best Grazing Method?

The best grazing method begins with the right stocking rate; that is, the number of animals on a given amount of land over a certain period of time without deterioration of the resource base. It is generally expressed as animal units per unit of land area. Stocking rate has a far more important effect on animal performance and on plant species composition in a pasture than any other consideration in a grazing system. It matters less whether all of the cattle are moved around from one pasture to another, effectively consuming grass at a high consumption level but in a short period of time and then resting for a longer period of time (rotational stocking), or whether the same number of cattle are spread out over the whole area to be grazed and left all of the time (continuous stocking). What does matter is that the number of cattle grazing (forage demand) is adjusted to the amount of consumable forage in the pasture. If this is not done, then the rancher allows the land to change from the impact of overstocking.

Grazing and Risk

In the decision to run cattle on a pasture or grazing unit, a rancher must consider the impact that cattle will have on the landscape. Cattle are a valuable part of a livestock operation, but the land's carrying capacity must be considered to achieve livestock production goals and sustainability of the land. A risk exists when running cattle if the land manager fails to adjust the stocking rate relative to the available foods produced.

Cattle will not eat all of the classes and kinds of plants growing in a pasture. The risk is exaggerated by the landowner who does not have an understanding of what cattle grazing will do to the land. Without this understanding, a landowner will claim to have problems with cattle competing with wildlife species such as white-tailed deer, pastures that do not grow grass anymore, brush and weeds that destroy the land, and drought that kills all the grass. Failure to understand cattle behavior and the impact of grazing can lead to ranch failure and rangeland degradation.

Grazing management involves a number of decisions, including the kinds and numbers of animals to be stocked and the distribution and timing of grazing. Annual stocking rate decisions are made before the year's forage production can be known. These decisions affect the nutritive value and quantity of the forage produced and the performance of livestock. Over time, cumulative grazing management decisions affect the productivity and health of the rangeland and the owner's financial solvency. The rangeland ecosystem is complex, and grazing mistakes can occur. Livestock markets can also change and vary from year to year.

In this changing environment, rangeland owners and managers can learn from their mistakes and make better decisions in the future. The most successful managers plan conservatively so that they can handle unforeseen situations, recognize the warning signs of unacceptable risks, and correct their management strategies before the rangeland resource is harmed.

People often equate livestock numbers with wealth and income level. Yet research shows that net economic returns are higher with moderate grazing. A land manager cannot afford to jeopardize long-term productivity for short-term economic gains. The ranching operation will not be sustainable if it harms the natural range ecosystem. Often in management, too much importance is placed on immediate gross returns from livestock and/or wildlife and not enough on maintaining rangeland health. What is done to the land today affects the future productivity and health of the land.

"Do what you can with what you have, where you are."
—Theodore Roosevelt

Wild and Managed Animal Populations

Prior to human intervention in Texas, natural forces such as fire and floods and grazing by bison and other wild animals kept most rangelands as open grassland speckled with a series of successional stages that allowed for diverse vegetation. Changes in vegetation were accompanied by shifts in the animal populations that resided on the area. As

Eighty remnants of the great Southern Plains bison herd enter their new 700-acre expanded range of restored native prairie at Caprock Canyons State Park near Quitaque. This herd comprises descendants of legendary Panhandle rancher Charles Goodnight's historic herd, which was introduced to the park in 1988. Courtesy of Texas Parks and Wildlife Department

climate has changed (long-term effect), the dietary source (vegetation) for herbivores has changed, which has led to new forms and behavior of animals. Ruminant species are varied in terms of size, anatomical and physiological characteristics, and behavior. Although all ruminants are cellulose utilizers, individual species occupied different niches to which they became adapted through competition. Ruminants of varying size and form (deer, antelope, bison, and elk) have distinct diet preferences and food-gathering habits.

Today's ranching industry attempts to manage both wild and domestic ruminants on the same range resource. Domestic animal systems differ from wild animal systems in that the domesticators and manager imposes restraints on the system to satisfy their needs. Although humans have always been a part of the system, they now assume a new role. For example, implementation of management on the Edwards Plateau and surrounding vegetation regions changed the natural system in three ways.

First, with the advent of fencing, animal movement was restricted and grazing patterns of animals altered. Thus, the opportunity to "eat and run" was removed, and animals were made to eat from the same area and from the same group of plants day after day. Second, the emphasis was shifted to level of "off-take." Higher numbers of animals forced into the system meant greater amounts of animal products that could be removed from the system. Third, the manager's view was short term. There was no way that humans could know the long-term impact of management decisions.

Consequently, Texas rangelands have become a **disclimax** community, which has general characteristics of a climax community but has been disturbed by various influences, usually humans and domestic animals. The more preferred plants were reduced and replaced by plants that could withstand repeated defoliation or were not preferred. Shorter perennial grasses, annual grasses and forbs, and mixed brush species increased. To a point, this vegetation shift has favored sheep and goat grazing. Continued abusive or too heavy utilization of remaining plants on many ranches with cattle, sheep, and goats has further reduced the vegetation to a simplified composition of short, opportunistic grasses and forbs and undesirable brush species.

The lands of Texas now present examples

Multiple species can be utilized in a complementary grazing system to take advantage of each grazer's habits and preferences of forage.

of various degrees of management, past and present. It is important to recognize that rangelands that produce more than one class of forage can provide for greater animal production if the grazing animal population can utilize the array of plant classes produced. This is not a new thought in relation to the previous discussion, but it takes on a new significance when related to domestic animal agriculture. Rangelands containing a combination of forage classes are best suited to grazing use by a combination of livestock. Thus, differences in grazing habits and forage preferences have led to the use of cattle, sheep, and goats in grazing combinations, referred to as complementary grazing systems. This practice of multiple-use grazing is as old as agriculture itself, but the utilization of an area in production of multiple livestock species has been new many times to many people.

Competition among Animals

Competition among animals is the mutual use of a resource in limited supply. Resources on the ranch include forage, water, cover, space (e.g., nesting sites, loafing areas, foraging areas, hiding or cover areas). Dietary overlap does not always mean that competition is occurring. This is true when we consider that dietary overlap does not account for forage availability. The greatest competition for a cow is another cow. This is called **intraspecific competition**. Cattle have been found to be complementary

Rangelands dominated by brush can be tailored to enhance habitat for wildlife species, such as white-tailed deer (*Odocoileus virginianus*), by designing brush manipulation to achieve the appropriate structure, spatial arrangement, and dispersion of brush. Courtesy of Texas Parks and Wildlife Department

when grazed with sheep, goats, and deer. Each species has its own feeding style determined by digestive capabilities and characteristics of its lips, tongue, lower incisor teeth, dental pad, mobility, and other physical characteristics.

Because of their feeding styles, animals are not direct competitors until the forage resource for a specific animal becomes limiting. As long as the primary sustaining foods of the individual species are readily available, competition will not occur. With this in mind, the rancher must strive to control the stocking rate, adjusting throughout the year, to keep primary foods for each animal available and not limiting.

What Should the Manager Do?

Leaving cattle in a pasture to "fend for themselves" when the forage supply is inadequate may permanently reduce carrying capacity, livestock and wildlife production, and net returns from the land. Overgrazing grasses can lead to plants with low vigor or a slow ability to recover from climatic conditions such as drought.

Weakening grasses and reducing the cover of litter and standing grass on a pasture can adversely affect the pasture's natural mineral and water cycle, thus reducing future grass production. The increase in bare ground in a pasture may also be conducive to the establishment of weed and brush species. Bare soil gives less chance to capture rainfall because of the lack of plant root systems or channels for directing the water downward into the soil. A lack of organic matter cover (litter and standing plant material) also increases the impact of raindrops on the soil surface and often leads to increased soil erosion.

The manager should learn how to grow the best grass possible, if livestock production is the goal. If wildlife management is the goal, a more diverse range of native grasses and forbs may be the desired end product. The manager should be flexible but prepared to make stocking rate decisions. Stocking rates should never be based on what was done in the past but determined by the forage that can be produced in years of median rainfall. Stocking rates should be based on 25% of annual forage production for rangeland; otherwise, there is a risk of overgrazing the land so that forage cannot recover sufficiently for the following year. Pastures should be checked frequently, but especially near the end of the normal forage growth cycle. This is an important time, as accumulated forage is needed to last until the start of the next growing season.

Stocking rates should also be based on the actual grazeable area of a pasture. This eliminates using ranch roads, steep cliffs, distance to water, rock cover, or heavily covered brush areas in the calculations. If these areas are used to calculate the stocking rate, the rate will be too high and the usable rangeland will be overstocked. The manager must build in pasture rest. Failure to defer pastures from grazing can also have a negative impact on both plant and animal performance.

Deferment is a grazing management practice that leaves an area ungrazed so that the forage can rest and recover before it is grazed again. Forage in deferred pastures will regain vigor and allow for reproduction. The manager should maintain a forage reserve to avoid getting caught short and having to destock when the market has also dropped.

Integrated Brush Management and Concepts for Rangeland

European settlement in Texas since the early 1800s has changed the state by farming, logging, overstocking, urban development, the lack of naturally occurring wildfires and other natural processes, and, it is thought, from an increase in atmospheric carbon dioxide. What we know about the landscape in the 1820s comes from the writings of early travelers who may have been teachers, writers, botanists, surveyors, or soldiers. Our conception of the landscape may be "brush" and unwanted plants that do not fit into the mental image we have for the land. Many native or naturally occurring plants do not fit into the goals or vision some landowners have for their land. Where do honey mesquite, greenbriar, persimmon, locust, and others fit into this picture? Why do unwanted brush species continue to spread? Do we really understand the ecology of brush? Some of the imbalance we see on the landscape has been caused by human activities and management decisions.

What Is Brush?

Brush has often been described as a dense growth of bushes, shrubs, and small trees. There is little question that brush has increased in density and distribution in areas that were once open grasslands. Some of our land management practices, such as overstocking with cattle and removing the historically frequent range fires, have contributed to the brush invasion. Where this has occurred, brush plants are usually labeled as pests, meaning these plants do not fit our vision for the land. Many regard honey mesquite as a pest, not a plant of value to humans, wildlife, or a healthy environment.

The value of a plant often lies in the eye of the beholder, and brushy plants may not always be pests. Certainly, brush competes with forage species for water, and shading by brush over a long period can change the forage species composition from warm-season grasses valued for livestock production to cool-season grasses that grow beneath the canopy of brush. In this case, cool-season grasses (such as Virginia wildrye, Canada wildrye, Texas wintergrass, and Texas bluegrass) can also be an asset for cattle production but a detriment to northern bobwhite production. They can be grazed in the early winter to late spring to reduce supplemental feed expenses for livestock or even be used by wildlife species such as turkey.

Other ecological shifts that may occur when brush invades grassland can also be beneficial. Brush stands alter the environment underneath their canopy and may provide a more nutrient-rich environment for other plants. Deep-growing roots can bring minerals to the soil surface where other plants may benefit through the recycling of leaf litter. Stands of plants with thorns can be barriers to grazing, such as dense mesquite or prickly pear, but these can protect desirable and more sensitive plants growing within them. Such protected areas allow these plants to survive as future seed sources for revegetating an area. Desirable woody plants also grow and establish inside the protective canopy of spiny or pest plants (like a nursery for infants).

Brush may increase the price of land being sold for rural and suburban development. In fact, acreage cleared of all brush may sell for up to 60% less than land where the brush is left intact. Developers, builders, and future buyers value an aesthetically pleasing view. Even honey mesquite and cedar may fulfill this role. When dealing with brush, it is wise to consider how the future value of a property may be affected. We often consider

The honey mesquite tree is one of the toughest, most invasive species of brush in the world. It thrives across the western two-thirds of Texas, both in rural pastures and on urban lots. Courtesy of Dale Rollins, Texas A&M AgriLife Extension Service

Prickly pear and other species of cacti may interfere with movement and handling of livestock and with forage utilization, cause serious livestock health problems, and compete with desirable forage plants.

the current situation without regard to the future. When making brush management decisions, we must ask if we have an expectation for the future value of our land.

Some woody plants have value other than for grazing, habitat, shade, or aesthetics. Honey mesquite, for example, can be cut for firewood or made into barbecue chips or charcoal briquettes, and heartwood of mesquite can be used for making fine furniture.

Brush often occurs in mixed stands, and it is necessary to identify the individual brush species when deciding whether there is a brush or pest problem. Simply classifying the plants as brush limits any understanding of their value or of the technique and strategies needed to manage the area. In Texas, no one plant is commonly named "brush." When an individual uses the word "brush" to describe plants growing on his or her land, this usually signifies that the individual does not know the name of the observed brush species. The value of brush, acceptable methods of control or management, and signs of ecological change are all tied to the name of the brush plant.

Brush Management Concept

The concept of brush management recognizes the potential value of some quantity of woody plants in range and pasture management. The term "brush management" is more appropriate than "brush control" because it describes current attitudes toward woody plants on rangeland. The development of a brush management concept has been closely tied to the realization that wildlife is an economic asset and that land management objectives should accommodate the habitat needs for wildlife. Increasing livestock production has usually been a high priority for landowners, but it should not be done at the expense of other products, such as wildlife.

Brush management strategies should be a part of an effort to manage the land resource for multiple uses, which include the production of quality water and air. In an integrated brush management program, we set management objectives based on an inventory of range resources. When problems are identified, economic and environmental analysis is used to describe alternative solutions. Effective brush management uses technology from a number of disciplines, including rangeland management, wildlife biology, animal science, weather, soil science, and economics. To carry out brush management planning, land managers have picked tools

A prescribed burn to eliminate brush. Courtesy of Natural Resources Conservation Service

of management from four broad categories: mechanical control, chemical control, biological control, and prescribed burning.

Choosing Best Management Practices

Brush management options are described in AgriLife Extension publication *Brush Management Methods* (http://wildlifehabitat.tamu.edu/Lessons/Mechanical-Treatments/Readings/Brush-Management-Methods.pdf). There is seldom one best method of brush management for any particular ranch, pasture, or landholding. Brush management is usually more effective and economical when a combination of methods is integrated over a period of several years. Integrated methods, for example, can increase the effectiveness and minimize the use of herbicides. Before selecting a method, feasible alternatives must be evaluated relative to

- the degree of control expected
- their characteristic weaknesses
- the expected life of the treatment
- possible secondary effects (i.e., increase of other undesirable brush or weed species)
- application requirements
- effect on wildlife habitat
- cost versus benefit
- safety and other regulations

Larry White, professor and extension range specialist with Texas A&M, along with C. Wayne Hanselka, also a range specialist, wrote that a successful rangeland manager should focus on the management of the climatic, biological, financial, and political risks of their operation. These would be much more important to their success than their capability to increase output of livestock and other products. However, "certain factors cannot be predicted or controlled. The contingency provisions of a plan are just as important as the specifications for things that are known. Risk and uncertainty is associated with every aspect of life. You must find ways to avoid, reduce, or manage risks and uncertainty if you are to be a sustainable rangeland owner/manager" (White 1999). Many landowners prefer to deal with symptoms rather than the problem. Others may pretend that no problem exists. Land managers must be pro-active. Treating symptoms may be a waste of financial resources and time. Determining the origin of the problem is the first step toward solving it.

Mesquite treated by a new chemical, Sendero, shows signs of morality. Courtesy of Texas A&M AgriLife Extension Service

Keep these points in mind for a successful brush management program:

- Determine the cause of a brush problem and then seek the methods or solutions to solving the problem first. Treating just signs of a problem (symptoms) guarantees that the problem will come back and may lead to more problems, which will cost more time and money to solve.
- When using chemicals as the method of control, match the target plant (know its name) to a chemical that is labeled for treating that brush species. If you cannot name the plant, seek help.
- Always read and follow the herbicide label directions. Remember, using a herbicide in a manner not consistent with the label is a violation of the law.

- The cost of a treatment escalates rapidly as the brush becomes denser or the number of basal stems per plant increases.
- Multiple-stemmed plants or rough-barked plants are more difficult to control using the individual plant treatments (IPT) such as the stem treatments. Smooth-barked plants are easiest to control.
- When using a stem treatment (best in areas with a low density of woody plants—fewer than 300 plants per acre), do not spray when the basal stems are wet. After mixing the herbicide with diesel in a mixture of 0.5% Remedy plus 0.5% Reclaim (also called the Brush Busters leaf spray), shake or agitate the mixture/solution vigorously and periodically during the application.
- Stem treatments and basal bark treatments are less effective if there is dense grass around the basal stems of a brush plant.

"The urge to comprehend must precede the urge to reform."
—Aldo Leopold

Rangeland Weed Management

The name "weed" has usually been associated with plants, both native and of foreign origin, that are not desirable. From the agronomic standpoint, a weed is described as a plant that can cause economic loss in a production unit. Many gardeners and home landscape managers will view a weed as a plant out of place, such as bermudagrass growing in a flower bed. Ecologically speaking, broad-leaved herbaceous plants are called "forbs," though laypeople generally call any broad-leaved plant a weed. From a consumer-based viewpoint, a weed is most often identified as an invader. Regardless of how we view weeds, in a natural setting forbs play an important role in the ecology of a land resource. Forbs are part of a natural process known as plant succession.

Texas Croton (*Croton texensis*), a native annual that many consider a weed in most rangelands. Courtesy of Texas A&M AgriLife Extension Service

"And what is a weed but a plant whose virtues have yet to be discovered?"
—Ralph Waldo Emerson

Weeds (both broad-leaved and grass species) are some of the earliest pioneer plants that appear over time in newly developing soils (**primary plant succession**). In this situation, weeds are able to withstand long periods of drought and grow where little soil exists. Weeds can produce an abundance of seeds. In early stages of succession, weeds provide cover to new soils and protection from wind and rain. A range manager's goal is for the weeds to cause changes in the soil and water and nutrient cycles and to provide a new environment that will in turn be conducive to growing larger plants higher in the ecological process or order.

In a wildlife manager's eyes, weeds are seen in a different light. Weed species come up in fields and pastures and are deemed to be "bad." Managers will classify weeds this way because weedy species or invaders may not meet the goals of landownership. In this case, weeds are a part of the natural process of **secondary succession**. Natural processes of change occur when the landowner or a natural event such as a fire, drought, or heavy grazing by bison has disturbed the soil and original established plant community (a plant community was present naturally on the land). These changes "set the plant community back," often to a less desirable state of production, depending on the manager's goals and objectives.

Human-caused disturbances of this system, such as plowing, raking, dozing, livestock grazing, and prescribed burning, can cause weeds to appear. Often the result is a soil and plant community that has an altered water and mineral cycle and less organic matter on the soil surface. Weeds appear as a natural process to stabilize the site and to provide protective cover for the soil surface. A good weed cover can actually help protect the soil from high summer temperatures, reduce evaporation of limited water in the upper soil profile, and reduce erosion from future rainfall events. Thus, weeds are a part of the natural function of rangelands and managed pastureland.

For this natural process to occur, the seed of weeds are already present in the top inch of soil in all pastures, yards, alleys, vacant lots, parks, roadsides, fence lines, and other sites. The seed of weeds lie in wait, and many of them are long-lived. For instance, the seed of annual or common broomweed can be viable in the soil for a minimum of 15 years, while the seed of woolly distaff thistle (a pest plant native to Italy) can have viable seed in the soil for up to 19 years. The land manager should interpret the presence of weeds correctly and know that they have responded to a condition of need in the natural ecosystem. When this is understood, management can work to alter the situation and continue to pursue land management goals.

Most of the weeds dealt with in wildlife land management are herbaceous plants. Many weeds are classified as "forbs" or "herbaceous" species and grasses, as previously discussed. Weeds may be annuals, living less than one year, or perennials that live for many years. Some weed species germinate in the fall, overwinter in a rosette stage, and go through stem elongation and flowering in the spring. This type of plant is considered a cool-season plant. Generally, warm-season annual weeds will germinate from seed in the spring (depending on temperature and available soil moisture), go through stem elongation during late spring and early summer, begin flowering in early to late summer, and then die in the fall or winter months. Knowing whether a weed is an annual or perennial, cool- or warm-season plant will help us understand the value and management of the plant.

Taking a range grass sample. Courtesy of Natural Resources Conservation Service

Weed Management Concept

Like all plants, weeds need sunlight, water, a growing space (soil), carbon dioxide in the atmosphere, and some or all of 20 primary and secondary nutrients in the soil. By eliminating one of these requirements, a manager may be able to control the population of weeds. But the grass growing on the rangeland has the same or similar needs. The manager must determine if responses to management are producing an environment conducive to weeds, their growth, and success.

The concept of weed management recognizes the potential value of some quantity of weedy plants in range and pasture management. Weeds must be recognized as a part of the natural system to give a soil protective cover when needed. In some instances, if the weeds were controlled, what would be left to grow even if the growing space and water were no longer needed by weeds? The truth may be that the plants growing on a piece of land today may be the best that the land will support under the current level of management.

Herbicide application either by tractor or hand pump can be effective control methods for annual and perennial weeds in Texas rangelands. Courtesy of Texas A&M AgriLife Extension Service

Managers often describe any plants that reduce forage availability to livestock as brush or weeds. However, while many native rangeland plants have no value for livestock production in a typical ranching or pasture environment, these plants may be essential to the survival of native wildlife, including game, nongame animals, birds, and even insects. Weed species provide wildlife with food, water, shelter, escape and nesting cover. In many instances, the presence of weeds is a life requirement for the survival of many wildlife species and therefore becomes a part of the overall ranch plan.

What is a weed under one management goal could be food under another goal. In the year-long diet of cattle, forbs make up about 12%, while sheep and goats consume 17% and 12%, respectively, in their diets (Lyons et al. 1996). Weeds or forbs are often noted to have higher levels of crude protein and phosphorus than any available grass known for grazing. Most forbs have a high cell content to cell wall ratio and are easily digested prior to the stage of flowering by all grazing livestock.

With the increased interest in ecotourism and management for native animals, the same manager who once made a living from livestock grazing may now be managing for more than just cattle. Research has indicated that white-tailed deer consume about 36% of their annual diet as forbs. Research also indicates that the seeds of broomweed and ragweed are in the top 10 seed foods eaten by quail and doves (Lyons et al. 1996). Weeds and forbs have taken on a new perspective in land management. A large portion of the 1,500 species of wildflowers that occur in Texas are agricultural or livestock industry weeds.

Control Recommendations for Specific Weeds Common in Texas

Control measures for annual and perennial weeds are similar. Following are specific recommendations.

Annual Weeds

Annual weeds (such as broomweed, bitter sneezeweed, croton, and buffalobur) are most effectively controlled by pulling them up by the root system. This ensures that the entire plant has been removed and killed. This method works well when just a few plants of a weed species are found growing in a pasture. For larger pastures, herbicide use may be desirable from a time and cost standpoint. Annual weeds are best controlled using herbicides in the spring when plants are 4 to 6 inches high and good moisture conditions exist. Allowing annual weeds to grow to this height will allow for enough leaf area to be present to take up a herbicide that has been broadcast on the pasture.

It is also practical to use biological control by grazing sheep and goats to help eliminate annual weeds. The manager must be careful not to let the sheep and goat grazing continue and be the source of the weed problem. The balance of forage demand (animal needs) must be matched with the amount of forage produced (production). Substituting sheep and goats for cattle may only create a more severe problem if the threshold of litter and ground cover is not watched.

Prescribed burning has been shown to be an effective tool for the control of annual weeds. Most often, the prescribed burn has been planned for and conducted in the late winter after most cool-season or winter weeds have emerged. If a good fine fuel cover exists, a properly conducted prescribed fire can eliminate most annual weeds. Again, it is important to know the names of the target weeds and learn about them. Some species of winter weeds can have a second germination period in the spring after the prescribed burn has been conducted. The reappearance of the unwanted weed pests by summer has led some to conclude that the prescribed burn did not control them. This is certainly the case with Texas broomweed, which can germinate both in the fall and spring.

Perennial Weeds

Many perennial weeds (such as bullnettle, Carolina horsenettle, upright prairie-coneflower, and yankeeweed) can be effectively controlled using herbicide or herbicide mixtures. The best time to spray is in the spring and always prior to flowering. Exceptions exist, though, as spray recommendations for bullnettle, Carolina nightshade or horsenettle, silverleaf nightshade, and western horsenettle are to treat in the spring when the plants begin to flower. Dogfennel and yankeeweed should be sprayed when the plants are 8 to 10 inches tall. Spray upright prairie-coneflower when plants are 2 to 6 inches tall and before flowering.

Perennial weeds that have been top-killed by grazing animals or a prescribed fire can resprout from the crown and return to normal growth. Most perennial weeds are not controlled through the use of grazing or fire, but they can be managed and/or suppressed. Seedling perennial weeds may be killed by grazing or with the use of a prescribed burn done at the appropriate time.

Get Your Money's Worth in Weed Management

Keep these points in mind to produce and have a successful weed management program:

1. Determine the cause of a weed problem and then seek the methods or solutions to solving the problem first. Just treating the symptoms guarantees that the problem will come back and may lead to more problems, which will cost more time and money to solve.

2. When using herbicides as the method of control, match the target plant (know its name) to a chemical that is labeled for treating that weed species. If you cannot name the plant, seek help.
3. Always read and follow the herbicide label directions.
4. Recognize that not all weeds react the same.
5. Conduct a survey to read the landscape and determine why weeds are coming in to the property.
6. Determine where the weeds are and target that area for treatment, not the whole pasture or unit.
7. Determine a desired level of control.
8. See if cutting off sunlight, water, or nutrients in the soil could help reduce the weed stand.
9. Develop a plan for weed control and change the current management to keep from having to do it all again next year.

Seeding Rangeland as a Management Practice

Sustaining renewable natural resources and productive environments such as Texas rangelands requires skilled, science-based management. The complexity of range ecosystems, market variability, weather, and human decision-making skills result in varying degrees of risks and management success and failure (White 1999). Native prairie restoration has also become popular with many managers interested in enhancing wildlife habitat for species ranging from ground-nesting birds to butterflies. Range seeding as a management tool has been used as a direct means of developing, altering, and improving the range ecosystem.

Range seeding is expensive, and the risk of failure is always present. In many cases though, seeding may be the most practical and environmentally sound practice available to land managers to meet stewardship goals to restore rangelands and missing ecosystem functions. The most common objective of range seeding has been to alter the vegetation composition to restore production potential or increase livestock grazing capacity. To restore the potential production through seeding is attractive to landowners with deteriorated range and less than profitable returns through ranching. However, seeding rangelands has often been oversold as a means to economically restore deteriorated range. It is not a cure or substitute for good rangeland management.

Many decision makers fail to assess the risks and determine the real causes for mistakes and problems (White 1999). How the range resource came to be in a deteriorated and lower productive state must be considered before seeding is selected. Seeding alone will not solve problems that previous management has created; nor is seeding always profitable in terms of forage produced.

Other objectives when seeding has been selected include

- revegetating barren or abandoned croplands
- revegetating after a prescribed fire
- providing a better seasonal balance in the forage supply
- improving the nutritive value and quantity of forage available
- reestablishing native plants that would not naturally become established
- providing cover or litter to prevent soil erosion and water runoff

In these cases, range seeding may be the tool to restore ecological properties and functions that serve and allow for sediment regulation, nutrient sinks, and filter strips between ecosystems. Seeding can be a successful tool to meet goals for landownership and values for the establishment of desirable vegetation on abandoned cropland and disturbed sites.

Risk exists in the interpretation of a successful seeding or established stand. What does a successful seeding look like? Native grass seeding rates are set at 20 live seeds planted per square foot. Under range improvement and land restoration, successful seeding or stand establishment is two established plants per square foot or 10%. Others may define a successful seeding as the mere introduction of a new plant species into the vegetation complex. Some set success as a seeding that resembles a planted row-crop field. Regardless, there is a major risk that the planted area will not resemble what was envisioned. Often patience is needed, as the grass seed may germinate over several years. Native grasses such as big bluestem may require three or more years to establish.

The greatest risk in range seeding comes from the inability to predict rainfall and other unforeseen conditions at planting and during the establishment period. Chances of seeding success decrease dramatically farther west and north because of low rainfall probabilities. One year in five may lead to successful seeding in the Trans-Pecos region of Texas, but success will be high most years where annual rainfall exceeds 35 inches. Additional risks are associated with the planting process and the selection of available seed to meet landowner goals. The how, why, when, and what to plant are explained well in the AgriLife Extension publication *Seeding Rangeland* (http://texnat.tamu.edu/about/ranchers-reference-guide/seeding-rangeland/).

Decision to seed: Land managers face economic, environmental, and policy-oriented questions each day as they work to sustain rangeland as a valuable and renewable resource. Determining whether a range can be restored by natural means or will require seeding is a matter of judgment. Improved management alone, particularly with livestock grazing, can restore some depleted ranges. Generally, if more than 10% of the vegetation is desirable native species, management can rely on natural succession. When the land or resource manager understands the cause or causes of range deterioration, natural revegetation and allowing secondary succession to occur can provide improvement in species composition and resource health over time. Seeding may be the best tool when insufficient desirable native plants remain. Allowing natural processes to occur may be cheaper than seeding but may take many years for deteriorated grazing or farming lands to recover. The outcome or final vegetation complex is also uncertain, as abused lands may never return to their historical state because of soil loss and other properties. Many times we have to accept what we get and adjust management to actual conditions. We do not have enough money to change nature.

Grass mixture versus monoculture: Because many landowners have one goal in mind, they do not always consider the effects land management practices may have on other aspects of the ecosystem. Loss of vegetation diversity will lead to a loss of native wildlife diversity. Likewise, planting a monoculture or single species stand can lead to habitat fragmentation for wildlife species. Planting one or several plant species on the land may make seeding easier, make the land easier to manage, or even meet the needs of a current livestock enterprise. A diversity or mixture of plants for seeding may provide a better ground cover, a more varied diet for animals, and less risk in getting a seeded stand established where the soil is heterogeneous. A diverse plant community is much more resilient to adverse climatic and biological (insects/diseases) changes than a monoculture. Planting a mixture of grasses and other kinds of plants can lead to greater flexibility for management and increased alternatives for land use and more successfully meets the variability of soils, moisture, and slope of a site.

Need for moisture: Successful seeding requires planning and use of proven procedures. To capitalize on moisture cycles, seeding should take place when needed moisture for germination and plant establishment is most likely to be present. For native, warm-season perennial grasses, planting is generally in the spring months of March and early April. Plans for seeding should be canceled if current soil moisture or the long-range forecast indicates inadequate moisture supplies. Seedling grasses need 29 to 30 days of appropriate temperature and moisture for establishment of root systems and nutrient storage to survive.

Seed selection and availability: A limited seed and variety resource is available to meet goals for range recovery and livestock and wildlife benefit. Not all of the species of native plants, ecotypes, and those best adapted to a local area are available or for sale. Planting commercial varieties or releases adapted to a local area usually increases the chances of success. Planting varieties not adapted to local conditions may not perform satisfactorily and may go dormant earlier, green up later, or be prone to increased damage from early or late frost or drier or wetter periods. For planting native grasses, seed varieties should be used that have an original selection origin of no more than 200 miles north or south and 100 miles east or west of the area for planting.

Native versus nonnative plants: Introduced plant species commonly function in the natural system as weeds. Risk is increased when the user of introduced plant species does not understand the invasive properties of weeds, that is, seed dispersal mechanisms, levels of competitiveness, or management required to sustain introduced plants. Many of the introduced grasses used today were selected for their resistance to overgrazing. They are extremely competitive with many of the native plant species and have become pest plants (examples include Johnsongrass, ryegrass, bahiagrass, common bermudagrass, King Ranch bluestem, Old World bluestem, medusahead, cheatgrass, and Caucasian bluestem). Similar actions and results have been noted with introduced forbs, legumes, and trees such as kudzu, Chinese tallowtree, kochia, Korean lespedeza, yellow sweetclover, Russian olive, lantana, and salt cedar.

Planting method: Over a large portion of Texas, seeding has been conducted as a valuable practice to follow various kinds of brush management, especially root plowing. Because of the large areas treated, methods such as aerial seeding have been employed to seed large and rough areas. Planting methods that do not give adequate soil/seed contact for improving seedling survival have a greater risk of failure than drilled seeds. Soil/seed contact may be improved with a soil disturbance such as roller chopping or "lite" raking. The same holds true for ground broadcast methods. When drilling of seed is not practical, broadcast methods can be used, but a greater risk exists. Native grass seeds are small and are generally planted from ⅛ to ¼ inch deep. Planting seeds deeper will increase the risk of seedlings not reaching the surface for sunlight and result in a weak or less than desirable stand.

Land preparation: When seeding is done on sites that have been plowed, the seedbed needs to be firm prior to planting to ensure adequate soil/seed contact. Recent plowed areas do not have time to settle and firm up naturally. Seeding in loose, fluffy, and air-filled soils does not reach the goal of good soil/seed contact, and the success of seeding may be low because seedlings do not survive. Seedbed preparation for planting in March should be done in late August or September to allow for natural settling and firming of the soil.

Weed control: When soil is disturbed for planting, it is natural for weeds to germinate and grow in a native seeded stand. Weed seeds are present naturally in soils to provide an emergency growth and cover of a disturbed site. The competition of these weeds with seeded grasses can be reduced through the use of disking between seeded rows or with chemicals. Risk of injury to young seedling grasses is reduced when the use of weed control chemicals is delayed until young grasses reach the four- to six-leaf stage of growth.

Range seeding is risky. You need to plan

accordingly and be prepared for adjustments in management to avoid future crises. The most profitable use of a seeding may require a shift in overall management of a land resource. It can be noted that native grass seeded areas usually require more intensive management of grazing and at least a one-year deferment from grazing during the establishment phase.

References

Allen, V. 1991. *Terminology for Grazing Lands and Grazing Animals.* Blacksburg, VA: Pocahontas Press. http://forages.oregonstate.edu/fi/topics/pasturesandgrazing/grazingsystemdesign/grazingterminology.

Allen, V. G., C. Batello, E. J. Beretta, J. Hodgson, M. Kothmann, X. Li, J. McIvor, J. Milne, C. Morris, A. Peeters, and M. Sanderson. 2011. An International Terminology for Grazing Lands and Grazing Animals. *Grass and Forage Science* 66:2–28. http://onlinelibrary.wiley.com/doi/10.1111/j.1365-2494.2010.00780.x/epdf.

Bentley, Henry Lewis. 1898. *Cattle Ranges of the Southwest: A History of Exhaustion of Pasturage and Suggestions for Its Restoration.* USDA Farmers Bulletin. Washington, DC: USDA.

Biggers, Don Hampton, and Seymour V. Connor. 2003. *Buffalo Guns and Barbed Wire: Two Frontier Accounts by Don Hampton Biggers.* Lubbock: Texas Tech University Press.

Box, Thad. 2001a. Listening to the Land: From the Dust of Shame. *Rangelands* 23 (3): 23.

———. 2001b. Listening to the Land: Ministers to the Land. *Rangelands* 23 (6): 46.

———. 2001c. Listening to the Land: Where the Buffalo Roamed. *Rangelands* 23 (2): 22.

Casper, Julie K. 2007. *Lands: Taming the Wilds.* New York: Infobase Publishing.

Holechek, Jerry L., Rex D. Pieper, and Carlton H. Herbel. 2001. *Range Management: Principles and Practices.* Upper Saddle River, NJ: Prentice Hall.

Kennedy, J. J., B. L. Fox, and T. D. Osen. 1995. Changing Social Values and Images of Public Rangeland Management. *Rangelands* 17:127–32.

Kothmann, Mort. 2001. Where Have We Come From? Where Are We, and Where Are We Going? *Rangelands: Society for Range Management* 23 (6): 47–48.

Lyons, Robert K., T. D. A. Forbes, and Rick Machen. 1996. *What Range Herbivores Eat—and Why.* Texas A&M AgriLife Extension Service B-6037. http://agrilifecdn.tamu.edu/animalscience/files/2012/04/B6037-rangeherbivores.pdf.

Stoddart, Laurence A., Arthur D. Smith, and Thadis W. Box. 1975. *Range Management.* New York: McGraw-Hill.

Welch, Tommy G. 2000. *Brush Management Methods.* Texas A&M AgriLife Extension Service E-44. http://wildlifehabitat.tamu.edu/Lessons/Mechanical-Treatments/Readings/Brush-Management-Methods.pdf.

White, Larry D. 1999. *Reducing Risk in Management Decision Making.* Risk Management for Texans Series RLEM No. 1. College Station: Texas A&M AgriLife Extension. http://cnrit.tamu.edu/cgrm/whatzhot/risk1.html.

UNIT 21

Urban Ecosystems

CLARK E. ADAMS
Professor, Department of Wildlife and Fisheries Sciences, Texas A&M University

KIERAN J. LINDSEY
Fellow and Associate Director of Online Programs, Center for Leadership in Global Sustainability, College of Natural Resources and Environment, Virginia Tech University

Unit Goals

After completing this unit, volunteers should be able to

- clearly differentiate the meaning of urban ecosystems, urban, urbanization, and urban sprawl
- compare urban and natural ecosystems in terms of diversity, interrelationships, cycles, and energy
- understand the unique ecology of urban ecosystems in terms of impacts on abiotic characteristics, nutrient cycles, and the water cycle; green and gray spaces; plants and animals
- determine the levels of plant and animal diversity in urban when compared to natural ecosystems

Introduction

For some students, the term "urban ecosystems" may seem to be an oxymoron. However, this unit demonstrates that using the prevailing definition of an **ecosystem**, "an interactive complex of communities and the abiotic environment affecting them within a particular area" (Wright and Boorse 2011, 36), the two terms are quite compatible. **Natural ecosystems** can be defined as any habitat without human influence—a rare bird indeed in the twenty-first century. **Urban ecosystems** have been a fascinating research subject for several decades. The direction and difficulties inherent in this field of study are examined throughout this unit. We begin with a brief history lesson and a few definitions.

The convergence of three societal events at the end of World War II set the stage for urban community development. First, automobiles and homes became more affordable and available, and returning soldiers had the means to purchase both. Second, Cold War mania provided a stimulus for the passage of the Highway Revenue Act of 1956, which created the Highway Trust Fund. The original political justification for extensive highway construction was to provide city dwellers a rapid escape mechanism in the event of nuclear attacks, and this legislation enabled the development of the network of superhighways through, around, and out of the cities. Third, America began to shift from a largely agrarian to a primarily urban society around 1945, as people moved away from family farms and self-contained communities to the city for work. Highways, affordable automobiles, really cheap gas (about 10 cents/gallon), and a population opting for city life turned into the most massive and sudden movement of humanity in its history (Adams and Lindsey 2010).

Urban, in this context, includes both cities and suburbs. Also known as the "built environment," the landscape includes places where most of the property is devoted to all things human-made and/or maintained: buildings of all shapes and sizes, manicured lawns and landscaped of-

Typical suburban landscaping causing simplification of habitat. Courtesy of Clark Adams

Typical metropolitan area with high-rise buildings, concrete surfaces, and roads. Courtesy of John Davis, TPWD

fice parks, cemeteries and vacant lots, strip malls and parking structures, elementary schools and college campuses, airports and warehouse districts. A substantial portion of this land is covered with some kind of impervious surface, in the form of either structures or pavement. The plant life is often native to other parts of the world or highly hybridized and thus requires much caretaking, such as mowing, pruning, weeding, watering, and applying herbicides, pesticides, and fertilizers. Urban can also be characterized as "large concentrations of people and industrial activity that consume more available energy and material than can be produced, and which produce more wastes than can be assimilated with the relatively small area they occupy" (Rees 1997, 64; Adams and Lindsey 2010, 112).

Urbanization is the process by which towns and cities are formed and become larger as more and more people begin living and working in central areas, that is, a spatial phenomenon: the concentration of population (McDonald and Marcotullio 2011). Over 5% of the surface area of the United States is covered by urban and other built areas. In the next 25 years, urban developed areas will increase to 9.2% of the total land base that is developed (McKinney 2006). Urbanization is an important driver of climate change and pollution and alters both biotic and abiotic ecosystem properties within, surrounding, and even at great distances from urban areas (Grimm et al. 2008).

"Urbanization can be characterized as an increase in human habitation, coupled with increased per capita energy and resource consumption and extensive modification of the landscape, creating a system that does not depend principally on local natural resources to persist" (McDonnell and Pickett 1990, 1232). McDonnell and Pickett's list of structural features unique to urbanization include dwellings, factories, office buildings, warehouses, roads, pipelines, power lines, railroads, channelized stream beds, reservoirs, sewage disposal facilities, landfills, and airports.

Urban ecology is "the study of humans in cities, of nature in cities, and the coupled relationship between humans and natural systems" (Marzluff et al. 2008, vii). The traditional scientific definition is used for studies of the distribution and abundance of organisms in and around cities and of the biogeochemical budgets of urban areas. For urban planners, urban ecology has focused on designing the environmental amenities of cities for people and on reducing environmental impacts of urban regions (Pickett et al. 2011). Bottom line—urban ecology research must include any and all anthropogenic influences within a human-dominated ecological system. The overarching goal is to understand how humans and ecological processes can coexist and help urban societies become more sustainable (Marzluff et al. 2008).

Urbanized areas and **urban clusters** now account for 80.7% of the US population (United Nations 2011). Urbanized areas ($N = 486$ nationwide) are defined as "a large central place and adjacent densely settled census blocks that together have a total population of 50,000 or more people." Urban clusters ($N = 3{,}087$ nationwide) consist of "at least 2,500 and less than 50,000 people" (United Nations 2011). The United States has a total land area of nearly 2.3 billion acres. Of this, 3% (61 million acres) is classified as urban land representing an increase of 1 million acres since 2002 (Nickerson et al. 2011). The US urban population increased by 12.1% from 2000 to 2010, outpacing the overall growth rate of 9.7% during the same period. There are 34 communities in Texas classified as urban, and 84.7% (22.7 million) of the Texas population resides in these urban communities (US Census Bureau 2010).

The post-WWII events previously discussed led to a phenomenon called **urban sprawl**, "the widespread expansion of metropolitan areas through buildings and shopping centers farther and farther from urban centers and lacing them together with more and more major highways, usually without planning" (Wright and Boorse 2011). Urban sprawl set the stage for a human- ecosystem conflict that had not existed before and reinforced a separation between people and much of the natural world (Adams and Lindsey 2010).

Disconnecting from Nature

So what does the shift from a primarily rural to urban population mean in terms of the majority of the Texas public becoming partners in urban ecosystem management? Even though many studies have demonstrated a connection between access to the natural world and improvements to health and quality of life, the "outdoors" is at a competitive disadvantage when trying to pull the public's attention away from smartphones and other mobile devices, laptop computers, and social network platforms, not to mention television, video games, and the shopping mall (Sterba 2012). There appears to be a growing public disconnect with nature, described by author Richard Louv as "nature deficit disorder" (2005, 10). One memorable quote from his book *Last Child in the Woods* came from a suburban fifth-grader who said, "I like to play indoors better 'cause that's where all the electrical outlets are." In addition to Louv's work, there are a number of books and other publications dedicated to examining the growing detachment of urbanites from the natural world. Two recent additions to the "must read" list for Master Naturalists are *Nature Wars* (Sterba 2012), and *Welcome to Subirdia* Marzluff (2014).

For most urbanites, gardens are a recreational pursuit rather than a food production necessity. It is probably safe to suggest that a majority of Texas residents have never eaten a meal they have produced "from the ground up." The entire concept of killing and butchering animals is met with abhorrence and disbelief that humans could exert such cruelty on another living organism.

In contrast, being raised on a farm exposed this author, quite early in life, to the basics of food production. These tasks were an absolute necessity given the lack of alternatives such as grocery stores and farmers' markets. For example, catching, beheading, removing feathers, gutting, and butchering were a necessity if one wanted to have fried chicken for dinner. This is in sharp contrast to the way most contemporary urbanites provide the family meal—purchasing frozen chicken chunks at the supermarket that may not even have a legitimate claim as being "made in America."

"There are two spiritual dangers in not owning a farm. One is the danger of supposing that breakfast comes from a grocery store, the other that heat comes from a furnace."
—Aldo Leopold, *A Sand County Almanac*

Ecological Principles of Ecosystem Structure and Function

Ecology is the study of interrelationships between the biotic and abiotic components of an ecosystem. It is a complex and complicated subject, summarized by Adams and Lindsey (2010) in terms of four principles, including diversity, interrelationships, cycles, and energy (DICE).

Diversity

Diversity can be defined as the variety of abiotic and biotic components within ecosystems. Natural ecosystems tend to be complex, highly diverse, and highly stable. The built environment, on the other hand, is the product of human manipulation, which tends to simplify and destabilize natural ecosystems. The previous photographs illustrate habitat simplification in suburban and metropolitan environments, respectively. The typical urban lawn is living testament to habitat simplification and destabilization. However, researchers are beginning to recognize that while the urban/suburban landscape includes large swaths of simplified habitat, urban ecosystems taken as a whole are far from simple, at least once construction ends and successional growth begins anew. The diversity of flora and fauna in well-established urban ecosystems appears to be on a par with at least some natural ecosystems (Adams 2015).

Some of the most compelling arguments for preserving biodiversity are those related to the effects of eroding biodiversity on human health. Both scientists and public health advocates have asserted that the preservation of biodiversity is crucial for present and future human health (Ostfeld and Keesing 2000). On the other hand, anthropogenic sources of species diversity in the urban landscape include introduction of nonnative species (a.k.a. exotics), modification of landforms and drainage networks, control or modification of natural disturbance agents, and the construction of massive and extensive infrastructures (Pickett et al. 1997, cited in Zipperer et al. 2000).

Diversity, interrelationships, cycles, and energy (DICE).

Interrelationships

"Everythingisconnectedtoeverythingelse" is a run-together sentence used as an analogy for ecological **interrelationships**. Ecosystems are composed of biotic (living) and abiotic (nonliving) components. The table provides several illustrations of how these components interact. Humans, in general, do not recognize how much their presence affects ecological relationships. Urban development, for example, increases the amount and types of pollutants released into the environment, changes the biotic and abiotic structure of aquatic and terrestrial habitats, and alters plant and animal relationships. Without question, ecosystems are complex. In order to really understand

Interrelationships between ecosystem components

Interrelationships	Example
abiotic × abiotic	temperature and rainfall = climate
abiotic × biotic	water temperature predicts fish species
biotic × abiotic	human pollution of the environment
biotic × biotic	predator/prey relationships, life cycles

this complexity, one needs to integrate population, community, and ecosystem processes across multiple scales (Ostfeld et al. 1998).

Cycles

Nitrogen, carbon, hydrogen, oxygen, phosphorus, and sulfur (N-CHOPS) are the fundamental and finite elements required by all living organisms. **Cycles** are the mechanisms that allow limited amounts of critical substances to remain infinitely available in natural ecosystems. The process of recycling each of these elements through producers, consumers, and decomposers, making them available forever in just the right amounts to sustain plant and animal life, could be referred to as the "circles of life."

In contrast, urban systems are usually designed around the principles of "too much of a good thing" and "one-way trips." Examples, respectively, are found in the overuse of fertilizers on lawns and gardens and the huge landfills for urban garbage where many recyclable products are thrown away, including metals, glass, plastics, and organic materials.

The water cycle is something of an exception; it provides a continuous supply of purified water using a system of three filters: air, soil, and plants. Urban development affects several aspects of the water cycle, including infiltration and runoff and the purification process (e.g., removal of pollutants from air and soil).

Energy

Energy becomes available to every aquatic and terrestrial ecosystem by trapping sunlight energy through the process of photosynthesis. Sunlight energy is free, everlasting (at least from a human life-span scale), and nonpolluting. Humans have not yet developed technology on a par with ability of photosynthesis to take full advantage of sunlight energy, and, as a result, the primary energy sources for urban ecosystems are fossil fuels (e.g., coal, natural gas, oil), which have adverse long-term effects on air, land, and aquatic ecosystems in both urban and rural settings.

The Ecology of Urban Ecosystems

Now that the four principal considerations of ecosystem structure and function have been introduced, they need to be examined in the context of urban ecosystems. Chace and Walsh provide a succinct summary of the status of information presently available on the topic of urban ecosystems: "The effect of urbanization can be immense, yet our understanding is rudimentary" (2006, 47). Their statement may sound overly pessimistic, but it is corroborated by a huge void separating what *should* be done compared to what *can* be done to address urban ecosystem management concerns. The fundamental questions that need to be answered are known, but as yet no coherent, repeatable research design exists to answer them. For the most part, there are no technological or intellectual tools to understand the complex dynamics of ecological systems that are in a constant state of flux at nearly every level of analysis.

Holling (1996) provides a summary of the four key characteristics of natural ecological systems: (1) change is episodic, not gradual; (2) spatial attributes are not uniform or scale invariant; (3) ecosystems are dominated by destabilizing forces preventing the establishment of equilibria in the long term; and (4) ecosystems do not respond to policies and management designed to achieve steady-state conditions. In contrast, the urban ecosystem, which is under constant human influence, is designed to (1) control change; (2) develop into neat and tidy habitat patches (residential and natural); (3) control or avoid the abiotic and biotic forces of ecosystem change; and (4) manage biota for predetermined types, functions, and numbers.

In fact, the urban systems are total contradictions to natural systems in terms of structure and function. The contradictions are largely the result of the human interventions and the ecological effects of urbanization. Specifically, "urbanization affects the structure and function of Earth's ecosystems through transformation of natural landscapes, alteration of biophysical processes and habitat, and modifications of major biogeochemical processes" (Alberti 2010, 178).

However, it is nearly impossible to conduct the type of research required to determine the effect of urbanization on the dynamics of natural ecosystems (Alberti 2010; Chace and Walsh 2006; Pickett et al. 2011). Urban ecosystems evolved over time and space as the outcome of dynamic interactions between **socioeconomic** and **biophysical** processes operating over multiple scales. Urban ecosystems need to be studied in the context of an integrated human-ecological (hybrid) phenomenon. However, past studies of urban systems have been parceled out to sociology, economics, ecology, and politics and examined separately rather than synthesized into one coherent theoretical framework by all vested interest groups (Alberti 2009).

"Ecological models of urban communities vastly simplify human processes"
—Marina Alberti, Advances in Urban Ecology

It must be obvious to the most casual observers that humans (*Homo sapiens*) have such profound effects on natural ecosystems they can be correctly labeled as a **keystone species** (Adams and Lindsey 2011), an organism that (1) affects the distribution or abundance of many other species; (2) can affect community structure by strongly modifying patterns of relative abundance among competing species; (3) affects community structure by affecting the abundance of species at multiple trophic levels; and (4) has disproportionately large impacts on communities (Waller and Alverson 1997; Power et al. 1996). The following human activities support consideration of the species as a keystone (O'Neill and Kahn 2000, O'Neill 2001, and Cunningham and Cunningham 2010, cited in Adams and Lindsey 2011):

- constructing both dispersal barriers and invasion pathways through habitat fragmentation
- introducing exotic species and causing mass faunal extinctions
- changing ecosystem stability by altering environmental constraints and biota
- manipulating disturbance regimes by suppressing or increasing probabilities of occurrence
- having an effect on communities that ripples across trophic levels
- changing competitive relationships

A keystone species has the capability of altering the abiotic and biotic components of the natural ecosystem to make them immediately less habitable to some species and more habitable to others, at least for as long as they are present. If humans were removed from the built environment, the urban ecosystem would change drastically, usually back to the ecosystem that existed prior to human presence.

We are able to measure anthropogenic effects on natural ecosystems in terms of what, when, where, why, and how the presence of *H. sapiens* leads to quantifiable

Environmentally and biologically relevant effects of urbanization

Physical and chemical environment	Population and community characteristics	Ecosystem structure and function
Air pollution	Altered assimilation rates	Altered decomposition rates
Hydrologic changes	Altered biological cycles	Altered nutrient retention
Local climate change	Altered disturbance regimes	Greater nutrient flux
Soil changes and movement	Altered reproductive rates	Increased habitat patches
Water pollution	Altered succession rates and direction	Habitat fragmentation and simplification
	Altered survival rates	Increased debris dams
	Altered growth rates	Increased sediment loading in streams
	Genetic drift and selection	Loss of biological diversity
	Introduced species	Loss of biological organization
	Landscape fragmentation	Loss of forest understory
	Population size and structure	Loss of plant productivity
	Reduced species diversity	Loss of redundant pathways for nutrient and energy transfer
	Social and behavioral changes	

Source: From McDonnell and Pickett (1990), cited in Adams and Lindsey (2010).

disturbances (Adams and Lindsey 2010). However, we do not know how to prevent or repair the damage resulting from these effects, nor do we know how resilient the human-created urban ecosystem is over time. Every plant and animal species, including humans, has but three choices under changing environmental conditions: (1) adapt—adjust and exploit the new situation; (2) move—disperse or migrate; or (3) die—become threatened, endangered, or extinct. Any one of these options can be used to develop a taxonomy of assemblages of flora and fauna present or missing in an urban ecosystem. Chace and Walsh (2006), citing many different publications, listed six factors that determine which species can coexist with humans:

1. Patch size and distribution of remnant native vegetation
2. Competition with exotic species that have a longer history of cohabitation with humans
3. Presence of nonnative predators
4. Structure and floristic characteristics of planted vegetation
5. Supplementary feeding by humans
6. Tolerance of residual pesticides

Evolution of Ecosystems

"We are changing Earth more rapidly than we are understanding it."
—Peter M. Vitousek, H. A. Mooney, J. Lubchenco, and J. M. Melillo, "Human Domination of Earth's Ecosystems"

There is always an orderly and ever-changing progression of events in the evolution of natural ecosystems. The existing abiotic structure predicts the plants, which predict the types of animals. Next, an orderly and progressive replacement of one community type by another takes place until a climax community is established—this process is known as **ecological succession**. The 10 ecological regions of Texas represent examples of climax community types.

ABIOTICS

(*e.g.*, hot and dry-desert)

PLANTS SPECIES

(cactus)

ANIMAL SPECIES

(desert tortoise)

How ecosystems are formed.

Urbanization often disrupts the progression of events that would predict or sustain a climax community by reversing the successional process to a simpler early-stage ecosystem. Fortunately, there is a built-in resiliency in nature that dampens the perturbations and destructive aspects of the urbanization process. This resiliency is illustrated in vacant lots or neglected cemeteries as they revert back to a version of the original ecosystem present prior to human interventions.

The abiotic structure of an environment, sometimes referred to as its inorganic components, is composed of various physical and chemical factors. It can be helpful to divide abiotic factors into two types: conditions and resources. **Conditions** include climate (e.g., temperature, moisture), pH (acidic or alkaline), turbidity, and wind (speed and direction). **Resources** include features such as chemical nutrients, light, oxygen, and space. The combination of conditions and resources determines which plant species exist in a particular area (Begon et al. 1996). The plant community then predicts the types of animals that will exist there. **Ecoregions** are classified based on the abiotic characteristics plus the dominant plant communities that result from the abiotic structure. Temperature and moisture (abiotic conditions) most often determine differences within vegetation regimes (e.g., rain forest, temperate forest, tundra), while soil nutrients (abiotic resources) influence the dominant vegetation type (e.g., trees, shrubs, grasses, or succulents).

Interestingly, it is rare to see a reference to climatic differences between urban environments (e.g., desert-urban, temperate-urban, tropical-urban) discussed in the literature, even though these variations certainly exist. Perhaps the reason is that the term "urban ecosystem" is relatively new and is often used as if the abiotic conditions within developed areas are monolithic. One need only visit the cities of Houston and El Paso, on opposite sides of this large state and in distinctly different ecoregions, Gulf Prairies and Trans-Pecos, respectively, to recognize that temperature and moisture variations are at work even in cities, resulting in species variation.

Abiotic factors

Conditions	Resources
pH (acidity vs. alkalinity)	Chemical nutrients (N, P, CO_2)
Salinity	Light (intensity and wavelength)
Temperature	Oxygen
Turbidity (cloudiness of water)	Space to live, feed, reproduce
Wind	Water or moisture

Often cities and even suburbs develop microclimates, with weather significantly different from that of the surrounding, less developed area. Cities become **heat islands**—areas where local temperatures are measurably higher than those in the nearby countryside. The heat island effect is the result of thermal mass (a.k.a. urban hardscape, such as brick, concrete, and asphalt) collecting heat during daylight hours and releasing it after dark, reflective heat from glass buildings and surface covers, and limited tree canopy and shade. Higher temperatures result in a longer growing season for plants. City lakes and ponds often remain ice-free longer during the winter than rural bodies of water, which can change wildlife behavior and habitat use. Some studies have shown that cities have more cloud cover and more precipitation than surrounding areas (although most of this moisture is quickly lost from increased runoff). Additionally, architectural features, such as tall buildings, affect wind speed within human-created landscapes (Adams and Lindsey 2010).

Urban Soils

The soil ecosystem provides a supportive substrate, as well as nutrients, water, and oxygen, to green plants. Soil is a mixture of four basic components (Adams and Lindsey 2010):

1. Inorganic materials, including rock, clay, silt, and sand that give structure to the soil
2. Organic matter, including living and decomposing organisms and plant parts, that supplies nutrients and helps hold moisture
3. Air that moves through the pore spaces, providing oxygen to plant roots
4. Water and dissolved nutrients that also move through the pore spaces and are important for a number of a plant's life processes (USDA 2001)

Soil Horizons

Soil consists of different layers called **horizons**. The arrangement and makeup of the horizons influence the amount and type of plant growth that can occur. The thickness of each layer will vary depending on the climate and region, and in developed areas the impacts of urbanization. The table describes the four general horizons in a soil profile. **Soil texture** refers to the relative proportions of each mineral type in a given soil; for example, roughly 40% sand, 40% silt, and 20% clay produce a soil classified as **loam**, considered to be the optimal mineral composition for a soil to facilitate healthy plant growth. Humus and other organic material from the O horizon will increase soil porosity, enhancing the water- and nutrient-holding abilities and the aeration qualities of soil.

As earthworms eat their way through the O, A, and sometimes the B horizons, they form open channels that connect the horizons, increase water infiltration and oxygen transfer from the surface, and, as a bonus, increase the humus content in the A horizon. Earthworms have an exceptional ability to displace large amounts of soil and play a major role in topsoil formation.

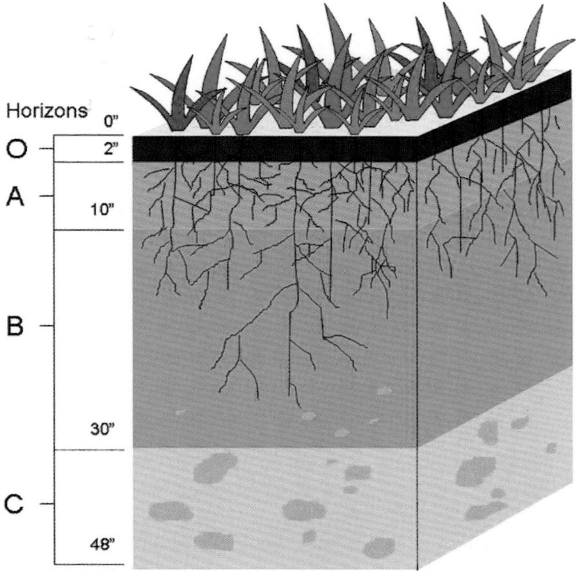

A typical soil profile showing the four horizons. Courtesy of US Department of Agriculture

Description of soil profiles

Horizon	Description
O	The top layer or organic horizon consisting of decaying plant material called "humus"
A	The most productive layer of soil commonly referred to as "topsoil," where most plant roots are found; composed primarily of a mixture of mineral and humus material and is where most soil functions occur
B	A subsoil layer formed by materials leached or moved from the A horizon, including clay, iron, aluminum, and some organic material
C	The lowest layer of soil composed of disintegrated parent material and other minerals

They can completely mix the top six inches of a humid grassland soil in 10–20 years (USDA 2001). Some of the same benefits are provided by burrowing mammals, such as moles and pocket gophers (Adams and Lindsey 2010).

The primary impacts of urbanization on the soil profile are to remove the O and most of the A horizons through scraping or grading, thus preparing the land for construction. Later, home and building owners will often attempt to replace the O horizon with purchased bags of mulch that contain decaying organic material. The A horizon is replaced with purchased bags or even truckloads of **topsoil** that may have been collected from some other development site, moving abiotic and/or biotic components far from their source in the process.

Soil grading and scraping to prepare soil for urban development. Courtesy of John M. Davis

Nutrients are constantly being recycled in our natural ecosystems. Organic matter is constantly being broken down and reused. However, some common urban activities eliminate this critical process. For example, grass, leaves, logs, and other organic matter that would ordinarily be recycled are instead raked, bagged, and hauled away. These practices remove nutrients and trace minerals from the system, so it may be necessary to add chemical fertilizers to offset the damage caused by their own attempts to keep the world outside their door neat and tidy. Unfortunately, commercial fertilizers do not replace all the nutrients plants need, and soil compaction and inappropriate application cause many of the chemicals to simply run off the surface and down the drain, negatively impacting the local watershed.

Soil Functions

Healthy soil ecosystems will support healthy plant growth aboveground if they contain ample supplies of oxygen, water, and nutrients. For these three key ingredients to be available to plants, soils must perform six critical functions simultaneously, regardless of region or climate (Scheyer and Hipple 2005):

1. Soils are sponges, soaking up rainwater and limiting runoff, playing a role in groundwater recharge and flood-control potentials in urban areas.
2. Soils are faucets, storing and releasing water and air for plants and animals to use.
3. Soils are supermarkets, providing valuable nutrients and air and water to plants and animals.
4. Soils are storage sites. Carbon is sequestered in soil, slowing its release into the atmosphere. Soils also store nutrients for future use by plants, animals, and microbes.
5. Soils are strainers, filtering and purifying water and air that flow through them.
6. Soils buffer, degrade, immobilize, de-

toxify, and trap pollutants, including oil, pesticides, herbicides, and heavy metals, and keep them from entering groundwater supplies.

These services are performed by topsoil, which forms as a result of three constantly interacting ecological processes: detritus decomposition, mineral leaching, and the detritus food web. No single soil function can be assigned to a single ecological process—each function is the result of all three, acting in concert. Imagine what might happen in terms of soil's ability to provide these critical functions when the O horizon (which includes detritus) is removed from the local soil ecosystem as a result of development. Without detritus the decomposer food chain shuts down, resulting in the loss of soil nutrients—the supermarket shelves are empty. No nutrients, no plants, and when they die, the root systems cannot hold the soil particles in place when it rains or the wind blows (Adams and Lindsey 2010).

Unique Features of Urban Soils

The general characteristics of urban soil are in stark contrast to those of natural soil ecosystems (Adams and Lindsey 2010) and include the following (Craul 1985; New York City Soil Survey Staff 2005):

- great vertical and spatial variability; for example, larger O horizons as a result of overmulching
- modified soil structure leading to compaction
- presence of surface crust on bare soil that is usually hydrophobic (repels water)
- modified soil reaction (e.g., pH is usually elevated)
- restricted aeration and water drainage
- interrupted nutrient cycling and a modified soil organism population and activity
- presence of anthropogenic materials and other contaminants
- highly modified soil temperature regimes

Taking Better Care of Urban Soil

These urban soil characteristics are interrelated—one condition leads to another. For example, modified soil structure can lead to presence of surface crust and restricted aeration and water drainage. The process of urbanization seriously alters or even removes some of the services provided by the soil ecosystem. It is important to understand value of a healthy soil ecosystem in sustaining a high-quality of life for all organisms. There are ways to restore and sustain the physical and biological properties of soil that benefit humans and all other organisms (USDA 2001). These are the golden rules of soil conservation:

1. Cover the soil.
2. Provide minimal or zero tillage.
3. Mulch for nutrients.
4. Maximize biomass production.
5. Maximize biodiversity.

Following the golden rules of soil conservation will produce productive soil that has a good supply of nutrients and nutrient-holding capacity; good infiltration and water-holding capacity that resists evaporative water loss; porous structure for aeration; near-neutral pH; and low salt content.

There are many sources of free information that provide strategies to restore soil fertility even in the most devastated urban soils. This information can be obtained from the state Extension Service, Producers Cooperative Association stores, and web-based resources, using the search term "urban soils." Restoring natural soil conditions provides economic benefits, including reduced need for watering and fertilizing, healthier plant growth, and more plant and animal diversity (Adams and Lindsey 2010).

Water Cycle

The water cycle purifies water through three processes: evapotranspiration (through

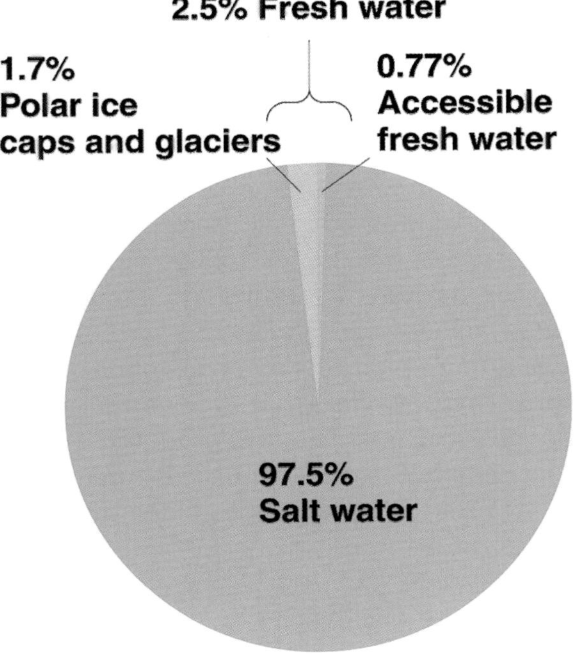

Earth's water. The earth has an abundance of water, but terrestrial ecosystems, humans, and agriculture depend on accessible fresh water, which constitutes only 0.77% of the total. From Wright and Boorse (2011, fig. 10.1)

plants); infiltration (through the soil); and evaporation (through air). The result is **potable** (drinkable) water. It is important to note that the water cycle does *not* produce more water; however, it does constantly recirculate and purify the water that sustains all life on earth. The graph of the earth's water may help you understand the importance of potable water—if all of the water present on earth would fill a one-gallon bucket, approximately one thimbleful (0.77%) would be drinkable.

Total surface water and groundwater withdrawals from 1950 to 2005 in the United States. From Kenny et al. (2009)

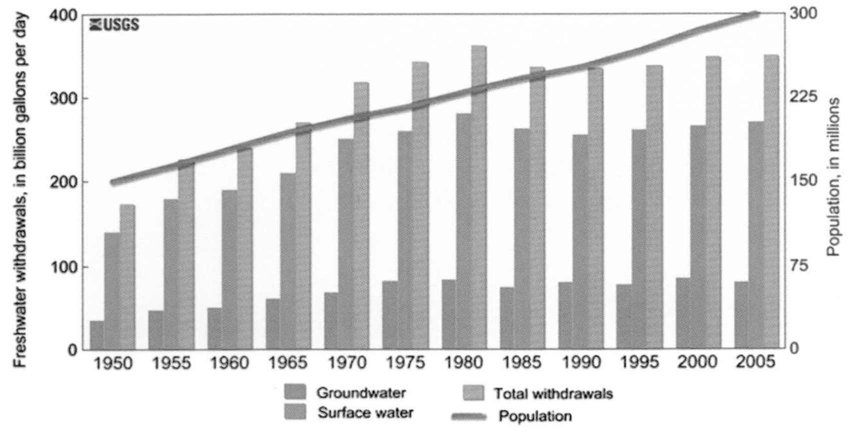

Impact of Urbanization on Water Resources

Life on earth depends on ecosystem health, which is inextricably connected to the water cycle; understandably, then, the water cycle must be protected. Yet the activities of people all over the world jeopardize this critical and delicate process through overuse, pollution, and disruption of the filtration process. This is particularly common in urban areas. Impervious surface covers (e.g., rooftops, parking lots, streets, sidewalks, and compacted soil) restrict or eliminate infiltration of water into the soil. Precipitation that once was absorbed into the soil, recharging groundwater supplies, now becomes runoff. Urbanization even amplifies the impact of drought; when rain does fall, it evaporates or becomes runoff without ever having a chance to infiltrate soils and recharge rivers, lakes, and aquifers.

Surface and groundwater supplies are the two major water sources for the majority of metropolitan areas, but the amount of fresh water withdrawn varies greatly by state and purpose. Surface water sources include lakes, river basins, and constructed impoundments, and the unit of measurement is an **acre-foot**, defined as the volume of one acre of surface area to a depth of one foot, or 325,851 gallons.

Texas' freshwater supply consists of 15 major river basins that contain 194 lakes or surface impoundments. According to the Texas Water Development Board (TWDB, n.d.), the state also has 9 major and 21 minor aquifers capable of producing potable groundwater. The annual consumption of two to three Texas households equals one acre-foot. Projected freshwater demand for Texas domestic uses is expected to increase from 18 million in 2010 to 19 million acre

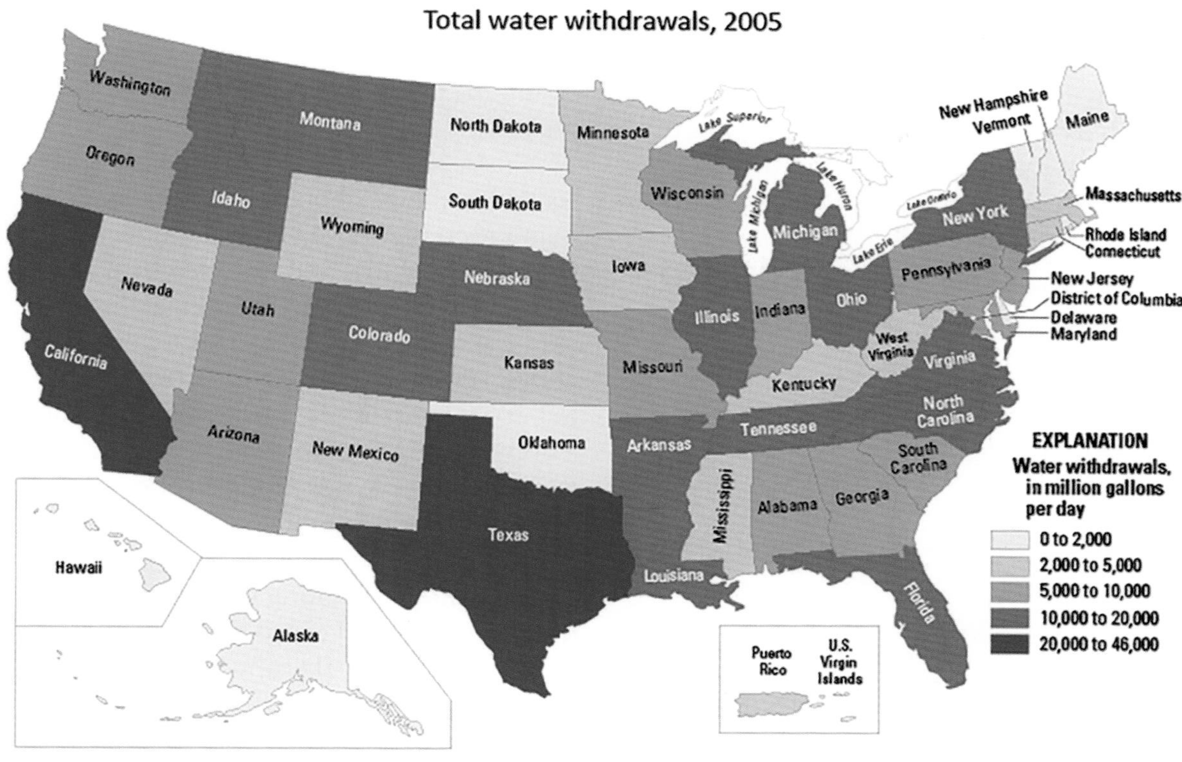

National summary of total water withdrawals in 2005. More recent data were not available. From Kenney et al. (2009)

feet by 2020 (TWDB 2011). Texas' population and, subsequently, water demand, are expected to continue growing until 2060. As of September 2014, 92 Texas lakes that provide fresh water to urban communities were below normal levels.

It is absolutely essential that water conservation measures become the norm in the daily life styles of urban residents, including

- using less than 100 gallons/capita/day for day-to-day activities such as bathing (e.g., two-minute showers), toilets, cooking, and cleaning; landscaping irrigation (e.g., use native plant species rather than exotic grasses); and recreational activities (e.g., swimming pools)
- capturing stormwater runoff in constructed urban wetlands
- using captured "gray" water resources in a community to irrigate public parks, golf courses, athletic fields, and other municipal properties
- developing enforceable community water conservation rules or laws
- eliminating or minimizing point and non-point sources of water pollution

To make these suggestions a reality, we need public education and community outreach programs on water conservation using best management practices and, in particular, providing evidence of the cost effectiveness of these measures.

Water Contaminants

Contaminants affect the entire water cycle by killing plants, entering surface water impoundments and streams, and traveling through the soil to contaminate aquifers.

National summary of methods of utilization of freshwater withdrawals in 2005. More recent data were unavailable. From Kenney et al. (2009)

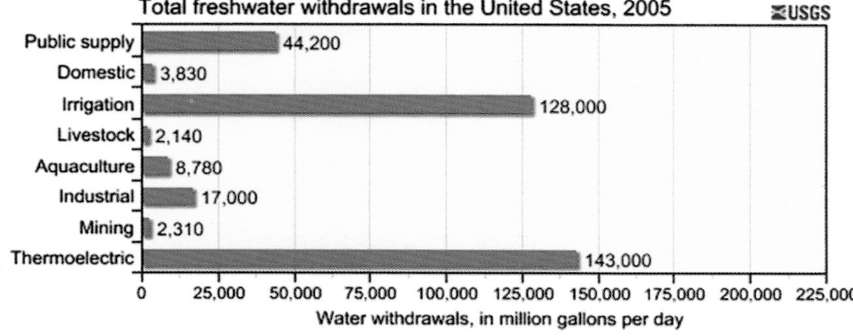

Even the air can become contaminated with sulfur monoxide (SO) radicals from burning fossil fuels and thus producing acid rains. Elevated concentrations of many types of chemicals can be found in urban surface waters, including mercury (Hg), lead (Pb), and aluminum (Al), along with pesticides (e.g., DDT, PCB) and other compounds that cannot be assimilated or tolerated by living organisms.

Lakes and other surface impoundments in the 15 river basins in Texas

River basin	Number of lakes or surface impoundments
Brazos	42
Canadian	3
Colorado	31
Cypress	10
Guadalupe	5
Lavaca	1
Neches	10
Nueces	3
Red	24
Rio Grande	7
Sabine	12
San Antonio	4
San Jacinto	6
Sulphur	4
Trinity	32
Total	194

Source: Texas Water Development Board (2015).

What is not shown in the table is organic waste—millions of pounds of solid and liquid excrement from companion animals, flocking songbirds and waterfowl, and even humans when water treatment facilities divert raw sewage into streams. Organic waste and fertilizer can cause surface waterways to become **eutrophic**, the process by which a body of water becomes highly enriched in dissolved nutrients, such as phosphates, that stimulate the growth of aquatic plant life, including phytoplankton and macrophytes, usually resulting in the depletion of dissolved oxygen. Loss of native species of aquatic animal life disrupts the aquatic food chain:

Aquatic food chain = phytoplankton → zooplankton → fish larvae → small fish → large fish → fish-eating birds

Urban water can be contaminated by point and nonpoint pollution sources. **Point source pollution** can be traced to a specific

Types of chemicals found in elevated concentrations in urban streams and their sources

Chemical	Source
Phosphorus	Wastewater and fertilizer runoff from lawns
Nitrate and ammonium	Wastewater and fertilizer runoff from lawns
Metals: Pb, Zn, Cr, Cu, Mn, Ni, Cd, Hg, As, Fe, B, Co, Ag, Sr, Sb, Sc, Mo, Li, Sn	Industrial discharge, brake linings, metal alloys, and accumulations on roads and parking lots
Pesticides and herbicides	Urban use around homes and workplaces and lawn and golf course management
Polychlorinated biphenyls (PCBs), polycyclic aromatic hydrocarbons (PAHs), petroleum-based aliphatic hydrocarbons	Stormwater runoff from industrial point sources, episodic spills, oil and gasoline spills
Pharmaceuticals: antibiotics, chemotherapeutic drugs, analgesics, narcotics, psychotherapeutic drugs	Hospital effluent and drug flushing down the toilet

Source: Paul and Meyer (2001).

Eutrophication in a freshwater pond. Courtesy of Texas A&M AgriLife Extension Service

location, such as discharge from a factory or wastewater treatment facility. This type of pollution is easy to monitor but still difficult to control. **Nonpoint source pollution** comes from many different sites throughout the watershed and is, therefore, difficult to monitor. Examples of nonpoint source pollution include fertilizers, pesticides, and organic waste from yards and petroleum residues from streets and parking lots. As water runoff travels across yards and paved surfaces, it picks up contaminants and carries them to the nearest watercourse.

Sediment loads in urban streams, ponds, and lakes are also a problem. Water runoff picks up sediment through erosion and carries it into watercourses. The increased stream volume and velocity caused by runoff and channelization scours the stream banks, releasing even more sediment. Streams become **turbid** (cloudy), which alters light penetration, which in turn affects the ability of aquatic vegetation to complete the process of photosynthesis. Sediment may also be deposited on the bottoms of the streams and ponds, covering gravel beds that once contained a rich diversity of invertebrate wildlife.

Channelization

Natural waterways are all sinuous curves; **channelization** is the process of carving the stream bank into a smooth, straight channel, usually removing trees and other vegetation at the same time. The channel may then be seeded with grass or lined with concrete. Converting natural streams into concrete channels is done to reduce erosion, at least in specific locations, and move water downstream more quickly to prevent flooding of roads and buildings. But channelizing a stream fixes one problem while creating a suite of new ones (Davis 2003):

1. **Stream channelization increases water velocity.** Smooth concrete walls increase the velocity of the water, causing significant erosion and flooding when the water exits at the end of the channel (Riley 1998).
2. **Stream channelization increases danger.** There have been documented cases of people being swept away when caught in water rushing down these smooth-walled channels.
3. **Stream channelization eliminates infiltration.** The concrete lining of the channel separates the water from the soil so it cannot soak into the soil (Riley 1998).
4. **Stream channelization eliminates pools and riffles.** Natural streams have a normal pattern of pools and riffles. Pools are deeper sections with slower-flowing currents. Riffles are shallow with faster currents. Since these habitats are different, they support different plant and animal species. When a stream is channelized, these habitats are destroyed along with the plant and animal species that depend on them.

5. **Stream channelization harms the food web.** Most stream systems rely on organic material carried in water from the surrounding landscape to form the basis of the food web. Channelization eliminates much of this resource.
6. **Stream channelization removes the native riparian (streamside) vegetation.** This eliminates habitat for treefrogs, kingfishers, herons, and other wildlife that depend on the vegetation.
   a. Replacing stream vegetation with concrete eliminates the natural beauty of the stream. People prefer to live adjacent to natural areas, and property values tend to be higher (Ferguson 1998).
   b. Removing the native vegetation along streams eliminates their water-polishing services, increasing the negative impact of excess nutrients and contaminants in urban waters (APWA 1981; Hammer 1997).
   c. Loss of vegetation along streams removes the cooling effect of shade. Water that flows down a shadeless concrete channel becomes overheated, resulting in low dissolved-oxygen levels and a reduced capacity for supporting life. Moreover, a change in water temperature of only a few degrees can have an adverse impact on populations of aquatic invertebrates and other animals.

An example of stream channelization. Courtesy of John Davis, TPWD

Nutrient Cycling

One of the most remarkable functions an ecosystem provides is recycling finite amounts of matter so they become an infinitely available resource for all living organisms. The simplicity of the process becomes evident when one studies how biogeochemical cycles work. The actors in this process are always the same: producers, consumers, and decomposers. These living organisms borrow the essential nutrients (e.g., nitrogen, carbon, hydrogen, oxygen, phosphorus, and sulfur) they need to live, but only for a limited period of time. The nutrients are released back into the ecosystem when the organism dies, to be used by another organism, and then another; round and round the wheel of life goes (and where it stops . . . we hope we never know!).

Humans, on the other hand, have established a throwaway culture in which matter is used once and then sealed off in landfills. Per capita food waste equals 33% of all edible food (Buzby and Hyman 2012) and 21% of municipal solid waste (4.38 pounds/capita/day) (EPA 2014). Landfills are the antithesis of properly functioning ecosystems. They represent a one-way-trip, a use-it-and-lose-it mentality. Given enough time, the matter contained in these mountains of waste will be broken down into other forms, but the decomposition process in landfills takes far longer than under more natural conditions. Many larger cities and municipal governments are attempting to reduce or even eliminate waste streams through recycling and reuse, realizing the potential value of landfill garbage and waste-to-energy (WTE) facilities. But we are far from realizing this lofty goal.

Urban Food Webs

The figure illustrates a natural and an urban food web. In the typical, if simplified, food web within a natural ecosystem, mice eat grass seeds, and owls eat mice. Of course, mice feed on other varieties of seeds as well as the occasional insect, just as owls may consume rabbits and squirrels in addition to mice (insects are even an important food for some smaller owl species, such as screech-owls).

Urban food webs paint quite a different picture, as can be demonstrated by constructing a web of common urban producers and consumers, both native and introduced. For example, common representatives of the producer level in a suburban area might include flowers, trees, and shrubs used in landscaping; as well as sunflower seed mix, sugar water, edible garbage, and pet food. Urban herbivore representatives would be rabbits, mice, deer, geese, squirrels, hummingbirds, and several species of granivore (seed-eating) birds. Humans, raccoons, and opossums are all urban omnivores, while urban carnivores include domestic dogs and cats, coyotes, foxes, raptors (e.g., meat-eating birds such as hawks and owls), and in some parts of the United States and Canada black bears, polar bears, and cougars.

Urban wildlife does its part to recycle matter; food wastes are a heavily exploited resource. In a typical urban food chain rats eat garbage, cats eat rats, and coyotes eat cats (urban residents often express shock when learning their pets may have been

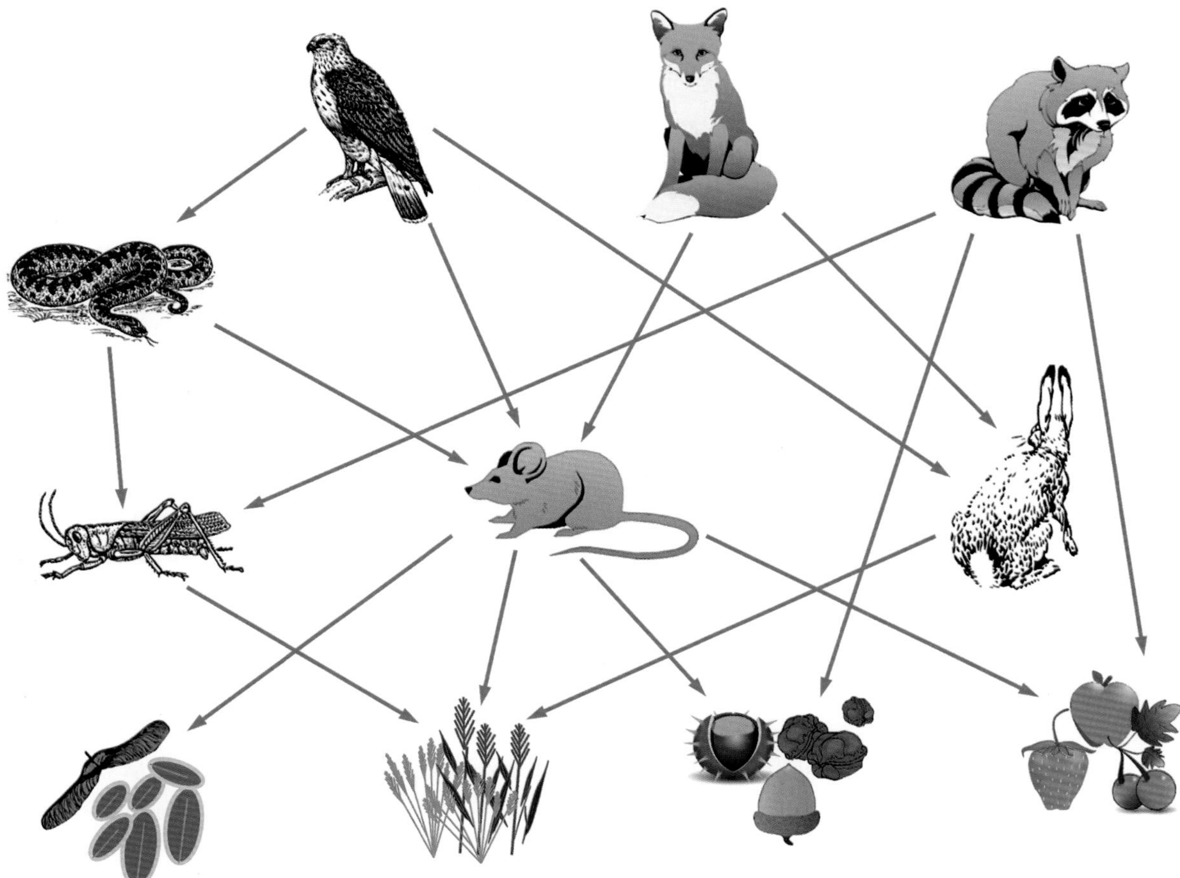

Natural ecosystem food web based on three trophic levels. From Adams and Lindsey (2012)

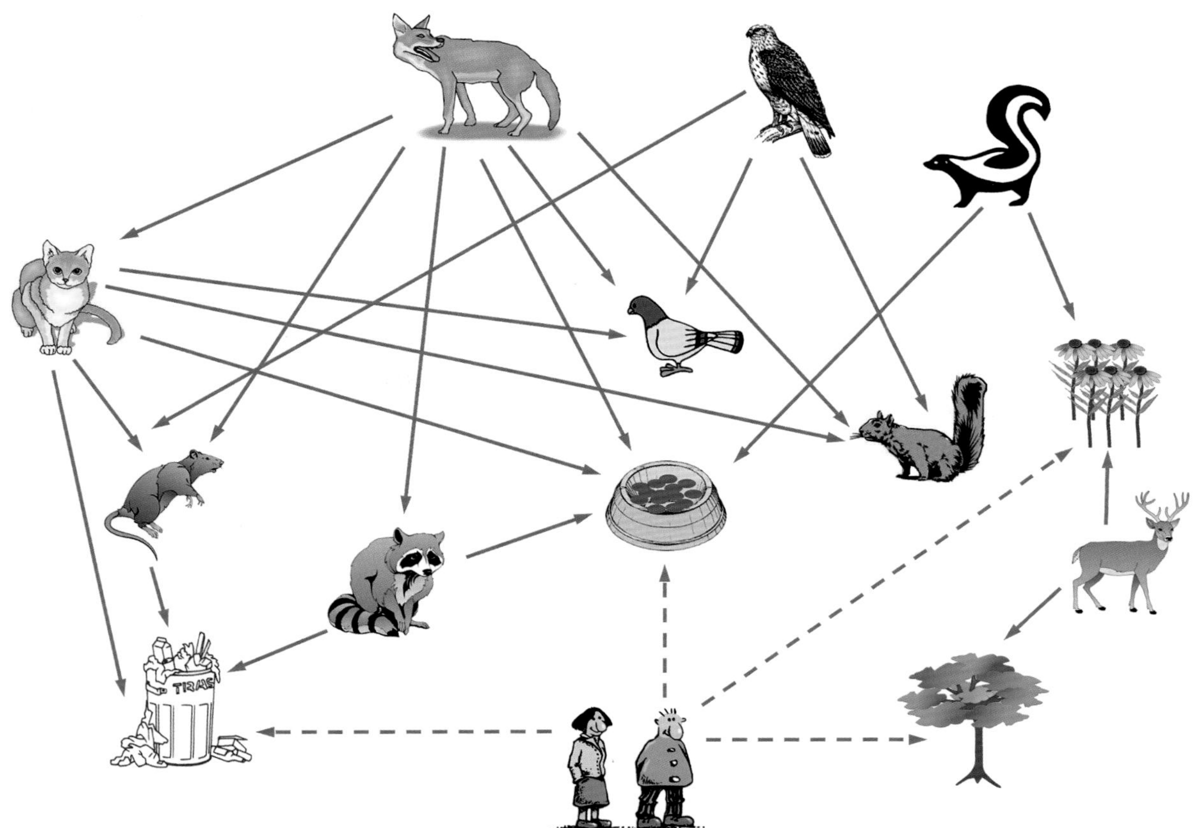

Urban ecosystem food web based on four trophic levels. From Adams and Lindsey (2010)

preyed upon by a coyote). However, cats and coyotes will also eat garbage—much less work than chasing down prey—and it is not uncommon to observe rats and cats feeding side by side near an overflowing dumpster (Sullivan 2004).

Urbanization Effects on Biotic Structure and Function

Urbanization affects both plant and animal communities.

Urban Plant Communities

Urban plants have some unique characteristics when compared to those in rural or natural areas (Pickett et al. 2011). The prevalence of native species decreases as one moves from the urban fringe to the city center, and nonnative exotics increase across the same continuum. One study found that in the period from 1894 to 1993, an urban park in Boston, Massachusetts, saw native species decrease by 84%, replaced by 64 new species (Drayton and Primack 1996).

Species richness is affected by the age of city, with older cities exhibiting more plant species diversity than younger cities. Also, the older, established areas of cities, such as cemeteries and early settlement neighborhoods, contain more vegetation variety and maturity than more recently developed neighborhoods. The number of plant species in urban areas correlates with human population size.

As an area undergoes urbanization, a pattern begins to emerge that allows us to categorize urban plant communities into three broad groups: natural remnants, derelict lands, and planted communities (Adams and Lindsey 2010).

Natural remnants of vegetation persist even in the midst of heavy development. These patches retain the characteristics of the native plant community that existed before urbanization, but they face many threats. As the patches fragment—becoming smaller in size and more widely spaced—pollination and dispersal of seeds become increasingly difficult for the resident plants. When forest remnants are carved up, species once found inside the relatively protected interior are forced to deal with the harsher conditions found at the newly created edge (e.g., increased wind, greater temperature fluctuations). Urbanization affects the local hydrology, which inevitably affects the plant communities. Species able to tolerate the changes may persist; those that cannot will disappear.

Derelict lands, sometimes referred to as vacant lots, are characterized by having been disturbed by construction at some point. Depending on how long it has been since the disturbance, the plants species likely to be found in these patches include invasive species and native pioneer species (e.g., ragweed). Like remnants, these small areas of habitat are fragmented and disconnected from one another. The biodiversity within these patches tends to be low, although those species represented may exist in large numbers.

Planted communities make up the majority of urban areas. They are largely artificial, making extensive use of high-maintenance species in a highly controlled manner. Many of the species found in planted communities come from Europe, Asia, and South America, including boxwood, nandina, crepe myrtle, photinia, ornamental pear, bermudagrass, and Asian jasmine (Davis 2003). An interesting activ-

Exotic plants and the native species they replace

Vegetation type	Exotic species	Native species
Forest systems	Chinese privet (*Ligustrum sinense*)	green ash (*Fraxinus pennsylvanica*)
	chinaberry (*Melis azedarach*)	flowering dogwood (*Cornus florida*)
	mimosa (*Albizia julibrissin*)	American elm (*Ulmus americana*)
	Siberian elm (*Ulmus pumila*)	sweet gum (*Liquidambar styraciflua*)
	Chinese tallow (*Sapium sibiferum*)	live oak (*Quercus virginiana*)
	Japanese honeysuckle (*Lonicera japonica*)	maple (*Acer* spp.)
Prairie systems	tall fescue (*Festuca arundinacea*)	big bluestem (*Andropogon gerardii*)
	Johnsongrass (*Sorghum halepense*)	indiangrass (*Sorghastrum nutans*)
	purple scabies (*Scabiosa atropurpurea*)	switchgrass (*Panicum virgatum*)
	sweetclover (*Melilotus officinalis* and *M. alba*)	rose gentian (*Sabatia campestis*)
	Japanese brome (*Bromus japonicus*)	prairie coneflower (*Ratibida pinnata*)
Aquatic systems	giant salvinia (*Salvinia molesta*)	pondweed (*Potamogeton* spp.)
	water hyacinth (*Eichhornia crassipes*)	water stargrass (*Heteranthera dubia*)
	hydrilla (*Hydrilla verticellata*)	arrowhead (*Sagittaria* spp.)
	parrot's feather (*Myriophyllum aquaticum*)	spatterdock (*Nuphar luteum*)
	Eurasian watermilfoil (*Myriophyllum spicatum*)	pickerel weed (*Pontederia cordata*)

Source: From Brockman (1986); Cushman and Jones (2004); Borman and Korth (1998); and Davis (2003).

ity for Master Naturalists would be to visit a local retailer; list all of the trees, shrubs, bushes, and flowers for sale; and then determine how many are native and how many are exotic species.

Land of Lawns

The typical urban landscape is really quite predictable. Just about every home or business will have a row of evergreen hedges around the perimeter of the building, called "foundation plantings." Unwanted views usually are "screened" with a row of evergreen hedges as well. With the exception of newly constructed developments, there will be large shade trees and some kind of groundcover, turfgrass being the most common. Often you will see a flower bed of some sort at the base of trees and along walkways, usually containing nonnative annuals and perennials to add color.

If traditional landscaping were ecologically sensitive, or even neutral, these practices would be a harmless cultural quirk, but the typical suburban lawn and garden create a myriad of ecological problems. Exotic plant species feature prominently in these settings, even though they tend to require more intensive maintenance to survive than would natives (and, ironically, often these same plants are marketed as "easy care"). For example, exotic plants generally require more moisture than native landscapes, which puts more pressure on community water supplies. Those species that do well can escape the confines of the yard and compete with endemic species. As native plants are lost, food and shelter resources are lost as well; this can have an adverse affect on resident wildlife.

The urban/suburban landscape is dominated by vast expanses of mowed turfgrass. Maintaining the perfect lawn is ecologically expensive. Running a lawn mower for one hour releases as much hydrocarbon into the air as driving a car for 11.5 hours (Schultz 1999, cited in Davis 2003). In the absence of irrigation and fertilization, most species of grass would not be able to grow and compete with native vegetation in most of the conterminous United States (Milesi et al. 2005). Turfgrass needs pesticides, herbicides, and fertilizers to achieve the preferred deep green color and lush texture, all of which significantly decrease water quality. According to Schultz (1999), 70 million pounds of chemicals are applied to US lawns each year. The majority of these chemicals are washed into local streams and reservoirs by rain and sprinkler systems. A "healthy" lawn endangers the ecosystem health.

Yet the residential lawn is the most conspicuous representation of human manipulation of the natural habitat. Vinlove and Torla (1995) set out to determine how much US land had been converted to lawn, based on the number of housing units and median lot size, and came up with an estimate of between 14 and 18 million acres. A later study (Milesi et al. 2005) using satellite imaging calculated that as much as 40,475,861 acres are cultivated with turfgrasses in the continental United States—three times that of irrigated cropland. Urban landscapes in Texas, including golf courses, account for 1.7 million acres (Cabrera et al. 2013).

A checklist of Texas amphibians, reptiles, birds, and mammals found in urban centers around the state has been compiled by the author and his team of urban ecologists. This resource is an impressive summary of the biodiversity that can be found even in the most urban of environments. To obtain a copy of this checklist, please download it from the Texas Master Naturalist website: http://txmn.org/about/curriculum/.

Urban Animal Communities

The presence of various species of wildlife found in urban ecosystems was predicated on the characteristics of the "urban wildlife syndrome (UWS)" (Pickett et al. 2011). The UWS, when applied to animals living in urban ecosystems, suggested that they have certain characteristics, conditions, or behaviors:

- generalists with high reproductive capacity (i.e., R-strategists)
- high dispersal abilities
- high rates of innovation
- high level of risk taking
- rapid life histories
- biotic homogenization
- elevated densities associated with human subsidies
- reduced wariness
- increased intraspecific aggression
- increased tolerance of human presence

Urbanization has a profound impact on the predevelopment wildlife community, most of which moves out of the area during construction. The species that return or move in once the bulldozers and landscapers have left are either fortunate, adaptable, or both. The fortunate ones include Canada geese, who just happen to share with humans a preference for broad expanses of grass, a lack of understory that provides a hiding place for predators, and bodies of water with gentle entry slopes: in other words, a typical park, golf course, or business park.

Raccoons, on the other hand, are the adaptability poster children; intelligent, omnivorous, dexterous—they not only tolerate life in human settlements but exploit the situation to great advantage. Killdeer are both fortunate and adaptive. Their luck comes in the form of parking lots that offer a wide, flat terrain similar to their native open uplands, not to mention insect-attracting lights that cause food to fall from the sky to the pavement like manna from heaven. In undeveloped areas, killdeer are primarily **diurnal** (active during the day), but the urban populations have adapted to the night shift and are often observed foraging for food late at night, when the cars are gone and the lights are on. Species that are neither lucky nor resilient simply disappear. There are plenty of others moving in to take their place.

As a result, urban wildlife communities are actually far more diverse than once thought (Adams 2015). In fact, there are vast assemblages of vertebrate fauna (amphibians, reptiles, birds, and mammals) residing in US urban areas alone, including a significant number of both native and alien species from each taxonomic class. Resources used to construct national and state vertebrate species do not always agree in terms of numbers or taxonomy and may not always included sampling from urban habitats. The initial challenge in developing lists of urban vertebrate fauna is identifying studies (formal and informal) that concentrate specifically on this landscape (Adams and Lindsey 2010), so indirect methods of identifying urban vertebrate wildlife have been used:

1. Road-kill data
2. Websites that provide national- and state-specific lists of amphibians, reptiles, birds, and mammals, for example:
   - AmphibiaWeb (http://www.amphibiaweb.org)
   - The Center for North American Herpetology (http://www.cnah.org/stateList.aspx)
   - What Bird (http://www.whatbird.com)
   - Smithsonian National Museum of Natural History: North American Mammals (http://nmnh-arcgis01.si.edu/nam/)
   - Texas Urban Species Checklist (Adams and Kiernan 2015; http://txmn.org/about/curriculum/)
3. Peer-reviewed literature sources listing urban fauna (Chace and Walsh 2006; Adams and Lindsey 2010)
4. Lists of urban amphibians, reptiles, birds, and mammals provided by citizen science groups
5. Intake records from wildlife rehabilitation

centers based in major US metropolitan areas
6. Field guides (Dixon 2000; Schmidly 2004; Tipton et al. 2012)

Road-Kill Data

One method of determining which wildlife species are present in urban communities was to examine the literature containing censuses of road-killed animals (Glista et al. 2008). Road- kill data are not an entirely accurate portrait of the wildlife community because the data will vary based on a species' ability to cross the road (e.g., roadrunners versus tortoises); the road's location, number of lanes, and speed limit; and the scale of analysis. Because of the slow movements of amphibians and reptiles, as well as the relative distance smaller animals must travel to cross the pavement, these groups are more likely to be road-kill victims (Adams and Lindsey 2010).

The table presents data from a census of road-killed animals over 7.4 miles of suburban roads in Indiana from March 2005 to July 2006 conducted by Glista et al. (2008). The researchers combined their tally of road-killed herptofauna with two other studies, resulting in a total of 42,502 dead amphibians and reptiles over 488 survey days. Note that over 7,000 road-killed amphibians could not be identified. One way to interpret these data is that roads may be having as much an effect on the loss of herptofauna populations as habitat destruction (to which, of course, roads contribute), climate change, infectious diseases, and UV radiation (Barbour et al. 1999, cited in Adams and Lindsey 2010).

To offset the road-kill carnage, wildlife crossings are being built in the United States and Europe to provide safe passage over and under major highway systems. These crossings may consist of bridges covered with native vegetation to make the passage more inviting to wildlife than bare concrete. Another approach to wildlife crossings is a box culvert or a riparian corridor under the highway. Fencing can be used, as appropriate, to funnel wildlife into these safe passages rather than cross in heavy traffic. Depending on their design, however, these structures may also efficiently funnel prey species toward waiting predators. More information on wildlife crossings can be obtained by accessing the Wildlife Crossings Toolkit (http://www.fs.fed.us/wildlifecrossings/library/) developed by the USDA Forest Service (Adams and Lindsey 2010).

Urban Fish

Fish communities are a kind of "canary in the coal mine" for the environmental health of our waterways. Polluted urban streams are characterized by fish communities that lack intolerant species, significant numbers of nonnative or introduced species, and low abundance and diversity of the native species. These conditions indicate poor fish habitat and significant ecological disturbances (Paul and Meyer 2001).

The biological and ecological effects of urbanization on fish communities (i.e., species present and relative abundance) are given special attention here for the following reasons:

1. Fish are useful long-term indicators of aquatic habitat conditions because they are relatively long-lived (e.g., several years) and mobile.
2. Fish communities generally include representative species from a variety of trophic levels (e.g., herbivores, omnivores, insectivores, detritivores, planktivores, and piscivores).
3. Fish are at the top of the aquatic food web and are, in some cases, consumed by humans, making them important for assessing contamination.
4. Fish are relatively easy to collect and identify to the species level. More common species can be sorted and identi-

Vertebrate species recorded along four Tippecanoe County, Indiana, survey routes, March 8, 2005–July 31, 2006

A. Mammalia

Scientific name	Common name	Total
Blarina brevicauda	northern short-tailed shrew	14
Canis familiaris	domestic dog	1
Canis latrans	coyote	1
Didelphis virginiana	opossum	79
Felis catus	domestic cat	5
*Lasiurus borealis**	eastern red bat	1
Marmota monax	woodchuck	1
Mephitis mephitis	striped skunk	16
Microtus ochrogaster	prairie vole	1
Microtus pennsylvanicus	meadow vole	15
Mus musculus	house mouse	2
Mustela vison	mink	6
Odocoileus virginianus	white-tailed deer	4
Ondatra zibethicus	muskrat	10
Peromyscus spp.	deer/white-footed mouse	39
Procyon lotor	raccoon	43
Scalopus aquaticus	eastern mole	4
Sciurus carolinensis	eastern gray squirrel	23
Sciurus niger	eastern fox squirrel	27
Sorex cinereus	masked shrew	1
Spermophilus tridecemlineatus	13-lined ground squirrel	6
Sylvilagus floridanus	eastern cottontail	37
Tamiasciurus hudsonicus	red squirrel	6
Tamias striatus	eastern chipmunk	7
Vulpes vulpes	red fox	1
?	unknown bat	2
?	unknown mammal	8
Total		**360**

B. Aves

Scientific name	Common name	Total
Agelaius phoeniceus	red-winged blackbird	8
Branta canadensis	Canada goose	2
Butorides virescens	green heron	1
Cardeulis tristis	American goldfinch	1
Cardinalis cardinalis	northern cardinal	9
Chaetura pelagica	chimney swift	36
Colaptes auratus	northern flicker	1
Dumetella carolinensis	gray catbird	1
Eremophila alpestris	homed lark	1
Hirundo rustica	barn swallow	5
Melanerpes erythrocephalus	red-headed woodpecker	2
Melospiza melodia	song sparrow	9
Molothrus ater	brown-headed cowbird	2
Otus asio	eastern screech-owl	6
Passer domesticus	house sparrow	15
Passerina cyanea	indigo bunting	3
Phasianus colchicus	ring-necked pheasant	2
Porzana carolina	sora	1
Quiscalus quiscula	common grackle	6
Spizella passerina	chipping sparrow	1
Sturnella magna	eastern meadowlark	2
Sturnus vulgaris	European starling	11
Tachycineta bicolor	tree swallow	1
Troglodytes aedon	house wren	1
Turdus migratorius	American robin	18
Zenaida macroura	mourning dove	4
?	unknown bird	56
Total		**205**

C. Amphibia

Scientific name	Common name	Total
Ambystoma tigrinum	eastern tiger salamander	142
Bufo americanus	American toad	111
Hyla spp.	treefrog	1
Pseudacris crucifer	spring peeper	8
Rana catesbeiana	bullfrog	1,671
Rana clamitans	green frog	172
Rana palustris	pickerel frog	18
*Rana pipiens**	northern leopard frog	74
Rana spp.	unknown ranid	7,602
?	unknown frog	10
Total		**9,809**

D. Reptilia

Scientific name	Common name	Total
Chelydra serpentina	snapping turtle	23
Chrysemys picta	Midland painted turtle	28
Elaphe obsoleta	black ratsnake	5
Elaphe vulpina	fox snake	9
Graptemys geographica	northern map turtle	1
Nerodia sipedon	northern watersnake	1
Storeria dekayi wrightorum	Midland brown snake	191
Terrapene carolina	eastern box turtle	
Thamnophis sirtalis	common garter snake	35
Trachemys scripta	red-eared slider	13
?	unknown snake	4
?	unknown turtle	2
Total		**141**

Source: Glista et al. (2008).

Note: Overall total = 10,515 road kills.

* Indicates species of special conservation concern in Indiana.

fied in the field by experienced fisheries professionals and subsequently released unharmed.

5. The environmental requirements of the most common species are well known. Life history information is extensive for many game and forage species, and information on fish distributions is readily available.
6. Water quality standards are typically characterized in terms of fisheries (e.g., cold water, cool water, warm water, sport, forage). Monitoring fish provides direct evaluation of "fishability" and "fish propagation," which emphasizes the importance of fish to anglers and commercial fishermen.
7. Fish account for nearly half of the endangered vertebrate species and subspecies in the United States (Barbour et al. 1999).
8. Fish provide many ecosystem services (Holmlund and Hammer 1999).

Fish species in urban stream communities tolerant of wide ranges in chemical and physical changes

Common name	Scientific name	Trophic designation*
banded killifish	*Fundulus diaphanous*	I
black bullhead	*Amerus melas*	O
blacknose dace	*Rhinichthys atratulus*	G
bluegill	*Lepomis macrochirus*	I
bluntnose minnow	*Pimephales notatus*	O
brown bullhead	*Ameiurus nebulosus*	I
catfish	*Ictalurus spp.*	G
central mudminnow	*Umbra limi*	I
comely shiner	*Notropis amoenus*	I
common carp	*Cyprinus carpio*	O
creek chub	*Semotilus atromaculatus*	G
eastern mudminnow	*Umbra pygmaea*	G
fathead minnow	*Pimephales promelas*	O
golden shiner	*Notemigonus crysoleucas*	O
goldfish	*Cariassius auratus*	O
green sunfish	*Lepomis cyanellus*	I
largescale sucker	*Catostomus macrocheilus*	O
northern squawfish	*Ptychocheilus oregonensis*	P
red shiner	*Cyrpinella lutrensis*	O
redear sunfish	*Lepomis microlophus*	O
reticulate sculpin	*Cottus perplexus*	I
rudd	*Scardinius erythrophthalmus*	O
silver carp	*Hypophthalmichthys molitrix*	O
spotfin chub	*Cyprinella monacha*	I
western mosquito fish	*Gambusia affinis*	O
white sucker	*Catostomus commersoni*	O
yellow bullhead	*Ameiurus natalis*	I

Source: Barbour et al. (1999).

*G = generalist—plant and animal material; I = insectivore—opportunistic predator on aquatic insects; O = omnivore—bottom feeder; P = piscivore—opportunistic predator on other fish.

Increasing urbanization is related to declines in fish diversity and abundance and a rise in the relative abundance of tolerant taxa increases with increasing urbanization. The number of invasive fish species rises in the more urbanized reaches of streams. Extensive fish kills are more common in urban streams after storms thanks to the extensive influx of pollutants from impervious surface cover runoff. The extirpation of fish species is not uncommon in urban river systems. Wastewater treatment effluent selects for fish species that have wide tolerances for changes in dissolved-oxygen concentration, temperature, and siltation.

The *Field Guide to Freshwater Fishes* by Page and Brooks (1991) lists 790 freshwater species native to the United States. Each of the 27 species listed in the table are also on the US Geological Survey's freshwater invasive species list (http://nas.er.usgs.gov/queries/SpeciesList.aspx?Group=Fishes), and the majority of species listed have a trophic classification denoting a broad range of feeding habits characteristic of tolerant and potentially invasive species. The report, *Nonindigenous Aquatic Species*, suggests 435 native species (55%) have become invasive through introductions outside their native range. How did this happen, and what are some of the ecological impacts?

Rahel (2002) discusses the occurrence and ecological impacts of invasive fish species in terms of **biotic homogenization**—the increased similarity of biotas over time caused by the replacement of native species with nonindigenous species, usually as a result of introductions by humans. In human-created habitats, endemic species typically are replaced by cosmopolitan species, resulting in a high level of similarity between ecosystems in disparate geographic locations. The interacting mechanisms that result in homogenization are (1) introductions of nonnative species, the key factor homogenizing fish faunas; (2) extirpations of native species; and (3) habitat alterations (e.g., abiotics, stream flow patterns, sedimentation) that facilitate the first two processes. Nonnative species are usually pollutant tolerant and have a wide range of tolerance to a host of abiotic conditions at the extreme end of the spectra (e.g., low dissolved-oxygen concentrations, high temperatures). Native endemic species are usually highly specialized, having adapted to a relatively narrow set of abiotic conditions. The table illustrates both the causes of nonnative species introductions and suggested strategies to reduce the rate of biotic homogenization.

A primary source of invasive fish species is the aquarium industry, which generates seven billion dollars annually (Holmlund and Hammer 1999). Each year, more than 2,000 nonnative fish species, representing nearly 150 million exotic freshwater and marine fishes, are imported into the United States for use in the aquarium trade. Dumping aquaria fish into the nearest body of water when they are no longer wanted creates a problem for the native fish species and for ecosystems in general (Phipps 2001).

Causes of nonnative species introductions and suggested responses

Causes of species introduction	Strategies for reducing homogenization
Deliberate transfers (e.g., stocking by sport fishing industry and state agencies)	Stop deliberate transfers and by-product introductions
By-product introductions (e.g., canal building, ballast water discharge, aquaculture operations)	Minimize habitat alterations (e.g., restore natural flow regimes)
Human introductions in urban landscape designs (e.g., garden ponds)	Increase public education concerning the magnitude of the problem and ecological ramifications
	Use sterile hybrids
	Remove naturalized populations of nonnative species prior to reestablishing native species

Urban Amphibians

Amphibians are a unique taxonomic group. They were the first species in the evolutionary history of vertebrates to leave the aquatic habitat and occupy land, at least for some portion of their life cycle. Exposure to moisture (directly, vegetational, or ambient) is an absolute requirement for survival. This is due to the unique respiratory anatomy and physiology of amphibians—they use both their lungs and skin for respiration.

It is instructive to compare the number of amphibian species found in each state in the United States because it provides clues about how the abiotic and biotic characteristics of states predict or preclude the existence of amphibians. For example, it should come as no surprise that states like Arizona (with extreme heat and lack of moisture) or Alaska (frigid temperatures) have relatively fewer amphibians than Louisiana.

Hammer and McDonnell (2008) have provided a helpful comprehensive review of the current literature on the ecology and conservation of amphibians in urban and suburban landscapes. Urbanization currently threatens over one-third of the world's known amphibian species due to habitat loss and/or fragmentation and degradation of habitat quality. This has led to a decrease in species richness and abundance of individual species as one moves toward the city center. More research to determine the proximate causes of amphibian response to human modification of the landscape is needed (Hammer and McDonnell 2008). We suggest this research begin by conducting a rigorous inventory of amphibian species

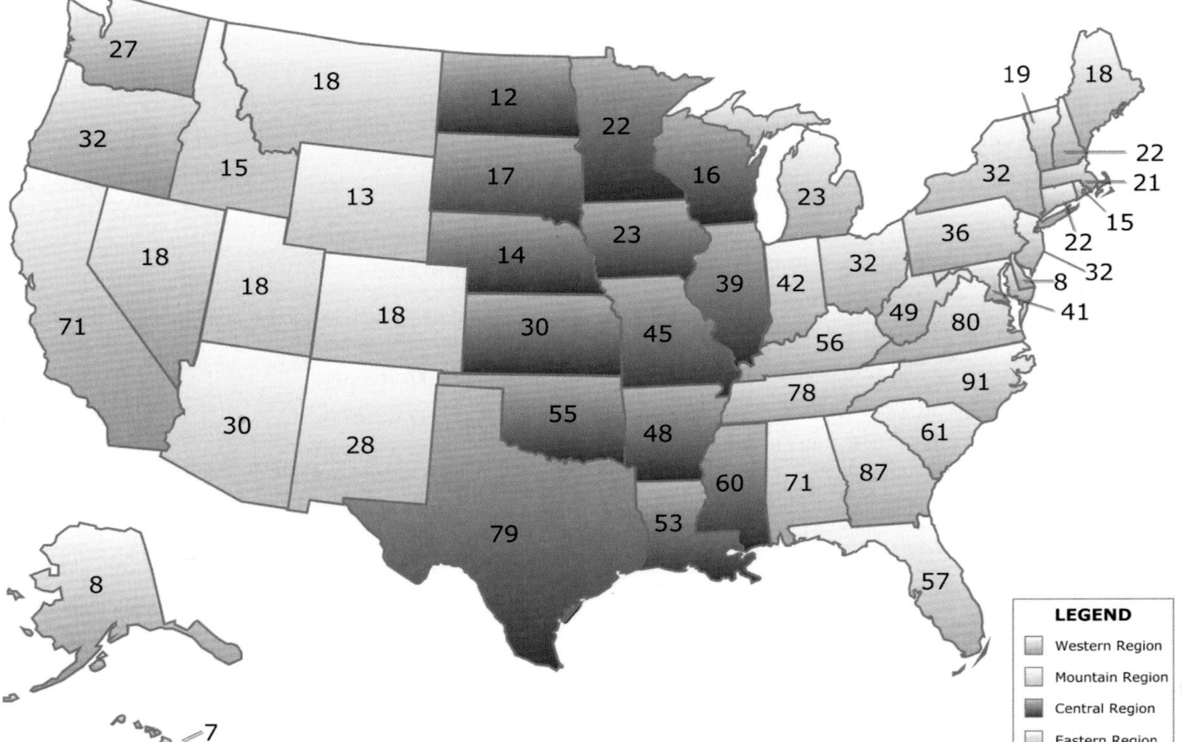

Comparative analysis of number of amphibian species found in each state. Courtesy of Cassandra La Fleur

that exist from the urban fringe to the urban core.

In the absence of a readily available comprehensive list of urban amphibian species in Texas, we attempted to construct such a list. One overarching problem when using species lists in general, and particularly for amphibians, is the inconsistency of taxonomic nomenclature for common or scientific names between lists for the same state (Smith and Chiszar 2006). For example, the American toad is listed as both *Anaxyrus* and *Bufo americanus*. Another hurdle when attempting to develop a list of urban species using national and state lists is that they may not include sampling from urban landscapes. So we relied, largely, on reports by citizen science groups and intake data from the Texas Wildlife Rehabilitation Coalition (TWCR) in Houston. These data were augmented by personal observations of the authors or lists from peer-reviewed articles and recorded in the Amphibians table of the "Texas Urban Species Checklist," which is housed on the Texas Master Naturalist website, http://txmn.org/about/curriculum/." Finally, we compared our list to the official state list of Texas amphibians.

We hypothesized that if the species commonly occurs in 50% or more of the continental United States, it will probably also be present in urban areas, based on the observations that "amphibian species that are habitat generalists or have relatively low dispersal requirements appear to be better able to survive in urban and suburban landscapes" (Hammer and McDonnell 2008, 2432); and urban ecosystems are a common denominator for all states, regardless of geographic or ecological region (e.g., western, mountain, central, or eastern).

Of the 79 species of amphibians known to exist in Texas, 67% (n = 53) have been observed in one or more of four metropolitan areas—Dallas–Fort Worth, El Paso, Houston, and Austin. Of the 53 urban amphibian spe-

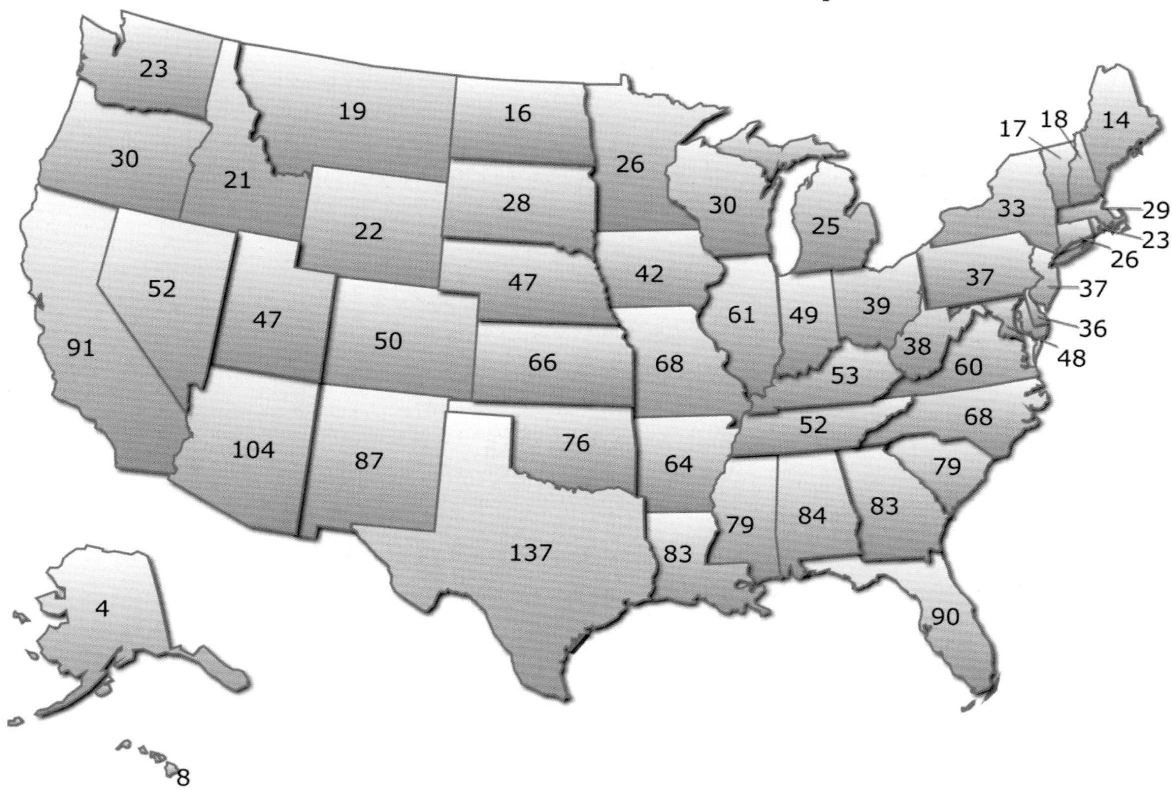

Comparative analysis of number of reptilian species found in each state. Courtesy of Cassandra La Fleur

cies found in Texas, 28% (n = 15) were also located in 24 or more states in the United States. Our findings for Texas amphibians only partially supported the proposed hypothesis; there were higher correlations when we completed our analysis for reptiles, birds, and mammals.

Urban Reptiles

Texas could legitimately claim to be "the reptile state" thanks to the large number (137) of species present and compared to all of the other states. Reptiles are **ectothermic**—their body temperature is influenced by the ambient temperature. As a result, they must find cool or warm spots within their habitat to regulate body temperature using outside sources and often prefer warmer climates.

Of the reptilian species found in Texas (n = 28) 20% were also located in urban communities, and 39% (n = 10) were also found in 24 or more states. There were not many sources of information from citizen science or naturalist organizations located in major metropolitan areas in Texas, and the official lists may well underrepresent their presence in urban communities.

Urban Birds

Birds are some of the most noticeable terrestrial vertebrates in the urban landscape, especially when they are overabundant or missing. People seem to have a special attraction to avian species. The imagery connected to birds includes both delicacy and fragility (e.g., the bee hummingbird, *Mellisuga helenae*) and raw power (e.g., the harpy eagle, *Harpia harpyja*). Birds are often less secretive than wild mammals, living out their lives seemingly with little regard for the people among them, allowing us to easily observe and enjoy their songs, colorful plumage, feeding, brood rearing, and interactions with other one another. However, our actions often contradict our professed

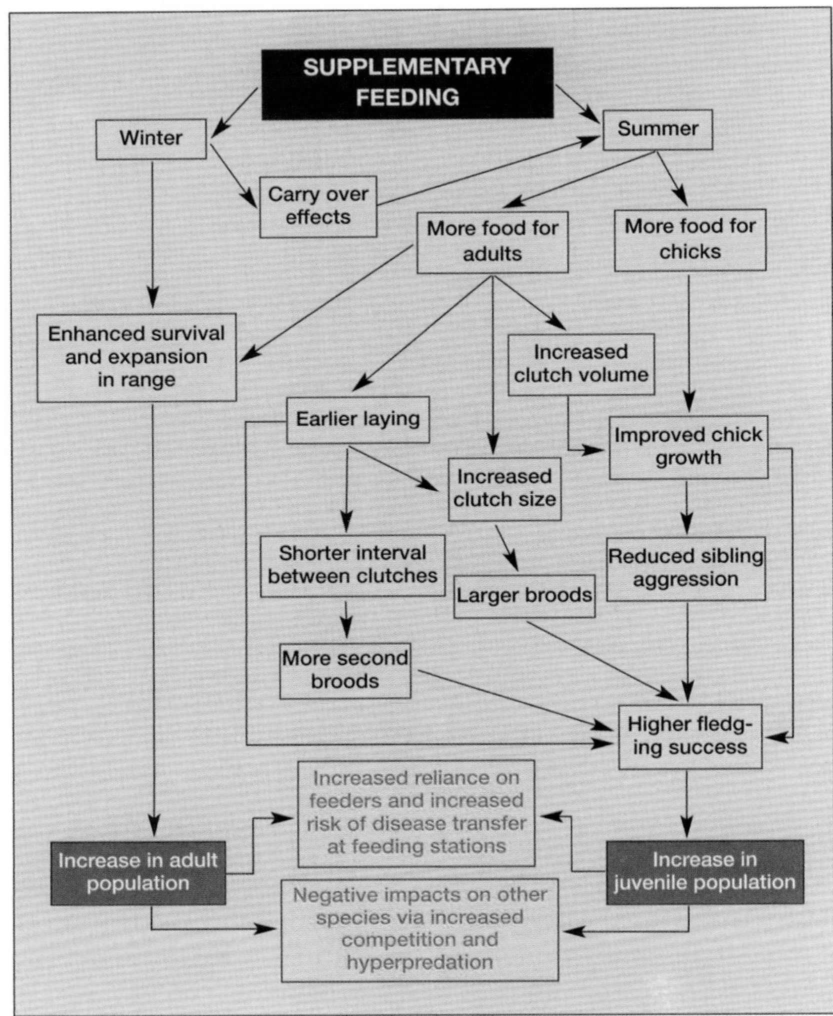

Impacts of supplementary feeding on the population dynamics of birds. The potential impacts of supplementary feeding during winter and the summer breeding season are shown, with arrows indicating the direction of the influence. The overall impact on the population—an increase in both adult and juvenile numbers—is shown by the gray boxes. Negative impacts are shown in red. From Robb et al. (2008)

love of birds, particularly in urban environments where our activities accidentally or intentionally have a negative impact (Adams and Lindsey 2010).

Even though the activities of some bird species can create conflict with their human neighbors, the overall attitudes of humans toward birds tends to be positive, as evidenced by the time and money they spend to get close to birds. A popular activity among urban residents that promotes the abundance of wild birds in urban ecosystems is the provision of supplemental food sources and other accoutrements (e.g., water for drinking and bathing, nest boxes). Over 52.8 million individuals (74%) of all wildlife watchers in 2011 fed wildlife around their home, and 41.3 million reported observing birds around their homes as backyard birders and/or at their bird feeders (United States Census Bureau 2011). Since 2006, bird food sales have increased from approximately \$3.6 billion to nearly \$4.1 billion, an increase of 21% in less than a decade. At the same time, nest box, feeder, and birdbath expenditures combined have gone up from $790 million to almost $970 million (23%).

Urban residents willingly pay to see birds up close and personal, but the tab at Wild Birds Unlimited is not the only cost. Supplementary feeding can be a driver for ecological change in avian populations (Robb et al. 2008). For example, easy access to near limitless food offers a survival advantage to certain species (e.g., granivores, nectivores), while also encouraging larger congregations of birds that facilitate disease transmission and increased predation. Robb et al. provided a diagrammatic and succinct overview of supplemental feeding on the population dynamics of birds.

An examination of the taxonomic classifications of birds captures the complexity of form and function within this group of vertebrates. One mid-twentieth-century estimate by Mayr (1946) included 2,600 different genera and 8,616 different species, discounting for subspecies and hybridization between species. A twenty-first-century estimate puts the number at over 10,000 species worldwide, with the United States accounting for approximately 925.

Physiological variations in avian taxonomic groups demonstrate adaptations to virtually every habitat, including terrestrial and aquatic (fresh water and salt water), rain forest and desert, the tropics as well as arctic (Adams and Lindsey 2010). Texas is second only to California in the number of bird species in the United States. The majority (94%, $n = 204$) of Texas urban bird species were also found in 24 or more states. These data suggest it is only logical to assume that any species known to occupy half or more of the states can likely be classified as urban. However, this statement needs further examination in terms of rigorous biological inventories in the major metropolitan communities in Texas.

Urban environments should no longer be viewed as lost habitat; rather, the built envi-

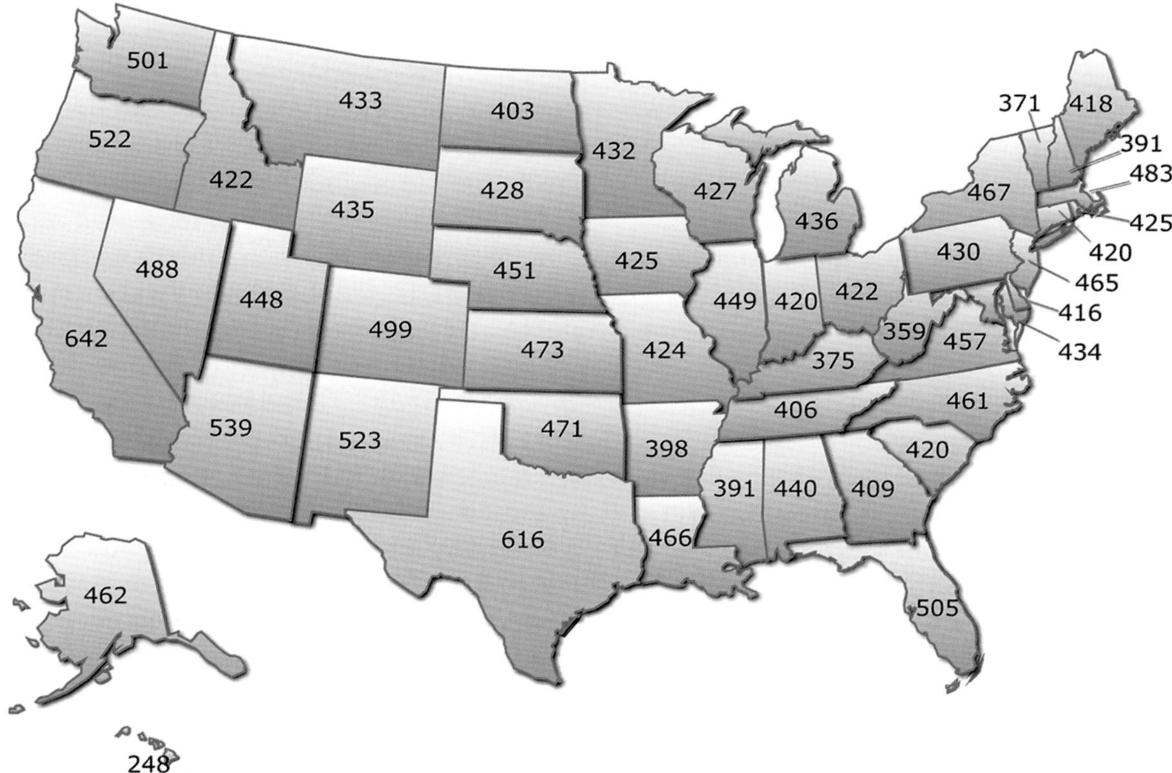

Comparative analysis of number of bird species found in each state. Courtesy of Cassandra La Fleur

ronment is a transformed habitat that, with proper management, has the potential to support diverse bird communities (Schochat et al. 2010). Blair (1996) has divided avian communities into three major classes based on their response to urbanization: urban avoiders, suburban adaptable, and urban exploiters. Urban settings normally have higher bird abundances than wildland settings for the following reasons (Schochat et al. 2010):

- abundant food resources (both natural and anthropogenic sources)
- prevalence of both native and invasive species
- habituation to the presence of humans, as well as anthropogenic noise and light
- extended breeding seasons because of the heat island effect
- exploitation of urban structures for nesting and safety
- low predation pressure

"Over increasingly large areas of the United States, spring now comes unheralded by the return of the birds, and the early mornings are strangely silent where once they were filled with the beauty of bird song."
—Rachel Carson, ca. 1964

Given all of the positive contributions of birds to human health and economics, it seems logical that conserving bird diversity would be a high priority in urban wildlife management. Unfortunately, this has not been and is not currently the case. There are astounding bird losses due to anthropogenic causes, primarily collisions with human-made structures. One study estimated 500 million to over 1 billion birds are killed annually in the United States alone (Erickson et al. 2005). There are at least 15 urban and exurban features that have lethal effects on migratory birds. In numerical order, these features are

1. Windows
2. Cats
3. Automobiles
4. Electric transmission line collisions
5. Agriculture
6. Urban development
7. Communication towers
8. Stock tank drowning
9. Oil and gas exploration
10. Logging and strip mining
11. Commercial fishing
12. Electrocution
13. Hunting
14. Wind towers
15. High-rise buildings

Bird kills in categories 5, 6, 9, and 10 are probably associated with chemical pollution (the DDT story revisited) and habitat loss. Many bird deaths have been associated with categories 8 and 9, but there do not appear to be any field studies that provide actual numbers.

The numbers provided in the table are estimates or extrapolations from direct counts as explained in the footnotes. Thus, there will be differences in the reported number of bird fatalities in the literature. Nevertheless, the loss of tens of millions of birds each year due to human alterations or activities in natural and urban areas begs the question of how some species of birds survive as reproducing populations at all. Is it possible that natural selection mechanisms that facilitated the evolutionary explosion of one of the most diverse classes of terrestrial vertebrates on earth will again function to provide those adaptations necessary to survive the structural impediments of urbanization?

Urban Mammals

Mammals are vertebrates with hair or fur—a characteristic that proved to be detrimental to the survival of many in the eighteenth, nineteenth, and early twentieth centuries, when "fur" clothing was all the rage. Beaver, bear, mink, coyote, deer, and raccoon populations were all decimated during the era of unregulated commercial harvest. Hard as it may be to believe now, there was a time in the early 1900s you would have been hard

Summary of predicted annual avian mortality

Mortality source	Annual mortality estimate	Percentage composition
Buildings[a]	550 million	58.2
Power lines[b]	130 million	13.7
Cats[c]	100 million	10.6
Automobiles[d]	80 million	8.5
Pesticides[e]	67 million	7.1
Communications towers[f]	4.5 million	0.5
Wind turbines[g]	285,000	<0.01
Airplanes	25,000	<0.01
Oil spills, oil seeps, fishing by-catch	not calculated	not calculated

Source: Erickson et al. (2005).

[a] Midrange of fatality estimates reported from Klem (1990); 1–10 bird fatalities per house, extrapolated to 100 million residences.

[b] Based primarily on a study in the Netherlands (Koops 1987), extrapolated to 500,000 miles of bulk transmission line in United States.

[c] One study in Wisconsin estimated 40 million (Coleman and Temple 1996); there are 60 million cats claimed as pets in the United States.

[d] Based primarily on one study in England (Hodson and Snow 1965; Banks 1979) that estimated 15.1 fatalities/mile of road each year; no searcher efficiency or bias adjustments in that study; updated based on increase in vehicle registrations.

[e] Conservative estimate using low range of empirical fatality rate (0.1 to 3.6 birds/acre); studies typically adjusted from search efficiency and scavenging.

[f] Estimates from models derived by Manville and Evans (M. Manville, pers. comm.)

[g] Midrange per turbine and per MW estimates derived from empirical data collected at several wind projects.

pressed to find a single white-tailed deer in Texas, but what a difference 100 years can make. In the twenty-first century, most of these mammals have not only recovered; their populations are thriving, reaching and even surpassing pre-eighteenth-century levels (Sterba 2012). Texas now lists 184 native wild mammal species, of which 25% ($n = 47$) have been observed or collected in urban areas, and 68% ($n = 125$) of these also occurred in 24 or more states. What happened?

Recovery by wild mammals is the direct result of urbanization and the subsequent changes in human perceptions, interest, and utilization of wild animals. US society moved from a primarily utilitarian to an appreciative valuation of wildlife. In addition, urbanization created abundant alternative food, water, and shelter resources for any mammal that could adapt.

Newly abundant and visible urban wildlife, particularly large, medium, and small mammals—has spawned an entirely new industry, referred to as Nuisance Wildlife Control, a contemporary form of harvesting wildlife for profit. Urban residents may be drawn to green spaces and a greater connection to nature, but they are, by and large, totally unprepared intellectually, emotionally, and financially to deal with the consequences of getting what they want. "Nuisance" is in the eye of the beholder, of course, so any attempt to create a comprehensive list of problem urban mammals would likely include nearly every species that calls the urban landscape home. When humans and wildlife live in closer and closer proximity, the potential for some kind of negative interaction rises. The best go-to strategy during these encounters is to re-

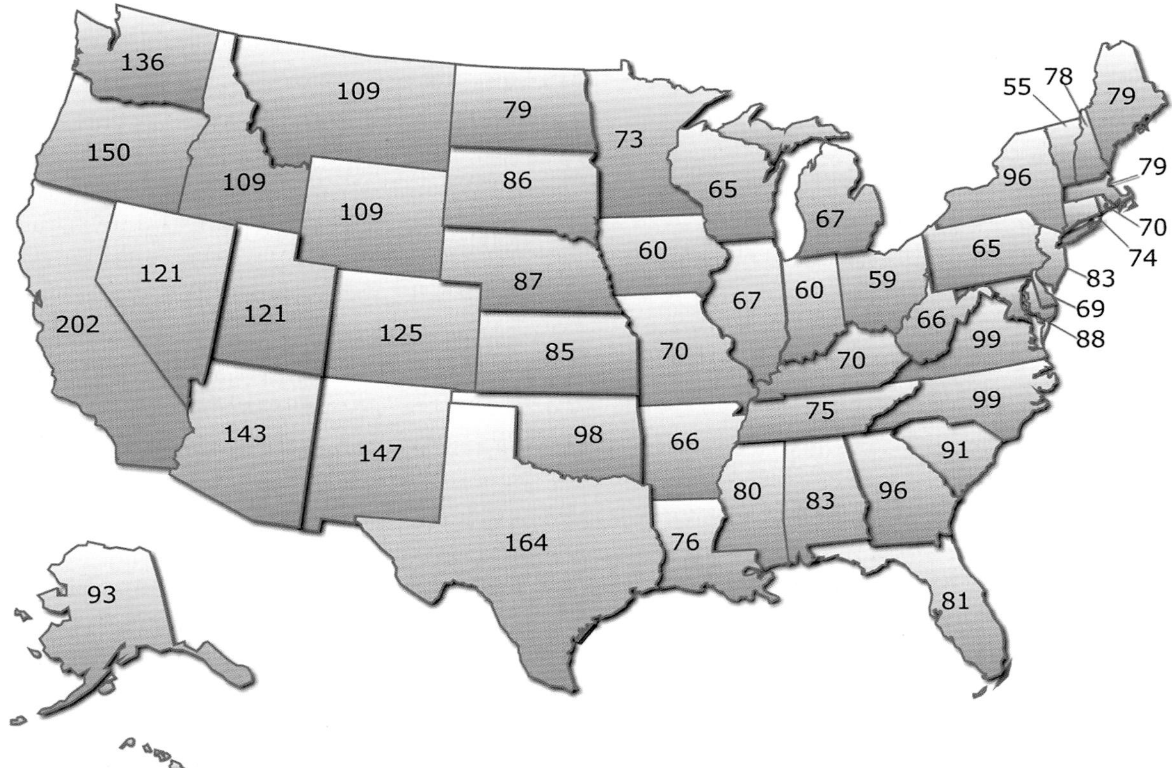

Comparative analysis of number of mammalian species found in each state. Courtesy of Cassandra La Fleur

treat, particularly if there is some perceived danger (e.g., coyote, bobcat, or cougar). To be covered in detail, the issue of human-wildlife conflict management deserves an entire lesson for Master Naturalists.

Urban Gray Spaces

Gray spaces are ubiquitous in the urban landscape and include dwellings, factories, office buildings, warehouses, roads, pipelines, power lines, railroads, channelized stream beds, reservoirs, sewage disposal facilities, landfills, and airports (Adams and Lindsey 2010). Wildlife encounters with urban gray spaces may be positive, negative, or neutral. Positive encounters include examples such as birds and bats using bridges and overpasses as nesting sites and safe havens from predation and adverse weather conditions. Negative impacts include habitat fragmentation by roads, wildlife-vehicle (automobiles and aircraft) collisions, and bird strikes on glass buildings and wind turbines.

Urbanization replaces natural habitats with four types of altered habitat that become progressively more common toward the urban core (McKinney 2002):

1. **Built habitat:** Buildings and sealed surfaces, such as roads and parking lots, that cover over 80% of central urban area
2. **Managed vegetation:** Residential, commercial, and other regularly maintained green spaces
3. **Ruderal vegetation:** Empty lots, abandoned farmland, and other green space that are cleared but not managed
4. **Natural remnant vegetation:** Remaining islands of original vegetation (usually subject to substantial nonnative plant invasion

Roads and Highways

Urban sprawl and resultant habitat fragmentation begin and are perpetuated by roads. In fact, one of the most widespread forms of modifications of the natural landscape during the past century has been 3.9 million miles of road construction. Trombulak and Frissell (2000) estimated an average loss of 11.8 million acres of land and water bodies that formerly supported plants, animals, and other organisms. In 2009 there were 97,117 miles of urban roads in Texas (US Department of Transportation 2009).

Roads can be built into forests, grasslands, deserts, or any other habitat accessible by road-building technology. When this happens, a large piece of habitat is fragmented into smaller (often square or rectangular) pieces to accommodate residential areas, business districts, parkland, and recreational, educational, and industrial zones. Roads make cities a mixture of built habitats and green spaces. Roads can facilitate access or become barriers for wildlife attempting to negotiate the fragmented pieces of habitat that was once in one piece. It is important to note that corridors, fragments, and barriers are all interrelated. A strip of woodland stretching across grassland to connect two forest fragments acts as a travel corridor for the woodland species, but it also acts as a barrier that fragments the grassland habitat. As habitat is fragmented, "edge" is created. Edge is the zone where two biomes (or habitat types) meet, for example, where forest meets grassland.

Urban sprawl could not have occurred without the Highway Trust Fund (HTF), created by the Highway Revenue Act of 1956 to ensure a dependable source of financing for the National System of Interstate and Defense Highways and the Federal-Aid Highway Program. The HTF provided each state with the resources to build a massive interstate highway system throughout the United States.

With the continuing growth in the size of highways (e.g., number of lanes) and higher traffic volume, there is a growing threat that affects a wide range of wildlife species and presents an almost impassable barrier for many species of reptiles, amphibians, and small mammals (Jackson 2000). At first, Forman (2000) estimated a "road-effect zone" (area affected ecologically by roads and associated vehicular traffic) that encompassed 19% of the total area of the continental United States. In a later publication, Forman et al. (2002) revised that estimate downward, reporting the area covered by roads, roadsides, and medians was equivalent to 1% of the US land base, a surface area equivalent to the state of South Carolina.

Buildings

Wildlife is most noticed by urban residents when the animal appears inside or in close proximity to the areas where we live, work, or recreate. The famous cliché "build it and they will come" is as appropriate to the built environment and wild animals as it is to baseball diamonds and ballplayers. Some wild species are selective in terms of what part of the building they prefer (e.g., roof, attic, walls, basement, inside, or outside), while others are generalists that occupy any available spaces to which they have access (Adams and Lindsey 2010). To be covered in detail, the issue of urban gray spaces deserves an entire lesson for Master Naturalists.

Conclusion

Our primary goals for this first examination of urban ecosystems are to establish a learning environment that awakens students' curiosity about the urban world in which they live; to stimulate students' desire to expand their knowledge about the urban world and how it works; to offer students an opportunity to measure their growth in knowledge (content) and understanding (application of content); and to challenge students to translate their new knowledge and understanding into personal actions and self-realizations. The following critical concepts were covered in this unit:

1. The fundamental ecological principles are DICE (diversity, interrelationships, cycles, and energy).
2. Urbanization impacts both the abiotic and biotic structure and function of ecosystems.
3. Urban soils generally have greater compaction, have a higher pH, and are less aerated than undisturbed soils.
4. Urban water systems have great variation in dissolved oxygen, turbidity, and contaminants over shorter periods of time than their counterparts in less urbanized areas because of the prevalence of impermeable surfaces in the built environment.
5. Urban food webs feature more predictable, more consistent, and more plentiful nutrient sources than food webs in undeveloped areas because of anthropogenic contributions (i.e., intentional and accidental supplemental feeding).
6. Urban plant communities include a relatively high number of nonnative species, which require a great deal of maintenance (e.g., water, fertilizers, pesticides) to survive, and invasive species, both of which crowd out native species.
7. Urban wildlife communities feature a large number of species with high levels of behavioral adaptability.
8. Urban green spaces include planted communities, derelict lands, and natural remnants.
9. Urban gray spaces include buildings, transportation infrastructure (e.g., highways, railroads, and airports), and altered waterways.

References

Adams, C. E. 2015. *Urban Wildlife Management*. 3rd ed. Boca Raton, FL: CRC Taylor and Francis Press.

Adams, C. E., and Kiernan. 2015. Texas Urban Species Checklist. Texas Master Naturalist. http://txmn.org/about/curriculum/.

Adams, C. E., and K. J. Lindsey. 2010. Urban Wildlife Management. 2nd ed. Boca Raton, FL: CRC Taylor and Francis Press.

———. 2011. Anthropogenic Ecosystems: The Influence of People on Urban Wildlife Populations. In *Urban Ecology: Patterns, Processes, and Applications*, ed. J. Niemela, 116–28. Oxford: Oxford University Press.

Alberti, M. 2009. *Advances in Urban Ecology*. New York: Springer.

———. 2010. Maintaining Ecological Integrity and Sustaining Ecosystem Function in Urban Areas. *Current Opinion in Environmental Sustainability* 2:176–84.

APWA. 1981. *Urban Storm Water Management*. Special Report No. 49. Chicago: American Public Works Association.

Banks, R. C. 1979. *Human Related Mortality of Birds in the United States*. Special Scientific Report, Wildlife No. 215. Washington, DC: Fish and Wildlife Service, US Department of the Interior.

Barbour, M. T., J. Gerritsen, B. D. Snyder, and J. B. Stribling. 1999. *Rapid Bioassessment Protocols for Use in Streams and Wadeable Rivers: Periphyton, Benthic Macroinvertebrates and Fish*. 2nd ed. EPA 841-B-99–

002. Washington, DC: US Environmental Protection Agency, Office of Water.

Begon, M., J. L. Harper, and C. R. Townsend. 1996. *Ecology: Individuals, Populations, and Communities*. Oxford, UK: Blackwell Press.

Blair, R. B. 1996. Land Use and Avian Species Diversity along an Urban Gradient. *Ecological Applications* 6:164–70.

Borman, S., and R. Korth. 1998. *Through the Looking Glass: A Field Guide to Aquatic Plants*. Stevens Point: University of Wisconsin–Stevens Point Foundation.

Brockman, C. F. 1986. *Trees of North America: A Field Guide to the Major Native and Introduced Species North of Mexico*. Racine, WI: Golden Press.

Buzby, J. C., and J. Hyman. 2012. Total and Per Capita Value of Food Loss in the United States. *Food Policy* 37:561–70.

Cabrera, R. I., K. L. Wagner, B. Wherley, and L. Lee. 2013. *Urban Landscape Water Uses in Texas: A Special Report by the Texas Water Resources Institute*. TWRI EM-116. College Station: Texas A&M University.

Chace, J. F., and J. J. Walsh. 2006. Urban Effects on Native Avifauna: A Review. *Landscape and Urban Planning* 74 (1): 46–79.

Coleman, J. S., and S. A. Temple. 1996. On the Prowl. Wisconsin Natural Resources (December). http://dnr.wi.gov/wnrmag/html/stories/1996/dec96/cats.htm.

Craul, P. J. 1985. A Description of Urban Soils and Their Desired Characteristics. *Journal of Arboriculture* 11:330–39.

Cunningham, W. P., and M. A. Cunningham. 2010. *Environmental Science: A Global Concern*. New York: McGraw-Hill.

Cushman, R. C., and S. R. Jones. 2004. *Peterson Field Guides: The North American Prairie*. New York: Houghton Mifflin.

Davis, J. M. 2003. Urban Systems. In *Texas Master Naturalist Statewide Curriculum*, 1st ed., ed. M. M. Haggerty. College Station: Texas Parks and Wildlife Department.

Dixon, J. R. 2000. *Amphibians and Reptiles of Texas*. College Station: Texas A&M University Press.

Drayton, B., and R. B. Primack. 1996. Plant Species Lost in an Isolated Conservation Area in Metropolitan Boston from 1894 to 1993. *Conservation Biology* 10:30–39.

EPA (Environmental Protection Agency). 2014. *Municipal Solid Waste Generation, Recycling, and Disposal in the United States: Facts and Figures for 2012*. EPA-530-F-14-001. http://www.epa.gov/wastes/nonhaz/municipal/pubs/2012_msw_fs.pdf.

Erickson, W. P., G. D. Johnson, and D. P. Young. 2005. *A Summary and Comparison of Bird Mortality from Anthropogenic Causes with an Emphasis on Collisions*. USDA Forest Service Gen. Tech. Rep. PSW-GTR-191. Washington, DC: USDA Forest Service.

Ferguson, B. K. 1998. *Introduction to Stormwater*. New York: John Wiley and Sons.

Forman, R. T. T. 2000. Estimate of the Area Affected Ecologically by the Road System in the United States. *Conservation Biology* 14:31–35.

Forman, R. T. T., D. Sperling, J. Bissonette, *A. P. Clevenger, C. D. Cutshall, V. H. Dale, L. Fahrig, R. France, C. R. Goldman, K. Heanue, J. A. Jones, F. J. Swanson, T. Turrentine, and T. C. Winter*. 2002. *Road Ecology: Science and Solutions*. Washington, DC: Island Press.

Glista, D. J., T. L. DeVault, and J. A. DeWoody. 2008. Vertebrate Road Mortality Predominantly Impacts Amphibians. *Herpetological Conservation and Biology* 3:77–87.

Grimm, N. B., D. Foster, P. Groffman, J. M. Grover, C. S. Hopkinson, K. J. Nadelhoffer, D. E. Pataki, and D. Peters. 2008. The Changing Landscape: Ecosystem Responses to Urbanization and Pollution across Climatic and Societal Gradients. *Frontiers in Ecology and the Environment* 6:264–72.

Hammer, A. J., and M. J. McDonnell. 2008. Amphibian Ecology and Conservation in an Urbanizing World. *Biological Conservation* 141:2432–49.

Hammer, D. A. 1997. *Creating Freshwater Wetlands*. 2nd ed. Boca Raton, FL: CRC Press.

Hodson, N. L., and D. W. Snow. 1965. The Road Deaths Enquiry, 1960–61. *Bird Study* 9:90–99.

Holling, C. S. 1996. Surprise for Science, Resilience for Ecosystems, and Incentives for People. *Ecological Applications* 6:733–35.

Holmlund, C. M., and M. Hammer. 1999. Ecosystem Services Generated by Fish Populations. *Ecological Economics* 29:253–68.

Jackson, S. D. 2000. Overview of Transportation Impacts on Wildlife Movements and Populations. In *Wildlife and Highways: Seeking Solutions to an Ecological and Socio-economic Dilemma*, ed. T. A. Messmer and B. West, 7–20. Bethesda, MD: The Wildlife Society.

Kenny, J. F., N. L. Barber, S. S. Hutson, K. S. Lindsey, J. K. Lovelace, and M. A. Maupin. 2009. *Estimated Use of Water in the United States in 2005*. US Geological Survey Circular 1344. http://pubs.usgs.gov/circ/1344/pdf/c1344.pdf.

Klem, D., Jr. 1990. Bird Injuries, Cause of Death, and Recuperation from Collisions with Windows. *Journal of Field Ornithology* 6:115–19.

Koops, F. B. J. 1987. *Collision Victims of High-Tension Lines in the Netherlands and Effects of Marking*. KEMA Report 01282-MOB 86–3048.

Louv, R. 2005. *Last Child in the Woods: Saving Our Children from Nature-Deficit Disorder*. Chapel Hill, NC: Algonquin Books.

Marzluff, J. M. 2014. *Welcome to Subirdia*. New Haven, CT: Yale University Press.

Marzluff, J. M., E. Schulenberger, W. Endlicher, W. Simon, M. Alberti, G. Bradley, C. Ryan, C. ZumBrunnen, and U. Simon, eds. 2008. *Urban Ecology: An International Perspective on the Interaction Between Humans and Nature*. New York: Springer-Verlag.

Mayr, E. 1946. The Number of Species of Birds. *Auk* 69:64–69.

McDonald, R., and P. Marcotullio. 2011. Global Effects of Urbanization on Ecosystem Services. In *Urban Ecology: Patterns, Processes, and Applications*, ed. J. Niemela, 193–205. Oxford: Oxford University Press.

McDonnell, M. J., and S. T. A. Pickett. 1990. Ecosystem Structure and Function along the Urban- Rural Gradients: An Unexploited Opportunity for Ecology. *Ecology* 71:1232–37.

McKinney, M. L. 2002. Urbanization, Biodiversity, and Conservation. *BioScience* 52:883–90.

———. 2006. Urbanization as a Major Cause of Biotic Homogenization. *Biological Conservation* 127:247–60.

Milesi, C., S. W. Running, C. D. Elvidge, J. B. Dietz, B. T. Tuttle, and R. R. Nemani. 2005. Mapping and Modeling the Biogeochemical Cycling of Turfgrasses in the United States. *Environmental Management* 36:426–38.

New York City Soil Survey Staff. 2005. *New York City Reconnaissance Soil Survey*. Staten Island, NY: USDA, Natural Resources Conservation Service.

Nickerson, C., R. Ebel, A. Borchers, and F. Carriazo. 2011. *Major Uses of Land in the United States, 2007*. USDA Economic Information Bulletin Number 89. http://www.ers.usda.gov/media/188404/eib89_2_.pdf.

O'Neill, R. V. 2001. Is It Time to Bury the Ecosystem Concept? (With Full Military Honors of Course!). *Ecology* 82:3275–84.

O'Neill, R. V., and J. R. Kahn. 2000. *Homo economus* as a Keystone Species. *BioScience* 50:333–37.

Ostfeld, R. S., and F. Keesing. 2000. Biodiversity and Disease Risk: The Case of Lyme Disease. *Conservation Biology* 14:722–28.

Ostfeld, R.S., F. Keesing, C. G. Jones, C. D. Canham, and G. Lovett. 1998. Integrative Ecology and Dynamics of Species in Oak Forests. *Integrative Biology* 1:178–86.

Page, M., and B. M. Brooks. 1991. *A Field Guide to Freshwater Fishes*. New York: Houghton Mifflin.

Paul, M .J., and J. L. Meyer. 2001. Streams in the Urban Landscape. *Annual Review of Ecology and Systematics* 32:333–65.

Phipps, R. 2001. Got Fish? Already Tired of That Holiday Gift Aquarium? Think before You Dump and Create an Even Bigger Problem. USGS News Release.

Pickett, S. T. A., W. R. Burch Jr., S. E. Dalton, T. W. Foresman, J. M. Grove, and R. A. Rowntree. 1997. A Conceptual Framework for the Study of Human Ecosystems in Urban Areas. *Urban Ecosystems* 1:185–201.

Pickett, S. T. A., M. L. Cadenasso, J. M. Grove, C. G. Boone, P. M. Groffman, E. Irwin, S. S. Kaushal, V. Marshall, B. P. McGrath, C. H. Nilon, R. V. Pouyat, K. Szlavecz, A. Troy, and P. Warren. 2011. Urban Ecological Systems: Scientific Foundations and a Decade of Progress. *Journal of Environmental Management* 92:331–62.

Power, M. E., D. Tilman, J. A. Estes, B. A. Menge, W. J. Bond, L. S. Mills, G. Daily, J. C. Castilla, J. Lubchenco, and R. T. Paine. 1996. Challenges in the Quest for Keystones. *BioScience* 46:609–20.

Rahel, F. J. 2002. Homogenization of Freshwater Faunas. *Annual Review of Ecology and Systematics* 33:291–315.

Rees, W. E. 1997. Urban Ecosystems: The Human Dimension. *Urban Ecosystems* 1:63–75.

Riley, A. 1998. *Restoring Streams in Cities: A Guide for Planners, Policymakers, and Citizens*. Washington, DC: Island Press.

Robb, G. N., R. A. McDonald, D. E. Chamberlain, and S. Bearhop. 2008. Food for Thought: Supplementary Feeding as a Driver of Ecological Change in Avian Populations. *Frontiers in Ecology and the Environment* 6:476–84.

Scheyer, J. M., and K. W. Hipple. 2005. *Urban Soil Primer*. Lincoln, NE: USDA, Natural Resources Conservation Service, National Soil Survey Center.

Schmidly, D. J. 2004. *Mammals of Texas: Revised Edition*. Austin: University of Texas Press.

Schochat, E., S. Lerman, and E. Fernandez-Juricic. 2010. Birds in Urban Ecosystems: Population Dynamics, Community Structure, Biodiversity and Conservations. In *Urban Ecosystem Ecology*, ed. J. Aitkenhead-Peterson and A. Volder, 75–86. Agronomy Monograph 55. Madison, WI: American Society of Agronomy.

Schultz, W. 1999. *A Man's Turf: The Perfect Lawn*. New York: Clarkson Potter.

Smith, H. M., and D. Chiszar. 2006. Dilemma of Name-Recognition: Why and When to Use New Combinations of Scientific Names. *Herpetological Conservation and Biology* 1:6–7.

Sterba, J. 2012. *Nature Wars*. New York: Crown Publishers.

Sullivan, R. 2004. *Rats: Observations on the History and Habitat of the City's Most Unwanted Inhabitants*. London: Bloomsbury.

Tipton, B. L., T. L. Hibbits, T. D. Hibbits, T. J. Hibbits, and T. J. LaDuc. 2012. *Texas Amphibians: A Field Guide*. Austin: University of Texas Press.

Trombulak, S. C., and C. A. Frissell. 1999. Review of Ecological Effects of Roads on Terrestrial and Aquatic Communities. *Conservation Biology* 14:18–30.

TWDB (Texas Water Development Board). n.d. Texas Aquifers. Accessed April 10, 2015. https://www.twdb.texas.gov/groundwater/aquifer/.

———. 2011. Water for Texas: Summary of the 2011 Regional Water Plans. 82nd Legislative Session. Accessed April 10, 2015. http://www.twdb.texas.gov/waterplanning/rwp/regions/doc/2011RWPLegislativeSummary.pdf.

———. 2015. River Basins. Accessed March 17, 2015. http://www.twdb.state.tx.us/surfacewater/rivers/river_basins/index.asp.

United Nations. 2011. *World Urbanization Prospects: The 2011 Revision*. New York: United Nations. http://esa.un.org/wpp/ppt/CSIS/WUP_2011_CSIS_4.pdf.

United States Census Bureau. 2010. 2010 Census Data. Accessed April 10, 2015. http://www.census.gov/2010census/.

———. 2011. *National Survey of Fishing, Hunting and Wildlife-Associated Recreation*. Washington, DC: United States Government Printing Office.

US Department of Agriculture. 2001. *Urban Soils*. Lincoln, NE: Natural Resources Conservation Service, National Soil Survey Center.

US Department of Transportation, Federal Highway Administration. 2009. Highway Statistics 2009. Accessed April 10, 2015. http://www.fhwa.dot.gov/policyinformation/statistics/2009/.

Vinlove, F. K., and R. F. Torla. 1995. Comparative Estimations of US Home Lawn Area. *Journal of Turf Management* 1:83–97.

Vitousek, P. M., H. A. Mooney, J. Lubchenco, and J. M. Melillo. 2008. Human Domination of Earth's Ecosystems. In *Urban Ecology: An International Perspective on the Interactions between Humans and Nature*, ed. J. M. Marzluff, E. Shulenberger, W. Endlicher, U. Simon, C. ZumBrunen, M. Alberti, G. Bradley, and C. Ryan, 3–13. New York: Springer.

Waller, D. W., and W. S. Alverson. 1997. The White-Tailed Deer: A Keystone Herbivore. *Wildlife Society Bulletin* 25 (2): 217–26.

Wolf, A. J., E. C. Hellgren, V. Bogosian III, and R. W. Moody. 2013. Effects of Habitat Disturbance on Texas Horned Lizards: An Urban Case Study. *Herpetologica* 69:265–81.

Wright, R. E., and D. F. Boorse. 2011. *Environmental Science: Toward a Sustainable Future*. 11th ed. San Francisco: Pearson Benjamin Cummings.

Zipperer, W. C., J. Wu, R. V. Pouyat, and S. T. A. Pickett. 2000. The Application of Ecological Principles to Urban and Urbanizing Landscapes. *Ecological Applications* 10:685–86.

UNIT 22

Laws, Regulations, and Ethics

MICHAEL MITCHELL
Game Warden, Law Enforcement, Texas Parks and Wildlife Department

CONTRIBUTOR:
RICHARD HEILBRUN
Texas Parks and Wildlife Department

Unit Goals

After completing this unit, volunteers should be able to

- explain the differences between Texas laws and Texas regulations
- describe who owns Texas wildlife
- be familiar with some early history of conservation law
- define situations Texas Master Naturalists may face and how to best deal with them
- broadly understand the federal and state permitting process
- demonstrate the working relationship between conservation law enforcement, Master Naturalists, and the general public
- identify why ethical standards are important for Texas Master Naturalists

Defining Laws, Regulations, and Ethics

Master Naturalists are typically inspired to want to collect, hold, and display all sorts of natural items, especially those from wild animals, and rightfully so. This can include owl feathers, alligator skins, and bird nests. The same excitement and interest in these natural items are what causes many to become involved in the Texas Master Naturalist program. But the reality is that these animals and birds, and their skins, feathers, claws, and teeth, are protected. Unfortunately, the way the laws are written, just saying, "I'm a Master Naturalist," or just collecting these natural items out of interest and exploration does not allow the laws to be circumvented. Simultaneously, that same set of laws does not exist to punish a minor child who innocently puts feathers on her hat. This section provides background on why these laws exist, who they are intended for, and how permits and exceptions may be obtained. Master Naturalists should follow the rules of the three-legged stool and consider each of the following when participating in volunteer programs and representing the Texas Master Naturalist program: federal, state, and local laws; the rules and regulations of the program; the ethics both of the program and of their personal natural resource ownership.

The Texas Master Naturalist Code of Ethics and Standards of Conduct contain

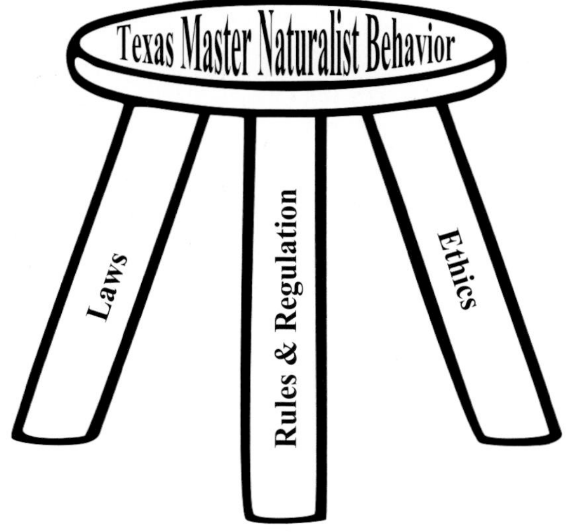

The three "stool legs" that Texas Master Naturalists should consider as they engage with their programs are federal, state, and local laws; the rules and regulations of the program; and the ethics of both the program and their personal natural resource ownership.

language about never inappropriately disturbing or harassing wildlife, never inappropriately removing natural objects, avoiding dishonesty, respecting others, and being responsible. For example, if a volunteer is to enter someone's property without permission and collect specimens, how would that reflect upon the Master Naturalist and the program as a whole? Is that illegal? How could it be appropriately done?

"We abuse land because we see it as a commodity belonging to us. When we see land as a community to which we belong, we may begin to use it with love and respect."
—Aldo Leopold

Ownership of Wildlife

Texas law clearly states that all wild animals, fur-bearing animals, wild birds, and wild fowl inside the border of this state are the property of the people of this state. The law also extends to fish and aquatic life, beds and bottoms of waters, and the like. The law further states that all public fresh water shall remain open to the public and that landowners' fences may be built to any height.

This standard of public ownership likely goes all the way back to the Magna Carta, 1215, which established royal authority and ownership over the forests, waterways, fisheries, and wildlife. That concept was reinforced in 1647 with the Colonial Ordinance, in which early Americans reinforced government oversight of natural resources but very strongly established public ownership of wildlife.

Wildlife traveling within Texas state boundaries is not owned by landowners or the government but rather by the people of the state of Texas. Texas has a strong history of wildlife management and conservation:

- 1861: Texas enacts its first game laws, establishing a two-year closed season on northern bobwhite on Galveston Island.
- 1874: Texas enacts its first trespass statute, protecting enclosed lands from trespass by "shooting, hunting, fishing or fowling."
- 1879: Texas enacts its first general game laws, protecting songbirds, and establishes a season for dove and quail hunting.
- 1883: Around 130 counties claim an exemption from all game laws.
- 1895: Texas Fish and Oyster Commission established.
- 1897: Law enacted making it illegal to take fish through the use of poison, lime, or explosives.
- 1900: Federal Lacey Act prohibits interstate transfer of wildlife.
- 1903: Texas legislature creates a five-year closed season on antelope, mountain sheep, and deer and sets bag limits on turkey, quail, and dove. Headlight hunting made illegal.
- 1907: Texas Game, Fish, and Oyster Commission established.
- 1909: First hunting licenses are required of those who hunt outside their home or in an adjoining county; 5,000 sold that first year.
- 1916: Federal Migratory Bird Treaty Act passes.
- 1919: First game wardens hired; six war-

Texas law allows fences to be built to any height. This has implications on the wildlife owned by the people of Texas. Courtesy of Clinton J. Faas, cjfaas@gmail.com

dens are employed to patrol the entire state.
- 1925: Texas legislature approves a game preserve act empowering the Game, Fish, and Oyster Commission to lease land from private landowners to create sanctuaries where hunting would be restricted and populations could recover.

In 1963 the Texas Parks and Wildlife Department (TPWD) was created, having evolved over time from various-named agencies. Today that agency has over 3,500 employees in 11 divisions. It receives funding from a myriad of sources, from hunting license sales to boat registrations to federal excise taxes upon firearms, ammunition, fishing tackle, and boat motor fuels. The legislature placed authority for managing fish and wildlife resources in all Texas counties with the TPWD when it passed the Wildlife Conservation Act in 1983. Previously, commissioners courts had set game and fish laws in many counties, and other counties had veto power over department regulations.

"No man is above the law and no man is below it; nor do we ask any man's permission when we require him to obey it. . . . Obedience to the law is demanded as a right; not asked as a favor."
—Theodore Roosevelt, Message to Congress, December 1903

Law Characteristics

Laws are a basic system of rules to govern our behavior. Texas has a complex set of laws, ranging from the Penal Code to the Texas Water Code. They cover many topics, from whether a child can ride in a pickup truck bed to how two railroad trains will meet at a railroad crossing. The laws are derived from the State Constitution.

Each legislative session, thousands of laws and law changes are submitted through the legislative process. They are referred to and considered by committees. Some make it to the House and Senate floor and, if passed, are then signed or vetoed by the governor. Of the thousands proposed each legislative session, typically only a few hundred make it. Those that do pass become the laws of Texas and are codified in statutes. But each law starts as a suggestion by anyone: concerned citizen, special-interest groups, state agencies, or the governor, for example. Following are some Texas laws that apply to resource conservation:

- Texas Penal Code, Title 7, Chapter 30: Burglary and Criminal Trespass. Outlines Texas' rules prohibiting an individual entering property, including agricultural land, without effective consent of the owner.
- Texas Parks and Wildlife Code, Title 5, Chapter 64: Birds. Protects nongame bird plumage and nests.
- Texas Health and Safety Code, Title 5, Chapter 365: Litter. Explains Texas' litter laws and, for example, that for-profit businesses will receive extra penalties if caught dumping for profit.

Obviously there are also federal, county, and city laws (often called **ordinances**). A discussion of federal laws is highly relevant, because so many parts of the environment cross state and political boundaries. Specifically, migratory birds can cross state lines quite easily as they progress on their annual journeys. Thus, Master Naturalists should be aware of some highly relevant federal laws:

- **Migratory Bird Treaty Act:** First passed in 1916, this law is enforced primarily by the US Fish and Wildlife Service and makes it illegal for anyone to take, possess, import, export, transport, sell, purchase, barter, or offer for sale, purchase, or barter any migratory bird or the parts, nests, or eggs of such a bird except under the terms of

Many birds migrate across state and even national boundaries, in this case the roseate spoonbill (*Platalea ajaja*). Courtesy of Texas Parks and Wildlife Department

a valid permit issue pursuant to federal regulations.

- **Endangered Species Act:** First passed in 1973, this law is also enforced primarily by the US Fish and Wildlife Service. It protects imperiled species and the ecosystems upon which they depend.

These laws can sound intimidating at first, but Master Naturalists are strongly encouraged to learn why the laws exist and not to fear them but appreciate their intentions. Exceptions and permits are routinely granted for appropriate purposes such as environmental education; there is simply a process that must be followed.

As an example, the Lacey Act of 1900 and the Migratory Bird Treaty Act of 1916 were enacted to address the loss of wildlife populations caused by market hunting for bird feathers. Ladies' hats at the turn of the century were often decorated with feathers from migratory birds. Though many states enacted laws to limit such market hunting, only the federal government could prevent the interstate commerce of these animal parts. Today these acts are used to limit poachers from transporting illegally obtained animal parts between states and across our international borders.

Regulations are declarations made by authorities. They are very similar to laws; however, rather than derive from legislative bills, they typically come from a rule-making process. For example, in Texas the legislature meets every two years. That is not nearly frequently enough for Texas to update its rules regarding hunting and fishing. Problems like droughts can make huge environmental changes over short periods of time, and the rules would need to be changed quickly. Thus, under state law, Texas has a Parks and Wildlife Commission, a nine-member board that meets several times throughout the year to update Texas' regulations regarding conservation protection. These regulations outline the start of dove season, the annual bag limits, the price of fishing licenses, the size of a keeper bass, the number of oysters that may be harvested in a day, and so on. They are published in the *Texas Register* and are contained within the Texas Administrative Code.

Implications for Naturalists

Texas Master Naturalists will likely find themselves in positions where their knowledge of conservation-related laws, regulations, and ethics is important. First, in their roles as ambassadors and teachers to the community, they may receive questions that, for example, would be best suited for the local game warden. Second, Master Naturalists may find themselves putting together displays and needing to understand how to properly collect and possess feathers, for example. Third, Master Naturalists' actions will speak louder than words when they organize field trips, for example, and will be examined as they are placed into ethical situations, such as crossing fences to get a better view.

Obtaining Permits

There are two general categories of permits for holding wildlife or their parts: federal and state permits. Broadly speaking, **federal permits** are required for federally protected species; **state permits** are required for state-protected species. Sometimes they overlap, and two concurrent permits are required. This is admittedly a complex topic. In this unit, a general overview is given because laws, regulations, and contacts change, but the general principles remain the same.

Federal permits are issued by the US Fish and Wildlife Service, which uses them to enable the public to engage in specific activities. These permits are required, for example, to possess migratory bird feathers. For additional information about permits, check the agency website (http://www.fws.gov/permits) or call its Migratory Birds Division in Albuquerque, New Mexico (505–248–6878). Allow 60–90 days to receive permits. There is a fee required.

State permits are issued by the Wildlife Division of TPWD. Permits are required to possess, display, care for, propagate, collect, transport, or sell protected wildlife species. For additional information about laws pertaining to these species or any of the permits discussed, check the agency website (http://www.tpwd.state.tx.us/business/permits/) or call the Wildlife Information Desk (800–792–1112). Cities or counties may also have rules regarding holding live wild animals.

The Wildlife Diversity Team at TPWD issues 10 types of state permits. Here only the **Educational Display permit** is discussed. If you have questions specific to this permit, please call the Wildlife Information Desk at 800–792–1112. A description of this program can be found on the agency website (http://www.tpwd.state.tx.us/business/permits/land/wildlife/educational/).

The state's Educational Display permit is required to hold or collect protected wildlife, or parts of protected wildlife, for educational purposes. For example, using a properly collected mammal skull for classroom and educational festival displays requires a permit. It is only issued to agents of accredited primary, secondary, or postsecondary educational institutions, governmental entities, or nonprofit educational organizations. There is a fee required. State permit application packets must be obtained from TPWD, completed, and returned along with two letters of recommendation from individuals in an appropriate biological or professional field. If you wish to collect or hold an endangered species, you must provide written justification explaining how the species will benefit from the proposed activity. The Educational Display permit does not allow the sale or propagation of animals. Permits are issued for three years, and a report is required each year in order to maintain the permit.

Texas game wardens check oyster harvests in Texas bays. Courtesy of Texas Parks and Wildlife Department

Law Enforcement Relationship

Laws and regulations may be enforced by a myriad of authorities. Federal officers enforce federal laws. State officers enforce state laws. All Texas laws can be enforced by the more than 64,000 sworn peace officers from more than 2,600 Texas police agencies. But some officers cannot enforce environmental-type regulations based on their own decisions or agency policies. County and city ordinances can be enforced

Example situations with risks and suggested outcomes

Situation in which the Master Naturalist . . .	and needs to . . .	Suggested best course of legal and ethical action
receives detailed questions about wildlife rules	understand the risk of taking on a role where misinformation could cause the recipient to receive a legal penalty	Refer the question to the local game warden or TPWD Wildlife Information Line (800-792-1112).
hears about a wild animal being held or requiring rehabilitation	place that animal into the hands of a permitted or appropriate rehabilitator	Check the TPWD website under the Wildlife tab for the nearest rehabilitator; then refer the animal holder to that person (http://www.tpwd.state.tx.us/huntwild/wild/rehab/).
gets information about trespassing or poaching	not take the risk of acting as the third party on that information	Direct the tipster to Operation Game Thief (800-792-GAME) or to the local game warden.
obtains feathers and wants to integrate them into an educational display	hold the proper permit(s) for this to be legal	Contact the permits team at TPWD and ensure the Master Naturalist has the correct permits or have a permittee receive the feathers. This may also require federal permits from the US Fish and Wildlife Service.
is leading a group on a hike and finds some feathers on the ground	teach the group the appropriate course of action	Explain that migratory bird parts may not be possessed, but nonmigratory animal parts, like turkey feathers or mammal skulls, can be collected when found on lands where the landowner has given permission to collect.
takes a group on a hike and wants to cross a fence to see an impressive natural site	cross a fence line of a piece of private property to get there, without having the landowner's prior consent	Do not cross the fence, and make this a teachable moment. Prep the next hike by contacting the landowner in advance and seeking permission (and waivers, if appropriate).
is discussing land-use rules while over an aquifer that happens to be regulated, for example, the Edwards Aquifer	give the best answers for an area that is regulated, which may be a referral to an agency	Contact the appropriate regulatory authority—in the case of the Edwards Aquifer, the Edwards Aquifer Authority and the Texas Commission on Environmental Quality. Groundwater conservation districts are regulatory agencies that exist all over Texas.

only by county and city officers, deputies, sheriffs, constables, and other official public safety officers.

The TPWD is unique. Due to stringent Texas laws regarding conservation enforcement, state park peace officers can enforce any state laws inside or outside parks, and Texas game wardens can enforce not only all state laws but also relevant federal conservation laws, as they hold dual commissions as deputy federal agents under the US Department of Interior and US Department of Commerce. In those capacities, game wardens typically initiate investigative action and then refer those cases to the appropriate federal agents.

Sharing Ethics

"What is popular is not always right, and what is right is not always popular."
—Howard Cosell, American sports journalist

Ethics are the moral principles that govern a person or group's behavior. The Texas Master Naturalist program has an ethical conviction and outlines that in its charter. Its individual members also have individual ethics. The two interplay but are highly likely to be closely examined during educational demonstrations and exhibitions. Ethics are particularly challenging because they govern not only what people see you do but often what choices you make while not being observed.

It is at the very core of the Texas Master Naturalist program to help others develop their own personal environmental ethics. This includes not only becoming more knowledgeable about our state's natural resources but acting as a steward to help others learn about them and how to preserve and protect them for future generations.

Becoming a Texas Master Naturalist is an exciting experience and with that title comes a responsibility. It includes knowing about the laws and regulations concerning nature. It also includes setting the standard in conservation ethics, a standard that will be viewed and discussed by many with whom the Master Naturalist interacts. It is hoped that graduates will know and demonstrate the appropriate principles.

"The land ethic simply enlarges the boundaries of the community to include soils, waters, plants, and animals, or collectively: the land. . . . In short, a land ethic changes the role of Homo sapiens from conqueror of the land-community to plain member and citizen of it. It implies respect for his fellow-members, and also respect for the community as such."
—Aldo Leopold

Website Resources

Texas Legacy Project. Time and Events in Conservation History. http://www.texaslegacy.org/m/timeline.html.

Texas Legislature. How to Follow a Bill Using TLO. Texas Legislature Online. http://www.capitol.state.tx.us/resources/FollowABill.aspx.

Texas Parks and Wildlife Department. Wildlife Permits. http://www.tpwd.state.tx.us/publications/pwdpubs/media/pwd_br_w7000_0637.pdf.

Texas Secretary of State. Texas Administrative Code. http://www.sos.state.tx.us/tac/.

Texas Water Development Board. Groundwater Conservation Districts. http://www.twdb.state.tx.us/groundwater/conservation_districts/.

US Fish and Wildlife Service. Permits Vision Document. http://www.fws.gov/permits/.

UNIT 23

Volunteers as Teachers

SHIRLEY JONES
Interpretive Specialist, Texas Parks and Wildlife Department (retired)

LINDA HEDGES
Regional Interpretive Specialist, Texas Parks and Wildlife Department

Unit Goals

After completing this unit, volunteers should be able to

- discuss the meaning of interpretation
- discuss types of interpretation
- identify and understand components of an interpretive experience
- understand the differences between a topic and a theme and the importance/functions each serves
- demonstrate audience management techniques

"In the end, we conserve only what we love. We love only what we understand. We understand only what we are taught."
—Baba Dioum Dioum, Senegalese poet

"To the dull mind nature is leaden. To the illuminated mind the whole world burns and sparkles with light."
—Ralph Waldo Emerson

Introduction

It is Saturday morning, and you are waiting at the benches near the trailhead at the local nature center. A number of your nature hike participants have already arrived—a boisterous group of Scouts and a family group with two children, both probably under the age of six. Headed toward you is a young couple holding hands, followed by a mature woman with two or three guidebooks tucked under her arm. The hands of your watch reach 10:00 a.m.—time to start the hike.

> This unit focuses on a challenging category—interpretation. It is a broad, rapidly changing field. The information presented here is meant only to introduce Texas Master Naturalists to interpretation and provide starting points for developing interpretive experiences and materials.

Sound familiar? Many Texas Master Naturalists will fulfill their service hours working directly with the public as volunteer guides for local sites or as program presenters for schools, summer camps, or other public functions. This kind of public contact work may be broken into three broad areas of function:

- **Orientation:** Greeting visitors to a site, collecting fees, directing visitors to site opportunities, and providing operational information.
- **Education:** Formalized experiences and transfer of information that meet specific learning objectives, usually within a nonvoluntary setting. Participants may be driven by external motivations, such as grades or certifications.
- **Interpretation:** Informal experiences and transfer of information, within a voluntary setting. Participants are internally motivated by an intrinsic satisfaction with their experience, with the experience viewed as another opportunity. Also central to the concept of interpretation is that

A group of learning Texas Master Naturalists. Courtesy of Leroy Williamson

participants find personal relevance and meaning in the material being presented. Interpretation has the power to enhance the experience, facilitate appreciation of the resource, and influence behaviors.

"By learning you will teach; by teaching you will learn."
—Latin proverb

What Is Interpretation?

The term **interpreter** came into common use in the 1930s. It is a confusing term (interpreters are often asked, "What languages do you speak?"); however, it is still considered the best one for the profession. After all, the secrets of nature and history are often quite "foreign" to our audiences.

While many mark the birth of interpretation with Freeman Tilden's classic work *Interpreting Our Heritage* (originally published in 1957), others point to Enos Mills's *Adventure of a Nature Guide and Essays in Interpretation* as the philosophical foundation of the profession. Enos Mills, a close friend of John Muir, was an interpretive guide in the Rocky Mountains from the late 1880s to the early 1920s. He published *Adventures of a Nature Guide* in 1920—he was a pioneer in the development of interpretation as a profession. The principles set forth by Tilden and Mills have many things in common and remain standard in the field today. The following definitions of **interpretation** may offer insight into the profession:

> An educational activity which aims to reveal meanings and relationships through the use of original objects, by firsthand experience, and by illustrative media, rather than simply to communicate factual information. (Tilden 1977, 9)

> Interpretation is the translation of the technical or unfamiliar language of the environment into lay language, with no loss in accuracy, in order to create and enhance sensitivity, awareness, understanding, appreciation, and commitment. . . . The goal of interpretation is a change in behavior of those for whom we interpret. (Risk 1994, 37, 40)

> Interpretation is a process, a rendering, by which visitors see, learn, experience and are inspired firsthand. . . . Interpretation is revelation based upon information." (Beck and Cable 1998, xxii, xxiii; 2011, xxi)

There are some newer definitions: "Interpretation is a mission-based communication process that forges intellectual and emotional connections between the interests of the audience and the meaning inherent in the resource" (National Association for Interpretation, n.d.). Sam Ham took the definitions of Tilden and the National Association for Interpretation and adopted the following working definition, which captures what makes interpretation different from other forms of information transfer. "Interpretation is a mission-based approach to communication aimed at provoking in audiences the discovery of personal meaning and the forging of personal connections with things, places, people, and concepts" (2013, 8).

Six Principles of Interpretation

The operative words seem to be *reveal, provocation, experiences, meanings, art, approach, whole,* and *relationships.* Good interpretation is always based on factual information, but it goes much further. Sam Ham put it this way: "Tilden saw interpretation as an approach to communicating in which the primary aim is the construction of meanings and the revelation of relationships in the visitor's mind rather than the mastering of isolated facts and figures. Although, any interpreter will use factual information to illustrate points and clarify meanings; according to Tilden, it's the points and meanings that interpreters should care about most—not the facts. This is what distinguishes interpretation from conventional instruction" (1992, 7). This communication, coupled with a quality experience, forms memorable interpretation. More recently, Ham has said, "Interpretation attempts to communicate in a thought-provoking way to an audience that's completely free to ignore it" (2013, 1).

In *Interpreting Our Heritage,* Tilden defined six principles of interpretation:

1. Any interpretation that does not somehow **relate** what is being displayed or described to something within the personality or experience of the visitor will be sterile.
2. Information, as such, is not interpretation. Interpretation is **revelation** based upon information. They are entirely different things. However, all interpretation includes information.
3. Interpretation is an **art**, which combines many arts, whether the materials presented are scientific, historical or architectural. Any art is in some degree teachable.
4. The chief aim of interpretation is not instruction but **provocation**.
5. Interpretation should aim to present a **whole** rather than a part, and must address itself to the whole person rather than any phase.
6. Interpretation addressed to children should not be a dilution of the presentation to adults, but should follow a fundamentally different **approach**. To be at its best it will require a separate program. (1977, 9)

Forms of Interpretations

In general, interpretation takes one of two forms. The names of these forms may vary from author to author, but the categories remain the same:

A nature tour. Courtesy of Texas Parks and Wildlife Department

- **Static interpretation:** Any interpretive contact that does not involve a living person to facilitate the contact. Brochures, signs, exhibits, and posters are all examples of static interpretive items. Keep in mind that your resource base—the plants, buildings, artifacts, landscapes, smells, and sounds—is, in itself, a static interpretive display.
- **Personal services interpretation** (also known as dynamic interpretation): Interpretive contacts that are facilitated by a living person. Guided tours, slide shows, living history demonstrations, and campfire talks are common examples.

While this unit focuses on dynamic interpretation, the "thinking process" relates to static items as well. Practiced interpreters find that an organized thinking process becomes second nature to program or materials development.

One specific type of interpretation that would be most utilized by the Master Naturalist volunteer is the **heritage interpretation**. This is the communication of information about, or the explanation of, the nature, origin, and purpose of historical, natural, or cultural resources, objects, sites and phenomena using personal or nonpersonal methods. Heritage interpretation may be performed at dedicated interpretation centers or at museums, historic sites, parks, art galleries, nature centers, zoos, aquarium, botanical gardens, nature reserves, and a host of other heritage sites (Tilden 1977).

"One generation plants trees . . . another gets the shade."
—Chinese proverb

Components of an Interpretive Experience

The information you present is only a part of the total interpretive experience. To be truly effective, you must consider the factors that will impact your presentation. Each component is worthy of separate study. Examination of the visitor component can include marketing, sociology, psychology, learning theory, and demographics. The presentation component includes the mechanics of speech, audiovisual aids, personal presentation styles, and organization of information. Resource components can include safety information, access, conservation, and multiple-use issues, in addition to the natural and cultural resources themselves.

The Visitor Component

New interpreters are frequently advised to "know the visitor"—who they are, where they are from, basic cultural orientation, and other demographic information. In practice, this is no simple matter. Sites frequently operate for years without gathering specific visitor information. If you are working with a more homogeneous group, such as a school or hobby club, you may already know about your visitor.

For many interpreters, the first glimpse of the visitor comes when he or she arrives for the program. One thing is known about all visitors—they come to a site or program for their own reasons. Interpreters must acknowledge and respect the validity of those reasons. For example, learning about animals may not be why people visit a zoo. They may be more interested in being with family. Rather than give them instruction, interpreters should try to provide inspiration to help visitors learn more on their own: "That which people discover for themselves generates a special and vital excitement and satisfaction" (Veverka, 1994, n.d.).

Think about the diverse group described in the introduction and list possible reasons for their attendance at the fictional hike. The Scouts may be earning a badge or enjoying a visit with a friend, the young couple may wish to share some time in a pleasant setting, the mature woman might wish to see a new bird, and Mom and Dad may be seeking a diversion for active children. Awareness of these motivations helps the interpreter better understand the visitor.

Visitors bring their own set of "baggage" with them when they attend a presentation. Meaning is inherent in people, not in words or terms. Your idea of a tall tree depends on your mental picture of all the trees you have ever seen. It would not mean the same to a visitor from the Kansas plains or the redwood forests of the Pacific Coast. Thus, good interpreters frequently use comparisons to common objects to accurately describe characteristics. This simple technique helps close the experience gap in very diverse groups of visitors.

"The art of teaching is the art of assisting discovery."
—Mark Van Doren

"Let nature be your teacher."
—William Wordsworth

The Presentation Component

Even experienced interpreters benefit from an occasional review of good public speaking practices, and there are many manuals available for this purpose. Most important, however, is the mind-set of the interpreter, who must never forget that the interpretive experience is not about the presenter but about the visitor and the resource. The interpreter is not the experience but only interprets—acting as a conduit, facilitator, and intermediary—between the visitor and the resource. Think about your own interpretive experiences. Chances are the most memorable were those where the interpreter was not the focus of attention.

Credibility is a major factor in the presentation component. Commentary and experiences based on fact, not perception or personal bias, will establish credibility. This can be more difficult than it appears on the surface. Examine the facts you plan to present. Can you actually point to a documented source for that information? Just as visitors see everything through their own experience, so does the interpreter. It is acceptable to express an opinion or to include undocumented oral traditions in a presentation, but be sure to present them as such. Balanced presentations fairly represent all sides of an issue or topic and can actually increase the amount of support for an important idea by establishing the credibility of the speaker.

The Resource Component

To be effective, the information you are presenting should be solidly rooted in the resource confronting the visitor. One experienced interpreter expressed this as an interpretive rule: "If you can't see it, you don't get to talk about it." While some may see this as a limiting factor (how can you talk about prescribed burning when standing in a green field six months after the last burn?), it actually helps interpreters identify creative avenues for presenting complex information. For instance, the interpreter might bring some photographs of the field prior to the burn, or a week after the burn, to show the progression of that fire-disturbed area. The interpreter could then challenge the group to predict changes for the area, based on what they now know. Pointing out charred bits of stumps, heightened canopy, lack of dense, dead vegetation, and other clues can help visitors visualize the fire and

Teaching to a group. Courtesy of Leroy Williamson

Teaching a group of kids. Courtesy of Leroy Williamson

feel successful in their ability to discover evidence that the fire was there. The more you can root your presentation in the immediate resource, the higher your chances of facilitating a memorable, effective experience.

"The most important task, if we are to save the earth, is to educate."
—Peter Scott

Take inventory of all the available resources. Stretch your mental resource inventory beyond concrete plants, animals, buildings, and artifacts. Landscape vistas, smells, sounds (or even quiet), and reflective space may be valuable resources that help your visitor visualize and internalize the information you present.

"Tell me and I will forget. Show me and I will remember. Involve me and I will understand."
—Confucius, 450 BC

An Approach to Developing Interpretive Experiences

Like any other skill, program planning involves practice, evaluation, correction, and more practice. Although each individual has his or her own formula for program development, many perform the following steps at some point:

Review the site mission. Why is the site or resource there, and why is it accessible to the public? Keep this vision and mission in mind. Your program should be a part of the larger whole for the site. Interpretation that does not relate/benefit/integrate with other site functions is likely to fall victim to a lack of budget, staffing, support, and visitor interest.

Inventory the resource. What resources will the visitor contact, and what do you have to work with? Do not rely solely on your own impressions, especially if you are very familiar with the site. Often, familiarity blinds us to the resources in front of us. Invite a friend who has not been to the site to walk through. What does your friend notice? What generates questions, invokes interest, or is appealing?

Here is another critical consideration: What does the condition of the resource communicate to the visitor? Studies reveal that visitors believe what they see and pay less attention to what they are being told. For example, a tour through a historic site mentally includes the grounds around any buildings. If the grounds, plants, and arrangements do not accurately reflect the time period being interpreted, we unconsciously send the message that "this is the way it was," even though we may say something different. Similarly, an eroded, poorly maintained nature trail sends the subliminal message that "this is okay; this is nature." Make sure that what you are saying is accurately reflected by the resource in front of the visitor. Carefully weigh the risks of interpreting degraded resources or consider integrating a "call to action" into your presentation.

Choose specific ideas and outcomes. This is absolutely the most important part of your program or experience, and it is frequently bypassed in the development process. Choose one specific big idea or theme and then decide what you want the visitor to feel, learn, or do as a result of your program. "If you don't want them to use the information, they why are you doing the program?" (Ververka, n.d.). This kind of evaluation can be very simple: Did the visitors ask any questions? Did they interact among themselves about the topic at hand? Did the visitors model the interpreter's behavior, such as picking up trash, avoiding a dangerous plant, or actively listening to bird calls?

If you do not know why visitors attended or what they enjoyed about your presentation, simply ask them occasionally. Beverly Serrell, a well-known authority on static exhibits, put it bluntly: "I used to think evaluation was optional. It's not. It's mandatory" (1996, x). Outcomes for an interpretive program will fall somewhere along the continuum shown, depending on what you want your visitors to learn, feel, or do. Sam Ham says that the end game of interpretation (as provocation) is to make people think and find personal meaning. An indicator of success is based on the number and kinds of thoughts provoked. This can be measured subjectively by the sorts of questions that are asked during and after a presentation and in general by the amount and type of conversation that is generated.

Develop a theme, and focus all activity on that theme. A theme is the central idea of any presentation. Frequently, novice interpreters mistake a topic for a theme, failing to narrow, focus, and support a single idea that the visitor can "get a handle on." Ham defines *theme* in this way: "For the interpreter, a theme is the overarching idea she or he is trying to develop. Synonyms are message, main point, moral to the story, and premise. For the audience, themes are the thoughts they're provided to think as a result of interpretation—that is, the conclusions they

Awareness
Appreciation
Action
Advocacy

A continuum of involvement: Awareness, Appreciation, Action, Advocacy. Courtesy of Mary Pearl Meuth, Texas A&M AgriLife Extension Service

Hands-on experiences are vital for engaging volunteers, like this coastal studies field trip to South Padre Island for the Rio Grande Valley Chapter. Courtesy of Barbara Lindley, Rio Grande Valley Chapter

draw, the inferences they make, the impressions they form, and the personal morals of the story they extract from an interpretive encounter" (2013, 256).

For example, the interpreter may choose to do a program on trees. "Trees" is a topic and a body of subject matter. A theme is a specific message about the subject matter, such as "Trees in Sam Houston State Park were the Wal-Mart for the pioneers," or "The trees surrounding you are apartment buildings for local wildlife." Note that themes are complete thoughts and sentences; topics are not. The process of narrowing and focusing encourages interpreters to select interesting, unusual, important facts for their presentations and avoid generalizations. Good themes make the rest of the program's development simple. Experienced interpreters know that when they are struggling to find good visitor activities or fun information to include, they need to reexamine their program theme.

Sam Ham makes several points about themes: "Thinking thematically focuses your attention and therefore reduces your work. . . . Most audiences find thematic communication easier to comprehend and more interesting. When audiences know in advance what your theme is going to be, they are able to see the relevance of the rest of the information you give them. [Ham references another researcher, Thorndyke.] . . . Most audiences will remember the theme, along with five or fewer main ideas used to present it, but they'll forget most of the rest" (1992, 40–42).

Begin your presentation with a clear, interestingly worded statement of your theme. End your presentation with a reinforcing restatement of that theme. This is one approach: the "sandwich model" with theme stated at the beginning and end and the meat of the presentation in the middle. Other techniques are the emergent theme model, where the theme is implied but

Volunteer orientation at the Mercedes Library of the Rio Grande Valley Chapter. Courtesy of Barbara Lindley, Rio Grande Valley Chapter

Students from Floresville North Elementary third grade learn how to use binoculars during a field trip to Helton Nature Park with the San Antonio River Authority. Courtesy of Kayla Gasker, San Antonio River Authority and Alamo Area Chapter

never actually stated, and the theme-at-the-end model, which is revelatory. These are considered more advanced techniques than the sandwich model.

Select resource contacts and methods to support the theme. What can your visitors actually do to help them reach the outcomes you identified earlier in the process? If you have a good theme, this part should be less difficult. As an example, for the "Trees as Wal-Mart" theme, you might pass around chunks of wood from the local tree species. Allow visitors to examine the grain, feel the weight, and predict the use for that kind of wood. Is it dense, and therefore good for furniture, or is it a light, fast-growing species good for fuel?

"Anyone can count the seeds in an apple, but no one can count the apples in a seed."
—Anonymous

Challenge visitors to look above and below eye level for shape and length—which trees might be best for fence posts, floor planks, or windbreaks (deciduous versus evergreen—which will break the winter winds)? For the informed interpreter, this approach provides plenty of room for solid scientific fact. Note how this kind of theme-first thinking keeps the interpreter focused on a central idea rather than lets isolated facts clutter the mental landscape. Allow the visitors' personal experiences and opinions to become part of the program and provide opportunities for them to see how the information relates to them personally. Challenge yourself to greater creativity. Try laying your initial program activities aside, place them off limits in your mind, and think of other ways to make your point. You can always come back to an initial idea, but you may miss an opportunity if you are too easily satisfied.

Avoid the temptation to "tell it all." Beck and Cable quoted Anatole France: "Do not try to satisfy your vanity by teaching a great many things. Awaken people's curiosity. It is enough to open minds; do not overload them. Put there just a spark. If there is some good inflammable stuff, it will catch fire" (1998, 9). Another interpreter put it in modern terms: "Sometimes, asking an interpreter a question is like trying to get a drink from a fire hydrant with a teacup." The recipe for good interpretation includes a few good ideas, supported by credible facts, presented with direct resource contact.

Present your program with confidence and enthusiasm; show respect for the visitor, the resource, and yourself. The visitor has chosen to spend this time with your program, for whatever reason. Beck and Cable express it this way: "We feel a sense of obligation, out of respect for the resource and for those who have come to enjoy it, to craft a worthy interpretation of the place. . . . Through our passion for the resources we interpret, we may bring out a similar passion in those we interpret to. To draw visitors into a full appreciation of the interpretive setting, the interpreter displays an affinity for the resource and a respect for humanity. We introduce visitors to something we love, not something we own" (Beck and Cable 1998, xxvi).

"A teacher affects eternity; he can never tell where his influence stops."
—Henry Adams, American historian and educator

Audience Management Techniques

The following are a few techniques for live, service-oriented interpretive programs. Good technique can also be gained from auditing tours and programs at your site or at similar sites. Take some tours and participate in a few programs, with your focus on the presenter's technique and the audience responses. Observe how visitors interact with the presenter and with each other.

Know your audience and plan your presentation accordingly. This topic keeps coming up because it is so important. Well-planned programs that accommodate audience motivations and needs have few problems. When faced with the generic general public audience, arrive at the program ahead of time and visit informally with the group. Be prepared to change a technique or include different information based on your observations. One experienced interpreter advises presenters to have 10 times the information needed for the planned program.

Sit down whenever you can. Commentary that exceeds two minutes makes standing a real problem. Shuffling feet, heads bobbing to gain a better view, "personal space" adjustments, and talking will inevitably occur and distract from the presentation.

Consider viewing perspectives and sound qualities. This is especially important on guided walks and nature tours. When you practice your walk, take time to stoop down or climb a little higher to look at your object from differing heights. Plan stops so that when you must talk for two or more minutes, sound will not be a problem. If you must point out an object at any distance, use some simple focusing tools, such as a cardboard tube, or other "frame."

Create a distinct physical environment to focus attention. All sorts of stimuli are dive-bombing your audience all the time. Create physical parameters for the audience. Allow shrubbery to form a wall, or use unusual seating objects or simple visual cues to form a distinct space for the visitor's experience. This focuses attention and makes the audience more confident about their role.

Avoid giving too many directions or instructions at a time. This is critical with younger groups as well as mixed groups with wide variations in ages. Groups led through an action may be very unfamiliar with it and may have trouble with things that have become simple to you. Break instructions into groupings that make sense, taking care not to talk down to your group.

Modeling behavior is a powerful tool. Your persona will affect the group. Your speech pacing, body language, and actions will be reflected in the group, especially if they perceive you as an "expert." Act the way you want them to act, do the things you want them to do, and feel the things you want them to feel. Challenge yourself to design interpretive communications that require no words.

Integrate cultural and natural history. Look for ways to add the "people story" to any interpretation of natural history, and vice versa. Always strive to show people that they are part of the overall picture and that they are significant to the topic of your presentation.

Team up. Presentations that use two interpreters can add interest, keep pacing lively, and short-circuit problems, especially with large groups.

Watch out when passing things around. We want folks to touch and handle objects, but it can be problematic, especially with younger groups. Kids often become more worried about getting to touch the object than participating in the experience. Use multiples, teams, or other methods to control this.

"If you can't see it, don't talk about it." Try to find some analogy, example, or other physical manifestation for every topic, even the most complex.

References

Beck, L., and T. Cable. 1998. *Interpretation for the 21st Century*. Champaign, IL: Sagamore Publishing.

———. 2011. *The Gifts of Interpretation: Fifteen Guiding Principles for Interpreting Nature and Culture*. 3rd ed. Urbana, IL: Sagamore Publishing.

Ham, S. 1992. *Environmental Interpretation—Practical Guide for People with Big Ideas and Small Budgets*. Golden, CO: North American Press.

———. 2013. *Interpretation: Making a Difference on Purpose*. Golden, CO: Fulcrum Publishing.

Mills, Enos. 1920. *Adventures of a Nature Guide and Essays in Interpretation*. Garden City, NY: Doubleday, Page.

National Association for Interpretation. n.d. Accessed March 27, 2015. http://www.interpnet.com/NAI/interp/About/What_We_Believe/nai/_About/Mission_Vision_and_Core_Values.aspx?hkey=ef5896dc-53e4-4dbb-929e-96d45bdb1cc1.

Risk, Paul H. 1994. Interpretation: A Road to Creative Enlightenment. *CRM: The Journal of Heritage Stewardship* 17 (2): 37, 40.

Serrell, B. 1996. *Exhibit Labels, an Interpretive Approach*. Walnut Creek, CA: Altamira Press, Sage Publications.

Tilden, F. 1977. *Interpreting Our Heritage*. 3rd ed. Chapel Hill: University of North Carolina Press.

Veverka, J. 1994. *Interpretive Master Planning*. Helena, MT: Falcon Press.

———. n.d. Language of Live Interpretation—Making Contact. Accessed April 24, 2015. http://www.heritageinterp.com/language.htm.

UNIT 24

Citizen Science

CULLEN HANKS
Texas Nature Tracker Biologist, Texas Parks and Wildlife Department

MARSHA MAY
Wildlife Diversity, Texas Parks and Wildlife Department

MICHAEL WARRINER
Nongame and Rare Species Program, Texas Parks and Wildlife Department

REVISIONS ALSO PROVIDED BY ROB STEVENSON
Department of Biology, University of Massachusetts Boston

Unit Goals

After completing this unit, volunteers should be able to

- define citizen science and describe its historical development
- be familiar with the tools and technology available to citizen scientists
- develop a citizen science project for their local chapter
- be familiar with the goals of the Texas Nature Trackers program
- become familiar with the Texas Quail Index program

What Is Citizen Science?

Citizen science refers to the engagement of amateur naturalists in scientific investigations—asking questions, collecting data, or interpreting results (Miller-Rushing et al. 2012). There is a rich tradition of amateur naturalists contributing to our knowledge of natural history. Today, their contribution is often described as "citizen science," but the term is relatively new and is often used in very different ways. This unit describes citizen science programs that the amateur naturalist community is using to advance our understanding and stewardship of biodiversity.

While the tools we are using are new, the **amateur naturalist** has always been essential to our understanding of the natural world. The word *amateur* is based on the Latin word *amator*, or "lover." By definition, amateur naturalists are unpaid and pursue their interest out of passion for nature. In the 1800s, amateur naturalists made significant contributions both large and small. Many scientific journals depended on contributions from amateur naturalists. Likewise, amateur collectors were an important source of specimens for growing natural history collections. However, amateur naturalists did more than contribute small pieces to a larger puzzle; they revolutionized it. The best example is none other than Charles Darwin. Not only was he not paid for his work, but he added to his research by writing thousands of letters soliciting data, in effect an early form of crowd-sourcing.

During the last 25 years the revolution in information technology has fundamentally changed our ability to document and share information about the natural world and led to an explosion of new citizen science projects. Today, instead of collecting and killing a representative specimen, we can capture images and audio recordings. Rather than send a letter, we can post our observations online where they are accessible to everyone

Charles Darwin, an amateur naturalist who helped revolutionize our understanding of biology. Photo by Julia Margaret Cameron, 1868

instantaneously. What has not changed is that the amateur naturalist community is making critical contributions, and we do it out of a passion for nature.

We currently face unprecedented conservation challenges, such as habitat fragmentation, invasive species, and climate change. Good policy and stewardship depend on our understanding of how wild populations are changing and the connection between these wild populations and our communities. Citizen science is going to continue to play a crucial role in both aspects. There will never be enough professional biologists to sufficiently monitor wild populations, and there is no better way to develop and maintain a connection with wild populations than through citizen science.

As a naturalist, there are more ways to engage in citizen science than ever before. There are many crowd-sourcing efforts managed by professional biologists where you can participate simply by reporting your observations: Citizen Science 1.0. Such efforts allow biologists to tap into the potential of the naturalist community, and by participating, you will be improving your knowledge and abilities as a naturalist. However, amateur naturalists are not limited to collecting data; they are actively contributing by taking part in every aspect of the scientific process: Citizen Science 2.0. By digging into research, asking questions, collecting data, compiling results, and sharing their knowledge, amateur naturalists continue to push the frontier of what we know about the natural world and improve our stewardship of biodiversity.

This is an exciting time for citizen science because we are realizing that it is not only critical to generating data but also essential for sustaining a community's connection to wild populations and stewardship of habitat.

Citizen Science 1.0: Collecting Data

In 1900, a professional ornithologist, Frank Chapman, wrote an editorial in *Bird-Lore* magazine encouraging bird enthusiasts to spend a few hours counting birds on Christmas afternoon. Chapman proposed the "Christmas Bird Census" as an alternative to the holiday tradition of seeing who could shoot the most species, and in the process he initiated one of the largest and longest-running citizen science efforts in history. In 1900, 27 people documented 90 species across 25 different locations. In 2012–13, over 71,000 people participated in more than 2,300 locations.

Christmas Bird Counts (CBCs), now administered by the National Audubon Society in conjunction with the Cornell Laboratory of Ornithology, produce an invaluable data set for tracking winter bird populations and documenting change over time. These data are used by organizations such as the US Fish and Wildlife Service (USFWS) and the American Bird Conservancy, as well as the

National Audubon Society, to evaluate the health of wild populations and prioritize conservation efforts.

CBCs have also proved invaluable in the way they bring together the birding community every year. Each CBC is a survey of all the birds within an established 15-mile circle. Most counts divide the circle into different sections with a leader for each section. While the size of the area is consistent, the number of participants varies depending on the count. Some counts have just a couple of people, while others can have over a hundred participants. While the effort is not standardized, the benefit is that CBCs are open to anyone who wants to participate. Thus, CBCs are an excellent opportunity for the novice to spend time in the field with more experienced birders. In many areas it has become a tradition where all the participants get together for a countdown dinner at the end of the day. In this way, CBCs not only create data that are important to conservation efforts; they have also helped create and support a community of birders who are invested in the success of those conservation efforts.

The CBCs have been an invaluable tool for documenting wintering populations, but they could not address the status of breeding birds. To address this shortcoming, Chandler Robbins of the USFWS launched the **North American Breeding Bird Survey (BBS)** in 1966. Each BBS route consists of 50 point counts along 24.5 miles, conducted by a single observer, making it a more systematic survey than a CBC. This effort is one of the most important sources of data on breeding birds in North America; in 2013 more than 3,000 routes were surveyed. The BBS and CBCs are the principal source of quantitative data on population trends for birds in North America during the twentieth century.

While these programs stand out in their geographic scale and the magnitude of

Three birders ready for a day of counting birds on the Mad Island Christmas Bird Count. Courtesy of Cullen Hanks

community engagement, amateur naturalists continued to contribute in many traditional ways throughout the twentieth century. Amateur naturalists continued to publish books and journal articles describing new species and undocumented behavioral observations. They continued to be an important source of specimens for natural history collections, and the records of trophies harvested by hunters and fishermen contributed to the description of species.

Just as amateur naturalists continued to push the frontier of our knowledge on natural history, they also banded together to support the naturalist community itself. One of the largest communities to develop was the birding community, in part fueled by access to modern binoculars and field guides. The birding community created checklists for parks, cities, and regions that provided a valuable complement to the field guide for the novice birder. They set up rare bird alerts that allowed people to call in rare birds and alert others who might want to see the species.

Birders also pushed the frontier on how amateur naturalists set goals, detect, and document wild species. The life list has proven to be a valuable tool for many a novice birder. County lists challenge birders to develop a better understanding of local patterns in habitat use. Big days, big sits, yard lists, and other challenges have become useful tests of a person's ability to find and identify different species. While not all of these efforts have contributed to science, in many ways they set the stage for the powerful innovations in citizen science that we are experiencing today.

Contributing as You Learn

Like all parts of our lives, the information technology revolution is fundamentally changing the way we generate and share information. Mobile technology, the Internet, social media, crowd-sourcing, digital cameras, and global positioning systems are all being incorporated into the naturalist tool kit. These tools are not only more efficient; they are also allowing us to accomplish multiple goals at the same time. The tools that we use to learn about nature are also the tools we use to track our progress and set personal goals. They are also the tools we use to contribute to conservation. Not surprisingly, the birding community has been paving the way with the guidance of the Cornell Laboratory of Ornithology and the development of eBird.

Started in 2002, **eBird** is an online platform that birders can use to submit and track their observations. There is also a mobile app (BirdLog) that allows users to use their smartphones to submit observations to eBird in the field. By doing so, they can monitor how many species they have observed at a discrete site, county, state, or country. They can also track how many species they have seen in a particular month or year. This is a convenient tool for setting goals and tracking progress. For example, the Texas Ornithological Society has established the Century Club, challenging Texas birders to find 100 species in 100 different counties in Texas.

In Texas alone, birders have logged close to 10 million observations. Just as this platform can be a powerful tool for tracking personal observations, the data collected have become essential to trip planning, migration alerts, and learning for birders. Based on what has been reported, eBird automatically creates seasonal abundance charts for each region. As a result, birders can see how the abundance of a species changes over the course of the year in their county and state. Birders were creating these tools before eBird, but now they are automatically updated every time an eBird user posts observations. Birders can also sign up for alerts when a rare bird is detected in a particular area, replacing the way birders have traditionally used telephones and answering machines to share rare bird observations.

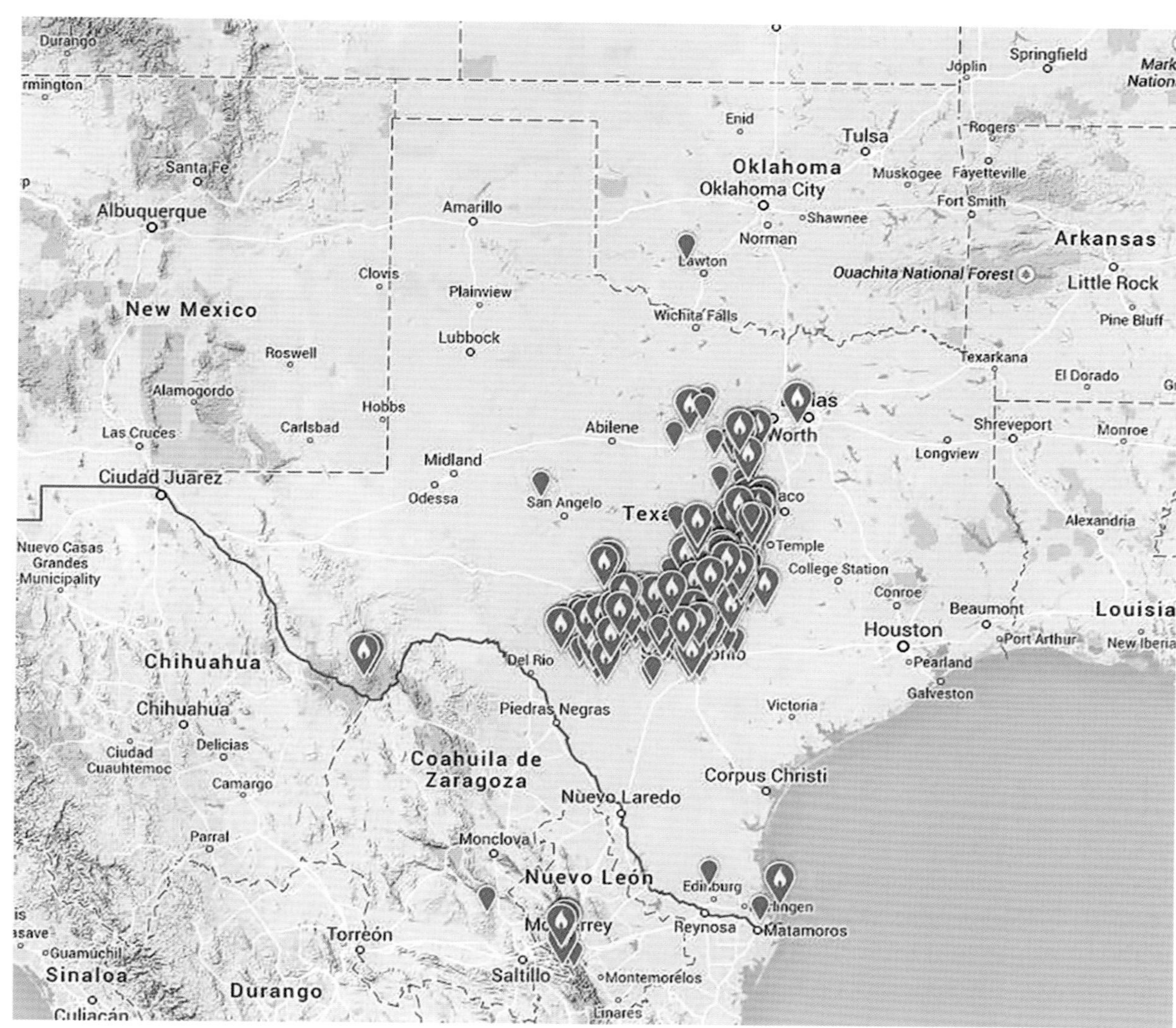

Map of golden-cheeked warbler (*Setophaga chrysoparia*) observations reported to eBird.

The Cornell Laboratory of Ornithology is continuing to develop the eBird platform and the functionality that serves the birding community.

While eBird has demonstrated the potential of crowd-sourcing in citizen science, birders are not the only group of naturalists to take advantage of modern technology in innovative ways. Online forums, digital cameras, and social media have powered innovative tools for reporting and identifying other taxa. This has been particularly important to the community of naturalists interested in insects and other invertebrates.

One of the great challenges to the amateur naturalist regarding insects is the ability to identify species and connect observations with additional information. One issue is the incredible diversity; there are estimated to be over one million species of insects on earth and just 10,000 species of birds. In Texas, there are more than 30,000 species of insects and approximately 600 species of birds. As a result, many different forums and online field guides have emerged that make insect identification more accessible to the amateur naturalist. One of the best examples is the platform **BugGuide**, which allows naturalists to post images of insects and other invertebrates in North America. BugGuide harnesses the power of the online community to help identify submissions, and the posted image is incorporated into the online field guide. In the process, these observations are augmenting our knowledge of species distribution and phenology.

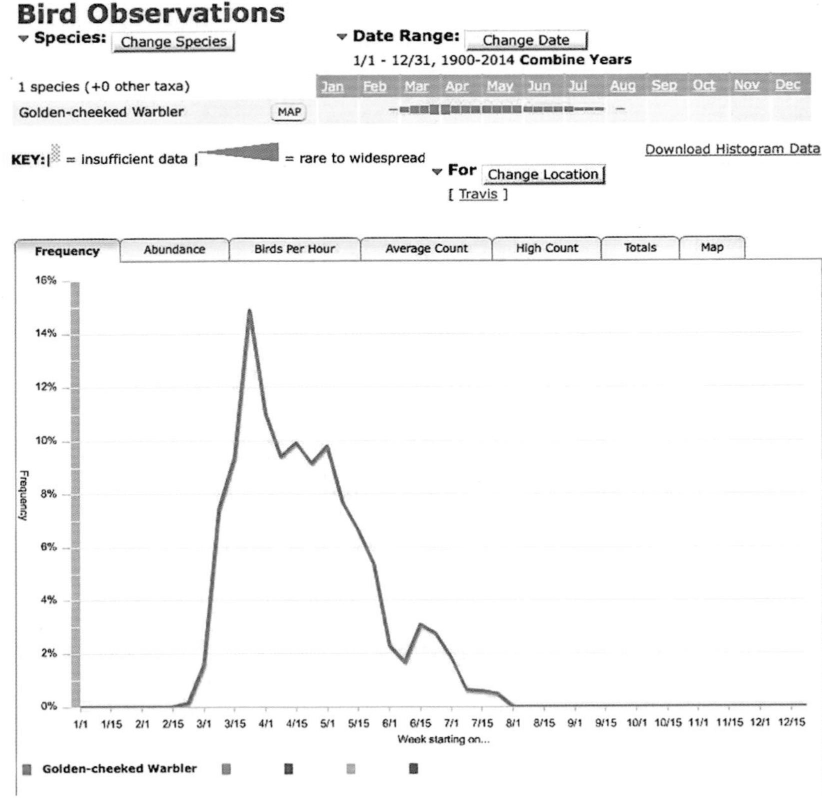

Seasonal bar chart and detection rate for golden-cheeked warbler (*Setophaga chrysoparia*) in Travis County.

A biologist records an observation of prairie lizard (*Sceloporus consobrinus*) at Gus Engeling Wildlife Management Area.

Prairie lizard (*Sceloporus consobrinus*) at Gus Engeling Wildlife Management Area.

One of the most powerful tools to emerge recently is **iNaturalist**, which brings together many recent innovations into a single platform for any species of plant or animal anywhere in the world. You can post observations on iNaturalist along with images or audio recordings. As on eBird, you can view your life list at different regional and temporal scales, making it a valuable tool to track your personal progress with all species.

Like other online field guides, this platform uses social media to discuss and validate the identification of each observation. In effect, iNaturalist takes the challenge of validating the data and turns it into a learning opportunity. The platform takes advantage of GPS technology to assign coordinates to every observation. This information is used to automatically create photographic field guides and checklist areas ranging in size from a local park to a state or country. In addition, this platform allows amateur naturalists, along with professional biologists, to initiate and establish a data-collecting project for a particular issue. For example, Texas Parks and Wildlife Department's Wildlife Diversity Program is using this platform for a number of different efforts across the state, ranging from research on urban predators to the detection of populations of rare species in Texas.

There is no doubt that technology is going to continue to revolutionize our ability to tap the potential of the naturalist community for research and conservation efforts. As you explore and document the natural world around you, consider how you can contribute by using one of the available platforms that will power our knowledge of wild populations in the twenty-first century. As we face unprecedented changes to natural habitats and wild populations of plants and animals, all of our observations and checklists will help tell the story of how things are changing and inform what we can do to have a positive impact on stewardship.

Texas Nature Trackers

The **Texas Nature Trackers (TNT)** program provides opportunities for naturalists to contribute to conservation and research efforts throughout Texas. While the slate of TNT projects is ever changing, it has opportunities for all skill levels throughout the state. Many naturalists participate by monitoring hummingbird activity in their backyard through the Texas Hummingbird Roundup, while others conduct systematic surveys for amphibians at local wetlands through the Texas Amphibian Watch. There is also a project specifically for whooping cranes, Texas Whooper Watch, where trained volunteers are helping to detect and monitor habitat use by migratory and wintering whooping cranes.

In addition to our traditional watch programs, TNT is collaborating with iNaturalist to document wild populations of plants and animals. In 2011 the Herps of Texas project (HoTX) was set up on iNaturalist to record observations of all species of reptiles and amphibians in Texas. This project, which is curated by three professional herpetologists, generated more than 10,000 observations from more than 600 members during the first two years. Through this project over 95% of the amphibian and reptile species in the state have been documented, and there is at least one observation in over 90% of the counties in Texas. The encouraging success of HoTX has led to the development of other projects focusing on mammals, birds, plants, and other taxa. Herpetologists and those interested in the HoTX project can participate in the annual Snake Days event, held every year in Texas around the celebrated World Snake Day, July 16 (www.snakedays.com).

Data from HoTX and other projects are already benefiting research and conserva-

A participant in Snake Days photographs a western diamondback rattlesnake (*Crotalus atrox*). Courtesy of Cullen Hanks

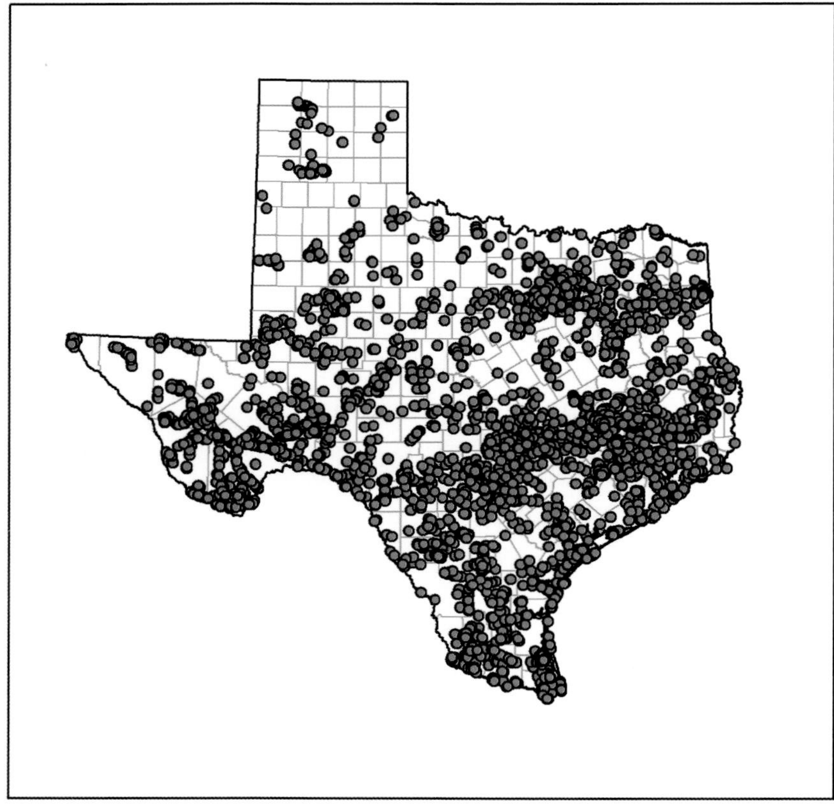

Herps of Texas observations from iNaturalist. In the first two years the Herps of Texas project documented more than 10,000 observations.

tion efforts in a number of ways. Over 15% of the observations are high-priority species as specified by the Texas Conservation Action Plan, and these data will be added to the Texas Natural Diversity Database (TXNDD). Environmental consultants and the Texas Parks and Wildlife Department's environmental review team use the TXNDD to evaluate the potential impact of development projects such as new roads or pipelines. Another use of the TXNDD is by biologists at Texas Parks and Wildlife, who use this database to rank the status of species in the state. Data from TNT projects are available to others conducting research in Texas. For example, observations have been incorporated into distribution models that can predict habitat with undetected populations.

Looking forward, the TNT program is looking for innovative ways to detect new populations of rare species, as well as docu-

While kayaking the Colorado River, Todd Jackson and Cullen Hanks discovered a new population of a rare plant, *Physostegia corellii*. The population was documented with an iNaturalist observation and added to the TXNDD. Because this is a threatened species, the location is obscured by about 6 miles (10 kilometers).

ment how the ranges of species are changing. To get involved, visit the Texas Nature Trackers website for information on tools, training opportunities, and the current slate of projects.

• • • • • • • • • • • • • • •

THE TEXAS QUAIL INDEX: CITIZEN SCIENCE IN ACTION

Rebekah Ruzicka, Extension Associate, Quail Decline Project, Texas A&M AgriLife Extension Service

The Texas Quail Index (TQI) is a program designed to use citizen scientists to monitor wild quail populations throughout the state of Texas. It is organized by Texas A&M AgriLife Extension Service and run at the county level using the local county extension agents (CEAs). The program is designed to educate land managers, hunters, and others about population dynamics, habitat requirements, and other factors affecting bobwhite and scaled quail in Texas, while at the same time providing useful data to give biologists a snapshot of quail populations statewide. The TQI provides an important opportunity to use citizen science statewide to help monitor the abundance of quail and bring attention to their importance, plight, and needs.

It starts by recruiting the Texas A&M AgriLife CEA for a particular county to participate in the TQI. The agent, in turn, finds a ranch or other suitable property willing to serve as the demonstration site. The CEA is also responsible for recruiting other members of the team from the community. This team could be the hunters who have a lease on the property, a former QuailMaster in the area, a former Bobwhite Brigade stu-

Texas Master Naturalists from Burnet County doing a call county survey for the Texas Quail Index program with Wade Hibler, Burnet County AgriLife Extension Unit. Courtesy of Becky Ruzicka, Texas A&M AgriLife Extension Service

dent, a Master Naturalist, agency personnel (Natural Resources Conservation Service or Texas Parks and Wildlife Department), and ideally a member of the local media. Each team leader goes through an intensive two-day training course to learn the data-collection methods employed. This training session is crucial to ensure that the data collected are comparable among sites statewide.

The teams are then responsible for following a standardized protocol and collecting data on quail abundance, predator abundance, and habitat quality on the participating site. They do this by using a variety of techniques throughout the year. To start off the breeding season, teams use spring call counts to assess breeding potential of the quail population. During nesting season (April–October), teams will use dummy nests to estimate the impact of predators on nesting quail in the area and assess the availability of quality nesting locations (i.e., the density of bunchgrasses and/or suitable prickly pear). Next, teams use game cameras to create an index of predator abundance on the property. This information can be used in conjunction with the results from the dummy nests to determine whether nest depredation may be a limiting factor on that property.

During the summer, teams assess the habitat quality on the property, using a guideline that takes into account all aspects

A male bobwhite quail (*Colinus virginianus*) calling on a mesquite perch. Courtesy of Becky Ruzicka, Texas A&M AgriLife Extension Service

of habitat that are important to quails: food availability, woody cover, nesting cover, and water availability. In September, teams use roadside counts as another marker of quail abundance. Roadside counts are used by Texas Parks and Wildlife Department for its annual quail forecast in each ecoregion. Fall covey call counts conducted in October are the last measure of the population going into hunting season and can be helpful in planning where to hunt and what habitat types the quail are using. Finally, harvest data are used as another index of abundance and a measure of production for that year by comparing the adult to juvenile ratio and coveys flushed per hour of hunting effort.

All these data collected at the county level are then submitted to a central database managed by Texas A&M AgriLife Extension Service to be analyzed on a statewide level. By combining all the observations, we can identify patterns in quail abundance across the state or answer other questions such as the relationship between different aspects of habitat quality (e.g., nest site availability) and quail abundance. Maybe most important though, the TQI will get people from across the state involved and thinking about what can be done to help in their area—citizen science is what makes it possible.

• • • • • • • • • • • • • • •

Citizen Science 2.0: Asking Questions and Analyzing Data

While platforms like eBird and iNaturalist make it easier than ever to contribute to the efforts of professional scientists, it is also easier than ever for the amateur naturalist to participate in all aspects of the scientific process. By developing your own questions, and digging for the answers, you deepen your appreciation for the natural world and find unique ways to contribute. Even better, a citizen science project is also an excellent project for a Texas Master Naturalist chapter.

Whether you are interested in a species, a place, or a system, the first step is to do research. In most cases, a little research will answer your question but lead to multiple new questions. Fortunately, it is easy to conduct basic research online. Citizen science tools like eBird, iNaturalist, and other reporting platforms allow you to explore the data. The Audubon Society allows you to download the data by species, count, region, and date range. This is very helpful for looking at significant trends in winter bird populations.

If you are interested in how a habitat or a population has changed, a little historical research can be invaluable. Today, the data in specimen collections are more valuable than ever, and most collections are posting their records online. Many collections allow you to peruse their records online. There are also a number of data portals that are compiling records from all of the different online collections, such as **VertNet**. On VertNet you can download specimen records for vertebrates from many different institutions at once. For example, if you are interested in which species of reptiles have been found in your county, you can download a list of all of the reptile specimens that have been collected within that region. Most often each record has a locality, which could allow you to revisit the area to see if the species is persisting. Alternatively, if you are interested in a particular location, such as a stream or a park, you could search for any specimen records from that location. Another valuable portal is **Fishes of Texas**; although it is restricted to fish, it has a user-friendly interface and a higher degree of quality control.

Another valuable resource is historic books and photographs that can be found online, in local libraries, or at local museums and historic societies. Historic books and articles may provide you with places that you can revisit to document change. Historic photographs can provide a trove of valuable information about the history of land use and habitats that influence present-day habitats. Together, they can provide a context that will add meaning to the observations we can make today.

When setting up a project, here are some things to think about:

Identify your hypothesis and assumptions. Even if you have a general question, it is good to articulate your hypothesis and the assumptions involved. Doing so will force you to think about how you can prove your hypothesis and minimize your assumptions. For example, if your question is when is the best time of year to see moths, your hypothesis might be that May is the best time to see moths. Your assumptions may be that moth activity is the same regardless of weather or phase of moon. However, you may want to standardize or at least document either condition.

Make it fun. Make sure that data collection is something that you actually want to do. As naturalists, we are motivated by our passion, and the projects that support that passion are the most likely to succeed. If your project involves others, think about how to make it social and engaging.

Validate your data. The data you collect will be much more valuable if validated in some way. One of the most obvious tools is to document observations with photographs or sound recordings. If you can use iNaturalist in your data collection, you will be automating the validation by having fellow naturalists confirm identifications. Posting your observations on iNaturalist will allow others to use your data for other projects.

Communicate your results. Share your results with your Texas Master Naturalist chapter or publish them in a way that they can be found in the future. Think about the naturalists who will follow 100 years from now; your observations and results will only become more valuable over time as long as they can be found by those who follow.

As a naturalist, you can easily develop a project in your backyard, in your local park, or in your county. For example, with just a black light you could do a weekly survey of moths and produce a chart of how moth diversity or abundance changes over the course of the year. You could develop a similar survey for pollinators at a backyard wildscape, or you could collect data on the relative pollinator diversity at different species of plants.

For your local park, just documenting biodiversity is a valuable contribution to your community. Species lists can be useful for demonstrating the value of stewardship and advocating for better management of habitats. To add value to your survey, standardize and document how you are conducting your survey; this will allow naturalists to replicate your effort and compare the results at points in the future. An even more sophisticated approach could involve surveying similar habitats with different management. For example, in some cases riparian areas are regularly mowed. You could set up a regular survey of mowed and unmowed riparian areas in a park to demonstrate the impact of mowing on habitat.

At the county level, you can add valuable information to how our ecological communities are changing. One interesting subject is the impact of nonnative species or species with expanding ranges. Currently, there is a new species of *Anolis* lizard, the brown anole, which has been introduced in Texas. Although it is found along the coast, this lizard is just now arriving in San Antonio, Austin, and other locations. This might be a valuable opportunity to document the abundance of our native green anole in these cities before it has been much affected by the new species. Other projects might involve historic specimens that have not been detected in your county in many years. An amateur naturalist could look up where they were last found and survey these locations at the appropriate time of year. In many cases, we do not even realize what has been lost, and by shining a light on that loss, you can raise awareness to change that we unconsciously perpetuate.

There are so many potential projects; the key is to follow your passion and your curiosity. Despite centuries of work by naturalists, there are many discoveries to be made just outside your door. While you may see more species if you travel far, your careful observations around where you live could prove to be more meaningful and more beneficial to our ability to conserve biodiversity. But whether you are a globe-trotting naturalist always looking to add a new species to your life list, or someone who enjoys watching the natural world from the front porch, citizen science is not only a good way to contribute

Three naturalists at an insect-attracting light in Anderson County. Black lights and other insect-attracting lights are a great way to survey nocturnal insects, and they can be set up anywhere. Courtesy of Cullen Hanks

but an excellent investment in your passion for the natural world. It will help sustain your sense of discovery for a lifetime.

References

Miller-Rushing, Abraham, Richard Primack, and Rick Bonney. 2012. The History of Public Participation in Ecological Research. *Frontiers in Ecology and the Environment* 10:285–90.

Additional Resources

North American Bird Conservation Initiative. 2014. *All-Bird Bulletin.* http://www.nabci-us.org/bulletin/bulletin-fa112014.pdf.

Silvertown, J. A. 2009. A New Dawn for Citizen Science. *Trends in Ecology & Evolution* 24:467–71. doi: 10.1016/j.tree.2009.03.017.

Tweddle, J. C., L. D. Robinson, M. J. O. Pocock, and H. E. Roy. 2012. *Guide to Citizen Science: Developing, Implementing and Evaluating Citizen Science to Study Biodiversity and the Environment in the UK.* Wallingford, UK: NERC/Centre for Ecology & Hydrology.

Website Resources

Audubon Christmas Bird Count: http://birds.audubon.org/christmas-bird-count

Cornell Lab of Ornithology, Citizen Science Toolkit: http://www.birds.cornell.edu/citscitoolkit/toolkit

eBird: http://ebird.org

Fishes of Texas: http://www.fishesoftexas.org

Flora of Texas Database: http://www.biosci.utexas.edu/prc/Tex.html

iNaturalist: http://www.inaturalist.org

Monarch Watch: http://www.monarchwatch.org

National Phenology Network: https://www.usanpn.org

Scistarter: http://scistarter.com/

Spotlight on Amateur Naturalists, Smithsonian National Museum of Natural History: http://www.mnh.si.edu/vz/vz_libraries/index.html

Texas A&M AgriLife, Biodiversity Research and Teaching Collections: http://brtc.tamu.edu/

Texas Parks and Wildlife, Texas Nature Trackers: http://www.tpwd.state.tx.us/huntwild/wild/wildlife_diversity/texas_nature_trackers/

VertNet: http://www.vertnet.org

Index